Blackwell Handbook of Early Childhood Development

Blackwell Handbooks of Developmental Psychology

This outstanding series of handbooks provides a cutting-edge overview of classic research, current research and future trends in developmental psychology.

- Each handbook draws together 25–30 newly commissioned chapters to provide a comprehensive overview of a sub-discipline of developmental psychology.
- The international team of contributors to each handbook has been specially chosen for its expertise and knowledge of each field.
- Each handbook is introduced and contextualized by leading figures in the field, lending coherence and authority to each volume.

The *Blackwell Handbooks of Developmental Psychology* will provide an invaluable overview for advanced students of developmental psychology and for researchers as an authoritative definition of their chosen field.

Published

Blackwell Handbook of Infant Development
Edited by Gavin Bremner and Alan Fogel

Blackwell Handbook of Childhood Social Development
Edited by Peter K. Smith and Craig H. Hart

Blackwell Handbook of Childhood Cognitive Development
Edited by Usha Goswami

Blackwell Handbook of Adolescence
Edited by Gerald R. Adams and Michael D. Berzonsky

The Science of Reading: A Handbook
Edited by Margaret J. Snowling and Charles Hulme

Blackwell Handbook of Early Childhood Development
Edited by Kathleen McCartney and Deborah Phillips

Forthcoming

Blackwell Handbook of Language Development
Edited by Erika Hoff and Marilyn Shatz

Blackwell Handbook of Early Childhood Development

Edited by

Kathleen McCartney and Deborah Phillips

Blackwell
Publishing

BLACKWELL PUBLISHING
350 Main Street, Malden, MA 02148-5020, USA
9600 Garsington Road, Oxford OX4 2DQ, UK
550 Swanston Street, Carlton, Victoria 3053, Australia

First published 2006 by Blackwell Publishing Ltd

1 2006

Library of Congress Cataloging-in-Publication Data

Blackwell handbook of early childhood development / edited by Kathleen McCartney and Deborah
Phillips.
    p. cm.—(Blackwell handbooks of developmental psychology)
  Includes bibliographical references and index.
  ISBN-13: 978-1-4051-2073-9 (hardcover : alk. paper)
  ISBN-10: 1-4051-2073-8 (hardcover : alk. paper)   1. Child psychology. 2. Child
development. I. Title: Handbook of early childhood development. II. McCartney,
Kathleen. III. Phillips, Deborah. IV. Series.

BF721. B44 2006
305.231—dc21

                              2005029124

A catalogue record for this title is available from the British Library.

Set in 10.5 on 12.5 pt Adobe Garamond
by SNP Best-set Typesetter Ltd, Hong Kong
Printed and bound in the United Kingdom
by TJ International, Padstow, Cornwall

For further information on
Blackwell Publishing, visit our website:
www.blackwellpublishing.com

Contents

List of Tables and Figures

Tables

Figures

Notes on Contributors

Sally Atkins-Burnett is Assistant Professor of Early Childhood Special Education at the University of Toledo.

Catherine C. Ayoub is Associate Professor of Education at the Harvard Graduate School of Education and Associate Professor of Psychology at the Harvard Medical School.

Rachel Barr is Assistant Professor of Psychology at Georgetown University.

Daniel Berry is a doctoral student in Human Development and Psychology at the Harvard Graduate School of Education.

Karen L. Bierman is Distinguished Professor of Psychology at Pennsylvania State University.

Marc H. Bornstein is Senior Investigator and Head of Child and Family Research at the National Institute of Child Health and Human Development.

Katherine Cahill is a doctoral student in Psychology at the University of Oregon.

Sandra L. Calvert is Professor of Psychology at Georgetown University and Director of the Children's Digital Media Center.

Susan B. Campbell is Professor of Psychology at the University of Pittsburgh.

Joanna Cannon is a postdoctoral fellow in Developmental Psychology at the University of Chicago.

Rachel Chazan-Cohen is Senior Research Analyst at the Office of Planning, Research and Evaluation, Administration for Children and Families, US Department of Health and Human Services.

Jane W. Couperus is the Foundation for Psychocultural Research – Hampshire College Program in Culture, Brain, and Development Assistant Professor of Developmental Cognitive Neuroscience.

Eric Dearing is Assistant Professor of Psychology at the University of Wyoming.

Kirby Deater-Deckard is Professor of Psychology at Virginia Polytechnic Institute and State University.

Janet Eisenband is a doctoral student in Cognitive Studies in Education at Teachers College, Columbia University.

Stephen A. Erath is a student in Child Clinical Psychology at the Pennsylvania State University.

Richard A. Fabes is a Professor in the Department of Family and Human Development at Arizona State University.

Kurt W. Fischer is Charles Bigelow Professor of Education at the Harvard Graduate School of Education.

Nathan A. Fox is Professor of Human Development at the University of Maryland.

Sarah L. Friedman is a staff member of the National Institute of Child Health and Human Development. She is Scientific Coordinator of the NICHD Study of Early Child Care and Youth Development.

Bridget M. Gaertner is a doctoral student in Family Science at the Arizona State University.

Susan A. Gelman is Associate Dean for Social Sciences and Frederich G. L. Huetwell Professor of Psychology at the University of Michigan.

Abigail H. Gewirtz is Assistant Professor of Psychology at the University of Minnesota.

Herbert P. Ginsburg is Jacob H. Schiff Foundations Professor of Psychology and Education at Teachers College, Columbia University.

Susan Goldin-Meadow is Irving B. Harris Professor of Psychology at the University of Chicago.

Megan R. Gunnar is Professor of Child Development at the University of Minnesota.

Michael J. Guralnick is Director of the Center on Human Development and Disability and Professor of Psychology and Pediatrics at the University of Washington.

Erika Hoff is Professor of Psychology at Florida Atlantic University.

Jessica Kieras is a doctoral student in Psychology at the University of Oregon.

Kristin H. Lagattuta is Assistant Professor of Psychology at the University of California, Davis.

John M. Love is a senior fellow at Mathematica Policy Research Inc., Princeton, NJ.

Kathleen McCartney is Gerald S. Lesser Professor of Early Childhood Development at the Harvard Graduate School of Education.

Jennifer N. Martin is a doctoral student in Human Development at the University of Maryland.

Ann S. Masten is Distinguished McKnight University Professor and Distinguished University Professor of Child Psychology at the University of Minnesota.

Samuel J. Meisels is President of the Erikson Institute.

Charles A. Nelson is Richard David Scott Chair of Pediatrics at the Harvard Medical School and Research Director of the Developmental Medicine Center at Boston Children's Hospital.

Lana Nenide is a doctoral student at the University of Wisconsin.

Sandra Pappas is a doctoral student in Developmental Psychology at Teachers College, Columbia University.

Deborah Phillips is Professor of Psychology at Georgetown University.

Robert C. Pianta is Professor and William Clay Parrish Jr. Chair in Education at the University of Virginia.

Tierney K. Popp is a doctoral student in Child Development and Family Studies at Arizona State University.

Michael I. Posner is Professor Emeritus at the University of Oregon and Adjunct Professor at the Weill Medical College in New York (Sackler Institute).

Helen Raikes is Professor, Department of Family and Consumer Sciences, University of Nebraska, Lincoln.

M. Jamila Reid is Co-Director of the Parenting Center and a research psychologist at the Department of Family and Child Nursing, at the University of Washington.

Sara Rimm-Kaufman is Assistant Professor of Educational Psychology at the University of Virginia.

Mary K. Rothbart is Professor Emeritus at the University of Oregon.

Jeanette Sawyer is a doctoral student in Clinical Psychology at Columbia University.

Lisa D. Settles is a member of the clinical faculty in the Department of Psychiatry and Neurology at Tulane University Health Sciences Center.

Anna T. Smyke is Research Instructor of Child and Adolescent Psychiatry at Tulane University.

Catherine E. Snow is Henry Lee Shattuck Professor of Education at the Harvard Graduate School of Education.

Susan J. Spieker is Professor of Family and Child Nursing at the University of Washington.

Amy Sussman is a researcher and adjunct faculty member in the Psychology Department at Georgetown University.

Louisa Banks Tarullo is a senior researcher at Mathematica Policy Research, Inc. in Washington, DC.

Ross A. Thompson is Professor of Psychology at the University of California, Davis.

Sara J. Van Winkle is a graduate student at the University of Wisconsin.

Deborah Lowe Vandell is a Professor in the Department of Educational Psychology at the University of Wisconsin-Madison.

Jane Waldfogel is Professor of Social Work and Public Affairs at Columbia University.

Carolyn Webster-Stratton is Professor and Director of the Parenting Clinic at the Department of Family and Child Nursing, University of Washington.

Marilyn C. Welsh is Professor of Psychology at the University of Northern Colorado.

Martha Zaslow is the Vice President for Research and Area Director for the Early Child Development content area at Child Trends.

Charles H. Zeanah is Professor of Psychiatry and Pediatrics and Director of Child and Adolescent Psychiatry at Tulane University.

Preface

In the first two years of life, infants develop amazing competencies across development, from controlled movements to representational thought to goal-directed attachment relationships. Our story picks up from this point through about age 7, the early childhood years. Early childhood, like infancy, represents a time of emerging skills – skills that make the 7-year-old seem more like an adult than an infant. In early childhood, children exchange magical and egocentric thinking for a theory of mind, the ability to execute a plan of action, and a rudimentary logic. Over time, "terrible" 2-year-olds become young children who can exhibit self-control by delaying gratification and inhibiting inappropriate responses. In a stunning feat, by the end of early childhood, children master most of the grammatical rules that adults use. Parents and teachers respond to these kinds of noticeable changes by using reasoning, encouraging independence, arranging play dates, and providing explicit opportunities for learning in their dealings with young children. Soon, children are reading, counting, developing friendships, choosing to engage in favorite activities, and more.

There are two main ways to study development at any age. The first is to chart the milestones that reflect changes observed in the average child, while the second is to assess individual differences among children. Both perspectives inform the knowledge base on early childhood development. Individual differences are of particular interest to those concerned with applied problems. For this reason, an understanding of early childhood necessitates an investigation of the contexts of development, what we refer to here as the social ecology of early development, including the family, peers, poverty, child care, and the media. To some extent, research on early childhood has informed policy issues, as reflected in work on assessment as well as evaluations of early interventions for children and parents. Comparative studies reveal vast differences across cultures in policies for children and families, which are more likely to reflect public will than research *per se*.

We began our editing task by reflecting on the emerging competencies in early childhood, the approaches social scientists use to study it, and methodological issues in the field. Then we constructed topics that represent our view of the landscape in early childhood development. We recruited leading scholars in developmental science to write relatively short, albeit comprehensive, reviews of the literature from both a theoretical and a conceptual perspective. To give the volume a unified voice, we asked authors to consider four organizing themes in their reviews: the role of early experiences as they shape the course of development; contributions of the cultural contexts within which children grow up; individual differences in developmental trajectories; and applications of development science to issues of practice and policy.

The result is a Handbook that we have organized into seven parts: Part I, Conceptual Frameworks; Part II, Early Biological and Physiological Development; Part III, Cognitive Development; Part IV, Language and Communicative Development; Part V, Social, Emotional, and Regulatory Development; Part VI, The Social Ecology of Early Development; and Part VII, Policy Issues. The four conceptual frameworks that open the Handbook provide a foundation for the field through their discussions of how to describe the interplay of genes and environments, how research on children's vulnerability and resilience informs our understanding of individual differences, how the study of normal and atypical development can enhance our understanding of developmental processes, and how domains of development intersect.

Our aim, like that of other editors in this Blackwell series, is to provide a Handbook that is accessible to a broad audience, from students to researchers to practitioners. Each chapter offers an independent overview of a topic, which can be read as a stand-alone piece. Note, however, that the authors liberally reference other chapters in the volume to help readers make important connections across the field. Indeed, several authors read one another's first drafts to discover not only common ground, but also points of diversion. One can easily imagine organizing an early childhood seminar around cross-chapter discussions of key developmental issues. In the final analysis, our aim has been to assemble a Handbook that will be useful to all within our field who seek to understand the developing child, to move the knowledge base forward, and apply this knowledge toward constructive policies and programs for all children.

Kathleen McCartney
Deborah Phillips

PART I

Conceptual Frameworks

1

Nature and Nurture in Early Childhood

Kirby Deater-Deckard and Katherine Cahill

Human development is shaped by dynamic transactions between genes and environments – genetic and environmental influences that can be independent or correlated, and additive or interactive in their effects. These effects cannot be elucidated without understanding how these transactions may be operating throughout the lifespan. The focus in developmental science has shifted toward testing models of how genes and environments work together to create human variability, as part of a much broader trend toward investigating biological and environmental factors in brain growth, functioning, and plasticity.

In the current chapter, we present research investigating the interplay between nature and nurture in early childhood development. We begin with an overview of the techniques used to ascertain genetic and environmental influences, and then turn to a description of what we know about the etiology of individual differences. We concentrate on the domains of physical development, cognitive and language skills, temperament, and the early signs of developing psychopathology. In addition, we consider recent developments in the study of gene–environment processes and molecular genetics, as they apply to early childhood.

Methods in Research on Gene–Environment Processes

Human genes and environments share remarkable similarities across populations. Indeed, humans share much of their genotype with many other species. However, there also is awesome variability in the form and function of genes and environments that give rise to equally remarkable variability across individuals, and it is the examination of the etiology of these individual differences that is at the root of contemporary quantitative and molecular genetics research (Plomin, DeFries, McClearn, & McGuffin, 2001). With few exceptions, behavioral and molecular genetic data are correlational. However, even correlational genetic designs yield data that are useful in pointing toward likely causal mechanisms, because they control for potential confounds between genetic and environmental influences – confounds that go undetected in most developmental studies of genetically related family members. Behavioral and molecular genetics research, in addition to experimental and quasi-experimental studies of the effects of familial and extra-familial experiences in development, are important contemporary approaches to understanding the contributions of both genes and environments to human development (Collins, Maccoby, Steinberg, Hetherington, & Bornstein, 2000).

Molecular genetic techniques

The Human Genome Project revealed that there are around 30,000 functional human genes – far fewer than the 100,000 that researchers expected to find. Genes are the functional parts of chromosomes that synthesize proteins. These proteins act as enzymes that are the building blocks for neurotransmitters, hormones, and other bio-chemicals. Human chromosomes come in pairs, and people have one allele (i.e., form) of a gene on one chromosome and one allele on the second. There are variations in alleles; some are longer or shorter or more complex than others, and these differences correspond to differences in protein synthesis and the production of chemicals involved in guiding human behavior. Base pairs are the unit of analysis in genome scans, and variability in base pairs at specific gene loci is related to variability in the production, destruction, and expression of enzymes. For instance, single base pair substitutions/single nucleotide polymorphisms (SNPs) and simple sequence repeats (SSRs) are structural variations that are associated with complex trait expression (Craig & McClay, 2003).

Consider as an example the dopamine receptor D4 gene (DRD4), which plays a role in determining the number of dopamine receptors in the brain. Having more dopamine receptors typically translates into greater dopamine activity in the brain, which is related to novelty seeking, attention problems – and, in more extreme cases, schizophrenia and disorganized attachment (Ebstein, Benjamin, & Belmaker, 2003). DRD4 alleles come in at least ten forms (Kluger, Siegfried, & Ebstein, 2002), but the most common are the 4- and 7-repeat alleles, often referred to as the short and long forms of DRD4, respectively. The long form is associated with higher levels of novelty seeking (Ebstein et al., 2003). DRD4 and the serotonin transporter 5-HTTLPR gene have received substantial attention in molecular genetics research, because they are thought to have widespread effects on complex human behaviors.

Molecular genetic techniques allow scientists to identify specific genes involved in the expression of complex human traits and behaviors, based on the analysis of structural differences in DNA like the differences just described in the DRD4 gene. Linkage and association approaches to studying genetic similarity (e.g., allele sharing and allelic frequency at specific locations on chromosomes) among family members have vastly increased our knowledge about individual genes implicated in some of the most widely studied human attributes, including how those genes are differentially expressed in individuals. More recent advances in molecular genetics have focused on understanding the complex processes involved in gene structure and functional expression.

A small number of genes involved in individual differences in early childhood have been identified, and little is understood about the intricacies of the expression of these genes in terms of their products (i.e., proteins, enzymes) and the effects of those gene products. Nevertheless, this research is progressing rapidly, and the work that has been done already greatly enriches our appreciation for the importance of examining gene–environment processes. The decades ahead will be filled with major discoveries regarding variation in structure and function of genes and networks of genes, their products, and the transactions between these and non-genetic factors. These will include discoveries arising from the search for relevant genes (based on genome scans) as well as from investigations of candidate genes in particular neurotransmitter systems implicated for specific attributes (based on existing knowledge from the human and animal biopsychology literatures).

Quantitative genetic techniques

Unlike molecular genetic approaches, quantitative genetic techniques are based on mathematical models that employ principles of population genetics to estimate the proportions of variance that are accounted for by genetic and environmental factors. Studies of sibling and parent–offspring pairs that vary in their genetic similarity (e.g., biological and non-biological relatives in intact, step, and adoptive families; twins; families that have used egg or sperm donation) allow for estimation of genetic, shared environmental, and non-shared environmental effects on outcomes of interest. If family members who are more genetically similar (e.g., identical versus fraternal twins) are more similar on a trait, then genetic variance or heritability is said to account for the greater similarity. If genetic similarity is controlled and family members continue to show similarity, shared environmental variance is said to be present. Non-shared environmental variance includes effects of all the non-genetic influences that lead to dissimilarity among family members, and includes measurement error (Reiss, Neiderhiser, Hetherington, & Plomin, 2000).

The overwhelming majority of research on the effects of nature and nurture in early childhood has employed quantitative techniques, but that trend is changing as molecular genetic techniques become more accessible (Plomin & Rutter, 1998). With this in mind, we turn to review the research on the contributions of genes and environments to children's early physical, cognitive, and psychosocial development.

Stature and Physical Development

A good place to start in considering research on gene–environment processes is with the literature on indices of stature – most scientists agree on what these observable attributes (i.e., *phenotypes*) are, and how they are best measured. There is also consensus on how these should be measured, and if used correctly, the measurement tools yield data that are highly reliable and valid. Quantitative genetics research has indicated substantial genetic variance in children's height, weight, and body mass index (BMI). Several twin and adoption studies have revealed heritability estimates that increase from early to middle childhood (e.g., Cardon, 1994; Phillips & Matheny, 1990). A study of 14- to 36-month-old twins showed that, even at these young ages, an average of two-thirds of the variance was attributed to genetic factors. Shared environmental variance was highest at 20 and 24 months for all measures, but remained modest, with the exception of moderate shared environment for BMI at 20 and 24 months (Chambers, Hewitt, Schmitz, Corley, & Fulker, 2001).

Environmental effects on BMI are reflected in rapid generational changes, evidenced as increases in the rates of obesity in children in the US. From 1988 to 1994, the rate of obesity in 2- to 5-year-olds rose from 7.2% to 10.4% (Ogden, Flegal, Carroll, & Johnson, 2002). Environmental conditions are implicated because genetic influences do not change this rapidly. Correlational research revealing that breastfeeding in infancy reduces children's risk for childhood obesity also points to the importance of early environmental experiences in physical development (Dietz, 2001). Yet the changing social conditions that promote overeating and sedentary lifestyle probably interact with genetic risk for obesity in some children (see below for more discussion of gene–environment interaction). It is to be hoped that researchers will continue to concentrate on identifying genetic variation as it interacts with environmental factors that put some children at increased risk for obesity and related health problems.

Cognitive Development

We now consider some of the psychological attributes in early childhood that have been investigated in genetically informative studies. Individual differences in children's cognitive development include a number of interrelated domains of skill and performance, ranging from processing speed and capacity, to complex problem solving, to language understanding and use. We concentrate in the following section on the two areas of inquiry that have received the most attention among researchers studying early childhood development – general cognitive ability (e.g., intelligence or IQ) and verbal communication skills.

General cognitive ability

Typically, general cognitive ability is estimated to be moderately heritable, based on twin and adoption studies of preschoolers. Longitudinal studies also suggest that genetic influences on general cognitive ability increase over early and middle childhood, while shared environmental effects are modest and often disappear by middle childhood (Bishop, Price, Dale, & Plomin, 2003; Cherny, et al., 2001; McCartney, Harris, & Bernieri, 1990; Petrill et al., 1998; Plomin et al., 2001; Wilson, 1983). This may reflect developmental changes arising from shifts in the degree to which children have more control, and parents less control, over their environments and daily experiences (Scarr & McCartney, 1983). Nevertheless, interventions for improving cognitive performance have been shown to be effective (Ramey & Haskins, 1981), and it is important to emphasize that about half of the variance in cognitive abilities is accounted for by non-shared environmental influences.

Single-gene disorders and chromosomal abnormalities are the most common causes of major deficits in general cognitive ability. Down's syndrome is a chromosomal abnormality characterized by the presence of a third twenty-first chromosome, and it is the most widespread cause of mental retardation in both males and females. The single-gene disorders of Fragile X syndrome and Rett syndrome are responsible for the second largest number of cases of mental retardation in males and females, respectively (Plomin et al., 2001). The single-gene disorder PKU is caused by a mutation of the PAH gene, and provides a clear example of how genes and environments work together. The mutation of the PAH gene prevents proper breakdown of phenylalanine, a substance commonly ingested through red meat and other foods. When phenylalanine levels build up, it damages the developing brain and leads to mental retardation and other symptoms. Maintaining a strict diet can prevent the great majority of the effects of PKU. Discovering the genes involved in disorders and how they function can open doors to developing environmental interventions that reduce or alleviate the effects of genetic problems (Plomin et al., 2001).

Language and communication

Many components of language and literacy development are moderately heritable. In this domain, the effects of the shared environment are often more evident, compared to the domain of general cognitive ability. Expressive language skills – compared to receptive skills – appear to be more genetically variable, and more of this genetic variance overlaps with genetic influences on general cognitive ability. In contrast, shared environmental influences appear to be more prominent for receptive language skills, compared with expressive skills (Young, Schmitz, Corley, & Fulker, 2001). Dale, Dionne, Eley, and Plomin (2000) reported heritability estimates of .25 and .39 for lexical and grammatical development, respectively, in 2-year-olds. Shared environmental effects were estimated at .69 for grammar and .48 for lexical development.

Common genetic and environmental processes are thought to underlie lexical and grammatical development, but it is less clear whether general verbal and non-verbal language development shares genetic and environmental influences (Dale et al., 2000). Verbal and non-verbal skills in 2-year-olds are moderately correlated, and less than half of this similarity is accounted for by common genetic influences (Price et al., 2000). Similarly, Dale et al. found low to moderate correlations between lexical and grammatical development and non-verbal skills. However, in contrast, Colledge et al. (2002) found extensive overlap in the genetic influence on verbal and non-verbal skills in 4-year-olds.

Genetic factors appear to be highly influential when it comes to more severe language and communication problems and disorders (Plomin et al., 2001). Dale et al. (1998)

found that heritability in vocabulary development was greater, and shared environmental variance smaller, among those scoring in the lowest 5% of the performance range in their large and diverse sample of 2-year-old twins. Similarly, variance in vocabulary scores for children with *persistent* language problems in early childhood was largely accounted for by genetic factors, whereas variance in vocabulary scores for children with *transient* language problems was more likely to be accounted for by environmental factors (Bishop et al., 2003). The genetic basis of dyslexia and other reading and communication disorders is currently under intense study, and the results of this research will allow for a clearer understanding of how genes and environments work together in shaping children's language development (Plomin et al., 2001).

To summarize, genetic variance is moderate to substantial in studies of cognitive and language functioning and performance in early childhood. There also is evidence for shared environmental influences; these are largest in early childhood, and dissipate with development. In contrast, non-shared environmental influences are present from early in life, and persist into middle childhood and beyond.

Temperament

Next, we consider temperament and its component parts, as the domain of social-emotional development that has received the most attention in behavioral genetic research. The estimates of heritable and genetic variance in these studies vary to some degree, due to differences across study designs (e.g., measurement, twin or adoption study).

Temperament is the framework for personality. It is rooted in biologically based individual differences, is moderately stable over time and across settings, and is modified by gene–environment processes. Individual differences in temperament are observable from infancy and are implicated in many crucial aspects of children's development and adaptation (Emde & Hewitt, 2001; Prior, 1999). Rothbart's theory of temperament posits that there are multiple dimensions of behavior that represent reactivity to stimuli and regulation of those reactions (Rothbart & Bates, 1998). Relevant domains in this literature that we highlight here include negative affectivity, effortful control, extraversion/surgency, sociability, and adaptability (see Rothbart, Posner, & Kieras, this volume).

Negative affectivity

The temperament dimension of Negative affectivity includes anger, sadness, discomfort, and low soothability. Quantitative genetic research indicates that approximately one-third to two-thirds of the variance in negative affectivity is heritable (Goldsmith, Buss, & Lemery, 1997; Oniszczenko et al., 2003; Plomin, Pedersen, McClearn, Nesselroade, & Bergeman, 1988). Angry reactions to restraint and the initiating of fights are estimated to be heritable, and this genetic variance appears to contribute mainly to the observable stability of individual differences (Emde, Robinson, Corley, Nikkari, & Zahn-Waxler,

2001). Some evidence for shared environmental influence also has been found, and environmental sources of variance (shared and non-shared) contribute to both continuity and change in these behaviors across infancy and the preschool years (Emde et al., 2001).

Molecular genetic research has implicated dopamine and serotonin genes in negative emotionality. Infants who have at least one long DRD4 allele display less negative emotionality (Ebstein, Levine, Geller, Auerbach, Gritsenko, & Belmaker, 1998) and less anger in response to restraint (Auerbach, Faroy, Ebstein, Kahana, & Levine, 2001). Mothers' reports of high levels of aggression in 4-year-olds were also found to be associated with the presence of the long form of DRD4 (Schmidt, Fox, Rubin, Hu, & Hammer, 2002). Twelve-month-olds who have two copies of the short form of the serotonin transporter 5-HTTLPR gene showed less pleasure than others during free play (Auerbach et al., 2001).

Effortful control

The dimension of Effortful control includes anticipation and enjoyment of low-intensity stimulation, perceptual sensitivity, and enhanced control of attention and impulses. High levels of effortful control are correlated with lower levels of negative emotionality (Rothbart, Ahadi, & Evans, 2000). Many studies have indicated moderate heritability in the components of effortful control, including task orientation, persistence, and related aspects of "difficult" temperament (Goldsmith et al., 1997; Lemery & Goldsmith, 2002; Manke, Suadino, & Grant, 2001). Molecular genetics research has linked the DRD4 gene to attentional control (Fan, Fossella, Sommer, Wu, & Posner, 2003), but this finding has not yet been replicated in young children. Shared environmental effects stemming from family socio-economic status and observed maternal warmth account for some of the variability in task persistence in early childhood (Petrill & Deater-Deckard, 2004).

Extraversion or surgency

The dimension of Extraversion or Surgency includes activity level, novelty seeking, positive affect, and low shyness. Activity level refers to the amount and intensity of physical movement and it is one of the most thoroughly researched dimensions of early childhood temperament. Overall, activity level has been found to be moderately heritable and to be relatively uninfluenced by shared environmental factors (Goldsmith et al., 1997). Among children at the extremes of activity level, the strength of genetic effects may increase (Manke et al., 2001), and the genetic effects on activity level appear to be moderately to highly stable across time points from infancy to 3 years of age (Saudino & Cherny, 2001). Variance in positive affect and general cheerfulness also appears to be mainly accounted for by heritability and non-shared environmental factors (Eid, Reimann, Angleitner, & Borkenau, 2003; Robinson, Emde, & Corley, 2001).

Research with newborns has identified genes in the serotonin and dopamine systems that are linked with temperament, especially components of temperament that relate to surgency. Among 2-week-olds, the presence of one or two alleles of the long form of the DRD4 gene was associated with higher scores on orientation, range of state, motor organization, and regulation of state (Ebstein et al., 1998). Additionally, an interaction between the DRD4 gene and the serotonin transporter 5-HTTLPR gene was found. Neonates without the long form of DRD4, and who also had only the short form of 5-HTTLPR, had significantly lower orientation scores than other infants (Ebstein et al., 1998). In a follow-up study of the infants in the Ebstein et al. study, Auerbach and colleagues (2001) found that the presence of the long form of DRD4 was associated with higher activity level at 12 months of age.

Sociability

The temperament dimension of Sociability refers to the enjoyment of interpersonal interaction (contrasted with shyness and enjoyment of being alone). Sociability is moderately heritable, with one-quarter to three-quarters of the variance attributed to genetic influences. Some studies also show evidence of shared environmental effects (Eid et al., 2003; Plomin et al., 1988; Schmitz, 1994). Genetic effects on sociability and shyness are moderately to substantially stable across 14 to 36 months of age (Saudino & Cherny, 2001). As with surgency, the heritability of more extreme forms of sociability is greater than that found for moderate sociability (Manke et al., 2001). Molecular genetic research on shyness implicates the 5-HTTLPR gene in increased shyness in second graders (Arbelle et al., 2003), but related serotonin genes have not been found to predict shyness in 4-year-olds (Schmidt et al., 2002).

Adaptability

The dimension of Adaptability is often identified as an important component of temperament, and it includes flexibility, distress in response to novelty, emotional regulation, and high soothability. Adaptability is moderately heritable, and evidence for modest shared environmental effects is sometimes found (Oniszczenko et al., 2003; Rusalov & Biryukov, 1993). Goldsmith, Lemery, Buss, and Campos (1999) reported substantial shared environmental influence in 3- to 16-month-olds' soothability scores. However, genetic effects accounted for all of the twin similarity in distress to novelty. The Ebstein et al. (1998) finding that the presence of the long form of DRD4 was associated with increased regulation of state in neonates suggests that genetic variation in the dopamine system also may play a role in adaptability.

To summarize, like the research on cognitive and language abilities, there is ample evidence of genetic influences in young children's temperament attributes. These findings include moderate heritability estimates as well as associations with specific dopamine and serotonin genes. Also like the research on cognitive and language abilities, there is ample non-genetic variation – much of this is non-shared, but again there is evidence of some shared environmental variance depending on the particular attribute in question.

Psychopathology

We turn briefly away from consideration of typical variation in cognitive and socio-emotional outcomes toward early indicators of psychopathology among young children. The environmental and genetic influences on psychopathology in early childhood vary depending on the type of symptom being examined, child age, and gender. The evidence for genetic variance is greatest and most consistent for externalizing problems. Internalizing problems (i.e., depression, anxiety, somatic problems) are moderately heritable throughout early and middle childhood, but the effects of the shared environment are less consistent (Murray & Sines, 1996; Schmitz, Fulker, & Mrazek, 1995). In one study, nearly one-quarter of the variance in girls' internalizing problems from ages 4 through 12 years was attributed to the shared environment, but there were no shared environmental influences found for boys (Murray & Sines, 1996). With respect to age differences, Schmitz et al. showed that the effects of the shared environment decreased and the effects of genetics increased on both internalizing and externalizing problems (i.e., aggression, non-compliance, delinquency, attention problems) from early to middle childhood (but see Gjone, Stevenson, & Sundet, 1996, who did not find this pattern for externalizing problems). Other investigations of externalizing problems in early childhood converge to show similarly moderate to high heritability estimates (Arseneault et al., 2003; Dionne, Tremblay, Boivin, Laplante, & Perusse, 2003; van den Oord, Verhults, & Boomsma, 1996; van der Valk, van den Oord, Verhulst, & Boomsma, 2001; van der Valk, Verhulst, Stroet, & Boomsma, 1998; Zahn-Waxler, Schmitz, Fulker, Robinson, & Emde, 1996).

Molecular genetics research has revealed potential gene–gene interactions that affect certain aspects of early childhood psychological health. Gene–gene interaction is said to occur when the effect of one gene's expression on a trait is moderated by the effect of another gene. One example is found in a study of disorganized infant–caregiver attachment. Infants from a low-risk sample were found to have four times the risk for a disorganized attachment classification if they had a specific form of the DRD4 gene. In addition, the presence of a particular SNP on the DRD4 gene had no main effect on attachment classification but increased the risk of disorganized attachment for children who also had the risk allele to ten times that of children who had neither the risk allele nor the risk SNP (Lakatos et al., 2002).

Gene–Environment Transactions

Up to this point, we have summarized findings regarding additive genetic and non-genetic effects on individual differences measures. However, these effects are not independent, nor do they operate in isolation from each other. Contemporary genetic theories of development place an emphasis on transactions between the genotype and the environment – specifically, gene–environment correlations and interactions.

Gene–environment correlation

Gene–environment correlation (r_{g-e}) refers to the non-independence of individuals' genetic make-up and the environments in which they exist. The pairing of genetic and environmental factors that interact to influence individual development is not random. Passive and non-passive types of r_{g-e} have been identified using quantitative genetic techniques (Plomin, 1994). Gene–environment correlation can be estimated through quantitative genetic models that include actual measures of the environmental variables of interest, and not just measures of the developmental outcome of interest (Plomin, 1994).

Passive r_{g-e} occurs when biological parents provide environmental conditions for their children that are correlated with their genetic make-up. For example, children who are highly sociable are more likely to have biological parents who also are fairly sociable because sociability is moderately heritable. These parents may expose their children to more people and social interaction than do other parents, and so these children will have many opportunities to further enhance their social skills. These children may develop to experience high levels of social interaction and positive reinforcement from others, and this may appear to be a result of their early exposure to high levels of interpersonal interaction. However, because the experiences they had may have arisen in part from genetic influences, so too do their later outcomes. Often, results from studies of related family members lead to conclusions of environmental causation, but the same findings could also indicate the presence of passive genetic influence. For instance, maternal education has been found to predict aspects of preschoolers' theory of mind development (Pears & Moses, 2003). One might conclude that well-educated mothers interact with their children in ways that promote their understanding of others' minds. Alternatively, the same genetically influenced cognitive abilities that facilitated the mothers' educational attainment might promote early theory of mind understanding in the children. Determining the appropriate interpretation of such findings can be resolved only by using genetically informative study designs that measure the outcomes and relevant environmental factors of interest (Petrill & Deater-Deckard, 2004).

Non-passive r_{g-e} arises when individuals either seek out environments and experiences that are correlated with their genetically based propensities (active r_{g-e}) or elicit responses based on their genetically based attributes that further reinforce those attributes (evocative or reactive r_{g-e}). As an example of active r_{g-e}, children who are low in activity level, a partially heritable trait, may select hobbies and peers that do not promote physical activity. These environmental factors are consistent with their genetically influenced tendencies and may make it less likely that their activity levels increase. Evocative r_{g-e} may be experienced by children struggling with early reading skills, partly on the basis of their genetic make-up, who elicit negative attention from their teachers in a way that serves to further dampen their persistence with and interest in reading. Evocative r_{g-e} also has been implicated in children's externalizing problems. Children's genetically influenced aggressive and inattentive behavior typically evokes harsh discipline or rejection from parents, teachers, and peers (Anderson, Lytton, & Romney, 1986; O'Connor, Deater-Deckard, Fulker, Rutter, & Plomin, 1998). These social responses may reinforce and promote continued growth in behavioral problems.

Maternal expression of warmth toward children is another process that appears to include evocative r_{g-e}. Mothers' reports of their positive feelings toward each of their children, as well as their observed warmth and responsiveness with each of their children, vary as a function of how genetically similar sibling children are to each other. Genetically unrelated adoptive siblings receive only modestly correlated levels of warmth from their adoptive mothers, whereas fraternal twins receive moderately similar levels of warmth from their mothers. Identical twins tend to receive warmth from their mothers that is very highly correlated. This pattern suggests that differences in children's genetically influenced responsiveness and engagement with their mothers elicit different levels of maternal warmth and emotional reciprocity with their children (Deater-Deckard & O'Connor, 2000; Deater-Deckard & Petrill, 2004).

Gene–environment interaction

Gene–environment interaction ($g \times e$) occurs when environmental conditions moderate the effects of genes or when genes moderate the effects of environmental conditions. There are many ways in which gene–environment interactions can affect how children's temperament, cognitive skills, and psychological health develop. Children at genetic risk for a "poor" outcome on a particular variable may develop in a typical way if the environmental conditions they experience reduce the genetic effect. Alternatively, risk-inducing environmental conditions may compound the obstacles faced by children already at genetic risk for certain problems, more than for children without that genetic risk. Many children are likely to also experience resilience as an outcome of $g \times e$. The effects of problematic environmental circumstances may be weakened or eradicated by protective genetic factors.

The best examples of $g \times e$ in human developmental science come from Caspi et al.'s (2002) work in the Dunedin Multidisciplinary Health and Development Study. Variation in the form and function of a gene involved in synthesizing monoamine oxidase A (MAOA), which metabolizes a neurotransmitter that is central to the control of emotion and behavior, appears to interact with children's experiences of maltreatment. For males who had the form of the gene that is related to adequate levels of MAOA production, childhood maltreatment was only modestly predictive of adult antisocial behavior. For males who had the form of the gene that is related to inadequate levels of MAOA production, childhood maltreatment was a strong predictor of adult antisocial behavior (Caspi et al., 2002).

Caspi et al. (2003) also reported evidence for another $g \times e$ involving protection against stressful life events; it is an important representative study, although its relevance to $g \times e$ in early childhood is less clear than the other finding just described above. Among young adults who had experienced stressful life events, those who had two copies of a particular form of a gene involved in the production of serotonin were less likely than those with one or no copies of the form of the gene to have developed depression. These examples clearly demonstrate the important role genetic variation can play in providing protection against environmental risk. Continuing to identify $g \times e$ processes that occur in early childhood and carry protection or risk for individuals should be one of the central goals of genetics research in developmental science.

Genetically Informative Studies Clarify Environmental Mechanisms

The gene–environment transactions described above should not be interpreted to indicate that genes are more important than environments in determining how children develop. Indeed, genetically informative studies elucidate the ways in which non-genetic influences operate in development, by providing tools for identifying with much greater precision the transactions between specific environmental factors and general genetic influence effects. As molecular genetic techniques lead to replications of findings with respect to specific genes, those genetic variables can then be added to these gene–environment process models, leading to even further precision (Plomin & Rutter, 1998).

Estimates of heritability obviously implicate genetic influences, but potential causal roles of environmental factors that are correlated and interacting with the involved genes cannot be dismissed. In addition, environmental changes likely produce changes in the gene–environment transactions that shape children's attributes and experiences. Furthermore, the gene–environment transactions underlying individual differences on any particular trait may not be uniform across populations and historical eras. For instance, shared environmental variance is typically negligible in quantitative genetic studies of cognitive performance by the time participants are school-age, but shared environmental effects may be far more pronounced in populations living in more extremely deprived environmental conditions arising from poverty or social exclusion (Turkheimer, Haley, Waldron, D'Onofrio, & Gottesman, 2003). Developmental science will only benefit from a broadening of the research base in a way that includes participants from more socio-economic and ethnic groups, although doing so raises challenges, both ethical and methodological.

Quantitative genetic research reveals that a considerable amount of the variance in young children's developmental outcomes arises from non-shared environmental influences. The environment has profound influence on children's development, and this can be seen particularly well in behavioral genetic studies in which genetic similarity among family members is employed statistically in the computations of effects (Plomin, 1994). These powerful non-shared environmental effects can be accounted for by using genetically informative designs (Reiss et al., 2000).

One aspect of young children's environments that has received a great deal of attention as a potential source of non-shared environmental influence is sibling differences in their experiences of interaction with the same shared parents. Our own study of 3-year-old identical twins indicated that the differences in mothers' warmth with each of their children predicted up to one-quarter of the difference in behavior problems within twin pairs (Deater-Deckard et al., 2001). The twin in each pair who received more maternal warmth tended to be happier, less aggressive, and more compliant than his or her sibling. This difference does not arise from genetic differences between the twins, because they are genetically identical.

Cataloging the mechanisms involved in non-shared environmental variation in outcomes of interest will help to explain why family members are often so dissimilar. Nevertheless, doing so will be difficult. Non-shared environment estimates also include error variance and non-genetic influences that operate in a non-systematic (and therefore unpredictable) way (Reiss et al., 2000; Turkheimer & Waldron, 2000). Also, the most direct test for these influences involves examining identical-twin differences, and because these sibling pairs are unique compared to all others (e.g., always same sex, same age, physically very similar), the findings may not generalize to non-identical-twin populations.

Shared environmental influences – those aspects of the environment that make family members similar – also can be identified using quantitative genetic methods. During early childhood, general cognitive ability includes moderate shared environmental variance. The same twin study of 3-year-olds just described revealed that much of the shared environmental variance in the preschool-aged twins' cognitive ability was due to overlapping variance between task orientation (an aspect of temperament), family socio-economic status, and maternal warmth (Petrill & Deater-Deckard, 2004). In general, developmental research investigating family processes will be improved to the extent that the measurement captures both global and child-specific environments within families. Such measures, when incorporated into quantitative genetic designs, will allow for more precise specification of shared and non-shared environmental mechanisms.

Change and Development

Gene–environment processes are not static over time. Environments evolve, and the expressions of genes change as well. For example, in spite of very clear evidence of genetic variance in measures of temperament in early childhood, these genetic signals are not apparent in neonates (Reise, 1990) – a developmental period when infant temperament can play a powerful role in the quality of the parent–child relationship when it is first being established. Nevertheless, this genetic signal grows in strength over the first two years of life (Matheny, 1983).

The correlations and interactions between genes and environments also can change. Gene–environment processes also vary between population groups and across eras within populations. This dynamism requires that if the interplay between genes and environments is to be fully understood, investigations of gene–environment processes must be conducted within a developmental context and with serious consideration to the environmental, historical, and systemic conditions of the population under study.

Therefore, research examining gene–environment transactions must be guided by developmental theories. Scarr and McCartney (1983) proposed one such framework, in which predictions were made regarding developmental shifts in the relative contribution of various forms of gene–environment correlation mechanisms. According to their theory, as children become more self-controlled and competent, they exercise a greater deal of control over their own environments. As a result, the theory states that passive forms of gene–environment correlation will wane as non-passive forms (implicated in the elicitation of and selection into certain types of experiences) become more influential. There have been very few explicit tests of this hypothesis (for a rare example, see McCartney et al., 1990), yet if it is true, it has major implications for the way in which we interpret findings based on family studies in early versus late childhood. For example, research has shown fairly consistent evidence of a modest-to-moderate positive correlation between parental use of physical punishment and child aggressive behavioral problems (Gershoff, 2002). Most researchers believe that this correlation reflects a bi-directional process between parent and child – the parent who is harsh elicits escalating problem behaviors in the child, and the child who is more difficult to manage elicits harsher treatment by the parent. However, it also is possible that this bi-directional process may be primarily parent-driven when children are very young, but primarily child-driven when those children get older. Furthermore, these interpersonal processes may reflect complex gene–environment correlation and interaction mechanisms. Only genetically sensitive designs incorporating longitudinal data can be used for drawing such conclusive inferences about the nature of bi-directional gene–environment transactions in development.

Where the Environment Lives: Subjective Experience

Children's subjective experiences are another environmental arena that is correlated with and interacts with genetic influences. Siblings who are more genetically similar report more similar retrospective accounts of their rearing environments and relationships with their parents, compared to less genetically similar siblings (Plomin, 1994). This may be due to evocative and passive gene–environment correlation effects. However, it is plausible that there are genetic influences on social information-processing mechanisms involved in selective attention and memory – mechanisms that influence how it is that children perceive and construe their experiences. Quantitative and molecular genetics research that focuses on children's perceptions of their family environments will be able to test whether this is the case.

Measuring young children's subjective experiences is a topic that has received renewed attention in recent years. Children's styles of social information processing, especially with respect to understanding other people's intentions, have been implicated in the explanation as to why some at-risk children show increasing tendencies toward aggression over time while others do not (Crick & Dodge, 1994). The internal environments children construct also likely contribute to the non-shared environmental variance often revealed in quantitative genetic studies. Recent research demonstrates that children's self-reported social cognitions offer similar and improved predictive validity compared to parent and teacher reports (Measelle, Ablow, Cowan, & Cowan, 1998). Developmental researchers should take seriously the assessment of both the external/objective and internal/subjective components of children's experiences if at all possible when investigating gene–environment transactions that shape early childhood development.

Conclusion

The evidence from quantitative genetic and, more recently, molecular genetic studies is clear in showing that genetic and environmental influences are operating together to produce the wide variations that we see between children in their physical and psychological functioning. However, much more work needs to be done. Researchers of early childhood must prepare themselves for integrating findings and research methods from molecular biology with the very best procedures currently used in mainstream developmental psychology. We should continue to refine even more precisely our operationalizations of the developmental outcomes that are of the utmost importance, as well as the environmental factors that are of greatest influence and that are most amenable to intervention.

We are at an important and very exciting crossroad in developmental science with regard to how we proceed in theorizing and empirically testing hypotheses regarding biological and environmental influences. There are many possible routes to choose from – some strongly emphasize biological or environmental determinism, and others strongly emphasize theories of integrative nature–nurture effects. Our view is that the latter approach will be the most fruitful one, and to this end we hope that the current chapter represents a useful roadmap.

References

Anderson, K., Lytton, H., & Romney, D. M. (1986). Mothers' interactions with normal and conduct-disordered boys: Who affects whom? *Developmental Psychology, 22,* 604–609.

Arbelle, S., Benjamin, J., Golin, M., Kremer, I., Belmaker, R. H., & Ebstein, R. P. (2003). Relation of shyness in grade school children to the genotype for the long form of the serotonin transporter promoter region polymorphism. *American Journal of Psychiatry, 160,* 671–676.

Arseneault, L., Moffitt, T. E., Caspi, A., Taylor, A., Rijsdijk, F. V., Jaffee, S. R., Ablow, J. C., & Measelle, J. R. (2003). Strong genetic effects on cross-situational antisocial behaviour among 5-year-old children according to mothers, teachers, examiner-observers, and twins' self-reports. *Journal of Child Psychology and Psychiatry, 44,* 832–848.

Auerbach, J. G., Faroy, M., Ebstein, R., Kahana, M., & Levine, J. (2001). The association of the dopamine D4 receptor gene (DRD4) and the serotonin transporter promoter gene (5-HTTLPR) with temperament in 12-month-old infants. *Journal of Child Psychology and Psychiatry, 42,* 777–783.

Bishop, D. V. M., Price, T. S., Dale, P. S., & Plomin, R. (2003). Outcomes of early language delay: II. Etiology of transient and persistent language difficulties. *Journal of Speech, Language, and Hearing Delay, 46,* 561–575.

Cardon, L. R. (1994). Height, weight, and obesity. In J. C. DeFries, R. Plomin, & D. W. Fulkner (Eds.), *Nature and nurture during middle childhood* (pp. 165–172). Cambridge, MA: Blackwell Publishers.

Caspi, A., McClay, J., Moffitt, T. E., Mill, J., Martin, J., Craig, I. W., Taylor, A., & Poulton, R. (2002). Role of genotype in the cycle of violence in maltreated children. *Science, 297,* 851–854.

Caspi, A., Sugden, K., Moffitt, T. E., Taylor, A., Craig, I. W., Harrington, H., McClay, J., Mill, J., Martin, J., Braithwaite, A., & Poulton, R. (2003). Influence of life stress on depression: Moderation by a polymorphism in the 5-HTT gene. *Science, 301,* 386–389.

Chambers, M. L., Hewitt, J. K., Schmitz, S., Corley, R. P., & Fulker, D. W. (2001). Height, weight, and body mass index. In R. N. Emde & J. K. Hewitt (Eds.), *Infancy to early childhood: Genetic and environmental influences on developmental change* (pp. 292–306). New York: Oxford University Press.

Cherny, S. S., Fulker, D. W., Emde, R. N., Plomin, R., Corley, R. P., & DeFries, J. C. (2001). Continuity and change in general cognitive ability from 14 to 36 months. In R. N. Emde & J. K. Hewitt (Eds.), *Infancy to early childhood: Genetic and environmental influences on developmental change* (pp. 206–220). New York: Oxford University Press.

Colledge, E., Bishop, D. V. M., Koppen-Schomerus, G., Price, T. S., Happe, F. G. E., Eley, T. C., Dale, P. S., & Plomin, R. (2002). The structure of language abilities at 4 years: A twin study. *Developmental Psychology, 38,* 749–757.

Collins, W. A., Maccoby, E. E., Steinberg, L., Hetherington, E. M., & Bornstein, M. H. (2000). Contemporary research on parenting: The case for nature and nurture. *American Psychologist, 53,* 218–232.

Craig, I. W., & McClay, J. (2003). The role of molecular genetics in the postgenomic era. In R. Plomin, J. C. DeFries, I. W. Craig, & P. McGuffin (Eds.), *Behavioral genetics in the postgenomic era* (pp. 19–40). Washington, DC: American Psychological Association.

Crick, N., & Dodge, K. A. (1994). A review and reformulation of social information-processing mechanisms in children's social adjustment. *Psychological Bulletin, 115,* 74–101.

Dale, P. S., Dionne, G., Eley, T. C., & Plomin, R. (2000). Lexical and grammatical development: A behavioral genetic perspective. *Journal of Child Language, 27,* 619–642.

Dale, P. S., Simonoff, E., Bishop, D. V. M., Eley, T. C., Oliver, B., Price, T. S., Purcell, S., Stevenson, J., & Plomin, R. (1998). Genetic influence on language delay in two-year-old children. *Nature Neuroscience, 1,* 324–328.

Deater-Deckard, K., & O'Connor, T. G. (2000). Parent–child mutuality in early childhood: Two behavioral genetic studies. *Developmental Psychology, 36,* 561–570.

Deater-Deckard, K., & Petrill, S. A. (2004). Parent–child dyadic mutuality and child behavior problems: Gene–environment processes. *Journal of Child Psychology and Psychiatry, 45,* 1171–1179.

Deater-Deckard, K., Pike, A., Petrill, S. A., Cutting, A., Hughes, C., & O'Connor, T. G. (2001). Nonshared environmental processes in social-emotional development: An observational study of identical twin differences in the preschool period. *Developmental Science, 4,* F1–F6.

Dietz, W. H. (2001). Breastfeeding may help prevent childhood overweight. *Journal of the American Medical Association, 285,* 2506–2507.

Dionne, G., Tremblay, R. E., Boivin, M., Laplante, D., & Perusse, D. (2003). Physical aggression and expressive vocabulary in 19-month-old twins. *Developmental Psychology, 37,* 261–273.

Ebstein, R. P., Benjamin, J., & Belmaker, R. H. (2003). Behavioral genetics, genomics, and personality. In R. Plomin, J. C. DeFries, I. W. Craig, & P. McGuffin (Eds.), *Behavioral genetics in the postgenomic era* (pp. 365–423). Washington, DC: American Psychological Association.

Ebstein, R., Levine, J., Geller, V., Auerbach, J., Gritsenko, I., & Belmaker, R. (1998). Dopamine D4 receptor and serotonin transporter promoter in the determination of neonatal temperament. *Molecular Psychiatry, 3,* 238–246.

Eid, M., Riemann, R., Angleitner, A., & Bornenau, P. (2003). Sociability and positive emotionality: Genetic and environmental contributions to the covariation between different facets of extraversion. *Journal of Personality, 71*, 319–346.

Emde, R. N., & Hewitt, J. K. (2001). *Infancy to early childhood: Genetic and environmental influences on developmental change.* New York: Oxford University Press.

Emde, R. N., Robinson, J. L., Corley, R. P., Nikkari, D., & Zahn-Waxler, C. (2001). Reactions to restraint and anger-related expressions during the second year. In R. N. Emde & J. K. Hewitt (Eds.), *Infancy to early childhood: Genetic and environmental influences on developmental change* (pp. 127–140). New York: Oxford University Press.

Fan, J., Fossella, J., Sommer, T., Wu, Y., & Posner, M. I. (2003). Mapping genetic variation of executive attention onto brain activity. *Proceedings of the National Academy of Sciences, 100*, 7406–7411.

Gershoff, E. T. (2002). Corporal punishment by parents and associated child behaviors and experiences: A meta-analytic and theoretical review. *Psychological Bulletin, 128*, 539–579.

Gjone, H., Stevenson, J., & Sundet, J. M. (1996). Genetic influence on parent-reported attention-related problems in a Norwegian general population twin sample. *Journal of the American Academy of Child and Adolescent Psychiatry, 35*, 588–596.

Goldsmith, H. H., Buss, K. A., & Lemery, K. S. (1997). Toddler and childhood temperament: Expanded content, stronger genetic evidence, new evidence for the importance of environment. *Developmental Psychology, 33*, 891–905.

Goldsmith, H. H., Lemery, K. S., Buss, K. A., & Campos, J. J. (1999). Genetic analyses of focal aspects of infant temperament. *Developmental Psychology, 35*, 972–985.

Kluger, A. N., Siegfried, Z., & Ebstein, R. P. (2002). A meta-analysis of the association between DRD4 polymorphism and novelty seeking. *Molecular Psychiatry, 7*, 712–717.

Lakatos, K., Nemoda, Z., Toth, I., Ronai, Z., Ney, K., Sasvari-Szekely, M., & Gervai, J. (2002). Further evidence for the role of the dopamine D4 receptor (DRD4) gene in attachment disorganization: Interaction of the exon III 48-bp repeat and the −521 C/T promoter polymorphisms. *Molecular Psychiatry, 7*, 27–32.

Lemery, K. S., & Goldsmith, H. H. (2002). Genetic and environmental influences on preschool sibling cooperation and conflict: Associations with difficult temperament and parenting style. *Marriage and Family Review, 33*, 77–99.

Manke, B., Suadino, K. J., & Grant, J. D. (2001). Extremes analyses of observed temperament dimensions. In R. N. Emde & J. K. Hewitt (Eds.), *Infancy to early childhood: Genetic and environmental influences on developmental change* (pp. 52–72). New York: Oxford University Press.

McCartney, K., Harris, M. J., & Bernieri, F. (1990). Growing up and growing apart: A developmental meta-analysis of twin studies. *Psychological Bulletin, 107*, 226–237.

Matheny, A. P. (1983). A longitudinal twin study of stability of components from Bayley's Infant Behavior Record. *Child Development, 54*, 356–360.

Measelle, J. R., Ablow, J. C., Cowan, P. A., & Cowan, C. P. (1998). Assessing young children's views of their academic, social, and emotional lives: An evaluation of the self-perception scales of the Berkeley Puppet Interview. *Child Development, 69*, 1556–1576.

Murray, K. T., & Sines, J. O. (1996). Parsing the genetic and nongenetic variance in children's depressive behavior. *Journal of Affective Disorders, 38*, 23–34.

O'Connor, T. G., Deater-Deckard, K., Fulker, D. W., Rutter, M., & Plomin, R. (1998). Gene–environment correlations in late childhood and early adolescence. *Developmental Psychology, 34*, 970–981.

Ogden, C. L., Flegal, K. M., Carroll, M. D., & Johnson, C. L. (2002). Prevalence and trends in overweight among US children and adolescents. *Journal of the American Medical Association, 288*, 1728–1732.

Oniszczenko, W., Zawadzki, B., Strelau, J., Riemann, R., Angleitner, A., & Spinath, F. M. (2003). Genetic and environmental determinants of temperament: A comparative study based on Polish and German samples. *European Journal of Personality, 17,* 207–220.

Pears, K. C., & Moses, L. J. (2003). Demographics, parenting, and theory of mind in preschool children. *Social Development, 12,* 1–19.

Petrill, S. A., & Deater-Deckard, K. (2004). Task orientation, parental warmth and SES account for a significant proportion of the shared environmental variance in general cognitive ability in early childhood: Evidence from a twin study. *Developmental Science, 7, 25–32.*

Petrill, S. A., Saudino, K., Cherny, S. S., Emde, R. N., Fulker, D. W., Hewitt, J. K., & Plomin, R. (1998). Exploring the genetic and environmental etiology of high general cognitive ability in fourteen- to thirty-six-month-old twins. *Child Development, 69,* 68–74.

Phillips, D., & Matheny, A. P. (1990). Quantitative genetic analysis of longitudinal trends in height: Preliminary results from the Louisville twin study. *Acta Geneticae Medicae et Gemellogiae, 39,* 143–163.

Plomin, R. (1994). *Genetics and experience: The interplay between nature and nurture.* Thousand Oaks, CA: Sage.

Plomin, R., DeFries, J. C., McClearn, G. E., & McGuffin, P. (2001). *Behavioral Genetics* (4th ed.). New York: Worth Publishers.

Plomin, R., Pedersen, N. L., McClearn, G. E., Nesselroade, J. R., & Bergeman, C. S. (1988). EAS temperaments during the last half of the life span: Twins reared apart and twins reared together. *Psychology and Aging, 3,* 43–50.

Plomin, R., & Rutter, M. (1998). Child development, molecular genetics, and what to do with genes once they are found. *Child Development, 69,* 1223–1242.

Price, T. S., Eley, T. C., Dale, P. S., Stevenson, J., Saudino, K., & Plomin, R. (2000). Genetic and environmental covariance between verbal and nonverbal development in infancy. *Child Development, 71,* 948–959.

Prior, M. (1999). Resilience and coping: The role of individual temperament. In E. Frydenberg (Ed.), *Learning to cope: Developing as a person in complex societies* (pp. 33–52). Oxford: Oxford University Press.

Ramey, C. T., & Haskins, R. (1981). The modification of intelligence through early experience. *Intelligence, 5,* 5–19.

Reise, M. (1990). Neonatal temperament in monozygotic and dizygotic twin pairs. *Child Development, 61,* 1230–1237.

Reiss, D., Neiderhiser, J., Hetherington, E. M., & Plomin, R. (2000). *The relationship code: Deciphering genetic and social influences on adolescent development.* Cambridge, MA: Harvard University Press.

Robinson, J. L., Emde, R. N., & Corley, R. P. (2001). Dispositional cheerfulness. In R. N. Emde & J. K. Hewitt (Eds.), *Infancy to early childhood: Genetic and environmental influences on developmental change* (pp. 163–177). New York: Oxford University Press.

Rothbart, M. K., Ahadi, S. A., & Evans, D. E. (2000). Temperament and personality: Origins and outcomes. *Journal of Personality & Social Psychology, 78,* 122–135.

Rothbart, M. K. & Bates, J. E. (1998). Temperament. In N. Eisenberg (Vol. Ed.), *Handbook of child psychology: Vol. 3. Social, emotional, and personality development* (5th ed., pp. 105–176). New York: Wiley.

Rusalov, V. M., & Biryukov, S. D. (1993). Human behavioral flexibility: A psychogenetic study. *Behavior Genetics, 23,* 461–465.

Saudino, K. J., & Cherny, S. S. (2001). Souces of continuity and change in observed temperament. In R. N. Emde & J. K. Hewitt (Eds.), *Infancy to early childhood: Genetic and environmental influences on developmental change* (pp. 89–110). New York: Oxford University Press.

Scarr, S., & McCartney, K. (1983). How people make their own environments: A theory of genotype → environmental effects. *Child Development, 54*, 424–435.

Schmidt, L. A., Fox, N. A., Rubin, K. H., Hu, S., & Hammer, D. H. (2002). Molecular genetics of shyness and aggression in preschoolers. *Personality and Individual Differences, 33*, 227–238.

Schmitz, S. (1994). Personality and temperament. In J. C. DeFries, R. Plomin, & D. W. Fulkner (Eds.), *Nature and nurture during middle childhood* (pp. 120–140). Cambridge, MA: Blackwell Publishers.

Schmitz, S., Fulker, D. W., & Mrazek, D. A. (1995). Problem behavior in early and middle childhood: An initial behavior genetic analysis. *Journal of Child Psychology and Psychiatry, 36*, 1443–1458.

Turkheimer, E., Haley, A., Waldron, M., D'Onofrio, B., & Gottesman, I. I. (2003). Socioeconomic status modifies heritability of IQ in young children. *Psychological Science, 14*, 623–627.

Turkheimer, E., & Waldron, M. (2000). Nonshared environment: A theoretical,methodological, and quantitative review. *Psychological Bulletin, 126*, 78–108.

van den Oord, E. J. C. G., Verhulst, F. C., & Boomsma, D. I. (1996). A genetic study of maternal and paternal ratings of problem behaviors in 3-year-old twins. *Journal of Abnormal Psychology, 105*, 349–357.

van der Valk, J. C., van den Oord, E. J. C. G., Verhulst, F. C., & Boomsma, D. I. (2001). Using parental ratings to study the etiology of 3-year-old twins' problem behaviors: Different views or rater bias? *Journal of Child Psychology and Psychiatry, 42*, 921–931.

van der Valk, J. C., Verhulst, F. C., Stroet, T. M., & Boomsma, D. I. (1998). Quantitative genetic analysis of internalising and externalising problems in a large sample of 3-year-old twins. *Twin Research, 1*, 25–33.

Wilson, R. S. (1983). The Lousiville Twin Study: Developmental synchronies in behavior. *Child Development, 54*, 298–316.

Young, S., Schmitz, S., Corley, R. P., & Fulker, D. W. (2001). Language and cognition. In R. N. Emde & J. K. Hewitt (Eds.), *Infancy to early childhood: Genetic and environmental influences on developmental change* (pp. 221–240). New York: Oxford University Press.

Zahn-Waxler, C., Schmitz, S., Fulker, D., Robinson, J., & Emde, R. (1996). Behavior problems in 5-year-old monozygotic and dizygotic twins: Genetic and environmental influences, patterns of regulation, and internalization of control. *Development and Psychopathology, 8*, 103–122.

2

Vulnerability and Resilience in Early Child Development

Ann S. Masten and Abigail H. Gewirtz

Over the past four decades, the study of vulnerability and resilience has played a central role in the emergence of developmental psychopathology as an integrative framework for understanding pathways to positive and negative adaptation. Though distinct in meaning and history, the concepts of vulnerability and resilience both stem from observed differences in how well individuals adapt to the challenges posed by life, either in normative or in extraordinary situations. *Vulnerability* generally refers to the predisposition or susceptibility of some people to specific diseases or maladaptive development in the face of negative experiences. This concept originated in the idea of vulnerability to injury in battle, from the Latin verb *vulnerare* (to wound). *Resilience*[1] generally refers to positive adaptation that has been manifested in the face of negative experiences. This concept has origins in the idea of physical materials that withstand stress without breaking or cracking and also in the idea of springing back or recovery, stemming from the Latin verb *resilire* (to recoil or leap back).

Scientific interest in vulnerability and resilience emerged in the twentieth century from the search for causes of mental illness and developmental problems (Luthar, 2003; Masten, Best, & Garmezy, 1990; Masten & Garmezy, 1985). Once it became clear that mental disorders aggregated in families with patterns suggesting genetic influences, diathesis-stressor models of mental illness soon followed (see Gottesman & Shields, 1972, 1982). In these models, individuals inherited a susceptibility to a particular disorder, which was then potentiated by adverse experiences, eventually leading to the full manifestation of disorder such as schizophrenia. Around the same time, developmental scientists were observing that some infants and children appeared to be more sensitive or reactive to negative experiences. In their classic work on early personality development, beginning in the 1930s, Murphy and Moriarty (1976), for example, studied individual differences in infants and young children in response to stressful experiences, contrasting *primary vulnerabilities*, evident very early in development and present from birth, with *secondary vulnerabilities*, acquired through experiences after birth. There was great interest among investigators of this time in the possibility of differences in temperament that rendered some infants more vulnerable to stressful rearing environments, as articulated by Chess and Thomas, among others (Seifer, 2000; Thomas, Chess, & Birch, 1968).

The intensive search for etiologies of mental disorders in the twentieth century led to extensive research on *risk factors*, the measurable predictors of bad outcomes of concern or interest to individuals, families, and communities (Kopp, 1983; Masten, Morison, Pellegrini, & Tellegen, 1990). Groups of children "at risk" for specific problems (because they had one or more established risk factors for that problem) were eventually studied prospectively over time in an effort to figure out the causes of poor and good developmental outcomes. These studies typically revealed wide variations in outcome for most risk factors, ranging from premature birth to poverty, and also the tendency for risk factors to accumulate in the lives of children, so that the effects of any one factor were difficult to discern (Garmezy & Masten, 1994; Masten et al., 1990; Rutter, 1979; Sameroff, 2000; Sigman & Parmelee, 1979). The search became even more complex as developmental system theorists argued persuasively that the influences of risk factors were probably synergistic and transactional, resulting from joint influences and bi-directional effects of child and context interacting over time (e.g., Sameroff & Chandler, 1975).

It was not long before several key risk investigators who studied children noticed that there were significant numbers of children in various risk studies who appeared to be developing well, despite their high-risk status. These investigators recognized the potential significance of positive development in a context of risk, and began to draw attention to these phenomena that would eventually be given the umbrella term *resilience* (Anthony, 1974; Garmezy, 1971; Garmezy & Rutter, 1983; Murphy & Moriarty, 1976; Rutter, 1979; Werner & Smith, 1982). The insight of these pioneers was twofold, first in noticing the striking variability in the development of children at risk for various reasons, and second in recognizing that elucidation of protective processes in naturally occurring resilience might inform intervention efforts to prevent problems or alter the life course in more favorable directions.

Extensive research over the last quarter-century has provided many clues about the processes of risk, vulnerability, and resilience, as evident in diverse chapters of this handbook. This conceptual chapter focuses on a framework for integrating, applying, and advancing contemporary research on risk, vulnerability, and resilience in early child development. The first section provides a working vocabulary for discussing vulnerability and resilience, setting the stage for the subsequent section on models of continuity and change in adaptive success. The concluding section highlights implications of such models for research and applications designed to improve positive development.

The Challenge of Defining Vulnerability and Resilience

Research on vulnerability and resilience requires working definitions of multiple constructs linked to the phenomena encompassed by these terms, including the following:

risk and risk factors; adversity, stressors, coping, and stress; assets, promotive and protective factors; and competence in developmental tasks. In-depth discussion of these concepts is beyond the scope of this chapter, but we will address the most fundamental ideas and controversies concerning these terms as a guide to this extensive domain of research. A concise glossary defining these terms is provided in Table 2.1.

Developmental studies of vulnerability and resilience are concerned with variations in how people adapt and function in their lives, and what might account for unexpectedly poor or good adaptation in development. Implicitly, these constructs require judgments about healthy and unhealthy development and also about threats to positive development.

Table 2.1 Concise glossary of concepts related to vulnerability and resilience in development

Vulnerability	Susceptibility to a specified negative outcome in the context of risk or adversity
Risk	Elevated probability of a negative or undesirable outcome in the future
Risk factors	Measurable attributes of people, their relationships, or contexts associated with risk
Stressor	An experience or event expected or observed to have significant negative or disruptive effects on the adaptation of individuals or other systems (families, organizations)
Adversity	Lasting or repeated experiences expected or observed to have significant negative effects or disruptive effects on adaptation; multiple stressors usually involved
Stress	The state of disturbance in adaptation within an organism (or system) resulting from a stressor, often characterized by disequilibrium in functioning and efforts to restore adaptive functioning
Coping	Efforts to adapt to stress or other disturbances created by a stressor or adversity
Developmental tasks	Standards of performance or achievement in various domains of adaptation expected by a particular society or social group for individuals during different periods of development, and that vary by culture, gender, period in history, and situation
Resilience	Positive patterns of adaptation in the context of risk or adversity
Assets or promotive factors	Measurable attributes of people, their relationships, or contexts generally associated with positive outcomes or development (regardless of adversity or risk level)
Protective factors	Measurable attributes of individuals, their relationships, or contexts particularly associated with positive outcomes or development in the context of risk or adversity

Vulnerability: the potential for negative adaptation

Vulnerability is a probabilistic and conditional concept. It is conditional because one has vulnerability with respect to a specific outcome of concern (e.g., autism, schizophrenia) or to maladaptation generally defined, and with respect to a challenge of some kind that threatens adaptation or development, which also may be specific in nature (e.g., a traumatic event, divorce, death of parent) or generally adverse (e.g., growing up in poverty). It is probabilistic because it refers to the potential for adaptive difficulties in the future. It is possible to be vulnerable to a disorder or problem and never manifest any difficulties in development because the provoking agent or environmental hazard never occurs. A classic exemplar of biological vulnerability in mental health is provided by phenylketonuria (PKU), a disease caused by a recessive gene defect that interferes with the breakdown of an essential amino acid. Exposure to phenylalanine in the diet typically leads to mental retardation and other problems for those with this genetic vulnerability, which can be prevented by early diagnosis (the PKU blood test administered to newborns) followed by controlling phenylalanine in the diet. Thus, although PKU cannot (yet) be prevented by altering the genotype, the negative consequences of this genetic disorder can be prevented by environmental intervention.

Though some forms of vulnerability are genetically based, others may arise over the course of development, from experiences that create susceptibility to future hazards. This possibility is illustrated by studies of early deprivation or trauma suggesting altered reactivity of stress-response systems in young humans and other mammals, discussed further in the next section on models. The landmark volume published by the National Research Council, *Neurons to Neighborhoods: The Science of Early Child Development* (Shonkoff & Phillips, 2000), documented the importance of early experience in shaping vulnerabilities in individual children.

Developmental perspectives on vulnerability

Vulnerability may also change as a function of development. General periods of elevated vulnerability have been noted during particular periods of the lifespan; there could be a peak in susceptibility for some problem or hazard during a given window of development (Shonkoff & Marshall, 2000). Infant brains, for example, are more vulnerable to damage from shaking than adult brains. Infants who have already formed an attachment to a specific caregiver are more vulnerable to separation distress than younger infants who have not formed such a bond. Developmental "growth spurts" may create risks and vulnerabilities until necessary supports and protections catch up with new capabilities. New motor achievements in rolling, crawling, and walking in early motor development can temporarily increase risks for accidents and vulnerabilities to injuries until the establishment of basic protections provided by self-control and regulatory skills and learning from experience. Similarly, cognitive gains in memory may increase fears about separation, visiting health clinics, and other ordinary life experiences in early childhood until various strategies for coping with these situations catch up. Developmental transitions triggered by changes in the organism (e.g., puberty), context (e.g., school entry), or the nature of interaction of organism with context (e.g., learning to walk) may pose problems if there are inadequate normative supports required to make successful transitions in these situations. Caregivers adapt their monitoring to the fluctuating risks and vulnerabilities posed by such changes over the course of development, striking a balance between protection and the fostering of learning by experience.

Given that young children are more dependent than older individuals for their care, they can be viewed as generally more vulnerable than older children and adults to experiences beyond their control. It could be argued that an infant is not a self-regulating system to the same degree as an adult, or even an older child, but is part of a caregiver–infant system that serves to regulate and protect the infant. Bowlby (1969) eloquently captured this idea in his powerful book on attachment as an adaptive system shaped by evolution:

> In man's environment of evolutionary adaptedness it is clearly vital that the mother of a child under three or four years should know exactly where he is and what he is doing, and be ready to intervene should danger threaten; for him to keep advertising his whereabouts and activities to her and to continue doing so until she signals "message received" is therefore adaptive. (p. 247)

From this perspective, an infant's vulnerability could be conceptualized in terms of the vulnerability of the caregiver–infant system to perturbations and might depend to a large extent on the caregiver's adaptive capacity in the caregiving role.

Thus, for the infant who has not yet developed the ability to self-regulate, regulation is located in the caregiver–infant system; its is dyadic. It was in reference to this idea that Winnicott (1965) made the claim: "There is no such thing as an infant" (p. 39). According to attachment theory, the caregiver is a source of responsive, predictable, and comforting emotion regulation. When an attachment relationship is working well ("secure attachment"), the infant experiences relatively short periods of distress before being comforted, stimulation is appropriate to the infant's capacity to manage it, and the infant and caregiver develop a pattern of flexible physiological and emotional communication (Sroufe, 1996). These experiences of dyadic regulation provide the scaffolding for the child's development of internal self-regulation (Sroufe, 1996).

Conversely, unresponsive, frightening, and/or chaotic caregiving are associated with distorted dyadic regulatory processes that leave an infant vulnerable to harm from even ordinary stressors encountered in daily life, with limited capacity for regulating arousal and distress. Attachment theorists propose that this kind of vulnerability results in a prototype of dysregulation, as the vulnerability initially located within the dyadic relationship gradually manifests as a vulnerability of the child via the child's adoption of disturbed patterns of dyadic regulation in his/her own responses to the environment and stress (e.g., Sroufe, Carlson, Levy, & Egeland, 1999).

Recent studies of brain plasticity in relation to early social experiences also suggest that vulnerabilities in the developing child's capacity to respond adaptively to stress may be shaped by early experiences (Shonkoff & Phillips, 2000), as discussed further later in this chapter and also in other chapters in this volume. There is compelling convergence across levels of analysis implicating the role of the caregiving relationship as key to both vulnerability and protection in early development.

Resilience: positive adaptation in the context of risk or adversity

The concept of resilience is conditional, like the concept of vulnerability, but it is not probabilistic because it is judged on the basis of adaptive behavior that has already occurred. The identification of resilience requires two fundamental judgments, one about exposure to adversity and the other about how well an individual is doing in life. If there has been no unusual exposure to hazards, threats, or adversities of any kind, and the developmental outcome is poor, then it is logical to assume that something about the organism is abnormal. On the other hand, under benign rearing conditions, we would not infer resilience from observed good outcomes. Inferences that a person shows resilience require two kinds of evidence: (a) that a significant threat to development or adaptation has occurred and (b) that the organism is doing well despite this threat. Thus, while a person can be deemed vulnerable without encountering adversity (in which case a good outcome is expected), a person cannot be considered resilient without overcoming adversity. Therefore, studies of resilience require a focus on the criteria by which "doing OK" in life will be judged as well as assessments of the circumstances past or present that pose a significant threat to healthy development.

Symptoms and developmental tasks: criteria for judging adaptation

Psychopathology and *success in age-salient developmental tasks* are two popular categories for evaluating how well a child's life is going. These terms reflect judgments about poor and good adjustment or adaptation in relation to norms for behavior expected in a given society at a given time and history for particular groups of children (Masten & Curtis, 2000). Some studies of resilience have focused on the absence of symptoms of psychopathology while others have focused on positive behaviors. Some studies focus on how a child is doing (external adaptation) and others focus on how a child is feeling (internal adaptation), and still others require good functioning in both respects.

There has been considerable debate over the years about the best criteria for defining resilience, without a full resolution (Luthar, Cicchetti, & Becker, 2000; Masten, 1999). Nonetheless, many developmental investigators have focused on how well children are doing in meeting the expectations of society for children of their age, acknowledging that these expectations vary in different cultures, periods of history, and situations. These general expectations often have been called *developmental tasks*, following the terminology of Robert Havighurst (see Masten & Coatsworth, 1995). Some of these tasks appear to be universal, in the sense that they are expected for children in every society (e.g., learning language), while others are expected only for children in particular cultures and times (e.g., learning to hunt buffalo) or only for some children in a culture (e.g., only boys are expected to hunt buffalo). Examples of widely acknowledged developmental tasks of early childhood include: attachment to one or more specific adults; learning to sit, stand, walk, run, and jump; acquiring a language; obedience to simple commands and instructions of parents and teachers; toilet training; self-control of proscribed physical aggression (e.g., not biting people); and appropriate play with toys and other children. Whether the life of a child is on track developmentally can be evaluated according to how well a child is meeting expectations for engaging and mastering such developmental tasks as he or she grows up.

Risks and stressors: criteria for judging threats

Threats to child development have been described in a number of ways as well, including risk factors, cumulative risk, adversity, stressors, and stress. *Risk* is the broadest term, referring generally to any predictor of an undesirable outcome, and a term with historical roots in the insurance industry and actuarial prediction, as well as in public health (Masten & Garmezy, 1985). In recent years, however, risk terminology has been sharpened by Helena Kraemer and her colleagues in an incisive series of papers on the definition and statistical modeling of risk (Kraemer et al., 1997; Kraemer, Stice, Kazdin, Offord, & Kupfer, 2001; Kraemer, Wilson, Fairburn, & Agras, 2002). For example, Kraemer and colleagues (1997) have argued persuasively that correlates and risk factors need to be differentiated by the clear antecedent nature of a risk factor. If it cannot be established empirically that a potential risk factor predates the negative outcome of interest, then it is termed a correlate, concomitant, or consequence, rather than a risk factor. Kraemer et al. also suggested clear criteria for causal risk factors, where there is evidence that manipulating the factor changes the outcome. (Note that for the purposes of this chapter, the term *risk* will be used in the broader, historical sense of an established predictor of a future undesirable outcome, without requiring evidence of the absolute antecedence of risk factor to outcome, because temporal antecedence is quite difficult to determine in much of the research on complex behavior in development.)

Cumulative risk refers to the now common observation that risk factors tend to co-occur and aggregate in the lives of children and that child functioning tends to decline as a function of increasing risk, no matter what the exact nature of the individual risk factors may be (Masten et al., 1990; Sameroff, Seifer, & Bartko, 1997). Major risk factors such as poverty often implicate a high level of cumulative risk when possible risk factors associated with poverty, such as low maternal education, father absence, poor health care, environmental hazards, and other possible risk factors, are considered. Risk gradients are readily constructed by counting well-established risk factors in the lives of individuals and plotting risk level against a wide variety of indicators of healthy development across the lifespan, ranging from educational attainment to life expectancy. These gradients typically show a rising slope relating risk to problems. For example, academic achievement in the early school years is strongly related to preschool cumulative risk indices, and this achievement gap widens over time (e.g., Gutman, Sameroff, & Cole, 2003).

Many examples of risk gradients can be found in the developmental literature (Hart & Risley, 1995; Keating & Hertzman, 1999; Sameroff et al., 1997). Moreover, many of the same risk factors contribute to risk gradients predicting different problems and disorders, leading influential champions of child development to argue that comprehensive interventions are needed to reduce cumulative risks in the lives of children (Cicchetti, Rappaport, Sandler, & Weissberg, 2000; Coie et al., 1993; Cowen, 2000; Ramey & Ramey, 1998; Weissberg, Kumpfer, & Seligman, 2003).

Stressors are a subset of risk factors, referring to events or experiences that usually have negative effects in the lives of people. Stressors include minor and everyday experiences, such as getting stuck in traffic or mean remarks of peers, as well as traumatic and uncommon experiences, such as earthquakes or the murder of a parent. Many kinds of stressors have been studied in early childhood, including deprivations associated with maternal loss or orphanage life, divorce, maltreatment, and domestic or neighborhood violence. As in the case of risk factors more broadly defined, negative life events frequently pile up in the lives of children and measures often tally multiple events to create cumulative adversity scores.

Stressors can be distinguished by whether they are acute or chronic, arising within the family, school, community, or another context, and also by the degree to which they are influenced by the child's own behavior (Gest, Reed, & Masten, 1999; Grant et al., 2003; Masten, Neemann, & Andenas, 1994). Among older children, exposure to stressors can be increased or avoided by actions of the child. This is not so much the case among younger children, who have less free agency in their lives. Nonetheless, some negative events, such as falls or choking, can result from a child's own behavior.

In a living system, *stress* refers to a state of disequilibrium or disturbance resulting from a challenging experience or stressor that exceeds the capacity of the system to maintain good functioning. This term has been used to refer to physical states as well as psychological states of imbalance (see Gunnar, this volume). Attempts (automatic or deliberate) to restore good functioning in response to such disturbances are described variously as coping, adjusting, adapting, assimilation and accommodation, defending, and so on. Young humans have a repertoire of tools for coping with stress at many levels, but perhaps the most developmentally distinctive is their aptitude for signaling and eliciting help from adults, most notably caregivers, ranging from the piercing screams of a young infant that summon even strange adults for help to a distressed toddler running into the comfort of a parent's arms.

The specific attachment relationship that forms between human infants and caregivers is a powerful adaptive tool for stress regulation that functions to modulate stress in the child in changing ways over the course of development. Fear and perceived threats (perceived by the child or the caregiver) can activate this system, leading to proximity seeking, contact, and other attachment behaviors observed in young children under stress by Bowlby (1969). Such clinical observations led Bowlby to formulate his profoundly influential evolutionary theory of attachment. Young children also use information provided by caregivers to interpret the safety of situations, a form of social referencing (Hornik & Gunnar, 1988). Reciprocal emotional availability is critical for social referencing, particularly in infants from 9–18 months. The 'visual cliff' experiments provide a classic example of such phenomena, wherein the infant's behavior in this context depends on the caregiver's facial cues (Hornik & Gunnar, 1988; Sorce, Emde, Campos, & Klinnert, 1985). Such phenomena reflect the operation of a powerful protective system for human development, features of which have been observed in other social species as well, most notably primates (Suomi, 2000; see also Gunnar, this volume).

Assets and protective factors

The search for causes of better and worse outcomes in development also has resulted in the identification of many correlates of adaptation in young children. Positive correlates and predictors of desirable outcomes are often termed *assets, promotive factors*, or *resources*, in contrast to risks, adversities, or stressors, which indicate the presence of negative correlates or predictors. In the context of risks and stressors, it is assumed that such advantages may counteract or counterbalance the effects of negative conditions or experiences. For example, it is an asset to have good problem-solving skills or a good memory or a loving parent under all kinds of conditions, including dangerous ones.

In contrast, *protective factors* have a specific or greater effect under risky or hazardous conditions than they do under more benign circumstances. An infant car seat always offers the safety provided by confining a child to the seat during a car ride, but it is specially designed to protect an infant from devastating injuries during an accident. The classic protective factor for childhood diseases is vaccination, which has inspired the concept of "stress inoculation" – the idea that there might be some way to psychologically prepare children for stressful or traumatic experiences. To date, such preparation has been pursued most extensively in preparing children for highly specific situations, such as surgery, tornadoes, fires, and terrorism (e.g., the Red Cross Masters of Disaster curriculum for disaster preparedness in schools). Experimental data testing the effectiveness of such preparation with regard to disasters and terrorism are understandably scarce, and further research is needed in this area (Feerick & Prinz, 2003), though there is some evidence supporting programs designed for hospital procedures and for schools (e.g., Blount, Smith, & Frank, 1999; Dubow, Schmidt, McBride, Edwards, & Merk, 1993; Whelan & Kirkby, 1998).

Moderators of risk or adversity

Vulnerability and protective factors have in common the property of *moderating* risk or its impact on the organism. Vulnerabilities enhance or exacerbate the effects of adversities, whereas protective factors ameliorate or reduce the negative consequences of adversities. A special kind of protective effect occurs when the adversity or stressor itself is prevented. Providing crossing guards for kindergartners walking to school undoubtedly has lowered the risk of accidental deaths and injuries from children being hit by motor vehicles. Similarly, laws banning young children from riding on tractors and other large farm equipment can be enacted to reduce the level of risk for accidental injuries to children living on farms.

Much of the research on vulnerability and resilience in early childhood has been directed at identifying the moderators of risk in the hope of uncovering how to prevent or ameliorate the effects of risk and adversities on child development. Defining and operationalizing the assessment of risks, assets, vulnerability, and protective factors was an essential step, but models linking the ingredients together were also important. Initially such models tend to be descriptive and speculative, but eventually, the goal is causal models of processes that explain vulnerability and resilience and set the stage for interventions or policy changes that promote healthier development.

Models of Vulnerability and Resilience

Models of vulnerability and resilience move beyond theoretical or operational definition of *what* matters (key ingredients) for understanding adaptation in development to describing, hypothesizing, and testing *how* individual differences in adaptation come about and unfold over time in development (causal processes underlying connections observed among the key ingredients). Not only do such models of vulnerability and resilience represent causal theories and strategies of analysis, they also provide a framework for conceptualizing prevention and intervention. An illustrative sampling of such models follows.

Diathesis-stressor models

The diathesis-stressor models as a group describe individuals who have a predisposition of some kind that creates a vulnerability or liability for developing one or more problems or disorders when challenged by stressful life experiences. Diathesis-stressor models require statistical strategies suited to detecting conditional or interaction effects, because it is posited in these models that outcomes are worse in the context of a given experience when the vulnerability is also present. Historically, the most influential diathesis-stressor models in behavioral development were formulated by behavioral genetics researchers to explain the role of genes and experience in the etiology of mental disorders, most particularly schizophrenia, as noted earlier (Gottesman & Shields, 1972, 1982; Scarr & Kidd, 1983). In such models, a genetic liability to disorder was inherited (usually a polygenic liability) but the eventual expression of that liability in the phenotype (as a disorder) depended on negative life experiences (the stressors). In these models, vulnerability changed over the course of development as a result of assumed interactions of genes and context, with "net liability" rising and falling as a result of ongoing gene expressions and interactions, and of many levels of interaction within the organism and between the phenotype and environment.

There was a surge of research in the 1960s and 1970s attempting to identify biological markers of vulnerability for particular mental disorders; results were not encouraging, probably because the research questions had jumped far ahead of the basic science and methodology needed in molecular genetics, neurosciences, brain imaging, gene mapping, and so forth, to identify and test vulnerability markers (Garmezy, 1984; Masten

& Garmezy, 1985; Watt, Anthony, Wynne, & Rolf, 1984). The explosion of scientific knowledge and methodology on the human genome and brain development at the end of the twentieth and beginning of the twenty-first centuries has set the stage for a resurgence in attempts to study gene-related vulnerability in development. The paper published recently in *Science* by Caspi et al. (2002) may well be the harbinger of this resurgence. These investigators tested a diathesis-stressor model of genetic vulnerability in which the monoamine oxidase A (MAOA) gene appeared to moderate the development of antisocial behavior among children exposed to serious maltreatment, such that maltreated children with a genotype producing high levels of MAOA expression were less likely to develop antisocial problems than children with a genotype producing low levels of MAOA.

Another variation on the diathesis-stressor model is the idea that biological vulnerability to stressors may actually be *created* by early experiences, even in an initially normal organism. The basic idea in these models is that during periods of development when adaptive systems in the organism are emerging and organizing, bad experiences (as a result of trauma, neglect, abuse, etc.) can become instantiated in the biology of the organism, by influencing the way stress systems are set up or sensitized (see Gunnar, this volume; Gunnar & Donzella, 2002; Zeanah, Smyke, & Settles, this volume). Thus, it is conceivable that lifelong vulnerability can result from negative early experiences. This idea is not new – Sameroff and Chandler (1975) described the "caretaking casualties" that arise from bad rearing environments in their classic transactional model of development, while Murphy and Moriarty (1976) observed the acquisition of "secondary vulnerabilities." However, contemporary models specify the processes by which experience becomes biologically embedded in the organism as a lasting vulnerability to stress.

An illustration of vulnerability resulting from adaptations of the developing brain is provided by recent studies of deprivation or trauma in young children suggesting that early experiences may alter reactivity of stress-response systems, in particular, the limbic-hypothalamic-pituitary-adrenocortical (L-HPA) system regulating glucocorticoid activity. Secure attachment relationships appear to moderate this system in the very young, such that cortisol elevations in response to stress are inhibited in the presence of the caregiver (Gunnar, this volume). However, when caregiver support is inadequate, young children's stress-response systems are highly vulnerable to cortisol elevations. For example, during periods of active abuse, young children show higher cortisol levels suggestive of a hyper-responsive L-HPA system, which may return to average levels when the abuse ceases. Early adversity which manifests in severe distortions of the caregiving relationship (e.g., maltreatment or orphanage placement) may also produce long-term changes in activity of the child's L-HPA system (DeBellis et al., 1999; Gunnar, Bruce, & Hickman, 2001), sensitizing the system to later stress.

Compensatory and protective factor models

Diathesis-stressor models tend to focus on vulnerability, the negative consequences of stress, and disease outcomes, although early models included the possibility of positive influences that lowered "net liability" (Masten & Garmezy, 1985). Early resilience researchers, such as Lois Murphy, Norman Garmezy, Michael Rutter, and Emmy Werner, emphasized the positive ingredients, processes, and outcomes in models of adaptation to stress (Masten, 1989; Masten & Powell, 2003). Models with compensatory or promotive factors include positive effects of variables not typically included in diathesis-stressor models. Compensatory models attempt to allow for the possibility that the presence of "good" influences (provided by assets or resources in a person's life) could counterbalance the "bad" influences of negative factors (including stressful experiences). Interventions designed to eliminate or reduce risks and stressors, as well as interventions to add or boost the effects of assets, are explicitly or implicitly based on this kind of basic additive model of adaptation in development.

It is conceivable that young children with better parents, nutrition, health insurance, preschools, neighborhood services, or other assets do better in life, no matter what adversity comes their way, than do those who have less going for them. It is also the case, however, that children who contend with less risk or adversity in the form of poverty, danger, toxins, maltreatment, war, and so on, are more likely to develop well compared to children whose lives are burdened with many such risks. Werner (2000), among other resilience investigators, has pointed out that children growing up with many risk factors can do well if there is a favorable balance of positive factors to offset the risks. In living organisms, she reminds us, this balance is continually shifting over the course of life and development.

Models with protective factors focus on the possibility that there are moderators of stress or risk with the potential to affect outcomes in a *positive* way. *Moderator models* of positive effects include those triggered into action by the threat (e.g., antibodies, airbags, and child-protection systems) and those that always are operating but that in the presence of specific challenges or general stress serve to ameliorate the effects of the challenge on the person's functioning (e.g., an easy-going personality, an optimistic outlook on life). In either case, the effect is viewed as protective when the result is a reduction in the impact of the stressor or risk factor on the child's life. Clearly, a moderator could be protective at the positive end (calm disposition) and exacerbate stress at the negative end (stress-reactive disposition). It is also conceivable that the same attribute could function as a protective factor for one kind of risk or outcome and a vulnerability factor for a different situation or outcome. Extremely inhibited children, for example, could be vulnerable to fear or anxiety in new situations but protected from the hazards of risk-taking behaviors (Masten & Coatsworth, 1998).

Within the moderator model, interventions can be conceptualized with the aim of activating available moderators, putting new moderators into place, or moderating the moderators. Installing a new 911 emergency system or crisis nursery program in a community would be an example of attempting to add protective services with the intent of ameliorating dangers to children before or as they occur. School programs to teach children what to do in the event of terrorist attacks, fires, or tornadoes are analogous to inoculations that boost antibodies to ward off disease in the event of an infection. These kinds of interventions seek to provide threat-activated protective systems. Interventions to reduce the stress-reactivity of an individual so that the response to current or future adversity is reduced are targeting a presumed vulnerability to stress and trying to alter the vulnerability, which is a different strategy. Still other interventions might be designed to boost general adaptability by, for example, improving skills for accessing information whenever needed or self-regulation skills to control arousal. Adding a mentor or good foster parent to the life of a high-risk child who has little social capital can be conceptualized in this model as adding a general protective system that promotes positive development and also may serve to buffer the child in the event of adverse experiences.

The possibility that the impact of adversity on children is mediated by parents or by the cognitive appraisals of individual children – mediator models of adversity – has led to another resilience model, in which the aim is to protect or moderate the mediator. Interventions can be aimed at shoring up or altering the processes of mediation to reduce the impact of adversity on the child. Interventions to protect or help parents handle stress or to help children reframe stressful situations through cognitive therapy would be examples of interventions aiming to moderate the mediator. In these cases of deliberate intervention at the mediator level, the intervention itself is the protective factor. Naturally occurring analogs would be the efforts made by friends, family, and neighbors who spontaneously take action to help parents undergoing stress in carrying out their parenting responsibilities. It is probably common for family and friends to intervene in this manner to protect children from the impact of adversity on parents.

Adaptive pathways and dynamic developmental models of resilience

Still missing in most models of assets and risks, vulnerability and protection processes, including those described above, is a dynamic portrait of individual lives through time, of the organism continuously interacting with his or her context, shaping and being shaped by experience. The problem, of course, lies in the complexity of development in a living system (Ford & Lerner, 1992; Thelen & Smith, 1998). Some attempts have been made to capture the patterns of adaptation in the lives of individuals over time, both in case accounts of vulnerability and resilience (Masten & O'Conner, 1989) and in abstract diagrams of developmental pathways toward and away from positive adaptation and psychopathology (Masten & Reed, 2002; Sroufe, 1997). Recent methodological advances in statistical strategies for modeling individual growth and change provide exciting new tools for addressing questions about natural maladaptation and resilience, as well as new tools for experimental intervention studies. However, the potential of these powerful new statistics for developmental research on resilience remains a promissory note at this time.

A Resilience Framework for Promoting Positive Development in Early Childhood

Research on risk, vulnerability, and resilience and the models and data associated with this work has led to a revolution in thinking about the nature, purpose, and scope of efforts to address risk and vulnerability, providing a framework for prevention and intervention (Cicchetti et al., 2000; Coie et al., 1993; Cowen, 2000; Luthar & Cicchetti, 2000; Masten & Garmezy, 1985; Masten & Powell, 2003; Sandler, Wolchik, Davis,

Haine, & Ayers, 2003; Weissberg et al., 2003; Wyman, 2003; Wyman, Sandler, Wolchik, & Nelson, 2000; Yates & Masten, 2004). The emerging framework is influencing the mission, models, measures, and methods of those who seek to promote positive development, prevent psychopathology, and redirect the course of development in more positive directions among children at risk for many different reasons and for many different problems (Masten, 2001; Masten & Powell, 2003).

The shift is profound, and we can highlight only a few features of the change here. However, the transformation is evident in many chapters of this handbook. Most fundamentally, perhaps, intervention models have moved away from deficit- or disease-based approaches to strength-based, competence-focused, and/or empowerment models. As this shift occurs, the goals of intervention are conceptualized in more positive terms (e.g., promoting positive development), positive as well as negative predictors and outcomes are measured, and methods of intervention are broadened to target assets, protective factors, health, and competence along with risks, vulnerabilities, and problems (Masten & Powell, 2003).

From a resilience framework perspective, interventions must not only be conceptualized in terms of both positive and negative outcomes, but they must also be developmentally and ecologically valid, taking into account the multiple, interrelated, bi-directional influences on a child and family over time. As noted earlier, it is increasingly recognized that, particularly for young children facing cumulative and/or chronic risks, interventions need to be multi-level, individually tailored in intensity, targeting multiple domains of competence, and of sufficient length to promote lasting change (Farran, 2000; Shonkoff & Meisels, 2000; Shonkoff & Phillips, 2000). These interventions may aim to reduce risk, alter vulnerability, and promote resilience by adding assets, reducing risk in a child's life, or by changing the moderators of risk (such as social competence, self-regulation, attachment, etc.) to enhance protections for children. Many interventions, particularly comprehensive models that target multiple domains of development, utilize two or more of the above strategies. For example, an intervention to boost assets may also enhance protection if the intervention alters parenting processes that mediate risk effects on children's functioning.

Asset-focused intervention strategies

There are many examples of interventions designed to boost assets in the lives of young children as a method for counterbalancing risks that are already present or expected to affect the child. Such interventions are wide-ranging in focus and level of intervention, from the individual or family to the community. Examples include: well-baby clinics; nutrition programs for pregnant mothers and young children; home visiting nurses for families with new babies; family education and school-readiness programs; nursery schools and quality day care; child health insurance; and neighborhood revitalization with new schools, playgrounds, libraries, or farmers' markets. Library and bookstore story time and reading incentive programs for parents and children encourage the development of cognitive and pre-reading skills in children directly and also build parenting assets by supporting parents in reading to their children. WIC (Women, Infant, Children nutritional program) and Head Start are among the best-known examples of large-scale efforts in the

United States implemented in recent decades to increase resources for low-income children with the goal of improving developmental outcomes. Many such efforts have been reviewed recently by Shonkoff and colleagues (Shonkoff & Phillips, 2000; Shonkoff & Meisels, 2000; Farran, 2000), and additional examples can be found in other chapters of this volume.

There are also examples of efforts to boost the effectiveness of a key asset or potential asset in the life of a young child, such as the caregiver, by improving the functioning of the asset in some way. Early childhood family education programs often aim to improve parenting as a means to healthier child development in a community. Programs for new parents, such as childbirth preparation, baby care classes, and general parenting education, increase resources for children via their influence on parents' caregiving skills and resources. In early development, risk factors and stressors often have their greatest effect on children indirectly – they are mediated by effects on key resources, especially caregivers. When the effects of risks (e.g., poverty) are largely mediated by their influence on child assets (e.g., quality of parenting and schooling), it becomes particularly crucial to consider intervening in this way. The "Triple P" parenting program, which originated in Australia, provides an example of an empirically validated, multi-level, national prevention effort, aimed at preventing child maltreatment and child problems, with a particular focus on parenting practices (Bor, Sanders, & Markie-Dadds, 2002; Sanders, Turner, & Markie-Dadds, 2002). Triple P interventions are calibrated to the needs of individual families, with components ranging from nationally televised universal parenting education programs to more targeted intensive small-group interventions for families and individual parenting interventions.

Risk-focused intervention strategies

It is important to remember that some of the most effective interventions for young children have targeted risk, in an effort to lower risk rates or eliminate risk factors altogether. Risk-focused interventions also come in many forms directed at many levels. Examples include: removal of landmines, lead, or asbestos from child environments; recommendations for infants to sleep on their backs; programs to reduce smoking and drinking in pregnant women; firearm regulations; metal detectors in schools; education about shaken baby syndrome; and prenatal care and nutrition programs to reduce premature births, low birth weight, and birth defects. Some risk-focused intervention strategies lower risk for both child and parent. Efforts to treat postpartum depression function to improve the parenting experienced by the infant at the same time as they reduce the risk of suicide or functional difficulties for the mother.

Protection-focused intervention strategies

Interventions also can be designed to add a moderator into a child's life or to moderate the moderator (e.g., improve the effectiveness of a positive moderator or reduce vulnerability). Examples of protection-focused interventions include the following: infant car seats; crossing guards; crisis nurseries; respite care; foster care; domestic violence shelters; 911 telephone services and safety planning for children related to violence, abduction, or sexual abuse; guardian ad litem programs; and international child inoculation programs. Mentoring programs are designed to add a protective factor into the lives of children who have insufficient access to caring adults. Many parenting programs are designed to boost the protective capabilities of the caregiver or to protect parenting in the context of risk or adversity, resulting in improvements in children's adaptation. For example, the Parenting Through Change program (PTC; Forgatch & DeGarmo, 1999) is a fourteen-week group parenting program for single separating mothers, aimed at enhancing positive parenting and reducing coercive parenting. Three-year follow-up data indicate the success of PTC in reducing children's behavior problems, improving school achievement, and reducing the incidence of maternal depression. Similarly, interventions can be designed to mobilize the pleasure-in-mastery or self-efficacy motivation systems (Bandura, 1997; Emde & Robinson, 2000; Shonkoff & Phillips, 2000). Some achievement and confidence-building programs for young disadvantaged or deprived children are designed explicitly or implicitly to boost or re-activate the fundamental systems believed to drive adaptive behaviors such as curiosity, exploration, learning, and persistent efforts to adapt in the face of difficulty (Masten & Coatsworth, 1995, 1998).

Vulnerability-focused intervention strategies – a look to the future

As knowledge about processes underlying biological vulnerability (genetic and experiential) becomes more specific, new possibilities for intervention will undoubtedly arise. Gene therapy to correct genetic anomalies (such as PKU) is one possibility. Another option becoming conceivable is the manipulation of gene expression through chemical or behavioral interventions. Such interventions would require extensive ethical debate and research to develop, test, and implement, but it is clear that interventions to alter vulnerability at the most basic levels of human functioning are becoming a reality.

Multi-focused strategies

Many of the most effective intervention programs incorporate more than one strategy described above, utilizing a multi-faceted model that addresses risks, assets, and protective or vulnerability processes in a comprehensive package, often designed to operate at multiple levels in the individual, family, classroom, school, community, or the larger society. Intervention scientists have argued that the pile-up of risks and the paucity of assets and protections in the lives of many children require a multi-focused strategy (Coie et al., 1993; Masten & Coatsworth, 1998; Wyman et al., 2000). The Triple P program in Australia (Sanders, Cann, & Markie-Dadds, 2003), mentioned above, like Project Head Start (Zigler & Muenchow, 1992) and the Abecedarian Early Intervention Project (Ramey & Ramey, 1998), uses a multi-focused, comprehensive approach to interventions for young children, providing a variety of social, health, and educational services to children and their families.

Conclusion

At the outset of the twenty-first century, it is clear that developmental theories about vulnerability and resilience and their application in prevention science or policy are becoming more complex, dynamic, multi-level, multidisciplinary, and systems-oriented. These trends are evident across the chapters of this handbook as well as the early childhood literature and they bode well for the future. Exciting new work on the neurobiology of vulnerability and resilience is emerging, as investigators capitalize on new tools for assessment and analysis, and new knowledge in molecular genetics and neuroscience, to probe gene–environment interaction and co-action, the boundaries of brain plasticity, and the processes by which early experience (good and bad) alters gene expression or sets biological regulatory systems (Boyce, in press; Curtis & Cicchetti, 2003; Gunnar, this volume; Rutter, in press). There is growing attention to cultural and contextual differences, as investigators study more diverse cultures and consider context-specific risk and protective factors along with the possibility of context-by-context interactions (Riley & Masten, 2005; Wright & Masten, 2004; Wyman, 2003). Long-neglected, culturally based protective systems, including religion and many other cultural traditions and practices, are garnering more empirical attention. Multi-level dynamics are taking center stage, as investigators from different disciplines team up to examine how interactions across system levels (from genes to person to family, media, or national policy) co-regulate human development and adaptation in the face of challenge (Dahl & Spear, 2004; Masten, in press; Steinberg et al., in press).

At the same time, interventions to promote resilience are becoming more evidence-based, theoretically informative, and embedded in community systems (Yates & Masten, 2004; Wright & Masten, 2004; Weissberg et al., 2003). Though there is much work to be done, basic research on vulnerability and resilience is beginning to provide a sturdier evidence base for policies and interventions designed to promote better developmental outcomes among young children with significant risk or vulnerabilities. Promising interventions designed within a resilience framework can now be tested and evaluated, not only to improve practice, but also to refine theories about the processes underlying risk and protection. Moreover, future interventions may well be informed by advances in the science of vulnerability and plasticity, making it possible to plan more strategically targeted and timed preventive interventions. Ultimately, the objectives of basic and applied research on vulnerability and resilience in development converge to serve a common purpose: the positive development of children who embody the human capital for the future of families and societies.

Note

1   *Resiliency* has been used by some behavioral scientists (as well as the general public) to refer to the individual capacity for resilience, a trait-like ability to rebound from adversity; however, that term is avoided in this chapter because it is fraught with misleading connotations (see Luthar, Cicchetti, & Becker, 2000; Masten, 1999; Riley & Masten, 2005). *Ego-resiliency* is a

broad personality trait construct describing the general capacity to adapt one's behavior to contextual demands (see Block & Block, 1980; Masten & Coatsworth, 1995).

References

Anthony, E. J. (1974). The syndrome of the psychologically invulnerable child. In E. J. Anthony & A. Koupernik (Eds.), *The child in his family: Children at psychiatric risk* (pp. 529–545). New York: Wiley.

Bandura, A. (1997). *Self-efficacy: The exercise of control.* New York: Freeman and Company.

Block, J., & Block, J. H. (1980). The role of ego-control and ego-resilience in the organization of behavior. In W. A. Collins (Ed.), *Minnesota Symposium on Child Psychology: Vol. 13. Development of cognition, affect, and social relations* (pp. 39–101). Hillsdale, NJ: Erlbaum.

Blount, R. L., Smith, A. J., & Frank, N. C. (1999). Preparation to undergo medical procedures. In A. J. Goreczny & M. Hersen (Eds.), *Handbook of pediatric and adolescent health psychology* (pp. 305–326). Boston: Allyn and Bacon.

Bor, W., Sanders, M. R., & Markie-Dadds, C. (2002). The effects of the Triple P-Positive Parenting Program on preschool children with co-occurring disruptive behavior and attentional/hyperactive difficulties. *Journal of Abnormal Child Psychology, 30*, 571–587.

Boyce, W. T. (in press). The biology of misfortune: Stress reactivity, social context, and the ontogeny of psychopathology in early life. In A. S. Masten (Ed.), *The Minnesota Symposia on Child Psychology: Vol. 34. Multilevel dynamics in developmental psychopathology: Pathways to the future.* Mahwah, NJ: Erlbaum.

Bowlby, J. (1969). *Attachment and loss.* New York: Basic Books.

Caspi, A., McClay, J., Moffitt, T. E., Mill, J., Martin, J., Craig, I. W., et al. (2002). Role of genotype in the cycle of violence in maltreated children. *Science, 297*, 851–854.

Cicchetti, D., Rappaport, J., Sandler, I., & Weissberg, R. P. (Eds.). (2000). *The promotion of wellness in children and adolescents.* Washington, DC: CWLA Press.

Coie, J. D., Watt, N. F., West, S. G., Hawkins, J. D., Asarnow, J. R., Markman, H. J., et al. (1993). The science of prevention: A conceptual framework and some directions for a national research program. *American Psychologist, 48*, 1013–1022.

Cowen, E. L. (2000). Psychological wellness: Some hopes for the future. In D. Cicchetti, J. Rappaport, I. Sandler, & R. P. Weissberg (Eds.), *The promotion of wellness in children and adolescents* (pp. 477–503). Thousand Oaks, CA: Sage Publications.

Curtis, W. J., & Cicchetti, D. (2003). Moving research on resilience into the 21st century: Theoretical and methodological considerations in examining the biological contributors to resilience. *Development & Psychopathology, 15*, 773–810.

Dahl, R. E., & Spear, L. P. (Eds.). (2004). *Adolescent brain development: Vulnerabilities and opportunities.* New York: New York Academy of Sciences.

De Bellis, M. D., Baum, A. S., Birmaher, B., Keshavan, M. S., Eccard, C. H., Boring, A. M., Jenkins, F. M., & Ryan, N. (1999). Developmental traumatology, Part 1: Biological stress systems. *Biological Psychiatry, 9*, 1259–1270.

Dubow, E., Schmidt, D., McBride, J., Edwards, S., & Merk, F. (1993). Teaching children to cope with stressful experiences: Initial implementation and evaluation of a primary prevention program. *Journal of Clinical Child Psychology, 22(4)*, 428–440.

Emde, R., & Robinson, J. O. (2000). Guiding principles for a theory of early intervention: A developmental-psychoanalytic perspective. In J. P. Shonkoff & S. J. Meisels (Eds.), *Handbook of early childhood intervention* (2nd ed., pp. 160–178). New York: CPU.

Farran, D. C. (2000). Another decade of intervention for children who are low income or disabled: What do we know now? In J. P. Shonkoff & S. J. Meisels (Eds.), *Handbook of early childhood intervention* (2nd ed., pp. 510–548). New York: Cambridge University Press.

Feerick, M. M., & Prinz, R. J. (2003). Next steps in research on children exposed to community violence and terrorism. *Clinical Child and Family Psychology Review*, 6, 303–305.

Ford, D. H., & Lerner, R. M. (1992). *Developmental systems theory: An integrative approach.* Newbury Park, CA: Sage Publications.

Forgatch, M. S., & DeGarmo, D. S. (1999). Parenting through change: An effective prevention program for single mothers. *Journal of Consulting and Clinical Psychology*, 67, 711–724.

Garmezy, N. (1971). Vulnerability research and the issue of primary prevention. *American Journal of Orthopsychiatry*, 41, 101–116.

Garmezy, N. (1984). Risk and protective factors in children vulnerable to major mental disorders. In L. Grinspoon (Ed.), *Psychiatry 1983* (Vol. III, pp. 99–104, 159–161). Washington, DC: American Psychiatric Press.

Garmezy, N., & Masten, A. S. (1994). Chronic adversities. In M. Rutter, L. Herzov, & E. Taylor (Eds.), *Child and adolescent psychiatry* (pp. 191–208). Oxford: Blackwell Scientific Publications.

Garmezy, N., & Rutter, M. (1983). *Stress, coping and development in children.* New York: McGraw-Hill.

Gest, S. D., Reed, M., & Masten, A. S. (1999). Measuring developmental changes in exposure to adversity: A life chart and rating scale approach. *Development and Psychopathology*, 11, 171–192.

Gottesman, I. I., & Shields, A. (1972). *Schizophrenia and genetics: A twin study vantage point.* New York: Academic Press.

Gottesman, I. I., & Shields, J. (1982). *Schizophrenia: The epigenetic puzzle.* New York: Cambridge University Press.

Grant, K. E., Compas, B. E., Stuhlmacher, A. F., Thurm, A. E., McMahon, S. D., & Halpert, J. A. (2003). Stressors and child and adolescent psychopathology: Moving from markers to mechanisms of risk. *Psychological Bulletin*, 129, 447–466.

Gunnar, M., Bruce, J., & Hickman, S. E. (2001). Salivary cortisol measures in infant and child assessment. In T. Theorell (Ed.), *Everyday biological stress mechanisms* (Vol. 22, pp. 52–60). Basel: Karger.

Gunnar, M. R., & Donzella, B. (2002). Social regulation of the L-HPA axis in early human development. *Psychoneuroendocrinology*, 27, 199–220.

Gutman, L. M., Sameroff, A. J., & Cole, R. (2003) Academic growth curve trajectories from 1st grade to 12th grade: Effects of multiple social risk factors and preschool child factors. *Developmental Psychology*, 39, 777–790.

Hart, B., & Risley, T. R. (1995). *Meaningful differences in the everyday experiences of young American children.* Baltimore: Brookes.

Hornik, R., & Gunnar, M. R. (1988). A descriptive analysis of infant social referencing. *Child Development*, 59, 626–634.

Keating, D. P., & Hertzman, C. (1999). *Developmental health and the wealth of nations: Social, biological, and educational dynamics.* New York: Guilford.

Kopp, C. B. (1983). Risk factors in development. In M. M. Haith & J. J. Campos (Eds.), *Handbook of child psychology: Vol. 2. Infancy and developmental psychobiology* (4th ed., pp. 1081–1188). New York: Wiley.

Kraemer, H. C., Kazdin, A. E., Offord, D., Kessler, R. C., Jensen, P. S., & Kupfer, D. (1997). Coming to terms with the terms of risk. *Archives of General Psychiatry*, 54, 337–343.

Kraemer, H. C., Stice, E., Kazdin, A., Offord, D., & Kupfer, D. (2001). How do risk factors work together? Mediators, moderators, and independent, overlapping, and proxy risk factors. *American Journal of Psychiatry, 158*, 848–856.

Kraemer, H. C., Wilson, G. T., Fairburn, C. G., & Agras, W. S. (2002). Mediators and moderators of treatment effects in randomized clinical trials. *Archives of General Psychiatry, 59*, 877–883.

Luthar, S. S. (Ed.). (2003). *Resilience and vulnerability: Adaptation in the context of childhood adversities*. New York: Cambridge University Press.

Luthar, S. S., & Cicchetti, D. (2000). The construct of resilience: Implications for interventions and social policies. *Development and Psychopathology, 12*, 857–885.

Luthar, S. S., Cicchetti, D., & Becker, B. (2000). The construct of resilience: A critical evaluation and guidelines for future work. *Child Development, 71*, 543–562.

Masten, A. S. (1989). Resilience in development: Implications of the study of successful adaptation for developmental psychopathology. In D. Cicchetti (Ed.), *The emergence of a discipline: Rochester Symposium on Developmental Psychopathology* (Vol. 1, pp. 261–294). Hillsdale, NJ: Lawrence Erlbaum Associates.

Masten, A. S. (1999). Resilience comes of age: Reflections on the past and outlook for the next generation of research. In M. D. Glantz, J. Johnson, & L. Huffman (Eds.), *Resilience and development: Positive life adaptations* (pp. 289–296). New York: Plenum.

Masten, A. S. (2001). Ordinary magic: Resilience processes in development. *American Psychologist, 56*, 227–238.

Masten, A. S. (Ed.). (in press). *The Minnesota Symposia on Child Psychology: Vol. 34. Multilevel dynamics in developmental psychopathology: Pathways to the future*. Mahwah, NJ: Erlbaum.

Masten, A. S., Best, K. M., & Garmezy, N. (1990). Resilience and development: Contributions from the study of children who overcome adversity. *Development and Psychopathology, 2*, 425–444.

Masten, A. S., & Coatsworth, J. D. (1995). Competence, resilience, and psychopathology. In D. Cicchetti & D. J. Cohen (Eds.), *Developmental psychopathology: Vol. 2. Risk, disorder, and adaptation* (pp. 715–752). New York: Wiley.

Masten, A. S., & Coatsworth, J. D. (1998). The development of competence in favorable and unfavorable environments: Lessons from research on successful children. *American Psychologist, 53*, 205–220.

Masten, A. S., & Curtis, W. J. (2000). Integrating competence and psychopathology: Pathways toward a comprehensive science of adaptation in development. *Development and Psychopathology, 12*, 529–550.

Masten, A. S., & Garmezy, N. (1985). Risk, vulnerability, and protective factors in developmental psychopathology. In B. B. Lahey & A. E. Kazdin (Eds.), *Advances in clinical child psychology* (Vol. 8, pp. 1–52). New York: Plenum Press.

Masten, A. S., Morison, P., Pellegrini, D., & Tellegen, A. (1990). Competence under stress: Risk and protective factors. In J. Rolf, A. S. Masten, D. Cicchetti, K. Nuechterlein, & S. Weintraub (Eds.), *Risk and protective factors in the development of psychopathology* (pp. 236–256). New York: Cambridge University Press.

Masten, A. S., Neemann, J., & Andenas, S. (1994). Life events and adjustment in adolescents: The significance of event independence, desirability, and chronicity. *Journal of Research on Adolescence, 4*, 71–97.

Masten, A. S., & O'Connor, M. J. (1989). Vulnerability, stress, and resilience in the early development of a high risk child. *Journal of the American Academy of Child and Adolescent Psychiatry, 28*, 274–278.

Masten, A. S., & Powell, J. L. (2003). A resilience framework for research, policy, and practice. In S. S. Luthar (Ed.), *Resilience and vulnerability: Adaptation in the context of childhood adversities* (pp. 1–25). New York: Cambridge University Press.

Masten, A. S., & Reed, M.-G. J. (2002). Resilience in development. In C. R. Snyder & S. J. Lopez (Eds.), *Handbook of positive psychology* (pp. 74–88). London: Oxford University Press.

Murphy, L. B., & Moriarty, A. E. (1976). *Vulnerability, coping, and growth: From infancy to adolescence.* New Haven: Yale University Press.

Ramey, C. T., & Ramey, S. L. (1998). Early intervention and early experience. *American Psychologist, 53,* 109–120.

Riley, J. R., & Masten, A. S. (2005). Resilience in context. In R. DeV. Peters, B. Leadbeater, & R. J. McMahon (Eds.), *Resilience in children, families, and communities: Linking context to practice and policy* (pp. 13–25). New York: Kluwer Academic/Plenum.

Rutter, M. (1979). Protective factors in children's responses to stress and disadvantage. *Annals of the Academy of Medicine, Singapore, 8,* 324–338.

Rutter, M. (in press). Gene–environment interplay and developmental psychopathology. In A. S. Masten (Ed.), *The Minnesota Symposia on Child Psychology: Vol. 34. Multilevel dynamics in developmental psychopathology: Pathways to the future.* Mahwah, NJ: Erlbaum.

Sameroff, A. J. (2000). Developmental systems, and psychopathology. *Development and Psychopathology, 12,* 297–312.

Sameroff, A. J., & Chandler, M. J. (1975). Reproductive risk and the continuum of caretaking casualty. *Review of Child Development Research, 4,* 187–244.

Sameroff, A. J., Seifer, R., & Bartko, W. T. (1997). Environmental perspectives on adaptation during childhood and adolescence. In S. S. Luthar, J. A. Burack, D. Cicchetti, & J. R. Weisz (Eds.), *Developmental psychopathology: Perspectives on adjustment, risk, and disorder* (pp. 507–526). New York: Cambridge University Press.

Sanders, M. R., Cann, W., & Markie-Dadds, C. (2003). The Triple P-Positive Parenting Programme: A universal population-level approach to the prevention of child abuse. *Child Abuse Review, 12,* 155–171.

Sanders, M. R., Turner, K. M. T., & Markie-Dadds, C. (2002). The development and dissemination of the Triple P-Positive Parenting Program: A multi-level, evidence-based system of parenting and family support. *Prevention Science, 3,* 173–189.

Sandler, I., Wolchik, S., Davis, C., Haine, R., & Ayers, T. (2003). Correlational and experimental study of resilience in children of divorce and parentally bereaved children. In S. Luthar (Ed.), *Resilience and vulnerability: Adaptation in the context of childhood adversities* (pp. 213–242). Cambridge: Cambridge University Press.

Scarr, S., & Kidd, K. K. (1983). Developmental behavior genetics. In P. H. Mussen (Ed.), *Handbook of child psychology* (Vol. 2, pp. 345–433). New York: Wiley.

Seifer, R. (2000). Temperament and goodness of fit: Implications for developmental psychopathology. In A. Sameroff, M. Lewis, & S. M. Miller (Eds.), *Handbook of developmental psychopathology* (2nd ed., pp. 257–276). New York: Kluwer Academic.

Shonkoff, J. P., & Marshall, P. C. (2000). The biology of developmental vulnerability. In J. P. Shonkoff & S. J. Meisels (Eds.), *Handbook of early childhood intervention* (2nd ed., pp. 35–53). New York: Cambridge University Press.

Shonkoff, J. P., & Meisels, S. J. (Eds.). (2000). *Handbook of early childhood intervention* (2nd ed.). New York: Cambridge University Press.

Shonkoff, J. P., & Phillips, D. A. (Eds.). (2000). *From neurons to neighborhoods: The science of early childhood development.* Washington, DC: National Academy Press.

Sigman, M., & Parmelee, A. M., Jr. (1979). Longitudinal evaluation of the preterm infant. In T. M. Field, A. M. Sostek, S. Goldberg, & H. H. Shuman (Eds.), *Infants born at risk: Behavior and development* (pp. 193–217). New York: Spectrum.

Sorce, J. F., Emde, R. N., Campos, J., & Klinnert, M. D. (1985). Maternal emotional signaling: Its effect on the visual cliff behavior of 1-year olds. *Developmental Psychology, 21,* 195–200.

Sroufe, L. A. (1996). *Emotional development: The organization of emotional life in the early years.* New York: Cambridge University Press.

Sroufe, L. A. (1997). Psychopathology as an outcome of development. *Development and Psychopathology, 9,* 251–268.

Sroufe, L. A., Carlson, E. A., Levy, A. K., & Egeland, B. (1999). Implications of attachment theory for developmental psychopathology. *Development and Psychopathology, 11,* 1–13.

Steinberg, L., Dahl, R., Keating, D., Kupfer, D. J., Masten, A. S., & Pine, D. (in press). The study of developmental psychopathology in adolescence: Integrating affective neuroscience with the study of context. In D. Cicchetti & D. Cohen (Eds.), *Handbook of developmental psychopathology* (2nd ed.). New York: Wiley.

Suomi, S. J. (2000). A biobehavioral perspective on developmental psychopathology: Excessive aggression and serotonergic dysfunction in monkeys. In A. Sameroff, M. Lewis, & S. M. Miller (Eds.), *Handbook of developmental psychopathology* (2nd ed., pp. 237–256). Dordrecht: Kluwer Academic Publishers.

Thelen, E., & Smith, L. (1998). Dynamic systems theories. In R. M. Lerner (Ed.), *Handbook of child psychology: Vol. 1. Theoretical models of human development* (5th ed., pp. 563–634). New York: Wiley.

Thomas, A., Chess, S., & Birch, H. G. (1968). *Temperament and behavior disorders in children.* New York: New York University Press.

Watt, N. F., Anthony, E. J., Wynne, L. C., & Rolf, J. E. (1984). *Children at risk for schizophrenia: A longitudinal perspective.* New York: Cambridge University Press.

Weissberg, R. P., Kumpfer, K. L., & Seligman, M. E. P. (2003). Prevention that works for children and youth. *American Psychologist, 58,* 425–432.

Werner, E. E. (2000). Protective factors and individual resilience. In J. P. Shonkoff & S. J. Meisels (Eds.), *Handbook of early intervention* (2nd ed., pp. 115–132). New York: Cambridge University Press.

Werner, E. E., & Smith, R. S. (1982). *Vulnerable but invincible: A study of resilient children.* New York: McGraw-Hill.

Whelan, T. A., & Kirkby, R. J. (1998). Advantages for children and their families of psychological preparation for hospitalisation and surgery. *Journal of Family Studies, 4*(1), 35–51.

Winnicott, D. W. (1965). The theory of the parent–infant relationship. In D. W. Winnicott (Ed.), *The maturational processes and the facilitating environment* (pp. 37–55). London: Hogarth Press.

Wright, M. O'D., & Masten, A. S. (2004). Resilience processes in development: Fostering positive adaptation in the context of adversity. In S. Goldstein & R. Brooks (Eds.), *Handbook of resilience in children* (pp. 17–37). New York: Kluwer Academic/Plenum.

Wyman, P. A. (2003). Emerging perspectives on context-specificity of children's adaptation and resilience: Evidence from a decade of research with urban children in adversity. In S. S. Luthar (Ed.), *Resilience and vulnerability: Adaptation in the context of childhood adversities* (pp. 293–317). New York: Cambridge University Press.

Wyman, P. A., Sandler, I., Wolchik, S., & Nelson, K. (2000). Resilience as cumulative competence promotion and stress protection: Theory and intervention. In D. Cicchetti, J. Rappaport, I. Sandler, & R. P. Weissberg (Eds.), *The promotion of wellness in children and adolescents* (pp. 133–184). Thousand Oaks, CA: Sage Publications.

Yates, T. M., & Masten, A. S. (2004). Fostering the future: Resilience theory and the practice of positive psychology. In P. A. Linley & S. Joseph (Eds.), *Positive psychology in practice* (pp. 521–539). Hoboken, NJ: Wiley.

Zigler, E., & Muenchow, S. (1992). *Head Start: The inside story of America's most successful educational experiment.* New York: Basic Books.

3

Family Influences on Early Development: Integrating the Science of Normative Development, Risk and Disability, and Intervention

Michael J. Guralnick

The focus of this chapter is on family patterns of interaction that influence the social and intellectual competence of young children. It is the development of social and intellectual competencies that enables children to pursue their own goals as effectively as possible and to do so in the context of larger family values, expectations, and routines. Of importance, the development-enhancing qualities of family patterns of interaction can and do differ substantially across families, and many of these variations can materially alter children's developmental trajectories, especially during the early childhood years. Indeed, families challenged by various combinations of environmental and psychosocial stressors or risk factors often establish family patterns of interaction that are far from optimal with respect to their development-enhancing features (Belsky & Fearon, 2002; Burchinal, Roberts, Hooper, & Zeisel, 2000; Liaw & Brooks-Gunn, 1994; Sameroff, Seifer, Barocas, Zax, & Greenspan, 1987).

From another perspective, and the one emphasized in this chapter, owing to genetic conditions, infectious agents, or other biologically based causes, many children exhibit uneven and unusual developmental characteristics that pose significant challenges to optimal family patterns of interaction for even the most conscientious and devoted of families. Nevertheless, as will be seen, irrespective of the nature and origin of stressors to optimal family patterns of interaction, a common developmental framework can be useful in understanding factors influencing children developing typically as well as those children who are vulnerable to developmental problems as a consequence of biological or environmental factors. Moreover, it is this same developmental framework that can serve as a guide to design and evaluate the effectiveness of early interventions intended to maximize the development-enhancing features of family patterns of interaction for vulnerable children. In fact, our understanding of development can be substantially enriched by a thoughtful integration of our knowledge of the developmental science of normative development, the developmental science of risk and disability, and intervention science (Cicchetti & Cohen, 1995; Guralnick, 1998, 2001a). Each of these topics is examined in this chapter in relation to family patterns of interaction.

Developmental Science of Normative Development

One major task of the science of normative development is to identify and organize those critical features of family patterns of interaction that influence the healthy development of young children. As one might imagine, this is a complex and demanding enterprise. Potential influential factors need to be sorted out and grounded theoretically, and measures must be established that capture the essence of the many dynamic processes of interest. A special challenge for developmental science, particularly when focusing on the early years, is to develop measurement systems for constructs that take into account the major developmental changes that are occurring even during this relatively brief period of a child's life. Moreover, determining whether, and the extent to which, specific family patterns of interaction actually influence children's social and intellectual competence demands sophisticated longitudinal studies and equally sophisticated statistical analyses. Fortunately, investigators who study family patterns of interaction have been able to identify many of these influences and establish their importance as contributors to children's social and intellectual competence (Collins, Maccoby, Steinberg, Hetherington, & Bornstein, 2000).

Three general types of family patterns of interaction have been clearly associated with child developmental outcomes (Guralnick, 1998). The first is the quality of *parent–child transactions*. These transactions constitute the substance of everyday exchanges between parents and children and may be said to be part of a mutually interacting system in which each participant exerts influence over the other (Sameroff & Fiese, 2000). As will be discussed shortly, a number of "relationship constructs" have been identified, the most important of which can best be referred to as "sensitive-responsiveness" to children's actions – an interaction pattern that has been clearly linked to children's social and intellectual competence.

The second family pattern of interaction focuses on *family-orchestrated child experiences*. Included here are the routines families establish, the introduction of the child to the family's social network, organizing educational experiences for the child, including the provision of developmentally appropriate toys, selecting an appropriate child care setting, arranging play dates, and involving the child in community activities consistent with his or her interests or even special needs should they arise.

The third and final family pattern of interaction consists of those parental activities relevant to ensuring the *health and safety of the child*. Providing proper nutrition, minimizing exposure to toxins, ensuring that immunization schedules are followed, and protecting the child from injury or from violence are some of the important aspects of this family pattern of interaction. A summary of some of the specific features of these three patterns and how they exert their influence on children's social and intellectual competence is discussed next.

Parent–child transactions

With respect to fostering young children's intellectual competence, the ability of parents to gauge their interactions so that they are consistent with their child's developmental level and motivational state is central to the development-enhancing aspects of the construct captured by the term "sensitive-responsiveness" (see Ainsworth, Blehar, Waters, & Wall, 1978). Clearly, for optimal interactions to occur, a highly developed sensitivity to and understanding of the cues children display are required. Over the years, a number of important dimensions of this construct have been identified, sometimes exerting their effects independently, but more often in an interrelated and interdependent fashion (see Bornstein & Tamis-Lemonda, 1989). An especially important aspect of sensitive-responsiveness is contingent responsiveness consisting of two dimensions: the ability to respond to the child in a timely and predictable fashion, and to organize the content of the transaction so as to be relevant and appropriate (see Martin, 1989). The timing of contingent responsiveness, in particular, is needed to maintain the social exchanges at a proper pace and to communicate to the child that his or her desires, interests, and interactions make a difference and exert an influence with respect to what happens next. High levels of sensitive-responsiveness also encourage social exchanges to flourish, often creating a lively "discourse" between parents and young children – highlighting salient features of the exchange and providing a context for elaborating upon topics of mutual interest. In many respects, this discourse context also allows parents to "scaffold" information by gradually extending their child's knowledge or guiding their child's skilled actions just beyond the child's current level of development (Vygotsky, 1978). "Zone of proximal development" is the term Vygotsky used to describe this process. This important dimension produces a motivating challenge to foster a child's intellectual competence and requires an appropriate level of sensitivity to a child's current state of development in addition to an interest in advancing the child's level of development (Wood, 1998). A final dimension of sensitive-responsiveness is one which requires interactions to be affectively warm, thereby demonstrating enthusiasm, attention, and affection (Steelman, Assel, Swank, Smith, & Landry, 2002) as well as highlighting critical features of the interaction.

These development-enhancing dimensions of parent–child transactions can be contrasted with those in which parents themselves control the timing and content of the exchanges – interactions that are often poorly linked to their children's needs or interests (e.g., not following the child's attentional focus). Here, parents tend to be highly directive, exerting control when it is not appropriate to do so. This intrusiveness, in the form of redirecting a child's activities or exerting excessive and inappropriate control through unnecessary restrictions on behavior, can clearly constrain many aspects of development (e.g., Parpal & Maccoby, 1985; Tomasello & Farrar, 1986).

Findings from numerous studies directly observing parent–child transactions in natural and laboratory settings have consistently obtained positive associations between the development-enhancing dimensions of sensitive-responsiveness and children's intellectual competence (e.g., Bornstein & Tamis-Lemonda, 1989; Landry, Smith, Miller-Loncar, & Swank, 1997; Landry, Smith, Swank, & Miller-Loncar, 2000; Lewis & Goldberg, 1969; Tomasello & Farrar, 1986; Wood, 1998). The precise contribution of the various dimensions of sensitive-responsiveness to child development may differ across developmental periods (e.g., more direct guidance or control may be of value early on but is detrimental to development if the pattern continues), and specific dimensions may be linked to specific aspects of a child's competence (e.g., responsiveness to children's vocalizations is associated with children's language development) (Bornstein & Tamis-Lemonda, 1989; Tamis-Lemonda, Bornstein, Baumwell, & Damast, 1996). Moreover, sensitive-responsiveness can wax and wane across developmental periods, but consistency over time provides the best outcomes (Landry, Smith, Swank, Assel, & Vellet, 2001).

A number of theoretical positions have been advanced to account for how these development-enhancing parent–child transactions support a child's development that is sustained over time. Strengthening the broader psychological make-up of the child through these exchanges, including numerous aspects of early emerging competence such as self-regulation and capacities that allow children to explore and learn more effectively and efficiently across varying development periods, is certainly one likely explanation (see Haley & Stansbury, 2003). These development-enhancing features may also be linked to the ability of the parent–child dyad to draw closer to one another. In so doing, expertise is gained with respect to knowledge of their child's development and interests (from the parents' perspective) and how best to capture the parents' attention (from the child's perspective). Of course, the consistency of sensitive-responsiveness of parents contributes as well.

Although the level of sensitive-responsiveness will vary over time, it nevertheless remains moderately stable (Bradley, 1989) and likely correlates positively with many other development-enhancing features of family interaction patterns to be discussed later in this chapter. Of importance, a major challenge for parents is to find the proper balance and developmental timing of these various dimensions in order to maximize their development-enhancing features. This balance surely depends on many factors, some of which are discussed below. One key factor is the developmental characteristics of the child, including the existence of any risk factors or disabilities. Clearly, this constitutes a circumstance that may require substantial adaptations to maintain optimal sensitive-responsiveness.

As might be expected, many of these same dimensions of parent–child transactions linked to intellectual competence are also development-enhancing with respect to children's social competence (e.g., Landry, Smith, Miller-Loncar, & Swank, 1998; Landry et al., 2001). After all, becoming socially competent has many problem-solving components as children attempt to pursue their interpersonal goals. The more qualitative dimension of sensitive-responsiveness, affective warmth, may be an especially important contributor to children's developing social competence if properly gauged to the child's developmental and motivational level (Steelman et al., 2002). Even specialized dimensions such as the way emotional arousal is modulated during parent–child play are related to children's emerging social competence (see Parke, Cassidy, Burks, Carson, & Boyum, 1992; and Thompson & Lagattuta, this volume). Finally, these development-enhancing interactions represented by the sensitive-responsiveness construct also underlie the formation of powerful and secure emotional attachments to caregivers (Ainsworth et al., 1978; Carlson, Sampson, & Sroufe, 2003). It is these secure attachments that serve both as a safe haven to allow the child to explore the world and as the prototype for mental representations of relationships or "internal working models" that can guide the formation of subsequent relationships (see Thompson, 1999). In fact, this positive orientation and set of expectations established by a secure attachment support socially competent functioning with adults and even carry over to relationships with peers (see Guralnick & Neville, 1997; Schneider, Atkinson, & Tardif, 2001).

In contrast, the absence of adequate levels of sensitive-responsiveness often leads to the formation of various types of problematic relationships, including insecure attachments. These insecure attachments do not in and of themselves preordain later developmental problems of a social and emotional nature, but rather constitute a major risk factor for their occurrence (see Carlson et al., 2003). Correspondingly, abundant evidence suggests that low levels of parental sensitive-responsiveness during the early years are predictive of future social and emotional difficulties (Wakschlag & Hans, 1999), with their expected detrimental effects on social competence. Unusually low levels of sensitive-responsiveness or interaction patterns incompatible with sensitive-responsiveness impair many and diverse aspects of children's social competence (see Guralnick & Neville, 1997; LaFreniere & Dumas, 1992). Indeed, lower levels of social competence prevent children from becoming productively involved in social relationships, in general, including relationships with peers (Guralnick, 2001c; Parker, Rubin, Price, & DeRosier, 1995).

Family-orchestrated child experiences

Parents are also primarily responsible for organizing a variety of experiences in both the home and the larger community environment that establish the conditions for other important development-enhancing experiences for their child. These include such diverse parental activities as providing an appropriately stimulating environment, for example selecting developmentally appropriate toys and materials (Bradley, 2002; Bradley et al., 1989). The orchestration of family routines and rituals involving the child provides the context for diverse and productive parent–child transactions (see Fiese, 2002). These routines, which may range from bedtime reading and other home literacy experiences, to involvement in family chores and activities, frequently serve as the occasion for development-enhancing parent–child transactions, especially the provision of spontaneous diverse use of language directed to the child (Griffin & Morrison, 1997; Hart & Risley, 1995). The sheer amount of language directed to young children, which varies enormously across families, turns out to be a powerful predictor of children's developing vocabularies and perhaps other aspects of development as well (Hart & Risley, 1995).

Even when parents are unavailable, they nevertheless are responsible for orchestrating the quality of development-enhancing experiences. Introducing their child to their own social network is one example. Selecting child care so that it constitutes a development-enhancing experience is, of course, a critical and difficult decision for families. Although the overall effects of child care on children's intellectual competence may be relatively small, an influence is nevertheless evident (NICHD Early Child Care Research Network, 2003; NICHD Early Child Care Research Network & Duncan, 2003). Parent-orchestrated child experiences also include community activities arranged by parents, both recreational and educational, which provide numerous development-enhancing opportunities (Dunst, Hamby, Trivette, Raab, & Bruder, 2000). A critical feature here is for parents to organize those activities consistent with their child's special interests or, as discussed later, with their child's special needs. It is also the case, as revealed by a substantial body of evidence, that parents can influence their child's social competence, particularly in connection with peers, through a variety of parent-orchestrated activities. Beneficial effects are associated with parental arranging and monitoring of even young children's experiences with peers (e.g., playdates) and through direct advice and instruction provided by parents with respect to managing relationships with peers (Ladd & Hart, 1992; Ladd & Pettit, 2003; Russell & Finnie, 1990).

Health and safety provided by the family

The third family pattern of interaction focuses on the crucial ability of families to attend to their child's basic needs with respect to health and safety. Maintaining a child's good health, with an emphasis on preventive health (e.g., immunizations), enables children to take advantage of many of the other development-enhancing aspects of family patterns of interaction described above. Similarly, maintaining proper nutrition is essential for optimal intellectual competence, although the processes through which this factor operates are complex (Georgieff & Rao, 1999; Gorman, 1995; Lozoff, De Andraca, Castillo, Smith, Walter, & Pino, 2003). Finally, protection from violence or even witnessing violence constitute important family responsibilities for many reasons, including the fact that these events can influence children's social and intellectual competence (Farver, Natera, & Frosch, 1999; Koenen, Moffitt, Caspi, Taylor, & Purcell, 2003; Osofsky, 1995).

Developmental Science of Biological Risk and Disability

Research has not yet determined precisely which of the many possible combinations of family patterns of interaction and their various dimensions will result in optimal or near optimal child development. Clearly, there are many diverse paths that families can take to optimize children's social and intellectual competence. The actual range is likely to be quite considerable and, judging by child outcomes, the vast majority of families fall well within that range. However, circumstances arise that make this task far more challenging, such as when families have inadequate financial resources, when mothers have experienced abuse or neglect themselves, when families have limited social supports, or when a parent has a mental health problem. In fact, the challenges or stressors to establishing optimal family patterns of interaction can be so severe as to place a child at risk for developmental delays and related problems. There is, in fact, a substantial literature in which several of the mechanisms through which this occurs have been identified (Duncan, Brooks-Gunn, & Klebanov, 1994; Guralnick, 1998, 2005b; Yeung, Linver, & Brooks-Gunn, 2000). Much of this information is addressed in other chapters in this volume.

Stressors to optimal family patterns of interaction also arise when children are at biological risk for developmental problems, such as those born prematurely at low birth weight, as well as for children with established developmental disabilities whose cognitive, motor, communicative, affective, or sensory systems are substantially compromised. Children with established disabilities frequently receive diagnoses such as cerebral palsy, autism, mental retardation (cognitive or intellectual delay for young children), hearing or visual impairment, or specific language disorder. The etiologies for many of these disorders are genetic, such as for children with Down's syndrome or Fragile X syndrome (Hagerman, 1999). In the case of children with established disabilities, typical developmental trajectories are, of course, not likely, nor are they expected.

Yet, any disruptions to optimal family patterns of interaction, unrelated to pre-existing family environmental or psychosocial stressors, may further compromise a child's development. Unfortunately, as discussed below, it appears that these disruptions occur regularly as a consequence of information needs that are generated, interpersonal and family stress that is experienced, additional resources that must be gathered, and confidence threats related to parenting that must be addressed (Guralnick, 1998). Of additional importance, available evidence suggests that the various dimensions and activities associated with the three family patterns of interaction identified for children developing typically are just as relevant and important for children at biological risk and for those with established disabilities. For example, sensitive-responsiveness manifested in its various dimensions is also a key to maximizing the development of these young children (Barnard, 1997; Landry et al., 1997; McCollum & Hemmeter, 1997; Spiker, Boyce, & Boyce, 2002; Yoder & Warren, 1999). Consequently, it is essential to identify the kinds of stressors associated with the characteristics of children at biological risk and those with established disabilities that may perturb family patterns of interaction. This, in turn, can lead to interventions designed to maintain or restore optimal family patterns of interaction.

Information needs

First, and perhaps most notable, children's specific developmental characteristics and related circumstances create information needs for families focused primarily on their child's current level of health and development as well as anticipated needs. The range of information needs turns out to be quite extraordinary, varying across developmental periods and children's particular risk or disability profiles. For example, early on, parents of children born prematurely must learn about highly sophisticated medical procedures in the neonatal intensive-care unit and the possible impact of these procedures on their child's development (Als, 1997; Als et al., 2003; Meyer et al., 1995). Even when these children are able to move from the hospital to home, differences in child responsiveness, sleep–wake cycles, and numerous other emotional and physiological regulation issues arise that substantially challenge optimal family interaction patterns, particularly parent–child transactions (Minde, 2000; Singer et al., 2003). Information is clearly needed in order to achieve optimal patterns.

The developmental delays of children with established disabilities and their sometimes highly atypical behavior, such as that which occurs for some children with autism, tend to create enormous challenges requiring parents to acquire considerable information to both understand and address these issues. Children's interactive abilities, in particular, are often perplexing for parents, frequently resulting in mismatches between their behavior and that of their child's or missed opportunities during parent–child transactions (see McCollum & Hemmeter, 1997). It is far more difficult for parents of young children with disabilities to read their child's cues accurately and to understand their needs. Broadly speaking, these children tend to be less emotionally expressive, less responsive to others, initiate social exchanges less frequently, and process information in unusual ways (Spiker et al., 2002). Many of these difficulties in parent–child transactions are apparent in the context of family routines, which potentially contain considerable development-enhancing value. This is especially the case when opportunities exist to share experiences through joint attention routines or when children are in situations in which they are uncertain as to their safety or comfort and could benefit from parental guidance (generally referred to as social referencing) (Guralnick, 2002; Kasari, Freeman, Mundy, & Sigman, 1995; Mundy & Stella, 2000; Sigman & Ruskin, 1999).

Information needs also arise in connection with the other two family patterns of interaction – ensuring optimal parent-orchestrated child experiences and the health and safety of their child. For example, parents must keep themselves informed with respect to the best programs and experts and keep current with respect to possible treatments and interventions (see Sontag & Schacht, 1994). Similarly, parents often find it difficult to provide appropriate experiences outside the family for their child with a disability. Playdates are very difficult to arrange for children with disabilities yet, unless parents make these arrangements, few experiences with peers result (Guralnick, Connor, Neville, & Hammond, 2002). This contrasts sharply with typically developing children, who frequently make their own arrangements with peers. Clearly, parents require information with respect to the best approaches to establishing experiences for their child with peers and to promoting their child's peer-related social competence (Guralnick, 1999).

The unusual difficulties parents of children with disabilities have in arranging child care exacerbates this lack of experience with peers (see Booth & Kelly, 1998). Obtaining information concerning those child care providers knowledgeable and sensitive to a young child's special needs is a major challenge for many families. Moreover, many children with disabilities, in particular, are at increased risk for a variety of health problems, which parents must become knowledgeable about. They must also remain vigilant, urging health care providers to be especially attentive to these risks (e.g., Roizen & Patterson, 2003). Although many parents are able to adjust appropriately to their child's atypical developmental patterns or seek out relevant information on their own to enable them to engage in development-enhancing parent–child transactions, others find this task to be extremely difficult.

Interpersonal and family distress

A second stressor to optimal family patterns of interaction comes in the form of inter-personal and family distress. Families are called upon, often rather abruptly, to reassess and reconsider many of their goals and expectations individually and as a family unit, and to substantially adjust their family routines. Sources for this type of stressor are seem-ingly ubiquitous, easily triggered by the diagnostic process, transition points in programs, or missed developmental milestones, and are even associated with the actual process of coping with relevant problems (Affleck and Tennen, 1993; Atkinson et al., 1999; Pianta, Marvin, Britner, & Borowitz, 1996). Family distress and accompanying social isolation can also arise as a consequence of a feeling of "sharing a stigma" associated with a child with a disability (Goffman, 1963), or by experiencing similar feelings of distress associated with the birth of a child at biological risk (Minde, 2000; Singer et al., 2003). Felt personal stress is also common, such as feelings of depression or role restriction occurring as the full meaning of coping with a child with a disability emerges (Roach, Orsmond, & Barratt, 1999). For children with disabilities, accompanying child behavior problems are perhaps the most stressful (Baker, Blacher, Crnic, & Edelbrock, 2002) and require the most extensive accommodations by families (Gallimore, Keogh, & Bernheimer, 1999). Again, although many families adjust well, others experience levels of interpersonal and family distress sufficient to adversely affect family patterns of interaction and further compromise a child's social and intellectual competence.

Resource needs

Resource needs generated by a child at biological risk or with a disability, the third category of potential stressors, are equally important. Child characteristics often disrupt typical family routines, placing numerous unexpected time and financial demands on family members (e.g., Bristol, 1987; Dyson, 1993). In the United States, for example, despite federal and state programs and private insurance that share the responsibility for many helpful services and supports for young children, the financial burden on families should not be underestimated, as out-of-pocket costs can be considerable (Birenbaum, Guyot, & Cohen, 1990; Shannon, Grinde, & Cox, 2003). All of these factors related to resource needs have the potential to disrupt one or more of the three family patterns of interaction (see Guralnick, 2004).

Confidence threats

Finally, the constancy and pervasiveness of many of these stressors can create a crisis of confidence in a family's ability to properly parent their child. Measures of parental stress are often elevated with regard to perceived competence in carrying out the parenting role (e.g., Roach et al., 1999). It is critical that families maintain a sense of mastery and control over all aspects of decision making, as only they are capable of acquiring and integrating information and resources as well as mitigating distress and social isolation in a manner that is compatible with family goals, values, priorities, and routines (Gallimore, Weisner, Bernheimer, Guthrie, & Nihira, 1993).

Intervention Science

For children at risk for developmental problems as well as for those with established disabilities, the developmental framework outlined above and the accompanying developmental science provide direction for the design of early intervention programs intended to help maximize children's development. Indeed, in the United States, numerous federal, state, and local programs have been established over the years to provide services, supports, and related resources to young vulnerable children and their families. Some are designed to be preventive in nature: that is, identifying children at risk (biological, environmental, or both) and then seeking to minimize that risk from being realized in the form of less than optimal child developmental outcomes. Other programs focus on children with established disabilities and are designed to maximize children's social and intellectual competence.

The most comprehensive of these programs is the state-administered but federally authorized Individuals with Disabilities Education Act (IDEA) (see Guralnick, in press). In actuality, this system consists of two major components: one focusing on infants and toddlers (Part C of IDEA), the other on preschool-age children (Part B). Encouraged by this legislation passed in the late 1980s, states first worked to integrate various service programs already in existence, such as those providing speech and language or physical therapy. This was followed by the development of new programs and services needed to ensure the availability of a comprehensive and coordinated set of services and supports for children and families within each community. Many structural components of early intervention systems were mandated by IDEA, such as creating an early identification and referral mechanism and ensuring that children make appropriate transitions from one program to another. Also contained within IDEA were certain principles to guide the system, such as those related to the importance of centering services on families (especially for infants and toddlers) and to ensuring that services are provided in ways that minimize the separation of children and families from their community (i.e., principles of natural environments and inclusion). The precise forms and nature of the community-based early intervention programs that have emerged within the framework of IDEA have varied substantially from state to state, but all are informed to some extent by both the developmental science of normative development and the developmental science of risk and disability.

Knowledge base

The complexity of the task of integrating and utilizing information from the developmental science of normative development and the developmental science of risk and disability to design early intervention programs is considerable. It is, of course, possible that we may actually be heading in the wrong direction. After all, establishing causal relationships in developmental science poses an unusual set of challenges (Shonkoff & Phillips, 2000). Moreover, there may have been important influences on children's development that were not assessed in the developmental science studies noted earlier in this chapter that were responsible for some of the patterns obtained. Besides the prospect of having failed to identify important features or dimensions of family interaction patterns, we must also consider the possibility that intrinsic child characteristics were the driving force for many of the developmental relationships that were found.

Fortunately, intervention science provides an opportunity to examine and evaluate the influence of these suggested family patterns of interaction on child development more directly. That is, experimental tests can be arranged by manipulating the factors of interest (e.g., a program to improve sensitive-responsiveness) and determining whether the expected outcomes occur. In essence, developmental science provides a theory of change and intervention science allows us to test that theory. When combined with clinical expertise and experience, the various aspects of developmental and intervention science can work together to provide a more accurate portrayal of family influences on children's development and generate feasible practices that can be applied in community settings that are effective in fostering children's social and intellectual competence.

Available evidence from intervention science now permits us to be more specific about how such early intervention programs should be organized and, as it turns out, that evidence is entirely consistent with the goal of minimizing the stressors to family patterns of interaction discussed in this chapter. Indeed, results from numerous studies, many very well controlled from a scientific perspective, suggest that when resource supports, social supports, and information and services are provided in the context of organized early intervention programs that are responsive to the stressors outlined above, both short- and long-term benefits with respect to children's social and intellectual competence can be achieved (Guralnick, 1997, 1998; Hill, Brooks-Gunn, & Waldfogel, 2003). To obtain these child developmental outcomes, services and supports responsive to assessments of stressors to family patterns of interaction are carefully individualized and implemented in a manner intended to strengthen families. Important features of these model interventions include administrative procedures to integrate and coordinate the diverse services that may be needed. Indeed, families have considerable access to services such as audiology, assistive technology, transportation, family counseling, family training, genetic counseling, and evaluation. These are in addition to more traditional health and therapeutic services (e.g., physical therapy). Clearly, coordination and integration are critical.

Some model programs that have been evaluated as part of intervention science have provided a unique array of services and supports. For example, in the United States, the Infant Health and Development Program is a preventive intervention program focusing on children born prematurely at low birth weight (Infant Health and Development Program, 1990). A critical component of that program was offering intervention-oriented day care in which a specific child-focused curriculum was implemented. The curriculum was pegged to children's developmental skill areas organized into themes related to cognitive and fine motor, social and self, motor, and language. It consisted primarily of games and activities easily integrated into established routines, along with strategies to develop the skills of adults to provide development-enhancing activities for the child. Other specialized programs include highly intensive applied behavioral analysis techniques for young children with autism (National Research Council, 2001). In this instance, carefully structured environments are created in which basic behavioral patterns and skills, such as imitation, are established through direct instruction and reward systems to provide the foundation for the establishment of more complex behavioral repertoires.

To be sure, much work remains in order to thoughtfully and sensitively design assessment protocols for stressors to family patterns of interaction, but considerable progress is being made (Guralnick, 2001b, 2005a). Nevertheless, among the lessons learned from intervention science are that interventions will only be successful if they are compatible with a family's culture, values, and priorities, particularly as they are realized through their own family structure and family routines. This requires thoughtful individualization of services and supports as each stressor successfully addressed contributes to the eventual positive outcome. Moreover, the intensity of service provided has emerged as a central element of effective interventions (see Guralnick, 1998). This requires a strong commitment of resources and the persistence of all those involved. Accordingly, the results from intervention science suggest we are clearly on the right track and point to directions for future refinements.

Summary and Future Directions

This chapter has outlined the important family influences on young children's social and intellectual competence based on developmental science. Three categories of family patterns of interaction were identified that independently or in concert influence children's developmental trajectories. Also discussed was the fact that it is difficult for parents to provide the development-enhancing features of these family patterns of interaction when challenged by stressors emanating from certain family or child characteristics. Fortunately, research and theory from the developmental science of normative development and the developmental science of risk and disability have enabled child developmentalists to gain a firm understanding of how these processes operate and how each influential factor relates to the others.

It was further suggested that a common developmental framework can be applied to children developing typically as well as to children at risk for developmental problems and those with established disabilities. This is a critically important point, as this developmental framework can serve as a guide to providing supports and services to families with vulnerable children. Most directly, it appears that successful efforts with respect to prevention or intervention will be those that strengthen families by minimizing stressors to family patterns of interaction. As noted, available evidence from intervention science supports this contention. Clearly, much can be learned from the integration of developmental and intervention science, as each informs the other as to the validity of its assumptions and assertions and suggests future directions to better understand the influences governing children's development and the best ways to enhance that development.

The fact that there is so much variability in response to early interventions, however, creates a sense of urgency to achieve an even better understanding of the developmental processes involved and the types of interventions that are most effective. Developmental and intervention science are hard at work on this "specificity" issue. Indeed, as we learn more about the responsiveness, or lack thereof, to existing early intervention programs of certain identifiable subgroups of children at risk and those with established disabilities, the form and intensity of interventions can be adjusted accordingly.

To gain more information, researchers and clinicians in the fields of genetics and neuroscience have joined with behavioral scientists in order to identify these subgroups of children and families and to characterize the developmental processes that may be uniquely associated with each (Bailey, Phillips, & Rutter, 1996; Nelson, 2000). Of importance, these collaborations are helping us to understand some of the "core deficits" affecting various subgroups of children. In turn, this information will be used as a form of "translational research" to inform child-focused and even family-based interventions which will be evaluated using the techniques of intervention science.

Finally, it is important to point out that developmental and intervention scientists have an important responsibility to maintain close contact with clinicians and community programs. Unfortunately, despite many excellent community-based systems and individual early intervention programs, services and supports for vulnerable children are not nearly as state-of-the-art or as evidence-based as we would like (Guralnick, 2005b, in press; Spiker, Hebbeler, Wagner, Cameto, & McKenna, 2000). Indeed, in the United States and elsewhere fragmentation of services remains a critical problem (Shonkoff & Phillips, 2000). This early intervention systems development issue constitutes one of the most formidable challenges to fostering the well-being of vulnerable children and their families.

References

Affleck, G., & Tennen, H. (1993). Cognitive adaptation to adversity: Insights from parents of medically fragile infants. In A. P. Turnbull, J. M. Patterson, S. K. Behr, D. L. Murphy, J. G. Marquis, & M. J. Blue-Banning (Eds.), *Cognitive coping, families, and disability* (pp. 135–150). Baltimore: Brookes.

Ainsworth, M. D. S., Blehar, M. C., Waters, E., & Wall, S. (1978). *Patterns of attachment: A psychological study of the strange situation.* New York: Wiley and Sons.

Als, H. (1997). Earliest intervention for preterm infants in the Newborn Intensive Care Unit. In M. J. Guralnick (Ed.), *The effectiveness of early intervention* (pp. 47–76). Baltimore: Brookes.

Als, H., Gilkerson, L., Duffy, F. H., McAnulty, G. B., Buehler, D. M., Vandenberg, K., Sweet, N., Sell, E., Parad, R. B., Ringer, S. A., Butler, S. C., Blickman, J. G., & Jones, K. J. (2003). A three-center, randomized, controlled trial of individualized developmental care for very low birth weight preterm infants: Medical, neurodevelopmental, parenting, and caregiving effects. *Journal of Developmental and Behavioral Pediatrics, 24,* 399–408.

Atkinson, L., Chisholm, V. C., Scott, B., Goldberg, S., Vaughn, B. E., Blackwell, J., Dickens, S., & Tam, F. (1999). Maternal sensitivity, child functional level, and attachment in Down syndrome. *Monographs of the Society for Research in Child Development, 64*(3, Serial No. 258).

Bailey, A., Phillips, W., & Rutter, M. (1996). Towards an integration of clinical, genetic, neuro-psychological, and neurobiological perspectives. *Journal of Child Psychology and Psychiatry, 37,* 89–126.

Baker, B. L., Blacher, J., Crnic, K. A., & Edelbrook, C. (2002). Behavior problems and parenting stress in families of three-year-old children with and without developmental delays. *American Journal on Mental Retardation, 107,* 433–444.

Barnard, K. E. (1997). Influencing parent–child interactions for children at risk. In M. J. Guralnick (Ed.), *The effectiveness of early intervention* (pp. 249–268). Baltimore: Brookes.

Belsky, J., & Fearon, R. M. P. (2002). Infant–mother attachment security, contextual risk, and early development: A moderational analysis. *Development and Psychopathology, 14,* 293–310.

Birenbaum, A., Guyot, D., & Cohen, H. J. (1990). Health care financing for severe developmental disabilities. *Monographs of the American Association on Mental Retardation, 14.*

Booth, C. L., & Kelly, J. F. (1998). Child-care characteristics of infants with and without special needs: Comparisons and concerns. *Early Childhood Research Quarterly, 13,* 603–622.

Bornstein, M. H., & Tamis-Lemonda, C. S. (1989). Maternal responsiveness and cognitive development in children. *New Directions for Child Development, 48,* 49–61.

Bradley, R. H. (1989). HOME measurement of maternal responsiveness. In M. H. Bornstein (Ed.), *Maternal responsiveness: Characteristics and consequences* (pp. 63–74). San Francisco: Jossey-Bass.

Bradley, R. H. (2002). Environment and parenting. In M. H. Bornstein (Ed.), *Handbook of parenting: Vol. 2. Biology and ecology of parenting* (2nd ed., pp. 281–314). Mahwah, NJ: Lawrence Erlbaum.

Bradley, R. H., Caldwell, B. M., Rock, S. L., Barnard, K. E., Gray, C., Hammond, M. A., Mitchell, S., Siegel, L., Ramey, C. T., Gottfried, A. W., & Johnson, D. L. (1989). Home environment and cognitive development in the first 3 years of life: A collaborative study involving six sites and three ethnic groups in North America. *Developmental Psychology, 25,* 217–235.

Bristol, M. M. (1987). The home care of children with developmental disabilities: Empirical support for a model of successful family coping with stress. In S. Landesman & P. M. Vietze (Eds.), *Living environments and mental retardation* (pp. 401–422). Washington, DC: American Association on Mental Retardation.

Burchinal, M. R., Roberts, J. E., Hooper, S., & Zeisel, S. A. (2000). Cumulative risk and early cognitive development: A comparison of statistical risk models. *Developmental Psychology, 36,* 793–807.

Carlson, E. A., Sampson, M. C., & Sroufe, L. A. (2003). Implications of attachment theory and research for developmental-behavioral pediatrics. *Developmental and Behavioral Pediatrics, 24,* 364–379.

Cicchetti, D., & Cohen, D. J. (1995). Perspectives on developmental psychopathology. In D. Cicchetti & D. J. Cohen (Eds.), *Developmental psychopathology: Vol. 1. Theories and methods* (pp. 3–20). New York: Wiley.

Collins, W. A., Maccoby, E. E., Steinberg, L., Hetherington, E. M., & Bornstein, M. H. (2000). Contemporary research on parenting: The case for nature and nurture. *American Psychologist, 55,* 218–232.

Duncan, G. J., Brooks-Gunn, J., & Klebanov, P. K. (1994). Economic deprivation and early childhood development. *Child Development, 65,* 296–318.

Dunst, C. J., Hamby, D., Trivette, C. M., Raab, M., & Bruder, M. B. (2000). Everyday family and community life and children's naturally occurring learning opportunities. *Journal of Early Intervention, 23,* 151–164.

Dyson, L. L. (1993). Response to the presence of a child with disabilities: parental stress and family functioning over time. *American Journal on Mental Retardation, 98,* 207–218.

Farver, J. M., Natera, L. X., & Frosch, D. L. (1999). Effects of community violence on inner-city preschoolers and their families. *Journal of Applied Developmental Psychology, 20*, 143–158.

Fiese, B. H. (2002). Routines of daily living and rituals in family life: A glimpse at stability and change during the early child-raising years. *Zero to Three, 22*(4), 10–13.

Gallimore, R., Keogh, B. K., & Bernheimer, L. P. (1999). The nature and long-term implications of early developmental delays: A summary of evidence from two longitudinal studies. In L. M. Glidden (Ed.), *International review of research in mental retardation* (Vol. 22, pp. 105–135). San Diego: Academic Press.

Gallimore, R., Weisner, T. S., Bernheimer, L. P., Guthrie, D., & Nihira, K. (1993). Family responses to young children with developmental delays: Accommodation activity in ecological and cultural context. *American Journal on Mental Retardation, 98*, 185–206.

Georgieff, M. K., & Rao, R. (1999). The role of nutrition in cognitive development. In C. A. Nelson & M. Luciana (Eds.), *Handbook of developmental cognitive neuroscience* (pp. 491–504). Cambridge, MA: MIT Press.

Goffman, E. (1963). *Stigma.* Englewood Cliffs, NJ: Prentice-Hall.

Gorman, K. S. (1995). Malnutrition and cognitive development: Evidence from experimental/quasi-experimental studies among the mild-to-moderately malnourished. *Journal of Nutrition, 125*, 2239S–2244S.

Griffin, E. A., & Morrison, F. J. (1997). The unique contribution of home literacy environment to differences in early literacy skills. *Early Child Development and Care, 127–128*, 233–243.

Guralnick, M. J. (Ed.). (1997). *The effectiveness of early intervention.* Baltimore: Brookes.

Guralnick, M. J. (1998). The effectiveness of early intervention for vulnerable children: A developmental perspective. *American Journal on Mental Retardation, 102*, 319–345.

Guralnick, M. J. (1999). Family and child influences on the peer-related social competence of young children with developmental delays. *Mental Retardation and Developmental Disabilities Research Reviews, 5*, 21–29.

Guralnick, M. J. (2001a). Connections between developmental science and intervention science. *Zero to Three, 21*(5), 24–29.

Guralnick, M. J. (2001b). A developmental systems model for early intervention. *Infants and Young Children, 14*(2), 1–18.

Guralnick, M. J. (2001c). Social competence with peers and early childhood inclusion: Need for alternative approaches. In M. J. Guralnick (Ed.), *Early childhood inclusion: Focus on change* (pp. 481–502). Baltimore: Brookes.

Guralnick, M. J. (2002). Les jeunes enfants trisomiques 21 dans leurs relations avec des pairs: Caractéristiques de développement et interventions envisageables [The peer relations of young children with Down syndrome: Developmental characteristics and intervention approaches]. *Journal de la Trisomie, 21*(4), 18–27.

Guralnick, M. J. (2004). Family investments in response to the developmental challenges of young children with disabilities. In A. Kalil & T. Deleire (Eds.), *Family investments in children: Resources and behaviors that promote success* (pp. 119–137). Mahwah, NJ: Lawrence Erlbaum.

Guralnick, M. J. (Ed.). (2005a). *The developmental systems approach to early intervention.* Baltimore: Brookes.

Guralnick, M. J. (Ed.). (2005b). An overview of the developmental systems approach to early intervention. In M. J. Guralnick (Ed.), *The developmental systems approach to early intervention* (pp. 3–28). Baltimore: Brookes.

Guralnick, M. J. (in press). The system of early intervention for children with developmental disabilities: Current status and challenges for the future. In J. W. Jacobson & J. A. Mulick (Eds.), *Handbook of mental retardation and developmental disabilities.* New York: Plenum.

Guralnick, M. J., Connor, R. T., Neville, B., & Hammond M. A. (2002). Mothers' perspectives of the peer-related social development of young children with developmental delays and communication disorders. *Early Education and Development, 13*, 59–80.

Guralnick, M. J., & Neville, B. (1997). Designing early intervention programs to promote children's social competence. In M. J. Guralnick (Ed.), *The effectiveness of early intervention* (pp. 579–610). Baltimore: Brookes.

Hagerman, R. J. (1999). *Neurodevelopmental disorders: Diagnosis and treatment.* New York: Oxford University Press.

Haley, D. W., & Stansbury, K. (2003). Infant stress and parent responsiveness: Regulation of physiology and behavior during still-face and reunion. *Child Development, 74*, 1534–1546.

Hart, B., & Risley, T. R. (1995). *Meaningful differences in the everyday experience of young American children.* Baltimore: Brookes.

Hill, J. L., Brooks-Gunn, J., & Waldfogel, J. (2003). Sustained effects of high participation in an early intervention for low-birth-weight premature infants. *Developmental Psychology, 39*, 730–744.

Infant Health and Development Program. (1990). Enhancing the outcomes of low-birth-weight, premature infants: A multisite, randomized trial. *Journal of the American Medical Association, 263*, 3035–3042.

Kasari, C., Freeman, S., Mundy, P., & Sigman, M. D. (1995). Attention regulation by children with Down syndrome: Coordinated joint attention and social referencing looks. *American Journal on Mental Retardation, 100*, 128–136.

Koenen, K. C., Moffitt, T. E., Caspi, A., Taylor, A., & Purcell, S. (2003). Domestic violence is associated with environmental suppression of IQ in young children. *Development and Psychopathology, 15*, 297–311.

Ladd, G. W., & Hart, C. H. (1992). Creating informal play opportunities: Are parents' and preschoolers' initiations related to children's competence with peers? *Developmental Psychology, 28*, 1179–1187.

Ladd, G. W., & Pettit, G. S. (2003). Parenting and the development of children's peer relationships. In M. H. Bornstein (Ed.), *Handbook of parenting: Vol. 3. Status and social conditions of parenting* (2nd ed., pp. 269–309). Mahwah, NJ: Lawrence Erlbaum.

LaFreniere, P. J., & Dumas, J. E. (1992). A transactional analysis of early childhood anxiety and social withdrawal. *Development and Psychopathology, 4*, 385–402.

Landry, S. H., Smith, K. E., Miller-Loncar, C. L., & Swank, P. R. (1997). Predicting cognitive-language and social growth curves from early maternal behaviors in children at varying degrees of biological risk. *Developmental Psychology, 33*, 1040–1053.

Landry, S. H., Smith, K. E., Miller-Loncar, C. L., & Swank, P. R. (1998). The relation of change in maternal interactive styles to the developing social competence of full-term and preterm children. *Child Development, 69*, 105–123.

Landry, S. H., Smith, K. E., Swank, P. R., & Miller-Loncar, C. L. (2000). Early maternal and child influences on children's later independent cognitive and social functioning. *Child Development, 71*, 358–375.

Landry, S. H., Smith, K. E., Swank, P. R., Assel, M. A., & Vellet, S. (2001). Does early responsive parenting have a special importance for children's development or is consistency across early childhood necessary? *Developmental Psychology, 37*, 387–403.

Lewis, M., & Goldberg, S. (1969). Perceptual-cognitive development in infancy: A generalized expectancy model as a function of mother–infant interaction. *Merrill-Palmer Quarterly, 15*, 81–100.

Liaw, F.-R., & Brooks-Gunn, J. (1994). Cumulative familial risks and low birth weight children's cognitive and behavioral development. *Journal of Clinical and Child Psychology, 23*, 360–372.

Lozoff, B., De Andraca, I., Castillo, M., Smith, J. B., Walter, T., & Pino, P. (2003). Behavioral and developmental effects of preventing iron-deficiency anemia in healthy full-term infants. *Pediatrics, 112*, 846–854.

McCollum, J. A., & Hemmeter, M. L. (1997). Parent–child interaction intervention when children have disabilities. In M. J. Guralnick (Ed.), *The effectiveness of early intervention* (pp. 549–576). Baltimore: Brookes.

Martin, J. A. (1989). Personal and interpersonal components of responsiveness. In M. H. Bornstein (Ed.), *Maternal responsiveness: Characteristics and consequences* (pp. 5–14). San Francisco: Jossey-Bass.

Meyer, E. C., Garcia Coll, C. T., Seifer, R., Ramos, A., Kilis, E., & Oh, W. (1995). Psychological distress in mothers of preterm infants. *Journal of Developmental and Behavioral Pediatrics, 16*, 412–417.

Minde, K. (2000). Prematurity and serious medical conditions in infancy: Implications for development, behavior, and intervention. In C. H. Zeanah, Jr. (Ed.), *Handbook of infant mental health* (2nd ed., pp. 176–194). New York: Guilford.

Mundy, P., & Stella, J. (2000). Joint attention, social orienting, and communication in autism. In A. M. Wetherby & B. M. Prizant (Eds.), *Autism spectrum disorders: Vol. 9. A transactional developmental perspective* (pp. 55–77). Baltimore: Brookes.

National Research Council. (2001). *Educating children with autism.* Committee on Educational Interventions for Children with Autism. Washington, DC: National Academy Press.

Nelson, C. A. (2000). The neurobiological bases of early intervention. In J. P. Shonkoff & S. J. Meisels (Eds.), *Handbook of early childhood intervention* (2nd ed., pp. 204–277). Cambridge: Cambridge University Press.

NICHD Early Child Care Research Network. (2003). Does quality of child care affect child outcomes at age 4½? *Developmental Psychology, 39*, 451–469.

NICHD Early Child Care Research Network, & Duncan, G. J. (2003). Modeling the impacts of child care quality on children's preschool cognitive development. *Child Development, 74*, 1454–1475.

Osofsky, J. D. (1995). The effects of violence exposure on young children. *American Psychologist, 50*, 782–788.

Parke, R. D., Cassidy, J., Burks, V. M., Carson, J. L., & Boyum, L. (1992). Familial contributions to peer competence among young children: The role of interactive and affective processes. In R. D. Parke & G. W. Ladd (Eds.), *Family–peer relationships: Modes of linkage* (pp. 107–134). Mahwah, NJ: Erlbaum.

Parker, J. G., Rubin, K. H., Price, J. M., & DeRosier M. E. (1995). Peer relationships, child development, and adjustment: A developmental psychopathology perspective. In D. Cicchetti & D. J. Cohen (Eds.), *Developmental psychopathology: Vol. 2. Risk, disorder, and adaptation* (pp. 96–161). New York: Wiley.

Parpal, M., & Maccoby, E. (1985). Maternal responsiveness and subsequent child compliance. *Child Development, 56*, 1326–1334.

Pianta, R. C., Marvin, R. S., Britner, P. A., & Borowitz, K. C. (1996). Mothers' resolution of their children's diagnosis: Organized patterns of caregiving representations. *Journal of Infant Mental Health, 17*, 239–256.

Roach, M. A., Orsmond, G. I., & Barratt, M. S. (1999). Mothers and fathers of children with Down syndrome: Parental stress and involvement in childcare. *American Journal on Mental Retardation, 104*, 422–436.

Roizen, N. J., & Patterson, D. (2003). Down's syndrome. *Lancet, 361*, 1281–1289.

Russell, A., & Finnie, V. (1990). Preschool children's social status and maternal instructions to assist group entry. *Developmental Psychology, 26*, 603–611.

Sameroff, A. J., & Fiese, B. H. (2000). Models of development and developmental risk. In C. H. Zeanah, Jr. (Ed.), *Handbook of infant mental health* (pp. 3–19). New York: Guilford.

Sameroff, A. J., Seifer, R., Barocas, R., Zax, M., & Greenspan, S. (1987). Intelligence quotient scores of 4-year-old children: Social-environmental risk factors. *Pediatrics, 79*, 343–350.

Schneider, B. H., Atkinson, L., & Tardif, C. (2001). Child–parent attachment and children's peer relations: A quantitative review. *Developmental Psychology, 37*, 86–100.

Shannon, P., Grinde, L. R., & Cox, A. W. (2003). Families' perceptions of the ability to pay for early intervention services. *Journal of Early Intervention, 25*, 164–172.

Shonkoff, J. P., & Phillips, D. A. (Eds.). (2000). *From neurons to neighborhoods: The science of early child development.* Washington, DC: National Academy Press.

Sigman, M., & Ruskin, E. (1999). Continuity and change in the social competence of children with autism, Down syndrome, and developmental delays. *Monographs of the Society for Research in Child Development, 64*(1, Serial No. 256).

Singer, L. T., Fulton, S., Davillier, M., Koshy, D., Salvator, A., & Baley, J. E. (2003). Effects of infant risk status and maternal psychological distress on maternal–infant interactions during the first year of life. *Journal of Developmental and Behavioral Pediatrics, 24*, 233–241.

Sontag, J. C., & Schacht, R. (1994). An ethnic comparison of parent participation and information needs in early intervention. *Exceptional Children, 60*, 422–433.

Spiker, D., Boyce, G. C., & Boyce, L. K. (2002). Parent–child interactions when young children have disabilities. In L. M. Glidden (Ed.), *International review of research in mental retardation* (Vol. 25, pp. 35–70). San Diego: Academic Press.

Spiker, D., Hebbeler, K., Wagner, M., Cameto, R., & McKenna, P. (2000). A framework for describing variations in state early intervention systems. *Topics in Early Childhood Special Education, 20*, 195–207.

Steelman, L. M., Assel, M. A., Swank, P. R., Smith, K. E., & Landry, S. H. (2002). Early maternal warm responsiveness as a predictor of child social skills: Direct and indirect paths of influence over time. *Journal of Applied Developmental Psychology, 23*, 135–156.

Tamis-LeMonda, C. S., Bornstein, M. H., Baumwell, L., & Damast, A. M. (1996). Responsive parenting in the second year: Specific influences on children's language and play. *Early Development and Parenting, 5*, 173–183.

Thompson, R. A. (1999). Early attachment and later development. In J. Cassidy & P. Shaver (Eds.), *Handbook of attachment: Theory, research, and clinical applications* (pp. 265–286). New York: Guilford.

Tomasello, M., & Farrar, M. J. (1986). Joint attention and early language. *Child Development, 57*, 1454–1463.

Vygotsky, L. S. (1978). *Mind in society.* Cambridge, MA: Harvard University Press.

Wakschlag, L. S., & Hans, S. L. (1999). Relation of maternal responsiveness during infancy to the development of behavior problems in high-risk youths. *Developmental Psychology, 35*, 569–579.

Wood, D. J. (1998). Teaching the young child: Some relationships between social interaction, language, and thought. In P. Lloyd & C. Fernyhough (Eds.), *Lev Vygotsky: Critical assessments. The zone of proximal development* (pp. 259–275). New York: Routledge.

Yeung, W. J., Linver, M. R., & Brooks-Gunn, J. (2002). How money matters for young children's development: Parental investment and family processes. *Child Development, 73*, 1861–1879.

Yoder, P. J., & Warren, S. F. (1999). Maternal responsivity mediates the relationship between prelinguistic intentional communication and later language. *Journal of Early Intervention, 22*, 126–136.

4

Developmental Pathways and Intersections among Domains of Development

Catherine C. Ayoub and Kurt W. Fischer

Conceptual Framework for the Intersections of Domains

The defining feature of development is the emergence of new forms – "development" is the property of change, and change is never more rapid than in early childhood. As a result of both its speed and complexity, the study of early development has often moved forward through concentration on specific domains. Domain-specific focus as well as issues of discontinuity and individual variation complicate the process of mapping developmental pathways in early childhood. Concepts of development have historically favored linear progressions that oversimplify and tend to homogenize development (Fischer et al., 1997; Piaget, 1983; Freud, 1933/1965; Kohlberg, 1969). In contrast to these linear models, we propose that a person develops along a web of multiple strands and that different people develop along different pathways or webs. At the same time, different people's webs can be similar, or they can be very different. The focus of this chapter is on the differences between webs as well as the processes by which strands separate and integrate within a web.

Secondly, the study of development has increasingly moved toward the fragmentation or splitting of the human organism into investigable units or domains – biology, behavior, culture, genetics, cognition, relationships, innate modules of mind, etc. – resulting in the inevitable loss of the *person* as an integrated, embodied center of agency and action (Fischer & Biddell, 1998; Lerner, Anderson, Balsano, Dowling, & Bobek, 2003; Overton, 2003). Though researchers acknowledge that development occurs across multiple integrated biological and behavioral levels (Susman, 1998), most scientific knowledge is generated and interpreted within distinct disciplinary boundaries, making our understanding of the person *as a whole* opaque.

Domain-specific exploration, although critically important to the advancement of scientific understanding, has the continued potential to isolate processes that occur simultaneously within the child. As a response to this fragmentation, a number of theorists have begun to think across domains, placing the young child's various developmental processes in context over time. For example, the notion of cognition and emotion as a set of dynamic and integrated systems is becoming a new powerful theory that bridges psychological and neurobiological conceptions of both thinking and feeling (Fischer & Biddell, 1998). Add to this equation the development of critical communication, motivational, and self-regulation skills, and the transformations in the "whole child" during the first five years of life are the most extraordinary across the lifespan.

We will use the examples of the alternate developmental pathways for shy, autistic, and maltreated children to highlight the importance of examining the intersections of domains from a developmental perspective. Assumptions about the child's cognitive, language, or social development, made in the absence of context and without attention to domain intersections, can lead to the erroneous belief that the child, for example, has a cognitive delay rather than an adaptive difference. The practical result is often that the assumed cognitive delay is addressed without acknowledgment of the child's actions as adaptive and developmentally maturing responses to an adversarial condition or environment.

Using an integrative pathways approach results in understanding the behavior of young children as adaptive and complex rather than simply delayed or dysfunctional. It is our perspective that the simplistic mischaracterization of delay in each group of "different" children we describe stems from the persistent view that development occurs in a domain-general and unidirectional way, regardless of context. This field is ready to accurately describe the variation in children's development with a "child-in-context" framework that emphasizes the enormous variation in human development, using the constructs of the developmental web and the central role of adaptation to the environment in the service of survival. As we present our three examples of young children who are "different," that is, shy, autistic, and maltreated, respectively, we will explore their developmental trajectories through considering their functioning both within and across developmental domains; it is the interface of this functioning that we will characterize as an alternative developmental pathway.

One promising contribution to this integrative approach of describing developmental pathways in early childhood is dynamic systems. The power of dynamic systems theory derives from analyzing stability as principles of order within variation. A system's development occurs through the dynamic link between the stability of a state and the variation around that state. Thelen and Smith (1998) describe the formation of relatively stable biological and behavioral states that can be reliably predicted; they also describe the constant variation around this stability. It is this holistic construct that serves as the basis for considering the interface of multiple domains of development – cognition, emotion, attachment – and their corollaries – motivation, verbal and non-verbal communication, and regulation – in the young child. This perspective argues for the integration of biology and behavior at a theoretical level that must focus on the stability and variability within each domain as well as the integration and timing of each with the other. It is through this lens that this chapter has been constructed.

Several assumptions about the nature of development and the pathway transgressed by any given child are important to consider at this point. Our understanding of the changes and continuities of the developmental process is based on assumptions about the nature of developmental pathways. We propose that development forms a web of multiple pathways or strands rather than the more common assumption that development proceeds along a single ladder of stages. This developmental web is the norm for the full range of skills, from relationships to reading (see Figure 4.1).

Additionally, this model assumes that people do not have integrated, fundamentally logical minds, but instead have naturally fractionated strands of the web that can be potentially integrated over time (Fischer & Ayoub, 1994). The nature of the developmental process across the lifespan is to continue to integrate these strands as well as to further create as well as to differentiate them. The conclusion here is that although emotions, regulatory processes, and communication skills as well as complex cognitive schemas like working models of close relationships develop systematically through a series of skill levels, such skills will vary across the strands in the web and will not necessarily form a unified whole. This whole, be it unified or segmented, is the child's developmental pathway. In young children, the variation observed is in good part due to the variety of patterns of integration and differentiation in the web and the timing and context of the expression of each skill set. However, skill theory allows for developmental synchrony across skills as well as disconnection or splitting of skill sets within the individual; each is an adaptive move within the developmental process (Fischer & Bidell, 1998).

On the side of thinking and learning, the cyclical changes in capacity in given domains are not evident in young children in everything that they do because most of their acting, thinking, and learning does not push the limit of their capacities. These new capacities can be matched with growth cycles of the brain, especially the cerebral cortex (Case, 1991; Fischer & Rose, 1998). This rich biological concept of recurring growth cycles that predict both behavior and brain changes occurs in repeating patterns of common developmental

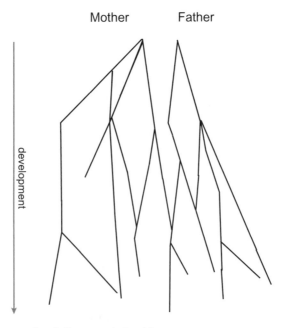

Figure 4.1　Developmental web for two relationships.

progress called a developmental level. In the last few years, new discoveries about brain functioning have led to evidence of recurring cortical growth cycles and the striking parallels of these cortical cycles with the cognitive-developmental cycles for levels and tiers. Derived from a neo-Piagetian frame, the nested cognitive developmental tiers include reflexes, actions, representations, and abstractions. Within each tier there are processes that organize thinking in the context of single units – mappings and systems of each of the four tiers (Fischer & Rose, 1998).

However, when a new developmental level emerges, optimal performance along most strands shows discontinuity, reflected in growth spurts and reorganizations, which are marked by changes in direction, forks, and intersections of strands in the web. These changes do not occur all at once, but are distributed across a specific age period or zone. With the development of each level, the young child can build new, more complex kinds of skills or understandings in diverse domains. Usually a child only produces this optimal level with strong contextual support – like that from a parent or teacher. Without such support, most thinking and learning occurs at lower levels, not at the optimal level. These phenomena contribute to the diversity and dynamic movement within pathways as both stability and adaptation continue to play off of each other, resulting in variation in the behavioral presentation of the young child at any given moment.

In order to consider the interface of cognition, emotion, motivation, and attachment interactions, one must first review the constructs that apply to each developmental process and then examine their intersections. Because development depends upon both stability and flexibility, both within and across domains, these two constructs are the cornerstones for understanding the developmental interface that describes for each child the way in which early development potentially influences later functioning.

Affective development and attachment constructs

The primacy of sensory and affective development for the first year and a half of life (Lyons-Ruth, 1998; Schore, 1994) provides a foundation for the cognitive and relational learning that moves so quickly through the preschool years. One of the very first tasks of infants is to develop affective attunement to their caregivers (Stern, 1983). Such attunement protects infants from the helplessness that is characteristic of the first two years of life. In their early forms, working models primarily incorporate young children's own motives and experiences in attachment relationships. However, by 1 to 2 years of age, children begin to recognize that their attachment figure's emotions and motives can differ from theirs. At this point, children's attachments become goal-corrected partnerships in which their working models incorporate their own intentions and desires as well as their understandings of others' intentions and emotions (Marvin & Britner, 1999). Working models of close relationships depict development, maintenance, and dissolution of attachments in terms of general role relationships specifying particular types of interactions and accompanying emotions.

The notion that attachment in its most popular form treats working models as divided into three organized categories – secure, ambivalent, or avoidant – as well as a disorganized fourth category, should be regarded as a starting point rather than the basis for models developing over time. In contrast we suggest that the analyses of developing relationships in young children are much more differentiated than these four categories and should include attention to context and culture as well as to security in the development of working models of relationships (LeVine & Miller, 1990). These diverse components of working models are all needed to describe the interface of emotion and cognition as well as the development of alternative pathways of development.

As evidence of the biological and affective interface, we can explore how early object relations directly influence the emergence of the frontolimbic system in the right hemisphere (Schore, 1994). A related way to map the young child's move from helplessness to competence is through the study of systems of physiological and emotional self-regulation (Shonkoff & Phillips, 2000). Self-regulatory tasks encompass the management of physiological arousal, emotions, and attention. The acquisition of behavioral, emotional, and ultimately cognitive self-control has been proposed as the fundamental stone of competent functioning (Bronson, 2000; Kopp, 2000). Arousal is regulated through attachment relationships as well as temperamental characteristics (van der Kolk, 1996).

Regulation is deeply embedded in early relationships. Over time, cognition and emotion flow together into the development of these patterns of interaction. As the young child gains cognitive maturity through a series of transformations in thinking, working models of relationships are also transformed to reflect the complexity of this acquisition of increasingly complex skills. However, individuals' worldview, that is, their view of themselves and others in the context of a vision of life as a primarily positive versus a negative or threatening experience, has its roots in the nature and continuity of the infant and toddler's primary nurturing relationships with key adults. We propose that the templates for coping skills developed from these primary relationships in early childhood are incorporated into the child's emotional structure. At each step they are transformed by the cognitive maturation of the child into adulthood as "working models" that contribute to a unique developmental path. Children who experience significant and repeated trauma in early childhood – for example, the trauma of physical abuse or the pain associated with the loss of a primary parenting figure – are likely to alter their socio-emotional perspective of relationships in fundamental ways (Ayoub, Fischer, & O'Connor, 2003). These alternations, in turn, also impact on the child's cognitive focus, motivation, and attention skills. These negative experiences, if they are severe or prolonged, can fundamentally alter the young child's developmental trajectory across domains in a way that reinforces such negativity. Two central organizers of developing close relationships that are potentially re-organized as a result of negative life experience, for example, are the positive–negative dimension of emotions and the natural patterns in differentiation and integration. Such patterns occur with developmental growth and lead to increasingly complex cognitive thought (Fischer & Ayoub, 1994). It is these two organizing principles which we will examine in exploring the interface of developmental domains and the development of individual working models and, ultimately, pathways across early childhood in our three examples of shyness, autism, and maltreatment.

Emotion and self-regulation constructs

Emotional expression and regulation are tasks that begin in infancy and are consolidated throughout early childhood. In infancy, expression and regulation center on engaging with and responding to the senses. The infant feels hungry, sleepy, cold or hot, alert or fussy. But as children grow, their physical states become much less powerful in predicting their emotions, and feelings hinge on the interpretation of experience in the context of causal understanding and relationships. Both individual and cultural meanings affect how children construe and react to their environments (Miller, 1994; Miller, Fung, & Mintz, 1996). Throughout early childhood the frontal neocortex matures and becomes interconnected in order to aid in more accurate emotional appraisal and emotional self-regulatory functions. The infant soon differentiates a cry – one for pain, one for discomfort, and one for hunger – and, likewise, the toddler quickly refines those responses into differentiated feelings of anger, fear, guilt, joy, and love that continue to be elaborated through the preschool years. Young children identify and differentiate negative emotions more specifically than positive emotions during the first three years of life, and the bias toward differentiation of negative emotions continues into adulthood (Shaver, Schwartz, Kirson, & O'Connor, 1987). This imbalance supports the need for self-preservation of the organism in its relatively helpless state.

One of the central organizers of developing thinking and relationships is the positive–negative dimension of emotions, which produces natural affective splitting of development into separate strands. Biases or constraints growing from positive and negative experiences organize action and thought from birth and thus shape development (Fischer, Shaver, & Carnochan, 1990). One of the most obvious ways in which the evaluation dimension organizes behavior is affective splitting, in which a person separates two events, people, objects, or aspects of a situation into positive and negative, even though to another observer the things are neither truly separate nor simply positive and negative (Harter & Buddin, 1987). Affective splitting is normative in the developmental process; splitting is also important for development of psychopathology, and in cases of recurrent negative life experience, it can serve as one coping strategy that results in a different personality organization or path. Recent work in the area of trauma and psychopathology supports a connection between the repeated trauma of early child abuse, for example, and a pervasive array of changes in thinking and emotion that produce serious disturbance (Terr, 1991). Symptoms include basic fragmentations in a person's sense of self and malignant feelings of inner badness at the core of beliefs about self and world.

Learning to understand emotions and being able to regulate them are primary tasks of early childhood. Although emotional understanding develops as a foundation for cognitive learning, it also grows in concert with the development of other forms of knowledge. Children's developing frameworks for inferring what other people are thinking, believing, intending, and feeling as well as for making predictions about how they will respond are evident in toddlers (Astington, 1993; Flavell & Miller, 1998) and continue to develop during the preschool years. The connection between emotion and expectation, the roots of "theory of mind" – for example, the glee of the young child in "fooling" the adult – offers evidence of the young child's ability to make these connections across domains and to act on them in complex ways (see Barr, this volume).

Another component of affective development in the early years is the emergence of executive functioning, which can also be mapped to early frontal lobe development (Schore, 1994). Hypothesis testing, impulse control, and planning are all characteristics that develop during this early period. Each is influenced by attention, memory, and concentration. Here the overlaying boundaries between cognition and emotion are most obvious (see Welsh, Friedman, & Spieker, this volume).

Cognitive and motivational constructs

Children from birth begin to make sense of the world in many ways, including spatial reasoning, physical causality, problem solving, categorization, and counting and quantification. These are the major tasks that have been associated with core intellectual competence in early childhood. Learning in these areas provides the foundation for complex reasoning. Infants become attuned to causal relationships and can distinguish causal sequences as well as the effects of their own behaviors on others (Mangelsdorf, 1992). Toddlers can recognize that other people have different tastes or preferences, and by age 4 young children can recognize everyday categories. By age 5, children can predict another person's intentions and recognize deception. Interestingly, the most varied differences in children beginning kindergarten are their skills in executive functioning. Although they may universally be able to understand causality, adopt another's perspective, and sort objects by categories, kindergarten children differ tremendously in their ability to learn, sequence, organize, and self-regulate their emotions; these differences often account for the most common problems described by their kindergarten teachers (Lyon, 1996).

Young children develop these cognitive abilities through orderly sequences of skills or concepts, showing abrupt stage-like discontinuities under some circumstances, and demonstrating some synchronies across tasks and contexts. In addition, children operate in a developmental range along each strand of the web. As a result different children often develop along different pathways and their ability to express and sustain their pathways becomes increasingly complex with age.

Early childhood is a critical time for the development, refinement, and consolidation of self-organizing motivational processes. Many 2- and 3-year-old children prefer and enjoy taking the role of a mean aggressive character, who often has more power and controls the action in a story or game. They also tend to understand these vivid negative roles better than positive roles (Fischer et al., 1997). By age 4, however, most children have given up the negative and mean for the positive characterization of people and events close to them. Furthermore, in pretend play the preschooler will often call on the "super-hero" – the super-good, all-powerful entity – to save the situation and vanquish the evil "other."

However, genetic predisposition, context, and attachment models can lead to differences in self-organizing motivation. Children who are quite inhibited temperamentally have more difficulty with negative appraisals (Fischer & Ayoub, 1994). Children who have experienced serious and repeated negative life events like child maltreatment may have negative and conflicted working models of self in relationship to other that will affect their self-appraisal. Finally, cultural differences come into play to re-orient appraisals within positive or negative categories. For example, in Chinese cultures shame is a powerful negative emotion (Li, Wang, & Fischer, 2004) associated with self-appraisal, while in western cultures guilt is more common.

Communication constructs

Whereas for the young child language serves primarily social goals, such as negotiating intimacy with the parent, defining a self separate from the parent, communicating needs and desires, and representing one's own point of view, increasingly over the preschool years language is used as the mechanism for gaining access to information about the physical and social world. The vocabulary spurt that typically occurs late in the second year of life presages an increasing focus by the learner on acquiring new words that in turn index access to new domains of knowledge, ranging from the biological (e.g., animal names, bodily functions) to the social (e.g., kinship terms, games) to the psychological (e.g., inner state words, relationships). Beginning around age 2, substantial individual and social class differences in rate of vocabulary acquisition begin to emerge, such that there are striking differences in total vocabulary size even before children enter kindergarten (Hart & Risley, 1995).

As children start to develop language, they begin to form a history of the self (i.e., autobiographical memory). Parents and other caregivers help regulate children's affective experience and assist in the development of a coherent life story and a cohesive self (Palombo, 1992). There is growing evidence that preschool children who have been exposed to significant and persistent negative experiences are at risk for constructing a lexicon of negative affect states related to the self (Nathanson, 1992) and are less adept at behavioral and affective regulation (Shields, Cicchetti & Ryan, 1994). They may develop rigid and controlling ways of interacting with others (Fischer et al., 1997). Adult caregivers influence children's expressive systems by helping solidify links between their cognitive problem solving, emotions, and language use. Parents who talk about feelings and conflicts tend to have children who develop a better understanding of emotion (Bretherton, Ridgeway, & Cassidy, 1990); those who encourage appropriate expression of negative emotions have children who tend to be more sympathetic and socially competent (Eisenberg & Fabes, 1992).

Constitutional contributions of the child

Study of the evolution of developmental pathways would not be complete without understanding the individual differences that the child brings to the process. Genetic predispositions, specifically temperament, are one such consideration. Most attention has been paid to those children who are inhibited, anxious, and uncomfortable with other children (Fox, Henderson, Rubin, Calkins, & Schmidt, 2001; Kagan, Reznick, & Snidman,

1987). These are children who appear overly sensitive to negative affect and wary of interaction with peers. However, many inhibited infants do not remain so (Fox et al., 2001). Some of these children need more time to develop relationships, but are able to do so if given extended opportunity (Asendorpf, 1989). Interestingly, children who tend to feel things more intensely than their peers – feelings like anger, sadness, or fear – but manage to control their emotions do not have as many problems as their counterparts with similar levels of emotional sensitivity who cannot control their emotions and actions (Fabes et al., 1999). It is not inhibition alone that predicts the differences in children's functioning, but the interface of inhibition and self-regulatory skills mediated by environmental supports.

Interface of Developmental Domains: Examples Based on Differences in Temperament, Disability, and Negative Life Experience

In this section we offer a series of examples of the interface of developmental domains, which serve as the basis for the development of varied pathways in young children. Our aim is to offer a set of extended examples of a "child-in-context" perspective to demonstrate how conventional concepts of and approaches to the study of domains in early development have mischaracterized children as delayed, immature, disorganized, or disoriented. Through the research literature and our own data, we identify distinct, complex and, in some contexts, adaptive developmental pathways exhibited by young inhibited, autistic, and maltreated children.

Diversity in normal development: the role of inhibited temperament

Webs of different shapes are produced by variations in emotional state and the child's ability to regulate those states. The first distinctive feature of alternative developmental paths has to do with the changes in the balance of positive and negative valences and biases that develop over the first six years of life. Anger facilitates control of complex mean interactions, and happiness facilitates control of nice ones. Each emotion evokes a preemptive social script in young children that biases them toward the positive (self-organizing motivation), including a certain interpretation of other people's behavior. An anger script (resulting from working models that include significant anger) biases the child toward taking offense at another person's actions, and therefore toward seeing someone else as mean and in turn acting mean. On the other hand, a joy script or a working model with positive and nurturing components will bias the child toward the positive, including a tendency to interpret actions as nice and in turn to act nice. This understanding will become more complex over time as the child moves from simple actions to mappings and systems of actions followed by representational thinking. Shifts in the child's ability to coordinate positive and negative emotion may assist the young child in regulation (see Figure 4.2).

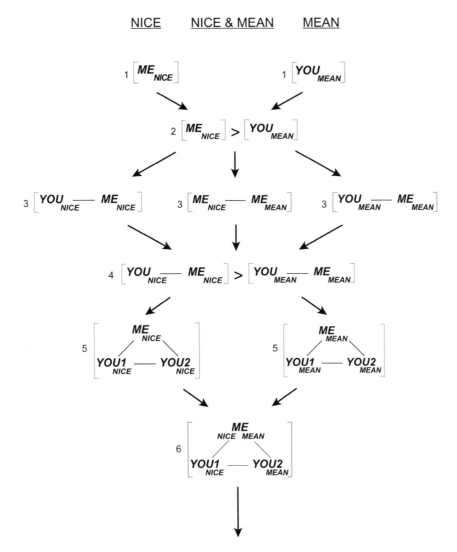

Figure 4.2   Developmental web for normative mean and nice social interactions. The numbers to the left of each set of brackets indicate the complexity ordering of the skill structures. The words and symbols with the brackets indicate the components of a skill structure. The arrows indicate order in the developmental pathway.

For example, children who are shy or behaviorally inhibited (Fox et al., 2001; Kagan et al., 1987) show a bias toward the positive and avoidance of the negative even during the toddler and preschool years. In a longitudinal study of inhibited and outgoing children, highly inhibited children have shown bias toward nice when telling stories about both nice and mean interactions. These inhibited children avoid the mean interactions much more strongly than their non-inhibited counterparts, especially when the stories involve the character identified as the child herself acting mean (Fischer & Ayoub, 1994).

This avoidance of mean persisted even when the inhibited children were specifically asked to imitate a story about a mean interaction. The inhibited children's reactions to the mean stories were less well regulated and more intense, or they seemed unable to understand the mean stories. This included identifying both simple mean tasks and those that included both nice and mean actions. The delay was specific to mean stories and was not present in other developmental measures. In terms of an alternative developmental pathway, the shy child showed a shift in the web that favored the positive and delayed the negative (see Figure 4.3). The shift is predicted to be especially evident for representations of self, where negative evaluations are rigidly shunned. The normative course of negativity bias until at least 3 years of age does not hold for the shy child. We can speculate about how this might impact the child by considering developmental trajectories in other domains. For example, inhibited children who are sensitized to mean avoidance and who are also unable to regulate their emotions may be at more risk than inhibited children who react with withdrawal, but do not create negative situations and suffer rejection by peers. In this case, however, the sensitivity to negative in inhibited children may increase the potential impact of disruption in other developmental processes as well as the children's innate abilities. Their vulnerability due to their heightened sensitivity to mean interactions may also be protective in some situations as well as make them more prone to distress in others.

Diverse pathways in the face of disability: the role of autism

A second distinctive feature in the development and maintenance of diverse developmental pathways relates to the presence of alternative patterns of fractionation and integration of skills across domains. Development is naturally fractionated in a kind of passive dissociation, with skills organized independently in terms of domain, task, context, and emotional state. A child's mind contains a number of different control systems that are not connected to each other. Naturally, this is most true during the child's early years. Because of the pervasiveness of fractionation, young children frequently cannot even represent the coexistence of certain elements in the world, such as that people are both good and bad (until they are capable of representational mapping). Fractionation of particular domains need not remain permanent, however, because skills can be integrated, and are as development proceeds. Active coordination of more and more complex skills occurs as the child gains the cognitive ability to connect them in increasingly complex ways. Integration occurs across emotional domains as well, including coordination of positive and negative categories.

However, children can use coordination as an adaptive mechanism for active separation between domains as well as for integration. Controlled separation or dissociation is pervasive and is typically seen in situations in which children are exposed to recurrent negative life experiences. In addition, although dissociation is sometimes totally unconscious, it can involve degrees of consciousness, in both normal and pathological situations. The separation can produce a misleading appearance that a person's skills are low-level and uncoordinated, although they in fact may involve high-level coordination for the purpose

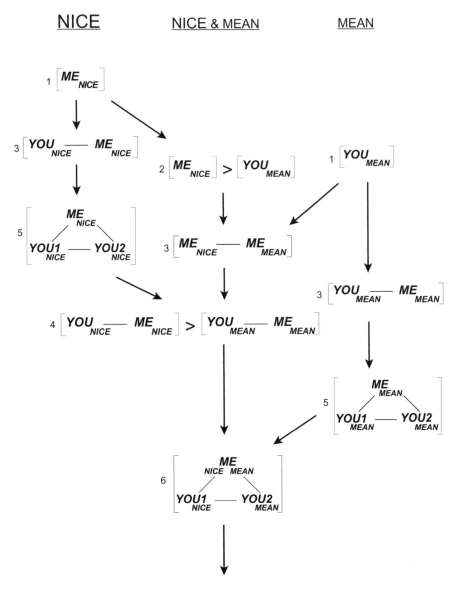

Figure 4.3 Developmental web biased toward nice interactions due to inhibited temperament. The numbers to the left of each set of brackets indicate the complexity ordering of the skill structures. The words and symbols with the brackets indicate the components of a skill structure. The arrows indicate order in the developmental pathway.

of dissociation. On the other hand, other pathways may include children who use extreme control through nurturance to manage their worlds and thereby present themselves as more competent and integrated than they actually are.

Autism offers an example of how a disability can promote an alternative pathway in response to functional genetic differences coupled with environmental responses. Although many have believed that autistic children are globally delayed, their presentations may instead be examples of alternative pathways given their severe impairments in understanding their emotions, other people, and relationships. These deficits, based on abnormal brain development (Kanner, 1943; Minshew & Pettegrew, 1996), impact the child across domains. Children with autism typically miss the relational connections in speech and gesture and are unable to identify the meaning of basic signals of emotions (facial expression, tone of voice, words). These deficits seem specific to feelings, other people, and social relationships, and do not involve general retardation or developmental delay. Indeed, a number of autistic children are extremely intelligent and can acquire sophisticated, specialized skills.

Donna Williams, in *Nobody Nowhere* (1992), has written a compelling account of her early life and experience as a developing person with autism. Few autistic individuals have written autobiographies, but Williams describes her different pathway vividly. She provides a valuable resource for moving beyond normative interpretations of autistic behavior in the context of the interface of multiple developmental domains. In conjunction with autistic people's difficulties in understanding and relating to others, they often have difficulty in comprehending spoken language. Williams describes the experience of hearing language as a young child as if the sound had to go through some "complicated checkpoint procedure" (p. 69) with her segmentation of the sounds often producing a strange and unintelligible message. Her problem is not deafness or emotional distress, but analysis of language. This might explain why some autistic individuals benefit from using an alternative form of language such as American Sign Language (Bonvillian & Nelson, 1978).

Williams's descriptions of her early life and the evolution of her thinking provide a basis for understanding the "different" integration of her developmental path. Especially important characteristics of her development were her difficulty in integrating socio-emotional information, her hypersensitivity to too much sensory stimulation, including touch, and her strong ability to tune out events around her. A simple example of her skill and her deficit was her reaction to someone commenting on her singing as a young child. After hearing the comment, she stopped singing in front of other people, evidencing remarkable self-control in order to avoid being heard, but she did not realize that people could hear her even if she could not see them.

Central to Williams's developmental adaptation was the construction of agents or shells both to communicate with others and to protect herself from the outside world. These compartmentalized agents indicated increasingly complicated skills starting at an early age and continuing through adulthood. For example, by age 3 years she had constructed an agent she called Willie to protect her from frightening people and situations. Willie was described as having a "hateful glaring eye, a pinched-up mouth, a rigid corpse-like stance, and clenched fists. Willie stamped his foot, Willie spat when he didn't like things, but the look of complete hatred was the worst weapon" (p. 11). Already during the preschool years, Williams had become skilled at purposely turning herself into Willie ("losing myself") when she needed protection.

When viewed from a single domain or from the perspective of normalcy, deficits in autistic children appear everywhere, but such analysis fails to capture the real development across domains that is occurring in autism. The socio-emotional and perceptual deficits are genuine, but so are the accomplishments growing out of the autistic framework. The final important point to make is that Williams's behavior made use of the skills she had in ways that aimed at mastery and adaptation in the best way she knew how.

Diversity in the face of environmental trauma: the role of child maltreatment

Conventional views on psychopathology following early maltreatment experiences assume immaturity or developmental delay resulting from fixation or regression. This perspective has been elaborated in the empirical literature, as methodological approaches to the study of developmental psychopathology have been built on traditional concepts of development that favor unidirectional, homogeneous growth regardless of context (e.g., Eigsti & Cicchetti, 2004; Veltman& Browne, 2001). Contrary to this view, we propose that maltreated children have been shown to demonstrate complex skills requisite with their particular, unique experience and on a par with their non-maltreated age-mates, even when psychopathology is evident (Fischer et al., 1997).

The attachment literature offers a helpful example. Abusive or neglectful behavior by a parent often results in the formation of an insecure attachment between the child and parent (Crittenden, 1985; Schneider-Rosen, Brunwald, Carlson, & Cicchetti, 1985). As a result, maltreated children's behavior toward abusive parents has most often been described as disorganized and erratic, shifting between approach and avoidance strategies. This pattern of interaction with the parent may become generalized and elaborated in the child's other relationships with adults and peers, such that abused children may appear unpredictable, volatile, and rigid (Darwish, Esquivel, Houtz, & Alfonso, 2001; Mueller & Silverman, 1989). Researchers have theorized that maltreated children typically evidence disorganized and disoriented attachment (Cicchetti, 1991; Crittenden, 1985).

However, we propose that the behaviors of "disorganized attachments" are neither disorganized nor disoriented. Instead, they represent a trauma dance composed of adaptive fight–flight coping mechanisms that evolve in response to trauma and physical threat and that eventually produce distinctively complex developmental pathways of highly sophisticated adaptation to traumatic environments. From the child's perspective, approach–avoidance behavior is self-protective, organized in the context of an environment where the primary caregiver is both abusive and nurturing. In contrast to traditional psychoanalytic theory, maltreated children do not demonstrate developmental delay or fixation of their relational models, nor do they show incoherence (Solomon & George, 1999). Instead their socio-emotional development follows a fundamentally different relationship pathway, which in its own terms is both developmentally advanced and coherent, adapted to the shifting behavior and inconsistency that they experience with their caregivers.

With development, these skills become even more sophisticated as children hone their defenses. This increasing complexity and sophistication puts abused children on a par with their healthy peers with respect to their relative complexity of cognitive skills but at risk for psychopathology, including depression, oppositionality, dissociation, and peer relationship problems (Briere, 1992). In this way, the abused child's behavior is both adaptive and maladaptive, depending upon the circumstance, making survival in the home possible but survival in other contexts challenging.

If maltreated children's behavior can be characterized as both adaptive and complex, why does developmental psychology persist in labeling these children as delayed? It is our perspective that this mischaracterization stems from the persistent view that development occurs in a domain-general and unidirectional way, regardless of context. The result is a lack of recognition of the child's "different" developmental pathway. In order to illustrate this fully we present a study of young maltreated children that specifically considers their functioning in several developmental domains and their interface (see Schlichtmann & Ayoub, in press). In contrast to the more "normative" positivity bias described at the beginning of the chapter, children who grow up in abusive and violent homes have been shown to develop a powerful and pervasive negativity bias in their play and early relationships (Fischer et al., 1997). This bias is likely the developmental precursor to the negative worldview so often described in traumatized adults.

To better understand this alternate developmental pathway we observed maltreated and non-maltreated toddlers and preschoolers during structured story telling assessments (Fischer, Hencke, Hand, Ayoub, & Russell, 2001). Fifty-three children, from 22 to 73 months, were interviewed for this study: half the participants were maltreated and the comparison participants matched on socio-economic status and ethnic group membership. Children were asked to retell and/or act out a series of seventeen nice, mean, and combined nice and mean stories that describe interactions between a self doll and several friend dolls. The stories began simply with a nice interaction between the self doll and a friend doll at the level of single representations. Stories were told in order of increasing complexity, forming a developmental sequence based on Fischer's dynamic skills theory. Children's performance on each story was coded on two variables. First, participants were coded on whether or not they successfully retold the story. Children could successfully pass either by verbally telling the story, or by acting the story out with dolls, or both. To successfully pass a story at a particular level of complexity the participant must be able to attend to the story and accurately represent, verbally or non-verbally, the characters as nice or mean and the various component parts of the story. The interviewer continued through the series until the participant failed to correctly retell three stories in a row. The participant received a score (skill level) for correct completions corresponding to the last correct completion prior to three failures. Second, participants' stories were coded for complexity of representation regardless of whether or not the story was retold correctly. A participant, for example, might switch who was nice and who was mean, or make a nice story mean, resulting in a "failure" to correctly retell the story, but tell a highly complex story nonetheless. Children were given a score corresponding to the complexity of the story with which they exhibited the highest skill level regardless of whether or not the story was told correctly.

A history of maltreatment affected the complexity of children's storytelling performance, but only for the structured component of the assessment. That is, children with a maltreatment history tended to successfully complete fewer accurate retelling story tasks prior to three failures than did their non-maltreated peers. This "gap" between the maltreated and non-maltreated performances was larger among older children. Maltreated children differed the most from their non-maltreated counterparts in the retelling of nice stories – they reproduced nice stories only half as often as did their non-maltreated peers. Importantly, there were no differences in the complexity of stories told between maltreated and non-maltreated participants when correct story replication was not taken into account.

For example, Donald, in modeling a nice interaction of the self doll with the other doll, says forcefully, "Guy, you wanna fight? I'll knock you down. He fight him. They fight. You wanna fight. I'm gonna fight you. Fuck my butt, fuck it." The examiner who reminds him that the task is to construct a nice story then supports him. With this social support, Donald is able to say, "Have some playdough, guy, don't leave me." Donald at first is unable to repeat a nice story; his story is an elaborate mean interaction from the beginning. Support from the examiner does enable Donald to give a positive response, but this response is followed by an abandonment theme ("don't leave me").

It is not that the maltreated children are "delayed," rather they exhibit an alternate developmental path commensurate with their early experience, demonstrating more skill with, and selective attention to, negative situations and relationships (Fischer et al., 1997) and selective inattention to positive tasks. This developmental pathway seems to hinder attention and persistence on structured school-like tasks (Porter, 2003), especially for tasks that do not capitalize on these children's honed skills around threat-related signals (Pollak & Tolley-Schell, 2003). As skill development involves complexity as its central dimension, change over this dimension clearly illustrates how maltreated children, like non-maltreated children, are capable of the same level of skill complexity but in a different context and with different biases based on emotional and contextual schemas.

Conclusion

The presence of alternate developmental pathways for inhibited, autistic, and maltreated children highlights the point that research in human development that focuses on only one instance or even a few instances of individual and contextual variation is not useful for understanding the development of all children. In these cases assumptions about the child's cognitive and social development, made in the absence of context and assessment of domain intersection, leads to the erroneous assumption that the child has a cognitive difficulty or delay. The practical conclusion leads practitioners to consider an illusive cognitive delay that is addressed without acknowledgment of the child's actions as adaptive and developmentally maturing responses to an adversarial environment. Furthermore, policies and programs in education stemming from research that assumes a unidirectional, homogeneous course of growth for all children will not be appropriate for all individuals across contexts.

A view across domains of development in early childhood allows the observer to begin to understand the complexity of the interface between the strands of skills that make up the developmental web and the organization of those strands that can be characterized as a variety of developmental pathways. An integrative approach to early development promotes the ability to assess and support the whole child by examining the child's holistic functioning without losing site of the interaction of domains one with another. Distinctive developmental pathways constructed by the young child in response to constitutional, environmental, or cultural conditions are not developmentally primitive or delayed. To the contrary, they are sophisticated adaptations in which these young children construct powerfully different affective-cognitive-communication organizations. Whether these adaptations stem from culture, family, or body, scientists and practitioners need to appreciate the complexity and effectiveness of pathways of variation within functional and pathological processes. Only then can we truly consider effective intervention and prevention.

Note

The authors thank Gabrielle Rappolt Schlichtmann, Catherine Snow, Barbara Pan, Erin O'Connor, Michael Connell, Pamela Raya, and Travis Wright for their contributions to the work on which this chapter is based. The research described in this chapter was made possible in part by the Roche Relief Fund, the Milton Fund, the Spencer Foundation, Frederick and Sandra Rose, and the harvard Graduate School of Education.

References

Asendorpf, J. (1989). Individual, differential, and aggregate stability of social competence. In B. Schneider & G. Attili (Eds.), *Social competence in developmental perspective* (pp. 71–90). New York: Kluwer Academic/Plenum.

Astington, J. W. (1993). *The child's discovery of the mind.* Cambridge, MA: Harvard University Press.

Ayoub, C., Fischer, K., & O'Connor, E. (2003). Analyzing development of working models for disrupted attachments: The case of family violence. *Attachment & Human Development, 5*(2), 97–120.

Bonvillian, J. D., & Nelson, K. E. (1978). Development of sign language in language-handicapped individuals. In P. Siple (Ed.), *Understanding language through signlanguage research* (pp. 187–212). New York: Academic Press.

Bretherton, I., Ridgeway, D., & Cassidy, J. (1990). The role of internal working models in the attachment relationship. In M. Greenberg, D. Cicchetti, & E. Cummings (Eds.), *Attachment during the preschool years* (pp. 273–308). Chicago: University of Chicago Press.

Briere, J. (1992). *Child abuse trauma: Theory and treatment of the lasting effects.* Newbury Park, CA: Sage Publications.

Bronson, M. B. (2000). *Self-regulation in early childhood: Nature and nurture.* New York: Guilford Press.

Case, R. (1991). *The mind's staircase: Exploring the conceptual underpinnings of children's thought and knowledge.* Hillsdale, NJ: Erlbaum.

Cicchetti, D. (1991). Fractures in the crystal: Developmental psychopathology and the emergence of self. *Developmental Review, 11,* 271–287.

Crittenden, P. (1985). Maltreated infants: Vulnerability and resilience. *Journal of Child Psychology and Psychiatry, 26,* 85–96.

Darwish, D., Esquivel, G., Houtz, J., & Alfonso, V. (2001). Play and social skills in maltreated and non-maltreated preschoolers during peer interactions. *ChildAbuse and Neglect, 25,* 13–31.

Eigsti, I., & Cicchetti, D. (2004). The impact of child maltreatment on expressive syntax at 60 months. *Developmental Science, 7,* 88–102.

Eisenberg, N., & Fabes, R. (1992). Emotion, regulation, and the development of social competence. In M. Clark (Ed.), *Review of personality and social psychology: Vol. 14. Emotion and social behavior* (pp. 119–150). Newbury Park, CA: Sage.

Fabes, R., Eisenberg, N., Jones, S., Smith, M., Guthrie, I., Poulin, R., Shepard, S., & Friedman, J. (1999). Regulation, emotionality, and preschoolers' socially competent peer interactions. *Child Development, 70*(2), 432–442.

Fischer, K., & Ayoub, C. (1994). Affective splitting and dissociation in normal and maltreated children: Developmental pathways for self in relationships. In D. Cicchetti & S. Toth (Eds.), *Rochester Symposium on Development and Psychopathology: Vol. 5. Disorders and dysfunctions of the self* (pp. 149–222) Rochester, NY: University of Rochester Press.

Fischer, K., Ayoub, C., Singh, I, Noam, G., Maraganore, A., & Raya, P. (1997). Psychopathology as adaptive development along distinctive pathways. *Development and Psychopathology, 9,* 749–779.

Fischer, K. W., & Bidell, T. R. (1998). Dynamic development of psychological structures in action and thought. In R. M. Lerner (Ed.), *Handbook of child psychology: Vol. 1. Theoretical models of human development* (5th ed., pp. 467–561). New York: Wiley.

Fischer, K., Hencke, R., Hand, H., Ayoub, C., & Russell, C. (2001). *Mean and Nice Interaction Scale: Peers.* Cognitive Developmental Laboratory, Harvard University.

Fischer, K. W., & Rose, D. (1998). Growth cycles of the brain and mind. *Educational Leadership, 11,* 56–60.

Fischer, K. W., Shaver, P. R., & Carnochan, P. (1990). How emotions develop and how they organize development. *Cognition and Emotion, 4*(2), 81–127.

Flavell, J. H., & Miller, P. H. (1998). Social cognition. In W. Damon (Ed.), *Handbook of child psychology: Vol. 2. Cognition, perception and language* (5th ed., pp. 851–898). New York: Wiley.

Fox, N. A., Henderson, K. H., Rubin, S. D., Calkins, S. D., & Schmidt, L. A. (2001).Continuity and discontinuity of behavioral inhibition and exuberance: Psychopathological and behavioral influences across the first four years of life. *Child Development, 72*(1), 1–21.

Freud, S. (1965). *New introductory lectures on psychoanalysis* (J. Strachey, Trans.). New York: Norton. (Original work published 1933.)

Hart, B., & Risley, T. (1995). *Meaningful differences in the everyday experience of young American children.* Baltimore: Brookes.

Harter, S., & Buddin, B. (1987). Children's understanding of the simultaneity of two emotions: A five-stage developmental sequence. *Developmental Psychology, 23,* 388–399.

Kagan, J., Reznick, J. S., & Snidman (1987). The physiology and psychology of behavioral inhibition in children, *Child Development, 58,* 1459–1473.

Kanner, L. (1943). Autistic disturbances of affective contact. *Nervous Child, 2,* 217–250.

Kohlberg, L. (1969). Stage and sequence: The cognitive developmental approach to socialization. In D. A. Goslin (Ed.), *Handbook of socialization theory and research* (pp. 347–480). Chicago: Rand McNally.

Kopp, C. B. (2000). Self-regulation in children. In J. J. Smelser & P. B. Baltes (Eds.), *International encyclopedia of the social and behavioral sciences* (pp. 187–212). Oxford: Elsevier.

Lerner, R., Anderson, P., Balsano, A., Dowling, E., & Bobek, D. (2003). Applied developmental science of positive human development. In R. Lerner, M. Easterbrooks, & Mistry, J (Eds.), *Handbook of psychology: Vol. 6. Developmental psychology* (pp. 535–558). Hoboken, NJ: Wiley.

LeVine, R. A., & Miller, P. M. (1990). Commentary (for section Cross-cultural validity of attachment theory). *Human Development, 33,* 73–80.

Li, J., Wang, L., & Fischer, K. W. (2004). The organization of Chinese shame concepts. *Cognition and Emotion, 18*(6), 767–797.

Lyon, R. (1996). Methodological issues and strategies for assessing developmental change and evaluating response to intervention. In D. Speece & B. Keogh (Eds.), *Research on classroom ecologies: Implications for inclusion of children with learning disabilities* (pp. 213–227). Hillsdale, NJ: Lawrence Erlbaum Associates.

Lyons-Ruth, K. (1998). Implicit relational knowing: Its role in development and psychoanalytic treatment. *Infant Mental Health Journal, 19*(3), 282–289.

Mangelsdorf, S. C. (1992). Development changes in infant stranger interactions. *Infant Behavior and Development, 15*(2), 191–208.

Marvin, R., & Britner, P. (1999). Normative development: The ontogeny of attachment. In J. Cassidy & P. Shaver (Eds.), *Handbook of attachment: Theory, research and clinical applications* (pp. 44–68). New York: Guilford Press.

Miller, P. J. (1994). Narrative practices: Their role in socialization and self-construction. In U. Neisser & R. Fivush (Eds.), *The remembering self: Construction and accuracy in the self-narrative* (pp. 158–179). Cambridge: Cambridge University Press.

Miller, P. J., Fung, H., & Mintz, J. (1996). Self-construction through narrative practices: A Chinese and American comparison of early socialization. *Ethos, 24*, 1–44.

Minshew, N. J., & Pettegrew, J. W. (1996). Nuclear magnetic resonance spectroscopic studies of cortical development. In R. Thatcher, G. R. Lyon, J. Ramsey, & N. Krasnegor (Eds.), *Developmental neuroimaging: Mapping the development of brain and behavior* (pp. 107–125). New York: Academic Press.

Mueller, E., & Silverman, N. (1989). Peer relations in maltreated children. In D. Cicchetti & V. Carlson (Eds.), *Child maltreatment: Theory and research on the causes and consequences of child abuse and neglect* (pp. 529–578). New York: Cambridge University Press.

Nathanson, D. (1992). *Shame and pride: Affect, sex, and the birth of self.* New York: W. W. Norton.

Overton, W. (2003). Development across the lifespan. In R. Lerner, M. Easterbrooks, & J. Mistry (Eds.), *Handbook of psychology: Vol. 6. Developmental psychology* (pp. 13–42). Hoboken, NJ: Wiley.

Palombo, J. (1992). Narratives, self-cohesion, and the patient's search for meaning. *Clinical Social Work Journal, 20*, 249–270.

Piaget, J. (1983). Piaget's theory. In W. Kessen (Ed.), *Handbook of child psychology: Vol. 1. History, theory and methods* (pp.103–126). New York: Wiley.

Pollak, S., & Tolley-Schell, S. (2003). Selective attention to facial emotion in physically abused children. *Journal of Abnormal Psychology, 112*(3), 323–338.

Porter, C. (2003). *Neurobehavioral sequelae of child sexual abuse.* Unpublished doctoral dissertation, Brigham Young University, Utah.

Schlichtmann, G. R., & Ayoub, C. (2004). *Adaptive and complex developmental pathways: The example of maltreated children.* Paper presented at Building Usable Knowledge in Mind, Brain, and Education Conference. Cambridge, MA.

Schneider-Rosen, K., Braunwald, K., Carlson, V., & Cicchetti, D. (1985). Current perspectives in attachment theory: Illustration from the study of maltreated infants. In I. Bretherington & E. Waters (Eds.), *Monographs of the Society for Research in Child Development: Growing points of attachment theory and research, 50*(Serial No. 209), 194–210.

Schore, A. (1994). *Affect regulation and the origin of self.* Hillsdale, NJ: Erlbaum.

Shaver, P., Schwartz, J., Kirson, D., & O'Connor, C. (1987). Emotion knowledge: Further exploration of a prototype approach. *Journal of Personality and Social Psychology, 52*, 1061–1086.

Shields, A., Cicchetti, D., & Ryan, R. (1994). The development of emotional and behavioral self-regulation and social competence among maltreated school-age children. *Development and Psychopathology, 6,* 57–75.

Shonkoff, J. P., & Phillips, D. A. (Eds.). (2000). *From neurons to neighborhoods: The science of early childhood development.* Washington, DC: National Academy Press.

Solomon, J., & George, C. (1999). The measurement of attachment security in infancy and childhood. In J. Cassidy & P. Shaver (Eds.), *Handbook of attachment: Theory, research, and clinical applications* (pp. 287–316). New York: Guilford.

Stern, D. (1985). *The interpersonal world of the infant: A view from psychoanalysis and developmental psychology.* New York: Basic Books.

Susman, E. (1998). Biobehavioural development: An integrative perspective. *International Journal of Behavioral Development, 22*(4), 671–679.

Terr, L. (1991). Childhood traumas: An outline and overview. *American Journal of Psychiatry, 148*(1), 10–19.

Thelen, E., & Smith, L. B. (1998). Dynamic systems theory. In W. Damon & W. Lerner (Eds.), *Handbook of child psychology: Vol. 1. The theoretical models of human development* (5th ed., pp. 563–634). New York: Wiley.

van der Kolk, B. (1996). The body keeps score: Approaches to the psychobiology of post-traumatic stress disorder. In B. van der Kolk, A. McFarlane, & L. Weisaeth (Eds.), *Traumatic stress: The effects of overwhelming experience on mind, body, and society* (pp. 214–241). New York: Guilford Press.

Veltman, M., & Browne, K. (2001). Three decades of child maltreatment research: Implications for the school years. *Trauma, Violence & Abuse, 2*(3), 215–239.

Williams, D. (1992). *Nobody nowhere: The extraordinary autobiography of an autistic.* New York: Avon Books.

PART II

Early Biological and Physiological Development

5

Early Brain Development and Plasticity

Jane W. Couperus and Charles A. Nelson

Over the past several decades there has been an explosion of research into brain development, and a recognition by those in the field of child psychology that understanding brain development can shed new light on our understanding of development in general. Historically changes in the brain were thought to influence development through maturation. Arguments in child psychology often focus on determining the roles of maturational forces versus experience in influencing the course of development. However, this dichotomous view has not answered questions about development in a satisfactory way. Instead, there is growing support for the idea that changes in the brain are inexorably linked to changes in the environment. Not only do changes in the environment, including experience, alter the brain, but changes in the brain alter behavior, which in turn can change the child's interaction with the environment. This understanding is modifying the questions that are asked. Current research often focuses on plasticity, the ability and extent to which the brain can be altered, rather than simply the periods of time that appear to be critical for particular behaviors to develop. This emphasis on plasticity is important in that it recognizes that brain development is not predetermined; it is shaped through both genetics and the environment during the prenatal months as well as after birth and across the lifespan. Thus it is critical for child psychologists to have some understanding of how the brain develops and functions and what aspects of the brain can and cannot be altered through experience (Nelson, de Haan, & Thomas, in press).

While it was once enough for researchers alone to understand the role of the brain in development, it is now becoming more and more important for the general public to understand as well. The reason for this shift is that as knowledge is disseminated, it influences everything from baby toys to public policy. For example, walking down the 0–3-year-old aisle in a toy store, it is impossible to ignore products advertised as creating smarter babies. Having an understanding of how the brain develops allows for more informative research and an informed public that can make use of the knowledge learned not only in the classroom, but also through research publications and mass media, to make better decisions about child development and education.

To have a firm understanding of how the brain influences development it is essential to understand the mechanisms that foster brain development. Shortly after conception there is an exponential change that takes place in embryonic development. Emerging from a thin layer of cells that occupy the outermost layer of the embryo comes what will be the highly complex brain, an organ that will continue to develop and change throughout the lifespan. Brain development is most dramatic prenatally, when enormous change occurs on the order of days, not simply in biology, but in the behaviors that can then be expressed. The purpose of this chapter is to introduce the basic mechanisms of brain development, anatomical changes, and the factors that influence the brain in both typical and atypical development. The brain is composed of billions of cells, primarily of two types, neurons and myelin. The main function of neurons is to process and communicate information within the brain. It is helpful to think of neurons as a tree, made up of a cell body and two ends, axons and dendrites. If the cell body is the trunk, the axons at one end look like leaves sending out information, while at the other end, the dendrites pick up information from other cells like roots (see Figure 5.1). The area where the axon of one cell and the dendrite of another meet is called a synapse. The second type of cell, a class of cells collectively called myelin, act as support cells, assisting the flow of information in the brain. It is the development and alteration of these two types of cells as well as their connections that are the focus of this chapter. Specifically, this chapter will address the basic formation of the brain through processes termed neural induction and neurulation; growth of the brain through proliferation and migration; development of connections within the brain through axonal and dendritic growth, as well as the refining of these connections through synaptogenesis, apoptosis, synaptic pruning, and myelination.

The mechanisms of brain development function in an open system affected by both internal and external influences. Changes within the developing brain can range from minute to extreme, emerging immediately or over time. The extent and flexibility of those

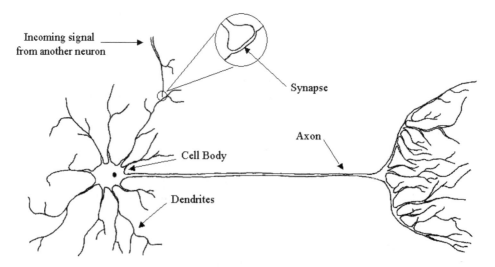

Figure 5.1   Neuron including cell body, axon, dendrites, and synapse.

changes reflects the plasticity of the brain. While earlier changes in brain development are more dramatic, they are also less plastic, meaning that, once in place, they are difficult to alter. Later alterations in brain development, while more subtle, may also be more plastic, with greater room for change.

To understand these changes this chapter will present a basic framework of brain development as derived from molecular, anatomic, and systems-level research, the majority of which is based on studies of non-human species. Using this framework we will then present the mechanisms though which modifications occur both pre- and postnatally and explore the factors that influence these changes.

The Basic Building Blocks

Neural induction and neurulation

The formation of the brain begins sixteen days after conception (O'Rahilly & Gardner, 1979). Within the span of seven months the brain transforms from a small group of cells to a highly complex organism that has the form, if not the function, of the mature brain. Understanding how the structure develops sheds light on not only the conditions that occur when something goes wrong, but also the miraculous nature of the process itself.

Early in development the organism is composed of three layers. The outermost layer (the dorsal side of the ectoderm) will eventually become the brain, starting as an area described as the neural plate. The neural plate is formed when cells in the outermost layer are specified through a process termed neural induction. Once the neural plate develops it is then transformed from a plate into a tube. During this process, called neurulation, the neural plate buckles and folds inwards, and the edges rise up, fusing to form a tube. This process begins on approximately day twenty-two (Keith, 1948), fusing first at the midsection and progressing outward in either direction until approximately day twenty-six (Sidman & Rakic, 1982). One end of the tube eventually forms the brain and the other develops into the spinal cord. The neural tube is important in the development of the central nervous system (CNS) because it is comprised of progenitor (or stem) cells that give rise to neurons and glia (including myelin) – the cells that are the foundation of the CNS.

Perturbations in the development of the neural tube can lead to devastating congenital birth defects. Among these are spina bifida and anencephaly when portions of the neural tube fail to close. While the most severe cases often result in the spontaneous reabsorption of the embryo (i.e., spontaneous abortion), milder cases result in lifetime disabilities. Anencephaly occurs when the end of the tube that forms the brain fails to close. In contrast, when the portion of the tube that will eventually become the spine fails to close, spina bifida results. Occurring in approximately 1 in every 1000 births (Lewis, 2003), spina bifida can result in portions of the spine protruding from the back, exposed and unprotected. As is the case with spinal cord injuries, the resulting paralysis is determined by the location and extent of the region that failed to close. This most basic alteration in development of the brain and spinal cord is not the result of genetic factors alone. The environment also plays a pivotal role (Finnell, Junker, Wadman, & Cabrera, 2002; Gos & Szpecht-Potocka, 2002). For example, epidemiological studies suggest that the recent public health campaign that advises pregnant women to supplement their diets with folic acid has reduced the incidence of neural tube defects, suggesting that folic acid may play a role in neurulation. While environmental changes during the process of neural tube development may affect the presence of neural tube abnormalities, once these abnormalities exist they are difficult to change. In the case of spina bifida, while surgery can close the open back in order to protect the spine, little more can be done to prevent paralysis. In the case of anencephaly, there are no current treatments, and in the more extreme cases the fetus does not survive.

Mechanisms of Brain Development

Proliferation and migration

Once the basic structure of the brain is formed, development shifts to the creation of new cells in what is termed proliferation. Once cells, specifically neurons – the basic functional cells of the brain – are born they travel to their final home in the brain through migration. Starting as a relatively small number of stem cells, new cells are created at an astounding rate. This exponential increase in the number of cells is critical to normal development because any alterations can have drastic effects on brain function. Alterations in proliferation and migration are implicated in structural brain abnormalities that are associated with mental retardation.

The process of proliferation can occur in two ways: symmetrically, when one cell becomes two identical cells, and asymmetrically, when one cell creates a replica of itself and another that will not replicate further (Rakic, 1988; Smart, 1985; Takahashi, Nowakowski, & Caviness, 1994). Initially cell division is symmetric, occurring within the innermost portion of the neural tube in an area termed the ventricular zone (Chenn & McConnell, 1995). During the initial phase of symmetric proliferation new neural cells travel back and forth between the inner and outer portions of the ventricular zone as they duplicate. The second phase of proliferation, asymmetric proliferation, stretches from the 7th prenatal week until midgestation (Rakic, 1978). It is during this time that neurons begin to form. When a non-proliferating cell is formed during asymmetric proliferation, the non-proliferating, or what is called the postmitotic, cell migrates towards its final destination (Rakic, 1988). This postmitotic cell will eventually become a neuron or other type of brain cell.

The neuronal process of migrating from where they are born to their final home in the brain is a complex phenomenon. Migration in human embryos begins around 8 prenatal weeks (Sidman & Rakic, 1973) and continues through at least 4.5 postnatal months when the last postmitotic neurons are created through asymmetric proliferation (Rakic, 1978). The process of migration is important because the adult brain (specifically the cortex or outer brain) consists of six unique layers. Neurons must find their home in these layers through migration. Migrating neurons follow an inside-out pattern of movement. Neurons that are produced earlier in development migrate to lower (or inner) cortical layers, whereas those produced later travel over other neurons for destinations in the outer cortex (Rakic, 1974, 2002). Eventually, neurons from the ventricular zone find their final destination in the inner layers, 4, 5, and 6, while later-developing neurons from the subventricular zone find their home in the outer layers, particularly 2 and 3. One exception to this pattern is those neurons that reside in the outermost layer, those in layer 1. These neurons are among the earliest to develop and are found in the ventricular zone. It is hypothesized that these neurons, along with those in the innermost layers, may act as scaffolding upon which future neurons travel (Chong, Babcook, Salamat, Nemzik, Kroeker, & Ellis, 1996).

Anatomical changes. The effect of proliferation and migration on the anatomy of the developing embryo is extensive. During the first phase of proliferation the cells of the ventricular zone begin dividing and multiplying. This can be seen as a bulging of different areas of the neural tube, creating three distinct areas (O'Rahilly & Muller, 1994). These areas are the proencephalon (forebrain), mesencephalon (midbrain), and rhombencephalon (hindbrain). As proliferation continues, these areas divide further, with the proencephalon splitting into the telencephalon and diencephalon, and the rhombencephalon into the metencephalon and meylencephalon. The mesencephalon does not divide. This process of enlarging forces the tube to buckle and round, eventually forming the shape of the adult brain. By approximately 7 months the brain has taken on the shape of the adult brain with six layers of cortex (Martin & Jessell, 1991).

Errors and their consequences. Whereas errors in neural tube development result in gross anatomical abnormalities, errors of proliferation and migration result in more subtle structural abnormalities (e.g., McBride & Kemper, 1982; Norman, 1980; Volpe, 1995). However, these deficits are no less profound. For example, reduced proliferation can result in microencephaly – a small-sized brain. Microencephaly in turn may lead to mental retardation and in some cases seizures (Volpe, 1995). There are multiple diseases and environmental influences that can result in microencephaly, including rubella, irradiation, maternal alcoholism, excessive vitamin A, and human immunodeficiency virus (HIV) (Kozlowski et al., 1997; Warkany, Lemire, & Cohen, 1981). In addition to microencephaly, research suggests that errors of cell proliferation and/or migration may be involved in such disorders as Down's syndrome and autism (Acosta & Pearl, 2003; Bambrick, Yarowsky, & Krueger, 2003). While direct connections between errors and their consequences can be seen with neural tube deficits, the nature of errors of proliferation and migration makes them more difficult to track. For example, recent evidence suggests that errors in cell migration may play a role in structural abnormalities in the cerebellum of people with autism (Fatemi, Stary, Halt, & Realmuto, 2001). However, how these structural abnormalities affect behavior is more difficult to pinpoint. The cerebellum has been associated with such varied processes as implicit (or non-conscious) learning and movement. Additionally, the complexity of autistic behavior further clouds connections between brain and behavior as the source problems in behavior and learning are difficult to define.

The exact mechanisms that alter proliferation and migration are still being explored, but progress is being made. For example, it has been suggested that in the case of micro-encephaly associated with maternal alcoholism, one mechanism that may contribute to errors of proliferation is the introduction of ethanol into the developing brain. It is theorized that ethanol may inhibit the proliferation of some types of neuronal cells, resulting in an overall reduction in the size of the brain (Costa & Guizzetti, 2002). Despite the progress that has been made there are many unanswered questions about how the environment affects proliferation as well as how the overproduction of neurons affects development. Additionally, because these changes occur early in the development of the brain, and the majority of these processes do not continue after birth, the alterations created are difficult to influence once in place and are thus relatively non-plastic.

Summary. Over the course of prenatal development the building blocks of the brain are put into place. Through the processes of proliferation and migration, a small cluster of cells develops into a tube, segments, expands, and grows into what will become the brain. There are often multiple intricate processes that interact over the course of development to make this happen. This allows for greater flexibility in development as well as greater vulnerability to insult, the consequences of which can be profound (Monk, Webb, & Nelson, 2001). However, simply creating neural cells and giving them a home in the brain is not enough. The brain is not composed of disconnected cells, but is a vast array of connections and systems that work together; it is the formations of these connections that will be the focus of the next section.

Connections and Prenatal Plasticity

Axonal and dendritic growth

Once neuronal cells reach their final destination in the brain, they must develop connections with the cells around them as well as with cells much farther away. This is a crucial aspect of development as precise connections between neurons are necessary for the purposes of communication and normal functioning. If you think of the brain as billions of people who need to talk to each other, the connections between them are like phone lines. It is important that each person be able to communicate with the other people important to their lives regardless of if they are near or far, and the connections must be exact. For example, when Sally in Chicago wants to reach Sam in Cleveland it is important that she only connect with Sam, not his neighbor and the 500,000 people who live in the area. These connections are made in the brain via axons and dendrites.

Axons. Neurons send signals to other neurons through a part of the neuron called an axon that extends outwards from the cell body to connect with other cells, often extending several centimeters (Tessier-Lavigne & Goodman, 1996; see Figure 5.1). Growth cones, sitting atop developing axons, are a key player in this process.[1] First described by Cajal about 100 years ago, growth cones play an important role both in the growth of the axon and in its navigation (Raper & Tessier-Lavigne, 1999). Using cues in the environment surrounding the neuron, the growth cone directs axons toward some cues and away from others, guiding their way to their final destinations. These environmental cues can be found both in the extracellular matrix (the matter found between cells) and on the surface of cells along the pathway (Jessell, 1988).

Dendrites. As axons reach out, many seek connections with dendrites, the receptor portion of neurons that receive signals (see Figure 5.1). While axonal growth can be complex, determined by a number of different factors, dendrite growth is simplistic. The growth of dendrites may be initiated by spontaneous electrical activity of receptors on the neuronal body or by contact from incoming axons (Mrzljak, Uylings, Van Eden, & Judas, 1990).

The first dendrites appear as thick processes extending from the cellular body. Along these processes are spines – the areas of dendrites that axons connect with at junctions called synapses. As dendrites mature, the number of spines increases and they become thicker, increasing in number and providing greater area for synaptic connections.

Anatomical changes. The growth of axons and dendrites from neurons to various areas of the brain is an immense task during gestation. While the physical changes on a macroscopic scale are subtle, at a microscopic level they are dramatic. The timing of axonal development varies as a function of the area in which axons are developing. For example, in some areas axons reach their final destinations at 15 weeks, and in others, at 32 weeks (Mrzljak, Uylings, Kostovic, & Van Eden, 1988). The timing of dendritic growth is tightly connected with axonal growth. Dendritic sprouting begins to occur at approximately 15 weeks, about the same time that axons begin to reach their final destinations. This sprouting continues well after birth through the 24th postnatal month in some cortical regions (Mrzljack et al., 1990).

While the production of neurons appears to occur primarily during prenatal development, the production of many axons and dendrites continues postnatally. For example, dendrites of a type of neuron called pyramidal neurons reach a peak in the second year of life (Mrzljak et al., 1990). Additionally, there appears to be an overproduction of both axons and dendrites during development, with the final number achieved through a process of competitive elimination.

Errors and their consequences. There are several factors that may result in the disruption of axonal and dendritic growth. Among the factors influencing axonal growth are physical barriers (e.g. tissue scaring due to injury), damage to the target neuron, as well as anoxia (lack of oxygen), toxins, malnutrition, and genetic anomalies (Webb, Monk, & Nelson, 2001). An example of this are children with X-linked aqueductal stenosis, a disorder in which a connection between two fluid-filled cavities in the brain (lateral ventricles) is too narrow, causing pressure in the brain (hydroencephaly). These children show a deficit in axonal connections in some areas of the brain as a function of physical restriction (Chow, Halliday, Anderson, Danks, & Fortune, 1985). Similar factors may influence dendritic growth. For example, abnormal dendritic development may be influenced by inappropriate cell location, abnormal axon placement, ingestion of neurotoxins, and malnutrition (Webb et al., 2001). Genetic disorders such as angelman syndrome, fragile X syndrome, autism and Duchenne muscular dystrophy also show possible errors in dendritic development (Volpe, 1995). The end result of these errors in axonal and dendritic growth are varied, ranging from learning disorders to mental retardation to disorders of movement.

Unlike earlier processes such as proliferation and migration, axonal and dendritic growth continue to some extent after birth. This may lead to greater plasticity, particularly during the development process. However, the ability of axons to re-grow is limited and thus far evidence has found axonal re-growth primarily in the case of damaged axons in the peripheral nervous system (i.e. nerves that allow for physical sensations) (e.g. Grill, Murai, Gage, & Tuszynski, 1997). Alterations in initial axonal and dendritic growth appear to be difficult to alter later in development.

Synaptogenesis. As axons and dendrites come together, connections form so that information can pass between neurons. These connections are called synapses and they are the basis for communication within the brain. Synapses generally form between axons and dendrites, but can also form between dendrites or between axons. Additionally, synapses can form between axons and the body of the neuron (or soma). This process is called synaptogenesis. Synapses come in two forms, electrical and chemical. Electrical synapses – for example, gap junctions – allow for the rapid transmittal of information by passing electric current from one neuron to the next. While we know a little about the mechanisms of gap junction formation in adults (e.g., Ahmad, Martin, & Evans, 2001), we don't know as much about the formation of electrical synapses in development (Webb, Monk, & Nelson, 2001). On the other hand, chemical synapse development is better understood. Chemical synapses translate electrical signals, called action potentials, arriving at the axon terminals (i.e., the end of the axon) into chemical messengers by signaling the release of chemicals called neurotransmitters from the axon. These chemical messengers pass through the space between axon and dendrite (i.e., synaptic cleft), bind to receptors on the dendrite, and trigger a series of events that either promote or inhibit action potentials in the receiving neuron (Okabe, 2002). Thus, cells can communicate either a "pass this along" signal or a "don't pass this along" signal; the various combinations of these signals from different neurons create a message.

The formation of synapses is likely to involve two processes. The first involves genetic programming for the development of the components necessary for synapses (Rakic, Bourgeois, Eckenhoff, Zecevic, & Goldman-Rakic, 1986). The second is environmental neuronal activity that triggers the development and maturation of synapses.

The initial development of synapses is tenuous. Most synapses become stabilized as appropriate coordinated signals are received from incoming neurons. Those synapses that do not receive such information are eliminated or reabsorbed (Changeux & Danchin, 1976). The stabilization of synapses (as well as incoming axons) depends on chemical communication (e.g., Huang & Reichardt, 2001; Katz & Shatz, 1996; Thoenen, 1995). In this way the brain becomes organized with some connections strengthened while others are eliminated. Relating this back to the telephone example, a line that connects Sally to both Sam and Simon will eventually only connect Sally to Sam, as those communications are appropriate while those to Simon are not. However, who needs to connect with whom

can change over time thus new lines are created and those that fall into disuse are eliminated. Thus synaptogenesis is one of the most plastic mechanisms in the brain across
development.

Anatomical changes. The timing of the initial development of synapses is difficult to
pinpoint due to difficulties defining when a synapse is functional versus mature. However,
by about 23 weeks the first mature synapses can be found (Molliver, Kostovic, & Van
der Loos, 1973). Synapse production continues throughout gestation and throughout
the lifespan; however, peak levels of synapses appear to occur early during the first year
of life (Webb et al., 2001). Additionally, different areas of the brain reach their synaptic peak at different times. For example, in areas associated with vision (i.e., the visual
cortex) peak synaptogenesis occurs between 2.5 and 8 postnatal months (Huttenlocher
& de Courten, 1987), whereas in other areas (e.g., the middle frontal gyrus in the
prefrontal cortex) the peak synaptic density is not achieved until after 15 postnatal
months (Huttenlocher & Dabholkar, 1997). However, the peak density of synapses
during development is higher than eventual synapse density in the adult. There are
many potential explanations for this overproduction that will be addressed in later sections of this review.

Errors and their consequences. Errors in synapse production and function are a potential
factor in a multitude of disorders, including Fragile X (O'Donnell & Warren, 2002),
schizophrenia (Eastwood, Law, Everall, & Harrison, 2003), Retts syndrome (Johnston,
Jeon, Pevsner, Blue, & Naidu, 2001), and Down's syndrome (Weitzdoerfer, Dierssen,
Fountoulakis, & Lubec, 2001). In these disorders there may be alterations in signaling
between neurons. For example, abnormal synapses may show a reduction in activity,
heightened activity, or a lack of plasticity (i.e., the ability to change). In addition to
alterations in the synapses themselves, lack of, or overproduction of, synapses may be a
secondary effect of errors in axonal and dendritic growth. In other words, if there are no
axons between two areas that should be communicating, there will be no synapses to pass
the information along either. The consequences of these alterations may be subtle or
profound. However, exactly how errors in synaptogenesis relate to disorder is unclear.
Alterations of synaptogenesis on a larger scale involve the overproduction or underproduc-
tion of synapses which is related to the processes of synapse elimination, apoptosis (programmed neuron cell death), and pruning.

Apoptosis

In the course of development there is a large overproduction of neurons. Of the cells
produced, roughly half die due to a variety of factors (Raff et al., 1993; Zakeri & Ahuja,
1997). One of the factors involved in cell death is apoptosis or programmed cell death.
Cells that are eliminated in this way shrink (rather than degrade) and are then absorbed
into other cells (Jacobson, Weil, & Raff, 1997). The primary factor that regulates apoptosis is the presence of neurotrophic factors. Neurotrophic factors are substances (e.g.,

proteins) that promote neuronal and axonal outgrowth and survival. When the levels of neurotrophins are too low, molecules within the cell trigger degeneration (Bergeron & Yuan, 1998).

Anatomical changes. While anatomical changes are relatively easy to see with the growth of neurons and their connections, the effects of apoptosis are subtle. With the continual growth and death of cells it is difficult to see large changes. However, the same is not true when there are errors in apoptosis.

Errors and their consequences. Errors in apoptosis have been linked to such varied consequences as profound mental retardation (Engidawork & Lubec, 2003) and emotional and behavioral disorders (Anand & Scalzo, 2000). The typical error in apoptosis is heightened apoptotic activity. While we understand the consequences of reduced numbers of neurons through heightened apoptotic activity, we don't know as much about the consequences of a lack in neural apoptosis. For example, in the case of Down's syndrome, research suggests that a reduction in the number of neurons is due to increased apoptosis (Sawa, 1999). As neurons are the basic foundation of communication, a reduction in the overall number has a large effect on mental functioning. Without neurons there are not axons, dendrites, or synapses to carry out communication in the brain. However, what would be the effect of an overproduction of neurons that was not reduced through apoptosis? Would this result in a smarter individual? This is unlikely as there has yet to be a study that links intelligence with greater neuronal density. Moreover, there are rare genetic conditions in which cell proliferation is not turned off, resulting in macrocephaly, in which there are too many neurons. This always results in mental retardation, frequently accompanied by seizures.

Synaptic pruning

The loss of neurons through apoptosis by default reduces the number of synapses. However, there is also another mechanism that leads to the loss of synapses (without the loss of the neuron) that is a normal part of development. This is important because there is an overproduction of synapses in addition to an overproduction of neurons. It has been proposed that overproduction of synapses may allow for recovery and adaptation following injury and allows for adaptation to the environment. However, it is not the overproduction of synapse formation alone that assists development. Instead it is the selective elimination of some synapses while others are strengthened that allows for plasticity and adaptation.

The time course for the pruning or retraction of synapses differs considerably from the overproduction of synapses. Whereas the overproduction of synapses begins prenatally and is completed in the first 1–2 postnatal years, the retraction of synapses begins in the first postnatal year and continues into adolescence. Synaptogenesis in early infancy leads to levels of synapses higher than those of adults, and these levels remain high until late in childhood and adolescence (Huttenlocher & Dabholkar, 1997). From the peak levels of synapses reached in childhood to the levels reached as an adult, the number of synapses is reduced by 40% (Huttenlocher, 1975; Huttenlocher & de Courten, 1987). The timing of synapse reduction varies as a function of the brain structure involved. For example, areas involved in auditory perception (i.e., the auditory cortex) reach adult density in childhood, with pruning ending before 12 years of age. However, in areas associated with higher cognitive functions (e.g., the prefrontal cortex), pruning continues through mid-adolescence (Huttenlocher & Dabholkar, 1997; see Figure 5.2).

The process of synaptic pruning is highly dependent on the communication between neurons, with both the neuron sending the signal (the presynaptic neuron) and the neuron receiving the signal (the postsynaptic neuron) playing a role. The progress of pruning appears to function by more active synapses being strengthened and less active synapses being weakened or even eliminated (Chechik, Meilijson, & Ruppin, 1999). Neurons organize and support synaptic contact through the type of information they receive (in the form of various chemicals) and the amount of information they receive. For example, the release of neurotransmitters may strengthen a synapse, while the lack of neurotransmitters may drive elimination (Diebler, Farkas-Bargeton, & Wehrle, 1979). A second type of chemical that may regulate synapses are neurotrophins, those chemicals that encourage growth. Synapses where neurotrophins are present are spared, while those without regular contact with other cells do not receive these neurotrophic factors and are thus eliminated (Changeux & Danchin, 1976). The adjustments that are made can either be quantitative (reducing the overall number of synapses) or qualitative (refining connections such that incorrect or abnormal connections are eliminated). Thus the changes that result from synaptic pruning are less global and act more as fine tuning.

Anatomical changes. Anatomical changes due to synaptic pruning are seen primarily at the molecular level. However, changes in the density of the brain due to pruning can be

Human Brain Development

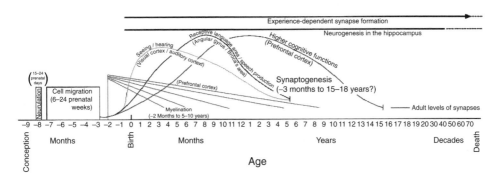

Figure 5.2 Developmental trajectories of mechanisms of brain development. Copyright © 2001 by the American Psychological Association. Reprinted with permission.

seen using structural imaging techniques (Sowell, Thompson, Tessner, & Toga, 2001). While there does not appear to be significant overall brain growth between childhood and adolescence, this may be due to the fact that continued growth is accompanied simultaneously with reduction and refinement of connections within the brain (Sowell et al., 2001).

Errors and their consequences. Similar to errors of synaptogenesis, errors in pruning may have consequences leading to disorder (e.g., schizophrenia; Rapoport et al., 2001). However, fewer disorders have been linked to pruning errors versus errors in synaptogenesis itself. One of the reasons for this is that pruning occurs throughout the lifespan, not just in relation to the overproduction of synapses but also in the daily functioning of the brain. Synapses are created and eliminated as a function of learning and thus are the greatest mechanisms for change and plasticity within the brain. This plasticity will be addressed in the final section of this chapter.

Myelination

The final mechanism involved in connections and communication within the brain is myelination. Myelination is the process by which a type of cells, called myelin, surround and insulate the axons of neurons in the brain. Myelin has often been overlooked in relation to brain development as it was thought to function primarily as insulation. The brain uses this insulation to increase the speed and efficiency at which information can travel (Webb et al., 2001). However, myelin may also play a role in the transfer of energy to neurons and may also support neuronal functioning. Moreover, it may actually be involved in communication between neurons (Fields & Stevens-Graham, 2002; Zahs & Newman, 1997). Thus, while we are still in the infancy of understanding the role of myelin in the brain, it is important to begin understanding how its development relates to behavior.

The process of myelination is protracted. Myelin is first visible only under the microscope, but as it continues to develop it becomes visible to the naked eye, eventually reaching adult density levels. The appearance of myelin appears early in development, but different areas of the brain reach maturity at different times, with some areas involved with higher cognitive functions (e.g., the prefrontal cortex) not reaching maturity until late in development (Fuster, 2002).

Although our understanding of myelination is limited, it appears that the process occurs in different areas of the brain at different times. Those areas with the earliest myelination correspond to areas associated with behavior systems that also function early in development. For example, primary sensory and motor areas involved in abilities such as vision and movement are myelinated before areas involved in higher cognitive functions such as association areas (Gibson, 1991). This correlates with what we've known about the process of development from a psychological perspective for many years. Higher cognitive skills such as those associated with Piaget's formal operations don't develop until middle to late childhood. The timing of this parallels myelination that occurs in the prefrontal cortex, an area that is associated with higher cognitive functions (Fuster, 2002). Additionally, the patterning of myelination follows what we understand about the flow of information in the brain. Information in the world enters the brain through one of the five senses (touch, taste, smell, vision, and audition) and follows a distinct path of processing. For example, light enters the eye and is coded into activity in the brain that first travels to the primary sensory areas, where it is initially processed (in this case the occipital cortex toward the rear of the brain). Then, once basic features of the light are processed, the information travels to secondary sensory areas, where it is further processed, and finally to association areas, where the final images are linked to concepts. Cortical areas involved in early processing of incoming stimuli (i.e., primary sensory areas) develop before areas involved in later processing (i.e., association areas) (Benes, Turtle, Khan, & Farol, 1994).

Anatomical changes. The prolonged process of myelination results in anatomical changes that must be viewed on a larger time scale. There are some systems that become myelinated prenatally. These include systems involved in posture, orientation, and the vestibular system (i.e., balance). However, the majority become myelinated after birth. For example, while the major tracts involved in vision begin myelinating before birth, maturity is not reached until approximately 9 months of age (Brody, Kinney, Kloman, & Gilles, 1987). Higher cognitive processes, involving the frontal cortex, are among the last to become myelinated (Fuster, 2002).

Errors and their consequences. Not all axons are myelinated, although the majority are (excluding those in the autonomic nervous system), and thus the lack of myelination can lead to disorder. Disruption in myelination may be caused by a range of factors, from deficiencies of amino acids or organic acids to congenital hypothyroidism, lack of enzymes (e.g., fatty aldehyde dehydrogenase, Willemsen et al., 2001), undernutrition, and periventricular leukomalacia (a consequence of prematurity; see Volpe, 1995). The consequences of these factors include mental retardation and disorders of movement such as adrenoleukodystrophy (ALD) and Sjogren-Larsson syndrome (Barkovich, 2000; Di Biase & Salvati, 1997; Willemsen et al., 2001). In these disorders communication between neurons is disrupted, either slowing or altering that communication. Additionally, even when myelination occurs normally, it can be the target of disease. Such is the case with diseases such as multiple sclerosis and phenylketonuria (PKU) (Huttenlocher, 2000). In these diseases, as with disorders of myelination, mental retardation, as well as disorders of movement and sensory systems, occurs. (For an overview of brain development, see Figure 5.2.)

In the preceding section three basic components of communication within the brain were discussed: axons and dendrites, synapses, and myelin. Each one of these components is essential for communication: axons and dendrites to carry the information across distances within the brain, synapses to pass that information between neurons, and myelin to support that communication. Consequences of alterations in the development of these components can be subtle or profound, affecting all aspects of behavior. Additionally, the timing of the development of these components influences their plasticity, with the growth of axons and dendrites being less plastic than synapses. It is this plasticity that will be addressed in the final section of this chapter.

Plasticity and the Environment

The brain not only grows and changes as a function of development, but it also retains considerable plasticity well into the lifespan. Once the building blocks of the brain are in place and the connections established, the brain continually interacts with itself and the environment, adapting to achieve an optimal functional state. This ongoing adaptation is termed plasticity, the ability to change and adapt in response to change in the brain or environment. However, some brain systems are more plastic than others, and are more plastic at some points in time than are others. For example, in the case of strabismus, one eye may be deviated outward. This deviation leads to competing and conflicting signals being sent to the visual cortex as this system is developing. As a result the brain effectively begins to ignore the non-dominant eye, and if not corrected early enough (i.e., the first few years), there will always be a strabismus-related perceptual deficit (Crawford, Harwerth, Smith, & von Noorden, 1993). Thus, while the visual system is plastic early in development, once established it is less plastic. In contrast, language association areas may retain plasticity through middle childhood. Evidence shows that children who suffered large lesions to language areas at or around the time of birth or who undergo hemispherectomy in the infancy period can have normal language expression. Unfortunately the same is not true for adults, who can recover some language but not nearly to the same extent (Bates et al., 2001; Woods & Teuber, 1978).

Mechanisms of plasticity

There are multiple mechanisms through which plasticity occurs. Some of these mechanisms are primarily gene-driven, while others rely more heavily on the environment. As discussed earlier, the brain is built through neurogenesis, proliferation, and migration. These processes, occurring primarily (although not fully) during prenatal development, are highly gene-driven. Thus, they are less plastic in relation to influences from the environment. Processes more amenable to change as a function of the environment (i.e., environmentally driven) are those involved in communication within the brain – synaptogenesis and pruning.

   As discussed previously, once the building blocks of the brain are in place, there is a protracted period of time in which the brain wires itself for normal functioning through the development of communication systems. Early overproduction of synapses allows the brain to be more plastic, maintaining those synapses that are functional and eliminating those that are non-functional or unnecessary (Huttenlocher, 1994) through apoptosis and pruning. There are two paths through which environmentally driven plasticity occurs: experience-expectant plasticity and experience-dependent plasticity (Greenough & Black, 1992).

Experience-expectant plasticity

The development of communicating brain systems requires intricate wiring within and between various brain systems. In order to develop normally, some systems require specific environmental input. Moreover, it is necessary for this input to occur during a window of time during which the brain is prepared to receive the input for normal development to occur. This type of environmentally driven plasticity is termed experience-expectant plasticity (Greenough & Black, 1992). As normal development will not occur without these experiences, they are assumed to be common to all members of the species (Nelson, 2000). For example, the visual system develops normally if an intact visual system (i.e., one without impairments) is exposed to a normal visual environment (e.g., patterned light information). In this case the visual input is "expected" in the environment. Lack of this input can have major effects on development, ranging from lack of vision to perceptual deficits. The primary mechanism through which experience-expectant plasticity occurs is thought to be the overproduction of synapses followed by retraction (Black, Jones, Nelson, & Greenough, 1998). Thus, while this is an environmentally driven process, it is also dependent on genetic factors. The combination of environmental and genetic mechanisms that occurs in experience-expectant plasticity results in change that is less plastic later in development.

Atypical development. When the normal expected environment is not present, atypical development occurs. Once atypical development has occurred through this mechanism it is relatively stable and immutable to change. For example, while it would be unethical to experiment with humans, deprivation experiments with cats have shown that if you light-deprive cats early in life they show multiple alterations in subsequent visual development. There are behavioral, physiological, and structural abnormalities in the visual pathways as a function of the timing and duration of deprivation (Wiesel & Hubel, 1965). Unfortunately, as these systems are experience-expectant in nature, once the system becomes stable, visual deficits remain throughout the lifespan. However, experience-dependent processes are far more plastic, as we describe below.

Experience-dependent plasticity

In contrast to experience-expectant plasticity, experience-dependent plasticity involves the brain's adaptation to information in the environment that is unique to individuals rather than common across the species (Greenough & Black, 1992). Thus the mechanisms through which experience-dependent plasticity occurs are different than those involved in experience-expectant plasticity. One of the primary mechanisms of experience-dependent plasticity is ongoing synaptogenesis and pruning. The greater plasticity seen in experience-dependent processes is a direct function of these mechanisms as they occur throughout the lifespan. For example, learning is highly experience-dependent. While all typically developing children are capable of learning how to make cookies, not all children do. Learning of this information is highly variable and often individualized. Additionally, whereas timing is critical in experience-expectant plasticity, the same is not true of experience-dependent plasticity. However, this does not mean that experience-dependent plasticity can occur at any time. Instead there may be necessary sequential dependencies on prior development (Black et al., 1998). This prior development can be either experience-expectant (i.e., the development of manual dexterity necessary for cookie making) or experience-dependent (i.e., learning to read instructions on how to make cookies). Thus, typically, experience-expectant and dependent processes do not occur in isolation; rather they interact across development.

Atypical development. While it is easy to appreciate alterations in development that might be considered "atypical" when discussing experience-expectant plasticity, the same is not true of experience-dependent plasticity. As experience-dependent plasticity relates to individual differences, atypical development is individual in nature. For example, exposure to a stressful environment such as an environment of maltreatment may alter the structure, function, and organization in such a way that behavior becomes atypical (Cicchetti & Cannon, 1999). Additionally, these alterations, albeit atypical, can be both negative and positive (Nelson, 1999). For example, studies with rats have shown that complex environments can lead to positive changes in structure and function of the brain (Greenough & Black, 1992).

Experience-expectant versus -dependent plasticity: caveats

While the utility of the experience-expectant versus -dependent plasticity distinction is clear, there are some important caveats. Many types of plasticity do not fall clearly into this dichotomy. For example, while general language development may represent an experience-expectant process, the nuances of language, such as the development of vocabulary, clearly represent an experience-dependent process. Similarly, because of the immaturity of our species' young, the formation of an attachment relationship between infant and caregiver may represent an experience-expectant process, whereas the *quality* of that relationship likely represents an experience-dependent process. Finally, from a methodological perspective, it is currently impossible to distinguish in the living child's or adult's brain synapses that reflect experience-expectant processes from those that reflect experience-dependent ones.

Conclusions and Future Directions

Over the course of early brain development structures form, connections develop, and the brain begins to be shaped not only by the process of development itself, but by the interplay between the brain and the environment. Developing systems are open because they are in progress, adjusting to the current conditions as they form. This allows for the plasticity and adaptability necessary to achieve optimal functioning.

While much is known about how the brain is assembled, how it is sculpted by genes and experience represents an area of relatively uncharted territory. We know the processes of development and change, but we do not have a clear understanding of how they relate to behavior (for elaboration, see Nelson & Bloom, 1997; Nelson, Bloom, Cameron, Amaral, Dahl, & Pine, 2002). Our understanding of connections between changes at the molecular level and the behavioral level are few and far between. While strides have been made in connecting adult behavior (e.g., language) to functioning brain systems (e.g., Broca's area), the same cannot be said for connecting brain development and changes in behavior. For example, it is thought that changes in cognition (e.g., development of abstract thinking) are related to changes in the brain (e.g., development of the prefrontal cortex) (Fuster, 2002). However, making direct connections between neurological change and behavioral change is difficult. Presently imaging techniques are utilized in research to relate brain and behavior at static points in development. This provides snapshots of brain–behavior relations, but does not reflect the mechanisms by which change in neural substrates alters behavior. Future study should examine changes in the brain in relation to changes in development using dynamic techniques where change can be followed over time. By examining the brain through change we may develop a better understanding of both brain and behavior, as well as their interaction. Additionally, studies relating higher-order concepts such as social understanding and culture and their relation to the developing brain is a topic that has not yet appeared on the radar screen of most investigators. This is an important area of research as these constructs affect a multitude of behaviors throughout development. Taking unconventional approaches to studying these topics will be necessary if we are to increase our understanding of plasticity and early brain development.

Notes

The writing of this chapter was made possible by grants from the National Institutes of Health to the second author (NS329976 and NS34458), and the graduate school of the University of Minnesota to the first author.

1　Investigation of the molecular mechanisms of growth cones is performed primarily with invertebrate and lower mammals; however, the mechanisms are thought to be the same as those for humans as they have been conserved through evolution.

References

Acosta, M. T., & Pearl, P. L. (2003). The neurobiology of autism: New pieces of the puzzle. *Current Neurology & Neuroscience Reports, 3*(2), 149–156.

Ahmad, S., Martin, P. E., & Evans, W. H. (2001). Assembly of gap junction channels: Mechanism, effects of calmodulin antagonists and identification of connexin oligomerization determinants. *European Journal of Biochemistry, 268*(16), 4544–4552.

Anand, K. J., & Scalzo, F. M. (2000). Can adverse neonatal experiences alter brain development and subsequent behavior? *Biology of the Neonate, 77*(2), 69–82.

Bambrick, L. L., Yarowsky, P. J., & Krueger, B. K. (2003). Altered astrocyte calcium homeostasis and proliferation in theTs65Dn mouse, a model of Down syndrome. *Journal of Neuroscience Research, 73*(1), 89–94.

Barkovich, A. J. (2000). Concepts of myelin and myelination in neuroradiology. *American Journal of Neuroradiology, 21*(6), 1099–1109.

Bates, E., Reilly, J., Wulfeck, B., Dronkers, N., Opie, M., Fenson, J., Kriz, S., Jeffries, R., Miller, L., & Herbst, K. (2001). Differential effects of unilateral lesions on language production in children and adults. *Brain & Language, 79*(2), 223–265.

Benes, F., Turtle, M., Khan, Y., & Farol, P. (1994). Myelination of a key relay zone in the hippocampal formation occurs in the human brain during childhood, adolescence, and adulthood. *Archives of General Psychiatry, 51*, 477–484.

Bergeron, L., & Yuan, J. (1998). Sealing one's fate: Control of cell death in neurons. *Current Opinion in Neurobiology, 8*, 55–63.

Black, J. E., Jones, T. A., Nelson, C. A., & Greenough, W. T. (1998). Neuronal plasticity and the developing brain. In N. E. Alessi, J. T. Coyle, S. I. Harrison, & E. Spencer (Eds.), *Handbook of child and adolescent psychiatry, Vol. 6: Basic psychiatric science and treatment* (pp. 31–53). New York: John Wiley & Sons.

Brody, B., Kinney, H., Kloman, A., & Gilles, F. (1987). Sequence of central nervous system myelination in human infancy: I. An autopsy study of myelination. *Journal of Neuropathology & Experimental Neurology, 46*, 283–301.

Changeux, J., & Danchin, A. (1976). Selective stabilization of developing synapses as a mechanism for the specification of neuronal networks. *Nature, 64*(5588), 705–712.

Chechik, G., Meilijson, I., & Ruppin, E. (1999) Neuronal regulation: A mechanism for synaptic pruning during brain maturation. *Neural Computation, 11*(8), 2061–2080.

Chenn, A., & McConnell, S. K. (1995). Cleavage orientation and the asymmetric inheritance of Notch 1 immunoreactivity in mammalian neurogenesis. *Cell, 82*, 631–641.

Chong, B. W., Babcook, C. J., Salamat, M. S., Nemzik, W., Kroeker, D., & Ellis, W. G. (1996). A magnetic resonance template for normal neuronal migration in the fetus. *Neurosurgery, 39*, 110–116.

Chow, C., Halliday, J., Anderson, R., Danks, D., & Fortune, D. (1985). Congenital absence of pyramids and its significance in genetic diseases. *Acta Neuropathology, 65*, 313–317.

Cicchetti, D., & Cannon, T. (1999). Neurodevelopmental processes in the ontogenesis and epigenesis of psychopathology. *Development and Psychopathology, 11*, 375–393.

Costa, L. G., & Guizzetti, M. (2002). Inhibition of muscarinic receptor-induced proliferation of astroglial cells by ethanol: Mechanisms and implications for the fetal alcohol syndrome. *Neurotoxicology, 23*(6), 685–691.

Crawford, M. L., Harwerth, R. S., Smith, E. L., & von Noorden, G. K. (1993). Keeping an eye on the brain: The role of visual experience in monkeys and children. *Journal of General Psychology, 120*, 7–19.

Di Biase, A., & Salvati, S. (1997). Exogenous lipids in myelination and myelination. *Kaohsiung Journal of Medical Sciences, 13*(1), 19–29.

Diebler, M., Farkas-Bargeton, E., & Wehrle, R. (1979). Developmental changes of enzymes associated with energy metabolism and the synthesis of some neurotransmitters in discrete areas of human neocortex. *Journal of Neurochemistry, 32*, 429–435.

Eastwood, S. L., Law, A. J., Everall, I. P., & Harrison, P. J. (2003). The axonal chemorepellant semaphorin 3A is increased in the cerebellum in schizophrenia and may contribute to its synaptic pathology. *Molecular Psychiatry, 8*(2), 148–155.

Engidawork, E., & Lubec, G. (2003). Molecular changes in fetal Down syndrome brain. *Journal of Neurochemistry, 84*(5), 895–904.

Fatemi, S. H., Stary, J. M., Halt, A. R., & Realmuto, G. R. (2001). Dysregulation of Reelin and Bcl-2 proteins in autistic cerebellum. *Journal of Autism & Developmental Disorders, 31*(6), 529–535.

Fields, R. D., & Stevens-Graham, B. (2002). New insights into neuron–glia communication. *Science, 298,* 556–562.

Finnell, R. H., Junker, W. M., Wadman, L. K., & Cabrera R. M. (2002). Gene expression profiling within the developing neural tube. *Neurochemical Research, 27*(10),1165–1180.

Fuster, J. M. (2002). Frontal lobe and cognitive development. *Journal of Neurocytology, 31*(3–5), 373–385.

Gibson, K. R. (1991). Myelination and behavioral development: A comparative perspective on questions of neoteny, altriciality and intelligence. In K. R. Gibson & A. C. Petersen (Eds.), *Brain maturation and cognitive development: Comparative and cross-cultural perspectives. Foundations of human behavior* (pp. 29–63). New York: Aldine de Gruyter.

Gos, M., & Szpecht-Potocka, A. (2002). Genetic basis of neural tube defects. I. Regulatory genes for the neurulation process. *Journal of Applied Genetics, 43*(3), 343–350.

Greenough, W. T., & Black, J. E. (1992). Induction of brain structure by experience: Substrates for cognitive development. In M. R. Gunnar & C. A. Nelson (Eds.), *The Minnesota Symposia on Child Psychology: Vol. 24. Developmental behavioral neuroscience* (pp. 155–200). Mahwah, NJ: Lawrence Erlbaum.

Grill, R., Murai, K., Gage, F. H., & Tuszynski, M. H. (1997). Cellular delivery of neurotrophin-3 promotes corticospinal axonal growth and partial functional recovery after spinal cord injury. *Journal of Neuroscience, 17*(14), 5560–5572.

Huang, E. J., & Reichardt, L. F. (2001). Neurotrophins: Roles in neuronal development and function. *Annual Review of Neuroscience, 24,* 677–736.

Huttenlocher, P. R. (1975). Synaptic and dendritic development and mental defect. In N. Buchwalk & M. Brazier (Eds.), *Proceedings of a conference in the series on mental retardation sponsored by the National Institute of Child Health and Human Development mental retardation research centers series: Vol. 18. Brain mechanisms in mental retardation* (pp. 123–40). New York: Academic Press.

Huttenlocher, P. R. (1994). Synaptogenesis, synapse elimination, and neural plasticity in human cerebral cortex. In C. A. Nelson (Ed.), *The Minnesota Symposia on Child Psychology: Vol. 27. Cognition, perception, and language* (pp. 35–54). Hillsdale, NJ: Lawrence Erlbaum Associates.

Huttenlocher, P. R. (2000). The neuropathology of phenylketonuria: Human and animal studies. *European Journal of Pediatrics, 159*(Suppl. 2), S102–106.

Huttenlocher, P. R., & Dabholkar, A. S. (1997). Regional differences in synaptogenesis in human cerebral cortex. *Journal of Comparative Neurology, 387*(2), 167–178.

Huttenlocher, P. R., & de Courten, C. (1987). The development of synapses in striat cortex of man. *Human Neurobiology, 6,* 1–9.

Jacobson, M. D., Weil, M., & Raff, M. C. (1997). Programmed cell death in animal development. *Cell, 88,* 347–354.

Jessell, T. (1988). Adhesion molecules and the hierarchy of neural development. *Neuron, 1,* 3–13.

Johnston, M. V., Jeon, O. H., Pevsner, J., Blue, M. E., & Naidu, S. (2001). Neurobiology of Rett syndrome: A genetic disorder of synapse development. *Brain & Development, 23*(Suppl. 1), S206–S213.

Katz, L., & Shatz, C. (1996). Synaptic activity and construction of cortical circuits. *Science, 274,* 1133.

Keith, A. (1948). *Human embryology and morphology.* London: Edward Arnold and Co.

Kozlowski, P. B., Brudkowska, J., Kraszpulski, M., Sersen, E. A., Wrzolek, M. A., Anzil, A. P., Rao, C., & Wisniewski, H. M. (1997). Microencephaly in children congenitally infected with human immunodeficiency virus: A gross-anatomical morphometric study. *Acta Neuropathologica, 93*(2), 136–145.

Lewis, V. (2003). *Development and disability.* Malden, MA: Blackwell Publishers.

McBride, M. C., & Kemper, T. L. (1982). Pathogenesis of four-layered microgyric cortex in man. *Acta Neuropathologica, 57,* 93–98.

Martin, J. H., & Jessell, T. M. (1991). Development as a guide to the regional anatomy of the brain. In E. R. Kandel, J. H. Schwartz, & T. M. Jessell (Eds.), *Principles of neural science* (3rd ed., pp. 296–308). Norwalk, CT: Appleton & Lange.

Molliver, M., Kostovic, I., & Van der Loos, H. (1973). The development of synapses in the human fetus. *Brain Research, 50,* 403–407.

Monk, C. S., Webb, S. J., & Nelson, C. A. (2001). Prenatal neurobiological development: Molecular mechanisms and anatomical change. *Developmental Neuropsychology, 19*(2), 211–236.

Mrzljak, L., Uylings, H. B. M., Kostovic, I., & Van Eden, C. (1988). Prenatal development of neurons in the human prefrontal cortex: A qualitative golgi study. *Journal of Comparative Neurology, 271,* 355–386.

Mrzljak, L., Uylings, H. B. M., Van Eden, C., & Judas, M. (1990). Neuronal development in human prefrontal cortex in prenatal and postnatal stages. *Progress in Brain Research, 85,* 185–222.

Nelson, C. A. (1999). Change and continuity in neurobehavioral development: Lessons from the study of neurobiology and neural plasticity. *Infant Behavior & Development, 22*(4), 415–429.

Nelson, C. A. (2000). Neural plasticity and human development: The role of early experience in sculpting memory systems. *Developmental Science, 3*(2), 115–136.

Nelson, C. A., & Bloom, F. E. (1997). Child development and neuroscience. *Child Development, 68,* 970–987.

Nelson, C. A., Bloom, F. E., Cameron, J., Amaral, D., Dahl, R., & Pine, D. (2002). An integrative, multidisciplinary approach to the study of brain-behavior relations in the context of typical and atypical development. *Development and Psychopathology, 14,* 499–520.

Nelson, C. A., de Haan, M., & Thomas, K. M. (in press). Neural bases of cognitive development. In W. Damon, R. Lerner, D. Kuhn, & R. Siegler (Eds.), *Handbook of child psychology: Vol. 2. Cognition, perception and language* (6th ed.). New York: John Wiley & Sons.

Norman, M. G. (1980). Bilateral encephaloclastic lesions in a 26 week gestation fetus: Effect on neuroblast migration. *Canadian Journal of Neurological Sciences, 7,* 191–194.

O'Donnell, W. T., & Warren, S. T. (2002). A decade of molecular studies of fragile X syndrome. *Annual Review of Neuroscience, 25,* 315–338.

Okabe, S. (2002). Birth, growth and elimination of a single synapse. *Anatomical Science International, 77*(4), 203–210.

O'Rahilly, R., & Gardner, E. (1979). The initial development of the human brain. *Acta Anatomica, 104,* 123–133.

O'Rahilly, R., & Muller, F. (1994). *The embryonic human brain: An atlas of developmental stages.* New York: Wiley-Liss.

Raff, M. C., Barres, B. A., Burne, J. F., Coles, H. S., Ishizaki, Y., & Jacobson, M. D. (1993). Programmed cell death and the control of cell survival: Lessons from the nervous system. *Science, 262,* 695–699.

Rakic, P. (1974). Neurons in rhesus monkey visual cortex: Systematic relation between time of origin and eventual disposition. *Science, 183,* 425–427.

Rakic, P. (1978). Neuronal migration and contact guidance in the primate telencephalon. *Postgraduate Medical Journal, 54*(Suppl. 1), 25–40.

Rakic, P. (1988). Specification of cerebral cortical areas. *Science, 241,* 170–176.

Rakic, P. (2002). Neurogenesis in adult primates. *Progress in Brain Research, 138,* 3–114.

Rakic, P., Bourgeois, J., Eckenhoff, M., Zecevic, N., & Goldman-Rakic, P. (1986). Concurrent overproduction of synapses in diverse regions of the primate cerebral cortex. *Science, 232,* 232–235.

Raper, J. A., & Tessier-Lavigne, M. (1999). Growth cones and axon pathfinding. In M. J. Zigmond, F. E. Bloom, S. C. Landis, J. L. Roberts, & L. R. Squire (Eds.), *Fundamental neuroscience* (pp. 519–546). Boston: Academic Press.

Rapoport, J. L., Castellanos, F. X., Gogate, N., Janson, K., Kohler, S., & Nelson, P. (2001). Imaging normal and abnormal brain development: New perspectives for child psychiatry. *Australian & New Zealand Journal of Psychiatry, 35*(3), 272–281.

Sawa, A. (1999). Neuronal cell death in Down's syndrome. *Journal of Neural Transmission. Supplementum, 57,* 87–97.

Sidman, R., & Rakic, P. (1973). Neuronal migration, with special reference to developing human brain: A review. *Brain Research, 62,* 1–35.

Sidman, R., & Rakic, P. (1982). Development of the human central nervous system. In W. Haymaker & R. D. Adams (Eds.), *Histology and histopathology of the nervous system* (pp. 3–143). Springfield, IL: Thomas.

Smart, I. H. M. (1985). A localized growth zone in the wall of the developing mouse telencephalon. *Journal of Anatomy, 140,* 397–402.

Sowell, E. R., Thompson, P. M., Tessner, K. D., & Toga, A. W. (2001). Mapping continued brain growth and gray matter density reduction in dorsal frontal cortex: Inverse relationships during postadolescent brain maturation. *Journal of Neuroscience, 21*(22), 8819–8829.

Takahashi, T., Nowakowski, R. S., & Caviness, V. S., Jr. (1994). Mode of cell proliferation in the developing mouse neocortex. *Proceedings of the National Academy of Sciences of the United States of America, 91,* 375–379.

Tessier-Lavigne, M., & Goodman, C. S. (1996). The molecular biology of axon guidance. *Science, 274,* 1123–1133.

Thoenen, H. (1995). Neurotrophins and neuronal plasticity. *Science, 279,* 593–598.

Volpe, J. J. (1995). *Neurology of the newborn* (3rd ed.). Philadelphia: Saunders.

Warkany, J., Lemire, R. J., & Cohen, M. M. (1981). *Mental retardation and congenital malformations of the central nervous system.* Chicago: Year Book Medical.

Webb, S. J., Monk, C. S., & Nelson, C. A. (2001). Mechanisms of postnatal neurobiological development: Implications for human development. *Developmental Neuropsychology, 19*(2), 147–171.

Weitzdoerfer, R., Dierssen, M., Fountoulakis, M., & Lubec, G. (2001). Fetal life in Down syndrome starts with normal neuronal density but impaired dendritic spines and synaptosomal structure. *Journal of Neural Transmission. Supplementum, 61,* 59–70.

Wiesel, T. N., & Hubel, D. H. (1965). Comparison of the effects of unilateral and bilateral eye closure on cortical unit reponses in kittens. *Journal of Neurophysiology, 28,* 1029–1040.

Willemsen, M. A., IJlst, L., Steijlen, P. M., Rotteveel, J. J., de Jong, J. G., van Domburg, P. H., Mayatepek, E., Gabreels, F. J., & Wanders, R. J. (2001). Clinical, biochemical and molecular genetic characteristics of 19 patients with the Sjogren-Larsson syndrome. *Brain, 124*(Pt 7), 1426–1437.

Woods, B. T., & Teuber, H. L. (1978). Changing patterns of childhood aphasia. *Annals of Neurology, 3,* 273–280.

Zakeri, Z. F., & Ahuja, H. S. (1997). Cell death/apoptosis: Normal, chemically induced, and teratogenic effect. *Mutation Research, 396*(1–2), 149–161.

Zahs, K. R., & Newman, E. A. (1997). Asymmetric gap junctional coupling between glial cells in the rat retina. *GLIA, 20*(1), 10–22.

6

Social Regulation of Stress in Early Child Development

Megan R. Gunnar

Stress is a fact of life beginning in earliest development. Successful adaptation requires both responding to stressful events and regulating stress reactions. Evidence from a variety of mammalian species indicates that during early development stress regulation is embedded in caregiver–infant interactions. Furthermore, the effectiveness of those interactions in regulating stress responding, both behaviorally and physiologically, influences the ontogeny of the neural systems that process threat information and activate defense responses. While most of this evidence is derived from animal studies, it is increasingly clear that, in some form, early caregiving also programs the development of the human stress system. The purpose of this chapter is to provide a brief overview of the neurophysiology of stress, to summarize the animal studies that motivate research on early experience and stress in human development, to briefly review the current state of research on social regulation of stress, and, finally, to examine the impact of failures of early caregiving on stress system activity later in childhood.

The Neurobiology of Stress

General principles

Stress results when demands exceed readily available resources. The nature of these demands varies from ones that threaten homeostasis (i.e., systemic stressors, e.g., blood volume loss, fever) to those that threaten the individual's psychological well-being (i.e., psychological stressors, e.g., emotional loss, anticipation or threats of physical or social harm) (Pacak & Palkovits, 2001). Although Selye (1946), the father of stress research, argued that stressors, regardless of their source, produce the same general pattern of biological response, we now know that this is not true. Infection, pain, energy needs, and psychological challenges operate through stressor-specific pathways to stimulate reactions that are to some extent specific to different classes of stressors (Pacak & Palkovits, 2001).

Stress is often viewed as bad for the body and brain, but this view is also too limited (de Kloet, 2003). The capacity to activate the body's stress system is essential to survival. Furthermore, a general principle of stress biology is that the mechanisms of acute, rapid stress responding are invariably paired with slower, more persistent mechanisms for terminating stress responses and organizing rest and restoration. When each mode (activation followed by termination and restoration) is functioning efficiently, stressors can foster positive development. Organisms become vulnerable to stressors when the mechanisms involved in activation or termination/restoration are impaired.

McEwen (1998) uses the term "allostasis" (maintaining stability through change) to describe the general function of stress responses. In practice, effective responses to stress involve shifting resources from everyday functioning absent a threat or challenge toward mobilization in the presence of threat. Accordingly, stress biology promotes survival by shifting where the organism puts it energy – away from behavioral (e.g., exploration) and physiological (e.g., physical growth) processes that prepare the organism to meet future demands, and toward behavioral (e.g., heightened vigilance) and physiological (e.g., breaking down of energy stores) processes needed for immediate survival. Mechanisms involved in termination and restoration shift energy resources back to future-oriented (non-threat) processes. Thus, when stress reactions are infrequent and efficient (i.e., "a system that readily turns on and off its behavioral, autonomic, and endocrine responses to stressors," de Kloet, 2003, p. 52), they are generally growth promoting. But, when frequent, prolonged, or chronic, stress responses have costs (allostatic load) which increase risks for disordered functioning, including disordered functioning of the stress system itself. Disordered and potentially harmful patterns of stress activity are characterized as responding too sluggishly or too strongly and/or terminating responding too slowly or too rapidly (de Kloet, 2003; McEwen, 1998).

The autonomic nervous system and stress

Two systems orchestrate many components of the stress response: the sympathetic nervous system (SNS), discussed in this section, and the hypothalamic-pituitary-adrenocortical (HPA) system, discussed in the next section (Johnson, Kamilaris, Chrousos, & Gold, 1992). The SNS produces norepinephrine from sympathetic synapses and epinephrine from the adrenal medulla. Along with the norepinephrine circuits of the brain, the SNS mediates many acute or "fight/flight" reactions to stressors. Activation of the SNS induces gycogenolysis in the liver and lipolysis in adipose tissue to increase blood glucose levels, raises blood pressure and increases heart rate, increases blood supply to the muscles and brain at the expense of the gastrointestinal tract and skin, and increases dilation of the pupils and the bronchioles to improve vision and increase oxygen consumption. Each of these changes mobilizes the body and brain to respond to stress.

SNS actions are balanced and reversed by actions of the parasympathetic nervous system (PNS). The PNS acts to lower heart rate and blood pressure, contracts the pupils and bronchioles, and facilitates digestion of food to restore depleted energy stores by increasing saliva production, diverting blood to the gastrointestinal tract, and increasing gastric motility. These actions serve to terminate the stress response and restore everyday, growth-promoting functioning. PNS cell bodies lie in the brainstem and leave the brain through several cranial nerves. Porges (1995a, 1995b) argues that the tenth or vagus nerve, particularly the efferent (brain to body) tract originating from the nucleus ambiguus, regulates cardiac and vocal activity related to competent stress and emotion regulation. In addition, the afferent (body to brain) projections from the vagus travel back to the brain via the nucleus tractus solitarius, feeding information about the state of peripheral organs to higher brain centers involved in stress and emotion.

While the SNS and PNS generally serve opposing – and thus related – functions, they respond independently. Porges (1995a) notes that the PNS plays a critical role in stress responding because rapidly decreasing vagal tone is an effective and energy-efficient means of allowing sympathetic influences to dominate. Furthermore, he notes that low baseline vagal tone indexes vulnerability to stressors, while failure to appropriately modify vagal tone under conditions of challenge or threat reflects deficits in adaptive capacities. Cacioppo and colleagues (Cacioppo, Uchino, & Berntson, 1994) argue that stress-vulnerable individuals regulate heart rate by increasing sympathetic input to the heart, where less stress-vulnerable individuals do so by merely decreasing vagal tone.

Cardiac activity has been used to study stress and emotion regulation in young children. Heart rate, however, does not allow one to distinguish between SNS and PNS contributions because heart rate can change because of changes in either sympathetic or vagal input, or both. For decades, developmental researchers have used measures of respiratory sinus arrhythmia (RSA) to index vagal tone (Porges, 1995b). RSA indexes the variability in heart rate associated with breathing, a variability regulated by the vagus nerve traveling from the nucleus ambiguus to the heart. Because the SNS and PNS are not locked into reciprocal activation, measures of vagal tone do not permit inference of sympathetic activity. Recently, developmental researchers have begun to measure pre-ejection period (PEP). PEP indexes the latency between the onset of the electro-mechanical systole (heart says to pump) and the onset of left-ventricular ejection (heart actually pumps). This latency is regulated largely by the SNS, with shorter latencies (lower or shorter PEP) reflecting greater SNS activity (Cacioppo et al., 1994). To date, very little work on either vagal tone or PEP has addressed the role of social relationships in stress regulation. Rather, this work has focused on individual differences among children in temperament and emotion regulation (e.g. Buss, Davidson, Kalin, & Goldsmith, 2004; Calkins & Fox, 2002).

The HPA system and stress

Unlike epinephrine and norepinephrine produced by activation of the SNS, glucocorticoids, the major stress hormones of the HPA system, cross the blood–brain barrier (although see work on 11β-HSD reviewed in de Kloet, 2003). In the brain, as elsewhere in the body, the way glucocorticoids operate is by affecting gene transcription. That is, they play a role in regulating the activation of genes. Because they affect the ways in which many of the genes that act in the brain are regulated, the HPA system and related systems of neuropeptides and receptors have been the focus of much of the research on stress and early experiences.

Activation and regulation of stress is largely orchestrated in the brain through two families of corticotropin-releasing hormone(CRH)-related peptides and receptors (Holsboer, 2003). CRH molecules operating through one type of CRH receptor (type 1) stimulate sympathetic, HPA, and behavioral defense reactions. A slower-acting system operating through another related peptide hormone (urocortins) works through another type of CRH receptor (type 2) to promote recovery and adaptation (for review, see de Kloet, 2003). Behaviorally, the effects of CRH via the first type of receptors (type 1) trigger and support stress and anxiety, while those of urocortins operating through the other type of CRH receptor (type 2) trigger and support calming and stress recovery.

CRH is produced not only in the hypothalamus, as described below, but in other brain regions involved in defensive responding. We know that the amygdala is an important region in sensing and organizing responses to threat. For example, when something happens that causes you to freeze, feel your hair stand on end, experience your heart racing, and so on, this is due to activation of the amygdala. Information comes into the amygdala and gets relayed to its center (central nucleus) to trigger these reactions. The central nucleus of the amygdala produces CRH, and it is through production and release of this brain peptide that many of these reactions are organized. The type of CRH receptors (type 1) that organize fear behavior also lie in many of the brain regions that organize anxious/fearful behavior. Furthermore, chronic exposure to glucocorticoids causes the amygdala to produce more CRH and changes the number of type 1 (fear/anxiety) CRH receptors. This is one mechanism through which activity of the HPA stress system can heighten stress reactivity over time. It is notable that early maternal deprivation in animal models increases CRH-1 receptors (fear/anxiety type) and reduces CRH-2 receptors (calming type), tipping the balance to reactivity over regulation of the stress system.

With regards to the HPA system proper, cells that a particular region of the hypothalamus (called the PVN) manufacture and release CRH into a small blood connection that runs between the hypothalamus and the anterior part of the pituitary gland (see Figure 6.1) (Herman & Cullinan, 1997). Once released, CRH stimulates specialized cells in the anterior pituitary to produce adrenocorticotropic hormone (ACTH). ACTH is carried through the bloodstream to the cortex of the adrenal glands, leading to the production of glucocorticoids (cortisol in humans and other primates; corticosterone in rats and mice). Glucocorticoids produce their effects by binding to two types of specialized receptors called MRs and GRs, for reasons that are not relevant here (de Kloet, 2003). Similar to type 1 and 2 CHR receptors, these two types of glucocorticoid receptors do somewhat opposing things. They also have different affinities for glucocorticoids. What this means is that it is easier for glucocorticoids to bind with and thus turn on one of these types of receptors than it is for them to bind with the other. MRs have higher affinity for glucocorticoids than do GRs. Thus, given the same amount of glucocorticoids hormone, MRs will be bound (turned on) more than GRs. What this means is that MRs are bound or turned on when glucocorticoids are in basal or non-stress ranges, while GRs only really get bound (turned on) when glucocorticoids rise into stress ranges.

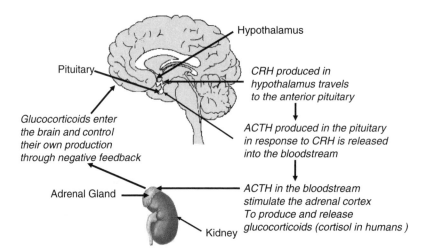

Figure 6.1   Schematic of the hypothalamic-pituitary-adrenocortical (HPA) system. CRH produced by cells in the hypothalamus travels to the anterior pituitary, where (along with other biochemicals not discussed) it stimulates the production and release of adrenocorticotropic hormone (ACTH). ACTH is released into the bloodstream, where it stimulates cells in the cortex of the adrenal gland to produce glucocorticoids (cortisol in humans). Glucocorticoids have widespread effects on tissues throughout the body and brain. Glucocorticoids cross the blood–brain barrier, affecting brain functioning. In addition, glucocorticoids regulate their own production through negative feedback at multiple levels of the brain.

MRs tend to promote the health of neurons, making them more sensitive to their neurotransmitters (including norepinephrine), helping them take in glucose to run the work of the nerve cell, and helping them to recover and get ready to fire again. Because basal levels of glucocorticoids are needed to stimulate MRs, when glucocorticoids are too low and have been that way chronically (as in chronic fatigue syndrome), the brain responds very sluggishly to threat. Chronically high basal levels of glucocorticoids, on the other hand, create a brain poised to respond rapidly and strongly to threat. GRs, the other type of glucocorticoids receptor, tend to do the opposite of MRs. This is why some researchers view rapid increases of glucocorticoids during the "stress" response as actually being important for turning off the brain's (and body's) stress reactions. In addition, the GRs that are turned on when glucocorticoids rise up to stress levels play a role in activating NMDA receptors. These are the receptors that are important for learning and memory. These (NMDA) receptors, however, produce substances that can damage nerve cells if they are maintained at high levels in the nerve cell. Glucose is needed to run the machinery that clears out these toxic substances. MRs, recall, help to get glucose into cells. GRs do the opposite. So, if glucocorticoids are in stress ranges for long periods of time, cells become very vulnerable to damage. Clearly, the biology of stress is complex and it is way too simple-minded to measure changes in glucocorticoids and label big responses bad and small responses good. It is also way too simplistic to measure glucocorticoid levels and label low levels as good and high levels as bad. The system operates within parameters such that moderate basal levels are probably important for supporting health, strong brief elevations are important for regulating stress reactions, and chronic and/or very frequent large elevations may put the organism at risk. While this picture certainly holds for adult individuals, special adjustments in these views may be necessary for understanding how glucocorticoids affect developing organisms whose brains may be shaped by both the typical levels of the hormone present and the frequency and duration of stress elevations in the hormone.

Since basal levels of the hormone seem to be significant in promoting healthy brain development, it is important to understand something about the daily rhythm in this hormone system. Glucocorticoids are high when we wake up and very low when we go to sleep at night (or in the morning, for nocturnal animals). Light is one of the most important "time givers" driving the day–night rhythm in the HPA system and in other systems that follow a circadian or day–night rhythm. However, social stimuli related to feeding and social patterns (i.e., when the family sleeps, wakes, etc.) also play important roles (van Esseveldt, Lehman, & Boer, 2000). In young children, the day–night HPA rhythm can be detected as early as the 6th postnatal week, but is not fully mature until children give up their daytime naps around 4 or 5 years of age (see review, Gunnar & Donzella, 2002). Adequately measuring the basal and stress response of the HPA system means knowing where the child is in his or her day–night HPA rhythm.

The antagonistic relation between MR- and GR-mediated effects functions to first promote and then reverse the physiological and behavioral processes set into motion as part of the acute, fight/flight response. Consistent with their effects of turning off brain stress reactions, GRs also terminate the HPA stress response. So, as glucocorticoids rise into stress ranges, one effect is for them to bind to GR and send signals to the hypothalamus to stop producing CRH (and thus ACTH and from there glucocorticoids). This is called *negative feedback* (de Kloet, 2003). Interestingly, the brain location responsible for turning off the HPA response depends, in part, on the kind of stress being experienced. If the kind is systemic (i.e., blood volume loss, fever), then the site that turns off the response is very deep in the brain, typically at the levels of the hypothalamus. However, if the type of stress requires thinking about it (i.e., anticipation of threat or loss), then the site that is important shifts to higher brain regions, including areas in the frontal cortex that are also involved in emotion regulation (Diorio, Viau, & Meaney, 1993). What this means is that if we want to know about how the brain regulates stress in studies of emotion regulation, for example, we probably shouldn't study glucocorticoid responses to a physical stressor.

The relation between MR- and GR-mediated effects helps explain an inverted U-shaped function that is frequently noted between glucocorticoids and adaptive outcomes. When glucocorticoids are too low to provide adequate MR activation, the reactivity-promoting effects of glucocorticoids are not actualized; as glucocorticoids rise, this tends to support behavioral and physiological organization and adaptation; while when glucocorticoids are very high for prolonged periods, this begins to impair organism functioning (e.g. Sapolsky, Romero, & Munck, 2000). Disturbing the balance of MRs to GRs can produce stress vulnerability (de Kloet, 2003). Notably, maternal deprivation in rodent studies has been found to decrease GRs but not MRs, resulting in a system poised for acute stress responses, but impaired in the ability to terminate and reverse these reactions (Heim, Owen, Plotsky, & Nemeroff, 1997).

Frontal Regulation of Stress

Regulation of stress by frontal regions of the brain that are also important for emotion regulation is a newer frontier in stress research. It has long been recognized that particular regions in the front of the brain play critical roles in regulating autonomic and emotional behavior; however, we are increasingly recognizing the importance of these frontal brain regions in regulating neuroendocrine facets of stress responding (Sullivan & Gratton, 2002). The orbital frontal cortex (OFC) has numerous reciprocal connections to other limbic regions, allowing the organization of behavior in relation to reward and the social context (Happaney, Zelazo, & Stuss, 2004). The OFC is believed to mediate the attachment relationship's function in regulating autonomic, behavioral, and neuroendocrine responses to stressful stimulation (Schore, 1996); however, the anterior cingulate cortex and other as yet less studied frontal nuclei (e.g., Mayberg et al., 1999) are also likely to be important in contextualizing and regulating stress and emotional functioning. Indeed, the anterior cingulate cortex appears to have a cognitive (dorsal) and affective (rostral, ventral) division which may reciprocally inhibit one another such that under conditions of threat, cognition becomes more automatic, rapid, and emotionally toned (Bush, Luu, & Posner, 2000).

Finally, based on a wide range of methods, the left and right prefrontal cortices appear to play different roles in emotion and stress regulation, with the right being more involved in withdrawal-oriented and the left with approach-oriented emotions (Davidson & Irwin, 1999). Concern over right frontal asymmetry (i.e., greater right relative to left prefrontal cortical activity) is consistent with evidence that there is a right bias in the reactive components of the stress system. Thus, in rats it is the right more than the left frontal cortex (medial region) that regulates neuroendocrine and autonomic responsivity to stressors (Sullivan & Gratton, 2002). Similarly, both the SNS (Kagan, Arcus, Snidman, Peterson, Steinberg, & Rimm-Kaufman, 1995) and PNS show a right cortical bias (Porges, 1995b). Hyperactivity in right frontal regions thus may reflect a bias not only to negative emotions, but also to hyperactivation of the stress system. As with research on autonomic activity in children, most emotion-related research on the prefrontal cortex has focused on temperamental differences (e.g., Fox, 1994). Less attention has been paid to early social experience effects on the development of the frontal systems involved in stress reactivity and regulation (however, see Dawson & Ashman, 2000). Given the protracted development of the prefrontal cortex in humans, it is highly likely that much of the human early experience stress story will involve development of this brain region and its connections to other areas of the brain involved in stress and emotion.

Animal Models of the Social Regulation of Stress

In the mid-1950s, Levine (see review, 2003), using a procedure termed *handling*, demonstrated that removing rat pups from their mothers over the first weeks of life for only a minute or so daily permanently altered the pups' stress reactivity and regulation. The half-century since this early work was published has seen remarkable advances in animal research on stress and early experience. During the first two postnatal weeks in the rat, the HPA system is relatively hypo-responsive to stress. That is, it is hard to produce elevations in glucocorticoids to stressors that will readily produce stress levels of the hormone in older animals. Although glucocorticoids are low during this time, marked stressor responses can be observed in the hypothalamus and higher brain regions. Thus, although it is often called the "stress hypo-responsive period," this is a misnomer, as the hypo-responsiveness is more focused on low levels of activity of the HPA system at the pituitary and adrenal level. Maternal stimulation is essential to maintaining the stress hypo-responsive period. Specifically, maternal licking and the provision of milk maintain the HPA system in this relatively quiescent state (Rosenfeld, Suchecki, & Levine, 1992). During these same postnatal weeks, because proteins that bind (and thus inactivate) glucocorticoids are low, most of the hormone in circulation is biologically active (Henning, 1978). The low levels of glucocorticoids maintained by maternal licking and nursing, therefore, are more than sufficient to serve needed adaptive functions. Elevations of glucocorticoids during this period can have dramatic effects on brain development, affecting maturations of neurons in the cerebral cortex, limbic system, and spinal cord and globally inhibiting neurogenesis, gliogenesis, cell division, and myelination (see Couperus & Nelson, this volume) while increasing apoptosis or programmed cell death (McEwen, 2000).

Early *handling* enhances maternal licking and appropriate nursing of her pups and results in offspring that are less fearful and exhibit more efficient stress responding. The opposite effects are observed when perturbations to the nest impair maternal licking and nursing stimulation in paradigms termed *maternal separation* or *maternal deprivation* (see review by Sanchez, Ladd, & Plotsky, 2001). The terminology in this field is a bit confusing as all of the manipulations involve separation and handling of the pups. The reasons are historical, but they beg the question of why some handling and separation promote more vigorous and organized maternal behavior and others disturb and disrupt maternal behavior. Some have suggested that the answer lies in what is typical for the species. Mother rats do leave their nests to go to find food. These bouts of separation are normal and typically quite brief. When mother returns she reorganizes her nest and feeds her young. Brief separation (called handling) mimics this species-typical experience. Long periods of forced separation, though, are not typical, and if such occur, they would probably signal to the mother that she needs to move her nest. Her inability to do so in the confines of a laboratory may be what disturbs and disrupts her maternal programming. This *story* is just that, a story that reasonably accounts for the different effects of different manipulations. What is more critical is evidence that, whatever is done, most of the effect seems to flow through how it affects mother–pup interactions when the mother is with her pups. Some of the effects of these early manipulations are permanent, involving permanent silencing of genes regulating the production of the GR (Weaver et al., 2004), while others can be modified by enriching the animal's experiences later in life (Bredy, Humpartzoomian, Cain, & Meaney, 2003).

Monkeys have also been used to study the effects of early social experiences on stress reactivity and regulation (Coplan et al., 1996). As in the rat, manipulations that disrupt maternal care and/or deprive infant monkeys of maternal stimulation are associated with the development of anxiety, fearfulness, and hyper-reactive stress responding (Suomi, 1995). Unlike rats, but similar to humans, infant monkeys form specific attachments. The opportunity to achieve maternal contact, even sometimes only distal contact, serves as a powerful buffer of stress responses in monkeys (Bayart, Hayashi, Faull, Barchas, & Levine, 1990). Many of the paradigms used to disturb mother–infant interaction in monkeys are imposed at a point when the infant is eating on its own and often spends much of its day playing at a distance from the mother. Disturbances in maternal behavior, therefore, are not likely to have their primary impact via reductions in tactile stimulation (reminiscent of rodent licking) or feeding. Instead, they may have their effects, at least in part, through disturbing response-contingent maternal care (i.e., maternal sensitivity and responsivity). Indeed, in a paradigm in which infants were reared with other infants (*peer-only* rearing), providing response-contingent pleasant (treats, toys) stimulation helped to ameliorate the fearfulness typically produced by peer-only rearing (Mineka, Gunnar, & Champoux, 1986). Thus, in non-human primates, the opportunity to contact the mother and the experience of response-contingent care serve as powerful regulators of stress responding during early development and affect the development of the stress–emotion system.

Psychobiological Studies of Stress and Emotion in Children

Human developmental studies of stress biology are relatively new. Until the early 1980s, developmental researchers were largely limited to examining heart rate–behavior associations (see, for review, Gunnar, 1986). After 1980, psychobiological studies in children burgeoned, a phenomenon readily traced to the availability of salivary assays for cortisol and theoretical and technical advances in psychophysiology. Here we will first trace key early periods of stress system development, and then discuss research on social regulation of stress in the first few years of life. Because the predominant glucocorticoid in humans is cortisol, from here on cortisol, rather than glucocorticoids, will be used in the text whenever the data refer to humans.

Early development of the stress system

Pre- and perinatal period. The ontogeny of the human stress system begins well before birth (Giannakoulpoulous, Sepulveda, Kourtis, Glover, & Fisk, 1994). With increased gestational age, fetal basal HPA activity increases and heart rate decreases, becomes more variable and more coupled with fetal movement (DiPietro, Hodgson, Costigan, Hilton, & Johnson, 1996). Experience begins to shape the infant's stress system before birth. In animal models, a wide range of environmental (e.g., loud noises) or psychosocial (e.g., entry into new social groups) stressors during pregnancy result in offspring who are more behaviorally and physiologically stress reactive (Weinstock, 2001). Activity of the maternal HPA axis appears to be the mediating factor, as inhibiting maternal glucocorticoid elevations prevents these effects (Barbazanges, Piazza, Moal, & Maccari, 1996).

The maternal glucocorticoid effects may be partly mediated by increases in placental corticotropin-releasing hormone induced by elevated maternal glucocorticoids (Schulkin, 1999).

Proving that maternal stress influences fetal development in humans is hampered by our inability to perform experiments. Nonetheless, there is now evidence that, controlling statistically for numerous obstetric risk factors, perceptions of high stress and low social support during pregnancy predict higher maternal HPA activity, higher maternal plasma levels of corticotropin-releasing hormone (which are of placental origin), fetuses with higher heart rates and less heart rate variability, newborns delivered earlier with lower birth weights, and higher scores on measures of infant fearfulness or behavioral inhibition (Wadhwa, Sandman, & Garite, 2001).

Although still preliminary, these studies suggest a transactional view of the fetal origins of infant stress reactivity and regulation. The placenta, which is of fetal origin, expresses genes that both influence and are influenced by maternal cortisol levels. Maternal cortisol levels, in turn, are influenced by obstetric factors and by the mother's reactions to the challenges of her daily existence. These influences, impinging on the developing fetus, affect activity of its developing stress system in ways that appear to contribute to the organization of postnatal temperament. Undoubtedly this is a vast oversimplification of highly complex processes; furthermore, it is likely that the stress–behavior system remains highly plastic after birth.

Healthy, full-term newborns mount behavioral, endocrine, and autonomic responses to aversive medical procedures that are not "all or none" but increase with the severity of the stressor (see review by Gunnar, 1992). Furthermore, they are remarkably capable of regulating stress. Stressors such as heel-stick blood draws, circumcision, and physical exams produce increases in heart rate, decreases in vagal tone, and elevate cortisol several fold; however, following such stressors, the parameters of these systems rapidly return to baseline. As a reflection of stress activation followed by rest and restoration, the healthy newborn tends to withdraw into the most restorative type of sleep following activation of the stress system. In addition to sleep, feeding and tactile stimulation appear to serve stress-regulatory functions for the newborn (Blass & Watt, 1999). Sucking and swallowing are complex motor acts that engage and are regulated by the vagal system (DiPietro & Porges, 1991). Thus vagal regulation may be partially responsible for the behavioral calming produced by non-nutritive sucking. In contrast, the calming and analgesic effects of pleasant tastes appear to be mediated by the natural opiates (e.g., endorphins) produced by the body that stimulate opiate receptors in the brain (Blass & Watt, 1999). In addition to activating opioid-mediated analgesic pathways, pleasant tastes also produce facial expressions of positive affect and increased left-sided frontal brain activity (Davidson & Fox, 1982). The regulatory roles for feeding and non-nutritive sucking have led Blass (Blass & Watt, 1999) to argue that during the early postnatal period the mother serves as a shield to buffer the infant from pain and facilitate the restoration of normal growth processes following periods of stress.

Infancy. It has been suggested that there are two periods of biobehavioral reorganization in the first postnatal year (Emde, Gaensbauer, & Harmon, 1976). The first, between 2 and 4 months, has been described as the 3-month revolution, when almost every facet of infant functioning exhibits reorganization. The second is during the latter half of the first year, when the emergence of independent locomotion appears to produce dramatic neurobehavioral changes. This latter is also the period associated with the emergence and organization of secure base behavior and inhibition of approach to novel or strange events and people (Bowlby, 1969). Both of these periods are associated with marked changes in stress reactivity and regulation.

Several research groups have used well-baby examinations and childhood inoculations in developmental studies of stress in infancy (Gunnar, Brodersen, Krueger, & Rigatuso, 1996; Lewis & Ramsay, 1995). As in the newborn period, during the first two postnatal months, cortisol increases, vagal tone decreases, and fussing/crying increases markedly during physical exams and inoculations (White, Gunnar, Larson, Donzella, & Barr, 2000). Around 3 months of age, however, cortisol responses begin to dissociate from cardiac and behavioral reactions under such mild stress conditions (Larson, White, Cochran, Donzella, & Gunnar, 1998). Specifically, while vagal tone decreases and behavioral distress increase, cortisol no longer elevates. It is not clear whether responsive caregiving has already begun to dampen HPA stress responsivity, or whether this decrease in HPA activity reflects maturation of negative feedback mechanisms.

The PNS also undergoes changes over these early months. Basal vagal tone is relatively low in the newborn period and increases across early childhood. Recently, research on vagal tone has shifted from an exclusive focus on baseline tone to interest in the dynamics of vagal regulation. According to Porges's (1995a) polyvagal theory, suppression of vagal tone allows increases in sympathetic activity, whereas increases allow the infant to engage in social approach while remaining calm. Modulating vagal tone, therefore, is viewed as a necessary support for social and attentional regulatory strategies. However, there is evidence that it is not until around 3 months of age that infants are able to regulate the vagal to support social interaction and soothing (Huffman et al., 1998).

In sum, the systems that influence stress reactivity and regulation undergo rapid maturation during the early months of life. By 3 months, mild stressors no longer produce elevations in cortisol. Baseline vagal tone increases and infants show increased competence in using vagal regulation to engage the social environment and to use social stimulation to sooth behavioral distress.

Between 4 months and 1 year, developmental changes in stress reactivity and regulation continue to be observed (for review see Gunnar, 2000). For example, elevations in cortisol to inoculation procedures are roughly comparable at 4 and 6 months of age; however, by the second year (i.e., 12, 15, or 18 months), most infants do not exhibit elevations in cortisol during these procedures. Similarly, psychosocial stressors such as a few minutes of maternal separation provoke elevations in cortisol, on average, prior to but not after 12 months for most infants. By the end of the first year, the human infant appears to have entered the functional equivalent of the rodent stress hypo-responsive period. As we will see, as in other primates, this "hypo-responsivity" actually reflects a buffering of the HPA system mediated by responsive relationships with caregivers.

Toddler and preschool periods. The diurnal rhythm of the HPA axis continues to develop during the toddler and preschool periods. Although an early morning peak and evening nadir in cortisol production is detected early in infancy, over the rest of the first year and up until the preschool period, cortisol levels do not gradually decline over the mid-portion of the day. Instead, we begin to see this more adult-type diurnal pattern as children give up their afternoon naps sometime during the preschool period (Watamura, Donzella, Kertes, & Gunnar, 2004). The emergence of a more adult-like diurnal rhythm over the daytime hours also seems to correspond to a decrease in the sensitivity of the HPA axis daytime rhythm to variations in caregiving contexts. Beginning at least as early as the toddler period, we have observed that young children who spend the day in out-of-home child care settings are very likely to exhibit rising patterns of hormone production over the day (Dettling, Gunnar, & Donzella, 1999; Dettling, Parker, Lane, Sebanc, & Gunnar, 2000; Watamura, Donzella, Alwin, & Gunnar, 2003; Watamura, Sebanc, Donzella, & Gunnar, 2002). This is not the pattern observed at home, and, indeed, increases in cortisol over the child care day have been judged against children's own cortisol production pattern at home on days when they do not go to child care. These increases in cortisol appear partly to reflect the quality of the child care, with larger increases observed in poorer-quality care settings (Dettling et al., 2000). Age, however, is also a significant predictor, with toddlers producing larger increases over the child care day than preschoolers (Watamura et al., 2003; Dettling et al., 1999).

A number of factors might account for these age changes in the capacity of a full day in group care settings to produce elevations in children's cortisol levels. Chief among these factors may be the development of anterior cortical regions that both support the development of social competence and allow better regulation of autonomic and neuroendocrine activity (Sullivan & Gratton, 2002). Thus, we have found that, even controlling for age, children who score higher on effortful control, a competency that may involve the development of the anterior cingulate cortex and dorsal lateral prefrontal cortex, have lower levels of cortisol over the day (Watamura et al., 2004). We have also noted that children who score lower on effortful control and who are more negative in emotionality exhibit larger increases in cortisol over the child care day (Dettling et al., 1999). Such children also have problems in peer relations (Eisenberg, Fabes, Guthrie, & Reiser, 2000), and we have found that peer rejection is associated with elevated cortisol levels in group care settings among preschoolers (Gunnar, Sebanc, Tout, Donzella, & van Dulmen, 2003).

In summary, although, as will be discussed in the next section, by the end of the first year of life children appear to have entered a period when it is difficult to elevate cortisol to many potentially threatening stimuli, when children are in group care settings we tend to observe an HPA axis whose activity appears highly reactive. Elevations in cortisol over the child care day are observed, except in very high-quality settings, and these elevations are larger among toddlers than older children. With development over the preschool years, the child's diurnal rhythm becomes more adult-like as sleep–wake behavior begins to approximate adult patterns, and the child seems better capable of maintaining basal cortisol activity (i.e., smaller rises in cortisol over the child care day). Increases in social competence that may make it easier for children to negotiate the complex peer landscape and maturation of anterior cortical systems that likely support social competence and physiologic regulation seem likely candidates for mediators of better HPA axis regulation when children are in group care settings. Why group care settings may be particularly challenging for HPA axis regulation in young children, however, reflects what we now know about the importance of social buffering or social regulation of this stress system as it emerges over the infancy period.

Social regulation of stress in infant and young child

In young children, studies of attachment have yielded strong evidence for social regulation of the stress system. Secure attachment relationships buffer or prevent stress responses under many conditions (see review, Gunnar, 2000). Some of the work supporting this argument has used the Strange Situation both to assess attachment security and to activate SNS/PNS and HPA stress responses. Generally speaking, in secure attachment relationships infants do not show elevations in cortisol during the Strange Situation, even when they exhibit increases in heart rate and behavioral distress. In contrast, infants in insecure attachment relationships exhibit elevations in cortisol that correlate with increases in heart rate and crying.

When attachment security is used to predict cortisol responses to situations other than the Strange Situation, similar results have been obtained. For example, Ahnert and colleagues (Ahnert, Gunnar, Lamb, & Barthel, 2004) recently noted that when mothers were required to help their toddlers adapt to their first child care by accompanying them for the first few days, toddlers in insecure relationships exhibited elevations in cortisol that were as large as when they were first at child care without the mother present. In contrast, toddlers in secure relationships did not show marked cortisol responses as long as the mother was with them. Similarly, in another study (Gunnar, Brodersen, Nachmias, Buss, & Rigatuso, 1996), toddlers who continued to produce elevations in cortisol during exam inoculations at 15 months tended to be insecurely attached to the parent who was with them. Likewise, toddlers who were wary and fearful of strange, arousing stimuli exhibited elevations in cortisol if they were insecurely, but not if they were securely, attached to the parent who was present (Nachmias, Gunnar, Mangelsdorf, Parritz, & Buss, 1996).

Attachment security is a relationship variable that reflects both child and parent contributions. Thus, the results reported above may merely mean that securely attached toddlers are simply less stress-reactive, perhaps temperamentally. However, several analyses of parental behavior suggest that it is the parent's sensitivity and responsiveness that influences both the security of the relationship and the child's cortisol responses to potential threat in the parent's presence. Thus, in the exam inoculation study, parents who were low in sensitivity and responsivity during doctor visits at 2, 4, and 6 months had infants who as toddlers tended to be insecurely attached and who continued to produce elevations in cortisol during the exam inoculation experience (Gunnar et al., 1996). Likewise, parents who were intrusive, controlling, and overprotective when their toddlers were exposed to arousing, potentially threatening events had toddlers who were likely to be insecurely attached and to exhibit larger increases in cortisol even after controlling for their behavioral reactions to the strange, arousing events (Nachmias et al., 1996). Caregiver sensitivity and responsivity, therefore, appears to be an important determinant of whether the caregiver's presence and availability serve to buffer activity of the HPA axis during the second year of life. It is noteworthy that this has also been documented for substitute caregivers such as babysitters and child care providers (see, for review, Gunnar & Donzella, 2002).

During the first year, there is also evidence that caregiver sensitivity and responsiveness influence whether infants show increases in cortisol and heart rate during parent–infant interactions (Haley & Stansbury, 2003; Spangler & Schieche, 1994). Furthermore, by the second year of life, toddlers who interact with parents who are more unresponsive and intrusive (i.e., clinically depressed mothers) tend to exhibit greater right frontal asymmetry (Dawson & Ashman, 2000). Thus over the first two years of life, it appears that insensitive, intrusive care increases the likelihood that the child will frequently experience statistically significant activations of stress biology. We do not yet know whether the statistically significant, yet relatively small, increases that have been observed have the capacity to program the child's stress system. Questions about the impact of early experiences on later stress reactivity and regulation have, so far, been addressed solely for children who have experienced more markedly impaired early caregiving.

Early experiences and later stress reactivity

We are only beginning to explore whether adverse caregiving early in life has organizing effects on the stress system that persist later in development. Research has been conducted on the children of depressed mothers whose mental illness often interferes with the provision of sensitive and responsive care, physically and sexually maltreated children, and children reared in institutional settings. Mothers who are depressed during their children's first years have children who as preschoolers and at school age exhibit higher cortisol levels (Ashman, Dawson, Panagiotides, Yamada, & Wilkinson, 2002; Dawson & Ashman, 2000; Essex, Klein, Cho, & Kalin, 2002) and a greater right-sided bias in frontal EEG (Dawson & Ashman, 2000). However, these studies also suggest that in order for these effects to be observed, the mother may need to be depressed both early in the child's life and around the time when the physiological measures are obtained. Unfortunately, this makes it difficult to determine whether impairments in early caregiving heighten reactivity to later adversity or whether it is the chronicity of adverse caregiving that is the critical factor.

Studies of more severe failures of the caregiving system, nonetheless, tend to support the potential for early experiences to program the development of the stress system. For example, several researchers have now shown that severe maltreatment during the first years of life is associated with elevated catecholamine (E and NE) and cortisol production over the day in children several years after rescue (Carrion, Weems, Ray, Glaser, Hessl, & Reiss, 2002; de Bellis et al., 1999). Nonetheless, interpretation of these studies is complicated by the fact that only children with chronic post-traumatic stress disorder (PTSD) were studied. We do not know whether stress system disturbances would also be seen in maltreated children who do not develop PTSD or other behavior disorders, although work by Cicchetti and Rogosch (2001) suggests that HPA activity is disordered primarily for children with significant behavior problems (see also Heim, Newport, Bonsall, Miller, & Nemeroff, 2001). Of course, this may reflect more severe maltreatment or a family system that continues to be highly chaotic or dysfunctional.

Early institutional or orphanage rearing is a final type of early adverse caregiving that has been studied. Many previously institutionalized children are now entering families in the US or other countries through international adoption. Behavioral studies of post-institutionalized children reveal that years after adoption into caring families significant numbers exhibit problems in cognitive functioning, social relatedness, and attention/behavior regulation (Rutter, Kreppner, O'Connor, & the English and Romanian Adoptees Study Team, 2001). Toddlers still living in institutional care exhibit marked disturbances in diurnal HPA activity (Carlson & Earls, 1997). Many years after adoption, 7–11-year-old children adopted from the most severely depriving institutional settings exhibit significantly elevated basal cortisol levels (Gunnar, Morison, Chisholm, & Schuder, 2001; Kertes, Madsen, Bales, & Gunnar, 2005).

Thus there is evidence that when early caregiving is severely compromised, children are more likely to develop atypical patterns of stress system activity. Unfortunately, to date, nearly all of the work has focused on basal activity. We have very few studies in which stressors have been imposed and the reactivity and subsequent regulation of autonomic and neuroendocrine responses have been examined. Furthermore, because of the complexity of the environments of early adversity, we cannot be certain that lack of *sensitive and responsive* care is the factor mediating the impact of early adversity on the developing stress system.

Summary and Future Directions

Poor regulation of stress biology is associated with physical and emotional disorders. Decades of research using animal models have revealed that early experiences program the brain circuitry involved in activation, termination, and restoration in response to stressful events. Some of these effects appear to be permanent, involving the permanent silencing of genes in key stress-regulatory pathways, while others appear to be modifiable by later experiences. Notably, the animal studies indicate that social stimuli are critically involved in the postnatal programming of stress. Research on early human development now clearly indicates that there is a human chapter to this mammalian early experience and stress story. Sensitive and responsive caregiving buffers the developing child from activation of stress biology, particularly activity of the HPA system. Although there are currently relatively few studies of early severe disturbances in the caregiving system that have examined later stress system activity, what work there is suggests increased risk for altered and/or disordered stress system responding when these children are followed later in childhood.

While we are making headway in understanding the development of stress reactivity and regulation, there are significant gaps in our knowledge. Some children are undoubtedly more constitutionally vulnerable to disorganizing effects of poor early care. Identifying genes and epigenetic processes that increase vulnerability to inadequate care early in life is one major frontier in this research area that requires integration of research across different levels of analysis, molecular to social interaction, and integration of animal and human developmental research. Research is needed that helps unpack the layers of socio-psychological stimulation that contribute to stress activation, termination, and restoration as these processes develop and influence one another over the first years of life. This work is essential to predict when and in which ways such different experiences as rearing by a depressed caregiver, physical and sexual maltreatment, and institutional care will have similar and dissimilar impacts on stress biology. With human children, intervention studies are needed to help isolate cause and effect relations between qualities of early care and the programming of the stress system and to determine the degree of plasticity in stress biology at different points in development. Finally, because we can anticipate that frontal cortical regions play significant roles in stress regulation, we need more research in both animals and humans to help explicate the role of the PFC and infra-limbic cortex in stress reactivity and regulation and to trace the development of frontal regulation of stress. Given the protracted development of the prefrontal cortex in humans, this work will be particularly important in understanding how to intervene at later points in development to help stress-vulnerable children to achieve healthy outcomes.

Note

Preparation of this manuscript was supported by a National Institute of Mental Health Research Scientist Award (MH00946).

References

Ahnert, L., Gunnar, M. R., Lamb, M., & Barthel, M. (2004). Transition to child care: Associations with infant–mother attachment, infant negative emotion and cortisol elevations. *Child Development, 75*, 639–650.

Ashman, S. B., Dawson, G., Panagiotides, H., Yamada, E., & Wilkinson, C. W. (2002). Stress hormone levels of children of depressed mothers. *Development & Psychopathology, 14*, 333–349.

Barbazanges, A., Piazza, P. V., Moal, M. L., & Maccari, S. (1996). Maternal glucocorticoid secretion mediates long-term effects of prenatal stress. *Journal of Neuroscience, 16*, 3943–3949.

Bayart, F., Hayashi, K. T., Faull, K. F., Barchas, J. D., & Levine, S. (1990). Influence of maternal proximity on behavioral and physiological responses to separation in infant rhesus monkeys (*Macaca mulatta*). *Behavioral Neuroscience, 104*, 98–107.

Blass, E. M., & Watt, L. B. (1999). Suckling- and sucrose-induced analgesia in human newborns. *Pain, 83*, 611–612.

Bowlby, J. (1969). *Attachment and loss: Attachment* (Vol. 1). New York: Basic Books.

Bredy, T. W., Humpartzoomian, R. A., Cain, D. P., & Meaney, M. J. P. (2003). Partial reversal of the effect of maternal care on cognitive function through environmental enrichment. *Neuroscience, 118*(2), 571–576.

Bush, G., Luu, P., & Posner, M. I. (2000). Cognitive and emotional influences in anterior cingulate cortex. *Trends in Cognitive Sciences, 4*(6), 215–222.

Buss, K. A., Davidson, R. J., Kalin, N., & Goldsmith, H. H. (2004). Context-specific freezing and associated physiological reactivity as a dysregulated fear response. *Developmental Psychology, 40*, 583–594.

Cacioppo, J. T., Uchino, B. N., & Berntson, G. G. (1994). Individual differences in the autonomic origins of heart rate reactivity: The psychometrics of respiratory sinus arrythmia and pre-ejection period. *Psychophysiology, 31*, 412–419.

Calkins, S. D., & Fox, N. A. (2002). Self-regulatory processes in early personality development: A multilevel approach to the study of childhood social withdrawal and aggression. *Development and Psychopathology, 14*, 477–498.

Carlson, M., & Earls, F. (1997). Psychological and neuroendocrinological sequelae of early social deprivation in institutionalized children in Romania. *Annals of the New York Academy of Sciences, 807*, 419–428.

Carrion, V. G., Weems, C. F., Ray, R. D., Glaser, B., Hessl, D., & Reiss, A. L. (2002). Diurnal salivary cortisol in pediatric posttraumatic stress disorder. *Biological Psychiatry, 51*, 575–582.

Cicchetti, D., & Rogosch, F. A. (2001). Diverse patterns of neuroendocrine activity in maltreated children. *Development & Psychopathology, 13*, 677–720.

Coplan, J. D., Andrews, M. W., Rosenblum, L. A., Owens, M. J., Friedman, S., Gorman, J. M., & Nemeroff, C. (1996). Persistent elevations of cerebrospinal fluid concentrations of cortico-tropin-releasing factor in adult nonhuman primates exposed to early-life stressors: Implications for the pathophysiology of mood and anxiety disorders. *Proceedings of the National Academy of Sciences of the United States of America, 93*, 1619–1623.

Davidson, R. J., & Fox, N. A. (1982). Asymmetrical brain activity discriminates between positive and negative affective stimuli in human infants. *Science, 218*, 1235–1237.

Davidson, R. J., & Irwin, W. (1999). The functional neuroanatomy of emotion and affective style. *Trends in Neuroscience, 3*, 11–21.

Dawson, G., & Ashman, S. (2000). On the origins of a vulnerability to depression: The influence of early social environment on the development of psychobiological systems related to risk for affective disorder. In C. A. Nelson (Ed.), *The Minnesota Symposia on Child Psychology: Vol. 31. The effects of adversity on neurobehavioral development* (pp. 245–278). New York: Lawrence Erlbaum Associates.

de Bellis, M. D., Baum, A. S., Birmaher, B., Keshavan, M. S., Eccard, C. H., Boring, A. M., Jenkins, F. J., & Ryan, N. D. (1999). Developmental traumatology, Part 1: Biological stress systems. *Biological Psychiatry, 9*, 1259–1270.

de Kloet, E. R. (2003). Hormones, brain and stress. *Endocrine Regulations, 37*, 51–68.

Dettling, A. C., Gunnar, M. R., & Donzella, B. (1999). Cortisol levels of young children in full-day childcare centers: Relations with age and temperament. *Psychoneuroendocrinology, 24*(5), 519–536.

Dettling, A. C., Parker, S. W., Lane, S. K., Sebanc, A. M., & Gunnar, M. R. (2000). Quality of care and temperament determine changes in cortisol concentrations over the day for young children in childcare. *Psychoneuroendocrinology, 25*, 819–836.

Diorio, D., Viau, V., & Meaney, M. J. (1993). The role of the medial prefrontal cortex (cingulate gyrus) in the regulation of hypothalamic-pituitary-adrenal responses to stress. *Journal of Neuroscience, 13*, 3839–3847.

DiPietro, J. A., Hodgson, D., Costigan, K. A., Hilton, S. C., & Johnson, T. R. B. (1996). Fetal neurobehavioral development. *Child Development, 67*, 2553–2567.

DiPietro, J. A., & Porges, S. W. (1991). Vagal responsiveness to gavage feeding as an index of preterm status. *Pediatric Research, 29*(3), 231–236.

Eisenberg, N., Fabes, R. A., Guthrie, I. K., & Reiser, M. (2000). Dispositional emotionality and regulation: Their role in predicting quality of social functioning. *Journal of Personality & Social Psychology, 78*, 136–157.

Emde, R. M., Gaensbauer, T. J., & Harmon, R. J. (1976). *Emotional expressions in infancy: A biobehavioral study.* New York: International University Press.

Essex, M. J., Klein, M., Cho, E., & Kalin, N. H. (2002). Maternal stress beginning in infancy may sensitize children to later stress exposure: Effects on cortisol and behavior. *Biological Psychiatry, 52,* 776–784.

Fox, N. A. (1994). Dynamic cerebral processes underlying emotion regulation. In N. A. Fox (Ed.), *The development of emotion regulation: Behavioral and biological considerations. Monographs of the Society for Research in Child Development, 59*(2–3, Serial No. 240), 152–166.

Giannakoulpoulous, X., Sepulveda, W., Kourtis, P., Glover, V., & Fisk, N. M. (1994). Fetal plasma and beta-endorphin response to intrauterine needling. *Lancet, 344,* 77–81.

Gunnar, M. R. (1986). Human developmental psychoendocrinology: A review of research on neuroendocrine responses to challenge and threat in infancy and childhood. In M. Lamb, A. Brown, & B. Rogoff (Eds.), *Advances in developmental psychology* (Vol. 4, pp. 51–103). Hillsdale, NJ: Lawrence Erlbaum Associates.

Gunnar, M. R. (1992). Reactivity of the hypothalamic-pituitary-adrenocortical system to stressors in normal infants and children. *Pediatrics, 90*(3), 491–497.

Gunnar, M. R. (2000). Early adversity and the development of stress reactivity and regulation. In C. A. Nelson (Ed.), *The Minnesota Symposia on Child Psychology: Vol. 31. The effects of adversity on neurobehavioral development* (pp. 163–200). Mahwah, NJ: Lawrence Erlbaum Associates.

Gunnar, M., Brodersen, L., Krueger, K., & Rigatuso, J. (1996). Dampening of behavioral and adrenocortical reactivity during early infancy: Normative changes and individual differences. *Child Development, 67,* 877–889.

Gunnar, M. R., Brodersen, L., Nachmias, M., Buss, K., & Rigatuso, R. (1996). Stress reactivity and attachment security. *Developmental Psychobiology, 29,* 10–36.

Gunnar, M. R., & Donzella, B. (2002). Social regulation of the cortisol levels in early human development. *Psychoneuroendocrinology, 27,* 199–220.

Gunnar, M. R., Morison, S. J., Chisholm, K., & Schuder, M. (2001). Long-term effects of institutional rearing on cortisol levels in adopted Romanian children. *Development and Psychopathology, 13*(3), 611–628.

Gunnar, M. R., Sebanc, A. M., Tout, K., Donzella, B., & van Dulmen, M. M. H. (2003). Peer rejection, temperament, and cortisol activity in preschoolers. *Developmental Psychobiology, 43,* 346–358.

Haley, D., & Stansbury, K. (2003). Infant stress and parent responsiveness: Regulation of physiology and behavior during still-face and reunion. *Child Development, 74,* 1534–1546.

Happaney, K., Zelazo, P. D., & Stuss, D. T. (2004). Development of orbital frontal functions: Current themes and future directions. *Brain and Cognition, 55*(1), 1–10.

Heim, C., Newport, J. D., Bonsall, R., Miller, A. H., & Nemeroff, C. B. (2001). Altered pituitary-adrenal axis responses to provocative challenge tests in adult survivors of childhood abuse. *American Journal of Psychiatry, 158*(4), 575–581.

Heim, C., Owen, M. J., Plotsky, P. M., & Nemeroff, C. B. (1997). The role of early adverse life events in the etiology of depression and posttraumatic stress disorder: Focus on corticotropin-releasing factor. *Annals of the New York Academy of Sciences, 821,* 194–207.

Henning, S. (1978). Plasma concentrations of total and free corticosterone during development in the rat. *American Journal of Physiology, 23*(5), E451–E456.

Herman, J. P., & Cullinan, W. E. (1997). Neurocircuitry of stress: Central control of the hypothalamo-pituitary-adrenocortical axis. *Trends in Neurosciences, 20,* 78–84.

Holsboer, F. (2003). Corticotropin-releasing hormone modulators and depression. *Current Opinion in Investigational Drugs, 4,* 46–50.

Huffman, L. C., Brayn, Y. E., del Carmen, R., Pederson, F. A., Doussard-Roosevelt, J. A., & Porges, S. W. (1998). Infant temperament and cardiac vagal tone: Assessments at twelve weeks of age. *Child Development, 69,* 624–635.

Johnson, E. O., Kamilaris, T. C., Chrousos, G. P., & Gold, P. W. (1992). Mechanisms of stress: A dynamic overview of hormonal and behavioral homeostasis. *Neuroscience and Biobehavioral Reviews, 16,* 115–130.

Kagan, J., Arcus, D., Snidman, N., Peterson, E., Steinberg, D., & Rimm-Kaufman, S. (1995). Asymmetry of finger temperature and early behavior. *Developmental Psychobiology, 28*(8), 443–451.

Kertes, D., Madsen, N., Bales, M., & Gunnar, M. (2005). *Salivary cortisol levels in internationally adopted children.* Manuscript submitted for publication.

Larson, M. C., White, B. P., Cochran, A., Donzella, B., & Gunnar, M. R. (1998). Dampening of the cortisol response to handling at 3 months in human infants and its relation to sleep, circadian cortisol activity, and behavioral distress. *Developmental Psychobiology, 33,* 327–337.

Levine, S. (2003). Stress: An historical perspective. In T. Steckler, N. Kalin, & J. M. H. M. Reul (Eds.), *Handbook on stress, immunology and behavior* (pp. 3–23). Amsterdam: Elsevier.

Lewis, M., & Ramsay, D. S. (1995). Developmental change in infants' responses to stress. *Child Development, 66,* 657–670.

McEwen, B. S. (1998). Stress, adaptation, and disease. Allostasis and allostatic load. *Annals of the New York Academy of Sciences, 840,* 33–44.

McEwen, B. S. (2000). Protective and damaging effects of stress mediators: Central role of the brain. *Progress in Brain Research, 122,* 25–34.

Mayberg, H. S., Liotti, M., Brannan, S. K., McGinnis, S., Mahurin, R. K., Jerabek, P. A., Silva, J. A., Tekell, J. L., Martin, C. C., Lancaster, J. L., & Fox, P. T. (1999). Reciprocal limbic-cortical function and negative mood: Convergent PET findings in depression and normal sadness. *American Journal of Psychiatry, 156,* 675–682.

Mineka, S., Gunnar, M. R., & Champoux, M. (1986). Control and early socio-emotional development: Infant Rhesus monkeys reared in controllable vs. uncontrollable environments. *Child Development, 57,* 1241–1256.

Nachmias, M., Gunnar, M. R., Mangelsdorf, S., Parritz, R. H., & Buss, K. A. (1996). Behavioral inhibition and stress reactivity: The moderating role of attachment security. *Child Development, 67,* 508–522.

Pacak, K., & Palkovits, M. (2001). Stressor specificity of central neuroendocrine responses: Implications for stress-related disorders. *Endocrine Review, 22,* 502–548.

Porges, S. W. (1995a). Cardiac vagal tone: A physiological index of stress. *Neuroscience and Biobehavioral Reviews, 19,* 225–233.

Porges, S. W. (1995b). Orienting in a defensive world: Mammalian modifications of our evolutionary heritage. A polyvagal theory. *Psychophysiology, 32,* 301–318.

Rosenfeld, P., Suchecki, D., & Levine, S. (1992). Multifactorial regulation of the hypothalamic-pituitary-adrenal axis during development. *Neuroscience and Biobehavioral Reviews, 16,* 553–568.

Rutter, M., Kreppner, J. M., O'Connor, T. G., & the English and Romanian Adoptees Team. (2001). Specificity and heterogeneity in children's responses to profound institutional privation. *British Journal of Psychiatry, 179,* 97–103.

Sanchez, M. M., Ladd, C. O., & Plotsky, P. M. (2001). Early adverse experience as a developmental risk factor for later psychopathology: Evidence from rodent and primate models. *Development and Psychopathology, 13,* 419–449.

Sapolsky, R. M., Romero, L. M., & Munck, A. (2000). How do glucocorticoids influence stress responses? Integrating permissive, suppressive, stimulatory and preparative actions. *Endocrine Reviews, 21*(1), 55–89.

Schore, A. N. (1996). The experience-dependent maturation of a regulatory system in the orbital prefrontal cortex and the origin of developmental psychopathology. *Development and Psychopathology, 8,* 59–87.

Schulkin, J. (1999). Corticotropin-releasing hormone signals adversity in both the placenta and the brain: Regulation by glucocorticoids and allostatic overload. *Journal of Endocrinology, 161*(3), 349–356.

Selye, H. (1946). The general adaptation syndrome and the diseases of adaptation. *Journal of Clinical Endocrinology and Metabolism, 6,* 117–230.

Spangler, G., & Schieche, M. (1994, July). *The role of maternal sensitivity and the quality of infant–mother attachment for infant biobehavioral organization.* Paper presented at the 9th International Conference on Infant Studies, Paris.

Sullivan, R., & Gratton, A. (2002). Prefrontal cortical regulation of hypothalamic pituitary-adrenal function in the rat and implications for psychopathology: Side matters. *Psychoneuroendocrinology, 27,* 99–114.

Suomi, S. J. (1995). Influence of attachment theory on ethological studies of biobehavioral development in nonhuman primates. In M. S. R. Goldberg & J. Kerr (Eds.), *Attachment theory: Social, developmental, and clinical perspectives* (pp. 185–201). Hillsdale, NJ: Analytic Press.

van Esseveldt, L. K. E., Lehman, M. N., & Boer, G. J. (2000). The suprachiasmatic nucleus and the circadian time-keeping system revisited. *Brain Research, 33,* 34–77.

Wadhwa, P. D., Sandman, C. A., & Garite, T. J. (2001). The neurobiology of stress in human pregnancy: Implications for development of the fetal central nervous system. *Progress in Brain Research, 133,* 131–142.

Watamura, S. E., Donzella, B., Alwin, J., & Gunnar, M. (2003). Morning-to-afternoon increases in cortisol concentrations for infants and toddlers at child care: Age differences and behavioral correlates. *Child Development, 74,* 1006–1020.

Watamura, S. E., Donzella, B., Kertes, D. A., & Gunnar, M. R. (2004). Developmental changes in baseline cortisol activity in early childhood: Relations with napping and effortful control. *Developmental Psychobiology, 45,* 125–133.

Watamura, S., Sebanc, A., Donzella, B., & Gunnar, M. R. (2002). Naptime at childcare: Effects on salivary cortisol levels. *Developmental Psychobiology, 40,* 33–42.

Weaver, C., Cervoni, N., Champagne, F. A., D'Alessio, A. C., Sharma, S., Seckl, J. R., Dymov, S., Szyf, M., & Meaney, M. (2004). Epigenetic programming by maternal behavior. *Nature Neuroscience, 7,* 847–854.

Weinstock, M. (2001). Alterations induced by gestational stress in brain morphology and behaviour of the offspring. *Progress in Neurobiology, 62,* 427–451.

White, B. P., Gunnar, M. R., Larson, M. C., Donzella, B., & Barr, R. G. (2000). Behavioral and physiological responsivity, sleep and patterns of daily cortisol in infants with and without colic. *Child Development, 71,* 862–877.

7

Temperament

Jennifer N. Martin and Nathan A. Fox

Temperament is thought to reflect stable, constitutionally based differences in behavior that are instrumental in guiding affective regulation and behavioral adaptation. Temperament can also be viewed as a complementary framework to the study of normative development because of its focus on individual, rather than group, differences. In addition, recent formulations of temperament reveal its influence in multiple areas, including attention and emotion regulation.

Temperamental characteristics have also been found to be relevant to children's successful adjustment within academic, social, and personal situations. However, each context is associated with specific demands and expectations that determine the salience of different temperamental traits and associated outcomes (Keogh, 1986). Thus the influence of temperament within various situations can have direct and/or indirect effects on children's adaptation to specific environmental contexts (i.e., home, academic, or peer settings).

Historical Origins of Temperament

The concept of innate temperamental characteristics can be traced back to ancient Greece and the work of Hippocrates (4th century BC) and Galen (2nd century AD). Their respective works were the first to emphasize the biological nature of individual differences. Although Hippocrates made no direct reference to the construct of temperament, his explanation of innate biological processes resulting from a system of bodily humors was expanded upon and formed into a typology of temperament by Galen several centuries later. Galen specified four primary subtypes of temperament based upon the varying dominance of the four fluid humors: sanguine (blood), choleric (bile), melancholic (black bile), and phlegmatic (phlegm), with an "ideal temperament" resulting from a stable balance of these four qualities (Strelau, 1998). Personality, according to Galen, resulted from the shifting of the primary humors, which was the driving force behind individual differences in thoughts, moods, and emotions (Kagan, 1994).

These explanations of personality as the product of innate qualities were eventually overlooked with the passage of time until the work of Pavlov in the early 1900s revived interest in individual differences and the biological underpinning of temperament. Pavlov noted that there were differences among the animals he tested in the speed with which they were conditioned. He theorized that individual differences in both speed and strength of conditioned reflexes have a physiological basis in the nervous system. This notion of individual differences was subsequently adopted by Eastern European personality theorists (Strelau, 1998) and by the British personality theorist Hans Eysenck (1970).

Perhaps one of the most influential studies in the revival of temperament research in the West was a longitudinal investigation of infant temperament conducted by Thomas, Chess, and colleagues (Thomas, Chess, Birch, Hertzig, & Korn, 1963). They conducted a set of detailed observations of newborn infants and their families and followed the development of these infants over the first years of life. On the basis of the data they collected, Thomas and Chess organized a structure to individual differences in infant behavior around nine dimensions (activity level, rhythmicity, adaptability, approach/withdrawal, intensity, sensory threshold, mood, distractibility, and attention span/distractibility). Infants varied in these dimensions in the manner in which they responded to the everyday situations of caregiving and interaction. Temperament reflected the "how" of behavioral response. How intense was the baby's reaction to a bath? How adaptable was the baby to new foods? Thomas and Chess found that these characteristics were fairly stable over the first years of life and were associated with a general adaptive response to the environment.

In addition to identifying these nine dimensions of temperament, Thomas and Chess postulated that there were different types of infants who were the product of their position on these nine continua. Thus, for example, infants who were high on the dimensions of adaptability, rhythmicity, approach, and positive mood were characterized as "Easy" in temperament. Infants who were low on adaptability, rhythmicity, and positive mood were considered "Difficult" in temperament, and infants who were low on adaptability, low on initial approach, and low on activity level were considered "Slow to Warm Up" in temperament. The notion that there were different temperament types is similar to the classical notions described above. Indeed, a good deal of research has utilized this typology to examine relations between difficult temperament and maladaptive outcomes (Carey, 1985a; Caspi, Henry, McGee, Moffitt, & Silva, 1995; Guerin & Gottfried, 1994; Zeanah, Keener, & Anders, 1986).

Thomas and Chess were also keenly aware of the importance of environmental influences in affecting infant temperament. They proposed that the match between parent expectations for their infant and the infant's personality was critical for creating a harmonious parent–child interaction. They termed this match "Goodness of Fit," and speculated that positive developmental outcomes were more likely to occur when a match existed between an infant's temperament and the parent's expectations.

The writings of Thomas and Chess generated great interest in multiple communities. Pediatricians recognized the importance of these early individual differences in responsiveness and attempted to adapt this framework for their work with new parents (Carey, 1985b; Carey & McDevitt, 1995). And developmental psychologists interested in the emergence of personality utilized the notion of "difficult temperament" to assess risk for maladaptive outcomes (Bates, Maslin, & Frankel, 1985; Guerin, Gottfried, & Thomas, 1997). Researchers developed a number of parental report questionnaires designed to assess and classify infants, toddlers, and young children along the nine dimensions of temperament (i.e., Infant Characteristic Questionnaire: Bates, Freeland, & Lounsbury, 1979; Infant Temperament Questionnaire: Carey, 1970; Toddler Temperament Scale: Fullard, McDevitt, & Carey, 1984; Behavioral Style Questionnaire: McDevitt & Carey, 1978). There were attempts, as well, to develop questionnaire measures that would assess the goodness of fit between parent and infant (Bates, Olson, Pettit, & Bayles, 1982; Lerner, Palermo, Spiro, & Nesselmade, 1982). These initiatives and research met with mixed success. In general, the work relied heavily on parental questionnaires. The relation between these reports and infant or child behavior was generally low, and prediction of maladaptive outcomes was poor.

During this same period of resurgence of interest in infant temperament in the late 1970s and early 1980s, the work of Eastern European personality trait psychologists came to light. These researchers (Nebylitsyn, Rozhdestvenskays, & Teplov, 1960; Strelau, 1982) considered themselves heirs to the Pavlovian model, focusing on individual differences in nervous system reactivity as a guiding construct for individual differences. Mary Rothbart was one of the first of US researchers who recognized the importance of this work and who adapted it into a structure for understanding infant temperament. Rothbart proposed that temperament results from an individual's inherent physiological disposition to react to stimulation and that reactivity is influenced over time through both maturational and experiential processes. Infants differ in their responsivity to sensory stimuli, particularly to novel and intense stimulation. This can be assessed by measuring an infant's threshold to respond to a stimulus, intensity of response, and duration of responding. Such assessments can be made at the physiological or behavioral levels and can provide a window into the infant's temperament. Variations in reactivity influence an individual's capability to regain a state of homeostasis following stimulation. During the first year of life, infants have few resources with which to regulate their reactive responses. Over the next few years, during the toddler and early childhood period, and with maturation of certain neural systems, children gain the resources to regulate their reactive responses.

Rothbart and her colleagues have used the dual constructs of reactivity and regulation to investigate the role of early individual differences in infancy and their later influence on social, emotional, and cognitive development in childhood (Derryberry & Rothbart, 1997; Rothbart, Ahadi, & Hershey, 1994). Rothbart (1981) identified several central temperament components evident in infancy (i.e., activity level, soothability, fear, distress to limitations, smiling, and duration of orienting). These traits, which are associated with reactivity and regulation processes, regulate, and in turn are regulated by, interactions with others (Putnam, Sanson, & Rothbart, 2002; Rothbart, 1989). In addition, as a child matures, the reactive forms of self-regulation are also governed by more controlled forms of self-regulation (i.e., selective orienting and effortful control of attention). For further detail on these reactivity and regulation processes see the discussion by Rothbart and colleagues in chapter 17 of this volume.

Approach and Withdrawal Systems

Specific types of temperament styles are also discussed within the approach and withdrawal systems framework. Approach and withdrawal behaviors have been noted across various levels of phylogeny and are distinguishable based on the intensity of stimuli needed to invoke reactivity of these systems. Withdrawal behaviors are vigorous responses that occur in response to intense levels of stimulation, whereas approach behaviors are more subdued in nature and manifest in connection with weak stimuli (Schneirla, 1959). Although Eysenck (1970) initially examined the physiology of human approach and withdrawal behaviors within the context of basic neural excitation and inhibition, it is Gray's reinforcement sensitivity theory (inspired by Eysenck's work) which has received the most attention in regard to expression and development of individual differences.

Gray's (1979, 1982) approach to the study of temperament has a central focus on the responsiveness of the organism to reward and punishment. Specifically, the reinforcement sensitivity theory bases personality differences on two hypothesized brain systems termed the behavioral activation system (BAS) and the behavioral inhibition system (BIS), which are hypothesized to regulate approach–withdrawal behavior and incentive response. The BIS is reactive to punishment cues as well as stimuli that are novel, aversive, or fear-provoking. Owing to the nature of the conditions that activate the BIS, multiple animal and human models of anxiety and social withdrawal have been developed with this bio-logical substrate as a central component (i.e., Fowles, 1980; Newman, Wallace, & Schmitt, 1997). Of particular importance to the neural circuitry of the BIS are the amygdala and the brainstem. Specifically, the lateral nucleus of the amygdala processes aversive sensory input and transmits this information through the hippocampus, the thalamus, the cortex, and the amygdala's central nucleus. The central nucleus projects to the brainstem, which controls the activation of fearful behavior responses such as freezing, heightened startle, and autonomic changes (Derryberry & Rothbart, 1997).

In contrast to the BIS, the BAS is responsive to appetitive motivation, sensitive to reward signals, and is associated with approach-related behaviors. Gray postulated that the BAS is a major contributor to the experience of positive affect, including feelings of joy and trust (Carver & White, 1994). Activation of the BAS is also associated with relief and avoidance as well as impulsivity. The general neural circuitry involved with this particular system is the basolateral amygdala, which activates dopaminergic neurons in the brainstem that facilitate approach behavior toward rewarding or appetitive stimuli (Derryberry & Rothbart, 1997). Another segment of the approach system relates to emo-tions involving anger and aggression. The approach system can elicit these emotional responses when an organism's progression toward appetitive stimuli is hindered (Depue & Iacono, 1989). In general, the BAS is best described as facilitating the appetitive needs of an organism (Derryberry & Rothbart, 1997).

The notion of individual differences in approach and withdrawal tendencies associated with differential sensitivity to reward and punishment has also been linked to the expression of different discrete emotions. Activation of the neural substrates underlying the BIS is thought to be associated with negative affect, while activation of the neural substrates of the BAS is thought to facilitate positive affect. Theories linking emotion expression and approach–withdrawal systems (Davidson, 1992; Fox, 1991; Fox & Davidson, 1984) speculate that emotions serve as important behavioral signals of either approach or withdrawal. To the extent that differences exist between individuals in the strength or the disposition to approach or withdraw from novelty or threat, there will also be differences in the tendency to express emotions associated with these motivational biases.

The Neural Substrates of Temperament

Research linking the approach–withdrawal and emotion systems in humans has utilized measures of brain electrical activity and behavioral observation of both motivated behavior and emotion (Fox, 1991; Sutton & Davidson, 1997). This work has identified a pattern of differential electroencephalogram (EEG) activation between the left and right hemispheres as associated with the tendency to approach or withdraw from stimulation. This lateralized pattern was first identified as a unique individual difference factor in adults (Davidson, Schwartz, Saron, Bennett, & Goleman, 1979) and was associated with the tendency to approach or withdrawal from stimuli evoking either positive or negative affect. Fox and colleagues have gone on to demonstrate that the pattern of lateralized EEG activity recorded in infants and children over the prefrontal cortex is significantly associated with the temperamental disposition to either approach or withdraw.

The EEG reflects electrical activity that is recorded off the scalp using small sensors and a bioamplifier to pick up the very small electrical signals that are generated by ensembles of neurons in the brain. Berger first described the EEG in 1929. He found that the electrical signal recorded off the scalp oscillated at a certain rate (or frequency) and that the height or amplitude of that oscillation varied as a function of the psychological state of the individual. If the individual is alert and attentive, the height of the oscillation tends to be small. However, if the individual is quiet and at rest, the height of the oscillation will increase. Berger and others have suggested that during attentional states unique ensembles of neurons become engaged in specific areas of the brain. Consequently, the mass action of neurons in the cortex would de-synchronize and result in reduced amplitude of EEG activity. When the individual is relaxed, there is greater neural synchrony and hence heightened amplitude. Thus, amplitude and engagement (activation) are inversely related.

In studies of EEG laterality, researchers place sensors or electrodes on homologous sites over the left and right hemispheres. Measures of amplitude (or EEG power) are obtained and the difference in amplitude between left and right is thought to reflect asymmetry in activation. This methodological approach has been used successfully with adults, children, and infants in association with behavioral tasks thought to engage either approach or withdrawal motivation or elicit a variety of emotions. Across these studies, greater left frontal EEG activation is associated with approach and positive emotions whereas greater right frontal EEG activation is related to withdrawal, avoidance, and negative emotions. Individual differences in these patterns of frontal asymmetry have been hypothesized to reflect the tendency, or the "trait disposition," for motivational states (Fox, 1994; Fox, Henderson, Rubin, Calkins, & Schmidt, 2001; Fox, Schmidt, Calkins, Rubin, & Coplan, 1996).

For example, Fox and Davidson (1987) examined EEG asymmetry in relation to individual differences in infant responsivity during affect-eliciting events that included stranger approach, mother approach, and maternal separation episodes. During each event reliable changes in frontal EEG asymmetry were evident and these changes were correlated with infant vocalization such that infant vocalization was associated with greater left frontal baseline activation in response to maternal interaction episodes and increased right frontal region activity during the maternal separation episode. In a separate study, Davidson and Fox (1989) also found that the pattern of frontal EEG asymmetry was predictive of the behavioral response of 10-month-old infants to maternal separation. Infants displaying left frontal, as opposed to right frontal, EEG asymmetry prior to the separation were less likely to cry during separation.

The measure of EEG asymmetry has also been used to reflect temperamental dispositions. Calkins and colleagues (Calkins, Fox, & Marshall, 1996) selected infants at 4 months for their motor and emotional reactions to novel auditory and visual stimuli. Two groups of infants were identified: those high in negative affect and high in motor reactivity and those high in positive affect and high in motor reactivity. At 9 months of age, measures of EEG were collected. Infants selected for high negative affect and high motor reactivity displayed right frontal EEG asymmetry while those selected for high positive affect and high motor reactivity displayed left frontal EEG asymmetry. In subsequent follow-up of these infants, Fox and colleagues (Fox, Henderson, Rubin et al., 2001) report that infants who were selected at 4 months of age on behavioral reactions to novelty were more likely to exhibit behavioral inhibition at 14 months of age and reticent social behavior at 4 years of age. Henderson, Fox, and Rubin (2001) also found that the interaction of infant temperament and frontal EEG asymmetry best predicted social reticence at age 4. Specifically, infants displaying right frontal EEG asymmetry who were identified with negative temperaments were more likely to show social reticence at age 4.

Although the neural origin of individual differences in frontal asymmetry remains somewhat unclear, it has been hypothesized that connections between the prefrontal cortex (PFC) and the amygdala may be involved. Rats with lesions of the medial PFC have been found to have a delayed extinction to aversive stimuli (Gewitz, Falls, & Davis, 1997; Morgan, Romanski, & LeDoux, 1993), which suggests that a neural path may exist between the PFC and the amygdala that serves to inhibit amygdala function (Amaral, Price, Pitkanen, & Carmichael, 1992; Davidson, 2002). In humans, the left PFC has been implicated as the primary inhibitor of amygdala activation with a "dampening of negative affective" in adult imaging studies (Davidson, Jackson, & Kalin, 2000, p. 898).

Behavioral Inhibition and a Synthesis of Temperament and Neuroscience

Some twenty years ago, Kagan and his students (Garcia-Coll, Kagan, & Reznick, 1984) described a group of young children who displayed heightened vigilant behavior in unfamiliar situations, were likely to withdraw from novel stimuli, and in some instances displayed fearful behavior when confronted with unfamiliar persons or events. Kagan called these children behaviorally inhibited and stated that they represented a unique temperament. His subsequent research revealed that these characteristics maintained a high degree of stability within an extreme group of the population and that these children, as they got older, withdrew from social interaction with unfamiliar and sometimes familiar peers. Around the same time that Kagan was publishing his behavioral findings on inhibited children, Joseph LeDoux and Michael Davis, two neuroscientists, were separately publishing their experimental findings on a brain system underlying conditioned fear in laboratory animals (Davis, 1986; LeDoux, Iwata, Cicchetti, & Reis, 1988). This neural system had at its center the amygdala, and particularly the central nucleus of the amygdala, as a locus for the processing of sensory and perceptual information and as a gateway to other brainstem nuclei for the production of fear responses. For example, pathways from the central nucleus to other nuclei led to freezing behavior, enhanced startle response, and autonomic as well as neuroendocrine changes. Kagan and others viewed this work as directly linking to the phenomenology of behavioral inhibition. Studies were completed to examine whether behaviorally inhibited infants and children exhibited the particular physiological changes that were seen in the laboratory as a result of heightened amygdala activity. In the next sections we briefly describe the startle, autonomic, and endocrine systems, specifically addressing three areas: startle reflex, heart rate, and cortisol.

Startle reflex

The startle reflex (or blink reflex) is a motor response that is generated when an intense stimulus is presented in a sudden manner. This response is mediated at the neural level by the brainstem pathway, the reticular formation, and the central nucleus of the amygdala and it is a reflex that is conserved across all species of mammals (Davis, Falls, Campeau, & Kim, 1993; Schmidt & Fox, 1998). Within humans, the intensity of the startle reflex has been found to vary according to the nature of the stimulus or the manner in which a stimulus is presented. In particular, affective modalities have been found to alter the function of the startle reflex such that induced negative states lead to augmented responses in both adults and children (Bradley, Lang, & Cuthbert, 1993; Grillon et al., 1999; Schmidt, Fox, & Schulkin, 1999). Individual differences in emotional reactivity have also been found to influence the degree of startle potentiation such that individuals with a greater tendency toward negative affect reactivity produce greater amplitude startle responses than do individuals with less negative reactivity (Cook, Hawk, Davis, & Stevenson, 1991).

Since the startle reflex is an inherent defensive mechanism activated in response to aversive stimuli, it provides a unique methodological insight into the approach–withdrawal and fear systems (Bradley, Cuthbert, & Lang, 1999). For example, Snidman and Kagan (1994) examined children who were either temperamentally inhibited or uninhibited while they viewed affect-laden slides. The children who were inhibited had greater startle responses, regardless of the affective context of the slides, as compared to uninhibited children. Likewise, Schmidt and Fox (1998) found that infants selected for high motor reactivity and high negative affect at 4 months of age exhibited a significantly greater startle amplitude increase from baseline to a fear-potentiated condition (stranger approach) than the children selected for either high motor reactivity and high positive affect, or low motor reactivity and low affect. Interestingly, the increase in startle response amplitude was not present in the high motor–high positive affect children, suggesting that the stranger approach paradigm may have served as a positive rather than a fearful event for this temperament group. Since there are a variety of conditions that can be used to elicit the startle response, future work may be able to better clarify the extent to which individual differences in affective valence influence attentional processes and the startle reflex in early childhood.

Heart rate

Another measure of the approach–withdrawal systems that can easily be examined in infants and children is respiratory sinus arrhythmia (RSA; also known as vagal tone). RSA is reflective of the vagus nerve connections that slow heart rate during exhalation and increase heart rate during inhalation. These connections are influenced by the neurotransmitter acetylcholine such that changes in cholinergic balance can alter the tonus of the vagal nerve, which in turn is related to motor arousal, orienting, attention, and approach behaviors (Porges, 1995; Stifter & Fox, 1990). Specifically, RSA is postulated to measure autonomic functioning that is manifested in certain neural and behavioral reactivity patterns (Calkins, 1997).

In studies of young children, Porges and colleagues have found that RSA provides a measure of emotional and behavioral reactivity in infants (Stifter, Fox, & Porges, 1989) and it also predicts maternal report of temperamental difficultness (Porges, Doussard-Roosevelt, & Portales, 1994). Fox (1989) longitudinally investigated the association between emotional reactivity and RSA in a group of infants selected for either high or low heart rate variability in response to novel or slightly stressful events at 5 months of age. Infants with a high RSA at 5 months exhibited greater reactivity to both positive and stressful stimuli, and at 14 months, the infants who were initially categorized as having a high RSA expressed greater approach and social behaviors as compared to infants initially categorized as low in RSA.

Stifter and Fox (1990) elicited positive and negative reactivity in newborn infants and again 5 months later, during which electrocardiogram (EKG) and maternal rating of temperament were collected. There was no connection between newborn and 5 month RSA; however, RSA at 5 months of age was predictive of individual differences in reactivity. Specifically, high RSA infants displayed greater negative affect, more activity, and a general lack of fear regarding novel objects. Calkins (1997) and colleagues (Calkins, Dedmon, Gill, Lomax, & Johnson, 2002; Calkins, Smith, Gill, & Johnson, 1998) have also found that RSA in late infancy is predictive of temperamental frustration across the toddler and preschool years. Overall, research on RSA suggests that there is a significant connection between cardiac measures of the autonomic nervous system and individual differences in behavioral and emotional reactivity which develops over the course of the first year of life and through early childhood.

Cortisol

The hypothalamic-pituitary-adrenocortical system (HPA) also relates to individual differences in reactivity and arousal. In particular, this system's output, a corticosteroid hormone called cortisol, is the body's primary regulator of the metabolic stress response (Fox, Hane, Perez-Edgar, in press). Since cortisol provides a measure of stress reactivity and because it is a non-invasive measure (it can be collected via salivary samples), this methodology has become a popular means of assessing individual differences in autonomic arousal (Fox, Henderson, & Marshall, 2001; see also Gunnar, this volume). Theoretically, the HPA axis should be the most reactive in instances where an individual senses a lack of control and thereby produces the highest elevations of cortisol. This notion is particularly pertinent to infancy and early childhood since children are continuously experiencing novel challenges and stressful social situations during this time period, and because young children are also heavily dependent upon external resources (i.e., caregivers) to help regulate their perceptions of the environment (van Bakel & Riksen-Walraven, 2004).

Several studies have found that elevated cortisol, in both infants and young children, correlates with the temperament traits of inhibition and fearfulness (Kagan, Reznick, & Snidman, 1987; Nachmias, Gunnar, Mangelsdorf, Parritz, & Buss, 1996; Schmidt et al., 1999). Theoretically, these results suggest that temperamentally inhibited or fearful children may have a lower threshold of physiological stress activation. There is evidence to suggest that this association may also exist for temperament traits associated with the BAS, such as anger-proneness. For instance, greater cortisol reactivity has been found in 15-month-old infants who were rated as highly anger-prone (van Bakel & Riksen-Walraven, 2004). Additional BAS-related traits have been found to positively correlate with cortisol response. Specifically, infants who were rated as high in distress to limitations were found to have elevated levels of cortisol during parental separation (Gunnar, Larson, Hertsgaard, Harris, & Brodersen, 1992) and anger levels in preschool children have been positively correlated to cortisol reactivity in the context of novel and challenging situations (Donzella, Gunnar, Kruger, & Alwin, 2000). In particular, temperament traits known to increase peer rejection (i.e., aggression, high surgency, and low effortful control) have also been shown to correlate with high cortisol reactivity in peer group settings (Gunnar, Sebanc, Tout, Donzella, & van Dulmen, 2003). Overall, these studies indicate that social relations may moderate the association between temperament traits and HPA reactivity, which suggests a need for further investigation of the relations between individual differences and cortisol reactivity within social contexts.

Continuity of Temperament across Childhood

Children classified as temperamentally inhibited are qualitatively different in their behavioral reactions to novelty, in their emotional experiences, and in their social interactions. In particular, children with an inhibited temperament display a high degree of vigilance in the face of novelty and in challenging situations. Often this is accompanied by heightened negative affect (Fox, Henderson, & Marshall, 2001; Fox, Henderson, Rubin et al., 2001; Kagan, 1992). In order to address the issue of continuity of this type of temperament, it is important to note that the measures used to reflect an inhibited temperament vary across development. For example, 2-year-old inhibited toddlers may be fearful of a novel object. This is less likely the case for a 5-year-old, who may instead display inhibition only in unfamiliar social situations.

Caspi (1998) described a heterotypic form of continuity in which diverse behavioral phenotypes can be associated due to a common underlying genotype, so although temperamental reactivity may be displayed differently in infants and preschoolers, both forms of behavior are postulated to be driven by the same underlying substrates of temperament. For instance, inhibition in young children is often assessed in regard to their latency to approach or interact with novel stimuli. Over the course of time older children will gradually develop a greater sense of control of their environment due to increased experience with objects and toys, thus reactivity toward novel stimuli becomes a less salient measure of inhibition. In contrast, older children are still highly reactive to social situations where they are required to interact with a novel adult or peer. Although inhibition in older children is more often assessed in the social context, it remains a reflective measure of the same underlying temperamental style that influenced a child's reactivity to novel stimuli as an infant and toddler.

The research conducted thus far indicates that the expression of an inhibited temperament displays a high degree of plasticity throughout childhood, with longitudinal studies of temperament indicating variability in the expression of inhibited and uninhibited behaviors over time. Kagan and colleagues (1987) studied children from toddlers through preschoolers and found that children originally classified as inhibited were more likely to become non-inhibited, as opposed to more inhibited, over time. Furthermore, studies that began in infancy and tracked temperament across time indicate that approximately 10% of all children initially classified as high in reactivity and negative affect will be classified as continuously inhibited throughout childhood (Kagan, Snidman, & Arcus, 1998).

For instance, Pfeifer and colleagues (Pfeifer, Goldsmith, Davidson, & Rickman, 2002) studied the continuity of temperament for children selected as extremely inhibited, extremely uninhibited, or intermediate at 32 months of age to 7 years of age. This study found that even four years after initial classification, the majority of children in this study retained their initial temperamental ranking. At 7 years of age, previously inhibited children were the most likely to exhibit high levels of shyness while children initially classified as uninhibited were the most likely to demonstrate a high degree of boldness, impulsivity, and low inhibitory control as assessed by maternal report. Although there was some movement in both inhibited and uninhibited temperamental rankings from 32 months to 7 years of age, this change was mainly evident for the subjects in the middle of the sample distribution.

Similar results have also been found by Fox and colleagues (Fox, Henderson, Rubin et al., 2001), who examined the development of infants chosen for extreme levels of high and low reactivity and affect at 4 months of age. In this study children's inhibited behaviors were assessed at three time points. At 14 and 24 months, inhibited behaviors were assessed in response to unfamiliar stimuli at the laboratory, and at 48 months inhibition was measured within the context of a play session with an unfamiliar group of peers that also occurred in the laboratory setting. Children rated as highly reactive and negative as infants displayed significantly greater inhibition at 14 months than children who were either high in positive affect and high in reactivity or low in both reactivity and affect. Interestingly, these group differences disappeared by 24 months of age, and by 4 years of age the high negative infants were almost as likely to be non-inhibited as they were to display behavioral inhibition.

In an attempt to identify the factors that may influence the continuity or change in the expression of social behavior among the inhibited sample, Fox and colleagues (Fox, Henderson, Rubin et al., 2001) examined both within-child and contextual factors. An inspection of the patterns of frontal EEG asymmetry in inhibited infants who remained stable and in those who changed revealed that the former maintained a right frontal EEG pattern while the latter group, those who changed in the expression of their behavior by becoming less inhibited, displayed increasing left frontal EEG asymmetry. There was a trend, as well, for inhibited girls to be more likely to change over time than inhibited boys. This trend is echoed in the work of others (e.g., Stevenson-Hinde) who found that inhibited boys were more likely to show stability of that behavior over time compared to inhibited girls. Stevenson-Hinde (2000) has speculated that parents may be more likely to find behavioral inhibition salient and discrepant in their sons and thus may be more over-protective of them. In contrast, behavioral inhibition in girls may be less noticeable and hence parents would interfere less, providing greater opportunities for other factors to exert change in the expression of the behavior.

Among the contextual factors that were predictive of discontinuity in inhibited behaviors was the child's history of out-of-home care. Children receiving care outside of their home during the first 24 months of life were more likely to become less inhibited over time as compared to children cared for solely in the home. Fox and colleagues (Fox, Henderson, Rubin et al., 2001) speculated that children in day care were exposed to a range of caregivers and unfamiliar peers at an early age and these experiences may lead to a decrease in wary or fearful behaviors in response to unfamiliar social situations during the preschool years. Young children in these settings are faced early on with the challenge of developing the necessary social skills to participate in successful interactions with peers. However, current studies suggest that children who are temperamentally fearful and who are in full-day, center-based care with lower quality ratings (based on size and child to caregiver ratio) demonstrate greater stress reactivity with cortisol increases throughout the day. Similar results are found in family day care settings that have comparable quality ratings (Dettling, Parker, Land, Sebanc, & Gunnar, 2000; Tout, de Haan, Kipp-Campbell, & Gunnar, 1998). Although the concept of group child care implies that consistent and repetitive experience with peers should allow for increased practice and mastery of social skills, further research is needed to fully understand how the quantity and quality of the child care received influences the potential social benefits for individual children of various temperaments.

In line with the gender and day care findings, Rubin and colleagues (Rubin, Hastings, Stewart, & Henderson, 1997) have found evidence of parental influence over continuity and discontinuity in the behavioral expression of temperament with toddlers rated as highly fearful. Specifically, fearful toddlers who exhibited the greatest inhibition across three separate contexts (nonsocial, adult-social, and peer-social) were the children most likely to have mothers who displayed over-solicitous behavior. This speaks again to a pattern of caregiving involving over-protection and over-indulgence that may in fact exacerbate temperamental behavioral inhibition in young children.

Others have reported that over-controlling parenting styles contribute to the exacerbation of inhibited behaviors and poor social interaction with peers (Park, Belsky, Putnam, & Crnic, 1997; Rubin, Cheah, & Fox, 2001). Over-protective parents are characterized by exhibiting over-solicitous actions such as shielding their children or being highly affectionate at inappropriate times. This lack of sensitivity often results from the parents' desire to control situations that they assume will produce anxiety in their child. As a result of over-solicitous parenting, highly fearful children are not given the opportunity to use self-generated coping behaviors. Without the chance to practice these techniques, children with over-solicitous parents have neither the chance to develop adaptive self-regulating strategies nor the ability to "overcome their dispositional vulnerabilities" (Rubin et al., 1997, p. 470).

Although there is relatively little empirical evidence regarding what form of parenting behavior is most adaptive for socializing fearful and inhibited children, there is some evidence that maternal response orientation and high positive affect are factors that are beneficial at the level of regulatory development (Kochanska, 1997). Additional research also indicates that the quality of maternal care can influence a child's adjustment in relation to the experience of stress, with poor attachment relationships and unsupportive maternal care mitigating the cortisol stress response in children temperamentally predisposed to high levels of frustration or anxiety (Gunnar, Broderson, Nachmias, Buss, & Rigatuso, 1996; Gunnar et al., 1992; see also Gunnar, this volume).

Consequences of Individual Differences in Temperament

The question of continuity or discontinuity in temperament is important as we struggle to understand how specific child–environment interactions contribute to distinct developmental trajectories for children. Specifically, it has been hypothesized that certain temperament styles may predispose children to be vulnerable to certain maladaptive developmental outcomes. In fact, a small segment of children identified as temperamentally inhibited or exuberant at a young age have been found to experience negative developmental outcomes in the form of social withdrawal and internalizing symptoms or peer rejection and externalizing behaviors, respectively (Rubin, Burgess, & Coplan, 2002; Burgess, Marshall, Rubin, & Fox, 2003).

Moreover, a significant proportion of children categorized as inhibited in infancy have been found to retain their inhibited behavioral styles and continue to avoid unfamiliarity and experience some degree of anxiety and fearfulness in social situations throughout childhood (Kagan et al., 1998). Furthermore, a number of similarities have been identified between children with an inhibited temperament and subjects who are highly anxious, with both of these groups typically exhibiting withdrawal in social situations and an avoidant coping style in the face of stress (Lonigan, Vasey, Phillips, & Hazen, 2004). The common behavioral manifestations that characterize these two conditions suggest that an inhibited temperament in early childhood may be a serious risk factor for anxiety problems in later childhood and adolescence. Indeed, a small but growing literature is emerging which indicates that early temperamental inhibition and negative affect are associated with the developmental of subsequent psychopathology (Eisengberg, Fabes, & Guthrie, 2000; Frick, 2004).

Related to both temperament and anxiety research is the study of attentional processes, which are fundamental to the adaptive regulation of emotions and behaviors. Research suggests that temperamentally inhibited children, who are high in reactivity and negative affect, may express heightened levels of attentional vigilance and orienting in novel situations due to their negative emotional biases. In particular, these children appear to have difficulty disengaging their vigilant behavior in unfamiliar social situations. Increased fixation in these situations without any intervening self-regulation, such as shifting attention or self-distracting, may exacerbate inhibited children's feelings of wariness or anxiety in novel social situations, and it has been suggested that the ability to shift attention may serve a protective self-regulatory function by moderating the association between behavioral inhibition and development of social anxiety (Fox, Henderson, Marshall, Nichols, & Ghera, 2005). This type of dysregulated attentional pattern is consistent with attentional behavior in anxious adults, who have been shown to experience difficulty disengaging from threatening aspects of emotional stimuli in cognitive tasks such as the emotional Stroop and the dot probe paradigms (Derryberry & Reed, 2002).

Altogether, current research indicates a strong connection between the early withdrawal and negative affect characteristics of inhibited temperament and the emergence of problematic levels of anxiety in later childhood and adolescence (Kagan & Snidman, 1999; Schwartz, Snidman, & Kagan, 1999). For instance, children who are inhibited are diagnosed with social anxiety disorder at higher rates than are non-inhibited children (Biederman, Hirshfeld-Becker, & Rosenbaum, 2001). In addition, children whose parents are diagnosed with an anxiety disorder have been found to exhibit high levels of behavioral inhibition (Rosenbaum, Biederman, & Hirshfeld, 1991). Overall, the strongest support for the connection between temperament and the development of anxiety problems has been found in studies that use an extreme groups approach. This approach may provide the greatest insight regarding the relations between temperament and psychopathology since the associations between temperament and socio-emotional outcomes are postulated to be non-linear in nature (Kagan, Snidman, & McManis, 2002).

Throughout childhood, extremely inhibited children typically exhibit low levels of social competence and high levels of social anxiety. Owing to their social wariness, inhibited children have difficulty engaging in social activities and often display reticent behavior in structured laboratory peer play sessions. Reticent behavior is theorized to result from an approach–avoidance conflict in which a child lingers near a social group but does not attempt to join the play (Coplan, Rubin, Fox, Calkins, & Stewart, 1994). This form of withdrawn behavior is distinct from solitary-passive behavior, in which a child can constructively play alone with an object in the presence of peers, and solitary-active behavior, which involves sensorimotor activities and dramatic play with or without an object while in the presence of peers (Rubin, Burgess, & Hastings, 2002). Reticent children desire to join in play with peers but the prospect of engaging in social interaction produces high levels of anxiety.

Peer interactions have also been examined in temperamentally different children within the school setting. Gersten (1989) found that inhibited children in their first week of kindergarten spent more time away from their peers engaging in watchful behaviors, whereas uninhibited children were more likely to participate in higher numbers of social interactions. This pattern of social wariness was not attributable to the novelty of the first week of school as social wariness was found to be evident for the inhibited children throughout the course of the school year. Patterns of inhibited behavior may display relatively strong stability in the school setting, and it has also been suggested that inhibited children may be more likely to fall under the teacher's radar during classroom activities and less likely to be called upon to join in class discussions (Martin, Nagel, & Paget, 1983). Conversely, exuberant children who are high on surgency and approach behaviors may demand more attention in the classroom. However, without adequate self-regulating skills the attention received may be more negative in nature with exuberant children prone to impulsivity, low frustration tolerance, and aggression (Calkins et al., 1996).

In middle to late childhood, behaviorally inhibited children who become socially withdrawn experience increased social difficulties with their peers in the school setting. In particular, these children are often rejected by peers and are frequently the target of bullying and victimization (Boivin, Hymel, & Bukowski, 1995; Hanish & Guerra, 2000). Research indicates that socially withdrawn children are disliked by their classmates and are viewed by their peers as anxious and isolated (Ollendick, Ross, Weist, & Oswald, 1990). Rubin, Burgess, and Coplan (2002) postulate that particularly during the middle school and high school years socially withdrawn children may be seen as relatively easy targets for harassment, which may result in victimization by peers in the form of either physical or verbal aggression. Continual harassment may contribute to children's increased fear of peers and further self-isolation from potential social interaction. Overall, cycles of poor social interaction appear to create negative psychological perceptions in socially withdrawn children in relation to self-worth, social competence, and maladaptive psychological outcomes, including feelings of loneliness, depression, or anxiety (Hymel, Bowker, & Woody, 1993; Morison & Masten, 1991; Renshaw & Brown, 1993; Rubin, 1993).

Overall, inhibited children tend to experience greater levels of social stress through ineffective interactions with others and the inability to self-regulate negative emotions that produce wariness and anxiety in novel situations. These behavioral patterns may compromise early peer relations and are detrimental to the development of social competence. If behaviorally inhibited children continually experience high levels of social failures, over time they may attribute poor social outcomes to internal causes and increasingly perceive ambiguous social situations as threatening, thus predisposing these children to maladaptive outcomes (Rubin, Bukowski, & Parker, 1998). Although an inhibited temperament in children has been suggested to serve as a protective factor in deterring the development of externalizing problems, it may also carry the high cost of increased vulnerability to internalizing problems and anxiety-related psychopathology.

Conclusion

Although the influence of environmental factors on the behavioral outcomes of temperamentally different children seems to increase the complexity of the construct of temperament, it is imperative to continue to investigate the factors that shape the expression of temperamental traits over time in order to determine how to diminish the maladaptive outcomes which are often experienced by children who are either extremely inhibited or exuberant. Overall, further research will be necessary to more clearly ascertain the association between specific temperament styles and the expression of adaptive or maladaptive behaviors.

It is also clear that attentional and regulatory abilities are salient to the manifestation of particular behavior patterns; however, the interaction between these skills and temperament traits has not yet been fully explained. This is likely due to the large number of behaviors which are studied and also the disperse age ranges used across various investigations of temperament and behavioral outcomes. Instead of focusing primarily on models of linear effects, researchers should incorporate greater use of models that account for mediating processes in the relation between behavioral outcomes and temperamental traits since this approach may prove to be more informative of adjustment outcomes across early childhood. In turn, more effective interventions may then be designed that will help to decrease potential negative developmental outcomes, including social reticence and peer rejections, for children who are extremely inhibited or exuberant. Likewise, a greater understanding of the biological and environmental correlates of negative developmental trajectories for children of various temperaments may lead to the implementation of more effective school and day-care policies.

References

Amaral, D. G., Price, J. L., Pitkanen, A., & Carmichael, S. T. (1992). Anatomical organization of the primate amygdaloid complex. In J. P. Aggleton (Ed.), *The amygdala: Neurobiological aspects of emotion, memory, and mental dysfunction* (pp. 1–66). New York: Wiley.

Bates, J. E., Freeland, C. A. B., & Lounsbury, M. L. (1979). Measurement of infant difficultness. *Child Development, 50*, 794–803.

Bates, J. E., Maslin, C. A. & Frankel, K. A. (1985). Attachment security, mother–child interaction, and temperament as predictors of behavior-problem ratings at age three years. *Monographs of the Society for Research in Child Development, 50*(1–2, Serial No. 209).

Bates, J. E., Olson, S. L., Pettit, G. S., & Bayles, K. (1982). Dimensions of individuality in the mother–infant relationship at six months of age. *Child Development, 53*, 446–461.

Biederman, J., Hirshfeld-Becker, D. R., & Rosenbaum, J. F. (2001). Further evidence of association between behavioral inhibition and social anxiety in children. *American Journal of Psychiatry, 158,* 1673–1679.

Boivin, M., Hymel, S., & Bukowski, W. (1995). The roles of social withdrawal, peer rejection, and victimization by peers in predicting loneliness and depressed mood in childhood. *Development and Psychopathology, 7,* 765–785.

Bradley, M. M., Cuthbert, B. N., & Lang, P. J. (1999). Affect and the startle reflex. In M. E. Dawson, A. M. Schell, & A. H. Bohmelt (Eds.), *Startle modification: Implications for neuroscience, cognitive science, and clinical science* (pp. 157–183). Cambridge: Cambridge University Press.

Bradley, M. M., Lang, P. J., & Cuthbert, B. N. (1993). Emotion, novelty, and the startle reflex: Habituation in humans. *Behavioral Neuroscience, 107,* 970–980.

Burgess, K. B., Marshall, P. J., Rubin, K. H., & Fox, N. A. (2003). Infant attachment and temperament as predictors of subsequent externalizing problems and cardiac physiology. *Journal of Child Psychology and Psychiatry, 44,* 819–831.

Calkins, S. D. (1997). Cardiac vagal tone indices of temperamental reactivity and behavioral regulation in young children. *Developmental Psychobiology, 31,* 125–135.

Calkins, S. D., Dedmon, S., Gill, K., Lomax, L., & Johnson, L. (2002). Frustration in infancy: Implications for emotion regulation, physiological processes, and temperament. *Infancy, 3,* 175–198.

Calkins, S. D., Fox, N. A., & Marshall, T. R. (1996). Behavioral and physiological antecedents of inhibited and uninhibited behavior. *Child Development, 67,* 523–540.

Calkins, S. D., Smith, C. L., Gill, K. L., & Johnson, M. C. (1998). Maternal interactive style across contexts: Relations to emotional, behavioral and physiological regulation during toddlerhood. *Social Development, 7,* 350–369.

Carey, W. B. (1970). A simplified method for measuring infant temperament. *Journal of Pediatrics, 77,* 188–194.

Carey, W. B. (1985a). Interactions of temperament and clinical conditions. *Advances in Developmental & Behavioral Pediatrics, 6,* 83–115.

Carey, W. B. (1985b). Clinical use of temperament data in pediatrics. *Journal of Developmental & Behavioral Pediatrics, 6,* 137–142.

Carey, W. B., & McDevitt, S. C. (1995). *Coping with children's temperament: A guide for professionals.* New York: Basic Books, Inc.

Carver, C. S., & White, T. L. (1994). Behavioral inhibition, behavioral activation, and affective responses to impending reward and punishment: The BIS/BAS Scales. *Journal of Personality and Social Psychology, 67,* 319–333.

Caspi, A. (1998). Personality development across the life course. In E. Eisenberg (Ed.), *Handbook of child psychology: Vol. 3. Social, emotional and personality development* (5th ed., pp. 311–388). New York: Wiley.

Caspi, A., Henry, B., McGee, R. O., Moffitt, T. E., & Silva, P. A. (1995). Temperamental origins of child and adolescent behavior problems: From age three to age fifteen. *Child Development, 66,* 55–68.

Cook, E. W, Hawk, L. W, Davis, T. L., & Stevenson, V. E. (1991). Affective individual differences and startle reflex modulation. *Journal of Abnormal Psychology, 100,* 5–13.

Coplan, R. J., Rubin, K. H., Fox, N. A., Calkins, S. D., & Stewart, S. L. (1994). Being alone, playing alone, and acting alone: Distinguishing among reticence and passive and active solitude in young children. *Child Development, 65,* 129–137.

Davidson, R. J. (1992). Emotion and affective style: hemispheric substrates. *Psychological Science, 3,* 39–43.

Davidson, R. J. (2002). Anxiety and affective style: Role of prefrontal cortex and amygdala. *Biological Psychiatry, 51*, 68–80.

Davidson, R. J., & Fox, N. A. (1989). Frontal brain asymmetry predicts infants' response to maternal separation. *Journal of Abnormal Psychology, 98*, 127–131.

Davidson, R. J., Jackson, D. C., & Kalin, N. H. (2000). Emotion, plasticity, context, and regulation: Perspectives from affective neuroscience. *Psychological Bulletin, 126*, 890–909.

Davidson, R. J., Schwartz, G. E., Saron, C., Bennett, J., & Goleman, D. J. (1979). Frontal versus parietal EEG asymmetry during positive and negative affect. *Psychophysiology, 16*, 202–203.

Davis, M. (1986). Pharmacological and anatomical analysis of fear conditioning using the fear-potentiated startle paradigm. *Behavioral Neuroscience, 100*, 814–824.

Davis, M., Falls, W. A., Campeau, S., & Kim, M. (1993). Fear-potentiated startle: A neural and pharmacological analysis. *Behavioural Brain Research, 58*, 175–198.

Depue, R. A., & Iacono, W. G. (1989). Neurobehavioral aspects of affective disorders. *Annual Review of Psychology, 40*, 457–492.

Derryberry, D., & Reed, M. A. (2002). Anxiety-related attentional biases and their regulation by attentional control. *Journal of Abnormal Psychology, 111*, 225–236.

Derryberry, D., & Rothbart, M. K. (1997). Reactive and effortful processes in the organization of temperament. *Development and Psychopathology, 9*, 633–652.

Dettling, A. C., Parker, S. W., Lane, S. K., Sebanc, A. M., & Gunnar, M. R. (2000). Quality of care and temperament determine changes in cortisol concentrations over the day for young children in child care. *Psychoneuroendocrinology, 24*, 819–836.

Donzella, B., Gunnar, M. R., Krueger, W. K., & Alwin, J. (2000). Cortisol and vagal tone responses to competitive challenge in preschoolers: Associations with temperament. *Developmental Psychobiology, 37*, 209–220.

Eisenberg, N., Fabes, R. A., & Guthrie, I. K. (2000). Dispositional emotionality and regulation: Their role in predicting quality of social functioning. *Journal of Personality & Social Psychology, 78*, 136–157.

Eysenck, H. J. (1970). *The structure of human personality* (3rd ed.). London: Methuen.

Fowles, D. C. (1980). The three arousal model: Implications for Gray's two-factor learning theory for heart rate, electrodermal activity, and psychopathy. *Psychophysiology, 17*, 87–104.

Fox, N. A. (1989). Psychophysiological correlates of emotional reactivity during the first year of life. *Developmental Psychology, 25*, 364–372.

Fox, N. A. (1991). If it's not left, it's right: Electroencephalograph asymmetry and the development of emotion. *American Psychologist, 46*, 863–872.

Fox, N. A. (1994). Dynamic cerebral processes underlying emotion regulation. *Monographs of the Society for Research in Child Development, 59*(2–3, Serial No. 240).

Fox, N. A., & Davidson, R. J. (1984). Hemispheric substrates of affect: A developmental model. In. N. A. Fox & R. J. Davidson (Eds.), *The psychobiology of affective development* (pp. 353–381). Hillsdale, NJ: Erlbaum Press.

Fox, N. A., & Davidson, R. J. (1987). Electroencephalogram asymmetry in response to the approach of a stranger and maternal separation in 10-month-old infants. *Developmental Psychology, 23*, 233–240.

Fox, N. A., Hane, A. A., & Perez-Edgar, K. E. (in press). Psychophysiological methods in the study of developmental psychopathology. In D. Cicchetti (Ed.), *Developmental psychopathology* (2nd ed.). Hoboken, NJ: John Wiley & Sons Inc.

Fox, N. A., Henderson, H. A., & Marshall, P. J. (2001). The biology of temperament: An integrative approach. In C. A. Nelson & M. Luciana (Eds.), *Handbook of developmental cognitive neuroscience* (pp. 631–646). Cambridge, MA: MIT Press.

Fox, N. A., Henderson, H. A., Marshall, P. J., Nichols, K. E., & Ghera, M. A. (2005). Behavioral inhibition: Linking biology and behavior within a developmental framework. *Annual Review of Psychology, 56,* 235–262.

Fox, N. A., Henderson, H. A., Rubin, K. H., Calkins, S. D., & Schmidt, L. A. (2001). Continuity and discontinuity of behavioral inhibition and exuberance: Psychophysiological and behavioral influences across the first four years of life. *Child Development, 72,* 1–21.

Fox, N. A., Schmidt, L. A., Calkins, S. D., Rubin, K. H., & Coplan, R. J. (1996). The role of frontal activation in the regulation and dysregulation of social behavior during the preschool year. *Development and Psychopathology, 8,* 89–102.

Frick, P. J. (2004). Temperament and childhood psychopathology: Integrating research on temperament and childhood psychopathology: Its pitfalls and promise. *Journal of Clinical Child and Adolescent Psychology, 33,* 2–7.

Fullard, W., McDevitt, S. C., & Carey, W. B. (1984). Assessing temperament in one- to three-year-old children. *Journal of Pediatric Psychology, 9,* 205–217.

Garcia-Coll, C., Kagan, J., & Reznick, J. S. (1984). Behavioral inhibition in young children. *Child Development, 55,* 1005–1019.

Gersten, M. (1989). Behavioral inhibition in the classroom. In J. S. Reznick (Ed.), *Perspectives on behavioral inhibition* (pp. 71–91). Chicago: University of Chicago Press.

Gewirtz, J. C., Falls, W. A., & Davis, M. (1997). Normal conditioned inhibition and extinction of freezing and fear-potentiated startle following electrolytic lesions of medial prefrontal cortex in rats. *Behavioral Neuroscience, 111,* 712–726.

Gray, J. A. (1979). A neuropsychological theory of anxiety. In C. E. Izard (Ed.), *Emotions in personality and psychopathology* (pp. 301–355). New York: Plenum.

Gray, J. A. (1982). *The neuropsychology of anxiety.* New York: Oxford University Press.

Grillon, C., Merikangas, K. R., Dierker, L., Snidman, N., Arriaga, R. I., Kagan, J., Donzella, B., Dikel, T., & Nelson, C. (1999). Startle potentiation by threat of aversive stimuli and darkness in adolescents: A multi-site study. *International Journal of Psychophysiology, 32,* 63–73.

Guerin, D. W., & Gottfried, A. W. (1994). Temperamental consequences of infant difficultness. *Infant Behavior and Development, 17,* 413–421.

Guerin, D. W., Gottfried, A. W., & Thomas, C. W. (1997). Difficult temperament and behavior problems: A longitudinal study from 1.5 to 12 years. *International Journal of Behavioral Development, 21,* 71–90.

Gunnar, M. R., Brodersen, L., Nachmias, M., Buss, K., & Rigatuso, R. (1996). Stress reactivity and attachment security. *Developmental Psychology, 29,* 10–36.

Gunnar, M. R., Larson, M. C., Hertsgaad, L., Harris, M. L., & Brodersen, L. (1992). The stressfulness of separation among nine-month-old infants: Effects of social context variables and infant temperament. *Child Development, 63,* 290–303.

Gunnar, M. R., Sebanc, A. M., Tout, K., Donzella, B., & van Dulmen, M. M. H. (2003). Peer rejection, temperament, and cortisol activity in preschoolers. *Developmental Psychobiology, 43,* 346–358.

Hanish, L. D., & Guerra, N. G. (2000). Predictors of peer victimization among urban youth. *Social Development, 9,* 521–543.

Henderson, H. A., Fox, N. A., & Rubin, K. H. (2001). Temperamental contributions to social behavior: The moderating roles of frontal EEG asymmetry and gender. *Journal of the American Academy of Child & Adolescent Psychiatry, 40,* 68–74.

Hymel, S., Bowker, A., & Woody, E. (1993). Aggressive versus withdrawn unpopular children: Variations in peer and self-perceptions in multiple domains. *Child Development, 64,* 879–896.

Kagan, J. (1992). Temperamental contributions to emotion and social behavior. In M. S. Clark (Ed.), *Emotion and social behavior* (pp. 99–118). Thousand Oaks, CA: Sage Publications, Inc.

Kagan, J. (1994). *Galen's prophecy: Temperament in human nature.* New York: Basic Books.

Kagan, J., Reznick, J. S., & Snidman, N. (1987). The physiology and psychology of behavioral inhibition in children. *Child Development, 58,* 1459–1473.

Kagan, J., & Snidman, N. (1999). Early childhood predictors of adult anxiety disorders. *Biological Psychiatry, 46,* 1536–1541.

Kagan, J., Snidman, N., & Arcus, D. (1998). Childhood derivates of high and low reactivity in infancy. *Child Development, 69,* 1483–1493.

Kagan, J., Snidman, N., & McManis, M. (2002). One measure, one meaning: Multiple measures, clearer meaning. *Development & Psychopathology, 14,* 463–475.

Keogh, B. K. (1986). Temperament and schooling: Meaning of "goodness-of-fit"? In J. V. Lerner & R. M. Lerner (Eds.), *Temperament and social interaction during infancy and childhood* (pp. 89–108). San Francisco: Jossey-Bass.

Kochanska, G. (1997). Mutually responsive orientation between mothers and their young children: Implications for early socialization. *Child Development, 68,* 94–112.

LeDoux, J. E., Iwata, J., Cicchetti, P., & Reis, D. J. (1988). Different projections of the central amygdaloid nucleus mediate autonomic and behavioral correlates of conditioned fear. *Journal of Neuroscience, 8,* 2517–2529.

Lerner, R. M., Palermo, M., Spiro, A., & Nesselmade, J. B. (1982). Assessing the dimensions of temperamental individuality across the life span: The dimensions of temperament survey. *Child Development, 53,* 149–159.

Lonigan, C. J., Vasey, M. W., Phillips, B. M., & Hazen, R. A. (2004). Temperament, anxiety, and the processing of threat-relevant stimuli. *Journal of Clinical Child & Adolescent Psychology, 33,* 8–20.

McDevitt, S. C., & Carey, W. B. (1978). The measurement of temperament in 3–7 year old children. *Journal of Child Psychology & Psychiatry, 19,* 245–253.

Martin, R. P., Nagel, R., & Paget, K. (1983). Relationship between temperament and classroom behavior, teacher attitudes, and academic achievement. *Journal of Psychoeducational Assessment, 1,* 377–386.

Morgan, M. A., Romanski, L., & LeDoux, J. E. (1993). Extinction of emotional learning: Contribution of medial prefrontal cortex. *Neuroscience Letters, 163,* 109–113.

Morison, P., & Masten, A. S. (1991). Peer reputation in middle childhood as a predictor of adaptation in adolescence: A seven-year follow-up. *Child Development, 62,* 991–1007.

Nachmias, M., Gunnar, M. R., Mangelsdorf, S., Parritz, R. H., & Buss, K. (1996). Behavioral inhibition and stress reactivity: The moderating role of attachment security. *Child Development, 67,* 508–522.

Nebylitsyn, V. D., Rozhdestvenskaya, V. I., & Teplov, B. M. (1960). Concerning the interrelation between absolute sensitivity and strength of the nervous system. *Quarterly Journal of Experimental Psychology, 12,* 17–25.

Newman, J. P., Wallace, J. F., & Schmitt, A. (1997). Behavioral inhibition system functioning in anxious, impulsive and psychopathic individuals. *Personality and Individual Differences, 23,* 583–592.

Ollendick, T. H., Ross, W. G., Weist, M. D., & Oswald, D. P. (1990). The predictive validity of teacher nominations: A five-year follow up of at-risk youth. *Journal of Abnormal Child Psychology, 18,* 699–713.

Park, S., Belsky, J., Putnam, S., & Crnic, K. (1997). Infant emotionality, parenting, and 3-year inhibition: Exploring stability and lawful discontinuity in a male sample. *Developmental Psychology, 33,* 218–227.

Pfeifer, M., Goldsmith, H. H., Davidson, R. J., & Rickman, M. (2002). Continuity and change in inhibited and uninhibited children. *Child Development, 73,* 1474–1485.

Porges, S. W. (1995). Cardiac vagal tone: A physiological index of stress. *Neuroscience and Biobehavioral Reviews, 19*, 225–233.

Porges, S. W., Doussard-Roosevelt, J. A., & Portales, L. A. (1994). Cardiac vagal tone: Stability and relation to difficultness and infants and 3-year-olds. *Developmental Psychobiology, 27*, 289–300.

Putnam, S. P., Sanson, A. V., & Rothbart, M. K. (2002). Child temperament and parenting. In M. H. Bornstein (Ed.), *Handbook of parenting: Vol. 1. Children and parenting* (2nd ed., pp. 255–277). Mahwah, NJ:Lawrence Erlbaum Associates.

Renshaw, P. D., & Brown, P. J. (1993). Loneliness in middle childhood: Concurrent and longitudinal predictors. *Child Development, 64*, 1271–1284.

Rosenbaum, J. F., Biederman, J., & Hirshfeld, D. R. (1991). Further evidence of an association between behavioral inhibition and anxiety disorders: Results from a family study of children from a non-clinical sample. *Journal of Psychiatric Research, 25*, 49–65.

Rothbart, M. K. (1981). Measurement of temperament in infancy. *Child Development, 52*, 569–578.

Rothbart, M. K. (1989). Temperament and development. In G. A. Kohnstamm, J. Bates, & M. K. Rothbart (Eds.), *Temperament in childhood* (pp. 77–110). Chichester: Wiley.

Rothbart, M. K., Ahadi, S. A., & Hershey, K. L. (1994). Temperament and social behavior in childhood. *Merrill-Palmer Quarterly, 40*, 21–39.

Rubin, K. H. (1993). The Waterloo Longitudinal Project: Correlates and consequences of social withdrawal from childhood to adolescence. In K. H. Rubin & J. Asendorpf (Eds.), *Social withdrawal, inhibition and shyness in childhood* (pp. 291–314). Hillsdale, NJ: Erlbaum.

Rubin, K. H., Bukowski, W., & Parker, J. G. (1998). Peer interactions, relationships, and groups. *Handbook of child psychology: Vol. 3. Social, emotional, and personality development* (5th ed., pp. 619–700). New York: Wiley.

Rubin, K. H., Burgess, K. B., & Coplan, R. J. (2002). Social withdrawal and shyness. In P. K. Smith & C. H. Hart (Eds.), *Handbook of child social development* (pp. 329–352). Oxford: Blackwell.

Rubin, K. H., Burgess, K. B., & Hastings, P. D. (2002). Stability and social-behavioral consequences of toddlers' inhibited temperament and parenting behaviors. *Child Development, 73*, 483–495.

Rubin, K. H., Cheah, C. S. L., & Fox, N. A. (2001). Emotional regulation, parenting and display of social reticence in preschoolers. *Early Education and Development, 12*, 97–115.

Rubin, K. H., Hastings, P. D., Stewart, S. L., & Henderson, H. A. (1997). The consistency and concomitants of inhibition: Some of the children, all of the time. *Child Development, 68*, 467–483.

Schmidt, L. A., & Fox, N. A. (1998). Fear-potentiated startle responses in temperamentally different human infants. *Developmental Psychobiology, 32*, 113–120.

Schmidt, L. A., Fox, N. A., & Schulkin, J. (1999). Behavioral and psychophysiological correlates of self-presentation in temperamentally shy children. *Developmental Psychobiology, 35*, 119–135.

Schneirla, T. C. (1959). An evolutionary and developmental theory of motivation underlying approach and withdrawal. *Nebraska Symposium on Motivation, 7*, 1–42.

Schwartz, C. E., Snidman, N., & Kagan, J. (1999). Adolescent social anxiety as an outcome of inhibited temperament in childhood. *Journal of the American Academy of Child & Adolescent Psychiatry, 38*, 1008–1015.

Snidman, N., & Kagan, J. (1994). The contribution of infant temperament differences to acoustic startle response. [Abstract] *Psychophysiology, 31*, S92.

Stifter, C. A., & Fox, N. A. (1990). Infant reactivity: Physiological correlates of newborn and 5-month temperament. *Developmental Psychology, 26,* 582–588.

Stifter, C. A., Fox, N. A., & Porges, S. W. (1989). Facial expressivity and vagal tone in 5- and 10-month-old infants. *Infant Behavior and Development, 12,* 127–137.

Strelau, J. (1982). Biologically determined dimensions of personality or temperament? *Personality and Individual Differences, 3,* 355–360.

Strelau, J. (1998). *Temperament: A psychological perspective.* New York: Plenum Press.

Stevenson-Hinde, J. (2000). Shyness in the context of close relationships. In W. R. Crozier (Ed.), *Shyness, development, consolidation and change* (pp. 88–102), New York: Routledge.

Sutton, S. K., & Davidson, R. J. (1997). Prefrontal brain asymmetry: A biological substrate of the behavioral approach and inhibition systems. *Psychological Science, 8,* 204–210.

Thomas, A., Chess, S., Birch, H. G., Hertzig, M. E., & Korn, S. (1963). *Behavioral individuality in early childhood.* New York: New York University Press.

Tout, K., de Haan, M., Kipp-Campbell, E., & Gunnar, M. R. (1998). Social behavior correlates of adrenocortical activity in daycare: Gender differences and time of day effects. *Child Development, 69,* 1247–1262.

van Bakel, H. J. A., & Riksen-Walraven, J. M. (2004). Stress reactivity in 15-month-old infants: Links with infant temperament, cognitive competence, and attachment security. *Developmental Psychobiology, 44,* 157–167.

Zeanah, C. H., Keener, M. A., & Anders, T. F. (1986). Explorations of difficult temperament. *Journal of Developmental and Behavioral Pediatrics, 7,* 122–123.

PART III

Cognitive Development

8

Early Conceptual Development

Susan A. Gelman

The first few years of life are marked by an astonishing increase in the amount and variety of children's knowledge. Between roughly 2 and 7 years of age, children learn thousands of words, they learn to "read" subtle emotional and mental states of other people, they predict the trajectories of objects moving through space, they understand that plants and animals grow but that cars and clouds do not, they can count and reason numerically, and more (see Siegler & Alibali, 2004, for review). Some young children develop remarkable expertise in a given topic (dinosaurs, songbirds, Pokémon), with factual bases in these domains that rival those of adults. The varied and rich bodies of knowledge that children develop early in life enable them to navigate their social and non-social worlds with increasing skill. At the same time, throughout the early school years, children possess striking misconceptions about these very same topics, with predictable errors in reasoning about physics (a marble rolling off a table will fall straight down), biology (people aren't animals; clouds and bicycles are alive), psychology (a person will believe what is true, not what he or she has evidence for), mathematics (squashing a ball of clay increases its weight), and more. That is, children's knowledge in the preschool years is a curious mixture of early competence and conceptual re-organizations.

In order to understand cognition in early childhood, it is important to examine the concepts that comprise children's knowledge: ideas such as "dinosaur," "think," "five," "alive." Concepts are the mental representations that correspond to categories and individuals, and they are often called the building blocks of thought. By studying concepts, we can better address fundamental theoretical issues (e.g., How can we characterize early thought? How does it change over time?) as well as address practical concerns of importance to children's lives (e.g., How do children reason about important topics such as illness, morality, and gender? How best can we instruct children about science, mathematics, or reading?). This chapter first reviews some of the evidence for children's early conceptual competence. However, focusing on early competence does not tell us where this early competence comes from. We therefore also ask: What role does experience play? What individual differences are found in children's concepts? How does cultural variation influence the content and structure of early concepts?

Early Competence

On many traditional accounts, concepts are said to undergo a fundamental, qualitative shift with development. That is, children and adults are often said to occupy opposite endpoints of various dichotomies, moving from perceptual to conceptual (Bruner et al., 1966), from concrete to abstract (Piaget, 1951), or from similarity to theories (Quine, 1977). These developmental dichotomies are intuitively appealing, in part because children often do seem to reason in ways that are strikingly different from how adults reason. For example, in the well-known "conservation error" studied by Piaget, children under 6 or 7 years of age report that an irrelevant transformation leads to a change in quantity (e.g., concluding that the amount of a liquid increases when it is simply poured from a wide container into a taller, narrower container). Children appear to focus on one salient but misleading dimension – for example, the height of a container – forgoing a deeper conceptual analysis. Throughout the history of research on children's concepts, there have been many demonstrations that young children are "prone to accept things as they seem to be, in terms of their outer, perceptual, phenomenal, on-the-surface characteristics" (Flavell, 1977, p. 79).

However, as an account of what children are capable of doing, such developmental dichotomies as the "perceptual-to-conceptual shift" are inadequate (R. Gelman & Williams, 1998; Mandler, 2004). An over-arching theme of the past thirty years of research on cognitive development is that infants and young children are surprisingly skilled and competent. In contrast to the older view, concepts do not undergo qualitative change with age. *With appropriately sensitive tasks*, children can display abilities that do not appear in their everyday actions (R. Gelman & Baillargeon, 1983). Methodological advances have been important in this work, because behavioral limitations can so easily mask early knowledge. Difficulties with behavioral inhibition or executive functioning (Carlson & Moses, 2001; Welsh, Friedman, & Spieker, this volume; Zelazo, Muller, Frye, & Marcovitch, 2003) and cognitive flexibility (Deák, 2003) can stand in the way of optimal performance.

Non-obvious and non-concrete concepts

Some of the most well-known examples of early conceptual competence fall within the domains of numerical reasoning and theory of mind, which are already the focus of other chapters in this volume (see also Barr and Ginsburg, Cannon, Eisenband, & Pappas, this volume). Other prominent examples include early concepts in the physical domain (such as the object concept) and in the biological domain (such as animacy). For example, infants as young as 3½ months of age expect objects to exist even when they are out of sight (Baillargeon, 1993). Infants also distinguish animate from inanimate movements. In a series of studies, Woodward (1998) habituated 6- and 9-month-old infants to an event in which a hand and arm reached over the course of a directed path to grasp one of two toys. In the test events, the position of the two toys was reversed and infants witnessed the arm reach either along a different path for the same toy or along the same path for a different toy. During test, both age groups looked longer at the change-in-goal events than at the change-in-path events – thus, implicitly, categorizing as similar those two events for which the "actor" (i.e., the hand) had the same underlying goal, despite the fact that such events were physically dissimilar. Further support for this interpretation is that 6-month-olds responded differently when the appendage involved was not an animate hand and arm, but instead a mechanical claw. With regard to the mechanical limbs, infants looked longer at the events that depicted a path change than a goal change. In sum, infants selectively encode human action in line with more mature understandings of intentional or goal-directed action, and categorize events on this basis.

More generally, infants and young children form a range of concepts that are remarkably similar to those of adults. Before they have even begun to speak, infants form categories of faces, speech sounds, emotional expressions, colors, objects, animals, and mappings across modalities (see Rakison & Oakes, 2003, for review). These capacities belie the hypothesized "blooming, buzzing confusion" proposed by William James (1890/1983).

By preschool age, not only are children capable of forming varied and subtle concepts, they are also able to reason about concepts that are altogether non-obvious. These include: causality (Gopnik & Sobel, 2000); energy (Morris, Taplin, & Gelman, 2000; Shultz, 1982); internal bodily organs (R. Gelman, 1990; Gottfried & Gelman, 2005; Simons & Keil, 1995); contagion and contamination (Siegal & Peterson, 1999; Hejmadi, Rozin, & Siegal, 2004; Hirschfeld, 2002); goals and purpose (Kelemen, 2004; Opfer, 2002); inheritance (Springer, 1996); and mental entities such as thoughts and desires (Barr, this volume). For example, by preschool age, children quite accurately predict which tool can be used to obtain an out-of-reach goal, indicating that they can reason about intervening mechanisms (Bullock, Gelman, & Baillargeon, 1982). They understand that a pig and a horse are more alike on the inside, even though a pig and a piggybank look more alike on the outside (S. A. Gelman & Wellman, 1991). They realize that a glass of milk behind an orange filter *really is* milk even though it *looks like* orange juice (Flavell, Flavell, & Green, 1983). They know that people *want* and *know* things, and that common objects were designed *for* a purpose (Kelemen, 2004).

Although for most of these topics preschool children have very little in the way of detailed, concrete knowledge, they have begun to appreciate that these non-obvious constructs exist and how they affect other, more observable outcomes and behaviors. For example, even 3-year-olds have a core understanding that "germs" can cause illness, even when a food or object looks clean (Kalish, 1996). It is intriguing that children are capable of this understanding at an age when they have not yet learned anything about the mechanisms by which viruses and bacteria affect human physiology (Au & Romo, 1999). That preschool children are open to reasoning about these topics and that they do so with considerable accuracy, despite an impoverished knowledge base, argues strongly that non-obvious entities are not beyond their capacity. Young children's concepts do not seem to depend on concrete, perceptually apparent properties.

Concepts as the basis for inferences

What is perhaps most impressive is that, in addition to forming concepts, young children use their concepts in the service of gaining further knowledge and interpreting experience. One way this can be seen most clearly is with children's category-based inductive inferences. Induction involves reasoning beyond what one can know with certainty, and can be contrasted with deduction, which involves logical inferences that are assured. For example, if someone is told that all dogs have leukocytes inside them, then inferring that a particular dog has leukocytes inside it would be a deduction. However, if someone is told that one particular dog has leukocytes inside it, then inferring that a different dog has leukocytes inside it would be an induction. Both children and adults use categories to extend knowledge in their inductive inferences (Carey, 1985; S. A. Gelman & Markman, 1986). For example, 14-month-old infants' inductive inferences are guided by the theoretically significant distinction between animate and inanimate, so that an action such as placing a key on an entity is restricted to inanimates, whereas giving an entity something to drink is restricted to animates (Mandler & McDonough, 1996, 1998; see Mandler, 2004, and Rakison & Poulin-Dubois, 2001, for extended discussion of this and related work).

In addition to the inductive potential of the animate/inanimate distinction, concepts encoded in basic-level words (e.g., dog, dinosaur) also have enormous inductive potential. In a sense, we might wish to say that each basic-level kind functions as a mini-theory or Kuhnian paradigm: "object[s] for further articulation and specification under new or more stringent conditions" (Kuhn, 1970, p. 23). Years ago, S. A. Gelman and Markman (1986) demonstrated that categories have an inductive function even for preschool children, that is, they have the potential to generate novel inferences. For example, children are more likely to generalize a newly learned property from a brontosaurus to a triceratops (both "dinosaurs," though radically different in appearance) than from a rhinoceros to a triceratops (highly similar in appearance, though different kinds). These findings have been replicated and extended in intriguing ways to categories of different hierarchical levels (e.g., Waxman, Lynch, Casey, & Baer, 1997) and to categories in the social domain (Heyman & Gelman, 2000a, 2000b; Hirschfeld, 1996). These findings have also been extended downward in age to young 2-year-olds (Jaswal & Markman, 2002) and even 13-month-olds (using appropriately simpler items and methods; Welder & Graham, 2001).

Thus, children do not assume that labels are mere conveniences – ways of efficiently referring to perceptually encountered information in a short-hand way. Instead, they expect certain labels – and the categories to which they refer – to capture properties well beyond those they have already encountered. A variety of control studies showed that these effects were not simply a response bias due to hearing the same word for the two category members (see S. A. Gelman, 2003, for review). For example, children do not base inferences consistently on novel labels, nor do they generalize accidental properties, such as an animal's age, on the basis of category membership.

Concepts and causal reasoning

Another way in which concepts extend knowledge is by encouraging causal reasoning. Barrett, Abdi, Murphy, and Gallagher (1993) note that "Concept learning involves more than simply keeping a running tally of which features are associated with which concept" (p. 1612), and present data suggesting that children's intuitive theories help determine which properties and which feature correlations children attend to in their classifications. For example, when asked to categorize novel birds into one of two categories, elementary-school children noticed correlations that were supported by causal links, and used such correlations to categorize new members (e.g., correlation between brain size and memory). The children did not make use of features that correlated equally well but were unsupported by a theory (e.g., the correlation between structure of heart and shape of beak). Krascum and Andrew (1998) likewise found beneficial effects of causal information on category learning in children as young as 4 and 5 years of age. As the authors note, "the meaningfulness of individual features is not a significant factor in children's category learning, and instead, what is important is that attributes within a category can be linked in a theory-coherent manner" (p. 343).

Recent evidence from Gopnik and Sobel (2000; Schulz & Gopnik, 2004) extends the effect to even younger children. In their studies, 2-, 3-, and 4-year-olds learned that a novel object with a novel name (e.g., "a blicket") had a certain causal power (i.e., placing the object on a machine would [apparently] cause the machine to light up and play music). Results indicate that even 2-year-olds use causal information to guide both naming and induction. Importantly, they do so more than in a control condition, in which the blicket is *associated* with the machine setting off, but appears *not* to cause it. Thus, correlational information alone did not determine children's naming.

Ahn (1998) formulated a specific version of the causal hypothesis that she termed the "causal status hypothesis," in which causal features are more central than effect features. Thus, even given equal frequency, cause and effect features will be weighted differently. This is a particularly intriguing claim in that both cause and effect features participate in causal relations. Intuitive examples of adult categorization support such a claim. For example, illnesses are often categorized by the virus that causes the symptoms of that illness rather than by the symptoms alone. When the causal status of features is manipulated experimentally, adults weighted the identical feature more heavily when it served as a cause than when it served as an effect. Of particular interest to the present context, Ahn, Gelman, Amsterlaw, Hohenstein, and Kalish (2000) found evidence for the causal status effect in children 7–9 years of age. Children learned descriptions of novel animals, in which one feature caused two other features. When asked to determine which test item was more likely to be an example of the animal they had learned, children preferred an animal with a cause feature and an effect feature rather than an animal with two effect features.

Although induction and causal reasoning can be viewed as positive because they allow children to expand their knowledge base, they also pose some problems for young children when they draw inappropriately broad inferences. One problem that results is stereotyping. Preschoolers often treat social categories as if they were biological categories, assuming, for example, that members of a social category (a category that is based on gender or race) will be alike with respect to ability or occupation (Hirschfeld 1996; Taylor 1996). A second problem is that young children at times ignore relevant information about statistical variation within a category (Gutheil & Gelman, 1997; López, Gelman, Gutheil, & Smith, 1992). For example, 4-year-olds do not seem to realize that a property known to be true of five birds provides a firmer basis of induction than a property known to be true of only one bird. They also do not seem to realize that variability in a category is relevant to the kinds of inductions that are plausible (Heit & Hahn, 2001; Lo, Sides, Rozelle, Osherson, & Viale, 2002).

Summary and open questions

In sum, this section illustrates several important points: concepts are used by children and adults to extend known information to previously unknown cases through both inductive inference and causal reasoning. Such processes are not based on perceptual similarity alone. Naming is an important vehicle for conveying category membership and thus guiding induction. Thus, this function is a highly useful tool available to children by at least preschool age. Despite children's ability to use categories for induction, even in the preschool years, they do not always appropriately constrain these inferences.

How to interpret such capacities is still a matter of hot debate. At least three positions have been argued at length: innate modules, general induction, and domain-specific naïve theories (see Wellman & Gelman, 1998). The innate modularity view suggests that certain conceptual distinctions are innate, biologically mandated, with highly fixed and constrained outcomes. On this view, children are like little adults, with relatively little conceptual change over time. In contrast, the general induction view suggests that knowledge arises rather passively out of children's environmental inputs and experiences, that variability in outcome is quite high, and that domain-general capacities (such as frequency of experiencing words, percepts, and concepts in association) are the means by which conceptual change takes place. On this view, children are like universal novices, lacking in experience most of all. Finally, the theory view is a constructivist approach. The theory view suggests that children construct their understandings by trying to understand the causal/explanatory links among pieces of knowledge, starting out with broad skeletal principles that set broad constraints on children's knowledge but allowing for variability within these constraints. On this view, children are distinctly different from adults, with understandings that will undergo qualitative conceptual change over time.

The distinction among these three explanatory frameworks can be illustrated with the concept of animacy. How can we characterize the knowledge young children have about the distinction between animals and inanimate objects? Nativists point out that the animacy concept arises early in infancy (Rakison & Poulin-Dubois, 2001), appears to have neurophysiological substrates (Caramazza & Shelton, 1998), and is cross-culturally uniform (Atran, 1999). Empiricists note that the animacy distinction is richly reflected in perceptual cues and the language input children receive (Smith, Colunga, & Yoshida, 2003), that its boundaries are cross-culturally variable (Imai & Gentner, 1997; Yoshida & Smith, 2003), and that it undergoes important developmental changes (Rakison & Poulin-Dubois, 2001; Sloutsky & Fisher, 2004). Theory theorists note that perceptual cues to animacy are ambiguous (Mandler, 2004), that animacy is cued by theory-based inferences (Booth & Waxman, 2002), and that animacy is central to a broad array of more complex understandings, including causal interpretations of action (Spelke, Phillips, & Woodward, 1995), attributions of mental states (Baron-Cohen, 1995), and attributions of biological processes (Carey, 1985).

There may be no need to choose among these three theoretical positions. Elements of each are likely to have merit. There appear to be at least some innate constraints on the sorts of concepts young children find "natural" and easy to learn. Moreover, domain-general, low-level processes of association appear to be quite powerful for children and adults (see Saffran, Aslin, & Newport, 1996). However, children also display evidence for an early tendency to dig deeper in their conceptions, attempting to make causal links among their pieces of knowledge, and building domain-specific knowledge structures that one might wish to call "theories." (For further debate of these issues, see Gelman, 2003; Rakison & Oakes, 2003; Smith, 2000.)

Role of Experience

The standard image of conceptual learning, thanks in large part to Piaget, is that of the solitary child engaged in acts of *self*-discovery. Everyday interactions with the world afford opportunities to test hypotheses and come to new understandings. When a 1-year-old observes her own reflection in the mirror, this is hypothesized to lead to discoveries about the self. When a 4-year-old counts pebbles in the garden, this is hypothesized to lead to discoveries of mathematical transitivity. (It is also important to acknowledge, however, the cultural and material backdrop that permits these events to occur in the first place, including mirrors and a conventionalized counting system; see Rogoff, 2003.)

Why has this "solitary thinker" model of development had such a tight hold on the field of cognitive developmental research? In part, one is struck by children's seeming resistance to input. Time and again, young children seem to have difficulty grasping concepts that are straightforward to an older child. In one classic example, 4-year-olds in Piaget's conservation task report that liquid poured from a short, wide beaker into a tall, thin beaker increases in amount. In a more recent example, children are shown a container with unexpected contents, such as a crayon box that (unexpectedly) is revealed to contain a toy truck (Perner, Leekam, & Wimmer, 1987). Although 5-year-olds readily predict that someone who hasn't seen the box before will expect it to contain crayons, 3-year-olds predict that someone who hasn't seen the box before will expect it to contain a toy truck

– in other words, they have trouble understanding that someone else's perspective will differ from their own (Barr, this volume). A focus on self-discovery also reflects the apparent similarities across individual children. Two-year-olds generally do think and act in ways that differ from 6-year-olds, across a wide range of individuals and cultures. The basic insight that still holds, therefore, is that conceptual development is an active process. The child is most certainly not a passive receptacle.

More recently, however, there is a growing recognition that conceptual development is not so solitary a process, after all. This recognition follows from several lines of research demonstrating the role of early experiences in children's concepts and knowledge organization. I focus here on illustrative examples in two areas: childhood expertise and the role of language input.

Childhood expertise

Specialized knowledge can exert surprisingly powerful effects on cognition (Wellman & Gelman, 1998). Over 30 years ago, Chase and Simon (1973) found that chess experts have superior memory for the position of pieces on a chessboard, although they are no better than non-experts in their memory for digits. Soon afterward, Chi (1978) demonstrated the same phenomenon in children: child chess experts even outperform adult chess novices, which is an interesting reversal of the more usual developmental finding. In these examples, experts are not in general more intelligent or more skilled than novices. The effects are localized within the domain of expertise. Regarding concept development, too, the child's level of sophistication varies markedly by content area. In a set of classic demonstrations, Chi and her colleagues found that preschool dinosaur experts not only had a larger set of facts at their disposal, but also organized this knowledge into a more cohesive hierarchical network of knowledge that permitted inductive inferences (Chi, Hutchinson, & Robin, 1989; Chi & Koeske, 1983; Gobbo & Chi, 1986; see also Lavin, Gelman, & Galotti, 2001, for related findings with child Pokémon experts).

A particularly impressive example of the benefits of expertise can be found in Mervis, Pani, and Pani (2003), who report a detailed case study of a child bird expert between 10 and 23 months of age. This child had acquired thirty-eight labels for types of birds, organized them into appropriate hierarchical organization, and recognized the principle that baby animals must be the same species as their parents, even if they look like something else. Child experts also experience many other cognitive advantages in memory organization and problem solving (Chi et al., 1989; Gobbo & Chi, 1986). In the domain of theory of mind, children who have greater opportunity to engage in thinking about mental states develop more rapidly (Perner, Ruffman, & Leekam, 1994; Peterson & Slaughter, 2003).

The study of childhood experts demonstrates that environmental inputs can yield variation in children's concepts. However, this work does not separate out the difficult question of cause: are childhood experts' concepts the way they are *because* of the enriched input, or do children seek out enriched input because of other factors (e.g., individual differences in intelligence or personality)? Clearly a child cannot become an expert without the relevant inputs, but we cannot be sure that the input *per se* is sufficient to yield conceptual growth. Detailed studies of the input and its effects are therefore also critical.

Language input

The language that children hear from others is a promising arena for examining input effects on children's concepts. The field of cognitive development has demonstrated children's early and keen sensitivity to subtleties of language, and their effects on categorization (Bloom, 2000; Bowerman & Choi, 2001; Bowerman & Levinson, 2001; Gentner & Goldin-Meadow, 2003; Gopnik, Choi, & Baumberger, 1996; Hall & Waxman, 1993; Imai & Gentner, 1997; Waxman, 1999). Moreover, in the field of linguistic anthropology, language is recognized as a powerful socializing influence (Ochs & Schieffelin, 1984). It is one of the most ubiquitous, early-acquired, and powerful forms of cultural transmission available to our species. From this perspective, it would be surprising if the language that parents use did not have an effect.

In recent years, a range of scholars have been studying the role of language in conceptual development (Bowerman & Levinson, 2001; Gentner & Goldin-Meadow, 2003; Yoshida & Smith, 2003). Although concepts do not *require* a conventional language system (Baillargeon, 2004; Tomasello, Call, & Hare, 2003; see also Goldin-Meadow, this volume), language may play an organizing role in both language-universal and language-specific ways.

One of the ways in which language may influence conceptual development is by means of words, which provide a placeholder or "invitation" for children to form a concept (Waxman & Markow, 1995). Words for "basic-level" categories (at a middle level of abstraction, such as "dog" rather than "vertebrate" or "Border collie") appear to have a special function for children as early as 9 months of age. Waxman and Markow (1995) refer to count nouns as "invitations" to form categories and look for relevant conceptual correlates (Xu, 2002, 2003, 2005): common labels lead children to search for commonalities; distinct labels lead children to search for differences. For example, when hearing two items labeled with a word, even 9-month-olds are more likely to attend to relevant categorical similarities (Balaban & Waxman, 1997). They expect certain labels – and the categories to which they refer – to capture properties well beyond those they have already encountered.

Recently several researchers have proposed that children may honor a *division of labor* in their use of words and concepts. That is, children seem to appreciate that many of their concepts are incomplete, and need to be supplemented by the knowledge of experts (Danovitch & Keil, 2004; Lutz & Keil, 2002; Markman & Jaswal, 2003; see also Coley, Medin, Proffitt, Lynch, & Atran, 1999, for an important distinction between knowledge and expectations). A striking example is the fact noted earlier, that children readily accept experimenter-provided labels, even when such labels are surprising and counter-intuitive (Graham, Kilbreath, & Welder, 2004). This can be considered a division of labor, in that children rely on the knowledge of adults in their acceptance of a label that extends beyond the child's own knowledge base. In a detailed case study, Mervis et al. (2003) provide the example of a child who deferred to adults in the matter of naming, a process they refer to as the "authority principle," which seemed in place by about 20 months of age in the child under study (Ari). For example, when Ari's father said, "That birdie's a cardinal," Ari accepted that it was a subtype of bird, not a synonym for bird (p. 265).

It is also important to point out that the effects of language on concepts may be subtle and implicit, rather than resulting from explicit instruction. For example, when talking to children about animal categories, mothers rarely explain precisely how or why it is that certain classifications contrast with perceptual similarity (e.g., why an eel is not a snake; S. A. Gelman, Coley, Rosengren, Hartman, & Pappas, 1998). Instead, they suggest by indirection, using labeling routines (e.g., "This is an eel, not a snake") and generalizing statements suggesting that a category is coherent (e.g., "Eels live in water").

The contrast between explicit versus implicit talk may have implications for data and arguments that parents play a minimal role for the socialization of certain concepts (such as gender [Maccoby, 1998] or race [Hirschfeld, 1996]). For example, Lytton and Romney (1991) conducted a meta-analysis of 172 studies, and found that most studies of parent socializing effects find non-significant and very small effect sizes. However, gender social-izing may exist in subtle aspects of language that would not have been measured in past research. For example, we have examined mother–child conversations about gender, with children 2½, 4½, and 6½ years of age (S. A. Gelman, Taylor, & Nguyen, 2004). Although mothers in this middle-class sample rarely expressed gender stereotypes directly, they emphasized gender concepts indirectly, by referring to gender categories ("You think most girls don't like trucks?"), providing gender labels ("That's a girl"), contrasting males and females ("Is that a girl job or a boy job?"), and giving approval to their children's stereo-typed statements.

Such uses of language would presumably be universal, as all languages encode concepts in nouns (though the particular contents and linguistic structures vary). More work is needed, however, to determine how universal properties of language (such as lexicaliza-tion) can influence the kinds of concepts children acquire.

Additionally, there has recently been in some sense a return to the Sapir–Whorf hypothesis: the notion that different languages are organized in substantially different ways, with corresponding effects on conceptual structure (Hill & Mannheim, 1992). For example, compare a language (such as English) that obliges speakers to mark whether they are talking about one object or multiple objects (plurality) with a language (such as Mandarin Chinese) that does not provide any marking on the noun to distinguish between singular and plural (e.g., "doll" and "dolls" are expressed with the same word). We might therefore predict greater sensitivity to singular–plural differences in English than in Mandarin.

One finding is that speakers of different languages seem to notice different aspects of experience, and to draw conceptual boundaries differently from one another. For example, Lucy (1996; Lucy & Gaskins, 2003) studied speakers of Yucatec Mayan, who use a classifier system such that different-shaped things can receive the same name but with a different classifier attached. In Yucatec, the words for banana, banana leaf, and banana tree are all the same root word, varying only in the classifier. This pattern con-trasts with the English system of naming, for which shape is a fairly good predictor of how a count noun is used (e.g., bananas are all crescent-shaped; trees are all roughly a certain shape; and so on). Correspondingly, when asked to group objects on the basis of either shape or substance in a non-linguistic sorting task, English speakers are more likely to use shape whereas Yucatec Mayan speakers are more likely to use substance. Surprisingly, however, this differentiation does not appear until somewhere between 7 and 9 years of age, suggesting that perhaps metalinguistic awareness is partly responsible for the effect.

Other examples of language influences on children's concepts can be found in the work of Imai and Gentner (1997) and Yoshida and Smith (2003), both of whom find that Japanese-speaking children and adults draw the boundary between objects and substances differently than English-speaking children. Whereas both English and Japanese speakers agree that a complex object (such as a clock) is an individual and a continuous boundless mass (such as milk) is a substance, they differ when it comes to simple objects. A molded piece of plastic, for example, would be an object for the English speaker but a substance for the Japanese speaker.

Another line of work that demonstrates the importance of environment-specific cues (in contrast to universal innate concepts) comes from studying the acquisition of spatial concepts. Different languages organize the spatial domain quite differently. For example, whereas English distinguishes containment (*in*) versus support (*on*) relations, Korean distinguishes loose-fitting containment (*nehta*) versus tight-fitting containment (*kkita*). The relevant developmental evidence is that children, from their earliest word productions, use spatial language in a manner that conforms to the system presented by their language (Bowerman & Choi, 2003). Thus, English-speaking children and Korean-speaking children use spatial terms in cross-cutting ways, thereby apparently demonstrating contrasting conceptual frameworks. These data suggest that concepts that were once thought to be innate (e.g., in, on) turn out to be language-specific, thereby arguing against there being a small set of universal primitives – at least in this domain. And children from their earliest word learning acquire the spatial concepts provided by their language, not the spatial concepts provided by some universal conceptual set.

Spelke (2003) has recently argued that language may promote more far-reaching changes than those discussed above. She notes that innate concepts in humans are highly similar and overlapping with innate concepts in a range of other species. For example, object constancy and number tracking are found in human infants *and* in non-human animals. What seems to distinguish humans from non-human species is the ease with which we combine concepts across domains. For example, in navigating space we can combine geometric concepts (e.g., "to the left") with non-geometric concepts (e.g., "blue") to arrive at novel combinations ("to the left of the blue wall"). Strikingly, preverbal infants and non-human animals seem to lack the ability to construct such cross-domain concepts. When faced with a task that requires this sort of conceptual combination, only language-using humans can solve it. In further studies, Spelke has found that manipulating the use of language (either training children on a new linguistic expression, or preventing internal or external use of language in adults) directly affects a person's capacity to use these combinations. She uses this same model to explain conceptual change in the realm of number. Language provides only a limited degree of flexibility, however, as the constituent concepts of a linguistically mediated combination must be initially established within an innate module.

Summary

What do we conclude about the role of experience in early concepts? On the one hand, it has been overlooked in much of the past literature, and clearly is in need of more serious attention. I have provided a selective glimpse into the issue, reviewing some important results regarding expertise and language. Childhood expertise demonstrates the potential that intense and targeted experiences can have on a child's conceptual system. Studies of language effects demonstrate both language-universal and language-specific respects in which children's concepts are responsive to the language children are hearing.

On the other hand, it is important not to overstate the importance of environmental inputs on the rate of true conceptual change. Inflated claims of "easy fixes" to conceptual development fly in the face of scientific evidence (e.g., listening to Mozart has at best minimal and short-term effects on problem solving in adults; Jones & Zigler, 2002). Relatedly, it is important not to confuse *structured* activities with *instructional* activities. Children can and do learn enormously from non-structured, everyday interactions that include hearing a rich and varied vocabulary (e.g., Hart & Risley, 1995; Huttenlocher, Vasilyeva, & Cymerman, 2002), sharing in a parent's passion for bird-watching, or even playing Pokémon.

Conclusions

Three key themes have emerged from this overview of recent research on young children's concepts:

Theme 1. Concepts are tools and as such have powerful implications for children's reasoning – both positive and negative. We have focused primarily on positive effects, including children's use of concepts to expand knowledge by means of inductive inferences and causal reasoning. At the same time, it is important to keep in mind that concepts can have negative effects, including stereotyping of social categories (e.g., gender, race, and personal characteristics such as aggression or intelligence). The positive and negative implications of concepts are intertwined and present from earliest uses.

Theme 2. Children's early concepts are not necessarily concrete or perceptually based. Even preschool children are capable of reasoning about non-obvious, subtle, and abstract concepts. In contrast to the view that children rely on concrete, perceptually obvious features for categorizing their world, non-obvious properties are surprisingly salient in young children's categories. In part this can be seen in children's attention to function and causality; in part this can be seen in children's early-emerging conceptions of "germs" and other non-visible entities. Regardless, these findings undermine traditional views of development. The broader implication is that knowledge is not always built up out of the accretion of specific details or concrete observations, but can also arise from general expectations.

Theme 3. Children's concepts are not uniform across content areas, across individuals, across tasks, or across cultures. Although many prominent past theories have posited universalist claims about development, these appear to gloss over important variation that must be considered. A corollary to this conclusion is that experiences – both early and later experiences – are important to children's developing concepts.

Note

Writing of this chapter was supported by NICHD grant HD36043 to the author.

References

Ahn, W. (1998). The role of causal status in determining feature centrality. *Cognition, 69*, 135–178.

Ahn, W., Gelman, S. A., Amsterlaw, J. A., Hohenstein, J., & Kalish, C. W. (2000). Causal status effect in children's categorization. *Cognition, 76*, B35–B43.

Atran, S. (1999). Itzaj Maya folk-biological taxonomy. In D. Medin & S. Atran (Eds.), *Folkbiology.* Cambridge, MA: MIT Press.

Au, T. K., & Romo, L. F. (1999). Mechanical causality in children's "folkbiology". In D. L. Medin & S. Atran (Eds.), *Folkbiology* (pp. 355–401). Cambridge, MA: MIT Press.

Baillargeon, R. (1993). The object concept revisited: New direction in the investigation of infants' physical knowledge. In C. Granrud (Ed.), *Visual perception and cognition in infancy* (pp. 265–315). Hillsdale, NJ: Erlbaum.

Baillargeon, R. (2004). Infants' physical world. *Current Directions in Psychological Science, 13*, 89–94.

Balaban, M. T., & Waxman, S. R. (1997). Do words facilitate object categorization in 9-month-old infants? *Journal of Experimental Child Psychology, 64*, 3–26.

Baron-Cohen, S. (1995). *Mindblindness: An essay on autism and theory of mind.* Cambridge, MA: MIT Press.

Barrett, S. E., Abdi, H., Murphy, G. L., & Gallagher, J. M. (1993). Theory based correlations and their role in children's concepts. *Child Development, 64*, 1595–1616.

Bloom, P. (2000). *How children learn the meanings of words.* Cambridge, MA: MIT Press.

Booth, A. E., & Waxman, S. R. (2002). Word learning is "smart": Evidence that conceptual information affects preschoolers' extension of novel words. *Cognition, 84*, B11–B22.

Bowerman, M., & Choi, S. (2001). Shaping meanings for language: Universal and language-specific in the acquisition of spatial semantic categories. In M. Bowerman & S. C. Levinson (Eds.), *Language acquisition and conceptual development* (pp. 475–511). Cambridge: Cambridge University Press.

Bowerman, M., & Choi, S. (2003). Space under construction: Language-specific spatial categorization in first language acquisition. In D. Gentner & S. Goldin-Meadow (Eds.), *Language in mind: Advances in the study of language and thought* (pp. 389–427). Cambridge, MA: MIT Press.

Bowerman, M., & Levinson, S. C. (Eds.). (2001). *Language acquisition and conceptual development.* New York: Cambridge University Press.

Bruner, J. S., Olver, R. R., Greenfield, P. M., et al. (1966). *Studies in cognitive growth.* New York: John Wiley.

Bullock, M., Gelman, R., & Baillargeon, R. (1982). The development of causal reasoning. In W. J. Friedman (Ed.), *Development of time concepts* (pp. 209–253). New York: Academic Press.

Caramazza, A., & Shelton, J. R. (1998). Domain-specific knowledge systems in the brain: The animate–inanimate distinction. *Journal of Cognitive Neuroscience, 10,* 1–34.

Carey, S. (1985). *Conceptual development in childhood.* Cambridge, MA: MIT Press.

Carlson, S., & Moses, L. J. (2001). Individual differences in inhibitory control and children's theory of mind. *Child Development, 72,* 1032–1053.

Chase, W. G., & Simon, H. A. (1973). The mind's eye in chess. In W. G. Chase (Ed.), *Visual information processing* (pp. 215–281). New York: Academic Press.

Chi, M. T. H. (1978). Knowledge structures and memory development. In R. Siegler (Ed.), *Children's thinking: What develops?* (pp. 73–96). Hillsdale, NJ: Erlbaum.

Chi, M. T. H., Hutchinson, J. E., & Robin, A. F. (1989). How inferences about novel domain-related concepts can be constrained by structured knowledge. *Merrill-Palmer Quarterly, 35,* 27–62.

Chi, M. T. H., & Koeske, R. (1983). Network representation of a child's dinosaur knowledge. *Developmental Psychology, 19,* 29–39.

Coley, J. D., Medin, D. L., Proffitt, J. B., Lynch, E., & Atran, S. (1999). Inductive reasoning in folkbiological thought. In D. L. Medin & S. Atran (Eds.), *Folkbiology* (pp. 205–232). Cambridge, MA: MIT Press.

Danovitch, J. H., & Keil, F. C. (2004). Should you ask a fisherman or a biologist? Developmental shifts in ways of clustering knowledge. *Child Development, 75,* 918–931.

Deák, G. O. (2003). The development of cognitive flexibility and language abilities. In R. Kail (Ed.), *Advances in child development and behavior* (Vol. 31, pp. 271–327). San Diego: Academic Press.

Flavell, J. H. (1977). *Cognitive development.* Englewood Cliffs, NJ: Prentice Hall.

Flavell, J. H., Flavell, E. R., & Green, F. L. (1983). Development of the appearance–reality distinction. *Cognitive Psychology, 15,* 95–120.

Gelman, R. (1990). First principles organize attention to and learning about relevant data: Number and the animate–inanimate distinction as examples. *Cognitive Science, 14,* 79–106.

Gelman, R., & Baillargeon, R. (1983). A review of some Piagetian concepts. In J. H. Flavell & E. Markman (Eds.), *Cognitive development: Vol. 3. Handbook of child development* (pp. 167–230). New York: Wiley.

Gelman, R., & Williams, E. (1998). Enabling constraints for cognitive development and learning: Domain specificity and epigenesis. In D. Kuhn & R. Siegler (Eds.), *Handbook of child psychology: Vol. 2. Cognition, perception and language* (5th ed., pp. 575–630). New York: John Wiley.

Gelman, S. A. (2003). *The essential child: Origins of essentialism in everyday thought.* New York: Oxford University Press.

Gelman, S. A., Coley, J. D., Rosengren, K., Hartman, E., & Pappas, T. (1998). Beyond labeling: The role of parental input in the acquisition of richly-structured categories. *Monographs of the Society for Research in Child Development, 63*(1, Serial No. 253).

Gelman, S. A., & Markman, E. M. (1986). Categories and induction in young children. *Cognition, 23,* 183–209.

Gelman, S. A., Taylor, M. G., & Nguyen, S. (2004). Mother–child conversations about gender: Understanding the acquisition of essentialist beliefs. *Monographs of the Society for Research in Child Development, 69*(1, Serial No. 275).

Gelman, S. A., & Wellman, H. M. (1991). Insides and essences: Early understandings of the nonobvious. *Cognition, 38,* 213–244.

Gentner, D., & Goldin-Meadow, S. (Eds.). (2003). *Language in mind: Advances in the study of language and thought.* Cambridge, MA: MIT Press.

Gobbo, C., & Chi, M. (1986). How knowledge is structured and used by expert and novice children. *Cognitive Development, 1,* 221–237.

Gopnik, A., Choi, S., & Baumberger, T. (1996). Cross-linguistic differences in semantic and cognitive development. *Cognitive Development, 11*, 197–227.

Gopnik, A., & Sobel, D. M. (2000). Detecting blickets: How young children use information about novel causal powers in categorization and induction. *Child Development, 71*, 1205–1222.

Gottfried, G. M., & Gelman, S. A. (2005). Developing domain-specific causal-explanatory frameworks: The role of insides and immanence. *Cognitive Development, 20*, 137–158.

Graham, S. A., Kilbreath, C. S., & Welder, A. N. (2004). Thirteen-month-olds rely on shared labels and shape similarity for inductive inferences. *Child Development, 75*, 409–427.

Gutheil, G., & Gelman, S. A. (1997). Children's use of sample size and diversity information within basic-level categories. *Journal of Experimental Child Psychology, 64*, 159–174.

Hall, D. G., & Waxman, S. R. (1993). Assumptions about word meaning: Individual and basic-level kinds. *Child Development, 64*, 1550–1570.

Hart, B., & Risley, T. (1995). *Meaningful differences in everyday parenting and intellectual development in young American children.* Baltimore: Brookes.

Heit, E., & Hahn, U. (2001). Diversity-based reasoning in children. *Cognitive Psychology, 43*, 243–273.

Hejmadi, A., Rozin, P., & Siegal, M. (2004). Once in contact, always in contact: Contagious essence and conceptions of purification in American and Hindu Indian children. *Developmental Psychology, 40*, 467–476.

Heyman, G. D., & Gelman, S. A. (2000a). Preschool children's use of novel attributes to make inductive inferences about people. *Cognitive Development, 15*, 263–280.

Heyman, G. D., & Gelman, S. A. (2000b). Preschool children's use of traits labels to make inductive inferences about people. *Journal of Experimental Child Psychology, 77*, 1–19.

Hill, J. H., & Mannheim, B. (1992). Language and world view. *Annual Review of Anthropology, 21*, 381–406.

Hirschfeld, L. A. (1996). *Race in the making: Cognition, culture, and the child's construction of human kinds.* Cambridge, MA: MIT Press.

Hirschfeld, L. A. (2002). Why don't anthropologists like children? *American Anthropologist, 104*, 611–627.

Huttenlocher, J., Vasilyeva, M., & Cymerman, E. (2002). Language input and child syntax. *Cognitive Psychology, 45*, 337–374.

Imai, M., & Gentner, D. (1997). A cross-linguistic study of early word meaning: Universal ontology and linguistic influence. *Cognition, 62*, 169–200.

James, W. (1983). *The principles of psychology.* Cambridge, MA: Harvard University Press. (Original work published 1890)

Jaswal, V. K., & Markman, E. M. (2002). Children's acceptance and use of unexpected category labels to draw non-obvious inferences. In W. Gray & C. Schunn (Eds.), *Proceedings of the twenty-fourth annual conference of the Cognitive Science Society* (pp. 500–505). Hillsdale, NJ: Erlbaum.

Jones, S. M., & Zigler, E. (2002). The Mozart effect: Not learning from history. *Journal of Applied Developmental Psychology, 23*, 355–372.

Kalish, C. W. (1996). Preschoolers' understanding of germs as invisible mechanisms. *Cognitive Development, 11*, 83–106.

Kelemen, D. (2004). Are children "intuitive theists"? Reasoning about purpose and design in nature. *Psychological Science, 15*, 295–301.

Krascum, R. M., & Andrews, S. (1998). The effects of theories on children's acquisition of family-resemblance categories. *Child Development, 69*, 333–346.

Kuhn, T. S. (1970). *The structure of scientific revolutions* (2nd ed.). Chicago: University of Chicago Press.

Lavin, B., Gelman, R., & Galotti, K. (2001, June). *When children are the experts and adults the novices: The case of Pokémon*. Poster presented at the American Psychological Society.

Lo, Y., Sides, A., Rozelle, J., Osherson, D., & Viale, R. (2002). Evidential diversity and premise probability in young children's inductive judgment. *Cognitive Science, 26*, 181–206.

López, A., Gelman, S. A., Gutheil, G., & Smith, E. E. (1992). The development of category-based induction. *Child Development, 63*, 1070–1090.

Lucy, J. A. (1996). *Grammatical categories and cognition*. New York: Cambridge University Press.

Lucy, J. A., & Gaskins, S. (2003). Interaction of language type and referent type in the development of nonverbal classification preferences. In D. Gentner & S. Goldin-Meadow (Eds.), *Language in mind: Advances in the study of language and thought* (pp. 465–492). Cambridge, MA: MIT Press.

Lutz, D. J., & Keil, F. C. (2002). Early understanding of the division of cognitive labor. *Child Development, 73*, 1073–1084.

Lytton, H., & Romney, D. M. (1991). Parents' differential socialization of boys and girls: A meta-analysis. *Psychological Bulletin, 109*, 267–296.

Maccoby, E. E. (1998). *The two sexes: Growing up apart, coming together*. Cambridge, MA: Belknap/Harvard.

Mandler, J. M. (2004). *The foundations of mind*. New York: Oxford University Press.

Mandler, J. M., & McDonough. L. (1996). Drinking and driving don't mix: Inductive generalization in infancy. *Cognition, 59*, 307–335.

Mandler, J. M., & McDonough, L. (1998). Studies in inductive inference in infancy. *Cognitive Psychology, 37*, 60–96.

Markman, E. M., & Jaswal, V. K. (2003). Commentary on Part II: Abilities and assumptions underlying conceptual development. In D. H. Rakison & L. M. Oakes (Eds.), *Early category and concept development: Making sense of the blooming, buzzing confusion* (pp. 384–402). New York: Oxford University Press.

Mervis, C. B., Pani, J. R., & Pani, A. M. (2003). Transaction of child cognitive-linguistic abilities and adult input in the acquisition of lexical categories at the basic and subordinate levels. In D. H. Rakison & L. M. Oakes (Eds.), *Early category and concept development: Making sense of the blooming, buzzing confusion* (pp. 242–274). New York: Oxford University Press.

Morris, S. C., Taplin, J. E., & Gelman, S. A. (2000). Vitalism in naïve biological thinking. *Developmental Psychology, 36*, 582–595.

Ochs, E., & Schieffelin, B. (1984). Language acquisition and socialization: Three developmental stories. In R. Shweder & R. LeVine (Eds.), *Culture theory: Mind, self, and emotion* (pp. 276–320). Cambridge: Cambridge University Press.

Opfer, J. E. (2002). Identifying living and sentient kinds from dynamic information: The case of goal-directed versus aimless autonomous movement in conceptual change. *Cognition, 86*, 97–122.

Perner, J., Leekam, S. R., & Wimmer, H. (1987). Three-year-olds' difficulty with false belief: The case for a conceptual deficit. *British Journal of Developmental Psychology, 5*, 125–137.

Perner, J., Ruffman, T., & Leekam, S. R. (1994). Theory of mind is contagious: You catch it from your sibs. *Child Development, 65*, 1228–1238.

Peterson, C., & Slaughter, V. (2003). Opening windows into the mind: Mothers' preferences for mental state explanations and children's theory of mind. *Cognitive Development, 18*, 399–429.

Piaget, J. (1951). *Play, dreams, and imitation in childhood*. New York: Norton.

Quine, W. V. O. (1977). Natural kinds. In S. P. Schwartz (Ed.), *Naming, necessity, and natural kinds* (pp. 155–175). Ithaca, NY: Cornell University Press.

Rakison, D. H., & Oakes, L. M. (Eds.). (2003). *Early category and concept development: Making sense of the blooming, buzzing confusion*. New York: Oxford University Press.

Rakison, D. H., & Poulin-Dubois, D. (2001). The developmental origin of the animate–inanimate distinction. *Psychological Bulletin, 2*, 209–228.

Rogoff, B. (2003). *The cultural nature of human development.* New York: Oxford University Press.

Saffran, J. R., Aslin, R. N., & Newport, E. L. (1996). Statistical learning by 8-month-old infants. *Science, 274*, 1926–1928.

Schulz, L. E., & Gopnik, A. (2004). Causal learning across domains, *Developmental Psychology, 40*, 162–176.

Shultz, T. R. (1982). Rules of causal attribution. *Monographs of the Society for Research in Child Development, 47*(1, Serial No. 194).

Siegal, M., & Peterson, C. (Eds.). (1999). *Children's understanding of biology and health.* New York: Cambridge University Press.

Siegler, R. S., & Alibali, M. W. (2004). *Children's thinking* (4th ed.). Upper Saddle River, NJ: Prentice Hall.

Simons, D. J., & Keil, F. C. (1995). An abstract to concrete shift in the development of biological thought: The insides story. *Cognition, 56*, 129–163.

Sloutsky, V. M., & Fisher, A. V. (2004). Induction and categorization in young children: A similarity-based model. *Journal of Experimental Psychology: General, 133*, 166–188.

Smith, L. B. (2000). Avoiding association when it's behaviorism you really hate. In R. Golinkoff & K. Hirsh-Pasek (Eds.), *Breaking the word learning barrier* (pp. 169–174). New York: Oxford University Press.

Smith, L. B., Colunga, E., & Yoshida, H. (2003). Making an ontology: Cross-linguistic evidence. In D. H. Rakison & L. M. Oakes (Eds.), *Early category and concept development: Making sense of the blooming, buzzing confusion* (pp. 275–302). New York: Oxford University Press.

Spelke, E. S. (2003). What makes humans smart? In D. Gentner & S. Goldin-Meadow (Eds.), *Advances in the investigation of language and thought* (pp. 277–311). Cambridge, MA: MIT Press.

Spelke, E. S., Phillips, A., & Woodward, A. L. (1995). In D. Sperber, D. Premack, & A. Premack (Eds.), *Causal cognition: A multidisciplinary debate* (pp. 44–78). New York: Clarendon Press/Oxford University Press.

Springer, K. (1996). Young children's understanding of a biological basis of parent–offspring relations. *Child Development, 67*, 2841–2856.

Taylor, M. G. (1996). The development of children's beliefs about social and biological aspects of gender differences. *Child Development, 67*, 1555–1571.

Tomasello, M., Call, J., & Hare, B. (2003). Chimpanzees understand psychological states: The question is which ones and to what extent. *Trends in Cognitive Sciences, 7*, 153–156.

Waxman, S. R. (1999). The dubbing ceremony revisited: Object naming and categorization in infancy and early childhood. In D. L. Medin & S. Atran (Eds.), *Folkbiology* (pp. 233–284). Cambridge, MA: MIT Press/Bradford Books.

Waxman, S. R., Lynch, E. B., Casey, K. L., & Baer, L. (1997). Setters and samoyeds: The emergence of subordinate level categories as a basis for inductive inference. *Developmental Psychology, 33*, 1074–1090.

Waxman, S. R., & Markow, D. B. (1995). Words as invitations to form categories: Evidence from 12- to 13-month-old infants. *Cognitive Psychology, 29*, 257–302.

Welder, A. N., & Graham, S.A. (2001). The influence of shape similarity and shared labels on infants' inductive inferences about nonobvious object properties. *Child Development, 72*, 1653–1673.

Wellman, H. M., & Gelman, S. A. (1998). Knowledge acquisition. In D. Kuhn & R. Siegler (Eds.), *Handbook of child psychology: Vol. 4. Cognitive development* (5th ed., pp. 523–573). New York: John Wiley.

Woodward, A. L. (1998). Infants selectively encode the goal object of an actor's reach. *Cognition,* *69,* 1–34.

Xu, F. (2002). The role of language in acquiring object kind concepts in infancy. *Cognition, 85,* 223–250.

Xu, F. (2003). The development of object individuation in infancy. In H. Hayne & J. Fagen (Eds.), *Progress in infancy research* (Vol. 3, pp. 159–192). Mahwah, NJ: Lawrence Erlbaum.

Xu, F. (2005). Categories, kinds, and object individuation in infancy. In L. Gershkoff-Stowe & D. Rakison (eds.), *Building object categories in developmental time* (pp. 63–89). Mawah, NJ: Lawrence Erlbaum.

Yoshida, H., & Smith, L. B. (2003). Shifting ontological boundaries: How Japanese- and English-speaking children generalize names for animals and artifacts. *Developmental Science, 6,* 1–34.

Zelazo, P. D., Muller, U., Frye, D., & Marcovitch, S. (2003). The development of executive function in early childhood. *Monographs of the Society for Research in Child Development, 68*(3, Serial No. 274).

9

Executive Functions in Developing Children: Current Conceptualizations and Questions for the Future

Marilyn C. Welsh, Sarah L. Friedman, and Susan J. Spieker

Scientific interest in conceptualizing executive function, as it manifests in adulthood and across child development, is evidenced by the sheer number of empirical articles and authoritative chapters that have been published in recent years (Anderson, 2002; Espy & Kaufmann, 2002; Luciano, 2003; Welsh, 2001, 2002). However, as with any new area of inquiry, more questions than answers have emerged from the theoretical and empirical work on executive function. This is a chapter about a young, active, and evolving area of scientific investigation that has not yet settled on a definition of executive function. Despite the fact that there are different definitions and emphases, it seems that there is general agreement that executive function refers to cognitive processes that are necessary for purposeful, future-oriented behavior. These include, but are not limited to: regulation of attention; inhibition of inappropriate responses; coordination of information in working memory; and capacities to organize, sequence, and plan adaptive behavior (Blair, 2002; Eslinger, 1996; Klein, 2003; Shonkoff & Phillips, 2000; Welsh, 2002; Zelazo & Frye, 1998; Zelazo, Muller, Frye & Marcovitch, 2003).

An important over-arching objective of this chapter will be to examine critically the current scientific usefulness of the theoretical construct of executive function, given that the individual component skills and manifestations (e.g., planning, working memory, inhibition) have been studied in their own right for decades (Flavell, 1971; Friedman, Scholnick, & Cocking, 1987; Hynd & Obrzut, 1981; Luria, 1966; Zelazo, Craik, & Booth, 2004). To this end, we will provide the historical context and circumstances under which the construct of executive functions was "born": that is, the clinical investigations of the neuropsychological sequelae of frontal cortical damage and the constellation of cognitive skills that appeared to be compromised. Next, we will describe how the fields of cognitive and developmental science have extended this clinical research to an exploration of the nature of executive functions as manifested by the intact brain in normally functioning and developing individuals. The current debate regarding whether executive function should be viewed as a unitary construct or as a multi-faceted construct (i.e., executive function or executive functions) gets at the very heart of the question of whether this cognitive domain can be distinguished from the component cognitive skills (e.g., working memory) that comprise it. In our "working definition" of executive function, we will propose a conceptualization of the construct that both links it to the various component processes and distinguishes it from them, in a "whole is more than the sum of its parts" fashion. One way of distinguishing the domain of executive function from other cognitive processes is to examine the biological mechanisms that may make it unique. We will approach this in two ways: first, by exploring whether the normal development of executive function parallels what we know about the normal development of the prefrontal cortex; and, second, by discussing how new discoveries in molecular genetics have linked individual differences in executive function, or in its component processes, to specific genes in both normally functioning and clinically diagnosed individuals.

A second major focus of this chapter will be to propose several questions that, in our opinion, should be the focus of future research in the area of executive function. These questions include the following: How should one conceptualize and assess executive function? Do variations within age, across development, and within clinical cases occur along the same principles? How and to what degree do nature and nurture interact to influence executive function? The "answers" to these and other questions yielded by future research will be fundamental to the ever-evolving construct validation process for this nascent psychological concept.

Current Conceptualizations of Executive Function

Brain damage and the birth of executive functions

The clinical study of the cognitive and behavioral sequelae of brain damage throughout the twentieth century provided the scientific community with putative evidence that the brain is organized into modules (or systems) that subserve different discrete cognitive and behavioral functions, such as spatial perception, language comprehension, speech, and emotion processing (Fodor, 1986). It was precisely such clinical observations by pioneers like Tueber (1964) and Luria (1973) that documented the distinct difference between damage to the frontal cortex and damage to posterior areas of the brain. Decades ago, these clinicians were quite surprised to observe that adults who have sustained frontal damage could nevertheless perform within the normal range on tests of intelligence. If the frontal cortex subserved "higher psychological processes," how was it possible to perform at an average level on such tests? Indeed, it was documented that damage to the frontal lobe did not impair attention, memory, or language, *per se*, but, instead, the ability to marshal all of these cognitive skills, as well as others, in the pursuit of a future goal. Although the symptoms following frontal damage may at first appear wide-ranging, the unifying theme that emerges is one of a general deficit in future-oriented, goal-directed behavior. Therefore, one current way of conceptualizing the domain of executive function is to posit that it represents the set of cognitive processes that are necessary for goal-directed behavior and that are mediated by the prefrontal cortex of the brain.

The clinical neuropsychological literature has documented case histories of individuals who have suffered focal frontal damage and who subsequently were impaired in their future-oriented, goal-directed behavior (Eslinger, 1996; Espy & Kaufmann, 2002). Based on these clinical investigations, several influential neuropsychological models of executive function have emerged. It was observed that the behavior problems associated with pre-frontal damage were "supramodal" in that they cut across specific cognitive, sensory, and motor domains (Lezak, 1995). The frontal-damaged patients who were described lacked self-initiated, purposeful behavior based on the skills of anticipation, planning, and monitoring (Luria, 1966). Other documented cognitive sequelae following damage to the prefrontal cortex included: distraction by irrelevant stimuli, inability to flexibly switch mental sets (i.e., perseveration), failure to initiate appropriate activity, problems maintaining effort over time, inability to use feedback, and failure to plan and organize activity to attain goals (Stuss & Benson, 1984). Other processes attributed to the prefrontal cortex based on human lesion studies include: appreciation of context (Fuster, 1997; Pribram, 1969), novel problem solving (Duncan, Burgess, & Emslie, 1995), and "memory for the future" (Ingvar, 1985); the latter concept can be conceptualized as a plan to obtain a future goal. In sum, these clinical investigations have converged on the perspective of executive function as a multi-faceted, rather than unitary, cognitive domain (Goldstein & Green, 1995; Keil & Kaszniak, 2002).

The conceptualization of executive function as those cognitive processes subserved by the frontal cortex has been virtually impossible to decouple from the prefrontal cortex of the brain (Tranel, Anderson, & Benton, 1995). It is important to note here that the frontal cortex comprises over one-third of human cortical tissue and is composed of a variety of anatomical components, each with specialized cortical and subcortical connections (Damasio & Anderson, 1993). Therefore, it is more accurate to attribute executive processes to the *prefrontal* cortex, and even more specifically to two regions within the prefrontal cortex: dorsolateral and orbital-frontal (Iversen & Dunnett, 1990; cited in Barkley, 1997). More recently, the underlying neural mediation of executive functions has been viewed from a "systems perspective," implicating the involvement of entire fronto-sub-cortical circuits (Banfield, Wyland, Macrae, Munte, & Heatherton, 2004; Heyder, Suchan, & Daum, 2004; Roth & Syakin, 2004). For example, Banfield et al. (2004) suggest that the connections between the dorsolateral prefrontal cortex and subcortical structures, such as the basal ganglia and thalamus, mediate the so-called "cold" executive functions, such as planning, conceptual reasoning, strategic behavior, flexibility, and working memory. In contrast, the circuit that involves the ventromedial/orbitofrontal prefrontal cortex and basal ganglia and thalamic structures underlies what might be called "hot" executive functions, such as self-monitoring and regulation of emotion processing and emotional response. Such new research is important to our search for a conceptualization of executive function and suggests that the various component processes may have somewhat different neurologic mediation.

Despite these advances, after decades of systematic observations of the behavioral sequelae of frontal cortical damage, two major gaps in our understanding of executive function remain. First, the conceptualization of this domain was based on the symptoms following brain damage. The problems inherent in extrapolating from the brain-damaged case to understanding the normal brain have plagued the field of neuropsychology from its earliest days (Keil & Kaszniak, 2002). Second, clinical neuropsychologists utilized assessment tools that proved to be sensitive to brain damage (Halstead, 1947), but that lacked both a theoretical and empirical foundation. In particular, there has been a paucity of measures specifically designed to test frontal lobe function. The best-known and most widely used measure of frontal function, the Wisconsin Card-Sorting Test (WCST; Milner, 1964), has been the target of increasing criticism in recent years (Pennington, Benneto, McAleer, & Roberts, 1995). The task requires the participant to apply a current sorting rule for a time and then flexibly switch to a new rule, contingent upon the tester's feedback. This is called "set shifting." Individuals with frontal lobe damage tend to perseverate with the old rule despite clear instructions to change. They are unable to make a mental shift to a new response set. Cognitive scientists have pointed out that there are many cognitive functions demanded by the WCST, such as monitoring events in working memory, comparing tester feedback to information stored in working memory, detecting cues to the new response set and applying them to action, inhibiting the old response, and so on. Impaired performance is not easily interpreted, but the sequence of cognitive functions is beginning to be differentiated with new brain-imaging techniques (Monchi, Petrides, Petre, Worsley, & Dagher, 2001). In the next section, we will explore how cognitive and developmental scientists have sought to address these two knowledge gaps in our understanding of executive function.

From symptoms to cognitive processes

The "birth" of the construct of executive function may be deeply rooted in the tradition of clinical neuropsychology and inextricably linked to the sequelae of brain damage; however, the field of cognitive psychology met the challenge of describing the nature of executive function as mediated by the intact brain. These perspectives on the construct of executive function attempted to characterize, in cognitive terminology, the vast array of symptoms observed by clinical neuropsychologists following frontal lobe damage. For example, in his "adaptive coding model" of prefrontal cortical function, Duncan (2001) proposes that populations of neurons in this brain region are particularly reactive to important task parameters (e.g., contextual features) and that these networks of cells flexibly adapt to the changing characteristics of the task. Therefore, cognitive scientists have integrated information gleaned both from brain-damaged cases and from neuroscientific investigations of brain function and have interpreted these data within a cognitive framework.

An influential information-processing perspective on executive function has been proposed by Norman and Shallice (1986) and is directly based on the neuropsychological deficits characteristic of frontal lobe damage. In the Supervisory Attention System (SAS) model, these authors highlight the distinction between routine and non-routine environmental contingencies when defining the essence of executive function. Their model involves a two-level system including a lower-level contention-scheduling function and a higher-level supervisory attentional function. The contention-scheduling function is effective in familiar, routine, over-learned situations in which particular stimulus inputs trigger specific and appropriate behavioral outputs in a more or less automatic way. The general operation of the contention-scheduling function is overseen by the supervisory attentional function that modulates activation levels such that certain input–output units will be favored for selection over others. Norman and Shallice propose that the situations that require the supervisory attentional function include those involving: (1) planning or decision making, (2) error-detection or error-correction, (3) the generation of novel action sequences, or (4) the inhibition of strong, over-learned responses. The Norman and Shallice model highlights what is unique about executive function: cognitive processes recruited in relatively novel situations that require an analysis of the problem at hand, followed by strategy generation, monitoring, and flexible revision of these strategies based on feedback. These clearly are conscious, effortful processes that would be the domain of some sort of "supervisory" system, as opposed to more routinized, over-learned, and automatic stimulus–response associations.

Other cognitive conceptualizations of executive function are much less directly related to neuropsychological and neuroscientific examinations of brain function. Instead, these conceptualizations derive from classic information-processing theory and, therefore, focus on the temporally organized multiple cognitive components that are assumed to be called into play when the individual is confronted with a goal-oriented problem-solving or planning task. For example, Scholnick and Friedman (1987) and Borkowski and Burke (1996) have presented models of executive function that reflect an information-processing perspective. These models include three major attributes: (1) task analysis, (2) strategy selection and revision (i.e., control processes), and (3) strategy monitoring. All three components fit within the executive level of processing because they presumably draw from the long-term memory representations of similar tasks, previously successful strategies, and other relevant knowledge (i.e., the cognitive level of processing), as well as from the representations of one's own cognitive strengths and weaknesses (i.e., the metacognitive level of processing).

The attempt to generate age-appropriate definitions of executive function for children, and even infants, is a recent phenomenon; for decades it was a commonly accepted "fact" in the field of neuropsychology that the prefrontal cortex did not "turn on" until pre-adolescence (e.g., Golden, 1981). However, *when* in normal development one believes executive function emerges depends a great deal on *how* one defines this cognitive domain (Welsh & Pennington, 1988). Until recently, the cognitive functions mediated by the prefrontal cortex were defined by neuropsychologists as higher-level reasoning and conceptual flexibility, as measured by the WCST and other neuropsychological frontal lobe tasks, which children could not do. In fact, studies have identified age 10 years as the time when typically developing children show adult-level performance on the WCST (Welsh, Pennington, & Grossier, 1991). Moreover, for decades neuropsychologists noted that the cognitive processes disrupted after frontal lobe damage bore a strong resemblance to Piaget's formal operational stage of cognitive development, which also emerged at about age 10 to 11 years. Although there appears to be a relationship between executive functions and formal operational reasoning (Emick & Welsh, 2005), the fact that formal operations characterize *mature* executive function does not logically lead to the statement that this is the *only* form in which executive functions manifest across childhood.

The idea that planning and goal-directed behavior were not possible prior to preadolescence dominated the field of neuropsychology for most of its modern history, and it is only in the last two decades or so that two disciplines, neuropsychology and developmental psychology, have shared information to generate new and exciting views of executive function and how it may change across development. Today there is a general acceptance of the existence of executive function skills in childhood and an emerging appreciation for how these skills impact and are impacted by the daily lives of children (Friedman & Scholnick, 1997; Gioia & Isquith, 2004). Although there is a good deal of variation in the names given to the factors underlying executive function in children, there is a certain amount of convergence on cognitive processes such as inhibition, fluency, planning, and conceptual reasoning, with working memory undoubtedly affecting most, if not all, of these processes (Anderson, 2002).

The difficulties inherent in defining the executive function construct in developing children have been reviewed recently (Espy & Kaufmann, 2002). Most definitions of executive function include "higher order, integrative, control-type skills where the translation of the definition into measurement tools is somewhat more difficult than with a more discrete skill" such as language or visual-spatial processing (Espy & Kaufmann, 2002, p. 117). In addition, executive function tests often measure multiple skills simultaneously, a fact that led to questions about their validity. However, this criticism may be misplaced, given that it is precisely the coordination of multiple skills that makes executive function a unique cognitive domain. Still, developing age-appropriate cognitive measures of such integrative processing has presented a serious challenge to researchers, particularly those attempting to assess executive functions in infants and young children (Diamond, Werker, & Lalonde, 1994; Espy, Kaufmann, McDiarmid, & Gilsky, 1999). These measurement challenges will certainly be a focus of research in the next several decades, as discussed later in this chapter.

Executive function: one function or many?

The genesis of the construct of executive function in the clinical neuropsychology field resulted in a view of a multi-faceted cognitive domain involving relatively independent components (e.g., initiation, working memory, inhibition, planning), all in the service of achieving a future goal. Recently, cognitive scientists have asked whether there are more parsimonious (i.e., unitary) computational models of executive function that can account for the varied sequelae observed after prefrontal damage or dysfunction. These computational models involve sophisticated computer programs that are designed to solve particular executive function tasks as well as to allow for the "lesioning" of the program to mimic the deficits characteristic of frontal lobe damage. Computational or "connectionist" models are substantially influenced by neuroscientific evidence of the manner in which neurons communicate at the synapse, and typically conceptualize executive function in a unitary fashion rather than as a multi-faceted construct.

Examples of a unitary construct view of executive function have been proposed and tested by cognitive scientists who view executive function either as a limited-capacity working-memory system (Kimberg, Desposito, & Farah, 1998) or as a system that effectively represents and maintains contextual information (Cohen & Servan-Schreiber, 1992). The notion that the prefrontal cortex (and, by implication, executive function) serves the important function of context representation is consistent with the types of deficits seen in frontal patients, and recent cognitive models of executive function also echo this view (Waltz et al., 2004).

A prominent view of executive function in developing children that is consistent with this "single function" perspective has been offered by Zelazo and colleagues (Zelazo et al., 2004). The Cognitive Complexity and Control (CCC) model likens executive function to mental representation of logical rules (if–then) that are needed to solve novel, goal-oriented problems; in this model, age-related changes seen in executive function reflect the ability to represent and maintain increasingly complex, hierarchical rules systems. In the authors' own words, this process is "resource-demanding and effortful, as is maintaining rules in working memory so that they can be used to constrain inferences and guide behavior" (Zelazo et al., 2004, p. 169). This unitary construct view of executive function is strikingly similar to the "cognitive control" factor identified by Brookshire, Levin, Song, and Zhang (2004) in their study of children, and the "context representation" view of executive function proposed by Cohen and Servan-Schreiber (1992) and by Waltz et al. (2004) for adults.

The debate regarding whether executive function is best conceptualized in a unifactorial or multifactorial manner has been examined empirically in adults and in children through exploratory and confirmatory factor analysis. The underlying logic of such research is that, if executive function can be characterized as a single cognitive process, then performance on a set of separate executive function tests should intercorrelate in such a way as to be best explained by a single latent factor. However, if executive function is best understood as multi-faceted, then performance across tests should be best described by multiple latent factors. The unitary view of executive function was explicitly rejected by two recent factor analytic studies that examined adult performance (Miyake, Friedman, Emerson, Witzki, & Howerter, 2000; Welsh et al., 2002) and has not fared much better in studies of children. Exploratory factor analyses are consistent with a multi-faceted view of executive function. Welsh et al. (1991) identified three relatively independent factors: (1) organized, speeded, and sequenced responding; (2) hypothesis testing and impulse control; and (3) planning. Not only did the statistical analysis reveal multiple components comprising executive function, but there was also evidence for different patterns of developmental differences across these factors. Evidence such as this led Vickie Anderson (2002) to state rather unequivocally, "based on behavioral and imaging research plotting the normal development of executive function, and from work with samples of adult patients with brain damage, executive function can no longer be conceptualized as a unitary construct" (p. 69).

A working definition of executive function and perspectives on its development

One of the greatest challenges for researchers in any scientific domain, and perhaps particularly in psychology, is that of construct validity. After decades of research exploring executive function, there is still an active debate regarding the usefulness of this construct and the degree to which it can be distinguished from other cognitive domains, such as memory and problem solving, for which there is greater consensus on definition and measurement. Based on the preceding discussion of the conceptualizations of executive function from neuropsychological, cognitive, and developmental perspectives, we are offering a "working definition" for how we view the construct of executive function and what makes it unique compared with other cognitive constructs. We propose that executive function involves the process of integrating and combining separate, but collaborative, cognitive abilities in service of a future goal. Executive function is elicited when a person is presented with a novel or challenging task or placed in an unfamiliar situation for which he or she does not have routinized, automatic responses. This construct includes several core cognitive processes, including, but not limited to, attention, working memory, inhibition, and self-monitoring. These core processes work in coordination to allow for the more complex manifestations of executive function, such as planning, inductive reasoning, and flexible, strategic problem solving. The fact that one can observe similarities in the developmental trajectories of "executive function" and component skills, working memory, and inhibition (Welsh, 2002) speaks to the issue of what appears to make executive function a unique construct. Unlike the more traditional cognitive categories, executive function represents the incorporation of those core skills, as well as more complex manifestations (planning, self-monitoring, etc.), all working in coordination to achieve a future-oriented goal.

Nevertheless, much of the current research continues to explore the construct by primarily focusing on its constituent components. In human infants, the most widely studied measure of emerging prefrontal cortical function is Piaget's classic A-not-B version of the object permanence task (Piaget, 1936/1954), due to its similarity to a task found to be sensitive to prefrontal damage in non-human primates (Jacobsen, 1935). The task involves repeatedly hiding a preferred object in one location ("A") and requiring that the infant retrieve it there. Infants who are less than 12 months old are usually successful on this task but fail when the task becomes more complex. For example, when the object is subsequently hidden in a second location ("B") in full view, infants under 12 months of age frequently make the A-not-B error by searching in the first-baited location ("A") instead of the current location ("B"). Diamond (1990) found that 12- to 13-month infants could tolerate increasingly longer delays between hiding the object and the commencement of search without making the A-not-B error, presumably indicating the functional development of a working-memory system. Interestingly, Diamond observed that infants frequently indicated that they understood the correct location of the object, as reflected by direction of gaze and body orientation; however, they continued to reach to the previously correct location. This observation is strikingly similar to reports by Luria (1973), in which adults with frontal cortical damage stated the correct card-sorting rule, but, nevertheless, sorted according to rules that were previously, but not currently, in force. In the case of the infant and the adult, the information active in working memory is not effectively guiding motor behavior, particularly in the face of strong, prepotent (e.g., previously reinforced) response. Therefore, the A-not-B task and other infant measures, such as the object retrieval task (Diamond et al., 1994), are sensitive assessments of the core executive processes of working memory and response inhibition, and the degree to which the two processes are coordinated in service of a future goal (e.g., finding the hidden object, retrieving the object from a plexiglass box). Diamond and Goldman-Rakic (1989) demonstrated that the cognitive processes demanded by these measures depended on the integrity of the prefrontal cortex in non-human primates, and later research found associations between improvement in performance on these tasks with changes in frontal EEG activity (Bell & Fox, 1992, 1997). Therefore, the earliest manifestation of executive function in human development can be observed in the infant's budding ability to coordinate working memory and inhibitory control in the context of means–end problem situations.

In toddlers and preschoolers, developmental researchers have examined executive functions by continuing to focus on the coordination of working memory and inhibition, but in more complex contexts. Forty years ago, when delay of gratification abilities were examined in preschoolers, the findings were not discussed in terms of "executive function." However, it is clear that the primitive plans generated by young children presented with a delay task (e.g., pretending the marshmallows were inedible logs in order to inhibit the strong, prepotent response to touch the candy when warned in advance not to do so) reflect executive function. Even earlier in the history of developmental psychology it was noted (Luria, 1966; Vygotsky, 1978) that an important developmental transition involved the ability to generate verbally mediated rules (presumably in working memory) to effectively guide behavior. Today, a range of set-shifting and conflict tasks are designed to "pull for" the integration of working-memory and inhibitory control processes and indicate that there is continuity in these abilities from infancy through the preschool years (3 to 7 years) as the rules become increasingly complex and hierarchical (Diamond & Taylor, 1996). Another context in which developing executive functions can be observed is the emergence of theory of mind between the ages of 3 and 5 years (see Barr, this volume). This ability to "suspend" what one now knows, to examine what one once knew as well as what a naïve person may believe to be true, is presumed to place heavy demands on working-memory resources and inhibitory control. In addition, theory of mind development may require the more complex executive functions of inductive reasoning and self-monitoring.

It is between the years of 6 and 10 that executive functions may be undergoing their most dynamic phase of development (Welsh, 2002). Working-memory capacity appears to increase over these years, reflective of the efficiency and automatization of attention and strategic processes (Case, 1992), and new abilities such as introspection, self-monitoring, and conscious control over memory and problem solving emerge (Brown, 1978; Flavell, 1971). Problem-solving tasks such as the Tower of Hanoi and Tower of London have become increasingly popular measures of executive functions in both adults and children, in typical and clinical populations. These tasks require the participant to transform a starting stack of disks or balls to a goal configuration, by following an explicit set of rules. To be successful, children must generate a move sequence in working memory, inhibit maladaptive moves, induce the regularity of relevant move patterns, and self-monitor the effectiveness of their strategies. Adult-level performance on the Tower of Hanoi has been observed on the simplest problems as early as age 6 years (Welsh et al., 1991). However, on more difficult problems that require the coordination of working memory, inhibition, flexibility, and self-monitoring for successful planning performance, adult-level accuracy is still not achieved by age 12 (Levin, Eisenberg, & Benton, 1991; Luciano, 2003; Welsh et al., 1991).

Does brain development parallel behavioral manifestations of normative development of executive function?

It is axiomatic that anatomical development must precede functional development. Following from this assumption, neurodevelopmental events, such as dendritic arborization and synaptogenesis (i.e., the development of synaptic connections), should mark the minimal age of onset of function in a given neural system (Huttenlocher & Dabholker, 1997, p. 70). Therefore, it seems reasonable to explore what is known about the unfolding of these neurodevelopmental events in the prefrontal cortex across childhood and to examine the question, "Do changes in the behaviors assumed to be linked to this cortical region follow a similar developmental progression?" Given that this research is in a nascent stage of development, it is not surprising that there is a lack of agreement across researchers regarding the time-course of prefrontal cortical development in the childhood years (Fuster, 1997).

By far, the most widely discussed measure of ontogenetic brain changes is synaptogenesis and synapse elimination. It is this index of brain development that has spurred the most controversy regarding the timing of prefrontal development (Luciano, 2003; Welsh, 2001). Research conducted in the Huttenlocher laboratory for the past thirty years has examined synaptogenesis and synaptic elimination in Layer III of the middle frontal gyrus of human prefrontal cortex. In their reviews, Huttenlocher and Dabholkar (1997) compare the time-course of synaptogenesis in primary visual cortex, primary auditory cortex, and prefrontal cortex (Layer II of anterior middle frontal gyrus). Consistent with earlier findings in the laboratory, the review showed that the prefrontal cortical region exhibited a later peak in synaptic density, at about 3 years, than did the primary sensory areas. There is a gradual decrease in synaptic density after this point; however, an excess number (compared to the number in adult brains) of synaptic contacts is maintained throughout the childhood years. This pattern of synaptic development can be seen as counterintuitive in light of what we know about normal behavioral development (Huttenlocher & Dabholkar, 1997). The sharp increase and high point in synaptic contacts occur at an age when executive function processes are only just beginning to manifest in a child's behavior. In contrast, the protracted period of improvement in executive processes that is apparent across the school-age years actually parallels a gradual *decline* in synaptic density in the prefrontal region. It may be precisely this *decrease* in synaptic number that reflects the stabilization of the functional networks underlying advances in cognitive processing, as proposed in the theory of stabilization (Changeux, Heidmann, & Patte, 1984).

Huttenlocher's empirical evidence of later and more protracted synaptic development in the prefrontal region of human cerebral cortex contrasts with the findings of Goldman-Rakic and colleagues (Goldman-Rakic, Bourgeois, & Rakic, 1997), suggesting *concurrent* synaptogenesis across a range of cortical areas (including the prefrontal cortex) in the rhesus monkey. These researchers found a period of rapid increase in synaptic density perinatally, which peaks at about 2 months of age. This high level of synaptic contacts is maintained until about age 3 years (i.e., age of sexual maturation), after which it begins to decline to adult levels. This pattern of sharp increase and plateau of excess synaptic contacts between 2 months and 3 years for rhesus monkeys conforms to the pattern seen in the prefrontal cortex of humans between about 2 years and puberty by Huttenlocher. However, Goldman-Rakic and colleagues observed this pattern of synaptogenesis in *all* areas of the cortex examined. They have acknowledged that their findings of contemporaneous synaptogenesis across several cortical regions stands in stark contrast to the data from the Huttenlocher laboratory. Interestingly, *both* research groups suggest that their neurodevelopmental data are consistent with evidence of behavioral development of those processes presumed to be mediated by the prefrontal lobe. Huttenlocher and Dabholkar (1997) contend that earlier synaptogenesis in primary visual cortex than in prefrontal cortex is consistent with the relatively early emergence of visual abilities (e.g., stereopsis) as compared to the gradual emergence of executive functions across childhood and well into adolescence. In contrast, Goldman-Rakic et al. (1997) maintain that early and concurrent synaptogenesis across the cortex makes sense given behavioral data indicating integrative processing within a functioning working-memory system as early as infancy (Diamond et al., 1994). As Goldman-Rakic et al. (1997) write, "The whole-cloth view of the cortex as a woven tapestry in which the entire piece emerges by progressive addition of threads to all portions simultaneously derives from consideration of the comparative time course of synapse formation and synaptic density in diverse regions of the primate cortex" (pp. 33–34).

These discrepant positions are at least partly reflective of the wide range of perspectives on those behaviors controlled by the prefrontal cortex, a prominent theme in earlier sections of this chapter. If one defines executive function in terms of the core cognitive processes (e.g., working memory and inhibition), then one could argue that these processes can be observed early in life (Goldman-Rakic et al., 1997). However, if one defines executive function as the integration of core processes that subserve future-oriented, goal-directed behavior, then a later emergence and more protracted development of executive function also rings true (e.g., Huttenlocher & Dabholkar, 1997).

The degree to which the development of executive functions as identified in the empirical literature conforms to what we currently know about the neurophysiological development of the prefrontal cortex has been discussed in two recent chapters. Welsh (2001) uses the three cycles of cortical development proposed by Thatcher (e.g., Thatcher, 1997) as an organizing framework. Interpreting the findings of developmental studies examining executive functions, as well as working memory and inhibition specifically, Welsh (2001) identified the following developmental trends. During Cycle I, from approximately 18 months to 5 years of age, there is evidence for emerging, and sometimes proficient, working memory, inhibition, and simple flexibility, especially when the tasks rely heavily on motor responses for performance. Cycle II, 5 to 10 years of age, is perhaps the most dynamic period for executive function development. Depending on the task, developmental improvements in planning, working memory, inhibition, and flexibility have been observed as early as age 6 years and as late as age 10 years. Finally, it appears that performance on many executive function tasks does not reach adult-level performance by the end of Cycle II; instead it continues to develop during Cycle III (10 to 14 years) and probably beyond this age period. There are consistent findings that the executive skills of verbal working memory, inhibition, and flexibility mature between the ages of 10 and 12 years. Interestingly, those skills that appear to show a protracted period of development beyond age 12, visual working memory and the coordination of working memory and inhibition, may be just the processes underlying performance on many planning tasks. Performance on tasks presumed to require planning skills, such as the Tower of Hanoi and Tower of London, also show a similarly protracted period of development.

Genetic discoveries and individual differences in executive functions

As noted by Espy and Kaufmann (2002), there is a great deal more known about the development of executive function than about the within-age individual differences among healthy individuals. Genetic research, both quantitative and molecular, is designed to examine such inter-individual variation, as well as the extreme variation associated with behavioral disorders (e.g., attention deficit hyperactivity disorder, ADHD). Below we will explore the links between genetic variation and executive function. We presume that such links are mediated by subtle differences in brain structure and function and undoubtedly interact with environmental conditions surrounding the child to influence the manifestation of executive function. Empirical investigation of genetic links to executive function is a relatively recent phenomenon and has taken many forms, from the examination of the relative contributions of genetic and environmental factors (quantitative genetics) to the search for specific candidate genes that may mediate executive function in both normal and impaired functioning (molecular genetics).

Quantitative genetic studies have examined the relative contribution of unique and shared genetic variability and unique and shared environmental variability to the performance variance observed in a range of tasks that assess the component executive function processes in normally functioning adults. A common paradigm utilized to address this question is a statistical model-fitting procedure known as the Cholesky analysis (Neale & Cardon, 1992) that was employed in research by Luciano, Wright, Smith, Geffen, Geffen, and Martin (2001) and by Hansell, Wright, Geffen, Geffen, Smith, and Martin (2001). In these studies unique genetic factors linked to working-memory performance and prefrontal function were identified that were distinguished from genetic factors contributing to other cognitive functions mediated by other cortical regions. Examining the executive function component process of inhibition, Hur and Bouchard (1997) found a strong genetic link to the shared variance between impulsivity and sensation seeking, as well as a link from a unique genetic factor to impulsivity alone.

A second approach to studying the genetic links to executive function involves testing specific candidate genes that theory and past research suggest might be linked to these cognitive processes. For example, the candidate gene approach was applied to the study of the relation between dopamine levels and executive function (Diamond, Briand, Fossella, & Gehlbach, 2004). The COMT gene, which was implicated, codes for an enzyme responsible for catabolizing catecholamines, such as dopamine, released into the synaptic cleft. A mutation of the COMT gene, the methionine (Met) polymorphism, results in greatly reduced enzyme activity and, thus, an extended period of dopamine activity in the synaptic space. Diamond et al. (2004) found that normal children who were homozygous for the Met polymorphism outperformed children without this genetic mutation on a working-memory test (Egan et al., 2001). Thus, evidence exists for a specific gene directly impacting neurochemical function in a brain region, the prefrontal cortex. Similarly, Lee, Kim, and Hyun (2003) identified a functional polymorphism of the serotonin transporter (5-HTT) gene to be related to impulsivity in a heterogeneous group of Korean adolescents.

In summary, emerging evidence suggests a substantial contribution of genetic endowment to individual and group differences in executive skills in both typical and atypical populations, such as ADHD (Biederman & Farone, 2002). Again, one must be cognizant that these genetic factors do not operate in a vacuum and, instead, interact with the social context that impinges on the person, both before and after birth. (For a detailed review of what we know about the role of social context in cognitive development see Gauvain, 2001. For information about the small magnitude of environmental effects on attention, memory and planning see work conducted by NICHD Early Child Care Research Network, 2005.)

Future Questions for Executive Function Research

Question 1: How can we best conceptualize executive function and its development?

Only recently have neuroscientists, cognitive psychologists, and developmentalists begun to "compare notes" on their respective conceptualizations of executive function (Crnic & Pennington, 1987; Welsh & Pennington, 1988). Our review of the scientific literature suggests that there is a need for consensus among researchers regarding the conceptual and operational definition of this construct. Statistical approaches have generally converged on the conclusion that executive function is multi-faceted, rather than unitary; however, the degree to which we can distinguish executive function and its component processes from other more traditional cognitive domains (e.g., attention, memory) remains an elusive question. Our conceptualization proposes that it is not any single cognitive process (e.g., working memory), but the coordination of more than one cognitive process (e.g., working memory and inhibition, allowing for flexible, strategic action) that defines executive function.

Question 2: How can one design valid and reliable measures of executive function?

Clearly related to the debate over the most appropriate definition of executive function, a second critical issue facing researchers is that of measurement. Specifically, how can one measure the component processes underlying executive function individually, as well as separately from their coordination, to achieve the goal of the particular task? If the advantage of the executive function construct is that it represents the integration of different component skills, then tasks need to be devised that test for individual differences in such integration, as well as demonstrate that the integration skills are independent of individual differences in the component skills. What happens when the coordinating skills are intact but the component skills vary in terms of their level? Is it possible that normal individual differences and clinical variations in executive function are due to individual differences in the balance between the component skills and the integrating skills? Answers to these questions will emerge from a more careful design of executive tasks.

Finally, tests of executive function should vary on a continuum between "brain-teaser" puzzles that are completely unfamiliar to the child examined and tests that model real-life situations. Research on planning has shown that availability of real-life schemas for dealing with executive function tasks is an important determinant of the extent to which children show proficiency on these tasks (Friedman & Scholnick, 1997; Friedman et al., 1987). More specifically, very young children can plan a birthday party or perform well on an errand-running task, but have more difficulty on the abstract Tower of Hanoi task. In addition, social, emotional, and motivational considerations have also been shown to affect performance on planning tasks. Planning in a universe completely under the control of the planner is in some ways easier than planning in a social context where one's plans may be at odds with other people's plans. These facts must be taken into account when designing batteries of tasks to evaluate executive function.

Question 3: What are the potential nature–nurture interactions in the development of executive function?

One context in which to examine nature–nurture interactions (Anastasi, 1968) in the development of executive function is in the case of child clinical disorders in which the integrity of executive function skills is compromised. This active area of research typically focuses on the biological mechanisms (e.g., brain, genetics) involved in the specific clinical disorder as the primary explanation of the pattern of deficits seen in executive function. For example, there is substantial evidence that a compromised dopaminergic system in ADHD perturbs the function of the prefrontal cortex, thus resulting in executive deficits. However, a broader perspective suggests that impairments in executive function observed in the clinically diagnosed children are really the consequence of an interaction of both nature (the biological mechanisms) and nurture (the environmental conditions in which this child is developing). In another relevant clinical condition, early-treated phenylketonuria (PKU), many of the biological mechanisms underlying the observed executive function impairments have been investigated for decades (Diamond, 2001; Welsh, Pennington, Ozonoff, Rouse, & McCabe, 1990). However, less well understood are how particular social factors serve to moderate the biological influences that predispose a child to executive function difficulties. Research focused on children with no known deficits in executive function suggests that children improve their skills through carrying out tasks requiring these skills in the context of interaction with others who are more expert than themselves and who scaffold, model, and complement the activities of the child (Gauvain, 2001). This body of knowledge can serve as the base for future investigations of the interaction of nature and nurture in the development of executive function.

Question 4: What "real-world" behaviors of children (e.g. problem behavior, school adjustment) are predicted by developmental and individual variation in executive function?

An association between poor performance on executive function tasks and externalizing problems in school-age children is widely reported (Coolidge, Thede, & Young, 2000). Whether this association is causal or spurious is not clear. Certain child characteristics, such as executive function ability, could contribute to the eventual display of externalizing problems. Such child characteristics may have both direct (Pennington & Bennetto, 1993) and transactional (Moffitt, 1993) effects on later behavior. It has also been argued that the association is spurious, in that executive function and conduct problems are both influenced by the same early adverse environments or predispositions (Aguilar, Sroufe, Egeland, & Carlson, 2000; Mezzacappa, Kindlon, & Earls, 2001). Finally, it may be that the association between executive function deficits and externalizing problems is accounted for by the subgroup of children with externalizing problems who also have symptoms of ADHD. Executive function deficits are not characteristic of all children with externalizing problems (Clark, Prior, & Kinsella, 2002). The association between attention problems and deficits in executive function remains after controlling for oppositional behaviors, but the association between oppositional behaviors and executive functions disappears when controlling for attention problems (Wiers, Gunning, & Sergeant, 1998).

Blair (2002) notes that self-regulatory skills, a construct that has similarities with executive function, underlie many of the behaviors and attributes associated with successful school adjustment. Other studies have found that higher-order processes labeled "cognitive self-control," which also share characteristics with executive function, are associated with reading and mathematics skill acquisition (Kurdek & Sinclair, 2000). Gathercole and Pickering (2000) found that children with low levels of school achievement at 7 years showed marked impairments on measures of central executive function; in particular, in complex working-memory tasks.

Summary and Concluding Thoughts

In this chapter, our objective was to introduce the construct of executive function and its development to readers for whom it may be a new and confusing concept. We have distinguished executive function from more traditional cognitive domains, such as memory and language, by describing its unique historical roots in the clinical neuropsychological investigations of frontal lobe damage, and the more recent attempts by cognitive and developmental scientists to hone its definition further. Whereas our working definition of executive function acknowledges its multi-faceted nature, we propose that it is the coordination of these various cognitive components (e.g., attention, working memory, inhibition, planning) in service of a future goal that differentiates executive function from other cognitive constructs. The current view of the neurodevelopment of the frontal cortex appears to dovetail nicely with our systematic review of the scientific literature about the manner in which executive skills emerge in infancy, are practiced in early childhood, become more sophisticated in middle childhood, and begin to solidify in adolescence. We predict that cutting-edge work in quantitative and molecular genetics will provide a much-needed window on the nature of within-age individual differences in both normally developing and clinically diagnosed children. Although scientific investigations of executive function have developed a substantial knowledge base over the past few decades, there is still much that we do not know, and a second purpose of this chapter was to highlight these gaps in our understanding. Fundamentally, there is a need to reach consensus among researchers in the cognitive, developmental, and neurosciences on the most effective and parsimonious way to conceptualize executive function, and from this collaborative effort, age-appropriate behavioral measures of the construct should begin to evolve.

References

Aguilar, B., Sroufe, L. A., Egeland, B., & Carlson, E. (2000). Distinguishing the early-onset/persistent and adolescence-onset antisocial behavior types: From birth to 16 years. *Development and Psychopathology, 12*(2), 109–132.

Anastasi, A. (1968). Heredity, environment, and the question "How?" *Psychological Review, 65*, 197–208.

Anderson, V. (2002). Executive function in children: Introduction. *Child Neuropsychology, 8*, 69–70.

Banfield, J. F., Wyland, C. L., Macrae, C. N., Munte, T. F., & Heatherton, T. F. (2004). The cognitive neuroscience of self-regulation. In R. F. Baumeister & K. D. Vohs (Eds.), *Handbook of self-regulation: Research, theory, and applications* (pp. 62–83). New York: Guilford Press.

Barkley, R. A. (1997). Behavioral inhibition, sustained attention, and executive functions: constructing a unified theory of ADHD. *Psychological Bulletin, 121*, 65–94.

Bell, M. A., & Fox, N. A. (1992). The relations between frontal brain electrical activity and cognitive development during infancy. *Child Development, 63*, 1142–1163.

Bell, M. A., & Fox, N. A. (1997). Individual differences in object permanence performance at 8 months: Locomotor experience and brain electrical activity. *Developmental Psychobiology, 31*, 287–297.

Biederman, J., & Faraone, S. V. (2002). Current concepts on the neurobiology of Attention-Deficit/Hyperactivity Disorder. *Journal of Attention Disorders, 6*, Supplement 1: S7–16.

Blair, C. (2002). School readiness: Integrating cognition and emotion in a neurobiological conceptualization of children's functioning at school entry. *American Psychologist, 57*(2), 111–127.

Borkowski, J. G., & Burke, J. E. (1996). Theories, models, and measurements of executive functioning: An information processing perspective. In L. G. Reid & N. A. Krasnegor (Eds.), *Attention, memory, and executive function* (pp. 235–261). Baltimore: Paul H. Brookes.

Brookshire, B., Levin, H. S., Song, J. X., & Zhang, L. (2004). Components of executive function in typically developing and head-injured children. *Developmental Neuropsychology, 25*, 61–83.

Brown, A. L. (1978). Knowing when, where, and how to remember: A problem of metacognition. In R. Glaser (Ed.), *Advances in instructional psychology* (pp. 77–165). Hillsdale, NJ: Lawrence Erlbaum Associates.

Case, R. (1992). The role of the frontal lobes in the regulation of cognitive development. *Brain & Cognition, 20*, 51–73.

Changeux, J.-P., Heidmann, T., & Patte, P. (1984). Learning by selection. In P. Marler & H. S. Terrace (Eds.), *The biology of learning* (pp. 115–137). New York: Springer-Verlag.

Clark, C., Prior, M., & Kinsella, G. (2002). The relationship between executive function abilities, adaptive behaviour, and academic achievement in children with externalizing behaviour problems. *Journal of Child Psychology and Psychiatry and Allied Disciplines, 43*(6), 785–796.

Cohen, J. D., & Servan-Schreiber, D. (1992). Context, cortex, and dopamine: A connectionist approach to behavior and biology in schizophrenia. *Psychological Review, 99*, 45–77.

Coolidge, F. L., Thede, L. L., & Young, S. E. (2000). Heritability and the comorbidity of attention deficit hyperactivity disorder with behavioral disorders and executive function deficits: A preliminary investigation. *Developmental Neuropsychology, 17*(3), 273–287.

Crnic, L. S., & Pennington, B. F. (1987). Developmental psychology and the neurosciences: An introduction. *Child Development, 58*, 533–538.

Damasio, A. R., & Anderson, S. W. (1993). The frontal lobes. In K. M. Heilman, & E. Valenstein (Eds.), *Clinical neuropsychology* (3rd ed., pp. 409–460). New York: Oxford University Press.

Diamond, A. (1990). The development and neural bases of memory functions as indexed by the AB and delayed response tasks in human infants and infant monkeys. *Annals of the New York Academy of Sciences, 608*, 267–317.

Diamond, A. (2001). A model system for studying the role of dopamine in prefrontal cortex during early development in humans: Early and continuously treated phenylketonuria. In C. A. Nelson & M. Luciano (Eds.), *Handbook of developmental cognitive neuroscience* (pp. 433–472). Cambridge, MA: MIT Press.

Diamond, A., Briand, L., Fossella, J., & Gehlbach, L. (2004). Genetic and neurochemical modulation of prefrontal cognitive functions in children. *American Journal of Psychiatry, 161*, 125–132.

Diamond, A., & Goldman-Rakic, P. S. (1989). Comparison of human infants and rhesus monkeys on Piaget's AB task: Evidence for dependence on dorsolateral prefrontal cortex. *Experimental Brain Research, 74*, 24–40.

Diamond, A., & Taylor, C. (1996). Development of an aspect of executive control: Development of the abilities to remember what I said and to "do as I say, not as I do." *Developmental Psychobiology, 74*, 24–40.

Diamond, A., Werker, J. F., & Lalonde, C. (1994). Toward understanding commonalities in the development of object search, detour navigation, categorization, and speech perception. In G. Dawson & K. W. Fischer (Eds.), *Human behavior and the developing brain* (pp. 380–426). New York: Guilford Press.

Duncan, J. (2001). An adaptive coding model of neural function in the prefrontal cortex. *Nature Reviews Neuroscience, 2*, 820–829.

Duncan, J., Burgess, P., & Emslie, H. (1995). Fluid intelligence after frontal lobe lesions. *Neuropsychologia, 33*, 261–268.

Egan, M. F., Goldberg, T. E., Kolachana, B. S., Callicott, J. H., Mazzanti, C. M., Straub, R. E., Goldman, D., & Weinberger, D. R. (2001). Effect of COMT Val 108/158 Met genotype on frontal lobe function and risk for schizophrenia. *Proceedings of the National Academy of Sciences, USA, 98*, 6917–6922.

Emick, J. A., & Welsh, M. C. (2005). Association between formal operational thought and executive function as measured by the Tower of Hanoi-Revised. *Journal of Learning and Individual Differences, 15*, 177–188.

Eslinger, P. J. (1996). Conceptualizing, describing, and measuring components of executive function: A summary. In G. R. Lyon & N. A. Krasnagor (Eds.), *Attention, memory, and executive function* (pp. 367–395). Baltimore: Paul H. Brookes.

Espy, K. A., & Kaufmann, P. M. (2002). Individual differences in the development of executive function in children: Lessons from the delayed response and A-not-B tasks. In D. L Molfese & V. J. Molfese (Eds.), *Developmental variations in learning: Applications to social, executive function, language, and reading skills* (pp. 113–137). Mahwah, NJ: Lawrence Erlbaum Associates.

Espy, K. A., Kaufmann, P. M., McDiarmid, M. D., & Gilsky, M. L. (1999). Executive functioning in preschool children: Performance on A-not-B and other delayed response format tasks. *Brain and Cognition, 41*, 178–200.

Flavell, J. H. (1971). First discussant's comments. What is memory development the development of? *Human Development, 14*, 272–278.

Fodor, J. A. (1986). The modularity of mind. In Z. W. Pylyshyn & W. Demopoulos (Eds.), *Meaning and cognitive structures: Issues in the computational theory of mind* (pp. 3–18). Westport, CT: Ablex.

Friedman, S. L., & Scholnick, E. L. (Eds.). (1997). *Why, how and when do we plan? The developmental psychology of planning.* Hillsdale, NJ: Lawrence Erlbaum Associates.

Friedman, S. L., Scholnick, E. K. & Cocking, R. R. (1987). Reflections on reflections: What planning is and how it develops. In S. L. Friedman, E. K. Scholnick, & R. R. Cocking (Eds.), *Blueprints for thinking: The role of planning in cognitive development* (pp. 515–534). New York: Cambridge University Press.

Fuster, J. M. (1997). *The prefrontal cortex* (3rd ed.). New York: Raven Press.

Gathercole, S. E., & Pickering, S. J. (2000). Working memory deficits in children with low achievements in the national curriculum at 7 years of age. *British Journal of Educational Psychology, 70*(2), 177–194.

Gauvain, M. (2001). *The social context of cognition:* New York: Guilford Press.

Gioia, G. A., & Isquith, P. K. (2004). Ecological assessment of executive function in traumatic brain injury. *Developmental Neuropsychology, 25*, 135–158.

Golden, C. J. (1981). The Luria–Nebraska Children's Battery: Theory and formulation. In G. W. Hynd & J. E. Obrzut (Eds.), *Neuropsychological assessment and the school-aged child* (pp. 277–302). New York: Grune & Stratton.

Goldman-Rakic, P. S., Bourgeois, J.-P., & Rakic, P. (1997). Synaptic substrate of cognitive development: Life-span analysis of synaptogenesis in the prefrontal cortex of the nonhuman primate. In N. Krasnegor, G. R. Lyon, & P. S. Goldman-Rakic (Eds.), *Development of the prefrontal cortex: Evolution, neurobiology, and behavior* (pp. 27–47). Baltimore: Paul H. Brookes.

Goldstein, F. C. & Green, R. C. (1995). Assessment of problem solving and executive functions. In R. L. Mapou & J. Spector (Eds.), *Clinical neuropsychological assessment: A cognitive approach* (pp. 49–81). New York: Plenum Press.

Halstead, W. C. (1947). *Brain and intelligence.* Chicago: University of Chicago Press.

Hansell, N. K., Wright, M. J., Geffen, G. M., Geffen, L. B., Smith, G. A., & Martin, N. G. (2001). Genetic influence on ERP slow wave measures of working memory. *Behavioral Genetics, 31*, 603–614.

Heyder, K., Suchan, B., & Daum, I. (2004). Cortico-subcortical contributions to executive control. *Acta Psychologica, 115*, 271–289.

Hur, Y. M., & Bouchard, T. J. (1997). The genetic correlation between impulsivity and sensation seeking traits. *Behavioral Genetics, 27*, 455–463.

Huttenlocher, P. R., & Dabholkar, A. S. (1997). Developmental anatomy of prefrontal cortex. In N. Krasnegor, G. R. Lyon, & P. S. Goldman-Rakic (Eds.), *Development of the prefrontal cortex: Evolution, neurobiology, and behavior* (pp. 69–83). Baltimore: Paul H. Brookes.

Hynd, W. & Obrzut, J. E. (Eds.). (1981). *Neuropsychological assessment and the school-aged child.* New York: Grune & Stratton.

Iversen, S. D., & Dunnett, S. B. (1990). Functional organization of striatum with neural grafts. *Neuropsychologia, 28*, 601–626.

Jacobsen, C. F. (1935). Functions of frontal association area in primates. *Archives of Neurology and Psychiatry, 33*, 558–569.

Keil, K., & Kaszniak, A. W. (2002). Examining executive function in individuals with brain injury: A review. *Aphasiology, 16*, 305–335.

Kimberg, D. Y., D'Esposito, M., & Farah, M. J. (1998). Cognitive functions in the prefrontal cortex: Working memory and executive control. *Current Directions in Psychological Science, 6*, 185–192.

Klein, C. (2003). Assessing the development of executive functions. *International Society for the Study of Behavioural Development Newsletter, 43*(1), 8–11.

Kurdek, L. A., & Sinclair, R. J. (2000). Psychological, family, and peer predictors of academic outcomes in first- through fifth-grade children. *Journal of Educational Psychology, 92*(3), 449–457.

Lee, J. H., Kim, H. T., & Hyun, D. S. (2003). Possible association between serotonin transporter promoter region polymorphism and impulsivity in Koreans. *Psychiatry Research, 118*, 19–24.

Levin, H. S., Eisenberg, H. M., & Benton, A. L. (Eds.). (1991). *Frontal lobe function and dysfunction.* New York: Oxford University Press.

Lezak, M. D. (1995). *Neuropsychological assessment* (3rd ed.). New York: Oxford University Press.

Luciano, M. (2003). The neural and functional development of human prefrontal cortex. In M. de Haan & M. H. Johnson (Eds.), *The cognitive neuroscience of development* (pp. 157–180). New York: Psychology Press.

Luciano, M., Wright, M., Smith, G. A., Geffen, G. M., Geffen, L. B., & Martin, N. G. (2001). Genetic covariance among measures of information processing speed, working memory, and IQ. *Behavioral Genetics, 31*, 581–592.

Luria, A. R. (1966). *Higher cortical functions in man.* New York: Basic Books.

Luria, A. R. (1973). *The working brain.* New York: Basic Books.

Mezzacappa, E., Kindlon, D., & Earls, F. (2001). Child abuse and performance task assessments of executive functions in boys. *Journal of Child Psychology and Psychiatry, 42*(8), 1041–1048.

Milner, B. (1964). Some effects of frontal lobectomy in man. In J. Warren & K. Akert (Eds.), *The frontal granular cortex and behavior* (pp. 313–334). New York: McGraw Hill.

Miyake, A., Friedman, N. P., Emerson, M. J., Witzki, A. H., & Howerter, A. (2000). The unity and diversity of executive functions and their contributions to complex "frontal lobe" tasks: A latent variable analysis. *Cognitive Psychology, 41*, 49–100.

Moffitt, T. E. (1993). The neuropsychology of conduct disorder. *Development and Psychopathology, 5*(1–2), 135–151.

Monchi, O., Petrides, M., Petre, V., Worsley, K., & Dagher, A. (2001). Wisconsin Card Sorting revisited: Distinct neural circuits participating in different stages of the task identified by event-related functional magnetic resonance imaging. *Journal of Neuroscience, 21*, 7733–7741.

Neale, M. C., & Cardon, L. R. (1992). *Methodology for genetic studies of twins and families (NATO ASI Series D: Behavioral and Social Sciences, Vol. 67).* Dordrecht: Kluwer Academic.

NICHD Early Child Care Research Network. (2005). Predicting individual differences in attention, memory, and planning in first graders from experiences at home, child care, and school. *Developmental Psychology, 41*(1), 99–114.

Norman, D. A. & Shallice, T. (1986). Attention to action: Willed and automatic control of behavior. In R. J. Davidson, G. E. Schwartz, & D. Shapiro (Eds.), *Consciousness and self-regulation: Advances in research and theory* (Vol. 4, pp. 1–18). New York: Plenum.

Pennington, B. F., & Bennetto, L. (1993). Main effects of transactions in the neuropsychology of conduct disorder? Commentary on "The neuropsychology of conduct disorder." *Development and Psychopathology, 5*(1–2), 153–164.

Pennington, B. F., Bennetto, L., McAleer, O. K., & Roberts, R. J. (1995). Executive functions and working memory: Theoretical and measurement issues. In G. R. Lyon & N. A. Krasnegor (Eds.), *Attention, memory, and executive function* (pp. 327–348). Baltimore: Paul H. Brookes.

Piaget, J. (1954). *The construction of reality in the child* (M. Cook, Trans.). New York: Basic Books. (Original work published 1936)

Pribram, K. H. (1969). The amnestic syndrome: Disturbances in coding? In G. A.Talland & N. C. Waugh (Eds.), *The pathology of memory* (pp. 127–157). New York: Academic Press.

Roth, R. M., & Syakin, A. J. (2004). Executive dysfunction in attention-deficit/hyperactivity disorder: Cognitive and neuroimaging findings. *Psychiatric Clinics of North America, 27*, 83–96.

Scholnick, E. K., & Friedman, S. L. (1987). The planning construct in the psychological literature. In S. L. Friedman, E. K. Scholnick, & R. R. Cocking (Eds.), *Blueprints for thinking: The role of planning in cognitive development* (pp. 3–38). New York: Cambridge University Press.

Shonkoff, J. P., & Phillips, D. A. (Eds.). (2000). *From neurons to neighborhoods: The science of early child development.* Washington, DC: National Academy Press.

Stuss, D. T., & Benson, D. F. (1984). Neuropsychological studies of frontal lobes. *Psychological Bulletin, 95*, 3–28.

Thatcher, R. W. (1997). Human frontal lobe development: A theory of cyclical cortical reorganization. In N. Krasnegor, G. R. Lyon, & P. S. Goldman-Rakic (Eds.), *Development of the prefrontal cortex: Evolution, neurobiology, and behavior* (pp. 85–113). Baltimore: Paul H. Brookes.

Tranel, D., Anderson, S. W., & Benton, A. L. (1995). Development of the concept of executive function and its relationship to the frontal lobes. In F. Boller & J. Grafman (Eds.), *Handbook of neuropsychology* (Vol. 9, pp 126–148). Amsterdam: Elsevier.

Tueber, H. L. (1964). The riddle of frontal lobe function in man. In. J. Warren & K. Akert (Eds.), *The frontal granular cortex and behavior* (pp. 410–440). New York: McGraw-Hill.

Vygotsky, L. S. (1978). *Mind in society: The development of higher psychological processes.* Cambridge, MA: Harvard University Press.

Waltz, J. A., Knowlton, B. J., Holyoak, K. J., Boone, K. B., Back-Madruga, C., McPherson, S., Masterman, D., Chow, T., Cummings, J. L., & Miller, B. L. (2004). Relational integration and executive function in Alzheimer's Disease. *Neuropsychology, 18*, 296–305.

Welsh, M. C. (2001). The prefrontal cortex and the development of executive functions. In A. Kalverboer & A. Gramsbergen (Eds.), *Handbook of brain and behaviour development* (pp. 767–789). Dordrecht: Kluwer.

Welsh, M. C. (2002). Developmental and clinical variations in executive functions. In U. Kirk & D. Molfese (Eds.), *Developmental variations in language and learning* (pp. 139–185). Mahwah, NJ: Lawrence Erlbaum Associates.

Welsh, M. C., Huzinga, M., Granrud, M., Cooney, J., Adams, C., & van der Molen, M. (2002, February). *A structural equation model of executive function in normal young adults.* Paper presented at the annual meeting of INS, Toronto, Ontario, Canada.

Welsh, M. C., & Pennington, B. F. (1988). Assessing frontal lobe functioning in children: Views from developmental psychology. *Developmental Neuropsychology, 4*, 199–230.

Welsh, M. C., Pennington, B. F., & Groisser, D. B. (1991). A normative-developmental study of executive function: A window on prefrontal function in children. *Developmental Neuropsychology, 7*, 131–149.

Welsh, M. C., Pennington, B. F., Ozonoff, S., Rouse, B., & McCabe, M. (1990). Neuropsychology of early-treated phenylketonuria: Specific executive function deficits. *Child Development, 61*, 1697–1713.

Wiers, R. W., Gunning, W. B., & Sergeant, J. A. (1998). Is a mild deficit in executive functions in boys related to childhood ADHD or to parental multigenerational alcoholism? *Journal of Abnormal Child Psychology, 26*, 415–430.

Zelazo, P. D., Craik, F. I. M., & Booth, L. (2004). Executive function across the life span. *Acta Psychologica, 115*, 167–183.

Zelazo, P. D., & Frye, D. (1998). Cognitive complexity and control: II. The development of executive function in childhood. *Current Directions in Psychological Science, 7*(4), 121–126.

Zelazo, P. D., Muller, U., Frye, D., & Marcovitch, S. (2003). The development of executive function in early childhood. *Monographs of the Society for Research in Child Development, 68* (3, Serial No. 274).

10

Developing Social Understanding in a Social Context

Rachel Barr

Theory of mind (TOM) is a multi-faceted construct that captures the capacity to make inferences about others' mental states, such as intentions, emotions, desires, and beliefs. Over time, children come to realize that such mental activity is not obvious to another person. They use this information about mental states to interpret behavior in others and to regulate social interactions (Astington, 1993; Astington & Gopnik, 1991a).

Although there is considerable interest in this pivotal social construct, there is also a great deal of theoretical controversy. The origin of the term "theory of mind" is based on the "theory theory" explanation that children literally are "little scientists," constructing a working theory of the contents of other people's minds (Bartsch & Wellman, 1995). Harris (1991) criticizes the theory theory approach by arguing that people do not systematically develop a theory the way that scientists do, nor do they make and test hypotheses. He argues instead that others' behavior is interpreted via a comparison with one's own mental states or imagination of another's mind. That is, TOM develops because thoughts, feelings, and desires experienced by the child are projected onto other people or simulated (Harris, 1991). This approach is termed simulation theory. Additional controversy exists over whether TOM is a unique ability or whether it is part of a larger representation system. Perner (2001) argues that TOM is not an independent socio-cognitive ability but is part of a complex representational system that involves increasing memory, language, executive functioning, and problem-solving abilities. In contrast, Leslie (1987) posited an independent theory of mind module that is domain-specific and maturational in nature, along the lines of a linguistic module.

Taken together, current findings do not unequivocally support any one of the theories. Given the state of the art, Wellman (2002) recommends searching for their commonalities. Theory theories and modular theories both agree that simulation is an important component. In addition, general abilities such as memory are also commonly thought to play a role in the development of TOM. Although TOM is a social construct, only recently has the focus of the research broadened from limitations on cognitive processing to studying the development of TOM within the child's social context. Naïve psychology theorists claim the development of any type of theory cannot form independent of the social context in which it is being derived (Astington & Olson, 1995; Lillard, 1998).

Diverse theoretical perspectives have led to a multi-faceted approach to the study of TOM, and each perspective has its own specific empirical focus. Theory theory has led to an emphasis on the development of false belief and in particular on precursors such as understanding of other people's desires, emotions, knowledge, and true belief. Simulation theory has led to an emphasis on the role of pretend play in TOM development. Representational theory has led to an emphasis on the cognitive abilities that emerge alongside TOM, particularly memory, executive functioning, and language. Modular theory has led to a focus on biological factors that might provide starting states for environmental input that will lead to TOM development, or, in the case of autism, disruption of TOM development. Finally, the naïve psychology approach has led to a focus on social factors such as family structure and cultural differences that might contribute to individual differences in TOM acquisition. This chapter will, therefore, cover how TOM is measured, how it develops, and how it is related to other developing abilities, individual differences in social context, and what happens when TOM does not develop, as in the case of autism. Although the term "theory of mind" has been widely criticized for presupposing a belief that humans act on the basis of a naïve theory (Astington, 1998; Harris, 1991; Lillard, 1998; Nelson, Plesa, & Henseler, 1998), it will be used throughout the chapter because it is so widely employed.

How Is TOM Measured?

Many tasks have been developed to assess TOM development in preschool children, but the false belief tasks are by far the most commonly used. These tasks are typically told in picture-book story form or are acted out with puppets. In order to succeed on the false belief tasks, children have to suspend their own knowledge of the real location of an object and report the thoughts/representation of another person. That is, children have to demonstrate that they can hold information that differs from that of another person, rather than take the egocentric view that another person has the same knowledge as they do.

Change in location or unexpected transfer task

In this classic task (Wimmer & Perner, 1983) the child has to predict where a character will look for an object that the child sees moved to a new location, but the character has not seen moved. To ensure that failure on the task is not due to difficulty processing the task, the experimenter also asks two memory questions. First, does the child remember the original location of the object, and second, does the child remember that the character has no knowledge that the object has been moved (Perner, Leekam, & Wimmer, 1987).

The unexpected contents task

In this task, developed by Perner and colleagues (1987), an experimenter presents the children with a candy box and asks what is in the box. The experimenter opens the box to reveal pencils rather than candy and asks what another child who has not seen what is inside the box would think it contains (other condition). The child might also be asked what he/she thought was inside the box before it was opened (self condition) (Gopnik & Astington, 1988; Perner et al., 1987).

What Develops?

Piaget (1929) was the first to propose that children under the age of 7 years had difficulty separating the physical and mental world. Since then, researchers have been trying to map out how a number of different skills that develop during early childhood contribute to the emergence of a fully fledged TOM (Butterworth, 1991; Meltzoff, 2002; Perner, 1991; Tager-Flusberg, 2003; Wellman, 1991, 2002; Zaitchik, 1990). The latest data suggest that children progress from imitating others and attending to others' goals and intentions during infancy, to understanding that others have different desires during toddlerhood, to understanding that others have different emotions, different knowledge, and different beliefs during early childhood. The defining TOM ability for a 4-year-old is the ability to pass the false belief task and understand that others can hold false beliefs that conflict with the real world. Beyond false belief understanding is higher-order understanding of embedded beliefs, sarcasm, and faux pas. Each developmental phase is described below.

Phase I – infancy: understanding intentionality – the role of imitation and joint visual attention

In phase I, perspective taking and intentionality begin to develop as a result of imitation (Gopnik & Meltzoff, 1993) and joint visual attention (JVA; Baron-Cohen, 1995; Butterworth, 1991).

Imitation. Before language, imitation is a critical form of non-verbal communication. At birth infants engage in face-to-face imitation games. Adults respond to this early imitation by imitating their infants' vocal play and facial gestures (Meltzoff, 1990; Papousek & Papousek, 1977; Trevarthen, 1993). Infants also recognize when they are being imitated (Meltzoff, 1990). Meltzoff and Gopnik (1994) argue that such parent–infant imitation games give infants practice in social interaction and communication, and as such are a "theory of mind tutorial."

Meltzoff and Moore (1977, 1983, 1989, 1992) found that newborn, 1-, and 3-month-old infants were able to imitate a range of adult gestures, including mouth opening, tongue protrusion, and head movement displays. They also demonstrated that 6-week-old infants remember the specific facial gestures modeled by a specific experimenter after a 24-hour delay. That is, infants may be able to use imitation to identify others around them (Meltzoff & Moore, 1994). Based on these findings, Meltzoff (2002) concluded that the neonate can recognize equivalence between his or her behavior and the behavior of other humans. Such a "starting state nativism" means that infants come into the world with the ability to map others' facial gestures onto their own via imitation and thereby detect that they are like other people.

Joint visual attention. JVA refers to "looking where someone else is looking," or "follow-ing the direction of attention of another person to the object of their attention" (Butterworth, 1991, p. 213). In order for JVA to occur, infants must look toward the face of another person. Face preference typically emerges very early during the neonatal period. Newborns prefer to look at faces more than any other visual stimuli (Hainline, 1978), preferentially gaze at a face with open eyes rather than a face with closed eyes (Batki, Baron-Cohen, Wheelwright, Connellan, & Ahluwalia, 2000), and discriminate facial expressions (Field, Woodson, Greenberg, & Cohen, 1982).

Over the first few months, the social contingency of face play becomes increasingly reinforcing to the infant. Infants display greater capillary dilation to social than non-social stimuli at 1 and 4 months of age (Fitzgerald, 1968). By 3 months infants are also devel-oping non-verbal communication which involves hand gestures, pre-speech oral move-ments, and bidirectional turn taking with their caregivers (Trevarthen, 1993). At this stage infants engage in dyadic (infant–other) eye-to-eye contact with their caregivers (Butterworth, 2001).

Beginning at around 6 months of age, attention extends beyond face-to-face interactions to other objects in the world and becomes triadic (infant–object–other) (Butterworth, 2001). At 6 months infants follow the direction of gaze to one side of space or another but cannot specifically locate an object. Nine- to 12-month-olds can locate a specific object in space, follow head and trunk movements, and begin social referencing. During social referencing they alternate their gaze between the jointly attended object and the adult gaze to assess the adult's perception of the object to help them decide whether to approach or avoid the object. These actions demonstrate that they are begin-ning to understand another's behavior as goal-directed (Butterworth, 2001).

An even more sophisticated coordinated JVA emerges at about 12 months. By this stage infants can point and can follow adult points. Pointing is important because it indicates that infants expect others to understand their goals. That is, infants expect others to follow their line of sight to a desired object in order to get the object or simply to share attention, and they understand when another person is trying to direct their attention as well. By 18 months they will even jointly attend to an object that is behind them.

Although studies of joint attention imply that infants have intentions and understand that others have intentions, direct studies of intentionality understanding are difficult in pre-verbal children (Heyes, 1996; Rovee-Collier, 1997). Several studies have, however, shown rudimentary understanding of intentionality during infancy (Meltzoff, 1995, 1999; Woodward, 1998). In a behavioral re-enactment paradigm, for example, 15- and 18-month-old infants, but not 9-month-olds, imitated pulling apart a dumbbell (the intended actions of an adult model) when the adult had attempted but failed to pull it apart (Meltzoff, 1995, 1999). When the action was demonstrated by an inanimate object, however, infants did not imitate pulling apart the dumbbell (the failed action) but did imitate pulling apart the dumbbell if the inanimate object demonstrated the completed action (Meltzoff, 1995). Meltzoff (1995) reported that during the second year of life infants are making distinctions between animate agents that have goals and intentions and inanimate agents that do not.

Taken together, studies of joint attention suggest that there is a long developmental progression between infants' first face preference to the understanding of others as intentional beings. JVA is, however, a fundamental step toward understanding others' minds in a social context and forms the foundation for the later ability to follow a conversation and interpret others' behavior based on their intentions (Bruner, 1995; Tomasello, 1995).

Phase II – Toddlerhood: understanding desire and pretend play

In phase II, 1½- to 2-year-old toddlers begin to understand the desires of others and start to engage in pretend play (Leslie, 1987; Wellman, 1994, 2002).

Desire. By 18 months, infants understand that an adult might desire something that is undesirable to them. In Repacholi and Gopnik's (1997) study, an adult tastes a piece of broccoli and a goldfish cracker. In one condition the adult indicates (through facial expressions and sounds) that she prefers the cracker (consistent with the infant's preference), and in another condition she indicates that she prefers the broccoli (inconsistent with the infant's preference). When asked to give the adult some more food, the infant chooses the food that the adult preferred (either the cracker or the broccoli), even if it is inconsistent with the infant's preference.

Bartsch and Wellman (1995) found that by 2 years of age children communicated desires using the verb "want" in their everyday conversations. Verbs like believe, think, and know do not routinely enter into everyday conversation until one year later. More parental talk about desire leads to earlier understanding of belief and more child talk about desire leads to earlier belief talk (Bartsch & Wellman, 1995).

Pretend play. It has been argued that social pretend and false beliefs develop in parallel because both require the ability to translate non-literal instances to understand the other person's perspective. Pretend play involves understanding another's emotions, thoughts, and beliefs during the pretend situation and may help the child to relate the mental and physical worlds (Dunn, 1991; Leslie, 1987; Wellman, 2002). A number of studies have demonstrated an association between specific aspects of pretend play and TOM task performance. First, children with imaginary friends have very high levels of pretend play and have an earlier onset of false belief understanding than other children (Taylor & Carlson, 1997). Second, Astington and Jenkins (1995) found an association between TOM performance and two specific aspects of pretend play: planned discussion of the pretend scenario and role assignment. Those children who planned the game more and assigned roles more often were more likely to pass false belief tasks, independent of age and language ability. The authors concluded that children who were more aware that others may have different thoughts or beliefs were also more likely to clarify the pretend situation with their peers. Third, Tan-Niam, Wood, and O'Malley (1998) found that level of shared meaning during pretend play was related to level of TOM when they studied pairs of children. If one member or both members of the pair had passed a false belief task, there was more shared meaning in pretend play.

Phase III – the 3-year-old's emerging understanding of knowledge and belief

There are a number of distinctions that 3-year-olds make that suggest they are taking a mentalistic approach, that is, thinking about thinking or beliefs. First, 3-year-olds can distinguish between pretend and real events (Wellman & Estes, 1986). A 3-year-old understands that a real cookie can be shared or eaten but that an imagined cookie cannot, and that an imagined cookie but not a real cookie can be transformed into something else. Second, Woolley and Wellman (1990) found that while children could not pass standard appearance–reality questions at 3 years of age, they could report that a toy was a pretend version of a real object even if it appeared similar to the real object. Third, 3-year-olds can recognize that seeing leads to knowing. Pratt and Bryant (1990) showed children two boxes with one person looking inside one and the other merely lifting the other box. The 3-year-olds reported that the person who had looked in the box "knows" the contents of the box but the other person who merely lifted it does not.

Although children cannot necessarily pass the false belief task before the age of 4 years, there are some occasions when 3-year-olds can both predict and explain behavior on the basis of understanding beliefs so long as false belief or conflicting truths are not involved (Bartsch & Wellman, 1989; Wellman & Estes, 1986; Zaitchik, 1990). In the change in location task, if the object is placed in two locations and the child is told that the character thinks that it is in only one of the two locations, children predict that the character will look in the location where the character thinks that it is. If they are told that the character changed his or her belief, children make a prediction based on the changed belief (Wellman & Bartsch, 1988). When the false belief task is simplified such that children are asked to explain the character's looking behavior, rather than to predict where the character will look, then they are more likely to explain correctly (Bartsch & Wellman, 1989). In a direct comparison of a prediction and explanation task only 31% passed the prediction test, while 66% of 3- and 4-year-olds gave explanations based on false beliefs. Bartsch and Wellman (1989) argued that providing explanations for behaviors might be easier than making predictions about behavior because there is no need to override conflicting thoughts about beliefs and desires of the character. The character has already failed to find the object of desire and this requires an explanation. Although it would be equally easy for children to explain actions from a behavioral perspective, the majority of children's explanations involved discussion about what another person thought or believed (Wellman & Bartsch, 1988; Wellman & Estes, 1986). Overall, the 3-year-old is in the final stages of the apprenticeship to understanding that others hold different beliefs.

Phase IV: Four-year-olds' understanding of the false belief task

Four years is considered a watershed in TOM development. The final developmental step during this phase is that children begin to understand misrepresentation or conflicting truths (Wellman, 2002). By 4 years children typically can explain another person's behavior on the basis of his or her false belief and thereby pass the false belief task. In a recent meta-analysis of 178 false belief studies Wellman, Cross, and Watson (2001) found that there was a systematic progression of children going from failing to passing the tasks between 2½ and 5 years of age. Typically children under 4 years do not pass the standard false belief tasks even though 98% correctly answer the memory questions (Perner et al., 1987; Wellman et al., 2001). Wellman and colleagues (2001) found that children under 3.5 years performed below chance, committing the false belief error, 3½- to 4-year-olds performed at chance, while 4-year-olds performed significantly above chance. This finding is consistent across tasks, question types, presentation mode, and linguistic forms for questions (Astington & Gopnik, 1991a; Wellman et al., 2001). Nevertheless, some factors do increase performance: (1) framing the question as deception toward another; (2) asking children to be active participants by changing the location of the object in the story; (3) having the object disappear instead of changing location; or (4) enhancing the salience of the initial belief. Wellman et al. (2001), however, argue against an early competence interpretation of the data. Although these factors increase performance, children systematically improve with age, suggesting that there is a conceptual change in the ability to process false belief information during the preschool years.

Phase V: second- and third-order representations

TOM continues to develop well into childhood, but investigation in children over 5 years is scarce (rare examples are Astington, 2003; Keenan, 2003). When studied, researchers focus on the development of second- and third-order representations. Second-order belief representations examine whether children can understand embedded beliefs, that is, that people have beliefs about beliefs in others' minds, which can also be true or false (see Astington, Pelletier, & Homer, 2002; Perner & Wimmer, 1985). A third-order representational task used with adults is the "faux pas" test (Stone, Baron-Cohen, Calder, Keane, & Young, 2003). The faux pas task looks at whether the participant understands that the faux pas was unintentionally hurtful to another participant in the vignette. Children typically do not succeed on this task until 11 years, but performance is highly correlated with their ability to pass first- and second-order false belief tasks.

How is TOM Related to Other Abilities?

A number of other representational abilities emerge at about the same time that children pass the false belief task. It has been argued that an increasingly sophisticated representation system is necessary to pass the false belief task because it contributes to the ability to hold different perspectives in mind (Perner, 2001).

Representational abilities

At around the same time that children pass the false belief task, they can pass a variant of the task, a false photograph task. The false photograph task is the same as the false belief task except that rather than the person and an object being moved, a photograph is taken and then afterwards an object is moved (Zaitchik, 1990). The child is asked where the object is in the photograph. Children pass the false photograph task when they correctly report that the photograph will show the object in the original position not in the new position. Here the child must distinguish between a representation of the room and the current state of the room.

When children first succeed on false belief tasks they also improve on three aspects of memory processing, source monitoring, metamemory skills, and free recall (Perner, 2001). Metamemory is one's knowledge of one's own memory ability. Once children gain metamemory skills they also begin to utilize rehearsal techniques and therefore can keep track of more information and the source of information hence an increase in both free recall and source monitoring. This also makes children less susceptible to misinformation, making it easier to hold conflicting truths or false beliefs in mind.

Their increasing ability to hold conflicting truths in mind also enhances their performance on the appearance–reality task. In the appearance–reality task the child is shown an object that looks or appears to be one thing but on closer examination is really another. For example, an object that looks like a rock is really a sponge. Those under 4 years old tend to make errors, and, as in the false belief task, performance on appearance–reality distinctions improves dramatically between 3 and 5 years (Flavell, Flavell, & Green, 1983). Gopnik and Astington (1988) found a significant correlation between the appearance–reality task and the false belief performance.

Executive functioning

To process the sequence of events in the false belief task, children need adequate working memory and the ability to inhibit their tendency to refer to their own knowledge base. Such working memory and inhibition is called executive functioning. Executive functioning as measured by the Zelazo card-sorting test, a children's version of the Wisconsin Card-Sorting Test and a measure of inhibition, is correlated with false belief performance (Frye, Zelazo, & Palfai, 1995; see also Welsh, Friedman, & Spieker, this volume).

Language ability

With respect to language ability, some argue that syntax demands in some TOM tasks mask earlier comprehension of false belief (Bretherton & Beeghly, 1982; Clements &

Perner, 1994). Clements and Perner (1994), for example, found that while 80% of children under 3½ years fail the verbal question about the location of the object, 80% look in the correct location. Furthermore, in a longitudinal study assessing language ability and false belief performance in 3-year-olds at three time points across a seven-month period, language ability predicted false belief performance, but not vice versa (Astington & Jenkins, 1999). In particular, syntactic ability was the strongest predictor. There are two possible ways to interpret these data. First, performance on a verbally based task requires a certain level of verbal ability before it can be passed. A stronger interpretation of the data, and the one that Astington and Jenkins favor, is that TOM depends upon language development. That is, learning the structure of language gives the child the symbolic representations in which to frame the understanding of the mind. Even if a weaker interpretation of the data is correct, Astington (2003) argues for the importance of controlling for language ability when assessing false belief understanding.

The Role of Social Context

Recently, there has been renewed interest in the role that social interaction might play in shaping children's TOM. Put simply, how children come to understand others must be considered within the context of their social experience (Dunn, 1992). False belief tasks may underestimate the child's real-world understanding of others' beliefs and intentions, and, as such, performance may in fact be better under naturalistic conditions (Astington, 2003; Astington & Jenkins, 1995; Astington & Olson, 1995; Barr & Hayne, 2003; Bartsch & Wellman, 1995; Dunn, 1992; O'Neill, 1996). Conflicting results from naturalistic studies, which tend to produce earlier reports of TOM understanding than experimental studies, do not necessarily mean that the different study designs measure different phenomena; instead they may capture different aspects or gradual developments of the same ability (Astington & Olson, 1995).

It has been argued that the narrative environment itself may also play a pivotal role in predicting TOM development (Astington, 2003; Bartsch & Wellman, 1995; Dunn, Brown, Slomkowski, Tesla, & Youngblade, 1991; Lewis, Freeman, Kyriakidou, Maridaki-Kassotaki, & Berridge, 1996; Nelson et al., 1998; Perner, Ruffman, & Leekam, 1994). Research on everyday conversations shows that children begin discussing emotions and desires during the second year of life and mental states of "thinking" and "knowing" during the third year (Bartsch & Wellman, 1995; Brown & Dunn, 1991). This understanding of others, found in naturalistic speech, occurs almost a year before children pass the false belief task.

Sibling status

It is now well recognized that social interaction with parents, other significant adults, siblings, and peers helps to shape the course of cognitive development during infancy and childhood (Farrant & Reese, 2000; Lamb, 1978; Sutton-Smith & Rosenberg, 1970; Teti,

Bond, & Gibbs, 1986; Zukow, 1990). Older siblings, like parents, often alter their behavior to meet the needs of younger children, providing the scaffold that is necessary for young children to learn (Dunn & Kendrick, 1982).

Dunn argues (e.g., Youngblade & Dunn, 1995) that sibling interactions are particularly important in TOM development. Three- to 4-year-old children with siblings pass a standard false belief task earlier than children without siblings (Jenkins & Astington, 1996; Lewis et al., 1996; Perner et al., 1994; Peterson, 2001; Ruffman, Perner, Naito, Parkin, & Clements, 1998; but see Arranz, Artamendi, Olabarrieta, & Martin, 2002; Cole & Mitchell, 2000). Peterson (2001) found that age of the non-target sibling was important, such that having an infant sibling or an adolescent sibling did not enhance false belief understanding. Cole and Mitchell (2000) found no effect of sibling status but found that socio-economic index (SEI) was in fact predictive of TOM performance, such that children from lower SEI families scored lower on false belief tasks than other children, controlling for age and language ability. In addition Lewis and colleagues (1996) found that the number of contacts children had with other relatives and the amount of time they spent with relatives who lived in close proximity uniquely predicted variance in false belief performance, along with age of the child and the number of younger and older siblings. Furthermore, Peterson and Siegal (2002) found that when a child (whether he or she is popular or unpopular with his/her peers) has a strong mutual stable friendship, the child will have a higher TOM score. Taken together, these findings suggest that it is the nature of the social interactions in which the child engages that are critical for TOM development.

There are a number of potential reasons why increased interaction with siblings, peers, or adults might enhance false belief understanding. First, sibling interaction in particular provides a rich source of information about mental representation, particularly in the form of joint pretend play (Barr & Hayne, 2003; Dunn, 1989; Dunn & Dale, 1984; Leslie, 1987; Meltzoff & Gopnik, 1994; Perner et al., 1994; Piaget, 1962). Youngblade and Dunn (1995) found that higher levels of pretend play with older siblings when children were 33 months old correlated with their false belief performance at 40 months of age even when children's mean length utterance (a measure of language production) was taken into account. In general more discussion about feelings was also positively related to levels of joint pretense.

Although children may be active participants in joint pretend play by 2 years of age, entry into pretend play may initially be imitative (Abramovitch, Corter, & Lando, 1979; Barr & Hayne, 2003; Dunn & Dale, 1984; Piaget, 1962; Zukow, 1990). The fact that children with siblings exhibit advanced levels of symbolic play may be due, at least initially, to their increased opportunity for imitation of the pretend play exhibited by their older siblings (Barr & Hayne, 2003). In a diary study on the effect of older siblings on the development of imitation, Barr and Hayne (2003) found that higher levels of joint pretend play characterized imitation by 12- to 18-month-old infants with siblings. An intriguing possibility is that other forms of peer–peer play may also facilitate the emergence of joint pretend play and TOM, in particular child care. It is important to note that types of sibling conflict resolution are also correlated with TOM performance (Bartsch & Wellman, 1995; Foote & Holmes-Lonergan, 2003; Lewis et al., 1996; Peterson, 2001). Specifically, those who scored higher on TOM were more likely to use persuasion and negotiating during sibling conflict situations (Foote & Holmes-Lonergan, 2003).

Finally, early talk about emotions and desires predicts earlier false belief understanding (Arranz et al., 2002; Bartsch & Wellman, 1995; Dunn et al., 1991). Dunn and colleagues (1991) found that mother–sibling–child conversations about feelings and causality when children were 33 months old correlated with their false belief performance and affect labeling at 40 months. Children's performance was also influenced by the relationships between the mother and older sibling and between the siblings, demonstrating the influence of complex social interactions. Youngblade and Dunn (1995) also noted that mothers and siblings talk about feelings with children differently. Mothers focus on discussing children's feelings, while siblings focus on shared feelings when playing make-believe or teasing. The fact that children with older siblings receive social information not only from multiple sources, but in a fashion that is complementary rather than redundant makes it even less surprising that younger siblings pass the false belief task at an earlier age than children without older siblings. Taken together, increased pretend play, other-focused conflict resolution, and discussion of emotions in positive relationships during the first three years of life significantly increases performance on false belief tasks in children with older siblings.

When theory of mind does not emerge: autism

Children with autism have a socio-cognitive deficit in the ability to perceive others as social beings with intentionality and a consequent deficit in sharing attention and experience (Baron-Cohen, 1991; Butterworth, 2001; Tomasello, 1995). In a seminal study, Baron-Cohen, Leslie, and Frith (1985) tested groups of typically developing children, children with Down's syndrome, and children with autism on a false belief task. They found that 85% of typically developing children and those with Down's syndrome passed the test while only 20% of children with autism passed. It is important to note that children with autism passed the control questions on memory, reality, and naming, demonstrating that their failure was not due to poor memory, linguistic problems, or simple inattention to the task (see Baron-Cohen, 1994). Many of the abilities that develop in typically developing children prior to a fully fledged TOM system do not develop in children with autism. Specifically, children with autism do not develop the typical phase I and phase II TOM abilities such as gaze monitoring (Baron-Cohen, 1994) or face preference. Dawson and colleagues (2002) found that 3- and 4-year-olds with autism could not differentiate between familiar and unfamiliar faces as did both typically developing and developmentally delayed children without autism; however, they could differentiate between familiar and unfamiliar objects, suggesting that a face recognition deficit is present early in development. Such a deficit may place these children on a trajectory where they also miss facial emotions.

Children with autism also show impairments in pointing (for review see Baron-Cohen, 1991, 1994). They tend to use proto-imperative pointing (e.g., pointing commands) and contact gestures (taking another person by the hand); however, they do not use proto-declarative pointing (e.g., pointing for shared interest) and they have difficulty interpreting such gestures (see Baron-Cohen, 1991; Dawson et al., 2002; Tomasello &

Camaioni, 1997). The absence of proto-declarative pointing is now one of the key diagnostic criteria for early identification of autism (Osterling & Dawson, 1994; Robins, Fein, Barton, & Green, 2001). Children with autism do, however, learn gestures such as hand clapping, waving bye, and shaking the head no. This may have to do with the repetitive and relatively unchanging nature of these gestures (Dawson, personal communication, 1996). They may in fact only be mimicking these gestures without fully understanding their conventional meaning (Tomasello & Camaioni, 1997). Owing to these large and very early deficits, Baron-Cohen (1991) attributes most of the subsequent deficits in the understanding of others to an initial primary deficit in joint attention functioning.

Children with autism also have deficits in imitation and play (Dawson & Adams, 1984). This is despite the fact that the social input of parents who have children with autism is not different from other parents (Baron-Cohen, 1991). Baron-Cohen (1987) found that only 20% of children with autism exhibited spontaneous pretend play in a free play situation while 80–90% of children with Down's syndrome and typically developing children did so.

Children with autism also fail on representational and language tasks that typically developing children pass at about the same time they pass the false belief task. They fail a pragmatic language task where they cannot regulate the conversation to keep in mind the knowledge that their conversational partners already have (Perner, Frith, Leslie, & Leekam, 1989). They exhibit limited use of mental state language terms (Tager-Flusberg, 1993), limited understanding of emotions in others when the emotions are more cognitive or belief-based (Baron-Cohen, 1991), and are impaired on recognizing the expression of surprise (Baron-Cohen, Spitz, & Cross, 1993). Perner and colleagues (1989) also found that children with autism failed a seeing-leads-to-knowing task. On appearance–reality tasks, such children are unable to report the difference between what an object looks like and what it really is. They seem to have extreme difficulty holding two representations in mind at once and focus on the perception rather than the knowledge of the object (Baron-Cohen, 1994).

An intriguing finding, however, is that while children with autism routinely fail false belief tasks, they pass the false photograph task (Leekam & Perner, 1991, see above). Children with autism can report the position of the original object in the photograph even though the object has been subsequently moved after the photograph was taken. That is, they can form an absent physical representation but not an absent social representation.

Baron-Cohen (1995) coined the term "mindblindness" and suggested that the major deficit in autism was a deficit in empathizing, which included deficits in joint attention, processing of intentions, recognizing emotions, pretense, and TOM. In the case of autism such a deficit in one or more of these abilities means that the pathway to adaptive social interaction is vastly divergent from typically developing children.

Are there cross-cultural differences?

There has been considerable debate over whether TOM is maturational and can develop independent of the environment. It has been hypothesized that TOM is a module, much like a linguistic device, that will emerge systematically in every child (Leslie, 1987). If performance is uniform across cultures, then this would be unequivocal support for the maturational account. On the other hand, it has been hypothesized that TOM is based on socialization or enculturation of attitudes and behaviors (Astington & Gopnik, 1991a, 1991b; Bruner, 1995; Lillard, 1998; Nelson et al., 1998). That is, scripts or narratives are internalized from the environment and are used to interpret others' behavior in analogous situations. If TOM is present in some and not other cultures, then this would be unequivocal support for the social construction account. Socialization differences in terms of sibling status, home discourse, and narration of events reported above strongly suggest that neither account is entirely plausible. More recently the strict maturational or modular approach has been modified and now uses starting states rather than innate modules to explain early predispositions. Starting states provide constraints on the infant's behavior to increase the chances that the environmental input and interaction patterns with others will be sought after in order for TOM to develop (Meltzoff, 2002). Those interaction patterns are constructed in a larger social sphere, and the cultural and group processes in its development also need to be considered (Astington, 2003; Lillard, 1998; Moghaddam, 2003). Lillard (1998) argues, in particular, that theory theory needs to be revised to allow for the impact of cultural variation on TOM. She asserts that culture itself is a source of evidence, and that variation in culture will lead to variation in the personal theory that is developed. For example, owing to differences in schooling and emphasis on individual versus collective norms, some cultures do not place as much importance on the mind, desires, or intentions (for review see Lillard, 1998). There are also vast cultural differences in the conception of self, on the effect of emotion on behavior, and on whether or not external, magical, or ancestral forces can directly influence behavior.

Cross-cultural data have shown remarkable consistency in the presence of a TOM across cultures but differences in developmental pathways and timelines. Although the bulk of studies have been conducted on white middle-class children from the US, the UK, Canada, Germany, and Austria, TOM studies have also been conducted in China, Turkey, Greece, Japan, the United Arab Emirates, and a traditional pre-literate hunter-gatherer sub-Saharan Baka tribe (Avis & Harris, 1991; Wellman et al., 2001). Although children from every culture pass a variant of the false belief task, there are, however, some variations in timing of false belief task solving from as early as the commonly reported 4 years to 6 to 7 years (Avis & Harris, 1991; Wellman et al., 2001).

Only recently have there been studies conducted that assess what might account for age variations. Holmes, Black, and Miller (1996) studied TOM development in children attending Head Start programs, where the sample consisted primarily of low-income African-American children. They found that children in their sample performed significantly worse on false belief tasks than other samples. In particular, a majority of children did not pass the false belief task until 5 years of age, one year later than in studies with white middle-class children.

One potential factor that might mediate cultural differences is parenting style. A widely accepted classification of parenting styles is authoritarian, authoritative, and permissive. Authoritarian parents focus on discipline while authoritative parents stress the importance of questioning and reasoning. Prior cross-cultural differences have demonstrated that a particular parenting style in one cultural context leads to academic success, but the same parenting style within a different cultural context does not. Vinden (2001) examined the association between parenting style and TOM development in Korean-American and Anglo-American families. She found significantly higher levels of authoritarian parenting in Korean-American families than in Anglo-American families. For Anglo-American families, authoritarian parenting was correlated with poorer performance on TOM tasks but the association did not hold for Korean-American families. In fact, while there was no difference in performance at 3 and 4 years, 5-year-old Korean children performed significantly better than Anglo-American children. Vinden argued that cultural priority differences, such as an emphasis on social expectations and norms combined with an encouraging parenting style, led to TOM performance that exceeded Anglo-Americans. The authoritarian style in Anglo-American families, with individual goals rather than collective goals, impaired TOM performance.

Why is Theory of Mind Development Important?

People use information about mental states to interpret behavior in others and to regulate social interactions (Astington, 1993; Astington & Gopnik, 1991b). Understanding of others' minds, and in particular false belief, is important for understanding morals, sarcasm, jokes, manipulation, Machiavellianism, lies, mistakes, and deception and to develop coherent autobiographical memory (Astington, 1993; Lagattuta & Wellman, 2001; Perner, 2001; Perner et al., 1987; Repacholi, Slaughter, Pritchard, & Gibbs, 2003; Wimmer & Perner, 1983). There is some evidence that newer pedagogical methods, which take developing TOM into account, may be more effective than traditional methods because they help children construct knowledge of their world and to reflect on their own individual learning (Astington, 1993).

A potential negative outcome of poor TOM development is peer rejection, poor communication, and aggressive behavior. For example, Capage and Watson (2001) found that TOM performance was a good predictor of social competence such that higher TOM scores were related to lower aggression scores in 3½- to 6-year-olds when age and language ability were controlled. Badenes, Estevan, and Bacete (2000) referred to development of a maladaptive TOM in children who are being abused whereby actions by others would be interpreted as aggressive acts. In the short term this would serve a protective function for the abused child, but in the long term it would lead to many difficulties with relationship formation.

Conclusions

Early competencies such as joint attention, imitation, understanding desires, pretend play, and representational skills are all critical for developing a TOM. Such abilities are building blocks for understanding others' mental states, an ability that continues to develop well beyond the preschool years. Autism research provides the best example that social input alone is not enough. Children require the social cognitive skills to decouple reality from pretend (Leslie, 1987), to recognize intentions (Meltzoff, 1995), and to hold multiple representations (Perner, 2001). Therefore, starting states in the child necessarily provide some constraints on the system. In particular, to develop a TOM, children must have a starting state that primes them to be attuned to others (Baron-Cohen, 1994; Meltzoff & Gopnik, 1994; Perner, 2001; Wellman, 2002). To use Bartsch and Wellman's (1995) analogy, children are like science students – they have an inherent interest in the social world around them and are surrounded by others who have a vested interest in helping them navigate that world. In a supportive social context, children learn the rules of the social world. Acknowledging that there are multiple contributions to the developing TOM will lead to a more sophisticated analysis of developmental pathways, and such findings will have important implications for early childhood development.

Note

This research was funded by grant number HD043047–01 from the National Institute Child Health and Development to Rachel Barr. I thank Amaya Garcia and Kimberley Price for assistance with the research.

References

Abramovitch, R., Corter, C. M., & Lando, B. (1979). Sibling interaction in the home. *Child Development, 50*(4), 997–1003.
Arranz, E., Artamendi, J., Olabarrieta, F., & Martin, J. (2002). Family context and theory of mind development. *Early Child Development & Care, 172*(1), 9–22.
Astington, J. W. (1993). *The child's discovery of the mind.* Cambridge, MA: Harvard University Press.
Astington, J. W. (1998). Theory of mind, Humpty Dumpty, and the icebox. *Human Development, 41*(1), 30–39.
Astington, J. W. (2003). Sometimes necessary, never sufficient: False-belief understanding and social competence. In B. Repacholi & V. Slaughter (Eds.), *Individual differences in theory of mind: Implications for typical and atypical development* (pp. 13–38). New York: Psychology Press.
Astington, J. W., & Gopnik, A. (1991a). Developing understanding of desire and intention. In A. Whiten (Ed.), *Natural theories of mind: Evolution, development and simulation of everyday mindreading* (pp. 39–50). Cambridge, MA: Blackwell.
Astington, J. W., & Gopnik, A. (1991b). Theoretical explanations of children's understanding of the mind. *British Journal of Developmental Psychology, 9*(1), 7–31.
Astington, J. W., & Jenkins, J. M. (1995). Theory of mind development and social understanding. *Cognition & Emotion, 9*(2–3), 151–165.
Astington, J. W., & Jenkins, J. M. (1999). A longitudinal study of the relation between language and theory-of-mind development. *Developmental Psychology, 35*(5), 1311–1320.
Astington, J. W., & Olson, D. R. (1995). The cognitive revolution in children's understanding of mind. *Human Development, 38*(4–5), 179–189.

Astington, J. W., Pelletier, J., & Homer, B. (2002). Theory of mind and epistemological development: The relation between children's second-order false-belief understanding and their ability to reason about evidence. *New Ideas in Psychology, 20*(2–3), 131–144.

Avis, J., & Harris, P. L. (1991). Belief–desire reasoning among Baka children: Evidence for a universal conception of mind. *Child Development, 62*(3), 460–467.

Badenes, L. V., Estevan, R. A. C., & Bacete, F. J. (2000). Theory of mind and peer rejection at school. *Social Development, 9*(3), 271–283.

Baron-Cohen, S. (1987). Autism and symbolic play. *British Journal of Developmental Psychology, 5*(2), 139–148.

Baron-Cohen, S. (1991). Precursors to a theory of mind: Understanding attention in others. In A. Whiten (Ed.), *Natural theories of mind: Evolution, development and simulation of everyday mindreading* (pp. 233–251). Cambridge, MA: Blackwell.

Baron-Cohen, S. (1994). From attention–goal psychology to belief–desire psychology: The development of a theory of mind, and its dysfunction. In S. Baron-Cohen, H. E. Tager-Flusberg, & D. J. Cohen (Eds.), *Understanding other minds: Perspectives from autism* (pp. 59–82). London: Oxford University Press.

Baron-Cohen, S. (1995). The eye direction detector (EDD) and the shared attention mechanism (SAM): Two cases for evolutionary psychology. In C. Moore & P. J. Dunham (Eds.), *Joint attention: Its origins and role in development* (pp. 41–59). Hillsdale, NJ: Erlbaum.

Baron-Cohen, S., Leslie, A. M., & Frith, U. (1985). Does the autistic child have a "theory of mind"? *Cognition, 21*(1), 37–46.

Baron-Cohen, S., Spitz, A., & Cross, P. (1993). Do children with autism recognise surprise? A research note. *Cognition & Emotion, 7*(6), 507–516.

Barr, R., & Hayne, H. (2003). It's not what you know, it's who you know: Older siblings facilitate imitation during infancy. *International Journal of Early Years Education, 11*(1), 7–21.

Bartsch, K., & Wellman, H. (1989). Young children's attribution of action to beliefs and desires. *Child Development, 60*(4), 946–964.

Bartsch, K., & Wellman, H. M. (1995). *Children talk about the mind.* London: Oxford University Press.

Batki, A., Baron-Cohen, S., Wheelwright, S., Connellan, J., & Ahluwalia, J. (2000). Is there an innate gaze module? Evidence from human neonates. *Infant Behavior & Development, 23*(2), 223–229.

Bretherton, I., & Beeghly, M. (1982). Talking about internal states: The acquisition of an explicit theory of mind. *Developmental Psychology, 18*(6), 906–921.

Brown, J. R., & Dunn, J. (1991). "You can cry, mum": The social and developmental implications of talk about internal states. *British Journal of Developmental Psychology, 9*(2), 237–256.

Bruner, J. (1995). The cognitive revolution in children's understanding of mind: Commentary. *Human Development, 38*(4–5), 203–213.

Butterworth, G. (1991). The ontogeny and phylogeny of joint visual attention. In A. Whiten (Ed.), *Natural theories of mind: Evolution, development and simulation of everyday mindreading* (pp. 223–232). Cambridge, MA: Blackwell.

Butterworth, G. (2001). Joint visual attention in infancy. In G. Bremner & A. Fogel (Eds.), *Blackwell handbook of infant development* (pp. 213–240). Malden, MA: Blackwell.

Capage, L., & Watson, A. C. (2001). Individual differences in theory of mind, aggressive behavior, and social skills in young children. *Early Education & Development, 12*(4), 613–628.

Clements, W. A., & Perner, J. (1994). Implicit understanding of belief. *Cognitive Development, 9*(4), 377–395.

Cole, K., & Mitchell, P. (2000). Siblings in the development of executive control and a theory of mind. *British Journal of Developmental Psychology, 18*(2), 279–295.

Dawson, G., & Adams, A. (1984). Imitation and social responsiveness in autistic children. *Journal of Abnormal Child Psychology, 12*(2), 209–225.

Dawson, G., Carver, L., Meltzoff, A. N., Panagiotides, H., McPartland, J., & Webb, S. J. (2002). Neural correlates of face and object recognition in young children with autism spectrum disorder, developmental delay and typical development. *Child Development, 73*(3), 700–717.

Dunn, J. (1989). Siblings and the development of social understanding in early childhood. In P. G. Zukow (Ed.), *Sibling interaction across cultures: Theoretical and methodological issues* (pp. 106–116). New York: Springer-Verlag.

Dunn, J. (1991). Understanding others: Evidence from naturalistic studies of children. In A. Whiten (Ed.), *Natural theories of mind: Evolution, development and simulation of everyday mindreading* (pp. 51–61). Cambridge, MA: Blackwell.

Dunn, J. (1992). Siblings and development. *Current Directions in Psychological Science, 1*(1), 6–9.

Dunn, J., Brown, J., Slomkowski, C., Tesla, C., & Youngblade, L. (1991). Young children's understanding of other people's feelings and beliefs: Individual differences and their antecedents. *Child Development, 62*(6), 1352–1366.

Dunn, J., & Dale, N. (1984). I a daddy: 2-year-olds' collaboration in joint pretend with sibling and with mother. In I. Bretherton (Ed.), *Symbolic play* (pp. 131–157). New York: Academic Press.

Dunn, J., & Kendrick, C. (1982). The speech of two- and three-year-olds to infant siblings: "Baby talk" and the context of communication. *Journal of Child Language, 9*, 579–595.

Farrant, K., & Reese, E. (2000). Maternal style and children's participation in reminiscing: Stepping stones in children's autobiographical memory development. *Journal of Cognition & Development, 1*(2), 193–225.

Field, T. M., Woodson, R., Greenberg, R., & Cohen, D. (1982). Discrimination and imitation of facial expressions by neonates. *Science, 218*(4568), 179–181.

Fitzgerald, H. E. (1968). Autonomic pupillary reflex activity during early infancy and its relation to social and nonsocial visual stimuli. *Journal of Experimental Child Psychology, 6*(3), 470–482.

Flavell, J. H., Flavell, E. R., & Green, F. L. (1983). Development of the appearance–reality distinction. *Cognitive Psychology, 15*(1), 95–120.

Foote, R. C., & Holmes-Lonergan, H. A. (2003). Sibling conflict and theory of mind. *British Journal of Developmental Psychology, 21*(1), 45–58.

Frye, D., Zelazo, P. D., & Palfai, T. (1995). Theory of mind and rule-based reasoning. *Cognitive Development, 10*(4), 483–527.

Gopnik, A., & Astington, J. W. (1988). Children's understanding of representational change and its relation to the understanding of false belief and the appearance–reality distinction. *Child Development, 59*(1), 26–37.

Gopnik, A., & Meltzoff, A. (1993). Words and thoughts in infancy: The specificity hypothesis and the development of categorization and naming. *Advances in Infancy Research, 8*, 217–249.

Hainline, L. (1978). Developmental changes in visual scanning of face and nonface patterns by infants. *Journal of Experimental Child Psychology, 25*(1), 90–115.

Harris, P. L. (1991). The work of the imagination. In A. Whiten (Ed.), *Natural theories of mind: Evolution, development and simulation of everyday mindreading* (pp. 283–304). Cambridge, MA: Blackwell.

Heyes, C. M. (1996). Genuine imitation? In C. M. Heyes & B. G. Galef, Jr. (Eds.), *Social learning in animals: The roots of culture* (pp. 371–389). San Diego: Academic Press.

Holmes, H. A., Black, C., & Miller, S. A. (1996). A cross-task comparison of false belief understanding in a Head Start population. *Journal of Experimental Child Psychology, 63*(2), 263–285.

Jenkins, J. M., & Astington, J. W. (1996). Cognitive factors and family structure associated with theory of mind development in young children. *Developmental Psychology, 32*(1), 70–78.

Keenan, T. (2003). Individual differences in theory of mind: The preschool years and beyond. In V. E. Slaughter & B. Repacholi (Eds.), *Individual differences in theory of mind: Implications for typical and atypical development* (pp. 121–142). New York: Psychology Press.

Lagattuta, K. H., & Wellman, H. M. (2001). Thinking about the past: Early knowledge about links between prior experience, thinking, and emotion. *Child Development, 72*(1), 82–102.

Lamb, M. E. (1978). The development of sibling relationships in infancy: A short-term longitudinal study. *Child Development, 49*(4), 1189–1196.

Leekam, S. R., & Perner, J. (1991). Does the autistic child have a metarepresentational deficit? *Cognition, 40*(3), 203–218.

Leslie, A. M. (1987). Pretense and representation: The origins of "theory of mind." *Psychological Review, 94*(4), 412–426.

Lewis, C., Freeman, N. H., Kyriakidou, C., Maridaki-Kassotaki, K., & Berridge, D. M. (1996). Social influences on false belief access: Specific sibling influences or general apprenticeship? *Child Development, 67*(6), 2930–2947.

Lillard, A. (1998). Ethnopsychologies: Cultural variation in theories of mind. *Psychological Bulletin, 123*(1), 3–32.

Meltzoff, A. N. (1990). Foundations for developing a concept of self: The role of imitation in relating self to other and the value of social mirroring, social modeling, and self practice in infancy. In D. Cicchetti & M. Beeghly (Eds.), *The self in transition: Infancy to childhood* (pp. 139–164). Chicago: University of Chicago Press.

Meltzoff, A. N. (1995). Understanding the intentions of others: Re-enactment of intended acts by 18-month-old children. *Developmental Psychology, 31*(5), 838–850.

Meltzoff, A. N. (1999). Origins of theory of mind, cognition and communication. *Journal of Communication Disorders, 32*(4), 251–269.

Meltzoff, A. N. (2002). Imitation as a mechanism of social cognition: Origins of empathy, theory of mind, and the representation of action. In U. Goswami (Ed.), *Blackwell handbook of childhood cognitive development* (pp. 6–25). Malden, MA: Blackwell.

Meltzoff, A., & Gopnik, A. (1994). The role of imitation in understanding persons and developing a theory of mind. In S. Baron-Cohen, H. E. Tager-Flusberg, & D. J. Cohen (Eds.), *Understanding other minds: Perspectives from autism* (pp. 335–366). London: Oxford University Press.

Meltzoff, A. N., & Moore, M. (1977). Imitation of facial and manual gestures by human neonates. *Science, 198*(4312), 75–78.

Meltzoff, A. N., & Moore, M. (1983). Newborn infants imitate adult facial gestures. *Child Development, 54*(3), 702–709.

Meltzoff, A. N., & Moore, M. (1989). Imitation in newborn infants: Exploring the range of gestures imitated and the underlying mechanisms. *Developmental Psychology, 25*(6), 954–962.

Meltzoff, A. N., & Moore, M. (1992). Early imitation within a functional framework: The importance of person identity, movement, and development. *Infant Behavior & Development, 15*(4), 479–505.

Meltzoff, A. N., & Moore, M. (1994). Imitation, memory, and the representation of persons. *Infant Behavior & Development, 17*(1), 83–99.

Moghaddam, F. M. (2003). Interobjectivity and culture. *Culture & Psychology, 9*(3), 221–232.

Nelson, K., Plesa, D., & Henseler, S. (1998). Children's theory of mind: An experiential interpretation. *Human Development, 41*(1), 7–29.

O'Neill, D. K. (1996). Two-year-old children's sensitivity to a parent's knowledge state when making requests. *Child Development, 67,* 659–677.

Osterling, J., & Dawson, G. (1994). Early recognition of children with autism: A study of first birthday home videotapes. *Journal of Autism & Developmental Disorders, 24*(3), 247–257.

Papousek, H., & Papousek, M. (1977). The first social relationships: A chance for development or a pathogenic situation? *Praxis der Psychotherapie, 22*(3), 97–108.

Perner, J. (1991). *Understanding the representational mind.* Cambridge, MA: MIT Press.

Perner, J. (2001). Episodic memory: Essential distinctions and developmental implications. In C. Moore & K. Lemmon (Eds.), *The self in time: Developmental perspectives* (pp. 181–202). Mahwah, NJ: Erlbaum.

Perner, J., Frith, U., Leslie, A. M., & Leekam, S. R. (1989). Exploration of the autistic child's theory of mind: Knowledge, belief, and communication. *Child Development, 60*(3), 689–700.

Perner, J., Leekam, S. R., & Wimmer, H. (1987). Three-year-olds' difficulty with false belief: The case for a conceptual deficit. *British Journal of Developmental Psychology, 5*(2), 125–137.

Perner, J., Ruffman, T., & Leekam, S. R. (1994). Theory of mind is contagious: You catch it from your sibs. *Child Development, 65*(4), 1228–1238.

Perner, J., & Wimmer, H. (1985). "John thinks that Mary thinks that . . .": Attribution of second-order beliefs by 5- to 10-year-old children. *Journal of Experimental Child Psychology, 39*(3), 437–471.

Peterson, C. C. (2001). Influence of siblings' perspectives on theory of mind. *Cognitive Development, 15*(4), 435–455.

Peterson, C. C., & Siegal, M. (2002). Mindreading and moral awareness in popular and rejected preschoolers. *British Journal of Developmental Psychology, 20*(2), 205–224.

Piaget, J. (1929). *The child's conception of the world.* Oxford: Littlefield, Adams.

Piaget, J. (1962). *Play, dreams, and imitation in children.* London: Routledge & Kegan Paul. (Original work published in French in 1927)

Pratt, C., & Bryant, P. (1990). Young children understand that looking leads to knowing (so long as they are looking into a single barrel). *Child Development, 61*(4), 973–982.

Repacholi, B. M., & Gopnik, A. (1997). Early reasoning about desires: Evidence from 14- and 18-month-olds. *Developmental Psychology, 33*(1), 12–21.

Repacholi, B., Slaughter, V., Pritchard, M., & Gibbs, V. (2003). Theory of mind, Machiavellianism, and social functioning in childhood. In B. Repacholi & V. Slaughter (Eds.), *Individual differences in theory of mind: Implications for typical and atypical development* (pp. 67–97). New York: Psychology Press.

Robins, D. L., Fein, D., Barton, M. L., & Green, J. A. (2001). The Modified Checklist for Autism in Toddlers: An initial study investigating the early detection of autism and pervasive developmental disorders. *Journal of Autism & Developmental Disorders, 31*(2), 131–144.

Rovee-Collier, C. (1997). Dissociations in infant memory: Rethinking the development of implicit and explicit memory. *Psychological Review, 104*(3), 467–498.

Ruffman, T., Perner, J., Naito, M., Parkin, L., & Clements, W. A. (1998). Older (but not younger) siblings facilitate false belief understanding. *Developmental Psychology, 34*(1), 161–174.

Stone, V. E., Baron-Cohen, S., Calder, A., Keane, J., & Young, A. (2003). Acquired theory of mind impairments in individuals with bilateral amygdala lesions. *Neuropsychologia, 41*(2), 209–220.

Sutton-Smith, B., & Rosenberg, B. G. (1970). *The sibling.* Oxford: Holt, Rinehart & Winston.

Tager-Flusberg, H. (1993). Autistic children's talk about psychological states: Deficits in the early acquisition of a theory of mind. *Child Development, 63*(1), 161–172.

Tager-Flusberg, H. (2003). Exploring the relationship between theory of mind and social-communicative functioning in children with autism. In B. Repacholi & V. Slaughter (Eds.), *Individual differences in theory of mind: Implications for typical and atypical development* (pp. 197–212). New York: Psychology Press.

Tan-Niam, C. S., Wood, D., & O'Malley, C. (1998). A cross-cultural perspective on children's theories of mind and social interaction. *Early Child Development & Care, 144,* 55–67.

Taylor, M., & Carlson, S. M. (1997). The relation between individual differences in fantasy and theory of mind. *Child Development, 68*(3), 436–455.

Teti, D. M., Bond, L. A., & Gibbs, E. D. (1986). Sibling-created experiences: Relationships to birth-spacing and infant cognitive development. *Infant Behavior & Development, 9*(1), 27–42.

Tomasello, M. (1995). Joint attention as social cognition. In C. Moore & P. J. Dunham (Eds.), *Joint attention: Its origins and role in development* (pp. 103–130). Hillsdale, NJ: Erlbaum.

Tomasello, M., & Camaioni, L. (1997). A comparison of the gestural communication of apes and human infants. *Human Development, 40*(1), 7–24.

Trevarthen, C. (1993). The self born in intersubjectivity: The psychology of an infant communicating. In U. Neisser (Ed.), *The perceived self: Ecological and interpersonal sources of self-knowledge* (pp. 121–173). New York: Cambridge University Press.

Vinden, P. G. (2001). Parenting attitudes and children's understanding of mind. A comparison of Korean American and Anglo-American families. *Cognitive Development, 16*(3), 793–809.

Wellman, H. M. (1991). From desires to beliefs: Acquisition of a theory of mind. In A. Whiten (Ed.), *Natural theories of mind: Evolution, development and simulation of everyday mindreading* (pp. 19–38). Cambridge, MA: Blackwell.

Wellman, H. M. (1994). Early understanding of mind: The normal case. In S. Baron-Cohen, H. E. Tager-Flusberg, & D. J. Cohen (Eds.), *Understanding other minds: Perspectives from autism* (pp. 10–39). London: Oxford University Press.

Wellman, H. M. (2002). Understanding the psychological world: Developing a theory of mind. In U. Goswami (Ed.), *Blackwell handbook of childhood cognitive development* (pp. 167–187). Malden, MA: Blackwell.

Wellman, H. M., & Bartsch, K. (1988). Young children's reasoning and beliefs. *Cognition, 30*(3), 239–277.

Wellman, H. M., Cross, D., & Watson, J. (2001). Meta-analysis of theory-of-mind development: The truth about false belief. *Child Development, 72*(3), 655–684.

Wellman, H. M., & Estes, D. (1986). Early understanding of mental entities: A reexamination of childhood realism. *Child Development, 57*(4), 910–923.

Wimmer, H., & Perner, J. (1983). Beliefs about beliefs: Representation and constraining function of wrong beliefs in young children's understanding of deception. *Cognition, 13*(1), 103–128.

Woodward, A. L. (1998). Infants selectively encode the goal object of an actor's reach. *Cognition, 69*(1), 1–34.

Woolley, J. D., & Wellman, H. M. (1990). Young children's understanding of realities, nonrealities, and appearances. *Child Development, 61*(4), 946–961.

Youngblade, L. M., & Dunn, J. (1995). Individual differences in young children's pretend play with mother and sibling: Links to relationships and understanding of other people's feelings and beliefs. *Child Development, 66*(5), 1472–1492.

Zaitchik, D. (1990). When representations conflict with reality: The preschooler's problem with false beliefs and "false" photographs. *Cognition, 35*(1), 41–68.

Zukow, P. G. (1990). Socio-perceptual bases for the emergence of language: An alternative to innatist approaches. *Developmental Psychobiology, 23*(7), 705–726.

11

Mathematical Thinking and Learning

Herbert P. Ginsburg, Joanna Cannon, Janet Eisenband, and Sandra Pappas

Over the past thirty years or so, psychologists and educators have conducted an impressive body of investigations on early mathematical thinking and learning (Baroody, Lai, & Mix, 2006; Geary, 1994; Ginsburg, Klein, & Starkey, 1998; Nunes & Bryant, 1996). This research not only sheds light on fundamental issues of cognitive development but also can provide guidance for current efforts at early childhood mathematics education. Our chapter draws selectively upon the extensive research literature to examine basic issues of early mathematical thinking and learning. First, we present a theoretical framework showing that the confluence of biology and environment guarantees the almost universal construction of a relatively powerful everyday mathematics. Second, the largest part of the chapter discusses young children's interest in and knowledge of number, shape, pattern, measurement, and space. Third, we present a brief account of mathematics teaching experiments. And finally we use recent research findings and theory to address issues of early childhood mathematics education.

How Does Mathematical Knowledge Develop?

Academic mathematical knowledge, like written column addition, is almost always acquired, often badly, through a process of direct instruction in school. But everyday mathematical knowledge – such as intuitive ideas of more and less, taking away, shape, size, location, pattern and position – is an essential and even inevitable feature of the child's cognitive development. Like other aspects of the child's cognition, such as theory of mind or critical thinking, everyday mathematical knowledge develops in the ordinary environment, usually without direct instruction. Indeed, everyday mathematical knowledge is so fundamental a feature of the child's cognition that it is hard to see how children could function without it.

Several factors guarantee that virtually all children develop key features of everyday mathematical knowledge. First, as Piaget (1952b) maintained, "general heredity," a kind of instinct to learn, ensures that all children attempt to assimilate and accommodate to their environments. As Gelman (2000) put it, "we can think of young children as self-monitoring learning machines who are inclined to learn on the fly, even when they are not in school and regardless of whether they are with adults" (p. 26).

Second, some writers posit a biological basis for specific mathematical concepts. For example, Gelman (2000) proposes that "we are born with number-relevant mental structures that promote the development of principles for counting" (p. 36). Similarly, Geary (1996) argues that all children, regardless of background and culture, are endowed with "biologically primary" abilities including not only number, but also basic geometry. These kinds of abilities are universal to the species (except perhaps for some retarded or otherwise handicapped children) and require only a minimum of environmental support to develop. The evidence for claims like these is mainly of two types. One is that some mathematical concepts seem to emerge very early in infancy (Wynn, 1992) and even in animals (Spelke, 2003). The other is that many everyday mathematical concepts appear to be universal (Klein & Starkey, 1988).

Third, the physical environment offers abundant food for thought. All children develop in an environment containing a multitude of quantitative phenomena and events (Ginsburg & Seo, 1999). Children are universally provided with common "supporting environments" for at least some aspects of mathematical development (Gelman, Massey, & McManus, 1991). All environments contain objects to count, shapes to discriminate, and locations to identify. No doubt some environments are richer than others and thus favor the acquisition of everyday mathematics. But all normal environments afford the learning of basic mathematical ideas.

Fourth, the social environment supports the development of mathematical thinking in several different ways. Almost all cultures offer children at least one basic mathematical concept and tool – namely counting. Even groups lacking formal education have developed elaborate counting systems (Zaslavsky, 1973). In many cultures, parents engage in various *informal* activities that may promote mathematics learning. Thus, they read storybooks, many of which require and may promote understanding of mathematical notions: Goldilocks encounters three bears varying in size, three bowls of porridge, and three beds whose size is correlated with the bears' (Ginsburg & Seo, 1999). Parents play board and card games with their children (Saxe, Guberman, & Gearhart, 1987). In some cultures, television shows like *Sesame Street*, computer programs, and various toys make elementary mathematics available to young children. Many US states now mandate preschool mathematics instruction and some schools use mathematics curricula (Sophian, 2004).

As a result of the natural tendency to learn, possible biological foundations for learning key concepts, and the rich physical and social environments in which they live, all normal children have the capacity, opportunity, and motive to acquire basic mathematical knowledge. Consider next young children's mathematical competence and then what they can be taught.

What Do Young Children Know about Mathematics?

Number

Early in life, children exhibit various everyday mathematical concepts and skills, ranging from basic notions of magnitude to adding and taking away.

Magnitude. Several naturalistic studies indicate that young children have a vital practical interest in differences and changes in magnitude. As Bloom (1970) shows, among the first words spoken by many babies is "more." Toddlers use the words "a lot" and "more" when consuming food and drink, for example using "more" to request extra helpings (Walkerdine, 1988). Similarly, 2- and 3-year-olds often indicate without counting that some collections have "a lot" or "many" (Wagner & Walters, 1982, p. 140). Young children are vitally concerned with growing both bigger and older (Corsaro, 1985). Indeed, mathematical thought may be said to provide a cognitive foundation for competition ("my tower is bigger than yours") and desire ("I want more cookies"), and is at the very least associated with these motives.

Experimental studies provide further evidence of children's competence in magnitude. Many years ago, Binet presented his 4-year-old daughter Madeleine with problems in which she was asked to determine quickly which of two haphazardly arranged groups of objects had "more" than the other. Although unable to count beyond three, Madeleine did well at comparisons involving much larger numbers of objects (Binet, 1969). An item based on the Binet task is used in the Test of Early Mathematics Ability (Ginsburg & Baroody, 2003), and normative data show that almost all children master it by the age of 3 or so. Intuitions of this type appear as early as infancy (Brannon, 2002). Low- and middle-income children, African-American and White, perform with approximately equal skill on Binet's task (Ginsburg & Russell, 1981).

How do children solve tasks of this sort? Many of the comparisons involve numbers (like 8) for which children have no words. According to Binet, Madeleine's judgment was based on the relative space covered by the two collections: she designated as "more" the set that covered the larger area, even when it had *fewer* elements. Although this strategy is sometimes ineffective, as in the Piagetian number conservation tasks, where the child mistakenly maintains that the longer of two equal lines of objects has the greater number, judgments based on relative space are often useful, as when one decides that one flock of geese flying overhead is greater in number than another because the former occupies more space than the latter.

Finally, although the intuition of "more" may be widespread, and even universal (Posner, 1982), it is far from perfect. A child (or adult) may be able to determine quickly that a set of six objects has more than a set of three, but only more precise methods like counting will reliably produce the judgment that a haphazardly arranged set of thirty-six is greater than one of thirty-five.

Counting words. Although intuitions provide an essential (but limited) basis for mathematical thinking, counting words are a cultural legacy providing children with a tool useful for further mathematical thought and precise calculation. Hearing number words in the everyday environment, young children actively engage in learning them, just as they learn other forms of language. From age 2 or 3, children spontaneously recite the counting words, with 3-year-old children sometimes reaching numbers as high as "ten" (Durkin, Shire, Riem, Crowther, & Rutter, 1986). Later, young children enjoy counting up to relatively large numbers, like 100 (Irwin & Burgham, 1992). Children even have an abstract interest in counting: they want to know what is the "largest number" (Gelman, 1980).

In almost all languages, the first ten or so number words are essentially nonsense syllables, with no underlying structure or meaning (Ginsburg, 1989), and must therefore be memorized in a rote fashion. But after that point, virtually all languages exhibit some degree of structure. For example, once reaching "twenty" in English, the child need only learn to repeat this number and append to it, in order, the numbers one to nine, and so on until "twenty-nine." Thus, learning to say the number words involves not only rote memory but also the induction of a system of generative rules built around the base ten system. Ironically, although English number words below "twenty" are harder to learn than those above it (particularly the irregular numbers from "thirteen" to "nineteen," which logically ought to be something like "ten-three, ten-four," etc., as they are in Chinese), we often restrict young children's learning to the difficult low numbers and delay teaching the easier higher numbers.

Enumeration. As young children learn to say the number words, they also struggle with counting things. At first, children's enumeration is extremely inaccurate: 2- and 3-year-olds can enumerate only very small sets (two, three, or even four objects) and may make errors like, "one, two, four" or skipping objects as they count (Fuson, 1991). But over time, children gradually learn to enumerate larger sets with increasing accuracy. This much is obvious to any parent. But what is less apparent is that from the age of 3 or so, children's counting, even when inaccurate, seems to be constrained by important counting principles (Gelman & Gallistel, 1986). For example, children seem to know the *one-to-one principle* – one and only one number word should be assigned to each object. Children also seem to know the *stable order principle* – number words should be said in the same order (correct or incorrect) all the time. Thus children may make the mistake of saying "one, two, four," but consistently use that order. Other guides to enumeration include the *cardinal principle* (the last number enumerated indicates the total value of the set); the *abstraction principle* (anything can be counted, from stones to unicorns); and the *order-irrelevance principle* (enumeration may begin with any object in the set so long as each is counted once and only once).

In brief, young children's enumeration, like their rule-based learning of the counting words, is far from mechanical. Enumeration embodies basic concepts of number and is less of a rote activity than Piaget (1952a) maintained when he asserted that pre-operational children's counting lacks meaning. In fact, hearing number words attached to objects may prompt the child to develop new concepts (Mix, 2002). Learning that both two apples and two dogs are designated as "two" may lead the child to focus on the abstract "two-ness" that the sets share.

Addition and subtraction. Perhaps building on their efforts at enumeration, children also display a spontaneous interest in addition and related topics like the partitioning of numbers. Anderson (1993) reports that her 3-year-old daughter wanted to know "What's another way to make five?" She then held up four fingers and one more, as well as other combinations (p. 28). At age 5, she created addition problems, asking, "Two and three, how many's that?" (Anderson, 1993, p. 28).

Intuitions. Before learning to calculate exact sums or differences, young children understand that the operation of addition results in an increase in number and subtraction a decrease (unless of course zero is added or subtracted). Three- and 4-year-olds possess a general understanding of how adding increases and subtracting decreases set size (Bertelli, Joanni, & Martlew, 1998). Indeed, children as young as 24 months have intuitions about adding and taking away (Sophian & Adams, 1987).

Accuracy. By the age of 3, young children can perform addition and subtraction calculations. However, success depends upon whether the problems contain small numbers (e.g., 2 + 1, 3 − 1), the context is meaningful, and manipulatives are available (Starkey & Gelman, 1982). Also, preschoolers' performance improves when non-verbal responses are permitted, and low-income children perform as well as middle-income children on non-verbal, but not verbal, problems (Jordan, Huttenlocher, & Levine, 1994).

Strategy. Young children use various informal strategies to solve addition and subtraction problems. Further, children can develop these strategies without adult assistance (Groen & Resnick, 1977). The strategies are of three general types varying in complexity: *direct modeling* with manipulatives (e.g., representing sets with blocks and then counting them), *counting strategies* without physical representations (e.g., remembering the number of the first set and then counting on the value of the second set, as in "five . . . six, seven" for five plus two), and *retrieval* of number facts (i.e., simply remembering that five plus two is seven) (Baroody & Tiilikainen, 2003). Retrieval may be considered a rote skill, but learning the number facts to be retrieved requires practice over time. In general, development progresses from direct modeling to counting strategies and finally to retrieval. Yet the course of development is not simple or smooth. At any one point, children typically use several different strategies and do not make clear progress from one major "stage" to the next (Crowley, Shrager, & Siegler, 1997).

Metacognition. The development of metacognition – the awareness of thinking and its uses (Kuhn, 2000) – is a fundamental task for young children. Children who exhibit key aspects of metacognition, including recognizing mistakes (Garofalo & Lester, 1985), evaluating the efficacy of their strategies, and expressing themselves while problem solving (Carr & Jessup, 1997), tend to perform better in school. Metacognitive skills begin to develop in children as young as 4 or 5years of age (Pappas, Ginsburg, & Jiang, 2003). A substantial proportion of these children recognized and corrected mistakes, adapted more effective strategies when encountering difficulty, and generated partial and/or full descriptions of their thinking.

Written symbolism. Written symbols are a culturally derived tool for representing mathematical ideas. Asked to represent quantities on paper, children produce several useful types of written responses. For example, Hughes (1986) found that children between the ages of about 3 and 7 years typically represent quantities using four types of responses. Older children are likely to rely on iconic (e.g., tallies) and symbolic (e.g., numerals) responses, while younger children exhibit idiosyncratic (e.g., scribble) and pictographic (e.g., drawing blocks) responses.

Although children as young as 3 can successfully represent quantities on paper, they have difficulty in representing addition and subtraction operations. Hughes (1986) assessed whether children could represent both the problem's initial quantity and its transformation (e.g., "show that first we had two bricks and then we added two more"). Children produced a variety of responses (e.g., representing the initial, added, or sub-tracted amounts), but few could represent the transformed sets. Instead most children represented the final quantity and often excluded information about the addition or subtraction operation.

Conclusions on number. Researchers have focused more on number than on any other aspect of young children's mathematics. The topic is rich, ranging from children's first attempts at saying number words to the use of written symbols. We derive three general conclusions. One is that the understanding of number is enormously complex. Young children do far more than rote counting to ten: they use rules to count; they employ abstract principles to enumerate; they develop and use various strategies for addition. Young children's approach to number is both concrete (as when they initially use objects to add) and abstract (as when they consider the nature of infinity in counting). The second conclusion is that the understanding of number does not proceed in a simple progression from one major "stage" to another: children employ many different strategies at any given point in time. The third conclusion is that young children manage to accomplish much of this learning on their own, usually without direct parental or other instruction.

Shape

Two theories influence our understanding of early shape comprehension: the first addresses children's mental representation of shapes (Piaget & Inhelder, 1967), and the second describes their developing geometric reasoning skills (Clements & Battista, 1992; van Hiele, 1986). Piaget and Inhelder argued that to have a true understanding of a shape, a child must be able to represent it in its absence. The researchers examined children's tactile exploration of hidden shapes and their attempts to match them to visible shapes. They proposed that children construct representations of shapes based on topological properties such as openness and continuity before they are able to incorporate information about the shapes' projective (e.g., rectilinear or curvilinear) and Euclidean (e.g., angle- or dis-tance-related) characteristics.

Although some subsequent experiments confirm an initial focus on topological features (Clements & Battista, 1992), other studies (Kato, 1986) have shown that children are able to attend to Euclidean features in some situations (for example, when smaller, more familiar shapes are used). Thus young children are not limited to topological features when constructing representations of shapes (Clements & Battista, 1992). However, even older children seem to focus on topological properties: thus, elementary-school students described the physical "morphing" of shapes into other shapes (e.g., a pentagon becoming a square when its top is pushed down) (Lehrer, Jenkins, & Osana, 1998).

Van Hiele also described stages of thinking about shapes. However, unlike Piaget, he addressed broad aspects of geometric reasoning, not only representations, in the context of instruction and social environment. Van Hiele proposed that children first identify shapes based on their appearance, at the "visual" level (e.g., a shape is a rectangle because it looks like a door). Later, at the "descriptive" level, children are able to incorporate properties of shapes (e.g., number of sides and corners) into their identification criteria. Eventually, students begin to demonstrate advanced levels of geometric thinking involving formal logical reasoning.

For the most part, preschoolers seem to behave according to the first van Hiele level, identifying and reasoning about shapes based on appearance. This is evidenced by their rejection of non-prototypical shapes (e.g., inverted triangles) in identification tasks (Clements, Swaminathan, Hannibal, & Sarama, 1999; Lehrer et al., 1998) and by the order in which they typically learn to recognize shapes: circles, followed by squares, then rectangles and triangles (Satlow & Newcombe, 1998). Shapes that are easiest to learn are those that vary the least in form (for example, a circle can only vary in size). However, there is some evidence that preschoolers also have knowledge of geometric properties and can use them to identify shapes (Clements et al., 1999). The general finding is that preschool and older children display behavior from a mix of the van Hiele levels, and that type of reasoning varies with different shapes (Burger & Shaughnessy, 1986).

Further, Clements and colleagues (Clements & Battista, 1992; Clements et al., 1999) argue that the van Hiele model fails to describe a key stage in the development of geometric thinking. In this "pre-recognitive" stage, which occurs prior to the van Hiele "visual" stage, children are unable to attend to key characteristics of shapes and therefore cannot yet form mental prototypes to which to compare shapes that they encounter.

In brief, while Piaget and van Hiele provide useful descriptions of trends in the ways that children represent and reason about shapes, both theorists' stage theories tend to underestimate the complexity of children's thinking.

Pattern

Many educators advocate work with repeating patterns in early childhood (e.g., learning to construct a line of blocks with systematic color alternation), asserting its value in fostering logical reasoning skills and algebraic thinking (e.g., making predictions and abstracting rules) and as a tool for teaching mathematical concepts such as measurement, arithmetic, and probability (Clements, 2004b). Unfortunately, few experimental studies have been conducted on the subject; in particular there has been little research on preschoolers' underlying understanding of patterns or the cognitive skills they gain from patterning activities.

Most relevant research assesses children's abilities to create or manipulate (e.g., duplicate, extend, or fill in) linear sequences composed of repeating iconic elements (often colored blocks). Such studies show that in the preschool years children become increasingly proficient at creating, duplicating, and extending patterns (Garrick, Threlfall, & Orton, 1999; Pieraut-Le Bonniec, 1982), but that these tasks can be difficult even for 5-year-olds (Klein & Starkey, 2004).

Variations in pattern tasks can significantly improve or hinder children's performance. For example, in extension tasks, children show more competence when they are provided with enough blank spaces to append the entire repeating unit (e.g., ABCABCABC_ _ _) than when given insufficient space (e.g., ABCABCABC_ _); in the second situation some children fill in the spaces by repeating the most recent element or by leaving them blank (Threlfall, 1999). We have observed that when asked to extend a pattern that ends in the middle of the repeating unit (e.g., ABCABCABCA_ _) preschoolers' common response is to begin the extension with the sequence's first element (ABCABCABCA<u>ABC</u>). The reason for this is unclear: does the extra "A" at the end confuse children and make it difficult for them to identify the repeating unit? Or are children merely being "trained" to extend a pattern by copying the elements starting at the beginning of the sequence, no matter what the last element is?

The different strategies children use also shed light on their understanding of pattern. Some argue that many of children's strategies do not necessitate recognition of the repeating unit and therefore appreciation of the pattern's rule (Threlfall, 1999). For example, children can extend or fill in gaps in a pattern by correcting an uneven distribution of its elements (e.g., in the sequence ABCAB_, there are not enough "C"s); in this situation some children have explained the need to provide a "partner" to a "lonely" element (Klahr & Wallace, 1970). Children also extend patterns by reciting all of the elements of a sequence in a rhythmic "chant" (e.g., red, blue, green, red, blue, green. . .) until the missing element is reached. Although this technique calls for the utterance of the repeating unit (repeatedly), it does not necessitate its recognition (Threlfall, 1999).

Lastly, we can gain insight from children's criteria for identifying patterns. In a study in which 4- to 6-year-olds classified household items (such as fabric, wrapping paper, and toys) as patterns or "non-patterns," many children insisted that patterns must be symmetrical and/or contain more than one color (Rawson, 1993). Further, children tended to accept materials resembling patterns seen in classrooms (such as child-constructed sequences of shapes) even if the items neither repeated nor followed a rule, and they rejected patterned arrays that contained elements not often seen in repeating patterns, such as numbers. Thus children appear to have biases when identifying patterns, possibly toward items associated with classroom instruction.

Measurement

What skills or understandings must children possess to measure? To illustrate, consider the following scenario. A child is asked to determine whether his classroom or the classroom next door built the taller tower. In addition, his tower is on the floor while the tower in the other room is on a desk. To accurately make such a comparison, the child must use an intervening measure, for example a ruler, to determine the height of each tower.

According to Piaget, Inhelder, and Szeminska (1960), measurement of this type requires the coordination of multiple relations, including an understanding of transitive inference: if tower A = C (in length) and tower B < C, then tower B < tower A. Piaget found that, given these conceptual demands, children could not accurately measure before the age of 7 or 8 years.

Yet in recent years, a substantial body of research has shown that young children know quite a bit about measurement. Infants possess a perceptual form of measurement ability; they can discriminate between two different continuous amounts (e.g., length, weight, area) when both objects are present (Mounoud & Bower, 1974; Tan & Bryant, 2000). Until grade school (about age 5 or 6), the most frequent method young children use for measuring such differences is direct visual or tactile comparison (Huntley-Fenner, 2001). When they do not have to use comparative vocabulary (e.g., say which of two lines is "longer"), preschoolers can use non-verbal means to accurately specify differences in continuous amounts (Miller, 1984). Further, although children might have difficulty utilizing comparative vocabulary in specified contexts, even toddlers frequently use such terms as *bigger* and *taller* in everyday life, indicating an awareness of these discriminations (Sera & Smith, 1987).

There is also evidence that preschoolers have a preliminary understanding of some fundamental measurement principles, which may involve knowing how to coordinate relations to measure continuous amounts. For instance, sophisticated measurement entails realizing that there is an inverse relation between unit size and number of units (i.e., the larger the unit of measurement, the smaller number of units will be assigned), a skill that requires coordinating relations between two different dimensions. When provided with training, preschoolers can begin to understand these principles, particularly when measurement scenarios are grounded in everyday activities and objects (Sophian, 2002).

Preschoolers can even use intervening measures when they are not required to employ comparative vocabulary like "longer" (Miller, 1989). Nonetheless, preschoolers' understanding of such ideas is clearly tenuous. It is not until elementary school that children can coordinate relations in measurement readily and without special supports. In particular, children's ability to measure complex continuous phenomena (e.g., volume) increases with age (Miller, 1984).

Space

Next we consider children's knowledge of two important components of mature spatial sense: specifying location and making sense of spatial representations. Adults use a variety of methods to specify spatial location, sometimes locating an object by reference to their own position and at other times by determining angles and distances from external landmarks. Even infants possess early perceptual forms of these abilities. By 22 months, infants can use landmarks to find the location of an object hidden in a space (e.g., they may use a sofa to locate a toy hidden behind it) (Newcombe & Learmonth, 1999).

With age, children's ability to specify location using various reference systems strengthens. Thus, 3-year-olds can accurately answer questions about the locations of objects relative to their own and other vantage points (Newcombe & Huttenlocher, 1992). Preschoolers can also use external guides such as an X and Y axis to help specify location (Clements, 2004a). However, there are limitations to this understanding. In particular, both infants and children have difficulty using distance information to specify location when they must coordinate conflicting reference systems (Newcombe, Huttenlocher, & Learmonth, 1999). For example, when asked to choose among pictures of different perspectives, preschoolers have a hard time specifying the location of an object from a vantage point different from their own. In this situation, the imagined frames of reference depicted in the pictures conflict with the perceptually present frame of reference. Young children's ability to specify location using distance from landmarks also varies depending on other features of the spatial task such as the nature of the space; children display greater skill in smaller and more familiar spaces (Newcombe & Learmonth, 1999).

Another important component of spatial understanding is the ability to interpret and use spatial representations such as maps and models. Preschoolers show some facility with such representations; they can understand what very simple maps or models stand for and use them to navigate represented space. Thus, shown a simple model of a room with a small figure representing a hidden object, 2½-year-olds could use the model to find the object in the represented space (DeLoache, 2002).

However, this ability is quite fragile. Not only can children's difficulties specifying location hinder their use of such representations, but also the introduction of representations like maps presents children with additional challenges: for example, recognizing the correspondence between items in the representation and the real objects they stand for. Preschoolers can focus too strongly on representational symbols, losing sight of their purely symbolic function. For instance, a preschooler stated that a line on a map could not represent a road because the line was too narrow for cars to fit on it (Liben & Downs, 2001). Children's understanding of spatial representations can be facilitated through the use of simple representations with symbols that were few in number and conveyed some meaning on their own (e.g., using a cube, not a toy car, to stand for a chair) (DeLoache, 2002).

Children also experience difficulties with distance and perspective. Asked to reconstruct a space from a map or model, children's reconstructions tend to maintain the relative position among objects but not the absolute position (e.g., the reconstructions are off-center, too small or too large), indicating a difficulty understanding how to translate distance information (Uttal, 1996). Children also struggle to coordinate frames of reference when a representation and space portray different perspectives (Liben & Downs, 2001).

How common are early mathematical activities?

The research reviewed to this point shows that children have a wide variety of mathematical skills, ranging from counting to spatial relations. But it is hard to tell from such research how frequently mathematical activity occurs in children's everyday lives. One study attempted to determine the nature and frequency of young children's everyday mathematical activities and the extent to which they are associated with socio-economic status (Seo & Ginsburg, 2004). The investigators videotaped (for 15 minutes each) the everyday mathematical behavior of ninety individual 4- and 5-year-old children drawn about equally from lower-, middle-, and upper-SES families during free play in their day care/preschool settings. Inductive methods were used to develop a coding system intended to capture the mathematical content of the children's behavior. Three categories of mathematical activity occurred with some frequency. *Pattern and shape* (exploration of patterns and spatial forms) occurred during an average of about 21% of the 15 minutes; *magnitude* (statement of magnitude or comparison of two or more items to evaluate relative magnitude) during about 13% of the minutes; and *enumeration* (numerical judgment or quantification) during about 12% of the minutes. No significant SES differences emerged in mathematical activity. In brief, regardless of SES, young children spontaneously and relatively frequently engage in forms of everyday mathematical activity ranging from counting to pattern.

The research also showed that mathematical activity occurred most frequently during block play. Froebel originally created the "gift" of blocks to stimulate engagement in geometric activities, and since then many types of blocks have been developed for young children (Hewitt, 2001). Blocks are an unnatural (they do not appear in nature) artifact (that is, a specially crafted, artificial device) originally designed to promote mathematical thinking. Leeb-Lundberg (1996) offers interesting anecdotal information concerning the mathematical richness of preschoolers' independent block play. For example, children often use blocks to make constructions symmetrical in three dimensions. Children use blocks to create patterns involving regular repetitions of shapes (for example, castles with tall cylinders topped by triangular prisms at regular intervals). Children frequently group similar shapes together and talk about how some blocks are bigger than others or what is on top and what is underneath. In brief, Froebel's gift does indeed seem to promote an abundance of mathematical and related activity.

Conclusions on mathematical knowledge

The research leads to several conclusions. First, young children are interested and have some degree of competence in many aspects of mathematics, not only number. Second, everyday mathematics occurs fairly frequently and is widespread, if not universal. Third, children's competence is variable: sometimes children appear more competent than usually supposed, as when they construct symmetry in three dimensions; sometimes clear patches of incompetence are evident, as in the case of the number conservation tasks, where young children typically maintain that the longer of two equal lines of objects has the greater number. Fourth, development in the different areas of knowledge is complex, and does not fit the straightforward stage progression that Piaget (1952a) originally proposed. Fifth, despite this inadequacy, Piaget's theory still offers important insights: in general the research indicates a developmental trend from "perceptual" to "logical." In many cases, children's early mathematics in different content areas begins with a relatively simple perceptual judgment, as in determining that sticks vary in length. Only later does the child supplement these judgments with more complex reasoning, for example by invoking the logic of transitivity to accomplish standard measurement.

Teaching Experiments

The research reviewed to this point has dealt almost exclusively with what Vygotsky (1978) called the child's "actual developmental level" (p. 85), the current state of mathematical knowledge. Although useful and important, research of this type ignores the child's "dynamic mental state" (p. 87) or potential for learning. In this view, research should focus not only on what the child knows *now*, but also on what the child *could* know given stimulating conditions for learning. Such research would examine children's performance over a period of time in a rich environment involving adult guidance designed to support and extend mathematical knowledge.

Although research of this type is rare, a study of "arithmetic-counting" (Zur & Gelman, 2004) is illuminating. The work began with a felicitous observation of a classroom number game. The teacher began by placing several felt "donuts" on an upright flannel board and asking the class to determine "how many" donuts were in the collection. Next, after a child added or subtracted a certain number of donuts from the array, the other children were asked to determine the sum. Many called out the answers without having counted. One child wisely asked the teacher to count to get the result. Instead, the teacher requested that the children do so.

Seeing its potential as a research method, Zur and Gelman (2004) then modified the game for use in experiments with 4- and then 3-year-olds. The procedure involved first asking children to count in order to determine "how many" objects were in a set, with amounts as large as fifteen for 4-year-olds. Generally, the children's enumeration was quite accurate. Then, as the children watched, one, two, or three objects (and in one condition as many as five) were added to or subtracted from the initial set, which was then hidden from view. The children were asked to "predict" how many objects were now in the set. Although many children had not previously used the word "predict," they caught onto its meaning very quickly. The experimenter then said, "Let's check your prediction," but did not explicitly suggest counting as a method for doing so.

Several results of this series of studies are notable. First, almost all 4-year-olds accurately determined the cardinal value of the sets (as large as twelve) in the initial presentation. Second, the children's predictions of the result of addition or subtraction were almost always in the right direction; they understood that adding makes more and subtracting less and were able to give reasonable (although not always exactly correct) answers. Third, children who quickly predicted the sum tended to be more accurate than those who responded slowly. The writers speculate that the fast responders used a mental addition or subtraction strategy to get the answer. Fourth, although not instructed to do so, all children used counting to check their prediction. Fifth, even the 3-year-olds achieved good levels of success on similar tasks involving smaller numbers.

The Zur and Gelman (2004) study is instructive in several respects. First, it illustrates the virtues of basing research on careful observation of children's everyday environments and appreciation of a skillful teacher's wisdom. Second, it shows that under supportive conditions the children could do more than normally expected. Third, it offers clear suggestions for education: to teach addition and subtraction, use counting and checking games involving relatively large numbers of objects.

Other work tells a similar story. When immersed in a challenging mathematics environment, young children exhibit a wide range of mathematical skills. They count to 100 and beyond; they investigate shape and space; and they learn to *talk* mathematics, using terminology like "hexagon" and communicating their ideas to teachers and peers (Greenes, 1999). Similarly, Zvonkin (1992) reports an interesting collection of activities he developed for his 4-year-old son and friends, including a game that fostered deep exploration of symmetries. For example, one player uses chips to construct a pattern on one half of a game board and the other player has to construct the pattern's mirror image (across the line of symmetry) on the other half.

Early Childhood Mathematics Education

In the US, many education professionals, parents, and policy makers are concerned that American children's mathematics performance is weaker than it should be. East Asian children outperform their American counterparts in mathematics achievement, perhaps as early as kindergarten (Stevenson, Lee, & Stigler, 1986). Also, within the US, low-income and disadvantaged minority children show lower average levels of academic achievement than do their middle- and upper-income peers (Denton & West, 2002).

One approach to ameliorating these problems is to strengthen preschool education. A solid foundation in preschool education, including mathematics, can help to improve academic achievement for children in general and for low-income children in particular (Bowman, Donovan, & Burns, 2001). Research shows that "readiness" is not an issue; children are already interested in and learning a mathematics that is often more genuine than what is later taught in school. Many states and other education agencies have therefore introduced new literacy and mathematics programs for preschool children. Many countries around the world are also emphasizing early childhood mathematics education (ECME). In view of these developments, the major question is not whether to teach early mathematics, but how to do so properly and effectively.

In response to the need for sound and effective ECME, several researchers have become involved in creating early mathematics programs (Casey, Kersh, & Young, 2004; Griffin, 2004; Serama & Clements, 2004; Sophian, 2004; Starkey, Klein, & Wakeley, 2004). No program has yet been extensively evaluated, although some are beginning the process. Here we briefly describe the program with which we are most familiar, namely our own, Big Math for Little Kids (BMLK) (Greenes, Ginsburg, & Balfanz, 2004), and discuss general issues it raises.

Created with the help of teachers over a four-year period, primarily in low-SES child care settings, BMLK is a comprehensive curriculum with separate materials for 4- and

5-year-olds. BMLK was developed with particular attention to low-SES children, but was meant to be challenging for all children. At both age levels, BMLK uses activities and stories to develop skills and ideas about number, shape, pattern, measurement, operations on number, and space. Sometimes instruction takes place during circle time, with the whole class present; sometimes the lead teacher, assistant teacher, and aides work with small groups of children or individuals; and sometimes children work alone with program materials during free play. The curriculum introduces skills and ideas in a carefully sequenced fashion and stresses accurate use of language. The activities are designed to be enjoyable. For example, children learn to count by jumping up and down as they say the numbers from 1 to 9; raise an arm as they say the numbers from 10 to 19; and growl like a lion from 20 to 29. The activities are also designed to be challenging: 4-year-olds often count to 100; construct symmetrical figures; add and subtract small numbers; and learn to read maps describing spatial locations.

BMLK was based on several principles emerging from the scientific literature:

- Research showing that young children already have considerable mathematical knowledge suggests that ECME should build on it and on the developmental trajectories of key concepts and skills (Baroody, 2004). For example, BMLK introduces a sequence of addition activities that proceed from concrete modeling to more mature strategies.
- Research showing that young children's mathematical thinking covers a wide range of topics and interests implies that ECME can and should cover the comprehensive content basic to mathematics, including number, geometry, space, pattern, and measurement. BMLK covers a wide variety of topics, not only number.
- Research showing that young children's mathematics involves not only behaviors but also important concepts, principles, and strategies suggests that ECME should promote mathematical thinking and concepts basic to the discipline of mathematics. BMLK introduces mathematical ideas, like the structure of the counting numbers or the idea of ascending pattern.
- Teaching experiments show that carefully designed activities can promote significant mathematics learning. ECME should therefore also employ adult-designed activities, and even a curriculum, in the sense of systematic, coherent, and planned activities that organize children's learning over time (National Association for the Education of Young Children and National Council of Teachers of Mathematics, 2002). BMLK does this by offering activities for every day of the academic year, organized in a carefully designed sequence.
- Research shows that although young children learn a great deal on their own, they do not learn as much as they could with adult guidance (Vygotsky, 1978). Children learn from play and play is wonderful; but it is not enough to ensure the learning we aim for. Early childhood teachers therefore should teach. In BMLK teachers take the initiative in guiding learning.
- Research shows that although low-SES children show relatively poor mathematics achievement (Denton & West, 2002) and may have special difficulty with verbal addition and subtraction problems, they perform as well as middle-SES children on

222 Herbert P. Ginsburg et al.

non-verbal forms of these tasks (Jordan et al., 1994). Further, anecdotal evidence (Greenes, 1999) suggests that stimulating teaching may produce impressive mathematics learning in low-SES children. Hence, educators should provide low-SES children with challenging early mathematics, perhaps emphasizing language. BMLK does this, for example, by introducing activities involving deductive logic and by encouraging children to describe in words their problem-solving methods.

• A final principle, deriving more from our values than from the research, is that children should appreciate from the outset that learning mathematics can be fun, challenging, and satisfying. BMLK tries not to bore children, not to make them feel helpless about learning mathematics, and not to make them dislike it, as too often happens in later schooling.

The principles described above may help to get us started and to guide our efforts, but they do not guarantee success. We need to examine critically and empirically our efforts at ECME. Implementing BMLK has raised many important issues for further research:

• We learned that the variability among and within children makes it difficult to teach a sequenced curriculum to a large group of young children. During circle time activity, some children do not pay attention or seem lost. The same child may seem confused one day but knowledgeable the next. Sometimes children seem to forget what they have just learned; sometimes they give evidence of knowing something they did not seem to learn. Little children are highly variable. (Of course, the same is true, perhaps to a lesser extent, of older children.) Research is needed to examine the extent and nature of this variability and how to cope with it.

• We came to the view that repetition and practice are highly desirable, particularly in view of the immense variability just described. Yet research on young children's mathematics does not seem to provide much guidance on this issue. Research needs to examine how repetition and practice, within an activity-oriented curriculum, can be used to promote learning.

• We began to question current views of children's competence. Throughout the development and field testing of BMLK, we observed children learning at a higher level than we expected. For example, as some children played BMLK mathematical games, they appeared to develop the ability to think in conditional terms, that is, to consider alternative moves and the consequences of those moves. Of course it is possible that we simply observed a few unusually precocious children. Yet because most research has not examined learning under stimulating conditions, it is possible that young children are capable of more than we expect, that we may have to rethink developmental trajectories, and that we should introduce more challenging mathematics than now seems appropriate. Only further research can settle these issues.

• We observed that BMLK seemed to have a major effect on children's language. In BMLK, children are encouraged to describe their thinking, to share their opinions, to explain and justify their ideas, and to read stories containing rich language. Our observation was that under these conditions, children's mathematical and non-mathematical language improved dramatically. Research is needed to examine the hypothesis that learning mathematics is tied to the development of mathematical vocabulary, expression of thinking, and general fluency.

- We observed that low-SES children seemed to learn a great deal from BMLK. Some teachers felt that their low-SES students were not ready to learn BMLK at their age level. Hence, such teachers of 5-year-olds began by implementing the program designed for 4-year-olds. But many teachers persisted, brought the children up to age-level expectations, and felt that their children did extremely well. Research is needed to examine more closely the effectiveness of the program for low-SES children. But this in turn raises the following issue.

- Implementation of BMLK taught us that it is hard to determine the current success of an ECME program. Young children are notoriously hard to assess, and few appropriate mathematics tests are available for them. Clearly, research is needed to provide new tests that are appropriate for young children; that cover relevant content (for example, pattern as well as number); and that measure important aspects of children's learning, like strategies, concepts, metacognition, language, and enjoyment. At present, such tests do not exist; as a result, evaluation of children's learning in experimental programs may not be meaningful.

- Finally, the biggest challenge in implementing BMLK is professional development. Many early childhood professionals are unfamiliar with teaching mathematics; after all they have received little training in ECME. Teachers need to understand young children's learning and thinking and how to teach. Researchers should help them to do this. Journal articles or chapters like these are not the solution. The great challenge is to find ways to help teachers to make productive use of psychological knowledge to gain insight into young children's learning, particularly low-SES children's, and to inform instruction (Ginsburg et al., 2005).

Conclusions on ECME

This is an exciting time in ECME. Research has shown that learning and teaching early mathematics is developmentally appropriate; researchers have contributed to the development of promising curricula; and evaluation efforts are underway. But several caveats are in order.

First, in addition to preparing children for the future, ECME should foster young children's current mathematical interests. As Dewey (1938) put it, the child should get "out of his present experience all that there is in it for him at the time in which he has it. When preparation is made the controlling end, then the potentialities of the present are sacrificed to a suppositious future" (p. 49).

Second, overly narrow evaluation may inhibit efforts to create an effective, enjoyable, and age-appropriate ECME. Measuring what can now be "scientifically" measured can result in ignoring what is most important about children's mathematics learning. Teaching to the limited test is as harmful at the preschool level as it is later.

Third, we should not only recognize the value of research, but also understand its limitations. Most of it is restricted to analysis of children's actual developmental level and fails to illuminate children's potential for learning mathematics under stimulating conditions.

Fourth, we need to understand that research alone does not produce good curriculum or teaching. The imagination of educators must supplement research findings and principles.

Next Steps

Research on early mathematical thinking and learning has already made important contributions to our understanding of children and to our attempts to improve their education. But much more needs to be done.

First, ECME can benefit from investigations of how children learn in a stimulating environment (which includes the teacher). Research on children's current knowledge is not sufficient.

Second, researchers should study a topic about which we know virtually nothing, namely the processes of teaching mathematics to young children. Partly because mathematics is seldom taught in early childhood, research on teaching at this age level is virtually non-existent. Vague appeals to "constructivism" do not help. Research on teaching may.

Note

The authors express their appreciation to Professor Arthur Baroody for his insightful comments on a draft of the chapter.

References

Anderson, A. (1993). Wondering – One child's questions and mathematics learning. *Canadian Children, 18*(2), 26–30.

Baroody, A. J. (2004) The developmental bases for early childhood number and operations standards. In D. H. Clements, J. Sarama, & A.-M. DiBiase (Eds.), *Engaging young children in mathematics: Standards for early childhood mathematics education* (pp. 173–219). Mahwah, NJ: Lawrence Erlbaum Associates.

Baroody, A. J., Lai, M., & Mix, K. S. (2006). The development of young children's early number and operation sense and its implications for early childhood education. In B. Spodek & O. Saracho (Eds.), *Handbook of research on the education of young children* (Vol. 2, pp. 187–221). Mahwah, NJ: Lawrence Erlbaum Associates.

Baroody, A. J., & Tiilikainen, S. H. (2003). Two perspectives on addition development. In A. J. Baroody & A. Dowker (Eds.), *The development of arithmetic concepts and skills: Constructing adaptive expertise* (pp. 75–125). Mahwah, NJ: Lawrence Erlbaum Associates.

Bertelli, R., Joanni, E., & Martlew, M. (1998). Relationship between children's counting ability and their ability to reason about number. *European Journal of Psychology of Education, 13*(3), 371–384.

Binet, A. (1969). The perception of lengths and numbers. In R. H. Pollack & M. W. Brenner

(Eds.), *Experimental psychology of Alfred Binet* (pp. 79–92). New York: Springer Publishing Co.

Bloom, L. (1970). *Language development: Form and function in emerging grammars.* Cambridge, MA: MIT Press.

Bowman, B. T., Donovan, M. S., & Burns, M. S. (Eds.). (2001). *Eager to learn: Educating our preschoolers.* Washington, DC: National Academy Press.

Brannon, E. M. (2002). The development of ordinal numerical knowledge in infancy. *Cognition, 83*, 223–240.

Burger, W. F., & Shaughnessy, J. M. (1986). Characterizing the Van Hiele levels of development in geometry. *Journal for Research in Mathematics Education, 17*(1), 31–48.

Carr, M., & Jessup, D. L. (1997). Gender differences in first-grade mathematics strategy use: Social and metacognitive influences. *Journal of Educational Psychology, 89*, 318–328.

Casey, B., Kersh, J. E., & Young, J. M. (2004). Storytelling sagas: An effective medium for teaching early childhood mathematics. *Early Childhood Research Quarterly, 19*(1), 167–172.

Clements, D. H. (2004a). Geometric and spatial thinking in early childhood education. In D. H. Clements, J. Serama, & A.-M. DiBiase (Eds.), *Engaging young children in mathematics: Standards for early childhood mathematics education* (pp. 267–297). Mahwah, NJ: Lawrence Erlbaum Associates.

Clements, D. H. (2004b). Major themes and recommendations. In D. H. Clements & J. Sarama (Eds.), *Engaging young children in mathematics: Standards for early childhood mathematics education* (pp. 7–72). Mahwah, NJ: Lawrence Erlbaum Associates.

Clements, D. H., & Battista, M. T. (1992). Geometry and spatial reasoning. In D. A. Grouws (Ed.), *Handbook of research on mathematics teaching and learning* (pp. 420–464). Reston, VA: National Council of Teachers of Mathematics.

Clements, D. H., Swaminathan, S., Hannibal, M. A. Z., & Sarama, J. (1999). Young children's concepts of shape. *Journal for Research in Mathematics Education, 30*(2), 192–212.

Corsaro, W. A. (1985). *Friendship and peer culture in the early years.* Norwood, NJ: Ablex.

Crowley, K., Shrager, J., & Siegler, R. S. (1997). Strategy discovery as a competitive negotiation between metacognitive and associative mechanisms. *Developmental Review, 17*, 462–489.

DeLoache, J. S. (2002). Early development of the understanding and use of symbolic artifacts. In U. Goswami (Ed.), *Blackwell handbook of childhood cognitive development* (pp. 206–226). Oxford: Blackwell.

Denton, K., & West, J. (2002). *Children's reading and mathematics achievement in kindergarten and first grade.* Washington, DC: National Center for Education Statistics.

Dewey, J. (1938). *Experience and education.* New York: Collier Books.

Durkin, K., Shire, B., Riem, R., Crowther, R. D., & Rutter, D. R. (1986). The social and linguistic context of early number word use. *British Journal of Developmental Psychology, 4*, 269–288.

Fuson, K. C. (1991). Children's early counting: Saying the number word sequence, counting objects, and understanding cardinality. In K. Durkin & B. Shire (Eds.), *Language in mathematical education: Research and practice* (pp. 27–39). Milton Keynes: Open University Press.

Garofalo, J., & Lester, F. K. (1985). Metacognition, cognitive monitoring, and mathematical performance. *Journal for Research in Mathematics Education, 16*, 163–176.

Garrick, R., Threlfall, J., & Orton, A. (1999). Pattern in the nursery. In A. Orton (Ed.), *Pattern in the teaching and learning of mathematics* (pp. 1–17). London: Cassell.

Geary, D. C. (1994). *Children's mathematical development: Research and practical applications.* Washington, DC: American Psychological Association.

Geary, D. C. (1996). Biology, culture, and cross-national differences in mathematical ability. In R. J. Sternberg & T. Ben-Zeev (Eds.), *The nature of mathematical thinking* (pp. 145–171). Mahwah, NJ: Lawrence Erlbaum Associates.

Gelman, R. (1980). What young children know about numbers. *Educational Psychologist, 15*, 54–68.

Gelman, R. (2000). The epigenesis of mathematical thinking. *Journal of Applied Developmental Psychology, 21*(1), 27–37.

Gelman, R., & Gallistel, C. R. (1986). *The child's understanding of number.* Cambridge, MA: Harvard University Press.

Gelman, R., Massey, C. M., & McManus, M. (1991). Characterizing supporting environments for cognitive development: Lessons from children in a museum. In L. B. Resnick, J. M. Levine, & S. D. Teasley (Eds.), *Perspectives on socially shared cognition* (pp. 226–256). Washington, DC: American Psychological Association.

Ginsburg, H. P. (1989). *Children's arithmetic: How they learn it and how you teach it* (2nd ed.). Austin: Pro Ed.

Ginsburg, H. P., & Baroody, A. J. (2003). *The test of early mathematics ability* (3rd ed.). Austin: Pro Ed.

Ginsburg, H. P., Kaplan, R. G., Cannon, J., Cordero, M. I., Eisenband, J. G., Galanter, M., & Morgenlander, M. (2005). Helping early childhood educators to teach mathematics. In M. Zaslow & I. Martinez-Beck (Eds.), *Critical issues in early childhood professional development* (pp. 171–202). Baltimore: Brookes Publishing.

Ginsburg, H. P., Klein, A., & Starkey, P. (1998). The development of children's mathematical thinking: Connecting research with practice. In I. Sigel & A. Renninger (Eds.), *Handbook of child psychology* (5th ed., Vol. 4, pp. 401–476). New York: John Wiley & Sons.

Ginsburg, H. P., & Russell, R. L. (1981). Social class and racial influences on early mathematical thinking. *Monographs of the Society for Research in Child Development, 46*(6, Serial No. 193).

Ginsburg, H. P., & Seo, K.-H. (1999). The mathematics in children's thinking. *Mathematical Thinking and Learning, 1*(2), 113–129.

Greenes, C. (1999). Ready to learn: Developing young children's mathematical powers. In J. Copley (Ed.), *Mathematics in the early years* (pp. 39–47). Reston, VA: National Council of Teachers of Mathematics.

Greenes, C., Ginsburg, H. P., & Balfanz, R. (2004). Big Math for Little Kids. *Early Childhood Research Quarterly, 19*(1), 159–166.

Griffin, S. (2004). Building number sense with Number Worlds: A mathematics program for young children. *Early Childhood Research Quarterly, 19*(1), 173–180.

Groen, G., & Resnick, L. B. (1977). Can preschool children invent addition algorithms? *Journal of Educational Psychology, 69*, 645–652.

Hewitt, K. (2001). Blocks as a tool for learning: Historical and contemporary perspectives. *Young Children, 56*(1), 6–13.

Hughes, M. (1986). *Children's invention of written arithmetic.* Oxford: Basil Blackwell.

Huntley-Fenner, G. (2001). Why count stuff? Young preschoolers do not use number for measurement in continuous dimensions. *Developmental Science, 4*(4), 456–462.

Irwin, K., & Burgham, D. (1992). Big numbers and small children. *The New Zealand Mathematics Magazine, 29*(1), 9–19.

Jordan, N. C., Huttenlocher, J., & Levine, C. S. (1994). Assessing early arithmetic abilities: Effects of verbal and nonverbal response types on the calculation performance of middle- and low-income children. *Learning and Individual Differences, 6*(4), 413–432.

Kato, Y. (1986). Development of spatial recognition in preschool children: On Piaget and Inhelder's hypothesis of topological space. *Perceptual and Motor Skills, 63*(2), 443–450.

Klahr, D., & Wallace, J. G. (1970). The development of serial completion strategies: An information processing analysis. *British Journal of Psychology, 61*(2), 243–257.

Klein, A., & Starkey, P. (1988). Universals in the development of early arithmetic cognition. In G. Saxe & M. Gearhart (Eds.), *Children's mathematics* (pp. 5–26). San Francisco: Jossey-Bass.

Klein, A., & Starkey, P. (2004). Fostering preschool children's mathematical knowledge: Findings from the Berkeley Math Readiness Project. In D. H. Clements & J. Sarama (Eds.), *Engaging young children in mathematics: Standards for early childhood mathematics education* (pp. 343–360). Mahwah, NJ: Lawrence Erlbaum Associates.

Kuhn, D. (2000). Metacognitive development. *Current Directions in Psychological Science, 9*(5), 178–181.

Leeb-Lundberg, K. (1996). The block builder mathematician. In E. S. Hirsch (Ed.), *The block book* (pp. 34–60). Washington, DC: National Association for the Education of Young Children.

Lehrer, R., Jenkins, M., & Osana, H. (1998). Longitudinal study of children's reasoning about space and geometry. In R. Lehrer & D. Chazan (Eds.), *Designing learning environments for developing understanding of geometry and space* (pp. 137–167). Mahwah, NJ: Lawrence Erlbaum Associates.

Liben, L. S., & Downs, R. M. (2001). Geography for young children: Maps as tools for learning environments. In S. L. Golbeck (Ed.), *Psychological perspectives on early childhood education: Reframing dilemmas in research and practice* (pp. 220–252). Mahwah, NJ: Lawrence Erlbaum Associates.

Miller, K. F. (1984). The child as the measurer of all things: Measurement procedures and the development of quantitative concepts. In C. Sophian (Ed.), *Origins of cognitive skills* (pp. 193–228). Hillsdale, NJ: Lawrence Erlbaum Associates.

Miller, K. F. (1989). Measurement as a tool for thought: The role of measuring procedures in children's understanding of quantitative invariance. *Developmental Psychology, 25*(4), 589–600.

Mix, K. S. (2002). The construction of number concepts. *Cognitive Development, 17*, 1345–1363.

Mounoud, P., & Bower, T. G. R. (1974). Conservation of weight in infants. *Cognition, 3*, 29–40.

National Association for the Education of Young Children and National Council of Teachers of Mathematics. (2002). *Position statement. Early childhood mathematics: Promoting good beginnings.* www.naeyc.org/resources/position_statements/psmath.htm

Newcombe, N., & Huttenlocher, J. (1992). Children's early ability to solve perspective-taking problems. *Developmental Psychology, 28*(4), 635–643.

Newcombe, N., Huttenlocher, J., & Learmonth, A. E. (1999). Infants' coding of location in continuous space. *Infant Behavior and Development, 22*(4), 483–510.

Newcombe, N., & Learmonth, A. (1999). Change and continuity in early spatial development: Claiming the radical middle. *Infant Behavior and Development, 22*(4), 457–474.

Nunes, T., & Bryant, P. E. (1996). *Children doing mathematics.* Oxford: Basil Blackwell.

Pappas, S., Ginsburg, H. P., & Jiang, M. (2003). SES differences in young children's metacognition in the context of mathematical problem solving. *Cognitive Development, 18*(3), 431–450.

Piaget, J. (1952a). *The child's conception of number* (C. Gattegno &. F. M. Hodgson, Trans.). London: Routledge & Kegan Paul.

Piaget, J. (1952b). *The origins of intelligence in children* (M. Cook, Trans.). New York: International Universities Press.

Piaget, J., & Inhelder, B. (1967). *The child's conception of space* (F. J. Langdon & J. L. Lunzer, Trans.). New York: W. W. Norton & Company.

Piaget, J., Inhelder, B., & Szeminska, A. (1960). *The child's conception of geometry* (E. A. Lunzer, Trans.). New York: Basic Books.

Pieraut-Le Bonniec, G. (1982). From rhythm to reversibility. In G. E. Forman (Ed.), *Action and thought: From sensorimotor schemes to symbolic operations* (pp. 253–263). London: Academic Press.

Posner, J. K. (1982). The development of mathematical knowledge in two West African societies. *Child Development, 53,* 200–208.

Rawson, B. (1993). Searching for pattern. *Education 1–13, 22*(1), 3–13.

Satlow, E., & Newcombe, N. (1998). When is a triangle not a triangle? Young children's developing concepts of geometric shape. *Cognitive Development, 13,* 547–559.

Saxe, G. B., Guberman, S. R., & Gearhart, M. (1987). Social processes in early number development. *Monographs of the Society for Research in Child Development, 52*(2, Serial No. 216).

Seo, K.-H., & Ginsburg, H. P. (2004). What is developmentally appropriate in early childhood mathematics education? Lessons from new research. In D. H. Clements, J. Sarama, & A.-M. DiBiase (Eds.), *Engaging young children in mathematics: Standards for early childhood mathematics education* (pp. 91–104). Hillsdale, NJ: Lawrence Erlbaum Associates.

Sera, M., & Smith, L. B. (1987). Big and little: "Nominal" and relative uses. *Cognitive Development, 2,* 89–111.

Serama, J., & Clements, D. H. (2004). *Building Blocks* for early childhood mathematics. *Early Childhood Research Quarterly, 19*(1), 181–189.

Sophian, C. (2002). Learning about what fits: Preschool children's reasoning about effects of object size. *Journal for Research in Mathematics Education, 33*(4), 290–302.

Sophian, C. (2004). Mathematics for the future: Developing a Head Start curriculum to support mathematics learning. *Early Childhood Research Quarterly, 19*(1), 59–81.

Sophian, C., & Adams, N. (1987). Infants' understanding of numerical transformations. *British Journal of Developmental Psychology, 5,* 257–264.

Spelke, E. S. (2003). What makes us smart? Core knowledge and natural language. In G. Gentner & S. Goldin-Meadow (Eds.), *Language in mind: Advances in the study of language and thought* (pp. 277–311). Cambridge, MA: MIT Press.

Starkey, P., & Gelman, R. (1982). The development of addition and subtraction abilities prior to formal schooling in arithmetic. In T. P. Carpenter, J. M. Moser, & T. A. Romberg (Eds.), *Addition and subtraction: A cognitive perspective.* Hillsdale, NJ: Lawrence Erlbaum Associates.

Starkey, P., Klein, A., & Wakeley, A. (2004). Enhancing young children's mathematical knowledge through a pre-kindergarten mathematics intervention. *Early Childhood Research Quarterly, 19*(1), 99–120.

Stevenson, H., Lee, S. S., & Stigler, J. (1986). The mathematics achievement of Chinese, Japanese, and American children. *Science, 56,* 693–699.

Tan, L. S., & Bryant, P. (2000). The cues that infants use to distinguish discontinuous quantities: Evidence using a shift-rate recovery paradigm. *Child Development, 71*(5), 1162–1178.

Threlfall, J. (1999). Repeating patterns in the early primary years. In A. Orton (Ed.), *Pattern in the teaching and learning of mathematics* (pp. 18–30). London: Cassell.

Uttal, D. H. (1996). Angles and distances: Children's and adults' reconstruction and scaling of spatial configurations. *Child Development, 67*(6), 2763–2779.

van Hiele, P. M. (1986). *Structure and insight: A theory of mathematics education.* Orlando: Academic Press.

Vygotsky, L. S. (1978). *Mind in society: The development of higher psychological processes.* Cambridge, MA: Harvard University Press.

Wagner, S. H., & Walters, J. (1982). A longitudinal analysis of early number concepts: From numbers to number. In G. E. Forman (Ed.), *Action and thought: From sensorimotor schemes to symbolic operations* (pp. 137–161). New York: Academic Press.

Walkerdine, V. (1988). *The mastery of reason: Cognitive development and the production of rationality*. London: Routledge.

Wynn, K. (1992). Addition and subtraction by human infants. *Nature, 358*, 749–750.

Zaslavsky, C. (1973). *Africa counts: Number and pattern in African culture*. Boston: Prindle, Weber & Schmidt.

Zur, O., & Gelman, R. (2004). Young children can add and subtract by predicting and checking. *Early Childhood Research Quarterly, 19*(1), 121–137.

Zvonkin, A. (1992). Mathematics for little ones. *Journal of Mathematical Behavior, 11*(2), 207–219.

PART IV

Language and Communicative Development

12

Language Experience and Language Milestones During Early Childhood

Erika Hoff

Overview

During the first four years of life, children progress from the newborn state, in which they neither speak nor understand any language, to being young children who comment, question, and express their ideas in the language of their community. One goal of this chapter is to describe the major milestones on this journey to linguistic competence. A second goal of this chapter is to describe the role played by children's experiences in this achievement. The nature of children's language experiences is part of what makes language acquisition possible, and it is part of what explains why children differ in the rate and course of their language development. A full description of the process of language development must, therefore, include a description of how that process is supported and shaped by children's experience.

This focus on the role of experience does not deny the internal contribution to language development. There must be innate characteristics of children that explain why only they, and not the young of any other species, can acquire language. Innate characteristics of children no doubt also contribute to explaining why language development is practically inevitable across the range of environments in which children develop – this is the resilience of language discussed by Goldin-Meadow (this volume). That notwithstanding, universal properties of human environments may also play a role in explaining the universal fact of language acquisition, and differences in children's environments clearly create differences in their language development. Language development reaches the same endpoint in all children (i.e., is characterized by equifinality) only in the sense that all children learn a language and all languages share certain characteristics. Children learn different languages, depending on the languages that they hear. Children who learn different languages then differ in the sounds they can distinguish and produce, in the sound–meaning mappings they make, in the grammatical rules they follow in producing and understanding speech, and in the social rules they follow in communicating. Among children acquiring the same language, there are differences in the rate and style of language development such that at every age, children differ in the size and composition of their vocabularies, in the complexity of their sentence structure, and in the skill and style with which they communicate. A full account of language development also requires an explanation of these individual differences. (This argument admittedly begs the issue(s) of when language acquisition reaches its endpoint and what sort of differences in language competence exist among adults who speak the same language. Here we focus on the differences in language development and language achievement in early childhood.)

In describing the milestones of language development and the role of experience in their achievement, it is useful to consider separately the several subcomponents of language: *phonology* comprises the sounds and sound system of language, the *lexicon* consists of words and their associated knowledge, *morphology* is the system for combining units of meaning into words, and *syntax* is the system for combining words into sentences. Together, knowledge of these components constitutes a child's (or adult's) linguistic competence. The ability to use this system to communicate is typically referred to as *communicative competence*, and it too has identifiable subcomponents. We will focus on two in this chapter: (1) the foundational understanding that language can be used in order to communicate, and (2) skill at producing connected discourse in conversation and story telling.

Phonological Development

The course of phonological development

Language competence depends upon the ability to discriminate different speech sounds, and this ability is present in infancy. By 6 months of age, infants' basic auditory capacities are nearly adult-like and infants this age or younger have demonstrated the ability to discriminate virtually all the sounds that languages use – regardless of whether those contrasts are present in the ambient language (Aslin, Jusczyk, & Pisoni, 1998).

The production of speech sounds also begins in infancy – well before speech itself – and milestones in speech sound production are achieved in a predictable sequence (see Table 12.1). At first, newborns produce only cries and noises that are termed vegetative sounds (such as burping and sneezing). Cooing (happy-sounding, vowel-like sounds) appears at 6 to 8 weeks, and laughter appears around the age of 16 weeks. Between 16 weeks and 30 weeks infants begin to combine different sounds into increasingly long and complex series, in what has been termed vocal play (Stark, 1986). Sometime around 6 to 9 months of age, the quality of infants' vocalizations changes as they start to babble. Canonical babbling, which is distinguished from the vocalizations that precede it by the presence of true syllables, is typically produced in reduplicated series of the same consonant and vowel combination (Oller, 1986). The appearance of canonical babbling is followed by a period of non-reduplicated, or variegated, babbling in which the range of consonants and vowels infants produce expands further. Prosody – the intonation contour of speech – becomes

Table 12.1   Milestones of phonological development in production

6–8 weeks	Cooing appears
16 weeks	Laughter and vocal play appear
6–9 months	Reduplicated (canonical) babbling appears
1 year	First words use a limited sound repertoire
18 months	Phonological processes (deformations of target sounds) become systematic
18 months–7 years	Phonological inventory completion

particularly noticeable at the stage of variegated babbling. Around 1 year children produce their first words, but this is not a major milestone in phonological development. The particular sounds that appear in first words are the same sounds that were evidenced in children's late babbling and transitional forms (Ingram, 1999). Children's vocalizations at this point are most frequently single syllables, with some two-syllable productions.

A new milestone in phonological development is reached at approximately 18 months of age when children's productions become consistent, although not adult-like. Prior to this point, the way children articulate particular sounds may vary from word to word. After this point, children appear to have developed systematic ways in which they alter the sounds of the target language so that they fit within the repertoire of sounds they can produce. These systematic transformations are called phonological processes (Menyuk, Menn, & Silber, 1986). Many phonological processes are common to all children acquiring the same language, and they give young children's speech certain characteristic features, such as transforming /r/ to /w/ and reducing consonant clusters such as "pl" to /p/ so that "Please Mr. Rabbit" is produced as "Pease Mr. Wabbit," for example.

It has been proposed that what underlies this change in production is a change in how children mentally represent the sounds of words. Initially, phonological representations are global whole-word representations, and thus the way a particular sound is represented may vary from word to word. After 18 months, children develop a system for representing words phoneme by phoneme, and thus the same phonemic representation for a particular sound is part of the mental representation of every word that has that sound. One factor that may underlie this change is vocabulary growth. The argument has been made that as vocabulary size grows, children's initial whole-word representations start to overlap in their acoustic properties and finer-grained representations are necessary in order to keep different words apart. This pushes children to a phonological analysis of their language and to the representation of a phonological system (see Gerken, 1994; Walley, 1993). (That is, distinguishing "bike" from "like" requires a level of phonological representation that is not need for distinguishing "bike" and "dog," and the bigger the child's vocabulary, the more likely it is to contain pairs of minimally different words.) Not all the data fit this story, however. There may be as much overlap in small vocabularies as in larger ones (Coady & Aslin, 2003), and studies of infants' word processing have found evidence that their word representations have more phonetic detail than the global/whole-word account would suggest (Swingley & Aslin, 2000). It is an open question at this point just what developmental changes occur in children's phonological representations and what might cause any such changes.

Language experience and phonological development

The sound properties of the speech addressed to children differ from the properties of speech addressed to adults in ways that arguably aid children's learning of the sounds and sound patterns of language. When talking to babies, adults use a higher-pitched voice, a wider range of pitches, longer pauses, and shorter phrases (Fernald & Simon, 1984; Fernald, Taeschner, Dun, Papousek, De Boysson-Bardies, & Fukui, 1989; and see summary in Gerken, 1994). Infant-directed speech is also produced at a slower tempo than adult-directed speech, with the result that vowels are prolonged. In child-directed speech, vowels also vary less than in adult-directed speech, thus children hear particularly clear examples of the sounds of their language (Kuhl & Meltzoff, 1997; Kuhl, Williams, Lacerda, Stevens, & Lindblom, 1992).

Experience also creates language-specific differences in the early perception and production of speech sounds. By 10 to 12 months, infants lose their initial ability to discriminate all speech sounds and become, like adults, less able to discriminate some consonant contrasts that are not used in their ambient language (Werker & Tees, 1984). Similar effects on vowel discrimination have been demonstrated in infants as young as 6 months old (Kuhl et al.,1992). It appears that even before babies know anything about the meanings of the sounds they hear, they are paying attention to the acoustic properties of those sounds, noticing what portions of the acoustic space their language uses, and forming categories around clusters of frequently occurring acoustic signals. These categories then guide perception such that within-category variation is ignored and between-category variation is attended to (Maye, Werker, & Gerken, 2002). With respect to production, "babbling drift" is the term given to the changes that occur in infants' babbling as influenced by properties of the target language (R. Brown, 1958). For example, Japanese and French babies use more nasal sounds in their babbling than Swedish and English babies do (de Boysson-Bardies, Halle, Sagart, & Durand, 1989; de Boysson-Bardies et al., 1992). These differences are subtle, however, and for the most part babbling sounds similar the world over (Oller & Eilers, 1998).

Relatively little is documented regarding individual differences in phonological development or potential environmental sources of such differences. The finding that phonological development is less affected by socio-economic status than are lexical or grammatical development suggests that environmental influences may play less of a role in phonological development than in the development of other language components (Dollaghan et al., 1999; Oller, Eilers, Basinger, Steffens, & Urbano, 1995). On the other hand, children's ability to hear (and thus the amount or fidelity of their input) does affect early phonological development. Infants who experience frequent ear infections, with associated hearing loss, have been found to be delayed in the onset of canonical babbling and to be different from infants without such a medical history in the quality of the vowels they produce in babbling (Rvachew, Slawinski, Williams, & Green, 1999), and deaf infants are substantially delayed in the onset of canonical babbling (Oller & Eilers, 1988). An important part of what infants hear that contributes to phonological development may be their own productions. In vocal play, infants may be discovering the correspondence between what they do with their vocal apparatus and the sounds that come out, and thus, without feedback, productive development is hampered (Kuhl & Meltzoff, 1988).

Lexical Development

The course of lexical development

Infants may understand their first word as young as 5 months. There are both anecdotal reports and experimental evidence of children selectively responding to their own name at this age (Mandel, Jusczyk, & Pisoni, 1995). At around 8 months, children begin to understand a few phrases, such as "Give me a hug," " Stop it," and "Come here" (Fenson, Dale, Reznick, Bates, Thal, & Pethick, 1994). Data from the MacArthur Communicative Inventory, which assesses children's comprehension and production vocabularies from mothers' reports, reveals that 10-month-old children's comprehension vocabularies range from an average of 11 words (for the bottom 10% of children tested) to an average of 154 words (for the top 10%). Children usually produce their first words sometime between 10 and 15 months of age (Benedict, 1979; Fenson et al., 1994), although some first words may be tied to particular contexts and therefore not truly referential. For example, one little boy said "duck" only in the context of knocking ducks off the edge of the tub. For this child, "duck" was part of an activity rather than a word that stood for a referent (Barrett, 1986). But if not initially, then soon, children's words start to be truly referential, and, as was the case for phonological development, there is a predictable sequence of milestones in the growth of a productive lexicon (see Table 12.2).

Word learning is typically slow at first, but for many children lexical development seems to shift into a different gear at the achievement of a fifty-word productive vocabulary (Benedict, 1979; L. Bloom, 1973; Nelson, 1973). This acceleration of lexical growth is known as the word spurt; however, there is disagreement as to whether all children show this pattern or whether such a thing as a spurt exists at all. Goldfield and Reznick (1990) have claimed that only some children show a spurt and that other children show more even rates of vocabulary development. Paul Bloom (2000) has claimed that the word spurt is a myth. Children do increase the rate at which they acquire new words, but, Bloom argues, the change for most children is a gradual increase rather than an abrupt change in rate. One thing that is clear about the rate of lexical growth is that it varies tremendously among children, with the result that vocabularies of children of the same age vary enormously in size. The MacArthur Inventory data (Fenson et al., 1994), for example, show that even excluding the top and bottom 15% of children, the range in production vocabulary size among 16-month-olds is between 0 and 160 words, and the range for 24-month-olds is between 50 and 550 words.

In terms of content, the vocabularies of very young children are not just small versions of the vocabularies of older children and adults; they differ in the kinds of words they contain. Not surprisingly, children's first words reflect their experiences. They know names for people, food, body parts, clothing, animals, and household items and expressions that are involved in their daily routines (Clark, 1979). First verbs include labels for actions

Table 12.2   Milestones of lexical development in production

10–15 months	First word is produced
15–18 months	50-word vocabulary is reached, vocabulary growth "spurts"
18–30 months	200-word vocabulary is reached
6 years	Vocabulary averages 14,000 words*

* From Templin (1957).

that are part of children's routines (e.g., *eat, drink, kiss, sing*) and verbs with more general meanings that are frequent in children's input (*look, go, come, do*) (Naigles & Hoff, in press). One feature of early vocabularies that has received a great deal of attention is the predominance of nouns (Bates et al., 1994; Benedict, 1979; Gentner, 1982; Gentner & Boroditsky, 2001). For English-speaking children with vocabularies between twenty and fifty words, fully 45% of their vocabulary consists of nouns compared to 3% for verbs (Caselli et al., 1995).

Language experience and lexical development

To learn a new word, the child must isolate that word from the continuous stream of speech and then must figure out the word's meaning. Properties of the way in which people talk to children arguably make both these tasks easier than they would be other-wise. The exaggerated stress patterns that characterize child-directed speech may make the segmentation problem easier. As evidence for this, one study found that adults learned words in a foreign language more readily if the words were presented with the intonation of infant-directed rather than adult-directed speech (Golinkoff & Alioto, 1995). Child-directed speech is also highly redundant and tends to be about the here-and-now, making the referents of new words available and giving children multiple opportunities to map new words onto their meanings. In addition to providing labels for things, adults also provide children with information about the things they are labeling (e.g., bats live in a cave; squirrels eat acorns; seals like the water) (Gelman, Coley, Rosengren, Hartman, & Pappas, 1998), thus supporting the child in filling out the meaning portion of new lexical entries.

The way in which languages and individuals present new words to children has consequences for their lexical development. Children acquiring Korean, Japanese, and Mandarin (Chinese) show less of a noun bias in their speech than children acquiring English (Fernald & Morikawa, 1993; Gopnik & Choi, 1995; Tardif, Gelman, & Xu, 1999), arguably because in these Asian languages, a verb is often the final word in a sentence, thus making verbs salient. Also, English-speaking American adults – at least middle-class mothers, who are the most frequently studied – spend a great deal of time labeling objects for their babies, whereas Japanese mothers do so much less frequently (Fernald & Morikawa, 1993).

Variability in the amount of language children hear also has an effect on vocabulary development. Children exposed to more speech develop vocabulary at a faster rate than children exposed to less speech (Hart & Risley, 1995; Hoff & Naigles, 2002; Hutten-locher, Haight, Bryk, Seltzer, & Lyons, 1991). This may be part of the explanation of findings that children from higher socio-economic strata have bigger vocabularies than children from lower socio-economic strata – mothers with higher levels of education talk more to their children than mothers with lower levels of education (Hoff, 2003; Hoff, Laursen, & Tardif, 2002). Socio-economic status (SES)-related differences in children's language can be quite large, with lower-SES children being a year or more behind higher-SES children by the age of 4 (Snow, 1999), although factors other than maternal speech may contribute to these differences (Hoff, 2003). Differences among children in the amount of adult speech they hear may underlie the effects of two other predictors of vocabulary development: children who attend child care centers with high adult–child ratios develop vocabulary more rapidly than children who attend child care centers with lower adult–child ratios (McCartney, 1984; NICHD Early Child Care Research Network, 2000), and first-born children develop vocabulary more rapidly than later-born children (Fenson et al., 1994; Hoff-Ginsberg, 1998; Pine, 1995).

Not just the amount, but also the nature of the speech children hear has effects on vocabulary development. Hearing a rich vocabulary that includes many different words and rare or sophisticated words is associated with more rapid vocabulary development than hearing a more restricted and simpler vocabulary (Hoff & Naigles, 2002; Weizman & Snow, 2001). This is another property of child-directed speech that varies as a function of maternal education and contributes to the SES-related differences in children's vocab-ularies (Hoff, 2003). It also helps, particularly for children under 18 months, if the timing of speech is responsive to child verbalizations and if the content of the speech is related to the child's focus of attention (Tamis-LeMonda, Bornstein, Kahana-Kalman, Baumwell, & Cyphers, 1998; Tomasello & Todd, 1983). In older children, vocabulary growth is predicted by the informativeness of the context in which new words are presented. The information can be provided explicitly, as when adults point out referents of new words (e.g. "This is a *car*"), indirectly, in the way a new word is paired with its referent (e.g., "Don't make that *gulping* noise" [following gulping]) (Weizman & Snow, 2001), or via the structure of the sentence (e.g., "*Give* the ball to Mommy" suggests that *give* is a verb of transfer) (Naigles & Hoff-Ginsberg, 1998).

Morphosyntactic Development

The course of morphosyntactic development

Morphemes are the smallest units of meaning. They include words and word parts with their own meanings, such as the "s" or "es" that marks the plural, the "ed" that marks past tense, and the "s" that marks the possessive. Morphology is the system for combining morphemes into words, and syntax is the system for combining words into sentences. Development of these sorts of knowledge is referred to as morphosyntactic development, and, like phonological and lexical development, it follows a predictable sequence (see Table 12.3). For children acquiring English, word combinations are the

Table 12.3   Milestones of morphosyntactic development in production

18–24 months	First word combinations appear
24–36 months	Speech is initially telegraphic, grammatical morphology develops
36 months	Full sentences are produced and range of sentence types (e.g., questions, negatives) increases
48 months	Full range of complex sentence types produced

first sign of morphosyntactic development. After several months of talking in single-word utterances, children begin to put two words together in sentences like "Daddy shirt," "Off TV," and "Pretty tower." These first word combinations tend to be missing function words, such as determiners, and bound morphemes. Because these are rather bare strings of content words, this type of speech has been termed "telegraphic" (R. Brown & Fraser, 1963).

Next, children start to combine three and more words into short sentences, and they begin to add the function words and bound morphemes that were missing in their first word combinations. As children gradually master the grammar of their language, they become able to produce increasingly long utterances. This is true not only when length is counted in words but even more so when length is counted in morphemes. For example, a telegraphic sentence such as "I watch it" has a length of three words and three morphemes. A non-telegraphic version of that sentence, "I am watching it," has a length of four words and five morphemes; *-ing* is a separate morpheme although not a separate word. Because length in morphemes is a good index of the grammatical complexity of an utterance, and because children tend to follow similar courses of development in adding complexity to their utterances, the average length of children's utterances (counted in morphemes) has been widely used as a measure of their syntactic development. Children's first sentences are usually simple active declarative sentences; negative sentences and questions, for example, appear later. The last major syntactic development is the production of multi-clause sentences. The development of these complex sentences usually begins some time before the child's second birthday and is largely complete by the age of 4 years.

Children differ in both the rate and the course of grammatical development. The differences in rate are the most obvious. Some children produce multi-word utterances at 18 months, whereas others do not start combining words until they are 2 years old. (Because rates of development vary so much, mean length of utterance is a much better index of young children's levels of language development than age is.) Less obvious than differences in when children start to combine words are differences in the kinds of multi-word utterances children produce. Some children's early multi-word utterances are rote-learned as wholes; other children's are combinations of separate words from the start. Most children include both unanalyzed chunks and smaller units in their early sentences, but children vary in how much they rely on one versus the other strategy of language analysis and production (Bretherton, McNew, Snyder, & Bates, 1983; Peters, 1986; Pine & Lieven, 1993).

Language experience and morphosyntactic development

Speech to children has properties that may support children's acquisition of language structure. For one, it is highly repetitious. Caregivers say things like, "Put the doll in her crib. Yes, the doll. That's right, in her crib." They also repeat and expand children's utterances (*Child*: Milk. *Adult*: You want some milk?). These repetitions and expansions of children's incomplete utterances might serve as little language lessons, revealing the component structures that make up sentences. The exaggerated prosodic features of speech may also provide cues to syntactic structure. For example, pauses and changes in intonation tend to occur at phrase boundaries. Infants appear to notice this correspondence between pauses and structure as evidenced by their preference to listen to speech in which pauses correspond to phrase boundaries over speech with pauses inserted elsewhere (Kemler Nelson, Hirsh-Pasek, Jusczyk, & Wright Cassidy, 1989). Open-class words (i.e., the nouns, verbs, adjectives, adverbs) tend to receive stress, and closed-class words (i.e., the determiners, auxiliary verbs) tend to be unstressed, providing cues to that grammatical distinction. Additionally, nouns and verbs differ: nouns tend to have first syllable stress, and verbs have second syllable stress (for example, compare the noun and verb versions of the word *record*) (Kelly, 1996). The hypothesis that children use these phonological cues to break into grammatical structure is known as the phonological bootstrapping hypothesis. Often, because prosodic cues seem particularly important, it is known as the prosodic bootstrapping hypothesis (see Morgan & Demuth, 1996, for a full discussion of this hypothesis).

It has been argued that these features of child-directed speech cannot carry much explanatory burden in accounting for language acquisition because in many cultures of the world people do not talk to prelinguistic children (Bavin, 1992; P. Brown, 1998; Heath 1983, 1990), yet these children acquire language too. (This argument applies to other aspects of language development as well, but the argument has centered on the acquisition of grammar.) Lieven (1994) has suggested a way to reconcile the fact that some children acquire language without being spoken to by adults with the hypothesis that adults' child-directed speech significantly contributes to grammatical development. One part of the solution is to point out that siblings and older children may talk to young children, and thus they are a source of input. (Although, interestingly, siblings appear not to be as good a source of input as adults [Hoff-Ginsberg & Krueger, 1991], perhaps explaining why first-borns and singletons are advantaged in some aspects of language development compared to later-born children and twins.) Another part of the solution is to suggest that children who learn language from the speech they overhear are more likely to learn grammar through rote-learning large chunks and then later analyzing their internal structure (Lieven, 1994). Finally, Lieven proposes that in cultures where children are not directly talked to, they may learn to talk more slowly as a result, and there is evidence in support of this proposal (Bavin, 1992; P. Brown, 2001). If children who are not directly addressed by adults acquire grammar in a different way or less rapidly than do children who are directly addressed, then the fact that they do acquire language does not mean that input plays no role when it is available. To the contrary, if differences in grammatical development are associated with differences in input, input is likely to be playing a role.

Variability in amount of language experience does show some relation to individual differences in the rate of grammatical development. The effects of adult contact in child care and birth order that were observed for vocabulary development are also observed for grammatical development (McCartney, 1984; NICHD Early Child Care Research Network, 2000). Experimental work has demonstrated that extra experience with certain structures results in earlier acquisition of those structures (Shatz, Hoff-Ginsberg, & MacIver, 1989; Valian & Lyman, 2003). Even the acquisition of a feature of grammar that is supposed to be specified in Universal Grammar is affected by exposure to input. In English, the sentence "Who do you think has green eyes?" is grammatical and "Who do you think that has green eyes?" is ungrammatical. In Spanish, the opposite (in translation) is true. According to many syntactic theories, this difference between Spanish and English is in the setting of a parameter and should be quickly learned from minimal input. In fact, however, it appears that a fair amount of input must be accrued for acquisition of these structures because Spanish–English bilingual children master these just a little later in each of their languages than do monolingual Spanish or English learners (Gathercole, 2002).

As was the case for vocabulary development, not just the amount, but also particular properties of the speech children hear predict grammatical development (Hoff-Ginsberg & Shatz, 1982; Richards, 1994). The frequency with which mothers produce partially repetitious sequences (like "Put the doll in the crib. That's right, the doll") and the frequency with which mothers expand or slightly change their children's prior utterance are associated with more rapid grammatical development in 2-year-olds (Hoff-Ginsberg, 1985, 1986; see review in Hoff-Ginsberg & Shatz, 1982). Among 5- and 6-year-olds, children who hear more complex speech later perform better on tests of the ability to understand complex speech, and this is true even when the sources of input (teachers) are genetically unrelated to the language learners (Huttenlocher, Vasilyeva, Cymerman, & Levine, 2002). The structural properties of children's verb use depend on structural properties of the utterances in which those verbs appear in child-directed speech (Naigles & Hoff-Ginsberg, 1998).

Communicative Development

The course of communicative development

Before children use language to communicate, they must have the intention to communicate. A central point to make in discussing the development of communicative intentions is that such intentions are not present from birth. Although adults can interpret babies' cries and other noises, the baby does not produce them with the intention of sending a message – at least not initially. The major milestones of communicative development are indicated in Table 12.4, with the first indication of intentional communication appearing at about 10 months. The change in behavior that occurs around this time is illustrated in the following two vignettes reported by Bates, Camaioni, and Volterra (1975), first at 9 months of age:

Table 12.4 Milestones of communicative development

9–10 months	Communicative intentions first appear
10–15 months	Joint attention skills develop
12 months >	Range of expressed communicative purposes expands
18 months >	Conversation skills develop
36 months >	Narrative skills develop

> In an effort to obtain a box that her mother is holding in her arms, Carolotta pulls at the arms, pushes her whole body against the floor, and approaches the box from several angles. *Yet during the entire sequence she never looks up into her mother's face.* (p. 214; italics added)

In contrast, at 11 months:

> Carolotta, unable to pull a toy cat out of the adult's hand, sits back up straight, *looks the adult intently in the face*, and then tries once again to pull the cat. (p. 215; italics added)

What underlies this change has been described as the development of the capacity for secondary intersubjectivity or the capacity for joint attention. Secondary intersubjectivity is the ability to share one's experiences with others – as opposed to primary intersubjectivity, which is the more limited capacity to share oneself with others (Trevarthen & Hubley, 1978). The term "joint attention" also refers to the state in which the child and communicative partner are both attending to a third object (Carpenter, Nagell, & Tomasello, 1998). Children's development of the capacity for joint attention and the role of joint attention in language acquisition have been the topic of substantial research attention. A key notion in this work is the idea that when infants seek joint attention with another they are demonstrating an understanding that other people are like them, and they are seeking contact with another mind. This understanding of other minds is argued to be a prerequisite for intentional communication (see Barr, this volume).

After passing this milestone at about 10 months, children's communicative behavior increases – in frequency, in the range of communicative intents they express, and in the number of different linguistic forms they use to realize each intention. One longitudinal study of children between 14 and 32 months found that the frequency of communicative intents increased from an average of 4 to 11 per minute; the proportion of communicative attempts that were interpretable increased from .47 to .94. At 14 months, children's communicative behavior occurred largely to serve four communicative different functions: directing the hearer's attention, negotiating immediate activity, discussing joint focus, and marking the event (e.g., with a "sorry" or "Thank-you"). At 32 months, twelve different communicative functions occurred with some regularity across children, including new types such as discussing clarification of action, discussing hearer's thoughts and feelings, and discussing things and events not present (Snow, Pan, Imbens-Bailey, & Herman, 1996).

Using language to communicate typically involves either participating in conversation or producing a monologue. It often appears that conversations, if not monologues, begin in infancy, but the "conversations" that occur between mothers and babies depend upon mothers' building a conversational structure around their children's behavior, and do not reflect infants' interactive skill (Shatz, 1983). There is no clear landmark that signifies children's entry into conversational participation. Rather, the relative burdens carried by the adult and the child in sustaining conversation gradually become more equal as children develop an understanding that they have responsibilities as conversational participants, as they learn what is required of them to fulfill these responsibilities in different linguistic contexts, and as they master the linguistic devices for meeting those requirements (Shatz, 1983).

Children's first understanding about the rules of conversation is that they are supposed to respond to another speaker's utterance. An early strategy that children employ to fulfill this conversational obligation is to respond with action. Gradually, children start to respond more frequently to talk with talk and also to respond differently to different kinds of utterances (Shatz & McCloskey, 1984). Children also become more skilled at initiating conversational topics. For conversation to be sustainable for very long, each party's contribution must be relevant to the previous speaker's turn. With development, children increase the contingency of their conversational contributions (Bloom, Rocissano, & Hood, 1976).

The most studied sort of monologue is the narrative, which is a verbal description of a past event. In ordinary language, narratives are stories. Children's first narratives occur in the context of conversation and are typically elicited and maintained by an adult. The adult provides the scaffolding for children's reports of past experience by introducing a past event as a topic ("Did you go to the zoo?") and then eliciting more information on the topic ("What did you see there?"). In these early narratives, most of the content of the narrative is supplied by the adult, and the child supplies single-word responses to the adult's questions. With development, children come to depend less on the scaffolding of adults' questions, and the children's contributions are longer and introduce new information, although reports of past events tend initially to be general descriptions of a kind of familiar event rather than specific descriptions of particular events. In the third phase, children's narratives depend less on either conversational support or general event knowledge, and they include more information that is unique to the particular event being recounted (Eisenberg, 1985).

In addition to the growing independence from adult support, other developmental trends in children's early narrative production include increases in the frequency of spontaneous mention of past events, increases in the length of the narratives produced, increases in the remoteness of the past event, increases in the structural complexity of the stories told, and increases in the use of narrative devices such as orienting to time and place and evaluating the events in the narrative (Haden, Haine, & Fivush, 1997; Miller & Sperry, 1988; Umiker-Sebeok, 1979).

Language experience and communicative development

The interest in meeting other minds that may be a foundation of normal communicative development appears to be a biologically based characteristic of humans. Environments meet this human characteristic by showing children that language can be used to communicate and by providing children with potential communicative partners (Crago, Allen, & Hough-Eyamie, 1997; Lieven, 1994). In fact, a potential communicative partner may be the only experiential requirement, as evidenced by deaf children who invent sign systems if they have no language model to learn from (Goldin-Meadow, this volume). The necessity of a communicative partner is suggested by the evidence that socially isolated children do not invent symbolic systems to represent their ideas (Shatz, 1994), although such cases of children locked in rooms or abandoned in woods can never provide conclusive evidence.

The responsiveness of one's communicative partner appears to have an influence on language development. Children whose mothers are more responsive to their early attempts to communicate do acquire language more rapidly than do children with less responsive mothers. This is not just a general benefit of responsive caregiving – the effect of responsivity to verbalization is specific to language development (Tamis-LeMonda & Bornstein, 1994; Tamis-LeMonda et al., 1998).

Turning to specific discourse skills, there is also evidence that experience plays a supportive and shaping role. Conversational skill appears to benefit from the availability of a model. For example, later-born children produce more contingent responses in conversation than same-aged first-born children do, even though their linguistic skills are not more advanced (Hoff-Ginsberg, 1998). Relatedly, Dunn and Shatz (1989) found that children with older siblings develop the ability to intrude into the conversation between the older sibling and the mothers. Between 2 and 3 years of age, the younger children's intrusions become more frequently relevant to the ongoing conversation and more frequently successful at gaining the child entry into the conversation. Thus, it may also be that children learn the communicative competencies the situation requires – first-born children have attentive mothers who will converse with them regardless of what they do, but second-born children need to learn conversational skills if they want to be included. The development of narrative skill clearly benefits from the support adults provide. Children whose parents ask useful, elaborative questions when the children are 2 years old produce better narratives when they are 3 (McCabe & Peterson, 1991), and the complexity and structure of the narratives mothers produce in conversation with their 2-year-olds are related to the complexity and structure of those children's narratives a year later (Fivush, 1991).

Conclusions

The accomplishment of language acquisition poses an explanatory challenge: what process can explain how the newborn who speaks no language becomes the 4-year-old who communicates with the world around him or her, speaking in complex sentences and making use of a vocabulary of hundreds, if not thousands, of words? The facts that no other species can do this at all, that humans can hardly be prevented from doing this, and that the development of language follows – at least in broad outline – a regular developmental course all suggest a biological basis. There are also, however, universal features of children's environments that may contribute to the universal acquisition of language. All environments in which language development occurs normally provide children with communicative partners and with a language model, and when environments differ in the degree to which they provide these supports, there is correlated variability in children's language development.

Correlations between properties of the language experiences that different environments provide and measures of language development could, in principle, have three underlying sources: effects of experience on language, effects of children's language skill on the language they elicit, and, in the case of correlations between maternal speech and child language growth, a common genetic basis. Some of the correlations between children's input and language development may reflect both genetic effects and effects of children on their environments to some degree. On the other hand, there are many findings of effects of input on language growth that do not admit of either of these accounts. Shared genes cannot underlie effects of adult–child ratios in child care centers or of birth order (Fenson et al., 1994; Hoff-Ginsberg, 1998; McCartney, 1984; NICHD Early Child Care Research Network, 2000; Pine, 1995), whereas differences in the amount of adult speech children that hear is a plausible explanation. Neither genetics nor child effects on input can explain effects of experimenter-created variability in exposure to vocabulary (Schwartz & Terrell, 1983) or correlations between how particular words appear in input and the order of those words' appearance in child speech (Huttenlocher et al., 1991; Naigles & Hoff-Ginsberg, 1998). Furthermore, the specificity of some correlations – for example, that the frequency of auxiliaries in questions in input predicts the acquisition of auxiliaries used in other ways (Newport, Gleitman, & Gleitman, 1977) – renders genetic or child-effect accounts implausible.

Another sort of argument for interpreting the correlations between language experience and language development as causal is that the observed relations are consistent with an account of the processes underlying development. The evidence that maternal responsiveness to infant verbalizations is associated with language development suggests that communicative interaction lays the foundation for language development. The evidence that the amount and nature of input predict the course and rate of language development suggests that language acquisition is also the result of the child's analysis of data collected in the course of communicative interaction.

To conclude, a description of the course of language development and of experiential correlates of its rate, course, and outcome suggests the following account: biology provides the human child with the capacity to turn language experience into language knowledge. Language development is the reliable result of the mental processes set in motion when children's language experiences meet that human capacity. The nature of those experiences, in turn, shapes the course and outcome of those processes.

References

Aslin, R. N., Jusczyk, P. W., & Pisoni, D. (1998). Speech and auditory processing during infancy: Constraints on and precursors to language. In D. Kuhn & R. S. Siegler (Eds.), *Handbook of child psychology: Vol. 2. Cognition, perception, and language* (5th ed., pp. 147–198). New York: John Wiley and Sons.

Barrett, M. D. (1986). Early semantic representations and early word usage. In S. A. Kuczaj & M. D. Barrett (Eds.), *The development of word meaning* (pp. 39–67). New York: Springer-Verlag.

Bates, E., Camaioni, L., & Volterra, V. (1975). The acquisition of performatives prior to speech. *Merrill-Palmer Quarterly, 21*, 205–226.

Bates, E., Marchman, V., Thal, D., Fenson, L., Dale, P., Reznick, J. S., Reilly, J., & Hartung, J. (1994). Developmental and stylistic variation in the composition of early vocabulary. *Journal of Child Language, 21*, 85–124.

Bavin, E. L. (1992). The acquisition of Walpiri. In D. I. Slobin (Ed.), *The crosslinguistic study of language acquisition* (Vol. 3, pp. 309–371). Hillsdale, NJ: Lawrence Erlbaum Associates.

Benedict, H. (1979). Early lexical development: Comprehension and production. *Journal of Child Language, 6*, 183–200.

Bloom, L. (1973). *One word at a time.* The Hague: Mouton.

Bloom, L., Rocissano, L., & Hood, L. (1976). Adult–child discourse: Developmental interaction between information processing and linguistic knowledge. *Cognitive Psychology, 8*, 521–552.

Bloom, P. (2000). *How children learn the meanings of words.* Cambridge, MA: MIT Press.

Bretherton, I., McNew, S., Snyder, L., & Bates, E. (1983). Individual differences at 20 months: Analytic and holistic strategies in language acquisition. *Journal of Child Language, 10*, 293–320.

Brown, P. (1998). Conversational structure and language acquisition: The role of repetition in Tzeltal adult and child speech. *Journal of Linguistic Anthropology, 8*, 1–25.

Brown, P. (2001). Learning to talk about motion UP and DOWN in Tzeltal: Is there a language-specific bias for verb learning? In M. Bowerman & S. C. Levinson (eds.), *Language acquisition and conceptual development* (pp. 512–543). Cambridge: Cambridge University Press.

Brown, R. (1958). *Words and things.* New York: Free Press.

Brown, R., & Fraser, C. (1963). The acquisition of syntax. In C. N. Cofer & B. S. Musgrave (Eds.), *Verbal behavior and learning* (pp. 158–196). New York: McGraw-Hill.

Carpenter, M., Nagell, K., & Tomasello, M. (1998). Social cognition, joint attention, and communicative competence from 9 to 15 months of age. *Monographs of the Society for Research in Child Development, 63*(4, Serial No. 255).

Caselli, M. C., Bates, E., Casadio, P., Fenson, J., Fenson, L., Sanders, L., & Weir, J. (1995). A cross-linguistic study of early lexical development. *Cognitive Development, 10*, 159–199.

Clark, E. V. (1979). Building a vocabulary: Words for objects, actions, and relations. In P. Fletcher & M. Garman (Eds.), *Language acquisition* (pp. 149–160). Cambridge: Cambridge University Press.

Coady, J. A., & Aslin, R. N. (2003). Phonological neighbourhoods in the developing lexicon. *Journal of Child Language, 30*, 441–471.

Crago, M. B., Allen, S. E. M., & Hough-Eyamie, W. P. (1997). Exploring innateness through cultural and linguistic variation: An Inuit example. In M. Gopnik (Ed.), *The biological basis of language* (pp. 70–90). Oxford: Oxford University Press.

de Boysson-Bardies, B., Halle, P., Sagart, L., & Durand, C. (1989). A crosslinguistic investigation of vowel formants in babbling. *Journal of Child Language, 16*, 1–17.

de Boysson-Bardies, B., Vihman, M., Roug-Hellichius, L., Duramd, C., Landberg, I., & Arao, F. (1992). Material evidence of infant selection from target language: A cross-linguistic study. In C. A. Ferguson, L. Menn, & C. Stoel-Gammon (Eds.), *Phonological development* (pp. 369–391). Timonium, MD: York Press.

Dollaghan, C. A., Campbell, T. F., Paradise, J. L., Feldman, H. M., Janosky, J. E., Pitcairn, D. N., & Kurs-Lasky, M. (1999). Maternal education and measures of early speech and language. *Journal of Speech, Language, and Hearing Research, 42*, 1432–1443.

Dunn, J., & Shatz, M. (1989). Becoming a conversationalist despite (or because of) having an older sibling. *Child Development, 60*, 399–410.

Eisenberg, A. (1985). Learning to describe past experiences in conversation. *Discourse Processes, 8*, 177–204.

Fenson, L., Dale, P. S., Reznick, J. S., Bates, E., Thal, D. J., & Pethick, S. J. (1994). Variability in early communicative development. *Monographs of the Society for Research in Child Development, 59*(5, Serial No. 242).

Fernald, A., & Morikawa, H. (1993). Common themes and cultural variations in Japanese and American mothers' speech to infants. *Child Development, 64*, 637–656.

Fernald, A., & Simon, T. (1984). Expanded intonation contours in mothers' speech to newborns. *Developmental Psychology, 20*, 104–113.

Fernald, A., Taeschner, T., Dun, J., Papousek, M., de Boysson-Bardies, B., & Fukui, I. (1989). A cross-language study of prosodic modifications in mothers' and fathers' speech to preverbal infants. *Journal of Child Language, 16*, 477–501.

Fivush, R. (1991). The social construction of personal narratives. *Merrill-Palmer Quarterly, 37*, 59–81.

Gathercole, V. C. M. (2002). Monolingual and bilingual acquisition: Learning different treatments of *that*-trace phenomena in English and Spanish. In D. K. Oller (Ed.), *Language and literacy in bilingual children* (pp. 220–254). Clevedon: Multilingual Matters, Ltd.

Gelman, S. A., Coley, J. D., Rosengren, K. S., Hartman, E., & Pappas, A. (1998). Beyond labeling: The role of maternal input in the acquisition of richly structured categories. *Monographs of the Society for Research in Child Development, 63*(1, Serial No. 253).

Gentner, D. (1982). Why nouns are learned before verbs: Linguistic relativity versus natural partitioning. In S. A. Kuczaj (Ed.), *Language development: Syntax and semantics* (pp. 301–334). Hillsdale, NJ: Erlbaum.

Gentner, D., & Boroditsky, L. (2001). Individuation, relativity, and early word learning. In M. Bowerman & S. Levinson (Eds.), *Language acquisition and conceptual development* (pp. 215–256). Cambridge: Cambridge University Press.

Gerken, L. (1994). Child phonology: Past research, present questions, future directions. In M. Gernsbacher (Ed.), *Handbook of psycholinguistics* (pp. 781–820). San Diego: Academic Press.

Goldfield, B. A., & Reznick, J. S. (1990). Early lexical acquisition: Rate, content, and the vocabulary spurt. *Journal of Child Language, 17*, 171–184.

Golinkoff, R. M., & Alioto, A. (1995). Infant-directed speech facilitates lexical learning in adults hearing Chinese: Implication for language acquisition. *Journal of Child Language, 22*, 703–726.

Gopnik, A., & Choi, S. (1995). Names, relational words, and cognitive development in English and Korean speakers: Nouns are not always learned before verbs. In M. Tomasello & W. E. Merriman (Eds.), *Beyond names for things: Young children's acquisition of verbs* (pp. 83–90). Hillsdale, NJ: Erlbaum.

Haden, C. A., Haine, R. A., & Fivush, R. (1997). Developing narrative structure in parent–child reminiscing across the preschool years. *Developmental Psychology, 33*, 295–307.

Hart, B., & Risley, T. R. (1995). *Meaningful differences in the everyday experience of young American children.* Baltimore: Paul H. Brookes.

Heath, S. B. (1983). *Ways with words.* Cambridge: Cambridge University Press.

Heath, S. B. (1990). The children of Trackton's children: Spoken and written language in social change. In J. W. Stigler, R. A. Shweder, & G. Herdt (Eds.), *Cultural psychology: Essays on comparative human development* (pp. 496–519). Cambridge: Cambridge University Press.

Hoff, E. (2003). The specificity of environmental influence: Socioeconomic status affects early vocabulary development via maternal speech. *Child Development, 74,* 1368–1378.

Hoff, E., Laursen, B., & Tardif, T. (2002). Socioeconomic status and parenting. In M. H. Bornstein (Ed.), *Handbook of parenting* (2nd ed., pp. 231–252). Mahwah, NJ: Lawrence Erlbaum Associates.

Hoff, E., & Naigles, L. (2002). How children use input in acquiring a lexicon. *Child Development, 73,* 418–433.

Hoff-Ginsberg, E. (1985). Some contributions of mothers' speech to their children's syntax growth. *Journal of Child Language, 12,* 367–385.

Hoff-Ginsberg, E. (1986). Function and structure in maternal speech: Their relation to the child's development of syntax. *Developmental Psychology, 22,* 155–163.

Hoff-Ginsberg, E. (1998). The relation of birth order and socioeconomic status to children's language experience and language development. *Applied Psycholinguistics, 19,* 603–630.

Hoff-Ginsberg, E., & Krueger, W. (1991). Older siblings as conversational partners. *Merrill-Palmer Quarterly, 37,* 465–481.

Hoff-Ginsberg, E., & Shatz, M. (1982). Linguistic input and the child's acquisition of language. *Psychological Bulletin, 92,* 3–26.

Huttenlocher, J., Haight, W., Bryk, A., Seltzer, M., & Lyons, T. (1991). Early vocabulary growth: Relation to language input and gender. *Developmental Psychology, 27,* 236–248.

Huttenlocher, J., Vasilyeva, M., Cymerman, E., & Levine, S. (2002). Language input and child syntax. *Cognitive Psychology, 45,* 337–374.

Ingram, D. (1999). Phonological acquisition. In M. Barrett (Ed.), *The development of language* (pp. 73–98). Hove: Psychology Press.

Kelly, M. (1996). The role of phonology in grammatical category assignments. In J. L. Morgan & K. Demuth (Eds.), *Signal to syntax: Bootstrapping from speech to grammar in early acquisition* (pp. 249–262). Mahwah, NJ: Lawrence Erlbaum Associates.

Kemler Nelson, D. G., Hirsh-Pasek, K., Jusczyk, P. W., & Wright Cassidy, K. (1989). How the prosodic cues in motherese might assist language learning. *Journal of Child Language, 16,* 55–68.

Kuhl, P. K., & Meltzoff, A. N. (1988). Speech as an intermodal object of perception. In A. Yonas (Ed.), *The Minnesota Symposia on Child Psychology: Vol. 20. Perceptual development in infancy* (pp. 235–266). Hillsdale, NJ: Erlbaum.

Kuhl, P. K., & Meltzoff, A. N. (1997). Evolution, nativism and learning in the development of language and speech. In M. Gopnik (Ed.), *The inheritance and innateness of grammars* (pp. 7–44). New York: Oxford University Press.

Kuhl, P. K., Williams, K. A., Lacerda, F., Stevens, K. N., & Lindblom, B. (1992). Linguistic experience alters phonetic perception in infants by 6 months of age. *Science, 255,* 606–608.

Lieven, E. V. M. (1994). Crosslinguistic and crosscultural aspects of language addressed to children. In C. Gallaway & B. J. Richards (Eds.), *Input and interaction in language acquisition* (pp. 56–73). Cambridge: Cambridge University Press.

McCabe, A., & Peterson, C. (1991). Getting the story: A longitudinal study of parental styles in eliciting narratives and developing narrative skill. In A. McCabe & C. Peterson (Eds.), *Developing narrative structure* (pp. 217–253). Hillsdale, NJ: Lawrence Erlbaum Associates.

McCartney, K. (1984). Effect of quality of day care environment on children's language development. *Developmental Psychology, 20,* 244–260.

Mandel, D. R., Jusczyk, P. W., & Pisoni, D. B. (1995). Infants' recognition of the sound patterns of their own names. *Psychological Science, 6,* 314–317.

Maye, J., Werker, J. F., & Gerken, L. (2002). Infant sensitivity to distributional information can affect phonetic discrimination. *Cognition, 82,* 101–111.

Menyuk, P., Menn, L., & Silber, R. (1986). Early strategies for the perception and production of words and sounds. In P. Fletcher & M. Garman (Eds.), *Language acquisition* (2nd ed., pp. 198–222). Cambridge: Cambridge University Press.

Miller, P. J., & Sperry, L. L. (1988). Early talk about the past: The origins of conversational stories of personal experience. *Journal of Child Language, 15*, 293–315.

Morgan, J. L., & Demuth, K. (1996). *Signal to syntax: Bootstrapping from speech to grammar in early acquisition.* Mahwah, NJ: Lawrence Erlbaum Associates.

Naigles, L., & Hoff, E. (in press). Verbs at the very beginning: Parallels between comprehension and input? In K. Hirsh-Pasek & R. Golinkoff (Eds.), *Action meets word: How children learn verbs.* Oxford: Oxford University Press.

Naigles, L. R., & Hoff-Ginsberg, E. (1998). Why are some verbs learned before other verbs? Effects of input frequency and structure on children's early verb use. *Journal of Child Language, 25*, 95–120.

Nelson, K. (1973). Structure and strategy in learning to talk. *Monographs of the Society for Research in Child Development, 38*(1–2, Serial No. 149).

Newport, E. L., Gleitman, H., & Gleitman, L. (1977). Mother, I'd rather do it myself: Some effects and non-effects of maternal speech style. In C. E. Snow & C. A. Ferguson (Eds.), *Talking to children: Language input and acquisition* (pp. 109–150). Cambridge: Cambridge University Press.

NICHD Early Child Care Research Network (2000). The relation of child care to cognitive and language development. *Child Development, 71*, 960–980.

Oller, D. K. (1986). Metaphonology and infant vocalizations. In B. Lindblom & R. Zetterstrom (Eds.), *Precursors of early speech* (pp. 21–35). New York: Stockton Press.

Oller, D. K., & Eilers, R. E. (1988). The role of audition in infant babbling. *Child Development, 59*, 441–449.

Oller, D. K., & Eilers, R. E. (1998). Interpretive and methodological difficulties in evaluating babbling drift. *Parole, 7/8*, 147–164.

Oller, D. K., Eilers, R. E., Basinger, D., Steffens, M. L., & Urbano, R. (1995). Extreme poverty and the development of precursors to the speech capacity. *First Language, 15*, 167–188.

Peters, A. M. (1986). Early syntax. In P. Fletcher & M. Garman (Eds.), *Language acquisition* (2nd ed., pp. 307–325). Cambridge: Cambridge University Press.

Pine, J. M. (1995). Variation in vocabulary development as a function of birth order. *Child Development, 66*, 272–281.

Pine, J. M., & Lieven, E. V. M. (1993). Reanalysing rote-learned phrases: Individual differences in the transition to multi-word speech. *Journal of Child Language, 20*, 551–573.

Richards, B. J. (1994). Child directed speech and influences on language acquisition: Methodology and interpretation. In C. Gallaway & B. J. Richards (Eds.), *Input and interaction in language acquisition* (pp. 74–106). Cambridge: Cambridge University Press.

Rvachew, S., Slawinski, E. B., Williams, M., & Green, C. L. (1999). The impact of early onset otitis media on babbling and early language development. *Journal of the Acoustic Society of America, 105*, 467–475.

Schwartz, R. G., & Terrell, B. Y. (1983). The role of input frequency in lexical acquisition. *Journal of Child Language, 10*, 57–64.

Shatz, M. (1983). Communication. In P. H. Mussen (Ed.), *Handbook of child psychology* (pp. 841–889). New York: Wiley.

Shatz, M. (1994). *A toddler's life: Becoming a person.* New York: Oxford University Press.

Shatz, M., Hoff-Ginsberg, E., & MacIver, D. (1989). Induction and the acquisition of English auxiliaries: The effects of differentially enriched input. *Journal of Child Language, 16*, 121–140.

Shatz, M., & McCloskey, L. (1984). Answering appropriately: A developmental perspective on conversational knowledge. In S. Kuczaj (Ed.), *Discourse development* (pp. 19–36). New York: Springer-Verlag.

Snow, C. E. (1999). Social perspectives on the emergence of language. In B. MacWhinney (Ed.), *The emergence of language* (pp. 257–276). Mahway, NJ: Lawrence Erlbaum Associates.

Snow, C. E., Pan, B., Imbens-Bailey, A., & Herman, J. (1996). Learning how to say what one means: A longitudinal study of children's speech act use. *Social Development, 5*, 56–84.

Stark, R. E. (1986). Prespeech segmental feature development. In P. Fletcher & M. Garman (Eds.), *Language acquisition* (2nd ed., pp. 149–173). Cambridge: Cambridge University Press.

Swingley, D., & Aslin, R. N. (2000). Spoken word recognition and lexical representation in very young children. *Cognition, 76*, 147–166.

Tamis-LeMonda, C. S. & Bornstein, M. H. (1994). Specificity in mother–toddler language–play relations across the second year. *Developmental Psychology, 30*, 283–292.

Tamis-LeMonda, C., Bornstein, M. H., Kahana-Kalman, R., Baumwell, L., & Cyphers, L. (1998). Predicting variation in the timing of language milestones in the second year: An events history approach. *Journal of Child Language, 25*, 675–700.

Tardif, T., Gelman, S. A., & Xu, F. (1999). Putting the "noun bias" in context: A comparison of Mandarin and English. *Child Development, 70*, 620–635.

Templin, M. (1957). *Certain language skills in children.* University of Minnesota Institute of Child Welfare Monograph Series 26. Minneapolis: University of Minnesota Press.

Tomasello, M., & Todd, J. (1983). Joint attention and lexical acquisition style. *First Language, 4*, 197–212.

Trevarthen, C., & Hubley, P. (1978). Secondary intersubjectivity: Confidence, confiding and acts of meaning in the first year. In A. Lock (Ed.), *Action, gesture and symbol: The emergence of language* (pp. 182–229). New York: Academic Press.

Umiker-Sebeok, D. J. (1979). Preschool children's intraconversational narratives. *Journal of Child Language, 6*, 91–109.

Valian, V., & Lyman, C. (2003). Young children's acquisition of wh-questions: The role of structured input. *Journal of Child Language, 30*, 117–144.

Walley, A. C. (1993). The role of vocabulary development in children's spoken word recognition and segmentation ability. *Developmental Review, 13*, 286–350.

Weizman, Z. O., & Snow, C. E. (2001). Lexical input as related to children's vocabulary acquisition: Effects of sophisticated exposure and support for meaning. *Developmental Psychology, 37*, 265–279.

Werker, J. F., & Tees, R. C. (1984). Cross-language speech perception: Evidence for perceptual reorganization during the first year of life. *Infant Behavior and Development, 7*, 49–63.

13

How Children Learn Language: A Focus on Resilience

Susan Goldin-Meadow

Children learn language in varied linguistic environments, and these environments can have an impact on how language-learning proceeds, particularly on the rate at which certain properties of language are learned (see Hoff, this volume). The goal of this chapter, however, is to explore the properties of language whose development is *not* beholden to the vagaries of environmental input but are, instead, robustly over-determined and expressed in almost all language-learning environments. Any particular manipulation of the environmental conditions under which language-learning takes place has the potential to alter the language-learning outcome. To the extent that a property of language is *unaffected* by a given manipulation, it can be said to be developmentally *resilient* – its developmental course is impervious to the change in input conditions. The more radical the manipulation is – that is, the more different the conditions are from the conditions that surround the typical language-learning situation – the more impressive it is that a given property of language continues to crop up.

To begin to identify the properties of language that are resilient across environmental variation, we examine language-learning in a variety of naturally occurring circumstances – when children learn different languages, when children learn language in a different modality, and when children get different amounts of input in their language. We also explore whether there is convergence across these manipulations in the properties identified as resilient. It is an empirical question as to whether the same property of language will survive a variety of input manipulations – that is, whether it will be resilient across a range of learning conditions. If so, we can be that much more certain that this particular property of language is fundamental to human communication. Thus, the chapter describes what we can learn about a child's preparation for language-learning from naturally occurring variations in learning conditions. I begin with a brief description of the steps children follow in a typical language-learning environment and then turn to language-learning in environments that vary from the norm.

Out of the Mouths of Babes

Starting with the word

Children produce their first words between 10 and 15 months, typically using each word as an isolated unit. They then proceed in two directions, learning (1) that the word can be composed of smaller, meaningful parts (morphology), and (2) that the word is a building block for larger, meaningful phrases and sentences (syntax).

But what is a word? Consider a child who wants a jar opened and whines while attempting to do the deed herself. This child has conveyed her desires to those around her, but has she produced a word? A word does more than communicate information – it stands for something; it's a symbol. Moreover, the mapping between a word and what it stands for is arbitrary – "dog" is the term we use in English for furry four-legged canines, but the term is "chien" in French and "perro" in Spanish. There is nothing about the form of each of these three words that makes it a good label for a furry creature – the word works to refer to the creature only because speakers of each language act as though they agree that this is what it stands for.

At the earliest stages of development, children may use a sequence of sounds consistently for a particular meaning, but the sequence bears no resemblance to the sound of any word in their language. These "proto-words" (Bates, 1976) are transitional forms that are often tied to particular contexts. For example, a child uses the sound sequence "brmm-brmm" every time he plays with or sees his toy truck. In fact, a child's proto-word need not be verbal at all – gesture works quite well. For example, a child smacks her lips every time she feeds her fish (Acredolo & Goodwyn, 1988). Indeed, some children rely heavily on gestural "words" to communicate with others at the early stages.

Learning that words are made of parts

Words in all languages are composed of parts. For example, the word "dogs" refers to more than one furry creature, but it does so systematically – "dog" stands for the animal, "s" stands for many-ness. We know this, in no small part, because we know that words like "cats," "shoes," "books," all refer to more than one cat, shoe, or book. We have extracted (albeit not consciously) what the words have in common – the "-s" ending in their forms and "plural" in their meanings – to form what is called a morpheme, a consistent pairing between a form and a meaning.

At the earliest stages, children seem to learn morphologically complex words as unanalyzed wholes, "amalgams" (MacWhinney, 1978). How can we tell when a child has analyzed "dogs" into its morphemic parts? One key piece of evidence, possible only when the pattern in the language the child is learning is not completely regular, comes from children's over-regularizations – errors in which children make exceptions to the adult pattern (e.g., feet) conform to the regular pattern (e.g., foots). Children who produce the incorrect form "foots" must have extracted the plural morpheme "-s" from a variety of other regular forms in their system, and added it to the noun "foot." Similarly, children who produce "eated" must have extracted the past tense morpheme "-ed" from verbs like "walked" and "stopped" and added it to the verb "eat" (Marcus, 1995). Creative errors of this sort also indicate that children know the difference between nouns and verbs; children add the "-ed" ending to verbs like "eat" or "walk" but rarely to nouns like "foot" or "shoe."

English does not have a very rich morphological system, unlike a language like Turkish, whose words contain many morphemes. For example, *ellerimde* is a single word in Turkish meaning "in my hands"; the word is composed of four meaningful parts, that is, four morphemes – *el* 'hand', *-ler* 'plural', *-im* 'first person possessive', *-de* 'locative' (Aksu-Koc & Slobin, 1985). Children learning languages rich in morphology turn out to learn the parts of words earlier in the course of language development than do children acquiring morphologically impoverished languages (Berman, 1985). And a morphological system that is regular is particularly easy to master. The inflectional system in Turkish is not only rich, it is predictable and perceptually salient. Children learning Turkish begin to produce words containing grammatical morphemes even before they produce words in sentences (Aksu-Koc & Slobin, 1985). In contrast, children acquiring English generally do not begin to learn the morphemes of their language until after they begin to combine words into sentences.

Combining words into ordered sentences

At about 18 months, children begin to produce two-word strings that have at least two characteristics in common (Bloom, 1970; Bowerman, 1973a; Brown, 1973). First, the content is the same. Children note the appearance and disappearance of objects, their properties, locations, and owners, and comment on the actions done to and by objects and people. Second, the words in these short sentences are consistently ordered (Braine, 1976). The particular orders children use mirror the orders provided by the language models they experience. Even when the languages they are learning have relatively free word order, children tend to follow a consistent pattern (based on a frequently occurring adult order; Slobin, 1966).

Moreover, before they produce two-word combinations, children have some understanding of word order. Children who only produce single words, when shown two scenes (Big Bird washing Cookie Monster versus Cookie Monster washing Big Bird), will look reliably longer at the scene that matches the sentence they are listening to – the first scene for the sentence "Big Bird is washing Cookie Monster" and the second for "Cookie Monster is washing Big Bird" (Hirsh-Pasek & Golinkoff, 1991). The order of words must be conveying information to the child about who is the doer (agent) and who is the done-to (patient) of the action.

Syntactic versus semantic categories

Young children produce words in consistent orders as soon as they combine them and, in this sense, adhere to a syntax. But is it the syntax of adults? Adult regularities are formulated in terms of syntactic categories (e.g., subjects precede verbs in English declarative sentences). However, the earliest sentences that children produce can be described at a semantic level and thus do not *require* a syntactic analysis (Angiolillo & Goldin-Meadow, 1982). For example, the sentence "baby drink" can be described as "agent precedes action" rather than "subject precedes verb." Indeed, the fact that young children often interpret sentences like "babies are pushed by dogs" to mean the babies are the *pushers* (not the *pushees*) suggests that, for these children, the first word is an agent, not a subject (i.e., it's defined in terms of its role in the action rather than its role in the syntactic structure of the sentence).

A description in terms of syntactic categories is needed when the words that fill the subject position are no longer restricted to a single semantic category (Bowerman, 1973b; e.g., "bottle falls" – bottle is not affecting an object and thus is not an agent) and when other aspects of the sentence depend on this non-semantic category (e.g., subject–verb agreement). It is not until children begin to fill in their telegraphic utterances with grammatical morphemes (e.g., verb endings that must agree in number with the subject – bottle falls versus bottles fall) that we have clear evidence for syntactic categories. However, the fact that children use their grammatical morphemes appropriately as soon as they appear in their repertoires suggests that the groundwork for syntactic categories may have been laid quite early, perhaps from the start (cf. Valian, 1986).

Underlying predicate frames

Children who are limited to two words per sentence in their talk nevertheless know something about the larger predicate frames that underlie their short sentences. They produce, at times, all of the appropriate arguments (semantic elements) that a given predicate allows. For example, at one time or another a given child produces "baby" or "juice" with the verb "drink" (i.e., both arguments associated with the *drink* predicate – actor, patient) and "mommy," "juice," or "baby" with the verb "give" (the three arguments associated with the *give* predicate – actor, patient, endpoint). Moreover, for children at the two-word stage, the rate at which a semantic element is put into words depends on the predicate frame underlying the sentence (Bloom, Miller, & Hood, 1975). If a predicate frame underlying a two-word sentence is relatively small (like the *drink* frame), an element in that structure will be more likely to be produced as one of the two words in the sentence than will an element that is part of a larger predicate frame (the *give* frame) – there's less competition for one of the two word slots in a sentence with a smaller versus a larger predicate frame. Thus, for example, children are more likely to produce "juice" with "drink" (a predicate with a two-argument underlying frame) than with "give" (a predicate with a three-argument underlying frame) simply because there is less competition for one of the two word slots in a sentence with two versus three underlying arguments (Goldin-Meadow, 1985; Goldin-Meadow & Mylander, 1984). The fact that the child's rate of production of a given element in a sentence varies systematically according to the size of the predicate frame hypothesized to underlie that sentence is evidence for the existence of the predicate frame itself.

In addition, when provided with sentences that differ in their argument structures, children can make the appropriate inferences about the type of action described. For example, children will look longer at a scene in which Cookie Monster is making Big Bird turn (as opposed to one in which each is turning independently) when they hear the two-argument sentence, "*Cookie Monster* is turning *Big Bird*," than when they hear the one-argument sentence "*Cookie Monster* is turning with Big Bird" (Hirsh-Pasek, Golinkoff, & Naigles, 1996).

Complex sentences

Children go on to enlarge their sentences in two ways. They elaborate one element of a single proposition: e.g., "baby drinking big bottle," where "big" modifies the object of the sentence, "bottle." They combine propositions to produce complex or compound sentences. For example, English-learning children produce sentences with object comple-ments ("I hope I don't hurt it"), embedded clauses ("that a box that they put it in"), coordinate clauses ("maybe you can carry that and I can carry this"), and subordinate clauses ("I gave him some so he won't cry"). The advent of two-proposition constructions brings with it the problem of relating the propositions. Who is doing the climbing in the sentence "the lion pushes the bear after climbing the ladder"? Children under 6 incor-rectly think it's the bear that climbs rather than the lion (Hsu, Cairns, Eisenberg, & Schlisselberg, 1989; but see de Villiers, Roeper, & Vainikka, 1990, for signs of some remarkably subtle judgments about complex sentences even at age 3).

Having taken a brief tour of language-learning under unremarkable circumstances, we turn to more varied conditions. Any change in the environmental conditions under which language is learned could, at least in theory, alter the course and even the outcome of the learning process. To the extent that a property of language is unaffected by a particular change, it can be said to be developmentally resilient, or buffered, against that change.

Language-Learning by Hand

Deaf individuals around the globe use sign languages as their primary means of com-munication and those sign languages are structured like all natural languages – despite the fact that they are processed by hand and eye rather than mouth and ear. The first question to ask is whether deaf children exposed to a sign language from birth acquire that language in the same way that hearing children acquire spoken language.

First signs

Deaf children produce their first recognizable signs slightly earlier in development than hearing children produce their first recognizable words (Meier & Newport, 1990) –

presumably because sign production requires less fine motor control than word production. However, these early signs do not appear to be used referentially (Bonvillian &
Folven, 1993). It is not until approximately 12 months that deaf children clearly use their
signs in referential contexts (i.e., to name or indicate objects and actions in their worlds)
– precisely the age at which hearing children produce their first recognizable words in
referential contexts (Petitto, 1988). Thus, although it may be easier to produce signs than
words, it is not easier to use those signs symbolically. This important step in the language-
learning process is taken at the same developmental moment, whether the child is learning a signed or spoken language.

Moreover, the iconicity present in parts of all sign languages appears to have little effect
on language-learning. Signs like "drink" (a cupped hand tilted at the mouth) are easy to
remember and are very often the first signs learned by *adults* acquiring American Sign
Language (ASL) as a second language. However, children do not take advantage of the
iconicity in the signs they are learning. Only one-third of the first signs that children
produce are iconic (Bonvillian & Folven, 1993), and the meanings of those signs are no
different from the words that one-word speakers initially produce (Newport & Meier,
1985).

Another example of how deaf children learn sign languages just like hearing children
learn spoken language comes from the acquisition of pronouns. Pronouns for *me* and *you*
are produced in ASL by pointing either at oneself (first person) or the addressee (second
person). We might expect these first- and second-person pronouns to be acquired early
simply because they resemble pointing gestures. However, they turn out to be relatively
late acquisitions, learned at about the same age that children learn first- and second-person
pronouns (*I* and *you*) in spoken languages (Petitto, 1987).

The parts of signs

Like words in spoken languages, signs turn out to be constructed out of morphemes (T.
Supalla, 1982). For example, an inverted V-hand representing a person can be simultaneously combined with a linear path representing forward movement to indicate someone
moving forward. However, as this example illustrates, signs often resemble the events they
represent. Sign-learning children might then guess wrong and assume that these signs are
pictures with no internal structure. If so, we might expect them to acquire signs of this
sort early. Alternatively, if children do not make use of the iconicity that underlies these
multi-morphemic forms, they should treat the signs as complex combinations of smaller
units from the start and thus acquire them relatively late. This is precisely what deaf
children learning ASL do (T. Supalla, 1982). Even by age 5, deaf children do not produce
all of the morphemes required in complex signs. As in a hearing child's acquisition of a
morphologically complex spoken language, morpheme acquisition continues in deaf
children until at least age 6.

Many verbs in sign languages (both the productive signs just described and the "frozen"
signs whose stems are unanalyzable wholes) are inflected to agree with their noun arguments. For example, the ASL verb "give" agrees with the nouns filling the x and z slots
in the frame "x gives y to z." In its uninflected form, "give" is produced in neutral space

(at chest level), with a short outward movement. To indicate "I give to you," the signer moves the sign from herself toward the addressee. To indicate "you give to me," the signer reverses the movement, beginning the sign at the addressee and moving it toward herself (Padden, 1983).

Iconicity could play a role in the deaf child's acquisition of verb agreement system. After all, the sign "I-give-you" is largely identical to the motor act children actually perform when they give a small object to an addressee. The agreement system should be relatively easy to acquire if iconicity is playing a role. However, if children are treating a sign like "I-give-you" not as a holistic representation of the giving act, but as a verb with markings for two arguments (the giver and the givee), the sign will be morphologically complex in their eyes and should therefore be acquired relatively late. And indeed it is not until between 3 and 3½ that deaf children use agreement widely and consistently (Meier, 1982). Moreover, the path of acquisition children follow seems to adhere to morphological principles rather than iconic ones – signs that agree with two arguments (e.g., "give") are acquired *later* than signs that agree with only one argument. Any iconic hypothesis ought to predict that "give" would be an early acquisition.

Combining signs into sentences

Children learning sign begin to produce two-sign sentences around the middle of the second year – approximately the same time that children learning spoken language produce their two-word sentences. Despite the differences in the modality of the languages they are learning, sign-learning children express approximately the same range of semantic relations in these early sentences as children learning spoken languages. Moreover, particular semantic relations emerge in about the same order as they do for English-learning children: existence relations appear early, followed by action and state relations, then locative relations, and finally datives, instruments, causes, and manners of action (Newport & Meier, 1985).

Deaf children learning sign language from their deaf parents use consistent word order as a syntactic device for marking role early in development, despite the fact that adult signers do not always do so. Thus, for example, whereas an adult signs "I-give-you" by moving the sign from herself toward the addressee, a deaf child produces three separate signs and produces them in a consistent order (point at self, give, point at addressee; Newport & Ashbrook, 1977). As in children learning spoken languages, children pick up the least marked or pragmatically most neutral orders in the sign languages they are exposed to: for example, subject–verb–object (SVO) in ASL (Hoffmeister, 1978) and subject–object–verb (SOV) in the Sign Language of the Netherlands (Coerts, 2000).

To summarize thus far, children are sufficiently flexible that, if presented with a language system processed by hand and eye, they will not only learn that system but they will do so without a hitch. Whatever predispositions children bring to the task of language-learning, they must be broad enough to work in the manual or the oral modality.

Language-Learning Around the Globe

Languages vary around the globe. Do the differences across languages make a difference to the language-learning child? If they do, we should see differences in the way children who are exposed to different languages progress through the language-learning stages. If they don't, we should see similarities across children despite the fact that they are exposed to different languages. Similarities of this sort are good candidates for the resilient properties of language.

For the most part, children accept the different constructions that appear across languages from the earliest stages. For example, English and Korean present children with different ways of talking about joining objects. Placing a videocassette in its case or an apple in a bowl are both described as putting one object "in" another in English. However, Korean makes a distinction that highlights the fit of the objects – a videocassette placed in a tight-fitting case is described by the verb "kkita," whereas an apple placed in a loose-fitting bowl is described by the verb "nehta." Young children have no trouble learning to talk about joining objects in terms of containment in English or fit in Korean (Choi & Bowerman, 1991). However, there are times when children seem to over-ride the linguistic input they receive, and these are the cases that we focus on in this section.

Privileged meanings

At times, children learning different languages express a particular meaning without apparent regard for the varied forms the meaning takes across the languages. For example, children learning English, Italian, Serbo-Croatian, and Turkish all follow the same developmental pattern when learning to talk about location – "in" and "on" precede "under" and "beside," which precede "between," "back," and "front" for objects that have an inherent front–back orientation (e.g., cars, houses), which precede "back" and "front" for objects that do not have an inherent orientation (e.g., plates, blocks; Johnston & Slobin, 1979). Importantly, the forms used to express these meanings differ across the languages – prepositions (English, Italian), prepositions and case inflections (Serbo-Croatian), and postpositions and case inflections (Turkish). The absolute ages for these developments differ across children learning each language. However, the *order* of development remains the same, suggesting that this order may be determined by the children themselves (for example, by changes in their understanding of locations and spatial relations independent of language).

There are other ways in which children can convince us that they are playing an active role in constructing their language. The range of meanings children express with a given form may be *broader* than the adult range. For example, children often use the same grammatical form for both animate and inanimate reference points in a locative relation, despite the fact that adult talk makes a distinction between the two. German-learning children incorrectly generalize "zu," the preposition used to express location (a relation involving an inanimate recipient), to express possession (a relation involving an animate recipient and conveyed by the preposition "von" in adult talk; Mills, 1985). As another example, English-learning children at times confuse "give," which adults use to refer to moving objects toward a person, and "put," which adults use to refer to moving objects to a place – "give some ice in here, mommy," and "can I go put it to her?" (Bowerman, 1982). The children are effectively ignoring animacy distinctions that are present in the adult language to which they are exposed.

In addition to broadening the meaning of an adult grammatical marking, children also *narrow* the meanings of adult grammatical forms, presumably to focus on distinctions that are conceptually salient for the child. For example, children around the globe begin by grammatically marking agent–patient (i.e., doer–done to) relations in basic causal events (Slobin, 1985). These are events in which an agent carries out a physical and perceptible change of state in a patient, by means of either direct body contact or an instrument – what Hopper and Thompson (1980) call *highly transitive* events. In Russian, a particular linguistic marker called an accusative inflection must be placed on all words that fill the syntactic slot *direct object*, regardless of the type of event conveyed. However, children acquiring Russian initially use the accusative inflection only for direct objects in sentences describing manipulative physical actions (giving, putting, throwing). In sentences describing actions that are less obviously operating on an object (e.g., seeing), young children use a noun without any inflection at all (Gvozdev, 1928/1961, as described in Slobin, 1985).

Children's initial use of tense reflects the same narrowing focus on events that bring about visible change of state. For example, children first use past-tense verb inflections on a select set of verbs – verbs that name momentary events resulting in a visible change of state or location (e.g., *find, fall, break*), and not on verbs that name events extending over time without an immediate and clear result (e.g., *play, hold, ride, write*; Bloom, Lifter, & Hafitz, 1980). Only later do children develop a more general past tense that applies to all verbs, including those describing events that do not result in visible changes of state. Moreover, the focus on results may bring with it a tendency to concentrate on marking patients at the expense of agents. For example, Italian-learning children will make the past participle of transitive verbs agree in number and gender with the direct object/patient, not the subject/agent – despite the fact that, in the input language, the participle agrees with neither object nor subject of a transitive verb, and agrees with the subject (actor) of an intransitive verb (Antinucci & Miller, 1976). The close relation between objects and results in the real world may encourage the child to create grammatical structure where there is none.

Privileged forms

In addition to *meanings* that appear to be privileged in the early stages of child language, there are *forms* that children apparently find easy to incorporate into their language. For example, children use consistent word order in their early sentences even when the language they are learning has relatively free word order (Bates, 1976; MacWhinney, 1977; Slobin, 1966). As another example, children place one-argument verbs in two-argument predicate frames whether or not the alternation is permissible in their language. For example, an English-learning child said "Kendall fall that toy" to mean that she dropped the toy (Bowerman, 1982). By placing "fall" in a "*y* __ *x*" frame rather than the correct "*x* __" frame, Kendall is giving the word a transitive meaning (action on an object) rather than an intransitive meaning (action with no object). Comparable examples have been reported in children learning French, Portuguese, Polish, Hebrew, Hungarian, and Turkish – even in languages where the input does not model this possibility (Slobin, 1985).

Children are sensitive to regularities of form not only within sentences but also across sentences. They detect regularities across word sets called *paradigms*. As an example of a paradigm, the various forms that verbs can take (*walk – walks – walked*) constitute a verb paradigm. We saw earlier that English-learning children detect regularities within paradigms, and often attempt to "regularize" any ill-fitting forms they find. For example, children alter the past tense form for "eat" so that it conforms to the paradigm constructed on the basis of the regular verbs in their language (*eat – eats – eated* rather than *eat – eats – ate*). Morphological paradigms in English are rather simple compared to paradigms in other languages but children are equally capable of regularizing the more complex morphological systems. For example, in Spanish, nouns that are masculine take the indefinite article *un* and the definite article *el* and generally end in *-o*; in contrast, nouns that are feminine take the articles *una* and *la* and generally end in *-a*. Spanish-learning children learn these regularities early, as is evident from the fact that they will attempt to "clean up" any nouns that happen to violate this paradigm: for example, they produce "una mana" rather than the irregular, but correct, form, "una mano" (= hand, feminine), and "un papelo" rather than the irregular correct form, "un papel" (= paper, masculine; Montes Giraldo, 1976, as described in Clark, 1985).

To summarize thus far, we find that children do exhibit commonalities in the early steps they take in the language-learning process despite differences in the languages to which they are exposed. These commonalities could well constitute "conceptual starting points for grammaticized notions" (Slobin, 1997). Starting points are just that – a place to begin. In the longer term, children are clearly able to cope with the wide diversity across languages, learning whatever system is put before them. The job of any theory of language acquisition is to account for the developmental progression that takes children from their starting point to such very different endpoints. If the endpoint language matches the child's starting point in a particular domain, that domain is likely to be relatively easy to learn. If, however, the endpoint language uses categories that are wider, or narrower, than the categories with which the child starts the language-learning process in a domain, that domain is likely to be more difficult to learn. Where the rough and easy spots are in the developmental process may thus depend on how the particular language a child is learning overlaps with the child's starting point.

Does More or Less Input Matter?

Some children hear a lot of talk, others hear much less. Do differences of this sort make a difference? To address this question, we need to observe variations in how a particular language – English, for example – is used across families, and then explore whether those variations have an impact on child language-learning.

The natural variation in language input that children receive

The sentences spoken to children are, by and large, short, usually consisting of a single clause; they are clearly spoken and therefore intelligible; they almost never contain grammatical errors; and they tend to focus on events that are taking place in the here-and-now and involve objects that are visible (Snow, 1972). All adults – and even 4-year-old children (Shatz & Gelman, 1973) – simplify their speech in these ways when addressing younger children. However, adults vary in how much they simplify their speech, and in how much they talk at all. The question is whether this variability in input is related in any way to child language-learning.

Newport, Gleitman, and Gleitman (1977) conducted the first of the studies designed to explore the impact of linguistic variation on child language-learning by taking a large number of measures of parental input at time 1, and relating these measures to changes in child language from time 1 to time 2. In general, frequency in the input a child receives seems to matter for both vocabulary- and syntax-learning. The amount of talk mothers address to their children is directly related to the number and types of words (Huttenlocher, Haight, Bryk, Seltzer, & Lyons, 1991; Naigles & Hoff-Ginsberg, 1998) and complex sentences (Barnes, Gutfreund, Satterly, & Wells, 1983; Huttenlocher, Vasilyeva, Cymerman, & Levine, 2002) that children acquire.

However, frequency is not the whole story. One of the most robust findings across a variety of studies is that the development of auxiliaries (e.g., *is, can, do, will*) is related to adult speech (Furrow, Nelson, & Benedict, 1979; Hoff-Ginsberg, 1985; Newport et al., 1977). But the relation is not a straightforward one. The rate at which adults use auxiliaries is *not* related to the child's use of auxiliaries. What does predict child use is mothers' use of *yes/no* questions – questions in which the auxiliary appears at the front of the sentence: for example, "*are* you coming over here?" (Newport et al., 1977). Thus, it is not just how often mothers produce auxiliaries that matters; it is how often auxiliaries are produced in salient positions in the sentence that predicts acquisition (where "salient" is defined in terms of the child's information-processing biases). Children thus appear to bring "learning filters" to the linguistic input they receive, and those filters determine whether input becomes "uptake" (Harris, 1992).

To make the story even more complicated, children are not merely "copying" (Valian, 1999) the input they receive. The fast auxiliary learners tend to hear auxiliaries in first position of sentences addressed to them. However, they first produce auxiliaries in the *middle* of their own sentences, even for questions (e.g., "what he *can* ride in?" "how he *can* be a doctor?"; Klima & Bellugi, 1966). Thus, what linguistic input does is provide opportunities for learning the language system – but it is up to the child to do the inductive work to figure out what that system is.

Enriching the input to children

We can increase the range of variation in the input children receive by providing richer linguistic environments than those found in nature. Experimenters can provide children with concentrated input by expanding particular aspects of the child's utterance. For example, a child says "you can't get in" and the experimenter turns the utterance into a question, manipulating auxiliaries in the process, "no, I can't get in, can I?" (Nelson, 1977). Overall, enrichment works – at least when it comes to auxiliaries. Moreover, enrichment works selectively. When children are provided with enriched input in predicate constructions, their predicates (including auxiliaries) become more complex, but the average length of their utterances and their noun phrases don't change at all (Nelson, Carskaddon, & Bonvillian, 1973).

Enrichment studies can provide clear data on the positive effects of linguistic input on language acquisition, that is, on properties of language that are *sensitive* to the effects of environment. However, enrichment studies cannot provide unequivocal data on the negative effects of linguistic input on acquisition, that is, on the environment-*insensitive* properties of language. If the language children naturally hear already provides enough input for a given linguistic property to develop, enriching their input is not likely to have a further effect on the development of that property.

To avoid this problem, we need to *reduce* the input children typically receive. If there is a threshold level of linguistic input necessary for certain language properties to develop, these properties should *not* develop in a child who lacks linguistic input. If, however, linguistic input is not necessary for a set of language properties to develop, these properties ought to emerge in the communications of a child without input. Note that, in studies of speech in natural and enriched environments, non-effects of linguistic input must be inferred from negative results – a property is assumed to be environment-insensitive if input *does not* affect its development. In contrast, in a deprivation study, the presence of a particular property in a child's language is positive evidence for environment-insensitive properties of language – a property is assumed to be environment-insensitive if it *does* appear in the deprived child's repertoire. These are language properties whose development is not affected by linguistic input. They therefore might be properties that children themselves are able to introduce into linguistic systems.

Degrading the input to children

It is unethical to remove a child's language input. Nevertheless, circumstances have arisen in which children have been deprived of linguistic input. For example, a young girl was discovered at age 13, after having been isolated and confined to a small room with no freedom of movement and no human companionship. This child, called "Genie," was deprived of not only linguistic input but also physical and social stimulation. Not surprisingly, she did not develop language or any other form of communication during her years of isolation and deprivation (Curtiss, 1977; Fromkin, Krashen, Curtiss, Rigler, & Rigler, 1974). Children do not develop human language under developmental conditions this extreme, suggesting that there are limits on the resilience of language.

But radical deprivation studies cannot tell us whether linguistic input is essential to language-learning. To address this question, we need to locate children experiencing normal social environments except for their impoverished linguistic input. For a variety of reasons, deaf children are often exposed to less-than-perfect linguistic input yet live in a supportive social world. Consider the case described by Singleton and Newport (2004). The child, Simon, was born to deaf parents, but his parents were late-learners of sign and thus did not have complete mastery of ASL morphology. Simon was exposed only to this imperfect model yet he developed morphological structure that was more complex than that of his parents and comparable in many respects to the morphological structure developed by deaf children exposed to complete models of ASL. Simon was not limited by his linguistic input.

The newly developing Nicaraguan Sign Language (NSL) provides further evidence of children going beyond their linguistic input. Opening the first school for the deaf in Managua in the late 1970s created an opportunity for Nicaraguan deaf children to inter- act with one another for the very first time. The children in this situation created a new sign language, which was initially very simple and had many irregularities. However, the language became the input for the next group of young signers, who developed new and more complex linguistic structures (Senghas & Coppola, 2001).

We also see linguistic creativity when deaf children are exposed not to a naturally evolving sign language (such as ASL or NSL) but rather to Manually Coded English (MCE), a sign system invented by educators to map English surface structure onto the visual/gestural modality. Deaf children find it difficult to process MCE and end up alter- ing the system, introducing grammatical devices reminiscent of those found in ASL (S. Supalla, 1991). Thus, when provided with *inadequate* linguistic input, children are capable of transforming that input and constructing a rule-governed system of their own.

An even more remarkable example of the resilience of language comes from children who have had *no exposure* to a conventional language model whatsoever. These children are born with hearing losses so severe that they cannot acquire spoken language and born to hearing parents who have not exposed them to a model of a sign language (either ASL or MCE). Such children are, for all intents and purposes, deprived of a usable model for language – although, importantly, they are not deprived of other aspects of human social interaction. Despite their lack of linguistic input, deaf children in these circumstances use gesture to communicate. This, by itself, is not striking. What is noteworthy is that the gesture systems these deaf children create are structured like natural language (Goldin- Meadow, 2003a). Table 13.1 lists the properties of language that have been found thus far in the deaf children's gesture systems. There may, of course, be many others not yet discovered. The table lists properties at the word- and sentence-levels, as well as properties of language use, and details how each property is instantiated in the deaf children's gesture systems.

In terms of word-level structure, the deaf children's gesture-words have five properties found in all natural languages. The gestures are *stable* in form, although they needn't be. It would be easy for the children to make up a new gesture to fit every new situation. However, the children develop a stable store of forms which they use in a range of situ- ations – they develop a lexicon, an essential component of all languages. Moreover, the gestures they develop are composed of parts that form *paradigms*, or systems of contrasts. When the children invent a gesture form, they do so with two goals in mind – the form must not only capture the meaning they intend (a gesture-to-world relation), but it must also contrast in a systematic way with other forms in their repertoire (a gesture-to-gesture

Table 13.1 The resilient properties of language

The resilient property	As instantiated in the deaf children's gesture systems
Words	
Stability	Gesture forms are stable and do not change capriciously with changing situations
Paradigms	Gestures consist of smaller parts that can be recombined to produce new gestures with different meanings
Categories	The parts of gestures are composed of a limited set of forms, each associated with a particular meaning
Arbitrariness	Pairings between gesture forms and meanings can have arbitrary aspects, albeit within an iconic framework
Grammatical functions	Gestures are differentiated by the noun, verb, and adjective grammatical functions they serve
Sentences	
Underlying frames	Predicate frames underlie gesture sentences
Deletion	Consistent production and deletion of gestures within a sentence mark particular thematic roles
Word order	Consistent orderings of gestures within a sentence mark particular thematic roles
Inflections	Consistent inflections on gestures mark particular thematic roles
Recursion	Complex gesture sentences are created by recursion
Redundancy reduction	Redundancy is systematically reduced in the surface of complex gesture sentences
Language use	
Here-and-now talk	Gesturing is used to make requests, comments, and queries about the present
Displaced talk	Gesturing is used to communicate about the past, future, and hypothetical
Generics	Gesturing is used to make generic statements, particularly about animals
Narrative	Gesturing is used to tell stories about self and others
Self-talk	Gesturing is used to communicate with oneself
Metalanguage	Gesturing is used to refer to one's own and others' gestures

relation). In addition, the parts that form these paradigms are *categorical.* The manual modality can easily support a system of analog representation, with hands and motions reflecting precisely the positions and trajectories used to act on objects in the real world. But, again, the children don't choose this route. They develop categories of meanings that, although essentially iconic, have hints of *arbitrariness* about them (the children don't, for example, all share the same form–meaning pairings for handshapes). Finally, the gestures the children develop are differentiated by *grammatical function.* Some serve as nouns, some as verbs, some as adjectives. As in natural languages, when the same gesture is used for more than one grammatical function, that gesture is marked (morphologically and syntactically) according to the function it plays in the particular sentence.

In terms of sentence-level structure, the deaf children's gesture sentences have six properties found in all natural languages. Underlying each sentence is a *predicate frame* that determines how many arguments can appear along with the verb in the surface structure of that sentence. Moreover, the arguments of each sentence are marked according to the thematic role they play. There are three types of markings that are resilient: (1) *deletion* – the children consistently produce and delete gestures for arguments as a function of thematic role; (2) *word order* – the children consistently order gestures for arguments as a function of thematic role; and (3) *inflection* – the children mark with inflections gestures for arguments as a function of thematic role. In addition, *recursion,* which gives natural languages their generative capacity, is a resilient property of language. The children form complex gesture sentences out of simple ones. They combine the predicate frames underlying each simple sentence, following systematic, and language-like, principles. When there are semantic elements that appear in both propositions of a complex sentence, the children have a systematic way of *reducing redundancy,* as do all natural languages.

Finally, in terms of language use, the deaf children use their gestures for six central functions that all natural languages serve. They use gesture to make requests, comments, and queries about things and events that are happening in the situation – that is, to communicate about the *here-and-now.* Importantly, however, they also use their gestures to communicate about the non-present – *displaced* objects and events that take place in the past, the future, or in a hypothetical world. In addition to these rather obvious functions that language serves, the children use their gestures to make category-broad statements about objects, particularly about natural kinds – to make *generic* statements. They use their gestures to tell stories about themselves and others – to *narrate.* They use their gestures to communicate with themselves – to *self-talk.* And finally, they use their gestures to refer to their own or to others' gestures – for *metalinguistic* purposes.

The properties of language found in the deaf children's gesture system are resilient in the sense that their development does not require input from a conventional language model. Moreover, even though the deaf children's hearing parents produce gestures when they talk to their children (as do all hearing speakers; Goldin-Meadow, 2003b), the parents' gestures do not exhibit the linguistic properties found in the deaf children's gestures. Thus, the children themselves are inventing the linguistic structures.

Interestingly, and perhaps not surprisingly, the deaf children's gesture systems exhibit the privileged meanings and privileged forms that children around the globe develop when exposed to conventional linguistic input. For example, the deaf children's grammatical systems are constructed around highly transitive events and focus on the results of events with little attention to animacy. In addition, the deaf children construct grammatical systems that have structure within sentences (e.g., ordering patterns, underlying predicate frames), as well as structure across sentences (e.g., word sets or paradigms), as do all children learning conventional languages. It is these forms and meanings that children themselves seem prepared to develop. If a model for these properties is not present in their input, children will invent them – operationally defining the resilient properties of language.

Is Language Innate?

The fact that all known human groups (even those incapable of hearing) have developed language is reason enough to consider the possibility that language-learning is innate. And the fact that human children can invent components of language even when not exposed to any linguistic input makes it more likely still that language-learning ought be considered innate. However, the problem in even beginning to address this issue is finding a comfortable definition of "innate."

One might naïvely think that if learning is involved in the development of a behavior, the behavior cannot be innate. However, we'd like our definition of innate to be more subtle – some learning is involved in the acquisition of all human skills, even one as basic as walking (Thelen & Ulrich, 1991). The issue is not whether learning has occurred but whether learning is guided by the organism as much as, if not more than, by the environment. A study by Marler (1990) best exemplifies the point. Two closely related species of sparrows were raised from the egg in identical environments and exposed to a collection of songs containing melodies typical for each species. Despite their identical input, the two species learned different songs. Each species learned only the songs in the collection that adult members of its own species typically sing. Similarly, Locke (1990) argues that to a certain extent human infants select the sounds they learn preferentially, often learning frequently heard phonemes relatively late and infrequently heard phonemes quite early. Birds and children both learn from the input they receive, but their learning is selective.

Another way of saying this is that the range of possible outcomes in the learning process is narrowed, and the organism itself does the narrowing. This narrowing, or "canalization," is often attributed to genetic causes (cf., Waddington, 1957). However, canalization can also be caused by the environment. For example, exposing a bird to a particular stimulus at one point early in its development can narrow the bird's learning later on – the bird becomes particularly susceptible to that stimulus, and buffered against responding to other stimuli, at later points in development (Gottlieb, 1991). Thus, for any given behavior, we need to investigate the causes of canalization rather than assume a genetic base.

In human studies, we cannot freely engineer organisms and environments, and developmental histories are quite complex. It is therefore difficult to attribute canalization to either genetic or environmental causes. Does this difficulty render the notion "innate" meaningless? Not necessarily. The definition of "innate" need not be anchored in genetic mechanisms. Indeed, of the large number of criteria that have, over many years and many disciplines, been applied to the term "innate," Wimsatt (1986) argues that the one that is *least* central to the notion's core is having a genetic base (see also Block, 1979; Spelke & Newport, 1998). In his view, a more fundamental definition is developmental resilience. A behavior that is developmentally resilient is one whose development is, if not inevitable, certainly one that each organism in the species is predisposed to develop under widely varying circumstances. Language seems to be a prime example of such a behavior.

We have seen in this chapter that language is resilient in the face of variations *external* to the organism. Interestingly, language-learning is also resilient in the face of variations *internal* to the organism. For example, grammar-learning in the earliest stages can proceed in a relatively normal manner and at a normal rate even in the face of unilateral ischemic brain injury (Feldman, 1994). As a second example, children with Down's syndrome have numerous intrinsic deficiencies that complicate the process of language acquisition; nevertheless, most acquire some basic language reflecting the fundamental grammatical organization of the language to which they are exposed (Fowler, Gelman, & Gleitman, 1994). Finally, and strikingly given the social impairments that are at the core of the syndrome, autistic children who are able to learn language are not impaired in some aspects of their grammatical development, specifically syntax or morphology, although they do often have deficits in the communicative, pragmatic, and functional aspects of their language (Tager-Flusberg, 1994).

Thus, language development can proceed in humans over a wide range of environments and a wide range of organic states, suggesting that the language-learning process is buffered. It looks as though there is a basic form that human communication naturally gravitates toward and a variety of developmental paths that can be taken to arrive at that form. In this sense, language development in humans can be said to be characterized by "equifinality" – a term coined by the embryologist Driesch (1908/1929, as reported in Gottlieb, 1996) to describe a process by which a system reaches the same outcome despite widely differing input conditions.

Of course, not all language users are alike. There are differences across individuals in what they do with language and perhaps even how much they know about language (e.g., Gleitman & Gleitman, 1970; see Hoff, this volume, for a discussion of factors that might lead to such individual differences). But there are some fundamental properties that are found in *all* human language users (properties like having a stable lexicon or using order to signal who does what to whom). It is these resilient properties that have been the focus of this chapter. Whatever developmental mechanisms we come up with to account for the aspects of language-learning that vary across individuals must also be able to account for the equifinality that characterizes the resilient properties of language.

Language is not a unitary whole, particularly when it comes to issues of resilience and innateness. Deaf children inventing their own gesture systems develop some but not all of the properties found in natural human languages (Goldin-Meadow, 2003a). The absence of a conventional language model appears to affect some properties of language more than others. Even when linguistic input is present, that input is more likely to affect rate of acquisition for certain properties of language than for others (e.g., auxiliaries more than complex sentences; Newport et al., 1977). Further, when language is acquired "off-time" (i.e., relatively late in the ontogenetic timespan), certain properties of language are more likely to be acquired (word order, complex sentences) than others (auxiliaries; Curtiss, 1977; Newport, 1991). Interestingly, it appears that the *same* properties of language may be resilient across many different circumstances of acquisition. For example, word order and the production of complex sentences are two properties that seem to be resilient across acquisition without a conventional language model, acquisition with varying input from a language model, and acquisition late in development after puberty (Goldin-Meadow, 1978, 1982). It is these resilient properties that form the bedrock of language-learning when it follows a typical course, and that may be able to serve as the starting point for intervention when language-learning goes awry.

In closing, I suggest that innateness is best evaluated through the perspective of developmental resilience. Innateness is operationalized by specifying the range of environments in which certain aspects of language-learning develop. There clearly are limits on language development in humans – children raised without human interaction do not develop language. But, as we have seen throughout this chapter, language development can proceed even in the face of deviations from typical learning environments. By exploring this resilience, we learn that certain aspects of language are central to humans – so central that their development is virtually guaranteed, not necessarily by a particular gene but by a variety of combinations of genetic and environmental factors. It is in this sense that language is innate.

References

Acredolo, L. P., & Goodwyn, S. W. (1988). Symbolic gesturing in normal infants. *Child Development, 59*, 450–466.

Aksu-Koc, A. A., & Slobin, D. I. (1985). The acquisition of Turkish. In D. I. Slobin (Ed.), *A cross-linguistic study of language acquisition: Vol. 1. The data* (pp. 839–878). Hillsdale, NJ: Erlbaum.

Angiolillo, C., & Goldin-Meadow, S. (1982). Experimental evidence for agent–patient categories in child language. *Journal of Child Language, 9*, 627–643.

Antinucci, F., & Miller, R. (1976). How children talk about what happened. *Journal of Child Language, 3*, 167–189.

Barnes, S., Gutfreund, M., Satterly, D., & Wells, G. (1983). Characteristics of adult speech which predict children's language development. *Journal of Child Language, 10*, 65–84.

Bates, E. (1976). *Language and context: The acquisition of pragmatics.* New York: Academic Press.

Berman, R. A. (1985). The acquisition of Hebrew. In D. I. Slobin (Ed.), *A cross-linguistic study of language acquisition: Vol. 1. The data* (pp. 256–371). Hillsdale, NJ: Erlbaum.

Block, N. (1979). A confusion about innateness. *Behavioral and Brain Sciences, 2*, 27–29.

Bloom, L. (1970). *Language development: Form and function in emerging grammars.* Cambridge, MA: MIT Press.

Bloom, L., Lifter, K., & Hafitz, J. (1980). Semantics of verbs and the development of verb inflections in child language. *Language, 56*, 386–412.

Bloom, L., Miller, P., & Hood, L. (1975). Variation and reduction as aspects of competence in language development. In A. Pick (ed.), *The Minnesota Symposium on Child Psychology* (Vol. 9, pp. 3–55). Minneapolis: University of Minnesota Press.

Bonvillian, J. D., & Folven, R. J. (1993). Sign language acquisition: Developmental aspects. In M. Marschark & M. D. Clark (Eds.), *Psychological perspectives on deafness* (pp. 229–265). Hillsdale, NJ: Erlbaum.

Bowerman, M. (1973a). *Early syntactic development: A cross-linguistic study with special reference to Finnish.* Cambridge: Cambridge University Press.

Bowerman, M. (1973b). Structural relationships in children's utterances: Syntactic or semantic. In T. Moore (Ed.), *Cognitive development and the acquisition of language* (pp. 197–213). New York: Academic Press.

Bowerman, M. (1982). Starting to talk worse: Clues to language acquisition from children's late speech errors. In S. Strauss (Ed.), *U-shaped behavioral growth* (pp. 11–36). New York: Academic Press.

Braine, M. D. S. (1976). Children's first word combinations. *Monographs of the Society for Research in Child Development, 41*(1, Serial No. 164).

Brown, R. (1973). *A first language.* Cambridge, MA: Harvard University Press.

Choi, S., & Bowerman, M. (1991). Learning to express motion events in English and Korean: The influence of language-specific lexicalization patterns. *Cognition, 41,* 83–121.

Clark, E. (1985). The acquisition of Romance, with special reference to French. In D. I. Slobin (Ed.), *A cross-linguistic study of language acquisition: Vol. 1. The data* (pp. 687–782). Hillsdale, NJ: Erlbaum.

Coerts, J. A. (2000). Early sign combinations in the acquisition of Sign Language of the Netherlands: Evidence for language-specific features. In C. Chamberlain, J. P. Morford, & R. Mayberry (Eds.), *Language acquisition by eye* (pp. 91–109). Mahwah, NJ: Erlbaum.

Curtiss, S. (1977). *Genie: A psycholinguistic study of a modern-day "Wild-Child."* New York: Academic Press.

de Villiers, J. G., Roeper, T., & Vainikka, A. (1990). The acquisition of long distance rules. In L. Frazier & J. G. de Villiers (Eds.), *Language processing and language acquisition* (pp. 257–297). Dordrecht: Kluwer.

Driesch, H. (1929). *The science and philosophy of the organism.* London: A. & C. Black. (Original work published 1908)

Feldman, H. M. (1994). Language development after early unilateral brain injury: A replication study. In H. Tager-Flusberg (Ed.), *Constraints on language acquisition: Studies of atypical children* (pp. 75–90). Hillsdale, NJ: Erlbaum.

Fowler, A. E., Gelman, R., & Gleitman, L. R. (1994). The course of language learning in children with Down Syndrome: Longitudinal and language level comparisons with young normally developing children. In H. Tager-Flusberg (Ed.), *Constraints on language acquisition: Studies of atypical children* (pp. 91–140). Hillsdale, NJ: Erlbaum.

Fromkin, V., Krashen, S., Curtiss, S., Rigler, D., & Rigler, M. (1974). The development of language in Genie: A case of language acquisition beyond the "Critical Period." *Brain and Language, 1,* 81–107.

Furrow, D., Nelson, K., & Benedict, H. (1979). Mothers' speech to children and syntactic development: Some simple relationships. *Journal of Child Language, 6,* 423–442.

Gleitman, L. R., & Gleitman, H. (1970). *Phrase and paraphrase: Some innovative uses of language.* New York: W. W. Norton & Co.

Goldin-Meadow, S. (1978). A study in human capacities. *Science, 200,* 649–651.

Goldin-Meadow, S. (1982). The resilience of recursion: A study of a communication system developed without a conventional language model. In E. Wanner & L. R. Gleitman (Eds.), *Language acquisition: The state of the art* (pp. 51–77). New York: Cambridge University Press.

Goldin-Meadow, S. (1985). Language development under atypical learning conditions: Replication and implications of a study of deaf children of hearing parents. In K. Nelson (ed.), *Children's language* (Vol. 5, pp. 197–245). Hillsdale, NJ: Erlbaum.

Goldin-Meadow, S. (2003a). *The resilience of language: What gesture creation in deaf children can tell us about how all children learn language.* NewYork: Psychology Press.

Goldin-Meadow, S. (2003b). *Hearing gesture: How our hands help us think.* Cambridge, MA: Harvard University Press.

Goldin-Meadow, S., & Mylander, C. (1984). Gestural communication in deaf children: The effects and non-effects of parental input on early language development. *Monographs of the Society for Research in Child Development, 49*(3–4, Serial No. 207).

Gottlieb, G. (1991). Experiential canalization of behavioral development: Results. *Developmental Psychology, 27,* 35–39.

Gottlieb, G. (1996). A systems view of psychobiological development. In D. Magnusson (Ed.), *The lifespan development of individuals: Behavioral, neurobiological and psychosocial perspectives: A synthesis* (pp. 76–103). New York: Cambridge University Press.

Gvozdev, A. M. (1961). Znacenie izucenija detskogo jazyka jlja jazykovedenija. In *Voprosy izucenija detskoj reci.* Moscow: Izd-vo Akademii Pedagogiceskix Nauk RSFSR. (Original work published 1928)

Harris, M. (1992). *Language experience and early language development: From input to uptake.* Hillsdale, NJ: Erlbaum.

Hirsh-Pasek, K., & Golinkoff, R. M. (1991). Language comprehension: A new look at some old themes. In N. A. Krasnegor, D. M. Rumbaugh, R. L., Schiefelbusch, & M. Studdert-Kennedy (Eds.), *Biological and behavioral determinants of language development* (pp. 301–320). Hillsdale, NJ: Erlbaum.

Hirsh-Pasek, K., Golinkoff, R. M., & Naigles, L. (1996). Young children's use of syntactic frames to derive meaning. In K. Hirsh-Pasek & R. M. Golinkoff (Eds.), *The origins of grammar: Evidence from early language comprehension* (pp. 123–159). Cambridge, MA: MIT Press.

Hoff-Ginsberg, E. (1985). Some contributions of mothers' speech to their children's syntactic growth. *Journal of Child Language, 12,* 367–385.

Hoffmeister, R. (1978). *The development of demonstrative pronouns, locatives and personal pronouns in the acquisition of American Sign Language by deaf children of deaf parents.* Unpublished Ph.D. dissertation, University of Minnesota.

Hopper, P. J., & Thompson, S. (1980). Transitivity. *Language, 56,* 251–299.

Hsu, J. R., Cairns, H. S., Eisenberg, S., & Schlisselberg, G. (1989). Control and coreference in early child language. *Journal of Child Language, 16,* 599–622.

Huttenlocher, J., Haight, W., Bryk, A., Seltzer, M., & Lyons, T. (1991). Early vocabulary growth: Relation to language input and gender. *Developmental Psychology, 27,* 236–248.

Huttenlocher, J., Vasilyeva, M., Cymerman, E., & Levine, S. (2002). Language and syntax. *Cognitive Psychology, 45,* 337–374.

Johnston, J. R., & Slobin, D. I. (1979). The development of locative expressions in English, Italian, Serbo-Croatian and Turkish. *Journal of Child Language, 6,* 529–545.

Klima, E. S., & Bellugi, U. (1966). Syntactic regularities in the speech of children. In J. Lyons & R. J. Wales (Eds.), *Pyscholinguistics papers* (pp. 183–208). Edinburgh: Edinburgh University Press.

Locke, J. L. (1990). Structure and stimulation in the ontogeny of spoken language. *Developmental Psychobiology, 23,* 621–643.

MacWhinney, B. (1977). Starting points. *Language, 53,* 152–168.

MacWhinney, B. (1978). The acquisition of morphophonology. *Monographs of the Society for Research in Child Development, 43*(1–2, Serial No. 174).

Marcus, G. (1995). Children's overregularization of English plurals: A qualitative analysis. *Journal of Child Language, 22,* 447–459.

Marler, P. (1990). Innate learning preferences: Signals for communication. *Developmental Psychobiology, 23,* 557–568.

Meier, R. P. (1982). *Icons, analogues, and morphemes: The acquisition of verb agreement in ASL.* Unpublished Ph.D. dissertation, University of California, San Diego.

Meier, R. P., & Newport, E. L. (1990). Out of the hands of babes: On a possible sign advantage in language acquisition. *Language, 66,* 1–23.

Mills, A. E. (1985). The acquisition of English. In D. I. Slobin (Ed.), *The crosslinguistic study of language acquisition: Vol. 1. The data* (pp. 141–254). Hillsdale, NJ: Erlbaum.

Montes Giraldo, J. J. (1976). El sistemas, la norma, y el aprendizaje de la lengua. *Thesaurus: Boletin del Instituto Caro y Cuervo, 31,* 14–40.

Naigles, L. R., & Hoff-Ginsberg, E. (1998). Why are some verbs learned before other verbs? Effects of input frequency and structure on children's early verb use. *Journal of Child Language, 25,* 95–120.

Nelson, K. E. (1977). Facilitating children's syntax acquisition. *Developmental Psychology, 13,* 101–107.

Nelson, K. E., Carskaddon, G., & Bonvillian, J. D. (1973). Syntax acquisition: Impact of experimental variation in adult verbal interaction with the child. *Child Development, 44,* 497–504.

Newport, E. L. (1991). Contrasting conceptions of the critical period for language. In S. Carey & R. Gelman (Eds.), *The epigenesis of mind: Essays on biology and cognition* (pp. 11–130). Hillsdale, NJ: Erlbaum.

Newport, E. L., & Ashbrook, E. F. (1977). The emergence of semantic relations in American Sign Language. *Papers and Reports on Child Language Development, 13,* 16–21.

Newport, E. L., Gleitman, H., & Gleitman, L. R. (1977). Mother, I'd rather do it myself: Some effects and non-effects of maternal speech style. In C. E. Snow & C. A. Ferguson (Eds.), *Talking to children: Language input and acquisition* (pp. 109–150). New York: Cambridge University Press.

Newport, E. L. & Meier, R. P. (1985). The acquisition of American Sign Language. In D. I. Slobin (Ed.), *The cross-linguistic study of language acquisition: Vol. 1. The data* (pp. 881–938). Hillsdale, NJ: Erlbaum.

Padden, C. (1983). *Interaction of morphology and syntax in American Sign Language.* Unpublished Ph.D. dissertation, University of California, San Diego.

Petitto, L. A. (1987). On the autonomy of language and gesture: Evidence from the acquisition of personal pronouns in American Sign Language. *Cognition, 27,* 1–52.

Petitto, L. A. (1988). "Language" in the prelinguistic child. In F. S. Kessel (Ed.), *The development of language and language researchers* (pp. 187–221). Hillsdale, NJ: Erlbaum.

Senghas, A., & Coppola, M. (2001). Children creating language: How Nicaraguan Sign Language acquired a spatial grammar. *Psychological Science, 12,* 323–328.

Shatz, M., & Gelman, R. (1973). The development of communication skills: Modifications in the speech of young children as a function of listener. *Monographs of the Society for Research in Child Development, 38*(5, Serial No. 152).

Singleton, J. L., & Newport, E. L. (2004). When learners surpass their models: The acquisition of American Sign Language from impoverished input. *Cognitive Psychology, 49,* 370–407.

Slobin, D. I. (1966). The acquisition of Russian as a native language. In F. Smith & C. Miller (Eds.), *The genesis of language: A psycholinguistic approach* (pp. 129–148). Cambridge, MA: MIT Press.

Slobin, D. I. (1985). Introduction: Why study acquisition crosslinguistically? In D. I. Slobin (Ed.), *A cross-linguistic study of language acquisition: Vol. 1: The data* (pp. 3–24). Hillsdale, NJ: Erlbaum.

Slobin, D. I. (1997). The universal, the typological, and the particular in acquisition. In D. I. Slobin (Ed.), *A cross-linguistic study of language acquisition: Vol. 5. Expanding the contents* (pp. 1–39). Hillsdale, NJ: Erlbaum.

Snow, C. E. (1972). Mothers' speech to children learning language. *Child Development, 43,* 549–565.

Spelke, E. S., & Newport, E. L. (1998). Nativism, empiricism, and the development of knowledge. In W. Damon (ed.), *Handbook of child psychology* (5th ed., Vol. 1, pp. 275–340). New York: John Wiley & Sons.

Supalla, S. (1991). Manually Coded English: The modality question in signed language development. In P. Siple & S. Fischer (Eds.), *Theoretical issues in sign language research: Vol. 2. Acquisition* (pp. 85–109). Chicago: University of Chicago Press.

Supalla, T. (1982). *Structure and acquisition of verbs of motion and location in American Sign Language.* Unpublished Ph.D. dissertation, University of California at San Diego.

Tager-Flusberg, H. (1994). Dissociations in form and function in the acquisition of language by autistic children. In H. Tager-Flusberg (Ed.), *Constraints on language acquisition: Studies of atypical children* (pp. 175–194). Hillsdale, NJ: Erlbaum.

Thelen, E., & Ulrich, B. D. (1991). Hidden skills: A dynamic systems analysis of treadmill stepping during the first year. *Monographs of the Society for Research in Child Development, 56*(1, Serial No. 223).

Valian, V. (1986). Syntactic categories in the speech of young children. *Developmental Psychology, 22,* 562–579.

Valian, V. (1999). Input and language acquisition. In W. C. Ritchie & T. K. Bhatia (Eds.), *Handbook of child language acquisition* (pp. 497–530). New York: Academic Press.

Waddington, C. H. (1957). *The strategy of the genes.* London: Allen & Unwin.

Wimsatt, W. C. (1986). Developmental constraints, generative entrenchment and the innate–acquired distinction. In W. Bechtel (Ed.), *Integrating scientific disciplines* (pp. 185–208). Dordrecht: Martinus Nijhoff.

14

What Counts as Literacy in Early Childhood?

Catherine E. Snow

Issues of literacy development are a major source of worry to American educators. Worries about whether US children read well enough emerge every time results of an international comparison are published. Not surprisingly, many of the provisions of the No Child Left Behind legislation are directed toward more stringent assessment and more effective instruction in literacy. Concerns about school readiness have led to efforts to expand preschool programs designed as prevention or intervention efforts for children of low-income parents, and to movements to publicly finance kindergarten classrooms for 4-year-olds.

Is all this attention really justified? What kinds of literacy skills do young children possess, and what is the evidence that those levels are unsatisfactory? The focus of this chapter is the many and varied child capacities that have been identified as related to literacy outcomes among children under the age of 8. The argument I will make is that conceptions of literacy, and definitions of what counts as literacy, vary enormously, and that those varying conceptions are reflected (a) in divergent claims about how well children are doing, (b) in differing conclusions about whether some early childhood accomplishments really matter to later literacy development, (c) in differing foci for the design of early childhood education and intervention programs, and (d) in varying emphases on skills selected for inclusion in the assessment of literacy in the early childhood period.

I start with a brief description of children's literacy development – what the mythical "average child" can do at various points in the preschool and early school years. Then I turn to a description of the disagreements among literacy researchers, the issues that divide them and that lead them to differing conceptions of literacy itself. I elaborate those differences by describing how they shape their advocates' answers to key questions about the central topics of interest: preschool literacy accomplishments, precursors to later literacy development, design of prevention/intervention programs, and assessment.

The Literate Child

Everyone agrees that literacy is a complex and multi-faceted skill which changes enormously as it is acquired. The Committee on the Prevention of Reading Difficulties in Young Children (National Research Council, 1998) outlined the literacy skills to be expected of children at different points up through grade 3. Table 14.1 presents a truncated version of the developmental guidelines they presented.[1] The typical 3-year-old can recognize some books by their covers, knows how to hold books upright and turn pages, listens when read to, expects to be able to understand pictures in books, may distinguish pictures from print, may recognize some letters, and produces purposeful-looking scribbles. The typical 4-year-old has learned to recite the alphabet and to recognize several letters, connects events in stories to "real life," understands that stories are different from notes or lists, may produce rhymes or alliterations, and may scribble, pretend-write, or draw with a communicative purpose. The typical kindergartner knows about titles and authors of books, may track the print when being read to from familiar simple books, can name all and write most of the letters, can recognize and spell some simple words, spontaneously questions events in stories and information books, and uses mostly invented spelling in writing. The typical first grader is starting to get a serious handle on the system of writing, is able to read accurately and fluently texts that include previously taught spelling patterns, uses letter–sound correspondence to sound out new words, spells with a combination of conventional and invented spelling, monitors her own writing and reading for correctness, and understands the differences among a wide variety of texts (informal notes, informative texts, stories, poems, slogans, lists, and so forth). In second and third grade, the typically developing child becomes increasingly accurate and fluent with an ever wider variety of spelling patterns, becomes able to tackle more complex texts independently, knows how to seek help from a dictionary or an adult with difficult words or ideas, writes a wide array of text-types increasingly conventionally and with ever greater capacity to revise independently, and infers the meanings of unfamiliar words encountered in otherwise comprehensible text. Of course, literacy growth continues after grade 3 – the capacity to read with different purposes, to learn from reading, to critique the text, to compare and contrast points of view when reading, and in other ways to produce and process complex tests may continue to develop through adulthood. But the skills acquired by third grade (acquired only, of course, if children enjoy home, preschool, and primary grade environments that support these learnings) constitute the firm foundation on which those more complex skills depend.

So How Do We Define Literacy?

The conceptions of literacy and literacy development that guide the work of prominent researchers and educators vary along a number of dimensions, in ways that are often implicit in the thinking and writing of their proponents. To help explicate the nature of the major controversies in the field of literacy development, I list some of those

Table 14.1 Examples of early literacy accomplishments in five domains

Domain	Birth–3	3–4	Kindergarten	Grade 1	Grade 2	Grade 3
Literacy concepts	Recognizes specific books by cover	Distinguishes print from pictures in books	Knows parts of books and their functions	Understands differences among genres, monitors own comprehension	Understands and applies many print conventions (punctuation, capitalization)	Understands and applies print conventions, uses indices, dictionaries, encyclopedias
Phonological awareness	Enjoys rhymes, nonsense words	Attends to beginning sounds and rhymes in words	Can identify and produce sound-based similarities in initial sounds, rhymes	Can blend and segment phonemes in most one-syllable words	Distinguishes regular from irregular spellings, can use sound patterns in writing	Distinguishes regular from irregular spellings, high-frequency from low-frequency pronunciations of spelling patterns
Print recognition	May name a few letters and numbers	Recognizes +/– 10 letters, including those in own name	Recognizes all upper- and lower-case letters	Recognizes all letters, tolerates some variation in font	Starts to use and read cursive, understands simple charts, diagrams, and graphs	Uses and reads increasingly complex charts, diagrams, and graphs
Reading	Labels objects in books	Recognizes some words, e.g. STOP or McDonald's	Reads some words by sight, reads familiar texts using print and pictures	Has a reading vocabulary of 300–500 words, reads simple texts fluently	Comprehends both fiction and nonfiction at grade level, reads independently and with motivation	Can summarize both fiction and nonfiction at grade level, reads independently and with motivation, can distinguish fact from opinion
Writing	Produces letter-like forms and scribbles	"Writes" lists, thank-you notes, etc., as part of play	Produces invented spellings, some conventional spellings	Uses combination of invented and conventional spelling to write independently	Writes in a variety of genres, revises own writing for spelling and mechanics, and for message and response to audience	Produces a variety of written forms, with attention to literary quality and to structure of the text, revises independently

Source: Adapted from National Research Council, 1998.

dimensions, with the caution that these various continua are certainly not independent of one another, and that a different parsing of the variation might be equally defensible.

Componential versus holistic

Literacy can be viewed as the product of an array of component skills, all of which are necessary to high-level performance. For example, phonological awareness, letter knowledge, automaticity in reading letter sequences, and lexical access could be identified as key component reading skills. Holistic thinkers see meaning-making as the central defining feature of good reading, are inclined to think of reading as a single, integrated capacity, and often deplore attention to isolated components in reading instruction or assessment.

Solitary versus social

Literacy can be viewed as an individual cognitive accomplishment, as an activity that is exemplified by "curling up with a book." Alternately, it can be viewed as an essentially interactive, collaborative activity embedded in social purposes, even when the act of reading itself is solitary. The solitary view sees reading and writing as primarily an inside-the-head psycholinguistic process, a process that involves the development of new neural pathways and organizations and that is subject to risk of failure due to factors of anatomy or neural processing. The social view brings in a political dimension – reading skill provides access to power and to knowledge, and failure can result from the unwillingness of those who hold power to share access.

Instructed versus natural

Literacy can be seen as dependent on instruction, with the corollary that quality of instruction is key. This view emphasizes the developmental nature of literacy – the passage of children through successive stages of literacy, in each of which the reading and writing tasks change qualitatively and the role of the instructor has to change accordingly (see Chall, 1996). Alternately, it can be seen as a natural product of growing up in a literate society, easy to acquire without explicit instruction if motivation and opportunities for practice are available. Those who hold the natural view minimize attention to developmental change by attributing equal value to various forms of participation in literacy.

Functional/technical versus transformational/cultural

Literacy can be viewed as a technical, functional accomplishment that simplifies tasks like participation in the workforce, accessing information, or navigating in a strange neighborhood. Functional views tend to focus on print-linked aspects of literacy, like filling in forms and deciphering signs. Alternately, literacy can be viewed as a factor in one's personal and social identity, a source of empowerment and reconstruction of the self, and a force in transforming the practices, rules, and relationships that constitute culture. This view emphasizes the consequences of literacy for ways of talking and thinking.

Singular/coherent versus multiple/varied

For some, the definition of reading is rather simple – it is what one does with a book or newspaper, it is what gets assessed on a high-stakes test. Others emphasize the contrast among, for example, the processes of reading a religious text that has been largely memorized and is meant to be believed literally, of reading a poem with an interpretive stance, of reading a contract with a critical stance, and of reading a bus timetable seeking specific information. In this multiple-literacies view, the variation across literacy tasks is more striking than the similarities among them.

School-focused versus home- and community-focused

For some, literacy tasks engaged in at school constitute the prototype for literacy, whereas others argue that most literacy activities and much literacy learning occur outside school, in the home, in the context of religious observance, daily life tasks, and community involvement.

Two Straw Persons

To understand how these various dimensions define contrasting conceptions of literacy, let us start simply by describing two views of literacy that might be located at the extremes of all these various continua. A group of scholars, including David Barton, James Gee, and Brian Street, have coined the term "The New Literacies" (Barton & Hamilton, 1998; Barton, Hamilton, & Ivanic, 2000; Gee, 1996; Street, 1995, 1999, 2001) in an attempt to emphasize their commitment to a notion of literacy that is social, community-based, culturally defined, varied, and potentially transformational. This view of literacy explicitly rejects a focus on individual skills, downplays the necessity of schooling or formal instruction, and tends to ignore information about development: for example, differences in how novice and expert readers interact with print. It accepts participation in a multi-party literacy event as evidence of being literate, without worrying about disparities in the skill levels or contributions of different individuals. Prototypical literacy events for those who hold this view might include "tagging" (spray-painting signatures on public surfaces), producing political banners, collaborating with friends to figure out a bus timetable, or contributing to an on-line discussion group.

In contrast, literacy as embodied in many of the policies associated with No Child Left Behind is viewed as an instructed skill, accomplished by the child operating individually, as a technical achievement exercised primarily and most crucially in school settings, analyzable into component skills, and unconnected to political or cultural commitments (Reyna, 2004). This is the view of literacy that might lead someone to say, "If you test a child on basic . . . reading skills, and you're 'teaching to the test,' you're teaching . . . reading" (Bush, 2001). It is a view of reading that promotes giving teachers explicit guidance about instruction focused on specific components within the reading process (Moats, 2004), and that operationalizes reading comprehension with tests of forced-choice answers to questions about brief passages. Prototypical literacy events within this view include reading a novel, studying for a test, or making a note to oneself.

Of course, in these descriptions both these positions are presented in a way that is somewhat stereotyped and exaggerated. Probably any reading researcher would insist on modifications and modulations of one of these positions before endorsing it. But it is these more unmodulated versions that often dominate policy and practice decisions, and that form the basis for the sometimes rabid political battles over reading instruction and curriculum design.[2] In the discussion that follows we will refer to the first of these views as the holistic and the second as the componential, though any of the other dimensions that differentiate them could also have been selected as the basis for naming each complex of beliefs.

Accepting these stereotyped descriptions, then, simply as markers for the range of variability in definitions of literacy, we turn to the major goals of this chapter. What are the implications of these varying views of literacy for thinking about young children's literacy accomplishments, and in particular about the nature of individual and group differences in these accomplishments? For deciding which early accomplishments are crucial to later success? For identifying the factors related to the development of literacy in young children, and thus making recommendations about the experiences young children should have, at home and in preschool and elementary classroom settings? And for making decisions about assessing literacy and establishing literacy goals for the society?

The Key Early Literacy and Precursor Skills

Young children, before they have had any formal literacy instruction, display many capacities and skills that can be viewed as directly relevant to their literacy development. Beliefs about exactly which of those capacities are crucial preliteracy skills, and which should be promoted by parents and preschool teachers, are, of course, determined by one's view of the nature of literacy itself.

There is general consensus that early emerging literacy-relevant skills include the capacity to recite the alphabet, to name and print letters, to spell simple words including one's own name, to recognize letters and signs in the environment, to identify books by their titles, and to handle books and other literacy artifacts appropriately (see table 14.1). These sorts of capacities are seen by more holistic thinkers as evidence that children are participating in authentic literacy activities, enacting the literacy practices they see their parents engaging in, or displaying cultural routines their parents value (Teale & Sulzby, 1986). They would, for example, view a child scribbling on a piece of paper, seated next to his mother while she makes a shopping list, as a full participant in a familial literacy practice, and would describe children "pretend reading" a familiar story book as displaying sophisticated literacy skills.

These same capacities are seen by componential thinkers as of varying importance. Certainly naming letters correctly and writing by using memorized or invented spellings are seen as important accomplishments; these reflect two skills that relate directly to later literacy outcomes: letter recognition and phonological analysis (Bond & Dykstra, 1967; see Bowey, 2005, for an extensive review). Reciting the alphabet and reading environmental print are not valued so highly by componential thinkers, as these accomplishments do not predict later literacy outcomes very robustly. The scribblings of the child helping his mom with a shopping list would be analyzed as representing a very early stage of literacy development – one in which the child understands that the graphic symbols which represent speech have unique features, but has not yet incorporated specific knowledge about letter shapes into his or her writing. Pretend reading might be seen as evidence that the child has had extensive book-reading experience (Sulzby, 1985), itself a predictor of good literacy outcomes, but not as offering much evidence about the child's actual literacy skills, because the child is probably using the pictures rather than the print as a guide in the performance.

Componential thinkers identify as crucial one set of skills that holistic thinkers are inclined to downplay – phonological analysis skills, leading to phonemic awareness (Byrne & Fielding-Barnsley, 1989). Phonemic awareness is the understanding that words are made up of smaller sounds, or phonemes. This is a key insight for children who will be learning to read in an alphabetic orthography, since the graphic symbols in such a system mostly represent phonemes. Thus, children with no awareness of phonemes will be puzzled by explanations of how to use print to represent speech. Phonological awareness is seen as one of the key early-emerging literacy-relevant skills, but it is of course a capacity which is rather remote from the construction of meaning that holistic thinkers focus on as the central literacy activity.

Holistic thinkers might, on the other hand, emphasize the importance of a number of accomplishments of "well-read-to" preschoolers that may seem on their surface to have little direct relation to literacy. Such accomplishments include, for example, the use of literary or formal language styles when engaging in pretend reading, or when dictating a text to an adult (Purcell-Gates, 1988, 1991). Other oral language skills likely to be possessed by children who will learn to read easily include academic language skills such as giving formal definitions or telling coherent narratives (Snow, Tabors, & Dickinson, 2001; Tabors, Roach, & Snow, 2001). Such capacities reflect the children's history of participation in a wide array of cultural practices related to literacy, including certain language forms and conventions. Listening to books read aloud, reciting religious texts, or pointing to the word *salad* while ordering a burger from the menu at McDonald's would all be treated as important evidence of emergent literacy by holistic thinkers.

Factors Related to Literacy Outcomes

As hinted above, early emerging capacities that seem conceptually to relate to literacy may not all be equally good as predictors of later literacy outcomes. Meta-analyses of longitudinal studies of literacy development (Scarborough, 1998) make clear that some early emerging skills are highly reliable predictors of later outcomes, whereas others, skills that seem on the face of it to be equally relevant to literacy, simply do not show such robust correlations.

The fact that some skills correlate with later literacy outcomes does not, of course, implicate those skills as the determinants of later literacy outcomes. Take letter knowledge as an example. The ability of 4-year-olds to name letters correlates with their tested second-grade reading scores at a level of about .60. But is that because naming letters is crucial to reading? Clearly not. In Russia, a country with high literacy achievement, young children are not expected to learn to recite the alphabet. In northern Europe (where children in general learn to read quite successfully) teaching young children letter names is avoided, on the theory that the letter names will interfere with the phoneme-value the letter signals. Letter names are typically syllables – the letter B is named *bee*, the letter F is named *eff*, and so on. Such correspondences can help children see sound–letter correspondences when the letter name is by chance homophonic with a segment of the word. For example, children have an easier time identifying the initial sound of *beet* than of *boat*, and recognizing the final sound of *deaf* than of *half* (Treiman, Tincoff, & Richmond-Welty, 1996). But if children used the letter-name strategy exclusively, trying to read by relying on letter names rather than letter sounds, this would cause great problems: *vide* the recollections of García Márquez (2003) about his early theories of orthography: "I had a hard time learning to read. It didn't seem logical to me that, given that the letter *m* was called *eme*, when it was followed by a vowel you were supposed to say *ma* and not *emea*. I couldn't read like that" (p. 112).

Knowing letter names may also contribute directly to reading skill by helping children differentiate and remember letters. Alternately, knowing letter names may simply reflect having had lots of experience with print and with book reading, on the basis of which children have learned many things that help them with reading. So perhaps the letter names simply serve as a proxy for other kinds of learning that are themselves causally related to better reading skills.

One of the most robust long-term predictors of good literacy outcomes that can be measured in early childhood is vocabulary. Children with large oral language vocabularies are very unlikely to have problems learning to read – a finding that renders the huge social class differences in vocabulary size among preschool-aged children (Hart & Risley, 1995) particularly important. The relationship of vocabulary to success in reading comprehension is easy to understand – clearly, it is hard to comprehend texts containing many words one does not know. In some studies vocabulary correlates more strongly with global comprehension than with word-reading measures even in second grade (Muter, Hulme, Snowling, & Stevenson, 2004), but in other studies (Snow, Tabors, Nicholson, & Kurland, 1995), the relationship between vocabulary and word recognition is also quite strong. Again, it is difficult to discern whether first graders with large vocabularies have better literacy skills simply because they come from homes and preschools that have provided richer environments for both language and literacy development, or whether knowing more words has a direct impact on the ease of learning to read. Walley (1993) and Goswami (2001) would argue for the latter claim, suggesting, for example, that phonological awareness is directly enhanced by knowledge of more words, since it provides the opportunity for more precise comparison among the sounds that differentiate phonemically similar words: for example, *hen, pen, ten,* but also *head, peck, tell* and *held, pecked, tent.*

Phonological awareness has been demonstrated to relate to literacy outcomes about as strongly as vocabulary in kindergarten and grade 1 (National Research Council, 1998). Again, the reasons for this seem obvious. The task facing early readers is figuring out, first, that letters represent sounds, and, second, which particular letters represent which particular sounds. That task presupposes that learners have some sense of what sounds are – yet the sounds that can be systematically related to letters are abstract, often unpronounceable, and difficult to think about. This fact differentiates alphabetic orthographies from syllabaries, in which the graphic symbols represent units like *fa, mo,* or *bu* that are relatively stable and psycholinguistically accessible. The capacity to think about phonemes, to recognize that at some level the /b/ sound in the three words *bat, tub,* and *trouble* is the same abstract entity (despite the many differences in the actual articulatory and acoustic features of /b/ in those three positions) is prerequisite to acquiring an understanding of alphabetic systems – in other words, that those three different sounds should all be represented by the letter B. Thus, whether children learn letter–sound correspondence from explicit phonics instruction ("This letter is a B, it makes a /b/ sound, we hear it at the beginning of words like *bat, bell, big, bop,* and *bug*") or from more meaning-focused instruction ("Let's all read together. This book is about *Bob the Big Bad Bug*"), having an understanding about phonemes as isolable units is likely to help. The helpfulness of phonemic awareness to children exposed to initial literacy instruction has led to calls for universal instruction in phonological awareness and considerable attention to phonological awareness within early reading curricula (National Institute of Child Health and Human Development, 2000). Unfortunately, such curricula have led in some cases to the notion that phonological awareness is an end in itself, rather than a stepping stone to better literacy learning. There is no evidence that learners need or benefit from phonological awareness curricula after grade 2; there is evidence that a total of about twenty hours of explicit attention to phonological awareness is sufficient to produce the desired effect in almost all children (Ehri, Nunes, Willows, Valeska Schuster, Yaghoub-Zadeh, & Shanahan, 2001); and there is evidence that supporting children to write with invented or estimated spelling generates phonological awareness as effectively as explicit curricula (Watt, 2001).

A striking and frustrating fact about literacy development is that it is much less likely to proceed in a trouble-free manner for certain large groups of children. Some sources of risk for literacy failure are unsurprising – mental retardation, hearing problems, language disorders, and dyslexia, for example. These individual risk factors should be responded to with extra attention to quality and intensity of literacy instruction.

Other sources of risk include social factors such as poverty, being a non-native speaker of the school language, and being a member of an ethnic or racial minority group

(National Research Council, 1998). Holistic and componential thinkers differ radically in their explanations for the heightened risk of these groups. Holistic thinkers attribute their greater probability of reading failure to political factors, arguing that it reflects the inequitable distribution of resources (nutrition, health care, safe and adequate housing, books, well-prepared teachers, adequately equipped school buildings), or alternately that it reflects the reduced value of literacy skills to members of groups that will not be given access to power even if they achieve well in school. Thus, they argue, improving reading outcomes for all requires a rethinking of power relations in society as a whole. Approaches to reading intervention that focus on providing more structured instruction are dismissed by holistic thinkers as irrelevant or even aligned with an agenda of preventing radical social change (Gee, 1999, 2000).

Componential thinkers are more likely to point out that children growing up in segments of the society more at risk of reading failure have less well-developed skills in key areas, such as understanding the functions of print, recognizing letters, manipulating phonemes, familiarity with the language of books, and rich vocabulary. It is these skill differences, they argue, that generate the risk of failure. Thus, rather than societal actions to redress social inequities (which might well, they would admit, be the source of the skill differences), they argue for direct intervention in the domains of deficit: teach letter names, phonological awareness, and vocabulary, as well as provide experiences with print.

Promoting Literacy Development at Home and in the Classroom

There have been many efforts to mount and evaluate prevention and early intervention programs designed to reduce the risks of poor literacy outcomes associated with poverty and minority status. These programs vary in the age range of the children they target, in the mode of delivery of services, and in sources of funding. Most importantly, though, they differ in the theories that inform them. It is thus, perhaps, instructive to describe examples of a few of these prevention/intervention efforts, from the perspective of their guiding presuppositions about literacy development. In this section I provide brief overviews of four widely disseminated early intervention programs: Early Head Start (EHS), Head Start, Home Instruction for Parents of Preschool Youngsters (HIPPY), and Project EASE. EHS and Head Start are both federally funded US programs, administered under local control but with increasingly stringent performance standards defining their services, and targeted at both children and their families. HIPPY and Project EASE are both programs designed basically to improve mothers' capacities to serve as teachers for their children; HIPPY was originally targeted at younger preschoolers, though it has now been extended to older preschoolers and kindergartners, and EASE was designed originally for kindergartners, but a preschool version is currently being developed as well.

These four interventions are of interest because of what they reveal about the covert or implicit theories of literacy development on which they are based. The original design of HIPPY and the central focus of Project EASE arise out of a componential view of early literacy development, but a componential view in which language skills are identified as the domain in which children at risk for literacy failure most need support and enrichment; print-related skills are included, but given less time than language. Early Head Start is highly convergent with the holistic view that improving familial resources across the board, including parental finances, employment, and health status, should generate improvement in child outcomes. That parent-empowerment model was a strong feature of Head Start programs during their first twenty to thirty years, but more recently the emphasis on particular child-outcomes, on enhanced attention to literacy preparation, and on the role of qualified teachers in Head Start classrooms has shifted the Head Start program toward embodying a componential view of literacy.

Early Head Start

In 1995 as part of the Head Start appropriations bill, the US Congress directed that 5% of Head Start funds be used for a new program targeted at families of infants and toddlers up to the age of 3, and that a randomized trial be launched on a subset of the first programs funded under the EHS vehicle. That study recruited seventeen sites and 3,001 families randomly assigned within site to treatment or control conditions. Data on the children in those families have been collected at child age 14, 24, and 36 months, and again prior to kindergarten entry. In addition, data were collected at those and/or other time points from family members, other care providers, and programs themselves. Because EHS was, like Head Start, charged to improve children's school performance, the child measures included assessments of language and cognition and school-readiness measures at the pre-kindergarten assessment.

Services varied across the programs that participated in the evaluation. Most programs used a case management system to provide a wide array of services to families, including guidance about finding child care, adult education services, medical care, transportation, and employment. However, regular attention to teaching parents about ways to improve children's pre-academic skills was prescribed as part of each home visit, and many programs also provided access to child group care settings designed to ensure growth in domains relevant to school readiness.

The measured child outcomes reflected these emphases on early school-related skills; child scores on measures of cognition and language were higher in the program than the control group (Love et al., 2002). Furthermore, participation in the program was associated with improved parenting practices across a variety of domains, including more stimulation of children's language and learning and less severe punishment strategies. In addition, program families showed higher levels of participation in education or job training during the program (Love et al., 2002).

Head Start

If popularity and continued congressional support were the metric, Head Start would have to be considered the most successful federal program ever launched. During its first forty years, nonetheless, Head Start underwent a couple of periods of dramatic change.

The first such period was close to its beginning. Head Start was founded with rather unrealistic expectations concerning the size of the effect that could be expected from relatively short-term, focused, and low-cost programs. It grew quickly in its early few years from a summer program focused on child learning to a year-round program that targeted health, nutrition, parent and community involvement as well as education. Some argued, in fact, that in this early period education was neglected in favor of all the other components, and that Head Start classrooms paid insufficient attention to providing the basis for literacy learning in kindergarten. For example, the emphasis on parental and community involvement was implemented by hiring many Head Start parents to work in the programs – with the result that the educational services being provided were not professional or even in many cases very enriched beyond what children would have received at home (see Love, Tarullo, Raikes, & Chazan-Cohen, this volume; Richmond & Ayoub, 1993; and Sigel, 2004).

The guidance provided to Head Start under the Bush administration, though, and the provisions of Early Reading First legislation shifted those priorities rather abruptly. Starting in 2003, Head Start programs were required to meet higher standards for the proportion of classrooms with qualified (professionally educated) teachers, and to report on their adherence to a variety of performance standards, which included standards for child knowledge of letters and other specific skills related to school readiness. The impact on instructional activities within the country's Head Start classrooms is not known, but it is very likely that teachers started spending considerably more time on measurable skills such as reciting the alphabet, counting, and recognizing letters and numbers. So far, this shift of attention has unfortunately not generated impressive increments in the skills of Head Start children (Whitehurst & Storch, 2001).

Interestingly, the enhanced skill focus has alarmed adherents of both views of the nature of literacy. Defenders of holistic views about literacy deplore efforts to teach 4-year-olds literacy skills explicitly, and many componential analysts would point out that emphasizing letter names and phonological awareness at the expense of attention to providing a rich language environment that would support vocabulary growth might be counterproductive (Snow & Páez, 2004).

HIPPY

The HIPPY model was devised first in Israel, as a way of intervening with immigrant groups with limited literacy and educational achievement (Lombard, 1994). It involves direct instruction to mothers about ways of using various toys and literacy materials – providing a rather structured set of activities and a relatively scripted way of interacting. A feature of HIPPY is that the maternal instruction is delivered by mothers from the same social class as the participants; this presumably promotes effective communication, ensures that the activities are not seen as being imposed by a distant group, and also provides newly enrolled mothers with evidence that people just like them learned and enjoyed such activities.

HIPPY has been internationally disseminated as a model for early intervention (Westheimer, 2003). It has been used, for example, in the US with low-income families, in the Netherlands with immigrant families, and in Turkey with rural and low-education mothers. Evaluations in those various settings have shown varied results – quite positive short- and longer-term impacts on children in Israel (Lombard, 1994) and in Turkey (Kagitcibasi, 1999), but no lasting documented effects on child outcomes in the Netherlands (Eldering & Vedder, 1999) and rather mixed and limited effects at various sites where it has been implemented in the US (see Home Instruction for the Parents of Preschool Youngsters, n.d.). The positive effects that have been documented include general performance in school, rather than literacy skills *per se*.

Project EASE

Project EASE was devised by Gail Jordan as a prevention program to improve the literacy outcomes of kindergartners attending schools serving a high proportion of children living in poverty in the White Bear Lake School District in Minnesota. It embodied the principle that the major domain in which parents could help their children was language, and that even low-income parents could be shown ways to engage in longer, lexically richer, and more extended conversations. Jordan devised curricular materials to support the desired types of interactions, invited parents to training sessions, and had kindergarten teachers assign activities for the parents to engage in with their children. A quasi-experimental study of the first implementation of Project EASE showed significant effects on children's language skills, including vocabulary, comprehension, and story telling (Jordan, Porche, & Snow, 2000).

Project EASE has subsequently been implemented in low-income schools in Ohio under the auspices of the Collaborative Language and Literacy Intervention Project. Comparison of participating children with those in similar schools that had not implemented EASE showed impacts on language skills similar to those found by Jordan and colleagues (2000; Porche & Pallante, 2004). An adaptation of the EASE program in Spanish has been implemented in Costa Rican kindergarten classrooms, and has been received with great enthusiasm by parents and children, though results concerning improved child outcomes are not yet available (Rolla San Francisco, Arias, & Villars, 2004).

Summary of insights from four interventions

All four of these interventions are strongly based in theory – but in somewhat different theories about what is the crucial prerequisite to literacy development, and where intervention needs to be targeted. HIPPY, Early Head Start, and Project EASE have also been evaluated using reasonably rigorous quasi-experimental or experimental procedures. The results suggest that HIPPY can work in some settings, and that both EHS and EASE work fairly robustly to improve those aspects of children's skills that they target, though their effect sizes are at best moderate. These programs all are based on a presupposition that effective intervention to reduce risk of literacy failure requires a broad definition of the precursors to literacy success, and requires changing patterns of linguistic and affective interaction as a context for language and literacy facilitation.

Assessing Individuals' Literacy Skills and Evaluating Literacy in Society

Perhaps the most significant source of evidence about one's commitment to a particular view of literacy is that reflected in a decision about how to assess literacy. High-level literacy is a multi-faceted skill, and devising a way to sample behavior that reflects that skill is not straightforward. Furthermore, the complexities of designing assessments lead many of us to draw conclusions from instruments that we know reflect the target domain inadequately.

Ultimately, the issue is that literate individuals are different from individuals with low levels of literacy, or with low involvement in literacy activities, in a wide array of different ways. Some of these are suggested by the findings of a research program showing widespread effects of exposure to print on many domains of knowledge (Stanovich, West, & Harrison, 1995). One ingenious study in this line of work (West, Stanovich, & Mitchell, 1993) compared two groups of adults selected to differ on literacy propensities. The members of the two groups were identified in airport waiting lounges, and were differentiated on the basis of whether they passed their time reading books or not (this study was carried out before the ubiquity of cell telephones eliminated the possibility of reading with comprehension in any public place). The quality of the book was not taken into consideration, so readers of Danielle Steele were as likely to be chosen as readers of William Faulkner. Nonetheless, the "reader group" scored significantly higher than the "nonreader group" on measures of vocabulary, world knowledge, author recognition, magazine recognition, and newspaper recognition. Of course, no one would seriously suggest that recognizing that *Field and Stream* is a real magazine while *Fitness Today* is not should be an acceptable test of literacy. But it does differentiate more from less literate adults.[3]

So what are the recommendations for assessing literacy in young children? One study, an effort to collect descriptive, longitudinal, multi-cohort data on the Head Start population, uses an instrument called FACES (Family and Child Experience Survey; Administration for Children and Families, n.d.). This survey assesses such child capacities as knowledge of letters, print concepts, vocabulary, and simple numerical skills, but it also collects considerable observational and interview data about the children included in the sample. The plans to use a test based on the FACES measure to draw conclusions about the progress of children in Head Start classrooms has been sharply criticized by Meisels, Barnett, Kagan, & Espinosa (2003) for its neglect of child diversity, because it risks narrowing the Head Start curriculum, and because of the time that would be invested in administering the instrument to every Head Start student.

But if one wanted a test to help identify preschoolers who would benefit from intervention or from access to above-average early literacy instruction, what should one use? Clearly, given the expectations of kindergarten teachers, children who do not know letters and who are completely unfamiliar with the notion that words could be classified by rhymes or by beginning sounds may run into trouble. Even more clearly, children who fall far below age expectations for vocabulary and for knowledge about topics of importance in kindergarten curricula (e.g., number, color, shape, botany, family, community, human biology) are less likely to thrive or to benefit from standard kindergarten teaching. These are domains that might well be assessed in a risk-screening assessment.

Coming to a View of Literacy That Can Inform Early Childhood Practitioners

So is there a correct conception of literacy? Clearly, neither of the extreme views presented earlier in this chapter is defensible in its entirety, and yet both those views make some useful claims. In particular, there are insights from both views that offer guidance for the design of optimally supportive environments for young children's literacy development. Let us return to the dimensions on which they differ to review what both positions might contribute to improved literacy practice with young children.

Componential versus holistic

There is considerable research evidence that several different domains of skill relate to literacy outcomes. In other words, children can encounter difficulty in learning to read because of deficits in letter recognition, phonemic awareness, automaticity of word reading, or vocabulary – evidence consistent with the componential view. But it is also clear that the essence of operating literately is the central process of constructing meaning, not simply the operation of the various components. It is also true that instruction should not focus on the components without linking them to the central purpose, comprehension. And the worry that children most at risk of literacy failure are also most likely to be provided print-component-focused instruction that fails to emphasize meaning has considerable basis in reality.

In thinking about the design of programs for young children, selecting components to focus on is key. Focusing a lot of time and attention on the limited-scope components (letter recognition, phonemic awareness) can undermine appropriate attention to the large-scope components (vocabulary, extended discourse, world knowledge) that ultimately will explain a good deal more of the variance in reading outcomes. Thus, in effect, both componential and holistic thinkers would strongly support the use of activities in early childhood classrooms that promote active involvement with meaningful literacy, such as reading books aloud and then talking about them, embedding reading and writing activities in language-rich play, and encouraging children to use mixtures of drawing and unconventional writing to express themselves.

Solitary versus social

Though literacy is ultimately, for the successful reader, an autonomous accomplishment with consequences for psycholinguistic processing and brain development, it remains a social activity for many, and social supports are crucial to its optimal development.

Consider the ubiquity of book discussion groups, the role of peer sociability in the popularity of Harry Potter volumes, the motivation to read associated with the expectation of discussing the topic with someone. Children from well-educated families with plenty of money can encounter difficulties learning to read, and when that happens it usually reflects a specific learning problem – a neurological or psycholinguistic cause. Children from poorly educated families with little money have a high probability of encountering difficulties learning to read, and the reasons for that can clearly be traced to political forces – an unwillingness to invest as much money and expertise in their learning as they need. However, it is possible to promote literacy achievement among the children of the politically powerless, and the best way to do so is to provide excellent, well-structured, and literacy-rich preschool programs, and good, structured, explicit instruction in the primary grades. Young children from homes where literacy experiences have been scarce might benefit especially from participation in preschool classrooms where interactions with books are valued social activities, not simply an opportunity for instruction.

Instructed versus natural

A small percentage of children simply learn to read, without explicit instruction, well before school age (Davidson & Snow, 1995). For such children, growing up in highly literate families, reading is indeed a natural product of development. Most children, though, need some help to figure out how reading works, and it is estimated (National Research Council, 1998) that a higher proportion of children fail to learn to read because they have not had adequate instruction than learn on their own, without instruction. For most children, literacy skills get reorganized many times over the course of development, and children's literacy knowledge changes qualitatively as they move from scribbling and pretend reading, to single-letter invented spellings and recognition of only a few familiar words, to more elaborated invented spellings and effortful decoding of regular words, to fluent writing and reading. Understanding those qualitative shifts in literacy skill is extremely important if preschool and primary teachers are to offer optimal, differentiated instruction and support.

Functional/technical versus transformational/cultural

Literacy skills are a primary predictor of employability and are strongly related to income (Murnane & Levy, 2004), evidence of their functionality. At the same time, learning to read can transform lives, in particular the lives of those who have suffered from the effects of illiteracy in a highly literate society (Jacobson, 2004). This is an issue on which both views of literacy are equally correct. Clearly, literacy involves both the accomplishment of technical, print-related skills and the capacity to learn, to write, and to talk in new ways. An excessive focus on the technical aspects of literacy can impoverish access to language and world knowledge in the educational environments of young children; that is a particular risk for children whose homes provide limited language and literacy stimulation.

Singular/coherent versus multiple/varied

Although different reading tasks call upon different skills and stances, they all require a common set of central skills – recognizing letters, translating print information into phonological information, and accessing meaning of lexical items. Thus, depending on whether one focuses on the decoding that is prerequisite to using texts actively or on the purposeful activity carried out with the text, one could well defend either position.

School-focused versus home- and community-focused

For many children, school is the primary place where they have rich encounters with literacy. For other children, the literacy activities they engage in outside of school are more interesting, more challenging, and more motivating than those available in their school settings. The existence of rich opportunities for literacy engagement outside of school could be exploited to support school learning, but the children whose reading and writing occur mostly in school need particular attention and support.

Conclusion

I have used major disagreements as a frame for understanding research on early literacy development because it is difficult to understand the discourse within the field of reading research without awareness of those disagreements. It is important to point out, though, that some of the virulent disagreements that have dominated the field of reading in previous periods have been resolved by the introduction of evidence into the argument. Thus, for example, arguments about whether reading was a top-down or a bottom-up process were finally settled by findings about the eye movements of skilled readers (see Snow & Juel, 2005), which demonstrated that they fixated on most of the letters on the page. Similarly, many of the points of disagreement noted in this chapter may well be resolved by the progress of research on questions such as what approaches to early intervention for reading difficulties are most effective, or the relative effectiveness of code-focused versus language-focused early literacy instruction for second-language learners and children growing up in poverty.

Notes

1   Even the selection of capacities to focus on in a table like this constitutes a theoretical commitment to a certain view of literacy. I attempt in this section, thus, to select for discussion a fairly wide array of relatively uncontroversial skills.
2   Perhaps the best way to learn about these straw-person positions is to read each side's characterization of the other. See, for example, the exchanges at *http://cars.uth.tmc.edu/debate/*

3   Readers interested in the nature of the debates between the more holistic and the more componential true believers should read Taylor's (1994) commentary on the Stanovich study; those interested in the study of tongue-in-cheek rhetoric should read Stanovich and West's (1994) response.

References

Administration for Children and Families. (n.d.). Head Start Family and Child Experiences Survey (FACES), 1997–2008. Retrieved January 11, 2005, from *http://www.acf.hhs.gov/programs/opre/hs/faces/index.html*

Barton, D. & Hamilton, M. (1998). *Local literacies: Reading and writing in one community.* London/New York: Routledge.

Barton, D., Hamilton, M., & Ivanic, R. (Eds.). (2000). *Situated literacies: Reading and writing in context.* London/New York: Routledge.

Bond, G. L., & Dykstra, R. (1967). The cooperative research program in first-grade reading instruction. *Reading Research Quarterly, 2,* 5–42.

Bowey, J. (2005). Predictors of individual differences in learning to read. In M. Snowling & C. Hulme (Eds.), *The science of reading: A handbook* (pp. 155–172). Oxford: Blackwell.

Bush, G. W. (2001). Message to Congress (Budget outline). Washington, DC. February 27.

Byrne, B., & Fielding-Barnsley, R. (1989). Phonemic awareness and letter knowledge in the child's acquisition of the alphabetic principle. *Journal of Educational Psychology, 81,* 313–321.

Chall, J. S. (1996). *Stages of reading development* (2nd ed.). Fort Worth, TX: Harcourt Brace College Publishers.

Davidson, R. G., & Snow, C. E. (1995). The linguistic environment of early readers. *Journal of Research in Childhood Education, 10,* 5–21.

Ehri, L. C., Nunes, S. R., Willows, D. M., Valeska Schuster, B., Yaghoub-Zadeh, Z., & Shanahan, T. (2001). Phonemic awareness instruction helps children learn to read: Evidence from the National Reading Panel's meta-analysis. *Reading Research Quarterly, 36,* 250–287.

Eldering, L., & Vedder, P. (1999). The Dutch experience with the Home Intervention Program for Preschool Youngsters (HIPPY). In L. Eldering & P. M. Leseman (Eds.), *Effective early education: Cross-cultural perspectives,* (pp. 235–258). New York: Falmer Press.

García Márquez, G. (2003). *Vivir para contarla.* New York: Vintage Books.

Gee, J. P. (1996). *Social linguistics and literacies: Ideology in discourses.* London/Bristol, PA: Taylor & Francis.

Gee, J. P. (1999). Reading and the new literacy studies: Reframing the National Academy of Sciences report on reading. *Journal of Literacy Research, 31,* 355–374.

Gee, J. P. (2000). The limits of reframing: A response to Professor Snow. *Journal of Literacy Research, 32,* 121–128.

Goswami, U. (2001). Early phonological development and the acquisition of literacy. In S. B. Neuman & D. K. Dickinson (Eds.), *Handbook of early literacy research* (pp. 111–125). New York: Guilford Press.

Hart, B., & Risley, T. (1995). *Meaningful differences in the everyday experience of young American children.* Baltimore: Paul H. Brookes.

Home Instruction for the Parents of Preschool Youngsters. (n.d.). HIPPY USA Research Summary. Retrieved January 11, 2005, from *http://www.hippyusa.org/Research/research_summary.html*

Jacobson, E. (2004). *Community building in Japanese adult basic education.* Unpublished doctoral thesis, Harvard Graduate School of Education.

Jordan, G., Porche, M., & Snow, C. (2000). Project EASE: The effect of a family literacy project on kindergarten students' early literacy skills. *Reading Research Quarterly, 45,* 524–546.

Kagitcibasi, C. (1999). Empowering parents and children: The case of the Turkish Early Enrichment Project. In L. Eldering & P. M. Leseman (Eds.), *Effective early education: Cross-cultural perspectives* (pp. 235–258). New York: Falmer Press.

Lombard, A. D. (1994). *Success begins at home: The past, present, and future of the Home Instruction Program for Preschool Youngsters* (2nd ed.). Guilford, CT: Dushkin Publishing Group.

Love, J., Kisker, E., Ross, C., Schoshet, P., Books-Gunn, J., Paulsell, D., Boller, K., Constantine, J., Vogel, C., Fuligni, A., & Brady-Smith, C. (2002). Making a difference in the lives of infants, toddlers, and their families: The impacts of Early Head Start. Princeton, NJ: The Mathematica Policy Research, Inc. Retrieved June 1, 2005 from *http://www.mathematica-mpr.com/publications/pdfs/ehsfinalsumm.pdf*

Meisels, S., Barnett, W. S., Kagan, S. L., & Espinosa, L. M. (2003, February 28). Retrieved on January 11, 2005 from *http://www.fairtest.org/nattest/Head_Start_Letter.html*

Moats, L. (2004). Science, language, and imagination in the professional development of teachers. In P. McCardle & V. Chhabra (Eds.), *The voice of evidence in reading research* (pp. 269–287). Baltimore: Paul H. Brookes.

Murnane, R., & Levy, F. (2004). *The new division of labor: How computers are creating the next job market.* Princeton: Princeton University Press.

Muter, V., Hulme, C., Snowling, M., & Stevenson, J. (2004). Phonemes, rimes, vocabulary, and grammatical skills as foundations of early reading development: Evidence from a longitudinal study. *Developmental Psychology, 40,* 665–681.

National Institute of Child Health and Human Development. (2000). *Report of the National Reading Panel. Teaching children to read: An evidence-based assessment of the scientific research literature on reading and its implications for reading instruction* (NIH Publication No. 00-4769). Washington, DC: US Government Printing Office.

National Research Council. (1998). *Preventing reading difficulties in young children.* Washington, DC: National Academy Press.

Porche, M. V., & Pallante, D. H. (2004, April). Sustained growth: A longitudinal analysis of a kindergarten intervention. In C. S. Snow (Chair), *Research into Practice: A Literacy Research and Intervention Case Study.* Paper presented at the American Educational Research Association Annual Meeting, San Diego.

Purcell-Gates, V. (1991). Ability of well-read-to kindergartners to decontextualize/recontextualize experience into a written-narrative register. *Language and Education: An International Journal, 5,* 177–188.

Purcell-Gates, V. (1988). Lexical and syntactic knowledge of written narrative held by well-read-to kindergarteners and second graders. *Research in the Teaching of English, 22,* 128–160.

Reyna, V. (2004). Why scientific research? The importance of evidence in changing educational practice. In P. McCardle & V. Chhabra (Eds.), *The voice of evidence in reading research* (pp. 47–58). Baltimore: Paul H. Brookes.

Richmond, J., & Ayoub, C. (1993). The evolution of early intervention philosophy. In D. Bryant & M. Graham (Eds.), *Implementing early intervention: From research to best practice* (pp. 1–17). New York: Guilford Press.

Rolla San Francisco, A., Arias, M., & Villars, R. (2004). *Evaluating the impact of different early literacy interventions on low-income Costa Rican kindergartners' academic skills.* Unpublished paper, Amigos del Aprendizaje, San Jose, Costa Rica.

Scarborough, H. S. (1998). Early identification of children at risk for reading disabilities: Phono-logical awareness and some other promising predictors. In K. Shapiro, P. J. Accardo, & A. J. Capute (Eds.), *Specific reading disability: A view of the spectrum* (pp. 77–121). Timonium, MD: York Press.

Sigel, I. (2004). Head Start – Revisiting a historical psychoeducational intervention: A revisionist perspective. In E. Zigler & S. Styfco (Eds.), *The Head Start debates* (pp. 45–60). Baltimore: Paul H. Brookes.

Snow, C. E., & Juel, C. (2005). Teaching children to read: What do we know about how to do it? In M. J. Snowling & C. Hulme (Eds.), *The science of reading: A handbook* (pp. 501–520). Oxford: Blackwell.

Snow, C. E., & Páez. M. (2004). The Head Start Classroom as an oral language environment: What should the performance standards be? In E. Zigler & S. Styfco (Eds.), *The Head Start debates* (pp. 215–244). Baltimore: Paul H. Brookes.

Snow, C. E., Tabors, P. O., & Dickinson, D. K. (2001). Language development in the preschool years. In D. K. Dickinson & P. O. Tabors (Eds.), *Beginning literacy with language* (pp. 1–25). Baltimore: Paul H. Brookes.

Snow, C. E., Tabors, P. O., Nicholson, P., & Kurland, B. (1995) SHELL: Oral language and early literacy skills in kindergarten and first grade children. *Journal of Research in Childhood Education, 10,* 37–48.

Stanovich, K., & West, R. (1994). Reply to Taylor. *Reading Research Quarterly, 29,* 290–291.

Stanovich, K. E., West, R. F., & Harrison, M. R. (1995). Knowledge growth and maintenance across the life span: The role of print exposure. Developmental Psychology, 31, 811–826.

Street, B. V. (1995). *Social literacies: Critical approaches to literacy in development, ethnography, and education.* London/New York: Longman.

Street, B. V. (1999). Literacy and social change: The significance of social context in the develop-ment of literacy programmes. In D. A. Wagner (Ed.), *The future of literacy in a changing world* (rev. ed., pp. 55–72). Cresskill, NJ: Hampton Press.

Street, B. V. (2001). Literacy empowerment in developing societies. In L. Verhoeven & C. Snow (Eds.), *Literacy and motivation* (pp. 291–300). Mahwah, NJ: Lawrence Erlbaum Associates.

Sulzby, E. (1985). Children's emergent reading of favorite storybooks: A developmental study. *Reading Research Quarterly, 20,* 458–481.

Tabors, P. O., Roach, K. A., & Snow, C. E. (2001). Home language and literacy environment final results. In D. K. Dickinson & P. O. Tabors (Eds.), *Beginning literacy with language* (pp. 111–138). Baltimore: Paul H. Brookes.

Taylor, D. (1994). The trivial pursuit of reading psychology in the "real world": A response to West, Stanovich, and Mitchell. *Reading Research Quarterly, 29,* 276–288.

Teale, W., & Sulzby, E. (1986). *Emergent literacy: Writing and reading.* Norwood, NJ: Ablex Publishing Corporation.

Treiman, R., Tincoff, R., & Richmond-Welty, D. (1996). Letter names help children to connect print and speech. *Developmental Psychology, 32,* 505–514.

Walley, A. (1993). The role of vocabulary development in children's spoken word recognition and segmentation abilities. *Developmental Review, 13,* 286–350.

Watt, H. C. (2001). *Writing in kindergarten teaches phonological awareness and spelling.* Unpublished doctoral dissertation, Harvard Graduate School of Education.

West, R. F., Stanovich, K. E., & Mitchell, H. R. (1993). Reading in the real world and its correlates. *Reading Research Quarterly, 28,* 34–50.

Westheimer, M. (Ed.). (2003*). Parents making a difference: International research on the Home Instruction for Parents of Preschool Youngsters (HIPPY) Program.* Jerusalem: The NCJW Research Institute for Innovation in Education, The Hebrew University.

Whitehurst, G., & Storch, S. A. (2001). The role of family and home in the literacy development of children from low-income backgrounds. In P. R. Britto & J. Brooks-Gunn (Eds.), *The role of family literacy environments in promoting young children's emerging literacy skills* (pp. 53–71). San Francisco: Jossey-Bass.

PART V

Social, Emotional, and Regulatory Development

15

Getting Along with Others: Social Competence in Early Childhood

Richard A. Fabes, Bridget M. Gaertner, and Tierney K. Popp

Basic and applied scientific interest in young children's social relationships can be traced to an assumption that is inherent in many of the theories that guided the developmental sciences of the twentieth century (Ladd, 1999). The theories of Mead, Freud, Bowlby, Erikson, Sullivan, Piaget, and Kohlberg all emphasize the fact that the nature and quality of children's social interactions have a significant impact on their development. During infancy, these social interactions primarily involve contact with parents, siblings, or adult caregivers. Although peer interactions increase during toddlerhood, it is during early childhood that children's social worlds expand dramatically beyond family interactions. These non-family interactions generally are qualitatively different than those with family members – they are increasingly more likely to involve peers and more likely to be freely chosen rather than necessitated. As a result, the establishment, maintenance, and quality of a child's social relationships are more dependent on the skills, attitudes, and charac-teristics that contribute to the dynamic nature of these relationships than is the case for family relationships. Non-familial interactional partners, especially young peers, are less forgiving of poor social behavior and are less likely to be motivated to interact in the future when poor-quality interactions occur than are family members (Rubin, Bukowski, & Parker, 1998).

Thus, it is during early childhood that the enhanced autonomous functioning of children plays a more critical role in determining the nature of social relationships and the subsequent consequences associated with these. This functioning includes a wide variety of behaviors and features – most of which are subsumed under the rubric of *social competence*. In addition, the increased cognitive, physical, and communicative skills that are gained over the course of early childhood facilitate the growth of a variety of social abilities (Howes, 1987b). As such, the study of children's social competence is a particu-larly important feature of research on social development during early childhood and has received considerable attention (Rose-Krasnor, 1997).

The present chapter reviews what we know about social competence in early child-hood, identifies its correlates, and discusses issues associated with its conceptualization and development during this period of the lifespan. Our focus is on social competence in typically developing young children (for a discussion of social competence in children with disabilities, see Diamond, 2002). Others in this volume touch on many aspects of social competence (see Vandell, Nenide, & Van Winkle and Thompson & Lagattuta).

Definition and Conceptualization of Social Competence

There are a wide variety of definitions of social competence that have been used and there is no consensus as to how it should be defined and/or measured (see Halberstadt, Denham, & Dunsmore, 2001; Rose-Krasnor, 1997; Topping, Bremner, & Holmes, 2000, for reviews). This is true despite the fact that most scholars share a sense of common understanding of the concept of social competence. Most conceptualizations – including ours – focus on the central notion that social competence reflects the degree of effective-ness in social interactions one has with others. There is, however, little specificity in the degree to which scholars agree beyond the general acceptance of the notion that social success is a key quality of social competence.

Despite the lack of a unitary definition of social competence, there are essential features that are generally agreed on that characterize competent social development in early child-hood. Primarily, these include the abilities to interact with others effectively and to develop positive relationships (Rubin et al., 1998). Over the course of early childhood, children should increasingly become able to initiate and maintain relationships with social partners, particularly their peers (Howes, 1987a). Children should become skilled at coordinating and communicating their actions and feelings with those of others, and should evidence more complex levels of play – they progressively engage in greater levels of cooperative and pretend play, and encounter social experiences in both dyadic and group contexts. Participation in these types of interactions requires the ability to enter into play with others, to coordinate one's actions with those of others, and to construct and communicate shared meanings (Howes, 1988). Children should become capable of controlling and adjusting their emotions and actions appropriately during the course of social interaction, and should generally show positive behaviors toward their peers, as well as decreasing negative behaviors such as aggression and withdrawal that may be markers of social problems as they age (Howes, 1987a; Saarni, 1990).

Relationships between children and their social environments are reciprocal and trans-actional (Lytton, 2000). Children may actively seek information, assistance, or interven-tion related to positive social interactions and relationships. Further, children possess a unique set of individual characteristics that they bring to social experiences, and these characteristics evoke particular reactions from their environment that promote and rein-force continued positive social interactions or, alternatively, may exacerbate existing social problems (Anderson, Lytton, & Romney, 1986). Children's characteristics may also influ-ence the attitudes and efforts adults, siblings, and peers adopt in socializing them. Although the evidence is limited, children's characteristics and socialization interact in predicting their adjustment outcomes. For example, maternal behavioral style has been found to moderate the relation between toddler temperament and later social behavior, such that when mothers were controlling and derisive, early inhibition predicted socially reticent behavior in preschool (Rubin, Burgess, & Hastings, 2002). Thus, socially competent children possess characteristics and qualities that affect the nature of their interactions with others. In turn, these interactions affect the skills and qualities that children acquire and retain. As such, it is difficult to tease out cause–effect relations in determining the antecedents and outcomes associated with social competence, but this remains an important and critical question in research on young children's social competence.

For the present purposes, we focus on the general notion that social competence reflects children's abilities to form positive, successful social relationships. Thus, socially competent children are seen playing often with other children and enjoying social interactions, and are sought out by their peers. This conceptualization is broad yet multi-faceted, and has significant implications for how we view both normative and atypical development, as well as the strategies, structures, and policies developed to promote successful social adaptation in children. We also hold the view that early childhood may represent a sensitive period in the development of social competence because it is during this time that most children encounter large groups of peers and other non-family members in social contexts where they are left more on their own to fend, defend, and manage for themselves (Fabes, Hanish, & Martin, 2004). Thus, how children cope with and adapt to the increasing demands on socially competent behavior that occur during early childhood may be particularly critical to subsequent adjustment and development (Fabes, Hanish, & Martin, 2003; Parker & Asher, 1987).

Predictors of Social Competence in Young Children

A prevailing line of inquiry in the study of early social development concerns the predictors of competent social behavior. Variation in children's biological characteristics, most notably their temperaments, may be significantly responsible for individual differences in the processes that support or hinder socially competent behaviors. Direct and indirect socialization by children's social partners also contribute to the development and utilization of these skills during the course of social interactions and the development of relationships.

Temperament

Temperament generally is used to refer to behaviors that are constitutionally based and account for individual differences in behavioral styles from the child's earliest years (Sanson & Hemphill, 2004). These behavioral styles reflect differences in emotional, motoric, and attentional reactivity to stimulation, as well as in patterns of self-regulation (Kagan, 2001; Marshall, Fox, & Henderson, 2000; Sanson, Hemphill, & Smart, 2002), and all of these behaviors have the potential to influence young children's abilities to form positive social relationships. Children who are prone to positive emotions relative to negative emotions, who are appropriately regulated and controlled in their social interactions, and who seek out rather than avoid or withdraw from others are more likely to be socially competent (Biederman et al., 2001; Eisenberg, 2002). Thus, children's temperamental qualities have the potential to affect their social competence.

Eisenberg and Fabes (1992) developed a heuristic model outlining the expected relations of social functioning with certain aspects of temperament. Specifically, they focused on the interaction of emotional intensity with three types of regulation. The types of regulation were characterized as: (a) highly inhibited (children high in behavioral inhibition but low in other types of regulation such as emotion regulation and instrumental coping), (b) under-controlled (children low in emotion regulation and emotion-related behavioral regulation, including the ability to deal instrumentally with the stressful context), and (c) optimally regulated (children high in various modes of adaptive regulation, moderately high in behavioral inhibition but not over-controlled, and flexible in their use of regulatory behavior).

Children who are optimally regulated were predicted to be high in social competence regardless of their level of emotional intensity. In contrast, children low in behavioral regulation, in the ability to cope instrumentally with the environment, and in the ability to regulate emotion were expected to be low in social competence and to be prone to externalizing problem behaviors. Internalizing problem behaviors and low social competence were expected to be predicted by the combination of high emotional intensity with low emotional regulation, low instrumental coping, and high levels of behavioral over-control. In general, support for these proposed patterns has been found, and this evidence has been shown with both younger and older children and in longitudinal relations over time (e.g., Eisenberg et al., 1997; Fabes et al., 1999), although sometimes these patterns are moderated by the sex of the child (Eisenberg et al., 1993) or by other characteristics of the child or the situation (e.g., how arousing it is; Fabes et al., 1999).

Socio-cognitive skills

As children's social arenas widen during early childhood, the nature of their play and interactions becomes more complex. To traverse the demanding and often unpredictable paths of social interaction, particularly with young peers of limited social abilities, children must learn to detect and interpret information about their partners and about the situation, and to behave and respond in a socially effective manner. This ability is aided by the development of early socio-cognitive skills that allow children to form a better understanding of what others likely are thinking, feeling, intending, and experiencing, as well as their own abilities to control and meet the demands of the situation. In particular, we focus on three important areas of socio-cognitive skills that are thought to underlie competent social behavior – theory of mind, emotional understanding, and social information processing.

The development of an understanding of the inner experiences of others represents an enormous accomplishment in the mental life of young children, and undoubtedly an important expansion of their social competence. Theory of mind research has been dominated by the study of the emergence of an understanding of others' beliefs and desires, which develops as children near school age (Astington & Gopnik, 1991; see Barr, this volume). Young children also develop an increasingly complex understanding of their own and others' mental states, including the recognition of perceptions, knowledge, desires, intentions, and emotions (Meltzoff, Gopnik, & Repacholi, 1999). Such knowledge is valuable in explaining and predicting the behaviors and intentions of others, and may enhance children's ability to engage more optimally in social interactions.

The socio-cognitive advances that emerge during early childhood allow children to view others as mental beings and to realize that their behaviors may be guided and motivated by such internal states. This abstract thinking requires children to utilize their mental understanding and perspective-taking abilities to predict or explain others' behaviors, and these abilities have been positively correlated with a number of aspects of social competence, including sophisticated pretend play behaviors (Maguire & Dunn, 1997), turn-taking in communication with peers (Slomkowski & Dunn, 1996), and positive peer relations and likeability (Watson, Nixon, Wilson, & Capage, 1999).

A growing body of research has also suggested that emotion understanding may be a fundamental component of social competence. Affective knowledge develops greatly over the course of early childhood in terms of young children's ability to notice, identify, and label observed emotional displays, and to predict and explain the emotional reactions of themselves and others (Saarni, 1999; see Thompson & Lagattuta, this volume). They have a greater understanding of the causes, meanings, appropriateness, and implications of emotions for social interaction. Children's ability to recognize and interpret the emotions of others is likely to enhance their ability to respond to them appropriately by helping them to organize and motivate their own behavior in response to their interpretations of their own and others' experiences (Lemerise & Arsenio, 2000). Knowledge of and about emotions may be particularly critical during early childhood as children experience a substantial broadening of their social world. Moreover, interpreting others' emotional states and needs is related to cooperative, empathic, and prosocial responses – responses that are core features of social competence (Eisenberg & Fabes, 1998).

There is much support for the connection between emotion understanding and social competence. Emotion understanding has been related to teacher- and peer-rated social competence (Denham et al., 2003), peer acceptance and likeability (Denham, McKinley, Couchoud, & Holt, 1990), and prosocial behaviors (Denham, 1986). However, young children may not be able to utilize these skills appropriately if they are experiencing intense emotional arousal and dysregulation, a proposition that fits with Eisenberg's and Fabes's (1992) heuristic model. Thus, other internal processes may mediate the links between children's social and emotional skills and their actual social behaviors.

There are several ways in which maladaptive social information processing – or children's appraisals of social cues and ensuing reactions – may lead to enhanced or impaired social competence. For instance, children who exhibit deficient interpersonal skills have problems in the ways in which they appraise the cues in their environment (Crick & Dodge, 1994). Socially competent behavior is contingent on the ability to accurately collect cues from the environment and to interpret and respond to them adaptively. However, maladaptive processing may occur in a variety of ways. Past experience or heightened emotional arousal can influence the ways in which children attend to social cues. Existing schemas, or knowledge bases, may influence the types of cues that children selectively attend to. Living in a hostile environment, for example, may cause children to be hypersensitive to negative cues. Further, emotional arousal may influence the types of stimuli on which children predominately focus their attention when encoding cues.

Given that social information-processing skills are typically developed in response to early experiences, they are best viewed as mediating variables in the relations between early experiences/skills and social competence. To date, most of the empirical research has focused on these relations in older children. However, social information-processing skills do indeed mediate between many early life experiences and social competence in young children. For example, early abuse appears to affect how children process and interpret information in social contexts, which in turn affects subsequent social competence (Dodge, Pettit, Bates, & Valente, 1995).

Communication skills

Language is the primary way in which children form relationships, regulate interactions with others, and make interpersonal contact. Children who have poor language skills may not be able to effectively engage others. Many important social skills are contingent upon receptive and expressive language abilities. The capacity to understand others and to adequately express one's own needs, ideas, and goals often hinges on linguistic competence. Indeed, coordinated pretend play – a hallmark of social competence during the preschool years – requires the ability to communicate shared meanings and representations. Children with enhanced expressive and receptive language ability demonstrate more social competence with their peers (Mendez, Fantuzzo, & Cicchetti, 2002). Alternatively, children who become frustrated by their inability to express themselves may limit their peer interactions or may resort to aggressive, non-verbal solutions to problems. With age, these types of interactions increasingly reflect low levels of social competence. Thus, children who are able to clearly communicate wants and needs – of their own and of others – increasingly are judged to be socially competent.

Children with poor language abilities may not be able to enter into interactions with others as easily or frequently. This decreased ability to interact with others may diminish children's peer acceptance, and lower the likelihood that other children will perceive them as worthwhile conversational and social partners (Brinton & Fujiki, 1993). Additionally, children with language impairments may show problems in conversational skills and social understanding, which may lead to peer rejection. The social interactions of children with specific language impairments look qualitatively different in regard to both frequency and quality of interactions than those of their age-mates with typical language abilities (Craig, 1993). Researchers have also found that children are more likely to initiate interactions with children who have normal language skills and much less likely to engage in interactions with children who have language difficulties (Rice, Sell, & Hadley, 1991). Further, children with specific language impairments engage in less positive interactions with their peers (Craig, 1993), possibly due to their inability to communicate effectively. Thus, both expressive and receptive language skills may have a substantial impact on children's socially competent behaviors.

Socialization Within the Family

As noted previously, much of children's early social experience occurs within the context of the family. As such, parents and siblings are powerful influences on the development of social competence in young children (Dunn, 1983; Maccoby, 1992). Parents deliberately teach their children about social behaviors, interactions, and relationships. Moreover, through more indirect processes, such as the nature of the relationships that children witness and experience within the family, as well as the overall emotional climate of the family, also implicitly demonstrate valued social attitudes and behaviors.

Parent–child interactions

One of the most direct ways in which parents contribute to the social development of their children is by explicitly teaching them social rules and expectations for behavior. This is a common part of everyday parent–child interaction from an early age, and a large body of literature has sought to identify the processes through which children internalize the values and lessons taught and displayed within the family (Maccoby & Martin, 1983). In addition, parents also talk with their young children about peer relationships. These conversations often consist of giving advice, feedback, teaching specific social strategies, and problem solving about children's peer encounters and concerns. This type of "coaching" has unique effects, over and above general parenting style, and has been positively related to peer acceptance and teacher-rated social competence (Mize & Pettit, 1997). Further, parents may also contribute to children's social competence through their facilitation of children's social interactions. Parents are in a position to provide a range of social opportunities and experiences and to structure the nature of these interactions. Parents may take an active role in children's peer interactions by initiating play opportunities or by scaffolding and supporting children's attempts at play engagement or conflict resolution (Ladd & Hart, 1992). Parent involvement may also be relatively less direct, including monitoring and supervising children's play. The importance of a direct parental role in peer relations may diminish over the preschool years as children gain more social experience and are capable of assuming more responsibility for their peer contacts and interactions.

Family relationships

Children are also indirectly introduced and integrated into the social world through their experiences and relationships within the family. Daily interactions between family members provide a wealth of opportunities for children to observe, learn, and practice the interpersonal skills that contribute to successful social relationships. For example, discourse about emotions and other mental states during everyday conversations may significantly contribute to children's emotion language and related socio-cognitive skills that contribute to their social competence (Fabes, Eisenberg, Hanish, & Spinrad, 2001).

Noting and identifying emotions in children and in others, providing information about the causes and meanings of emotional displays and other behaviors, and exploring differences in perspectives and potential responses may increase children's awareness of and sensitivity to the thoughts and feelings of others. In addition to natural conversations, parents may coach their children about emotions, perspectives, and behavioral causes. Maternal reports of disciplinary style that specifically encouraged children's thinking about a victim's feelings after wrongdoing were positively associated with children's performance on a theory of mind task – such as a false belief task (Ruffman, Perner, & Parkin, 1999). Overall, early talk about feelings and the causes of behaviors have consistently predicted children's concurrent and later social and emotional understanding (Dunn, Brown, Slomkowski, Tesla, & Youngblade, 1991).

It has been suggested that interpersonal conflict may be a particularly important context within which young children may make strides in advancing their social understanding (Dunn, 1988). Conflict between parents and children, increasingly common over the early years, may provide a framework for experiencing differing perspectives, for becoming aware of the needs and desires of others, and for learning and testing the strategies and skills that promote social competence. Additionally, the affective nature of conflict is likely to have particular significance for emotional understanding. The ways in which parents acknowledge and balance the simultaneous pursuit of competing goals during disputes with their children has been found to influence how children interact and resolve conflicts with their peers (Crockenberg, Jackson, & Langrock, 1996). Specific strategies that parents utilize during the course of conflict and resolution with their children – particularly explanations, compromise, reasoning, and discussion of emotions – often are used by their children in other social settings (Laible & Thompson, 2002).

Parents may socialize their children's emotions and emotion understanding in many other respects (see Eisenberg, Cumberland, & Spinrad, 1998). Particularly during early childhood, adults play a key role in supporting children's efforts at behavioral and emotional control (Kopp, 1989; see Rothbart, Posner, & Kieras, this volume). Moreover, parental attitudes and beliefs about emotions likely guide their socialization efforts and lead to differences in the way in which children view the appropriateness of emotional reactions, displays, and related behaviors. Specifically, the valence and nature of parental reactions to children's emotions, especially negative emotion, may have important implications for children's social competence (Fabes, Poulin, Eisenberg, & Madden-Derdich, 2003). Punitive and minimizing reactions (e.g., punishing the child or not recognizing the seriousness of the child's distress) have been found to be remarkably detrimental, and have been linked with regulation difficulties, poor social behaviors, and deficits in emotion understanding in preschoolers (Denham, Mitchell-Copeland, Strandberg, Auerbach, & Blair, 1997; Fabes, Leonard, Kupanoff, & Martin, 2001). Alternatively, more supportive, comforting parental reactions to children's negative emotions have been associated in some studies with positive social behaviors and relationships with peers (Denham et al., 1997; Fabes, Poulin et al., 2003). The relation between parental emotional socialization strategies and children's peer behaviors may also be mediated by children's physiological arousal and regulation capabilities (Eisenberg et al., 1998; Gottman, Katz, & Hooven, 1997).

A further indirect influence on children's social competence is the overall tendency for family members to display and express emotions (Halberstadt, Crisp, & Eaton, 1999). Parental emotional expressiveness may affect children's social competence by influencing children's own emotionality and regulation (Gottman et al., 1997) or by modeling patterns of emotional behavior and reactions that are socially optimal or maladaptive. Indeed, greater levels of observed and reported parental positive expressivity have been linked with children's emotion understanding (Denham, Zoller, & Couchoud, 1994) and social acceptance (Cassidy, Parke, & Braungart, 1992), whereas parental negative expressivity has been associated with lower levels of social competence (Isley, O'Neil, & Parke, 1999).

In addition to these variations in family emotional climate, the overall nature of different relationships within the family may contribute to the development of social competence in children. Attachment theorists propose that the relationship between child and caregiver creates an "internal working model" of the nature of relationships and of the self in relation to others (Bowlby, 1962). These cognitive representations are thought to then generalize to other relationships and guide children's expectations, interpretations, and behaviors in other social situations. Variations in children's attachment histories have been associated with differences in their concurrent and later social competence. Securely attached children exhibit enhanced negative emotion understanding (Laible & Thompson, 1998), improved friendship quality (Kerns, 1994), and positive social behaviors with peers (Bohlin, Hagekull, & Rydell, 2000). Furthermore, modest but significant effect sizes have been reported for children's attachment security and their peer relations (Schneider, Atkinson, & Tardif, 2001). In contrast, parental mental health problems, which are likely to disrupt the parent–child relationship, have been associated with children's behavior problems (Harnish, Dodge, Valente, & the Conduct Problems Prevention Research Group, 1995).

The spousal relationship may also have implications for children's social competence. In particular, marital discord may have a detrimental impact on children's social functioning, although this may be modified by qualities of marital conflict (e.g., frequency, intensity) and resolution (e.g., constructive, destructive). Children's cognitive and emotional interpretations and responses to marital conflict have been hypothesized to mediate the links with their social functioning (Davies & Cummings, 1998; Grych & Fincham, 1990). Witnessing of conflict may chronically heighten emotional arousal in children or may demonstrate hostile or at the very least ineffectual conflict resolution strategies. Hostile, withdrawn, or detached patterns of marital communication have been related to later externalizing and internalizing problems in children (Katz & Woodin, 2002). Alternatively, the effects of marital conflict on children's social competence may be mediated or moderated by alterations in parenting behaviors.

Culture, socialization, and social competence

A central function of family relationships involves the transmission of cultural norms and preferences, which also contribute to differences in what is considered socially competent behavior. For instance, in most western cultures, parents and other adult social agents emphasize children's independence and autonomy as important elements of effective social behavior. Social competence is based on socializing how children are different from one another and on the importance of children asserting themselves. In contrast, the Japanese representation of social competence is based on fitting in with others and the importance of being connected with them (Markus & Kitayama, 1991). Thus, the factors that contribute to positive social competence for American and Japanese children differ according to the cultural values and practices to which they are exposed. Japanese culture values the development of cooperation and the yielding of personal autonomy (White & LeVine, 1986). Unlike western cultures, the Japanese do not view such behaviors as signs of inappropriateness or weakness – they are thought to reflect maturity and social competence. In western cultures, however, independence and autonomy are highly valued and social competence is characterized in part by the degree to which children reflect these valued characteristics.

Sibling relationships

Sibling relationships may present unique socialization experiences related to social competence for young children because they differ in qualitative ways from other types of relationships, and sibling interactions increase greatly during the preschool years (Brown & Dunn, 1992). Although sibling relationships generally involve an age difference between siblings, roles are often more parallel in nature, similar to children's experiences with peers (Dunn, 1983). The content of sibling interactions also differs from parent–child exchanges, with greater emphasis on explaining and understanding others' perspectives and feelings (Brown & Dunn, 1992). However, unlike peer interactions, sibling relationships also include the emotional closeness of a family bond (Dunn, 1996). As evidence of the potentially socializing effects of sibling relationships, the presence of siblings – particularly older and more numerous siblings – as well as the frequency of pretend play with siblings, has been linked with children's earlier and enhanced performance on tasks of social and emotional understanding (Ruffman, Perner, Naito, Parkin, & Clements, 1998). This finding is not always consistent, and it has been argued that the quality of the sibling relationship may be more predictive of children's social skills and competence than the mere presence of siblings in the home (Cutting & Dunn, 1999). Indeed, qualitative differences in the warmth and conflict experienced within the sibling relationship have been linked with children's social and emotional behaviors in the peer setting.

Socialization by Peers

During early childhood, peer interactions increasingly become part of children's social worlds. As such, it is during this period that peers become greater socialization influences than during infancy and toddlerhood. Clearly, the relation between social competence and peer interactions is complex and reciprocal – socially competent children have more positive interactions with peers, and more positive interactions with peers enhance social competence by maintaining and facilitating social contact, social skills, and socialization experiences. Conversely, children with low social competence are at risk for poor peer interactions, rejection, and unacceptance, reducing their opportunities to gain social skills and positive socialization experiences (Ladd, 1999).

Although much is known about the characteristics of popular versus unpopular or rejected/withdrawn children (Asher, Parkhurst, Hymel, & Williams, 1990; Rubin et al., 1998), little is known about the ways in which children socialize behaviors related to social competence. Moreover, the context for learning about socially competent behaviors during early childhood reflects the context in which children encounter the majority of their peers – namely, that peer interactions and experiences occur most often in the context of same-sex interactions, and this sex segregation is one of the most powerful and pervasive developmental social phenomenon known to exist in early childhood (Maccoby, 1990). Sex segregation begins around the age of 3 years and escalates over childhood. Young boys and girls show strong and consistent preferences for same-sex peers over other-sex peers (Fabes, Hanish, & Martin, 2003) and this preference increases through the elementary-school years (Maccoby & Jacklin, 1987). Interestingly, same-sex play partner preferences are primarily child-driven rather than adult-driven. That is, the strongest sex segregation occurs in settings where children are allowed to make their own choices and when adults are not immediately present or involved in children's play (Maccoby, 1990; Maccoby & Jacklin, 1987; Thorne, 2001). Moreover, these preferences are difficult to change. For instance, when teachers provided reinforcement to preschool children for playing with other-sex peers, the amount of cross-sex play increased while the contingency was in effect. When the reinforcement was discontinued, the children quickly returned to baseline levels of segregated play (Serbin, Tonick, & Sternglanz, 1977). Such findings suggest that peer influences, particularly same-sex peer influences, represent important socializing influences for young children's socially competent behavior (Fabes et al., 2004).

The strength of sex segregation has led to cogent speculation about the short- and long-term consequences of playing with girls and boys (Leaper, 1994), but little research has actually addressed this critical issue. Based on the consistency and strength of sex segregation, the idea has been promoted that girls and boys develop within different cultures from which they derive widely different social experiences. Because many aspects of play are different among boys and among girls, the impact that same-sex peer groups have on young boys' and girls' socially competent behavior and skills should be manifested in different ways.

Playing with boys provides different opportunities and experiences than playing with girls. Boys' groups are larger, and they tend to play in more public places with less proximity to, and supervision from, adults than do girls (Fabes, Martin, & Hanish, 2003; Smith & Inder, 1993). Boys' play also tends to be rougher and more active than girls' play, and it more often involves physical contact, fighting, and taunting. Boys quickly establish a hierarchical pecking order, and this order tends to remain stable over time (Maccoby & Jacklin, 1987). In contrast, dominance hierarchies in girls' groups are more fluid and less stable. Girls often emphasize cooperation and verbal interaction among play partners and use enabling forms of communication that promote group harmony.

Compared to boys' groups, girls' groups are more likely to select activities that are adult-structured and that are governed by strict social rules (Leaper, 1994).

The experiences that boys and girls have in their segregated peer groups contribute to many aspects of social competence in both positive and negative ways, and this contribution is likely to be above and beyond the individual difference variables that lead children to initially select themselves into same-sex peer groups (Martin & Fabes, 2001). Experiences gained within boys' and girls' same-sex peer groups foster different behavioral norms and interaction styles that contribute to socially competent behaviors and interactions. Children who violate these norms by engaging in cross-sex behavior may be at risk for low social competence, particularly for boys (Sroufe, Bennett, Englund, & Urban, 1993). Over time, repeated exposure to these different behavioral and motivational norms and interaction styles may promote the development of different skills, attitudes, motives, interests, and behaviors (Leaper, 1994). As such, same-sex peer groups represent a potentially powerful context for socialization for social competence in early childhood, particularly as it applies to development in the early years when peer relationships and peer group dynamics are just forming (Fabes, Hanish, & Martin, 2003).

Interventions for Young Children's Social Competence

Much of the research on early social competence has been fueled by a growing awareness that childhood social experiences and peer relations are linked with a host of short- and long-term adjustment outcomes, including social and behavioral problems, school adaptation, and psychopathology (Buhs & Ladd, 2001; Coie, Terry, Lenox, & Lochman, 1995). Children's social behaviors with peers show remarkable stability from early childhood to school age (Howes, 1983), and thus it is likely that social experiences and opportunities during the early years set children on a trajectory of positive or negative development that will continue over time. Consequently, a growing number of intervention programs have been developed for enhancing social competence in young children who are at risk for or are exhibiting maladaptive social development early in life.

Interventions designed to improve children's social competence during early childhood have focused not only on the promotion of socially acceptable behaviors and appropriate interpersonal skills, but also on the prevention or reduction of aversive or negative behaviors such as aggression and other antisocial conduct. These programs have utilized a variety of methods, differing in goals, intensity, and comprehensiveness. Some have targeted children with indicated behavioral problems likely to interfere with positive social interactions and peer relations, whereas others have provided universal (e.g., class-wide) services to all children.

The most common intervention approach is direct training – involving explicit instruction, practice, and reinforcement of relevant social skills, such as emotion understanding, problem solving, and play strategies, or efforts to address children's socio-cognitive orientations and processes. Skills and strategies are taught using various techniques, including discussion, modeling, group activities, coaching, and role playing. Some interventions are designed to be implemented by the teacher and used within the school setting. In these approaches, social competence lessons are incorporated into everyday classroom experiences and interactions. Other programs, particularly those targeting young children who already demonstrate social problems, utilize sessions with trained clinicians (e.g., Webster-Stratton, Reid, & Hammond, 2001b). Social training intervention programs have shown some evidence of success in improving preschoolers' and toddlers' observed social behaviors (Denham & Burton, 1996; Zanolli, Paden, & Cox, 1997) and reducing aggression and behavior problems (Webster-Stratton, Reid, & Hammond, 2001a).

In contrast to individual-level interventions, which are designed to influence children directly, contextual approaches alter aspects of the social environment to generate desired effects in children (Durlak, 1997). Most notably, parent training programs provide caregivers with information and strategies about parenting skills and behaviors (e.g., discipline practices, affective and communicative styles) that support the development of social competence in children (see Webster-Stratton & Reid, this volume). Parent training programs have been fairly successful in improving the behavior of many young children with early conduct problems (e.g., Hartman, Stage, & Webster-Stratton, 2003). In another context, Harrist and Bradley (2003) implemented a successful program aimed at affecting social competence by changing the kindergarten classroom environment – they targeted the class-wide attitudes toward and practice of social exclusion.

Some programs have incorporated both home and school components, offering social skills training, parent training, and family support. Two such programs beginning at the transition to school and designed to prevent the development of antisocial behaviors are First Steps to Success (Golly, Sprague, Walker, Beard, & Gorham, 2000) and Fast Track (Conduct Problems Prevention Research Group, 2002). Both of these programs have demonstrated positive effects on children's social behaviors lasting several years. Similarly, broad interventions such as Head Start also utilize a comprehensive approach that targets children's development in a number of domains in order to promote overall health and well-being, with children's social competence as a significant goal (Raver & Zigler, 1997). In general, sustained, multi-faceted, and multi-component intervention programs appear to be most effective in producing positive outcomes related to social competence in young children as compared to those that target isolated goals. However, examinations of the long-term maintenance of these effects are sorely needed.

In addition, it is important to better understand which children are most at risk for social maladjustment. Typically, children who live in adverse conditions experience multiple stressors, which may interfere with the development of social competence. High levels of family and environmental stress or financial strain may lead to negative parenting practices or home experiences that undermine healthy social development (Linver, Brooks-Gunn, & Kohen, 2002; Schmidt, DeMulder, & Denham, 2002). Indeed, children who benefit most from intervention efforts are often those with the most to gain initially (i.e., those most lacking in social competence) and those facing the highest levels of risk for poor social outcomes (Webster-Stratton et al., 2001b).

Finally, it is difficult to identify emerging social problems until children become integrated into formal group settings, most notably school environments. Whereas interventions directed at social competence are abundant for school-aged children, they are more limited for preschoolers and scant during the toddler years. Moreover, the nature of the interventions shifts with increasing age – from a focus on promotion of positive, socially

competent behaviors in young children to a greater emphasis on the reduction and prevention of socially inappropriate behaviors such as aggression and other behavior problems in older children (August, Realmuto, Hectner, & Bloomquist, 2001). Given the
developmental continuity in social behaviors during early childhood, it is important to
examine the origins of both positive and negative behaviors with very young children and
to intervene in maladaptive processes as early as possible.

Summary and Conclusion

Clearly, many aspects of development during early childhood are relevant to our understanding of how young children come to form smooth and effective relationships with
those outside of their own family. The entrance into preschool and formal schooling
brings about critical changes in the social context and ecology of children's lives, and these
changes increase the demands and stress placed on them for acting and behaving appropriately with others, particularly with their peers.

Researchers of social competence during early childhood have employed a wide variety
of measures and methods. As children move through this age period and develop more
mature socio-cognitive and communicative abilities, they are better able to tell us about
their own and others' social qualities, preferences, and status. However, owing to the
fact that young children are particularly sensitive to demand characteristics and social desirability when questioned about their social behavior with others, careful attention to such
measurement issues is warranted. To fully assess differences in young children's social
competence and peer-related experiences also requires extensive observations of their social
interactions. Thus, there is a critical need for research that examines more intensively the
diverse everyday behaviors and interactions of young children and how these affect social
competence (Ramey & Ramey, 1997). Additionally, there is a critical need for studying the
processes that underlie the transactional dynamics associated with socially competent
interaction. As such, there may be a need to employ more dynamic types of analyses and
conceptualizations of social competence (Martin, Fabes, Hanish, & Hollenstein, in press).

Studies of the antecedents and correlates of social competence, as well as the link of
early experiences to competence, also are important for a better understanding of early
social competence. Inconsistencies in the corpus of research reflect the difficulties in
conceptualizing and measuring social competence in early childhood and in determining
the specific skills and qualities associated with the development of positive social relationships. Thus, it remains unclear how the various aspects of social competence develop
during early childhood and how these affect short- and long-term adjustment. Research
that addresses the multi-dimensional qualities of social competence and how these vary
across diverse contexts is necessary to provide a more integrated and synthesized understanding of its development. Moreover, although we know that cultural processes play a
role in determining socially competent behavior, more research is needed, particularly in
regard to subcultural processes that may contribute to variability within, as well as
between, cultures. What is clear, however, is that the nature of social competence, the
behaviors that reflect it, and the qualities that affect it change dramatically over early

childhood. Given the widening social environments in which young children find themselves, being, doing, and getting along with others are key features of this important developmental period.

.˙.

Note

Support for Richard A. Fabes came from a grant from the National Institute of Child Health and Human Development (1 R01 HD45816-01A1). Tierney K. Popp was supported by an Interdisciplinary Doctoral Training Grant in Early Intervention from the US Department of Education. Bridget M. Gaertner was supported by a Cowden Research Fellowship from the Department of Family and Human Development.

References

Anderson, K. E., Lytton, H., & Romney, D. M. (1986). Mothers' interactions with normal and conduct-disordered boys: Who affects whom? *Developmental Psychology, 22*, 604–609.

Asher, S. R., Parkhurst, J. T., Hymel, S., & Williams, G. A. (1990). Peer rejection and loneliness in childhood. In S. R. Asher & J. D. Coie (Eds.), *Peer rejection in childhood* (pp. 253–273). New York: Cambridge University Press.

Astington, J. W., & Gopnik, A. (1991). Theoretical explanations of children's understanding of the mind. *British Journal of Developmental Psychology, 9*, 7–31.

August, G. J., Realmuto, G. M., Hectner, J. M., & Bloomquist, M. L. (2001). An integrated components preventive intervention for aggressive elementary school children: The Early Risers Program. *Journal of Consulting & Clinical Psychology, 69*, 614–626.

Biederman, J., Hirshfeld-Becker, D. R., Rosenbaum, J. F., Herot, C., Friedman, D., Snidman, N., Kagan, J., & Faraone, S. V. (2001). Further evidence of association between behavioral inhibition and social anxiety in children. *American Journal of Psychiatry, 158*, 1673–1679.

Bohlin, G., Hagekull, B., & Rydell, A. (2000). Attachment and social functioning: A longitudinal study from infancy to middle childhood. *Social Development, 9*, 24–39.

Bowlby, J. (1962). *Attachment and loss: Vol. I. Attachment.* New York: Basic Books.

Brinton, B., & Fujiki, M. (1993). Language, social skills, and socioemotional behavior. Clinical Forum: Language and social skills in the school age population. *Language Speech, and Hearing Services in Schools, 24*, 194–198.

Brown, J. R., & Dunn, J. (1992). Talk with your mother or your sibling? Developmental changes in early family conversations about feelings. *Child Development, 63*, 336–349.

Bush, E. S., & Ladd, G. W. (2001). Peer rejection as an antecedent of young children's school adjustment: An examination of mediating processes. *Child Development, 37*, 550–560.

Cassidy, J., Parke, R. B. L., & Braungart, J. (1992). Family–peer connections: The roles of emotional expressiveness within the family and children's understanding of emotions. *Child Development, 73*, 603–618.

Coie, J., Terry, R., Lenox, K., & Lochman, J. (1995). Childhood peer rejection and aggression as predictors of stable patterns of adolescent disorder. *Development and Psychopathology, 7*, 697–713.

Conduct Problems Prevention Research Group. (2002). The implementation of the Fast Track Program: An example of a large-scale prevention science efficacy trial. *Journal of Abnormal Child Psychology, 30*, 1–17.

Craig, H. K. (1993). Social skills of children with specific language impairment: Peer relationships. *Language, Speech, and Hearing Services in Schools, 24*, 206–215.

Crick, N. R., & Dodge, K. A. (1994). A review and reformulation of social information-processing mechanisms in children's social adjustment. *Psychological Bulletin, 115*, 74–101.

Crockenberg, S., Jackson, S., & Langrock, A. M. (1996). Effects of parenting and gender on children's social competence. In M. Killen (Ed.), *Children's autonomy, social competence, and interactions with adults and other children* (Vol. 73, pp. 41–56). San Francisco: Jossey-Bass.

Cutting, A. J., & Dunn, J. (1999). Theory of mind, emotion understanding, language, and family background: Individual differences and interrelations. *Child Development, 70*, 853–865.

Davies, P. T., & Cummings, E. M. (1998). Exploring children's emotional security as a mediator of the link between marital relations and child adjustment. *Child Development, 69*, 124–139.

Denham, S. A. (1986). Social cognition, prosocial behavior, and emotion in preschoolers: Contextual validation. *Child Development, 57*, 194–201.

Denham, S. A., Blair, K., DeMulder, E., Levitas, J., Sawyer, K., Auerbach-Major, S., & Queenan, P. (2003). Preschool emotional competence: Pathway to social competence? *Child Development, 74*, 238–256.

Denham, S. A., & Burton, R. (1996). A social-emotional intervention for at-risk 4-year-olds. *Journal of School Psychology, 34*, 225–245.

Denham, S. A., McKinley, M., Couchoud, E. A., & Holt, R. (1990). Emotional and behavioral predictors of preschool peer ratings. *Child Development, 61*, 1145–1152.

Denham, S. A., Mitchell-Copeland, J., Strandberg, K., Auerbach, S., & Blair, K. (1997). Parental contributions to preschoolers' emotional competence: Direct and indirect effects. *Motivation and Emotion, 21*, 65–86.

Denham, S. A., Zoller, D., & Couchoud, E. A. (1994). Socialization of preschoolers' emotion understanding. *Developmental Psychology, 30*, 928–936.

Diamond, K. E. (2002). The development of social competence in children with disabilities. In P. K. Smith & C. H. Hart (Eds.), *Blackwell handbook of childhood social development* (pp. 572–587). Malden, MA: Blackwell.

Dodge, K. A., Pettit, G. S., Bates, J. E., & Valente, E. (1995). Social information processing patterns partially mediate the effect of early physical abuse on later conduct problems. *Journal of Abnormal Psychology, 104*, 632–643.

Dunn, J. (1983). Sibling relationships in early childhood. *Child Development, 54*, 787–811.

Dunn, J. (1988). *The beginnings of social understanding.* Cambridge, MA: Harvard University Press.

Dunn, J. (1996). Siblings: The first society. In N. Vanzetti & S. Duck (Eds.), *A lifetime of relationships* (pp. 105–124). Pacific Grove, CA: Brooks/Cole.

Dunn, J., Brown, J., Slomkowski, C., Tesla, C., & Youngblade, D. (1991). Young children's understanding of other people's feelings and beliefs: Individual differences and their antecedents. *Child Development, 62*, 1352–1366.

Durlak, J. A. (1997). *Successful prevention programs for children and adolescents.* New York: Plenum Press.

Eisenberg, N. (2002). Emotion-related regulation and its relation to quality of social functioning. In W. W. Hartup & R. A. Weinberg (Eds.), *The Minnesota Symposium of Child Psychology: Vol. 32. Child psychology in retrospect and prospect* (pp. 133–171). Mahwah, NJ: Erlbaum.

Eisenberg, N., Cumberland, A., & Spinrad, T. L. (1998). Parental socialization of emotion. *Psychological Inquiry, 9*, 241–273.

Eisenberg, N., & Fabes, R. A. (1992). Emotion, regulation, and the development of social competence. In M. S. Clark (Ed.), *Emotion and social behavior* (Vol. 14, pp. 119–150). Newbury Park, CA: Sage.

Eisenberg, N., & Fabes, R. A. (1998). Prosocial development. In W. Damon & N. Eisenberg (Eds.), *Handbook of child psychology: Vol. 3. Social, emotional, and personality development* (pp. 701–778). New York: Wiley.

Eisenberg, N., Fabes, R. A., Bernzweig, J., Karbon, M., Poulin, R., & Hanish, L. (1993). The relations of emotionality and regulation to preschoolers' social skills and sociometric status. *Child Development, 64*, 1418–1438.

Eisenberg, N., Guthrie, I. K., Fabes, R. A., Reiser, M., Murphy, B. C., Holgren, R., Maszk, P., & Losoya, S. (1997). The relations of regulation and emotionality to resiliency and competent social functioning in elementary school children. *Child Development, 68*, 295–311.

Fabes, R. A., Eisenberg, N., Hanish, L., & Spinrad, T. (2001). Preschoolers' spontaneous use of emotion language: Relations to social status. *Journal of Early Education and Development, 12*, 11–17.

Fabes, R. A., Eisenberg, N., Jones, S., Smith, M., Guthrie, I. K., Poulin, R., Shepard, S. A., & Friedman, J. (1999). Regulation, emotionality, and preschoolers' socially competent peer interactions. *Child Development, 70*, 432–442.

Fabes, R. A., Hanish, L. D., & Martin, C. L. (2003). Children at play: The role of peers in understanding the effects of childcare. *Child Development, 74*, 1039–1043.

Fabes, R. A., Hanish, L. D., & Martin, C. L. (2004). The next 50 years: Considering gender as a context for understanding young children's peer relationships. *Merrill-Palmer Quarterly, 50*, 260–273.

Fabes, R. A., Leonard, S. A., Kupanoff, K., & Martin, C. L. (2001). Parental coping with children's negative emotions: Relations with children's emotional and social responding. *Child Development, 72*, 907–920.

Fabes, R. A., Martin, C. L., & Hanish, L. D. (2003). Qualities of young children's same-, other-, and mixed-sex play. *Child Development, 74*, 921–932.

Fabes, R. A., Poulin, R., Eisenberg, N., & Madden-Derdich, D. (2003). The Coping with Negative Emotions Scale: Psychometric properties and relations with social competence. *Marriage & Family Review, 34*, 285–310.

Golly, A., Sprague, J., Walker, H. M., Beard, K., & Gorham, G. (2000). The First Step to Success program: An analysis of outcomes with identical twins across multiple baselines. *Behavioral Disorders, 25*, 170–182.

Gottman, J. M., Katz, L. F., & Hooven, C. (1997). *Meta-emotion: How families communicate emotionally.* Mahwah, NJ: Erlbaum.

Grych, J. H., & Fincham, F. D. (1990). Marital conflict and children's adjustment: A cognitive-contextual framework. *Psychological Bulletin, 108*, 267–290.

Halberstadt, A. G., Crisp, V., & Eaton, K. (1999). Family expressiveness: A retrospective and new directions for research. In P. Philippot, R. S. Feldman, & E. Coats (Eds.), *Social contexts of nonverbal behavior* (pp. 109–155). New York: Cambridge University Press.

Halberstadt, A. G., Denham, S. A., & Dunsmore, J. C. (2001). Affective social competence. *Social Development, 10*, 79–119.

Harnish, J. D., Dodge, K. A., Valente, E., & the Conduct Problems Prevention Research Group. (1995). Mother–child interaction quality as a partial mediator of the roles of maternal depressive symptomatology and socioeconomic status in the development of child behavior problems. *Child Development, 66*, 739–753.

Harrist, A. W., & Bradley, K. D. (2003). "You can't say you can't play": Intervening in the process of social exclusion in the kindergarten classroom. *Early Childhood Research Quarterly, 18*, 185–205.

Hartman, R. R., Stage, S. A., & Webster-Stratton, C. (2003). A growth curve analysis of parent-training outcomes: Examining the influence of child risk factors (inattention, impulsivity, and hyperactivity problems), parental and family risk factors. *Journal of Child Psychology and Psychiatry and Allied Disciplines, 44*, 388–398.

Howes, C. (1983). Patterns of friendship. *Child Development, 54*, 1041–1053.

Howes, C. (1987a). Social competence with peers in young children: Developmental sequences. *Developmental Review, 7*, 252–272.

Howes, C. (1987b). Social competency with peers: Contributions from child care. *Early Childhood Research Quarterly, 2*, 155–167.

Howes, C. (1988). Peer interaction of young children. *Monographs of the Society for Research in Child Development, 53*(1, Serial No. 217).

Isley, S. L., O'Neil, R. C., D., & Parke, R. D. (1999). Parent and child expressed affect and children's social competence: Modeling direct and indirect pathways. *Developmental Psychology, 35*, 547–560.

Kagan, J. (2001). Temperamental contributions to affective and behavioral profiles in childhood. In S. G. Hoffman & P. M. DiBartolo (Eds.), *From social anxiety to social phobia: Multiple perspectives* (pp. 216–234). Needham Heights, MA: Allyn & Bacon.

Katz, L. F., & Woodin, E. M. (2002). Hostility, hostile detachment, and conflict engagement in marriages: Effects on child and family functioning. *Child Development, 73*, 636–651.

Kerns, K. A. (1994). A longitudinal examination of links between mother–child attachments and children's friendships in early childhood. *Journal of Social and Personal Relationships, 11*, 379–381.

Kopp, C. B. (1989). Regulation of distress and negative emotions: A developmental view. *Developmental Psychology, 25*, 343–354.

Ladd, G. W. (1999). Peer relationships and social competence during early and middle childhood. *Annual Review of Psychology, 50*, 333–359.

Ladd, G. W., & Hart, C. H. (1992). Creating informal play opportunities: Are parents' and preschoolers' initiations related to children's competence with peers? *Developmental Psychology, 28*, 1179–1187.

Laible, D., & Thompson, R. (1998). Attachment and emotional understanding in preschool children. *Developmental Psychology, 34*, 1038–1045.

Laible, D., & Thompson, R. (2002). Mother–child conflict in the toddler years: Lessons in emotion, morality, and relationships. *Child Development, 73*, 1187–1203.

Leaper, C. (1994). Exploring the consequences of gender segregation on social relationships. In C. Leaper (Ed.), *Childhood gender segregation: Causes and consequences* (pp. 67–86). San Francisco: Jossey-Bass.

Lemerise, E., & Arsenio, W. (2000). An integrated model of emotion processes and cognition in social information processing. *Child Development, 71*, 107–118.

Linver, M. R., Brooks-Gunn, J., & Kohen, D. E. (2002). Family processes as pathways from income to young children's development. *Developmental Psychology, 38*, 719–734.

Lytton, H. (2000). Toward a model of family-environmental and child-biological influences on development. *Developmental Review, 20*, 150–179.

Maccoby, E. E. (1990). Gender as a social category. In S. Chess & M. E. Hertzig (Eds.), *Annual progress in child psychiatry and child development* (pp. 127–150). New York: Brunner/Mazel.

Maccoby, E. E. (1992). The role of parents in the socialization of children: An historical overview. *Developmental Psychology, 28*, 1006–1017.

Maccoby, E. E., & Jacklin, C. N. (1987). Gender segregation in childhood. In H. W. Reese (Ed.), *Advances in child development and behavior* (Vol. 20, pp. 239–287). Orlando: Academic Press.

Maccoby, E. E., & Martin, J. A. (1983). Socialization in the context of the family: Parent–child interaction. In P. H. Mussen & E. M. Hetherington (Eds.), *Handbook of child psychology: Vol. 4. Socialization, personality, and social development* (pp. 1–101). New York: Wiley.

Maguire, M. C., & Dunn, J. (1997). Friendships in early childhood, and social understanding. *International Journal of Behavioral Development, 21,* 669–686.

Markus, H. R., & Kitayama, S. (1991). Culture and the self: Implications for cognition, emotion, and motivation. *Psychological Review, 98,* 224–253.

Marshall, P. J., Fox, N. A., & Henderson, H. A. (2000). Temperament as an organizer of development. *Infancy, 1,* 239–244.

Martin, C. L., & Fabes, R. A. (2001). The stability and consequences of young children's same-sex peer interactions. *Developmental Psychology, 37,* 431–446.

Martin, C. L., Fabes, R. A., Hanish, L. D., & Hollenstein, T. (in press). Social dynamics in preschool. *Developmental Review.*

Meltzoff, A. N., Gopnik, A., & Repacholi, B. M. (1999). Toddlers' understanding of intentions, desires and emotions: Explorations of the dark ages. In P. D. Zelazo & J. W. Astington (Eds.), *Developing theories of intention: Social understanding and self-control* (pp. 17–41). Mahwah, NJ: Erlbaum.

Mendez, J., Fantuzzo, J., & Cicchetti, D. (2002). Social competence of low-income African-American preschool children: Multivariate relationships and individual differences. *Child Development, 73,* 1085–1100.

Mize, J., & Pettit, G. S. (1997). Mothers' social coaching, mother–child relationship style, and children's peer competence: Is the medium the message? *Child Development, 68,* 312–332.

Parker, J. G., & Asher, S. R. (1987). Peer relations and later personal adjustment: Are low-accepted children at risk? *Psychological Bulletin, 102,* 357–389.

Ramey, C., & Ramey, S. (1997). *The development of universities and children.* Cambridge, MA: Harvard Project on Schooling and Children.

Raver, C. C., & Zigler, E. F. (1997). Social competence: An untapped dimension in evaluating Head Start's success. *Early Childhood Research Quarterly, 12,* 363–385.

Rice, M. L., Sell, M. A., & Hadley, P. A. (1991). Social interactions of speech- and language-impaired children. *Journal of Speech and Hearing Research, 34,* 1299–1307.

Rose-Krasnor, L. (1997). The nature of social competence: A theoretical review. *Social Development, 6,* 111–135.

Rubin, K. H., Bukowski, W., & Parker, J. G. (1998). Peer interactions, relationships, and groups. In W. Damon & N. Esienberg (Eds.), *Handbook of child psychology: Vol. 3. Personality and social development* (pp. 619–700). New York: Wiley.

Rubin, K. H., Burgess, K. B., & Hastings, P. D. (2002). Stability and social-behavioral consequences of toddlers' inhibited temperament and parenting behaviors. *Child Development, 73,* 483–495.

Ruffman, T., Perner, J., Naito, M., Parkin, L., & Clements, W. (1998). Older (but not younger) siblings facilitate false belief understanding. *Developmental Psychology, 34,* 161–174.

Ruffman, T., Perner, J., & Parkin, L. (1999). How parenting style affects false belief understanding. *Social Development, 8,* 395–411.

Saarni, C. (1990). Emotional competence: How emotions and relationships become integrated. In R. A. Thompson (Ed.), *Socioemotional development* (Vol. 36, pp. 115–182). Lincoln: University of Nebraska Press.

Saarni, C. (1999). *The development of emotional competence.* New York: Guilford Press.

Sanson, A. V., & Hemphill, S. A. (2004). Connections between temperament and social development: A review. *Social Development, 13,* 142–170.

Sanson, A. V., Hemphill, S. A., & Smart, D. (2002). Temperament and social development. In P. K. Smith & C. H. Hart (Eds.), *Handbook of childhood social development* (pp. 97–116). Oxford: Blackwell.

Schmidt, M. A., DeMulder, E. K., & Denham, S. (2002). Kindergarten social-emotional competence: Developmental predictors and psychosocial implications. *Early Child Development & Care*, *172*, 451–462.

Schneider, B. H., Atkinson, L., & Tardif, C. (2001). Child–parent attachment and children's peer relations. *Developmental Psychology*, *37*, 86–100.

Serbin, L. A., Tonick, I. J., & Sternglanz, S. H. (1977). Shaping cooperative cross-sex play. *Child Development*, *48*, 924–929.

Slomkowski, C., & Dunn, J. (1996). Young children's understanding of other people's beliefs and feelings and their connected communication with friends. *Developmental Psychology*, *32*, 441–447.

Smith, A. B., & Inder, P. M. (1993). Social interaction in same and cross gender pre-school peer groups: A participant observation study. *Educational Psychology*, *13*, 29–42.

Sroufe, L. A., Bennett, C., Englund, M., & Urban, J. (1993). The significance of gender boundaries in preadolescence: Contemporary correlates and antecedents of boundary violation and maintenance. *Child Development*, *64*, 455–466.

Thorne, B. (2001). Girls and boys together but mostly apart: Gender arrangement in elementary school. In R. Satow (Ed.), *Gender and social life* (pp. 152–166). New York: Wiley.

Topping, K., Bremner, W., & Holmes, E. A. (2000). Social competence: The social construction of the construct. In R. Bar-On & J. D. A. Parker (Eds.), *The handbook of emotional intelligence* (pp. 28–39). San Francisco: Jossey-Bass.

Watson, A. C., Nixon, C. L., Wilson, A., & Capage, L. (1999). Social interaction skills and theory of mind in young children. *Developmental Psychology*, *35*, 386–391.

Webster-Stratton, C., Reid, J., & Hammond, M. (2001a). Preventing conduct problems, promoting social competence: A parent and teacher training partnership in Head Start. *Journal of Community Psychology*, *30*, 283–302.

Webster-Stratton, C., Reid, J., & Hammond, M. (2001b). Social skills and problem-solving training for children with early-onset conduct problems: Who benefits? *Journal of Child Psychology and Psychiatry and Allied Disciplines*, *42*, 943–952.

White, M., & LeVine, R. A. (1986). What is ii ko (good child)? In H. Stevenson, H. Azuma, & K. Hakuta (Eds.), *Child development and education in Japan* (pp. 55–62). New York: Freeman.

Zanolli, K. M., Paden, P., & Cox, K. (1997). Teaching prosocial behavior to typically developing toddlers. *Journal of Behavioral Education*, *7*, 373–391.

16

Feeling and Understanding: Early Emotional Development

Ross A. Thompson and Kristin H. Lagattuta

Emotional development in early childhood offers a window into the psychological growth of the child. Young children's efforts to comprehend emotions reveal their developing grasp of the workings of the mind and the influence of emotion on personal well-being and social relationships. Their everyday struggles to manage strong feelings, particularly negative emotions, reflect their awareness of the need to regulate intense emotions and to abide by social and cultural conventions. The appearance of self-conscious emotions, such as guilt, pride, and shame, reflects the powerful connection between children's emotional lives and their developing sense of self. Each of these conceptual achievements is intimately connected to everyday family experiences and relationships in which young children learn about emotions, including their causes and consequences. Emotional development thus both contributes to children's growing social competence and derives from their advancing psychological understanding. This is contrary to a theoretical tradition in psychology that regards emotions as disorganizing or inimical to sophisticated thought or behavior.

Contemporary research on early emotional development highlights both the sophistication of young children's thinking about emotion, and the depth and vulnerability of their emotional lives. Children's conceptual understanding of emotions develops early because emotional experiences comprise a salient, powerful, and central force in their everyday lives and relationships. Children learn about emotion in family climates, some of which offer a secure setting for emotion communication and understanding, while others impose emotional challenges that threaten to exceed children's coping capacities and compromise their developing knowledge and skills. Contrary to a tradition that has viewed young children as simple emotion thinkers who lack capacities for the depths of sadness or grief that adults experience, contemporary scholarship highlights that young children have surprisingly complex emotion concepts, and early experiences can, for some, create enduring vulnerability to emotion-related problems in childhood and in the years that follow.

Emotions are among the most biologically basic features of human functioning that are deeply rooted in the developing brain (Panksepp, 1998). At the same time, emotional development reflects the most important conceptual and relational influences in early childhood. Our purpose is to survey the landscape of this expanding research field. We begin by discussing the conceptual foundations of emotional development in infancy and early childhood, describing how children's earliest knowledge about the causes of emotions are based on broader, richer forms of psychological understanding. Recognizing that young children do not achieve these conceptual insights on their own, we then consider how the emotional climate of the family influences children's emotional capacities, understanding, and communication to others. Because one of the signal achievements in early childhood is the development of a sense of self, we consider the appearance of self-referential emotions such as pride, shame, guilt, and embarrassment in a third section, along with children's growing empathic capacities. Finally, we describe recent discoveries in children's ability to regulate their emotions.

Emotion Understanding

Early in infancy, babies convey a surprisingly rich tapestry of emotions, including happiness, sadness, fear, anger, and surprise, that are often accompanied by compelling vocal expressions (Izard, 1991). Anyone who has been around a crying infant, for example, knows the urgency with which caregivers attempt to soothe the baby. During the months and years that follow, children's emotional expressions become increasingly organized to convey a broader variety of more subtle emotional messages (Camras, 2000). One of the most interesting features of emotional development, however, is the growth of emotion understanding. As with the development of emotional expressions, there are surprisingly early and sophisticated achievements in children's comprehension of emotion during infancy and the preschool years.

Infant and toddler years

Critical foundations for children's emotion understanding are formed during the infant and toddler years. Indeed, before children are able to talk about and reflect on emotional experiences, they develop the ability to identify facial and vocal displays of emotion and to recognize how people's emotions are connected to their actions. As a result, infants begin to look to the emotional expressions of caregivers to guide their behavior in unfamiliar situations.

During the first year, infants develop an awareness of how different emotions "look" and "sound." Starting around 5 to 7 months of age, infants can distinguish between facial displays of some negative (sad, mad, afraid) and positive/neutral (happy, surprise) emotions, and they prefer displays in which emotional voices and facial emotion expressions are congruent versus incongruent (Bornstein & Arterberry, 2003; Walker-Andrews, 1997; Walker-Andrews & Dickson, 1997). Remarkably, recent research has shown that even

3½-month-olds can discriminate between facial displays of happiness, sadness, and anger when they are posed by their mothers instead of by strangers (Montague & Walker-Andrews, 2002). Infants as young as 5 months also react differentially to negative and positive emotions conveyed through speech. Young infants respond with positive affect to happy "approval" vocalizations (speech with melodic, exaggerated rise–fall F_o contours) and they express negative affect to angry "prohibition" vocalizations (speech with a sharp, staccato vocal intonation) – even when the utterances are spoken in non-native languages (Fernald, 1996). Although these early emotion concepts are immature relative to older children's and adults' conceptual knowledge, these nascent emotion categories likely enable very young children to more efficiently encode, store, and retrieve emotion-related information, much the same way as any type of category functions.

By 9 to 12 months, infants know that people's emotions are often directed towards objects, people, or events in the environment, and convey useful information about how to respond (Moses, Baldwin, Rosicky, & Tidball, 2001; Phillips, Wellman, & Spelke, 2002). For example, if a mother emotes positively toward an novel object (e.g., an unfamiliar toy), infants are more likely to approach the object, whereas if the mother exhibits fear, the infant is more likely to avoid that object and/or stay close to the mother. This phenomenon is commonly known as "social referencing" (Saarni, Mumme, & Campos, 1998). Interestingly, maternal "anger" expressions often lead to uncertainty in the infant about whether to approach or avoid the object (Barrett, Campos, & Emde, 1996). Not only do infants "socially reference" emotion information in response to another's facial expressions of emotion, but they also do so in response to emotionally expressive vocalizations (Mumme, Fernald, & Herrera, 1996).

This transition to knowing that people's emotions are often directed toward people, objects, or events in the world (e.g., "He likes cats"; "She's mad at her mom") is a watershed in children's emotion understanding and in their developing psychological knowledge more broadly. Indeed, the development of "secondary intersubjectivity" (i.e., sharing knowledge or emotions about objects or people beyond the caregiver–infant dyad; Trevarthen, 1998) is one of the hallmark achievements in children's early understanding of people's mental states – what another person wants, intends, knows, thinks, and feels emotionally (see Baldwin & Moses, 1996; Malle, Moses, & Baldwin, 2001; Wellman & Lagattuta, 2000). Further evidence that 9- to 12-month-olds are becoming increasingly interested in people's emotional evaluations about objects or events is their increased sensitivity to people's eye gaze direction (e.g., Butterworth, 1991), their use of a pointing gesture to call attention to nearby objects (e.g., Woodward & Guajardo, 2002), and their motivation to establish joint attention, or "shared looking," with social partners at an object or event (Adamson & Bakeman, 1991). The absence of these behaviors at this age can, in fact, signal developmental delays that may warrant professional attention. The first birthday also heralds the emergence of toddlers' comprehension of other people as intentional agents who act in planful ways (Tomasello & Rakoczy, 2003).

After several months of this pointing, gesturing, vocalizing, and emoting about objects and people in everyday social interactions, 18-month-olds reveal an entirely new level of emotion understanding. They realize that not everyone reacts the way they do. People can differ in their preferences and emotions (Meltzoff, Gopnik, & Repacholi, 1999). Repacholi and Gopnik (1997) presented 14- and 18-month-olds with two bowls: one containing broccoli, the other, goldfish crackers. Not surprisingly, nearly all children clearly preferred the goldfish crackers. Next, children watched the experimenter facially and verbally express emotions that either agreed with the toddler's preferences (i.e., "match" condition – delight with the goldfish and disgust with the broccoli) or disagreed with the child's preferences ("mismatch" condition – disgust with the goldfish and love of broccoli). The experimenter then extended her hand to the child and said, "I want more, can you give me some more?" Results showed that the 18- but not 14-month-olds reliably gave the experimenter the food she desired in both the match and mismatched condition. In contrast, the 14-month-olds overwhelmingly offered the tasty goldfish crackers – what they, themselves, desired.

Eighteen-month-olds' recognition that people can have different emotional evaluations of the same object coincides with several other advances in young children's emotional and psychological knowledge that we discuss later, including greater interest in and talk about people's mental and emotional states, the emergence of self-awareness and the subsequent development of self-conscious emotions like pride, guilt, and shame, and the development of empathy. Taken together, toddlers have become psychologically minded in a way that heralds the beginnings of deeper forms of emotional understanding.

Preschool years

As preschoolers develop more sophisticated ideas about the causes of emotion, they often focus on the situations that evoke emotion, or how emotions can be caused by *external events* (e.g., falling down, receiving a present, having an argument). Children as young as age 3 to 4 can pair these kinds of familiar situations with appropriate emotional reactions. Interestingly, "happy situations" are the easiest for them to identify (see Denham, 1998, for a review). Harris (1989) argues that young children learn to pair emotions with situations based on their experiences with a "two-part script." If preschoolers are given one part of the script, either the emotion or the situation, they can fill in the other part. For example, young children can easily reason that getting presents make a person happy, and that a person will feel sad if their pet dies. But preschoolers' range of emotion scripts is limited, and they are not very good at matching up more complex emotions that have no distinctive facial expressions, such as guilty, disappointed, relieved, grateful, and jealous (see Harris, Olthof, Terwogt, & Hardman, 1987). This capacity emerges after the preschool years.

Although knowledge about common eliciting situations for basic emotions is an essential foundation for the early development of young children's knowledge about feelings (Denham, 1998), such a "script-like" understanding of emotion falls short in explaining why individual people often have different, and even opposite, emotional reactions to the same event. In order to explain such *person-specific* emotions (e.g., why Mary is sad, but Jill is happy upon seeing a dog), children must understand that specific emotions are elicited by the meaning that events have for individuals in relation to their prior intentions, desires, beliefs, thoughts, and memories. Thus, children's ability to understand the person-specific nature of emotions is critically connected to their developing understanding of people as *psychological* beings with internal mental lives, what is known as a "theory of mind" (see Wellman & Lagattuta, 2000, and Barr, this volume). Indeed, recent research on preschoolers' emotion understanding reveals that early emotion concepts are inter-twined with children's developing understanding about the psychological world.

Starting around 2 to 3 years of age, children develop an understanding that what people *desire* affects how they feel. They recognize that people feel good, for example, when they get what they want and feel bad when they do not (e.g., Wellman & Banerjee, 1991; Wellman & Bartsch, 1988; Yuill, 1984). Wellman and Woolley (1990) showed 2-year-olds a series of vignettes where a character wanted to find a particular object (e.g., a cat). The character either finds what he or she wanted, finds nothing, or finds an attractive substitute (e.g., a bunny). Children were asked to predict whether the person felt happy or sad. Results showed that even 2-year-olds consistently predicted that the person would feel happy if they found the desired object (100% correct predictions), but feel sad if he or she found nothing (91% correct predictions) or found a substitute (72% correct predictions). When 3- to 5-year-olds (and adults) are asked to describe prototypic "happy" or "sad" situations, the large majority of their scenarios describe getting or doing what one desires as the cause of happiness, and not getting or doing what one wants as leading to sadness (Harter & Whitesell, 1989). Importantly, however, 3- to 5-year-olds experience difficulty reasoning about desire–emotion links in situations where a person has a negative desire (e.g., a child wants to hit a classmate with a ball) or when the means for fulfilling a desire is immoral or prohibited (Arsenio & Lover, 1995; Lagattuta, in press; Yuill, 1984; Yuill, Perner, Peerbhoy, & Emde, 1996).

Young children also come to understand that emotions can be influenced by people's knowledge or beliefs about a situation. For example, Wellman and Banerjee (1991) pre-sented 3- and 4-year-olds with stories such as this: "Jeff visited his grandma and when he got to her house he saw that it was purple. He was very surprised." When asked to explain the cause of Jeff's surprise, preschoolers often appealed to the character's beliefs (e.g., "He's surprised because he didn't think it would be purple"). Thus, young children evidence knowledge that the emotion of "surprise" is based on a person not knowing or expecting a certain outcome. Related studies by Harris and his colleagues (e.g., Harris, Johnson, Hutton, Andrews, & Cooke, 1989) have further shown that, starting around the ages of 5 and 6, children appreciate that emotions can even be based on mistaken beliefs about the world. That is, they know that even if Ellie's favorite drink is not in the cup, she will feel happy (before drinking it) if she *thinks* it is there (see also Hadwin & Perner, 1991; Ruffman & Keenan, 1996).

Adult knowledge about the psychological causes of emotions goes beyond just under-standing that people's desires and beliefs about *current* circumstances influence people's emotions. We recognize that emotions are also frequently caused by thinking or being reminded about *past* experiences. In a series of studies, Lagattuta, Wellman, and Flavell (1997) examined developmental changes in children's knowledge about the connections between people's emotions, their thoughts, and their individual life histories. They pre-sented 3- through 6-year-olds with scenarios featuring characters who experience a sad event (e.g., doll broken by circus clown) and then, many days later, start to feel the same negative emotion after seeing a reminder of that past experience (e.g., seeing the clown that broke the doll, the doll's bottle, a photograph of the doll). Children were asked to explain the cause of the characters' current sadness. Results showed that many 3-year-olds, the majority of 4-year-olds, and nearly all 5- and 6-year-olds could explain that a person's emotions were elicited by thinking about the past for at least one story trial (e.g., "She's sad because she remembers her dolly"), with the consistency of these "thinking explanations" increasing significantly over the preschool years. In a separate task, children as young as 3 years demonstrated understanding that changes in thought can cause changes in emotion. That is, they consistently predicted that people who experienced a negative event (e.g., losing a cat) would "feel better" if they thought about a distracting activity (e.g., what snack they were going to eat) and "feel worse" if they thought most about the negative event.

Additional studies by Lagattuta and Wellman (2001) further examined the situations where 3- to 7-year-olds do and do not make such life-historical, mental explanations for emotions. Scenarios varied in whether the event made the target character feel "happy" versus "sad"/"mad," whether or not the target character's current emotion was typical or atypical for the current circumstances (e.g., Anne feels mad after the clown gives her a balloon, versus Anne feels mad after the clown soaks her with a water balloon), and whether or not two people in the same situation experienced the same or different emotions. Results indicated that young children (3- to 5-year-olds) only provided cognitively based emotion explanations for someone who was experiencing a *negative* emotion that *mismatched* a current, typically positive situation (e.g., Anne feels mad after the clown gives her a balloon). Not until the ages of 6 to 7 years did children consistently demonstrate knowledge about the connections between thoughts and emotions in other contexts (e.g., matched or mismatched positive emotions, matched negative emotions). Interestingly, then, although children younger than 7 or 8 rarely suggest mental strategies (e.g., thinking positive thoughts) to feel better or cope in negative situations (Harris, 1989), they do develop early knowledge about how negative thoughts can make a person feel bad even in a positive situation.

Young children's developing psychological and emotional knowledge is reflected not only in their responses to hypothetical story tasks, but also in how they talk about emotions during their everyday conversations. Between the ages of 2 and 5 years, children's receptive and productive vocabulary to describe emotions expands significantly (Bretherton & Beeghly, 1982; Bretherton, Fritz, Zahn-Waxler, & Ridgeway, 1986; Dunn, Bretherton, & Munn, 1987). Children also talk more often about emotions of people besides themselves (Smiley & Huttenlocher, 1989), and comment more frequently about emotions experienced in the past or expected for the future (Kuebli & Fivush, 1992; Lagattuta & Wellman, 2002). Moreover, children's talk about emotions expands beyond simple labels and descriptions (e.g., "He's sad") to focus more on explaining the causes of emotions (e.g., "He's sad because nobody will play with him"), or seeking emotion explanations from others (e.g., "Why is he sad?") (Bretherton & Beeghly, 1982; Dunn & Brown, 1993; Lagattuta & Wellman, 2002). During the same period, children also begin conversing more frequently about mental states, including discussing causal connections between people's internal psychological states and their emotions or behaviors (e.g., "He's sad because he thought he would get a toy, but didn't") (Bartsch & Wellman, 1995; Hickling & Wellman, 2001; Lagattuta & Wellman, 2002). Notably, parents and children more often focus these rich conversations about the causes of emotions, past emotions, and mind–emotion connections on negative as opposed to positive emotions, perhaps because they are more troubling and arousing (see Lagattuta & Wellman, 2002). We will return to the significance of negative emotions in our later section on emotion communication and regulation in the family.

In summary, during the preschool and early grade-school years, children's expanding language skills afford them frequent opportunities to talk about, explain, reflect on, and learn about their own emotional experiences and the feelings of people around them. Between the ages of 3 and 5, children reveal understanding about the situational determinants of emotions. Yet, contrary to previous conclusions that preschoolers are simple "situationists" when it comes to understanding emotion causes, many recent studies indicate that young children achieve remarkably early insights into how people's minds – including their desires, beliefs, and thoughts – can influence their emotional well-being. Moreover, young children not only recognize that emotions are elicited by events or appraisals of the "here and now," but they also understand that current emotions can be meaningfully shaped by people's unique past experiences. Research on parent–child conversations suggests that talk about and reflection on negative emotions may play an especially important role in the development of children's early understanding of emotions.

Emotional Development and Close Relationships

How do young children develop such a sophisticated understanding of emotion? Certainly one reason is that emotional experiences are highly salient events that young children strive to comprehend. Witnessing a sibling's distress or trying to manage fear focuses a child's attention on the causes and consequences of strong feelings. Children are not alone in their efforts to understand emotion, however. Emotional development is significantly shaped by the broader emotional climate of the family (Gottman, Katz, & Hooven, 1997), including how parents and children talk about their own and others' emotional experiences.

The most salient emotional experiences of newborns and young infants often occur during periods of social interaction with a caregiver, such as during feeding, comforting, holding, and playing (Saarni et al., 1998). Beginning in infancy, a parent's sensitive responsiveness to the child's emotional signals (such as crying and smiling) and support during everyday routines and stressful experiences encourage the growth of security and emotional well-being (Cassidy, 1994; Thompson, 1994). Over the course of the first year, infants begin to expect their parents to share their positive feelings and intervene helpfully when they are distressed (Capatides & Bloom, 1993; Thompson, 1998). These kinds of sensitive, responsive transactions and secure parent–child relationships together help regulate developing emotions and psychobiological stress systems. In fact, a toddler's physiological arousal to stressful situations is buffered by the presence of a sensitive parent (Gunnar & Donzella, 2002). In stressful situations with a parent present, toddlers with a secure relationship with the parent did not show elevations in cortisol, while toddlers with an insecure relationship with the parent showed cortisol elevations (Gunnar & Donzella, 2002; see also Gunnar, this volume; Nachmias, Gunnar, Mangelsdorf, Parritz, & Buss, 1996).

One way this buffering occurs is through "social referencing." As earlier noted, infants and toddlers are attuned to the emotional expressions of others, and frequently turn to – or "socially reference" – those they trust for emotional guidance when faced with upsetting, frightening, confusing, or other challenging circumstances. Young children respond to these situations more positively and competently when adults provide reassuring emotional cues (e.g., smiles, soothing words, a relaxed posture) compared to when the emotional signals they receive from parents are negative or ambivalent (see Saarni et al., 1998). Moreover, adults who are sensitive to a toddler's emotional signals also more effectively guide their child's efforts to cope with new challenges or situations (Nachmias et al., 1996). In general, a secure parent–child attachment relationship is associated with enhanced emotion understanding, greater cooperation, less negativity and decreased aggression in close relationships, as well as other indications of positive emotional growth in early childhood (see Thompson, 1999, for a review).

The emotional climate of the home consists not only of how parents respond to a child's emotions, but also how emotion is expressed among family members (Denham, 1998; Eisenberg, Cumberland, & Spinrad, 1998). Parents are salient models of emotional responsiveness to their offspring. By their behavior, they help children define acceptable forms of emotional expression and self-control, including the appropriate emotional responses for specific situations (such as when disagreeing with another). Parents' negative emotions provide particularly salient lessons in how and whether disturbing emotions such as anger are confronted and resolved, as well as the degree to which close relationships are preserved or strained by intense emotional exchanges (Cummings & Davies, 1994). Parents also provide salient examples of when emotions must be masked, muted, or accentuated. These types of parental behaviors foster in children more generalized styles of responding to the emotions of others (e.g., in sympathetic, avoidant, dismissing, denigrating, or other ways) and the capacity to adapt their emotional reactions to widely varying circumstances.

For all of these reasons, the findings of an extensive research literature are unsurprising: children tend to be more positive and exhibit greater emotional well-being in families characterized by positive emotional expressivity and, conversely, are more emotionally negative in family settings saturated with conflict and in which parents respond dismissively or punitively to children's emotional expressions (Denham, 1998; Eisenberg et al., 1998; Halberstadt & Eaton, 2002). In one study, for example, preschoolers who showed high amounts of negative emotionality during free play with peers had parents who responded punitively, harshly, and with distress to the child's negative emotion at home (Fabes, Leonard, Kupanoff, & Martin, 2001). These children were not only negative but were also low in social competence with peers, as independently indexed by teacher reports.

Children learn not only by observing their parents' emotional actions and reactions but also through conversations in which emotion is the central topic or through direct instruction. During their everyday conversations with parents, young children frequently label, describe, ask questions, provide explanations, and learn about the causes and consequences of people's feelings. Not surprisingly, then, parents who discuss emotions more frequently and with greater elaboration have children with more accurate and richer conceptualizations of emotion (Denham, 1998; Denham, Zoller, & Couchoud, 1994; Dunn, 1996; Dunn, Brown, Slomkowski, Tesla, & Youngblade, 1991; Thompson, Laible, & Ontai, 2003).

Parent–child conversations support the development of emotional understanding in many ways. In discussions about past experiences, witnessed events, or while reading stories, parents can help interpret what another person is feeling, clarify the causes of someone's emotions, link emotion in another person to the child's own experience, ask questions of children that further their understanding of the consequences of emotional arousal, and coach children in strategies for managing feelings (Thompson et al., 2003). Parents and children devote considerably more effort to discussing the causes of negative in comparison to positive emotions because negative emotion is conceptually more complex and is also more troubling, and thus there is a stronger inherent urgency to regulate or prevent intense negative feelings (Lagattuta & Wellman, 2002). Some research indicates that parents also talk about emotion differently with daughters than with sons: they use more elaboration and have a greater relational focus in their emotion-related conversations with daughters (Fivush, 1998).

When discussing emotion with their children, parents frequently incorporate the cultural beliefs, moral evaluations, and assumptions about causality that are part of how people think about their feelings in everyday circumstances. These cultural beliefs and values embedded in everyday conversation influence the early development of emotion understanding. Children in western and non-western cultures differ, for example, in their beliefs about whether anger or shame is the more appropriate emotional response to interpersonal difficulty, and whether it is suitable to express negative feelings in such situations (Cole, Bruschi, & Tamang, 2002). As a consequence, children learn about emotion in conversations that link emotion to standards of conduct and social awareness. This likely explains why parental conversational references to feelings are an even more significant predictor of early conscience development than are parents' explicit references to rules (Laible & Thompson, 2000).

Parents also directly coach emotion and emotional self-control in offspring, especially in circumstances when the child's emotional demeanor is important to manage (such as during religious services, birthday parties, or a doctor's visit). More broadly, the general emotional climate of the family defines the daily emotional demands with which young children must cope: how regularly young children encounter another family member with strong feelings (of anger, happiness, sadness, or other emotions), how children's emotional responses are affected by the emotions around them (e.g., feeling anxious in a conflicted family environment), and the sense of emotional security that is either fostered or undermined by the overall emotional quality of family interaction (Cummings & Davies, 1994).

A young child's emotional growth is socialized not only by parent–child interaction but also by encounters with siblings at home and with peers outside the home. Indeed, young children talk about feelings and thoughts more frequently with friends and siblings than they do with their mothers (Brown, Donelan-McCall, & Dunn, 1996), and these conversations contribute to children's developing psychological and emotional understanding (Hughes & Dunn, 1998). Sibling interactions provide unique contexts for promoting the growth of emotion expression and understanding, such as pretend play that permits animated role-taking of feelings and coping strategies (Dunn et al., 1991; Youngblade & Dunn, 1995), sibling conflict that involves negotiating desires and needs with other family members (Dunn & Herrera, 1997), and sibling jealousy that provokes siblings to compete with each other for parental attention and affection (Volling, McElwain, & Miller, 2002). Young children can also observe the causes and consequences of the salient emotions evoked by peer interactions. This is especially important in view of the significance of emotional understanding for social competence (Rubin, Coplan, Nelson, Cheah, & Legace-Seguin, 1999). Emotional understanding with peers enhances the incentives for prosocial behavior and buffers aggressive conduct among preschoolers, contributes to the quality of social skills that elicit peer acceptance or rejection, and fosters the emergence of enduring friendships in early childhood (Dunn, 2004; Rubin et al., 1999). Indeed, because young peers are much less accepting and accommodating social partners than are parents and other adults, peer groups are likely to provide unique incentives for children to learn how to comprehend and respond appropriately to others' feelings (see also Fabes, Gaertner, & Popp, this volume).

These social influences are important because emotion understanding is a foundation for social competence in early childhood. Individual differences in preschoolers' emotional competence – defined as capability in emotional expressiveness, emotion regulation, and emotion knowledge – predict teacher and peer measures of social competence both concurrently and in kindergarten (Denham, Blair, DeMulder, Levitas, Sawyer, Auerbach-Major, & Queenan, 2003). The emergence of individual differences in "emotional competence" (Saarni, 1999) or "affective social competence" (Halberstadt, Denham, & Dunsmore, 2001) in the preschool years is important in shaping children's social skills and dispositions in ways that have implications not only for friendship and peer status but also for academic competence, self-image, and emotional well-being (Thompson & Raikes, in press).

Early Emotional Vulnerability

The importance of the family environment as a laboratory of early emotional development is underscored by the realization that even young children can experience the severity of trauma, depths of sadness and grief, and capacities for uncontrollable anger and aggression that traditionally were viewed as possible only at older ages (Shonkoff & Phillips, 2000). Young children who are witnesses to domestic violence, for example, are more likely to exhibit internalizing symptoms (such as depression and anxiety) and externalizing symptoms (such as aggression) as well as showing signs of post-traumatic stress disorder (Rossman, Bingham, & Emde, 1997; Rossman, Hughes, & Rosenberg, 2000). Comparable symptomatology can be observed in young children who have been maltreated (Cicchetti & Toth, 2000; Macfie, Cicchetti, & Toth, 2001). Young children also exhibit symptomatology of depression (Robinson & Garber, 1995), anxiety disorders (Vasey & Dadds, 2001), conduct and behavioral disorders (Owens & Shaw, 2003; Shaw,

Gilliom, Ingoldsby, & Nagin, 2003), and other serious forms of affective psychopathology. The risk of serious psychological problems increases when children are in threatening or traumatizing circumstances like those described above, but psychological symptomatology certainly is not inevitable, and many children in these situations do not develop serious problems, especially when they have available to them social support and other resources for effective coping.

The emotional climate of the home is often a significant contributor to these emotional vulnerabilities in young children (Thompson & Calkins, 1996; Thompson, Flood, & Goodvin, in press). Children in homes characterized by marital conflict, for example, often seek to re-establish the emotional security they have lost by intervening in parental arguments, monitoring parental moods, and otherwise striving to manage their emotions in a conflicted home environment (Cummings & Davies, 1994; Davies & Forman, 2002). Frequent coercive and negative family interactions sometimes extend beyond the home to antagonistic peer interactions (Reid, Patterson, & Snyder, 2002).

Young children of parents with affective disorders like depression are also at heightened risk of emotional problems because of the caregiver's limited accessibility as a source of emotional support for the child (Goodman & Gotlib, 1999). For example, Dawson and her colleagues showed that infants of depressed mothers were more likely to exhibit affective and neurobiological disturbances when interacting with their mothers as well as with a non-depressed caregiver. As preschoolers, these children continued to exhibit behavioral and brain differences when compared with the offspring of non-depressed mothers or mothers whose depression had remitted (Dawson et al., 2003). Other studies have further shown that harsh parenting is an important predictor of which children will later develop behavioral problems, especially as parenting interacts with the child's temperamental vulnerability (Rubin, Burgess, Dwyer, & Hastings, 2003; Owens & Shaw, 2003; Shaw et al., 2003).

In short, the sensitivity of young children to the family emotional climate is a double-edged sword. In well-functioning families it enhances the development of skills in emotion understanding and self-regulation, but in families torn by parental psychopathology, domestic violence, or other significant disorders, it can contribute to enduring emotional vulnerability.

Although the emotional problems arising in children in these circumstances are not typically self-correcting, they can be remediated through therapeutic efforts emphasizing family assistance, social support to the child, and efforts to help children recover age-appropriate coping skills. For young children exposed to domestic violence, for example, programs that provide parenting support to mothers and that assist young children in comprehending their family experiences have proven beneficial (Graham-Berman & Hughes, 2003).

Emotional Development and the Self

Emotional development in early childhood is deeply related to a child's growing sense of self. As young children develop self-awareness and self-understanding late in the second year and in the third year, their emotional repertoire broadens to encompass self-conscious emotions like pride, shame, guilt, and embarrassment (Barrett, 1998; Lewis, 2000). The indications of developing self-awareness during this period are readily observable (Thompson, 1998). Toddlers begin to recognize their mirror images before the second birthday, revealing an objective awareness of their physical appearance. Between 18 and 36 months, children increasingly refer to themselves verbally ("Andy big!"), ascribe emotions to themselves, describe themselves by gender and by other characteristics or behaviors, assert their competence by doing things for themselves, and become more interested in how they are evaluated by others (see Thompson & Goodvin, 2005, for a review).

The emergence of self-conscious emotions derives from the enhanced self-awareness of the young child. As a result, the simple joy of success becomes accompanied by looking and smiling to an adult and calling attention to the feat (pride), and sadness in the presence of a disapproving adult grows into efforts to avoid the caregiver's approbation (shame) or make amends (guilt). Young children's experience of the self-conscious emotions deepens in the fourth and fifth years with further growth in self-understanding, especially as children begin to attribute psychological characteristics or traits to themselves, such as describing themselves as shy (Eder, 1989).

Self-conscious evaluative emotions like pride, shame, and guilt require not only self-awareness, but also an external standard against which the child's characteristics or performance is evaluated (Thompson, Meyer, & McGinley, 2006). Young children appear to be particularly sensitive to the behavioral expectations of people who matter to them, and may even view these expectations as normative obligations in a manner resembling what Piaget called "moral absolutism" (Thompson, et al., 2006; Wellman & Miller, in press). The young child's search for normative standards of conduct coincides with the salient reactions of parents, whose responses to the successes and failures of their offspring not only directly induce feelings of pride, guilt, or shame, but also cognitively structure the child's understanding of the causes of these emotions (Stipek, 1995). Parents do this by explicitly linking their response to the standards the parent has previously conveyed ("You know better than to hit your sister!"), invoking salient attributions of responsibility ("Why did you hit her?"), and often directly inducing the self-referent evaluation and emotion ("Bad boy!"). Kochanska's research on the development of conscience and guilt has shown that parental reactions to children's behavior as well as the child's personal capacities for self-regulation critically contribute to the growth of the child's "moral self" (e.g., Kochanska, Gross, Lin, & Nichols, 2002).

Parental and personal responses to others' negative feelings also influence the development of empathy in early childhood (Zahn-Waxler, 2000). The sight and sound of another's distress, fear, or anger is a motivationally complex and stressful event for young children because of their limited understanding of its causes and its threats to their personal security. Consequently, young children may respond with sympathetic feelings and prosocial assistance to the upset person, or, alternatively, they may seek personal comfort or ignore, laugh at, or even aggress toward the other person. When adults can assist the children's understanding of the emotions they are witnessing, especially by clarifying causality and responsibility, raw empathic arousal is more likely to become channeled into prosocial versus antisocial initiatives, including admitting culpability or feeling guilt when the child is responsible (Zahn-Waxler & Robinson, 1995).

Another achievement in emotional development during this period also relates to the growth of self-understanding and psychological awareness. At age 4 to 5, when advances in their emerging "theory of mind" enable young children to comprehend how people act on the basis of beliefs that may, or may not, be correct, they begin to appreciate their own capacities for emotional deception. As young as age 4, therefore, they begin to manage their emotional expressions in social situations, using the "display rules" that cause them to feign delight in a disappointing gift, or look nonchalant in the face of teasing (Banerjee, 1997; Cole, 1986). Although it is not until middle childhood that children's understanding of display rules and their functioning flourishes (Jones, Abbey, & Cumberland, 1998; Saarni, 1999), their growing appreciation of the social deception of one's emotional expressions contributes to a broader discovery: one can disguise one's true feelings and thus retain the privacy of emotional experience. In light of how cultural values concerning the self and the social world vary, it is unsurprising that children in western and non-western cultures differ from the age of 6 in their understanding of the social conventions governing the social expression of positive and negative emotions (Cole et al., 2002; Cole & Tamang, 1998). Even within western cultures the display rules conveyed to boys and girls differ. It is more appropriate for girls than for boys, for example, to display feelings of sadness or fear (Fivush, 1998).

Development of Emotion Regulation

During early childhood, competencies in emotion regulation emerge (Cole, Martin, & Dennis, 2004; Eisenberg & Morris, 2002; Thompson, 1994). Emotion regulation consists of the external aids (such as another's comfort) and internal strategies (such as redirecting disturbing thoughts) for managing emotional arousal. Young children have diverse motives for managing their emotions: to feel better in stressful circumstances (such as during family conflict), elicit support (e.g., after a tricycle crash), manage fear and act courageously (such as when confronting a bully), affirm relationships (by managing the frustration of taking turns), comply with social rules (such as remaining quiet in church), and for many other reasons. At the same time that young children are learning to manage the *expression* of emotions by using display rules, therefore, they are also acquiring skills at regulating emotional *arousal* itself.

Initially, parents are primarily responsible for managing the emotions of infants and young children. They do so by directly intervening to soothe a distressed baby, responding appropriately and helpfully to the toddler's emotional signals, regulating the emotional demands of the home and other familiar settings, altering the child's construal of emotionally arousing experiences (such as trips to the dentist or exciting playground rides), and coaching children on social expectations or strategies for emotional management (Thompson, 1990). At the same time, the security and confidence that young children derive from their relationships with caregivers offer support for emotion regulation because the adult's supportive companionship and assistance provide immediate reassurance (Cassidy, 1994; Thompson, 1998). The parent's immediate intervention in a stressful experience and the general security of the parent–child relationship each contribute to helping infants and young children regulate their feelings.

As children grow older, they become more capable of managing emotions for themselves. Besides knowing when and how to seek comfort from an adult, preschoolers can also be observed making active efforts to avoid or ignore emotionally arousing situations, redirecting their attention or activity in more emotionally satisfying ways, substituting new goals for those that have been frustrated, using distraction or reassuring self-talk, seeking further information about challenging situations, and in other ways (see review by Thompson, 1990). Furthermore, as they proceed into middle childhood, children become proficient at enlisting more internally directed, psychological strategies for emotional self-regulation, such as altering their thoughts or attributions of motives. In these ways, skills of emotion self-regulation follow the development of more sophisticated forms of emotional understanding – enlisting children's increased understanding of the situational and mental determinants of emotion.

Like emotional understanding, a child's capacity for emotional self-regulation is critical to social competence and peer acceptance because skills of emotional self-control are necessary for managing aggressive impulses, responding appropriately to peers' feelings, maintaining friendship, and cooperating with a group (Rubin et al., 1999). Emotional self-regulation is also important for academic success because capacities to follow instructions, focus attention, and cooperate with teachers and peers in a classroom require managing feelings and behaviors (Thompson & Raikes, in press). In one study with socio-economically disadvantaged preschool boys, for example, Gilliom and colleagues found that children's emotion regulation strategies during a frustrating task at age 3½ – such as shifting attention away from the sources of frustration or seeking information about the situation – predicted children's cooperativeness and externalizing behavior at school age (Gilliom, Shaw, Beck, Schonberg, & Lukon, 2002). Conclusions such as these underscore the significance of the emotional skills that children acquire in early childhood for understanding and managing their emotions in multiple contexts.

Conclusion

Emotional development is intimately connected to the most fundamental facets of psychological growth in early childhood. Young children's developing understanding of the causes and consequences of emotion is related to their broader comprehension of how people's desires, needs, thoughts, and intentions affect behavior. Young children's capacities to interpret and respond adaptively to emotions are also deeply tied to their experience in family relationships that socialize emotional experience in complex ways. Their experience of self-conscious emotions, together with their developing capacities for empathy and their growing understanding of display rules, are each related to a young child's unfolding self-understanding. As young children develop emotional capacities and become increasingly aware of the causes and consequences of emotional experiences, their skills of emotional self-regulation emerge, built on the incentives for emotional self-control found in close relationships.

Because emotional growth is intimately related to the most psychologically constructive features of early development, individual differences in emotional development index
many of the child's broader psychological competencies. When the emotional climate of
the home is troubled, as we have noted, children reveal these difficulties in affective
problems or difficulties in emotional self-control. Thus, even very young children can
experience the peaks of emotional delight as well as the depths of intense fear, anxiety,
and depression. High levels of emotional negativity in the family not only create emotional vulnerabilities for young children but also can jeopardize their ability to form
successful social relationships outside of the home. Children who are frequently rejected
or disliked by their peers, for example, often exhibit deficiencies in their capacities to
appropriately "read" and respond to the feelings of other children. For these reasons,
understanding better the bases of individual differences in early emotional development
is important not just because of the strong connections between emotional growth and
other facets of psychological growth, but also because emotional disturbances are often
the first and most apparent index of other difficulties in children's lives.

These conclusions, based on current research on early emotional development, are an
important and welcomed contrast to traditional views of emotion in young children,
which have typically emphasized the disorganizing, irrational features of early emotional
experience, and the inability of young children to experience emotion with the depth or
intensity of adults. This growing awareness of the sophistication of young children's
understanding of emotions and of the complexity of feeling that young children are
capable of experiencing, together with the importance of children's close relationships for
emotional growth, mandates vigorous further research in this area.

References

Adamson, L. B., & Bakeman, R. (1991). The development of shared attention during infancy. In
    R. Vasta (Ed.), *Annals of child development* (Vol. 8, pp. 1–41). London: Kingsley.

Arsenio, W., & Lover, A. (1995). Children's conceptions of sociomoral affect: Happy victimizers,
    mixed emotions, and other expectancies. In M. Killen & D. Hart (Eds.), *Morality in everyday
    life: Developmental perspectives* (pp. 87–128). Cambridge: Cambridge University Press.

Baldwin, D. A., & Moses, L. J. (1996). The ontogeny of social information gathering. *Child
    Development, 67*, 1915–1939.

Banerjee, M. (1997). Hidden emotions: Preschoolers' knowledge of appearance–reality and emotion
    display rules. *Social Cognition, 15*, 107–132.

Barrett, K. (1998). The origins of guilt in early childhood. In J. Bybee (Ed.), *Guilt and children*
    (pp. 75–90). San Diego: Academic Press.

Barrett, K., Campos, J. J., & Emde, R. N. (1996). Infants' use of conflicting emotion signals.
    Cognition and Emotion, 10, 113–135.

Bartsch, K., & Wellman, H. (1995). *Children talk about the mind.* Oxford: Oxford University
    Press.

Bornstein, M. H., & Arterberry, M. E. (2003). Recognition, discrimination, and categorization of
    smiling by 5-month-old infants. *Developmental Science, 6*, 585–599.

Bretherton, I., & Beeghly, M. (1982). Talking about internal states: The acquisition of an explicit
    theory of mind. *Developmental Psychology, 18*, 906–921.

Bretherton, I., Fritz, J., Zahn-Waxler, C., & Ridgeway, D. (1986). Learning to talk about emotions: A functionalist perspective. *Child Development, 57,* 529–548.

Brown, J. R., Donelan-McCall, N., & Dunn, J. (1996). Why talk about mental states? The significance of children's conversations with friends, siblings, and mothers. *Child Development, 67,* 836–849.

Butterworth, G. (1991). The ontogeny and phylogeny of joint visual attention. In A. Whiten (Ed.), *Natural theories of mind* (pp. 223–232). Oxford: Blackwell.

Camras, L. A. (2000). Surprise! Facial expressions can be coordinative motor structures. In M. Lewis & I. Granic (Eds.), *Emotion, development, and self-organization* (pp. 100–124). New York: Cambridge University Press.

Capatides, J. B., & Bloom, L. (1993). Underlying processes in the socialization of emotion. In C. Rovee-Collier & L. P. Lipsitt (Eds.), *Advances in infancy research* (Vol. 8, pp. 99–135). Norwood, NJ: Ablex.

Cassidy, J. (1994). Emotion regulation: Influences of attachment relationships. In N. A. Fox (Ed.), *The development of emotion regulation and dysregulation: Biological and behavioral aspects. Monographs of the Society for Research in Child Development, 59*(2–3, Serial No. 240), 228–249.

Cicchetti, D., & Toth, S. L. (2000). Developmental processes in maltreated children. In D. J. Hansen (Ed.), *Nebraska Symposium on Motivation: Vol. 46. Motivation and child maltreatment* (pp. 85–160). Lincoln: University of Nebraska Press.

Cole, P. M. (1986). Children's spontaneous control of facial expression. *Child Development, 57,* 1309–1321.

Cole, P. M., Bruschi, C. J., & Tamang, B. L. (2002). Cultural differences in children's emotional reactions to difficult situations. *Child Development, 73,* 983–996.

Cole, P. M., Martin, S. E., & Dennis, T. A. (2004). Emotion regulation as a scientific construct: Methodological challenges and directions for child development research. *Child Development, 75,* 317–333.

Cole, P. M., & Tamang, B. L. (1998). Nepali children's ideas about emotional displays in hypothetical challenges. *Developmental Psychology, 34,* 640–646.

Cummings, E. M., & Davies, P. (1994). *Children and marital conflict: The impact of family dispute and resolution.* New York: Guilford.

Davies, P. T., & Forman, E. M. (2002). Children's patterns of preserving emotional security in the interparental subsystem. *Child Development, 73,* 1880–1903.

Dawson, G., Ashman, S. B., Panagiotides, H., Hessl, D., Self, J., Yamada, E., & Embry, L. (2003). Preschool outcomes of children of depressed mothers: Role of maternal behavior, contextual risk, and children's brain activity. *Child Development, 74,* 1158–1175.

Denham, S. A. (1998). *Emotional development in young children.* New York: Guilford.

Denham, S. A., Blair, K. A., DeMulder, E., Levitas, J., Sawyer, K., Auerbach-Major, S., & Queenan, P. (2003). Preschool emotional competence: Pathway to social competence. *Child Development, 74,* 238–256.

Denham, S. A., Zoller, D., & Couchoud, E. A. (1994). Socialization of preschoolers' emotion understanding. *Developmental Psychology, 30,* 928–936.

Dunn, J. (1996). The Emanuel Miller Memorial Lecture 1995. Children's relationships: Bridging the divide between cognitive and social development. *Journal of Child Psychology & Psychiatry, 37,* 507–518.

Dunn, J. (2004). *Children's friendships: The beginnings of intimacy.* Oxford: Blackwell.

Dunn, J., Bretherton, I., & Munn, P. (1987). Conversations about feelings between mothers and their young children. *Developmental Psychology, 23,* 132–139.

Dunn, J., & Brown, J. R. (1993). Early conversations about causality: Content, pragmatics, and developmental change. *British Journal of Developmental Psychology, 11,* 107–123.

Dunn, J., Brown, J. R., Slomkowski, C., Tesla, C., & Youngblade, L. (1991). Young children's understanding of other people's feelings and beliefs: Individual differences and their antecedents. *Child Development, 62,* 1352–1366.

Dunn, J., & Herrera, C. (1997). Conflict resolution with friends, siblings, and mothers: A developmental perspective. *Aggressive Behavior, 23,* 343–357.

Eder, R. A. (1989). The emergent personologist: The structure and content of 3½-, 5½-, and 7½-year-olds' concepts of themselves and other persons. *Child Development, 60,* 1218–1228.

Eisenberg, N., Cumberland, A., & Spinrad, T. L. (1998). Parental socialization of emotion. *Psychological Inquiry, 9,* 241–273.

Eisenberg, N., & Morris, A. S. (2002). Children's emotion-related regulation. In R. Kail (Ed.), *Advances in child development and behavior* (Vol. 30, pp. 190–229). San Diego: Academic.

Fabes, R. A., Leonard, S. A., Kupanoff, K., & Martin, C. L. (2001). Parental coping with children's negative emotions: Relations with children's emotional and social responding. *Child Development, 72,* 907–920.

Fernald, A. (1996). Approval and disapproval: Infant responsiveness to vocal affect in familiar and unfamiliar languages. *Child Development, 64,* 657–674.

Fivush, R. (1998). Gendered narratives: Elaboration, structure, and emotion in parent–child reminiscing across the preschool years. In C. P. Thompson & D. J. Herrmann (Eds.), *Autobiographical memory: Theoretical and applied perspectives* (pp. 79–103). Mahwah, NJ: Erlbaum.

Gilliom, M., Shaw, D. S., Beck, J. E., Schonberg, M. A., & Lukon, J. L. (2002). Anger regulation in disadvantaged preschool boys: Strategies, antecedents, and the development of self-control. *Developmental Psychology, 38,* 222–235.

Goodman, S. H., & Gotlib, I. H. (1999). Risk for psychopathology in the children of depressed mothers: A developmental model for understanding mechanisms of transmission. *Psychological Review, 106,* 458–490.

Gottman, J. M., Katz, L. F., & Hooven, C. (1997). *Meta-emotion: How families communicate emotionally.* Mahwah, NJ: Erlbaum.

Graham-Berman, S. A., & Hughes, H. M. (2003). Intervention for children exposed to interparental violence (IPV): Assessment of needs and research priorities. *Clinical Child and Family Psychology Review, 6,* 189–204.

Gunnar, M. R., & Donzella, B. (2002). Social regulation of the cortisol levels in early human development. *Psychoneuroendocrinology, 27,* 199–220.

Hadwin, J., & Perner, J. (1991). Pleased and surprised: Children's cognitive theory of emotion. *British Journal of Developmental Psychology, 9,* 214–234.

Halberstadt, A. G., Denham, S. A., & Dunsmore, J. C. (2001). Affective social competence. *Social Development, 10,* 79–119.

Halberstadt, A. G., & Eaton, K. L. (2002). A meta-analysis of family expressiveness and children's emotion expressiveness and understanding. *Marriage & Family Review, 34,* 35–62.

Harris, P. L. (1989). *Children and emotion: The development of psychological understanding.* Oxford: Blackwell.

Harris, P. L., Johnson, C. N., Hutton, D., Andrews, G., & Cooke, T. (1989). Young children's theory of mind and emotion. *Cognition and Emotion, 3,* 379–400.

Harris, P. L., Olthof, T., Terwogt, M. M., & Hardman, C. E. (1987). Children's knowledge of the situations that provoke emotion. *International Journal of Behavioral Development, 10,* 319–343.

Harter, S., & Whitesell, N. R. (1989). Developmental changes in children's understanding of single, multiple, and blended emotion concepts. In C. Saarni & P. L. Harris (Eds.), *Children's understanding of emotion* (pp. 81–116). Cambridge: Cambridge University Press.

Hickling, A. K., & Wellman, H. M. (2001). The emergence of children's causal explanations and theories: Evidence from everyday conversation. *Developmental Psychology, 37*, 668–683.

Hughes, C., & Dunn, J. (1998). Understanding mind and emotion: Longitudinal associations with mental-state talk between young friends. *Developmental Psychology, 34*, 1026–1037.

Izard, C. E. (1991). *The psychology of emotions.* New York: Plenum.

Jones, D. C., Abbey, B. B., & Cumberland, A. (1998). The development of display rule knowledge: Linkages with family expressiveness and social competence. *Child Development, 69*, 1209–1222.

Kochanska, G., Gross, J. N., Lin, M. H., & Nichols, K. E. (2002). Guilt in young children: Development, determinants, and relations with a broader system of standards. *Child Development, 73*, 461–482.

Kuebli, J., & Fivush, R. (1992). Gender differences in parent–child conversations about past emotions. *Sex Roles, 27*, 683–698.

Lagattuta, K. H. (2003). When you shouldn't do what you want to do: Young children's understanding of desires, rules, and emotions. *Child Development.*

Lagattuta, K. H., & Wellman, H. M. (2001). Thinking about the past: Young children's knowledge about links between past events, thinking, and emotion. *Child Development, 72*, 82–102.

Lagattuta, K. H., & Wellman, H. M. (2002). Differences in early parent–child conversations about negative versus positive emotions: Implications for the development of emotion understanding. *Developmental Psychology, 38*, 564–580.

Lagattuta, K. H., Wellman, H. M., & Flavell, J. H. (1997). Preschoolers' understanding of the link between thinking and feeling: Cognitive cuing and emotional change. *Child Development, 68*, 1081–1104.

Laible, D. L., & Thompson, R. A. (2000). Mother–child discourse, attachment security, shared positive affect, and early conscience development. *Child Development, 71*, 1424–1440.

Lewis, M. (2000). Self-conscious emotions: Embarrassment, pride, shame, and guilt. In M. Lewis & J. M. Haviland-Jones (Eds.), *Handbook of emotions* (pp. 563–573). New York: Guilford.

Macfie, J., Cicchetti, D., & Toth, S. L. (2001). The development of dissociation in maltreated preschool-aged children. *Development and Psychopathology, 13*, 233–254.

Malle, B. F., Moses, L. J., & Baldwin, D. A. (Eds.). (2001). *Intentions and intentionality: Foundations of social cognition.* Cambridge, MA: MIT Press.

Meltzoff, A. N., Gopnik, A., & Repacholi, B. M. (1999). Toddlers' understanding of intentions, desires and emotions: Explorations of the dark ages. In P. D. Zelazo & J. W. Astington (Eds.), *Developing theories of intention: Social understanding and self-control* (pp. 17–41). Mahwah, NJ: Erlbaum.

Montague, D. P., & Walker-Andrews, A. S. (2002). Mothers, fathers, and infants: The role of person familiarity and parental involvement in infants' perception of emotion expressions. *Child Development, 73*, 1339–1352.

Moses, L. J., Baldwin, D. A., Rosicky, J. G., & Tidball, G. (2001). Evidence for referential understanding in the emotions domain at twelve to eighteen months. *Child Development, 72*, 718–735.

Mumme, D. L., Fernald, A., & Herrera, C. (1996). Infants' responses to facial and vocal emotional signals in a social referencing paradigm. *Child Development, 67*, 3219–3237.

Nachmias, M., Gunnar, M., Mangelsdorf, S., Parritz, R. H., & Buss, K. (1996). Behavioral inhibition and stress reactivity: The moderating role of attachment security. *Child Development, 67*, 508–522.

Owens, E. B., & Shaw, D. S. (2003). Predicting growth curves of externalizing behavior across the preschool years. *Journal of Abnormal Child Psychology, 31*, 575–590.

Panksepp, J. (1998). *Affective neuroscience.* London: Oxford University Press.

Phillips, A. T., Wellman, H. M., & Spelke, E. S. (2002). Infants' ability to connect gaze and emotional expression to intentional action. *Cognition, 85*, 53–78.

Reid, J. B., Patterson, G. R., & Snyder, J. (2002). *Antisocial behavior in children and adolescents: A developmental analysis and model for intervention.* Washington, DC: American Psychological Association.

Repacholi, B., & Gopnik, A. (1997). Early reasoning about desires: Evidence from 14- and 18-month-olds. *Developmental Psychology, 33*, 12–21.

Robinson, N. S., & Garber, J. (1995). Social support and psychopathology across the life span. In D. Cicchetti & D. J. Cohen (Eds.), *Developmental psychopathology: Vol. 2. Risk, disorder, and adaptation* (pp. 162–209). New York: Wiley.

Rossman, B. B. R., Bingham, R. D., & Emde, R. N. (1997). Symptomatology and adaptive functioning for children exposed to normative stressors, dog attack, and parental violence. *Journal of the American Academy of Child & Adolescent Psychiatry, 36*, 1089–1097.

Rossman, B. B. R., Hughes, H. M., & Rosenberg, M. S. (2000). *Children and interparental violence: Impact of exposure.* Philadelphia: Taylor & Francis.

Rubin, K. H., Burgess, K. B., Dwyer, K. M., & Hastings, P. D. (2003). Predicting preschoolers' externalizing behaviors from toddler temperament, conflict, and maternal negativity. *Developmental Psychology, 39*, 164–176.

Rubin, K. H., Coplan, R. J., Nelson, L. J., Cheah, C. S. L., & Lagace-Seguin, D. G. (1999). Peer relationships in childhood. In M. H. Bornstein & M. E. Lamb (Eds.), *Developmental psychology: An advanced textbook* (4th ed., pp. 451–501). Mahwah, NJ: Erlbaum.

Ruffman, T., & Keenan, T. R. (1996). The belief-based emotion of surprise: The case for a lag in understanding relative to false belief. *Developmental Psychology, 32*, 40–49.

Saarni, C. (1999). *The development of emotional competence.* New York: Guilford.

Saarni, C., Mumme, D. L., & Campos, J. J. (1998). Emotional development: Action, communication, and understanding. In N. Eisenberg (Ed.), *Handbook of child psychology: Vol. 3. Social, emotional and personality development* (5th ed., pp. 237–309). New York: Wiley.

Shaw, D. S., Gilliom, M., Ingoldsby, E. M., & Nagin, D. S. (2003). Trajectories leading to school-age conduct problems. *Developmental Psychology, 39*, 189–200.

Shonkoff, J. P., & Phillips, D. A. (Eds.). (2000). *From neurons to neighborhoods: The science of early childhood development.* Washington, DC: National Academy Press.

Smiley, P., & Huttenlocher, J. (1989). Young children's acquisition of emotion concepts. In C. Saarni & P. L. Harris (Eds.), *Children's understanding of emotion* (pp. 27–49). Cambridge: Cambridge University Press.

Stipek, D. (1995). The development of pride and shame in toddlers. In J. P. Tangney & K. W. Fischer (Eds.), *Self-conscious emotions* (pp. 237–252). New York: Guilford.

Thompson, R. A. (1990). Emotion and self-regulation. In R. A. Thompson (Ed.), *Nebraska Symposium on Motivation: Vol. 36. Socioemotional development* (pp. 383–483). Lincoln: University of Nebraska Press.

Thompson, R. A. (1994). Emotion regulation: A theme in search of definition. In N. A. Fox (Ed.), *The development of emotion regulation and dysregulation: Biological and behavioral aspects. Monographs of the Society for Research in Child Development, 59*(2–3, Serial No. 240), 25–52.

Thompson, R. A. (1998). Early sociopersonality development. In N. Eisenberg (Ed.), *Handbook of child psychology: Vol. 3. Social, emotional, and personality development* (5th ed., pp. 25–104). New York: Wiley.

Thompson, R. A. (1999). Early attachment and later development. In J. Cassidy & P. Shaver (Eds.), *Handbook of attachment: Theory, research, and clinical applications* (pp. 265–286). New York: Guilford.

Thompson, R. A., & Calkins, S. (1996). The double-edged sword: Emotional regulation for children at risk. *Development and Psychopathology, 8*(1), 163–182.

Thompson, R. A., Flood, M. F., & Goodvin, R. (in press). Social support and developmental psychopathology. In D. Cicchetti & D. Cohen (Eds.), *Developmental psychopathology: Vol. III. Risk, disorder, and adaptation* (2nd ed.). New York: Wiley.

Thompson, R. A., & Goodvin, R. (2005). The individual child: Temperament, emotion, self, and personality. In M. Bornstein & M. E. Lamb (Eds.), *Developmental psychology: An advanced textbook* (5th ed., pp. 391–428). Mahwah, NJ: Erlbaum.

Thompson, R. A., Laible, D. J., & Ontai, L. L. (2003). Early understanding of emotion, morality, and the self: Developing a working model. In R. V. Kail (Ed.), *Advances in child development and behavior* (Vol. 31, pp. 137–171). San Diego: Academic.

Thompson, R. A., Meyer, S., & McGinley, M. (2006). Understanding values in relationship: The development of conscience. In M. Killen & J. Smetana (Eds.), *Handbook of moral development.* (pp. 267–297). Mahwah, NJ: Erlbaum.

Thompson, R. A., & Raikes, H. A. (in press). The social and emotional foundations of school readiness. In J. Knitzer, R. Kaufmann, & D. Perry (Eds.), *Early childhood mental health.* Baltimore: Paul H. Brookes.

Tomasello, M., & Rakoczy, H. (2003). What makes human cognition unique? From individual to shared to collective intentionality. *Mind & Language, 18*, 121–147.

Trevarthen, C. (1998). The concept and foundations of infant intersubjectivity. In S. Braten (Ed.), *Intersubjective communication and emotion in early ontogeny* (pp. 15–46). New York: Cambridge University Press.

Vasey, M. W., & Dadds, M. R. (Eds.). (2001). *The developmental psychopathology of anxiety.* London: Oxford University Press.

Volling, B. L., McElwain, N. L., & Miller, A. L. (2002). Emotion regulation in context: The jealousy complex between young siblings and its relations with child and family characteristics. *Child Development, 73*, 581–600.

Walker-Andrews, A. S. (1997). Infants' perception of expressive behaviors: Differentiation of multimodal information. *Psychological Bulletin, 121*, 437–456.

Walker-Andrews, A. S., & Dickson, L. R. (1997). Infants' understanding of affect. In S. Hala (Ed.), *The development of social cognition* (pp. 161–186). Hove: Psychology Press.

Wellman, H. M., & Banerjee, M. (1991). Mind and emotion: Children's understanding of the emotional consequences of beliefs and desires. *British Journal of Developmental Psychology, 9*, 191–214.

Wellman, H. M., & Bartsch, K. (1988). Young children's reasoning about beliefs. *Cognition, 30*, 239–277.

Wellman, H. M., & Lagattuta, K. H. (2000). Developing understandings of mind. In S. Baron-Cohen, H. Tager-Flusberg, & D. Cohen (Eds.), *Understanding other minds: Perspectives from developmental cognitive neuroscience* (2nd ed., pp. 21–49). New York: Oxford University Press.

Wellman, H. M., & Miller, J. G. (in press). Including deontic reasoning as fundamental to theory of mind. *Psychological Review.*

Wellman, H. M., & Woolley, J. D. (1990). From simple desires to ordinary beliefs: The early development of everyday psychology. *Cognition, 35*, 245–275.

Woodward, A. L., & Guajardo, J. J. (2002). Infants' understanding of the point gesture as an object-directed action. *Cognitive Development, 17*, 1061–1084.

Youngblade, L. M., & Dunn, J. (1995). Individual differences in young children's pretend play with mother and sibling: Links to relationships and understanding of other people's feelings and beliefs. *Child Development, 66*, 1472–1492.

Yuill, N. (1984). Young children's coordination of motive and outcome in judgments of satisfaction and morality. *British Journal of Developmental Psychology, 2,* 73–81.

Yuill, N., Perner, J., Pearson, A., Peerbhoy, D., & Emde, J. (1996). Children's changing understanding of wicked desires: From objective to subjective and moral. *British Journal of Developmental Psychology, 14,* 457–475.

Zahn-Waxler, C. (2000). The development of empathy, guilt, and internalization of distress: Implications for gender differences in internalizing and externalizing problems. In R. J. Davidson (Ed.), *Anxiety, depression, and emotion* (pp. 222–265). New York: Oxford University Press.

Zahn-Waxler, C., & Robinson, J. (1995). Empathy and guilt: Early origins of feelings of responsibility. In J. P. Tangney & K. W. Fischer (Eds.), *Self-conscious emotions* (pp. 143–173). New York: Guilford.

17

Temperament, Attention, and the Development of Self-Regulation

Mary K. Rothbart, Michael I. Posner, and Jessica Kieras

Self-regulation has been defined as the modulation of thought, affect, and behavior, involving deliberate as well as automated mechanisms (Karoly, 1993). It is related to emotional control and planning as well as the control of one's own behavior. The toddler and preschool years are basic to the development of self-control, emotion regulation, and planning. In this chapter, we present an integrated review of studies on the development of self-regulation from infancy to the early school years, focusing particularly on aspects of temperament, including individual differences in attention. We have defined temperament as constitutionally based individual differences in reactivity and self-regulation in emotion, activity, and attention (Rothbart & Bates, in press; Rothbart & Derryberry, 1981). By constitutional, we mean biologically based, and influenced over time by genes, environment, and experience. Reactivity refers to the onset, intensity, and duration of emotional, motor, and orienting reactions. Self-regulation refers to processes that serve to modulate reactivity. Both reactive and regulative aspects of temperament are involved in the development of self-regulation.

Development of attention, including the control of orienting and the development of executive attention, provides a major basis for the development of self-regulation (Rueda, Posner, & Rothbart, 2004). In our view, executive attention provides a neural substrate for developing temperamental effortful control, with effortful control defined as the ability to inhibit a dominant response in order to perform a subdominant response, to detect errors, and to engage in planning. Our original discovery of effortful control as a broad dimension of temperament came from factor analyses of the Children's Behavior Questionnaire (CBQ; Rothbart, Ahadi, Hershey, & Fisher, 2001) assessing temperament in children age 3 to 7. This research identified three broad factors, including a general factor of Effortful Control (with loadings from attentional shifting, attentional focusing, inhibitory control, and perceptual sensitivity), distinct from factors of Surgency/Extraversion (with loadings from activity level, positive anticipation, high-intensity pleasure/sensation seeking, impulsivity, smiling and laughter, and a negative loading from shyness) and Negative Emotionality (with loadings from shyness, discomfort, fear, anger/frustration, sadness, and a negative loading from soothability/falling reactivity) (Ahadi, Rothbart, & Ye, 1993; Rothbart et al., 2001). Similar broad factors have also been identified in the toddler period (Putnam, Ellis, & Rothbart, 2001), and we have also found intercorrelations among measures of attentional focusing, attentional shifting, and inhibitory control in adults' effortful control (Derryberry & Rothbart, 1988; Rothbart, Ahadi, & Evans, 2000).

In our review of the development of self-regulation and its links to temperament, we begin with the early months of life, when modulation of distress occurs through selective orienting. Early in development, the caregiver uses soothing techniques that include distracting the infant through orienting of attention; these may provide a basis for later self-regulation in both orienting and executive attention. In development beyond infancy, children are able to make increasingly difficult adjustments in their thought and behavior through effortful control. We regard executive attention as a neural mechanism that underlies effortful control, and examine efforts to design tasks that can trace the development of executive attention. Effortful control is basic to socialization in the family and with peers; it is also important in children's transition to the school environment.

Development of Self- and Other-Regulation

Infant studies

The early life of the infant is concerned with the regulation of state, including regulation of distress (Sander, 1962). Orienting, the selection of information from sensory input, is a major mechanism for this regulation. Caregivers provide a hint as to how attention is used to regulate the state of the infant when they attempt to distract their infants by bringing their attention to other stimuli (Halsted, 1991). As infants orient, they are often quieted, and their distress appears to diminish.

We have conducted a systematic study of orienting and soothing in 3- to 6-month-old infants (Harman, Rothbart, & Posner 1997). Infants were first shown a sound and light display; about 50% of the infants became distressed by the stimulation, but then strongly oriented to interesting visual and auditory soothing events when these were presented. While the children oriented, facial and vocal signs of distress disappeared. However, as soon as the orienting stopped – for example, when the object was removed – the infants' distress returned to almost exactly the levels shown prior to presentation of the soothing object. An internal system, which we termed the *distress keeper*, which we believe involves the amygdala, appears to hold a computation of the initial level of distress, so that it returns if the infant's orientation to the novel event is lost. In our later studies, infants were quieted by distraction for as long as one minute, without changing the eventual level of distress reached once orienting ended (Harman et al., 1997).

For young infants, the control of orienting is at first largely in the hands of caregiver presentations. By 4 months, however, infants have gained considerable control over disengaging their gaze from one visual location and moving it to another, and greater orienting skill in the laboratory is associated with lower temperamental negative emotion and greater soothability as reported by parents (Johnson, Posner, & Rothbart, 1991). Related phenomena appear to be present in preschool and older children as well as adults, and they provide an important aspect of self-regulation. Adults and adolescents who report themselves as having good ability to focus and shift attention also say they experience less negative affect (Derryberry & Rothbart, 1988), and negative emotion and effortful control are inversely related in parent reports of temperament in toddlers and early school-age children (Putnam et al., 2001). Indeed, many of the ideas of both modern cognitive therapy and eastern methods for controlling the mind are based upon using attention to reduce the intrusion of negative ideation.

Longitudinal studies

We have studied the development of regulatory behaviors in a longitudinal study of 66 children seen at 3, 6, 10, and 13 months of age (Rothbart, Ziaie, & O'Boyle, 1992). The infants were presented with stimuli varying in intensity and predictability to assess their temperamental reactivity, but we were struck by the degree of active coping with distress and arousal shown by the infants. We therefore coded their self-regulatory behaviors and grouped the codes into larger functional categories. These included *active avoidance* (including the codes: arch back, arm retraction, leave chair, lean away, push back, and remove hand), *orientation to the mother* (look toward mother, lean toward mother, and leave chair toward mother), *disengagement of attention* (gaze aversion, look down, look away, turn head, and look toward experimenter), *approach* (lean forward, reach, reach point, and inhibited reach), *attack* (bang toy, pounding, and push toy away), *body self-stimulation* (arm movement, banging, body movement, kicking, and repeated hand movement), *tactile self-soothing* (hand–mouth, mouthing, touch ear–head, and clasp hands), and *respiration* (heavy breathing, sighs, and yawns).

As in our study (Rothbart et al., 1992), Murphy's (1962) observations of self-regulation and coping in infancy included stimulus selection through orienting, physical means of selection through approach, avoidance, attack, and obtaining the assistance of another person. These strategies are present in infancy, but they may persist through early childhood and into later development. Murphy described the strategies in this way:

> We can see here something of the early backgrounds for devices of managing stimulation: shutting out stimuli that come at an unwanted time, by turning away so as not to see, covering up ears, protesting; rejecting stimuli that cannot be handled successfully; diminishing or terminating stimulation that is too much for pleasure, or after satiation; or in greater extremity, destroying or attacking painful stimuli. On the positive side of stimulus management we see the beginnings not only of choice and selection, approach and seeking, but of techniques for evoking response, getting more of interpersonal stimulation as well as impersonal stimuli; restructuring or merely organizing stimuli to enhance the satisfaction from exchanges with the environment. (pp. 338–339)

A number of changes in self-regulation occurred across the period of our observation (Rothbart et al., 1992). First, children increasingly looked to their mothers during the presentation of arousing stimuli such as masks and mechanical toys. Children's disengagement of attention from arousing stimuli was also related to lower levels of negative affect by 13 months. Stability from 10 to 13 months was also found in infants' use of disengagement, mouthing, hand to mouth (e.g., thumb sucking), approach, and withdrawing the hand, suggesting that some of the infants' self-regulation strategies were becoming habitual. Over the period of 3 to 13 months, passive self-soothing decreased and more active approach, attack, and body self-stimulation increased. Infants who showed the greatest distress at 3 months tended to persist in a very early form of regulation, self-soothing. Once a coping mechanism develops, it may persist, because it brings relief, even though more sophisticated coping mechanisms are now available.

More recent studies have found direct links between infants' self-regulated disengagement of attention and concurrent decreases in negative affect (Stifter & Braungart, 1995). Correlations also have been found between infants' use of self-regulation in anger-inducing situations and their later preschool ability to delay responses (Calkins & Williford, 2003). Further support of the idea that mechanisms used early to cope with negative emotion may later be transferred to the control of cognition and behavior was reported by Mischel and his colleagues (Sethi, Mischel, Aber, Shoda, & Rodriguez, 2000). Toddlers were briefly separated from their mothers, and at age 5, their behavior was observed in a situation where they could delay gratification in order to receive a more valued reward. Toddlers whose use of distraction strategies increased over the period of separation were at age 5 able to delay longer.

Temperament and early self-regulation

Some children will be more subject to over-stimulation and negative emotion than others, and will therefore need to decrease stimulation; other, more surgent and extraverted children seek excitement (Murphy, 1962; Rothbart & Bates, in press). Children also differ in effortful control, and we expect that the efficiency of effortful control depends in part on the strength of the dominant response (the one most likely to be made in the absence of instructions). Our only predictor of childhood effortful control from laboratory measures in infancy (we could not as yet measure this system early in life) was the speed with which children grasped high-intensity toys in the laboratory (Rothbart, Ahadi, & Evans, 2000). Those who grasped the toys quickly showed higher impulsivity, anger/frustration, and aggression at 7 years, and tended to be lower in attentional and inhibitory control. Thus, strong approach tendencies may constrain the application of effortful control (Rothbart, Derryberry, & Hershey, 2000). If we use an analogy of approach tendencies as the "accelerator," and inhibition tendencies as the "brakes" on behavior and emotional expression, stronger acceleration would be expected to weaken the braking influence of fear and effortful inhibitory control.

Fear as a control system. Late in the first year, some infants also begin to demonstrate fear in their inhibited approach to unfamiliar and intense stimuli (Rothbart, 1988; Schaffer, 1974), and fearful behavioral inhibition shows considerable longitudinal stability across childhood and into adolescence (Kagan, 1998). Fearful inhibition developing late in the first year of life allows inhibitory control of behavior. In our longitudinal work, infant fear assessed in the laboratory predicted childhood fear, sadness, and shyness at 7 years (Rothbart, Derryberry, & Hershey, 2000). Fear did not predict later frustration/anger, but was inversely related to later approach, impulsivity, and aggression. These findings suggest that fear is also involved in the self-regulation of approach-related and aggressive tendencies (Gray & McNaughton, 1996).

More fearful infants also later showed greater empathy, guilt, and shame in childhood (Rothbart, Ahadi, & Hershey, 1994). These findings suggest that fear might be involved in the early development of moral motivation, and Kochanska (1995, 1997) has indeed found that temperamental fearfulness predicts conscience development in preschool-age children. On the other hand, extreme fear may lead to problems in children's rigid over-control of behavior, as reflected in the Blocks' description of inflexible patterns of response that can limit children's positive experiences (J. H. Block & Block, 1980; Kremen & Block, 1998). Thus, the temperamental dimension of fearfulness within the first year of life allows the first major control system of behavior, but it is a reactive one that can lack flexibility. During the toddler and preschool years, development of executive attention underlying effortful control allows the child greater control of stimulation and response, including the ability to select responses in a conflict situation, and we now discuss this development.

In recent exciting work by Aksan and Kochanska (2004), children who were more fearful and inhibited at 33 months showed more volitional inhibitory control at 45 months. They suggest that more fearful and inhibited children have a greater opportunity to foster their own self-control during periods of slow approach to novel situations.

Self-Regulation in the Toddler and Preschool Years

Approach motivation related to surgency/extraversion and inhibition related to fear are both temperamental dispositions, yet we know that we can also approach the things we fear and avoid the things that promise reward. How does this come about? Effortful control provides a mechanism for this important flexibility. During the second year, language and increasing impulse control become available to the child, bringing with them the possibility of improved communication and improved self-regulation (Kopp, 1992). There is also increasing understanding of the self as an independent being in potential control of events, and there are increased attempts to influence objects and others (Harter, 1999). Two-year-olds have few self-regulatory skills and little patience, however, and when their expectations are not met, they often respond with anger, sometimes crying or showing temper tantrums (Kopp, 1992). Temperamental differences in anger are also reliably positively related to individual differences in approach or surgency/extraversion (Rothbart & Derryberry, 2002). Bronson (2000) notes the toddlers' increasing awareness of the possibility of control; the actual skills of consciously controlling one's own behavior will be developing during the preschool and school years, and one mechanism for this accomplishment is the development of temperamental effortful control.

Kochanska, Murray, and Harlan (2000) have characterized the construct of effortful control as being "situated at the intersection of the temperament and behavioral regulation literatures" (p. 220). What does effortful control mean for temperament and development? It means that unlike early theoretical models of temperament that emphasized how people are moved by their positive and negative emotions or level of arousal, we are not always at the mercy of affect. Using effortful control, we can more flexibly approach situations we fear and inhibit actions we desire. The efficiency of control, however, will depend on the strength of the emotional processes against which effort is exerted (Rothbart et al., 2000). For example, when the child must delay an approach response to an appealing toy, the child with a stronger disposition to approach will require greater effortful control to succeed.

Effortful control can support the internalization of competence-related goals (e.g., being kind to others, school performance), and their achievement, and is also involved in the inhibition of immediate approach with the goal of a larger reward later, in Jack Block's (2002) "hedonism of the future." Effortful control allows the activation of behavior that would otherwise not be performed due to threatened punishment. In general, it allows the person to act "on principle." Effortful control is not itself a basic motivation, but rather the means to effectively satisfying desired ends. It is similar to the attentional capacities underlying Block's (2002) construct of ego resiliency, allowing for the flexible ability to shift levels of control depending on the situation.

Evidence for stability of effortful control has been found in research by Mischel and his colleagues (Mischel, Shoda, & Peake, 1988; Shoda, Mischel, & Peake, 1990). Preschoolers were tested on their ability to wait for a delayed treat that was preferable to a readily accessible, but less preferred treat. Preschoolers better able to delay gratification were found to have better self-control and an increased ability to deal with stress, frustration, and temptation. Their delay of gratification in seconds also predicted later parent-reported attentiveness, concentration, competence, planfulness, and intelligence during adolescence. In addition, seconds of preschool delay predicted academic competence in SAT scores, even when controlling for intelligence. In follow-up studies when the participants were in their thirties, preschool delay predicted goal-setting and self-regulatory abilities (Ayduk et al., 2000), suggesting remarkable continuity in these dimensions of self-regulatory skills.

Effortful control plays an important role in the development of conscience, with internalized conscience greater in children high in effortful control (Kochanska, Murray, Jacques, Koenig, & Vandegeest, 1996; Kochanska, Murray, & Coy, 1997; Kochanska et al., 2000). Thus, both the reactive temperamental control system of fear and the attentionally based system of effortful control appear to regulate the development of moral thought and behavior, with the influence of fear found earlier in development. At Oregon, we found that children 6 to 7 years old who were high in effortful control were also high in empathy and guilt/shame, and low in aggressiveness (Rothbart, Derryberry, & Posner, 1994). Effortful control may support empathy by allowing children to attend to the other child's condition instead of focusing only on their own sympathetic distress. Eisenberg, Fabes, Nyman, Bernzweig, and Pinulas (1994) found that 4- to 6-year-old boys with good attentional control tended to deal with anger by using non-hostile verbal methods rather than overt aggression.

Inhibitory aspects of effortful control have been related to observations of committed compliance (ready and positive acceptance of the maternal agenda) in the toddler and preschool years (Kochanska, Coy, & Murray, 2001; Kochanska et al., 1997). In this research, links were stronger in tasks where the children were asked to inhibit an enjoyable action, such as playing with attractive but prohibited toys, than in those where the child was required to initiate and sustain an activity, such as cleaning up the toys after a free play situation. Effortful control has also been related to preschool peer- and teacher-reported agreeableness (including helpfulness, sharing, and niceness) (Cumberland-Li, Eisenberg, & Reiser, 2004). In addition to social competence, effortful control has also been found to be related to children's adjustment (see reviews by Eisenberg, Smith, Sadovsky, & Spinrad, 2004; Vohs & Ciarocco, 2004).

Finally, individual differences in effortful control are related to aspects of metacognitive knowledge, such as theory of mind, that is, knowing that people's behavior is guided by their beliefs, desires, and other mental states (Carlson & Moses, 2001). Moreover, tasks that require the inhibition of a prepotent response are correlated with performance on theory of mind tasks even when other factors, such as age, intelligence, and working memory, are factored out (Carlson & Moses, 2001). Inhibitory control and theory of mind share a similar developmental time course, with advances in both areas between the ages of 2 and 5. Because of the centrality of effortful control to the broad range of abilities in executive functioning, such as planning, memory, and problem solving, we focus on the development of executive attention in the next section.

Executive Attention

Functional neuroimaging has allowed many cognitive tasks to be analyzed in terms of the brain areas they activate, and attention has been examined in this way (Corbetta & Shulman, 2002; Driver, Eimer, Macaluso, & van Velzen, 2004; Posner & Fan, in press). Imaging data support the presence of three networks related to different aspects of attention: alerting, orienting, and executive attention (Posner & Fan, in press). Alerting refers to achieving and maintaining a state of high sensitivity to incoming stimuli; orienting refers to the selection of information from sensory input; and executive attention includes mechanisms for monitoring and resolving conflict among thoughts, feelings, and responses. Executive attention is seen to provide the neural basis for effortful control.

The anterior cingulate gyrus, one of the main nodes of the executive attention network, has been linked to a variety of specific functions related to self-regulation These include the monitoring of conflict (Botvinick, Braver, Barch, Carter, & Cohen, 2001), control of working memory (Duncan et al., 2000), regulation of emotion (Bush, Luu, & Posner, 2000), and response to error (Holroyd & Coles, 2002). In emotion studies, the cingulate is often seen as part of a network involving orbital frontal cortex and the amygdala that regulates our emotional response to input. Activation of the anterior cingulate is observed when people are asked to control their natural reactions to strong positive

(Beauregard, Levesque, & Bourgouin, 2001) or negative emotions (Ochsner, Bunge, Gross, & Gabrieli, 2002).

Development of executive attention

Assessments of executive attention have focused on situations of conflict and delay tasks in which it is easy to identify the dominant (inhibited) and subdominant (activated) responses. For example, in the standard Stroop task, where words for different colors are printed in conflicting ink colors, naming the color of ink, which is a subdominant response, requires longer reaction times for a skilled reader than does naming the word, which is a dominant response. Since reading is learned rather late, a number of conflict tasks have been developed for younger children, such as the Day/Night Stroop task (Gerstadt, Hong, & Diamond, 1994), where children are asked to say "day" when they see a picture associated with night (e.g., moon and stars) and "night" when they see a picture associated with day (e.g., sunshine).

Another example is the spatial conflict task, in which object identity and spatial location of a stimulus are placed in conflict. In this task the child has two response keys, labeled with pictures of stimuli. The stimuli are presented on a computer screen and the child is instructed to press the key that corresponds to the picture that is presented. Conflict trials are those in which the stimulus appears on the side opposite the corresponding key (Gerardi-Caulton, 2000; Simon, 1969). Another example is the flanker task, in which the response to a target is in conflict with surrounding stimuli, such as pressing a key corresponding to a fish that is facing one direction, while several fish on either side of it are facing the opposite direction (Eriksen & Eriksen, 1974; Rueda, Fan, et al., 2004). Both the spatial conflict task and the flanker task have been linked to functioning of the brain's executive attention network (Fan, Flombaum, McCandliss, Thomas, & Posner, 2003), and can be used as model tasks for its development.

Figure 17.1 provides a timeline illustrating changes in children's performance on tasks that assess executive attention or executive functioning during early childhood. Different tasks have been used at different ages. The ranges above the timeline represent periods where there has been significant improvement in children's performance on the tasks. The arrows below the timeline indicate the age at which children typically can perform each task successfully. Performance was considered typical for children of a given age when either: (1) the authors of the referenced paper stated that most children of this age could perform the task successfully or that successful performance was typical at that age, or (2) data indicated that the majority of children could perform the task successfully. A bold box indicates that the arrow points to the earliest age at which most children can do the task: here, the referenced paper reported that children of the previous age on the timeline could not perform the task successfully.

The tasks discussed involve two different types of responses: those that are reflexive and non-arbitrary (such as reaching along the line of sight), and those that are based on an arbitrary rule (such as sorting red cards on the left and blue cards on the right). The difficulty of delay and conflict tasks and the developmental course of their successful

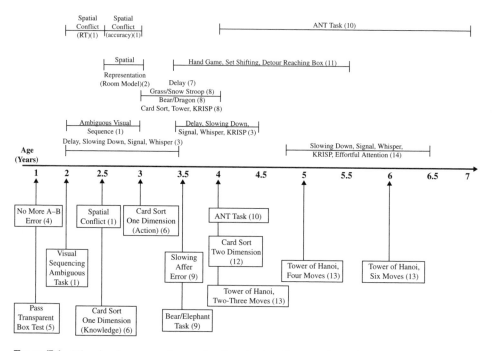

Figure 17.1   The development of executive functioning. Ranges above the timeline represent significant improvements in children's performance on the tasks. Arrows below the timeline indicate the age at which children can typically perform each task successfully. A bold box indicates that the arrow points to the earliest age at which most children can do the task. In these cases, the referenced paper found that children of the previous age on the timeline could not perform the task successfully. For example, children were able to perform the action version of the one-dimensional card sort task at age 3, but not at age 2½. A non-bolded box indicates that the previous age was not tested.

The numbers next to the tasks correspond to the following references: (1) Rothbart, Ellis, Rueda, & Posner (2003); (2) Sharon & DeLoache (2003); DeLoache (1995); (3) Kochanska et al. (1996); (4) Diamond (1991); (5) Diamond, Cruttenden, & Neiderman (1994); (6) Zelazo & Reznick (1991); (7) Thompson, Barresi, & Moore (1997); (8) Carlson & Moses (2001); (9) Jones, Rothbart, & Posner (2003); (10) Johnson et al. (1991); (11) Hughes (1998); (12) Zelazo, Muller, Frye, & Marcovitch (2003); (13) Klahr & Robinson (1981); and (14) Kochanska et al. (1997).

completion depend in part on the strength and automaticity of the response to be inhibited, and the arbitrariness of the non-dominant response.

Years 1 to 3

Non-conflicting responses can be learned as early as 3 to 4 months. At this age, infants can move their eyes in anticipation of a visual event that has repeatedly occurred at a particular location (Haith, Hazan, & Goodman, 1988). They can also execute a series of eye movements in anticipation of locations when the next location is unambiguous (e.g., positions 1, 2, 3, 1, 2, 3). However, if conflict is induced (e.g., in the sequence 1, 2, 1, 3, where a 1 is followed by a 2 early in the sequence, but by a conflicting 3 later in the sequence), children are unable to successfully resolve the ambiguity until about 2 years of age (Clohessy, Posner, & Rothbart, 2001).

During the first year of life, children learn to resolve conflict between reaching along the line of sight and detour reaching in a three-sided, transparent plexiglas box (Diamond et al., 1994). Late in the first year, children can also pass the A ~ B task, showing that they are able to over-ride an automatic (non-arbitrary) dominant response (repeating a previously rewarded motor movement toward an object) and replace it with another relatively automatic but initially subdominant response (reaching and looking toward the location where the object was just hidden) (Diamond, 1991).

Between 30 and 36 months, children learn to perform the spatial conflict key press task described above. This task requires inhibiting the dominant response toward a spatial location, in order to make a response based on matching identity (Gerardi-Caulton, 2000; Rothbart et al., 2003). At 24 months, children are only able to carry out the task when the stimulus is on the same side of the computer screen as the matching response key (congruent condition), but by 30 months, most children can handle the incongruent trials where the matching target is on the opposite side of the stimulus (adults are also slowed by this condition). Children performing better on spatial conflict have also been rated by their parents as having relatively higher levels of temperamental effortful control and lower levels of negative affect (Rothbart et al., 2003), and children at 30 months who performed well on the spatial conflict task also performed well on the eye movement conflict task. Two-year-old children who were unable to complete the spatial conflict task were described by their parents as having lower effortful control and higher negative affectivity on the CBQ measure of temperament (Rothbart et al., 2003). These findings are consistent with the idea that the capacity to engage in rule-based action supports responding to social rules and regulating emotion.

Games of young children like "Simon Says" or "Mother May I?" give children practice under conflict in inhibitory control (Reed, Pien, & Rothbart, 1984), and a somewhat more difficult conflict task involves asking the child to follow the well-learned instruction of one puppet, while inhibiting the instruction when given by another puppet (Simple Simon game) (Jones et al., 2003), an arbitrary instruction. At 36–38 months children were unable to avoid responding to both puppets, and showed no slowing following making an error. However, at 39–41 months most children were correct on both kinds of trials and also slowed their responses after a mistaken compliance, indicating they had detected an error. Physical responses often provide the means of self-regulation in these inhibition tasks. In the Simple Simon game, for example, rather than using verbal means of self-regulation, preschool children frequently physically prevented their actions by sitting their hands or holding down one hand with the other (Jones et al., 2003).

Thirty-six-month-old children can sort cards based on an arbitrary one-dimensional rule (e.g., blue cards go on the right, red cards on the left). Frye, Zelazo, and Palfai (1995) found that 30-month-old children could demonstrate they knew a card-sort rule, but they were not able to sort cards based on that rule until about 3 years of age. For example, children might be told that red cards are to be placed in a pile on the left and blue cards in a pile on the right. When asked "which pile do the red (or blue) cards go in?" most children of 30 months can indicate the location correctly. However, when asked to put each card in its place, most of them are unable to do so. Children who correctly answer the knowledge questions continue to make errors on the actual sorting task until about 36 months. Most of the errors involve putting a card in the pile where a card was placed on the previous trial. This is similar to the A ~ B error, in that the children have a tendency to repeat a motor movement in spite of a change in the stimulus context. However, in this case, the task involved arbitrary sorting rules, rather than more reflective or automatic response tendencies. In summary, from infancy to age 3, children first learn to regulate conflict in relation to reflexive actions, and later begin to develop the ability to behave in ways that are consistent with arbitrary cognitively represented rules.

Years 3 to 6

Between 3 and 5 years of age, children develop the ability to succeed in tasks where the subdominant responses directly conflict with the dominant responses. These include saying "day" for a picture of night and vice versa (Carlson & Moses, 2001; Gerstadt et al., 1994). Diamond, Kirkham, and Amso (2002) tested children on the day/night task and a modified version, where children were told to say "pig" or "dog" for the day and night picture stimuli. Children performed more poorly on the day/night version than on the pig/dog version, indicating that conflict of the response contributed to the difficulty of the task. They also include making a conflicting motor response in the hand game (Hughes, 1998). In this game, children first repeat the hand movements of the experimenter, either making a fist or placing the hand flat on the table. Later, children are asked to make the fist when the experimenter puts the hand down flat, and vice versa.

Correct performance on two-dimensional card sorts is not seen until 4 to 5 years (Zelazo et al., 2003). In this case, the dominant response is arbitrary (e.g., color) and has been learned during the pre-switch phase, which can be as short as only one trial. The subdominant response follows a new arbitrary set of rules (e.g., shape). Children tend to perseverate on the pre-switch rules when they are in conflict with the post-switch rules. Improvement during these years may be due in part to children's ability to organize rules into a hierarchical system, where the child switches from one set of rules to another, depending on a specific condition, reducing conflict between the pre- and post-switch rules (Zelazo et al., 2003).

Tasks measuring children's abilities to suppress a dominant response (inhibitory control) are often included in effortful control batteries (Kochanska et al., 1996, 1997). The subdominant conflicting response is always to inhibit an action, so the difficulty of the task depends on how strong the dominant response is. A number of inhibitory control tasks require the child to wait for a signal before responding. For example, in the Pinball task, children are asked to hold onto the plunger that releases a ball until the experimenter says "go" (Reed et al., 1984). The goal here is to inhibit the dominant response, which is releasing the plunger and shooting the ball into the game. Another set of tasks used to assess inhibitory control involves slowing down motor activity (Kochanska et al., 1996).

Different variants of these tasks have been used to study children between ages 2 and 6. Generally, children are asked to perform a motor task, such as walking down a strip of tape on the floor or drawing a line on a piece of paper, and are then asked to perform the same task again, only as slowly as possible. Children's times on the two sets of trials are compared to get a measure of their abilities to slow down their motor activity. As shown in Figure 17.1, children show improvement in waiting for a signal and slowing down motor activity tasks and other inhibitory tasks between 2 and 6 years of age (Kochanska et al., 1996, 1997; Reed et al., 1984).

Summary

In summary, as executive attention develops, there are changes in the conflicts that children are able to resolve. Children by a year of age can over-ride a strong, natural, or non-arbitrary tendency, provided that the subdominant response is also somewhat natural; children at age 2 can resolve conflicts related to spatial locations; children older than 2½ can apply a matching rule and over-ride a tendency to reach in the direction of the original stimulus when pressing a key; and between 3 and 5 years, children learn to resolve conflicts in which the subdominant and dominant responses are in conflict with one another. Children's skills at conflict resolution as measured on flanker tasks continue to improve at least until age 7 (Rueda, Fan, et al., 2004). When tasks involve other executive functions, such as the ability to retain multiple dimensions in working memory, or planning several steps ahead, as in the Tower of Hanoi problem (Klahr & Robinson, 1981), development occurs later and may be more protracted. Improved performance on more complex conflict-related tasks can be observed up to middle childhood, and full development of these skills may not take place until early adulthood (Rothbart & Rueda, 2005).

Environmental and Genetic Influences on Effortful Control

Social environment

What social experiences might facilitate the development of effortful control? Although it is difficult to separate the direction of influence in these studies, 18-month-olds' use of distraction and constructive coping during frustration is related to their mothers' guidance by positive rather than negative, directive, or controlling behavior (Calkins & Johnson, 1998). This correlation was found concurrently at 18 months, and mothers' behavior at 18 months predicted their children's self-regulation at 24 months (Calkins, Smith, Gill, & Johnson, 1998). Similar findings have linked warm and supportive parenting to later inhibitory and attentional control (Gilliom, Shaw, Beck, Schonberg, & Lukon, 2002; Kyrios & Prior, 1990). Kochanska et al. (2000) found that mothers' responsiveness at 22 months predicted effortful control at 22 and 33 months, whereas mothers' use of power-assertive discipline was linked to low levels of effortful control. The relation between parental power assertion and children's later conscience development has also been found to be mediated by children's level of effortful control, with mothers' power assertion negatively predicting child effortful control, which continued to predict conscience even though the effect of power assertion dropped to non-significance (Kochanska & Knaack, 2003).

Although the direction of influence could be from mother to child in these studies, it is important to remember that the direction of influence may also be reversed, so that children who are difficult to regulate may require more controlling efforts from parents at the earlier ages, and children who are more self-regulated may elicit more warmth and approval. This raises the question of possible genetic influences on the development of executive attention and effortful control.

Genes

Goldsmith, Buss, and Lemery (1997) have found evidence for both genetic and shared family influences on CBQ effortful control scales in childhood, and Fan, Wu, Fossella, & Posner (2001) have found evidence for heritability of executive attention in adulthood. Links have also been reported between specific genes related to dopamine and norepinephrine function and individual differences in the efficiency of executive attention (Diamond, Briand, Fossella, & Gehlbach, 2004; Fossella, Posner, Fan, Swanson, & Pfaff, 2002). In infants, specific genes have also been linked to lower orientation and higher distress scores (Auerbach et al., 1999; Ebstein et al., 1998). Suomi and his colleagues have recently reported interactions between genes and environment in rhesus monkey studies. In these studies, the effect of specific genes depended on peer versus mother rearing, with a short allele of the 5-HTTLR gene linked to lower orientation scores, but only for monkeys who had been reared with peers, not for mother-reared monkeys (Barr et al., 2003; Bennett et al., 2002). One interpretation of these findings is that mothers may buffer their infants' experience so as to moderate the expression of the genetic characteristic. This work may serve as a model for future research in understanding the development of self-regulation.

Training

We have tested whether a specific educational intervention during development of executive attention in 4- and 6-year-olds can influence the efficiency of children's attention (Rueda, Rothbart, McCandliss, Saccamanno, & Posner, 2005). Since a central aspect of the executive attention network is the ability to deal with conflict, we used this feature to design a set of training exercises adapted from efforts to train rhesus monkeys for space travel (Rumbaugh & Washburn, 1995), which had resulted in monkeys' ability to resolve conflict in a Stroop-like task (Washburn, 1994). Our exercises began with training the child to control the movement of an animated cat on a computer screen by using a joystick. Other exercises involved prediction of where an animated figure would move, given its initial trajectory, retention of information for a matching to sample task, and the resolution of conflict.

We tested the efficacy of a very brief five days of attention training with children brought to the laboratory over seven days for sessions lasting about forty minutes and conducted over a two- to three-week period. The first and last days were used to assess the effects of the training on the attention network test (Rueda, Fan, et al., 2004), which assesses the efficiency of the alerting, orienting, and executive network, and was performed while recording 128 channels of electroencephalogram (EEG) activity recorded from scalp electrodes. In addition we used a general test of intelligence (the K-BIT; Kaufman & Kaufman, 1990) to determine how well the learning might generalize, and a temperament scale (CBQ; Rothbart et al., 2001).

We randomly assigned 4- and 6-year-old children to experimental groups, that underwent the five days of training or to control groups that had only pre and post tests or that came in for five days to work with interactive videos. The trained children showed better overall scores in the executive network than either control group, but this difference was not significant owing to extreme variability. However, the training generalized to overall IQ and to the matrix sections of the K-BIT test; tests quite different from the training. EEG evidence suggested that the children after training had more adult-like event-related potentials in comparison to what was found prior to training or in either of the control groups. There were no main effects of training on temperament scores, but we are examining the role of temperament and of genes in the pre–post differences and in the rate of learning during training. These results provide evidence of some ability to train the executive attentional network. How replicable and general these effects are and how long they would last are still unknown.

Somewhat similar forms of training involving working memory for older children with attention deficit hyperactivity disorder have also improved performance on the same aspects of the K-BIT as we found (Klingberg, Forssberg, & Westerberg, 2002). An additional functional magnetic resonance imaging paper (Olesen, Westerberg, & Klingberg, 2004) reported increased prefrontal and parietal activity after training of working memory in these children.

Future Prospects in Self-Regulation Research

While our understanding of the biology of socialization is still very incomplete, we know that the neural networks underlying the control of thoughts and emotions develop strongly during early childhood. We also have evidence of the influence of genes in laying down the common structure of these networks and influencing individual differences in their efficiency, as well as influences provided by specific early experiences. The task remains to understand these developments more fully, to expand the range of attention training and socialization, and to link them in detail to the improvement in task performance during early childhood, as documented in Figure 17.1.

It will also be important to further link children's attentional skills to the kind of emotional self-regulation and coping mechanisms they develop early and later in life. This will of necessity require longitudinal research that takes into account individual differences in temperament, and links early coping strategies to those used later in development.

A related concern will be to follow the ways in which fearful self-regulation, in combination with strong effortful control, may be unhelpful for adaptation, when reflected in rigid and self-limiting control of thought, emotion, and behavior (J. Block & Kremen, 1996), and interactions between fearful inhibition and effortful control (Rothbart & Bates, in press; Rothbart & Posner, in press).

Note

This research was funded by the National Institute of Mental Health (NIMH): grants MH43361 and MH01471 to the first author.

References

Ahadi, S. A., Rothbart, M. K., & Ye, R. M. (1993). Children's temperament in the U.S. and China: Similarities and differences. *European Journal of Personality, 7*, 359–378.

Aksan, N., & Kochanska, G. (2004). Links between systems of inhibition from infancy to preschool years. *Child Development, 75*, 1477–1490.

Auerbach, J., Geller, V., Letzer, S., Shinwell, E., Levine, J., Belmaker, R. H., & Ebstein, R. P. (1999). Dopamine D4 receptor (D4DR) and serotonin transporter promoter (5-HTTLPR) polymorphisms in the determination of temperament in 2-month-old infants. *Molecular Psychiatry, 4*, 369–374.

Ayduk, O., Mendoza-Denton, R., Mischel, W., Downey, G., Peake, P. K., & Rodriguez, M. (2000). Regulating the interpersonal self: Strategic self-regulation for coping with rejection sensitivity. *Journal of Personality and Social Psychology, 79*, 776–792.

Barr, C. S., Newman, T. K., Becker, M. L., Parker, C. C., Champoux, M., Lesch, K. P., Goldman, D., Suomi, S. J., & Higley, J. D. (2003). The utility of the non-human primate for studying gene by environment interactions. *Genes, Brain, and Behavior, 6*, 336–340.

Beauregard, M., Levesque, J., & Bourgouin, P. (2001). Neural correlates of conscious self-regulation of emotion. *Journal of Neuroscience, 21*, RC 165.

Bennett, A. J., Lesch, K. P., Heils, A., Long, J. C., Lorenz, J. G., Shoaf, S. E., Champoux, M., Suomi, S. J., Linnoila, M. V., & Higley, J. D. (2002). Early experience and serotonin transporter gene variation interact to influence primate CNS function. *Molecular Psychiatry, 7*, 118–122.

Block, J. (2002). *Personality as an affect-processing system: Toward an integrative theory*. Mahwah, NJ: Erlbaum.

Block, J., & Kremen, A. (1996). IQ and ego-resiliency: Their conceptual and empirical connections and separateness. *Journal of Personality and Social Psychology, 70*, 349–361.

Block, J. H., & Block, J. (1980). The role of ego-control and ego-resiliency in the organization of behavior. In W. A. Collins (Ed.), *The Minnesota Symposium on Child Psychology: Vol. 13. Development of cognition, affect and social relations* (pp. 39–101). Hillsdale, NJ: Erlbaum.

Botvinick, M. M., Braver, T. S., Barch, D. M., Carter, C. S., & Cohen, J. D. (2001). Conflict monitoring and cognitive control. *Psychological Review, 108*, 624–652.

Bronson, M. B. (2000). *Self-regulation in early childhood: Nature and nurture*. New York: Guilford.

Bush, G., Luu, P., & Posner, M. I. (2000). Cognitive and emotional influences in the anterior cingulate cortex. *Trends in Cognitive Science, 4*, 215–222.

Calkins, S. D., & Johnson, M. C. (1998). Toddler regulation of distress to frustrating events: Temperamental and maternal correlates. *Infant Behavior and Development*, *21*, 379–395.

Calkins, S. D., Smith, C. L., Gill, K. L., & Johnson, M. C. (1998). Maternal interactive style across contexts: Relations to emotional, behavioral, and physiological regulation during toddlerhood. *Social Development*, *7*, 350–369.

Calkins, S. D., & Williford, A. (2003, April). *How infants regulate negative emotions: What is effective? What is adaptive?* Paper presented at the Society for Research in Child Development conference held in Tampa, FL.

Carlson, S. T., & Moses, L. J. (2001). Individual differences in inhibitory control in children's theory of mind. *Child Development*, *72*, 1032–1053.

Clohessy, A. B., Posner, M. I., & Rothbart, M. K. (2001). Development of the functional visual field. *Acta Psychologica*, *106*, 51–68.

Corbetta, M., & Shulman, G. L. (2002). Control of goal-directed and stimulus-driven attention in the brain. *Nature Neuroscience Reviews*, *3*, 201–215.

Cumberland-Li, A., Eisenberg, N., & Reiser, M. (2004). Relations of young children's agreeableness and resiliency to effortful control and impulsivity. *Social Development*, *13*, 193–212.

DeLoache, J. S. (1995). Early understanding and use of symbols: The model model. *Current Directions in Psychological Science*, *4*, 109–113.

Derryberry, D., & Rothbart, M. K. (1988). Arousal, affect, and attention as components of temperament. *Journal of Personality and Social Psychology*, *55*, 958–966.

Diamond, A. (1991). Neuropsychological insights into the meaning of object concept development. In S. Carey & R. Gelman (Eds.), *The epigenesis of mind: Essays on biology and cognition* (pp. 67–110). Hillsdale, NJ: Erlbaum.

Diamond, A., Briand, L., Fossella, J., & Gehlbach, L. (2004). Genetic and neurochemical modulation of prefrontal cognitive functions in children. *American Journal of Psychiatry*, *161*, 125–132.

Diamond, A., Cruttenden, L., & Neiderman, D. (1994). AB with multiple wells: I. Why are multiple wells sometimes easier than two wells? II. Memory or memory + inhibition? *Developmental Psychology*, *30*, 192–205.

Diamond, A., Kirkham, N., & Amso, D. (2002). Conditions under which young children can hold two rules in mind and inhibit a prepotent response. *Developmental Psychology*, *38*, 352–362.

Driver, J., Eimer, M., Macaluso, E., & van Velzen, J. (2004). Neurobiology of human spatial attention: Modulation, generation, and integration. In N. Kanwisher & J. Duncan (Eds.), *Attention and performance XX: Functional neuroimaging of visual cognition* (pp. 267–300). Oxford/New York: Oxford University Press.

Duncan, J., Seitz, R. J., Kolodny, J., Bor, D., Herzog, H., Ahmed, A., Newell, F. N., & Emslie, H. (2000). A neural basis for general intelligence. *Science*, *289*, 457–460.

Ebstein, R. P., Levine, J., Geller, V., Auerbach, J., Gritsenko, I., & Belmaker, R. H. (1998). Dopamine D4 receptor and serotonin transporter promoter in the determination of neonatal temperament. *Molecular Psychiatry*, *3*, 238–246.

Eisenberg, N., Fabes, R. A., Nyman, M., Bernzweig, J., & Pinulas, A. (1994). The relations of emotionality and regulation to children's anger-related reactions. *Child Development*, *65*, 109–128.

Eisenberg, N., Smith, C. L., Sadovsky, A., & Spinrad, T. L. (2004). Effortful control: Relations with emotion regulation, adjustment, and socialization in childhood. In R. F. Baumeister & K. D. Vohs (Eds.), *Handbook of self-regulation: Research, theory, and applications* (pp. 259–282). New York: Guilford.

Eriksen, B. A., & Eriksen, C. W. (1974). Effects of noise letters upon the identification of a target letter in a nonsearch task. *Perception & Psychophysics, 16,* 143–149.

Fan, J., Flombaum, J. I., McCandliss, B. D., Thomas, K. M., & Posner, M. I. (2003). Cognitive and brain consequences of conflict. *NeuroImage, 18,* 42–57.

Fan, J., Wu, Y., Fossella, J. A., & Posner, M. I. (2001). Assessing the heritability of attentional networks. *BMC Neuroscience, 2,* 1–7.

Fossella, J., Posner, M. I., Fan, J., Swanson, J. M., & Pfaff, D. W. (2002). Attentional phenotypes for the analysis of higher mental function. *The Scientific World Journal, 2,* 217–223.

Frye, D., Zelazo, P. D., & Palfai, T. (1995). Theory of mind and rule-based reasoning. *Cognitive Development, 10,* 483–527.

Gerardi-Caulton, G. (2000). Sensitivity to spatial conflict and the development of self-regulation in children 24–36 months of age. *Developmental Science, 3,* 397–404.

Gerstadt, C. L., Hong, Y. J., & Diamond, A. (1994). The relationship between cognition and action: Performance of children 3½–7 years old on a Stroop-like daylight test. *Cognition, 53,* 129–153.

Gilliom, M., Shaw, D. S., Beck, J. E., Schonberg, M. A., & Lukon, J. L. (2002). Anger regulation in disadvantaged preschool boys: Strategies, antecedents, and the development of self-control. *Developmental Psychology, 38,* 222–235.

Goldsmith, H. H., Buss, K. A., & Lemery, K. S. (1997). Toddler and childhood temperament: Expanded content, stronger genetic evidence, new evidence for the importance of environment. *Developmental Psychology, 33,* 891–905.

Gray, J. A., & McNaughton, N. (1996). The neuropsychology of anxiety: Reprise. In D. A. Hope (Ed.), *Nebraska Symposium on Motivation: Vol. 43. Perspectives on anxiety, panic, and fear* (pp. 61–134). Lincoln: University of Nebraska Press.

Haith, M. M., Hazan, C., & Goodman, G. S. (1988). Expectation and anticipation of dynamic visual events by 3.5-month-old babies. *Child Development, 59,* 467–479.

Halsted, N. (1991). Developmental mechanisms of soothing and orienting in infancy. *Dissertation Abstracts International, 51*(11-B), 5605.

Harman, C., Rothbart, M. K., & Posner, M. I. (1997). Distress and attention interactions in early infancy. *Motivation and Emotion, 21,* 27–43.

Harter, S. (1999). *The construction of the self: A developmental perspective.* New York: Guilford.

Holroyd, C. B., & Coles, M. G. H. (2002). The neural basis of human error processing: Reinforcement learning, dopamine and the error-related negativity. *Psychological Review, 109,* 679–709.

Hughes, C. (1998). Finding your marbles: Does preschoolers' strategic behavior predict later understanding? *Developmental Psychology, 34,* 1326–1339.

Johnson, M. H., Posner, M. I., & Rothbart, M. K. (1991). Components of visual orienting in early infancy: Contingency learning, anticipatory looking, and disengaging. *Journal of Cognitive Neuroscience, 3,* 335–344.

Jones, L. B., Rothbart, M. K., & Posner, M. I. (2003). Development of executive attention in preschool children. *Developmental Science, 6,* 498–504.

Kagan, J. (1998). Biology and the child. In N. Eisenberg (Ed.), *Handbook of child psychology: Vol. 3. Social, emotional, and personality development* (5th ed., pp. 177–235). New York: Wiley.

Karoly, P. (1993). Mechanisms of self-regulation: A systems view. *Annual Review of Psychology, 44,* 23–52.

Kaufman, A. S., & Kaufman, N. L. (1990). *Kaufman Brief Intelligence Test.* Manual Circle Pines, MN: American Guidance Service.

Klahr, D., & Robinson, M. (1981). Formal assessment of problem-solving and planning processes in preschool children. *Cognitive Psychology, 13,* 113–148.

Klingberg, T., Forssberg, H., & Westerberg, H. (2002). Training of working memory in children with ADHD. *Journal of Clinical and Experimental Neuropsychology, 24,* 781–791.

Kochanska, G. (1995). Children's temperament, mothers' discipline, and security of attachment: Multiple pathways to emerging internalization. *Child Development, 66,* 597–615.

Kochanska, G. (1997). Multiple pathways to conscience for children with different temperaments from toddlerhood to age 5. *Developmental Psychology, 3,* 228–240.

Kochanska, G., Coy, K. C., & Murray, K. T. (2001). The development of self-regulation in the first four years of life. *Child Development, 72,* 1091–1111.

Kochanska, G., & Knaack, A. (2003). Effortful control as a personality characteristic of young children: Antecedents, correlates, and consequences. *Journal of Personality, 71,* 1087–1112.

Kochanska, G., Murray, K., & Coy, K. C. (1997). Inhibitory control as a contributor to conscience in childhood: From toddler to early school age. *Child Development, 68,* 263–277.

Kochanska, G., Murray, K. T., & Harlan, E. T. (2000). Effortful control in early childhood: Continuity and change, antecedents, and implications for social development. *Developmental Psychology, 36,* 220–232.

Kochanska, G., Murray, K., Jacques, T. Y., Koenig, A. L., & Vandegeest, K. A. (1996). Inhibitory control in young children and its role in emerging internalization. *Child Development, 67,* 490–507.

Kopp, C. B. (1992). Emotional distress and control in young children. In N. Eisenberg & R. A. Fabes (Eds.), *New directions for child development, No. 55: Emotion and its regulation in early development* (pp. 41–56). San Francisco: Jossey-Bass.

Kremen, A. M., & Block, J. (1998). The roots of ego-control in young adulthood: Links with parenting in early childhood. *Journal of Personality and Social Psychology, 75,* 1062–1075.

Kyrios, M., & Prior, M. (1990). Temperament, stress, and family factors in behavioral adjustment of 3–5-year-old children. *International Journal of Behavioral Development, 13,* 67–93.

Mischel, W., Shoda, Y., & Peake, P. K. (1988). The nature of adolescent competencies predicted by preschool delay of gratification. *Journal of Personality and Social Psychology, 54,* 687–696.

Murphy, L. B. (1962). *The widening world of childhood: Paths toward mastery.* New York: Basic Books.

Ochsner, K. N., Bunge, S. A., Gross, J. J., & Gabrieli, J. D. E. (2002). Rethinking feelings: An fMRI study of the cognitive regulation of emotion. *Journal of Cognitive Neuroscience, 14,* 1215–1229.

Olesen, P. J., Westerberg, H., & Klingberg, T. (2004). Increased prefrontal and parietal activity after training of working memory. *Nature Neuroscience, 7,* 75–79.

Posner, M. I., & Fan, J. (in press). Attention as an organ system. In J. Pomerantz (Ed.), *Neurobiology of perception and communication: From synapse to society. The IVth De Lange Conference.* Cambridge: Cambridge University Press.

Putnam, S. P., Ellis, L. K., & Rothbart, M. K. (2001). The structure of temperament from infancy through adolescence. In A. Eliasz & A. Angleitner (Eds.), *Advances in research on temperament* (pp. 165–182). Lengerich: Pabst Science.

Reed, M., Pien, D., & Rothbart, M. K. (1984). Inhibitory self-control in preschool children. *Merrill-Palmer Quarterly, 30,* 131–148.

Rothbart, M. K. (1988). Temperament and the development of inhibited approach. *Child Development, 59,* 1241–1250.

Rothbart, M. K., Ahadi, S. A., & Evans, D. E. (2000). Temperament and personality: Origins and outcomes. *Journal of Personality and Social Psychology, 78,* 122–135.

Rothbart, M. K., Ahadi, S. A., & Hershey, K. L. (1994). Temperament and social behavior in childhood. *Merrill-Palmer Quarterly, 40,* 21–39.

Rothbart, M. K., Ahadi, S. A., Hershey, K., & Fisher, P. (2001). Investigations of temperament at three to seven years: The Children's Behavior Questionnaire. *Child Development, 72*, 1394–1408.

Rothbart, M. K., & Bates, J. E. (in press). Temperament. In N. Eisenberg (Vol. Ed.), *Handbook of child psychology: Vol. 3. Social, emotional and personality development* (6th ed). New York: Wiley.

Rothbart, M. K., & Derryberry, D. (1981). Development of individual differences in temperament. In M. E. Lamb & A. L. Brown (Eds.), *Advances in developmental psychology* (Vol. 1, pp. 37–86). Hillsdale, NJ: Erlbaum.

Rothbart, M. K., & Derryberry, D. (2002). Temperament in children. In C. von Hofsten & L. Bäckman (Eds.), *Psychology at the turn of the millennium. Vol. 2: Social, developmental, and clinical perspectives* (pp. 17–35). Hove: Psychology Press.

Rothbart, M. K., Derryberry, D., & Hershey, K. (2000). Stability of temperament in childhood: Laboratory infant assessment to parent report at seven years. In V. J. Molfese & D. L. Molfese (Eds.), *Temperament and personality development across the life span* (pp. 85–119). Hillsdale, NJ: Erlbaum.

Rothbart, M. K., Derryberry, D., & Posner, M. I. (1994). A psychobiological approach to the development of temperament. In J. E. Bates & T. D. Wachs (Eds.), *Temperament: Individual differences at the interface of biology and behavior* (pp. 83–116). Washington, DC: American Psychological Association.

Rothbart, M. K., Ellis, L. K., Rueda, M. R., & Posner, M. I. (2003). Developing mechanisms of temperamental effortful control. *Journal of Personality, 71*, 1113–1143.

Rothbart, M. K., & Posner, M. I. (in press). Temperament, attention, and developmental psychopathology. In D. Cicchetti & D. J. Cohen (Eds.), *Developmental psychopathology* (2nd ed.). New York: Wiley.

Rothbart, M. K., & Rueda, M. R. (2005). The development of effortful control. In U. Mayr, E. Awh, & S. W. Keele (Eds.), *Developing individuality in the human brain* (pp. 167–188). Washington, DC: American Psychological Association.

Rothbart, M. K., Ziaie, H., & O'Boyle, C. G. (1992). Self-regulation and emotion in infancy. In N. Eisenberg & R. A. Fabes (Eds.), *New directions for child development, No. 55: Emotion and its regulation in early development* (pp. 7–23). San Francisco: Jossey-Bass Publishers.

Rueda, M. R., Fan, J., McCandliss, B., Halparin, J. D., Gruber, D. B., Pappert, L., & Posner, M. I. (2004). Development of attentional networks in childhood. *Neuropsychologia, 72*, 1029–1040.

Rueda, M. R., Posner, M. I., & Rothbart, M. K. (2004). Attentional control and self-regulation. In R. F. Baumeister & K. D. Vohs (Eds.), *Handbook of self-regulation: Research, theory, and applications* (pp. 357–370). New York: Guilford.

Rueda, M. R., Rothbart, M. R., McCandliss, B., Saccamanno, L., & Posner, M. (2005). Training, maturation and genetic influences on the development of executive attention. *Proceedings of the National Academy of Sciences of the US, 102*(41), 14931–14936.

Rumbaugh, D. M., & Washburn, D. A. (1995). Attention and memory in relation to learning: A comparative adaptation perspective. In G. R. Lyon & N. A. Krasengor (Eds.), *Attention, memory, and executive function* (pp. 199–219). Baltimore: Brookes Publishing Co.

Sander, L. W. (1962). Issues in early mother–child interaction. *Journal of the American Academy of Child Psychiatry, 1*, 141–166.

Schaffer, H. R. (1974). Cognitive components of the infant's response to strangeness. In M. Lewis & L. A. Rosenblum (Eds.), *The origins of fear* (pp. 11–24). New York: Wiley.

Sethi, A., Mischel, W., Aber, J. L., Shoda, Y., & Rodriguez, M. L. (2000). The role of strategic attention deployment in development of self-regulation: Predicting preschoolers' delay of gratification from mother-toddler interactions. *Developmental Psychology, 36*, 767–777.

Sharon, T., & DeLoache, J. S. (2003). The role of perseveration in children's symbolic understanding and skill. *Developmental Science, 6,* 289–296.

Shoda, Y., Mischel, W., & Peake, P. (1990). Predicting adolescent cognitive and self-regulatory competencies from preschool delay of gratification: Identifying diagnostic conditions. *Developmental Psychology, 26,* 978–986.

Simon, J. R. (1969). Reaction toward a source of stimulation. *Journal of Experimental Psychology, 81,* 174–176.

Stifter, C. A., & Braungart, J. M. (1995). The regulation of negative reactivity in infancy: Function and development. *Developmental Psychology, 31,* 448–455.

Thompson, C., Barresi, J., & Moore, C. (1997). The development of future-oriented prudence and altruism in preschoolers. *Cognitive Development, 12,* 199–212.

Vohs, K. D., & Ciarocco, N. J. (2004). Interpersonal functioning requires self-regulation. In R. F. Baumeister& K. D. Vohs (Eds.), *Handbook of self-regulation: Research, theory, and applications* (pp. 392–407). New York: Guilford.

Washburn, D. A. (1994). Stroop-like effects for monkeys and humans: Processing speed or strength of association? *Psychological Science, 5,* 375–379.

Zelazo, P. D., Muller, U., Frye, D., & Marcovitch, S. (2003). The development of executive function in early childhood. *Monographs of the Society for Research in Child Development, 68*(3, Serial No. 274).

Zelazo, P. D., & Reznick, J. S. (1991). Age-related asynchrony of knowledge and action. *Child Development, 62,* 719–735.

18

Maladjustment in Preschool Children: A Developmental Psychopathology Perspective

Susan B. Campbell

Temper tantrums, defiance, fights over toys, a high level of activity, picky eating, sibling jealousy, excessive shyness, and separation anxiety – these behaviors are familiar to any child care provider, preschool teacher, or parent with young children. But to what degree are these behaviors normative and age-related, a reaction to transitory stress in the face of a developmental challenge or transition, or a marker of an emerging problem? This question has been at the forefront of attempts to identify children at risk for emotional and behavior disorders in early childhood in order to track the developmental course of problem behavior and provide prevention or early intervention programs (Beckwith, 2000; Campbell, 2002; Cowan & Cowan, 2002; Reid, 1993). Although some young children showing these potentially symptomatic behaviors will indeed go on to have serious problems that worsen with development, the majority of non-referred pre-schoolers showing hard-to-manage or shy and withdrawn behavior at home and/or child care will overcome their early difficulties (Bennett, Lipman, Racine, & Offord, 1998; Campbell, Pierce, Moore, Marakovitz, & Newby, 1996; Mathiesen & Sanson, 2000). Research suggests that only a small proportion of children showing problem behavior in early childhood will continue on a pathway toward serious adjustment problems in middle childhood. The major task for the researcher and clinician alike becomes one of identifying which shy or hard-to-manage preschoolers are really at risk for continuing problems, in contrast to those who are going through a difficult developmental transition, or are showing behaviors that, despite the concerns of parents or other adults, are well within the normal range.

In this chapter, I will first briefly describe some of the main developmental tasks of the preschool period and how they are reflected in positive adjustment in order to provide a contrast with problem behaviors; next I will attempt to define clinically significant behavior problems in young children. Dimensions and categories (diagnoses) of problem behavior will be described and discussed to clarify distinctions between serious and potentially chronic problems and more normative behaviors. The developmental psychopathology perspective will serve as an organizing framework to help to identify which problem preschoolers are most likely to be at risk for continuing problems (Campbell, 2002; Campbell, Shaw, & Gilliom, 2000; Cicchetti & Cohen, 1995; Cummings, Davies, & Campbell, 2000; Sameroff, 2000). Next, individual differences in preschool children, and individual differences in families and parenting, will be discussed as they converge with social context effects to predict different adjustment outcomes. Finally, the implications for prevention and intervention are touched on briefly.

More serious disorders that also may be identified in the preschool period, including those that are primarily biologically based, such as autism spectrum or pervasive developmental disorders (Rutter, 2000), will not be addressed in this chapter. Similarly, I will not focus on serious disorders with more obvious etiologies, that is, disorders that appear to result from extremes of pathological caregiving and/or deprivation, or from the experience of catastrophic and frightening events, such as physical or sexual abuse, war, natural disasters, or other atypical events, that is, disorders like reactive attachment disorder (Zeanah & Boris, 2000; Zeanah & Fox, 2004) or post-traumatic stress disorder (Scheeringa & Gaensbauer, 2000). Rather, this chapter emphasizes more typical problem behaviors evident in the preschool period that may or may not be related to later adjustment difficulties.

Developmental Tasks and Problem Behaviors

The period from 2 to 5 is one of rapid developmental change and transformation. During this period children learn to regulate their emotions and generally to control their own behavior to some degree, with decreasing reliance on adult intervention; self-regulatory abilities emerge concomitant with children's increasing engagement with other children, and these skills allow for independent play in dyads and groups with some adult monitoring, but not constant supervision. Young children's greater ability to plan and to use language both to communicate with others and to guide their own behavior also facilitates positive interactions with other children. Well-functioning preschool children are interested in the world around them, invested in exploration and socio-dramatic play, and able to modulate arousal and impulses. This is reflected not only in major strides in cognitive and language development, but also in children's ability to focus attention and regulate both positive and negative emotions, especially anger and aggression. In the peer group, the well-functioning 4-year-old is able to take turns, share toys, engage in reciprocal conversation, coordinate play with peers, and resolve disputes without disrupting the interaction.

By age 4, most preschoolers are able to negotiate role assignments and joint goals in order to engage in mutually agreed-upon pretend play scenarios that involve perspective taking and awareness of inner states in self and others – both real and imagined. In addition to competence in the peer group, the well-functioning preschool child also shows age-appropriate social and cognitive development that is reflected in positive parent–child relationships, emerging school-readiness skills, and the willingness to follow directions and cooperate with reasonable adult requests in group settings such as child care or preschool. There is a profound transformation from the 2-year-old with relatively rudimentary language, self-regulation, and cooperative play skills to the 4- or 5-year-old with quite sophisticated conversational ability, self-control, and the social competence needed for complex reciprocal play with peers. It is during this major developmental transition between toddlerhood and age 5 that some problem behaviors emerge, either reflecting transient adjustment reactions or signs of more serious and entrenched responses to stress and challenge.

In contrast to the well-functioning preschooler, problems in preschool children are often evident in high levels of negative and angry affect, non-compliance and outright defiance with parents and other adults, frequent squabbles with siblings that may include physical aggression, difficulties in the peer group reflected in fights over toys and lack of cooperative play, and the failure to follow directions and comply with adult requests in preschool or child care. Such children may act without thinking, wander aimlessly in the preschool classroom, have difficulty playing alone or with others when unsupervised, and be highly active and disorganized in their play. Impulsivity, inattention, and over-activity may co-occur with tantrums and oppositional behavior (Barkley et al., 2002; Lavigne et al., 1996; Speltz, DeKlyen, Greenberg, & Dryden, 1995). Indeed, defiance, temper tantrums, and over-activity are among the most common reasons why young children are referred to mental health settings (Eyberg, 1992; Speltz et al., 1995); non-compliance and problems with peers, especially serious aggression, are frequent complaints of child care providers and preschool teachers, and when these problems are serious enough, the child may even be asked to leave the child care setting (Campbell, 2002). Parents may also be concerned about delayed or atypical language development which also co-occurs with defiance and aggression (Dietz, Lavigne, Arend, & Rosenbaum, 1997; Gadow, Sprafkin, & Nolan, 2001).

On the other hand, some young children may be especially fearful, anxious, sad, and socially withdrawn, although in general these problems appear to be less likely in young children (Gadow et al., 2001; Lavigne et al., 1996) in the absence of abuse, neglect, or other serious disruptions in parenting or other family problems; when these problems do occur in the absence of high levels of family stress, anxiety and related problems, they tend to be less stable (Lavigne et al., 1998; Mathiesen & Sanson, 2000). Thus, many problem behaviors that emerge in the preschool period appear to reflect extreme variations in the development of self-regulation (e.g., tantrums, aggression, hyperactivity, inattention), social competence (e.g., cooperation with peers, following directions), and emotional expression that impair the child's ability to function smoothly in the family, with peers, and in out of home settings such as child care or preschool.

Defining Clinically Significant Problems in the Preschool Child

Most children will show some problematic behavior at some point in early development, be it excessive shyness, finicky eating, clinginess, a high activity level, or tantrum behavior, thus blurring the line between typical and transient behaviors and serious problems (Koot, 1993; Richman, Stevenson, & Graham, 1982). Conversely, many of these behaviors that are common and relatively transient in most young children also define more serious problems that, under some circumstances, may merit mental health intervention. Developmental transitions and challenges during this period are sometimes marked by the appearance of behaviors that are annoying or of concern to adults. For example, it is not uncommon for young children to become defiant or clingy or to want to resume bottle feeding after the birth of a sibling (Dunn, 1985). Some young children may become upset after they experience a change in caregiver (e.g., a move from the toddler to the preschool room) or a move to a new child care setting; this upset may be expressed as tearfulness, separation anxiety, and/or angry outbursts. Still other children may become easily excited and over-active in group settings with peers and have difficulty modulating their behavior on their own, and thus require adult support to encourage positive peer interaction. These behaviors are usually transient and age-related, reflecting typical reactions to normative events in young children's lives that require reorganization and adaptation.

At the same time, many of these same behaviors are also *symptoms* of the childhood disorders to be discussed below: oppositional defiant disorder, attention deficit hyperactivity disorder, and separation anxiety disorder. This highlights the importance of understanding the developmental and social context when trying to distinguish between normative behavior and symptomatic behavior in young children. For this reason, a number of researchers recently have cautioned against over-pathologizing essentially typical and transient behavior in preschool children (Bennett et al., 1998; Campbell, 2002; McClellan & Speltz, 2003). Because children show such enormous changes in the ability to regulate activity, attention, impulses, and the expression of negative affect during the preschool period (Campbell, 2002; Eisenberg & Fabes, 1998; Kopp, 1989; Ruff, Capozzoli & Weissberg, 1998), differentiating normative, age-related behavior from symptoms of an incipient disorder can sometimes be a challenge.

Campbell (2002), therefore, proposed a definition of disorder in young children that includes a *cluster* of symptoms that have been troublesome for some time (to differentiate the behavior from a normative reaction to a stressful event or change), is evident in more than one situation or setting (e.g., home and child care) and across relationships (e.g., parents and caregivers), is relatively severe, and is likely to impede the child's ability to negotiate the important developmental tasks necessary for adaptive functioning in the family and the peer group. In addition, serious problems, for example, with separation or with angry defiance may sometimes be a sign of ongoing difficulties in the caregiving environment. Thus, it is not the presence of specific problem behaviors that differentiates "normal" from "abnormal," but their *frequency, intensity, chronicity, constellation, social context, and implications for future development.*

Thus, for example, tantrums would be interpreted as merely a transient developmental phenomenon if they were apparent in a preschool-age child with few other problems, and especially if they occurred primarily in specific stressful or challenging situations, when the child was over-tired, or soon after the birth of a sibling or after another life transition. On the other hand, tantrums might be considered symptomatic of a more serious and potentially more persistent problem if they occurred frequently, were intense, the child was difficult to control in other settings (e.g., fighting frequently with siblings and/or peers), and was showing a general pattern of non-compliance, aggression, and poor regulation of negative affect. In this situation, a consultation with a mental health provider skilled in work with young children and families would be appropriate. At a minimum parents and child care providers might need guidelines on how to manage the child's behavior, although the mental health professional would also need to assess aspects of the family and child care setting, including the amount of structure, support, and limit-setting provided to the child to understand the context in which the problem behaviors occur. The success of parent management programs for parents with young children (Eyberg, 1992; Hood & Eyberg, 2003; Nixon, 2002) suggests that tantrums and defiance often occur when children are overwhelmed or confused by inconsistent, overly harsh, or inadequate limit-setting. We now turn to a description of individual differences in the manifestations of problem behaviors in young children.

Dimensions and Categories of Childhood Disorders

Young children's problems are usually defined dimensionally in terms of *over-controlled or internalizing* behaviors that are reflected in worry, anxiety, sadness, and social withdrawal and represent self-focused expressions of distress. These are in contrast to *under-controlled* or *externalizing* behaviors such as tantrums, defiance, fighting with peers, impulsivity, and over-activity. These behaviors are typically high in annoyance value and/or the potential to hurt others and they are an outward manifestation of problems (Achenbach, 1991, 1992). At a categorical level, in terms of psychiatric diagnoses described in the *Diagnostic and Statistical Manual of Mental Disorders* (*DSM-IV*, American Psychiatric Association [APA], 1994, 2000), only a few categories of disorder would be applicable to preschool children (the exclusion of autism spectrum disorders and reactive attachment disorder from this discussion was already noted); these include oppositional defiant disorder (ODD), attention deficit hyperactivity disorder (ADHD), and separation anxiety disorder (SAD).

Although clear developmental guidelines are not provided in the *DSM*, there are age-related caveats that suggest caution in applying these diagnoses to very young children. In addition, the American Academy of Pediatrics (AAP) has published a companion volume to the *DSM* to assist primary care providers who must make diagnostic decisions daily, and it provides much clearer developmental guidelines for distinguishing among normal variations in behavior that may be annoying or of concern to parents, potentially transient problems that may suggest mild and time-limited difficulties, and problems that are likely to be more longstanding and to require intervention (*DSM-PC*, American Academy of Pediatrics [AAP], 1996). For example, the *DSM-PC* discusses normative presentations of non-compliance in early childhood, such as saying "no" to a request, in contrast to more serious and sustained presentations that include outright defiance and aggression. Even so, there has been an upsurge in diagnoses of mental disorders in preschool children with a concomitant increase in the use of psychoactive medications (Short, Manos, Findling, & Schubel, 2004; Zito et al., 2000), and this has prompted concerns about over-diagnosis and inappropriate treatment (Bennett et al., 1998; McClellan & Speltz, 2003; see Campbell, 2002, for a more thorough discussion of these issues).

Externalizing Disorders

Oppositional defiant disorder

The diagnostic criteria for ODD include the presence of four out of eight symptoms of uncooperative behavior and negative affect (loses temper, argues, defies or refuses to comply, deliberately annoys others, often blames others, touchy, angry, spiteful) that continue for at least six months and interfere with social and cognitive functioning. To be considered a clinically significant symptom, a behavior must "occur more frequently than is typically observed" in children of "comparable age and developmental level." Although the developmental guidelines for this diagnosis are vague, the duration and impairment criteria mean that it is less likely to be applied to children who are going through a short-lived developmental transition. As noted in the *DSM-IV* (APA, 1994), "Because transient oppositional behavior is very common in preschool children . . . caution should be exercised" (p. 92) in making this diagnosis.

Still, it is easy to imagine how parents might construe some of the typical behaviors of toddlerhood and the early preschool period, especially in families with more than one child (e.g., annoying others, spiteful), as meeting symptomatic criteria. Thus, it is necessary for the clinician to rule out, for example, typical sibling squabbles in evaluating the clinical significance of particular symptoms in young children. Given the overlap between the typical behaviors of preschoolers and the symptoms of oppositional disorder, it may be easy to over-diagnose age-appropriate but difficult behavior as a psychiatric disorder. The *DSM-PC* (AAP, 1996) provides some perspective on this issue by including a discussion of a number of issues like the birth of a sibling, family conflict, and other stressful life events that may lead to adjustment reactions in young children, expressed as problematic behaviors that overlap considerably with the symptoms of ODD. At the same time, parents who are dealing with a difficult developmental transition may well benefit from structured interventions geared to handling difficult children (Eyberg, 1992; Hood & Eyberg, 2003; Nixon, 2002), regardless of whether they actually meet the *DSM-IV* criteria for a diagnosis of ODD.

Despite these cautions, this diagnosis is clearly applicable to some 4- and 5-year-olds, and even some 3-year-olds with serious problems (Keenan & Wakschlag, 2000). For example, Lavigne and colleagues (1996), in one of the few studies to examine the prevalence of diagnoses in a non-clinical sample of preschool children, found that ODD was by far the most common diagnosis. In a sample of children attending primary care pediatric practices 16.8% met criteria for at least a probable diagnosis of ODD; of these, 8.1% were considered to be showing severe symptoms. More than twice as many boys as girls were considered ODD, with the rate peaking at age 3 and leveling off by age 5. In clinically referred samples of preschool children, ODD is also one of the most common diagnoses, and it is much more frequent in boys than girls (Gadow et al., 2001; Keenan & Wakschlag, 2000).

Follow-up data from the Lavigne et al. (1998) study indicated that about 50% of the children with disruptive diagnoses initially, at between ages 2 and 5, were likely to continue to receive a diagnosis at subsequent follow-up assessments one to three years later.

Children who were younger at the time of initial assessment were more likely to outgrow their problems, suggesting that this diagnosis becomes more valid by age 4 or 5, when more serious problems can be more easily differentiated from transient age-related difficulties with defiance, tantrums, and the regulation of negative affect. Lavigne et al. (1996) found the highest rates of ODD at age 3, a time when children are often struggling with issues of autonomy and self-regulation, and parents may feel frustrated as their child becomes less cooperative. This suggests that the elevated rate of ODD reported in this study at age 3 includes a large proportion of false positive cases, children who were experiencing a difficult developmental transition. By age 4 or 5, this cluster of behaviors is more likely to reflect the emergence of potentially persistent problems, but serious problems can sometimes be identified in 3-year-olds who are showing extreme levels of oppositional and angry behavior (Campbell et al., 2000; Keenan & Wakschlag, 2000). Across the preschool period, persistent problems are evident primarily in the context of family risk and adversity (Campbell, 2002; Campbell et al., 2000; Shaw et al., 1998) and when the difficult behaviors co-occur with symptoms of ADHD and/or cognitive deficits (Barkley et al., 2002; Greenberg, Speltz, DeKlyen, & Jones, 2001; Sonuga-Barke, Auerbach, Campbell, Daley, & Thompson, 2005).

Attention deficit hyperactivity disorder

Preschool children often reach clinical attention because of impulsive and over-active behavior, and these complaints also tend to be much more common in boys. Indeed, in a sample of consecutive clinical referrals of 3- to 6-year-olds, Gadow et al. (2001) found that ADHD was the most common diagnosis, with over half of the referred boys meeting criteria for ADHD. According to the *DSM-IV* (APA, 1994), six symptoms of inattention and/or six symptoms of hyperactivity/impulsivity must last for at least six months and be evident across settings, thereby ruling out children who might be showing situation-specific anxiety or upset that appears as fidgetiness and/or inattention. The six-month duration criterion also serves to rule out children who seem impulsive and over-active because they are going through a brief adjustment reaction to stressful life events such as entering child care or coping with the birth of a sibling.

Young children may easily meet criteria for the hyperactive-impulsive subtype which includes fidgeting, talking excessively, and having difficulty staying seated, taking turns, and playing quietly. This has raised concerns about the over-diagnosis of this disorder in younger children (Marshall, 2000). However, it is noteworthy that in the Lavigne et al. (1996) study ADHD was diagnosed rarely and it usually occurred with a diagnosis of ODD. The *DSM-IV* also provides an important caveat: "It is especially difficult to establish this diagnosis in children younger than 4 or 5 years" (APA, 1994, p. 81). However, the potential to over-diagnose this disorder in young children is a cause for concern, as it is sometimes difficult to make a clear diagnostic decision when confronted with a rambunctious, curious 3- or 4-year-old whose parents cannot cope with his behavior. Because of the increased use of stimulant medication in this age group (Short et al., 2004; Zito et al., 2000), the importance of an accurate diagnosis cannot be over-emphasized. We know little about the effects of stimulant medication on early brain development, so the use of medication in young children raises a number of ethical concerns (Marshall, 2000).

As noted in the *DSM-PC* (AAP, 1996), a diagnosis of ADHD is most likely to occur when there are also signs of cognitive deficits, poor language development, or oppositional behavior. The energetic toddler or preschooler with a sunny disposition is less likely to meet criteria for a diagnosis of ADHD than the child who is non-compliant and angry, consistent with Lavigne et al.'s (1996) observation that few children in their preschool sample received a diagnosis of ADHD in the absence of a co-occurring ODD diagnosis. Barkley and colleagues (2002) screened a large number of preschool children during the pre-kindergarten year and selected children with symptoms of both ADHD and ODD. Despite intervention, children with a combination of behavior problems, cognitive deficits, and high levels of functional impairment were doing quite poorly at a three-year follow-up. Furthermore, another important indicator of risk for ADHD (as opposed to transient problems) is a family history of ADHD symptoms, given the high genetic loading for this condition (Levy, Hay, McStephen, Wood, & Waldman, 1997). Sonuga-Barke and colleagues (2005) have posited that early symptoms of ADHD, even when potentially clinically significant, may be ameliorated by positive parent–child interaction, appropriate firm limit-setting, and positive school experiences, whereas early signs of ADHD may escalate when the child has an especially explosive and impulsive temperament and parent–child relations are coercive. In this scenario, co-occurring ADHD and ODD may become more severe by middle childhood, and the coercive parenting may well reflect genetic contributions to the more chronic form of the disorder.

Taken together, both ODD and ADHD in young children tend to co-occur, and these behavior problems are much more common in boys. Their early emergence together, especially in families with high levels of stress and negative, coercive parenting, predicts continuing problems that may persist to middle childhood and beyond (Campbell, 2002; Moffitt, 1990).

Internalizing (Emotional) Disorders

Much less is known about the internalizing disorders reflecting anxiety, social withdrawal, fearfulness, and sad mood in young children than about ODD and ADHD. This is partly because these behaviors must be more extreme than externalizing behaviors to be noticed and partly because they are often short-lived and transient. Thus, for example, many children show specific fears such as the fear of animals, the dark, or monsters (Campbell, 1986), and these are often age-related fears that do not impair functioning. Thus, it is unlikely that most children with specific fears would meet diagnostic criteria for a specific phobia. Indeed, in the Lavigne et al. (1996) study, out of 510 children, very few (<1%) met criteria for phobias or separation anxiety. Lavigne et al. (1996) comment on the very low rate of internalizing or emotional disorders in their sample. Even in a clinically referred sample, Gadow et al. (2001) identified relatively few cases of separation anxiety or other internalizing disorders. This is consistent with the caveats and developmental guidelines discussed in the *DSM-PC* (AAP, 1996), where it is noted that many of the symptoms of depression (e.g. sad mood, eating or sleeping problems) and anxiety disorders (worry, avoidance of social activities, shyness) are quite common and they may also be relatively brief reactions to specific life events or changes.

Moreover, in the *DSM-IV* (APA, 1994), with the exception of separation anxiety disorder, the other internalizing disorders (specific phobia, social phobia, generalized anxiety disorder, depression) use criteria meant to cut across the age range from childhood to adulthood and there is almost no discussion of developmental differences in clinical presentation. Developmental guidelines are provided in the *DSM-PC* (AAP, 1996), but it is of interest that the behaviors that may indicate fear, anxiety, or depression in young children such as crying, tantrums, clinging to an adult, or avoiding interactions with unfamiliar people are behaviors that may be triggered by a range of situations. Therefore, in the absence of a prolonged period of symptomatic behavior that interferes with the child's ability to progress developmentally and interact in the peer group, it is difficult to arrive at a specific diagnosis, except possibly the diagnosis of adjustment reaction or separation anxiety disorder.

Separation anxiety

Separation anxiety is the only anxiety disorder that is specific to childhood. It is described in the *DSM-IV* (APA, 1994) as "developmentally inappropriate and excessive anxiety concerning separation from home" (p. 113) or from "major attachment figures." Among the eight symptoms defining this disorder are "recurrent excessive distress" in anticipation of separation, worry about losing the attachment figure, school refusal, and fear of being alone or sleeping alone. Nightmares and physical symptoms may also be present. Only three symptoms of four weeks duration are required for a diagnosis, although the disturbance must cause significant distress and/or impairment in functioning. Developmental guidelines are not provided. However, it is suggested that separation anxiety is most likely to emerge after a life stress such as the loss of a relative or pet, a major illness, or the move to a new neighborhood.

In young children, then, without the cognitive capacities to understand sudden and/ or dramatic life change, it is not clear when we can reasonably talk about a "disorder" as opposed to an appropriate reaction to a stressful, confusing, and/or frightening event. Because young children may not be expected to cope easily with certain kinds of stressful events or to readjust quickly to a major life change, but instead may need the close support of an attachment figure to help them make the necessary transitions, the expression of anxiety through nightmares, physical symptoms, or separation protest may be normative rather than pathological. Thus, a 3-year-old who shows a strong reaction to a loss or other major life change or upsetting event that is expressed as clinginess, crying, and other signs of separation distress may be behaving in very predictable ways that do not merit a diagnosis of a *psychiatric disorder.* On the other hand, in the absence of any identifiable event in the life of a young child who becomes virtually panic-stricken at the prospect of separation, both a diagnosis and treatment may be warranted; at the least, this fearful and incapacitating behavior may be evidence that something serious is going on in the family or in the child care setting. It also seems reasonable that a diagnosis is less apt in 2- and 3-year-olds than in older preschool children, although in the face of a catastrophic event such as the death of a parent or marital separation such a reaction may hardly be surprising even in somewhat older children, concerned, for example, with being abandoned by the remaining parent. Children showing normative reactions to stressful events obviously require support and comfort from caring adults, who may themselves need guidance on the best ways to help their child cope with upsetting experiences.

Indeed, symptoms of extreme and prolonged clinginess and upset are more likely to reflect serious problems in the family and the child–caregiver relationship, if not outright deprivation or neglect (National Center for Clinical Infant Programs, 1994). Prolonged sad mood, excessive fear of strangers, excessive separation distress, and other intense fears are unlikely to occur on their own in very young children in the absence of a major loss, traumatic event, neglectful or abusive care, or in the context of a more serious disorder such as autism, reactive attachment disorder, or in reaction to trauma. These problems clearly warrant intervention for the child and family.

Parent–child problems

In recognition of the fact that many symptomatic behaviors in young children really reflect problems in the parent–child relationship or in parents' approaches to childrearing, the *DSM-IV* (APA, 1994) also includes "parent–child relational problem" as another "condition" that may require clinical attention and be the focus of treatment. This diagnosis is warranted when the primary problems revolve around parent management strategies, such as inconsistency or coercive parenting, or over-protectiveness. Surprisingly, this condition merits only a brief paragraph in the *DSM-IV* and it is not discussed explicitly in the *DSM-PC* despite the fact that this is a very common presenting complaint in pediatric primary care. Indeed, in the Lavigne et al. (1996) study, parent–child problem was the second most common classification (4.6%) after ODD and it was more than twice as common as ADHD. In addition, there were dramatic differences in prevalence as a function of age. In the sample of 2-year-olds, 9.2% presented with a parent–child problem as the "terrible twos" emerged, but by age 4 only 2.8% were considered parent–child problems, and by age 5, only one parent–child dyad was so classified. Because many problems of early childhood revolve around the quality of the parent–child relationship and issues of limit-setting and control, and this is by far the most widely researched area of early child social development, this topic clearly deserves more attention in diagnostic manuals for clinicians working with young children.

In summary, the major disorders of childhood including oppositional defiant disorder, attention deficit hyperactivity disorder, and separation anxiety disorder can be diagnosed in preschool children. However, many, if not most, children showing the symptoms of these disorders are likely to be showing less severe and more transient manifestations of problems, given the overlap between symptoms of disorder and typical reactions to stress and change. However, a developmental psychopathology perspective suggests additional issues to consider when attempting to differentiate between behavior that is normative and behavior that may be symptomatic of more serious and potentially chronic behavior problems in the preschool period.

A Developmental Psychopathology Perspective on Young Children's Problem Behavior

The developmental psychopathology perspective is based on the assumption that outcomes are probabilistic and are a function of converging child, family, and social context effects (Cicchetti & Cohen, 1995; Cummings et al., 2000; Sameroff, 2000). Thus, a child who is extremely active, defiant, and aggressive at age 3 is more likely to continue on a pathway toward ADHD and/or conduct problems in the future than is a more easy-going, cooperative child with good social skills. However, the potentially problematic 3-year-old may well be going through a difficult developmental transition such as adapting to the birth of a sibling, a move, entry into child care, or some other change that is associated with increased anxiety and non-compliance, and that same child may look fine by age 4. In contrast, the compliant 3-year-old may develop problem behaviors at a later date. On the other hand, some extremely difficult preschoolers may indeed continue on a pathway toward more serious problems. Continuity in problem behavior may or may not be evident. A complex mix of child, family, and social factors interact over time to predict pathways and outcomes (Campbell, 2002; Cummings et al., 2000; Deater-Deckard, Dodge, Bates, & Pettit, 1998; Greenberg et al., 1999).

Individual Differences in Child Behavior

As is evident from prior chapters, there are wide individual differences in behavior during infancy and toddlerhood that appear to be biologically based and to be reflected in variations in reactivity and regulation (Rothbart & Bates, 1998); these individual differences may be evident in children's activity level, attention, and positive and negative mood, as well as in their ability to regulate these behaviors and emotions appropriately in response to situational demands. Individual differences in temperament have long been considered potential precursors of early-emerging problems in adjustment (Thomas, Chess, & Birch, 1968). Thomas et al. (1968) discussed children who are "difficult," that is, especially irritable, and hard to soothe when upset or who do not readily settle into a routine, in contrast to relatively "easy" children and those who are "slow to warm up," as evidenced by negative reactions to new people or to changes in routine. More recent research on temperament has focused on extremes of inhibition and fearfulness in contrast to extremes of fearlessness and risk-taking, as well as the ability to regulate negative emotions, especially anger and sadness (Calkins, 1994; Frick, 2004; Kagan, 1997; Rothbart, Posner, & Hershey, 1995). These may be seen as precursors of internalizing (anxiety and depression) and externalizing problems (conduct problems, attention deficit hyperactivity disorder), although research on this remains equivocal (Frick, 2004; Rothbart et al., 1995).

In addition to individual differences in temperament or early-emerging personality characteristics, gender is associated with different patterns of adjustment and maladjustment. Patterns of gender differences are clearer by middle childhood, but even in the preschool period, externalizing problems appear to be more prevalent in preschool boys, whereas both boys and girls evidence internalizing problems; these findings are consistent across epidemiological, community, and clinical samples (Gadow et al., 2001; Keenan & Wakschlag, 2000; Lavigne et al., 1996; Richman et al., 1982). Cognitive problems and language delays, which are also more common in boys, are likewise associated with elevated rates of oppositional behavior and attention problems in preschool children (Barkley et al., 2002; Richman et al., 1982).

Taken together, there is evidence that some children are at higher risk than others for either externalizing or internalizing problems in early childhood by virtue of certain personality characteristics. Gender and language development are also associated with particular types of problems. However, there is also considerable evidence indicating that family context, especially parenting, makes a difference either by helping children overcome early anxiety or impulsivity, or conversely by exacerbating these maladaptive tendencies.

Family Influences

Children's problems do not emerge in a vacuum, but in the context of the family. It has been argued that emotional and behavior problems in early childhood (not including problems that are largely or entirely biologically based, like mental retardation or autism spectrum disorders) often signal difficulties in early parent–child relationships (Aguilar, Sroufe, Egeland, & Carlson, 2000; Carlson & Sroufe, 1995; Lieberman, Silverman, & Pawl, 2000). Whereas it is well documented that child abuse and neglect predict a range of adjustment problems in young children (Wolfe, 1999), it is also clear that less severe indicators of negative parenting including harsh, punitive, angry, detached, and rejecting parental behaviors are associated with high levels of child non-compliance, active defiance, temper tantrums, and aggression (Campbell et al., 1996; Crockenberg & Litman, 1990; McFayden-Ketchum, Bates, Dodge, & Pettit, 1996; Shaw et al., 1998; Spieker, Larson, Lewis, Keller, & Gilchrist, 1999). This association between negative parenting and behavior problems in early childhood may emerge in the context of an insecure attachment relationship (Moss, Bureau, Cyr, Mongeau, & St.-Laurent, 2004; Speltz, DeKlyen, & Greenberg, 1999), but this association also appears to reflect other aspects of the parent–child relationship that go beyond attachment (Moss et al., 2004).

Because research on parent–child interaction and behavior problems has generally been correlational in nature, and studies have not used genetically informed designs, these associations and transactions over time may be due to gene–environment correlation or interaction (Deater-Deckard & O'Connor, 2000; Rutter et al., 1997). For example, a more irritable, demanding, or difficult-to-soothe infant may elicit less sensitive and involved caretaking in early childhood which in turn is associated with an insecure attachment, especially when parents are themselves stressed or poorly adjusted. These bi-directional influences (a difficult infant and a less responsive or more irritable parent) may be a product of gene–environment correlation, since the irritable infant and the annoyed parent share half their genes. Moreover, this process may be exacerbated over time. Whereas a less irritable child may be less upset by negative or harsh parenting, some children may be especially reactive to harsh parental interventions (Belsky, Hsieh, & Crnic, 1998), but respond more positively to firm control (Bates, Pettit, Dodge, & Ridge, 1998), especially when it is paired with warmth and respect for autonomy (Kochanska, 1997). Thus, the escalating, coercive process described by Patterson, Debaryshe, and Ramsey (1989) may reflect not only bi-directional influences, but gene–environment interactions. Regardless of the underlying process, the link between harsh parenting and externalizing behavior is well documented and highlights the importance of considering family context when attempting to predict whether a hard-to-manage preschool child will continue on a pathway toward more severe and chronic problems (Campbell, 2002; Cowan & Cowan, 2002). Even though we cannot be sure what initially triggered the coercive interaction, many studies suggest that interventions that modify negative parenting can be effective, and especially so with preschool-age children (Cowan & Cowan, 2002; Hood & Eyberg, 2003).

Most research linking parenting and children's externalizing problems has focused on harsh, punitive discipline or on inconsistent discipline. However, evidence suggests that the lack of positive engagement may also be associated with higher levels of problem behavior (Gardner, 1987; Pettit, Bates, & Dodge, 1997). Greenberg, Speltz, and DeKlyen (1993) have argued that explosive, demanding, and non-compliant behavior may be one way in which some children attempt to gain attention from disengaged parents. In general, studies linking low levels of maternal involvement (Gardner, 1987; Pettit et al., 1997) or low maternal sensitivity in early childhood (NICHD Early Child Care Research Network [ECCRN], 1998, 2003, 2004) to externalizing behavior in preschool and beyond indicate that it is more than the presence of negative and harsh parenting that may be predicting externalizing problems. Lack of warmth, involvement, and proactive parenting are also associated with higher levels of behavior problems. Not surprisingly, in the absence of warmth and reciprocated positive affect, parents have a harder time obtaining cooperation from their preschool child, and engaging children in the mutually responsive style of parent–child interaction described by Kochanska (1997) that appears to facilitate childrearing, even when young children may be somewhat difficult to manage (Campbell, 2002; Denham, Workman, Cole, Weissbrod, Kendziora, & Zahn-Waxler, 2000; Gardner, 1987; Gardner, Sonuga-Barke, & Sayal, 1999).

It is noteworthy that successful interventions developed for parents of young children with oppositional problems begin by teaching them to play with their child and respond to their child's cues as a way of improving relationship quality (Eyberg, 1992). They also encourage proactive approaches to limit-setting that help parents anticipate trouble and redirect their children to positive activities when they may be about to lose control (Gardner et al., 1999). Although most research has focused on mother–child interaction, there is evidence that when fathers are involved with preschool boys referred for treatment, harsh and negative control also predicts more severe problems (DeKlyen, Speltz, &

Greenberg, 1998). Other recent studies have targeted more specific processes as potentially important in understanding the links between parent–child interaction and behavior problems, including modeling and coaching children in ways to control negative emotions (Cole, Teti, & Zahn-Waxler, 2003; Thompson, 1998).

In addition to more proximal aspects of parenting, more distal factors, including socioeconomic status indicators, especially poverty and low maternal educational level, marital conflict, maternal depressive symptoms, and single-parent status, have been associated both concurrently and predictively with the early onset of behavior problems, primarily externalizing problems, and with their persistence into middle childhood (Campbell et al., 1996; Deater-Deckard et al., 1998; Greenberg et al., 1999; McLoyd, 1990, 1998; NICHD ECCRN, 2004). The nature of these relationships is complex because negative and disengaged parenting often occurs in tandem with these other family stresses. Thus, many indicators of family climate are highly intercorrelated with each other as well as with methods of childrearing, and they may have direct effects on the child as well as indirect effects mediated through less involved or more negative parenting (McLoyd, 1990, 1998; Webster-Stratton & Hammond, 1999).

The developmental psychopathology perspective considers the child in the context of the family and community more generally and also takes into account the balance between risk and protective factors. A complex model of the emergence of behavior problems in preschool children must, therefore, include child characteristics, parenting behaviors, family composition and interaction patterns, and factors in the family's wider social environment (Campbell, 2002). In general, the transactions over time between child characteristics (including possible biological vulnerability, personality and temperamental dispositions, and developmental needs and competencies) and parenting factors (primarily the quality of parental affective involvement with the child and childrearing approaches, especially around limit-setting and control) are the strongest predictors of children's social and emotional functioning. However, family climate, as indexed by the quality of the marital relationship, family composition, and parental personality and psychological well-being, also appears to affect the child's psychosocial adaptation. Family climate appears to have both a direct impact on children and an indirect one, mediated through the effects of the family environment on parental availability, sensitivity, and childrearing strategies (Belsky, 1984). Finally, more general aspects of the psychosocial environment, including the quality and availability of social support for parents, the nature and availability of institutional supports, and the availability of material resources, affect the child both directly and indirectly (Bronfenbrenner, 1986). Such factors, however, have their greatest impact on the child via their effects on parental well-being, the level of stresses within the family, and the ability of parents to carry out their parenting functions.

Intervention/Prevention

This brief overview of behavior problems in preschool children and the family context in which they are more likely to persist highlights the importance of prevention and early intervention programs, especially since programs begun after school entry are not always that effective, even when they are comprehensive (Barkley et al., 2000). A thorough review of this topic is beyond the scope of this chapter; however, it is clear that there are a number of promising structured, didactic, skill-based parent training programs that emphasize positive parenting for high-risk families (Lyons-Ruth & Melnick, 2004) or for children with diagnosed ADHD (Sonuga-Barke, Daley, Thompson, Laver-Bradbury, & Weeks, 2001) or ODD (Eyberg, Boggs, & Algina, 1995; Nixon, 2002). These programs focus not only on child management, but also on parent–child relationship building. In general, treatment programs appear to be more successful with younger than older children; further treatment programs are generally more effective than prevention programs in modifying aggressive, non-compliant, and oppositional behavior, possibly because families in treatment are more motivated than those who have not necessarily self-identified as having a problem with their child. However, it is not always clear whether children's behavior is normalized post-treatment (Nixon, 2002). Depending on the severity of the problem and the degree of family turmoil that co-occurs with the children's problems, other interventions may also be necessary, including a focus on the mother's depression, the parents' marital difficulties, or other family problems (Cowan & Cowan, 2002; Patterson, DeGarmo, & Forgatch, 2004; Webster-Stratton & Hammond, 1999). In summary, there is growing evidence that young children's problems are often amenable to intervention, especially with structured parenting programs that provide parents with specific skills and also consider the wider family context. However, despite decades of research on this issue, there are still many hard-to-reach families without access to mental health interventions and many children and families falling through the cracks of service delivery systems. Clearly, the mental health, child care, child welfare, and educational systems need to collaborate to confront the serious problems that many young children face prior to school entry and to provide integrated services for young children showing serious behavior problems in early childhood.

References

Achenbach, T. M. (1991). *Manual for the Child Behavior Checklist/4–18 and 1991 Profile*. Burlington, VT: University of Vermont, Department of Psychiatry.

Achenbach, T. M. (1992). *Manual for the Child Behavior Checklist/2–3 and 1992 Profile*. Burlington, VT: University of Vermont, Department of Psychiatry.

Aguilar, B., Sroufe, L. A., Egeland, B., & Carlson, E. (2000). Distinguishing the early-onset/persistent and adolescent-onset antisocial behavior types: From birth to 16 years. *Development and Psychopathology, 12*, 109–132.

American Academy of Pediatrics. (1996). *The classification of child and adolescent mental diagnoses in primary care (DSM-PC)*. Elk Grove, IL: Author.

American Psychiatric Association (1994). *Diagnostic and statistical manual of mental disorders* (4th ed., *DSM-IV*). Washington, DC: Author.

American Psychiatric Association. (2000). *Diagnostic and statistical manual of mental disorders* (Text ed., *DSM-IV*). Washington, DC: Author.

Barkley, R. A., Shelton, T. L., Crosswaite, C., Moorehouse, M., Fletcher, K., Barrett, S., Jenkins, L., & Metavia, L. (2000). Multi-method psycho-educational intervention for preschool children with disruptive behavior: Preliminary results at post-treatment. *Journal of Child Psychology and Psychiatry, 41,* 319–332.

Barkley, R. A., Shelton, T. L., Crosswaite, C., Moorehouse, M., Fletcher, K., Barrett, S., Jenkins, L., & Metavia, L. (2002). Preschool children with disruptive behavior: Three-year outcome as a function of adaptive disability. *Development and Psychopathology, 14,* 45–67.

Bates, J. E., Pettit, G. S., Dodge, K. A., & Ridge, B. (1998). Interaction of temperamental resistance to control and restrictive parenting in the development of externalizing behavior. *Developmental Psychology, 34,* 982–995.

Beckwith, L. (2000). Prevention science and prevention programs. In C. Zeanah (Ed.), *Handbook of infant mental health* (2nd ed., pp. 439–456). New York: Guilford Press.

Belsky, J. (1984). The determinants of parenting: A process model. *Child Development, 55,* 83–96.

Belsky, J., Hsieh, K., & Crnic, K. (1998). Mothering, fathering, and infant negativity as antecedents of boys' externalizing problems and inhibition at age 3 years: Differential susceptibility to rearing experience? *Development and Psychopathology, 10,* 301–319.

Bennett, K. J., Lipman, E. L., Racine, Y. C., & Offord, D. R. (1998). Do measures of externalizing behavior in normal populations predict later outcome? Implications for targeted interventions to prevent conduct disorder. *Journal of Child Psychology and Psychiatry, 39,* 1059–1070.

Bronfenbrenner, U. (1986). Ecology of the family as a context for human development: Research perspectives. *Developmental Psychology, 22,* 723–741.

Calkins, S. (1994). Origins and outcomes of individual differences in emotion regulation. In N. A. Fox (Ed.), *The development of emotion regulation. Monographs of the Society for Research in Child Development, 5* (2–3, Serial No. 240), 53–72.

Campbell, S. B. (1986). Developmental issues. In R. Gittelman (Ed.), *Anxiety disorders of childhood* (pp. 24–57). New York: Guilford Press.

Campbell, S. B. (2002). *Behavior problems in preschool children: Clinical and developmental issues.* (2nd ed.) New York: Guilford Press.

Campbell, S. B., Pierce, E. W., Moore, G., Marakovitz, S., & Newby, K. (1996). Boys' externalizing problems at elementary school: Pathways from early behavior problems, maternal control, and family stress. *Development and Psychopathology, 8,* 701–720.

Campbell, S. B., Shaw, D. S., & Gilliom, M. (2000). Early externalizing behavior problems: Toddlers and preschoolers at risk for later maladjustment. *Development and Psychopathology, 12,* 467–488.

Carlson, E., & Sroufe, L. A. (1995). Contribution of attachment theory to developmental psychopathology. In D. Cicchetti & D. Cohen (Eds). *Developmental psychopathology: Vol. 1. Theory and methods* (pp. 581–617). New York: Wiley.

Cicchetti, D. & Cohen, D.J. (1995). Perspectives on developmental psychopathology. In D. Cicchetti & D. J. Cohen (Eds.), *Developmental psychopathology: Vol. 1. Theory and methods* (pp. 3–20). New York: Wiley.

Cole, P. M., Teti, L. O., & Zahn-Waxler, C. (2003). Mutual emotion regulation and the stability of conduct problems between preschool and early school age. *Development and Psychopathology, 15,* 1–18.

Cowan, P., & Cowan, C. (2002). Interventions as tests of family systems theories: Marital and family relationships in child development and child psychopathology. *Development and Psychopathology, 14,* 731–759.

Crockenberg, S., & Litman, C. (1990). Autonomy as competence in 2-year-olds: Maternal correlates of child defiance, compliance and self-assertion. *Developmental Psychology, 26,* 961–971.

374   *Susan B. Campbell*

Cummings, E. M., Davies, P. T., & Campbell, S. B. (2000). *Developmental psychopathology and family process.* New York: Guilford Press.

Deater-Deckard, K., Dodge, K. A., Bates, J. E., & Pettit, G. S. (1998). Multiple risk factors in the development of externalizing behavior problems: Group and individual differences. *Development and Psychopathology, 10,* 469–493.

Deater-Deckard, K., & O'Connor, T. G. (2000). Parent–child mutuality in early childhood: Two behavioral genetic studies. *Developmental Psychology, 36,* 561–570.

DeKlyen, M., Speltz, M. L., & Greenberg, M.T. (1998). Fathering and early onset conduct problems: Positive and negative parenting, father–son attachment, and marital conflict. *Clinical Child and Family Psychology Review, 1,* 3–22.

Denham, S. A., Workman, E., Cole, P. M., Weissbrod, C., Kendziora, K. T., & Zahn-Waxler, C. (2000). Prediction of externalizing behavior problems from early to middle childhood: The role of parental socialization and emotional expression. *Development and Psychopathology, 12,* 23–45.

Dietz, K., Lavigne, J. V., Arend, R., & Rosenbaum, D. (1997). Relations between intelligence and psychopathology among preschoolers. *Journal of Clinical Child Psychology, 26,* 99–107.

Dunn, J. (1985). *Siblings.* Cambridge, MA: Harvard University Press.

Eisenberg, N., & Fabes, R. (1998). Prosocial development. In N. Eisenberg (Ed.), *Handbook of child psychology: Vol. 3. Social, emotional, and personality development* (5th ed., pp. 701–778). New York: Wiley.

Eyberg, S. M. (1992). Assessing therapy outcome with preschool children: Progress and problems. *Journal of Clinical Child Psychology, 21,* 306–311.

Eyberg, S. M., Boggs, S., & Algina, J. (1995). Parent–child interaction therapy: A psychosocial model for the treatment of young children with conduct problem behavior and their families. *Psychopharmacology Bulletin, 31,* 83–91.

Frick, P. J. (2004). Integrating research on temperament and child psychopathology: Its pitfalls and promise. *Journal of Clinical Child and Adolescent Psychology, 33,* 2–7.

Gadow, K. D., Sprafkin, J., & Nolan, E. E. (2001). DSM-IV symptoms in community and clinic preschool children. *Journal of the American Academy of Child and Adolescent Psychiatry, 40,* 1383–1392.

Gardner, F. E. (1987). Positive interaction between mothers and conduct-problem children: Is there training for harmony as well as fighting? *Journal of Abnormal Child Psychology, 15,* 283–293.

Gardner, F. E., Sonuga-Barke, E. & Sayal, K. (1999) Parents anticipating misbehavior: An observational study of strategies parents use to prevent conflict with behavior problem children. *Journal of Child Psychology and Psychiatry, 40,* 1185–1196.

Greenberg, M. T., Lengua, L. J., Coie, J. D., Pinderhughes, E. E., Bierman, K., Dodge, K. A., Lochman, J. E., & McMahon, R. J. (1999). Predicting developmental outcomes at school entry using a multiple risk model: Four American communities. *Developmental Psychology, 35,* 403–417.

Greenberg, M. T., Speltz, M. L., & DeKlyen, M. (1993). The role of attachment in the development of disruptive behavior problems. *Development and Psychopathology, 5,* 191–214.

Greenberg, M. T. Speltz, M. L. DeKlyen, M. & Jones, K. (2001). Correlates of clinic referral for early conduct problems: Variable and person-oriented approaches. *Development and Psychopathology, 13,* 255–276.

Hood, K. K. & Eyberg, S. M. (2003). Outcomes of parent–child interaction therapy: Mothers' reports of maintenance three to six years after treatment. *Journal of Clinical Child and Adolescent Psychology, 32,* 419–429.

Kagan, J. (1997). Temperament and reactions to unfamiliarity. *Child Development, 68,* 139–143.

Keenan, K., & Wakschlag, L. S. (2000). More than the terrible twos: The nature and severity of behavior problems in clinic-referred preschool children. *Journal of Abnormal Child Psychology*, *28*, 33–46.

Kochanska, G. (1997). Mutually responsive orientation between mothers and their young children: Implications for early socialization. *Child Development*, *68*, 94–112.

Koot, H. M. (1993). *Problem behavior in Dutch preschoolers*. Rotterdam: Erasmus University.

Kopp, C. B. (1989). Regulation of distress and negative emotions: A developmental view. *Developmental Psychology*, *25*, 343–354.

Lavigne, J. V., Arend, R., Rosenbaum, D. Binns, H., Christoffel, K. K., & Gibbons, R. D. (1998). Psychiatric disorders with onset in the preschool years: I. Stability of diagnoses. *Journal of the American Academy of Child and Adolescent Psychiatry*, *37*, 1246–1254.

Lavigne, J. V., Gibbons, R. D., Christoffel, K. K., Arend, R., Rosenbaum, D., Binns, H., Dawson, N., Sobel, H., & Isaacs, C. (1996). Prevalence rates and correlates of psychiatric disorders among preschool children. *Journal of the American Academy of Child and Adolescent Psychiatry*, *35*, 204–214.

Levy, F., Hay, D. A., McStephen, M., Wood, C. & Waldman, I. (1997). Attention-deficit hyperactivity disorder: A category or a continuum? Genetic analysis of a large-scale twin study. *Journal of the American Academy of Child and Adolescent Psychiatry*, *36*, 737–744.

Lieberman, A. F., Silverman, R., & Pawl, J. H. (2000). Infant–parent psychotherapy: Core concepts and current approaches. In C. Zeanah (Ed.), *Handbook of infant mental health* (2nd ed., pp. 472–484). New York: Guilford Press.

Lyons-Ruth, K., & Melnick, S. (2004). Dose–response effect of mother–infant clinical home visiting on aggressive behavior problems in kindergarten. *Journal of the American Academy of Child and Adolescent Psychiatry*, *43*, 699–707.

McClellan, J. M., & Speltz, M. L. (2003). Psychiatric diagnosis in preschool children. *Journal of the American Academy of Child and Adolescent Psychiatry*, *42*, 127–128.

McFadyen-Ketchum, S. A., Bates, J. E., Dodge, K. A., & Pettit, G. S. (1996). Patterns of change in early childhood aggressive-disruptive behavior: Gender differences in predictions from early coercive and affectionate mother-child interactions. *Child Development*, *67*, 2417–2433.

McLoyd, V. C. (1990). The impact of economic hardship on Black families and children: Psychological distress, parenting, and socio-emotional development. *Child Development*, *61*, 311–346.

McLoyd, V. C. (1998). Socieconomic disadvantage and child development. *American Psychologist*, *53*, 185–204.

Marshall, E. (2000). Planned Ritalin trial for tots heads into uncharted waters. *Science*, *290*, 1280–1282.

Mathiesen, K., & Sanson, A. (2000). Dimensions of early childhood behavior problems: Stability and predictors of change from 18 to 30 months. *Journal of Abnormal Child Psychology*, *28*, 15–31.

Moffitt, T. E. (1990). Juvenile delinquency and attention deficit disorders: Boys' developmental trajectories from age 3 to age 15. *Child Development*, *61*, 893–910.

Moss, E., Bureau, J. F., Cyr, C., Mongeau, M., & St.-Laurent, D. (2004). Correlates of attachment at age 3: Construct validity of the preschool attachment classification system. *Developmental Psychology*, *40*, 323–334.

National Center for Clinical Infant Programs (1994). *0–3: Diagnostic classification of mental health and developmental disorders of infancy and early childhood*. Arlington, VA: Author.

NICHD Early Child Care Research Network (1998). Early child care and cooperation, compliance, defiance, and problem behavior at 24 and 36 months of age. *Child Development*, *69*, 1145–1170.

NICHD Early Child Care Research Network (2003). Does the amount of time spent in child care predict socioemotional adjustment during the transition to kindergarten? *Child Development*, *74*, 976–1005.

NICHD Early Child Care Research Network (2004). Trajectories of physical aggression from toddlerhood to middle childhood: Predictors, correlates, and outcomes. *Monographs of the Society for Research in Child Development*, *69*(4, Serial No. 278).

Nixon, R. D. V. (2002). Treatment of behavior problems in preschoolers: A review. *Clinical Psychology Review*, *22*, 525–546.

Patterson, G. R., Debaryshe, B., & Ramsey, E. (1989). A developmental perspective on antisocial behavior. *American Psychologist*, *44*, 329–335.

Patterson, G. R., DeGarmo, D., & Forgatch, M. S. (2004). Systematic changes in families following prevention trials. *Journal of Abnormal Child Psychology*, *32*, 621–633.

Pettit, G., Bates, J., & Dodge, K. (1997). Supportive parenting, ecological context, and children's adjustment: A seven-year longitudinal study. *Child Development*, *68*, 908–923.

Reid, J. (1993). Prevention of conduct disorder before and after school entry: Relating interventions to developmental findings. *Development and Psychopathology*, *5*, 243–262.

Richman, N., Stevenson, J., & Graham, P. J. (1982). *Preschool to school: A behavioural study*. London: Academic Press.

Rothbart, M. K., & Bates, J. E. (1998). Temperament. In N. Eisenberg (Ed.), *Handbook of child psychology: Vol. 3. Social, emotional, and personality development* (5th ed., pp. 105–176). New York: Wiley.

Rothbart, M. K., Posner, M., & Hershey, K. (1995). Temperament, attention, and developmental psychopathology. In D. Cicchetti & D. Cohen (Eds.), *Developmental psychopathology: Vol. 1. Theory and methods* (pp. 315–340). New York: Wiley.

Ruff, H. A., Capozzoli, M., & Weissberg, R. (1998). Age, individuality, and context as factors in sustained visual attention during the preschool years. *Developmental Psychology*, *34*, 454–464.

Rutter, M. (2000). Genetic studies of autism: From the 1970s into the millennium. *Journal of Abnormal Child Psychology*, *28*, 3–14.

Rutter, M., Dunn, J., Plomin, R., Simonoff, E., Pickles, A., Maughan, B., Ormel, J., Meyer, J., & Eaves, L. (1997). Integrating nature and nurture: Implications of person–environment correlations and interactions for developmental psychopathology. *Development and Psychopathology*, *9*, 335–364.

Sameroff, A. J. (2000). Dialectical processes in developmental psychopathology. In A. J. Sameroff, M. Lewis, & S. Miller (Eds.), *Handbook of developmental psychopathology* (2nd ed., pp. 23–40). New York: Plenum.

Scheeringa, M. S., & Gaensbauer, T. J. (2000). Post-traumatic stress disorder. In C. Zeanah (Ed.), *Handbook of infant mental health* (2nd ed., pp. 369–381). New York: Guilford Press.

Shaw, D. S., Winslow, E. B., Owens, E. B., Vondra, J. I., Cohn, J. F., & Bell, R. Q. (1998). The development of early externalizing problems among children from low-income families: A transformational perspective. *Journal of Abnormal Child Psychology*, *26*, 95–108.

Short, E. J., Manos, M. J., Findling, R. L., & Schubel, E. A. (2004). A prospective study of stimulant response in preschool children: Insights from ROC analyses. *Journal of the American Academy of Child and Adolescent Psychiatry*, *43*, 251–259.

Sonuga-Barke, E. J. S., Auerbach, J., Campbell, S. B., Daley, D., & Thompson, M. (2005). Varieties of preschool hyperactivity: Multiple pathways between risk and disorder. *Developmental Science*, *8*, 141–150.

Sonuga-Barke, E. J. S., Daley, D., Thompson, M., Laver-Bradbury, C., & Weeks, A. (2001). Parent-based therapies for preschool attention deficit/hyperactivity disorder: A randomized controlled trial with a community sample. *Journal of the American Academy of Child and Adolescent Psychiatry, 40*, 402–408.

Speltz, M. L., DeKlyen, M., & Greenberg, M. T. (1999). Attachment in boys with early onset conduct problems. *Development and Psychopathology, 11*, 269–286.

Speltz, M. L., DeKlyen, M., Greenberg, M. T., & Dryden, M. (1995). Clinical referral for oppositional defiant disorder: Relative significance of attachment and behavioral variables. *Journal of Abnormal Child Psychology, 23*, 487–507.

Spieker, S. J., Larson, N. C., Lewis, S. M., Keller, T. E., & Gilchrist, L. (1999). Developmental trajectories of disruptive behavior problems in preschool children of adolescent mothers. *Child Development, 70*, 443–458.

Thomas, A., Chess, S., & Birch, H. (1968). *Temperament and behavior disorders in children.* New York: New York University Press.

Thompson, R. A. (1998). Early socio-personality development. In N. Eisenberg (Ed.), *Handbook of child psychology: Vol. 3. Social, emotional, and personality development* (5th ed., pp. 25–104). New York: Wiley.

Webster-Stratton, C., & Hammond, M. (1999). Marital conflict management skills, parenting style, and early-onset conduct problems: Processes and pathways. *Journal of Child Psychology and Psychiatry, 40*, 917–927.

Wolfe, D. A. (1999). *Child abuse: Implications for child development and psychopathology.* Thousand Oaks, CA: Sage.

Zeanah, C. H., & Boris, N. W. (2000). Disturbances and disorders of attachment in early childhood. In C. Zeanah (Ed.), *Handbook of infant mental health* (2nd ed., pp. 353–368). New York: Guilford Press.

Zeanah, C. H., & Fox, N. (2004). Temperament and attachment disorders. *Journal of Clinical Child and Adolescent Psychology, 33*, 32–41.

Zito, J. M., Safer, D. J., dosReis, S., Gardner, J. F., Boles, M., & Lynch, F. (2000). Trends in the prescribing of psychotropic medications to preschoolers. *Journal of the American Medical Association, 283*, 1025–1030.

PART VI

The Social Ecology of Early Development

19

Family Systems

Marc H. Bornstein and Jeanette Sawyer

A once narrow focus in child development research on the individual child or the parent(*read*: mother)–child dyad as the sole subject of study has undergone a steady expansion and been replaced by emphases on *relationships* and *interactions* as well as *contexts* that reach beyond child and mother to encompass the full diversity of the child's social embeddedness. This inclusive research orientation reflects the growing awareness that fathers, extended family members, and significant others outside the family, as well as physical, social, and cultural contexts, interconnect and shape child development, parenting, and family life. The roles and functions of all family members are interdependent, and family members influence one another both directly and indirectly. "Models that limit examination of the effects of interaction patterns to only the father–child and the mother–child dyads and the direct effects of one individual on another are inadequate for understanding the impact of social interaction patterns in families" (Parke, 2002, p. 41).

Theoreticians and researchers alike are therefore challenged today to move beyond individual and dyadic foci to include larger spheres of influence, and, in recognizing the complexity of factors that influence child development, to find ways to examine both direct and indirect pathways of interaction. The *family systems* view provides a coherent foundation and framework for such forward-looking theory and research.

What Is a Family System?

> In essence, the structural approach to families is based on the concept that a family is more than the individual biopsychodynamics of its members. Family members relate according to certain arrangements, which govern their transactions. These arrangements, though usually not explicitly stated or even recognized, form a whole – the structure of the family. The reality of the structure is of a different order from the reality of the individual members. (S. Minuchin, 1974, p. 89)

Several variations of family systems theory share certain core principles and focus on multi-determined, complex, dynamic processes. Within the framework of a family systems model the family is understood to be a dynamical system. "Broadly defined, a dynamical system is simply a more-or-less self-contained set of elements that interact in complex, often nonlinear ways to form coherent patterns" (Vallacher & Nowak, 1994, p. xv). As such, a family system is principally characterized by wholeness and order, circular causality, a hierarchical structure, and adaptive self-organization.

First, the family system functions as an organized whole, comprised of interdependent elements or subsystems that include individuals as well as relationships among individuals. In other words, the family system encompasses subsystems that are systems in and of themselves (Golombok, 2002). These subsystems "organize themselves to fulfill their role in the functioning of the totality" (Magnusson, 1998, p. 2). Understood as an organized whole, the family has properties that are not reducible to its constituent parts (i.e., the whole is greater than the sum of its parts; Cox & Paley, 2003).

Research supports this essentially Gestalt notion applied to family functioning. Parenting behaviors in a parent–child dyadic context differ quantitatively and qualitatively from behaviors of the same dyad exhibited in the context of the entire family. For example, Deal, Hagan, Bass, Hetherington, and Clingempeel (1999) found that parents behaved one way when the whole family was together and another when each interacted one-on-one with their young child. When their child was present, couples were less hostile, coercive, warm, communicative, and self-disclosing in their behavior toward one another. Such comparative research within the family underscores the fact that unique phenomena may arise at the level of the family as a system.

Second, each element or subsystem within the family both affects and is affected by other elements; a change in any one aspect of the system can lead to changes in others. Causal relations among elements of the family system are understood to be circular rather than linear (Golombok, 2002). ("Multidirectional influences" may be more accurate still, as the term "causation" often lends itself to the interpretation of uni-directional influence.) Contemporary developmental science has long recognized bi-directional processes as central to family systems theory (Bell, 1968).

Third, intrinsically interconnected subsystems are organized in a hierarchical structure designating power alignments among family members and boundaries that define the rules for subsystem interactions (Golombok, 2002). The asymmetrical nature of the parent–child relationship exemplifies the parental "executive subsystem" in such a family hierarchy (P. Minuchin, 1985; S. Minuchin, 1974) that regulates family interactions and outcomes by managing family members' behaviors and relationships. This hierarchy is necessary for child development. According to Vygotsky (1978), the parent, being more advanced than the child, raises the child's level of competence through reciprocal interactions. The "dynamic systems perspective" posits that reciprocity between parent and child specifically facilitates higher forms of interaction.

Families have the ability to reorganize adaptively in response to change or challenge. The fourth family systems characteristic of "adaptive self-organization" allows the family system to continue to function in light of novel circumstances (Cox & Paley, 2003). Like other living systems, family systems continually strive to attain a dynamic balance amidst the experiences of growth and maturation, on the one hand, and the need for consistency, on the other. Stability or homeostasis is maintained, in part, by negative feedback, or "self-regulation," which serves to correct deviations from families' usual ways of functioning and so preserve continuity. "The family system, like any system, has self-stabilizing properties . . . families stabilize around habitual patterns of interaction; thus there is continuity over time in the familial forces that support the distinctive personality patterns of individual children" (Maccoby, 1984, p. 326). As each individual or subsystem within a family faces and responds to change, through the process of adaptive self-organization, new structures and patterns emerge (Cox & Paley, 2003), and, reciprocally, "when the structure of the family group is transformed, the positions of members in that group are altered accordingly. As a result, each individual's experiences change" (S. Minuchin, 1974, p. 2).

Adaptive self-organization is a key aspect of the family system and emphasizes the importance of examining transition points in the family life cycle. Systems undergoing change are especially volatile (Bogartz, 1994), and in the family system, one significant period of change is the transition to parenthood. Developmental scientists primarily interested in adult personality change have focused on the transition to parenthood for this reason (Heinicke, 2002). For example, new parents experience change in some aspects of adult personality (i.e., self-efficacy expectations, personal control, anxiety, and depression) and are more prone to mental disturbance and a decline in marital satisfaction. Generally during the transition to parenthood gender roles become more traditional, with women becoming the primary caregiver (C. P. Cowan & Cowan, 2000). As the family moves from one stage of the life cycle to the next, the equilibrium established during the former stage is disrupted by changes in one or more family members or in the context in which the family lives (Steinberg & Silk, 2002).

These four characteristics of family systems – wholeness and order; circular causality; a hierarchical structure; and adaptive self-organization – highlight the importance of examining the family *qua* system in addition to considering how each individual or subsystem responds.

Family Systems Research

Family systems research provides social scientists with new avenues of study in terms of understanding the social and emotional growth of children within families and larger social contexts. Although the complex, dynamic systems view of the family challenges research, in recent years some valuable empirical strides have been taken to test family systems theory. To understand variations in developing parent–child relationships and their effects on children's development, P. A. Cowan, Powell, and Cowan (1998) developed a six-domain model that describes connections among subsystems within a family system. These domains serve to organize an otherwise potentially overwhelming number of subsystems and relations among the subsystems that compose a family system. We turn now to a brief discussion of each of these domains within the family systems framework.

Individual characteristics

The family is at base composed of individuals. A comprehensive understanding of any one subsystem necessitates examining each individual's characteristics. In the parent–child domain, for example, parenting is shaped, in part, by biological processes (Corter & Fleming, 2002), transient emotional sensibilities, and enduring personality attributes of parents (Vondra, Sysko, & Belsky, 2005). Subtle as well as not-so-subtle characteristics of children also influence parenting (Hodapp & Ty, 2005; Karraker & Coleman, 2005). So-called "child effects" may be of different kinds. Some are universal and common to all children; others are unique to a particular child or situation. Lorenz (1935/1970) argued that physiognomic features of "babyishness" provoke adults to express nurturant reactions toward babies. Children's crying motivates adults to approach and soothe, and their smiling encourages adults to stay near (Ainsworth, Blehar, Waters, & Wall, 1978). Other structural characteristics of children also affect parenting and the quality of parent–child interaction; child health status, gender, and age are three significant factors. These examples highlight the importance of considering the influence of individual characteristics on the dynamic interplay amongst elements of the system.

Family systems research points to interactions between age and gender in determining children's reactions to marital conflict (Davies, Meyers, Cummings, & Heindel, 1999; Grych, 2002). Following children for two years after their parents' divorce, Hetherington, Cox, and Cox (1982) found that, when compared to "stable" homes, boys from divorced families were more hostile, aggressive, and disliked by peers, although girls did not differ in these respects. Research that examines family systems through a simpler lens that fails to encompass individual characteristics is bound to yield a much more limited understanding of parent–child relationships (Lerner, Rothbaum, Boulos, & Castellino, 2002).

The couple relationship

Couple-relationship quality, and the effect of marital quality on parenting and on child development, have become increasingly prominent topics of study in developmental science, as psychological research on the family has broadened from focusing primarily on parent–child interaction to investigating how individuals and relationships within the family influence one another (Gable, Belsky, & Crnic, 1992). This literature generally supports the family systems hypothesis that marital and parent–child relationships are interdependent (Grych, 2002) and that parents' marital quality links to the quality of parents' relationships with their children and their young children's development (Cox, Paley, & Harter, 2001; Cummings & Davies, 1994).

For example, marital discord and divorce affect children's psychological health and functioning (Cummings, Iannotti, & Zahn-Waxler, 1985; Grych & Fincham, 1990) such as child internalizing and externalizing behaviors and disorders, including antisocial behavior (P. A. Cowan, Cowan, Schulz, & Heming, 1994; Fincham, Grych, & Osborne, 1994) and problematic peer relationships (Kerig, 1996; Parke et al., 2001). Although links between parents' marital quality and, say, children's peer competence have been found, the mechanisms by which marital conflict exerts such influences have not been clearly delineated. The most popular hypothesis is that marital conflict "spills over" into parent–child relationships, with resulting negative effects on the child (Cummings & Davies, 1994; Erel & Burman, 1995; Wilson & Gottman, 2002). More specific hypotheses have been advanced to the effect that emotional security (Davies & Cummings, 1994) and emotion (dys)regulation patterns (Crockenberg & Langrock, 2001) explain the links between parents' interactions as a couple and children's difficulties with peers. Cummings and his colleagues (Cummings & Davies, 1995; Cummings & Wilson, 1999) proposed an emotional-security hypothesis consistent with a family systems view. They found that destructive marital conflict threatens the child's sense that she or he can feel safe and emotionally secure in the family. Marital problems could make it difficult for a parent to provide social support or act as a source of stress relief (Barth & Parke, 1993). Parental strife limits adults' emotional and physical availability, leaving children without support and potentially affecting their performance in school.

Children may be directly or indirectly affected by their parents' marital quality. A direct-effects model postulates that exposure to conflict influences children's behavior. For example, Erel and Burman (1995) documented changes in children's physiology, cognitions, and emotions in response to marital conflict. An indirect-effects model posits that the impact of marital conflict on children is mediated by changes in the parent–child relationship *per se* (Cummings & O'Reilly, 1997; Grych & Fincham, 2001). Marital conflict is associated with poor parenting (Katz & Kahen, 1993; P. A. Cowan et al., 1994). Affective change in the quality of parent–child relationships and lack of emotional availability have been implicated as potential mediating factors through which marital conflict affects parenting (Parke, 2002).

Feinberg (2003) proposed that coparenting, a special aspect of the marital relationship, affects child development more directly than parents' marriage quality in general. Coparenting refers to ways in which parents (or parental figures) relate to each other in the role of parent. The construct of coparenting grew from divorce research that indicated that children's adjustment might not be negatively affected by divorce *per se*, but rather by post-divorce factors, including ongoing interparental relations (Hetherington & Stanley-Hagen, 2002). The coparenting model (McHale, Khazan, Rotman, DeCourcey, & McConnell, 2002) is comprised of four interrelated components: agreement or disagreement on childrearing issues; division of (child-related) labor; support/undermining the coparental role; and the joint management of family interactions (Feinberg, 2003). A glimpse into the coparenting literature reveals some ways in which these dimensions might directly influence children. For example, parental childrearing disagreements are related to child behavior problems in preschool and kindergarten (Deal, Halverson, & Wampler, 1989), in adolescence (Feinberg, 2003), and longitudinally across these time periods (Vaughn, Block, & Block, 1988).

The impact of marital conflict and distress need not always be negative. Forehand, Armistead, and Klein (1995) pointed out that individual and family processes can buffer children from the negative impact of their parents' divorce. P. A. Cowan, Cowan, Ablow, Johnson, and Measelle (2005) further explore direct links between parents' marital quality and young children's adaptation, examine various individual and family processes that operate to protect children from the negative impact of their parents' unresolved conflict, and suggest some indirect mechanisms that link parents' marital quality with children's adjustment.

The quality of the relationship between each parent and child

Empirical research attests to the short- and long-term influences of parent-provided experiences in child development (Collins, Maccoby, Steinberg, Hetherington, & Bornstein, 2000). Not only do biological parents contribute to the genetic makeup of their children, parents directly shape their children's experiences and influence their children's development by both their beliefs and behaviors. Until recently, however, most empirical research investigating family climate did not fully reflect the fact that the majority of children throughout the world grow up in family systems where there is more than one significant parenting figure guiding more than one child's socialization at a time (McHale et al., 2002).

While "parenting" is often equated with "mothering," research continues to emphasize the need to distinguish father–child from mother–child relationships. Mothers and fathers interact with and care for children in distinctly different and oftentimes complementary ways (Barnard & Solchany, 2002; Parke, 2002).

Mothers. In the minds of many observers, mother is unique, the role of mother universal, and motherhood unequivocally principal in child development. Various responsibilities of parenting, like nurturance, social exchange, and teaching, may be distributed across various members of the culture; however, the ultimate responsibility for young children within the context of the nuclear or extended family usually, if not universally, falls to mother. Cross-cultural surveys attest to the primacy of biological mothers' caregiving (Leiderman, Tulkin, & Rosenfeld, 1977). Mothers tend and interact with babies and toddlers more than do fathers (Belsky, Gilstrap, & Rovine, 1984). Fathers may withdraw from their children when they are unhappily married; mothers typically do not (Kerig, Cowan, & Cowan, 1993). On average, mothers spend between 65 and 80% more time than fathers do in direct one-to-one interaction with their children (Parke, 2002). In research involving both traditional American families (Belsky, Garduque, & Hrncir, 1984) and traditional and non-traditional (father primary caregiver) Swedish families (Lamb, Frodi, Frodi, & Hwang, 1982), parental gender was found to exert the greatest influence on the quality of parent–child interaction.

Fathers. Fathers play their own role in their children's development, and the quality of paternal involvement is related to children's cognitive, emotional, and social growth (Cabrera, Tamis-LeMonda, Bradley, Hofferth, & Lamb, 2000). Easterbrooks and Goldberg (1984) found that young children's adaptation was promoted both by the amount of paternal involvement and by the quality or sensitivity of their fathers' behavior. In this connection, Isley, O'Neil, and Parke (1996) reported that, when maternal affect was controlled, fathers' affect and control predicted children's social adaptation; and

Koestner, Franz, and Weinberger (1990) found paternal childrearing involvement at age 5 was the strongest predictor of empathy in adulthood. Fathers evidently contribute uniquely to their children's development (Parke, 2002).

Western industrialized nations have witnessed increases in the amount of time fathers spend with their children (Yeung, Sandberg, Davis-Kean, & Hofferth, 2001). Despite the fact that men can be competent caregivers, it is still the case that, in comparison to mothers, fathers typically assume less responsibility for childcare and rearing, and that fathers are primarily helpers in these arenas (Cabrera et al., 2000; Parke, 2002). Paternal involvement appears to be partially mediated by fathers' beliefs in the biological basis of gender differences and their perceived capability (or lack thereof) to provide adequate care (Beitel & Parke, 1998). Russel (1983) found that most Australian fathers believed in a "maternal instinct" in regard to child care, and that fathers who endorsed that belief participated less in child care. Maternal attitudes about father involvement can also serve to limit father involvement. Allen and Hawkins (1999) developed the notion of "gate-keeping" to describe this effect, noting that fathers also engage in gatekeeping activities.

As researchers in child development have come to recognize multiple social influences on child development – maternal and paternal but also sibling and others – they have come to appreciate that many influences are indirectly mediated through complex paths and networks. Parke (2002) suggested that many paternal influences on child development are indirectly mediated through the father's impact on the mother, for example. In other words, even if the mother has the major direct influence on child development in a "traditional" family (in which the mother stays at home to care for and socialize her children while the father is a breadwinner), the father has important indirect influences.

Sibling relationships

Developmental research on family process has traditionally focused on a single child in the family (Hoffman, 1991), yet the vast majority of families have more than one child. Consistent with the principle of adaptive self-organization, the family system undergoes significant change with the birth of a second child (Belsky, Rovine, & Fish, 1989). The births of later children alter the roles of each family member and forever affect the ways in which each interacts with all others. As families have additional children, parents report having less free time, fewer financial resources, and they tend to feel more overwhelmed and tied down (Lundberg, Mardberg, & Frankenhaeuser, 1994). Parents who have more children would also be expected to feel increased strain at work due to the need to make more money, and more strain at home because of the need to care for additional children (Voydanoff & Donnelly, 1989).

Parents of second-born children are in many ways not the same as parents of first-borns, and so the family systems of first- and later-born children differ (Dunn & Plomin, 1991). Family structure has long been thought to play a significant role in the development and expression of individual differences in children (Adler, 1931). Indeed, Plomin and Daniels (1987) contended that the "effective environments of siblings are hardly any more similar than are the environments of strangers who grow up in different families"

(p. 15). They further argued that few "shared" environmental influences stem from being reared in the same house by the same parents (Reiss, Neiderhiser, Hetherington, & Plomin, 2000).

Successive foci on siblings' "shared" versus "non-shared" environments spotlight potential sources of similarities and differences in the experiences of first-born and later-born children growing up in the same family (Plomin & Daniels, 1987). Noting that parents do not act the same with each of their young children, Dunn (1995), Plomin (1994), and their colleagues (Hetherington, Reiss, & Plomin, 1994) have drawn attention to the importance of understanding variations in parent–child relationships within families for understanding non-shared environmental influences. Children in the same family may be treated differently because they differ in age, cognitive level, personality characteristics, or sex, for example. Combined with variation in genetic make-up, within-family variation in parenting offers a potent reason for why children in the same family differ from one another (Dunn & Plomin, 1990; Hetherington et al., 1994). Ward, Vaughn, and Robb (1988), for example, observed that mothers were more emotionally supportive and involved with their second-born 2-year-olds than their first-born 2-year-olds, and Moore, Cohn, and Campbell (1997) found that mothers were more affectively positive with second-born infants and second-born infants were themselves more positive than were first-borns. It is also the case that siblings may identify more or less with a given family member, and in the process de-identify with one another.

Beyond the nuclear family

When we move beyond the mother–father–sibling–child relationship (Fivaz-Depeursinge & Corboz-Warnery, 1999) to describe child socialization within extended family systems, we are faced with very different sets of circumstances concerning skills, resources, and roles. Family systems involving the child's biological parents and extended family members have usually been the norm rather than the exception throughout human history (Bateson, 2000). One advantage of the extended family not shared by isolated single-parent (Weinraub, Horvath, & Gringlas, 2002) or nuclear families is the vast repository of knowledge about parenting and childrearing afforded by others in the kin network. Indeed, taking a long historical view, it might be argued that societal circumstances at one time favored grandparents (Smith & Drew, 2002), rather than parents, to serve as primary parenting figures for young children once they had been weaned (McHale et al., 2002).

Moreover, increasing numbers of the world's children are today being reared in dual-family systems by biological parents and one or more step-parents (Hetherington & Stanley-Hagan, 2002), by foster parents (Haugaard & Hazen, 2002), by adoptive parents (Brodzinsky & Pinderhughes, 2002), by grandparents parenting alone or together with one or both biological parents (Smith & Drew, 2002) – as well as by aunts, uncles, kin, and in many other adaptive family systems (P. Minuchin, 2001). The dynamic influences of multi-generational households become readily evident in family systems analyses.

Today's teenage mother typically lives with her family of origin (Moore & Brooks-Gunn, 2002), and the body of literature concerned with adolescent parenting harbors much research on multi-generational households. A family systems approach looks at the impact of teen motherhood not only on the mother but on the entire family as well as on family climate and emotional quality (Chase-Lansdale, Wakschlag, & Brooks-Gunn, 1995).

Family systems theory is recognized as apt to grandparenting research, especially with the increased perception within society that grandparents are an integral part of the family unit. According to Smith and Drew (2002), the most direct form of grandparent–grandchild influence is through surrogate parenting. Based on data from the National Longitudinal Study of Youth (NLSY), Fuller-Thompson, Minkler, and Driver (1997) reported that 11% of grandparents were the primary caregivers of their grandchildren. Using data from the National Study of Families and Households, Baydar and Brooks-Gunn (1998) found that approximately 12% of grandmothers resided with a grandchild, and approximately 43% provided child care on a regular basis. A grandparent may have a direct influence on a grandchild by acting as emotional support during times of familial stress, and "observational studies show that grandparents can act as a source of secure attachment for young children" (Smith & Drew, 2002, p. 160). In families with teenage mothers, a healthy relationship with a grandmother may buffer a young child from under-developed maternal functioning.

Grandmothers also impact grandchildren indirectly in that they act as role models for their grandchildren's parents. In this sense, coresidence appears to benefit younger mothers. Chase-Lansdale, Brooks-Gunn, and Zamsky (1994) found that, when mothers were 16 years old or younger at the birth of their first child, coresiding mothers and grandmothers exhibited more positive and less harsh parenting than non-coresiding parents and grandparents. The Baltimore Multigenerational Family Study assessed the mother–grandmother relationship, and found that mothers who had interactions with their own mothers who were characterized as mature, flexible, and autonomous were more likely themselves to be emotionally supportive, affectively positive, and authoritative.

Research into intergenerational parenting concerns itself with the transmission of beliefs and behaviors across generations. For better or worse, parenting patterns are often passed down through generations. Ruoppila (1991) found significant correlations between grandparental and parental childrearing in a Finnish sample (Smith & Drew, 2002). Vermulst, de Brock, and van Zutphen (1991) examined parental functioning across generations in a Dutch sample of grandmother–mother dyads; approximately one-third of the variation in mothers' parental functioning could be explained in terms of earlier parental functioning of the grandmother. The use of physically aggressive and punitive techniques in the grandparent–parent generation predicts similar behavior in the parent–grandchild generation and antisocial behavior in grandchildren (Farrington, 1993; Murphy-Cowan & Stringer, 1999). When parents abuse their children, the children are at risk of repeating the pattern as adults with their own children (Newcomb & Locke, 2001; Pears & Capaldi, 2001). Sociological studies and meta-analyses find that adult children whose parents divorced are more likely to end their own marriages in divorce, for example (Amato, 1996). Similarly, maritally dissatisfied couples are more likely to have unhappily married parents (Amato & Booth, 2001; Schneewind & Ruppert, 1998), and marital violence in the family of origin tends to repeat in the successive generation (Stith et al., 2000).

The Adult Attachment Interview (AAI) assesses an adult's model of his or her own relationship with his or her parents. A strong predictive link has emerged between the child's attachment with the child's mother and the mother's AAI classification (Smith & Drew, 2002). Van IJzendoorn (1995) reviewed AAI studies that included 854 parent–child dyads and found 75% concordance between a child's secure/insecure classification in the Strange Situation and the child's parent's autonomous/non-autonomous classification on the AAI.

Together these findings support the hypothesis of a connection among intermediate family relationship mechanisms: parents' narratives about their family-of-origin relationships are associated with the quality of their relationships with their spouses and their children. We should not assume, however, that the intergenerational transmission of behavioral patterns occurs solely through environmental influences. In the case of divorce, for example, Pope and Mueller (1979) hypothesized that parent–offspring resemblance for divorce was due to social modeling. McGue and Lykken (1992), however, contended a genetic influence on risk of divorce. In a study of over 1500 same-sex twin pairs, they found the risk of divorce among monozygotic twins was substantially greater than the risk of divorce among dizygotic twins.

Ecological dimensions of family systems

The ecological perspective extends the family systems framework to examining the roles of extrafamilial and contextual factors (e.g., educational institutions, places of employment, legal and social norms, culture) in explaining individual adjustment and family processes. Like the family systems view, the ecological perspective "stresses the interactive and synergistic, rather than additive and competitive, nature of the links between the family and other influences" (Collins et al., 2000, p. 227). One of Bronfenbrenner's (Bronfenbrenner & Morris, 1998) central contributions to developmental science was to stimulate researchers to think about individual and family development from a systemic point of view by placing the study of individuals and families in the context of the wider society and culture. Outside the family, friends and social groups (Crockenberg, 1988) interact with the family system *per se*. For example, Parke and colleagues' (2002, 2004) extensive efforts to unravel patterns of influence between families and children's peer systems have revealed that they are highly interrelated.

Family systems always need to be considered in their socio-cultural contexts (Bornstein, 1991; Bornstein & Bradley, 2003; Bronfenbrenner & Morris, 1998; LeVine, 2003). As Hay and Nash (2002) pointed out, we continue to assume that the "traditional" nuclear family is the blueprint against which all other types of family should be compared – usually unfavorably. The challenge for future research is to acknowledge that investigators often focus too narrowly on households of predominantly Anglo-Saxon background (Tomlinson & Swartz, 2003), even though such families are in the minority, and contemporary study fails to adequately represent the cultural diversity and complexity of contemporary family life. A pervading critique of contemporary developmental science is that research in the field has tended to describe the constructs, structures, functions, and processes of child development and childrearing that accord with ideals only appropriate to middle-class, industrialized and developed, western societies (Bornstein, 2002).

Looking Toward the Future: Closing the Gap Between Family Systems Theory and Research

Virtually all of psychology's guiding theories depict child development and parenting as unfolding alone or within the context of dyadic parent–child relationships. With the rise in popularity of a family systems framework, important progress is being made by developmental scientists in moving beyond the individual and the dyad and to contextualizing relationships. The family systems perspective offers a refreshing and more realistic view of the family as an interdependent system wherein changes in family structure or in any family member or family subsystem prompt changes throughout the system. This perspective has led to examining relationships and adjustments within and between marital, parent–child, and sibling subsystems as well as to appraising family functioning in divorced and remarried families at the level of the whole family system. Family-level processes, such as adaptive family organization and family cohesion, have shown unique explanatory power over and above dyadic family interactions (Johnson, 2003; Johnson, Cowan, & Cowan, 1999; McHale, Johnson, & Sinclair, 1999).

Still missing, however, from this breaking wave of family systems research are studies that focus on the full family group as a unit. Few studies have investigated the role of family-level functioning in children's adjustment, although family research has long been guided by clinical family systems theories that advocate the importance of the whole family environment in children's development (e.g., S. Minuchin, 1974). A full understanding of child development, therefore, must take into consideration all the relationships among all family members and not only individual relationships. Studies of early childhood have found composite measures of whole-family functioning combining observed dyadic and triadic (e.g., mother–father–infant; mother–child–child) assessments of family processes to predict behavior across a variety of age groups in childhood (Johnson, 2003; Johnson et al., 1999; Lindahl, 1998; Lindahl & Malik, 1999).

Family systems models favor longitudinal study that is requisite to both observing and describing the causal processes that reflect reciprocal influences of various levels of the family system (Cox & Paley, 2003). Yet most family-level research still does not track changes in child and family functioning over time or, if it does scrutinize links between family functioning and children's behavior, move beyond the parent–child dyad. Future research should examine changes in whole-family functioning across extended periods of childhood (Johnson, 2003).

To appreciate fully the effects of family climate on child development and child–parent relationships requires multiple types of data representing multiple levels of analysis. Information about parents' attitudes, values, perceptions, and beliefs helps to explain when and why parents behave as they do and needs to complement observations of parenting in multiple caregiving situations. To better adjudicate among equally plausible rival hypotheses, family systems researchers also champion the use of complementary qualitative and quantitative approaches.

Family systems models show that child development results from dynamic transactions across multiple levels and instigate researchers to seek developmental effects at multiple levels of the organization of the family system. Furthermore, the implications of the family systems line of thinking for parenting interventions are noteworthy. Although offering direct help with parenting to mothers and fathers makes sense, the systemic view suggests any number of strategic intervention points to foster positive outcomes in parent–child relationships and the need to consider the family system as a whole.

Note

This chapter summarizes selected aspects of our research, and portions of the text have appeared in previous scientific publications cited in the references. We thank C. Varron for assistance.

References

Adler, A. (1931). *What life should mean to you.* Boston: Little, Brown.

Ainsworth, M. D. S., Blehar, M. C., Waters, E., & Wall, S. (1978). *Patterns of attachment: A psychological study of the Strange Situation.* Hillsdale, NJ: Erlbaum.

Allen, J. M., & Hawkins, A. J. (1999). Maternal gatekeeping: Mothers' beliefs and behaviours that inhibit greater father involvement in family work. *Journal of Marriage and Family, 61,* 199–212.

Amato, P. R. (1996). Explaining the intergenerational transmission of divorce. *Journal of Marriage and Family, 58,* 628–640.

Amato, P. R., & Booth, A. (2001). The legacy of parents' marital discord: Consequences for children's marital quality. *Journal of Personality & Social Psychology, 81,* 627–638.

Barnard, K. E., & Solchany, J. E. (2002). Mothering. In M. H. Bornstein (Ed.), *Handbook of parenting: Vol. 3. Status and social conditions of parenting* (2nd ed., pp. 3–25). Mahwah, NJ: Lawrence Erlbaum Associates.

Barth, J. M., & Parke, R. D. (1993). Parent-child relationship influences on children's transition to school. *Merrill-Palmer Quarterly, 39,* 173–195.

Bateson, M. (2000). *Full circles, overlapping lives: Culture and generation in transition.* New York: Random House.

Baydar, N., & Brooks-Gunn, J. (1998). Profiles of grandmothers who help care for their grandchildren in the United States. *Family Relations, 47,* 385–393.

Beitel, A., & Parke, R.D. (1998). Maternal and paternal attitudes as determinants of father involvement. *Journal of Family Psychology, 12,* 268–288.

Bell, R. Q. (1968). A reinterpretation of the direction of effects in studies of socialization. *Psychological Review, 75,* 81–95.

Belsky, J., Garduque, L., & Hrncir, E. (1984). Assessing performance, competence, and executive capacity in infant play: Relations to home environment and security of attachment. *Developmental Psychology, 20,* 406–417.

Belsky, J., Gilstrap, B., & Rovine, M. (1984). The Pennsylvania infant and child relations: A meta-analytic review. *Psychological Bulletin, 118,* 108–132.

Belsky, J., Rovine, M., & Fish, M. (1989). The developing family system. In M. Gunnar & E. Thelen (Eds.), *The Minnesota Symposium on Child Psychology: Vol. 22. Systems and development* (pp. 119–166). Hillsdale, NJ: Lawrence Erlbaum Associates.

Bogartz, R. S. (1994). The future of dynamic systems models in developmental psychology in the light of the past. *Journal of Experimental Child Psychology, 58*, 289–319.

Bornstein, M. H. (1991). Approaches to parenting in culture. In M. H. Bornstein (Ed.), *Cultural approaches to parenting* (pp. 3–19). Hillsdale, NJ: Lawrence Erlbaum Associates.

Bornstein, M. H. (2002). Toward a multiculture multiage multimethod science. *Human Development, 45*, 257–263.

Bornstein, M. H., & Bradley, R. H. (Eds.). (2003). *Socioeconomic status, parenting, and child development.* Mahwah, NJ: Lawrence Erlbaum Associates.

Brodzinsky, D. M., & Pinderhughes, E. (2002). Parenting and child development in adoptive families. In M. H. Bornstein (Ed.), *Handbook of parenting: Vol. 1. Children and parenting* (2nd ed., pp. 279–311). Mahwah, NJ: Lawrence Erlbaum Associates.

Bronfenbrenner, U., & Morris, P. A. (1998). The ecology of developmental processes. In W. Damon & R. M. Lerner (Eds.), *Handbook of child psychology: Vol. 1. Theoretical models of human development* (5th ed., pp. 993–1028). New York: Wiley.

Cabrera, N. J., Tamis-LeMonda, S., Bradley, R. H., Hofferth, S., & Lamb, M. E. (2000). Fatherhood in the twenty-first century. *Child Development, 71*, 127–136.

Chase-Lansdale, P. L., Wakschlag, L. S., & Brooks-Gunn, J. (1995). A psychological perspective on the development of caring in children and youth: The role of the family. *Journal of Adolescence, 18*, 516–556.

Chase-Lansdale, P. L., Brooks-Gunn, J., & Zamsky, E. S. (1994). Young African-American multigenerational families in poverty: Quality of mothering and grandmothering. *Child Development, 65*, 373–393.

Collins, W. A., Maccoby, E. E., Steinberg, L., Hetherington, E. M., & Bornstein, M. H. (2000). Contemporary research on parenting: The case for nature and nurture. *American Psychologist, 55*, 218–232.

Corter, C. M., & Fleming, A. S. (2002). Psychobiology of maternal behavior in human beings. In M. H. Bornstein (Ed.), *Handbook of parenting: Vol. 2. Biology and ecology of parenting* (2nd ed., pp. 141–181). Mahwah, NJ: Lawrence Erlbaum Associates.

Cowan, C. P., & Cowan, P. A. (2000). *When partners become parents: The big life change for couples.* Mahwah, NJ: Lawrence Erlbaum Associates.

Cowan, P. A., Cowan, C. P., Ablow, J., Johnson, V., & Measelle, J. (2005). *The family context of parenting in children's adaptation to elementary school.* Mahwah, NJ: Lawrence Erlbaum Associates.

Cowan, P. A., Cowan, C. P., Schulz, M. S., & Heming, G. (1994). Prebirth to preschool family factors in children's adaptation to kindergarten. In R. D. Parke & S. G. Kellam (Eds.), *Family research consortium: Advances in family research: Vol. 4. Exploring family relationships with other social contexts* (pp. 75–114). Hillsdale, NJ: Lawrence Erlbaum Associates.

Cowan, P. A., Powell, D., & Cowan, C. P. (1998). Parenting interventions: A family systems perspective. In W. Damon (Ed.), *Handbook of child psychology: Vol. 4. Child psychology in practice* (pp. 3–72). New York: Wiley.

Cox, M. J., & Paley, B. (2003). Understanding families as systems. *Current Directions in Psychological Science, 12*, 193–196.

Cox, M. J., Paley, B., & Harter, K. (2001). Interparental conflict and parent–child relationships. In J. H. Grych & F. D. Fincham (Eds.), *Interparental conflict and child development: Theory, research, and applications* (pp. 249–272). New York: Cambridge University Press.

Crockenberg, S. B. (1988). Social support and parenting. In H. E. Fitzgerald, B. M. Lester, & M. W. Yogman (Eds.), *Theory and research in behavioral pediatrics* (Vol. 4, pp. 141–174). New York: Plenum.

Crockenberg, S., & Langrock, A. (2001). *The role of emotion and emotional regulation in children's responses to interparental conflict.* New York: Cambridge University Press.

Cummings, E. M., & Davies, P. (1994). *Children and marital conflict: The impact of family dispute and resolution.* New York: Guilford Press.

Cummings, E. M., & Davies, P. T. (1995). The impact of parents on their children: An emotional security perspective. *Annals of Child Development, 10,* 167–208.

Cummings, E. M., Iannotti, R. J., & Zahn-Waxler, C. (1985). Influence of conflict between adults on the emotions and aggression of young children. *Developmental Psychology, 21,* 495–507.

Cummings, E. M., & O'Reilly, A. W. (1997). Fathers in family context: Effects of marital quality of child adjustment. In M. E. Lamb (Ed.), *The father's role in child development* (3rd ed., pp. 49–65). New York: Wiley.

Cummings, E. M., & Wilson, A. (1999). Contexts of marital conflict and children's emotional security: Exploring the distinction between constructive and destructive conflict from the children's perspective. In M. Cox & J. Brook-Gunn (Eds.), *Conflict and closeness in families: Causes and consequences* (pp. 105–129). Mahwah, NJ: Erlbaum.

Davies, P. T., & Cummings, E. M. (1994). Marital conflict and child adjustment: An emotional security hypothesis. *Psychological Bulletin, 116*(3), 387–411.

Davies, P. T., Meyers, R. L., Cummings, E. M., & Heindel, S. (1999). Adult conflict history and children's subsequent responses to conflict: An experimental test. *Journal of Family Psychology, 13,* 610–628.

Deal, J. E., Hagan, M. S., Bass, B., Hetherington, E. M., & Clingempeel, G. (1999). Marital interaction in dyadic and triadic contexts: Continuities and discontinuities. *Family Process, 38,* 105–115.

Deal, J. E., Halverson, C. F., Jr., & Wampler, K. S. (1989). Parental agreement on child-rearing orientations: Relations to parental, marital, family, and child characteristics. *Child Development, 60,* 1025–1034.

Dunn, J. (1995). *From one child to two.* New York: Fawcett Columbine.

Dunn, J., & Plomin, R. (1990). *Separate lives: Why siblings are so different.* New York: Basic Books.

Dunn, J., & Plomin, R. (1991). Why are siblings so different: The significance of differences in sibling experiences within the family. *Family Process, 30,* 271–283.

Easterbrooks, M. A., & Goldberg, W. A. (1984). Toddler development in the family: Impact of father involvement and parenting characteristics. *Child Development, 55,* 740–752.

Erel, O., & Burman, B. (1995). Interrelatedness of marital relations and parent family development project, I: Stability and change in mother–infant and father–infant interaction in a family setting at one, three, and nine months. *Child Development, 55,* 692–705.

Farrington, D. P. (1993). Understanding and preventing bullying. In M. Tonry (Ed.), *Crime and justice: An annual review of research* (Vol. 17, pp. 381–458). Chicago: University of Chicago Press.

Feinberg, M. (2003). The internal structure and ecological context of coparenting: A framework for research and intervention. *Parenting: Science and Practice, 3,* 95–131.

Fincham, F. D., Grych, J. H., & Osborne, L. N. (1994). Does marital conflict cause child maladjustment? Directions and challenges for longitudinal research. *Journal of Family Psychology, 8,* 128–140.

Fivaz-Depeursinge, E., & Corboz-Warnery, A. (1999). *The primary triangle: A developmental systems view of mothers, fathers, and infants.* New York: Basic Books.

Forehand, R., Armistead, L., & Klein, K. (1995). Children's school performance: The roles of interparental conflict and divorce. In B. A. Ryan, G. R. Adams, T. P. Gulotta, R. P. Weissberg, & R. L. Hampton (Eds.), *The family–school connection: Theory, research, and practice* (pp. 250–269). Thousand Oaks, CA: Sage.

Fuller-Thomson, E., Minkler, M., & Driver, D. (1997). A profile of grandparents raising grandchildren in the United States. *Gerontologist, 37,* 406–411.

Gable, S., Belsky, J., & Crnic, K. (1992). Marriage, parenting, and child development: Progress and prospects. *Journal of Family Psychology Special Issue: Diversity in Contemporary Family Psychology, 5,* 276–294.

Golombok, S. (2002). Parenting and contemporary reproductive technologies. In M. H. Bornstein (Ed.), *Handbook of parenting: Vol. 3. Status and social conditions of parenting* (2nd ed., pp. 339–360). Mahwah, NJ: Lawrence Erlbaum Associates.

Grych, J. H. (2002). Marital relationships and parenting. In M. H. Bornstein (Ed.), *Handbook of parenting: Vol. 4. Applied parenting* (2nd ed., pp. 203–225). Mahwah, NJ: Lawrence Erlbaum Associates.

Grych, J. H., & Fincham, F. D. (1990). Marital conflict and children's adjustment: A cognitive-contextual framework. *Psychological Bulletin, 108,* 267–290.

Grych, J. H., & Fincham, F. D. (Eds.). (2001). *Interparental conflict and child development.* New York: Cambridge University Press.

Haugaard, J., & Hazan, C. (2002). Foster parenting. In M. H. Bornstein (Ed.), *Handbook of parenting: Vol. 1. Children and parenting* (2nd ed., pp. 313–327). Mahwah, NJ: Lawrence Erlbaum Associates.

Hay, D., & Nash, A. (2002). Social development in different family arrangements. In P. K. Smith & C. Hart (Eds.), *Blackwell handbook of childhood social development* (pp. 238–261). Oxford: Blackwell.

Heinicke, C. M. (2002). The transition to parenting. In M. H. Bornstein (Ed.), *Handbook of parenting: Vol. 3. Status and social conditions of parenting* (2nd ed., pp. 363–388). Mahwah, NJ: Lawrence Erlbaum Associates.

Hetherington, E. M., Cox, M., & Cox, R. (1982). Effects of divorce on parents and children. In M. E. Lamb (Ed.), *Nontraditional families* (pp. 233–288). Hillsdale, NJ: Lawrence Erlbaum Associates.

Hetherington, E. M., Reiss, D., & Plomin, R. (Eds.). (1994). *Separate social worlds of siblings: Impact of nonshared environment on development.* Hillsdale, NJ: Lawrence Erlbaum Associates.

Hetherington, E. M., & Stanley-Hagan, M. M. (2002). Parenting in divorced and remarried families. In M. H. Bornstein (Ed.), *Handbook of parenting: Vol. 3. Status and social conditions of parenting* (2nd ed., pp. 287–315). Mahwah, NJ: Lawrence Erlbaum Associates.

Hodapp, R., & Ly, T. M. (2005). Parenting children with developmental disabilities. In T. Luster & L. Okagaki (Eds.), *Parenting: An ecological perspective* (2nd ed., pp. 177–201). Hillsdale, NJ: Lawrence Erlbaum Associates.

Hoffman, L. W. (1991). The influence of the family environment on personality: Accounting for sibling differences. *Psychological Bulletin, 110,* 187–203.

Isley, S., O'Neil, R., & Parke R. D. (1996). The relation of parental effect and control behavior to children's classroom acceptance: A concurrent and predictive analysis. *Early Education and Development, 7,* 7–23

Johnson, V. K. (2003). Linking changes in whole family functioning and children's externalizing behavior across the elementary school years. *Journal of Family Psychology, 17,* 499–509.

Johnson, V. K., Cowan, P. A., & Cowan, C. P. (1999). Children's classroom behavior: The unique contribution of family organization. *Journal of Family Psychology, 13,* 355–371.

Karraker, K. H., & Coleman, P. (2005). The effects of child characteristics on parenting. In T. Luster & L. Okagaki (Eds.), *Parenting: An ecological perspective* (2nd ed., pp. 147–176). Hillsdale, NJ: Lawrence Erlbaum Associates.

Katz, L. F., & Kahen, V. (1993, April). *Marital interaction patterns and children's externalizing and internalizing behaviors: The search for mechanisms.* Paper presented at the biennial meeting of the Society for Research in Child Development, New Orleans.

Kerig, P. K. (1996). Assessing the links between interpersonal low income African-American families. *Journal of African-American Men, 2,* 87–102.

Kerig, P. K., Cowan, P. A., & Cowan, C. P. (1993). Marital quality and gender differences in parent–child interaction. *Developmental Psychology, 29,* 931–939.

Koestner, R., Franz, C., & Weinberger, J. (1990). The family origins of empathic concern: A 26-year longitudinal study. *Journal of Personality and Social Psychology, 58,* 709–717.

Lamb, M. E., Frodi, A. M., Frodi, M., & Hwang, C. P. (1982). Characteristics of maternal and paternal behavior in traditional and nontraditional Swedish families. *International Journal of Behavioral Development, 5,* 131–141.

Leiderman, P. H., Tulkin, S. R., & Rosenfeld, A. (Eds.). (1977). *Culture and infancy: Variations in the human experience.* New York: Academic Press.

Lerner, R. M., Rothbaum, F., Boulos, S., & Castellino, D. R. (2002). Developmental systems perspective on parenting. In M. H. Bornstein (Ed.), *Handbook of parenting: Vol. 2 Biology and ecology of parenting* (2nd ed., pp. 285–309). Mahwah, NJ: Lawrence Erlbaum Associates.

LeVine, R. A. (2003). *Childhood socialization.* Hong Kong: University of Hong Kong.

Lindahl, K. M. (1998). Family process variables and children's disruptive behavior problems. *Journal of Family Psychology, 12,* 420–436.

Lindahl, K. M., & Malik, N. M. (1999). Observations of marital conflict and power: Relations with parenting in the triad. *Journal of Marriage and Family, 61,* 320–330.

Lorenz, K. (1970). *Studies in animal and human behavior* (R. Martin, Trans.). London: Methuen. (Original work published 1935)

Lundberg, U., Mardberg, B., & Frankenhaeuser, M. (1994). The total workload of male and female white-collar workers as related to age, occupation level, and number of children. *Scandinavian Journal of Psychology, 4,* 315–327.

Maccoby, E. E. (1984). Socialization and developmental change. *Child Development, 55,* 317–328.

Magnusson, D. (1998). The logic and implications of a person-oriented approach. In R. B. Cairns, L. R. Bergman, & J. Kagan (Eds.), *Methods and models for studying the individual* (pp. 33–64). Thousand Oaks, CA: Sage.

McGue, M., & Lykken, D. T. (1992). Genetic influence on risk of divorce. *Psychological Science, 3,* 368–373.

McHale, J. P., Johnson, D., & Sinclair, R. (1999). Family dynamics, preschoolers' family representations and preschool peer relationships. *Early Education & Development, 10,* 373–401.

McHale, J., Khazan, I., Rotman, T., DeCourcey, W., & McConnell, M. (2002). Co-parenting in diverse family systems. In M. H. Bornstein (Ed.), *Handbook of parenting: Vol. 3. Status and social conditions of parenting* (2nd ed., pp. 75–107). Mahwah, NJ: Lawrence Erlbaum Associates.

Minuchin, P. (1985). Families and individual development: Provocations from the field of family therapy. *Child Development, 56,* 289–302.

Minuchin, P. (2001). Looking toward the horizon: Present and future in the study of family systems. In J. McHale & W. Grolnick (Eds.), *Retrospect and prospect in the psychological study of families* (pp. 259–278). Mahwah, NJ: Lawrence Erlbaum Associates.

Minuchin, S. (1974). *Families and family therapy.* Cambridge, MA: Harvard University Press.

Moore, G. A., Cohn, J. F., & Campbell, S. B. (1997). Mothers' affective behavior with infant siblings: Stability and change. *Developmental Psychology, 33*, 856–860.

Moore, M. R., & Brooks-Gunn, J. (2002). Adolescent parenthood. In M. H. Bornstein (Ed.), *Handbook of parenting: Vol. 3. Status and social conditions of parenting* (2nd ed., pp. 173–214). Mahwah, NJ: Lawrence Erlbaum Associates.

Murphy-Cowan, T., & Stringer, M. (1999). Physical punishment and the parenting cycle: A survey of Northern Irish parents. *Journal of Community & Applied Social Psychology, 9*, 61–71.

Newcomb, M. D., & Locke, T. F. (2001). Intergenerational cycle of maltreatment: A popular concept obscured by methodological limitations. *Child Abuse & Neglect, 25*, 1219–1240.

Parke, R. D. (2002). Fathers and families. In M. H. Bornstein (Ed.), *Handbook of parenting: Vol. 3. Status and social conditions of parenting* (2nd ed., pp. 27–73). Mahwah, NJ: Lawrence Erlbaum Associates.

Parke, R. D., Dennis, J., Flyr, M., Morris, K. L., Killian, C., McDowell, D. J., & Wild, M. (2004). Fathering and children's peer relationships. In M. E. Lamb (Ed.), *The role of the father in child development* (4th ed., pp. 32–57). New York: Wiley.

Parke, R. D., Kim, M., Flyr, M., McDowell, D., Simpkins, S., Killian, C. M., & Wild, M. (2001). Managing marital conflict: Links with children's peer relationships. In J. Grych & F. Fincham (Eds.), *Child development and interparental conflict* (pp. 291–314). Thousand Oaks, CA: Sage.

Parke, R. D., Simpkins, S. D., McDowell, D. J., Kim, M., Killian, C., Dennis, J., Flyr, M. L., Wild, M., & Rah, Y. (2002). Relative contributions of families and peers to children's social development. In P. K. Smith & C. Hart (Eds.), *Blackwell handbook of childhood social development* (pp. 156–177). Oxford: Blackwell.

Pears, K. C., & Capaldi, D. M. (2001). Intergenerational transmission of abuse: A two-generational prospective study of an at-risk sample. *Child Abuse & Neglect, 25*, 1439–1461.

Plomin, R. (1994). *Genetics and experience: The interplay between nature and nurture.* Thousand Oaks, CA: Sage.

Plomin, R., & Daniels, D. (1987). Why are children in the same family so different from each other? *Behavioral and Brain Sciences, 10*, 1–16.

Pope, H., & Mueller, C. W. (1979). The intergenerational transmission of marital instability: Comparisons by race and sex. In G. Levinger & O. C. Moles (Eds.), *Divorce and separation* (pp. 99–113). New York: Basic Books.

Reiss, D., Neiderhiser, J. M., Hetherington, M., & Plomin, R. (2000). *The relationship code: Deciphering genetic and social influences on adolescent development.* Cambridge, MA: Harvard University Press.

Ruoppila, I. (1991). The significance of grandparents for the formation of family relations. In P. K. Smith (Ed.), *The psychology of grandparenthood: An interactional perspective* (pp. 123–139). London: Routledge.

Russell, G. (1983). *The changing role of fathers.* St. Lucia: Queensland University Press.

Schneewind, K. A., & Ruppert, S. (1998). *Personality and family development: An intergenerational longitudinal comparison.* Mahwah, NJ: Lawrence Erlbaum Associates.

Smith, P. K., & Drew, L. M. (2002). Grandparenthood. In M. H. Bornstein (Ed.), *Handbook of parenting: Vol. 1. Children and parenting* (2nd ed., pp. 103–133). Mahwah, NJ: Lawrence Erlbaum Associates.

Steinberg, L., & Silk, J. S. (2002). Parenting adolescents. In M. H. Bornstein (Ed.), *Handbook of parenting: Vol. 1. Children and parenting* (2nd ed., pp. 103–133). Mahwah, NJ: Lawrence Erlbaum Associates.

Stith, S. M., Rosen, K. H., Middleton, K. A., Busch, A. L., Lundeberg, K., & Carlton, R. P. (2000). The intergenerational transmission of spouse abuse: A meta-analysis. *Journal of Marriage and Family, 62*, 640–654.

Tomlinson, M., & Swartz, L. (2003). Imbalances in the knowledge about infancy: The divide between rich and poor countries. *Infant Mental Health Journal, 24*, 547–556.

Vallacher, R. R., & Nowak, A. (Eds.). (1994). *Dynamical systems in social psychology*. San Diego, CA: Academic Press.

van IJzendoorn, M. H. (1995). The association between adult attachment representations and infant attachment, parental responsiveness, and clinical status: A meta-analysis on the predictive validity of the Adult Attachment Interview. *Psychological Bulletin, 113*, 404–410.

Vaughn, B. E., Block, J. H., & Block, J. (1988). Parental agreement on child rearing during early childhood and the psychological characteristics of adolescents. *Child Development, 59*, 1020–1033.

Vermulst, A. A., de Brock, A. J. L. L., & van Zutphen, R. A. H. (1991). Transmission of parenting across generations. In P. K. Smith (Ed.), *The psychology of grandparenthood: An interactional perspective* (pp. 100–122). London: Routledge.

Vondra, J., Sysko, H. B., & Belsky, J. (2005). Developmental origins of parenting: Personality and relationship factors. In T. Luster & L. Okagaki (Eds.), *Parenting: An ecological perspective* (2nd ed, pp. 35–71). Mahwah, NJ: Lawrence Erlbaum Associates.

Voydanoff, P., & Donnelly, B. W. (1989). Work and family roles and psychological distress. *Journal of Marriage and Family, 51*, 923–932

Vygotsky, L. (1978). *Mind in society*. Cambridge, MA: Harvard University Press.

Ward, M. J., Vaughn, B. E., & Robb, M. D. (1988). Social-emotional adaptation and infant–mother attachment in siblings: The role of the mother in cross-sibling consistency. *Child Development, 59*, 643–651.

Weinraub, M., Horvath, D. L., & Gringlas, M. B. (2002). Single parenthood. In M. H. Bornstein (Ed.), *Handbook of parenting: Vol. 3. Status and social conditions of parenting* (2nd ed., pp. 109–140). Mahwah, NJ: Lawrence Erlbaum Associates.

Wilson, B. J., & Gottman, J. M. (2002). Marital conflict, repair, and parenting. In M. H. Bornstein (Ed.), *Handbook of parenting: Vol. 4. Applied parenting* (2nd ed., pp. 227–258). Mahwah, NJ: Lawrence Erlbaum Associates.

Yeung, W. J., Sandberg, J. F., Davis-Kean, P. E., & Hofferth, S. L. (2001). Children's time with fathers in intact families. *Journal of Marriage and Family, 63*, 136–154.

20

Poverty During Early Childhood

Eric Dearing, Daniel Berry, and Martha Zaslow

The 1990s were a time of historic decline in child poverty rates in the United States (Blank & Haskins, 2001). By 1999, welfare reform, a thriving economy, and federal benefits to the working poor such as the Earned Income Tax Credit (EITC) resulted in the lowest overall child poverty rate in twenty years and the lowest rate ever for black children (Haskins, 2001). Yet about one out of every six children in the country remains poor today, the highest rate among wealthy, industrialized countries (Mishel, Bernstein, & Allegretto, 2005; US Census Bureau, 2004).

From a developmental science perspective, understanding the sequelae of poverty has become increasingly sophisticated with respect to both the questions asked and methods used to address these questions. This sophistication has been facilitated by at least two important advances within the field. First, theory has emphasized the study of child development outside the laboratory, calling attention to the physical and psychosocial milieu in which children's growth is embedded both within and outside of the family (e.g., Bronfenbrenner & Morris, 1998; Magnusson & Stattin, 1998). Second, there has been a movement towards using interdisciplinary methodologies to investigate poverty effects, including methods from demography, economics, psychology, policy science, public health, and sociology, to name a few.

The result of such advances has been a well-established knowledge base defining poverty as a multi-faceted context with consequences that are often pervasive and most detrimental when experienced during early childhood. Further, many of the mechanisms relaying the harmful effects of poverty to children have been documented. Nonetheless, salient limitations and controversies within the field continue to exist. This chapter aims to integrate well-established knowledge and emerging evidence as well as address existing limitations in the study of poverty during early childhood. We make recommendations for future research by building on resolutions from science committees evaluating the study of child development in the context of poverty (American Psychological Association, 2000; Citro & Michael, 1995; Shonkoff & Phillips, 2000).

Incidence of Poverty During Early Childhood

According to the most recent US Census estimates, more than 17% of children under the age of 18 live in families with incomes falling below official poverty thresholds, which for a two-parent family of four was $18,660 in 2003 (US Census Bureau, 2004). The majority of these children are school-age and older. Poverty *rates*, however, are highest during early childhood, such that young children are more likely to be poor than any other age group (Douglas-Hall & Koball, 2004). In fact, the poverty rate for children under five (20.3%) was nearly twice that for adults (10.7%) in 2003 (US Census Bureau, 2004).

Risk of living in poverty during early childhood is associated with both ethnicity and family structure. Young children who are African–American or Latino–American and those living in single-parent households are at heightened risk, despite recent declines in the proportion of these children who are poor. More specifically, although poverty rates declined dramatically in the 1990s for young African-American and Latino-American children, they remain about twice as likely to be poor, compared with their European-American peers and they are three times more likely to be poor than their Asian-American peers. For children less than 5 years of age, for example, estimated poverty rates in 2003 were 8.4% for Asian-American children and 16.8% for European-American children, but 39.7% for African-American and 32.4% for Latino-American children (US Census Bureau, 2004). Furthermore, African-American and Latino-American children are significantly more likely to live in extreme poverty (i.e., less than 50% of the official poverty thresholds) than their European-American peers (US Census Bureau, 2004; Wertheimer, 1999).

Similarly, although the poverty rate decreased by about 18% over the last decade for children living in female-headed households in which a spouse was not present, almost half (49.3%) of children under 5 living in these households were poor in 2003 (Song & Lu, 2002; US Census Bureau, 2004). Comparatively, the risk of living in poverty was about five times less for children under 5 who lived with married parents (i.e., 9.9%). In addition, estimates from the Panel Study of Income Dynamics indicated that as many as 81% of children living in single-parent households have experienced at least one year in poverty (Rank & Hirschl, 2001).

Economic growth and welfare reform in the 1990s led to considerable increases in the number of young children living in *working* poor families. By 2000, in fact, more than half of poor families with children under 3 years of age relied entirely on earnings and no public assistance and three-quarters of all poor children under 3 had at least one working parent (Song & Lu, 2002). Potential explanations for the fact that many working families with young children have remained poor include: a movement of manufacturing jobs from the inner city to the suburbs; technological advances that have limited the skilled positions available to less educated persons; the relatively low value of the minimum wage when adjusted for inflation; and the fact that most employment gains during the 1990s were in the service sector and were often part-time and/or temporary positions (Autor, Levy, & Murnane, 2003; Seccombe, 2000, 2002).

It is important to note, however, that increased employment among poor mothers, beginning around 1994, did play an important role in child poverty rate reductions during the 1990s (Haskins, 2001). As Haskins (2001) has outlined, the positive effects of maternal employment were due, in large part, to changes in tax law that reduced income taxes for the poor and expanded the EITC. In 1999, in fact, federal payroll and income taxes accounted for a 10% reduction in the child poverty rate and this was largely due to the EITC (Haskins, 2001). Yet the effectiveness of maternal employment for raising children out of poverty via work incentives such as the EITC is inextricably linked with the strength of the economy. As job growth has slowed – especially among low-income workers – so has the effectiveness of such programs for reducing poverty; between 2000 and 2002, for example, real income among low-income, female-headed households fell by 8% (Mishel et al., 2005).

Nonetheless, chronically poor families who are continuously dependent on public assistance continue to be the exception rather than the rule as most families' poverty experiences are relatively short (i.e., one to three years) (Bane & Ellwood, 1986; Mishel et al., 2005; Rank & Hirshl, 2001). Once in poverty, however, the probability of experiencing reoccurring episodes is high (Rank & Hirschl, 2001). In addition, exposure to neighborhood poverty may be more likely to be long term, especially for African-American and female-headed families (Quillian, 2003). Further, the United States compares unfavorably with other industrialized nations in this regard such that, on average, poverty experiences in the US are twice as likely to be chronic as those in other industrialized countries (Mishel et al., 2005).

The Developmental Context of Poverty

Environmental risks permeate the homes, child care centers, preschools, and neighborhoods of young children living in poverty (for reviews, see Bradley & Whiteside-Mansell, 1997; Brooks-Gunn & Duncan, 1997; Evans, 2004; Leventhal & Brooks-Gunn, 2000; McLoyd, 1998). Compared with children who are not poor, for example, those who are poor live in contexts that are considerably less likely to include resources that stimulate or support development. Further, compared with their non-poor peers, poor children are more likely to be exposed to a wide variety of harmful agents that impede development.

At home, children living in poverty are less likely than their non-poor peers to have access to books, age-appropriate toys, computers, and high-quality playground equipment; a similar disparity in level of stimulating resources exists in the child care and preschool arrangements of poor versus non-poor children (e.g., Bradley, Corwyn, McAdoo, & Coll, 2001; NICHD Early Child Care Research Network, 1997). Compared with their peers who are not poor, young children in poverty are also less likely to visit learning environments outside their homes such as museums (e.g., Bradley et al., 2001). Further, young children in poverty are exposed to a variety of factors associated with the low quality of housing their families can afford, including: high levels of air and water pollutants (e.g., sulfur oxides), over-crowding, inadequate lighting conditions, and neighborhoods characterized by poor municipal services and few merchants or retail stores (Evans, 2004).

Beyond the physical features of their environments, the psychosocial environments of children in poverty are less stimulating and supportive on average, and filled with greater risk relative to those of children in higher-income families. For example, parents living in poverty spend less time engaged in learning-related activities with their young children, including: less time reading to their children, less time engaged in teaching (e.g., teaching the alphabet), and less time talking with their children (Bradley et al., 2001; Evans, 2004; Hart & Risely, 1995; Hoff, 2003). In addition, parents living in poverty are more likely to use punitive parenting strategies and are less likely to demonstrate high levels of responsiveness with their young children (e.g., Bradley et al., 2001; McLeod & Shanahan, 1993).

Risk of exposure to violence within both the family and neighborhood is also related to family income such that the poorest children are most likely to both witness and personally experience violent acts (e.g., Burgess, Leone, & Kleinbaum, 2000; Coulton, Korbin, Su, & Chow, 1995; Korbin, Coulton, Chard, Platt-Houston, & Su, 1998; Leventhal & Brooks-Gunn, 2000; Sampson, Raudenbush, & Earls, 1997). Further, children in low-income families are more likely than those in middle-income families to interact with aggressive peers. As early as 2 years of age, in fact, children in low-income families are more likely than children in middle-income families to interact with aggressive peers in both neighborhood and child care settings (Sinclair, Pettit, Harrist, Dodge, & Bates, 1994).

Developmental Sequelae of Poverty During Early Childhood

Environmental contexts and children's experiences within those contexts play a central role in cognitive, language, social-emotional, and neurobiological development during early childhood (Shonkoff & Phillips, 2000). Indeed, the context of poverty negatively influences functioning during early childhood in most areas of development. Poverty experiences during early childhood may, in fact, have more negative effects compared with poverty experiences during later life stages, and these effects may become increasingly negative the longer children live in poverty (Brooks-Gunn & Duncan, 1997; Duncan, Yeung, Brooks-Gunn, & Smith, 1998). Although poverty appears most detrimental for children's achievement, cognitive, and language development, physical health plays a unique role in the development of young children who are poor, primarily because health problems may exacerbate the consequences of poverty in other developmental domains (for reviews, see Aber, Jones, & Cohen, 2000; Brooks-Gunn & Duncan, 1997; Duncan & Brooks-Gunn, 1997; Luthar, 1999; McLoyd, 1998; Seccombe, 2000).

Health outcomes

Reviews have highlighted a wide variety of health risks associated with poverty during early childhood (e.g., Bolig, Borkowski, & Brandenberger, 1999; Brooks-Gunn & Duncan, 1997; Chen, Matthews, & Boyce, 2002). Compared with their non-poor peers, children living in poverty are more likely to experience abnormal patterns of physical development, including stunted growth, and are more likely to be exposed to environmental toxins such as lead. During early childhood, poverty is also associated with an increased probability of injury from accidents and an increased probability of acquiring diseases and illnesses such as AIDS, asthma, bacterial meningitis, and ear infections. And once acquired, illnesses are less likely to be treated and are more likely to become chronic conditions for poor children than for non-poor children (Seccombe, 2002).

Poverty is also associated with increased mortality rates during early childhood. Between the ages of 1 and 4, children living in families that are eligible for federal assistance may be more than four times as likely to die from unintentional, non-motor vehicle injuries compared with their peers living in families whose earnings are above federal eligibility thresholds (Nelson, 1992). Further, the effects of poverty on mortality and illness often appear largest during early childhood compared with middle childhood and adolescence (e.g., Halfon & Newacheck, 1993; Nelson, 1992). For example, in a sample of over 17,000 children who were representative of the US population and between the ages of 1 and 17, a higher proportion of poor children under the age of 5 had asthma compared with their non-poor peers, but there were no significant differences in asthma rates for 6- to 11-year-olds or for 12- to 17-year-olds (Halfon & Newacheck, 1993).

Understanding the health risks posed by poverty during early childhood, however, requires attention to child health and families' economic context during the prenatal and infancy periods. Pre- and postnatal health problems associated with poverty such as prenatal alcohol/drug exposure and low birthweight increase children's vulnerability to health risks associated with poverty during early childhood (Bolig et al., 1999). In addition, health problems associated with poverty during early childhood become risk factors themselves for developmental problems in later life, including problems in achievement, cognitive, language, social-emotional, and physical domains (Evans, 2003). Consider, for example, the direct effects of lead poisoning on intelligence and the indirect effect of illness on academic achievement via school absences.

It is also important to note that just as poverty increases children's susceptibility to health problems, health problems increase children's susceptibility to the negative effects of poverty. As Baumeister and colleagues have noted, "biological vulnerabilities, such as low birth weight, tend to combine with environmental contingencies, such as poverty, thus creating a synergistic effect in which their interaction is much more powerful than their main effects" (Baumeister, Kupstas, & Klindworth, 1991, p. 470). No doubt, such synergistic effects are compounded in severity by poor families' limited access to and use of health care services (US Department of Health and Human Services, 1998; Bell & Simkin, 1993). In summary, beyond the potential health risks associated with poverty experiences, the combined effects of poverty and poor health during early childhood increase the probability that children will experience developmental problems in other domains.

Achievement, cognitive, and language outcomes

Developmental differences between poor and non-poor children are often greatest in achievement, cognitive, and language domains (Duncan & Brooks-Gunn, 1997; McLoyd,

1998). Compared with their non-poor peers, young children living in poverty perform worse on a variety of achievement, intelligence, language, and school-readiness indicators. Persistence and depth of poverty have also proven to be important, such that children who live in persistently poor families and children who live in extremely poor families are at greatest risk for negative outcomes in these domains. In addition, early childhood appears to be a time of heightened sensitivity to the negative effects of poverty on achievement, cognition, and language.

By analyzing data from two longitudinal studies, Smith, Brooks-Gunn, and Klebanov (1997) were able to estimate the effects of poverty in a diverse sample with several indicators of achievement, including multiple verbal and full-scale intelligence measures. On average, children who lived in families that were persistently poor during the first four year of life scored between 40% and 60% of a standard deviation lower on these indicators than children who lived in families that were never poor. Children from families that experienced transient episodes of poverty also scored lower than those children from families that were never poor, but the difference between these two groups was not as large (i.e., on average, approximately 33% of a standard deviation) as the difference between the always poor and never poor groups (Smith et al., 1997).

As noted, the developmental consequences of poverty may be exacerbated for children with health risks. Considerable cognitive functioning differences have, in fact, been documented between children with health risks who are persistently poor and their non-poor peers. In a sample of children who were born premature and with a low birthweight, intelligence scores at age 5 for those who were persistently poor during early childhood were, on average, nearly three-quarters of a standard deviation lower than those for children who were never poor (Duncan, Brooks-Gunn, & Klebanov, 1994); intelligence scores for children who were poor for shorter periods of time were approximately one-quarter of a standard deviation lower than those for children who were never poor (Duncan et al., 1994).

Consistent with results on persistence of poverty, income indicators that capture average level of income (or average income relative to needs) during early childhood are more strongly associated with achievement, cognitive, and language outcomes during early childhood than income indicators that capture only a single year of children's lives (Blau, 1999; Taylor, Dearing, & McCartney, 2004). It should be noted, however, that researchers who have examined the effects of persistent poverty during the school years have reported mixed results (e.g., Ackerman, Brown, & Izard, 2004a).

Depth of poverty during early childhood also matters such that the effects of family economic resources appear greatest for the poorest families. Smith et al. (1997), for example, found that very poor children had lower levels of cognitive and language achievement than children closer to but still below the poverty line. More specifically, between the ages of 3 and 6, children living in families with incomes less than 50% of the official poverty threshold consistently scored more than a half standard deviation lower on cognitive and language outcomes than their peers who lived in families that were near poverty (i.e., 150% to 200% of the official poverty threshold). More generally, relations between family income and achievement, cognitive, and language outcomes appear to be nonlinear, such that developmental differences associated with family income differences are largest at the low end of the income distribution (Duncan et al., 1998; Taylor et al., 2004).

Finally, as noted above, detrimental effects associated with poverty on children's cognitive development and educational attainment often appear greatest during early childhood compared with other life stages (Brooks-Gunn & Duncan, 1997; Duncan et al., 1998; Guo, 1998; Haveman & Wolfe, 1994). Duncan and colleagues (1998), for example, found that income during the first five years of life was more strongly associated with high school completion than income during middle childhood or adolescence. In fact, $10,000 more income, averaged across early childhood, was associated with a 2.8-fold increase in the odds of completing high school. Further, researchers who have focused on the school years report the largest effect sizes at school entry and shortly thereafter, with diminishing effect sizes as children age (e.g., Ackerman, Brown, & Izard, 2004b). More generally, material deprivation during early childhood as measured by families' receipt of federal benefits and poor housing conditions is significantly associated with lower levels of achievement in adolescence and lower social status in adulthood, although cumulative deprivation from early childhood through adolescence is a better predictor of adult achievement than any individual developmental stage (Schoon, Bynner, Joshi, Parsons, Wiggins, & Sacker, 2002).

Social-emotional outcomes

During early childhood, children living in poverty are at risk in a number of social-emotional domains, although effect sizes are usually smaller than those for achievement outcomes (e.g., Brooks-Gunn & Duncan, 1997; Duncan & Brooks-Gunn, 1997; Linver, Brooks-Gunn, & Kohen, 2002; Luthar, 1999; McLeod & Shanahan, 1993; 1996; McLeod & Nonnemaker, 2000; McLoyd, 1998; Taylor et al., 2004; Yeung, Linver, & Brooks-Gunn, 2002). Based on parent, teacher, and child care caregiver reports, young children in poverty are more likely than their non-poor peers to display both externalizing (e.g., aggression, hyperactivity, and other conduct problems) and internalizing (e.g., anxiety, depression, and social withdrawal) problems. Further, children in poverty tend to display fewer positive behaviors (e.g., compliance) than their non-poor peers (e.g., Dearing, McCartney, & Taylor, 2001; Taylor et al., 2004).

As found with children's achievement, the association between family income and both positive and negative social behaviors appears to be non-linear, such that the effects of income are greatest at the low end of the income distribution (e.g., Taylor et al., 2004). Results regarding the effects of persistent poverty on social-emotional outcomes have been mixed, however. Although some researchers have found significantly greater risk associated with persistent poverty compared with intermittent poverty for behavior problems (e.g., Duncan et al., 1994), others have not (e.g., Korenman, Miller, & Sjaastad, 1995; also see Ackerman et al., 2004b, who considered the effects of persistent poverty across preschool and early school years).

It may be that the effects of persistent poverty vary by the types of social-emotional problems researchers assess. More specifically, there is some evidence that persistent poverty during early childhood increases risk for internalizing problems above and beyond contemporaneous poverty, but risk of developing externalizing problems is most strongly associated with contemporaneous poverty (McLeod & Shanahan, 1993). Further, in a recent study of school-age children, intermittent and recent economic deprivation was associated with a higher risk of developing externalizing problems than long-term, persistent deprivation (Ackerman et al., 2004a).

Considering that several theoretical perspectives on behavior dysregulation in response to adversity emphasize the accumulating negative effects of chronic exposure to risk (e.g., Cummings, Davies, & Campbell, 2000; Evans, 2004; Fergusson & Horwood, 2003; Hammen, 1992; Hart & Risley, 1995), the processes by which children's social and emotional functioning may become more sensitive to isolated bouts of poverty compared with chronic exposure remain less clear. Ackerman and colleagues (2004a) have suggested that children may be emotionally reactive to negative changes in family economic circumstances that are temporally recent because these experiences decrease both child and parent feelings of efficacy and control, thereby increasing feelings of stress within the family. Others have also emphasized the role of contemporaneous financial stress due to recent financial losses as a precursor to lessened feelings of control and increased mental health problems for parents, increased harsh parenting practices, and, in turn, social-emotional problems for children (e.g., Elder & Caspi, 1988). Few theorists, however, have directly addressed why reactivity to persistent versus intermittent and contemporaneous poverty experiences may vary by problem subtype (i.e., externalizing versus internalizing).

There is also little evidence that early childhood is a time of heightened social-emotional responsiveness to poverty. Unique risks during early childhood associated with immature coping abilities and relatively restricted access to social support mechanisms outside the family have been addressed theoretically (e.g., Luthar, 1999). Yet, despite some evidence that negative mental health effects associated with poverty experienced during early childhood can persist at least into middle childhood (McLeod & Shanahan, 1996), there is little empirical work addressing developmental variations in the social-emotional effects of poverty.

Mechanisms linking poverty and development during early childhood

Theorists have proposed two general pathways linking poverty and child outcomes: (1) family investments and (2) family stress. Developed primarily in the economics literature, family investment theories emphasize families' abilities, or lack thereof, to invest in resources that either stimulate or support growth (e.g., Becker, 1993; Becker & Tomes, 1979, 1986). Developed primarily in the developmental psychology literature, family stress theories emphasize impoverishment and financial loss as stressors for parents and children that deplete psychosocial resources and impair mental health (e.g., R. D. Conger et al., 2002; Elder & Caspi, 1988).

Within families, monetary expenditures on children are subject to several influences, including costs of goods and services, parental spending preferences, and the amount of economic resources families have to allocate (Kalil & DeLeire, 2004). By definition, families in poverty have few economic resources to invest in their children, although whether or not resource scarcity is the primary constraint on poor families' investments in their children is controversial (e.g., Chevalier & Lanot, 2002; Shea, 2000). Chevalier and Lanot (2002), for instance, argue that family characteristics such as parent education are stronger determinants of investments in children's education than family income. Nonetheless, there is substantial evidence that family investments in developmentally stimulating and supportive physical resources as well as family investments in time and effort associated with learning-related activities have proven to be important mediators of associations between poverty and child development, especially for cognitive, language, and achievement outcomes.

In a variety of national data sets, the level of cognitive stimulation provided in the home environment, as measured by learning materials (e.g., number of books) and learning-related parenting behaviors (e.g., amount of parent talk), has explained between 33% and 50% of the association between family income and child cognitive, language, and achievement outcomes during early childhood (Dearing et al., 2001; Klebanov, Brooks-Gunn, McCarton, & McCormick, 1998; Linver et al., 2002; Smith et al., 1997; Taylor et al., 2004; Yeung et al., 2002). In addition, there is some evidence that parent emotional distress and, in turn, punitive parenting may help explain associations between income and children's achievement, at least in verbal domains (Yeung et al., 2002). Researchers who have directly compared the role of family investment and family stress, however, report a larger role for investment processes compared with stress processes for cognitive, language, and achievement outcomes (Linver et al., 2002; Yeung et al., 2002). On the other hand, these researchers report a relatively larger role for family stress in linking poverty and child social-emotional distress in early childhood.

Theorists who emphasize family stress as a mediator linking family economics and child development have primarily focused their work on the potential effects of poverty on child social and emotional well-being (e.g., C. J. Conger, Rueter, & Conger, 2000; Elder & Caspi, 1988; McLoyd, 1989). According to family stress models, child social-emotional well-being suffers from economic hardship due to a chain of psychosocial events that begins with impaired parent psychological functioning. More specifically, poverty (or dramatic economic loss) is associated with parent emotional difficulties, including depressive symptoms and feelings of uncertainty, ambiguity, and loss of control. In turn, conflict between parents is posited to increase along with parents' use of harsh, punitive, and rejecting parenting strategies, thereby increasing emotion regulation problems for children.

Although most empirical support for the family stress model comes from studies of family economics during middle childhood (e.g., R. D. Conger et al., 2002; Solantaus, Leinonen, & Punamaki, 2004) and adolescence (C. J. Conger et al., 2000; Elder, Van Nguyen, & Caspi, 1985), replications have recently been extended to early childhood (Linver et al., 2002; Yeung et al., 2002; for one of the first studies of the family stress model during early childhood, see Elder & Caspi, 1988). Associations between family income and social-emotional functioning during early childhood are explained, in large part, by parent emotional distress and parenting behaviors. That is, there is consistent evidence of a pathway of mediation in which lower income is associated with higher levels of parent emotional distress, this emotional distress is associated with more punitive and less warm parenting strategies, and these parenting strategies are, in turn, associated with higher levels of child externalizing and internalizing problems.

There is potential for reciprocal, interactive, and cumulative effects of investment and stress processes, however. As Evans (2004) recently detailed, for example, the accumulation of risk factors that occur across physical (e.g., inadequate housing conditions) and psychosocial (e.g., low parental responsiveness) environments may be of relatively greater harm for both achievement and social-emotional outcomes of poor children than any single risk factor. During middle childhood, there is evidence that associations between poverty and children's physiological stress (i.e., neuroendocrinological and cardiovascular indices), psychological distress (i.e., maternal and self-report), and emotion regulation (e.g., delay of gratification) are either fully or partially mediated by exposure to multiple risk factors, some of which are associated with family investments and others of which are associated with family stress (Evans & English, 2002). It is not clear, however, whether cumulative risk exposure functions similarly during early childhood. Children's physiological stress and more limited emotion regulation may, over time, come to affect the kinds of interactions that they elicit from adults, thereby creating reciprocal patterns of effects.

Causal Inference and Practical Significance Dilemmas: Endogeneity, Effect Size, and Measurement Concerns

Despite being one of the most well-studied phenomena in the social sciences, much debate continues over the causal influences of family income on children's development and the practical significance of these effects. With regard to causal inference, potential endogeneity biases in non-experimental studies are of primary concern. With regard to practical significance, debates center on absolute and relative effect sizes of income and the feasibility of policy solutions.

Causal inference and potential endogeneity bias in poverty studies

Potential endogeneity bias, due to omitted variables, limits causal inferences in non-experimental poverty studies. In short, the question is whether poverty influences child development or whether an unobserved variable (e.g., genetics) influences both. Estimated income effects may be biased if determinants of both family income and child outcomes such as genetic endowments are not controlled. Often, researchers have estimated an assortment of child and family characteristics as statistical covariates to address this potential bias. As Duncan and colleagues (Duncan, Magnuson, & Ludwig, 2004) have detailed, this approach is often inadequate; estimating child and family covariates in ordinary least-squares regression models, for example, can result in either underestimated or overestimated income effects, and the direction of bias is often difficult to determine (Duncan et al., 2004).

More effective methods used by poverty researchers to control for potential endogeneity biases have included welfare experiments, natural experiments, and within-family analyses. Much of this work has been focused on school-age children or data that were collapsed across early childhood and later developmental stages. The negative income tax experiments conducted in the 1970s were, for example, focused primarily on school-age children (e.g., Maynard & Murnane, 1979). Nonetheless, there are notable exceptions in which researchers using these methods have focused on early childhood.

There have now been multiple experimental evaluations of differing approaches to welfare reform in which welfare applicants or recipients were randomly assigned to a traditional (usually Aid to Families with Dependent Children, AFDC) or new welfare approach. In the present context, it is of particular importance not only that impacts on children have been studied along with economic impacts in a number of these evaluations, but also that the welfare reform approaches studied have included those that have provided financial incentives for making the transition from welfare to work (by continuing to provide welfare benefits up to a point as earnings increased), as well as those that mandated work without providing such incentives. The programs that provided financial incentives for working, particularly if the incentives were strong, tended to increase both income and employment, while those that mandated employment without financial incentives tended to increase employment without increasing income.

Reviewers of these evaluation studies concluded that programs that increased both employment and income have tended to have favorable impacts on both cognitive and behavioral outcomes for young children, while programs that increased employment alone had fewer and more variable impacts on child outcomes (Magnuson & Duncan, 2004; Morris, Huston, Duncan, Crosby, & Bos, 2001; Zaslow et al., 2002). Underscoring the point that income effects appear to have differing implications in different periods of development, these studies have not found the same patterning of impacts for adolescents according to whether programs did or did not increase income (Brooks, Hair, & Zaslow, 2001; Zaslow et al., 2002). Indeed, a meta-analysis of results for adolescents concluded that overall there are small unfavorable effects of the welfare reform programs on adolescents' school outcomes (Gennetian et al., 2002).

Looking at the findings for young children, the evaluation of the Minnesota Family Investment Program (Gennetian & Miller, 2002) is particularly revealing because its design helps disentangle the role of financial incentives and of mandated employment in child impact results. In this evaluation poor, single-mother families with young children were randomly assigned to one of three welfare programs: (1) typical AFDC benefits and financial rules, (2) mandatory employment and financial incentives to encourage work (i.e., in addition to employment income, families kept a portion of their welfare financial supplements until income reached approximately 140% of the poverty threshold), and (3) financial incentives without mandatory employment. Across multiple measures, Gennetian and Miller (2002) found that both versions of the program involving financial incentives resulted in better academic performance and social-emotional outcomes for young children whose mothers had been long-term welfare recipients when they enrolled, although results were not as positive for children of recent welfare recipients assigned to these programs (for a discussion of differences in child impact results for short- and longer-term welfare recipients, see Tout et al., 2004).

Importantly, the improved child outcomes reported by Gennetian and Miller (2002) appeared to be primarily a function of increased income rather than increased employment. Consider, for example, that social competence scores were significantly better for children living in families who received only the financial incentives compared with those living in families who had mandatory employment combined with incentives. Children's performance in school was statistically indistinguishable for these two groups, but both of these groups performed significantly better than children in families receiving the traditional AFDC benefits. There was no evidence that combining work mandates with incentives improved child outcomes above and beyond incentives alone.

Turning to other approaches that help address potential endogeneity problems, Duncan and colleagues (1998) have used sibling models to estimate the effect of within-family variations in income on years of completed schooling. In their models, between-sibling differences in completed schooling were regressed on between-sibling differences in family income when children were between the ages of 0 to 5 years, 6 to 10 years, and 11 to 15 years. In other words, these analyses capitalized on differences in family economic context that non-twin siblings potentially experienced due to naturally occurring gains or losses in family income over time. The authors report a positive association between income during early childhood and years of completed schooling that was significantly larger than this association for the later age periods. It is important to note that unmeasured variables that were constant within families and, more specifically, that did not vary across siblings could not bias these estimated income effects.

Studies that capitalize on within-child variations in family economic context by estimating the association between changes in family income and changes in child outcomes are another way to control for potential biases that arise from time-invariant family, parent, or child characteristics that are not measured (Duncan et al., 1998, 2004). Using such models, Blau (1999) reported income effects that were, in general, statistically indistinguishable from zero, although these analyses were not focused on early childhood. On the other hand, significant effects of income and income changes during early childhood have been reported by researchers using simple change, that is, regressing child outcomes during early childhood on family income while controlling for earlier assessments of the outcomes of interest (Dearing et al., 2001; Duncan et al., 1994; also see Taylor et al., 2004, for income effects during early childhood using a random-effects estimator to control for potential endogeneity biases). Dearing et al. (2001), for example, reported that economic gains for children living in poverty were positively associated with cognitive and language performance at 36 months of age, controlling for cognitive performance during infancy.

Within-family analyses of income change have also been estimated for potential mediating contexts, including cognitive stimulation in the home environment and maternal depressive symptoms during early childhood. Votruba-Drzal (2003) used within-family estimators to demonstrate that gains in family income were associated with increases in cognitively stimulating resources in the home environment during early childhood. Similarly, Dearing, Taylor, and McCartney (2004) used within-family estimates to demonstrate that gains in family income and transitions out of poverty were significantly associated with decreases in maternal depressive symptoms in the first three years after childbirth. These authors also reported a significant indirect effect in which employment gains led to income gains and, thereby, decreases in depressive symptoms. In other words, their results were most consistent with a causal path leading from income change to depressive symptom change rather than the opposite.

The importance of within-family studies of income change extends beyond endogeneity concerns, however. Family income is often in flux, particularly for poor families (Bane & Ellwood, 1986; Duncan, 1998). Modeling these within-family changes in income can be useful for determining whether or not children and families can recover from impoverishment. In other words, within-family analyses are informative with regard to whether or not children and families are responsive to improvements in economic circumstances, a question of considerable relevance to developmental science and policy. Yet, for both within- and between-family analyses, questions of practical significance are also fundamental to determining the policy relevance of findings (McCartney & Rosenthal, 2000).

Practical significance: interpreting effect sizes in an empirical context with measurement error

Poverty researchers have increasingly focused on effect sizes to help determine the practical significance of income for children's life chances. When poor children are compared with their non-poor peers, effect sizes for early childhood outcomes often range from moderate to large, with the largest evident in achievement, cognitive, and language domains (for reviews of effect sizes, see Brooks-Gunn & Duncan, 1997; Duncan & Brooks-Gunn, 1997). On the other hand, effects are generally small in absolute size for associations between early childhood outcomes and income, *per se*. The estimated effect of increasing a poor family's income by $10,000, for example, has generally been associated with changes in child outcomes of less than 25% of a standard deviation (Taylor et al., 2004; for similar estimates that were not specific to, but included, early childhood outcomes, see Aughinbaugh & Gittleman, 2003; Blau, 1999).

Studies of poverty and child development usually rely on self-report data for family income. In many cases, parents are asked to report on multiple income components such as wages, cash benefits, and non-cash benefits. From these items, researchers often then form aggregate indicators of total annualized family income (e.g., for a discussion of aggregate income and poverty indicators in the National Longitudinal Survey of Youth, see Cole & Currie, 1994). It is likely that these indicators include substantial measurement error. Empirical estimates, in fact, have indicated that as much as 25% of the variance in observed income based on self-report may be due to measurement error (Sabelhaus & Groen, 2000). Although people appear able to reliably report such factors as work tenure and union status, self-reports of annualized income appear highly unreliable, and this problem may be particularly evident among the poor (Duncan & Hill, 1985; Meyer & Sullivan, 2003).

Considering the potential measurement error in income data, how should researchers interpret estimated income effects? McCartney and Rosenthal (2000) have argued that an over-reliance on absolute effect sizes can lead researchers to wrongfully dismiss findings as unimportant, because measurement error problems common to studies of children's development may bias effects towards zero. As such, these authors encourage researchers to consider effect sizes in context.

One way of establishing an empirical context for income effect sizes is to consider them *relative* to effect sizes for other well-established determinants of children's development (McCartney & Rosenthal, 2000). Using this approach, Taylor and colleagues (2004) compared effect sizes for family income with those for maternal verbal intelligence. Across a variety of achievement, cognitive, language, and social-emotional outcomes for children in poverty, income effect sizes were, on average, nearly 75% as large as those for maternal verbal intelligence; further, the income effect size was 30% larger than that for maternal verbal intelligence when considering associations with level of cognitive stimulation and parental support in the home environment (Taylor et al., 2004). Among poor children, effect sizes for family income also compare favorably with those for years of maternal education and Early Head Start intervention (Dearing et al., 2001; Taylor et al., 2004).

Given long-standing agreement among social scientists that maternal characteristics such as intelligence and education are of substantial practical importance for children's development via both environmental and genetic pathways, the practical importance of family income also appears to be considerable. Nonetheless, poverty researchers should not be satisfied with income data that are likely to have considerable measurement error. For researchers using secondary analyses of existing data, one suggestion for reducing measurement error is to disaggregate income composites into the specific items on which participants report (e.g., maternal wages, paternal wages, cash benefits) so that obvious inconsistencies may be corrected (Cole & Currie, 1994). For future studies, measures of household consumption appear to have less measurement error than those for family income and, as such, may be a useful alternative for capturing economic well-being and hardship (Deaton, 2003; Meyer & Sullivan, 2003). In addition, recent criticisms of the US Census Bureau's official poverty threshold as an inadequate criterion for tracking incidence of poverty should be noted by researchers interested in the developmental ramifications of economic deprivation (Citro & Michael, 1995).

Measuring Family Economic Resources

Household consumption

Simply put, household consumption is an index of family expenditures with adjustments for the value of services and minus investments in such factors as education, medical care, and pension plans as well as charitable giving (for a more complete discussion of forming consumption measures, see Meyer & Sullivan, 2003; US Census Bureau, 2003; for examples of empirical work using expenditure data, see Lundberg & Rose, 2004; Ziol-Guest, Kalil, & DeLeire, 2004). In their review and empirical examination of measures of family economic well-being, Meyer and Sullivan (2003) note several conceptual advantages to measures of family consumption compared with those for family income, including the fact that consumption measures more effectively capture access to credit, accumulating assets, and in-kind transfers such as Medicaid. As the National Research

Council (Citro & Michael, 1995) noted, consumption measures are also less likely than income measures to be influenced by short-term income fluctuations that have little effect on material well-being, primarily because families often use savings and credit to offset short-term income losses. In addition, incentives to under-report family income (e.g., a fear that an accurate reporting of income could lead to increased taxes or a loss of benefits) are unlikely to bias reports of consumption (Meyer & Sullivan, 2003).

Based on a variety of empirical comparisons of consumption and income measures, Meyer and Sullivan (2003) conclude that indicators of consumption appear to contain less measurement error than those for income. These authors also found that under-reporting of family income appears to occur disproportionately at the lower ends of the income distribution. Although the point of Meyer and Sullivan's work was not to address the implications of non-random under-reporting for estimated associations between income and child outcomes, we argue that under-reporting by lower-income families and more accurate reporting by higher-income families could bias the estimated effect of income on child outcomes toward zero.

As an example of this potential bias, consider two children: (1) a child with an IQ of 90 who lives in a family that earns $30,000 per year, but reports earning $20,000 per year; and (2) a child with an IQ of 110 who lives in a family that accurately reports earning $50,000. Based on the family reports, a twenty-point difference in child IQ is associated with a $30,000 difference in income (or every $10,000 is associated with just over one-third of a standard deviation in IQ). However, the true relation indicates that a twenty-point difference in child IQ is associated with a $20,000 difference in income (or $10,000 is associated with two-thirds of a standard deviation in IQ). To the extent that consumption measures avoid incentives for under-reporting among lower-income families and to the extent that they include less random measurement error, measures of family consumption are likely to provide more accurate estimates of the association between family economic well-being and child development than measures of family income.

On the other hand, family income data are easier to collect than consumption data. As such, there are often pragmatic reasons for using family income as an indicator of material well-being, especially in large surveys (Meyer & Sullivan, 2003). Although researchers using income data should be cautious in their interpretations of absolute effect sizes, the potential analytical strengths of income data in large, heterogeneous samples should not be overlooked. Given that many potential policy solutions to poverty, such as the EITC, target family income and not consumption *per se*, studies of income are policy-relevant despite measurement problems. However, regardless of whether researchers examine income or consumption data, there are dilemmas surrounding how poverty is defined and what thresholds accurately represent economic and material deprivation (Citro & Michael, 1995; US Census Bureau, 2003).

Experimental poverty thresholds

Researchers, advocacy groups, and policy makers have traditionally relied on official US Census poverty thresholds. Based on family size and the number of children within the household, the official poverty thresholds are estimates of the minimum income necessary to meet family financial needs; families with incomes below these thresholds are identified as poor. The National Research Council (NRC) Panel on Poverty and Family Assistance (Citro & Michael, 1995), however, outlined several weaknesses associated with the official thresholds. Weaknesses include, for example, inadequate accounting for variations in child care costs for working and non-working parents, health care needs and costs, differences in housing costs across geographic locations, changes in standards of living (beyond inflation) across historical periods, and policy initiatives that alter disposable income levels. In response to this critique, the US Census Bureau and poverty researchers have begun using alternative poverty thresholds.

Alternative thresholds, based on the NRC recommendations, are often referred to as experimental or quasi-relative poverty measures (e.g., Iceland, 2000, 2003). These measures make adjustments for taxes and tax credits, in-kind benefits (e.g., food stamps), and work-related expenses such as child care and out-of-pocket medical costs, as well as geographic variations in food, clothing, and shelter costs. Compared with the official threshold, experimental and quasi-relative measures result in estimates of the poverty population that are more similar to the total population in three important ways. First, compared with estimates using the official poverty measure, black children constitute a smaller percentage and white (non-Hispanic) children constitute a larger percentage of the poor population when using experimental measures (Iceland, Short, Garner, & Johnson, 2001; Short, 2001).

Second, working families make up a larger percentage and families receiving welfare make up a smaller percentage of the poor population when using experimental measures compared with official poverty measure (Citro & Michael, 1995). In particular, compared with the official measure, experimental measures increase the proportion of poor families with children who are working full-time relative to those who are working part-time or are unemployed (Short, 2001). This is primarily due to the fact that experimental measures account for child care and health care costs as well as social security taxes (Short, 2001). Third, children living in married-couple households account for a greater percentage of the poor and children living in single-parent female-headed households account for a smaller percentage of the poor when using experimental poverty thresholds rather than official poverty thresholds (Iceland et al., 2001). This third difference is largely due to the fact that, on average, married-couple families receive lower levels of government benefits and have higher work-related expenses (Iceland et al., 2001).

To date, empirical work with experimental poverty measures has been limited largely to demographic research. Much less is known about the ramifications of using experimental poverty measures in developmental studies. Because demographic characteristics of families identified as poor are considerably different when using experimental thresholds than when using the official US Census thresholds, empirical work using both is needed to determine what findings are peculiar to the official poverty threshold and what findings remain constant when using alternative specifications.

To the extent that alternative poverty measures result in demographically different poor samples and to the extent that findings vary across these poverty specifications, the importance of such factors as race, employment, and family structure across economic contexts could be clarified. Even so, more direct efforts at contextualizing poverty are necessary. Despite the empirical means to identify variations in poverty effects across unique life circumstances, poverty research has been constrained in large part to main effect questions: that is, what is the average effect of poverty across families?

Contextualizing Poverty During Early Childhood

Few poverty researchers have examined variations across children with regard to associations between family economics and child outcomes, despite the fact that poverty estimates are often taken from large samples that include diverse sets of families with regard to race, employment circumstances, family structure, geographic location (e.g., rural versus urban), parent education, and parent age as well as diverse sets of children with regard to gender, temperament, and health status, to name just a few characteristics. As noted above, the moderating effects of child age, depth of poverty, and persistence of poverty are exceptions to this rule. Nonetheless, present knowledge of the developmental consequences of poverty is based primarily on estimates averaged across children with variations in child, family, and community characteristics held constant. In other words, we understand the effects of poverty, all other things being equal. All other things, however, are not equal.

Given that family investment and stress appear to be the primary mechanisms linking poverty with child outcomes, life circumstances that alter patterns of investment and stress within or outside the family may alter developmental outcomes for poor children. Following this rationale, we argue that poverty researchers should be asking: what elements of poor children's lives are likely to: facilitate investment in developmental resources within the family or compensate for a lack of such resources; impede investment efforts within families or hamper children's abilities to take advantage of available resources; decrease or mitigate family stress; or heighten or exacerbate family stress? Importantly, the answers to these questions can help determine for whom poverty is most detrimental and, in turn, help guide intervention efforts. More specifically, from a policy perspective, concerns over intervention costs provide motivation to target interventions toward children at greatest risk and the mechanisms most likely to promote positive development (Magnuson & Duncan, 2004).

A recent study of the interactive effects of early child care quality, cognitive stimulation in the home, and child gender helps illustrate the benefits of examining moderators of family investment and stress for low-income children and families (Votruba-Drzal, Coley, & Chase-Lansdale, 2004). Votruba-Drzal and colleagues report, for example, that children living in low-income households who were in high-quality child care were less likely to display borderline or clinical levels of externalizing behavior problems than their peers in low-quality child care; importantly, these behavior problem differences associated with child care quality were greatest when children received low levels of cognitive stimulation in the home. These authors also found that child gender interacted with child care quality such that low-quality care was more strongly associated with risk of developing internalizing problems for boys compared with girls and high-quality care was more likely to protect boys than girls from developing externalizing problems.

As Votruba-Drzal and colleagues note, high-quality child care may increase the level of stimulating opportunities otherwise unavailable to low-income children (i.e., investment). High-quality child care may also be associated with decreased parenting stress in poor families (McCartney, Dearing, & Taylor, 2003). Regarding child gender, boys compared with girls may display higher levels of behavioral and physiological reactivity to environmental stressors during early childhood (Crockenberg, 2003).

Although an exhaustive list of potential moderators is beyond the scope of this review, the large literatures on child temperament, family structure, ethnicity, employment circumstances, and neighborhood conditions indicate that these are variables deserving special attention because of their relevancy to family investment and stress (e.g., Crockenberg & Leerkes, 2003; Crouter & Booth, 2004; Dunifon, Kalil, & Danziger, 2003; Garcia-Coll, Macmillan, McMorris, & Kruttschnitt, 2004; Leventhal & Brooks-Gunn, 2000; Meyer & Brillon, 1995; Ziol-Guest et al., 2004). Consider, for example, three findings from empirical work on family structure and poverty. First, change in partner status is one of the most common causes of families with young children entering and exiting poverty (Bane & Ellwood, 1986). Second, there is evidence that household expenditures and family stress both vary by marital status, independent of income differences across single, married, and divorced families (e.g., Amato, 1995; Hetherington, Bridges, & Insabella, 1998; Ziol-Guest et al., 2004). Third, the combined effects of single parenthood and poverty increase the probability that women will hold jobs that are low in prestige and task complexity, which are in turn associated with increased parent stress and more coercive parenting (Dunifon et al., 2003; Raver, 2003; Walter, 2002).

Above we have noted that recent financial loss appears to have different implications for children's social-emotional outcomes, especially externalizing behavior problems, than does persistent poverty. Examining the specific context surrounding financial loss may yield greater understanding of the patterns of child outcomes resulting from loss. For example, was the loss precipitated by marital disruption or for other reasons, such as the occurrence of a health problem preventing work? Family processes may be substantially different when financial loss occurs as a result of marital disruption rather than because of a newly occurring health problem.

We would have much greater understanding of why children have a tendency to show externalizing behavior problems with recent financial loss if we knew the proportion of families in which the recent loss was a result of marital disruption, and more specifically marital disruption involving overt conflict that children witnessed. In general, there is a need to move beyond status indicators such as whether a child comes from a family that is poor or not poor, or a family that is recently versus persistently poor. We believe that understanding the circumstances surrounding and precipitating income gains and losses for poor families, and how child outcomes vary across those circumstances, is an important next step for the field.

Conclusion

Following historic declines in child poverty during the late 1990s, more than 20% of children younger than 5 are estimated to be poor today in the United States. Environmental risks are ubiquitous for these children and their families, pervading developmental contexts within and outside the home. Indeed, more than two decades of empirical work has indicated that compared with their non-poor peers, children who are poor during early childhood have more health problems, display lower levels of achievement in cognitive and language domains, have more social-emotional problems, and lower levels of educational attainment in later life. Some evidence also suggests that compared with later childhood and adolescence, the effects of poverty during early childhood appear most detrimental. Two important mechanisms relaying these negative effects to children appear to be reduced family investments in physical and psychosocial resources that stimulate and support children's development and heightened family stress.

Until recently, a limitation of studies linking family economics and development during early childhood was a strong reliance on between-family comparisons (e.g., poor versus not-poor children) using non-experimental methods that had considerable potential for endogeneity problems. Welfare experiments and within-family analyses, however, have supported the general finding that poverty during early childhood limits children's life chances and that increased income can help ameliorate this harm. Yet determining the practical significance of family economic conditions remains controversial. Given measurement error problems such as under-reporting among poor families, *absolute* effect sizes for income appear less useful for determining practical importance than evaluations of *relative* effect sizes within an empirical context. Increased use of family consumption and expenditures as measures of economic well-being should further clarify questions of practical significance, because these indicators appear to have less random and non-random error compared with income indicators.

The incidence validity of empirical works on poverty during early childhood remains high, because the incidence of poverty during early childhood remains high (Fabes, Martin, Hanish, & Updegraff, 2000). So what should the focus be in future work? It is arguable that the additive effects of economic deprivation during early childhood are well understood. Consider, for example, that exposure to multiple environmental stressors appears more harmful to children than exposure to any one stressor associated with the context of poverty (Evans, 2004), that more time in poverty is associated with worse outcomes than less time (e.g., Duncan et al., 1994), and that greater economic deprivation is associated with more harmful effects than lesser economic deprivation (i.e., depth of poverty, e.g., Smith et al., 1997). On the other hand, interactive effects within the context of poverty have received less attention and are deserving of more work.

We know much about the average effects of poverty and family income, holding other aspects of children's lives constant, but we know much less about how child, family, and community characteristics may alter patterns of investment and stress associated with family economics, or how investment and stress may interact with one another. Unraveling moderating processes could be beneficial to intervention efforts in that understanding processes that magnify developmental risk associated with poverty could help identify children at greatest disadvantage, and understanding processes that minimize developmental risk associated with poverty could help identify mechanisms worthy of targeting with intervention.

References

Aber, J. L., Jones, S., & Cohen, J. (2000). The impact of poverty on the mental health and development of very young children. In C. H. Zeanah, Jr. (Ed.), *Handbook of infant mental health* (2nd ed., pp. 113–128). New York: Guilford Press.

Ackerman, B. P., Brown, E. D., & Izard C. E. (2004a). The relations between persistent poverty and contextual risk and children's behavior in elementary school. *Developmental Psychology, 40,* 367–377.

Ackerman, B. P., Brown, E. D., & Izard C. E. (2004b). The relations between contextual risk, earned income, and the school adjustment of children from economically disadvantaged families. *Developmental Psychology, 40,* 204–216.

Amato, P. R. (1995). Single-parent households as settings for children's development, well-being, and attainment: A social network/resources perspective. *Sociological Studies of Children, 7,* 19–47.

American Psychological Association. (2000). Resolution on poverty and socioeconomic status. *http://www.apa.org/pi/urban/povres.html*

Aughinbaugh, A., & Gittleman, M. (2003). Does money matter? A comparison of the effect of income on child development in the United States and Great Britain. *Journal of Human Resources, 38,* 416–440.

Autor, D. H., Levy, F., & Murnane, R. J. (2003). The skill content of recent technological change: An empirical exploration. *Quarterly Journal of Economics, 118,* 1279–1333.

Bane, M. J., & Ellwood, D. (1986). Slipping into and out of poverty: The dynamics of spells. *Journal of Human Resources, 21,* 1–23.

Baumeister, A. A., Kupstas, F. D., & Klindworth, L. M. (1991). The new morbidity: A national plan of action. *American Behavioral Scientist, 34,* 468–500.

Becker, G. S. (1993). *Human capital: A theoretical and empirical analysis, with special reference to education* (3rd ed.). Chicago: University of Chicago Press.

Becker, G. S., & Tomes, N. (1979). An equilibrium theory of the distribution of income and intergenerational mobility. *Journal of Political Economy, 87,* 1153–1189.

Becker, G. S., & Tomes, N. (1986). Human capital and the rise and fall of families. *Journal of Labor Economics, 4,* S1–39.

Bell, K., & Simkin, L. (1993). *Caring prescriptions: Comprehensive health care strategies for young children in poverty.* New York: National Center for Children in Poverty, Mailman School of Public Health Columbia University. *http://www.nccp.org/media/chc93-text.pdf*

Blank, R. M., & Haskins, R. (Eds.). (2001). *The new world of welfare.* Washington, DC: Brookings Institution Press.

Blau, D. M. (1999). The effect of income on child development. *Review of Economics and Statistics, 81,* 261–276.

Bolig, E. E., Borkowski, J., & Brandenberger, J. (1999). Poverty and health across the life span. In T. L. Whitman, T. V. Merluzzi, & R. D. White (Eds.), *Life-span perspective on health and illness* (pp. 67–84). Mahwah, NJ: Lawrence Erlbaum Associates.

Bradley, R. H., Corwyn, R. F., McAdoo, H. P., & Coll, C. G. (2001). The home environments of children in the United States part I: Variations by age, ethnicity, and poverty status. *Child Development, 72,* 1844–1886.

Bradley, R. H., & Whiteside-Mansell, L. (1997). Children in poverty. In R. T. Ammerman & M. Hersen (Eds.), *Handbook of prevention and treatment with children and adolescents: Intervention in the real world context* (pp. 13–58). New York: Wiley.

Bronfenbrenner, U., & Morris, P. A. (1998). The ecology of developmental processes. In W. Damon & R. M. Lerner (Eds.), *Handbook of child psychology: Vol. 1. Theoretical modes of human development* (5th ed., pp. 993–1028). New York: Wiley.

Brooks, J. L., Hair, E. C., & Zaslow, M. (2001). *Welfare reform's impact on adolescents: Early warning signs.* Washington, DC: Child Trends.

Brooks-Gunn, J., & Duncan, G. J. (1997). The effects of poverty on children. *The Future of Children, 7*(2), 55–71.

Burgess, R. L., Leone, J. M., & Kleinbaum, S. M. (2000). Social and ecological issues in violence toward children. In R. T. Ammerman & M. Hersen (Eds.), *Case studies in family violence* (2nd ed., pp. 15–38). Dordrecht: Kluwer Academic Publishers.

Chen, E., Matthews, K. A., & Boyce, W. T. (2002). Socioeconomic differences in children's health: How and why do these relationships change with age? *Psychological Bulletin, 128*, 295–329.

Chevalier, A., & Lanot, G. (2002). The relative effect of family characteristics and financial situation on educational achievement. *Educational Economics, 10*, 165–181.

Citro, C. F., & Michael, R. T. (Eds.). (1995). *Measuring poverty: A new approach.* Washington, DC: National Academy Press.

Cole, N., & Currie, J. (1994). *Reported income in the NLSY: Consistency checks and methods for cleaning the data* (Technical working paper No. 160). Cambridge, MA: National Bureau of Economic Research.

Coulton, C. J., Korbin, J. E., Su, M., & Chow, J. (1995). Community-level factors and child maltreatment rates. *Child Development, 66*, 1262–1276.

Conger, K. J., Rueter, M. A., & Conger, R. D. (2000). The role of economic pressure in the lives of parents and their adolescents: The family stress model. In L. J. Crockett & R. K. Silbereisen (Eds.), *Negotiating adolescence in times of social change* (pp. 201–223). New York: Cambridge University Press.

Conger, R. D., Wallace, L. E., Sun, Y., Simons, R. L., McLoyd, V. C., & Brody, G. H. (2002). Economic pressure in African American families: A replication and extension of the family stress model. *Developmental Psychology, 38*, 179–193.

Crockenberg, S. C. (2003). Rescuing the baby from the bathwater: How gender and temperament (may) influence how child care affects child development. *Child Development, 74*, 1034–1038.

Crockenberg, S. C., & Leerkes, E. (2003). Infant negative emotionality, caregiving, and family relationships. In A. Booth & A. C. Crouter (Eds.), *Children's influence on family dynamics: The neglected side of family relationships.* Mahwah, NJ: Lawrence Erlbaum Associates.

Crouter, A. C., & Booth, A. (Eds.). (2004). *Work–family challenges for low-income parents and their children.* Mahwah, NJ: Lawrence Erlbaum Associates.

Cummings, E. M., Davies, P. T., & Campbell, S. B. (2000). *Developmental psychopathology and family process: Theory, research, and clinical implications.* New York: Guilford Press.

Dearing, E., McCartney, K., & Taylor, B. A. (2001). Change in family income-to-needs matters more for children with less. *Child Development, 72*, 1779–1793.

Dearing, E., Taylor, B. A., & McCartney, K. (2004). Implications of family income dynamics for women's depressive symptoms during the first three years after childbirth. *American Journal of Public Health, 94*, 1372–1377.

Deaton, A. (2003). Household surveys, consumption, and the measurement of poverty. *Economic Systems Research, 15*, 135–159.

Douglas-Hall, A., & Koball, H. (2004). *Low-income children in the United States.* New York: National Center for Children in Poverty, Columbia University Mailman School of Public Health. *http://www.nccp.org/pub_cpf04.html*

Duncan, G. J. (1988). The volatility of family income over the life course. In P. Baltes, D. Featherman, & R. M. Lerner (Eds.), *Life-span development and behavior* (pp. 317–388). Hillsdale, NJ: Lawrence Erlbaum Associates.

Duncan, G. J., & Brooks-Gunn, J. (1997). Income effects across the life span: Integration and interpretation. In G. J. Duncan & J. Brooks-Gunn (Eds.), *Consequences of growing up poor* (pp. 596–610). New York: Russell Sage Foundation.

Duncan, G. J., Brooks-Gunn, J., & Klebanov, P. K. (1994). Economic deprivation and early childhood development. *Child Development, 65*, 296–318.

Duncan, G. J., & Hill, D. H. (1985). An investigation of the extent and consequences of measurement error in labor-economic survey data. *Journal of Labor Economics, 3*, 508–532.

Duncan, G. J., Magnuson, K. A., & Ludwig, J. (2004). The endogeneity problem in developmental studies. *Research in Human Development, 1*, 59–80.

Duncan, G. J., Yeung, J. W., Brooks-Gunn, J., & Smith, J. R. (1998). How much does poverty affect the life chances of children? *American Sociological Review, 63*, 406–423.

Dunifon, R., Kalil, A., & Danziger, S. K. (2003). Maternal work behavior under welfare reform: How does the transition from welfare to work affect child development? *Children and Youth Services Review, 25*, 55–82.

Elder, G. H., & Caspi, A. (1988). Economic stress in lives: Developmental perspectives. *Journal of Social Issues, 44*, 25–45.

Elder, G., Van Nguyen, T., & Caspi, A. (1985). Linking family hardship to children's lives. *Child Development, 56*, 361–375.

Evans, G. W. (2003). A multimethodological analysis of cumulative risk and allostatic load among rural children. *Developmental Psychology, 39*, 924–933.

Evans, G. W. (2004). The environment of childhood poverty. *American Psychologist, 59*(2), 77–92.

Evans, G. W., & English, K. (2002). The environment of poverty: Multiple stressor exposure, psychophysiological stress, and socioemotional adjustment. *Child Development, 73*, 1238–1248.

Fabes, R. A., Martin, C. L., Hanish, L. D., & Updegraff, K. A. (2000). Criteria for evaluating the significance of developmental research in the twenty-first century: Force and counterforce. *Child Development, 71*, 212–221.

Fergusson, D. M., & Horwood, H. L. (2003). Resilience to childhood adversity: Results of a 12-year study. In S. S. Luthar (Ed.), *Resilience and vulnerability: Adaptation in the context of childhood adversities* (pp. 130–155). New York: Cambridge University Press.

Garcia-Coll, C. T., Meyer, E. C., & Brillon, L. (1995). Ethnic and minority parenting. In M. H. Bornstein (Ed.), *Handbook of parenting: Vol. 2. Biology and ecology of parenting* (pp. 189–210). Mahwah, NJ: Lawrence Erlbaum Associates.

Gennetian, L. A., Duncan, G., Knox, V. W., Vargas, W. G., Clark-Kauffman, E., & London, A. S. (2002). *How welfare and work policies for parents affect adolescents: A synthesis of research.* New York: Manpower Demonstration Research Corporation.

Gennetian, L. A., & Miller, C. (2002). Children and welfare reform: A view from an experimental welfare program in Minnesota. *Child Development, 73*, 601–620.

Guo, G. (1998). The timing of the influences of cumulative poverty on children's cognitive ability and achievement. *Social Forces, 77*, 257–287.

Halfon, N., & Newacheck, P. W. (1993). Childhood asthma and poverty: Differential impacts and utilization of health services. *Pediatrics, 91*, 56–61.

Hammen, C. (1992). The family-environmental context of depression: A perspective on children's risk. In D. Cicchetti & S. L. Toth (Eds.), *Developmental perspectives on depression* (pp. 251–281). Rochester, NY: University of Rochester Press.

Hart, B., & Risley, T. R. (1995). *Meaningful differences in the everyday experiences of young American children.* Baltimore: Brookes.

Haskins, R. (2001). Effects of welfare reform on family income and poverty. In R. M. Blank & R. Haskins (Eds.), *The new world of welfare* (pp. 103–136). Washington, DC: Brookings Institution Press.

Haveman, R. H., & Wolfe, B. S. (1994). *Succeeding generations: On the effects of investments in children.* New York: Russell Sage Foundation.

Hetherington, E. M., Bridges, M., & Insabella, G. M. (1998). What matters? What does not? Five perspectives on the association between marital transitions and children's adjustment. *American Psychologist, 53,* 167–184.

Hoff, E. (2003). The specificity of environmental influence: Socioeconomic status affects early vocabulary development via maternal speech. *Child Development, 74,* 1368–1378.

Iceland, J. (2000). Poverty among working families: Findings from experimental poverty measures. US Census Bureau. *http://www.census.gov/prod/2000pubs/p23-203.pdf*

Iceland, J. (2003). Why poverty remains high: The role of income growth, economic inequality, and changes in family structure, 1949–1999. *Demography, 40,* 499–519.

Iceland, J., Short, K., Garner, T. I., & Johnson, D. (2001). Are children worse off? *Journal of Human Resources, 36,* 398–412.

Kalil, A., & DeLeire, T. (Eds.). (2004). *Family investments in children's potential: Resources and parenting behaviors that promote success.* Mahwah, NJ: Lawrence Erlbaum Associates.

Klebanov, P. K, Brooks-Gunn, J., McCarton, C., & McCormick, M. C. (1998). The contribution of neighborhood and family income to developmental test scores over the first three years of life. *Child Development, 69,* 1420–1436.

Korbin, J. E., Coulton, C. J., Chard, S., Platt-Houston, C., & Su, M. (1998). Impoverishment and child maltreatment in African American and European American neighborhoods. *Development and Psychopathology, 10,* 215–233.

Korenman, S., Miller, J., & Sjaastad, J. (1995). Long-term poverty and child development in the United States: Results from the NLSY. *Children and Youth Services Review, 17,* 127–155.

Leventhal, T., & Brooks-Gunn, J. (2000). The neighborhoods they live in: The effects of neighborhood residence on child and adolescent outcomes. *Psychological Bulletin, 126,* 309–337.

Linver, M. R., Brooks-Gunn, J., & Kohen, D. E. (2002). Family processes as pathways from income to young children's development. *Developmental Psychology, 38,* 719–734.

Lundberg, S., & Rose, E. (2004). Investments in sons and daughters: Evidence from the consumer expenditure survey. In A. Kalil & T. DeLeire (Eds.), *Family investments in children's potential: Resources and parenting behaviors that promote success* (pp. 163–180). Mahwah, NJ: Lawrence Erlbaum Associates.

Luthar, S. S. (1999). *Poverty and children's adjustment.* Thousand Oaks, CA: Sage.

McCartney, K., Dearing, E., & Taylor, B. A. (2003, April). *Is high-quality child care an intervention for children living in poverty?* Poster presented at the biennial meeting of the Society for Research in Child Development, Tampa, FL.

McCartney, K., & Rosenthal, R. (2000). Effect size, practical importance, and social policy for children. *Child Development, 71,* 173–180.

McLeod, J. D., & Nonnemaker, J. M. (2000). Poverty and child emotional and behavioral problems: Racial/ethnic differences in processes and effects. *Journal of Health and Social Behavior, 41,* 137–161.

McLeod, J. D., & Shanahan, M. J. (1993). Poverty, parenting, and children's mental health. *American Sociological Review, 58,* 351–366.

McLeod, J. D., & Shanahan, M. J. (1996). Trajectories of poverty and children's mental health. *Journal of Health and Social Behavior, 37,* 207–220.

McLoyd, V. C. (1989). Socialization and development in a changing economy: The effects of parental job and income loss on children. *American Psychologist, 44,* 293–302.

McLoyd, V. C. (1998). Socioeconomic disadvantages and child development. *American Psychologist*, *53*, 185–204.

Macmillan, R., McMorris, B. J., & Kruttschnitt, C. (2004). Linked lives: Stability and change in maternal circumstances and trajectories of antisocial behavior in children. *Child Development*, *75*, 205–220.

Magnuson, K. A., & Duncan, G. J. (2004). Parent- versus child-based intervention strategies for promoting children's well-being. In A. Kalil & T. DeLeire (Eds.), *Family investments in children's potential: Resources and parenting behaviors that promote success* (pp. 209–236). Mahwah, NJ: Lawrence Erlbaum Associates.

Magnusson, D., & Stattin, H. (1998) Person–context interaction theories. In W. Damon and R. M. Lerner (Eds.), *Handbook of child psychology: Vol. 1. Theoretical models of human development* (5th ed., pp. 685–759). New York: Wiley.

Maynard, R. A., & Murnane, R. J. (1979). The effects of a negative income tax on school performance: Results of an experiment. *Journal of Human Resources*, *14*, 463–476.

Meyer, B. D., & Sullivan, J. X. (2003). *Measuring the well-being of the poor using income and consumption* (Working paper No. 970). Cambridge, MA: National Bureau of Economic Research.

Mishel, M., Bernstein, J., & Allegretto, S. (2005). *The state of working America 2004–2005*. Ithaca, NY: Cornell University Press.

Morris, P. A., Huston, A. C., Duncan, G. J., Crosby, D. A., & Bos, J. M. (2001). *How welfare and work policies affect children: A synthesis of research*. New York: Manpower Demonstration Research Corporation.

Nelson, M. D. (1992). Socioeconomic status and childhood mortality in North Carolina. *American Journal of Public Health*, *82*, 1131–1133.

NICHD Early Child Care Research Network. (1997). Familial factors associated with the characteristics of non-maternal care for infants. *Journal of Marriage and the Family*, *59*, 389–408.

Quillian, L. (2003). How long are exposures to poor neighborhoods? The long-term dynamics of entry and exit from poor neighborhoods. *Population Research and Policy Review*, *22*, 221–249.

Rank, M. R., & Hirschl, T. A. (2001). The occurrence of poverty across the life cycle: Evidence from the PSID. *Journal of Policy Analysis and Management*, *20*, 737–755.

Raver, C. C. (2003). Does work pay psychologically as well as economically? The role of employment in predicting depressive symptoms and parenting among low-income families. *Child Development*, *74*, 1720–1736.

Sabelhaus, J., & Groen, J. A. (2000). Can permanent-income theory explain cross-sectional consumption patterns? *Review of Economics and Statistics*, *82*, 431–438.

Sampson, R. J., Raudenbush, S. W., & Earls, F. (1997). Neighborhoods and violent crime: A multilevel study of collective efficacy. *Science*, *277*, 918–924.

Schoon, I., Bynner, J., Joshi, H., Parsons, S., Wiggins, R. D., & Sacker, A. (2002). The influence of context, timing, and duration of risk experiences for the passage from childhood to midadulthood. *Child Development*, *73*, 1486–1504.

Seccombe, K. (2000). Families in poverty in the 1990s: Trends, causes, consequences, and lessons learned. *Journal of Marriage and Family*, *62*, 1094–1113.

Seccombe, K. (2002). "Beating the odds" versus "changing the odds": Poverty, resilience, and family policy. *Journal of Marriage and Family*, *64*, 384–394.

Shea, J. (2000). Does parents' money matter? *Journal of Public Economics*, *77*, 155–184.

Shonkoff, J. P., & Phillips, D. A. (2000). *From neurons to neighborhoods: The science of early childhood development*. Washington, DC: National Academy Press.

Short, K. (2001). Experimental Poverty Measures: 1999. In US Census Bureau, *Current Population Reports* (P60–216). Washington, DC: US Government Printing Office. Retrieved from *http://www.census.gov/prod/2001pubs/p60-216.pdf*

Sinclair, J., Pettit, G., Harrist, A., Dodge, K., & Bates, J. (1994). Encounters with aggressive peers in early childhood: Frequency, age differences, and correlates of risk for behavior problems. *International Journal of Behavioral Development, 17*, 675–696.

Smith, J. R., Brooks-Gunn, J., & Klebanov, P. K. (1997). Consequences of living in poverty for young children's cognitive and verbal ability and early school achievement. In G. J. Duncan & J. Brooks-Gunn (Eds.). *Consequences of growing up poor* (pp. 132–189). New York: Russell Sage Foundation.

Solantaus, T., Leinonen, J., & Punamaki, R. (2004). Children's mental health in times of economic recession: Replication and extension of the family economic stress model in Finland. *Developmental Psychology, 40*, 412–429.

Song, Y., & Lu, H. (2002). *Early childhood poverty: A statistical profile.* New York: National Center for Children in Poverty, Columbia University Mailman School of Public Health. *http://www.nccp.org/media/ecp02-text.pdf*

Taylor, B. A., Dearing, E., & McCartney, K. (2004). Incomes and outcomes in early childhood. *Journal of Human Resources, 39*, 980–1007.

Tout, K., Brooks, J., Zaslow, M., Redd, Z., Moore, K., McGarvey, A., & McGroder, S. (2004). *Welfare reform and children: A synthesis of impacts in five states. The Project on State-Level Child Outcomes.* Washington, DC: Administration for Children and Families and the Office of the Assistant Secretary for Planning and Evaluation, US Department of Health and Human Services.

US Census Bureau. (2003). *Supplemental measures of material well-being: Expenditures, consumption, and poverty 1998 and 2001. http://www.census.gov/prod/2003pubs/p23-201.pdf*

US Census Bureau (2004). *Current population survey.* Annual Demographic Survey: March Supplement (Pov01). *http://ferret.bls.census.gov/macro/032004/pov/new01_100.htm*

US Department of Health and Human Services (1998). *Chartbook on children's health insurance.* Office of the Assistant Secretary for Planning and Evaluation, Office of Health Policy. *http://aspe.hhs.gov/health/98chartbk/98-chtbk.htm*

Votruba-Drzal, E. (2003). Income changes and cognitive stimulation in young children's home learning environments. *Journal of Marriage and Family, 65*, 341–355.

Votruba-Drzal, E., Coley, R. L., & Chase-Lansdale, L. P. (2004). Child care and low-income children's development: Direct and moderated effects. *Child Development, 75*, 296–312.

Walter, M. (2002). Working their way out of poverty? Sole motherhood, work, welfare and material well-being. *Journal of Sociology, 38*, 361–380.

Wertheimer, R. (1999). *Trends in the well-being of America's children and youth: 1999.* Washington, DC: Child Trends.

Yeung, W. J., Linver, M. R., & Brooks-Gunn, J. (2002). How money matters for young children's development: Parental investment and family processes. *Child Development, 73*, 1861–1879.

Zaslow, M., Moore, K., Brooks, J., Morris, P., Tout, K., Redd, Z., & Emig, C. (2002). Experimental studies of welfare reform and children. *The Future of Children, 12*(1), 79–95.

Ziol-Guest, K. M., Kalil, A., & DeLeire, T. (2004). Expenditure decisions in single-parent households. In A. Kalil & T. DeLeire (Eds.), *Family investments in children's potential: Resources and parenting behaviors that promote success* (pp. 181–208). Mahwah, NJ: Lawrence Erlbaum Associates.

21

Orphanages as a Developmental Context for Early Childhood

Charles H. Zeanah, Anna T. Smyke, and Lisa D. Settles

Orphanages remain the most common form of care for orphaned and abandoned children in many parts of the world. Although numbers are difficult to ascertain, there is little question that millions of children are maintained in institutions, and many of them receive care that is of appallingly poor quality (Human Rights Watch, 2004). Institutions for young children are widely used in Russia and Eastern Europe, Central and Southeast Asia, and Central and South America, but institutions for young children are also used in most Western European countries (Browne & Hamilton-Giachritsis, 2004), as well as in the United States (Child Welfare League of America [CWLA], 2004).

Although institutions have been used as a form of care for young maltreated and abandoned children in the United States since the eighteenth century, they had almost disappeared by the late 1960s. This decline began near the turn of the twentieth century, as American welfare approaches increasingly relied on foster care, but institutions for young children never completely disappeared. In some large urban areas in the late 1980s they made a comeback in response to a crack cocaine epidemic. Large numbers of infants were removed at birth from mothers who tested positive for cocaine and were placed in care, and the numbers of infants requiring placement overwhelmed many foster care systems (Harden, 2002). Newborns continue to be placed in foster care in large numbers in the US, most often related to maternal substance use (Wulczyn, Hislop, & Harden, 2002). In some communities (e.g., Washington, DC), a significant proportion of infants are still cared for in large institutions rather than by families (CWLA, 2004).

Additional reasons for renewed interest in studying the effects of institutional care came about as a result of the fall of the Ceauşescu regime in Romania in 1989 and the opening of the Romanian orphanages to the world. Prospective adoptive parents from the West adopted children out of institutions which epitomized the problems with over-crowded, poor-quality, institutional care (Johnson, 2000). Despite serious developmental, socio-emotional, and health problems in these children, Rutter, Kreppner, and O'Connor (2001) have reported surprising variability in the degree to which children were affected by their institutional experience, and they documented substantial recovery from many early delays and deviant behavior.

In any case, the debate over orphanage care is not over. Even in the US, some have continued to advocate for use of orphanages rather than foster care (see McKenzie, 1999). Some religious groups have never given up orphanages and continue to advocate for their use. In 1994, the Speaker of the United States House of Representatives, Newt Gingrich, called for a return to orphanages to care for children whose mothers were unemployed but beyond the limits of lifetime welfare caps (London, 1999). This suggestion provoked intense reactions, including objections to institutional care based on higher rates of infection, poorer rates of growth, delays in cognitive development, aberrant social and emotional development, and higher prevalence of maltreatment (Frank, Klass, Earls, & Eisenberg, 1996).

In this chapter, we review the literature on young children raised in orphanages and consider the implications of this literature for questions from developmental theory and science. Which aspects of early development are more or less vulnerable to environmental deprivation? How much recovery is possible following attempts to remediate early deprivation? Does the nature of the deprivation (physical/health, cognitive stimulation, continuity of care) predict variation in outcomes? What does this tell us about the most important elements of caregiving? Does the extent and/or duration of deprivation matter? Are sensitive periods in development evident from studies of early deprivation?

Given the importance of the questions surrounding care for abandoned and maltreated young children, we begin by considering the ecology of institutional life for young children, noting that there is wide variability within and between institutions for young children.

Ecology of Institutional Life

Systematic study of the caregiving environment of orphanages has demonstrated both quantitative and qualitative deficiencies compared to the environment of children raised in families. One such study was the Bucharest Early Intervention Project (BEIP), the first randomized, controlled study of foster care as an intervention to remediate the developmental and socio-emotional effects of institutionalization in infants and toddlers (Zeanah et al., 2003). Using an adaptation of the Observational Record of the Caregiving Environment (ORCE; NICHD Early Child Care Research Network [ECCRN], 1996), for example, investigators in the BEIP found that the quality of the caregiving environment was significantly higher among infants and toddlers reared by their parents at home (Smyke, Koga, Johnson, Zeanah, & the BEIP Core Group, 2005). Parents of the home-reared infants and toddlers were available and interacted significantly more frequently with them than institutional caregivers did with the infants and toddlers in their care. Parents of home-reared children talked with them with significantly greater frequency than institutional caregivers talked with the children in their care. Not surprisingly, children's word-like utterances were also greater in number among the home-reared children.

Qualitative and descriptive studies over the years have articulated the actual experience of young children raised in institutional settings. Despite considerable variability in the quality of care between and even within institutions, both historical and contemporary descriptions have been consistent in noting certain interrelated features (Dennis & Najarian, 1957; Goldfarb, 1945a, 1945b; Muhamedrahimov, 2000; Provence & Lipton, 1962; Spitz, 1945; Zeanah et al., 2003). These include: a regimented daily schedule and paucity of stimulation; staffing limitations, including understaffing and the fact that caregivers work shifts and have relatively limited time with individual children; and non-individualized care and lack of caregiver psychological investment in children.

Schedule and stimulation

The daily schedule is regimented, and typically children are expected to conform to the institution's schedule. Thus, children are fed at mealtimes rather than when they are hungry, changed at changing time rather than when they are wet, and put down at nap- or bedtime rather than when they are sleepy. Such scheduling is not all bad, as young children often enjoy predictable environments, but the lack of flexibility for individual children may be concerning.

Beyond the routine, there is often little in the way of stimulation. According to Provence and Lipton's (1962) classic descriptions of an American orphanage in the mid-twentieth century, children remained inside nursery rooms for much of the time, often kept in their cribs for most of the day and night, experiencing human contact rarely and only for instrumental purposes such as diapering and feeding. There was often an eerily quiet atmosphere in rooms full of babies. The children were housed in rooms with children the same age and tended by overworked nurses who briskly changed and bathed them with little time for play or social interaction. Feeding consisted of propped bottles with formula early on to which pureed food was added as children grew older (Provence & Lipton, 1962). Cloth was sometimes placed around cribs, to prevent drafts, but it effectively reduced visual stimulation except for the area above the infant's crib (Dennis & Najarian, 1957). Many of these features are still found in Romanian and Russian institutions in the early twenty-first century (Muhamedrahimov, 2000; Zeanah et al., 2003).

Our observations of many orphanages for young children in Romania have reminded us of what is implicit in many descriptions of orphanage routines: that is, the paradoxical combination of a rigid routine combined with long stretches of time in which there are no structured activities. As a consequence, beyond the rigid schedule of daily activities, there are few if any demands placed on the children. Effectively, this creates an environment of non-contingency in which it is difficult for young children to learn about the consequences of their actions (Groze & Ileana, 1996; Hough, 2000; Levy, 1947). Feeding, changing of diapers, and being picked up by a caregiver just happen to these babies, without them doing anything that elicits the interaction (Provence & Lipton, 1962).

Caregiver to child ratios

Most institutions that have been studied have had high caregiver to child ratios. For example, in many studies ratios have ranged from 1:12 to 1:15, even for children less than 3 years old. Perhaps compounding the large ratios, children of similar ages are placed together, meaning that many children often have similar needs at the same time, stretching a caregiver's ability to respond reasonably. In keeping with earlier descriptive studies, in our own observations in contemporary Romania, there is little positive social interaction between caregivers and children, and children rarely spend time outside or away from the institution (Provence & Lipton, 1962).

Non-individualized care and limited psychological investment

It is perhaps not surprising that in an environment of high child to caregiver ratios, material deprivation, and low morale, there is often little in the way of caregiver psychological investment in individual children. In conducting studies involving interviews with caregivers about the behavior of young children, we learned that they sometimes did not know the ages, personalities, and behaviors of some of the children with whom they had worked for more than a year.

Mealtime is one of several times when perfunctory care is especially apparent. Typically, children sit in groups at tables or in high chairs. Younger children are fed a bite at a time out of a common bowl using the same spoon, each in turn. Older children feed themselves with limited adult supervision. There is almost no talking, and even this may be limited to gruff commands. In other words, feeding as a social experience is almost nonexistent (Muhamedrahimov, 2000).

Staffing limitations

Even in orphanages with more favorable child to caregiver ratios, there is still the problem of inconsistent caregiving. A given child may be cared for by fifteen to thirty different caregivers who worked rotating morning, evening, and night shifts (Levy, 1947; Smyke, Dumitrescu, & Zeanah, 2002; Tizard, 1977). Orphanages are often staffed by workers of lower socio-economic status who have little motivation to encourage the development of the children they care for (Brodbeck & Irwin, 1946; Provence & Lipton, 1962; Zeanah et al., 2003). Understaffing and frequent turnover exacerbate the problem of limited psychological investment by caregivers and severely limit opportunities for infants to be held or to experience meaningful interactions with their caregivers (Hunt, Mohandessi, Ghodssi, & Akiyama, 1976; Provence & Lipton, 1962).

In 1999, Smyke and colleagues (2002) took advantage of a natural quasi-experiment to demonstrate the importance of reducing the number of caregivers involved with young, institutionalized children. At a large Romanian institution, the director implemented a "pilot unit" in which the number of caregivers for each child during the times the child was awake was reduced from more than sixteen to four. Structured interviews with care-givers demonstrated fewer signs of aggression, stereotypies, and signs of attachment dis-order in children on the pilot unit compared to children on a standard unit in the same institution.

What seemed clear was that reducing the number of caregivers involved with the children had increased their psychological investment in the children. Each grouping of twelve to fifteen children in the "pilot unit" was named (e.g., the "cubs," the "kittens," etc.), and the caregivers referred to them in interviews as "my" children. This contrasted sharply with caregivers from the "standard" unit, who sometimes described having one or two "favorite" children, but beyond that, demonstrated no particular psychological investment in the children on their unit (Smyke et al., 2002).

Developmental Problems Associated with Institutionalization

Given the caregiving environment of most orphanages, it is not surprising that develop-mental differences have been well documented in institutionalized versus family-reared children. Family-reared comparison groups in various studies have included children being raised at home by their biological parents, children placed in foster homes after removal from their biological parents, and children who have been adopted. In reviewing studies of institutionalized children we will indicate which studies used foster care, adop-tion, or never institutionalized children as a comparison group. Nevertheless, the consis-tency of findings about developmental differences between children raised in these disparate types of family settings and children raised in institutions suggest that the most important distinction may be between children raised in some type of family setting versus children raised in an institutional setting.

Studies for the past sixty to seventy years have examined many domains of develop-ment, including physical growth, cognitive and language development, social develop-ment and attachment, motor development and behavior problems. Although many prenatal risk factors are evident in children in institutions, developmental problems in children in institutions are believed to result in part from the deprivation inherent in institutional care. These findings are reviewed below by domain of development, and the studies and samples we review are summarized in Table 21.1.

Physical development

One of the most frequently noted problem areas in institutionalized children is poor growth. Height, weight, and head circumference all have been noted to be compromised, sometimes severely. For example, young children in Romanian institutions are shorter, weigh less, and have smaller heads than their never institutionalized Romanian counter-parts (Smyke et al., 2005). Although many children who are raised in orphanages experi-ence prenatal malnutrition and are born at low birth weight, much of the growth failure appears to be related to deprivation in the institution itself. For example, the time a child

Table 21.1 Studies with multiple reports on the same sample (all studies not listed) followed by single-sample studies

Reference	Domain(s) assessed	Site/ Origin of subjects	Number of subjects	Age	Measures
Canada: Chisholm, Ames, and colleagues					
Chisholm et al. (1995)	Attachment, indiscriminate friendliness	CN Adopted from RO (RO) Adopted early from RO (EA) Family-reared from CN (CB)	RO: 46 EA: 30 CB: 46	30 mo.	Parent interview; attachment security; Parenting Stress Index
Morison et al. (1995)	Developmental screening	CN Adopted from RO (RO) Adopted early from RO (EA)	RO and EA matched (24 in each group)	27.3 mo. (range: 17–37)	Revised Denver Prescreening Developmental questionnaire; Revised Gesell
Fisher et al. (1997)	Behavior problems, physical growth	CN Adopted from RO (RO) Adopted early from RO (EA) Family-reared from CN (CB)	RO: 46 CB: 46 RO subsample: 29 EA: 29	31.5 mo. 31 mo. 25 mo. 25 mo.	Parent interview Parent interview; CBCL
Chisholm (1998)	Attachment, indiscriminate friendliness	CN Adopted from RO (RO) Adopted early from RO (EA) Family-reared from CN (CB)	RO: 46 EA: 30 CB: 46	T1: 30 mo. T2: 54 mo.	Parent interview; attachment security interview; separation–reunion procedure; Stanford–Binet; CBCL

Table 21.1 *Continued*

Reference	Domain(s) assessed	Site/ Origin of subjects	Number of subjects	Age	Measures
Canada: Other studies					
Benoit et al. (1996)	Development, behavioral, medical problems	CN Adopted from RO	22	T1: 19 mo. T2: 35 mo.	Medical/developmental history; developmental assessment; maternal–child interaction
Marcovitch et al. (1997)	Development, attachment, behavior problems	CN Adopted from RO at <6 mo. or ≥6 mo.	<6 mo.: 37 ≥6 mo.: 19	3–5 yrs	CBCL; Stanford–Binet; SSP
Netherlands: Hoksbergen and colleagues					
Hoksbergen et al. (2002)	Medical, behavioral, psychosocial problems, support for family	Netherlands Adopted from RO	83	6.8 yrs (range: 3.5–14.6)	Parent interview
Hoksbergen et al. (2003)	Post-traumatic stress disorder, behavior problems	Netherlands Adopted from RO	T1:74 T2:80	8 yrs (range: 4–15)	Parent interview; trauma questionnaire; CBCL
United Kingdom: O'Connor, Rutter, and colleagues					
Rutter & the ERA study team (1998)	Developmental deficit and catch-up	UK Adopted from UK Adopted from RO	UK < 6 mo.: 52 RO < 6 mo.: 58 RO 6–24 mo.: 59	4 yrs	Physical measurement: head circumference, weight, height; McCarthy, Denver scales

Study	Outcomes	Groups	Sample sizes	Ages	Measures
Rutter et al. (1999)	Quasi-autistic behavior	UK Adopted from UK Adopted from RO	UK < 6 mo.: 52 RO < 6 mo.: 58 RO 6–24 mo.: 53 RO > 24 mo.: 54	4 & 6 yrs 4 & 6 yrs 4 & 6 yrs 6 yrs	Parent interview; parent and teacher questionnaires; play session including separation–reunion; McCarthy, Denver scales; ASQ; ADI-R
O'Connor et al. (2000)	Cognitive development, physical growth	UK Adopted from UK Adopted from RO	UK < 6 mo.: 52 RO < 6 mo.: 58 RO 6–24 mo.: 53 RO > 24 mo.: 54	4 & 6 yrs 4 & 6 yrs 4 & 6 yrs 6 yrs	Physical measurement: head circumference, weight; McCarthy, Merrill-Palmer, Denver scales
Kreppner et al. (2001)	Inattention/ hyperactivity, attachment, IQ, conduct problems	UK Adopted from UK Adopted from RO	UK < 6 mo.: 52 RO < 6 mo.: 58 RO 6–24 mo.: 59 RO > 24 mo.: 48	4 & 6 yrs 4 & 6 yrs 4 & 6 yrs 6 yrs	Parent interview; family relationship, behavioral questionnaires; cognitive, developmental measures; child observation; teacher questionnaire
Rutter et al. (2001)	Attachment, inattention/ hyperactivity, emotional problems, autistic features, cognitive, peer problems, conduct problems	UK Adopted from UK Adopted from RO	UK < 6 mo.: 52 RO < 6 mo.: 58 RO 6–24 mo.: 53 RO > 24 mo.: 54	6 yrs	Parent interview; parent and teacher questionnaires; McCarthy; ASQ; ADI-R

Table 21.1 *Continued*

Reference	Domain(s) assessed	Site/ Origin of subjects	Number of subjects	Age	Measures
Beckett et al. (2002)	Post-institutionalized behavior patterns	UK Adopted from RO	144	6 yrs	Parent interview
O'Connor et al. (2003)	Attachment, cognitive development	UK Adopted from UK Adopted from RO	UK < 6 mo.: 52 RO < 6 mo.: 58 RO 6–24 mo.: 53	4 yrs	Caregiver interview; modified separation–reunion procedure conducted in home
United Kingdom: Tizard and colleagues					
Tizard & Rees (1974)	IQ, response to stranger	UK Institutionalized Adopted Restored to biol. family Comparison	IN: 26 AD: 24 RB: 15 C: 30	4½ yrs (± 1 mo.)	WPPSI; test behavior; response to stranger; caregiver/parent interview
Hodges & Tizard (1989a)	IQ, behavior problems	UK Institutionalized Adopted Restored to biol. family Comparison	IN: 5 AD: 17 RB: 11 C: 31	16 yrs	Parent interview; Wechsler Adult Intelligence Scale; behavior questionnaire; teacher questionnaire
Hodges & Tizard (1989b)	Family, non-family social relationships	UK Institutionalized Adopted Restored to biol. family Comparison	IN:5 AD: 17 RB: 11 C: 31	16 yrs	Parent interview; social difficulties questionnaire; teacher questionnaire

United States: Goldfarb

Study	Focus	Country / Sample	Sample size	Age	Measures
Goldfarb (1943)	Behavior, language, cognitive problems	US; Inst. for 3yrs → FC; FC from infancy	Group A, B (each) 20 In-FC 20 FC	A: 6yrs 9 mo. B: 8yrs 6 mo.	Development, behavior problem checklist
Goldfarb (1944)	Behavior problems related to placement change in FC	US; Inst. for 3yrs → FC; FC from infancy	40 In-FC 40 FC	7yrs 8 mo.	Record review
Goldfarb (1945a)	Cognitive, language, motor, adaptive development	US; Inst. for 3yrs → FC; FC from infancy	In-FC: 15 FC: 15	T1: 34–35 mo. T2: 43 mo.	Stanford–Binet; Merrill-Palmer; language scales; Vineland Social Maturity; motor coordination; Rorschach
Goldfarb (1945b)	Cognitive development, emotional problems	US; Inst. for 3yrs → FC; FC from infancy	In-FC/FC: 15 In-FC/FC: 20 In-FC/FC: 20 In-FC/FC: 15	T1: 3 yrs–3 yrs 7 mo. T2: 6 yrs 7 mo. T3: 8 yrs 5 mo. T4: 12 yrs 2 mo.	Stanford–Binet; Merrill-Palmer; language scales; Vineland Social Maturity; motor coordination; behavior checklist; Rorschach

Romania: Bucharest Early Intervention Project

Study	Focus	Country / Sample	Sample size	Age	Measures
Marshall et al. (2004)	Brain functioning	RO; Institutionalized and never-institutionalized infants and toddlers	IN: 104 NI: 46	22.4 mo. (±6.0) 21.0 mo. (±6.2)	Electroencephalogram (EEG)

Table 21.1 *Continued*

Reference	Domain(s) assessed	Site/ Origin of subjects	Number of subjects	Age	Measures
Parker & Nelson (2005)	Brain functioning, discrimination of facial expressions of emotion	RO Institutionalized and never-institutionalized infants and toddlers	IN: 72 NI: 33	22.4 mo. (±6.1) 20.9 mo. (±6.9)	Event-related potentials (ERP)
Smyke et al. (2005)	Physical, cognitive, speech & language development, behavior problems and competencies, caregiving environment	RO Institutionalized and never-institutionalized infants and toddlers	IN: 124 NI: 66	21.07 mo. (±7.29) 19.32 mo. (±7.16)	Physical measurements: HC, height, weight; BSID; REEL; RDLS; ITSEA; ORCE
Zeanah et al. (in press)	Attachment, attachment disorder	RO Institutionalized and never-institutionalized infants and toddlers	IN: 99 NI: 50	23.85 mo. (±4.85) 22.25 mo. (±5.01)	SSP; DAI; ITSEA; ORCE; BSID
Other studies in Eastern Europe and Russia					
Kaler & Freeman (1994)	Cognitive, social development	RO Orphanage Non-orphanage	OR: 25 NO: 11	35.2 mo. (±6.6) 36.6 mo. (±14.8)	BSID; Vineland; ESCS-mod.; mirror and rouge test; level of play; peer interaction
Muhamedrahimov (2000)	Institutional ecology in baby home institutions	Russia Children < 3 mo., 3–10 mo.	*n* not stated	<3 mo. 3–10 mo.	Observations of caregivers and their responses to children: duration of feeding, feeding rate, response to crying, etc.; caregiver questionnaire

Study	Outcomes measured	Location/Groups	N	Age	Method
Smyke et al. (2002)	Attachment disturbances, aggression, stereotypies, language	RO Institution Standard care Pilot unit Never-institutionalized	ST: 32 PI: 29 NI: 33	33 mo. (±11.4) 39.7 mo. (±11.2) 32.4 mo. (±10.2)	Caregiver/parent interview
Browne & Hamilton-Giachritsis (2004)	Rates of institutionalization	Europe	32 nations	Children < 3	Survey
Other studies					
Lowrey (1940)	Behavior problems, language, cognitive development	US Infant home (IN) children referred to psychiatrist	28	1–4 yrs	Review of records; caregiver/child interview
Spitz (1945)	Intelligence, perception, memory, social relations	Location unspecified Institution 1 Family-reared 1 Institution 2 Family-reared 2	IN1: 69 FR1: 11 IN2: 61 FR2: 23	0–12 mo.	Hetzer-Wolf baby tests; case review; observation
Brodbeck & Irwin (1946)	Language	Iowa, US Orphanage Family-reared	OR: 94 FR: 217	0–6 mo.	Speech sound measurement
Levy (1947)	Cognitive development	US Institution Boarding homes (FC)	<6 IN: 83 BH: 39 6–12 IN: 12 BH: 22 >12 IN: 6 BH: 68	<6 mo. 6–12 mo. >12 mo.	Gesell; Merrill-Palmer; Vineland; Stanford–Binet

Table 21.1 *Continued*

Reference	Domain(s) assessed	Site/ Origin of subjects	Number of subjects	Age	Measures
Dennis & Najarian (1957)	Cognitive	Lebanon Orphanage Family-reared	OR: 49 FR: 41	2–12 mo. 4½–6 yrs	Cattell; Goodenough draw-a-man; Knox cubes; Porteus maze
Provence & Lipton (1962)	Ecology of orphanage	US Institution Foster care	IN: 75 FC: 75	14–26 wks 27–39 wks 40–52 wks	Gesell developmental exam; physical, neurological exam; physical measurements; behavior observation; caregiver interview
Wolkind (1974)	Psychiatric disorder, "affectionless psychopathy"	UK Children's home (IN)	92	5 mo.–12 yrs 11 mo	Child interview; caregiver interview; chart review
Hunt et al. (1976)	Cognitive, effects of changes in stimulation and caregiver ratio	Iran Orphanage Wave 1: No intervention Wave 2–5: Intervention-varied levels of enrichment US Family-reared comparison	W1: 15 W2: 10 W3: 9 W4: 20 W5: 11 FR: 16	Selected at 4 wks	Uzgiris–Hunt Scales administered over first 3 yrs of child's life
Gindis (2000)	Review of language problems	US Adopted internationally Post-institutionalization			
Hough (2000)	Review of risk factors for language development	US Adopted from Eastern Europe and Russia Post-institutionalization			

Study	Focus	Location / Groups	Sample	Age	Measures
Johnson (2000)	Review of medical and developmental sequelae of institutionalization	US Adopted from Eastern Europe			
Johnson & Hostetter (2000)	Review of health problems in post-institutionalized children	US Adopted internationally			
Rojewski et al. (2000)	Behavior problems	US Adopted from China	45	46.9 mo. (±19.1)	Parent Rating Scale (BASC) questionnaire
Roy et al. (2000)	Emotional and behavioral disturbances, cognitive development	UK Residential Foster care Control for both groups drawn from each child's classroom (no out-of-home care)	R: 19 CC-R: 19 FC: 19 CC-FC: 19	80.4 mo. 79.8 mo. 80.6 mo. 81.3 mo.	WISC; caregiver and teacher questionnaires; caregiver and teacher interviews; classroom observations
Chugani et al. (2001)	Brain and neuropsychological functioning	US Adopted from RO Normal adults Family-reared US children with epilepsy	AD: 10 NO: 17 EP: 7	8.83 yrs 27.6 yrs 10.7 yrs	PET scan; neuropsychological evaluation; CBCL; parent interview
Harden (2002)	Cognitive, behavior problems, caregiving environment	US Congregate care Foster care	CC: 35 FC: 30	16.6 mo. (±5.8)	BSID; Toddler Behavior Checklist; Vineland; HOME; ITERS

Table 21.1 Continued

Reference	Domain(s) assessed	Site/ Origin of subjects	Number of subjects	Age	Measures
Johnson (2002)	Review of effects of adoption on: cognitive, attachment, behavior problems, social deficits, physical growth	US International and national adoption			
Vorria et al. (2003)	Attachment, cognitive development, quality of care	Greece Institutionalized Family-reared	IN: 86 FR: 41	M: 13 mo; F: 13.1 (range: 11–17.2) M: 13.6 mo; F: 14.1 (range: 11.1–17.6)	SSP; CCTI: BSID; observation of social behavior; ECERS
Roy et al. (2004)	Inattention/ hyperactivity, attachment to caregiver, peer attachment, dependency	UK Residential care Foster care	R: 19 FC: 19	80.4 mo. 80.6 mo.	WISC; caregiver and teacher questionnaires; caregiver interview

AD = adopted; ADI-R = Autism Diagnostic Interview-Revised; ASQ = Autism Screening Questionnaire; BASC = Behavior Assessment Scale for Children; BH = boarding home; BSID = Bayley Scales of Infant Development; C = comparison; CB = Canadian-born, family-reared; CBCL = Child Behavior Checklist; CC = congregate care; CC-FC = control group for foster care; CC-R = control group for residential; CCTI = Colorado Children's Temperament Inventory; CN = Canada; DAI = Disturbances of Attachment Interview; EA = adopted early into Canada; ECERS = Early Childhood Environment Rating Scale; EP = children with epilepsy; ESCS = Early Social Communication Scale (modified); F = female; FC = foster care; FR = family-reared; HC = head circumference; HOME = Home Observation for Measurement of the Environment; IN = institution; In-FC = institutionalized first and then placed in foster care; IQ = intelligence quotient; ITERS = Infant/Toddler Environment Rating Scale; ITSEA = Infant Toddler Social Emotional Assessment; M = male; NI = never-institutionalized; NO = normal adult; OR = orphanage; ORCE = Observational Record of the Caregiving Environment; PET = Positron Emission Tomography; PI = pilot unit – reduced caregiver/child ratio, four caregivers per unit; R = residential; RB = restored to biological family; RDLS = Reynell Developmental Language Scales; REEL = Receptive Expressive Emergent Language Test; RO = Romania; SSP = Strange Situation procedure; ST = standard institutional care; T1/T2 = Time 1/Time 2; W = wave; WISC = Wechsler Intelligence Scale for Children; WPPSI = Wechsler Preschool and Primary Scales of Intelligence.

spent in an orphanage was inversely related to the height of the child (Fisher, Ames, Chisholm, & Savoie, 1997). Johnson and Hostetter (2000) estimated that the psycho-social growth retardation of children raised in orphanages meant that children fell behind one month of growth for every three to four months they spent in an orphanage.

In their study of young children adopted out of Romanian institutions in the early 1990s, Fisher and colleagues found that 85% of the children fell below the tenth percentile for weight and 59% were below the fifth percentile for weight (McMullan & Fisher, 1995). At follow-up at age 4½ years, many of the adopted Romanian children were below the tenth percentile in weight and height (Fisher et al., 1997). Further, some catch-up of height and weight is evident when children are removed from institutions and placed in adoptive (Rutter et al., 1999) or foster families (Nelson, 2004). Nevertheless, catch-up remains incomplete, and children raised in institutions remain shorter, lighter, and have smaller heads than their never-institutionalized counterparts.

Motor development

Gross and fine motor delays, as well as more abnormal motor movements, have been associated with institutional care. Provence and Lipton (1962), for example, noted some delays as early as 3 to 4 months of age, and more were evident at older ages. They speculated that these delays were due to a lack of opportunities for exploration that would have been provided had caregivers held children more frequently. Sweeney and Bascom (1995) compared motor development on the Peabody Developmental Motor Scales between two groups of Romanian orphans, those diagnosed as Failure to Thrive (FTT; $n = 236$) and those without Failure to Thrive (NFTT; $n = 31$). The NFTT infants scored higher on both gross and fine motor skills than the FTT infants, but overall, both groups of infants performed below the sixth percentile in gross and fine motor skills. Stereotypies, such as body rocking, wrist flapping, and face guarding, have been observed (Cermak & Daunhauer, 1997), especially in infants who exhibited growth retardation (Sweeney & Bascom, 1995) and among children exposed to neglecting, under-stimulating institutional environments (Kaler & Freeman, 1994; Vorria et al., 2003).

Beckett and her colleagues (2002) examined the incidence of stereotypical behavior, self-injurious behavior, and atypical interests in a variety of sensory stimuli. Almost one-half of children adopted into the UK displayed stereotypical movements. The incidence of these behaviors decreased over time, but they did not disappear completely. Several children in the study also had problems with chewing and swallowing solid foods. Some of these difficulties persisted well into the preschool years (Beckett et al., 2002).

Cognitive development

Studies for the past sixty years comparing institution-reared children to children in some form of family care (foster care, adoption, or never-institutionalized children raised by their parents) have found average IQs that have ranged from ten to forty points lower in institutionalized children (Goldfarb, 1945a; Smyke et al., 2005; Spitz, 1945; Tizard &

Rees, 1974; Vorria et al., 2003; Zeanah et al., 2003). The effects are demonstrable early, as in a study in Lebanon comparing institutionalized children and children in foster care who were assessed throughout the first year of life. Delays were apparent as early as two months of age (Dennis & Najarian, 1957). Furthermore, the effects are sometimes lasting, as in a study by Goldfarb (1945b), in which children who were placed in foster care at age 3 years after early institutionalization had not caught up with a comparison group raised in foster care even by the early teen years. Further, there is some evidence of negative correlations between length of time institutionalized and cognitive performance, suggesting that the longer young children remain institutionalized, the more declines become apparent (Smyke et al., 2005).

In institutions that are more stimulating and that provide better caregiver to child ratios (Hodges & Tizard, 1989a; Hunt et al., 1976; Tizard, 1977; Tizard & Rees, 1974; Vorria et al., 2003), severe cognitive deficits are not always noted for children. Nevertheless, differences between institution-reared children and children reared in any type of family setting are still evident. In fact, an increasingly more stimulating caregiving environment was studied systematically in an orphanage in Iran in an effort to improve the infants' cognitive abilities (Hunt et al., 1976). Using the Uzgiris–Hunt ordinal scales to assess infant progress, infants who received more stimulating environments achieved higher levels on the scales than did those who experienced care at the first three levels.

Recovery from early deprivation in institutions also has been examined. A study by Tizard and her colleagues of children institutionalized in residential nurseries in England is instructive (Tizard, 1977). In this study, children were placed at or soon after birth, primarily for reasons of poverty or illegitimacy. They were maintained in small, mixed-age groups, in a stimulating environment that included books, instruction in the preschool years, and toys, as well as caregiver to child ratios that were more favorable than in most previous studies.

Between 2 and 4 years of age, 24 of the children were adopted, 15 were returned to their biological families, and another 26 remained institutionalized. At age 4 years, children who had been adopted had scores on the Wechsler Preschool and Primary Scales of Intelligence that were approximately one standard deviation (fifteen points) higher than those of children returned to their biological mothers or children who remained institutionalized. Despite these differences, scores of all three groups of children were within the average range, suggesting no severe cognitive delays in these children (Tizard & Rees, 1974).

More recent studies of children adopted out of Romanian institutions also have demonstrated large gains in cognitive development. Romanian infants who remained in institutions briefly (<4 months) and for longer periods (>8 months) and had been adopted into Canadian families were compared to Canadian children of matched gender and ages who were reared at home by their parents (Marcovitch et al., 1997; Morison, Ames, & Chisholm, 1995). Children adopted at older ages had more developmental delays when they first met their parents. The percentage of children experiencing delays over time decreased but still remained elevated. In contrast, children adopted before 4 months of age exhibited markedly fewer delays (Morison et al., 1995).

Rutter and colleagues (1999) evaluated two groups of children adopted into the United Kingdom from Romania – children adopted before age 6 months and children adopted after 6 months – and they were compared to a group of children adopted within the UK. Despite significant delays at the time of adoption (reported retrospectively by their adoptive parents), children adopted before 6 months of age had achieved almost complete developmental catch-up by 4 years of age. Those adopted after 6 months demonstrated significant catch-up but their mean cognitive index scores were seventeen points below those of children adopted within country.

Of course, children were not randomly assigned to adoption or to reunification with their biological families in this study, and the selection bias for children who were adopted may have affected outcomes. For example, children with family histories of epilepsy or schizophrenia, or those who had congenital or other defects, were not freed for adoption, so that they could be observed for emerging pathology (Tizard, 1977). Clearly, these non-random group differences have potential large effects on outcomes.

Language development

Particular deficits have been noted in language development (Dennis & Najarian, 1957; Goldfarb, 1945a; Provence & Lipton, 1962; Spitz, 1945) both in children in institutions and in children adopted out of institutions. Institutionalized infants were found to demonstrate lower frequencies of vocalizations and fewer types of vocalizations as early as 2 to 4 months of age, when compared to infants raised in their own families (Brodbeck & Irwin, 1946). Lack of imitation by caregivers and interaction with them were cited as likely contributors to this early differentiation in language skills. Further, the development of focused attachment relationships in the second half of the first year of life and the acquisition of beginning language skills are time-linked in the young infant's life (Goldfarb, 1945a). Interestingly, a few children in the institutional setting had language skills as good as, or better than, their family-reared counterparts. Although this was characterized as a rare occurrence, it was linked with "favorite" status, when a worker became fond of a given child, and tended to talk with and interact with the favorite child more frequently. Further, foster children who were institutionalized for the first three years of life showed more speech problems than children raised in foster homes (Goldfarb, 1943).

The importance of language as a means of interaction, but also as a means of organization for other types of cognitive skills, makes delays or deficits in this area especially salient (Gindis, 2000). Language not only contributes to the development of cognitive skills but is an important factor in the child's development of self-regulatory skills. Although we have highlighted the aspects of the institutional environment which impact overall development, it is important to recognize the specific aspects of the institutional ecology that function as risk factors for the development of this essential skill (Hough, 2000).

Children develop language in environments characterized by both stimulation and contingency (Stromswold, 1995; Tarabulsy, Tessier, & Kappas, 1996). It is not surprising, therefore, that in studies of children adopted into the United States from Eastern Europe, speech and language delay is one of the primary deficits (Hough, 2000). The foundations of language skills, such as turn-taking, are in the process of developing long before the child speaks his or her first word. Contingent responsiveness on the part of the caregiver is an integral part of this process. When the child vocalizes and the caregiver responds, the child becomes a partner in the language experience. In an institutional setting, harried caregivers who are responsible for changing a room full of children cannot make the time to respond to the communication attempts of each child, and eventually the infant's efforts at communication disappear (Provence & Lipton, 1962).

Institutionalized and post-institutionalized children routinely have been observed to have difficulty with speech and language skills, more so for expressive than for receptive skills, but delayed nonetheless. In several studies, rates of language delay have approached or exceeded 70% (Goldfarb, 1943; Lowrey, 1940) and these rates persisted even when children had been placed in foster care as preschoolers (Goldfarb, 1943). In the BEIP study, language quotient scores for institutionalized infants and toddlers also were reduced markedly when compared to children reared at home by their parents (Smyke et al., 2005). Expressive Language Quotients were on average twenty points lower than Receptive Language Quotients, suggesting that expressive language was particularly affected in the institutional environment. Children placed in foster care rather than institutions in early infancy did not exhibit marked delay in speech and language development (Goldfarb, 1943). More recently, infants and toddlers raised in congregate care had poorer communication skills than children raised in foster care (Harden, 2002), part of an overall pattern of greater competence among foster children.

Disturbances of Attachment and Institutional Care

Organizing an attachment to a small number of discriminated attachment figures is one of the essential tasks of early childhood. An attachment relationship between a young child and caregiver requires sufficient ongoing interaction between the two so that the child learns to seek comfort, support, and nurturance selectively from that caregiver. Institutional care, which limits to varying degrees the child's opportunities to form selective attachments, therefore, might be expected to be associated with disturbances of attachment.

Children living in institutions

The effects of institutional care on attachment were first examined by Barbara Tizard and her colleagues in a study of sixty-five young children placed in residential nurseries in London. Compared to institutions in many parts of the world, these facilities were smaller, with more favorable caregiver to child ratios, more adequate toys and stimulation, and they made some effort to individualize care (Tizard, 1977). As noted earlier, children either remained in the institutions, were placed in adoptive homes, or were returned to their birth families. In addition to studying the children's cognitive abilities at age 4 years, these children and sixty-five never-institutionalized children had their attachment to their caregivers assessed through caregiver interviews. Of importance, among the twenty-six continually institutionalized children, most had seriously disturbed attachments (Tizard & Rees, 1974).

Ten of these children were "overly friendly," that is, they approached unfamiliar adults as often as familiar adults. Evidence of reticence around unfamiliar adults was absent, and these children sometimes exhibited separation protest from strangers. They displayed attention-seeking behavior and were indiscriminate in seeking comfort. The children's attachment to others seemed superficial since adults seemed to be interchangeable.

Eight children from the continuously institutionalized group had even more seriously disturbed relatedness. They were emotionally withdrawn, odd, and unresponsive. They tended not to seek comfort when distressed nor to respond to comfort when it was offered. They demonstrated disturbances of emotion regulation as evidenced by diminished positive affect, and outbursts of fearfulness, irritability, or sadness for which precipitants were unclear.

These patterns of disturbed attachment had been observed in institutionalized children both in older descriptive studies (Provence & Lipton, 1962; Wolkind, 1974) and in more rigorous contemporary studies (Smyke et al., 2002; Zeanah et al., in press). In fact, these patterns of emotionally withdrawn, unresponsive behavior and indiscriminate behavior became the basis for the clinical phenomenology of disorders of attachment.

More recently, two studies have assessed attachments in institutionalized children using the Strange Situation Procedure (SSP; Ainsworth, Blehar, Waters, & Wall, 1978). This method has some advantages over interviews, in that it is observational and because it has been so thoroughly validated as the "gold standard" for assessment of attachment relationships in hundreds of studies throughout the world (Solomon & George, 1999). On the other hand, the SSP is used to assess qualities of extant attachment relationships. As noted, the assumption that an attachment even exists between a young child in an institution and a caregiver is unwarranted. Therefore, it is unclear whether the SSP is even appropriate to use when the presence or absence of an attachment relationship is not established.

In a sample of infants in a Greek institution, Vorria et al. (2003) reported that a majority of these infants (65%) had "disorganized" attachments to their caregivers. This is a classification of attachment derived from aberrant behavior that the child displays in the SSP which is associated with substantially increased risk for subsequent maladaptation. In a similar study of young children in institutions in Bucharest, Romania, 78% had failed to organize an attachment to their institutional caregivers (Zeanah et al., in press). In both samples, proportions were significantly different from ethnically similar, comparison children who were raised at home by their parents.

Disturbances of attachment among children reared in institutions, however, are not fully described merely by an increased probability of having disorganized attachments. Evidence of incompletely developed patterns of attachment in the institutionalized children has been noted in the Bucharest study (Zeanah et al., in press). After observing unusual behavior in children in the SSP that was not adequately captured by extant classifications, the investigators developed a continuous rating of the degree to which attachment had formed between child and caregiver. Coders were blind to whether the children were community children being raised by their parents or institutionalized children being seen with their institutional caregivers. They rated *all* of the community children as having fully developed attachment relationships with their mothers, but they rated fewer than 5% of institutionalized children as having fully developed attachments with their institutional caregivers. Many of the institutionalized children demonstrated only barely discernible differentiation between their familiar caregivers and a complete stranger.

Children adopted out of institutions

Three studies have examined patterns of attachment in preschool children adopted out of Romanian institutions. These studies all have found a high proportion of unusual classifications. Marcovitch et al. (1997) found that only 30% of young children adopted from Romania were securely attached (compared to 42% in a Canadian-born never-institutionalized comparison group) and 42% were insecure/controlling (compared to 10% in the comparison group). Chisholm (1998) reported more insecure attachments in Romanian adoptees (63%) than in Canadian-born comparison children (42%). Additionally, more than 21% of the Romanian adoptees displayed atypical insecure patterns, while none of the Canadian children did so. Finally, O'Connor et al. (2003) found that at age 6 years, following adoption into the UK out of Romanian institutions, 51% of children were classified as insecure/controlling or insecure/other compared to only 17% of children adopted within the UK (but never institutionalized). In addition, 36% of children adopted out of Romanian institutions, compared to only 13% of intra-UK adopted children, exhibited non-normative behavior in separations and reunions, such as extreme forms of emotional over-exuberance, nervous excitement, silliness, coyness, and excessive playfulness more typical of a much younger child.

Finally, there is presumptive evidence from children adopted out of institutions who develop attachments to their new families (Chisholm, 1998; O'Connor et al., 2003), although signs of reactive attachment disorder (RAD) may persist for years in some of these children and many have atypical insecure patterns of attachment. Because of lack of baseline assessments, it is unclear whether the children were or were not attached prior to adoption. A recent study that does include assessments of children's attachment prior to removal from institutions and placement in foster care is the Bucharest Early Intervention Project (Zeanah et al., 2003, cited above). In preliminary findings, signs of emotionally withdrawn/inhibited and indiscriminately social/disinhibited RAD were significantly reduced for children in foster care compared to those who remained in the institutional environment (Zeanah et al., in press). These preliminary results do not necessarily mean that the effects on attachment are reversed, however, as the quality of attachments that these children develop to their foster parents must be assessed to complete the picture.

Other Problems in Young Children Associated with Institutional Rearing

Problem behaviors

An important question is whether institutional care is associated with increased risk for internalizing and externalizing behavior problems. Some studies have suggested both increased aggression and increased withdrawal in institutionalized children (Smyke et al., 2002), but results are not consistent.

Children living in institutions. Behavior problems and signs of psychiatric disturbance have been reported in studies of institutionalized children for many years. In one early study, for example, a consistent pattern of aggressiveness, temper tantrums, speech problems, attention-seeking behavior, and over-eating or picky eating was noted (Lowrey, 1940). These problems are similar to those that have been noted in children who have been severely neglected (Smith & Fong, 2004).

Similarly, Goldfarb (1943) reported that children who had been institutionalized for the first three years of life demonstrated consistently greater levels of problem behaviors when they were compared to children raised in foster care, ranging from feeding and sleeping difficulties to problems with aggressive behavior and hyperactivity to marked over-dependence on adults with attention-seeking behavior. Wolkind (1974) also described "affectionless psychopathy" as a post-institutional syndrome.

Despite these early reports, recent studies have been less consistent in finding differences between institutionalized and family-reared children with regard to externalizing and internalizing problems. For example, infants and toddlers reared in congregate care in Washington, DC, were compared to children raised in traditional foster care, and reported behavior problems were similar for the two groups (Harden, 2002). Also, in the Bucharest study there were large differences between institutionalized and community children in physical, cognitive, language, and social characteristics, but no differences in levels of internalizing or externalizing behaviors (Smyke et al., 2005; Zeanah et al., in press). However, very young Greek children in residential care, which was likely not as neglecting an environment as the Romanian orphanages, were reported to have greater levels of aggression and non-involved behavior than did children cared for in their homes (Vorria et al., 2003).

Children adopted out of institutions. Early reports regarding children adopted out of Romanian institutions described a variety of developmental and behavioral problems (Doolittle, 1995; Groze & Ileana, 1996). These behaviors are assumed to be associated with the length of time in institutional care, which is inextricably confounded with age, and the level of deprivation in the institution, information usually gathered retrospectively from adoptive parents (Doolittle, 1995; Rutter et al., 2001). Rutter and his colleagues (2001) used parent and teacher reports regarding a range of behavioral problems, including emotional difficulties, conduct problems, and peer problems, and found no differences between a group of 6-year-olds adopted within the UK and a group adopted out of Romanian institutions. Using a checklist of behavior problems, Marcovitch and her colleagues (1997) compared children adopted into Canada prior to 6 months of age to children adopted into Canada at 6 months of age or older. Mean scores for both groups fell within the normal range, although the total problem behavior score was higher for children adopted later. Chinese children adopted into the US were identified as at risk for some behavior problems (Rojewski, Shapiro, & Shapiro, 2000), but their scores for eight problem areas were within normal limits.

Social competence

Social competence is an important index of adaptation in the early years (Sameroff, 2000). Infants and toddlers become competent in interacting with their environment through repeated experiences and under the guidance of a committed caregiver. Nevertheless, studies of competence among institutionalized children have been rare. Goldfarb (1945a, 1945b) documented poorer social competence among young institutionalized children compared to children in foster care. In the Bucharest Early Intervention Project, marked differences between institutionalized and never-institutionalized Romanian infants and toddlers were noted in competence skills such as mastery motivation, imitation/play, empathy, and prosocial peer relations as measured by caregiver report (Smyke et al., 2005). Clearly, this is an area deserving further study.

Psychiatric disturbances

Inattention/hyperactivity syndromes. Increased activity and difficulty attending are frequently reported in post-institutionalized children. In one early study, for example, 6-year-old children who had been raised in institutions for the first three years of their lives and then been placed in foster families displayed more hyperactivity, anxiety, and difficulty with attention than did their counterparts raised exclusively in foster care (Goldfarb, 1944). In the Tizard study, adopted children were less distractible and restless than either children remaining in the institution or those reunified with their families (Tizard & Rees, 1974). More recent studies of currently or previously institutionalized children have reaffirmed these earlier reports of restlessness, hyperactivity, and difficulty with attention (Doolittle, 1995; Kreppner, O'Connor, & Rutter, 2001; Roy, Rutter, & Pickles, 2000; Rutter et al., 2001), difficulties which have been proposed as a possible link to difficulty in establishing and maintaining selective attachments (Roy et al., 2000).

Autistic spectrum disorders. Based on clinical observations of hundreds of institutionalized children in Russia and Romania, Federici (1998) reported that some of the children appeared to display an unusual constellation of behaviors, including cognitive impairment, socially withdrawn and unresponsive behaviors, and stereotypies. He described this constellation as "institutional autism." Rutter and colleagues (1999) used state-of-the-art diagnostic procedures to evaluate 4-year-old children in their sample of Romanian orphans adopted into the UK, and they found that 6% met diagnostic criteria for autism and that another 6% had mild, often isolated, features of the disorder. Given that most children were placed in institutions at or shortly after birth, and given the proportion of children affected, it did not seem that this reflected a placement bias but rather that the experience of institutionalization produced a phenotype that was indistinguishable from autism. Interestingly, when re-evaluated at age 6 years, most of the children in this sample were much improved and no longer met criteria for autism, though some continued to exhibit unusual behaviors. Because the children had responded so dramatically to more favorable caregiving environments, the investigators described the syndrome as "quasi-autistic." What vulnerabilities in individual children might lead to such a clinical picture among institutionalized children and the processes through which the caregiving environment ameliorates such symptomatology remain to be elucidated.

Post-traumatic stress disorder (PTSD). Children who have spent two to three years in an adverse caregiving institutional environment may be at risk for post-traumatic stress disorder (PTSD; Federici, 1998). Hoksbergen and colleagues (2003) addressed issues of PTSD among children adopted from Romania into the Netherlands by comparing them to Dutch norms obtained from children living in their families. On average, the adopted children were almost 3 years of age when adopted, and at the time of the study their ages ranged from 4 to 15 ($M = 8$ years). Using a trauma questionnaire, parent interview, and a problem behavior checklist, Hoksbergen and colleagues (2003) found that when compared to a Dutch-born group, the children in this sample had significantly more internalizing, externalizing, and total problems; a third of the children adopted from Romania had scores in the clinical range. Total problem scores were plotted against scores on the trauma questionnaire, showing that when children were rated in the clinical range for total problems, the trauma score was also elevated.

Studies of brain functioning

To date, only three studies of brain functioning in institutionalized and formerly institutionalized children have been published. Chugani, Behen, Musik, Juhasz, Nagy, and Chugani (2001) used positron emission tomography to study ten children adopted out of Romanian institutions. As a group, the children had problems of attention deficits, impulsivity, and social abnormalities. Compared to healthy adults, they were found to exhibit reduced brain metabolism in the orbital prefrontal gyrus, the infralimbic prefrontal cortex, the amygdala, the lateral temporal cortex, and the hippocampus. Compared to 10-year-old children with refractory epilepsy, the Romanian children showed decreased metabolism in the left orbital frontal cortex. This study is important in pointing to possible areas of brain functioning abnormalities, particularly since these areas are all plausible neural substrates for the previously described behavioral abnormalities. Nevertheless, any conclusions about these findings must be tempered by concerns about selection factors that led to including these ten children in the study and the absence of adequate controls. In a study of electroencephalogram patterns, Marshall, Fox, and the BEIP Core Group (2004) reported increased low-frequency (theta) power in posterior scalp regions and decreased high-frequency (alpha and beta) power, particularly in frontal and temporal areas, in institutionalized compared to never-institutionalized Romanian children. These findings are compatible with a developmental delay model, or with a model suggesting that institutional care is associated with reduced brain electrical activity. Parker and Nelson (2004) studied event-related potentials to different facial expressions of emotion in the same sample studied by Marshall, Fox, and their colleagues. They replicated the findings of reduced power, and they found different patterns of response to fear and sad expressions in institutionalized and never-institutionalized Romanian children, implicating abnormalities in the neural circuitry underlying recognition of facial expressions of emotion. These preliminary studies of brain functioning point to possible abnormalities, but there is a clear need for more studies to link these preliminary findings more clearly to specific behavioral abnormalities.

Conclusions and Future Directions

For nearly three centuries, orphanages have existed to care for young children. Although wide variability among and even within orphanages is well documented, the literature is consistent in demonstrating that adverse developmental characteristics in children are clearly associated with institutional rearing. Certain features of institutional care, reviewed in this chapter, appear to militate against adequately individualized care, and even in more favorable institutions, some degree of developmental deficits is almost always documented.

From a policy perspective, the expense and the well-documented harmful effects of institutional rearing argue strongly against this form of care. We should note, however, that calls for the end of institutional care for young children date back at least to the late nineteenth century, and yet institutions for young children still exist in most of the developed countries in the world. From this staying power, we infer that orphanages must serve certain functions that societies find useful. Sequestering abandoned children from the rest of society is one possible function that comes to mind.

From a developmental science perspective, institutional rearing affords an opportunity to study development in conditions of social and sometimes material deprivation. Findings throughout the last fifty years about the effects of institutionalization are quite consistent, and some preliminary conclusions about the effects are warranted:

1. Institutional rearing leads to harmful effects on children's development. Although some of the developmental abnormalities associated with institutional rearing likely accrue from risk factors that precede institutional care, such as prenatal malnutrition and substance exposure, or possibly from genetic vulnerabilities, some of the effects are also likely due to the caregiving experience in institutions. Two lines of evidence point to this. First, even when no differences in background risk factors can be detected between children placed in foster care and children placed in institutions, children in institutions are more compromised (Roy, Rutter, & Pickles, 2004). Second, many children adopted out of institutions recover substantially from early abnormalities, even though prenatal risk factors and genetic vulnerabilities do not change.

2. Developmental domains are variably compromised by institutional rearing. Institutional care is associated with risks for serious developmental compromise in virtually every area studied. Still, some domains appear to be more vulnerable to insults and less likely to recover than others. Thus, in both Tizard's longitudinal study (Tizard, 1977) and Vorria's study (Vorria et al., 2003), both of which included more favorable ratios of caregivers to children, cognitive impairment was limited, but attachment was seriously compromised. Further, even in children adopted and who have normal intelligence, atypical patterns of attachment may be evident years later (Hodges & Tizard, 1989b; O'Connor et al., 2003).

This suggests that attachment is more vulnerable than cognition to the pernicious effects of institutional care.

Although substantial recovery from the effects of early institutional care occurs for most children (Rutter et al., 2001), some children remain compromised for many years, at least in some areas (Hodges & Tizard, 1989a, 1989b). Still, cognitive recovery appears to exceed social recovery in children raised in institutions. Furthermore, children adopted out of Romanian institutions may encounter more difficulties as they enter their teen years, though longitudinal data on this question are lacking (Gunnar & Kertes, 2003; O'Connor, 2003).

All recovery data, however, are limited by the fact that no studies published to date about recovery have used randomized designs. Adoption studies seem likely to include a non-representative sample of institutionalized children, and this bias may inflate any assessment of favorable outcomes. Comparing children raised in foster homes to those raised in institutions begs the question of what factors distinguish children who are placed in these two forms of care.

3. Quality of caregiving appears to be importantly related to both degree of insult and amount of recovery, with important caveats. First, individual differences in the quality of caregiving in institutions have been related to individual differences in child outcomes (Smyke et al., 2005). Second, when changes in levels of stimulation to institutionalized children were experimentally controlled, increasing stimulation was associated with more favorable outcomes (Hunt et al., 1976). Finally, when the number of caregivers assigned to a given child was reduced, but the ratio of caregivers to children was not changed, the children had fewer signs of disordered attachment (Smyke et al., 2002). All of these findings are compatible with the idea that higher quality of caregiving in conditions of deprivation may buffer some of the adverse developmental consequences, although much remains to be learned about which aspects of caregiving are most important for which developmental outcomes.

Further, most investigators assume that caregiving improves dramatically for young children adopted from institutions, even though systematic documentation of this improvement is largely lacking. In any case, it is clear that children who are adopted out of institutions have readily demonstrable developmental gains that are large. On the other hand, in the limited data available, most of the recovery appears to take place in the first year or two after placement (Rutter & O'Connor, 2004). Nevertheless, the paucity of studies, and particularly of long-term longitudinal studies, limits our confidence in this conclusion.

4. Earlier intervention for deprivation is more likely to be beneficial than later intervention. Questions of the timing of both developmental insults and interventions designed to ameliorate them are among the most compelling and vexing in psychology. One problem is that because the vast majority of institutionalized children are placed there at or soon after birth, the length of deprivation is nearly perfectly confounded with the age at which the intervention (placement in families) begins. Another problem is that extremely large samples will be required in order to test for specific critical or sensitive periods, and these are often not available.

O'Connor and his colleagues (2000) showed, for example, substantial recovery in cognitive functioning in children adopted into the UK from Romanian institutions.

Children adopted before 6 months had a general cognitive index that was on average twenty-five points higher at age 6 years than children adopted after 24 months (Rutter & O'Connor, 2004). Results were somewhat different for disinhibited attachment in that although this abnormal social behavior declined following adoption, it remained apparent in a significant minority of children after placement in adoptive homes. These results indicate that timing appears to matter, but its effects may be different in different domains of development.

These preliminary conclusions notwithstanding, there remain serious limitations and gaps in the literature that limit our understanding of developmental processes and limit our ability to develop sound child protection policies. These areas need additional exploration and elucidation. For example, although many studies have examined multiple domains of development, few have attempted to look at the interrelationships among these domains. That is, not only are questions about vulnerability and plasticity within specific domains important, but the interrelationships among the domains also may be vital to understand. Second, especially in the area of cognitive development, only gross measures of overall developmental level are typically reported rather than examining more specific constructs such as executive functioning or face and emotion processing. Similarly for communicative development, only receptive and expressive level are typically reported, rather than more specific constructs such as the initiation of and response to joint attention. Third, more within-country studies of the effects of institutionalization are needed so that effects resulting from the experience of adoption into another culture (and often a different language) can be disentangled from the effects of institutionalization itself. Fourth, there have been almost no studies of brain functioning, and we know far too little about structural or functional differences in brain development in children raised in institutions. Ultimately, behavioral plasticity and recovery from early abnormalities must involve neurobiological processes, but formidable challenges remain before we determine which ones. At this point, measures of brain functioning are often less available in settings that have large numbers of institutionalized children. Also, young children are challenging to study with functional imaging techniques in any setting. As our methods of studying brain functioning improve, so will our ability to examine brain and behavioral relationships. Finally, studies of methods to improve institutional quality and child outcomes also have a place (see McCall, Muhamedrahimov, Groark, Palmov, & Nikiforova, 2003), as institutional care for abandoned children is likely to remain widely used in many parts of the world for many years to come.

Note

Preparation of this chapter was supported in part by the MacArthur Foundation Research Network on Early Experience and Brain Development (Charles A. Nelson, Chair).

References

Ainsworth, M. D. S., Blehar, M. C., Waters, E., & Wall, S. (1978). *Patterns of attachment.* Hillsdale, NJ: Erlbaum.

Beckett, C., Bredenkamp, D., Castle, J., Groothues, C., O'Connor, T. G., Rutter, M., & the English and Romanian Adoptees (ERA) Study Team (2002). Behavior patterns associated with institutional deprivation: A study of children adopted from Romania. *Journal of Developmental and Behavioral Pediatrics, 23*, 297–303.

Benoit, T., Joycelyn, L. J., Moddemann, D. M., & Embree, J. E. (1996). Romanian adoption: The Manitoba experience. *Archives of Pediatric and Adolescent Medicine, 150*, 1278–1282.

Brodbeck, A. J., & Irwin, O. C. (1946). The speech behaviour of infants without families. *Child Development, 17*, 145–156.

Browne, K., & Hamilton-Ciachritis, C. (2004). Mapping the number and characteristics of children under three in institutions across Europe at risk of harm. *Daphne programme – Year 2002: Final report.* School of Psychology, University of Birmingham Centre for Forensic and Family Psychology.

Cermak, S. A., & Daunhauer, L. A. (1997). Sensory processing in the post-institutionalized child. *American Journal of Occupational Therapy, 51*, 500–507.

Child Welfare League of America. (2004). [Use of congregate care for infants and toddlers in the United States: State by state findings]. Unpublished raw data.

Chisholm, K. (1998). A three year follow-up of attachment and indiscriminate friendliness in children adopted from Romanian orphanages. *Child Development, 69*, 1092–1106.

Chisholm, K., Carter, M., Ames, E., & Morison, S. (1995). Attachment security and indiscriminately friendly behaviour in children adopted from Romanian orphanages. *Development and Psychopathology, 7*, 283–294.

Chugani, H. T., Behen, M. E., Musik, O., Juhasz, C., Nagy, F., & Chugani, D. C. (2001). Local brain functional activity following early deprivation: A study of postinstitutionalized Romanian orphans. *NeuroImage, 14*, 1290–1301.

Dennis, W., & Najarian, P. (1957). Infant development under environmental handicap. *Psychological Monographs: General and Applied, 71*, 1–13.

Doolittle, T. (1995). *The long-term effects of institutionalization on the behavior of children from Eastern Europe and the former Soviet Union: Research, diagnoses, and therapy options.* Parent Network for Post-Institutionalized Children. Retrieved July 17, 2004 from *http://www.mariaschildren.org/english/babyhouse/effects.html*

Federici, R. S. (1999). *Help for the hopeless child: A guide for families.* Alexandria, VA: Dr. Ronald S. Federici and Associates.

Fisher, L., Ames, E. W., Chisholm, K., & Savoie, L. (1997). Problems reported by parents of Romanian orphans adopted to British Columbia. *International Journal of Behavioral Development, 20*, 67–82.

Frank, D. A., Klass, P. E., Earls, F., & Eisenberg, L. (1996). Infants and young children in orphanages: One view from pediatrics and child psychiatry. *Pediatrics, 97*, 569–578.

Gindis, B. (2000). Language-related problems and remediation strategies for internationally adopted orphanage-raised children. In T. Tepper, L. Hannon, & D. Sandstrom (Eds.), *International adoption: Challenges and opportunities* (2nd ed., pp. 89–97). Meadow Lands, PA: Parent Network for the Post-Institutionalized Child.

Goldfarb, W. (1943). Infant rearing and problem behavior. *American Journal of Orthopsychiatry, 13*, 249–265.

Goldfarb, W. (1944). Infant rearing as a factor in foster home replacement. *American Journal of Orthopsychiatry, 14*, 162–173.

Goldfarb, W. (1945a). Effects of psychological deprivation in infancy and subsequent stimulation. *American Journal of Psychiatry, 102*, 18–33.

Goldfarb, W. (1945b). Psychological privation in infancy and subsequent adjustment. *American Journal of Orthopsychiatry, 15*, 247–255.

Groze, V., & Ileana, D. (1996). A follow-up study of adopted children from Romania. *Child and Adolescent Social Work Journal, 13*, 541–565.

Gunnar, M. R., & Kertes, D. A. (2003). *Early risk factors and development of internationally adopted children: Can we generalize from the Romanian case?* Paper presented in T. G. O'Connor & M. Rutter (Chairs), Psychological and biological evidence concerning the role of early experiences on development. Symposium at Society for Research in Child Development, Tampa, FL.

Harden, B. J. (2002). Congregate care for infants and toddlers: Shedding new light on an old question. *Infant Mental Health Journal, 23*, 476–495.

Hodges, J., & Tizard, B. (1989a). IQ and behavioral adjustment of ex-institutional adolescents. *Journal of Child Psychology, Psychiatry, and Allied Disciplines, 30*, 53–75.

Hodges, J., & Tizard, B. (1989b). Social and family relationships of ex-institutional adolescents. *Journal of Child Psychology, Psychiatry, and Allied Disciplines, 30*, 77–97.

Hoksbergen, R., ter Laak, J., van Dijkum, C., Rijk, S., Rijk, K., & Stoutjesdijk, F. (2003). Post-traumatic stress disorder in adopted children from Romania. *American Journal of Orthopsychiatry, 73*, 255–265.

Hoksbergen, R., van Dijkum, C., & Stoutjesdijk, F. (2002). Experiences of Dutch families who parent an adopted Romanian child. *Journal of Developmental and Behavioral Pediatrics, 23*, 403–409.

Hough, S. D. (2000). Risk factors for the speech and language development of children adopted from Eastern Europe and the former USSR. In T. Tepper, L. Hannon, & D. Sandstrom (Eds.), *International adoption: Challenges and opportunities* (2nd ed., pp. 99–119). Meadow Lands, PA: Parent Network for the Post-Institutionalized Child.

Human Rights Watch. (2004). *Children's rights: Orphans and abandoned children.* Retrieved July 13, 2004 from *http://www.hrw.org/abandoned.htm*

Hunt, J. M., Mohandessi, K., Ghodssi, M., & Akiyama, M. (1976). The psychological development of orphanage-reared infants: Interventions with outcomes. *Genetic Psychology Monographs, 94*, 177–226.

Johnson, D. E. (2000). Medical and developmental sequelae of early childhood institutionalization in Eastern European adoptees. In C. A. Nelson (Ed.), *The effects of early adversity on neurobehavioral development* (Vol. 31, pp. 113–162). Mahwah, NJ: Lawrence Erlbaum.

Johnson, D. E., & Hostetter, M. (2000). Planning for the health needs of your institutionalized child. In T. Tepper, L. Hannon, & D. Sandstrom (Eds.), *International adoption: Challenges and opportunities* (2nd ed., pp. 9–21). Meadow Lands, PA: Parent Network for the Post-Institutionalized Child.

Kaler, S., & Freeman, B. (1994). Analysis of environmental deprivation: Cognitive and social development in Romanian orphans. *Journal of Child Psychology and Psychiatry, 35*, 769–781.

Kreppner, J. M., O'Connor, T. G., & Rutter, M. (2001). Can inattention/hyperactivity be an institutional deprivation syndrome? *Journal of Abnormal Child Psychology, 29*, 513–528.

Levy, R. J. (1947). Effects of institutional vs. boarding home care on a group of infants. *Journal of Personality, 15*, 233–241.

London, R. D. (1999). The 1994 orphanage debate: A study in the politics of annihilation. In R. B. McKenzie (Ed.), *Rethinking Orphanages for the 21st Century* (pp. 79–102). Thousand Oaks, CA: Sage Publications.

Lowrey, L. G. (1940). Personality distortion and early institutional care. *American Journal of Orthopsychiatry, 10*, 576–585.

McCall, R. B., Muhamedrahimov, R. J., Groark, C. J., Palmov, O. I., & Nikiforova, N. V. (2003, April). *Research design and measurements in the St. Petersburg–USA Orphanage Project.* Paper presented in R. B. McCall (Chair), Improving stability and responsiveness of caregiving for children birth to four in St. Petersburg, Russia, orphanages. Symposium conducted at Society for Research in Child Development, Tampa, FL.

McKenzie, R. B. (Ed.). (1999). *Rethinking orphanages for the 21st century*. Thousand Oaks, CA: Sage Publications.

McMullan, S. J., & Fisher, L. (1995, April). *Developmental progress of Romanian orphanage children in Canada*. Paper presented at the Biennial Conference of the Society for Research in Child Development, Indianapolis.

Marcovitch, S., Goldberg, S., Gold, A., Washington, J., Wasson, C., Krekewich, K., & Handley-Derry, M. (1997). Determinants of behavioral problems in Romanian children adopted in Ontario. *International Journal of Behavioral Development, 20*, 17–31.

Marshall, P. J., Fox, N. A., & the BEIP Core Group (2004). A comparison of the electroencephalogram between institutionalized and community children in Romania. *Journal of Cognitive Neuroscience, 16*, 1327–1338.

Morison, S. J., Ames, E. W., & Chisholm, K. (1995). The development of children adopted from Romanian orphanages. *Merrill-Palmer Quarterly, 41*, 411–430.

Muhamedrahimov, R. (2000). New attitudes: Infant care facilities in Saint Petersburg, Russia. In J. D. Osofsky & H. E. Fitzgerald (Eds.), *WAIMH handbook of infant mental health: Vol. 1. Perspectives on infant mental health* (pp. 245–294). New York: Wiley.

Nelson, C. A. (2004, April). *The effects of early institutionalization on brain–behavior development: The Bucharest Early Intervention Project*. Symposium conducted at the Society for Research in Child Development, Tampa, FL.

NICHD Early Child Care Research Network. (1996). Characteristics of infant child care: Factors contributing to positive caregiving. *Early Childhood Research Quarterly, 11*, 269–306.

O'Connor, T. G. (2003). *Developmental programming effects for psychological outcomes: 11-year follow-up of children adopted from institutions in Romania*. Paper presented in T. G. O'Connor & M. Rutter (Chairs), Psychological and biological evidence concerning the role of early experiences on development. Symposium conducted at Society for Research in Child Development, Tampa, FL.

O'Connor, T. G., Marvin, R. S., Rutter, M., Olrick, J. T., Brittner, P. A., & the English and Romanian Adoptees (ERA) Study Team. (2003). Child–parent attachment following severe early institutional deprivation. *Development and Psychopathology, 15*, 19–38.

O'Connor, T. G., Rutter, M., Beckett, C., Keaveney, L., Kreppner, J. M., & the ERA Adoptees Study Team (2000). The effects of global severe privation on cognitive competence: Extension and longitudinal follow-up. *Child Development, 71*, 376–390.

Parker, S. W., & Nelson, C. A. (2004). *The impact of institutional rearing on the ability to discriminate facial expressions of emotion: An event-related potential study*. Manuscript submitted for publication.

Provence, S., & Lipton, R. C. (1962). *Infants in institutions*. New York: International Universities Press.

Rojewski, J. W., Shapiro, M. S., & Shapiro, M. (2000). Parental assessment of behavior in Chinese adoptees during early childhood. *Child Psychiatry and Human Development, 31*, 79–96.

Roy, P., Rutter, M., & Pickles, A. (2000). Institutional care: Risk from family background or pattern of rearing? *Journal of Child Psychology and Psychiatry, 41*, 139–141.

Roy, P., Rutter, M., & Pickles, A. (2004). Institutional care: Associations between overactivity and lack of selectivity in social relationships. *Journal of Child Psychology and Psychiatry, 45*, 866–873.

Rutter, M., Andersen-Wood, L., Beckett, C., Bredenkamp, D., Castle, J., Groothues, C., Kreppner, J., Keaveney, L., Lord, C., O'Connor, T. G., & the English and Romanian Adoptees Study

Team, et al. (1999). Quasi-autistic patterns following severe early global privation. *Journal of Child Psychology and Psychiatry, 40,* 537–549.

Rutter, M., & the English Romanian Adoptions Study Team (ERA). (1998). Developmental catch-up, and deficit, following adoption after severe global early privation. *Journal of Child Psychology and Psychiatry, 39,* 465–476.

Rutter, M., Kreppner, J. M., & O'Connor, T. (2001). Specificity and heterogeneity in children's responses to profound institutional privation. *British Journal of Psychiatry, 179,* 97–103.

Rutter, M., & O'Connor, T. (2004). Are there biological programming effects for psychological development? Findings from a study of Romanian adoptees. *Developmental Psychology, 40,* 81–94.

Sameroff, A. J. (2000). Developmental systems and psychopathology. *Development and Psychopathology, 12,* 297–312.

Smith, M. G., & Fong, R. (2004). *The children of neglect.* New York: Brunner-Routledge.

Smyke, A. T., Dumitrescu, A., & Zeanah, C. H. (2002). Disturbances of attachment in young children. I: The continuum of caretaking casualty. *Journal of the American Academy of Child and Adolescent Psychiatry, 41,* 972–982.

Smyke, A. T., Koga, S. F. M., Johnson, D. E., Zeanah, C. H., & the BEIP Core Group. (2005). *The caregiving context in institution reared and family reared infants and toddlers in Romania.* Manuscript submitted for publication.

Solomon, J., & George, C. (1999). The measurement of attachment security in infancy and childhood. In J. Cassidy & P. R. Shaver (Eds.), *Handbook of attachment: Theory, research, and clinical applications* (pp. 287–316). New York: Guilford.

Spitz, R. (1945). Hospitalism: An inquiry into the genesis of psychiatric conditions in early childhood. *Psychoanalytic Study of the Child, 1,* 53–74.

Stromswold, K. (1995). The cognitive and neural bases of language acquisition. In M. S. Gazzaniga (Ed.), *The cognitive neurosciences* (pp. 855–870). Cambridge, MA: MIT Press.

Sweeney, J. K., & Bascom, B. B. (1995). Motor development and self-stimulatory movement in institutionalized Romanian children. *Pediatric Physical Therapy, 7,* 124–132.

Tarabulsy, G. M., Tessier, R., & Kappas, A. (1996). Contingency detection and the contingent organization of behavior interactions: Implications for socioemotional development in infancy. *Psychological Bulletin, 120,* 25–41.

Tizard, B. (1977). *Adoption: A second chance.* London: Open Books.

Tizard, B., & Rees, J. (1974). A comparison of the effects of adoption, restoration to the natural mother, and continued institutionalization on the cognitive development of four-year-old children. *Child Development, 45,* 92–99.

Vorria, P., Papaligoura, Z., Dunn, J., van IJzendoorn, M. H., Steele, H., Kontopoulou, A., & Sarafidou, Y. (2003). Early experiences and attachment relationships of Greek infants raised in residential group care. *Journal of Child Psychology, Psychiatry and Allied Disciplines, 44,* 1208–1220.

Wolkind, S. N. (1974). The components of "affectionless psychopathy" in institutionalized children. *Journal of Child Psychology and Psychiatry, 15,* 215–220.

Wulczyn, F., Hislop, K., & Harden, B. J. (2002). The placement of infants in foster care. *Infant Mental Health Journal, 23,* 454–475.

Zeanah, C. H., Nelson, C. A., Fox, N. A., Smyke, A. T., Marshall, P., Parker, S. W., & Koga, S. F. (2003). Designing research to study the effects of institutionalization on brain and behavioral development: The Bucharest Early Intervention Project. *Development and Psychopathology, 15,* 885–907.

Zeanah, C. H., Smyke, A. T., Koga, S. F., & Carlson, E. (in press). Attachment in institutionalized children and community children in Romania. *Child Development.*

22

Peer Relationships in Early Childhood

Deborah Lowe Vandell, Lana Nenide, and Sara J. Van Winkle

The last thirty years have been marked by substantial progress in our understanding of peer relations during early childhood. Advances have occurred in three areas: (1) in describing normative developmental changes in peer relations during the first five years, (2) in identifying factors that influence the frequency and quality of different types of peer relations, and (3) in examining the effects of early peer relations on other areas of child functioning. In this review, our goal is to summarize some of the notable findings in each of these areas. Because of space limitations, our review is not comprehensive or exhaustive, but, rather, illustrative of central themes and findings. Less progress has been made in testing transactional models of peer relations during early childhood that reflect and integrate advances across the three areas. We argue that research that adopts transactional models is sorely needed.

A Conceptual Framework

Hinde's seminal work has served as a guide and organizational framework for a generation of peer research (Hartup, 1996; Hinde, 1976, 1979; Rubin, Bukowski, & Parker, 1998). Hinde argued that interpersonal relationships can be studied at four levels of complexity: individual social behaviors, social interactions between individuals, enduring social relationships, and social groups. At the individual level, social behaviors such as prosocial acts, vocalizations and verbalizations, and aggression acts are examined. These social behaviors are then embedded in social interactions that are characterized by social overtures (sometimes called "bids" or "initiation strategies") and social responses that vary as a function of the physical setting and characteristics of participants. For young children, social interactions have been studied as patterns or configurations of behaviors occurring during free play, pretend play, and conflicts with peers. Social interactions are then embedded in social relationships, which endure over time and have their own qualities and features. In the case of young peers, both friendships and mutual antipathies have been studied (Ross, Conant, Cheyne, & Alevizos, 1992). Dyadic relationships are then embedded in larger peer groups that have their own hierarchical structure and qualities (Hawley, 2002; Ross et al., 1992). At the group level, children's status within the peer group (whether children are accepted, rejected, neglected, popular), dominance hierarchies, and the characteristics of the peer group, such as its gender composition and behavioral similarities, are studied.

For the most part, individual investigators (or individual teams of researchers) have focused on a particular level within this hierarchy, so much of the literature has considered early sociability or friendships or peer groups, although some investigators (Denham & Holt, 1993; Dunn & Hughes, 1998; Fabes, Martin, Hanish, Anders, & Madden-Derdich, 2003; Howes, 1988) have studied the interplay among different levels of the peer system.

Another distinction that shapes much of the research of the last thirty years is whether peer relations are viewed as the dependent variable, i.e., the "outcome of interest," or as the independent variable, i.e., the "predictor" of other domains of interest. Those who have conceptualized peer relations as an "outcome" have considered individual child factors such as gender and temperament as predictors of the quality and quantity of children's behaviors with peers. Others interested in peer relations as a developmental outcome have examined effects of early parent–child relationships on early peer relations. Those who have focused on peer relations as the independent variable (or as a contributor to children's development) have framed the question differently. They consider ways in which early peer relations influence or affect child developmental outcomes such as their adjustment to school, cognitive problem solving, moral understanding, and feelings of loneliness.

In the sections that follow, we review findings from these three schools of research, beginning with normative descriptions of early social behaviors, interactions, relationships, and peer groups during early childhood. We then consider peer relations as a developmental outcome in early childhood and finally as a predictor of other developmental domains.

Descriptions of Early Peer Relations

Peer relations undergo substantial developmental changes during early childhood that are reflected at each level of analysis proposed by Hinde. In terms of individual social behaviors, interest in peers can be seen as early as age 2 months when infants share mutual gazes (Mueller & Vandell, 1979). By 6 months, babies look, vocalize, and smile at a peer (Vandell, Wilson, & Buchanan, 1980). Some of these behaviors have agonistic quality, such as when one infant pulls another's hair or pokes a finger in a peer's eye, which seem to reflect curiosity without negative intent. In studies of infants and toddlers, these "positive" and "negative" social behaviors are moderately correlated, suggesting that both types of behaviors are expressions of social interest (Brownell, 1990). During the preschool period, the frequency of positive social behaviors increases and the frequency of negative behaviors and aggression decreases (Levin & Rubin, 1983; Vaughn, Vollenweider, Bost, Azria-Evans, & Snider, 2003).

Individual social behaviors provide the building blocks for social interactions in which one child directs a social behavior to another child who responds with a behavior to which the first responds, and so forth. Interaction exchanges as long as six turns have been reported between 6-month-old infants (Vandell et al., 1980). Longer and more complex play exchanges have been recorded between toddler peers, including "games" of peek-a-boo, run-chase, and bang the drum (Mueller & Brenner, 1977) as well as simple pretend play (Howes, 1984). Conflicts also occur, particularly relatively sustained tussles over toys.

Several factors help to set the stage for these early social exchanges or interactions. Children often play near others, which positions children to move to a level of complex social interactions. In observations based on Parten's (1932) classic play categories (unoccupied, solitary, parallel, onlooker, associative, and cooperative), Rubin et al. (1998) report that being an onlooker (i.e., watching a peer) and playing alongside a peer (parallel play) served as a bridge or transition to associative and cooperative social play. Mutual imitation also sets the stage for more advanced cooperative play of preschoolers (Howes, 1992).

The frequency of peer interaction increases during the preschool period, and play becomes more complex as preschoolers engage in more extended episodes of cooperative pretend play involving scripts and complementary roles (Rubin et al., 1998). Communication also is more successful for preschoolers than for toddlers. Detailed sociolinguistic analyses reveal that approximately 60% of preschoolers' utterances are socially directed, comprehensible, and result in appropriate responses (Levin & Rubin, 1983; Mueller, 1972). Piaget's early argument (1959) that preschoolers are egocentric and socially unaware is belied by these careful observations.

Carollee Howes (1984, 1992; Howes & Matheson, 1992) has been instrumental in describing the processes and developmental significance of social pretend play with peers. Young children first engage in simple social pretend play, in which both children perform pretend acts without a script. In associate social pretend play, the second level she observed, young children engage in scripted pretend play composed of organized, multievent play sequences in which they arrange pretend acts into a meaningful sequence. In cooperative social pretend play, the most advanced pretend play, a script and complementary pretend roles are evident (e.g., Julie "feeds" Emma with a bottle, and Emma "drinks" and "cries" like a baby). The negotiation and discussion of these pretend play roles and scripts provide a context for mastering the communication of meaning, for learning to compromise, and for safely exploring issues related to intimacy and trust. Another marker of the growing sophistication of preschoolers' social interactions is relational aggression, in which children, particularly girls, attempt to control others by undermining their relationships with peers (Crick, Casas, & Ku, 1999).

Because infants and toddlers have limited language skills, early friendships and antipathies have been defined behaviorally. In an early study of a toddler playgroup, Vandell and Mueller (1980) specified three behavioral indicators of early friendships: mutual preferences between children for one another as play partners; social interactions marked by a predominance of positive affect or sharing; and the presence of early games (the most complex play observed in the playgroup). Using these criteria, children as young as 22 months appeared to be friends.

Howes and Philipsen (1992) defined toddler friendships similarly: playing within 3 feet, engaged in interactive social play, and expressed shared positive affect in 30% of the scans of a classroom. Using these criteria, Howes and Philipsen reported that most of the children whom they studied had a single friend at age 16 months, three or four friends as older toddlers, and five or six friends as preschoolers. These friendships were stable for as long as two years. The toddler friendships were equally likely to be mixed genders, whereas preschoolers were much more likely to have same-sex friends.

In their observations in an Israeli kibbutz, Ross et al. (1992) observed two groups of 20-month-old children over a two-month period and found that the children made special adjustments in their interactions with specific partners that would not be predicted based on the individual characteristics that these children displayed with others. Evidence of reciprocal relationships was found in both mutual positive exchanges and agonistic exchanges. Positive interactions are directed toward those who had directed positive initiations previously, and conflictual interactions were directed toward those with whom there had been previous conflicts, suggesting that both friendships and mutual antipathies were developing.

These observational data suggest that interactions of toddler friends differ from those of acquaintances in terms of their mutual preferences as playmates, which is arguably a sign of early commitment consistent with Hinde's distinguishing feature of relationships – mutual commitment. Another common element in all of these studies of early friendships is that they were observed in settings in which young children were regularly together with the same group of peers. Without the opportunity of regular contact, the friendships would not have been possible. Thus, child care opened up an opportunity for friendships in young children.

Preschool friendships have been assessed both behaviorally and by child and parent reports. During the preschool period, children direct more social overtures, engage in more social interactions, and play in more complex ways with "friends" compared to "non-friends" (Gottman, 1983; Hinde, Titmus, Easton, & Tamplin, 1985). Preschool friends also have more conflicts than do non-friends, and these conflicts are resolved differently (Hinde et al., 1985). Friends are more likely to negotiate a solution, to stay in proximity after the conflict, and to continue to interact. There also is evidence that preschool friendships can provide emotional support at stressful times such as the birth of a sibling (Vandell, 1987) and the transition to school (Ladd & Kochenderfer, 1996).

Preschool friendships also have been identified from children's reciprocated nominations of liked playmates. In a longitudinal study of children who attended a university laboratory school, Walden, Lemerise, and Smith (1999) found that 75% of the children had at least one reciprocated friendship nomination in the fall and 85% of the children had at least one reciprocated nomination in the spring, with significant stability in friendship choices from the fall and the spring of the school year. The friendships were typically between same-age, same-sex peers.

Other researchers have focused on peer groups in early childhood. Strayer and Strayer (1976), for example, observed preschool classrooms and identified stable dominance hierarchies in the classrooms based on object struggles, threats, and conflicts. Children who lost an object struggle rarely initiated conflicts with children with whom they had previously lost a conflict, resulting in less conflict over time in the classroom. Sociometric analyses of preschool classrooms also have been conducted. These studies have identified popular and rejected preschoolers based on peers' nominations or ratings, which are somewhat stable over time (Black & Logan, 1995; Denham & Holt, 1993; Ladd, Price, & Hart, 1988).

These normative descriptions of social behaviors, interactions, and relationships have provided a rich array of measures and formulations of peer relations in early childhood that could be applied to questions about individual differences. It is to the individual difference question that we now turn.

Peer Relations as a Developmental Outcome

A central question for many peer researchers is: "What factors influence the quality, quantity, and development of peer relations in early childhood?" Three sets of factors – the children's own characteristics, parent–child relations, and experiences in early child care – have received the most attention.

Child characteristics

Although gender differences are not seen in the social behaviors of infants and toddlers with their peers (Mueller & Vandell, 1979), consistent gender differences are evident in preschool-aged children. Girls display more prosocial orientations, empathy, and positive peer play whereas boys are more likely to engage in more rough-and-tumble play and to be perpetrators and victims of physical aggression (Clark & Ladd, 2000; Crick et al., 1999; NICHD Early Child Care Research Network [ECCRN], 2001; Smith, 2001). Preschool-aged girls are more accepted by their classmates; boys are viewed as more aggressive and are more rejected by their classmates (Clark & Ladd, 2000; Kerns, Cole, & Andrews, 1998; Smith, 2001).

In a series of elegant studies, Carol Martin and Richard Fabes (2001; Fabes et al., 2003) have studied the processes associated with these emerging gender differences. In this work, they find same-sex peer play increases over the school year, with the context of this play changing as girls begin to play closer to adults and boys begin to play farther away from adults as the year progresses. Boys become more physically active and engage in more rough-and-tumble play, a pattern that is exaggerated when boys are playing with a group of boys. Taken together, these observations suggest that boys and girls are affected by their interactions with their same-sex peers during the preschool period and that their behaviors become more distinct and gender-typed during this period.

Children's dispositional characteristics or temperament also predict the quality and quantity of peer relations in early childhood. Three temperamental dimensions – shyness, emotionality and emotional regulation, and activity – have received the most attention. Children with more "difficult" temperaments in infancy, as measured by high-intensity negative emotions and low adaptability, display less positive sociability and more negative/aggressive behaviors with peers as preschoolers (NICHD ECCRN, 2001). Children who are temperamentally difficult as infants also have more conflicts and exhibit more intense negative emotions during interactions with friends in the preschool period (O'Brien, Roy, Jacobs, Macaluso, & Peyton, 1999). Temperamental shyness, on the other hand, is associated with fewer social behaviors (both positive and negative) with peers during early childhood (Russell, Hart, Robinson, & Olsen, 2003).

Some have studied the particular processes by which early temperament impacts relations with peers. Calkins and colleagues (Calkins, Gill, Johnson, & Smith, 1999), for example, report that toddlers who have difficulty modulating their negative emotions as measured in a series of frustrating tasks in the laboratory and who responded to frustration by venting were later observed to have more conflicts with an unfamiliar peer. In contrast, toddlers who responded to the frustrating tasks by trying to distract themselves or to self-soothe had fewer conflicts with an unfamiliar peer, findings that are consistent with the proposition that negative emotionality increases the likelihood of aggression.

Similar issues have been investigated in preschool-aged children. Children who expressed more intense negative emotions on the playground and in the classroom early in the school year have been observed to spend more time in solitary play later in the school year (Fabes, Hanish, Martin, & Eisenberg, 2002), a finding consistent with the view that negative emotionality places children at risk for social withdrawal and social isolation as well as aggression.

There also is evidence that emotional regulation is linked to children's friendships and peer group affiliations. Preschool-aged children who are better regulated emotionally early in the school year have significantly more friendships later in the school year, even after controlling for number of fall friendships (Walden et al., 1999). Children who regulate negative emotions more easily tend to affiliate in more positive playgroups with other well-regulated children, whereas children who have difficulty regulating negative emotions tend to affiliate with peers who also have similar difficulties (Denham et al., 2001). Being part of a peer group characterized by anger and negative emotionality then predicts lower social competencies up to one year later.

Children's cognitive and language skills also are linked to early peer relations. During early childhood, children make substantial gains in cognitive and language skills, which enable them to interpret social situations more accurately and support the normative development of sophisticated interactions with peers, including complex fantasy play. Individual differences in cognitive and language skills and in social understanding also are linked to individual social behaviors, early interactions, and friendships. Toddlers and preschoolers who have more advanced cognitive and language skills are more socially competent with peers according to mothers and caregivers, and they are observed to be more socially skilled in interactions with a friend (NICHD ECCRN, 2001). Children's understanding of mental states, including identifying false beliefs and emotion states, predict quality interactions between preschool friends (Dunn, Cutting, & Demetriou, 2000). In contrast, lower language comprehension is found to predict more frequent and intense peer conflicts (O'Brien et al., 1999).

Parent–child and peer relationships in early childhood

Other research studies have focused on the linkages between parent–child and peer relationships. Although these studies are guided by a variety of perspectives – attachment, social learning, and social capital – all share the view that children's relations with their peers are grounded in the parent–child relationship.

Influenced by Bowlby's theory (1969) that infant–mother attachment provides an internal working model for other social relationships, a number of researchers have studied relations between the quality of early attachment relationships and children's social behaviors, social interactions, friendships, and peer group acceptance. These studies find that securely attached infants are more socially competent and popular as well as less aggressive in interactions with friends during early childhood. Insecurely attached infants display more negative emotions, hostility, and aggression and less assertive control during peer interactions in early childhood (McElwain, Cox, Burchinal, & Macfie, 2003; Rubin et al., 1998). Relations between attachment security and peer networks also are reported. Children with secure attachments tend to affiliate in positive playgroups with other securely attached children, whereas children with insecure parental attachments tend to affiliate with other insecurely attached children in playgroups characterized by more negative emotionality (Denham et al., 2001).

The robustness of the attachment findings is supported by a meta-analysis of sixty-three studies involving a combined sample of 3510 children that reported an overall effect size of .20 between attachment security and peer relations (Schneider, Atkinson, & Tardif, 2001). A larger mean effect size was detected between attachment quality and children's friendships (mean ES = .24) than between attachment and peer group status (mean ES = .13), suggesting that attachment is more closely linked to other intense, intimate relationships than it is to relations with peer groups. At the same time, the absolute effect is not large, indicating that attachment is only one of the factors associated with early peer relations.

Parenting practices is another factor believed to influence early peer relations. In his book *Friends and Enemies*, Schneider (2000) cites some thirty studies as detecting links between parenting practices and child aggression. Twelve of these studies include children who were under the age of 5 years. In these studies, punitive, coercive, and authoritarian parenting during early childhood predicts more aggressive behaviors with peers. Five studies are cited as detecting relations between parent–child interactions and children's positive sociability with peers. In particular, reciprocated positive affect, encouragement to initiate interactions, and explicit efforts to *explain* encounters with peers are linked to positive social behaviors with peers in early childhood. Finally, eighteen studies found associations between parental explanations, nurturance, and even-handed discipline and increases in peer acceptance and popularity and decreases in peer rejection during early childhood.

Most studies of parenting and peer relations have focused on maternal behavior, but a few investigators have considered the role of fathers as well as mothers. In one large study involving both American and Australian preschoolers, Russell et al. (2003) determined that both maternal and paternal parenting were associated with early peer relations. Paternal authoritarian parenting significantly predicted both physical and relational aggression with peers. MacDonald and Parke (1984) found positive associations between fathers' physical play with their young children and children's peer acceptance and popularity.

Attachment security and modeling are only two of the processes by which parents can influence their young children's peer relations. A third process is by creating opportunities for children to interact with peers and by providing advice about appropriate play strategies. Parke's tripartite model (Parke et al., 2002) is consistent with this social capital perspective. Two of the three paths in the tripartite model are related to parental facilitation of peer relations in which parents arrange opportunities for their children to interact with peers and then provide advice about peer choices and interactions. These paths are particularly important in early childhood when children have limited opportunities to seek out peers on their own. Studies show that parents who actively arrange "play dates" and who indirectly supervise those dates have children who are better liked by peers, exhibit more prosocial behaviors, and have more friends (Kerns, Cole, & Andrews, 1998; Parke et al., 2002; Rubin et al., 1998).

Others (Lindsey, Mize, & Pettit, 1997) have looked in close detail at early parent–child interactions as an opportunity to hone social skills that can then be used with peers. For example, children whose interactions with their mothers include more mutual compliance are rated by teachers as being more socially competent. Children whose interactions with their fathers reflect more mutual compliance are more accepted by their peers. The investigators argued that mother–child and father–child dyads that are able to achieve a balance in their efforts to influence the behaviors and play of the other provide young children with the groundwork for their social competencies with peers. Black and Logan's findings (1995) also are consistent with this interpretation. In that study, more balanced turn-taking and communication in the parent–child dyads was linked to more responsive communication with peers, which in turn predicted greater peer acceptance.

Linkages between child care and peer relations

Parent–child relationships are only one of the contexts in which social competencies with peers can be developed. Child care is another (see Phillips, McCartney, & Sussman, this volume). Child care settings provide young children with two types of social experiences that parent–child interactions cannot: sustained contact with other adults and sustained contact with familiar peers. Some scholars have emphasized the social opportunities afforded by early child care experiences in which social competencies and friendships are fostered by recursive exchanges that are co-constructed by familiar children over time (Howes, 2000; Mueller & Brenner, 1977). Other research has emphasized the roles of caregivers and teachers as attachment figures and sources of emotional security as well as language and cognitive stimulators (Howes, Hamilton, & Philipsen, 1998; Pianta, 1994). Others, however, have argued that early and extensive hours in child care are problematic and contribute to increased aggression and externalizing behaviors (Belsky, 2001).

Evidence of both positive and negative effects of early child care on early peer relations has been detected. With respect to caregiver–child relationships, more positive caregiving by child care providers predicts greater sociability with peers and fewer negative interactions, even after controlling for children's temperament, cognitive/language competencies, and gender, and for maternal sensitivity (NICHD ECCRN, 2001). Similar positive associations were detected in the Cost, Quality, and Outcome Study, another large prospective longitudinal study of child care. In that study, children who had attended child care centers in which they had closer teacher–child relationships were reported by their second-grade teachers to be more socially competent with peers (Howes, 2000). In a third longitudinal study (Howes et al., 1998), the quality of the attachment relationship with a first child care teacher predicted the quality of children's friendships in middle childhood. Children who had secure relationships with their caregiver had more positive relationships with friends at age 9.

There also is evidence that amount of time in early child care is related to children's behaviors with peers. At age 2 years, children who had spent more hours in child care were reported by caregivers to have more behavior problems and by mothers to be less socially competent; they were observed to have more negative interactions with peers (NICHD ECCRN, 1998). At age 4½ years and in kindergarten, similar differences were found, with children who had been in child care for more hours displaying more externalizing behaviors (NICHD ECCRN, 2003).

These relations did not appear to be solely mediated by mother–child interactions or attachment quality (at least as measured in this study) because the relations remained significant after controlling for these factors. Nor are they explained by quality of caregiver behaviors because the relation between hours and problem behaviors remained after controlling for this factor as well. A third possibility is that the quality of peer context may be important.

This third possibility is consistent with findings of Gunnar and colleagues (see Gunnar, this volume). These investigators have assessed cortisol levels across the day in child care and at home for children of varying ages and temperament. They observed that cortisol increased on those days in which children were in centers (the opposite of the typical circadian rhythm of cortisol), but not on days in which these same children were at home (Watamura, Donzella, Alwin, & Gunnar, 2003). The largest increases in cortisol were observed in children who were less involved in peer play (Watamura et al., 2003), who were less socially competent (Tout, de Haan, Kipp-Campbell, & Gunnar, 1998), who had the most difficulty regulating negative emotions and behavior (Dettling, Gunnar, & Donzella, 1999), and who were more fearful (Watamura et al., 2003). These findings suggest that toddlers and preschoolers who are learning to negotiate with peers are experiencing large peer groups as socially demanding and stressful.

Peer Relations as Predictors of Child Developmental Outcomes

A third set of research studies has examined the implications of early peer relations for other aspects of child functioning. Peer relations during middle childhood are associated with a wide variety of child developmental outcomes (Gifford-Smith & Brownell, 2003; Rubin et al., 1998; Schneider, 2000; Vandell, 2000). In his book *Friends and*

Enemies, Schneider (2000) referenced nineteen studies that detected relations between peer aggression in middle childhood and long-term adjustment problems including delinquency, drug use, and academic difficulties. Fourteen longitudinal studies examined links between social withdrawal and long-term adjustment, primarily anxiety and internalizing problems. Six studies were cited as finding links between friendships in middle childhood and children's well-being, including less depression and loneliness and better adjustment.

Less is known about the effects of early peer relationships on children's subsequent relations with peers or other developmental outcomes. Nonetheless, several of the relations between peer relationships in middle childhood and later child developmental outcomes are foreshadowed in early childhood. For example, overt aggression in preschoolers is associated with peer rejection (Ladd & Price, 1987; Ladd et al., 1988). Social withdrawal in early childhood is linked to introversion at age 9 years (Hagekull & Bohlin, 1998) and lower self-esteem at age 12 years (Asendorpf & van Aken, 1994).

It appears that peer experiences in early childhood (like peer experiences in middle childhood and adolescence) present children with distinct opportunities and challenges, which interactions with parents and teachers do not. In contrast to parent–child relationships, which are inherently asymmetrical and unequal, peer interactions are more symmetrical and place more "demands" on both partners to initiate, respond, and coordinate exchanges in order to keep social interactions going (Vandell & Wilson, 1987). During their interactions with peers, young children are pushed to recognize the needs of their social partners and to respond appropriately or the interactions will terminate.

In addition, as Hay (1985) observed twenty years ago, young peers have shared interests that parents and adult caregivers do not. Toddler peers, for example, tire much less quickly of games such as "jumping off a step" and "banging on pans" than do adults. Likewise, preschool peers enjoy repeating (and repeating) extended pretend play scripts that are less appealing to adults. Peers also are in a better position to understand the emotional life of their peers than are parents or children who are a different age because peers face the same transitions and operate at the same socio-cognitive level. Around age 4 years, children spend more time talking about mental states with siblings and friends than with their mothers (Brown, Donelan-McCall, & Dunn, 1996). As Salisch (2001) observed, "To put it simply: A ghost that frightens their child may not impress them very much. Even if a parent can understand why her child feels 'X,' she may discount the validity of her child's appraisal" (p. 312). These observations suggest that early peer experiences could foster the development of social competencies with peers as well as development in other domains.

In a series of studies conducted over a fifteen-year period, Howes (1984, 1988, 1992; Howes & Philipsen, 1998) examined continuity in social competencies that develop within the peer system. She has found children's interactions and play with peers to have developmental consequences. Preschoolers who engage in more complex play with peers are less aggressive and less socially withdrawn than preschoolers who engage in less complex peer play. In longitudinal analyses, children who engage in more complex peer play as toddlers are more prosocial, engaged in complex play, and were less withdrawn as preschoolers. Children who engaged in more complex peer play as preschoolers were less aggressive and withdrawn at age 9.

Judy Dunn and colleagues have focused on related issues in their studies of young friends. In a longitudinal study (Hughes & Dunn, 1998), the frequency that young friends engaged in mental-state talk during free play predicted performance on theory-of-mind tasks such as understanding false beliefs one year later. Others have found early friendships to predict child well-being. Children involved in mutual friendships at the beginning of the school year showed better classroom behavior and more involvement in cooperative pretend play and social play at the end of the school year (Taylor & Machida, 1994). Young children who lack friendships, in contrast, are at risk for poor emotion regulation (Walden et al., 1999).

In addition to the linkages with social outcomes, there is some evidence that peer relations in early childhood have implications for cognition. For example, in one experimental study, dyadic peer interactions were examined as possible promoters of learning and problem solving (Azmitia, 1988). Participants worked alone in a pre-test task that involved copying a complex Lego model that required spatial relations and breaking down a complex problem. "Novices" and "experts" were then randomly assigned to novice pairs, expert pairs, or mixed pairs. Collaboration was more conducive to learning than independent work, and children in mixed-ability pairs worked more accurately than children alone or in matched-ability pairs. In another experimental study, children who worked with a more skilled peer showed greater improvement in their logical inferential skills (Roazzi & Bryant, 1998).

A Transactional Perspective

For the most part, individual research studies have focused on peer relations either as a predictor or as an outcome. In a few instances, however, investigators have considered the interplay between peer relationships and other factors over time. This transactional approach is consistent with Sameroff's (1987) view of development as a dynamic and multi-directional interplay between child, family, and environmental factors. Several transactional pathways have been proposed (see Rubin et al., 1998).

One pathway is posited for a relatively easy-going child who, in combination with supportive and responsive parenting practices, develops a secure attachment that, in turn, influences social understanding and socially skilled interactions. Socially competent behaviors, in turn, influence peers' responses and reactions as manifested in sustained relationships with particular children and greater acceptance by groups of peers. Parent–child relationships are then nurtured and maintained by children's displays of social competencies with peers and adults and by success at school and extracurricular endeavors.

A second transactional pathway emphasizes evocative gene–environment effects (see Deater-Deckard & Cahill, this volume). This occurs when temperamentally difficult infants elicit less nurturing and responsive behaviors from parents, which set the stage for insecure attachment relationships. As preschoolers, these children are more likely to be aggressive with peers, which increases the likelihood of rejection by the peer group and conflictual interactions with teachers. Aggressive children also are more likely to elicit negative feedback from peers and to have more problems achieving academic success.

A third pathway may occur for temperamentally inhibited infants who are easily aroused and wary and who are difficult to soothe. There is evidence that behaviorally inhibited children are more likely to refrain from interacting, which hinders opportunities to develop social skills, and there is also some evidence that highly reactive infants are more likely to be insecurely (anxiously) attached. Parents may then respond by being over-protective and infantilizing or by being over-directive and controlling. There is some evidence that withdrawn children are more aggressive in middle childhood, perhaps because they lacked experiences with peers in which social skills are constructed.

These three pathways are only a subset of possible transactional processes. For children who attend child care or early education programs, evidence of interplays between teacher–child relationships and peer relationships also need to be considered (Howes et al., 1998; Pianta, 1994). For children who have siblings, these relationships also are associated with peer relations over time (Dunn & Hughes, 1998; Vandell & Wilson, 1987). Consideration of these more complex patterns requires that we move beyond simple causal models.

Conclusions

A substantial body of research has accumulated that documents the richness of peer relations in early childhood. This richness is evident in the diverse forms of social behaviors, interactions, friendships, and peer group relations that are observed during this period. Children's gender, temperamental dispositions, and cognitive/linguistic competencies play important roles in the variations in these early relations. The influence of parent–child relationships also is documented across multiple studies. Several processes and mechanisms that include attachment security, parenting practices, and parent–child communication have been linked to early interactions and relationships with peers. Child care experiences, including children's relationships with their child care providers and with peers, also have been related to the quality of peer relationships in early childhood. Finally, there is growing evidence that these variations in early relationships with peers have implications for children's emotional well-being, social understanding, and cognition. Further research is needed, however, to test transactional models that consider the interplay between child characteristics, parent–child relationships, teacher–child relationships, and peer relationships over time.

References

Asendorpf, J. B., & van Aken, M. A. G. (1994). Traits and relationship status: Stranger versus peer group inhibition and test intelligence versus peer group competence as early predictors of later self-esteem. *Child Development, 65,* 1786–1798.

Azmitia, M. (1988). Peer interaction and problem solving: When are two heads better than one? *Child Development, 64,* 430–444.

Belsky, J. (2001). Developmental risks (still) associated with early child care. *Journal of Child Psychology & Psychiatry, 42,* 845–859.

Black, B., & Logan, A. (1995). Links between communication pattern in mother–child, father–child, and child–peer interactions and children's social status. *Child Development, 66,* 255–271.

Bowlby, J. (1969). *Attachment and loss: Vol. 1. Attachment.* Harmondsworth: Penguin.

Brown, J. R., Donelan-McCall, N., & Dunn, J. (1996). Why talk about mental states? The significance of children's conversations with friends, siblings, and mothers. *Child Development, 67,* 836–849.

Brownell, C. (1990). Peer social skills in toddlers: Competencies and constraints illustrated by same-age and mixed age interactions. *Child Development, 61,* 838–848.

Calkins, S. D., Gill, K. L., Johnson, M. C., & Smith, C. L. (1999). Emotional reactivity and emotional regulation as predictors of social behavior with peers during toddlerhood. *Social Development, 8,* 310–334.

Clark, K. E., & Ladd, G. W. (2000). Connectedness and autonomy support in parent–child relationships: Links to children's socioemotional orientation and peer relationships. *Developmental Psychology, 36,* 485–498.

Crick, N. R., Casas, J. F., & Ku, H-C. (1999). Relational and physical forms of peer victimization in preschool. *Developmental Psychology, 36,* 376–385.

Denham, S. A., & Holt, R. W. (1993). Preschoolers' likeability as cause or consequence of their social behavior. *Developmental Psychology, 29,* 271–275.

Denham, S., Mason, T., Caverly, S., Schmidt, M., Hackney, R., Caswell, C., & DeMulder, E. (2001). Preschoolers at play: Co-socializers of emotional and social competence. *International Journal of Behavioral Development, 25,* 290–301.

Dettling, A. C., Gunnar, M. R., & Donzella, B. (1999). Cortisol levels of young children in full-day childcare centers: relations with age and temperament. *Psychoneuroendocrinology, 24,* 519–536.

Dunn, J., Cutting, A. L., & Demetriou, H. (2000). Moral sensibility, understanding others, and children's friendship interactions in the preschool period. *British Journal of Developmental Psychology, 18,* 159–177.

Dunn, J., & Hughes, C. (1998). Young children's understanding of emotions within close relationships. *Cognition and Emotion, 12,* 171–190.

Fabes, R. A., Hanish, L. D., Martin, C. L., & Eisenberg, N. (2002). Young children's negative emotionality and social isolation: A latent growth curve analysis. *Merrill-Palmer Quarterly, 48,* 284–307.

Fabes, R. A., Martin, C. L., Hanish, L. D., Anders, M. C., & Madden-Derdich, D. A. (2003). Early school competence: The roles of sex-segregated play and effortful control. *Developmental Psychology, 39,* 848–858.

Gifford-Smith, M. E., & Brownell, C. A. (2003). Childhood peer relationships: Social acceptance, friendships and peer networks. *Journal of School Psychology, 41,* 235–284.

Gottman, J. M. (1983). How children become friends. *Monographs of the Society for Research in Child Development, 48*(3, Serial Number 201).

Hagekull, B., & Bohlin, G. (1998). Preschool temperament and environmental factors related to the five-factor model of personality in middle childhood. *Merrill-Palmer Quarterly, 44,* 194–215.

Hartup, W. W. (1996). The company they keep: Friendships and their developmental significance. *Child Development, 67,* 1–13.

Hawley, P. H. (2002). Social dominance and prosocial and coercive strategies of resource control in preschoolers. *International Journal of Behavioral Development, 26,* 167–176.

Hay, D. (1985). Learning to form relationships in infancy: Parallel attainments with parents and peers. *Developmental Review, 5*, 122–161.

Hinde, R. A. (1976). On describing relationships. *Journal of Child Psychology and Psychiatry, 17*, 1–19.

Hinde, R. A. (1979). *Towards understanding relationships*. London: Academic Press.

Hinde, R. A., Titmus, G., Easton, D., & Tamplin, A. (1985). Incidence of "friendship" and behavior with strong associates versus nonassociates in preschoolers. *Child Development, 56*, 234–245.

Howes, C. (1984). Sharing fantasy: Social pretend play in toddlers. *Child Development, 56*, 1253–1258.

Howes, C. (1988). Peer interaction of young children. *Monographs of the Society for Research in Child Development, 53*(1, Serial No. 217).

Howes, C. (1992). *The collaborative construction of pretend*. Albany: State University of New York Press.

Howes, C. (2000). Social-emotional classroom climate in child care, child–teacher relationships and children's second grade peer relations. *Social Development, 9*, 191–204.

Howes, C., Hamilton, C. E., & Philipsen, L. C. (1998). Stability and continuity of child–caregiver and child–peer relationships. *Child Development, 69*, 418–426.

Howes, C., & Matheson, C. C. (1992) Sequences in the development of competent play with peers: Social and social pretend play. *Developmental Psychology, 28*, 961–974.

Howes, C., & Philipsen, L. (1992). Gender and friendship: Relationships within peer groups of young children. *Social Development, 1*, 230–242.

Howes, C., & Philipsen, L. (1998). Continuity in children's relations with peers. *Social Development, 7*, 340–349.

Hughes, C., & Dunn, J. (1998). Understanding mind and emotion: Longitudinal associations with mental-state talk between young friends. *Developmental Psychology, 34*, 1026–1037.

Kerns, K. A., Cole, A., & Andrews, P. B. (1998). Attachment security, parent peer management practices, and peer relationship in preschoolers. *Merrill-Palmer Quarterly, 44*, 504–522.

Ladd, G. W., & Kochenderfer, B. (1996). Friendship quality as predictor of young children's early school adjustment. *Child Development, 67*, 1103–1118.

Ladd, G., W., & Price, J. M. (1987). Predicting children's social and school adjustment following the transition from preschool to kindergarten. *Child Development, 58*, 1168–1189.

Ladd, G. W., Price, J. M., & Hart, C. H. (1988). Predicting preschoolers' peer status from their playground behaviors. *Child Development, 59*, 986–992.

Levin, E., & Rubin, K. H. (1983). Getting others to do what you wanted them to do: The development of requestive strategies. In K. Nelson (Ed.), *Child language* (Vol. 4, pp. 157–186). Hilllsdale, NJ: Erlbaum.

Lindsey, E. W., Mize, J., & Pettit, G. S. (1997). Mutuality in parent–child play: Consequences for children's peer competence. *Journal of Social and Personal Relationships, 14*, 523–538.

MacDonald, K., & Parke, R. D. (1984). Bridging the gap: Parent–child play interaction and peer interactive competence. *Child Development, 55*, 1265–1277.

McElwain, N. L., Cox, M. J., Burchinal, M. R., & Macfie, J. (2003). Differentiating among insecure mother–infant attachment classifications: A focus on child–friend interactions and exploration during solitary play at 36 months. *Attachment & Human Development, 5*, 136–164.

Martin, C. L., & Fabes, R. A. (2001). The stability and consequences of young children's same-sex peer interactions. *Developmental Psychology, 3*, 431–446.

Mueller, E. (1972). The maintenance of verbal exchanges between young children. *Child Development, 43*, 930–938.

Mueller, E., & Brenner, J. (1977). The origins of social skills and interactions among playgroup toddlers. *Child Development, 48*, 854–861.

Mueller, E., & Vandell, D. L. (1979). Infant–infant interaction. In J. Osofsky (Ed.), *Handbook of infant development* (pp. 591–622). New York: John Wiley & Sons.

NICHD Early Child Care Research Network. (1998). Early child care and self-control, compliance, and problem behavior at 24 and 36 months. *Child Development, 69*, 1145–1170.

NICHD Early Child Care Research Network. (2001). Child care and children's peer interactions at 24 and 36 months: The NICHD Study of Early Child Care. *Child Development, 72*, 1478–1500.

NICHD Early Child Care Research Network. (2003). Does amount of time spent in child care predict socioemotional adjustment during the transition to kindergarten? *Child Development, 74*, 976–1005.

O'Brien, M., Roy, C., Jacobs, A., Macaluso, M., & Peyton, V. (1999). Conflict in the dyadic play of 3-year-old children. *Early Education and Development, 10*, 289–313.

Parke, R. D., Simkins, S. D., McDowell, D. J., Kim, M., Killian, C., Dennis, J., Flyr, M. L., Wild, M., & Rah, Y. (2002). Relative contributions of families and peers to children's social development. In P. K. Smith & C. H. Hart (Eds.), *Blackwell handbook of child development* (pp. 156–177). Oxford: Blackwell.

Parten, M. B. (1932). Social participation among preschool children. *Journal of Abnormal Psychology, 27*, 243–269.

Piaget, J. (1959). *The language and thought of the child.* New York: Harcourt Brace.

Pianta, R. C. (1994). Patterns of relationships between children and their kindergarten teachers. *Journal of School Psychology, 32*, 15–31.

Roazzi, A., & Bryant, P. (1998). The effects of symmetrical and asymmetrical social interaction on children's logical inferences. *British Journal of Developmental Psychology, 16*, 175–181.

Ross, H. S., Conant, C., Cheyne, J. A., & Alevizos, E. (1992). Relationships and alliances in the social interactions of kibbutz toddlers. *Social Development, 1*, 1–17.

Rubin, K. H., Bukowski, W., & Parker, J. G. (1998). Peer interactions, relationships, and groups. In W. Damon & N. Eisenberg (Eds.), *Handbook of child psychology* (Vol. 3, pp. 619–700). New York: Wiley.

Russell, A., Hart, C. H., Robinson, C. C., & Olsen, S. F. (2003). Children's sociable and aggressive behavior with peers: A comparison of the US and Australia, and contribution of temperament and parenting styles. *International Journal of Behavioral Development, 27*, 74–86.

Salisch, M. V. (2001). Children's emotional development: Challenges in their relationships to parents, peers, and friends. *International Journal of Behavioral Development, 25*, 310–319.

Sameroff, A. (1987). The social context of development. In N. Eisenberg (Ed.), *Contemporary topics in developmental psychology* (pp. 273–291). New York: Wiley.

Schneider, B. H. (2000). *Friends and enemies: Peer relations in childhood.* London: Oxford University Press.

Schneider, B. H., Atkinson, L., & Tardif, C. (2001). Child–parent attachment and children's peer relations: A quantitative review. *Developmental Psychology, 37*, 86–100.

Smith, M. (2001). Social and emotional competencies: Contributions to young African-American children's peer acceptance. *Early Education & Development, 12*, 49–72.

Strayer, F. F., & Strayer, J. (1976). An ethological analysis of social agonism and dominance relations among preschool children. *Child Development, 47*, 980–989.

Taylor, A. R., & Machida, S. (1994). The contribution of parent and peer support to Head Start children early school adjustment. *Early Childhood Research Quarterly, 9*, 387–405.

Tout, K., de Haan, M., Kipp-Campbell, E., & Gunnar, M. (1998). Social behavior correlates of cortisol activity in child care: Gender differences and time-of-day effects. *Child Development,* 69, 1247–1262.

Vandell, D. L. (1987). Baby sister/baby brother: Reactions to the birth of a sibling and patterns of early sibling relations. In F. F. Schacter & R. K. Stone (Eds.), *Practical concerns about siblings: Bridging the research–practice gap* (pp. 13–37). New York: Haworth Press.

Vandell, D. L. (2000). Parents, peer groups, and other socializing influences. *Developmental Psychology,* 36, 699–710.

Vandell, D. L., & Mueller, E. (1980). Peer play and friendships during the first two years. In H. C. Foot, A. J. Chapman, & J. R. Smith (Eds.), *Friendships and social relationships in children* (pp. 181–208). New York: Wiley.

Vandell, D. L., & Wilson, K. S. (1987). Infants' interaction with mother, sibling, and peer: Contrasts and relations between interaction systems. *Child Development,* 58, 176–186.

Vandell, D. L., Wilson, K. S., & Buchanan, N. R. (1980). Peer interaction in the first year of life: An examination of its structure, content, and sensitivity to toys. *Child Development,* 51, 481–488.

Vaughn, B. E., Vollenweider, M., Bost, K. K., Azria-Evans, M. R., & Snider, J. B. (2003). Negative interactions and social competence for preschool children in two samples: Reconsidering the interpretation of aggressive behavior for young children. *Merrill-Palmer Quarterly,* 49, 245–278.

Walden, T., Lemerise, E., & Smith, M. C. (1999). Friendship and popularity in preschool children. *Early Education and Development,* 10, 351–371.

Watamura, S. E., Donzella, B., Alwin, J., & Gunnar, M. R. (2003). Morning-to-afternoon increase in cortisol concentrations for infants and toddlers at child care: Age differences and behavioral correlates. *Child Development,* 74, 1006–1121.

23

Child Care and Early Development

Deborah Phillips, Kathleen McCartney, and Amy Sussman

Child care has become part of the common fabric of young children's experiences prior to formal school entry. It provides early childhood education for young children, as well as early intervention for children at risk. It is a basic support for employed parents across the economic spectrum and a worksite for low-wage, predominantly female workers. For the vast majority of children in the US, child care serves as the environment where they first form relationships with adults other than their parents, learn to interact with children other than siblings on a regular basis, receive or fail to receive important inputs for early learning, and experience their initial encounter with a school-like environment. These experiences, along with those from the family context, provide a foundation for future development. We begin by reporting the demographics of child care use in the US. Then we review research on child care using Bronfenbrenner's ecological framework (Bronfenbrenner & Morris, 1998; McCartney & Galanopoulos, 1988). We start by discussing the child care context itself, that is, the *microsystem* experienced by the young child. We proceed to the *mesosystem* of the home–child care interface, the *exosystem* of supports for child care providers and regulatory systems directed at the safety and quality of care, and the *macrosystem* reflected in public policy and public attitudes in the US. At each ecological level, we summarize the developmental knowledge base in light of nested contexts that influence young children.

The Demographics of Child Care

In the past forty years, the most significant social change affecting young children, from infancy through the preschool years, has been the dramatic increase in maternal employment and associated increase in young children's participation in child care. This latter trend is compounded by the 32% of non-working mothers in the US who use some form of child care (National Center for Education Statistics [NCES], 2002). Parents' decisions regarding child care for their children are constrained by family income, access to public child care benefits, the hours and nature of their jobs, and the availability of child care in their communities. These constraints limit our ability to study the effects of child care, because family background variables are confounded with indicators of child care experience, for example age at entry into child care, amount of time in child care, type of child care, and quality of child care.

In the context of very modest US family leave policies (see Waldfogel, this volume), most working mothers return to work within the first few months of their child's birth. Accordingly, children typically begin care within the first six months of life (NICHD Early Child Care Research Network [ECCRN], 1997, 2005). And children in care are there for long hours, averaging between 25 and 31 hours per week even for infants (Ehrle, Adams, & Tout, 2001). Placement in full-time care (i.e., care for 35 or more hours per week) increases over the early childhood years such that 32% of children under 1 year of age and 43% of 2-year-olds are in child care full-time (Ehrle et al., 2001). This proportion is even greater for 3- and 4-year olds, with more than 45% of preschoolers in a child care or preschool setting full time (Capizzano & Adams, 2000a).

Most families rely on a patchwork of child care arrangements over the early childhood period. These arrangements include every conceivable combination of care by mothers and fathers, who juggle work and non-work schedules to maintain parental care; care by relatives, especially the grandmothers, aunts, and even siblings of the children in care; and care by non-relatives, including family child care providers, nannies, and center-based teachers. Accurate portrayals of this patchwork have eluded researchers, who typically focus on the primary arrangement, knowing that this results in a tremendous loss of information on children's experiences.

When mothers are employed, infant and toddler care is provided predominantly by parents (27%) and relatives (27%); care by family child care providers and center-based teachers is less prevalent, i.e., 17% and 22% respectively (Erhle et al., 2001). As children get older, they are more likely to be enrolled in center-based programs and less likely to be in exclusive parental care or cared for by relatives: that is, 45% of 3- and 4-year olds are in child care centers, 14% are in family child care homes, 17% are cared for by relatives, and 18% are cared for exclusively by their parents (Capizzano & Adams, 2000a). As these data suggest, child care is neither a stable nor a consistent experience for young children. On average, 34% of children under age 3 experience multiple arrangements, as do 44% of 3- and 4-year-olds (Capizzano & Adams, 2000b).

The forms of care that parents use vary quite systematically with some family characteristics. For example, Hispanic children and children growing up in single-mother families are much more likely to be cared for by relatives than are children of other races and family structures. Among two-parent families, those with lower incomes are least likely to rely on center care and nanny care, and more likely to use care by relatives and parents than their counterparts with more resources (Erhle et al., 2001). Children with disabilities tend to enter care at an older age, to be in informal arrangements with relatives and in home-based arrangements, and to make the transition to center-based arrangements at older ages in comparison to typically developing children (Booth & Kelly, 2002).

The Child Care Microsystem

A microsystem consists of the immediate experiences of an individual in a given context. With respect to child care, children's immediate experiences derive from their interactions with child care providers, teachers, and often peers, as well as with the materials present in their environment. Researchers have focused on two aspects of children's proximal experiences: child care quality and quantity. The latter is easily measured by an indicator of hours in care. The assessment of quality is more complex. Some instruments assess multiple dimensions of quality, including furnishings and displays for children, personal care routines, language and reasoning experiences, and adult needs, as is the case with the Early Childhood Environment Rating Scale (Harms, Clifford, & Cryer, 1998). Others, such as the Observational Record of the Caregiving Environment (NICHD ECCRN, 1996), focus on interactions between caregivers and children. Early childhood educators and developmentalists alike believe that quality is rooted in sensitive and responsive interactions between caregivers and children. Skilled caregivers, for example, offer activities that are appropriate for a child's age, ability, culture, and interests. They are sensitive and responsive to individual differences among children and understand how to manage peer interactions constructively. In addition, they provide children with generous amounts of attention and support. Other indicators of child care quality, for example materials or health and safety standards, typically co-vary with process quality. Structural indicators, including provider education and training, provider–child ratio, and group size, also predict process quality (NICHD ECCRN, 2002a; Phillipsen, Burchinal, Howes, & Cryer, 1997). Studies of process quality inform theoretical questions about early experiences, while studies of structural indicators of quality inform social policy questions, because governments can regulate teacher education and the like.

Research on the microsystem effects of child care on children's development has evolved in three phases: an early phase consisting of between-groups studies, a middle phase consisting of within-group quality studies, and the current phase of large-scale studies. Early between-group studies were designed to compare children in child care with children in exclusive parental care in order to determine whether child care *per se* (i.e., of any kind, quality, or amount) posed any risks for the developing child. These studies were typically flawed, in that researchers failed to consider family confounds of child care experience. Attempts to control for family confounds of child care selection (i.e., parent education, family income, maternal depression) exemplify within-group studies of children attending child care programs that vary in quality. The advantage of larger studies is that they enable researchers to move beyond findings that quality matters to explore moderators and mediators of effects. We agree with Lamb (1998) that it "appears likely that different children will be affected differently by various day care experiences, although we remain ignorant about most of the factors that modulate these differential effects" (p. 116).

Quality of child care

One of the most robust findings in the developmental literature concerns the relation between child care quality and children's cognitive, language, and social outcomes. This association has been documented in experimental studies of early childhood intervention studies, such as the Abecedarian Project (Ramey, 2000) and the Perry Preschool Project (Weikart, 1998). These intervention studies provide compelling evidence of the effectiveness of early care and education, because, in some cases, the effects last through adulthood. Moreover, cost–benefit estimates reveal that early childhood interventions are cost-effective because they reduce the need for subsequent services (Barnett, 1995). Because intervention effects are not generalizable beyond at-risk children and derive from exposure to model programs, studies of children in community child care programs provide complementary evidence that child care quality matters. Large-scale studies that control for potential family selection effects are most convincing.

This review will focus primarily on two such studies: the Cost, Quality, and Outcomes Study (CQO), a study of 418 children nested within 176 centers in four states, and the National Institute of Child Health and Human Development Study of Early Child Care and Youth Development (NICHD SECCYD), a prospective study of 1364 children from birth through 15 years. In these two studies, high-quality child care was associated with a range of cognitive and language outcomes, even when controlling for family background variables, including social class indicators (Cost, Quality, & Outcomes Team, 1995; NICHD ECCRN, 2000). There is some evidence that effects are strongest for language outcomes, including both receptive language (Burchinal, Cryer, Clifford, & Howes, 2002) and expressive language (NICHD ECCRN, 2000). The NICHD network found stronger effects when they focused their quality measure on language stimulation *per se*; moreover, quality effects continued through first grade (NICHD ECCRN, 2002b).

The NICHD network collaborated with economist Greg Duncan to explore a range of statistical models assessing child care effects on cognitive and language test scores. Using change models, they demonstrated that increases in child care quality between 24 and 54 months were associated with increases in cognitive test scores (NICHD ECCRN & Duncan, 2003). In change models, each child serves as his or her own control, and as such, the likelihood that the effect can be accounted for by a confound, for example some unmeasured aspect of the family, is reduced. The researchers also showed that amount of time spent in center care appeared to be an index of quality, because it, too, was associated with cognitive and language outcomes, probably because children in center care are more likely to be exposed to educated providers who offer an early childhood curriculum compared with children in less formal programs. Nevertheless, it is also the case that variation in quality among less formal settings, specifically home-based child care, is associated with higher cognitive and language assessments at 15, 24, and 36 months (Clarke-Stewart, Vandell, Burchinal, O'Brien, & McCartney, 2002). High quality is also related to a range of social outcomes. In the NICHD SECCYD, quality was negatively related to ratings of behavior problems and positively related to social competence (NICHD ECCRN, 1998), as well as positively related to positive peer interaction (NICHD ECCRN, 2001). The CQO study team has replicated the negative association between quality and behavior problems, where quality was indexed by teacher–child closeness (Peisner-Feinberg et al., 2001).

Some reviewers have dismissed child care effects as small (Blau, 1999; Scarr, 1998); however, this point has been disputed by McCartney and Rosenthal (2000), who noted that the child care effect sizes are sometimes equivalent to those for maternal education. Based on his review of this literature, economist James Heckman (2000) concluded that early childhood interventions, like child care, offered one of the best investments in human capital, primarily because "skill begets skill" (p. 50). In other words, early investment promotes later investment.

Structural indicators of quality are also related to a range of outcomes. One of the most consistent findings concerns providers' formal education. For example, a recent study of child care used by mothers working their way off of welfare reported that low-income children had higher cognitive skills when their providers had more education (Loeb, Fuller, Kagan, & Carrol, 2004). The CQO group found that college education for teachers was associated with children's receptive language skills (Burchinal et al., 2002). In an experimental study, Rhodes and Hennessy (2000) demonstrated that a 120-hour training course translated into gains in complex social and cognitive play. When centers meet professional standards for child–caregiver ratio, children score higher on cognitive and language tests (Burchinal et al., 2000; NICHD ECCRN, 1999). The NICHD network demonstrated that the association between structural indicators and child outcomes is mediated by process quality (NICHD ECCRN, 2002a). It is hardly surprising that caregivers can do a better job when they have had formal education and work in settings with lower child–caregiver ratios.

Quantity of child care

In a series of reviews, Belsky (1986, 2001) has drawn attention to the consistent finding that quantity of care is positively associated with behavior problems. Until recently, developmentalists wondered whether this association was mediated by child care quality. This seemed especially likely given the consistent finding that poor-quality care was associated with behavior problems (see previous section). Yet in the NICHD SECCYD, there is a clear linear association between hours in care and behavior problems, an association first detected at two years (NICHD ECCRN, 1998) and replicated through kindergarten (NICHD ECCRN, 2003). Quality of care mediated this effect, though not completely, and no interactions between quality and quantity were detected.

Despite the qualifications noted in the discussion of this NICHD ECCRN (2003) paper concerning the small effect size and the fact that children's behavior, on average, was well within the normal range, the findings caused quite a stir in academic circles and in the media. The paper was published along with a set of commentaries, no doubt because the implications of the quantity finding are important for parents and policy makers alike. For example, Fabes, Hanish, and Martin (2003) suggested that the association might be mediated by time spent with a large group of peers. Newcombe (2003) warned that any risks of child care hours for children must be weighed against the benefits of maternal employment, including increased family income and decreased maternal depression. And Love et al. (2003) failed to replicate the findings using three different data sets. In their study of children from families on welfare, a distinctly different sample from that studied in the NICHD SECCYD, Votruba-Drzal, Coley, and Chase-Lansdale (2004) found that extensive child care was a risk only for children in low-quality care arrangements. Long hours in child care for children from low-income families may buffer them from the effects of poverty. How quantity is measured may matter as well. For example, in a Swedish study, children who experienced more hours per week in care were rated as having lower social competence, while children who experienced more days per week in care were rated as having higher social competence. In future studies, it will be critical to identify the mechanisms through which child care hours pose a risk, as well as the children for whom extensive hours in child care pose a risk.

The Child Care Mesosystem

Bronfenbrenner used the term "mesosystem" to refer to interconnections among contexts that the developing child experiences. McCartney (in press) has recently outlined four kinds of research on the family–child care mesosystem: family selection of child care, the predictive power of the family across child care contexts, child care as a family support, and family moderators of child care effects. These four literatures demonstrate how important questions about the interconnections between the child care and family contexts can be lost when research attempts to isolate the effects of one from the other.

Family selection

A vast array of family selection variables has been studied, including those that reflect differences among families with respect to demographics, attitudes, and personality characteristics. One of the strongest selection factors is family income. Consider that, among families who pay for child care, these expenses constitute an average of 14% of earnings for low-income families and 18% of earnings for families living in poverty (Giannarelli, Adelman, & Schmidt, 2003). With respect to relative care and family child care, lower family income is associated with lower quality; with respect to center-based care, the relation between income and quality is U-shaped (Galinsky, Howes, Kontos, & Shinn, 1994; NICHD ECCRN, 1997; Phillips, Voran, Kisker, Howes, & Whitebook, 1994), with lower- and middle-income families receiving lower-quality care than families living in poverty or with high incomes. This appears to reflect access to public subsidies and programs, such as Early Head Start, Head Start, and state pre-kindergarten programs, which are targeted to very low-income families and tend to offer higher-quality care than community-based child care programs (NICHD ECCRN, 1997). Not surprisingly, parent satisfaction with child care arrangements also varies by income level such that lower-income mothers are more likely to express dissatisfaction. For example, 43% of low-income single mothers interviewed as part of the nationally representative National Child Care Survey reported that they would use a different child care arrangement if they could afford to do so (Brayfield, Deitch, & Hofferth, 1993). There is little doubt that parent choices are sometimes constrained by economic considerations (Fuller, Holloway, & Liang, 1995; Phillips & Adams, 2001).

Predictive power of the family across child care contexts

Because time in child care replaces time in the family, there have been several attempts to assess whether child care diminishes the effect of the family on children's development. In their Chicago study, Clarke-Stewart and colleagues examined a range of family factors and found no evidence for differential influence of the family across child care arrangements on a wide range of outcomes (Clarke-Stewart, Gruber, & Fitzgerald, 1994). The NICHD ECCRN (1998) compared associations between parenting variables and a range of child outcomes for two groups: children in exclusive parental care and children in full-time child care. They did not find significant differences between the predictor–outcome matrices for the two groups. Indeed, despite the fact that child care experience has pervasive effects on children's development, the influence of variables that capture the child's home environment, such as mother sensitivity, has been found uniformly to be greater than the influence of non-parental care indicators.

Perhaps the best evidence for the predictive power of the family when children are in child care comes from research on mother–child attachment. Daily separations have been hypothesized to reduce opportunities for "ongoing tuning of the emerging infant–caregiver interactive system" (Sroufe, 1988, p. 286). In the NICHD ECCRN (1998) study, there were no significant differences in attachment security related to child care participation as indexed by four parameters: age of entry into child care, continuity of care, amount of care, and quality of care. Even for children in extensive, early, unstable, or poor-quality care, the risk of insecure attachment was not higher than that for other children. Instead, attachment security was related to the mother's sensitivity and responsiveness. Interactions between low maternal sensitivity and low-quality care, more hours in care, and many care arrangements were associated with increased insecurity, findings that support a dual-risk model of development (Werner & Smith, 1992).

Child care as a family support

High-quality child care may actually serve a compensatory function for children with less sensitive mothers. There is now a substantial body of research documenting that child care can serve as a support for families, especially families at risk, via parent education and informal mentoring (Smith, Perou, & Lesesne, 2002; Webster-Stratton & Reid, this volume). Most parent education consists of the promotion of knowledge concerning child development. Formal education occurs via numerous mechanisms, including home visits, workshops, study groups, books and periodicals, organizational activities, and lectures (Bowman, 1997). Informal education occurs through conversations between parents and child care providers that typically occur during drop-off and pick-up times, as well as through modeling by providers of caregiving, teaching, and behavior management. In addition, parent education can extend beyond child development to job training and self-esteem programs (Benasich, Brooks-Gunn, & Clewell, 1992).

Family moderators of child care effects

There are a handful of recent studies documenting that child care quality matters more for children from families at risk. For example, using the NICHD SECCYD data set, McCartney, Dearing, and Taylor (2003) showed that high-quality child care protected children from the negative effects of low income with respect to school readiness, receptive language, and expressive language. Specifically, children at or near the poverty level who attended high-quality child care had higher scores on cognitive and language tests than did children in low-quality child care or children not in care. In the CQO study, a positive association between child care quality and math skills was stronger for children whose mothers had less education, and an association between teacher–child closeness and fewer behavior problems was more likely to be sustained through early elementary school for children whose mothers had less education (Peisner-Feinberg et al., 2001).

Two recent studies with low-income samples documented home environment–child care interactions. In their welfare sample, Votruba-Drzal et al. (2004) did not find main effects of child care quality on children's reading and math skill trajectories; however, when children were from stimulating home environments, high-quality child care was associated with significant increases in reading. It appears that some learning must be available in the home for children to profit from quality child care. Similarly, Bryant and colleagues found that children in higher-quality Head Start programs performed better on cognitive tests of problem solving and reasoning (Bryant, Burchinal, Lau, & Sparling, 1994). Because there is a restricted income range for welfare and Head Start samples, these home environment by child care interactions are all the more impressive. Further, there is some evidence that risk by child care interactions may extend to characteristics of children themselves. For example, in two studies, children with lower scores on tests of cognitive development profited more from high-quality care (NICHD ECCRN & Duncan, 2003; Ramey, Bryant, & Suarez, 1985).

The Child Care Exosystem

The child care that children receive in the US is highly conditioned by other systems and circumstances in the communities and states that surround it. The aspects of this exosystem that have received the most attention in research are conditions affecting the child care workforce and the regulatory structures that affect the safety and quality of child care.

Child care workforce

Child care is viewed and studied primarily as an environment for children. But it is also an adult workplace in which nearly 5 million individuals – 97–99% of them women –

work in any given week (Burton et al., 2002). The work is characterized by extremely low pay, low status, and high turnover. Data collected by the US Bureau of Labor Statistics (Center for the Child Care Workforce, 2004) indicate that child care providers and teachers typically earn between $8.37 and $10.67 per hour, as compared to $20.38 per hour earned by kindergarten teachers. This is of concern to developmentalists because wages appear to be a significant factor affecting the quality of care that children receive. In a recent analysis of center-based programs in three states, for example, the wages paid to the teachers were as strong a predictor of classroom quality (assessed with the Early Childhood Environment instruments described above) as were child–caregiver ratios (Phillips, Mekos, Scarr, McCartney, & Abbott-Shim, 2001). Others have also reported significant associations between wages and quality of care (Phillipsen et al., 1997; Scarr, Eisenberg, & Deater-Deckard, 1994).

Low wages fuel job turnover among child care teaching staff (Whitebook & Sakai, 2004). Turnover rates for child care providers (across all types of care) are among the highest of any segment of the labor force tracked by the Department of Labor, hovering at 30% per year (US Bureau of Labor Statistics, 1998). Studies of center-based teaching staff have found that 25% to 40% leave their jobs each year (Kontos, Howes, Shinn, & Galinsky, 1995; Whitebook, Howes, & Phillips, 1990). Comparable turnover rates (i.e., closures of family child care homes) have been found for home-based providers (Phillips, Whitebook, & Crowell, 2003). A recent longitudinal study of a center-based workforce in California reported that three-quarters of all teaching staff had left their jobs in just four years (Whitebook & Sakai, 2004).

Children cared for in settings characterized by high turnover are significantly more likely than children in stable child care settings to experience poor overall quality of care as well as more detached and harsh caregiving (Anderson, Nagel, Roberts, & Smith, 1981; Helburn, 1995; Howes & Hamilton, 1993; Kontos et al., 1995; Whitebook et al., 1990). Higher staff turnover is also associated with poor developmental outcomes for children, including lower vocabulary test scores (Howes, Phillips, & Whitebook, 1992). The mechanism hypothesized to account for the association between turnover and child outcomes is children's attachments to their caregivers; both security of attachment and positive outcomes are more likely under conditions of caregiver stability (Goossens & van IJzendoorn, 1991; Howes & Hamilton, 1992).

The regulatory context of child care

In every state, some, but by no means all, child care programs are required to comply with regulations that establish a threshold of quality below which children's safety and development are presumably compromised. Safety and health precautions figure prominently in these regulations, but they also include provisions regarding staff training, caregiver–child ratios, and maximum group sizes. States vary widely, however, in the stringency of these regulations and there are no national standards to ensure even a modicum of consistency (Marsland, Zigler, & Martinez, 2003; Phillips, Lande, & Goldberg, 1990; Young, Marsland, & Zigler, 1997). For example, ratio requirements in different states allow from three to twelve infants per teacher in center-based arrangements

(Hollestelle, 2000). It is not surprising that, across all types of care, adult–infant ratios have been observed to range from 1:1 to 1:13 (NICHD ECCRN, 1996). Although most states permit infants and toddlers to be cared for by staff who, on average, have not completed high school, a handful of states require at least some college-level training in child development or early childhood education.

Recent comprehensive reviews of state child care regulations based on professional standards, as well as proposed (but not implemented) federal guidelines, have revealed that half to two-thirds of states fail to require even minimally acceptable care (Marsland et al., 2003; Young et al., 1997). In addition, many care providers do not meet these requirements or are exempt from them and thus able to operate legally beyond the purview of state licensing laws (Brauner, Gordic, & Zigler, 2004; Gormley, 1995; Helburn & Bergmann, 2002). Twelve states exempt religious-based child care centers and twenty states exempt half-day nursery schools. The majority of family day care homes and virtually all smaller arrangements with relatives, friends, and nannies are exempt from regulation.

Studies of state-regulated child care centers show an association between stricter licensing standards and higher levels of sensitive and responsive caregiving (Whitebook et al., 1990; Howes, Smith, & Galinsky, 1995; Phillips, Howes, & Whitebook, 1992; Phillips et al., 2001). In addition, centers that voluntarily meet standards promulgated by the American Public Health Association and the American Academy of Pediatrics (1992) demonstrate higher levels of classroom quality (Phillips et al., 1992; Whitebook et al., 1990) and higher levels of cognitive and language development among the enrolled children (NICHD ECCRN, 2001). Regulations for family child care homes vary across states as well. The National Association for Family Child Care has devised an age-weighted group size index in an effort to offer a meaningful standard or guideline for states. According to this standard, caregivers can provide quality caregiving for a group of children that does not exceed 100 points, where each child under 2 represents 33 points, 2-year-olds represent 25 points, 3- to 6-year-olds represent 16 points, and children over 6 years represent 10 points (Modigliani & Bromer, 1997). This system was, in effect, evaluated by Clarke-Stewart and colleagues (2002), who demonstrated that caregivers in settings that met this recommended standard were more likely to provide positive caregiving, an index of child care quality operationalized by caregiver sensitivity, positive regard for the child, and ability to foster exploration of the environment.

The Child Care Macrosystem

Child care exists within a broader macrosystem of public policies and public attitudes that affect children's experiences and development in child care. In the past decade, the policy context has grown extremely complex as child care has become increasingly embedded in a broader array of early childhood education and income support policies. With respect to public attitudes, relatively new research is shedding light on the ambivalence with which the US public views child care.

There is no coherent national child care policy in the US. Rather, public policy for child care is highly dispersed across:

- *tax policy*: tax-paying families can receive a credit for their child care expenses;
- *early education policy*: numerous federal and state programs, ranging from Head Start to state-funded pre-kindergarten, both meet some families' child care needs and are explicitly coordinating their services with community-based child care programs;
- *higher education policy*: bears on college- and university-based training programs for child care teachers.
- *income support policy*: the major share of direct federal support for child care is now part of welfare reform legislation;
- *defense policy*: the US Military Child Care Act provides child care for military families that substantially exceeds the typical quality of care for non-military families; and
- *family leave policy*: enables some parents to stay home briefly with their infants or newly adopted children, and thus to rely on parental care.

Child care policy in the US is also highly decentralized, with the federal government's role largely restricted to providing funds (either directly or through the tax system). This leaves most decisions regarding the structure and quality of child care services (including, as noted above, decisions about child care regulation), eligibility for these services, and funding priorities (e.g., upgrade quality or serve more families) up to the states, in effect creating fifty child care systems. In all states, however, government child care support is almost exclusively directed to families living in or near poverty, a notably distinct feature of child care in the US compared to many other industrialized countries (see Waldfogel, this volume).

The developmental consequences of child care policies have gone largely unstudied, with one important exception. There is a growing body of research on the family and child effects of welfare reform, which includes a subset of studies examining child care. The Personal Responsibility and Work Opportunity Reconciliation Act (PRWORA), signed into law on August 22, 1996, not only dramatically altered the structure of the welfare system, but also consolidated four major federal child care programs for low-income families into a single funding stream authorized at more than $20 billion between 1997 and 2002. Child care was portrayed as an integral component of making work possible and "making work pay" (Phillips, in press).

The emerging research on child care funded through PRWORA is addressing two questions: (1) "What types and quality of child care are these subsidies purchasing?" and (2) "What are the developmental effects of child care purchased through this funding stream?" Families working their way off of welfare are disproportionately likely to rely on informal child care arrangements with relatives and friends (Capizzano, Adams, & Sonenstein, 2000; Giannarelli, Sonenstein, & Stagner, in press; McCabe, Brady-Smith, & Brooks-Gunn, in press; Robins, 2003), although a sizeable minority rely on center-based arrangements. Use of Head Start, in contrast, appears to decline as mothers make the transition from welfare to work (Gassman-Pines, 2003; Paulsell, Kisker, Raikes, Love, & Jerald, in press). The reasons for this trend are not understood but may involve the mismatch between part- and full-school-day Head Start hours and work-related hours when child care is needed. These trends are of concern in light of evidence, summarized above, that the observed quality of care received by low-income children is consistently poorer than that received by higher-income children except among those using center-based arrangements.

These findings have been replicated in studies of welfare reform, which document the inadequate care children receive while their mothers work to meet the requirements of welfare reform and/or to improve their family's economic circumstances (Coley, Li-Grining, & Chase-Lansdale, in press). For example, one study of the effects of welfare reform in three US cities has reported that the majority of child care centers used by low-income children provided developmentally beneficial child care, whereas only one-third of the home-based arrangements met this standard of care (Coley, Chase-Landsale, & Li-Grining, 2001).

Efforts to assess the effects of welfare reform, generally, on young children have failed to produce consistent evidence of either harmful or beneficial consequences (Morris, Gennetian, & Knox, 2002). Related efforts to assess the developmental implications of child care provided in the context of welfare reform are in their infancy. A study of children of mothers entering work-first programs in California, Connecticut, and Florida who had greater exposure to center-based programs (but not to home-based programs) received higher scores on tests of school readiness (Loeb et al., 2004). Researchers from the Welfare, Children, and Families Three-City Study have recently reported that young children in higher-quality child care arrangements, both centers and home-based, showed fewer behavior problems compared with children in lower-quality care (Votruba-Drzal et al., 2004). The investigators have speculated that care providers in higher-quality programs help young children learn to regulate their emotions, because they are consistent, warm, engaged, and able to support positive peer interactions. Similarly, a pair of reports looking across a set of random assignment studies of welfare reform has also found positive effects of center-based care both on teacher reports of reduced externalizing problems and on children's achievement in the early grades of elementary school (Crosby, Dowsett, Gennetian, & Huston, 2004; Gennetian, Crosby, Dowsett, & Huston, 2004).

These welfare studies are thus confirming long-standing evidence, reviewed above, that variation in child care quality has relatively greater developmental consequences for low-income children whose home environments may be less capable of compensating for inadequate child care. Somewhat ironically, detrimental effects of welfare reform that have been found for adolescents may be partially attributable to increased demands for them to provide child care for younger siblings, thus detracting from time spent on activities that would be directly beneficial for their own development (Clarke-Kauffman et al., 2002; Morris et al., 2002).

Public attitudes about child care

Research at the crossroads of psychology and communications is clarifying our understanding of public attitudes about child care, which have long been portrayed as ambivalent, at best. An examination of child care frames, or mental short-cuts that help us organize our thoughts on an issue, reveals that individuals relate child care to safety and work, which tie in to issues of personal and parental responsibility (Brauner et al., 2004; Frameworks Institute, 2002; Gilliam & Nall Bales, 2001; Nall Bales, 1999). Within the work frame, child care is seen as a vehicle facilitating maternal employment. Within the safety frame, child care evokes worries about negligence and abuse. Taken together, these frames cast child care as a service for parents, rather than an influential environment for children's development, and as a "kiddy container" where children need to be kept free from harm, rather than a setting where children learn and grow. Accordingly, parents typically identify child care quality with a place where their children will be left with "an affectionate and responsible provider and [in] a safe, orderly environment" (Farkas, Duffett, & Johnson, 2000, p. 17). This frame protects parents from worries that child care providers may usurp their role as their child's primary source of love and learning and preserves societal attitudes about the primacy of parents.

Relatedly, frames emphasizing maternal work and safety place child care squarely in the realm of personal rather than governmental or societal responsibility. It is only when low-income families need child care assistance to balance childrearing and employment responsibilities that a majority of the public condones a government role in child care (Farkas et al., 2000; Pew Research Center for the People and the Press, 1998; Sylvester, 2001). Support for public policy on child care is restricted to situations where there is a compelling economic reason for mothers to go to work (or become a public burden), and to the provision of financial support to parents as distinct from efforts to improve the child care that is available or create incentives for parents to use only certain types of child care.

Summary

Young children experience widely disparate types, patterns, qualities, and amounts of child care during the years prior to school entry. It is not surprising, then, that child care does not have uniform effects on early development. It can confer risk and/or protection depending on the circumstances and characteristics of the care arrangement and the providers, the family and the child, and the broader context of child care in the US. Child care exerts its influence on children's development through the quality of early care and education that children experience, as well as through the amount of time they spend in child care over their early years. Open questions include how these two features of child care interact to affect early development, whether there are any thresholds that can be identified, the mechanisms through which these influences operate, and which children growing up in which circumstances are most affected by child care experiences that vary in their quality and quantity.

If there is one central lesson from the last three decades of research on child care, it is that the developmental consequences of child care cannot be adequately understood absent consideration of family influences. These influences include the family's central role in selecting child care, the role that child care often plays as a source of family support, and important interactions that are now emerging between child care and family environments. Notably, across samples with a range of characteristics, child care environments have been found to have, at the very least, a modest, incremental influence on early development. For children growing up in relatively more adverse family circumstances due to poverty or non-optimal parenting, it appears that this influence may be even greater than for their more privileged peers.

The broader context of child care is characterized by a poorly paid, and thus unevenly prepared and very unstable, workforce; a regulatory system that provides minimal protection to young children; and growing government funding that is, however, largely restricted to families working their way off of welfare. This context places research on child care in the forefront of social change and both scientific and public controversy. Policy lags behind science and public ambivalence persists. Future research on child care thus bears the interrelated responsibility of advancing knowledge about child development and informing public debate so that children and their families can count on receiving care that protects and promotes early development.

Note

Support for Kathleen McCartney came from a grant from the National Institute of Child Health and Human Development (HD25451). We thank the National Institute of Child Health and Human Development Early Child Care Research Network for the dataset and Kristen L. Bub for her assistance with library research and editing suggestions.

References

American Public Health Association & American Academy of Pediatrics. (1992). *Caring for our children: National health and safety performance standards: Standards for out-of-home child care programs.* Ann Arbor, MI: Author.

Anderson, C., Nagel, R., Roberts, W., & Smith, J. (1981). Attachment to substitute caregivers as a function of center quality and center involvement. *Child Development, 52,* 53–61.

Barnett, W. S. (1995). Long-term effects of early childhood programs on cognitive and school outcomes. *The Future of Children, 5*(3), 25–50.

Belsky, J. (1986). Infant day care: A cause for concern? *Zero to Three, 6,* 1–9.

Belsky, J. (2001). Developmental risks (still) associated with early child care. *Journal of Child Psychology and Psychiatry, 42,* 845–859.

Benasich, A. A., Brooks-Gunn, J., & Clewell, B. C. (1992). How do mothers benefit from early intervention programs? *Journal of Applied Developmental Psychology, 13,* 311–362.

Blau, D. (1999). The effects of child care characteristics on child development. *Journal of Human Resources, 34,* 786–822.

Booth, C. L., & Kelly, J. F. (2002). Child care effects on the development of toddlers with special needs. *Early Childhood Research Quarterly, 17*(2), 171–196.

Bowman, B. T. (1997). Preschool as family support. In C. Dunst & M. Wolery (Eds.), *Advances in early education and day care* (pp. 157–172). Greenwich, CT: JAI Press.

Brauner, J., Gordic, B., & Zigler, E. (2004). Putting the child back into child care. *Social Policy Report, XVIII*(III), 5.

Brayfield, A., Deitch, S. G., & Hofferth, S. (1993). *Caring for children in low-income families: A substudy of the National Child Care Survey, 1990.* A National Association for the Education of Young Children Study, conducted by the Urban Institute. Washington, DC: Urban Institute Press.

Bronfenbrenner, U., & Morris, P. A. (1998). The ecology of developmental processes. In W. Damon & R. M. Lerner (Eds.), *Handbook of child psychology: Vol. 1. Theoretical models of human development* (5th ed., pp. 993–1028). New York: Wiley.

Bryant, D. M., Burchinal, M., Lau, L. B., & Sparling, J. J. (1994). Family and classroom correlates of Head Start children's developmental outcomes. *Early Childhood Research Quarterly, 9,* 289–309.

Burchinal, M. R., Cryer, D., Clifford, R. M., & Howes, C. (2002). Caregiver training and classroom quality in child care centers. *Applied Developmental Science, 6,* 2–11.

Burchinal, M. R., Roberts, J. E., Riggins, R., Zeisel. S., Neebe, E., & Bryant, M. (2000). Relating quality of center child care to early cognitive and language development longitudinally. *Child Development, 71,* 339–357.

Burton, A., Whitebook, M., Young, M., Bellm, D., Wayne, C., Brandon, R. N., & Maher, E. (2002, May). *Estimating the size and components of the US child care workforce and caregiving population. Key Findings from the Child Care Workforce Estimate.* Washington, DC: Center for the Child Care Workforce; and Seattle, WA: Human Services Policy Center, University of Washington.

Capizzano, J., & Adams, G. (2000a). The hours that children under five spend in child care: Variation across states. *New Federalism: National Survey of America's Families,* Series B (No. B-8). Washington, DC: Urban Institute.

Capizzano, J., & Adams, G. (2000b). The number of child care arrangements used by children under five: Variation across states. *New Federalism: National Survey of America's Families,* Series B (No. B-12). Washington, DC: Urban Institute.

Capizzano, J., Adams, G., & Sonenstein, F. (2000). Child care arrangements for children under five: Variation across states. *New Federalism: National Survey of America's Families,* Series B (No. B-7). Washington, DC: Urban Institute.

Center for the Child Care Workforce. (2004). *Current data on the salaries and benefits of the US early childhood education workforce, 2004.* Washington, DC: Author.

Clark-Kauffman, E., Duncan, G., Gennetian, L., Knox, V., London, A., & Vargas, W. (2002, May). *How welfare and work policies for parents affect adolescents: A synthesis of research.* New York: Manpower Demonstration Research Corporation.

Clarke-Stewart, K. A., Gruber, C., & Fitzgerald, L. (1994). *Children at home and in day care.* Hillsdale, NJ: Erlbaum.

Clarke-Stewart, K. A., Vandell, D. L., Burchinal, M., O'Brien, M., & McCartney K. (2002). Do regulable features of child-care homes affect children's development? *Early Childhood Research Quarterly, 17,* 52–86.

Coley, R. L., Chase-Lansdale, P. L., & Li-Grining, C. (2001). *Child care in the era of welfare reform: Quality, choices, and preferences.* Policy Brief 01–04. Johns Hopkins University, Baltimore.

Coley, R. L., Li-Grining, D. P., & Chase-Lansdale, P. L. (in press). Low-income families' child care experiences: Meeting the needs of children and families. In N. Cabrera, R. Hutchens, & H. E. Peters (Eds.), *From welfare to childcare: What happens to young children when mothers exchange welfare for work?* Mahwah, NJ: Erlbaum.

Cost, Quality, & Outcomes Team. (1995). *Cost, quality, and child outcomes in child care centers.* Denver: University of Colorado at Denver.

Crosby, D., Dowsett, C., Gennetian, L. A., & Huston, A. (2004). *The effects of center-based care on the problem behavior of low-income children with working mothers.* New York: Manpower Demonstration Research Corporation.

Ehrle, J., Adams, G., & Tout, K. (2001). *Who's caring for our youngest children: child care patterns of infants and toddlers.* Washington, DC: Urban Institute.

Fabes, R. A., Hanish, L. D., & Martin, C. L. (2003). Children at play: The role of peers in understanding the effects of child care. *Child Development, 74,* 1039–1043.

Farkas, S., Duffett, A., & Johnson, J. (2000). *Necessary compromises: How parents, employers and children's advocates view child care today.* New York: Public Agenda.

Frameworks Institute. (2002). *The frameworks perspective: Strategic frame analysis.* Retrieved from *http://www.frameworks.org/strategicanalysis/perspectives.html*

Fuller, B., Holloway, S. D., & Liang, X. (1995). *Which families use nonparental child care and centers? The influence of family structure, ethnicity, and parental practices.* Cambridge, MA: Department of Human Development and Psychology, Harvard University.

Galinsky, E., Howes, C., Kontos, S., & Shinn, M. (1994). *The study of children in family child care and relative care.* New York: Families and Work Institute.

Gassman-Pines, A. (2003, June). *The effects of welfare and employment policies on child care use by low-income young mothers.* Summary of Key Findings Working Paper No. 19. New York: Manpower Demonstration Research Corporation.

Gennetian, L., Crosby, D., Dowsett, C., & Huston, A. (2004). *Center-based care and the achievement of low-income children: Evidence using data from experimental employment-based programs.* New York: Manpower Demonstration Research Corporation.

Giannarelli, L., Adelman, S., & Schmidt, S. (2003). *Getting help with child care expenses.* Occasional Paper Number 62. Assessing the New Federalism. Washington, DC: Urban Institute.

Giannarelli, L., Sonenstein, F., & Stagner, M. (in press). Child care arrangements and help for low-income families with young children: Evidence from the National Survey of America's Families. In N. Cabrera, R. Hutchens, & H. E. Peters (Eds.), *From welfare to childcare: What happens to young children when mothers exchange welfare for work?* Mahwah, NJ: Erlbaum.

Gilliam, F. D., & Nall Bales, S. (2001). Strategic Frame Analysis: Reframing America's youth. *Social Policy Report, 15,* 3–14.

Goossens, G., & van IJzendoorn, M. (1991). Quality of infant attachments to professional caregivers: Relation to infant–parent attachments and day care characteristics. *Child Development, 61,* 832–837.

Gormley, W. T., Jr. (1995). *Everybody's children: Child care as public problem.* Washington, DC: Brookings.

Harms, T., Clifford, R. M., & Cryer, D. (1998). *Early Childhood Environment Rating Scale* (Rev. ed.). New York: Teachers College Press.

Heckman, J. (2000). Policies to foster human capital (with discussion). *Research in Economics, 54*(1), 3–56.

Helburn, S. W. (1995). Center structure: Staff policies and characteristics. In S. W. Helburn (Ed.), *Cost, quality, and child outcomes in child care centers: Technical report* (pp. 91–124). Denver: Economics Department, University of Colorado at Denver.

Helburn, S., & Bergmann, B. (2002). *America's child care problem: The way out.* New York: Palgrave for St. Martin's Press.

Hollestelle, K. (2000). *Child Care Center Licensing Study.* Washington, DC: Children's Foundation.

Howes, C., & Hamilton, C. (1992). Children's relationships with caregivers, mothers, and child care teachers. *Child Development, 63,* 859–866.

Howes, C., & Hamilton, C. (1993). The changing experience of child care: Changes in teachers and teacher–child relationships and children's social competence with peers. *Early Childhood Research Quarterly, 8,* 15–32.

Howes, C., Phillips, D., & Whitebook, M. (1992). Thresholds of quality in child care centers and children's social and emotional development. *Child Development, 63,* 449–460.

Howes, C., Smith, E., & Galinsky, E. (1995). *The Florida Child Care Quality Improvement Study: Interim report.* New York: Families and Work Institute.

Kontos, S., Howes, C., Shinn, M., & Galinksy, E. (1995). *Quality in family child care and relative care.* New York: Teachers College Press/Columbia University.

Lamb, M. E. (1998). Nonparental child care: Context, quality, correlates, and consequences. In W. Damon (Ed.), *Handbook of child psychology: Vol. 4. Child psychology in practice* (pp. 73–133). New York: Wiley.

Loeb, S., Fuller, B., Kagan, S. L., & Carrol, B. (2004). Child care in poor communities: Early learning effects of type, quality, and stability. *Child Development, 75,* 47–65.

Love, J. M., Harrison, L., Sagi-Schwartz, A., van IJzendoorn, M. H., Ross, C., Ungerer, J. A., Raikes, H., Brady-Smith, C., Boller, K., Brooks-Gunn, J., Constantine, J., Kisker, E. E., Paulsell, D., & Chazan-Cohen, R. (2003). Child care quality matters: How conclusions may vary with context. *Child Development, 74,* 1021–1033.

McCabe, L., Brady-Smith, C., & Brooks-Gunn, J. (in press). A tale of two American cities: Maternal employment and child care in fragile families with young children. In N. Cabrera, R. Hutchens, & H. E. Peters (Eds.), *From welfare to childcare: What happens to young children when mothers exchange welfare for work?* Mahwah, NJ: Erlbaum.

McCartney, K. (in press). The family–child care mesosystem. In A. Clarke-Stewart & J. Dunn (Eds.), *Families count: Effects on child and adolescent development.* Cambridge: Cambridge University Press.

McCartney, K., Dearing, E., & Taylor, B. A. (2003, April). *Is higher-quality child care an intervention for children from low-income families?* Paper presented at the Biennial Meeting of the Society for Research in Child Development, Tampa, FL.

McCartney, K., & Galanopoulos, A. (1988). Child care and attachment: A new frontier the second time around. *American Journal of Orthopsychiatry, 58,* 16–24.

McCartney, K., & Rosenthal, R. (2000). Effect size, practical importance, and social policy for children. *Child Development, 71,* 173–180.

Marsland, K., Zigler, E., & Martinez, A. (2003). *Regulation of infant and toddler child care: Are state requirements for centers adequate?* Unpublished manuscript. New Haven, CT: Yale University.

Modigliani, K., & Bromer, J. (1997). *The providers' self-study workbook: Quality standards for NAFCC accreditation.* Boston: Wheelock College Family Child Care Project.

Morris, P., Gennetian, L. A., & Knox, V. (2002, March). *Welfare policies matter for children and youth: Lessons for TANF reauthorization.* New York: Manpower Research Demonstration Corporation.

Nall Bales, S. N. (1999). Early childhood education and the framing wars. In Benton Foundation (Ed.), *Effective language for discussing early childhood education and policy* (pp. 2–6). Washington, DC: Benton Foundation.

National Center for Education Statistics. (2002). *The condition of education 2002.* (NCES 2002–025). Washington, DC: US Government Printing Office. Retrieved from *http://nces.ed.gov/pubs2002/2002025.pdf*

Newcombe, N. S. (2003). Some controls control too much. *Child Development, 74,* 1050–1052.

NICHD Early Child Care Research Network. (1996). Characteristics of infant child care: Factors contributing to positive caregiving. *Early Childhood Research Quarterly, 11*(3), 269–306.

NICHD Early Child Care Research Network. (1997). Child care in the first year of life. *Merrill–Palmer Quarterly, 43*(3), 340–360.

NICHD Early Child Care Research Network. (1998). Relations between family predictors and child outcomes: Are they weaker for children in child care? *Developmental Psychology, 43,* 1119–1128.

NICHD Early Child Care Research Network. (1999). Child outcomes when child care center classes meet recommended standards for quality. *American Journal of Public Health, 89,* 1072–1077.

NICHD Early Child Care Research Network. (2000). The relation of child care to cognitive and language development. *Child Development, 71,* 960–980.

NICHD Early Child Care Research Network. (2001). Nonmaternal care and family factors in early development: An overview of the NICHD Study of Early Child Care. *Journal of Applied Developmental Psychology, 22,* 559–579.

NICHD Early Child Care Research Network. (2002a). Child care structure, process, outcome: Direct and indirect effects of child care quality on young children's development. *Psychological Science, 13,* 199–206.

NICHD Early Child Care Research Network. (2002b). Early child care and children's development prior to school entry: Results from the NICHD Study of Early Child Care. *American Educational Research Journal, 39,* 133–164.

NICHD Early Child Care Research Network. (2003). Does amount of time spent in child care predict socioemotional adjustment during the transition to kindergarten? *Child Development, 74,* 976–1005.

NICHD Early Child Care Research Network (2005). Child care in the first yeat of life. In NICHD Early Child Care Research Network (Ed.), *Child care and child development: Results from the NICHD Study of Early Child Care and Youth Development* (pp. 39–49). New York: Guilford Press.

NICHD Early Child Care Research Network & Duncan, G. (2003). Modeling the impacts of child care quality on children's preschool cognitive development. *Child Development, 74,* 1454–1475.

Paulsell, D., Kisker, E. E., Raikes, H., Love, J. M., & Jerald, J. (in press). Child care in Early Head Start: Challenges, successes, and strategies for supporting quality. In N. Cabrera, R. Hutchens, & H. E. Peters (Eds.), *From welfare to childcare: What happens to young children when single mothers exchange welfare for work?* Mahwah, NJ: Erlbaum.

Peisner-Feinberg, E. S., Burchinal, M. R., Clifford, R. M., Culkin, M. L., Howes, C., Kagan, S. L., & Yazejian, N. (2001). The relation of preschool child-care quality to children's cognitive and social developmental trajectories through second grade. *Child Development, 72,* 1534–1553.

Pew Research Center for the People and the Press. (1998). *Deconstructing distrust: how Americans view government.* Washington, DC: Pew. Available at *http://people-press.org/trustrpt.htm*

Phillips, D. (in press). Child care as risk or protection in the context of welfare reform. In N. Cabrera, R. Hutchens, & H.E. Peters (Eds.). *From welfare to childcare: What happens to young children when single mothers exchange welfare for work?* Mahwah, NJ: Erlbaum.

Phillips, D., & Adams, G. (2001). Child care and our youngest children. *The Future of Children, 11*(1), 35–51.

Phillips, D., Howes, C., & Whitebook, M. (1992). The social policy context of child care: Effects on quality. *American Journal of Community Psychology, 20*(1), 25–51.

Phillips, D., Lande, J., & Goldberg, M. (1990). The state of child care regulation: A comparative analysis. *Early Childhood Research Quarterly, 5,* 151–179.

Phillips, D., Mekos, D., Scarr, S., McCartney, K., & Abott-Shim, M. (2001). Paths to quality child care: Structural and contextual influences on children's classroom environments. *Early Childhood Research Quarterly, 15,* 475–496.

Phillips, D., Voran, M., Kisker, E., Howes, C., & Whitebook, M. (1994). Child care for children in poverty: Opportunity or inequality? *Child Development, 65,* 472–492.

Phillips, D., Whitebook, M., & Crowell, N. (2003, April 24–7). *Who leaves? Who stays? Stability and quality of the child care workforce through time.* Paper presented at the meetings of the Society for Research in Child Development, Tampa, FL.

Phillipsen, L., Burchinal, M. R., Howes, C., & Cryer, D. (1997).The prediction of process quality from structural features of child care. *Early Childhood Research Quarterly, 12,* 281–304.

Ramey, C. (2000). Helping children get started right: The benefits of early childhood intervention. In K. Bogenschneider & J. Mills (Eds.), *Helping poor kids succeed: Welfare, tax and early intervention policies* (Wisconsin Family Impact Seminar Briefing Report No.14, pp. 21–28). Madison, WI: University of Wisconsin Center for Excellence in Family Studies.

Ramey, C., Bryant, D. M., & Suarez, T. M. (1985). Preschool compensatory education and the modifiability of intelligence: A critical review. In D. K. Detterman (Ed.), *Current topics in human intelligence: Vol: 1. Research methodology* (pp. 247–296). Norwood, NJ: Ablex.

Rhodes, S., & Hennessy, E. (2000). The effects of specialized training on caregivers and children in early-years settings: An evaluation of the foundation course in playgroup practices. *Early Childhood Research Quarterly, 15,* 559–576.

Robins, P. K. (2003, June). *The effects of welfare policy on child care decisions: Evidence from ten experimental welfare-to-work programs.* Summary of Key Findings Working Paper Series, No. 18. New York: Manpower Demonstration Research Corporation.

Scarr, S. (1998). American child care today. *American Psychologist, 53,* 95–108.

Scarr, S., Eisenberg, N., & Deater-Deckard, K. (1994). Measurement of quality in child care centers. *Early Childhood Research Quarterly, 9,* 131–151.

Smith, C., Perou, R., & Lesesne, C. (2002). Parent education. In M. H. Bornstein (Ed.), *Handbook of parenting: Vol. 4. Applied parenting* (2nd ed., pp. 389–410). Mahwah: NJ: Erlbaum.

Sroufe, L. A. (1988). A developmental perspective on day care. *Early Childhood Research Quarterly, 3,* 283–291.

Sylvester, K. (2001). Caring for our youngest: Public attitudes in the United States. *The Future of Children, 11*(1), 53–61.

US Bureau of Labor Statistics. (1998). *Occupational projections and training data.* Washington, DC: US Department of Labor.

Votruba-Drzal, E., Coley, R. L., & Chase-Landsale, P. L. (2004). Child care and low-income children's development: Direct and moderated effects. *Child Development, 75,* 296–312.

Weikart, D. P. (1998). Changing early childhood development through educational intervention. *Preventive Medicine, 27,* 233–237.

Werner, E. E., & Smith, R. S. (1992). *Overcoming the odds.* Ithaca, NY: Cornell University Press.

Whitebook, M., Howes, C., & Phillips, D. (1990). *Who cares? Child care teachers and the quality of care in America: Final report of the National Child Care Staffing Study.* Washington, DC: Center for the Child Care Workforce.

Whitebook, M., & Sakai, L. (2004). *By a thread: How child care centers hold on to teachers, how teachers build lasting careers.* Kalamazoo, MI: W. E. Upjohn Institute for Employment Research.

Young, Y. T., Marsland, K. W., & Zigler, E. (1997). The regulatory status of center-based infant and toddler child care. *American Journal of Orthopsychiatry, 67,* 535–544.

24

The Social Ecology of the Transition to School: Classrooms, Families, and Children

Robert C. Pianta and Sara Rimm-Kaufman

Beginning with the birth of Head Start and continuing in the 1990s with the National Education Goals, the United States' educational spotlight has been trained on young children for several decades (Carnegie Task Force, 1994; Meisels, 1999; Shonkoff & Phillips, 2000). A large part of the attention to the education of young children involves describing, understanding, and improving interactions and transactions that take place within and between the various settings experienced by young children that make up the social ecology of the transition period. Efforts related to early education are so prominent that policy (Katz, 1987; Vecchiotti, 2003), program development (National Association for the Education of Young Children, 1998; Schweinhart, Barnes, & Weikart, 1993; Southeastern Regional Vision for Education, 1995), and practice (Holtzman, 1992; Huffman & Speer, 2000) initiatives have themselves become part of the ecology of transition. In relation to the ecology of school transition, the present chapter addresses conceptualization, structural features of transition, the quality of early education settings, families and their associations with educational settings, and school-based policies and practices. At all levels – structural features, process, and practices – it will be evident that there is as much variation in the ecology of school transition as there is in children's skills and abilities as they proceed through this period.

A Conceptual Model of Early Schooling and Individual Differences

We consider the period of transition to school to be bounded, roughly, by the ages 3 and 7, during which attention increasingly is focused on children's "readiness for school" and the programs and practices that support such an outcome. In their approach to transition to school, Pianta and Walsh (1996) argued that it may be more accurate to characterize readiness as a property not of children, but, instead, of the *transition ecology*: an organized system of interactions and transactions among persons (parents, teachers, children), settings (home, school, child care), and institutions (community, governments) that are oriented to support developmental and educational progress of children during the period of 3–7 years of age. Distinguishing readiness from the ecology in which it emerges has been a source of great debate, and the resolution of the issues embedded in this debate often shape the actual practices and policies to which children are exposed in this period. Meisels (1999) argues convincingly that conceptualization of readiness and transition drives decisions about assessment and programming that can have dramatic effects on the educational opportunities to which children are exposed during this period. For this reason, we believe it is critical to elaborate on the argument of Pianta and Walsh (1996), to examine the conceptual models used to understand readiness and transition and identify the consequences of adopting such models for policy and practice.

Models of transition

Children's transitions into kindergarten can be thought about in a variety of ways. We describe here two models that have been used in conceptualizing readiness and transition (see Rimm-Kaufmann & Pianta, 2000, for a more complete discussion of these and other models). The more openly developmental and ecologically informed models appear best-suited to the current state of knowledge concerning the forces that shape children's progress through the transition period, although the complexity of such models often poses challenges to application.

In the Rimm-Kaufman and Pianta (2000) framework, a *skills-only* model is discussed as the predominant perspective influencing transition policy and practice. This model reduces the transition period to a focus on the abilities and skills the child displays at a given time. Adjustment during the transition period is understood in terms of child characteristics such as their readiness skills, chronological age, or level of maturation, with little to no focus on ecological, or even developmental, features. The skills-only model fails to acknowledge evidence indicating that children's skills are remarkably unstable during this period, both across time and across settings; stability for children's academic and cognitive skills from preschool to kindergarten is only moderate while for social skills, the effect size is even smaller (La Paro & Pianta, 2001). It is certainly conceivable that the developmental transformations taking place in this period are at least in part related to the ecology within which the transformations occur.

Despite its inadequacies, it is important to note that a wide range of policy and practice initiatives draw on the skills-only model in fundamental ways. The vast majority of states and school systems that employ developmental screenings or other forms of "readiness assessment" and then make decisions regarding children's suitability for educational programs or even attending kindergarten based on these assessments are in part adopting the "skills-only" model of transition. At the federal level this model is reflected in one of the more contentious legislative and policy decisions related to accountability in early childhood education: conducting individual assessments of skills in literacy and math for all children attending Head Start programs across the US, nearly 500,000 3- and 4-year-olds (Administration on Children, Youth and Families [ACYF], 2002; Meisels & Atkins-Burnett, 2000). In more basic form, the skills-only model is evident in policies that focus on age of the child as a marker for readiness, a focus of many discussions between parents and kindergarten teachers (NICHD Early Child Care Research Network [ECCRN], submitted). When accountability mechanisms focus attention on and regulate around "output" in terms of child skills rather than "input" in terms of program quality or educational practices, such mechanisms both reinforce and draw upon a view that the transition period can be reduced to readiness skills of children.

More developmentally and ecologically informed models of the transition period (Belsky & MacKinnon, 1994; Meisels, 1999; Rimm-Kaufman & Pianta, 2000; Shonkoff & Phillips, 2000) attend to the diverse set of inputs to the child during this period and the ways in which such inputs are linked with one another at any given time. Of these models, the most comprehensive attend to the integration of developmental and ecological considerations during this period. In a *developmental/ecological* model (see Figure 24.1), child, family, school, peer, and community factors are interconnected and interdependent with one another not only at a given time but throughout the transition period (Rimm-Kaufman & Pianta, 2000). This perspective considers the key changes in relationships among the child, school, family, and community as the child moves from pre-kindergarten experiences into formal schooling, and the ways in which these relationships figure prominently in the development and transformation of children's competencies. Thus, rather than understanding children's transition solely in terms of the child's skills, or influences on those skills at any given time, this perspective emphasizes the organization of assets within a social ecology, how this organization emerges and how it operates to support (or inhibit) child competence over time. In this way, efforts to assess and improve school readiness, following from this developmental/ecological definition, are broad-based and focused on the settings and resources to which children are exposed from very early in life (e.g., Bryant, Clifford, Saluja et al., 2002; Ripple, Gilliam, Chanana, & Zigler, 1999).

Recent initiatives related to "Ready Schools" apply the developmental/ecological model by focusing on preschool and school policies and practices in relation to transition, early childhood programming and assessment, and relationships with families and preschools. In fact, an often neglected aspect of the National Education Goals Panel's (NEGP) work on Goal One (the readiness goal) was to conceptualize and define "Ready Schools" and produce a guide for state and local policy makers that outlined key features of ready schools, nearly all of which were concerned with the ecology of school transition. In the report *Ready Schools*, the National Education Goals Panel (1998, p. 5) outlines ten keys to ready schools, at least three of which directly call attention to the importance of the transition ecology (Pianta & Walsh, 1996; Rimm-Kaufman & Pianta, 2000). These include: smoothing the transition between home and school, ensuring continuity between early care and education programs and elementary schools, and serving children in communities. Even though the focus of the Goals Panel's efforts was to call attention to the promotive effect of transition support, the report also suggests that effective transition practices may be particularly helpful for children and families at risk of disengagement.

The ready schools principles and framework are being implemented through initiatives supported by the Council of Chief State School Officers, High Scope Foundation, the

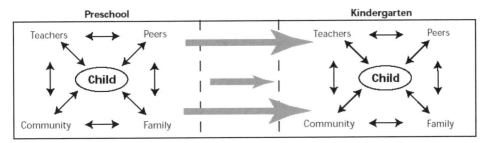

Figure 24.1   The ecological and dynamic model of transition.

Pathways Mapping Initiative (*http://www.PathwaysToOutcomes.org*) of the Project on Effective Interventions at Harvard University, and the National Governors Association Task Force on School Readiness (National Governors Association Center for Best Practices, 2004). Yet, despite recognition that success in the early years of school is reflective of, and embedded in, developmental and ecological processes, most efforts in relation to readiness and transition focus on whether children know their colors or their alphabet (Love, Logue, Trudeau, & Thayer, 1992; Meisels, 1999).

Structural features of the transition ecology

One aspect of the transition period that makes it unique is the collision of children's competencies with the structuring of resources that schools and communities offer in kindergarten (Pianta & Walsh, 1996). In fact, one might argue that the very nature of this as a *transition* period is due to this meshing of individual differences among children (and families) with variation in resources and structures of schools (and communities).

Pre-kindergarten programs are one example of the opening of new niches in the transition ecology; state funds allocated to pre-kindergarten programs increased from $200 million in 1988 to almost $2 billion by 1999 (Wohl, 2001), and in the 2000–2001 school year at least thirty-four states and the District of Columbia were offering pre-kindergarten programs, with many programs under the auspices of public schools (Bryant, Clifford, Saluja et al., 2002). Parents' decisions to enroll their children in an assortment of early education programs also open opportunities for children; the 2000 Current Population Survey indicated that 52% of parents reported their 3- and 4-year-old children were "in school"– some 4 million children overall, suggesting that many families consider center-based child care or community-based or private preschools as "school" of some sort (US Census Bureau, 2000). Clearly, for the majority of children in the United States, coming to kindergarten is not their first experience with formal programming directed at educationally relevant outcomes (Pianta & Walsh, 1996). If this is true, then the "transition" to school may have less to do with how much children change and more to do with how settings and environments, and their relations with one another, are structured and change during this period.

Structural features of transition ecologies differ as much as children do. This is quite clear when one considers policies that regulate access to educational opportunity. As just one example at the structural level, policies regulating kindergarten are highly variable across states: kindergarten attendance is mandatory in some states and optional in others (Vecchiotti, 2003); the age for compulsory school attendance in the United States ranges from 5 to 8 (Education Commission of the States, 2000); kindergarten lasts two and one-half hours in some states, and a full day (6–7 hours) in others (Vecchiotti, 2003), while, as just noted, in some states kindergarten attendance is not even mandatory; and state-funded pre-kindergarten programs range from as short as 2½ hours per day to as long as 10 hours per day (Bryant, Clifford, Saluja et al., 2002).

Who gets access to resources is another point of variation across states. Because early childhood education is costly (Dwyer, Chait, & McKee, 2000), states have to choose between providing more children with part-day pre-kindergarten or providing fewer, but needier children, with longer pre-kindergarten programs, thus cutting opportunity for some. Most states make this decision to limit access in terms of the "risk" level of the child or family: for example, 79% of states with pre-kindergarten programs chose to focus on the children who were most "at risk," yet universal access is a stated goal for many (Bryant, Clifford, Saluja et al., 2002).

Policies also shape the attributes and skills of the adults who staff elementary school and preschool educational settings. At the kindergarten level, nearly all states require a Bachelor's degree and some level of specialized training in education for adults to be certified to teach, and in practice this appears to be realized for well over 95% of the teachers in kindergarten classrooms (National Center for Education Statistics [NCES], 1994, 1999; Pianta, La Paro, Payne, Cox, & Bradley, 2002). However, in the preschool years, the teachers to whom children are exposed vary widely in their level of training and, on average, receive less training and education than their elementary-school counterparts. For example, states vary widely in the education level required to teach pre-kindergarten. Minimum requirements range from a Child Development Associate (CDA) certificate to an Associate's degree to a Bachelor's degree (Bryant, Clifford, Saluja et al., 2002). Furthermore, some states require that the two- or four-year degree be in early childhood education or child development, while others do not specify a field of study.

Findings from the National Center for Early Development and Learning's (NCEDL) Multi-State Pre-Kindergarten study (Clifford et al., 2005) show that unlike the elementary workforce, only 70% of pre-kindergarten teachers had at least a Bachelor's degree, while 15% had a two-year degree and 16% had no formal degree past high school. This study estimated that about half (51%) of pre-kindergarten teachers had attained a Bachelor's degree *and* certification to teach 4-year-olds, a figure of combined education and credentialing that is substantially lower than the parallel figure combining education and training for elementary-school teachers (NCES, 1999). For children who do not receive early education services in pre-kindergarten programs but who are enrolled in the less regulated ecology of family- or center-based child care, exposure to credentialed or degreed staff is even lower (Helburn, 1995; Phillipsen, Cryer, & Howes, 1995; NICHD ECCRN, 2002). By way of comparison, about 33% of teachers in Head Start have a Bachelor's degree or higher (ACYF, 2001) and 22% of teachers in Head Start have a Bachelor's degree or higher in early childhood education-related areas (ACYF, 2002).

Finally, to the extent that program access, length of program, and attributes of program staff reflect policy decisions that shape opportunities for children during the transition period, such opportunities appear more restricted or of lesser quality for children of color or children in poverty. One finding of the NCEDL Pre-Kindergarten study (Clifford et al., 2005) was that poor children were more likely to be taught by teachers with lower qualifications (e.g., less than a Bachelor's degree), and were more likely to be exposed to shorter-day programs. Children in poverty or children of color are more likely to experience structural discontinuities in the transition ecology in other ways as well. For example, pre-kindergarten and kindergarten children are much more likely to be African-American or Latino than their teachers (Clifford et al., in press; NCES, 1999) and far more likely to speak a language different than their teacher (Clifford et al., 2005) than other children.

How do early educational environments shape child competencies? Quality

Nearly every single piece of state legislation that provides support for the implementation and expansion of educational programs for young children, whether in the pre- or post-kindergarten years, emphasizes that such programs should be of high quality and use appropriate practices (e.g., Bryant, Clifford, Early et al., 2002; Clifford et al., 2005; NCES 2003; NEGP, 1995; Ripple et al., 1999). In this chapter we do not describe quality in child care settings, as that is a focus of the chapter by Deborah Phillips, Kathleen McCartney, and Amy Sussman in the present volume, but instead focus on pre-kindergarten and elementary-classroom quality.

Several large-scale observational research efforts related to early education report results pertaining to the quality of classroom experiences in pre-kindergarten, kindergarten, and first grade. These include the observations of: approximately 1000 children in first grade conducted by the NICHD Study of Early Child Care and Youth Development (NICHD ECCRN, 2002); the 240 pre-kindergarten classrooms in six states (Bryant, Clifford, Early et al., 2002) that are part of the NCEDL's Multi-State Pre-Kindergarten Study; and 223 kindergarten classrooms involved in the NICHD SECCYD observed in three states (Pianta et al., 2002). In addition, observations of global quality have been conducted in Head Start settings that are part of the Family and Child Experience Survey (FACES) and the Head Start Transition studies (ACYF, 1999, 2000, 2001, 2002; see also Love, Tarullo, Raikes, & Chazan-Cohen, this volume). As a set, these results capture the best estimate to date of the state of the classroom sector of the transition ecology in America.

There are two main conclusions that can be drawn from this work. First, despite variation from study to study, on average, the quality of the typical early education setting is mediocre with regard to the kind of interactions and stimulation known to produce developmental gains for children (NICHD ECCRN, 2002; La Paro, Pianta, & Stuhlman, 2004). Second, there is tremendous variation in quality offered to children from time to time or setting to setting; at times this variation is systematically related to factors such as family income or teacher characteristics and at times there is little or no relation between quality and the parameters used to regulate or influence it (Hamre & Bridges, 2004; NICHD ECCRN, 2002; Pianta et al., 2002).

The best available information on pre-kindergarten program quality and child out-comes is available in the NCEDL six-state study of pre-kindergarten, which reports marked variation in the nature and quality of educational experiences offered to children in pre-k, and that, on average, there is considerable room for improvement (Pianta et al., 2005). Importantly, the six states participating in the NCEDL study were chosen because they had all been implementing pre-kindergarten for some years and so were somewhat mature with regard to infrastructure. Across the 250 classrooms sampled in six states in the NCEDL study, overall average classroom quality was mediocre (below the "5" level on the Early Childhood Environment Rating Scale), with the full range of quality rep-resented. Ratings of classroom "productivity" and "emotional quality" using the Classroom Assessment Scoring System (Pianta, La Paro, & Hamre, 2004) were below the mid-point on a seven-point scale, and ratings of "quality of feedback" to students averaged a "2" despite teachers being fully credentialed, experienced, and using an organized curriculum (Pianta et al., 2005). Individual children in some pre-kindergarten classrooms were exposed to few, if any, instances of any form of literacy-focused activities, whereas in other classrooms children received more than an hour of exposure to literacy-related activities, including narrative story telling, practice with letters, rhyming games, and listening.

In kindergarten and first grade the pattern of low–moderate quality and variation is the same (NICHD ECCRN, 2002; Pianta et al., 2002). For example, although for the most part the typical child in an early elementary classroom receives instruction in whole-group experiences, in some classrooms children are never taught in a whole group while in others this is the mode of instruction all day. And although literacy instruction is the predominant activity offered to children in kindergarten and first grade, in a substantial number of classrooms children were offered no literacy activities at all. In some kinder-garten or first-grade classrooms, 100% of the activity observed in a morning-long block was organized as teacher-directed whole-group instruction. In others, none of the activi-ties observed could be coded as this form of instruction.

Despite this exceptional variability, the picture that emerges of the typical PreK-1 early education classroom is: whole-group instruction, a somewhat positive social environment, and low levels of productivity and engagement in learning-related activities. These envir-onments can be characterized as socially positive but instructionally passive: children listen and watch, much time is spent on routines or management of materials, and chil-dren have little direct contact with teachers in instructional or scaffolding-type interac-tions that stimulate learning. These classrooms appear low in "intentionality," a term that refers to directed, designed interactions between children and teachers in which teachers purposefully challenge, scaffold, and extend children's skills (Bryant, Clifford, Early et al., 2002; NICHD ECCRN, 2002; Pianta, 2003).

When examining the same children's experiences over time, it is evident that variation in classroom quality and experience remains the rule rather than the exception. Recent studies show that the associations between, for example, having a sensitive teacher prior to going to school and having one rated as sensitive in kindergarten, first grade, or third grade are barely significant (NICHD ECCRN, 2004, 2005). Furthermore, even in the same schools using the same curriculum, the same child moving through the early grades is not likely to be exposed to similar levels of instructional activities in reading or math (NICHD ECCRN, 2005).

Families and the transition ecology

The contribution of family processes to the competencies of young children as they enter school is well documented (Alexander & Entwisle, 1988; Barth & Parke, 1996; Pianta & Harbers, 1996). Families have direct effects on readiness; parental sensitivity and stimulation have a clear and frequently documented relation with early school success (Comer & Haynes, 1991; Estrada, Arsenio, Hess, & Holloway, 1985; Pianta & Harbers, 1996; Pianta, Smith, & Reeve, 1991; Ramey & Campbell, 1991). Parents' behaviors toward their children and the stimulation, materials, and routines they provide in the home environment support the self-regulatory skills, motivation, language, pre-literacy, and social skills that underlie most of what children are called upon to do in school (Belsky & MacKinnon, 1994; Bradley, Caldwell, & Rock, 1988; Pianta & Walsh, 1996). The evidence for a direct connection between family process variables and children's early school adjustment points to the causal impact of interactions within the family on the child's competencies.

But there are also less direct avenues by which families influence their children's early school success (Pianta & Walsh, 1996; Rimm-Kaufman & Pianta, 2000). For example, children from highly transient families may face a disadvantage because they are less likely to experience continuity in peer relationships (Masten, Miliotis, Graham-Bermann, Ramirez, & Neeman, 1993). Similarly, parent involvement, characterized by communication with teachers, coherence between home and school learning, mutual support, and cooperative decision making between parents and teacher, is also associated with children's success in school (Epstein, 1996; Rimm-Kaufman, Pianta, Cox, & Bradley, 2003). Family culture shapes early school transition outcomes by conveying academic values to their children: involved parents may reinforce school-based practices at home as they teach academic skills and reinforce attitudes and motivation to help children learn (Bempechat, 1990). There is very little doubt that family process and culture and family–school linkages are key components of the transition ecology.

Families' cultural background clearly plays a role in the transition ecology. Because school adjustment often refers to a set of specific competencies (e.g., the ability to sit still, to stay on-task), children who have not been socialized to this set of norms are often identified as having problems adjusting to school (Mokuau & Tauili'ili, 1998; Skinner, Bryant, Coffman, & Campbell, 1998). Cultural backgrounds also contribute to the types of relationships that develop between home and school as well as the perceptions and misperceptions that families and schools hold toward each other. Families from Latino cultures exemplify a notable paradox. Latino families have been described as holding strong values for education (Zuniga, 1998) and appear to hold very positive views of their children's teachers and school (Pew Hispanic Center/Kaiser Family Foundation, 2004), views that are more optimistic about school than those held by comparable African-American or European-American families. However, schools and teachers often do not perceive Latino families as involved and interested in their children's education. Often, families do not become actively involved in traditional family involvement activities because they experience a language barrier, while also feeling that they have little to offer since they view teachers as the professionals responsible for educating their children (Zuniga, 1998). Such problems are particularly prominent in the transition to kindergarten when families from other cultures begin to participate in the public school system and issues of language, expectations, and roles become critical features in the connection between home and school. Most teachers report little or no training in how to understand and communicate with families from diverse ethnic or cultural backgrounds.

The literature on parent–teacher or parent–school relationships provides a window on the dynamic nature of the transition to kindergarten. In theory and in practice, parent involvement with schooling forms the foundation for the home–school relationship and contributes to children's achievement, attitudes, and aspirations, even beyond the effects of family socio-economic status and student ability (Epstein, 1987; Izzo, Weissberg, Kasprow, & Fendrich, 1999). How does parent involvement work? Parents socialize their children academically when they promote expectations for success that are consistent with the school's goals and expectations. (Bempechat, 1990; Reynolds, 1989). If parents and teachers communicate about curriculum and homework, parents may monitor their children's progress more appropriately (Epstein, 1992; Slaughter-Defoe, Nakagawa, Takanishi, & Johnson, 1990). When parents and teachers create consistent contingencies for good behavior, parents may offer home-based reinforcements shown to improve school behavior (Barth, 1979). Overall, parents and teachers who create academic and social goals together enhance the continuity between home and school and create an integrated experience for the child (Comer & Haynes, 1991). Thus, the link between two contexts – home and school – may be an important influence on children's school success as a function of multiple pathways.

Communication, cooperation, mutual respect, and reciprocity are key features of the quality of the home–school relationship (Comer & Haynes, 1991) and probably other relationships in the transition ecology. In terms of communication, although both parents and teachers determine the quality of parent–teacher relationships, the primary initiator of contact shifts from the parent to the teacher as the child moves from preschool to kindergarten. Preschool programs are often designed to foster relationships between teachers and parents and initiate frequent contact with parents, something they do with great success (NCES, 2000). However, kindergarten programs typically emphasize parent contact less and initiate such contact with decreasing frequency and increasing selectivity (e.g., only for problems) and formality (e.g., conferences, meetings) (Rimm-Kaufman & Pianta, 1999). Thus, parents experience a shift and reorganization of their relationship with their child's educational setting when the child enters school.

Contact is often school-based and/or casual in preschool. Parents of preschool children are more involved in school-based activities (e.g., classroom volunteering, meeting with other parents to schedule activities for the school) than parents in kindergarten (Fantuzzo, Tighe, & Childs, 2000). Further, the families who are highly involved and communicate frequently with their child's preschool teachers are not necessarily the same as those who show high family involvement and communication in kindergarten (Rimm-Kaufman & Pianta, in press). Thus, one facet of the transition to school is a shift in the organization of contact in the parent–teacher relationship (Epstein, 1996), a shift that appear to be orchestrated by characteristics, priorities, and resources of the preschool and/or kindergarten programs (Oden & Ricks, 1990; Rimm-Kaufman & Pianta, in press).

Special educators have devoted considerable resources to understanding the transition to school and intervening both formally and informally to improve it for children (Fowler, Schwartz, & Atwater, 1991; Katims & Pierce, 1995; Repetto & Correa, 1996; Roberts, Akers, & Behl, 1996; Rous, Hemmeter, & Schuster, 1994). This literature emphasizes the ways in which quality transitions are defined by maintenance of relationships over time and among multiple contexts, including parents/family, preschool service providers, health service providers, school-based service providers, and others (Fowler et al., 1991). For example, parents move from being the primary coordinators of services to sharing this responsibility with child care specialists and ultimately to working more closely with educational agencies to coordinate and identify appropriate programming and special services (Alper, Schloss, & Schloss, 1996). Ideally, the successful coordination of services incorporates interagency collaboration, staff and family involvement in the transition process, as well as suitable preparation for the child (Rous et al., 1994).

For children with identified special needs, the formal nature of the transition ecology contrasts with the experience of most other children. During the period of transition, school-based programs are mandated to provide parents with information addressing their legal rights, placement options for their child, methods for family involvement, and approaches to prepare their child for transition (Rous et al., 1994). These formalized linkages emphasize informational connections across settings (Pianta & Kraft-Sayre, 2003) reflected in Individualized Education Program planning, transfer of assessment information and records, and careful attention to curriculum consistency. Although these more formalized, contextually sensitive approaches to transition are routinely implemented for children with special needs, they have seldom been translated into policy or practice for typically developing children.

Finally, the literature on family–school relationships and their development over time suggests the need to re-conceptualize how we think about the *outcomes* of early school transition. That home–school links are such an important part of the transition ecology that they contribute heavily to children's school competence during this and subsequent periods, *and* that the transition to school is a period in which every family (parent) of an entering child begins a new relationship with that child's school or teacher suggests that family–school links should indeed be considered an *outcome* of the early school transition, not a correlate or antecedent. Thus a child's competence in a kindergarten classroom may not be the only, or best, outcome measure of a successful transition; instead, the quality of the parents' relationships with teacher and school staff, and their relationship with the child's schooling, may be an equally valid indicator of transition outcome, and one that may forecast later school success.

School-based policies and practices in the transition to school

In the report *Ready Schools* (NEGP, 1998), the authors describe different aspects of the transition ecology from the perspective of elementary school actions:

> Some districts and schools reach out to local families well before the children reach age five. In written or personal communications, such districts and schools may suggest steps that

parents can take . . . to ensure that their children get off to a strong, healthy, start. . . . Many schools have found that home visits by teachers or principals before children enter school can have a substantial impact on kindergartners' adjustment . . . lively and reassuring orientation sessions for parents and children are also helpful . . . [and] should allow plenty of time for question-and-answer sessions. . . . Parents need to know that they have standing invitation to visit the school . . . . (pp. 6–7)

The language of the Goals Panel conveys a relationship focus in efforts to improve the transition ecology and emphasizes positive connections between home, preschool, and school that are based on personal contacts and ongoing communication concerning curriculum and activities. Pianta and Kraft-Sayre (2003) suggest two forms of linkage in the transition ecology: *social* (e.g., involving personal relationships, formal or informal social networks that address social and emotional needs of participants) and *informational* (connections that provide information to participants). However, despite the importance accorded the transition period by a large number of educational policy makers, practitioners, and researchers, there has been little research on the nature and course of children's transition experiences and the activities of schools, preschools, and families that form social and informational links in the transition ecology. Most studies, as the Goals Panel notes, lead to the conclusion that "transition activities . . . are the exception rather than the rule in our public schools" (NEGP, 1998, p. 7).

In the first systematic national survey of teachers' transition practices, Love et al. (1992), reported that roughly 20% of US schools had a range of transition activities that met the needs of families and students for information and personal contact with the school. This finding suggests that, at that time, transition activities were not a specific focus of educational practice or policy *per se*. In 1995 the NCEDL, building on the work of Love et al. (1992), conducted a comprehensive survey of kindergarten teachers' practices and attitudes related to transition and school readiness in a national sample of more than 3500 teachers in the United States. This survey was fielded as the first of the Center's initiatives to understand more systematically, and eventually intervene in, the transition ecology.

In one of the first sets of results from this survey, teachers reported on their use of practices related to the transition of children into kindergarten in the 1996–1997 academic year and barriers to implementing transition practices (Pianta, Cox, Early, & Taylor, 1999). Use of practices related to the transition into kindergarten was reported as near-universal; the most frequently reported practice (talking with the child's parent after school starts) was employed by 95% of the sample. As has been the case with other studies of transition (Love et al., 1992; Rathbun & Germino-Haushren, 2001) the most frequently reported practices are those that take place after the start of school and/or involve low-intensity, generic contact (e.g., flyers, brochures, group open-houses). Not surprisingly, practices that involved in-person contacts with children or families were used least often, as were practices that involved contact between schools and children or families before the start of school. As schools (or districts) become increasingly urban, have higher levels of minority and/or poverty representation, personal contacts are reported less often and low-intensity, after-the-start-of-school contacts are more common. More than 40% of teachers reported that their district did not have a plan or policy related to the transition into kindergarten.

The same NCEDL sample of regular education public school kindergarten teachers also provided information about transition practices for young children with special needs transitioning into regular education kindergarten and first-grade classrooms, a common occurrence in public education (Wolery, 1999). Although over 80% of regular education kindergarten teachers and over 50% of teachers used some form of transition practice for a special needs student, as was the case for non-special education students, the most frequently reported transition practice was sending a parent a letter after school started, or having children visit a first-grade classroom. Thus use of transition practices was nearly identical for teachers with and without children with special needs in their class; however, teachers with children with special needs in their class generally reported using more individual transition practices that occurred before school started or transition practices that involved coordinating meetings among personnel, a focus of compliance with legislation (Wolery, 1999).

On the whole, findings from surveying teachers suggest the typical transition for children in the United States consists of contact with school that is too little, too late, and too impersonal, a conclusion that is highly consistent with what parents report about the transition experience (Pianta & Kraft-Sayre, 2003). Parents regularly describe a lack of connection to the school, increasingly formalized and negative contact, and a lack of what they believe is information they would find useful for planning for their child's entry to school (Epstein, 2001; Pianta & Kraft-Sayre, 2003). Furthermore, preschool teachers and child care providers routinely report a lack of regular communication and programmatic linkage with school personnel and settings, the absence of integrated curricula and assessment procedures across the transition period, and the absence of transition planning mechanisms in the community (Love et al., 1992; Pianta & Kraft-Sayre, 2003; Rathbun & Germino-Hausken, 2001). To return to the developmental/ecological model of transition, to the extent that the typical transition ecology can be assessed in terms of social or information linkages among preschool staff, parents, and elementary educators, such linkages are scattered, non-systematic, and highly idiosyncratic. The level of variation and idiosyncrasy is so pronounced that some investigators have adopted a research strategy of case study methodology in attempts to describe these links (Epstein, 2001; Pianta & Kraft-Sayre, 2003).

Conclusions and Trends Shaping the Transition Ecology in the Future

Looking ahead, the large-scale investment in pre-kindergarten, the reality of accountability, serious concerns about equity and access to high-quality early educational programming, and the increased likelihood of parental choice and voucher systems as mechanisms for enrolling in school all have the potential to re-shape the ecology of school transition in the next decade.

Investment in preschool education and care programs, whether through public, state-supported pre-kindergartens, community-based preschool, or private center-based child care, has soared (Blank, Shulman, & Ewen, 1999). Increasingly, the worlds of early childhood and elementary education are merging; nearly half of public elementary schools now house a program for children younger than age 5 (Clifford, Early, & Hills, 1999), by the mid-1990s nearly a million children below the age of 5 were in programs in some way tied to schools (Clifford et al., 1999), and a large proportion of children are enrolled in formal, school-like private preschools and center-based childcare (NICHD ECCRN, 2002). Nearly every child goes to "school" before they go to kindergarten.

As the worlds of early education and child care merge, there is increasing pressure to create smooth, organized transitions across settings and across time, so that a child's educational program from ages 3–7 (and a family's experience of it) is *coherent* across settings and not fragmented as a function of location, staffing, or age (Hamre & Bridges, 2004). It is highly likely that the emerging 3–7 educational system will rest on a very wide range of providers and service delivery systems; thus if its potential to improve children's developmental success is to be realized, transition policies and practices will play an integral role in programming in this emergent system of early education services.

The unprecedented level of investment in and attention to early care and education also takes place in the context of a policy climate that emphasizes accountability. Regardless of one's position on the broader issue of accountability *per se*, accountability assessments even for early education and care settings currently rest on direct assessment of children and communication of those results to families and the general public. This is exemplified by the recent adoption of child outcome accountability assessments in Head Start, the use of standardized assessments and "benchmarks" for child performance in pre-kindergarten, and a growing interest on the part of parents in knowing what contributions center-based child care experiences make to their children's school readiness.

However, despite the universal recognition of the importance of quality during this era of accountability, there is a noticeable lack of systematic information, at state, local, or federal levels, gauging whether programs are indeed observed to offer high-quality experience or whether parents and teachers and providers are effectively linked. Although state legislation may mandate high program quality, regulations typically codify the legislative mandate in terms of distal quality indicators such as teacher credentialing or class size (Hamre & Bridges, 2004; Ripple et al., 1999). Yet these distal or structural indicators of quality are by no means equivalent to quality as experienced by children at home or in classrooms (Hamre & Bridges, 2004; NICHD ECCRN, 1999, 2002, 2005).

In conclusion, the transition ecology is a complex aspect of early education and care. This ecology is highly complex and variable; in fact aspects of the transition ecology vary as much as children do. Within the transition ecology, social and informational resources are transmitted across settings, persons, and time through relationships and interactions that have consequences for children's experiences and readiness outcomes. Yet, despite its apparent importance, the transition ecology has not been the subject of extensive research or intervention efforts, although such efforts hold promise for realizing a system of early education services in which children's education is coherent, systematic, and effective.

Note

The work reported herein was supported, in part, under the Educational Research and Development Centers Program, PR/Award Number R307A60004, as administered by the Office of

Educational Research and Improvement, US Department of Education to the National Center for Early Development and Learning. It was also supported by the National Institute of Child Health and Human Development (NICHD) to the NICHD Study of Early Child Care and Youth Development. The NICHD Study of Early Child Care and Youth Development is directed by a Steering Committee and supported by NICHD through a cooperative agreement (U10) that calls for a scientific collaboration between grantees and the NICHD staff. The contents do not necessarily represent the positions or policies of the National Institute on Early Childhood Development and Education, the Office of Educational Research and Improvement, the US Department of Education, or the National Institute of Child Health and Human Development, and endorsement by the federal government should not be assumed.

References

Administration on Children, Youth and Families. (1999). *Head Start program performance measures: Second progress report.* Washington, DC: US Department of Health and Human Services.

Administration on Children, Youth and Families. (2000). *Head Start program performance measures: Longitudinal findings from the FACES study.* Washington, DC: US Department of Health and Human Services.

Administration on Children, Youth and Families. (2001). *Head Start program performance measures: Third progress report.* Washington, DC: US Department of Health and Human Services.

Administration on Children, Youth and Families. (2002). *Head Start program information report* (National Level Summary, Report 5). Washington, DC: US Department of Health and Human Services.

Alexander, K. L., & Entwisle, D. R. (1988). Achievement in the first 2 years of school: Patterns and processes. *Monographs of the Society for Research in Child Development, 53*(2, Serial No. 218).

Alper, S., Schloss, P. J., & Schloss, C. N. (1996). Families of children with disabilities in elementary and middle school: Advocacy models and strategies. *Exceptional Children, 62*(3), 261–70.

Barth, R. (1979). Home-based reinforcement of school behavior: A review and analysis. *Review of Educational Research, 49*(3), 436–458.

Barth, J., & Parke, R. (1996). The impact of the family on children's early school adjustment. In A. J. Sameroff & M. M. Haith (Eds.), *The five to seven year shift: The age of reason and responsibility* (pp. 329–362). Chicago: University of Chicago Press.

Belsky, J., & MacKinnon, C. (1994). Transition to school: Developmental trajectories and school experiences. *Early Education and Development, 5*(2), 106–119.

Bempechat, J. (1990). The role of parent involvement in children's academic achievement: A review of the literature. *Trends and Issues No. 14.* New York: Columbia University, Institution for Urban and Minority Education. (ERIC Document Reproduction Service No. ED 322 285.)

Blank, H., Schulman, K., & Ewen, D. (1999). *Seeds of success: State pre-kindergarten initiatives, 1998–1999.* Washington, DC: Children's Defense Fund.

Bradley, R. H., Caldwell, B. M., & Rock, S. L. (1988). Home environment and school performance: A ten-year follow-up and examination of three models of environmental action. *Child Development, 59*, 852–867.

Bryant, D., Clifford, R., Early, D., Pianta, R., Howes, C., Barbarin, O., & Burchinal, M. (2002, November). *Findings from the NCEDL Multi-State Pre-Kindergarten Study.* Annual meeting of the National Association for the Education of Young Children, New York.

Bryant, D., Clifford, R., Saluja, G., Pianta, R., Early, D., Barbarin, O., Howes, C., & Burchinal,

M. (2002). *Diversity and directions in state pre-kindergarten programs.* Chapel Hill: University of North Carolina, FPG Child Development Institute, NCEDL. Available at *http://www.fpg.unc. edu/~ncedl/PDFs/diversity_direct.pdf*

Carnegie Task Force on Meeting the Needs of Young Children. (1994). *Starting points: Meeting the needs of our youngest children.* New York: Carnegie Corporation of New York.

Clifford, R., Barbarin, O., Chang, F., Early, D., Bryant, D., Howes, C., Burchinal, M., & Pianta, R. (2005). What is pre-kindergarten? Characteristics of public pre-kindergarten programs. *Applied Developmental Science, 9,* 126–143.

Clifford, R., Early, D. M., & Hills, T. (1999). Almost a million children in school before kindergarten. *Young Children, 54*(5), 48–51.

Comer, J. P., & Haynes, N. M. (1991). Parent involvement in schools: An ecological approach. *The Elementary School Journal, 91*(3), 271–277.

Dwyer, C. M., Chait, R., & McKee, P. (2000). *Building strong foundation for early learning.* Washington, DC: US Department of Education, Planning, and Evaluation Service.

Education Commission of the States. (2000). *Easing the transition to kindergarten* [On-line]. Retrieved from *http://www.ecs.org/clearinghouse/12/03/1203.htm*

Epstein, J. L. (1987). Parent involvement: What research says to administrators. *Education and Urban Society, 19*(2), 119–136.

Epstein, J. L. (1992). School and family partnerships. In M. Alkin (Ed.), *Encyclopedia of educational research* (6th ed., pp. 1139–1151). New York: Macmillan.

Epstein, J. L. (1996). Advances in family, community, and school partnerships. *New Schools, New Communities, 12*(3), 5–13.

Epstein, J. L. (2001). *School, family, and community partnerships.* Boulder, CO: Westview.

Estrada, P., Arsenio, W. F., Hess, R. D., & Holloway, S. D. (1985). Affective quality of the mother–child relationship: Longitudinal consequences for children's school-relevant cognitive functioning. *Developmental Psychology, 23*(2), 210–215.

Fantuzzo, J., Tighe, E., & Childs, S. (2000). Family involvement questionnaire: A multivariate assessment of family participation in early childhood education. *Journal of Educational Psychology, 92*(2), 367–376.

Fowler, S. A., Schwartz, I., & Atwater, J. (1991). Perspectives on the transition from preschool to kindergarten for children with disabilities and their families. *Exceptional Children, 58*(2), 136–145.

Hamre, B. K., & Bridges, M. (2004). *Early care and education staff preparation, quality, and child development: A review of the literature.* Manuscript submitted for review.

Helburn, S. W. (1995). Center structure: Staff policies and characteristics. In S. W. Helburn (Ed.), *Cost, quality, and child outcomes in child care centers: Technical report* (pp. 91–124). Denver: Economics Department, University of Colorado at Denver.

Holtzman, W. H. (1992). *School of the future.* Washington, DC: American Psychological Association.

Huffman, L. R., & Speer, P. W. (2000). Academic performance among at-risk children: The role of developmentally appropriate practices. *Early Childhood Research Quarterly, 15*(2), 167–184.

Izzo, C. V., Weissberg, R. P., Kasprow, W. J., & Fendrich, M. (1999). A longitudinal assessment of teacher perceptions of parent involvement in children's education and school performance. *American Journal of Community Psychology, 27*(6), 817–830.

Katims, D. S., & Pierce, P. L. (1995). Literacy-rich environments and the transition of young children with special needs. *Topics in Early Childhood Special Education, 15*(2), 219–234.

Katz, L. G. (1987). Early education: What should young children be doing? In S. L. Kagan & E. F. Zigler (Eds.), *Early schooling: The national debate* (pp. 151–167). New Haven: Yale University Press.

La Paro, K. M., & Pianta, R. C. (2001). Predicting children's competence in the early school years: A meta-analytic review. *Review of Educational Research, 70*(4), 443–484.

La Paro, K. M., Pianta, R. C., & Stuhlman, M. (2004). Classroom Assessment Scoring System (CLASS): Findings from the Pre-K Year. *Elementary School Journal, 104*(5), 409–426.

Love, J. M., Logue, M. E., Trudeau, J. V., & Thayer, K. (1992). *Transitions to kindergarten in American schools* (Contract No. LC 88089001). Portsmouth, NH: US Department of Education.

Masten, A., Miliotis, D., Graham-Bermann, S., Ramirez, M., & Neeman, J. (1993). Children in homeless families: Risks to mental health and development. *Journal of Consulting and Clinical Psychology, 61*(2), 335–343.

Meisels, S. J. (1999). Assessing readiness. In R. C. Pianta & M. J. Cox (Eds.), *The transition to kindergarten* (pp. 39–66). Baltimore: Brookes Publishing.

Meisels, S. J., & Atkins-Burnett, S. (2000). The elements of early childhood assessment. In J. P. Shonkoff & S. J. Meisels (Eds.), *Handbook of early childhood intervention* (2nd ed., pp. 231–257). New York: Cambridge University Press.

Mokuau, N., & Tauili'ili, P. (1998). Families with Native Hawaiian and Samoan roots. In E. W. Lynch & M. J. Hanson (Eds.), *Developing cross-cultural competence: A guide for working with young children and their families* (2nd ed., pp. 409–441). Baltimore: Brookes Publishing.

National Association for the Education of Young Children. (1998). *Accreditation criteria and procedures of the National Association for the Education of Young Children.* Washington, DC: Author.

National Center for Education Statistics. (1994). *School and Staffing Survey 1993–1994: Principal's Survey.* Washington, DC: US Department of Education.

National Center for Education Statistics. (1999). *America's kindergartners.* Washington, DC: US Department of Education.

National Center for Education Statistics. (2000). *America's Kindergartners.* Washington, DC: US Department of Education.

National Center for Education Statistics. (2003). *Overview and inventory of state education reforms: 1990–2000.* Washington, DC: US Department of Education, Institute of Education Sciences.

National Education Goals Panel. (1995). *National Education Goals Report Executive Summary: Improving education through family–school–community partnerships.* Washington, DC: Author.

National Education Goals Panel. (1998). *Ready schools.* Washington, DC: Author.

National Governors' Association Center for Best Practices. (2004). *NGA Task Force on School Readiness: A discussion framework.* Washington, DC: NGA.

NICHD Early Child Care Research Network. (1999). Child outcomes when child care center classes meet recommended standards for quality. *American Journal of Public Health, 89,* 1072–1077.

NICHD Early Child Care Research Network. (2002). Early child care and children's development prior to school entry: Results from the NICHD Study of Early Child Care. *American Educational Research Journal, 39,* 133–164.

NICHD Early Child Care Research Network. (2004). Does class size in first grade relate to changes in child academic and social performance or observed classroom processes? *Developmental Psychology, 40,* 651–664.

NICHD Early Child Care Research Network. (2005). A day in third grade: Observational descriptions of third grade classrooms and associations with teacher characteristics. *Elementary School Journal, 105,* 305–323.

NICHD Early Child Care Research Network. (submitted). Age of entry to kindergarten and children's academic achievement and socioemotional development. *Journal of Educational Psychology.*

Oden, S., & Ricks, J. (1990, April). *Follow-up study of Head Start's role in the lives of children and families: Interim report.* Paper presented at the annual meeting of the American Educational Research Association, Boston.

Pew Hispanic Center/Kaiser Family Foundation, 2004. *National Survey of Latinos: Education.* Available at *http://www.kff.org/kaiserpolls/3031.cfm*

Phillipsen, L. C., Cryer, D., & Howes, C. (1995). Classroom processes and classroom structure. In S. W. Helburn (Ed.), *Cost, quality and child outcomes in child care centers: Technical report* (pp. 125–158). Denver: Economics Department, University of Colorado at Denver.

Pianta, R. C. (2003). *Standardized classroom observations from pre-k to 3rd grade: A mechanism for improving classroom quality and practices, consistency of P-3 experiences, and child outcomes.* A Foundation for Child Development working paper. New York: Foundation for Child Development.

Pianta, R. C., Cox, M., Early, C., & Taylor, L. (1999). Kindergarten teachers' practices related to the transition to school: Results of a national survey. *Elementary School Journal, 100*(1), 71–86.

Pianta, R. C., & Harbers, K. (1996). Observing mother and child behavior in a problem-solving situation at school entry: Relations with academic achievement. *Journal of School Psychology, 34,* 307–322.

Pianta, R. C., Howes, C., Burchinal, M., Bryant, D., Clifford, R., Early, D., & Barbarin, O. (2005). Features of pre-kindergarten programs, classrooms, and teachers: Do they predict observed classroom quality and child–teacher interactions? *Applied Deveopmental Science, 9,* 144–159.

Pianta, R. C., & Kraft-Sayre, M. (2003). *Successful kindergarten transition.* Baltimore: Brookes Publishing.

Pianta, R. C., La Paro, K. M., & Hamre, B. K. (2004). *Classroom Assessment Scoring System (CLASS).* Unpublished measure, University of Virginia.

Pianta, R. C., La Paro, K. M., Payne, C., Cox, M. J., & Bradley, R. (2002). The relation of kindergarten classroom environment to teacher, family, and school characteristics and child outcomes. *Elementary School Journal, 102*(3), 225–238.

Pianta, R. C., Smith, N., & Reeve, R. (1991). Observing mother and child behavior in a problem-solving situation at school entry: Relations with classroom adjustment. *School Psychology Quarterly, 6,* 1–16.

Pianta, R. C., & Walsh, D. J. (1996). *High-risk children in schools: Constructing sustaining relationships.* New York: Routledge.

Ramey, C. T., & Campbell, F. A. (1991). Poverty, early childhood education, and academic competence: The Abecedarian experiment. In A. C. Huston (Ed.), *Children in poverty: Child development and public policy* (pp. 190–221). New York: Cambridge University Press.

Rathbun, A., & Germino-Hausken, E. (2001, April). *How are transition to kindergarten activities associated with parent involvement during kindergarten?* American Educational Research Association, Seattle.

Repetto, J. B., & Correa, V. I. (1996). Expanding views on transition. *Exceptional Children, 62*(6), 551–563.

Reynolds, A. J. (1989). A structural model of first-grade outcomes for an urban, low socioeconomic status, minority population. *Journal of Educational Psychology, 81*(4), 594–603.

Rimm-Kaufman, S. E., & Pianta, R. C. (1999). Patterns of family–school contact in preschool and kindergarten. *School Psychology Review, 28*(3), 426–438.

Rimm-Kaufman, S. E., & Pianta, R. C. (2000). An ecological perspective on the transition to kindergarten: A theoretical framework to guide empirical research. *Journal of Applied Developmental Psychology, 21*(5), 491–511.

Rimm-Kaufman, S. E., & Pianta, R. C. (in press). Family–school communication in preschool and kindergarten in the context of a relationship enhancing intervention. *Early Education and Development.*

Rimm-Kaufman, S. E., Pianta, R. C., Cox, M., & Bradley, R. (2003). Teacher-rated family involvement and children's social and academic outcomes in kindergarten. *Early Education and Development, 14*(2), 179–198.

Ripple, C. H., Gilliam, W. S., Chanana, N., & Zigler, E. (1999). Will fifty cooks spoil the broth? The debate over entrusting Head Start to the states. *American Psychologist, 54,* 327–343.

Roberts, R. N., Akers, A. L., & Behl, D. D. (1996). Family-level service coordination within home visiting programs. *Topics in Early Childhood Special Education, 16*(3), 279–301.

Rous, B., Hemmeter, M. L., & Schuster, J. (1994). Sequenced transition to education in the public schools: A systems approach to transition planning. *Topics in Early Childhood Special Education, 14*(3), 374–393.

Schweinhart, L. J., Barnes, H., & Weikart, D. P. (1993). *Significant benefits: The High/Scope Perry Preschool study through age 27.* Ypsilanti, MI: High/Scope Press.

Shonkoff, J., & Phillips, D. (Eds.). (2000). *From neurons to neighborhoods: The science of early childhood development.* Washington, DC: National Academy Press.

Skinner, D., Bryant, D., Coffman, J., & Campbell, F. (1998). Creating risk and promise: Children's and teachers' constructions in the cultural world of kindergarten. *The Elementary School Journal, 98*(4), 297–312.

Slaughter-Defoe, D. T., Nakagawa, K., Takanishi, R., & Johnson, D. J. (1990). Toward cultural/ecological perspectives on schooling and achievement in African- and Asian-American children. *Child Development, 61,* 363–383.

Southeastern Regional Vision for Education. (1995). *Passages: Providing continuity from preschool to school.* Atlanta, GA: Author

US Census Bureau. (2000). *Enrollment status of the population 3 years old and over, by age, sex, race, Hispanic origin, nativity, and selected educational characteristics.* (Population Paper Listing-148). Washington, DC: Author.

Vecchiotti, S. (2003). Kindergarten: An overlooked educational policy priority. *Social Policy Report, 17*(2), 3–19.

Wohl, F. (2001). Pre-kindergarten: Expanding the boundaries of education. *Principal, 80*(5), 22–25.

Wolery, M. (1999). Children with disabilities in early elementary school. In R. Pianta & M. Cox (Eds.), *The transition to kindergarten* (pp. 253–280). Baltimore: Brookes Publishing.

Zuniga, M. E. (1998). Families with Latino roots. In E. W. Lynch & M. J. Hanson (Eds.), *Developing cross-cultural competence: A guide for working with young children and their families* (2nd ed., pp. 209–250). Baltimore: Brookes Publishing.

25

Media and Early Development

Sandra L. Calvert

The media available to infants and very young children have undergone rapid changes in the past decade. From the beginnings of life, the worlds of infants and young children are embedded in screen media, including digital interactive media. We know that the content of these media has important effects during early childhood, but our knowledge about infants is still largely uncharted territory. In this chapter I explore infants' and young children's early access and media exposure patterns, how children learn from media, and the effects of media on early development. I then examine research germane to social policies that influence infants' and young children's media experiences.

Early Media Use: Access, Experiences, and Parental Attitudes

A 2003 survey conducted by the Henry J. Kaiser Family Foundation provides the first comprehensive data about early media use for children who are 6 months to 6 years old (see Calvert, Rideout, Woolard, Barr, & Strouse, 2005; Rideout, Vandewater, & Wartella, 2003; Vandewater et al., 2005). Using phone interviews, more than 1000 US parents were contacted about the media use patterns of their infants and young children during the spring of 2003. Children in the Henry J. Kaiser sample lived in a media-rich environment. Most of their homes had television sets (99%), DVD or videotape players (95%), cable or satellite options (78%), radios (98%), CD or tape players (93%), computers (73%), internet access (63%), and console (49%) and hand-held video game players (32%) (Rideout et al., 2003). Regardless of education, income, and family structure, Caucasian families were more likely to own computers than Latino families, and Caucasian families were more likely than African-American and Latino families to have internet access (Calvert, Rideout et al., 2005).

A typical day in the life of a young child

Media are a ubiquitous presence in the typical day of very young children. For all young children in the Henry J. Kaiser study (Rideout et al., 2003), using screen media (83%) and playing outside (83%) were their most frequent activities, followed by reading or being read to (79%) and listening to music (79%). When screen exposure was broken apart, children mainly watched television programs (73%) and videos or DVDs (73%), while computer use (18%) and video game play (9%) were less frequent activities. For children under age 2, their most frequent activities were to listen to music (81%) and read or be read to (71%). Sixty-eight percent of children under age 2 typically have some exposure to screen media on a daily basis. Most of that exposure was to television (59%) and to videos and DVDs (42%). Using a computer (5%) or playing a video game (3%) was relatively rare for children under age 2, but when they do use a computer children typically play games (Calvert, Rideout et al., 2005; Rideout et al., 2003).

If one examines the amount of time children spend in these various activities, the privileging of screen media becomes obvious. Children spent almost 2 hours each day with screen media, played outdoors for an additional 2 hours, listened to music about an hour a day, and spent only about 39 minutes reading or being read to (Rideout et al., 2003). For the screen media, children on a typical day spent just over an hour watching television, 38 minutes watching DVDs and videos, 10 minutes using a computer, and about 5 minutes playing video games. Even the 6-month- to 2-year-olds spent about 2 hours per day in front of a screen (Rideout et al., 2003).

Thirty-five percent of the children in the Henry J. Kaiser study lived in heavy media households where the television set was reportedly "on" either always or most of the time, even when no one was viewing it; these children watched more television, read or were read to less, and were less likely to read than the other children (Vandewater et al., 2005). Children who had television sets in their bedrooms also viewed more television programs and DVDs (Vandewater et al., 2005). Boys and girls did not differ in their early use of computers (Calvert, Rideout et al., 2005), but boys did play more video games than girls did, even at these young ages (Rideout et al., 2003). Even though African-American families in the Henry J. Kaiser study were less likely to have internet access than Caucasian families, African-American families were more likely to report computer use by their children on a typical day (Calvert, Rideout et al., 2005), a finding that is consistent with the heavier use of television by African-American than Caucasian families (Comstock, 1991). These findings suggest that African-Americans are heavy screen users across a wide range of media. Children's heavy time investment implicates screen media as a major socialization agent during early development.

Early media skills

Not only were very young children in the Henry J. Kaiser study frequently exposed to media, they were also making active choices about their exposure. Many young children had favorite programs and liked to watch the same DVDs repeatedly (Rideout et al.,

2003), an activity that improves early imitation (Barr, Chavez, Fujimoto, Muentener, & Strait, 2003). Although the entire sample of very young children was not using computers frequently on a daily basis, almost half of the sample had used a computer at some point. Specifically, 21% of 6-month- to 2-year-olds, 58% of 3- to 4-year-olds, and 77% of 5- to 6-year-olds had used a computer (Calvert, Rideout et al., 2005). Of these computer users, approximately 12–14% used a computer every day (Calvert, Rideout et al., 2005). For those families in the Henry J. Kaiser study who had computers, parents reported that toddlers began using computers during the second year of their lives, generally from a parent's lap (Calvert, Rideout et al., 2005). By the middle of their third year, most children with computers were capable of controlling the mouse to point and click, many could load CD-ROMs by themselves, and many could turn on the computer by themselves (Calvert, Rideout et al., 2005). Twenty-seven percent of 6-month- to 3-year-olds and 56% of the 4- to 6-year-olds can actually use a computer independently of parental support, operating the computer on their own at least some of the time (Rideout et al., 2003). The Henry J. Kaiser data suggest a considerable amount of autonomy for very young children, which enables an early start on the basic skills that will be needed along the digital highway.

Using the mouse may well be a key to independent computer use. If technologies are designed so that infants can use them, then much earlier control of a "mouse" emerges than was reported in the Henry J. Kaiser study. For instance, large hand switches with only a one-click option rather than two can be used as early as age 6 months, with most infants showing competency at ages 9–11 months, and 100% of 15- to 17-month-olds using such devices successfully (Swinth, Anson, & Dietz, 1993). These studies suggest that ergonomic issues prevent infants from using computers and that a new approach for pointing and clicking may foster very early computer literacy skills.

Parental attitudes about children's early media use

Interestingly, the Henry J. Kaiser study (Rideout et al., 2003) found that parents generally perceived media as being a constructive educational influence in their young children's development. However, perceptions varied by medium. As seen in Figure 25.1, parents view computers and television as being more helpful than hurtful to their children's educational development (Rideout et al., 2003). In contrast, parents were more likely to think that video games hurt than helped their child's educational development (Rideout et al., 2003). Parents who personally spent more time using specific media were most likely to perceive those particular media as constructive forces in their child's development, perhaps because they were more familiar with the content, or perhaps as a rationalization for letting their child use them (Rideout et al., 2003).

Books were parents' favorite choice for educational value, with 96% of parents rating traditional books helpful, compared with 62% for educational talking books, 58% for educational television, 49% for educational videos, 43% for educational computer games, and 31% for educational websites. Although they valued books the most, their children still spent more overall time with screen media than in reading activities (Rideout et al., 2003). While infants, toddlers, and children once moved from book to screen media,

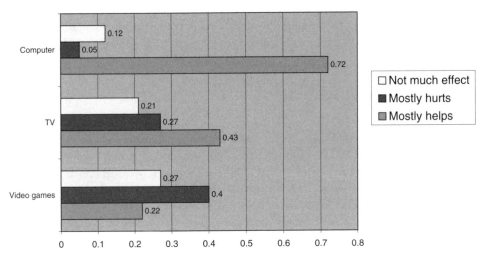

Figure 25.1 Percent of parents who say each medium mostly helps/hurts children's learning.

they now move from one screen medium to another screen medium. Overall, the findings suggest that books play a secondary role to screen media during early development.

How Do Children Learn from Media Presentations?

Representational capacities are at the heart of children's observations and interactions with media as children must decode symbolically presented material in order to process the content (Huston & Wright, 1983). Three major models have emerged to describe learning from media. The first perspective involves imitation, a process where infants and young children see another person depict a behavior and then copy it into their own behavioral repertoire. Imitative processes in the television area were originally described by Bandura (e.g., 1965) through processes of social learning that take place via observation of models, be they live or symbolically present. These ideas were later extended to the infant years by Meltzoff (2002), who embedded imitation within a "theory of mind" orientation (see Barr, this volume). More specifically, Melzoff (2002) theorized that infants learn about how others think and feel by imitating adults. The second perspective, the exploration-to-search model, describes a shift from an early interest and exploration of information associated with perceptually salient stimuli like movement to a later interest in less salient stimuli like dialogue where more informative content is found (Huston & Wright, 1983). These shifts occur because of maturation and experiences, particularly experiences involving media. The third perspective, the comprehensibility model, focuses on how well children can understand the language used in presentations, which, in turn, guides their attention to content that they think they can understand (Lorch, Anderson, & Levin, 1979). These three models dovetail with three tiers of representational skills: enactive (with the body), iconic (in pictures), and symbolic (in words) (Bruner, Olver, & Greenfield, 1966).

Imitation

During the first hours of life, infants can imitate adult facial expressions, such as sticking out their tongues (Meltzoff & Moore, 1983). This is an amazing skill because newborn infants have never seen their own faces, let alone their tongues. Meltzoff (2002) speculates that infants come prewired to look for others who are "like me"; with this recognition comes an innate tendency to imitate these people, thereby enhancing their own self-discovery as infants map their motor movements onto the movements they observe in others.

Meltzoff (2002) argues that a theory of mind framework is useful for understanding how the infant moves to an adult understanding of how the world works. Building on a nativist approach, Meltzoff explores three key premises: (1) infants are innately equipped to map adult movements into their own behavioral repertoires, primarily through imitation; (2) infants experience first-person links between their own emotional experiences and the associated bodily states, which allows them to learn about themselves; and (3) infants infer how others feel when looking at adults because they have experienced those bodily states themselves.

Infant imitation of live and symbolic models. A considerable amount of knowledge documents that both infants and young children use imitation to learn from live and televised models. The newborn skill of imitating facial expressions immediately after exposure (Meltzoff & Moore, 1983) is followed by 6-week-old infants' deferred imitation of a live adult's facial expressions 24 hours after exposure occurs (Meltzoff & Moore, 1994). Delayed, i.e., deferred, imitation is a particularly important process because it indicates that babies remember an event they observed earlier, an event that is now removed in time and place. Put another way, deferred imitation serves as an indicator of representational thought. In the media area, Meltzoff (1988) found that 14-month-old infants could later imitate filmed events that they had observed on a television monitor, such as manipulating a toy in a specific manner. However, these video manipulations were created by having an adult experimenter in the video presentation respond contingently to the actual actions of the infants, a process that is not possible when viewing a television program or a video created for a mass audience.

Although researchers have demonstrated both immediate and delayed infant imitation of televised events, infants' imitation of televised models generally lags behind their imitation of live models. For example, 18-month-old infants who saw video tapes performed at about the same level of competency as 12-month-olds who viewed a similar live presentation (Barr & Hayne, 1999). Infants may forget televised information because they do not initially encode the information accurately or because they forget the information during a delay. Research suggests that the problem is an encoding issue. For example,

Hayne, Herbert, and Simcock (2003) found that toddlers at ages 24 and 30 months did not remember targeted actions as well when they observed a television rather than a live presentation. Because infants failed at this task immediately after exposure, there is clearly an encoding issue. Moreover, one can improve babies' deferred imitation by adding an attention-getting feature like sound effects to highlight certain aspects of the presentation or by repeating the vignette; both approaches focus on ensuring that babies initially encode targeted information (Barr et al., 2003). The addition of sound effects to the presentation also points to some of the inherent problems in most studies that compare live and televised depictions: the televised depictions involved in most imitation studies do not take advantage of attention-getting features like sound effects that are an inherent part of media productions. Instead they reduce those comparisons to exactly what is being done by a live adult. Studies of programs made for infants that contain strong production values have more ecological validity.

Imitation of aggressive and prosocial behaviors during early childhood. By age 3, children can readily imitate film, video, and televised depictions. One of the classic areas of media study involved the role of aggressive video, film, or televised depictions in children's aggressive behavior. The earliest studies of media aggression involved the processes by which observing social models influenced young children's subsequent imitation of aggressive behaviors. In a classic experimental study (Bandura, 1965), pre-school-aged children were exposed to a film in a laboratory in which a model was rewarded, punished, or received no consequences for violent actions. After viewing, children, particularly boys, who saw the model rewarded for aggressive behavior were more likely to imitate the aggressive behaviors spontaneously than were those who saw the model punished. When children were offered incentives to reproduce the aggressive behavior, most could do so. In other words, there was a difference between learning and performance. Bandura (1965) concluded that children learned the aggressive action and stored that information for possible use later, even if it was not spontaneously imitated in the present situation.

Prosocial behavior can be imitated just as aggressive behavior can be. In a seminal field study (Stein & Friedrich, 1972), preschool-aged children's social behaviors in their child care settings were compared after being exposed to a diet of violent content from Superman and Batman cartoons, of prosocial content from *Mister Rogers' Neighborhood*, or of neutral content. Those who had viewed the prosocial *Mister Rogers' Neighborhood* programs demonstrated more prosocial behaviors. By contrast, children who viewed the violent cartoons acted more aggressively than did those who had viewed the prosocial or neutral television programs. Nonetheless, the less aggressive children may still have learned aggressive behavior, even if they did not spontaneously perform it. Subsequent meta-analyses of both violent (Paik & Comstock, 1994) and prosocial television programs (Mares, 1996) link these presentations to aggressive or prosocial acts, respectively.

Long-term effects of exposure to televised violence on subsequent aggressive behavior have been conducted, but comparable long-term studies in the prosocial area have not. Early identification with media characters and investment in television content, as measured by talking about television and using television in play themes during early childhood, is linked to later aggressive behavior during high school and adulthood (D. R.

Anderson, Huston, Schmitt, Linebarger, & Wright, 2001; Huesmann & Eron, 1986). However, viewing violent content at age 5 sometimes predicts teen aggressive attitudes (Eron, Lefkowitz, Huesmann, & Walder, 1972), but sometimes does not (D. R. Anderson et al., 2001). Similarly, intelligence has sometimes been found to serve as a moderator of aggression (Wiegerman, Kuttschreuter, & Baarda, 1992) and sometimes it has not (D. R. Anderson et al., 2001). More longitudinal research is needed that begins tracking different cohorts of children during infancy and follows them into adulthood.

Consistent with the television literature, studies find short-term outcomes after exposure to aggressive video game content. For example, preschool-aged children, particularly boys, who viewed an aggressive cartoon or who played an aggressive video game acted more aggressively immediately after exposure (Silvern & Williamson, 1987). Similarly, children who interacted with a violent karate video game played more aggressively immediately after exposure whereas those who interacted with an action-oriented non-violent video game imitated that behavior (Schutte, Malouff, Post-Garden, & Rodasta, 1988). Comparable studies about even short-term exposure to prosocial video games have not been conducted, and longitudinal studies in the aggressive and prosocial video game literature are notably absent.

Summary. Taken together, the studies suggest that imitation is the initial mechanism that allows children to understand televised and video game models. Studies suggest an early lag in imitating televised over live models but that the underlying skills to imitate prosocial or antisocial behaviors are clearly present at birth. Imitation occurs after exposure to television programs and video games. Early studies examined imitation in laboratory or field settings after exposure to violent or prosocial stimuli. Recent studies of imitation have begun to focus on the biological origins of imitation.

The exploration-to-search model

Formal features, the grammar of television, are visual and auditory production techniques that structure, mark, and represent content (Huston & Wright, 1983). The exploration-to-search model applied Berlyne's (1960) work on perceptual salience to television formal features. Berlyne argued that certain environmental stimuli were innately attention-getting due to perceptually salient qualities such as movement, contrast, incongruity, complexity, and surprise. We attend to these stimuli because they signal a change in the environment, and selective attention to changes increases the chances of survival. Huston and Wright (1983) argued that certain formal features were perceptually salient and others were not. Perceptually salient features like action, for example, embodied movement whereas visual and auditory special effects were characterized by incongruity, surprise, and novelty. By contrast, dialogue is not typically presented with perceptually salient features. Because television productions directed at young children often use perceptually salient features, young children were expected to pay attention to the content associated with those stimuli. With age and experience, attention to salient stimuli was expected to undergo a habituation process, leading to a search for meaningful content regardless of perceptual salience. With these developmental changes, dialogue, a non-salient verbal feature where most of the meaningful plot-relevant content is presented, was expected to become more attention-worthy, and, hence, older children were expected to learn more after exposure to televised content.

Early correlational research supported some facets of the exploration-to-search model. For instance, we (Calvert, Huston, Watkins, & Wright, 1982) initially studied children's attention to, and comprehension of, a prosocial children's television program. We found that perceptually salient formal features can assist preschoolers' and kindergarteners' visual attention as well as improve their comprehension of content. In the attention area, salient audio features like sound effects (e.g., zips and booms), loud music, and character vocalizations (e.g., Fat Albert, our main character, said "Hey, Hey, Hey") can initially affect visual attention by eliciting a *primitive orienting response*. With age and experience, those features can become *learned markers* of meaningful content.

Once formal features gain attention, comprehension can be improved by presenting important content contiguously. For example, Fat Albert would say "Hey, Hey, Hey, I've got something to say." Then he would immediately tell children something important about the story. Because the vocalization had elicited young children's visual attention, the *contiguous presentation* with key dialogue led to better comprehension of the important program messages (Calvert et al., 1982).

Formal features, particularly action and dialogue, can also serve as *modes to represent content*. As predicted, older more so than younger children did understand the non-salient language well when action was not present, especially for the adult, abstract dialogue. We expected and found benefits of action for preschoolers' and kindergarteners' comprehension, presumably because action parallels a visual, iconic form of thinking. However, even our 9- and 10-year-olds' comprehension benefited from action, a finding that we did not predict. It seems that visual modes of presentation continue to benefit children's learning at least through middle childhood.

Other researchers, by contrast, had found that action interfered with young children's memory of important television content. For example, Hayes and Birnbaum (1980) showed preschool-aged children a cartoon that mixed the visual and auditory tracks from two different programs. Preschoolers remembered the visually presented content at the expense of the verbally presented content, a phenomenon that became known as the visual superiority hypothesis. Pezdek and Hartman (1983) also found a visual superiority effect when the visual and audio tracks were mismatched, but the effect was not found when children viewed the original intact presentation. We argued that the visual track is more interesting and compelling to young children when it competes with the less salient audio track. That is, the visual track is more memorable when it conflicts with the audio track.

Subsequent experimental research demonstrated that visual action can serve as a supplement to language. Using a computer scenario of a park where features could be tightly manipulated, my colleagues and I (see Calvert, 1999 for a summary of these studies) manipulated action and dialogue in relation to objects (e.g., dog, cat). Then we examined the objects that children remembered. Young children remembered more moving than non-moving objects. In a related study, preschoolers were also more likely to *name* moving than non-moving objects, providing evidence that formal features can elicit an early rehearsal strategy that is typically absent in young children.

In summary, research supports the underlying premises of the exploration-to-search model in that: (1) perceptually salient audio techniques like sound effects and vocalizations can call attention to important television content, thereby resulting in better comprehension; and (2) perceptually salient features like action can supplement the audio track by providing children with dual modes to think about and represent content. Contrary to prediction, however, the beneficial effects of salient features continue into middle childhood. Moreover, dialogue about abstract events removed in time and place, rather than dialogue about concrete events, was most difficult for children to understand. Hence, not all dialogue is created equal.

The comprehensibility model

The comprehensibility model emerged from studies that examined the relation between visual attention and comprehension of televised content. Initially, researchers believed that if you wanted to enhance learning, the strategy was to enhance visual attention. That is, the more children attended to content, the more they should understand. That underlying premise was not always supported by the data. For example, Lorch et al. (1979) manipulated young children's visual attention to an episode of *Sesame Street* by creating a viewing situation where some children had toys and others did not. Although children who did not have toys watched twice as much of the program as those who did have toys, enhanced attention did not translate into better comprehension. Instead, children who looked at specific program points when the important content was being presented were more likely to understand that material. The researchers concluded that the comprehensibility of the content, primarily the dialogue track, was the primary determinant of visual attention. Children attend when they think that they can understand the content.

The comprehensibility hypothesis was then tested in two related studies where *Sesame Street* vignettes were used as the stimuli (D. R. Anderson, Lorch, Field, & Sanders, 1981). In the first study, 3- and 5-year-olds attended most to segments where dialogue was supported by visual content, followed by segments where there was no dialogue at all; dialogue with no visual referents had the least attention (e.g., someone talking on a phone). In the second study, the comprehensibility of an episode of *Sesame Street* was manipulated. Visual attention was highest for children who viewed the normal intact program followed by a version with randomly ordered scenes, a version where characters spoke a foreign language, and a version where the dialogue was spoken backwards, respectively. Five-year-olds were more sensitive to the dialogue manipulations, as indicated by their decreases in visual attention to the screen, than were 3-year-olds. In short, incomprehensible dialogue lost young children's attention.

Even infants are sensitive to dialogue manipulations that alter program comprehensibility. Frankenfield et al. (2004) applied the same procedures used by Daniel Anderson et al. (1981) in degrading *Sesame Street* vignettes to create vignette degrades in an episode of *Teletubbies*, a program designed for infants and toddlers. Eighteen- and 24-month-olds looked less when they viewed degraded rather than normal versions of the program. These results suggest that very young children are active strategic viewers in search of meaning-ful content.

Summary

Taken together, the research documents three main ways that infants and young children learn from media: (1) through imitation, in which infants and children observe others and copy another person's behaviors into their own repertoires; (2) through encoding and memory of content associated with perceptually salient stimuli; and (3) through compre-hensible dialogue which can guide children's visual attention to content that they can understand. Most of the literature involves naturalistic or experimental studies where data are collected immediately after exposure or after a short delay, and most of that literature involves television, not the newer interactive media. Little longitudinal research currently exists in any content domain except aggression.

The Educational Lessons of Media

Young children who view well-designed educational television programs, such as *Sesame Street, Mister Rogers' Neighborhood, Blue's Clues*, and *Dora the Explorer*, learn cognitive skills, cognitive knowledge, and prosocial lessons and behaviors. While these programs demonstrate promising outcomes for young children's cognitive and social development by age 3, there are other televised and interactive programs that have not been studied but which claim, either explicitly or implicitly, to benefit development. These include television programs directed at infants, such as *Baby Einstein*, as well as online games and interactive story books. In fact, Daniel Anderson and Tiffany A. Pempek (2005) argue that children may learn very little from screen media during the first two years of life, an issue that I will return to in the social policy section.

Sesame Street

Sesame Street is the gold standard by which educational success in television programs has historically been measured. From its inception, researchers examined the educational outcomes of this program on its young viewers. Early evaluations of the cognitive impact of *Sesame Street* ran into difficulties, however, because it was a hit.

The first evaluation study (Ball & Bogatz, 1970) included an encouragement and a no encouragement group. Parents of children in the encouragement group received toys about the program to stimulate their child's interest whereas the control group did not. Even so, children in the control group were just as likely to view the program as those in the treatment group. Consequently, the evaluators had to group the children by quar-tiles and conducted the analyses based on how much they viewed the series. Ball and Bogatz (1970) found that 3- to 5-year-old children who were the most frequent viewers of the series learned letters, numbers, classification, sorting, and knowledge about the parts of the body more than infrequent viewers did. There were no social class or gender differences in children's learning.

In a second evaluation study, Bogatz and Ball (1971) studied children who could only get *Sesame Street* by having a special cable to connect them to UHF channels which were not commonly available in homes at that time. Children in the treatment group received access to the UHF channels and hence *Sesame Street* while children in the control group did not receive UHF channels. Bogatz and Ball replicated their findings of cognitive benefits for the frequent viewers with this new sample, and also found differences in Peabody Picture Vocabulary scores which favored the treatment group. The evaluators also examined some of the children from the original study who were now beginning to go to school. Teachers, who did not know how much individual children had viewed *Sesame Street*, rated those who had seen the program more often as being better prepared for the classroom.

With success came criticism. Cook and his colleagues (1975) argued that the beneficial effects of *Sesame Street* came from maternal encouragement and involvement with their children rather than from simply viewing the program. When the data were reanalyzed using children who did not receive maternal encouragement, cognitive benefits remained, but they were more limited. Children improved in letter and number recognition, but not in the more advanced cognitive tasks. In addition, Cook et al. pointed out that middle-class children were more likely than poorer children to watch the program, thereby potentially increasing rather than decreasing the achievement gap across socio-economic status and racial groups.

As *Sesame Street* became better known, poorer children were just as likely to view the series as more affluent ones (Rice, Huston, Truglio, & Wright, 1990). Moreover, when maternal encouragement was eliminated in a subsequent evaluation of *Sesame Street*, beneficial effects of viewing remained (Wright et al., 2001). Wright and his colleagues (2001) tracked cohorts of 2- and 4-year-old children from low- and moderate-income families for three years. Frequent more so than infrequent viewers of educational programs, primarily *Sesame Street*, spent more time reading, participating in educational activities, and were better prepared for school, as indexed by higher scores in vocabulary and mathematics. By contrast, children who frequently viewed cartoons and general audience programs performed less well on academic tests than did those who viewed these programs infrequently. These effects occurred after controlling for family variables such as income and primary language spoken.

The most convincing evidence for academic benefits of *Sesame Street* viewing comes from a longitudinal follow-up of adolescents who differentially viewed educational programs during the preschool years (D. R. Anderson et al., 2001). Adolescents, particularly boys, who were frequent viewers of educational television programs like *Sesame Street* during their childhood performed better in their high school courses of mathematics, science, and English. The frequent viewers also had more favorable attitudes about academic success, including their own, they read more books, and they were more creative. Beneficial effects occurred even after controlling for family characteristics. Overall, the research suggests that one indicator of academic success is the kind of programs that very young children view.

Other educational television programs

Blue's Clues, an educational program about a blue animated dog, emphasizes flexible thinking, problem solving, and prosocial behavior. In each episode, which is broadcast multiple times, Blue leaves clues for his friend Steve or Joe to solve a problem with the assistance of their young audience. Pauses are built into the program, and the characters ask the audience for assistance. Daniel Anderson and his colleagues (2000) found that children will view the program repeatedly and that they learn more with each repetition of the program. The initial viewing of a particular episode generally results in attentive and quiet behaviors; as mastery occurs across repetitions, children become more interactive and answer the questions posed by the host. A longitudinal assessment of program effectiveness compared children with and without access to the series. Those who viewed the program showed improvements in cognitive skills such as solving riddles, creative thinking, and solving non-verbal matrices; children's expressive vocabulary was not affected by exposure to the program.

Just as found in evaluations of *Sesame Street*, encouragement to view influenced learning outcomes for two other educational television programs, *Allegra's Window* and *Gullah Gullah Island*. After six months' exposure to these series, caregivers reported increases in flexible thinking, problem solving, and prosocial behaviors for all children exposed to the series when compared to a control group, but effects were particularly strong for those who were encouraged to view (Bryant et al., 1995).

Rehearsal activities

Although children can learn many lessons of value on their own from educational television programs, learning is clearly enhanced when adults either label the content for children or use toys to role play with children about the important story content. Friedrich and Stein (1975) showed preschool-aged children episodes of *Mister Rogers' Neighborhood* with various rehearsal options: none; books that complemented the program content; toys that complemented the program content; and both books and toys. After viewing, an adult rehearsed the content with children through reading the books or guided role play about the content. Children, particularly girls, who had books as an aid understood the prosocial program content best. Children, particularly boys, who used puppets to role play and rehearse the content were best able to translate the program messages into their own behavioral repertoires. In a similar study with low-income children from Head Start (Friedrich-Cofer, Huston-Stein, Kipnis, Susman, & Clewett, 1979), prosocial behavior with peers increased the most when children viewed prosocial television programs and participated with teachers in rehearsal activities. By contrast, viewing the prosocial television programs alone had little effect on children's behaviors.

Effects are also greatest when live rather than televised models deliver the verbal labels and role play treatments. For example, preschool and kindergarten children who viewed a prosocial educational television program learned more of the important story content when a co-viewing adult interpreted the content for them than when his voice said the same content on the television audio track (Watkins, Calvert, Huston-Stein, & Wright, 1980). Similarly, live models were more effective than televised models in getting preschool-aged children, particularly boys, to engage in prosocial action, though the prosocial television did work better than exposure to neutral television programs (Ahammer & Murray, 1979). Imaginative play, which is generally disrupted by television viewing (van der Voort & Valkenburg, 1994), can increase when children view prosocial television programs, particularly when live adults help children translate the messages into their play (Friedrich-Cofer et al., 1979). Taken together, the results suggest the importance of live adults for maximizing children's benefits from prosocial television programs.

Engagement and Learning: Interactive Stories

Interactivity has been championed as the way in which newer media enhance young children's learning, particularly their early literacy skills. Our early findings suggest that interactivity is an engagement feature, one that pulls children into an activity and keeps them interested, but that interactivity does not necessarily enhance learning. For example, we (Calvert, Strong, & Gallagher, 2005) manipulated the amount of interactivity, defined as user *control*, which 4-year-old children had with an adapted online story. Over four exposures, children, particularly boys, lost attention and made increasing efforts to take control of the mouse or made requests to change the activity when the adult was solely in control. By contrast, children were attentive across the four sessions when they controlled the mouse. Although attention was affected by interactivity, learning the targeted words in the story was not. These findings are consistent with those reported by Chera and Wood (2003), who found that exposure to "talking books" enhanced children's phonological skills and even their story telling, but not their word recognition.

The literature on talking books may show mixed effects on learning in part because of the way in which interactive experiences draw attention to the story narrative versus other program elements. More specifically, game designers sometimes make the incidental content amusing and fun to play with by embellishing it with interesting production techniques (Calvert, Strong, & Gallagher, 2005). When the interactive experience emphasizes the story, children's story telling benefits; however, when the experience emphasizes the playful clicks on incidental story material, story telling suffers (Labbo & Kuhn, 2000). These findings offer important insights to those who create online stories and games for young children: that which is highlighted tends to be remembered.

Media, Gender, and Ethnicity

One of the key ways in which media may influence young children's development is by providing access to role models whom children may admire and imitate (Calvert, 1999). Those who are like children, in terms of gender and ethnicity, may be especially likely to influence behavior. Stereotyped patterns of males and females as well of different ethnic groups are pervasive in media depictions, thereby limiting exposure to non-traditional models, but even one positive depiction has the potential to create positive developmental outcomes.

Boys do not preferentially attend to male characters until about age 7, the age when gender constancy is achieved, and girls attend to both males and female characters even after gender constancy is achieved (Luecke-Aleska, Anderson, Collins, & Schmitt, 1995). Young girls avoid video games where the content is generally directed at male interests (Rideout et al., 2003).

The effects of media on young children from different ethnic backgrounds are largely unknown. In a study that we (Calvert, Strong, Jacobs, & Conger, 2005) conducted about *Dora the Explorer*, a prosocial program about an animated Latina girl, a television episode was edited to make it interactive at several program points and compared to various television versions of that program. We found that both the Latina and Caucasian preschool-aged girls identified more with Dora than boys did, primarily because Latino boys did not identify with the Latina female character. Although Caucasian children learned more story content than Latino children, the Latina girls learned the story content better when they had a computer interface to control the program rather than when they simply observed the program with a live adult. The results suggest the importance of having characters in television programs who are "like me." Additional research about the effects of television and interactive media on ethnic minority children's learning and social behavior is clearly needed.

Social Policy and Media Exposure

Policy issues have been and continue to be prevalent in the media area. These include the potential negative impact of any early screen exposure, exposure to advertising, and exposure to violence.

Early screen exposure

The American Academy of Pediatrics (1999) recommended no screen time for infants and toddlers who are under age 2. However, there were no empirical data about the role of media exposure on early development. That vacuum is now slowly being filled. A key issue is the kind of content children are viewing.

The video deficit model. Studies about infant exposure to television content draw a distinction between foreground and background television (D. R. Anderson & Pempek, 2005). Foreground television is made for infants and young children and generally gains their attention (D. R. Anderson & Pempek, 2005). By contrast, background television is made for an older audience, often adults, and plays while infants and younger children are present, but not necessarily viewing (D. R. Anderson & Pempek, 2005). Background television can disrupt infants' and toddlers' play activities (Evans, Pempek, Kirkorian,

Frankenfield, & Anderson, 2004). During early childhood, however, television viewing and play tend to co-occur, in part because children play as they view television (Huston, Wright, Marquis, & Green, 1999). The most deleterious effects of background television may occur because the video disrupts parent–child interaction, a known facilitator of early development, by pulling the parent's attention away from the infant and toward the video (A. C. Huston, personal communication, June 26, 2004).

Foreground television programs made explicitly for infants are the key to understanding the role of very early media exposure. Programs made for infants and young children gain their attentional interest very early in development. For example, 12- to 15-month-old infants are highly attentive to *Baby Mozart* and *Sesame Street Sing-along* videos, particularly those babies who had seen the programs previously (Spagnolo, Ruskis, Garcia Albert, & Barr, 2004). Similarly, 18- and 24-month-olds pay considerable attention to *Teletubbies*, and their attention drops when the program dialogue is incomprehensible (Frankenfield et al., 2004). These studies suggest that foreground television gains infants' visual attention and that they are sensitive to its language.

Even so, Daniel Anderson and Tiffany A. Pempek (2005) argue that infants and toddlers do not understand what they are viewing. They cite four lines of research for drawing this conclusion. The first evidence involves studies of infant imitation which find a delay for imitating a televised over a live model's actions (Barr & Hayne, 1999). However, these findings are eliminated when perceptually salient production techniques and repetition are added to the production (Barr et al., 2003), techniques that also make the stimuli more ecologically valid.

Anderson and Pempek's (2005) second argument involves studies about object retrieval tasks where a young child is shown a toy being hidden in a room that the child can see via a window or via a television screen. Then the child is taken into that room and asked to find the toy. Two-year-old children who watch the toy being hidden through a window can do this retrieval task, but those who see the video version do poorly at age 2, show mixed results at age 2½ years, and perform well at age 3 (Schmitt & Anderson, 2002; Troseth & DeLoache, 1998). These problems persist even when toddlers are given a felt-board version of the video, suggesting that it is not a problem in understanding images on a 2D screen (Evans, Crawley, & Anderson, 2004). Adult intervention facilitates successes, but only a live adult helps the child, not a closed-circuit experience where the adult speaks to them from a video screen (Evans et al., 2004). Interestingly, however, if 2-year-olds have personal experiences with closed-circuit television, then their performance improves on this task (Troseth, 2003). That they can learn to do these tasks tells us that biological limitations do not prevent toddlers from understanding screen media.

Language learning is the third line of evidence used to support the video deficit hypothesis (D. R. Anderson & Pempek, 2005). Although 2-year-olds can learn language from viewing videos (Rice et al., 1990), they learn labels better when a live rather than a televised model delivers the same message (Grela, Lin, & Krcmar, 2003). Anderson and Pempek's (2005) last line of evidence involves one study that examined how well infants learn emotional responses portrayed on video (Mumme & Fernald, 2003). One-year-olds avoided an object when it had been paired with fearful emotional expressions, but they did not approach the object when it had been paired with positive expressions; 10-month-olds showed no effects whatsoever (Mumme & Fernald, 2003). Overall, Anderson and Pempek (2005) find a video deficit in which live over video models are favored for learning during the first two and a half years of life.

Although Anderson and Pempek (2005) argued that very young children learn little from viewing educational television content, that may well depend on the program. For example, Linebarger and Walker (2005) found that 6- to 30-month-olds who were shown age-appropriate programs sometimes show positive and negative outcomes, depending on the linguistic content of the television programs that they were viewing. The researchers tracked babies from 6 months to 30 months of age. Babies were first interested in television programs at 9 months with a major jump in interest occurring at 18 months. Viewing programs like *Blue's Clues* and *Dora the Explorer*, which encourage active participation and provide ample time for the viewer to respond, as well as *Clifford the Big Red Dog* and *Arthur*, where clear models for the use of expressive language are provided, were all associated with gains in expressive language and greater vocabularies at 30 months of age. By contrast, viewers of *Sesame Street* and of *Teletubbies* had lower scores in both expressive language and vocabulary. The Teletubbies use baby talk, which may interfere with mature language development. However, it is unclear why there were negative effects for viewing *Sesame Street*, though the program is designed for an older target audience and so may be too difficult for infants and toddlers. Finally, *Barney* viewers had increases in expressive language, but vocabulary acquisition lagged. These results suggest that specific programs must be examined to disentangle this complex relationship between early development, screen media, and language development.

In summary, while the evidence thus far does support live over video models for learning, what remains to be answered are why these effects exist, what they mean, and how different they are from slightly older children's learning. For instance, while older children learn from video presentations, live adults who help them understand the content facilitate young children's learning during the preschool years, particularly in processing the verbal, linguistic content (Friedrich & Stein, 1975; Watkins et al., 1980). A video may simply be deficient to a live model throughout the early years. Secondly, video presentations that are constrained to fit into a live format do not take advantage of the production features that call attention to, and potentially help infants and young children to process, certain content. Thirdly, the effects of foreground television on infant learning may well depend on the particular program. Finally, toddlers show the same decrements to incomprehensible videos as 3-year-olds do; if variations in visual attention are a reliable index of comprehensibility at age 3, they should also be an accurate indicator at age 2. More research is needed in this area to determine the effects of early viewing of foreground and background television on infant and toddler learning, particularly longitudinal studies, since by age 3, young viewers begin to reap short- and very long-term benefits from viewing educational television programs. It remains unclear why an effect that is supposedly very negative suddenly turns very positive in a matter of a few months.

Attention deficits and early television viewing. Early exposure to television content has recently been linked to later attentional deficits. Christakis, Zimmerman, DiGiuseppe, and McCarty (2004) conducted a secondary analysis of data collected during the 1980s.

Parents indicated how much time their 1½- and 3½-year-olds had spent with television. The researchers later created an "attention deficit" index by asking parents several questions such as how well their children concentrated when these children were age 7. The top 10% of that distribution was said to have an attention deficit. Small positive correlations were found between the total amount of viewing at both ages and attention deficits. However, the researchers did not have an independent clinical diagnosis of attention deficits for these children, nor did they establish a causal relationship. For instance, parents with hyperactive children may well discover that television viewing is a way to quiet their children; therefore, the direction of the relation could be from hyperactivity to television viewing rather than the reverse. In addition, television programs for very young children were not made during the 1980s. Therefore, this sample was viewing background television programs that have been shown to have harmful effects. More research is needed to examine this relationship, particularly research involving early experiences with foreground televised and computer-based media that are designed to benefit very young children and infants.

Commercial advertising

A very long-standing social policy issue has been the effects of commercial advertising on very young children. Because of cognitive limitations inherent in the viewing audience, young children do not understand advertisements, nor are they capable of doing so. Until at least age 7, young children believe that advertisements are there to assist them in finding out more about products rather than to persuade them to buy certain brands (Robertson & Rossiter, 1974). Repetition of the message is often used to increase children's memory of the commercial content (Stewart & Ward, 1993). Because sugar-coated cereals and candy are often advertised to children, health risks, including dental problems and obesity, are potential problems. In fact, a recent Henry J. Kaiser Family Foundation (2004) review implicates food advertisements in the development of childhood obesity. Legislative action in the 1970s put several safeguards such as the separation principle in place that were supposed to help children make discriminations between the program content and the commercial advertisements (Ward, 1980). However, these separators have largely been ineffective (Palmer et al., 2004).

Media characters have also become the center of advertising strategies. In the Henry J. Kaiser report, Rideout et al. (2003) found that 97% of 6-month- to 6-year-olds had toys, clothes, or other products that were based on characters from television programs and movies. Originally referred to as program-based commercials, the ancillary products associated with the programs have increasingly become the revenue stream used to finance American children's television programs. While once illegal, the Federal Communications Commission under chair Mark Fowler made product-based programs an acceptable way of doing business (Fowler & Brenner, 1982). That policy was never reversed.

Problems associated with advertising also occurred online at websites where deceptive practices were used to sell to children, such as getting them to provide personally identifying information via a census at Batman's Gotham City (Montgomery & Pasnik, 1996). Such practices have now been regulated by the Children's Online Privacy Protection Act

(1998), which prevents advertisers from targeting children who are under age 13 (Montgomery, 2001). A side-effect of the Children's Online Privacy Protection Act was that there was no revenue stream to support the online programs that were being designed. Consequently, successful children's television programs subsidize their websites, an activity that many independent web producers were unable to afford.

Media violence

Another long-standing policy concern involves the role of media violence in children's antisocial behaviors. Young children are particularly susceptible to these influences because they do not understand intent as well as older children do, and they do not connect aggressive actions to consequences when there are commercial breaks between the aggressive action and the subsequent punishment (Collins, 1973). Playing aggressive video games yields similar negative outcomes on young children's social behaviors (C. Anderson & Bushman, 2001).

In spite of a considerable amount of data that links aggressive activity to children's antisocial behavior (e.g., Bandura, 1965; Huesmann & Eron, 1986; Paik & Comstock, 1994), social policies to curb children's exposure to violence have been ineffective. The media industry often uses its First Amendment rights, guaranteeing freedom of speech, to prevent any kind of "censorship." Labeling content as violent (e.g., "V" in television programs) has become one avenue for alerting parents about the potential problems with certain programs. In addition, the V-Chip has become a tool that parents can use to control access to violent programs by blocking programs with certain ratings, such as the "V" for violence. Jordan (2002), however, found that most parents do not use the V-Chip, even when given instructions about how to use it.

Conclusion

The effects of media on the developing infant and child are ubiquitous. Very young children view videos, listen to music, and play video games in their homes, their cars, and in airplanes. They are early computer users, initially sitting in their parents' lap, but soon have sufficient skills to use a computer on their own. Although books are still highly valued by parents, books now take a second place to screen media in early developmental experiences. Early media experiences can improve the well-being of children, preparing them for school entry and academic and social success. Or media can undermine successful developmental outcomes, resulting in aggressive behavior, consumerism, and perhaps even attentional problems. There are huge gaps in the literature about the newer interactive media, and about infancy and media effects, particularly how early media use affects reading skills, yet the implications for children's healthy development are quite clear. Early media experiences can set developmental trajectories into motion, affecting the kinds of people our children will be, both now and in the future, as well as the kind of society we are creating for generations yet to come.

Note

The author acknowledges the National Science Foundation (Grant no. 0126014) and the Stuart Family Foundation for their support of the Children's Digital Media Center during the writing of this chapter.

References

Ahammer, I. M., & Murray, J. P. (1979). Kindness in the kindergarten: The relative influence of role playing and prosocial television in facilitating altruism. *International Journal of Behavioral Development, 2,* 133–157.

American Academy of Pediatrics, Committee on Public Education. (1999). Media education. *Pediatrics, 104,* 341–342.

Anderson, C., & Bushman, B. (2001). Effects of violent videogames on aggressive behavior, aggressive cognition, aggressive affect, physiological arousal, and prosocial behavior: A meta-analytic review of the scientific literature. *Psychological Science, 12,* 353–359.

Anderson, D. R., Bryant, J., Wilder, A., Crawley, A., Santomero, A., & Williams, M. E. (2000). Researching *Blue's Clues*: Viewing behavior and impact. *Media Psychology, 2,* 179–194.

Anderson, D. R., Huston, A., Schmitt, K., Linebarger, D., & Wright, J. (2001). Early childhood television viewing behavior and adolescent behavior. *Monographs of the Society for Research in Child Development, 66*(1, Serial No. 264).

Anderson, D. R., Lorch, E. P., Field, D. E. & Sanders, J. (1981). The effects of TV program comprehensibility on preschool children's visual attention to television. *Child Development, 52,* 151–157.

Anderson, D. R., & Pempek, T. (2005). Television and very young children. *American Behavioral Scientist, 48,* 505–523.

Ball, S., & Bogatz, G. A. (1970). *The first year of Sesame Street: An evaluation.* Princeton, NJ: Educational Testing Service.

Bandura, A. (1965). Influence of models' reinforcement contingencies on the acquisition and performance of imitative responses. *Journal of Personality and Social Psychology, 1,* 589–595.

Barr, R., Chavez, V., Fujimoto, M., Muentener, P., & Strait, C. (2003, April). *Repeated exposure and cartoon sound effects enhance infant imitation from television.* Poster presented at the Society of Research on Child Development, Tampa, FL.

Barr, R., & Hayne, H. (1999). Developmental changes in imitation from television during infancy. *Child Development, 70,* 1067–1081.

Berlyne, D. E. (1960). *Conflict, arousal, and curiosity.* New York: McGraw Hill.

Bogatz, G. A., & Ball, S. (1971). *The second year of Sesame Street: A continuing evaluation.* Princeton, NJ: Educational Testing Service.

Bruno, J. S., Olver, R. S., & Greenfield, P. M., et al. (1966). *Studies in cognitive growth: A collaboration at the Center for Cognitive Studies.* New York: Wiley.

Bryant, J., McCallum, J., Maxwell, M., McGavin, L., Love, C., Raney, A., Mundorf, N., Mundorf, J., Wilson, B., & Smith, S. (1995, September). *Report 3: Effects of six-months' viewing of Allegra's Window and Gullah Gullah Island.* Tuscaloosa: University of Alabama, Institute for Communication Research.

Calvert, S. L. (1999). *Children's journeys through the information age.* Boston: McGraw-Hill.

Calvert, S. L., Huston, A. C., Watkins, B. A., & Wright, J. C. (1982). The relation between selective attention to television forms and children's comprehension of content. *Child Development, 53,* 601–610.

Calvert, S. L., Rideout, V. J., Woolard, J. L., Barr, R. F., & Strouse, G. A. (2005). Age, ethnicity, and socioeconomic patterns in early computer use: A national survey. *American Behavioral Scientist, 48,* 590–607.

Calvert, S. L., Strong, B., & Gallagher, L. (2005). Control as an engagement feature for young children's attention to, and learning of, computer content. *American Behavioral Scientist, 48,* 578–589.

Calvert, S. L., Strong, B., Jacobs, E., & Conger, E. (2005, August). *Gender, ethnicity and activity for young children's learning from media.* Poster presented at the American Psychological Association, Washington, DC.

Chera, P., & Wood, C. (2003). Animated multimedia "talking books" can promote phonological awareness in children beginning to read. *Learning and Instruction, 13,* 33–52.

Christakis, D. A., Zimmerman, F. J., DiGiuseppe, D. L., & McCarty, C. A. (2004). Early television exposure and subsequent attentional problems in children. *Pediatrics, 113,* 708–713.

Collins, W. A. (1973). Effects of temporal separation between motivation, aggression, and consequences: A developmental study. *Developmental Psychology, 8,* 215–221.

Comstock, G. (1991). *Television and the American child.* San Diego: Academic Press.

Cook, T. D., Appleton, H., Connor, R. F., Shaffer, A., Tamkin, G., & Weber, S. (1975). *Sesame Street revisited.* New York: Russell Sage Foundation.

Eron, L. D., Lefkowitz, M. M., Huesmann, L. R., & Walder, L. O. (1972). Does television violence cause aggression? *American Psychologist, 27,* 253–263.

Evans, M. K., Crawley, A. M., & Anderson, D. R. (2004). *Two-year-olds' object retrieval based on television: Testing a perceptual account.* Unpublished manuscript. University of Massachusetts at Amherst.

Evans, M. K., Pempek, T. A., Kirkorian, H. L., Frankenfield, A. E., & Anderson, D. R. (2004, May). *The impact of background television on complexity of play.* Presented at the biennial International Conference for Infant Studies, Chicago.

Fowler, M., & Brenner, D. (1982). A marketplace approach to broadcast regulation. *Texas Law Review, 60,* 207–257.

Frankenfield, A. E., Richards, J. R., Lauricella, A. R., Pempek, T. A., Kirkorian, H. L., & Anderson, D. R. (2004, May). *Looking at and interacting with comprehensible and incomprehensible Teletubbies.* Poster session presented at the biennial International Conference for Infant Studies, Chicago.

Friedrich, L. K., & Stein, A. H. (1975). Prosocial television and young children: The effects of verbal labeling and role playing on learning and behavior. *Child Development, 46,* 27–38.

Friedrich-Cofer, L. K., Huston-Stein, A. H., Kipnis, D. M., Susman, E. J., & Clewett, A. S. (1979). Environmental enhancement of prosocial television content: Effect on interpersonal behavior, imaginative play, and self-regulation in a natural setting. *Developmental Psychology, 15,* 637–646.

Grela, B., Lin, Y., & Krcmar, M. (2003, April). *Can television be used to teach vocabulary to toddlers?* Paper presented at the annual meeting of the American Speech Language Hearing Association, Chicago.

Hayes, D., & Birnbaum, D. (1980). Preschoolers' retention of televised events: Is a picture worth a thousand words? *Developmental Psychology, 16,* 410–416.

Hayne, H., Herbert, J., & Simcock, G. (2003). Imitation from television by 24- and 30-month-olds. *Developmental Science, 6,* 254–261.

Henry J. Kaiser Family Foundation. (2004). *The role of media in childhood obesity.* Menlo Park, CA: Author.

Huesmann, L. R., & Eron, L. D. (Eds.). (1986). *Television and the aggressive child: A cross-national comparison.* Hillsdale, NJ: Erlbaum.

Huston, A. C., & Wright, J. C. (1983). The informative functions of formal features. In J. Bryant & D. R. Anderson (Eds.), *Children's understanding of television: Research on attention and comprehension* (pp. 35–68). New York: Academic Press.

Huston, A. C., Wright, J. C., Marquis, J., & Green, S. B. (1999). How young children spend their time: Television and other activities. *Developmental Psychology, 35,* 912–925.

Huston, A. C., Wright, J. C., Rice, M. L., Kerkman, D., & St. Peters, M. (1990). The development of television viewing patterns in early childhood: A longitudinal investigation. *Developmental Psychology, 26,* 409–420.

Jordan, A. (2002, April). *V-Chip use.* Paper presented at the Summit on Children's Media Policy, St. Thomas, Virgin Islands.

Labbo, L. D., & Kuhn, M. R. (2000). Weaving chains of affect and cognition: A young child's understanding of CD-ROM talking books. *Journal of Literacy Research, 32,* 187–210.

Linebarger, D., & Walker, D. (2005). Infants and toddlers TV viewing and relations to language outcomes. *American Behavioral Scientist, 48,* 624–645.

Lorch, E. P., Anderson, D. R., & Levin, S. (1979). The relationship of visual attention to children's comprehension of television. *Child Development, 50,* 722–727.

Luecke-Aleska, D., Anderson, D. R., Collins, P. A., & Schmitt, K. L. (1995). Gender constancy and television viewing. *Developmental Psychology, 31,* 773–780.

Mares, M. L. (1996). Positive effects of television on social behaviour: A meta-analysis. *Publications in the Annenberg Public Policy Center's Report Series, 3,* 1–26.

Meltzoff, A. N. (1988). Imitation of televised models by infants. *Child Development, 59,* 1221–1229.

Meltzoff, A. N. (2002). Imitation as a mechanism of social cognition: Origins of empathy, theory of mind, and the representation of action. In U. Goswami (Ed.), *Blackwell handbook of childhood cognitive development* (pp. 6–25). Oxford: Blackwell.

Meltzoff, A. N., & Moore, M. K. (1983). Newborn infants imitate adult facial gestures. *Child Development, 54,* 702–719.

Meltzoff, A. N., & Moore, M. K. (1994). Imitation, memory, and the representation of persons. *Infant Behavior and Development, 17,* 83–99.

Montgomery, K. (2001). Digital kids: The new on-line children's consumer culture. In D. Singer & J. Singer (Eds), *Handbook of children and the media* (pp. 635–650). Thousand Oaks, CA: Sage.

Montgomery, K., & Pasnik, S. (1996). *Web of deception: Threats to children of online marketing.* Washington, DC: Center for Media Education.

Mumme, D. L., & Fernald, A. (1993). The infant as onlooker: Learning from emotional reactions observed in a television scenario. *Child Development, 74,* 221–237.

Paik, H., & Comstock, G. (1994). The effects of television violence on antisocial behavior: A meta-analysis. *Communication Research, 21,* 516–546.

Palmer, E., Cantor, J., Dowrick, P., Kunkel, D., Linn, S., & Wilcox, B. (2004). *Psychological implications of commercialism in the schools.* Washington, DC: American Psychological Association.

Pezdek, K., & Hartman, E. F. (1983). Children's television viewing: Attention and comprehension of auditory and visual information. *Child Development, 54,* 1015–1023.

Rice, M. L., Huston, A. C., Truglio, R. T., & Wright, J. C. (1990). Words from *Sesame Street*: Learning vocabulary while viewing. *Developmental Psychology, 26,* 421–428.

Rideout, V., Vandewater, E., & Wartella, E. (2003). *Zero to six: Electronic media in the lives of infants, toddlers, and preschoolers.* Menlo Park, CA: Henry J. Kaiser Family Foundation.

Robertson, T. S., & Rossiter, J. R. (1974). Children and commercial persuasion: An attribution theory analysis. *Journal of Consumer Research, 1,* 13–20.

Schmitt, K. L., & Anderson, D. R. (2002). Television and reality: Toddlers' use of visual information from video to guide behavior. *Media Psychology, 4,* 51–76.

Schutte, N., Malouff, J., Post-Garden, J., & Rodasta, A. (1988). Effects of playing video games on children's aggressive and other behaviors. *Journal of Applied Social Psychology, 18,* 454–460.

Silvern, S. B., & Williamson, P. A. (1987). The effects of video game play on young children's aggression, fantasy, and prosocial behavior. *Journal of Applied Developmental Psychology, 8,* 453–462.

Spagnolo, D., Ruskis, J., Garcia, A., Albert, S., & Barr, R. (April, 2004). *Infant attention and child–parent interactions during child-directed television program viewing.* Paper presented at the Eastern Psychological Association, Washington, DC.

Stein, A. C., & Friedrich, L. K. (1972). Television content and young children's behavior. In J. P. Murray, E. A. Rubenstein, & G. A. Comstock (Eds.), *Television and social behavior: Vol. II. Television and social learning* (pp. 202–317). Washington, DC: US Government Printing Office.

Stewart, D. W., & Ward, S. (1993). Media effects on advertising. In J. Bryant & D. Zillmann (Eds.), *Media effects: Advances in theory and research* (pp. 315–366). Hillsdale, NJ: Erlbaum.

Swinth, Y., Anson, D., & Deitz, J. (1993). Single-switch computer access for infants and toddlers. *The American Journal of Occupational Therapy, 47,* 1031–1038.

Troseth, G. (2003). TV guide: Two-year-old children learn to use video as a source of information. *Developmental Psychology, 39,* 140–150.

Troseth, G. L., & DeLoache, J. (1998). The medium can obscure the message: Young children's understanding of video. *Child Development, 69,* 950–965.

van der Voort, T. H., & Valkenberg, P. M. (1994). Television's impact on fantasy play: A review of research. *Developmental Review, 14,* 27–51.

Vandewater, E. A., Bickham, D. S., Lee, J. H., Cummings, H. M., Wartella, E. A., & Rideout, V. J. (2005). When the television is always on: Heavy television exposure and young children's development. *American Behavioral Scientist, 48,* 539–562.

Ward, S. (1980). The effects of television advertising on consumer socialization. In R. P. Adler, G. S. Lesser, & A. Dorr (Eds.), *Children and the faces of television: Teaching, violence, selling* (pp. 185–194). New York: Academic Press.

Watkins, B., Calvert, S. L., Huston-Stein, A., & Wright, J. C. (1980). Children's recall of television material: Effects of presentation mode and adult labeling. *Developmental Psychology, 16,* 672–674.

Wiegermann, O., Kuttschreuter, M., & Baarda, B. (1992). A longitudinal study of the effects of television viewing on aggressive and prosocial behaviors. *British Journal of Social Psychology, 31,* 147–164.

Wright, J. C., Huston, A. C., Murphy, K. C., St. Peters, M., Piñon, M., Scantlin, R., & Kotler, J. (2001). The relations of early television viewing to school readiness and vocabulary of children from low-income families: The Early Window Project. *Child Development, 72,* 1347–1366.

PART VII

Policy Issues

26

Evaluating Early Childhood Assessments: A Differential Analysis

Samuel J. Meisels and Sally Atkins-Burnett

Assessment consists of the process of obtaining information for the purpose of making evaluative decisions. In early childhood, assessment is fundamentally a positive process that holds the potential for enhancing teaching and improving learning by means of the information obtained – specifically, a child's likely membership in a high-risk group (identification), the best way to approach a teaching encounter (instructional improvement), how well a program is achieving its stated goals (evaluation), or whether children are learning what they are intended to learn (accountability).

Widespread testing of children below age 8, or grade 3, was not very prevalent in the US until the latter part of the twentieth century. Although reading-readiness tests have a history that is nearly a century old (see Cuban, 1992), they focused specifically on early reading skills, and served solely an instructional purpose – to assist teachers in preparing young children to learn to read. Otherwise, little formal testing of young children took place, with the exception of IQ tests, which were dominated by the Stanford–Binet and by group-administered tests. In the 1960s and 1970s a wide variety of readiness tests began to appear, but these tests were typically selected by classroom teachers, or occasionally by school districts, to ascertain children's relative preparedness for particular classroom programs (Meisels, 1987), rather than to evaluate a child's general developmental status.

During the late 1960s and early 1970s developmental screening tests emerged. One of the first such tests, and certainly the most widely used, was the Denver Developmental Screening Test (DDST; Frankenberg & Dodds, 1967). Although several other screening instruments are available (see Glascoe, Martin, & Humphrey, 1990; Meisels & Atkins-Burnett, 2005) and dismayingly large numbers of screening tests are developed "locally," without any known validation or standardization (Costenbader, Rohrer, & Difonzo, 2000), the DDST remains the most widely used screening test in the United States, if not the world (Glascoe et al., 1992). Unfortunately, the DDST has been one of the least accurate commercially available predictors of early development (see Meisels, 1988), under-referring as many as 95 out of 100 at-risk children in its first versions.

Some of the interest in the DDST and in developmental screening in general followed from the growth of testing for special needs in the mid-1970s and the 1980s in response to legislation that required states and local education agencies to find, identify, and serve children with special needs. These requirements, incorporated into the Education for All Handicapped Children's Act of 1975 (P.L. 94–142), first affected children as young as age 5. However, with subsequent reauthorizations of this law (now called the Individuals with Disabilities Education Act), children with suspected disabilities from birth onwards are eligible for assessment services (Meisels & Shonkoff, 2000).

The next major landmark in general early childhood testing occurred with the formulation of the National Education Goals in 1989 (National Education Goals Panel, 1991). The first of these goals stated that, "By the year 2000 all children will enter school ready to learn." Several task forces and resource panels were established not only to expli-cate these twelve words, but also to try to determine how we would know if children were ready (Meisels, 1999). Over the decade of the 1990s, the Goals Panel discussions did not result in the selection or development of a "readiness test." Rather, the Goals Panel agreed that, because of the inherent relativity in the concept of readiness, at best we can identify the domains of readiness behavior shown by the child – language, cogni-tion, social and emotional, physical, and approaches to learning – while recognizing that schools, families, and communities are also a critical part of the readiness equation. As Bruner (1966) said, it is a "mischievous half-truth" to assume that one waits for readiness to appear, since it "largely turns out that one teaches readiness or provides opportunities for its nurture" (p. 29).

Nevertheless, according to data reported by the National Center for Education Statis-tics, large numbers of children are being tested before or at entrance to kindergarten. In 1998–9, 69% of public schools administered entrance or placement tests prior to kindergarten. These tests were used by the schools to determine class placement, identify children who might need additional assessment, inform decisions about admission for children who were younger than the cut-off age, and help teachers to design individual-ized instruction. In addition, 27% of schools continue to use some form of formalized testing prior to kindergarten as a justification for delaying entry to kindergarten (Prakash, West, & Denton, 2003). This high-stakes use of testing in early childhood runs contrary to position statements issued by professional organizations (e.g., NAEYC & NAECS/SDE, 2003).

The current perspective on testing young children shows that it is marked by significant problems. A forum on preschool assessment convened at Temple University in January 2003 (Kochanoff, 2003) suggested the need to focus on creating new assessments that respect the contexts of minority children's lives; recognize the importance of naturalistic and process-oriented information; are broader than just literacy and numeracy, by includ-ing motor, problem-solving and other cognitive skills, and socio-emotional development; and establish integrative procedures that allow for a comprehensive understanding of children's learning and make it possible to evaluate the interaction among different devel-opmental domains.

Assessments should examine multiple areas of development in multiple contexts and include naturalistic and process-oriented information. Neisworth and Bagnato (2004) offer eight standards for developmentally appropriate assessments. Such assessments measure socially acceptable and worthy developmental indicators; use naturalistic methods; are useful for interventions, equitable for diverse children, and sensitive to small differences; examine the convergence of diverse information; are congruent with evidence-based findings; and include collaboration among parents and professionals.

Clearly, much work remains. Many children are not experiencing the benefits of fair, equitable, and well-constructed assessments. In what follows, we will provide an analytical discussion of the field as we know it today by adhering to a typology that categorizes four uses or roles for assessment in the preschool years: (1) identification, (2) instructional improvement, (3) program evaluation, and (4) accountability (Shepard, Kagan, & Wurtz, 1998). Our goal is to explore the limits of what we know about early childhood assessment so that new work can be undertaken and practices that employ the contributions of the past can become more effective.

Identification

Assessments for identification are intended to determine whether children are likely to be eligible for special services. In particular, developmental screening instruments seek to identify children who may be at high risk for school failure and/or developmental disabilities. As a procedure that seeks to identify at an early age those children who have a high probability of exhibiting delayed or abnormal development, screening tests carry significant consequences for individual children and, therefore, should be held to the highest psychometric standards (American Educational Research Association, American Psychological Association, & National Council on Measurement in Education, 1999; Bracken, 1987; Joint Committee on Testing Practices, 1988). Screening tests should be brief, efficient, inexpensive, objectively scored, reliable, valid, culture-fair, and broadly developmental in focus (Meisels & Atkins-Burnett, 2005). Screening tests do not provide definitive conclusions about a child's developmental status. Rather, the results of screening tests are roughly equivalent to those of a hypothesis that must be confirmed or disconfirmed by subsequent evaluation and further assessment.

If for no other reason than their brevity, screening tests invariably contain errors. The key question concerns the quantity and distribution of the erroneous identifications. Given the demonstrated value of early intervention (Shonkoff & Phillips, 2000), it is reasonable to assume that a higher proportion of false positives is preferable to false negatives, so that as few at-risk children as possible can be assumed to be not at risk (Meisels, Henderson, Liaw, Browning, & Ten Have, 1993). For this reason, screening should occur within a context of progressive or serial testing (e.g., 4, 8, 12, 18 months; 2, 3, 4, 5 years) so that if at-risk children are missed at one age, they can be identified later. Indeed, it is virtually an axiom of assessment at all age levels that no single measure administered on a single occasion can be used to determine eligibility for services or to make any other "high-stakes" decision (Heubert & Hauser, 1999). Since developmental disorders are generally attributable to multiple causes or multiple factors, screening and assessment of those at risk for non-optimal development should reflect multiple aspects of development and multiple assessment opportunities (Hemmeter, Joseph, Smith, & Sandall, 2001; NAEYC & NAECS/SDE, 2003).

A common confusion in early childhood assessment is that between screening and readiness testing. Stated very broadly, screening tests assess a child's ability to acquire the skills that are then measured on readiness tests. Readiness tests focus on current skill acquisition and performance, they are highly influenced by opportunity to learn, and they focus on criteria that are assumed to be prerequisite for later skills. Many of these tests are poor predictors of school performance, because children who have not been taught certain skills may acquire them easily in school and will then appear to be false positives (i.e., the test will indicate that they are "not ready" to perform in school when in fact they are, following instruction or modification of their experience) (Meisels, 1987). Although readiness tests provide a starting point for instruction, they often include tasks and probes that are unfamiliar to children, and as such, these tests should not be used to make placement decisions.

Screening instruments also should not be used to make placement decisions. When screening results indicate that more detailed assessment is needed, families should be invited to help plan and collect assessment information (Hemmeter et al., 2001). Primary caregivers have knowledge of children over time and can often help professionals understand the child's strengths and weaknesses. Parents observe their child's behavior in multiple environments and under many different circumstances. They can make important contributions to the screening and assessment process and should be included from planning the assessment through follow-up. Families can also contribute critical knowledge about cultural and linguistic differences that may affect interpretation of assessment data (Barona & Santos de Barons, 2000; Barrera, 1996).

It is important to keep in mind that every assessment can be an intervention in some respect, even screenings. Parents may pay attention to the questions asked and make inferences about whether their child should or should not be able to respond. Parental perceptions of children can be affected negatively if information and results are not shared appropriately and sensitively. "The professional's job is not to promote her or his view of the child to the parent but to join the parents and other professionals in viewing the child multidimensionally in order to contribute to the generation of strategies that will help the child make developmental advances and organize his or her world more adequately" (Meisels & Atkins-Burnett, 2000, p. 235).

Instructional Improvement

Assessment information that is collected in an ongoing manner in the preschool classroom can inform instruction and influence programming. Data collected longitudinally allow teachers to examine children's growth over time and consider the effects of different instructional techniques and curricula. In early childhood, the staple of assessment is observation of the child in the natural setting. These observations may be documented using anecdotal records, checklists, event sampling, running records, rating scales, socio-grams, or reflective diaries/logs/journals (McAfee & Leong, 2002). In addition, child behavior may be documented using video, audiotapes, photographs, and samples of work. Several commercially available assessments have been designed to help focus the teacher's observations and/or the collection of work (Dodge, Colker, & Heroman, 2001; High/Scope Research Foundation, 1992; Marazon, 1999; Meisels, Jablon, Marsden, Dichtel-miller, & Dorfman, 2001; Missouri Department of Elementary and Secondary Educa-tion, 1992). These assessment systems utilize developmental continua and rubrics (i.e., analyses of curriculum elements that demonstrate differential achievement of these cur-ricular objectives) to help teachers focus observations on important developmental goals and educational standards. They provide tools for documenting and collecting data. Well-developed rubrics guide teachers in observing the qualities and essential components of successful performance in a given area.

For some children and teachers, the rubrics included in some of these measures are so broad that the developmental change they encompass does not capture the growth that may occur in a single year (this is particularly true of children with special needs, who may progress in only small increments). Teachers need to document intermediate steps and recognize small changes. Expanded rubrics provide a means to collect data on these finer gradient changes.

Assessments that are useful for guiding instruction include checklists of behaviors that are important indicators of success in the curriculum or classroom, and/or represent specific developmental milestones. However, some developmental checklists include items that are markers of a child's current status, but are not suitable instructional goals for children. When developmental indicators are placed in order of difficulty without any reference to how they link to curriculum, teachers need to be very knowledgeable about the items included in the assessment and their relationship to different areas of develop-ment. Without reference to how items represent curriculum and/or early learning standards, teachers may be unable to interpret the relevance of a child's responses. The connection between assessment and instruction or intervention becomes very weak in such cases and may lead to inappropriate instruction.

Integral to the productive use of instructional assessment is the quality of a teacher's observational skills. Teachers must be capable of understanding individual differences among children, connecting these perceptions to a well-defined framework of develop-ment based on state standards, and using these observations to improve instruction and maximize students' learning (Meisels 1994, 1996a; Meisels, Liaw, Dorfman, & Nelson, 1995). Professional development in the use of observational assessments is extremely important.

Instructional assessments, no less than other types of assessment, should be subjected to rigorous validity studies. Studies examining the reliability and validity of observational assessments have demonstrated interrater reliability and consequential, construct, and predictive validity (Meisels, Atkins-Burnett, Xue, Bickel, Nicholson, & Son, 2003; Meisels, Bickel, Nicholson, Xue, & Atkins-Burnett, 2001; Meisels et al., 1995). In addi-tion, levels of teacher implementation, understanding, and satisfaction, and evaluations of parental understanding and satisfaction can be investigated by means of survey questionnaires and interviews (Meisels, Xue, Bickel, Nicholson, & Atkins-Burnett, 2001; Nicholson, 2000).

Fundamentally, instructional uses of early childhood assessment are intended to answer questions about how children can be helped, how children's accomplishments can be enhanced, and how adults can more adequately assist children in meeting their potential (Meisels & Atkins-Burnett, 2000). These questions can be answered only when the evidence helps uncover patterns in development and the reasons behind children's successes and failures. In order to perceive these patterns, information about the circumstances under which children are successful and unsuccessful must be collected. It is insufficient to record that a child did or did not exhibit particular behaviors. The environmental supports, level of engagement, qualities of the behavior (e.g., fluidity, spontaneity, control) and interactions that elicited behaviors also provide important information about the child's skills, knowledge, dispositions, interests, and growing abilities. To support their development, children should be evaluated based on their current performance in relation to their own prior performance, rather than on comparisons with other children.

In recent years, assessment and intervention (i.e., instruction) have begun to be considered jointly, rather than apart. When these two functions are fused, they can be used to support the child's ability to function successfully (Meisels, 1996b). Assessment facilitates instructional choices, and the child's responses to those instructional choices are correlative aspects of assessment evidence. In this way, assessment and instruction can be viewed as dynamic processes in which one informs the other.

Program Evaluation

Assessments are used in program evaluation studies to focus on the child, the environment, and the instruction or intervention. Evaluations are concerned with demonstrating how effectively a program has achieved its goals. When evaluating programs, measurement of implementation and of program quality should be the first priority on the evaluation agenda because the ultimate goal of a program evaluation is to ensure that programs serving young children and families are making a positive difference in their lives (Gilliam, 2000; Gilliam & Zigler, 2000). Toward that end, meaningful evaluations must go beyond collections of child outcomes to include careful examination of program variations that may be related to differences in child outcomes. Patton (1997) labels as "developmental evaluation" the model that utilizes the process of evaluation to continue to develop and refine the program in an "ongoing process of continuous improvement, adaptation, and intentional change" (p. 105). Such a formative evaluation is designed to pose continuous evaluative questions and to collect data to answer those questions. Program evaluations that follow this model are designed to answer such questions as what services are provided, who received the services, and whether the services produced anticipated outcomes (Gomby, 1999).

The fidelity to the intervention of the program must always be considered when assessing program effects in order to know how frequently and with what level of quality the recommended practices are implemented. Without this information, it is impossible to determine which features of a program that are measured are responsible for the outcomes (Solomon, 2002). Moreover, the interaction of program characteristics with community, family, and child contexts should be considered in examining program efficacy. Given the diversity among children and families, there may be differences in the type and intensity of services that will be helpful to particular groups of children. It may also be the case that some programs are not implemented as well or as intensively as developers had planned and the program evaluation may not be a fair test of the model, but, instead, an "evaluation of a poorly implemented shadow" (Gomby, 1999, p. 28). In this case, it may be difficult to tell if the program could indeed support development of a specific group of children when well implemented. Although child outcomes are often a key indicator of program evaluation, the critical determinant of program success should be change (i.e., what the child knows and can do after involvement with the program) rather than status (i.e., where the child ranks in relation to others).

Assessments that are included in evaluations must be tied closely to program goals. For example, with the current policy focus on literacy in early childhood, many early care and education programs are beginning to emphasize acquisition of early literacy skills. Researchers often ask parents about the frequency with which they read aloud to their child. However, they do not obtain similar information about the frequency and amount of reading aloud or the types of texts read in the classroom or the types of questions and comments made by teachers and children. Rating instruments such as the Early Childhood Environment Rating Scale-Revised Edition (ECERS-R; Harms, Clifford, & Cryer, 1998) and the Assessment Profile for Early Childhood Programs (Abbott-Shim & Sibley, 1998) are frequently used in large-scale evaluation studies. These instruments examine program quality across a wide range of dimensions (e.g., space, personal care, language/ reasoning, parents and staff, etc.). They do not entail in-depth, process-oriented observations of any single component and, as a result, they are difficult to target toward the specific goals of a program.

Similarly, child assessments should be chosen to assess the intended outcomes, rather than merely discrete skills that are related to an outcome. In an effort to save time and money, many large program evaluations commit the error of assessing only lower-level skills or including too few items to measure an area reliably. Relying on select subtests from a measure is another practice that should be used with caution. Although a full assessment may have good psychometric properties, the individual subtests may not be reliable or valid when administered in isolation. Another concern with current evaluation efforts is the way in which skills are sampled and assessed. Many current evaluation efforts attempt to address the issues that current policy makers consider important (letter naming and phonological awareness, for example), but ignore the interrelatedness of development and the multiple ways in which children – particularly children from differing cultural backgrounds – might demonstrate what they know and can do. The greatest concern with this narrow focus is that teachers will begin to teach only what they perceive is valued, based on what is assessed. Preschool is a time for building a rich resource of language and experiences upon which children may draw as they continue learning in formal education. Evaluation efforts should support, not hinder, teachers and programs in offering children rich and complex learning experiences.

Rather than sampling discrete (and often disconnected) skills within constructs, program evaluations should sample children and examine the complexity of their development and learning in order to understand the effects of the program on the child's functioning. In addition, analysis of program effects needs to account for the influence of familial factors and how the program affects them. Families continue to have a strong influence on the learning and development of young children even when they are in full day programs. Evaluations in the preschool years must examine how programs support diverse families in caring for and educating their children in ways that will have both short- and long-term results. Multi-dimensional, multi-method assessments are very expensive to collect, but can be feasible when representative samples of children are studied. Good evaluations consist of much more than lengthy enumerations of individual items and subtests from other assessments. Much more work in this area is needed if we are truly to understand the impact of programs on children's development.

Accountability

Recent years have witnessed an enormous growth in accountability testing in schools all across the US. With the passage of the No Child Left Behind Act (NCLB), introduced by President George W. Bush on his third day in office, every student from third to eighth grade is required to be tested annually in mathematics and reading. Targets for continuing improvement by individual schools on these assessments over a ten-year period are embedded in federal law, and sanctions, including transfer of pupils and closure of failing schools (as defined by results on the tests), are spelled out in the law as well. Never before in the nation's history has so much high-stakes testing taken place, nor have the stakes ever been any higher.

High-stakes tests are defined as those that are linked directly to decisions that are important to a child's future, such as retention or promotion, tracking into achievement groups, choice of curriculum, and so forth. High-stakes decisions also affect teachers and schools, as, for example, when the results of tests are relied upon to decide if a teacher will receive a bonus, a principal will be rehired, or a school will be closed (see Madaus, 1988; Mueller, 2002).

Under NCLB and the resulting accountability culture, attention to reporting and documenting success on achievement tests has grown exponentially. In the face of this near-obsession with making test scores the criterion of school success and a legislative commitment to the "stick" of penalties and sanctions rather than the "carrot" of high expectations and enhanced teaching methodologies, what is the role of accountability and high-stakes testing in early childhood?

To some extent, the answer to this question is moot. Referring to the work of the National Education Goals Panel, the Committee on Appropriate Test Use of the National Academy of Sciences noted, "In general, large-scale assessments should not be used to make high-stakes decisions about students who are less than 8 years old or enrolled below Grade 3" (Heubert & Hauser, 1999, p. 279). The Goal 1 Resource Group pointed out that "standardized achievement measures are not sufficiently accurate to be used for high-stakes decisions about individual children and schools" (Shepard et al., 1998, p. 31). Further, the resource panel suggests that "if direct measures are used before age 8 to monitor trends in learning, matrix sampling procedures should be used to . . . protect against the misuse of data to make decisions about individual children" (Shepard et al., 1998, p. 31).

Still another National Academy of Sciences panel echoed the same words. In 2001 the Committee on Early Childhood Pedagogy (Bowman, Donovan, & Burns, 2001), of which the first author was a member, stated that assessments used for purposes external to the classroom, rather than to improve practice, place a heavy burden on the assessments and the adults responsible for them. According to this report, tests used for high-stakes purposes must not be mistaken for statements about the learning trajectory of individual children.

Understanding the role that high-stakes testing and accountability can play in the first years of life calls for us to examine some fundamental assumptions. Three basic axioms of assessment of young children can be articulated. First, assessment is a dynamic process. It calls for information from multiple sources, collected over numerous time points, reflecting a range of experiences. Research of the past generation has demonstrated repeatedly that when it comes to risk and resilience, measurement does not occur in a vacuum. Multiple sources need to be taken into account (Sameroff & Fiese, 2000; Shonkoff & Phillips, 2000; Werner, 2000). Second, best practice suggests that a formal assessment is only the first of many steps that is followed by a cycle of intervention and re-evaluation. It is only when an assessment is embedded in a context of testing, teaching, and retesting that we can hope to improve the accuracy of our predictions from test scores (Greenspan & Meisels, 1996; Popham, 2005). Third, the meaning of an assessment is closely tied to its use – to decisions about what will happen next in a child's life. Indeed, we know that, to some extent, the validity of an assessment lies in how it is used (Messick, 1994). Without evidence that tests are valid, it is unacceptable for them to be used to decide unilaterally whether a child should be promoted or retained or "redshirted," whether a school or program should be allowed to function or to be closed, or whether a teacher or principal should be rewarded or punished.

These assumptions are all violated when high-stakes tests are used with young children. The complexity of assessment, its relationship to other elements of teaching and learning, and its appropriate uses are all ignored for the sake of policy directives that are highly questionable with young children. Furthermore, child development research tells us that young children are poor test takers – not only because they have not been taught to take tests or because they lack experience with tests, but because the formal test paradigm is at odds developmentally with how young children grow and develop.

Numerous difficulties occur when one tries to administer formal tests to young children. These include children's restricted ability to comprehend such assessment cues as verbal instructions and stimuli, situational cues, or written instructions. Further, the structure of some questions calls for children to give differential weights to alternative choices, distinguish recency from primacy, or follow the trail of multi-step directions – any of which may pose significant cognitive problems for many children. Finally, behavioral inhibitions or ability to defer or regulate responses are not uniformly distributed among young children. Hence, some may not be able to control their behavior to meet the demand characteristics of the assessment situation, and their behavior regulation may be impaired by boredom, fatigue, hunger, illness, or anxiety (Meisels, 1994).

Still another reason that conventional tests and measurements in early childhood may provide unreliable information is that children's opportunities to learn are vastly different in early childhood. "Opportunity to learn" concerns what children have been taught before coming to school. The diversity of opportunities to learn in early childhood describes a fundamental inequity that children must overcome when they enter school. Testing older children has its own challenges and pitfalls, but at least there is usually a period of common schooling before these children are assessed (even NCLB does not call for testing below grade 3). For young children this is rarely the case.

Finally, to assume that a test administered at the outset of the formal school experience (as, for example, in the administration of a school readiness test) can make valid predictions that may have long-term consequences for individual children assumes these inequities to be virtually immutable. But one of the tasks of schooling is to overcome inequities that are present on entry by providing an environment in which children can learn and begin to achieve. By ignoring the differences that may be attributable to opportunity to learn, as conventional accountability measures do, we are begging the question of what individual children need and how curricula can be fashioned to be responsive to those needs.

Further information about the problems of making predictions from early childhood assessments is available from a meta-analysis performed by LaParo and Pianta (2000). They report the results from seventy longitudinal studies that sought to correlate academic/cognitive and social/behavioral measures in preschool and kindergarten with like measures in first and second grade. They found that, on average, only 25% of the variance in early academic/cognitive performance is predicted from preschool or kindergarten cognitive status and only 10% or less of the variance in K-Grade 2 social/behavioral measures is accounted for by similar measures at preschool or kindergarten. The authors conclude that "instability or change may be the rule rather than the exception during this period" (p. 476).

Another important related study was conducted by Kim and Suen (2003). Using Hierarchical Linear Modeling (HLM), they performed a "validity generalization study" of 716 predictive correlation coefficients from 44 studies. Their purpose was to determine if the predictive validity coefficients of early assessments can be used to draw generalized conclusions about later achievement or success in school. Their study shows that predictive validity coefficients in early childhood are different in different situations. They conclude that "the predictive power of any early assessment from any single study is not generalizable, regardless of design and quality of research. The predictive power of early assessments is different from situation to situation" (p. 561). The authors are not saying that no early childhood test is predictive; after all the potential predictive coefficients of the tests in their study ranged from .12 to .81. What they are saying is that predictive validity coefficients vary as a function of test type, specific construct being assessed, length of prediction, and administration procedures. Moreover, if we were to average all adjusted predictive coefficients in order to obtain a "typical" overall prediction, we would be providing misleading information because this overall average coefficient, which conceals substantial unaccounted-for variation, is not representative and therefore is not meaningful. In short, this study arrives at conclusions that are very similar to LaParo and Pianta (2000): Instability is more the case than not in early childhood development, and tests of accountability that overlook the implications of this variability will mislead policy makers, the public, and children's teachers.

In the face of these results and other information that has been presented here, it is difficult to conclude that accountability testing in early childhood is a meaningful endeavor. Yet policy makers continue to call for such assessments, for much the same reason as they demand accountability data for programs for older students: to be able to prove that a program that receives public support is achieving its goals. This rationale has never been clearer than with the Head Start National Reporting System (NRS).

First administered in the fall of 2003, the NRS is the largest single testing ever mounted by the federal government – at any age level or any time. The NRS is a relatively narrow test of literacy and numeracy. Elsewhere we have criticized the construction and selection of items for the test (Meisels & Atkins-Burnett, 2004). Here we will mention three key psychometric principles that the NRS, similar to all other assessments, must satisfy (see American Educational Research Association et al., 1999). They include:

1. *External validity of the subtests*. There must be evidence to demonstrate that the particular subtests of a test measure what they purport to measure.
2. *Construct representativeness*. The test items must capture important aspects of the construct that the test is intended to measure.
3. *Reduce construct-irrelevant variance*. The test scores should not be influenced by factors that are irrelevant to the constructs the test is intended to measure, such as choice of vocabulary, selection of illustrations, language burden of particular items, or how the items appear on the page.

Not only are these psychometric characteristics of great consequence for the NRS and other candidates for accountability testing in early childhood, the broader issue is that secondary effects beyond conventional high-stakes can come into play when a high-stakes test is administered. Since the time of Skinner, it has been well known that "you teach what you test." In Head Start, it is likely that teachers will be strongly influenced to alter their teaching and curriculum to conform to the pedagogical model implicit in this test (this is widely known as "measurement-directed instruction"). Research tells us that when a teacher knows that the results of a test will be used to make decisions that may affect the program's continuation, teachers are sorely tempted to begin teaching to the test (Lynn, 2003; Padulla et al., 2003).

Research also informs us that a major portion of the variance in child development and academic achievement is accounted for by birth circumstances and differences in demographic characteristics (e.g., socio-economic status, race, family size, prenatal care, home language) (Camburn, Rowan, Atkins-Burnett, & Hayes, 2003; Entwisle & Alexander, 1990). Analysis of program effects needs to account for the influence of these factors and how the program affects family dynamics that might enhance long-term development. Relying solely on child performance at a single time point ignores the lessons learned from Head Start and many other interventions.

All of this is not to reject the importance of measuring outcomes. It is possible to construct assessments that provide fair and equitable information about what young children have learned, how they have been taught, and what those working with them can do next in order to advance growth and development (Meisels, 1999; Raver & Zigler, 2004). But simplistic approaches to outcome assessment that are uninformed by research, that attempt to compress all of a child's experience into a narrow set of achievement items, and that do not take into account the context in which children live and grow have the potential to do harm. The Hippocratic oath applies to assessment in early childhood as strongly as it does in other fields of human service.

If we accept the premises we have provided here that young children are developmentally not good test takers; that children's opportunities to learn differ greatly; that development in the first years of life is marked by variability and change; that predictive validity coefficients in early childhood cannot be generalized meaningfully; and that available tests are narrow and unresponsive to individual needs, the conclusion we draw is that high-stakes tests do not have a place in early childhood. Instead of constructing tests that are designed to focus on normative achievements of children, thus masking individual differences, we should try to develop assessments that highlight differences in development and that examine patterns of change. This will enable children to show their strengths and perform optimally rather than to point up their weaknesses and narrow their focus to areas for remediation (Gardner, 1993). The approach to assessment in early childhood with the highest probability of accomplishing this is repeated observational assessment (Meisels, 1996a). These are assessments that are based on systematic observations of children engaged in tasks that are part of their daily experience, and, responding to instruction and experiences, designed to scaffold learning. But clearly, this type of assessment is criterion-referenced, relies on teacher judgment, calls for relatively high levels of training and technical assistance, and cannot be used for high stakes without teachers' judgments being distorted.

It is for these reasons that if accountability is to be used in early childhood, it should be viewed as a system and not as a test. The National Research Council points out that tests are not perfect: "A test score is not an exact measure of a student's knowledge or skills" (Heubert & Hauser, 1999, p. 275). Although assessments have not been developed that are useful for accountability purposes in the early years of life, as more and better tests become available, we need to understand that our best hope continues to be multi-method, multi-dimensional assessments that combine normative and curriculum-embedded, or observational, assessments that are used in naturalistic environments. The normative measures would need to be representative of the complex tasks that we want children to be able to perform, instead of the atomistic low-level tasks currently used in many program evaluations and accountability efforts. The observational tools would help teachers to understand what part of a task presents difficulty for a particular child and what types of support the child needs to be successful. When the two approaches to assessment are linked, children may actually perform better on standardized measures because instruction can be targeted to the skills and needs of the learner by using the information gained from the ongoing observational assessment.

In short, there is no single way to demonstrate accountability – especially in early childhood. Child development cannot easily be "pinned down." Observational assessments provide a means for recording the context for learning, what has been taught, and what has been learned, as long as this is done in a low-stakes environment. High-stakes applications of judgment-based assessments will create intolerable conflicts of interest for teachers. Nevertheless, instructionally based information can be of extraordinary importance to policy makers and others who are responsible for the effectiveness of early childhood programs because they provide documentation of what is being taught and learned. Observational assessments collected on all children can be supplemented by comprehensive, individual, normative assessments of a sample of children in order to determine if the information from the observational assessments corresponds to expectations. In this way we can begin to construct a web or network of evidence that shows us not only what children are learning and how they are developing, but also how accurate our assessments are. Such a plan is ambitious, but it may be the only meaningful way to be accountable to and for young children.

Conclusion

Fundamentally, early childhood assessment concerns asking and answering questions about children's knowledge, skills, behavior, and personality. The information we acquire through assessment is then used to make evaluative decisions, in which evaluation consists of judging how closely something approximates a standard, whether the standard is highly objective and external or relatively subjective and open to interpretation.

With the advent of high-stakes testing, assessments have increasingly become instruments of reward and punishment. But for young children, there is no justification for this use. Standardized assessments assume that measurement error is randomly distributed. Social, cultural, linguistic, and ecological differences in early childhood are not randomly distributed. Until our methodologies advance to the point where they can account for the diversity and the volatility of development during the preschool years, any use of assessments for accountability purposes will be riddled with problems of invalidity.

We subscribe to two principles that we believe should influence assessment decisions in early childhood. First, meaningful measurements begin with meaningful interactions between assessors and children. These interactions are a necessary condition for obtaining useful information for making evaluative decisions about children. This calls for assessments that are contextualized and culturally appropriate, assessors who are well trained and can establish rapport with the children they are testing and their families, and decisions that are not based on a single point in time or a single context or a single source of information for decision making.

Our second principle concerns values, as implied by the word "evaluate." Assessment does not take place in a context that is free of values. What we assess generally suggests what we value. Indeed, those who select and administer assessments are engaged in making a value-bounded choice about their view of learning and development. However, too often, we assess what is easy, what is narrow, and what is expedient. The need is pressing for integrative assessment methodologies that will allow us to examine the interaction of different areas of development and the ways in which children can be successful in meeting the demands of home and school. It is particularly important that we attend to the constructs that we know to be important for later achievement and life outcomes, especially communication, problem solving, and socio-emotional development. More-over, these assessments need to be fair to children from diverse cultures and allow for the multiple ways in which children demonstrate their knowledge, skills, and abilities.

This chapter has described a number of achievable challenges: that of identifying children at risk for developmental delay or school failure; that of obtaining evaluative information from classroom settings that can be used effectively to inform instruction and improve learning; and that of designing evaluations that reflect the wide range of influences that affect child growth and development. Perhaps the greatest challenge of all is to act on the words of Stephen Jay Gould (1981), when he wrote about the "mismea-sure of man": "There are . . . few injustices deeper than the denial of an opportunity to strive or ever hope by a limit imposed from without, but falsely identified as lying within" (p. 28). Our task as consumers and developers of assessments is to meet the challenge of being as confident as possible that the information we are obtaining about each child is accurate and meaningful so that assessment can play a positive role in supporting children's development.

References

Abbott-Shim, M., & Sibley, A. (1998). *Assessment Profile for Early Childhood Programs: Research version*. Atlanta, GA: Quality Assist.

Administration for Children and Families (June 6, 2003). *Information Memorandum: Description of the NRS Child Assessment*. Accessed online on September 28, 2003 at *http://www.headstartinfo. or/publications/im03_07.htm*

American Educational Research Association, American Psychological Association, & National Council on Measurement in Education. (1999). *Standards for educational and psychological testing*. Washington, DC: American Educational Research Association.

Barona, A., & Santos de Barons, M. (2000). Assessing multicultural preschool children. In B. Bracken (Ed.), *Psychoeducational assessment of preschool children* (3rd ed., pp. 282–297). Boston: Allyn & Bacon.

Barrera, I. (1996). Thoughts on the assessment of young children whose sociocultural background is unfamiliar to the assessor. In S. J. Meisels & E. Fenichel (Eds.), *New visions for the develop-mental assessment of infants and young children* (pp. 69–84). Washington, DC: Zero to Three Press.

Bowman, B. T., Donovan, M. S., & Burns, M. S. (Eds.). (2001). *Eager to learn: Educating our preschoolers*. Washington, DC: National Academy Press.

Bracken, B. A. (1987). Limitations of preschool instrumentations and standards for minimal levels of technical adequacy. *Journal of Psychoeducational Assessment, 5*, 313–326.

Bruner, J. (1966). *Towards a theory of instruction*. Cambridge, MA: Harvard University Press.

Camburn, E., Rowan, B., Atkins-Burnett, S., & Hayes, A. (2003, April). *The effect of students' kindergarten instructional experiences on early literacy achievement*. Paper presented at the Annual Meeting of the American Educational Research Association, Chicago.

Costenbader, V., Rohrer, M., & Difonzo, N. (2000). Kindergarten screening: A survey of current practice. *Psychology in the Schools, 37*(4), 323–332.

Cuban, L. (1992). Why some reforms last: The case of the kindergarten. *American Journal of Education, 100*, 166–194.

Dodge, D. T., Colker, L. J., & Heroman, C. (2001). *A teacher's guide to using The Creative Curriculum® Developmental Continuum Assessment System.* Washington, DC: Teaching Strategies, Inc.

Entwisle, D., & Alexander, K. (1990). Beginning school math competence: Minority and majority comparisons. *Child Development, 61*, 454–471.

Frankenburg, W. K., & Dodds, J. (1967). The Denver Developmental Screening Test. *Journal of Pediatrics, 71*, 181–191.

Gardner, H. (1993). Assessment in context: The alternative to standardized testing. In H. Gardner, *Multiple intelligences: The theory in practice* (pp. 161–183). New York: Basic Books.

Gilliam, W. S. (2000). On overgeneralizing from overly-simplistic evaluations of complex social programs: In further response to Goodson, Layser, St. Pierre and Bernstein. *Early Childhood Research Quarterly, 15*(1), 66–71.

Gilliam, W. S., & Zigler, E. F. (2000). A critical meta-analysis of all evaluations of state-funded preschool from 1977 to 1998: Implications for policy, service delivery, and program evaluation. *Early Childhood Research Quarterly, 15*(4), 441–473.

Glascoe, F. P., Byrne, K. E., Ashford, L. G., Johnson, K. L., Chang, B., & Strickland, B. (1992). Accuracy of the *Denver-II* in developmental screening. *Pediatrics, 89*(6), 147–154.

Glascoe, F. P., Martin, E. D., & Humphrey, S. (1990). A comparative review of developmental screening tests. *Pediatrics, 86*(4), 547–554.

Gomby, D. S. (1999). Understanding evaluations of home visitation programs. *The Future of Children, 9*(1), 27–43.

Gould, S. J. (1981). *The mismeasure of man.* New York: Norton.

Greenspan, S. I., & Meisels, S. J. (1996). Toward a new vision for the developmental assessment of infants and young children. In S. J. Meisels & E. Fenichel (Eds.), *New visions for the developmental assessment of infants and young children* (pp. 11–26). Washington, DC: Zero to Three.

Harms, T., Clifford, R. M., & Cryer, D. (1998). *Early Childhood Environment Rating Scale – Revised edition.* New York: Teachers College Press.

Hemmeter, M. L., Joseph, G. E., Smith, B. J., & Sandall, S. (2001). *DEC recommended practices program assessment: Improving practices for young children with special needs and their families.* Missoula, MT: Division for Early Childhood of the Council for Exceptional Children.

Heubert, J. P., & Hauser, R. M. (Eds.). (1999). *High stakes: Testing for tracking, promotion, and graduation.* Committee on Appropriate Test Use. Washington, DC: National Academy Press.

High/Scope Research Foundation (1992). *Child observation record.* Ypsilanti, MI: Author.

Joint Committee on Testing Practices. (1988). *Code of fair testing practices in education.* Washington, DC: American Psychological Association.

Kim, J., & Suen, H. K. (2003). Predicting children's academic achievement from early assessment scores: A validity generalization study. *Early Childhood Research Quarterly, 18*, 547–566.

Kochanoff, A. T. (Ed.). (2003). *Report of the Temple University forum on preschool assessment: Recommendations for Head Start.* Philadelphia, PA: Temple University.

LaParo, K. M., & Pianta, R. C. (2000). Predicting children's competence in the early school years. A meta-analytic review. *Review of Educational Research, 70*(4), 443–484.

Lynn, R. L. (2003). Accountability: Responsibility and reasonable expectations. *Educational Researcher, 32*(7), 3–13.

McAfee, O., & Leong, D. (2002). *Assessing and guiding young children's development and learning* (3rd ed.). Needham Heights, MA: Allyn & Bacon.

Madaus, G. F. (1988). The influence of testing on the curriculum. In N. Tanner & K. J. Rehage (Eds.), *Critical issues in curriculum: Eighty-seventh yearbook of the national society for the study of education* (pp. 83–121). Chicago: University of Chicago Press.

Marazon, R. A. (1999). *The Marazon classroom system: Four easy steps to developmental planning and assessment.* Perrysburg, OH: Maps for Life.

Meisels, S. J. (1987). Uses and abuses of developmental screening and school readiness testing. *Young Children, 42,* 4–6, 68–73.

Meisels, S. J. (1988). Developmental screening in early childhood: The interaction of research and social policy. In L. Breslow, J. E. Fielding, & L. B. Lave (Eds.), *Annual review of public health* (Vol. 9, pp. 527–550). Palo Alto, CA: Annual Reviews, Inc.

Meisels, S. J. (1994). Designing meaningful measurements for early childhood. In B. L. Mallory & R. S. New (Eds.), *Diversity and developmentally appropriate practices: Challenges for early childhood education* (pp. 202–222). New York: Teachers College Press.

Meisels, S. J. (1996a). Performance in context: Assessing children's achievement at the outset of school. In A. J. Sameroff & M. M. Haith (Eds.), *The five to seven year shift: The age of reason and responsibility* (pp. 410–431). Chicago: University of Chicago Press.

Meisels, S. J. (1996b). Charting the continuum of assessment and intervention. In S. J. Meisels & E. Fenichel (Eds.), *New visions for the developmental assessment of infants and young children* (pp. 27–52). Washington, DC: Zero to Three.

Meisels, S. J. (1999). Assessing readiness. In R. C. Pianta & M. Cox (Eds.), *The transition to kindergarten* (pp. 39–66). Baltimore: Paul Brookes.

Meisels, S., & Atkins-Burnett, S. (2000). The elements of early childhood assessment. In J. P. Shonkoff & S. J. Meisels (Eds.), *Handbook of early intervention* (2nd ed., pp. 231–257). New York: Cambridge University Press.

Meisels, S. J., & Atkins-Burnett, S. (2004). The Head Start National Reporting System: A Critique. *Young Children, 59*(1), 64–66.

Meisels, S. J., & Atkins-Burnett, S. (2005). *Developmental screening in early childhood: A guide* (5th ed.). Washington, DC: National Association for the Education of Young Children.

Meisels, S. J., Atkins-Burnett, S., Xue, Y., Nicholson, J., Bickel, D. D., & Son, S. (2003). Creating a system of accountability: The impact of instructional assessment on elementary children's achievement test scores. *Education Policy Analysis Archives, 11*(9). *http://epaa.asu.edu/epaa/v11n9/*

Meisels, S. J., Bickel, D. D., Nicholson, J., Xue, Y., & Atkins-Burnett, S. (2001). Trusting teachers' judgments: A validity study of a curriculum-embedded performance assessment in Kindergarten – Grade 3. *American Educational Research Journal, 38*(1), 73–95.

Meisels, S. J., Henderson, L. W., Liaw, F., Browning, K., & Ten Have, T. (1993). New evidence for the effectiveness of the *Early Screening Inventory. Early Childhood Research Quarterly, 8,* 327–346.

Meisels, S. J., Jablon, J. R., Marsden, D. B., Dichtelmiller, M. L., & Dorfman, A. B. (2001). *The Work Sampling System.* New York: Pearson Early Learning.

Meisels, S. J., Liaw, F.-R., Dorfman, A. B., & Nelson, R. (1995). The Work Sampling System: Reliability and validity of a performance assessment for young children. *Early Childhood Research Quarterly, 10*(3), 277–296.

Meisels, S. J., & Shonkoff, J. P. (2000). Early childhood intervention: A continuing evolution. In J. P. Shonkoff & S. J. Meisels (Eds.), *Handbook of early intervention* (2nd ed., pp. 3–33). New York: Cambridge University Press.

Meisels, S. J., Xue, Y., Bickel, D. D., Nicholson, J., & Atkins-Burnett, S. (2001). Parental reactions to authentic performance assessment. *Educational Assessment, 7*(1), 61–85.

Messick, S. (1994). The interplay of evidence and consequences in the validation of performance assessments. *Educational Researcher*, *23*, 12–23.

Missouri Department of Elementary and Secondary Education. (1992). *Project construct: A framework for curriculum and assessment*. Jefferson City, MO: Author.

Mueller, J. (2002). Facing the unhappy day: Three aspects of the high stakes testing movement. *Kansas Journal of Law and Public Policy*, *11*, 201–278.

NAEYC & NAECS/SDE. (2003). *Early childhood curriculum, assessment, and program evaluation: Building an effective, accountable system in programs for children birth through age 8*. A joint position statement of the National Association for the Education of Young Children (NAEYC) and the National Association of Early Childhood Specialists in State Departments of Education (NAECS/SDE). Accessed online March 9, 2004 at *http://www.naeyc.org/resources/position_statements/pscape.pdf*

National Education Goals Panel. (1991). *The National Education Goals report*. Washington, DC: Author.

Neisworth, J. T., & Bagnato, S. J. (2004). The mismeasure of young children. *Infants & Young Children*, *17*(3), 198–213.

Nicholson, J. M. (2000). *Examining evidence of the consequential aspects of validity in a curriculum embedded performance assessment*. Unpublished doctoral dissertation, University of Michigan, Ann Arbor.

Padulla, J. J., Abrams, L. M., Madaus, G. F., Russell, J. K., Ramos, M. A., & Miao, J. (2003). *Perceived effects of state-mandated testing programs on teaching and learning: Findings from a national survey of teachers*. Chestnut Hill, MA: National Board on Educational Testing and Public Policy, Boston College.

Patton, M. Q. (1997). *Utilization-focused evaluation* (3rd ed.). Thousand Oaks, CA: Sage Publications.

Popham, W. J. (2005). *Classroom assessment: What teachers need to know* (4th ed.). Boston: Allyn & Bacon.

Prakash, N., West, J., & Denton, K. (2003, March). *Schools' use of assessments for kindergarten entrance and placement: 1998–99*. (NCES Statistics in Brief: NCES 2003–004). Washington, DC: National Center for Education Statistics.

Raver, C. C., & Zigler, E. F. (2004). Another step back? Assessing readiness in Head Start. *Young Children*, *59*(1), 58–63.

Sameroff, A. J., & Fiese, B. H. (2000). Transactional regulation: The developmental ecology of early intervention. In J. P. Shonkoff & S. J. Meisels (Eds.), *Handbook of early intervention* (2nd ed., pp. 135–159). New York: Cambridge University Press.

Shepard, L. A., Kagan, S. L, & Wurtz, E. (Eds.). (1998). *Principles and recommendations for early childhood assessments*. Washington, DC: National Education Goals Panel.

Shonkoff, J. P., & Phillips, D. A. (Eds.). (2000). *From neurons to neighborhoods: The science of early childhood development*. Washington, DC: National Academy Press.

Solomon, B. (2002). Accountability in public child welfare: Linking program theory, program specification, and program evaluation. *Children and Youth Services Review*, *24*(6/7), 385–407.

Werner, E. E. (2000). Protective factors and individual resilience. In J. P. Shonkoff & S. J. Meisels (Eds.), *Handbook of early intervention* (2nd ed., pp. 115–133). New York: Cambridge University Press.

27

Head Start: What Do We Know About Its Effectiveness? What Do We Need to Know?

John M. Love, Louisa Banks Tarullo, Helen Raikes, and Rachel Chazan-Cohen

Head Start has been the setting and source of a great deal of research over the four decades since the program's inception. As a federal program focusing on children in the years before formal schooling, most from families with economic, social, health, and/or mental health risk factors, it has served as a natural and national laboratory for a wide range of basic, prevention, early intervention, and program evaluation research. These research efforts have ranged in scale from individual case studies through large-scale national evaluations, and in methodology from qualitative, narrative profiles through rigorous experimental designs. As Head Start approaches its fifth decade and faces numerous policy and programmatic challenges, it is a crucial time to take stock of what has been learned about the program's effectiveness, its potential to make a difference in children's lives during and after the program, and the windows into early childhood development that the research has opened.

In this chapter we summarize previous reviews of Head Start research and then examine more recent (within the past fifteen years) outcome and impact studies that have not been systematically summarized. The recent research includes descriptive studies and randomized impact evaluations; it includes both studies that examine very large national data sets and small-scale studies of particular programs or in particular communities. The cumulative evidence provides lessons for the child development field about when and how program experiences affect children's development, as well as lessons for programs seeking to enhance their services. We exclude from our review evaluations of "Head Start-like" interventions, which many previous reviewers have merged with research on Head Start interventions. Even though broader reviews are useful for understanding the full range of early childhood interventions, we focus on studies of Head Start in the belief that the conclusions will be most useful to Head Start policy makers if we concentrate on research that has looked at programs implemented as part of the Head Start funding stream. We assert that although the extant research on Head Start is insufficient for certain purposes, it is sufficiently clear for others. We discuss the policy implications of the areas of sufficiency and the research implications for those areas that remain inconclusive. This review is necessarily selective; it provides a window on Head Start findings, not an exhaustive catalog of studies or findings.

It was an ambitious mandate to "strike at the basic cause of poverty," as President Johnson proclaimed Head Start's goal to be (Ross, 1979). In fiscal year 2004, Head Start spent $6.6 billion in federal funds to serve almost a million children from poverty-level families (and has served 21 million children since its inception). One reason why Head Start research has been targeted for criticism is that after an early disastrous experience with the hastily and poorly designed Westinghouse study (Cicirelli, 1969), the national program had not been subjected to a rigorous evaluation until the 1998 Congressional Head Start reauthorization mandated a national impact study. A preliminary report on the impact study's findings was released in June 2005, and we include a synopsis of the main findings here. Nevertheless, these findings are unlikely to bring the Head Start "debate" to a close. Before presenting the other research findings, however, we first describe the program and the families it serves and then briefly trace the development of the government's research agenda for Head Start. Both provide important contexts for understanding the full panorama of Head Start research.

The Head Start Program and the Families It Serves

The overall goal of Head Start is to bring about "a greater degree of social competence in preschool children from low-income families" (US Department of Health and Human Services [USDHHS], 1996). Social competence includes cognitive, intellectual, and social development, and physical and mental health. Later formulations of Head Start's goals for children have incorporated the National Education Goals Panel's "whole-child" view (Kagan, Moore, & Bredekamp, 1995) within the Head Start child outcomes framework (USDHHS, 2003) and have placed the term "school readiness" at the top of the Head Start performance measures pyramid (Administration for Children and Families [ACF], 2003b; Love, Aber, & Brooks-Gunn, 1994). Although Head Start services have traditionally focused on 3- to 5-year-olds, attention is increasingly given to development during the birth-to-3-year period. The Early Head Start program was launched in 1995 to serve this younger age group. Key principles of Head Start entail providing comprehensive services (education, including child development services, health, nutrition, and social services), fostering the parent's role as the principal influence on the child's development, encouraging parents to be involved in policy and program decisions, and establishing partnerships with community agencies to improve the delivery of services to children and families. The federal Head Start Bureau places a premium on quality through detailed program performance standards (USDHHS, 1996) and regular monitoring of compliance.

Over the years, Head Start has become the nation's primary federally sponsored child development program. In fiscal year 2003, 1670 grantees served 909,608 children (ACF,

2004b). Eighty-seven percent of the children served are 3 and 4 years old; 53% are 4-year-olds; 8% are infants and toddlers under 3, including families who enroll before the child's birth. About 12.5% are children with disabilities. Based on data from the 2003 Head Start Program Information Report (PIR), preschool Head Start children are about equally likely to be in full-day (6 hours or more, 48.9%) and part-day programs (44.6%). The great majority of preschool Head Start children are in center-based programs (93.5%). Program auspices are more than one-third private/public non-profit (34.6%), nearly one-third Community Action Agency or CAA (31.7%), and about one-fifth public school systems (19.7%). Smaller percentages of grantees are tribal governments (6.9%), government/non-CAA agencies (5.9%), and private/public for-profit organizations (1.2%) (USDHHS, 2004).

In fiscal year 2003, the annual federal cost per child was $7092, with an additional 20% of costs provided by the grantees as their "non-federal share," e.g., space, volunteer staff time, and professional services. To be eligible for Head Start, families must meet both the federal income eligibility criterion (i.e., family income at or below the federal poverty level), with 10% over-income permitted, and the age criterion (3–5 for regular Head Start, prenatal to 3 for Early Head Start). Other criteria relating to family characteristics are added by local grantees to help Head Start better serve community needs. Head Start is not an entitlement program and thus not all eligible families are served. The Congressional Research Service has estimated that in fiscal year 2002, Head Start served 49% of the eligible 3- and 4-year-olds and, through Early Head Start, 3% of the eligible population of infants and toddlers under age 3 (Gish, 2004, p. 7).

The families that Head Start serves are among the neediest of the poverty-level population, with typical associated risks. An in-depth profile of the families served is provided by the recent analysis of Head Start Program Information Report (PIR) data by the Center for Law and Social Policy (Hart & Schumacher, 2004). Although actual family incomes were not reported, Hart and Schumacher noted that 74% of enrolled families had incomes at or below the federal poverty level ($18,400 for a family of four in 2003) and 18% were receiving public assistance when they enrolled. One or both parents were employed in 72% of Head Start families. Twenty-one percent of families used public assistance (i.e., Temporary Assistance for Needy Families, or TANF), down from 45% in 1997. The majority (56%) of families were headed by a single parent, 61% of whom were working parents. In about three-quarters of families, neither parent had more than a high-school education. Hart and Schumacher noted the diversity of Head Start children: 32% were African-American, 31% Latino, 28% white, 3% American Indian or Alaskan Native, 2% Asian, 1% Hawaiian or other Pacific Islander, and 3% were described as bi- or multi-racial. Spanish was the primary language for 22% of Head Start children, and overall 27% of the children spoke a non-English primary language. Thirteen percent of the children were diagnosed with a disability, with the most common being speech or language impairments.

The PIR does not record psychological data, but the first wave of the Family and Child Experiences Survey (FACES) reported on a nationally representative sample of Head Start families and children in 1997 (Administration on Children, Youth and Families [ACYF], 2002). That study found that close to a third of the respondents (primarily mothers) reported symptoms that classified them as moderately or severely depressed. Further evidence of the at-risk nature of the population is seen in the finding that about one-quarter of the children were reported to have witnessed crime or domestic violence in their lives, and about one-fourth had a parent or other household member who had been involved in the criminal justice system. Yet, like more-advantaged parents with young children, Head Start families in the FACES sample were optimistic about their children's potential for educational attainment, and expressed belief in the strengths of their families to meet challenges. They were very involved in educational activities with their children at home and turned to Head Start staff as a major source of information and support regarding their children's development (ACYF, 2002).

The Federal Head Start Research Agenda

Head Start began in 1965 with not only an ambitious social agenda but also a strong commitment to research and evaluation. A review of the research on Head Start needs to be placed in the context of that segment of the research – indeed, a major segment – that is guided and sponsored by the federal government, currently under the auspice of the ACF in the US Department of Health and Human Services, as described in greater detail elsewhere (Love, Chazan-Cohen, & Raikes, in press). Head Start research entered a new era in the 1990s as the ACF responded to the advice of several key advisory panels: (1) the Advisory Panel for the Head Start Evaluation Design Project (also known as the "Blueprint Committee"; USDHHS, 1990); (2) the Advisory Committee on Head Start Quality and Expansion (USDHHS, 1993); and (3) the National Academy of Sciences Roundtable on Head Start Research in 1994 (Phillips & Cabrera, 1996). These advisory committees advocated an expanded role for research in program planning and stressed the need for integration among programmatic questions, research, and program improvement activities. They also emphasized the need to assess program quality and benefits of the program for children and families, and to explore whether outcomes vary across subgroups of children and families, defined by such factors as race and ethnicity, immigration status, maternal employment, and years in the program.

In part to be responsive to these advisory panels, Congress mandated several specific studies and cemented the role of the large national study within the research agenda. The 1994 reauthorization mandated development of specific performance measures, as well as descriptive longitudinal studies designed to examine progress that children and families make during their time in the program and beyond. This led to the study known as FACES, a longitudinal study following a representative group of children and families in Head Start, findings from which are cited in this chapter. The 1994 amendments to the Head Start Act also instituted a new programmatic effort aimed at pregnant women and families with infants and toddlers, which later became known as Early Head Start. When it authorized this new program, Congress mandated a national impact evaluation (also described later). Finally, as noted above, the 1998 reauthorization mandated a study that would provide a "national analysis" of the impact of Head Start to be designed by an independent panel of experts. Thus, rigorous random assignment impact studies of both Head Start and Early Head Start were undertaken during this time.

Since the 1990s, the federal research agenda has included plans to address questions that are important to both programs and policy makers through several mechanisms: basic field-initiated research, descriptive research aimed at identifying who is being served and how, and effectiveness or impact studies. Basic research aimed at illuminating developmental processes serves to inform strategies for enhancing developmental outcomes, resulting in promising programmatic approaches or curricula, which can then be tested and refined through demonstration projects. Descriptive studies at the national level identify characteristics of participants and programs and describe the links between services received and the outcomes achieved. Finally, effectiveness studies address questions of the program's impacts on participants, and both participant and program features that plausibly account for these impacts.

To place Head Start research in the broader context of what is known about Head Start-eligible children and families, the ACF also has supplemented national studies being conducted by other federal departments (and in some cases, other agencies have supplemented the ACF studies). Collaborations with the National Institute of Child Health and Human Development (NICHD – the NICHD Study of Early Child Care and Youth Development and the Early Head Start father studies) and the Department of Education (Early Childhood Longitudinal Studies, Birth and Kindergarten cohort studies) have ensured that measures, methods, and knowledge are shared. The most recent collaboration has been the Interagency School Readiness Consortium, a joint effort of NICHD, the ACF, and the Assistant Secretary for Planning and Evaluation (ASPE) in the US Department of Health and Human Services and the Office of Special Education and Rehabilitative Services (OSERS) in the US Department of Education. The initiative is designed to support research on the effectiveness of interventions, programs, and curricula in promoting school readiness for both typically and atypically developing children from birth through age 5.

What Previous Research Summaries Have Concluded About Head Start Effectiveness

Examinations of Head Start's short-term outcomes provide the most robust evidence of the program's effectiveness. In 1997, Devaney, Ellwood, and Love's (1997) review concluded that the "evidence accumulated from many different studies supports the conclusion that children who experience at least one year of [Head Start] show significant short-term benefits in their cognitive, social, and physical development and in receipt of health services" (p. 107). This evidence of beneficial effects is particularly important when considered in light of the poverty context in which the program operates. Substantial evidence suggests that, absent interventions, long-term poverty depresses the cognitive and social-emotional development of young children (Korenman, Miller, & Sjaastad, 1995).

The most complete and comprehensive review of Head Start research was completed in 1985. Across seventy-two studies included in a major meta-analysis of Head Start research available at that time (McKey et al., 1985), Head Start was found to have sizeable effects on children's cognitive development when measured at the end of the Head Start year; and this was true regardless of the particular outcome measures used. Furthermore, the twenty-one most rigorous studies (those that employed an experimental treatment-control group design) showed a mean effect size of 0.52 across all cognitive measures. This indicates that the average performance of the Head Start group was more than half a standard deviation above the mean for the control group. Although the interpretation of effect sizes is fraught with ambiguity (McCartney & Dearing, 2002; McCartney & Rosenthal, 2000), Barnett (1995) suggests that differences of this magnitude constitute "meaningful improvement in cognitive ability and can have important implications for children in terms of academic performance and placement in special education classes" (p. 27).

Head Start has also shown beneficial effects on children's social-emotional development at the end of the Head Start year. Across seventeen studies that assessed social-emotional outcomes, the Head Start synthesis report found benefits of Head Start participation on both achievement motivation and social behavior (McKey et al., 1985). These findings cannot be attributed to a particular outcome measure: the seventeen studies included eighteen different measures of achievement motivation and eleven measures of social behavior.

The Head Start goals of providing comprehensive health services and fostering healthy physical development have received far less emphasis in program evaluations. However, a random assignment evaluation in the mid-1980s in four counties with highly under-served populations found that, at the end of the year, Head Start children were much more likely than the controls to have received basic health services, enjoyed better access to health care services, experienced improved health status, eaten meals significantly higher in nutrient quality, and exhibited better motor coordination and development. Further, Head Start children who displayed pediatric problems upon program entry were less likely to have the same problems remaining one year later (Fosberg & Brown, 1984).

We are not aware of any more recent review or synthesis that approaches McKey et al. in comprehensiveness. However, reviews of the early childhood intervention litera-ture more generally often include some Head Start studies along with a larger focus on early childhood interventions that are not Head Start. Good examples are the recent reviews by Barnett (1995), Karoly et al. (1998), and Lynch (2004). Barnett reviewed twenty-one studies of "large-scale" public programs – sixteen of which were studies of city, county, or state Head Start programs, or studies with national samples – and fifteen studies of smaller model programs, including one Head Start study. All had followed their samples into elementary school, with follow-up assessments conducted at some point between grades 1 and 8. None of the large-scale studies employed a randomized design. Three of the sixteen Head Start studies found no effects; four found initial effects that were no longer present at third grade; but nine studies found persisting effects. Barnett noted that in general, the magnitude of effects was smaller in the larger-scale studies.

Karoly et al. reviewed a large number of program evaluations, but focused their analysis of benefits on nine that were selected as being large enough to ensure unbiased results, having matched control groups (typically through random assignment), and measuring a wide range of outcomes. None of the nine was a Head Start program evalu-ation, because "the numerous evaluations of Project Head Start are not readily summarized in the format used [in our tables]" (Karoly et al., 1998, p. 25). In their text, however, the authors discussed findings from the early Head Start studies, including the Westinghouse Report (Cicirelli, 1969), because of its historical – not scientific – significance. Most of the Head Start research they reviewed was included in the McKey et al. meta-analysis.

More recently, Lynch (2004) attempted a cost–benefit analysis of early childhood development programs, including a small number of the Head Start studies that are also summarized here. His general conclusions were that findings on the effectiveness of Head Start are "quite variable" (p. 33). His focus was on the larger number of non-Head Start early childhood intervention studies, and his evidence of the long-term benefits of Head Start was based on the same studies we report here.

Although Head Start program planners had hoped that their program efforts would sustain benefits well into the elementary-school years, a one-year program may not be sufficient to protect children from future risk. While a number of studies claim to show a "fade-out" effect (such that gains present at the end of the Head Start year are no longer found in second or third grade), their methodologies have not been sufficiently rigorous to support conclusions about the long-term effects of Head Start. In particular, Head Start follow-up studies have failed to take into account the fact that two of the benefits found – less grade retention and special education placements – meant that more of the low-achieving children in the comparison group were no longer in the research sample at a given grade level (Barnett, 1993, 2002, 2004).

Although most research has focused on the program's benefits for children, a number of studies have examined the "indirect" effects for families, staff, and communities. The synthesis report found several areas in which the benefits of Head Start programs extend beyond enhancing children's development (McKey et al., 1985). Head Start parents participate in various paid and volunteer program positions that range from clerical to classroom to policy making. In 1992, some 94% of enrolled families received needed support services through the program (Brush, Gaidurgis, & Best, 1993; McCall, 1993). Some studies have shown that parental childrearing practices have been positively affected by Head Start participation, but others have not (McKey et al., 1985). Career development is only secondary to Head Start's aims, yet some 35% of Head Start staff in 1992 were former children or parents of the enrolled Head Start children (Brush et al., 1993; McCall, 1993). Some policy makers have considered such employment opportunities to be an important program benefit as low-income parents seek alternatives to public assistance.

The few reviews that have been completed since 1985 have not changed the overall picture of Head Start's effectiveness. While both short- and long-term benefits have been documented, the evidence is uneven and, for some, unconvincing given the absence, until 2005, of a national randomized experimental study of Head Start. The most recent relevant compilation is not a single, systematic review, but a collection of fifty-three articles edited by Zigler and Styfco (2004). The article by Barnett is both a review – covering much of the territory already reported here – and an updated assessment of his earlier analyses of "fade-out" (Barnett, 2004). He concludes that "the weight of the evidence indicates that a wide range of preschool programs including Head Start can increase IQ scores during the early childhood years, improve achievement, and prevent grade retention and special education" (p. 242).[1] However, he also notes that Head Start has smaller effects than do model programs, and raises the concern that the large federal program lacks the necessary resources to match the quality and intensity of model programs.

We have not yet discussed the review that has had the greatest impact on Head Start research *policy* – the 1997 report from the US General Accounting Office[2] (US GAO, 1997) that led to the Head Start Impact Study. Supporting the report's subtitle (*Research Provides Little Information on Impact of Current Program*), the GAO reviewers examined twenty-two diverse studies (out of nearly 600 screened) that met their criteria, that is, were conducted since 1975, used a comparison group, and reported results of statistical significance tests. The GAO concluded that the number of impact studies (i.e., those estimating "differences in outcomes caused by Head Start participation") was too small to draw valid conclusions, and they all had methodological problems, the most serious of which were (1) non-comparability of the comparison groups (only one of the studies used random assignment, and some used only test norms as the basis for comparison) and (2) small samples. But perhaps the most serious concern raised by the GAO was the absence of studies using nationally representative samples. We now turn to reviewing more recent Head Start research, beginning with the study that responded to the GAO's concerns.

Recent Studies of Head Start Effects

National impact studies

Based on recommendations from the GAO (USGAO, 1997), requirements of the Head Start Reauthorization in 1998, and guidance from the 1999 Advisory Committee on Head Start Research and Evaluation, Head Start launched a study of the national impact of the preschool program in fall 2002. The study was designed to answer two central questions: (1) What difference does Head Start make to the key outcomes of development and learning (in particular, the multiple domains of school readiness) of the nation's low-income children? (2) Under what circumstances does Head Start work best and for which children? (ACF, 2003a).

The Head Start Impact Study (HSIS) sampled 4667 3- and 4-year-old children eligible for Head Start who applied to 383 centers across 84 nationally representative programs in fall 2002. Children were randomly assigned to either a group receiving Head Start services or a control group that did not receive Head Start services but that was permitted to enroll in other services selected by parents or to be cared for at home. Only communities that had more eligible applicants than could be served were included in the sample. Data collection began in fall 2002 and continues through spring of the children's first-grade year. Similar to FACES, the study includes direct child assessments, interviews, ratings from parents and teachers, and observations of the child's current Head Start or other care setting (ACF, 2003a).

Impact results from the first year showed that Head Start children (both 3- and 4-year-olds) were outperforming their control group peers on a range of developmental measures after nine months of program participation. For children who entered Head Start at age 4, in the cognitive domain, Head Start children scored significantly higher on letter–word identification, letter naming, spelling, and parent-reported literacy skills. Head Start children were also more likely to have received dental care and their parents read to their child more frequently. The study found no impacts on social-emotional measures among the 4-year-olds. Effect sizes for the significant impacts ranged up to one-third of a standard deviation (from 0.13 to 0.32) (ACF, 2005).

For children who entered Head Start at age 3, the program showed more than twice as many significant impacts, including letter–word identification, letter naming, draw-a-design, vocabulary, color naming, and parent-reported literacy skills. Unlike the 4-year-olds, the younger children showed significant reductions in behavior problems and hyperactive behavior when compared with the control group's 3-year-olds. Three-year-olds were also more likely to receive dental care and received higher ratings of overall health. Parents of the 3-year-olds read to them more often, scored higher on a family cultural enrichment scale, and showed lower use of physical discipline. Effect sizes for the significant impacts on 3-year-olds ranged up to one-third of a standard deviation (from 0.10 to 0.34) (ACF, 2005).

Subgroup analyses found that impacts were stronger for African-American and Hispanic 3-year-old children, but this was not true for 4-year-olds. Fewer impacts were found for children whose home language was not English. Some small differences in impacts were found based on mother's age when her first child was born (improved disciplinary practices for teenage mothers and more reading for older mothers) and mother's depressive symptoms at baseline (a decrease in cognitive impacts for 3-year-olds when mothers were more depressed). Future reports will examine subgroups of programs (e.g., part-day vs. full-day programs).

The second major national impact study was conducted with Head Start's newest program – Early Head Start. The Early Head Start Research and Evaluation Project was also undertaken in response to Congressional requirements; Congress wanted the newly funded Early Head Start program to be rigorously evaluated in its earliest stages. The ACF conducted the Early Head Start Research and Evaluation Project as an experimental-design study involving 3001 children and families in seventeen sites; families enrolled when children were 12 months of age or younger. Randomly assigned control group children were free to avail themselves of any services in the community other than Early Head Start. Children were assessed at 14, 24, and 36 months of age and were followed up in pre-kindergarten;[3] parent interviews, videotaped observations of parent–child interactions, and child care quality observations were completed in conjunction with the age-related assessments, and parents were interviewed about the extent of service use at regular intervals following random assignment.

When children were 24 months and again when they were 36 months of age, the evaluation reported a pattern of favorable impacts across a wide range of child outcomes, primary caregiver (i.e., parent, mostly mothers) outcomes, and primary caregiver self-sufficiency outcomes. Central findings for the Early Head Start children, contrasted with the control group, included higher scores on the Bayley Scales of Infant Development and the Peabody Picture Vocabulary Test, lower ratings of aggressive behavior problems, greater engagement of the parent in the interactive play situation, and more sustained attention with objects in the play context. Primary caregivers in the Early Head Start group were more supportive and less detached and intrusive with their children in the play context than control parents, provided home environments with greater warmth and supports for language and learning, were more likely to read to their child every day, and showed less negative parenting. In terms of their self-sufficiency, Early Head Start primary caregivers participated more in education and job training and were more often employed while they were in the program. Fathers were interviewed in twelve sites. The program fathers spanked less than control group counterparts and, in sites where fathers were observed in videotaped interactions of father–child play, Early Head Start fathers were less intrusive. Early Head Start had impacts on children's behavior in interaction with their fathers, as it did on their interactions with their mothers, such that program children, in contrast with those in the control group, demonstrated more positive interactions. Effect sizes of impacts in these overall analyses ranged from 0.09 to 0.20.

An important lesson from the Early Head Start study for other Head Start research is its subgroup findings. Impacts for children and families in a number of subgroups were notably larger than in the total-sample analyses just cited. For example, impacts were stronger for African-Americans, families who enrolled when the mother was pregnant, families with a moderate number of risk factors, and families in fully implemented mixed-approach programs; effect sizes for both child and primary caregiver outcomes were in the range of one-third to one-half of a standard deviation for many of these subgroup impacts. The findings related to implementing the Head Start Program Performance Standards are particularly policy-relevant: the more successful programs were in implementing the program requirements, the greater the impacts for children and families (ACF, 2002).

National descriptive studies

In the mid-1990s, pushed by the requirements of GPRA (Government Performance and Results Act, PL 103–92) and the 1994 Head Start Reauthorization (42 USC 9831 et seq.), Head Start began a comprehensive initiative to develop program performance measures to describe program quality and outcomes and the empirical links between them. The result was the Head Start FACES study, which features successive cohorts (1997, 2000, 2003) of a nationally representative sample of children, families, and programs. Based on a comprehensive, "whole-child" view of school readiness, FACES uses multiple sources of data on child characteristics and skills, including direct child assessment, classroom observation, and reports from parents and teachers. The study is currently following its third cohort of children, starting in fall 2003, from program entry through spring of kindergarten (ACF, 2003b). These cohorts provide successive descriptive pictures on stability and change in the population served, staff qualifications, observed classroom quality, and child and family outcomes.

Longitudinal data from the first two cohorts have demonstrated that children in Head Start entered preschool substantially below normative peers on most standardized assessments of cognitive abilities (ACF, 2003b). While they may have progressed at comparable or even better than average rates during the program year, they still failed to completely close the achievement gap. Final levels and rates of growth in child progress were related to measures of classroom quality. In addition, children's performance at the end of Head Start was predictive of their kindergarten performance, and both cognitive and behavioral factors were related to whether a child was promoted to first grade. More specific results are detailed below.

The majority of children surveyed in FACES entered Head Start at age 3 or 4 with early literacy and mathematics skills far below national averages: at the sixteenth percentile in receptive vocabulary and early writing, the twenty-first percentile in early math, and the thirty-first percentile in letter knowledge. However, the highest quarter of Head Start children were at or above the fiftieth percentile, indicating a wide range of skill levels within the program. In the 1997 cohort, children made vocabulary and early writing gains greater than those of the normative sample, and in 2000, children also showed greater than average gains in letter knowledge. Criterion-related findings provided data relative to the Congressional mandate that Head Start children should know ten letters of the alphabet: Children in 2000 entered Head Start knowing four letters and could identify nine by the end of the year. In addition, according to teacher report, children showed significant increases in social skills over the program year, and significant decreases in hyperactive behavior (ACF, 2003b).

During the kindergarten year, children who had participated in Head Start progressed further toward national averages (but did not meet them), with gains in effect-size terms ranging from about .3 to .5 standard deviation units in vocabulary, early math, and early writing. Head Start performance predicted achievement levels at the end of kindergarten: Head Start teacher ratings of behavior predicted kindergarten teacher ratings, as well as performance on cognitive assessments, over and above their Head Start cognitive scores. Interestingly, the trajectories of decoding or "inside-out" skills (Whitehurst et al., 1994; Whitehurst & Lonigan, 1998) and of comprehension or "outside-in skills" were different. While letter knowledge at the end of Head Start was the strongest predictor of kindergarten-level reading ability, vocabulary at the end of Head Start was the strongest predictor of general knowledge (ACF, 2003b).

By collecting detailed information from teachers about their skills, experience, and beliefs about early childhood practice, as well as objective observations of classroom quality, FACES has yielded provocative analyses of the factors that may influence child outcomes in early childhood environments (ACF, 2003b). Higher teacher salaries and the use of an integrated curriculum such as High/Scope or Creative Curriculum (the predominant curricula in Head Start programs) are related to greater gains in letter knowledge and cooperative classroom behavior. Children whose teachers had higher salaries also showed greater improvement in hyperactive behavior, and children in programs using the High/Scope curriculum showed greater improvement in both total behavior problems and hyperactive behavior relative to children in programs with other curricula. While higher teacher credentials were linked to greater gains in writing skills, and longer classroom days were linked to greater gains in both letter knowledge and early writing, other quality measures were not associated with greater gains. Scores on the Early Childhood Environment Rating Scale-Revised (ECERS-R) and child–adult ratios were not associated with differences in fall–spring achievement gains; arguably, because of Head Start performance standards, these quality measures fall within a narrower "good" quality range and do not show as much variation as has been seen in studies of other preschool programs (ACF, 2003b). Teacher knowledge and beliefs about child development emerged as a mediator between teacher educational credentials and observed classroom quality. The more educated the Head Start teacher, the more likely she was to endorse positive attitudes and knowledge of early childhood practice, and the higher the observed quality of her classroom (ACF, 2003b).

Studies using national data sets

Absent a national impact study of Head Start, researchers have turned to national data sets and innovative research designs to derive non-experimental estimates of Head Start's effectiveness. Among such efforts, Janet Currie, Duncan Thomas, and colleagues have conducted groundbreaking analyses of the National Longitudinal Study of Youth (NLSY), a study of young people begun in 1978 that added Head Start identifiers in 1988. Their research has been particularly important in discussions of Head Start program effectiveness because they are able to analyze national data (even though not collected for this purpose), they conduct creative analyses that provide sensible comparison "groups," such as siblings who did not attend Head Start, and they have been able to establish the most comprehensive set of findings that speak to long-term outcomes.

Using a sibling comparison design with the NLSY's Child–Mother files (NLS-CM), Currie and Thomas (1995) attempted to control for shared characteristics of family background. The authors found that among white children, those attending Head Start made significantly more progress in vocabulary and early reading scores than non-Head Start attendees, although there were apparently no similar benefits for African-American children. Further analyses (allowing for separate measurement at the time of program exit and any diminution over time) showed that when measured at age 5, benefits were in fact similar for both racial groups at the end of the program. However, while these effects persisted into adolescence for white children, they rapidly eroded for African-American children.

A companion analysis of the same NLSY data (Currie & Thomas, 1999) showed larger gains among Hispanics than among non-Hispanic whites. Efforts to understand these differences at program exit, which persisted into the early school grades, led to studies of both quality in Head Start and longer-term effects. Currie and Neidell (2003) again turned to the NLSY (1979 Child and Young Adult Data) to compare outcomes of Head Start children in higher- and lower-spending counties at the time the child was enrolled. This proxy for program quality was based on administrative data from PIR and Head Start budget (PCCost) data (USDHHS, 1999), which were analyzed in relation to child outcomes from the NLSY, such as cognitive scores, behavior problems, and grade retention. Compared with other children in the same area at age 4, across ethnic groups, Head Start children in programs in higher-spending counties had higher reading scores and were less likely to have been retained in grade than non-Head Start children. Interestingly, the effects were stronger for children in high-poverty counties (an analysis added to control for the issue of community resources as opposed to program-specific resources). Considering racial and ethnic subgroups, higher spending for white children results in less grade repetition for the Head Start children than non-Head Start children. Higher spending for African-American children leads to better results for Head Start than non-Head Start children on math, reading, and vocabulary assessments, but not on grade repetition. The authors also concluded that, on average, Head Start costs approximately 71% of the cost of the more intensive Perry Preschool intervention.

Using data from the Panel Study of Income Dynamics (PSID), Garces, Thomas, and Currie (2000) examined evidence of the effects of Head Start participation on longer-term outcomes such as educational attainment, earnings, and involvement in the criminal justice system using a sibling comparison design. The PSID featured special questions about Head Start beginning in 1995, allowed for controls on family background characteristics, and allowed for evaluation of typical programs funded at typical levels in the late 1960s and 1970s (as opposed to model programs such as the Perry Preschool and Abecedarian programs). Again, the researchers found differential trajectories to be associated with racial and ethnic group. Among white children, those who had attended Head Start showed a significantly greater likelihood of completing high school and attending college, as well as some evidence of higher earnings in early adulthood. On the other hand, among African-Americans, former Head Start participants were significantly less likely to have been charged with or convicted of a crime. In addition, there were some sibling differences in subgroups. African-American males who attended Head Start were more likely than their siblings to have completed high school.

To investigate possible reasons for these differential long-term effects, Currie and Thomas (2000) obtained a sample of 16,875 eighth-graders' data from the National Education Longitudinal Survey (NELS). They found that the "quality" of schools, defined as average test scores for the school, were different for African-American and white Head Start graduates: white Head Start children attended schools similar in quality to schools attended by other white children, whereas African-American Head Start children attended schools lower in quality than those attended by other African-American children. In other words, the "fade-out" effect may occur, in part, because "black Head Start children are more likely to subsequently attend schools of poor quality" (Currie & Thomas, 2000).[4] The authors caution that the findings using non-experimental data and retrospective report may have drawbacks. Barnett (2004) goes even further. Based on an alternative analysis of the same NLSY data, Barnett and Camilli (2000) found estimates of both short- and long-term effects of Head Start to be nearly identical for African-American and white non-Latino children. Barnett concludes that it is "unlikely that any valid estimates of Head Start effects could be produced using the NLS-CM data," due in part to the need to use cross-sectional analyses to estimate change over time (Barnett, 2004, p. 238). In our view, the program of research conducted by Currie, Thomas, and colleagues reveals important patterns of findings that should be explored further in prospective impact studies.

Smaller-scale research studies

In 1994, *Early Childhood Research Quarterly* published a special issue focusing on Head Start research. In his introduction to the collection of thirteen studies, Powell (1994) articulated the journal's purpose: "Refinements in our understanding of children and families involved in Head Start programs can be of significant benefit to decision-making about Head Start directions, especially when investigators are thoughtful about implications of their data for the ways in which programs are designed and implemented" (p. 242). None of the studies reported Head Start effects, either in experimental or quasi-experimental designs. Several of the researchers focused on how child outcomes are associated with such factors as home literacy environments, parent mental health, and parenting behaviors, which we summarize later in connection with lessons for child development and programs. However, it is important to note that the associations reported are in the context of the development of program children only, not in the context of any impacts of the program in changing the trajectories of Head Start children in comparison with those of a control or comparison group.

The ACF has sponsored site-specific and limited-scale cross-site research through partnerships between university-based researchers and programs, sometimes employing experimental designs. For example, in March 2001, Head Start funded eight five-year studies under the Head Start Quality Research Center (HSQRC) Consortium, designed to develop, test, refine, and disseminate interventions to enhance children's school readiness. Interventions ranged across enhancements to curriculum in literacy and social-emotional development, teacher training and mentoring, fostering parent involvement, and supporting assessment practices. Collecting data on outcomes using common cross-site measures derived from FACES allowed for pooling across sites, and consistent measurement over time allowed for pooling samples across annual cohorts.

Some findings have been notable. For example, children participating in interventions that focused on teacher training showed significantly greater progress than control group children in PPVT scores, book knowledge, and early math in the first cohort (2001–2), and significantly greater declines in parent ratings of hyperactive behavior in the second cohort (2002–3) (ACF, 2004c). Individual HSQRC studies with somewhat larger samples, such as one site testing two literacy-focused enhancements, have also shown important results. In a large program in New York state, Fischel and colleagues (2004) demonstrated that children in each intervention condition had significantly higher scores than children in comparison classrooms on number of letters known, letter–word identification, a literacy-readiness measure, and book knowledge. In addition, parental literacy practices and children's behavioral characteristics were linked with literacy outcomes at program exit.

Researchers frequently have difficulty implementing experimental designs. To test the feasibility of random assignment designs using wait-list controls, Abbott-Shim, Lambert, and McCarty (2003) examined school-readiness outcomes for Head Start-eligible children randomly assigned to a treatment (Head Start) or a wait-list control group in a southeastern, metropolitan community. Growth rates from fall to spring for the Head Start children were significantly higher than for control children in receptive vocabulary and phonemic awareness. There was no impact on a scale of social skills and positive approaches to learning, and a reduction in behavior problems occurred only for the control group (which was higher than the Head Start group at baseline). Parent reports of health outcomes showed that the Head Start children surpassed their control counterparts in important health and nutrition habits.

Studies exploring questions of Head Start impacts have often taken into account the quality of the early childhood or subsequent school experience. In terms of concurrent quality measures, Bryant and colleagues (Bryant, Burchinal, Lau, & Sparling, 1994) found that children in better-quality Head Start classrooms (measured by the ECERS) showed better performance on measures of achievement and pre-academic skills. However, in this study of 32 classrooms and 145 children, teacher education, experience, and attitudes were not found to be associated with observed classroom quality.

Lee and colleagues (Lee, Brooks-Gunn, & Schnur, 1988) found large initial group differences between Head Start children and those attending no preschool or another preschool, with Head Start children at a disadvantage in demographic and baseline cognitive performance. While Head Start children showed significant gains in both cognitive and non-cognitive measures over the program year, they still lagged behind their peers in cognitive levels. African-American children most at risk showed the greatest gains. At the time of kindergarten and first-grade follow-up, the effects were not as large as those found immediately after preschool (Lee, Brooks-Gunn, Schnur, & Liaw, 1990). When the children were followed into the middle-school years (Lee & Loeb, 1995), the quality factor once again emerged: controlling for family background characteristics, former Head Start attendees were in schools of significantly lower quality than were the comparison children.

The Long-Term Benefits of Head Start (LTBHS) study followed up former Head Start children seventeen years after they had participated in High/Scope's Head Start Planned Variation in Florida and Colorado (Oden, Schweinhart, & Weikart, 2000). Following the study's quasi-experimental design, the authors report a pattern of findings for these young adults, especially at the Florida site, that are in the same direction as those of more intensive interventions, such as the High/Scope Perry Preschool Study. In the Florida subgroup analyses, a higher proportion of Head Start girls had completed high school and fewer had been arrested compared to non-Head Start attendees. Stronger impacts were seen in Head Start programs that used integrated curricula such as High/Scope, similar to the findings of the national FACES study.

Finally, it is important to acknowledge the unique contribution of Slaughter-Defoe and Rubin's (2001) longitudinal study of a small sample of African-American children who enrolled in Head Start in summer 1965 and were followed up in 1972–3 and 1978. Their rich analysis of the changing family, community, and societal environments in which the children developed over time is unprecedented. Without addressing the complexities of the study's design, attrition analysis, and contextual analysis, what stands out is the importance of how children perceive themselves in terms of achievement motivation and the roles of their parents and teachers in the children's evolving motivations and expectations.

Lessons from Head Start Research about Children's Development

We began our review with the understanding that Head Start is important, not only as a mix of services and settings designed to accomplish particular goals, but also as a laboratory for the study of early childhood development in multiple contexts: families, care and education settings, and communities. Even studies with an effectiveness evaluation focus – to document whether Head Start works, whether it can be improved, and how – have also investigated developmental questions that span interdisciplinary inquiry. Investigators' research questions have ranged from the role of prenatal care in improving infant and maternal health, through the potential for mitigating the effects of community violence, to understanding the specific predictive factors in 3-year-olds that lead to becoming successful readers in third grade. From the breadth of Head Start research, much can be learned about the factors influencing the development of children from low-income families.

The broad array of discretionary grants awarded with Head Start research funds has resulted in substantial contributions to the field of child development. Important work in the domains of emergent literacy, social-emotional functioning, and infant development more generally, has contributed to our understanding of the developmental trajectories of low-income children, as well as of the kinds of environments at home and school that are most conducive to healthy patterns. The ACF's ongoing process of archiving evaluation studies' data for access by the child development research community contributes to expanding the potential for learning more. In addition, linkages with other national studies allows Head Start research and research on low-income populations to be put into a broader context. The ACF has supplemented national studies being conducted by other federal departments, and in some cases other agencies have supplemented ACF studies. For example, collaborations with the US Department of Education on the Early Childhood Longitudinal Studies, both the birth and the kindergarten cohorts, contribute to sharing measures, methods, and knowledge. Three areas of research (emergent literacy, social-emotional development, and Early Head Start) illustrate the potential for learning about child development in the context of Head Start research.

Emergent literacy

Whitehurst, Lonigan, and colleagues have developed a program of research that helps to map the connections between the emergence of the earliest skills in decoding and comprehension and later reading competence (Whitehurst & Lonigan, 1998). Interventions aimed at improving children's skills have used dynamic approaches to caregiver–child reading that were tested and refined with Head Start populations (Whitehurst et al. 1994, 1999). For example, one experimental study tested the effects of an interactive reading and phonemic awareness program on the emergent literacy skills of Head Start children through second grade, finding that they were stable through kindergarten but not beyond, and that variations in Head Start and school quality accounted for differences in growth from year to year (Whitehurst et al., 1999). A possible role for programs in supporting home literacy environments was shown in an earlier Head Start study that reported that from 12% to 18.5% of the variance in 4-year-olds' language scores was accounted for by home literacy environment variables, such as frequency of parent reading with the child, number of picture books in the home, and number of minutes the parent read to the child the previous day (Payne, Whitehurst, & Angell, 1994).

Social-emotional development and behavior

Over the years, Head Start has funded a variety of intervention studies focused on improving children's behavior and attitudes toward learning. Walker, Feil, and colleagues have shown promising results with a Head Start adaptation of their First Step to Success curriculum, designed to achieve primary and secondary prevention goals and outcomes in school readiness through both teacher- and peer-related forms of adjustment (Feil, Golly, Walker, & Severson, 2004). The treatment group decreased negative classroom behavior compared to the control group; in kindergarten follow-up, effects were maintained at a lower level, suggesting the need for "booster" sessions in the early school years.

Fantuzzo and colleagues (1995) have contributed substantially to understanding the social-emotional domain in urban Head Start children's lives through the development and refinement of a variety of measures geared specifically to low-income preschool populations, studies focusing on early identification of behavior problems, and interventions designed to improve classroom environments. For example, a recent study demonstrated the predictive dimensions of under-active and over-active behavior problems at program entry for learning and behavioral outcomes at the end of the school year. The authors also suggested that Head Start staff were likely to miss identification of children with behavior problems as a group, but also more likely to identify over-activity than under-activity (Fantuzzo, Bulotsky, McDermott, Mosca, & Lutz, 2003). Webster-Stratton and colleagues have developed and disseminated interventions aimed at improving children's behavioral interactions through improved parenting. For example, in a study of Head Start children and parents, teachers reported better parental involvement and child social competence in the intervention group (Webster-Stratton, 1998; Webster-Stratton & Reid, this volume). Webster-Stratton's focus has been on training practitioners to use the techniques she has developed to deal with "challenging behaviors" in the classroom. In a study of parental correlates of developmental outcomes among a Mexican-American Head Start migrant sample, Siantz and Smith (1994) found parenting style to account for a significant proportion of the variance in child behavior problems, with more-rejecting maternal parenting associated with higher rates of reported child behavior problems.

Many studies do not fall neatly into a category of outcomes studied or explanatory factors examined. For example, Hubbs-Tait and colleagues (2002) examined relationships among cumulative family risks, Head Start attendance, and three diverse child outcomes: receptive vocabulary, social competence as rated by the children's teachers, and how well children followed directions, also rated by teachers. Children in the higher-risk families benefited more from Head Start in vocabulary development.

Early Head Start

Secondary analyses of data collected in the national Early Head Start evaluation are beginning to yield a body of literature on the development and developmental contexts of children in low-income families from birth to school age. While much of this work is in preparation and review stages, it already has been featured in several special issues of scholarly journals (e.g., *Infant Mental Health Journal*, Fitzgerald, Love, Raikes, & Robinson, 2002; *Fathering*, Cabrera, 2004; *Parenting: Science and Practice*, Boller & Bradley, in press). Specific findings highlight paternal contributions to children's language and cognitive development, above and beyond maternal contributions (Tamis-LeMonda, Shannon, Cabrera, & Lamb, 2004), and relations among maternal intrusiveness, warmth, and relationship outcomes as a function of ethnicity and acculturation (Ispa et al., 2004). Methodological analyses are furthering understanding of measures in the context of a relatively large low-income population, and include studies of the factor structure of the HOME instrument (Home Observation for Measurement of the Environment; e.g., Fuligni, Han, & Brooks-Gunn, 2004), validity of parental language self reports (Pan, Rowe, Spier, & Tamis-LeMonda, 2004), and videotaped assessment of father– and mother–child interactions (Ryan, Brady-Smith, & Brooks-Gunn, 2004).

Lessons from Head Start Research for Programs

Over a decade ago, Powell concluded that "movement toward conclusive statements about the merits of particular Head Start designs or practices with specific populations requires research on program variables in context. Here the field consistently comes up short" (p. 242). The picture is much less bleak today. With a goal of continuous program improvement, Head Start's descriptive and experimental research programs have tried to answer questions about how best to improve program practice in order to support children's growth and development and to enhance the well-being of their families. A number of lessons have emerged.

Perhaps the strongest lesson is that quality matters in Head Start, just as research has demonstrated throughout the history of child care research (Love et al., 2003; Love, Schochet, & Meckstroth, 1996; NICHD Early Child Care Research Network & Duncan, 2003; Phillips, McCartney, & Sussman, this volume). First, Head Start program performance standards – the criteria that define Head Start programs – are associated with higher levels of quality than are commonly seen in preschool and child care environments (see, for example, Clifford et al., in press, for data on preschool environments). Head Start classroom quality has been shown to be in the "good" range over two cohorts of nationally representative Head Start samples in FACES, with few classrooms scoring below minimal quality and with a more limited range than found in several other national studies (ACF, 2003b) and in the HSIS (ACF, 2005). These findings were replicated in center-based Early Head Start sites (ACF, 2004d). Even stronger evidence for the importance of performance standards was found through the national Early Head Start evaluation's experimental design: implementing the Head Start Performance Standards was associated with a pattern of broader child and parent impacts (ACF, 2002; ACYF, 2001).

FACES has demonstrated that the factors contributing to observed quality in Head Start classrooms range from teacher education and beliefs to teacher salaries and use of integrated curricula. Some predicted links with child outcomes have also been found, such as the association between teacher salaries, length of school day, or use of a comprehensive curriculum and gains in children's cognitive and social-emotional development.

However, other expected relationships were not found: observed classroom quality using a standard measure (ECERS-R) and child–adult ratios was not associated with gains in children's achievement.

Program staff need advice on how to achieve best practices using their limited resources and working with increasingly challenged families in their communities. In an example of useful research, Baydar, Reid, and Webster-Stratton (2003) found that Head Start centers randomly assigned to a special parent training intervention (compared with centers in the control condition) improved parenting for families both with and without mental health risk factors. Such studies help programs understand ways of enhancing their ability to aid at-risk families.

Particularly important for agencies designing their service-delivery approach, the Early Head Start evaluation found that all program models (whether center-based, home-based, or a "mixed approach" that combines the two) showed positive impacts, but somewhat different patterns of effects. The mixed-approach programs demonstrated the strongest pattern of impacts, particularly when fully implementing the performance standards. However, other research has shown that programs that begin as home-based and change to a mixed approach encounter some challenges in making that transition (Gill, Greenberg, & Vazquez, 2002).

Research focused on the role of fathers in Early Head Start programs provides additional lessons for programs. As programs implement tested father involvement strategies, the participation of fathers increases (McAllister, Wilson, & Burton, 2004; Raikes & Bellotti, in press). Father involvement in programs is associated with positive child outcomes (Roggman, Boyce, Cook, Christiansen, & Jones, 2004), and father involvement can be enhanced by understanding fathers' perspectives on the supports that programs provide (Summers, Boller, & Raikes, 2004). Other studies have documented variations in enrollment of Early Head Start children into Part C programs for children with disabilities (Peterson et al., 2004) and evidence of a need for more intensive mental health services for all families and more intensive health services for Hispanics (ACF, 2004a).

This completion of the cycle of research from research-based practice through evaluation and continuous improvement feedback is a direct result of the federal research program. Phillips and White (2004) commented recently that Head Start is fulfilling its dual role as a social intervention and a research laboratory. We have seen through this research that social scientists, as Phillips and White characterize them, can be both hands-on program conceptualizers and arm's-length program evaluators.

Summary and Conclusions

While gaps and shortcomings in Head Start research necessarily remain, we have summarized a vibrant, continuous, and comprehensive array of studies. The attention recently paid to experimental designs on a national basis in both Head Start and its younger sibling, Early Head Start, has been particularly important for answering specific accountability questions. These include not simply whether the program is effective, but also for whom it is effective, under what conditions it is effective, and what conditions moderate its effectiveness. At the same time, as reported here, the large national databases generated from these impact studies have the potential to yield even richer lessons: for testing and refining best practices for programs, and for investigating conditions that influence the development of children from low-income families.

We conclude that Head Start research has journeyed far since the last major synthesis in the mid-1980s. There continues to be clear evidence from a sizeable body of research, as previous reviewers have noted and as the recent national impact study has confirmed (ACF, 2005), to demonstrate that the program provides immediate benefits for the children it enrolls: Head Start participants can begin kindergarten on a stronger footing than they would without the program. There is also evidence of the persistence of long-term gains – at least into elementary school and perhaps beyond when children attend good-quality elementary schools. But the credibility of that conclusion is much weaker, relying primarily on non-experimental evidence analyzed after the fact, rather than prospectively, and often using data originally collected for other purposes.

What next for Head Start research? To continue to promote research that contributes to the field of child development while supporting continuous program improvement, the Head Start research community should pursue a broad and diversified portfolio of research investments. One essential element involves continuing the ongoing, longitudinal descriptive study of the preschool program, to provide information on Head Start children's developmental progress in a rich context of family demographics, teacher qualifications, and observed classroom quality. As FACES has provided normative data on the Head Start preschool child, future descriptive work in Early Head Start could similarly seek to understand the characteristics, precursors, and correlates of infant and toddler development.

A logical next step is to conduct randomized control trials, testing research-based interventions in multiple sites, and varying interventions that enhance implementation of specific programmatic features in prescribed and carefully documented ways. For example, an initiative designed to train program staff in child assessment administration and interpretation could be systematically varied in terms of the staff targeted or mode of instruction offered to determine what works best. An intervention that has been shown to enhance early literacy skills with one low-income group could be adapted and tested for its effectiveness with English language learners, children with disabilities, children of migrant and seasonal farmworker families, or other special populations that Head Start increasingly serves.

Other key lessons are emerging from the rich data sets now available. Variability of findings by race/ethnicity, first language, and number of demographic and other risks suggests that developmental, contextual, and intervention processes may differ for subgroups attending Head Start. It will be important, therefore, to fine-tune our understanding of what works for whom and under what conditions. Now that Head Start can offer services from before birth until kindergarten, it will be important to discover how to obtain the best value for the available resources. What types and levels of services over this developmental period yield the best outcomes, given varying degrees of risk?

Although Head Start's supporters and critics have, since the beginning, provided external impetus for large-scale program evaluations, some of the most important work derives from an internal drive toward continuous program improvement, aimed at enhancing the existing program in ways large and small. So long as that movement continues to build capability in programs to participate in and learn from research, the field of child development and, more important, the well-being of children of poverty will be well served.

Notes

The content of this publication does not necessarily reflect the views or policies of the US Department of Health and Human Services.

1   The majority of studies Barnett reviewed were long-term follow-up studies of model programs, like Abecedarian and High/Scope Perry Preschool, or studies of local Head Start, Title I, state pre-kindergarten programs, other locally implemented programs, and analyses of Head Start samples within national data sets (the latter we summarized here).

2   In summer 2004, the agency was renamed the Government Accountability Office.

3   Findings from the pre-kindergarten follow-up are not yet available.

4   Currie and Thomas note that eighth-grade test scores are important predictors of future labor market outcomes (Murnane, Willett, & Levy, 1995). Lee and Loeb (1995) found similar results with the NELS data on five different quality indexes (average school socio-economic status, average achievement, safety, teacher–student relations, and academic climate).

References

Abbott-Shim, M., Lambert, R., & McCarty, F. (2003). A comparison of school readiness outcomes for children randomly assigned to a Head Start program and the program's wait list. *Journal of Education for Students Placed at Risk, 8*(2), 191–214.

Administration for Children and Families. (2002, June). *Making a difference in the lives of infants and toddlers and their families: The impacts of Early Head Start.* Washington, DC: US Department of Health and Human Services.

Administration for Children and Families (2003a). *Building futures: The Head Start Impact Study interim report.* Washington, DC: US Department of Health and Human Services.

Administration for Children and Families. (2003b). *Head Start FACES 2000: A whole-child perspective on program performance (Fourth progress report).* Washington, DC: US Department of Health and Human Services.

Administration for Children and Families (2004a, February). *Are families healthy and getting needed services? Health and disabilities services in Early Head Start.* Washington, DC: US Department of Health and Human Services.

Administration for Children and Families. (2004b, April). *Head Start Program Fact Sheet.*

Administration for Children and Families. (2004c). *Interim report for Quality Research Centers Data Coordination Center cross-sectional analyses.* Washington, DC: US Department of Health and Human Services.

Administration for Children and Families. (2004d, February). *The role of Early Head Start in addressing the child care needs of low-income families with infants and toddlers.* Washington, DC: US Department of Health and Human Services.

Administration for Children and Families. (2005, June). *Head Start Impact Study: First year findings.* Washington, DC: US Department of Health and Human Services.

Administration on Children, Youth and Families. (2001, June). *Building their Futures: How Early Head Start programs are enhancing the lives of infants and toddlers in low-income families.* Washington, DC: US Department of Health and Human Services.

Administration on Children, Youth and Families. (2002). *A descriptive study of Head Start families: FACES Technical Report 1.* Washington, DC: US Department of Health and Human Services.

Barnett, W. S. (1993, May 19). Commentary: Does Head Start fade out? *Education Week*, p. 40.

Barnett, W. S. (1995). Long-term effects of early childhood programs on cognitive and school outcomes. *The Future of Children, 5*(5), 3–27.

Barnett, W. S. (2002, September 13). *The battle over Head Start: What the research shows.* Paper presented at a Congressional Science and Public Policy briefing on the impact of Head Start, Washington, DC.

Barnett, W. S. (2004). Does Head Start have lasting cognitive effects? The myth of fade-out. In E. Zigler & S. J. Styfco (Eds.), *The Head Start debates* (pp. 221–250). Baltimore: Brookes.

Barnett, W. S., & Camilli, G. (1999). *Estimating Head Start effects.* (Working Paper). New Brunswick, NJ: Graduate School of Education, Rutgers University.

Baydar, N., Reid, M. J., & Webster-Stratton, C. (2003). The role of mental health factors and program engagement in the effectiveness of a preventive parenting program for Head Start mothers. *Child Development, 74*, 1433–1453.

Boller, K., & Bradley, R. (Eds.). (in press). Early Head Start Father Studies [Special issue]. *Parenting: Science and Practice.*

Brush, L., Gaidurgis, A., & Best, C. (1993). *Indices of Head Start program quality.* Washington, DC: Pelavin Associates.

Bryant, D. M., Burchinal, M., Lau, L. B., & Sparling, J. J. (1994). Family and classroom correlates of Head Start children's developmental outcomes. *Early Childhood Research Quarterly, 9*, 289–309.

Cabrera, N. (Ed.). (2004). Fathers in Early Head Start [Special issue]. *Fathering: A Journal of Theory, Research, and Practice About Men as Fathers, 2*(1).

Cicirelli, V. G. (1969). *The impact of Head Start: An evaluation of the effects of Head Start on children's cognitive and affective development* (Vols. 1–2). Washington, DC: National Bureau of Standards, Institute for Applied Technology.

Clifford, R. M., Barbarin, O., Chang, F., Early, D., Bryant, D., Howes, C., Burchinal, M., & Pianta, R. (in press). What is pre-kindergarten? Characteristics of public pre-kindergarten programs. *Applied Developmental Science.*

Currie, J., & Neidell, M. (2003, November). *Getting inside the "black box" of Head Start quality: What matters and what doesn't?* (NBER Working Paper 10091). Cambridge, MA: National Bureau of Economic Research.

Currie, J., & Thomas, D. (1995). Does Head Start make a difference? *American Economic Review, 85*(3), 341–364.

Currie, J., & Thomas, D. (1999). Does Head Start help Hispanic children? *Journal of Public Economics, 74*, 235–262.

Currie, J., & Thomas, D. (2000). School quality and the longer-term effects of Head Start. *Journal of Human Resources, 35*, 755–774.

Devaney, B., Ellwood, M., & Love, J. M. (1997). Programs that mitigate the effects of poverty on children. *The Future of Children, 7*(2), 88–112.

Fantuzzo, J., Bulotsky, R., McDermott, P., Mosca, S., & Lutz, M. (2003). A multivariate analysis of emotional and behavioral adjustment and preschool educational outcomes. *School Psychology Review, 32*, 185–203.

Fantuzzo, J., Sutton-Smith, B., Coolahan, K. C., Manz, P. H., Canning, S., & Debnam, D. (1995). Assessment of preschool play interaction behaviors in young low-income children: Penn Interactive Peer Play Scale. *Early Childhood Research Quarterly, 10*, 105–120.

Feil, E. G., Golly, A., Walker, H., & Severson, H. H. (2004, June). *Promoting Head Start children for social-emotional success at school: Followup results from the adaptation of First Step to Success.* Presented at Head Start's 7th National Research Conference, Washington, DC.

Fischel, J. E., Spira, E. G., Shaller, G. E., Fuchs-Eisenberg, A., Katz, S., & Storch, S. A. (2004, June). *The enhancement of emergent literacy skills in Head Start: Outcomes of classroom curriculum research.* Paper presented at Head Start's 7th National Research Conference, Washington, DC.

Fitzgerald, H., Love, J., Raikes, H., & Robinson, J. (Eds.). (2002). Early Head Start [Special issue]. *Infant Mental Health Journal, 23*(1–2).

Fosberg, S., & Brown, B. (1984). *The effects of Head Start health services: Report of the Head Start health evaluation.* Cambridge, MA: Abt Associates.

Fuligni, A. S., Han, W., & Brooks-Gunn, J. (2004). The Infant–Toddler HOME in the second and third years of life. *Parenting: Science and Practice, 4,* 139–159.

Garces, E., Thomas, D., & Currie, J. (2000). *Longer term effects of Head Start.* (NBER Working Paper 8094). Cambridge, MA: National Bureau of Economic Research.

Gill, S., Greenberg, M., & Vazquez, M. (2002). Changes in the service delivery model and home visitors' job satisfaction and turnover in an Early Head Start program. *Infant Mental Health Journal, 23*(1–2), 182–196.

Gish, M. (2004). *Head Start issues for the 108th Congress.* CRS Report for Congress. Washington, DC: Congressional Research Service, Library of Congress.

Hart, K., & Schumacher, R. (2004, June). Moving forward: Head Start children, families, and programs in 2003. *CLASP Policy Brief, Head Start Series,* No. 5.

Hubbs-Tait, L., Culp, A. M., Huey, E., Culp, R., Starost, H.-J., & Hare, C. (2002). Relation of Head Start attendance to children's cognitive and social outcomes: Moderation by family risk. *Early Childhood Research Quarterly, 17,* 539–558.

Ispa, J. M., Fine, M. A., Halgunseth, L. C., Harper, S., Robinson, J., Boyce, L., Brooks-Gunn, J., & Brady-Smith, C. (2004). Maternal intrusiveness, maternal warmth, and mother–toddler relationship outcomes: Variation across low-income ethnic and acculturation groups. *Child Development, 75,* 1613–1631.

Kagan, S. L., Moore, E., & Bredekamp, S. (1995). *Reconsidering children's early development and learning: Toward common views and vocabulary.* Washington, DC: National Education Goals Panel.

Karoly, L. A., Greenwood, P. W., Everingham, S. S., Houbé, J., Kilburn, M. R., Rydell, C. P., Sanders, M., & Chiesa, J. (1998). *Investing in our children: What we know and don't know about the costs and benefits of early childhood interventions.* Santa Monica, CA: Rand.

Korenman, S., Miller, J. E., & Sjaastad, J. E. (1995). Long-term poverty and child development in the United States: Results from the NLSY. *Children and Youth Services Review, 17*(1/2), 127–156.

Lee, V. E., Brooks-Gunn, J., Schnur, E., & Liaw, F. R. (1990). Are Head Start effects sustained? A longitudinal followup comparison of disadvantaged children attending Head Start, no preschool, and other preschool programs. *Child Development, 61,* 495–507.

Lee, V. E., Brooks-Gunn, J., & Schnur, E. (1988). Does Head Start work? A 1-year follow-up comparison of disadvantaged children attending Head Start, no preschool, and other preschool programs. *Developmental Psychology, 24,* 210–222.

Lee, V. E., & Loeb, S. (1995). Where do Head Start attendees end up? One reason why preschool effects fade out. *Educational Evaluation and Policy Analysis, 17,* 62–82.

Love, J. M., Aber, L., & Brooks-Gunn, J. (1994). *Strategies for assessing community progress toward achieving the first national educational goal.* Princeton, NJ: Mathematica Policy Research, Inc.

Love, J. M., Chazan-Cohen, R., & Raikes, H. (in press). Forty years of research knowledge and use: From Head Start to Early Head Start and beyond. In J. L. Aber, S. Bishop-Josef, S. Jones, K. McLearn, & D. Phillips (Eds.), *Child development and social policy: Knowledge for action*. Washington, DC: American Psychological Association.

Love, J. M., Harrison, L., Sagi-Schwartz, A., van IJzendoorn, M. H., Ross, C., Ungerer, J. A., Raikes, H., Brady-Smith, C., Boller, K., Brooks-Gunn, J., Constantine, J., Kisker, E. E., Paulsell, D., & R. Chazan-Cohen, R. (2003). Child care quality matters: How conclusions may vary with context. *Child Development, 74*, 1021–1033.

Love, J. M., Schochet, P. Z., & Meckstroth, A. L. (1996, May). *Are they in any real danger? What research does – and doesn't – tell us about child care quality and children's well-being*. Child Care Research and Policy Papers; Lessons from Child Care Research funded by the Rockefeller Foundation. Princeton, NJ: Mathematica Policy Research.

Lynch, R. G. (2004). *Exceptional returns: Economic, fiscal, and social benefits of investment in early childhood development*. Washington, DC: Economic Policy Institute.

McAllister, C. L., Wilson, P. C., & Burton, J. (2004). From sports fans to nurturers: An Early Head Start program's evolution towards father involvement. *Fathering: A Journal of Theory, Research, and Practice about Men as Fathers, 2*(1), 31–60.

McCall. R. B. (1993). *Head Start: Its potential, its achievements, its future: A briefing paper for policymakers*. Pittsburgh, PA: Office of Child Development, University of Pittsburgh.

McCartney, K., & Dearing, E. (2002). Evaluating effect sizes in the policy arena. *Evaluation Exchange, 8*(1), 4–7.

McCartney, K., & Rosenthal, R. (2000). Effect size, practical importance, and social policy for children. *Child Development, 71*, 173–180.

McKey, R., Condelli, L., Ganson, H., Barrett, B., McConkey, C., & Plantz, M. (1985, June). *The impact of Head Start on children, families and communities: Final report of the Head Start Evaluation, Synthesis and Utilization Project*. Washington, DC: CSR, Inc.

Murnane, R., Willett, J., & Levy, F. (1995). The growing importance of cognitive skills in wage determination. *Review of Economics and Statistics*, May.

NICHD Early Child Care Research Network & Duncan, G. J. (2003). Modeling the impacts of child care quality on children's preschool cognitive development. *Child Development, 74*, 1454–1475.

Oden, S., Schweinhart, L. J., & Weikart, D. P. (2000). *Into adulthood: A study of the effects of Head Start*. Ypsilanti, MI: High/Scope Educational Research Foundation.

Pan, B. A., Rowe, M. L., Spier, E., & Tamis-LeMonda, C. (2004). Measuring productive vocabulary of toddlers in low-income families: Concurrent and predictive validity of three sources of data. *Journal of Child Language, 31*, 587–608.

Payne, A. C., Whitehurst, G. J., & Angell, A. L. (1994). The role of home literacy environment in the development of language ability in preschool children from low-income families. *Early Childhood Research Quarterly, 9*, 427–440

Peterson, C. A., Wall, S., Raikes, H. H., Kisker, E. E., Swanson, M. E., Jerald, J., Atwater, J., & Qiao, W. (2004). Early Head Start: Identifying and serving children with disabilities. *Topics on Early Childhood Education Special Education, 24*(2), 76–88.

Phillips, D. A., & Cabrera, N. J. (Eds.). (1996) *Beyond the blueprint: Directions for research on Head Start's families*. Washington, DC: Roundtable on Head Start Research/Board on Children, Youths, and Families, National Research Council and Institute of Medicine.

Phillips, D. A., & White, S. H. (2004). New possibilities for research on Head Start. In E. Zigler & S. J. Styfco (Eds.), *The Head Start debates* (pp. 263–278). Baltimore: Brookes.

Powell, D. R. (1994). Head Start and research: Notes on a special issue. *Early Childhood Research Quarterly, 9*, 241–242.

Raikes, H. H., & Bellotti, J. (in press). Two studies of father involvement in Early Head Start programs: A national survey and a demonstration program evaluation. *Parenting: Science and Practice.*

Roggman, L., Boyce, L., Cook, G., Christiansen, K., & Jones, D. (2004). Playing with Daddy: Social toy play, Early Head Start, and developmental outcomes. *Fathering: A Journal of Theory, Research, and Practice about Men as Fathers, 2*(1), 83–109.

Ross, C. (1979). Early skirmishes with poverty: The historical roots of Head Start. In E. Zigler & J. Valentine (Eds.). *Project Head Start: A legacy of the war on poverty* (pp. 21–42). New York: Free Press.

Ryan, R. M., Brady-Smith, C., & Brooks-Gunn, J. (2004). Videotaped parent–child interactions in the Early Head Start Research and Evaluation Project: Focus on fathers. *Evaluation Exchange, X*(3), 24.

Siantz, M. L. deL., & Smith, M. S. (1994). Parental factors correlated with developmental outcome in the migrant Head Start child. *Early Childhood Research Quarterly, 9*, 481–503.

Slaughter-Defoe, D. T., & Rubin, H. H. (2001). A longitudinal case study of Head Start eligible children: Implications for urban education. *Educational Psychologist, 36*(1), 31–44.

Summers, J. A., Boller, K., & Raikes, H. (2004). Preferences and perceptions about getting support expressed by low-income fathers. *Fathering: A Journal of Theory, Research, and Practice about Men as Fathers, 2*(1), 61–82.

Tamis-LeMonda, C., Shannon, J., Cabrera, N., & Lamb, M. (2004). Fathers and mothers at play with their 2- and 3-year-olds: Contributions to language and cognitive development. *Child Development, 75*, 1613–1631.

US Department of Health and Human Services. (1990). *Head Start research and evaluation: A blueprint for the future. Recommendations of the Advisory Panel for the Head Start Evaluation Design Project.* Washington, DC: Author.

US Department of Health and Human Services. (1993). *Report of the Advisory Committee on Head Start Quality and Expansion.* Washington, DC: Author.

US Department of Health and Human Services. (1994). *The Statement of the Advisory Committee on Services for Families with Infants and Toddlers.* Washington, DC: Author.

US Department of Health and Human Services, Administration for Children and Families. (1996, November 5). Head Start Program Performance Standards. *Federal Register, 61*(215), 57186–57227.

US Department of Health and Human Services, Administration for Children and Families, Head Start Bureau. (1999, September). Head Start PCCost: The computerized version of the grant application package, SF424A Version 4.01 Y2K. Washington, DC: Author.

US Department of Health and Human Services, Administration for Children and Families (2003, September). *The Head Start leaders guide to positive child outcomes: Strategies to support positive child outcomes.* Washington, DC: Administration on Children, Youth and Families, Head Start Bureau.

US Department of Health and Human Services, Administration for Children and Families (2004). *Program Information Report, FY2003.* Washington, DC: Author.

US General Accounting Office. (1997). *Head Start: Research provides little information on impact of current program.* (GAO/HEHS-97–59). Washington, DC: Author.

Webster-Stratton, C. (1998). Preventing conduct problems in Head Start children: Strengthening parenting competencies. *Journal of Consulting and Clinical Psychology, 66*, 715–730.

Whitehurst, G. J., Epstein, J. N., Angell, A. C., Payne, A. C., Crone, D. A., & Fischel, J. E. (1994). Outcomes of an emergent literacy intervention in Head Start. *Journal of Educational Psychology, 86*, 542–555.

Whitehurst, G. J., & Lonigan, C. J. (1998). Child development and emergent literacy. *Child Development, 69*, 848–872.

Whitehurst, G. J., Zevenbergen, A. A., Crone, D. A., Schultz, M. D., Velting, O. N, & Fischel, J. E. (1999). Outcomes of an emergent literacy intervention from Head Start through second grade. *Journal of Educational Psychology, 91*, 261–272.

Zigler, E., & Styfco, S. J. (Eds.). (2004). *The Head Start debates.* Baltimore: Brookes.

28

Early Childhood Policy: A Comparative Perspective

Jane Waldfogel

Countries vary widely in the approaches they take to early childhood policy. How well do different countries meet the needs of children and families in the early childhood years? How does the US compare? Are there areas of early childhood policy where the US could learn from the example of other countries? In this chapter, I provide an overview of the approaches peer countries take to three major types of early childhood policies – parental leave, early childhood education and care, and child benefits – and contrast those approaches to the policy choices the US has made. I consider the relative merits of alternative policies in meeting the needs of children and families in the early childhood years, and conclude by drawing lessons for US policy. The countries that I consider here are the thirty advanced industrialized nations that make up the Organization for Economic Cooperation and Development (OECD). As developed countries, the OECD nations are appropriate peers for comparison with the US. They are frequently studied together, and comparable data tend to be readily available for them.

Within the OECD, analysts have identified three major types of social welfare state: Anglo-American, Continental European, and Nordic (Esping-Anderson, 1990). As the name suggests, the Anglo-American group includes the United Kingdom and its former colonies (Australia, Canada, New Zealand, and the United States). These countries tend to rely to a larger extent than others on the private market and employers for social welfare provision; they also tend to have less regulated labor markets and more income inequality. The Continental European countries (such as France, Germany, and Italy) are quite diverse but tend to follow a "corporatist" welfare state model, with both employers and the government playing an active role in social welfare provision; they also tend to have lower levels of income inequality than the Anglo-American group. The third group, the Nordic or Scandinavian countries (such as Denmark, Norway, and Sweden), are distinct in having the most active role for government in social welfare provision and in having the strongest commitment to reducing income inequality; this commitment is reflected in high progressive tax rates and low levels of wage inequality. Some member nations of the OECD do not fit into these groups but rather represent their own subgroups: the Asian countries (Japan, South Korea), transition economies (Czech Republic, Poland, Slovakia), and other newly industrializing countries (Mexico). These latter countries are quite heterogeneous, but have welfare states that tend to resemble the Anglo-American or Continental European countries.

As we shall see, the early childhood policies that have developed in these different groups of countries are quite distinct. So too are their other social welfare policies. Although this chapter will not consider those other social welfare policies, it is important to note that the early childhood policies considered here typically occur within the context of a wider array of health and social services programs that provide medical care for children and also support parents in their parenting role. Such policies, which include health insurance, well-baby and immunization services, home health visiting programs, child health programs, and so on, vary widely across countries, with the US tending to lag in their provision (Kamerman & Kahn, 1991, 1995).

Three Types of Early Childhood Policies

Governments have typically used three types of policies to support children and families during the early childhood years: parental leave, early childhood education and care, and child benefits. *Parental leave policies* – whether in the form of maternity leave (for mothers), paternity leave (for fathers), or parental leave (for mothers or fathers) – help parents who were employed before a birth to remain home for a period of time so that they can provide care for a child themselves. Usually, although not always, parental leave policies provide the right to a job-protected leave and to some income replacement during the leave. *Early childhood education and care policies*, in contrast, help parents pay for non-parental care and education for a child, by subsidizing the care that parents select or by providing care directly through public programs. Such policies may also influence the type of care and education that is offered and its quality. Early childhood education and care programs serve children of both working and non-working parents. Thus, they serve both a child development and day care function. A third type of policy which supports children and families in the early childhood years is *child benefits*. Many countries outside the US have historically had special maternity grants for families with newborns as well as child benefits for all families with children. In addition, several countries have recently instituted "early childhood benefits," which provide additional benefits to families with young children.

A country's choice of a policy or set of policies can influence the decisions parents make about care and education arrangements for their children. If a country offers generous parental leave but little support for child care or education, parents will be more likely to stay home with their children than to use non-parental care or education. Alternatively, if a country offers little parental leave but more generous support for child care and education, parents are likely to return to work early and place children in child care. Policy can also influence the type of child care or education in which children are placed and its quality.

Parental Leave Policies

Until 1993, the US was one of the few industrialized countries without maternity leave legislation. Even after the passage of the Family and Medical Leave Act (FMLA) in that year, the US still stands out as having particularly minimal legislation. This section reviews what we know from research about parental leave policies, summarizes the provisions of the FMLA and other legislation in the US, and then considers the policies that exist in other countries.

What do we know from research about parental leave policies and outcomes for children and families?

Although there is no consensus internationally as to how long parental leaves should last, mounting evidence supports the wisdom of allowing a parent to stay home for up to a year post-birth. However, lengthy leaves – extending beyond the first year of life into the second and third year and taken predominantly by women – may have fewer benefits, and greater costs.

With regard to the first year of life, there is a good deal of evidence that policies that allow new mothers to stay home beyond the first few weeks and months of life are associated with improved health outcomes for women and children. Research in the US has found that women who return to work later in the first year have better mental health (less depression) (Chatterji & Markowitz, 2004), and comparative studies have found that when paid leave periods are longer, infant mortality rates are lower (Ruhm, 2000; Tanaka, 2005). Unpaid leave does not have the same protective effect, presumably because parents are less likely to take it (Ruhm, 2000; Tanaka, 2005). These improvements in child health may come about because parents on leave are able to monitor their children's health and safety at home. There is also evidence that children whose mothers stay home longer in the first year of life are more likely to receive well-baby care and to be fully immunized (Berger, Hill, & Waldfogel, 2005). There may also be benefits associated with breast-feeding, since women who take leave are more likely to initiate breast-feeding, and to continue for longer (Berger et al., 2005; Cunningham, Jelliffe, & Jelliffe, 1991; Lindberg, 1996; Roe, Whittington, Fein, & Teisl, 1996).

There may also be links between longer leaves and improved child development outcomes. A number of studies in the US have found adverse effects on cognitive development or behavioral problems for children whose mothers work in the first year, particularly when mothers work early and/or long hours (Brooks-Gunn, Han, & Waldfogel, 2002; Shonkoff & Phillips, 2000; Smolensky & Gootman, 2003). Although these effects tend to be small, are not found for all children or in all studies, and may not all persist beyond the preschool years, this research nevertheless suggests that some children might do better along some dimensions if their mothers had the chance to stay home longer in the first year of life.

The evidence is less clear regarding leaves that extend beyond one year. Where adverse effects of maternal employment or non-parental child care have been found, these have tended to be concentrated in the first year. It is not clear that exclusive parental care in the second and third years of life would on average be more beneficial in terms of child health and development than a mixture of parental care and non-parental care and education. The answer is likely to depend on the circumstances of a particular child, family, and larger community. Moreover, long leaves raise issues in terms of gender equity, making it harder for women to maintain attachments to employers and to advance in careers, as well as potentially affecting employment or wages for women overall (Ruhm, 1998; Waldfogel, 2001b).

Thus, the research suggests that providing a year of job-protected and paid parental leave to all new parents, so that a parent can stay home for the first year if she or he chooses to do so, would have many positive benefits for children and their parents. The case is not so clear for extending leave into the second and third year of life. So, these considerations suggest providing a year of paid and job-protected leave to all new parents, followed in the next year or two by some support, but at a diminished level and alongside access to high-quality child care, so that parents can choose whether to stay home beyond the first year, use non-parental care or education, or combine the two.

Parental leave policy in the US

The FMLA provides the right to a short (twelve-week), job-protected parental leave for workers who meet qualifying conditions (i.e., those who work in firms of at least fifty workers and have worked at least 1250 hours in the prior year). Because of these qualifying conditions, fewer than half of the nation's private sector workers are eligible for leave guaranteed by the FMLA (Waldfogel, 1999a, 2001a). Moreover, the FMLA does not include any income replacement or pay during the leave; as a result, some workers who are eligible for leave do not take it (Commission on Family and Medical Leave, 1996; Cantor et al., 2001).

In spite of these limitations, the FMLA has had quite a dramatic impact on parental leave *coverage* in the United States, especially for men, few of whom previously had the right to a paternity leave (Waldfogel, 1999a). However, the impact of the law on parental leave *usage* has been less pronounced. Studies have found generally small effects of the US law on leave usage by new mothers (Han & Waldfogel, 2003; Klerman & Leibowitz, 1998; Ross, 1998; Waldfogel, 1999b) and no discernible effects on leave usage by new fathers (Han & Waldfogel, 2003). The fact that the law extended coverage but had so little impact on usage suggests that there are limits to the extent to which families are willing and able to use unpaid leave. Given the financial constraints that families with new children often face, taking leave without pay may simply not be an option for many of them.

In addition to the federal FMLA, there are also several state maternity or parental leave laws, including some which provide a longer leave period for at least some workers (Han & Waldfogel, 2003). However, like the federal law, these laws tend not to be universal but rather cover workers in larger firms or, in some instances, state employees only. Additionally, five states have temporary disability insurance (TDI) laws which provide a period of paid leave for workers with a temporary disability, including pregnancy and childbirth.

Under these TDI laws, new mothers are typically eligible for 6 to 8 weeks of leave, with some pay. Recently, California extended its TDI law to cover 12 weeks of parental leave, becoming the first state in the nation to offer paid parental leave (Smolensky & Gootman, 2003).

Leave policies in other nations

The parental leave policies in other OECD countries, summarized in Table 28.1, differ from those in the United States in four major respects (Kamerman, 2000b, 2000c; Moss & Deven, 1999; Waldfogel, 2001c). First, they tend to provide a longer period of leave – an average of 18 months of childbirth-related leave across the OECD. Second, they typically provide some form of wage replacement. Third, the policies tend to be universal, covering all new mothers (in the case of maternity leave), all new fathers (paternity leave), or all new parents (parental leave). Fourth, these policies tend to be operated on a social insurance basis, with funding for leave benefits coming from social insurance funds (to which all employees and employers contribute) rather than individual employers, so that when a woman goes out on maternity leave, her employer does not have to pay her salary. These cross-country differences reflect the historical origins of these policies. In countries other than the US, maternity leave policies were introduced more than a century ago, along with other social insurance programs, and were seen as a way to protect the health of women and children (Kamerman, 2000c).

When one compares the US to peer nations, the differences in parental leave policy are striking. Even among its fellow Anglo-American nations, the US is distinctive. Its closest neighbor, Canada, extended its leave coverage in 2002 and now offers a year of childbirth-related leave, and all but two weeks of the leave are paid, from a social insurance fund. The United Kingdom provides a year of job-protected maternity leave to all new mothers, with the first 6 months paid from social insurance funds (to be extended to 12 months under plans announced in December 2004). Australia and New Zealand provide a year of unpaid parental leave (New Zealand also provides 12 weeks of paid maternity leave). Thus, all the Anglo-American nations except the US now offer a year of job-protected parental leave, and all but Australia and US provide at least some paid leave.

In the Nordic and Continental European countries, the periods of leave – nearly all paid – are even longer, ranging up to 3 years or more in several countries. And, again, these leaves tend to be paid from social insurance funds, rather than by individual employers. In contrast, the Asian countries have short maternity leave periods along US lines, although Japan (since 1995) has a year of parental leave.

Take-up of these parental leave policies is very high, particularly on the part of women, and, as would be expected, leave policies significantly influence women's employment and leave-taking (Gregg, Gutierrez-Domenech, & Waldfogel, 2003; Ronsen, 1999). Men, in contrast, have been much less responsive to changes in leave policies – even in Sweden, the country that has made the greatest effort to promote paternity leave (Haas & Hwang, 1999). A number of countries are now experimenting with ways to induce fathers to take more leave. One provision that has been tried in the Nordic countries is the introduction

Table 28.1 Childbirth-related leave policies in the United States and other OECD nations

Country	Months	Type of leave and payment
Australia	12	52 weeks parental leave, unpaid.
Austria	40	16 weeks maternity leave, at 100% of prior earnings. Up to 3 years of child care allowance, at flat rate, with higher rate for single and low-income parents.
Belgium	7	15 weeks maternity leave, at 75–80% of prior earnings. 13 weeks parental leave, at flat rate.
Canada	12	17 weeks maternity leave, 15 weeks at 55% of prior earnings. 35 weeks parental leave, at 55% of prior earnings.
Czech Rep.	36	28 weeks maternity leave, at 69% of prior earnings. Parental leave until child is age 3, unpaid.
Denmark	19	18 weeks maternity leave, at 90% of prior earnings. 10 weeks parental leave, at 60% of prior earnings. 1 year child care leave, at 60% of prior earnings.
Finland	36	18 weeks maternity leave, at 65% of prior earnings. 26 weeks parental leave, at 65% of prior earnings. Childrearing leave until child is age 3, at flat rate.
France	36	16 weeks maternity leave, at 100% of prior earnings. Parental leave until child is age 3, unpaid for 1 child; paid at flat rate (income-tested) for two or more.
Germany	39	14 weeks maternity leave, at 100% of prior earnings. 3 years parental leave, at flat rate (income-tested) for 2 years, unpaid for 3rd year.
Greece	10	17 weeks maternity leave, at 50% of prior earnings. 26 weeks parental leave, unpaid.
Hungary	36	24 weeks maternity leave, at 70% of prior earnings. Childrearing leave until child is age 3, at flat rate.
Iceland	6	3 months maternity leave, at 80% of prior earnings. 3 months parental leave, at 80% of prior earnings.
Ireland	7	18 weeks maternity leave, at 70% of prior earnings. 14 weeks parental leave, unpaid.
Italy	15	5 months maternity leave, at 80% of prior earnings. 10 months parental leave, at 30% of prior earnings.
Japan	12	14 weeks maternity leave, at 60% of prior earnings. Parental leave until child is age 1, unpaid.

Table 28.1 *Continued*

Country	Months	Type of leave and payment
Korea	2	8 weeks maternity leave, unpaid.
Luxembourg	10	16 weeks maternity leave, at 100% of prior earnings. 6 months parental leave (or 12 months part-time), at flat rate.
Mexico	3	12 weeks maternity leave, at 100% of prior earnings.
Netherlands	10	16 weeks maternity leave, at 100% of prior earnings. 26 weeks parental leave, unpaid.
New Zealand	3	12 weeks parental leave, flat rate. Extended parental leave, unpaid.
Norway	24	52 weeks parental leave, at 80% of prior earnings (or 42 weeks at 100%). Childrearing leave until child is age 2, at flat rate.
Poland	28	16 weeks maternity leave, at 100% of prior earnings. 2 years of parental leave, at flat rate.
Portugal	30	26 weeks maternity leave, at 100% of prior earnings. Up to 2 years parental leave, unpaid.
Slovakia	36	28 weeks maternity leave, at 69% of prior earnings. Parental leave until child is age 3, unpaid.
Spain	36	16 weeks maternity leave, at 100% of prior earnings. Parental leave until child is age 3, unpaid.
Sweden	24	24 months parental leave, 18 months at 80% of prior earnings, 3 months flat rate, 3 months unpaid.
Switzerland	4	16 weeks maternity leave, pay varies by canton.
Turkey	3	12 weeks maternity leave, at 67% of prior earnings.
UK	12	52 weeks maternity leave, at 90% for 6 weeks and flat rate for 20 weeks, if sufficient work history; otherwise, flat rate for 26 weeks. Second 26 weeks unpaid. 13 weeks parental leave, unpaid, up to 4 weeks per year may be taken any time between birth and age 6.
US	3	12 weeks of family leave (which includes maternity leave), unpaid.
OECD average	18	

Sources: Clearinghouse on International Developments in Child, Youth, and Family Policies at Columbia University (2002), "Table 1. Maternity, Paternity, and Parental Leaves in the OECD Countries 1998–2002"; European Foundation for the Improvement of Living and Working Conditions (2004); and Tanaka (2004).

of "use it or lose it" policies that provide additional leave time for the family that can be used only by the father (Kamerman, 2000b; Smith & Pylkkanen, 2004).

Another fairly new development in other advanced industrialized countries is the introduction of policies giving parents of young children the right to return to work part-time (Gornick & Meyers, 2003; Sleebos, 2003). Sweden has since 1978 had a policy allowing parents of children under the age of 8 to work part-time (6 hours a day). In 1997, the European Union issued a part-time working directive. In some EU countries, parents of young children now have the right to work part-time; in others, employers are required to consider such requests, although they are not required to grant them.

Early Childhood Education and Care Policies

The second major way governments help children and families in the early childhood years is through early childhood education and care (ECEC) policies. This section reviews what we know from developmental science and research about the effects of child care and education on children and families (see chapter by Phillips, McCartney, & Sussman in this volume) and then offers a brief comparison of ECEC policies in the US and other nations.

What do we know from developmental science and research about ECEC policies and outcomes for children and families?

The single most important lesson from developmental science and research on early childhood education and care is that quality matters. Although most of the studies linking quality to improved child outcomes have been observational and thus cannot establish causality with certainty, the weight of the evidence suggests that better quality is associated with improved child outcomes (Blau, 2001; Shonkoff & Phillips, 2000; Smolensky & Gootman, 2003; Vandell & Wolfe, 2002). Quality can be measured in various ways, but the key element is that the care is sensitive and responsive to the individual child. The best way to measure quality is for trained observers to visit the setting and assess its "process quality" using a rating system specifically developed to measure the quality of care being provided along such dimensions of warmth, responsiveness, stimulation, and sensitivity. When this type of assessment is not possible, the second-best way is to document structural elements of quality that have been found to be associated with sensitive and responsive care. These elements include well-educated and well-compensated staff, low child:staff ratios, and small group sizes.

Whether quality is measured in terms of process or structural elements, the other striking conclusion from research is that the quality of care on offer in the United States ranges widely but on average is not very good (Smolensky & Gootman, 2003). The low average quality of care and education in the US helps explain why typical center-based child care programs in the US have not been found to have the same beneficial effects that high-quality model interventions have. Thus, while a series of randomized experiments have shown that high-quality early childhood interventions can boost children's cognitive attainment with neutral or even positive effects on their social and emotional development (see reviews in Currie, 2001; Karoly et al., 1998; Waldfogel, 2002), studies of day care have had more mixed results (see reviews in Shonkoff & Phillips, 2000; Smolensky & Gootman, 2003). Generally, such studies find that children who have attended center-based care at age 3 or 4 enter school with better reading and math skills. However, links between center-based care and more behavior problems have also been reported, particularly if children have entered that care early in childhood and for long hours. Quality plays a key role here, with care or education settings that are rated higher on quality having more positive effects. There may also be important individual differences among children, such that some children are more affected by group care than others (Shonkoff & Phillips, 2000).

So what are the implications of developmental science and research for ECEC? The main implication is the importance of promoting high-quality care and education for children throughout the early childhood years. At the same time, ECEC, like parental leave, should take into account individual differences among children and families, particularly when children are under age 3.

ECEC policies in the US

Early childhood education and care policies can be distinguished on at least three dimensions. The first has to do with auspices. Governments may provide child care and education directly, or they may subsidize or reimburse some of the costs of care and education that parents purchase from the private market. A second distinction has to do with universal versus targeted provision. Governments may offer child care or education services to all children, or may target their support to particular children. And third, the aims of child care and education may be seen as developmental, or as employment-related. Thus, ECEC can be seen as a service promoting child development, or as a service supporting parental employment.

ECEC policies in the US are distinctive along all three dimensions. First, the US tends to rely more than other countries on private market provision, and where the government does become involved, that involvement tends to mainly take the form of subsidizing or offsetting the costs of care (through subsidies, vouchers, or tax credits), rather than direct provision of care (Kamerman & Waldfogel, 2005). The US does have some measures aimed at promoting quality of care (such as regulations and licensing standards), but these vary widely across states and are generally weak (Gormley, 1995; Phillips & Mekos, 1993). Second, US policy in this area is, for the most part, targeted, rather than universal. With the exception of the new universal pre-kindergarten programs which Georgia, Oklahoma, and the District of Columbia have adopted, state and federal programs are mainly targeted, to low-income or disadvantaged families, or families with working mothers. Third, greater weight has been placed in the US on policies and programs to promote parental employment, rather than child development. This emphasis means that when resources are constrained, there is a tendency to favor programs that expand the quantity of care rather than its quality.

The policy choices that the US has made have implications in terms of the two criteria highlighted above – quality and parental choice. With a market system, the US offers parents a good deal of choice. However, for most families, that choice is constrained by the high costs of care. Moreover, US policy does little with regard to quality, with the exception of state regulatory and licensing activity, which, as discussed above, is relatively weak. The result is a system that is characterized by low average quality of care, and a good deal of inequality (Meyers, Rosenbaum, Ruhn, & Waldfogel, 2004). There are large gaps in enrollment in center-based care between children from higher- and lower-income families. There are also gaps in quality, with children from the highest-income families tending to receive the highest-quality care. Programs targeted to the lowest-income families help raise the enrollment of children from some of those families, and the quality of care in which they are enrolled, but such programs do not reach all low-income families (only about 15% receive subsidies), and provide little help to middle-income families (Meyers et al., 2004; Phillips, Voran, Kisker, Howes, & Whitebrook, 1994).

How do ECEC policies in other countries compare?

As we have seen, the US relies on a private market system, with the government getting involved mainly through subsidies and mainly on a targeted basis, and with child care being seen primarily as a service to support maternal employment rather than child development. Other countries differ on all three dimensions, tending to have more public sector provision, on a universal basis, and with a child development focus.

One striking trend across countries is the increasing share of children enrolled in ECEC as children approach school entry. Provision for children under the age of 3 varies a good deal across countries (we lack good comparable data on provision for this age group, but the data we do have indicate that the share of under 3s enrolled in some form of ECEC ranges from near zero to as much as half or more in the Nordic countries; OECD, 2001b, Table 4.7, p. 144). As children approach school entry, enrollment in some form of center- or school-based provision becomes more widespread. The latest figures for OECD countries indicate that in many countries enrollment is becoming universal, particularly in the year or two prior to school entry. In countries such as Belgium, Denmark, France, Italy, and the UK, 80% or more of 3- and 4-year-olds are enrolled, and close to 100% of 5-year-olds, in contrast to the US, where only 47% of 3- and 4-year-olds, and 79% of 5-year-olds are enrolled (OECD, 2001a, Figure 3.2, p. 188; OECD, 2003, Table C1.2, p. 254). These low enrollment rates for the US are particularly striking given that it has one of the earliest school starting ages, typically beginning at age 5, compared to age 6 or 7 in many other countries (OECD, 2001a, Table 3.1, p. 46).

Another difference across countries is in the share of children who are enrolled in care that is either publicly provided or at least partly subsidized or reimbursed by government. The US provides a generally lower level of child care support than other peer nations for which comparable data are available (Gornick & Meyers, 2003). Only 6% of US children under age 1 or 2, and only 53% of children age 3 to 5, are in publicly supported child care. (This latter figure may seem high given that only about 15% of eligible low-income families receive subsidized care, but about 17% of families receive some public support through the child and dependent care tax credit [Smolensky & Gootman, 2003], and about a third of 3- and 4-year-olds are enrolled in Head Start, publicly provided pre-schools, or kindergarten programs [Meyers et al., 2004].) Although the figures for the US's nearest neighbor, Canada, are comparable, the figures for other nations are considerably higher. In France, for instance, 20% of 1- and 2-year-olds are in publicly supported care, and 99% of 3- to 5-year-olds; the figures in Denmark are 74% and 90%. Even the UK, which has historically lagged behind other European countries in child care provision, has a higher share of children age 3 to 5 in publicly supported care – 77% as of 2000 – than the US, although few British children under age 3 are in publicly supported care. These high enrollments for 3- to 5-year-olds in the UK reflect the recent National Child Care Strategy, which made a publicly funded preschool place available to all 3- and 4-year-olds.

In countries where the public sector plays a larger role, governments spend more per child, and families pay a smaller share of the costs. Among the seven countries for which comparable data are available, the US spends the lowest amount per child – $679 as of 2000 – compared to $780 in the UK, $1369 in the Netherlands, $3161 in France, $3189 in Finland, $4050 in Denmark, and $4950 in Sweden (Gornick & Meyers, 2003, Table 7.6, p. 217). And parents in the US bear the largest share of the costs – on average about 60% of the cost of care for children under age 5 – in contrast to Continental European and Nordic countries, where parents pay between 0% and 45% of costs, and governments cover between 55% and 100% of costs, depending on the age of the child and the income of the family (Gornick & Meyers, 2003, Table 7.4, p. 214).

What accounts for these differences across countries in the proportions of children in care and education, and the share of the costs of care covered by government? In part, these differences are linked to the differences in parental leave policies that we saw in Table 28.1. Some countries, such as Germany, have historically offered lengthy parental leave in place of public support for ECEC. However, these differences in ECEC provision also reflect differing views of government's role.

In the US, the use of child care for preschool-age children has been seen as essentially a private decision, with the government bearing little or no obligation to help out with the costs, unless necessary to help a low-income parent remain employed or to prepare a disabled or disadvantaged child for school. Although the US does have subsidies and tax credits that help with child care expenses for working families, and although an increasing number of states are providing no-cost preschool services prior to kindergarten, the investment that the US makes in early childhood care and education pales by comparison to the investments being made by other countries.

In the Nordic countries and many Continental European countries, child care is seen as a public responsibility and a public good, like primary and secondary education. These countries have long had universal provision of preschool care for children age 3 and older, and the Nordic countries have recently moved to guarantee a child care place for all children age 1 or older who seek it (Kamerman, 2000a). Another difference from the US is that early childhood care and education is seen as a valuable end in itself, providing an important social experience for children.

It is clear that many countries do a better job than the US in providing access to a preschool education and in offsetting the costs of that provision. But what about quality – do other countries offer care of good quality, or are they sacrificing quality in order to serve larger numbers of children? Unfortunately, comparative data on quality are scarce. In particular, we lack data on process quality. The limited data we do have on items such as teacher education and training, child:staff ratios, and group sizes suggest that the quality of care varies a good deal across countries. The European Commission's Childcare Network recommends a ratio of not more than fifteen children to one teacher for children age 3 to 6. Of the twelve countries in a recent OECD study (OECD, 2001a), eight have regulations that set child:teacher ratios this low or lower, while four countries (including the US) allow ratios to be higher. With regard to teacher training and education, standards also vary widely (OECD, 2001a). In several countries, teaching staff in preschool settings must have a three- or four-year university degree, but staff in other child care settings are less highly trained and are lower paid. Other countries (such as Denmark, Finland, Sweden) have more integrated systems where all child care or education teachers (except family day care providers) must have a three- or four-year university degree (Italy is now moving in this direction as well). In the UK, as in the US, a large divide exists between early childhood care and education teachers working in child care or preschool settings, who tend to have low levels of training and pay, and teachers in school settings (such as nursery classes in the UK or pre-kindergarten programs in the US), who are more likely to have university degrees and to be paid on a par with primary school teachers.

Improving quality has been a focus of recent reforms in a number of countries (OECD, 2001a). In Australia, for instance, a new quality improvement and accreditation system (QIAS) was introduced in 1994 whereby early childhood education and care providers must meet specific process quality standards in order to be eligible for government subsidies. The QIAS process is participatory: providers first conduct a self-study and are then rated by a peer reviewer. Providers who do not pass the peer review are encouraged to develop a plan to come into compliance and are censured only if they fail to participate, or if they fail to pass after three tries. Improving quality has also been a priority in the UK, where preschoolers are served in many different types of settings of widely varying quality, as in the US. The government has tightened up regulations and standards for preschools and moved their monitoring to the same body that monitors primary and secondary schools. The government has also spelled out a recommended curriculum and learning goals for the early years.

Child Benefits

Another way to support children and families in the early childhood years is through the provision of child benefits. Although a comprehensive consideration of income support policies is beyond the scope of this chapter (see Kamerman & Kahn, 1991, 1995, for a more extended discussion), I briefly consider three major forms of child benefits: (1) universal child benefits; (2) special maternity grants or other special programs for infants;

and (3) early childhood benefits. This section briefly describes the evidence about the importance of income in early childhood, the system of cash benefits in place in the US, and the benefits offered in other countries.

What do we know from developmental science and research about the importance of income in early childhood?

There are many reasons why income in early childhood would matter for child development (Duncan & Magnuson, 2003). At a minimum, money allows parents to buy needed goods and services for their young children. In addition, when families have more income, the home environment they provide is more likely to be supportive of child health and development. Conversely, when families are in poverty or under financial strain, parents are at greater risk of depression and parental stress, which in turn negatively impacts their parenting and outcomes for their children. Although analysts disagree as to the extent to which these associations are causal and how important income is for child development (Duncan & Brooks-Gunn, 1997; Mayer, 1997), early childhood does seem to be the period when money matters the most. Evidence on this point comes from a series of studies coordinated by Duncan and Brooks-Gunn (1997), which found that income in early childhood was more strongly associated with child development and achievement than income in later childhood and adolescence. More recently, experimental studies in the US, from evaluations of welfare to work reforms, have provided further evidence that income matters for development in early childhood (Morris, Huston, Duncan, Crosby, & Bos, 2001). Preschool-age children in families exposed to welfare-to-work reforms that raised parents' employment and family income made larger gains in cognitive achievement than control-group children, whereas preschoolers in families exposed to reforms that raised parents' employment but without income gains did not.

Evidence on the impact of specific types of child benefits on child outcomes is less readily available. Although it is well documented that countries that have more generous child benefits have lower rates of post-tax-and-transfer child poverty, the effects on child outcomes have not been systematically studied (Waldfogel, 2004). One recent study examined how child health outcomes (in particular, infant mortality) were affected by the generosity of child benefits and maternity allowances across countries, and found that when countries had more generous maternity allowances, rates of infant mortality were lower (Tanaka, 2005).

Child benefits in the US

The US does not have a universal child benefit or child allowance that goes to all families with children. Instead, it relies primarily on means-tested cash (and in-kind) benefits for the lowest-income families, alongside a system of tax credits for other families (including, for example, a child care tax credit for families with an employed parent and who purchase child care). Most tax credits are limited to families with incomes high enough to owe taxes, but there are also some refundable tax credits for families with children, most notably the Earned Income Tax Credit, which has become a particularly important form of cash benefit for low-income families with a working parent. There have been several attempts in the US to institute a universal child benefit, or a fully refundable child tax credit. Recently, the child tax credit was made partially refundable. Its amount is low (a maximum of $500 per child in 2001, rising to $1000 per child over the next ten years), but it is reasonably well targeted to low- and moderate-income families with children, with the recent changes mainly benefiting families with annual incomes between $10,000 and $35,000 per year (see Sawhill & Thomas, 2001; Smolensky & Gootman, 2003).

The US has no special maternity grants or cash supports specifically targeted to families with newborns or young children. Until fairly recently, it did exempt families with newborns or young children from the welfare work requirements that applied to other families as a condition of receiving cash welfare assistance. However, this has changed in recent years, and since the passage of welfare reform in 1996, there is no longer any federal requirement that mothers of young children be exempted from welfare work requirements. As a result, state policies now vary a good deal, with twenty-seven states still exempting mothers from working until their child is at least a year old, but with twenty-three others requiring work at some point in the first year or having no exemptions at all (Brady-Smith, Brooks-Gunn, Waldfogel, & Fauth, 2001). There are also a few states that have instituted alternative programs to provide cash support to low-income families with newborns or young children. Two states have what they call "at-home infant child care" programs, which provide cash benefits to low-income families with a child under the age of one who stay home to care for their child themselves (Smolensky & Gootman, 2003).

Child benefits in other countries

Most industrialized countries have some form of universal child benefit (or child allowance) – a cash grant that goes to all families with children and that increases with the number of children. Many countries provide extra support to families with a new baby, through some form of maternity grant or allowance. These grants can be particularly important for families where the mother was not working prior to the birth and is therefore not eligible for maternity or parental leave benefits. In some instances, these benefits are provided universally; in others, they are provided to low-income families only.

A more recent innovation is "early childhood benefits" – cash grants provided to families with young children. As we saw earlier, many countries offer paid parental leave or childrearing benefits to families where the parent is not working in the labor market. Early childhood benefits, in contrast, are available to *all* parents with young children regardless of whether they work in the labor market. These benefits are explicitly designed to allow families to choose parental care or child care or some combination of the two. Only two countries currently offer this type of benefit.

Finland, in 1985, was the first to introduce an early childhood benefit. The grant is available to all families with a child under the age of 3 who are not using publicly funded child care. Given that Finland guarantees a publicly funded child care place for all children age 1 or older whose parents desire one, the early childhood benefit gives parents a full set of choices: to remain home and receive the childrearing benefit; work and use private child care and receive the childrearing benefit; or work and use public child care (instead of receiving the childrearing benefit). The first option appears to be most popular among families with infants, while the most popular option for families with toddlers remains publicly provided child care (Kamerman, 1994; Salmi & Lammi-Taskula, 1999). The policy seems not to have had a large impact on women's labor force participation (Salmi & Lammi-Taskula, 1999).

The other country with an early childhood benefit is Norway (Leira, 1999). (Sweden enacted a childrearing grant in 1994 but repealed it the following year before it came into effect, due to concerns about the law's impact on the country's commitment to publicly funded child care.) Norway enacted its childrearing grant in 1998, providing a cash benefit to parents of children age 12 months to 36 months. The benefit is roughly equal to the amount the government would pay for a publicly funded child care place and, as in Finland, it is provided on the condition that the child does not attend publicly funded child care. Norway's policy has been controversial (Leira, 1999). Although it was intended to give families more time to care for children and more choice in care arrangements, and to equalize the benefits offered to families who do and do not use publicly funded care for their under-3s, the law has also led to an expansion in the use of private care, and a slowing of the growth of publicly funded places. In the long run, then, the policy may shift children from public sector child care into private sector child care, which may or may not be desirable. Since the policy subsidizes parental care, it may also induce women to stay out of the labor force longer, which again may or may not be desirable.

Conclusions

The US clearly differs sharply from other countries in its early childhood policies. Given what we know from developmental science and research, what are the implications of these differences for US policy? Should the US be moving in the direction of extending parental leave rights, expanding support for early childhood care and education, and/or implementing some form of child benefit? The answers to these questions are not clear-cut. We still have more to learn about what care arrangements are best for children (keeping in mind that no one set of arrangements will be ideal for all children). Other impacts must also be considered. A strong gender thread runs through this discussion, because the parents who take parental leave are primarily women.

With these caveats in mind, several conclusions are clear. With regard to parental leave, extending the total duration of childbirth-related leave to 12 months (as Canada and the UK recently did) and providing universal and paid coverage (as most other countries do) would yield benefits for child health and development in the first year of life. In the area of early childhood care and education, providing more support for high-quality care for children under age 3 and moving toward universal and publicly funded high-quality preschool provision for 3- and 4-year-olds, as other nations have, would be two important steps that the US could take to better meet the needs of children and their families in early childhood. With regard to child benefits, several promising options are worthy of further study and trial.

The bottom-line message in the comparative data is clear: across the three main types of policies that countries enact to support children and families in the early childhood years – parental leave, early childhood care and education, and child benefits – the US provides less support to families with young children than its peers do. It is also true, as noted earlier, that the US has a weaker system of health and social services programs for families with young children than other countries. This lack of public support means that parents in the US bear a larger share of the costs of raising a young child than parents bear in other countries, and that the services a child receives are more closely linked to his or her parents' income. How to optimally provide more support for young children's care – through expanded parental leave, more support for early childhood care and education, and/or the introduction of early childhood benefits – and how to expand the US system of health and social services for families with children are excellent questions for further research and discussion. But enough is known now to identify useful next steps, and the US should not delay in making the commitment to take those steps.

Note

I am grateful for support from the National Institute of Child Health and Development, the John D. and Catherine T. MacArthur Foundation, and the Russell Sage Foundation. I am also grateful to the Centre for Analysis of Social Exclusion at the London School of Economics, where I was a visitor when this chapter was written.

References

Berger, L., Hill, J., & Waldfogel, J. (2005). Maternity leave, early maternal employment, and child outcomes in the US. *Economic Journal, 115*, F29–F47.

Blau, D. (2001). *The child care problem.* New York: Russell Sage Foundation.

Brady-Smith, C., Brooks-Gunn, J., Waldfogel, J., & Fauth, R. (2001). Work or welfare? Assessing the impacts of recent employment and policy changes on very young children. *Evaluation and Program Planning, 24*, 409–425.

Brooks-Gunn, J., Han, W., & Waldfogel, J. (2002). Maternal employment and child cognitive outcomes in the first three years of life: The NICHD Study of Early Child Care. *Child Development, 73*(4), 1052–1072.

Cantor, D., Waldfogel, J., Kerwin, J., Wright, M. M., Levin, K., Rauch, J., Hagerty, T., & Kudela, M. S. (2001). *Balancing the needs of families and employers: Family and medical leave surveys, 2000 update.* Rockville, MD: Westat.

Chatterji, P., & Markowitz, S. (2004). *Does the length of maternity leave affect maternal health?* (NBER Working Paper No. 10206). Cambridge, MA: National Bureau for Economic Research.

Clearinghouse on International Developments in Child, Youth, and Family Policies at Columbia University. (2002). *Early childhood education and care.* Retrieved January 6, 2004, from *http://www.childpolicyintl.org*

Commission on Family and Medical Leave. (1996). *A workable balance: Report to the Congress on family and medical leave policies.* Washington, DC: Women's Bureau, US Department of Labor.

Cunningham, A. S., Jelliffe, D. B., & Jelliffe, E. F. P. (1991). Breast-feeding and health in the 1980s: A global epidemiological review. *Journal of Pediatrics, 118*(5), 659–666.

Currie, J. (2001). Early childhood intervention programs. *Journal of Economic Perspectives 15*(2), 213–238.

Duncan, G., & Brooks-Gunn, J. (Eds.). (1997). *Consequences of growing up poor.* New York: Russell Sage.

Duncan, G., & Magnuson, K. (2003). Promoting the healthy development of young children. In I. Sawhill (Ed.), *One percent for the kids: New policies, brighter futures for America's children* (pp. 16–39). Washington, DC: Brookings Institution.

Esping-Anderson, G. (1990). *Three worlds of welfare capitalism.* Princeton, NJ: Princeton University Press.

European Foundation for the Improvement of Living and Working Conditions. (n.d.). *European Industrial Relations Observatory Online.* Retrieved February 11, 2004, from *http://www.eiro. eurofound.ie*

Gormley, W. T. (1995). *Everybody's children: Child care as a public problem.* Washington, DC: Brookings Institution.

Gornick, J., & Meyers, M. (2003). *Families that work: Policies for reconciling parenthood and employment.* New York: Russell Sage Foundation.

Gregg, P., Gutierrez-Domenech, M., & Waldfogel, J. (2003). *The employment of married mothers in Great Britain: 1974–2000.* (CEP Discussion Paper No. 596). London: Centre for Economic Performance, London School of Economics.

Haas, L., & Hwang, P. (1999). Parental leave in Sweden. In P. Moss & F. Deven (Eds.), *Parental leave: Progress or pitfall? Research and policy issues in Europe* (pp. 45–68). Brussels: CBGS Publications.

Han, W., & Waldfogel, J. (2003). Parental leave: The impact of recent legislation on parents' leave-taking. *Demography, 40(1)*, 191–200.

Kamerman, S. B. (1994). Family policy and the under-3s: Money, services, and time in a policy package. *International Social Security Review, 47*(3–4), 31–43.

Kamerman, S. B. (2000a). Early childhood education and care: An overview of developments in the OECD countries. *International Journal of Educational Research, 33*, 7–29.

Kamerman, S. B. (2000b). Parental leave policies: An essential ingredient in early childhood education and care policies. *Social Policy Report, 14*(2), 3–15.

Kamerman, S. B. (2000c). From maternity to parenting policies: Women's health, employment, and child and family well-being. *Journal of the American Women's Medical Association, 55*(2), 96–99.

Kamerman, S. B., & Kahn, A. J. (Eds.). (1991). *Child care, parental leave, and the under 3s: Policy innovation in Europe.* New York: Auburn House.

Kamerman, S. B., & Kahn, A. J. (1995). *Starting right: How America neglects its youngest children and what we can do about it.* New York: Oxford University Press.

Kamerman, S. B., & Waldfogel, J. (2005). Market and non-market institutions in early childhood education and care. In R. Nelson (Ed.), *Market and non-market institutions.* New York: Russell Sage Foundation.

Karoly, L., Greenwood, P., Everingham, S., Houbé, J., Kilburn, R., Rydell, P., Sanders, M., & Chiesa, J. (1998). *Investing in our children: What we know and don't know about the costs and benefits of early childhood interventions.* Santa Monica, CA: Rand.

Klerman, J. A., & Leibowitz, A. (1998, April). *FMLA and the labor supply of new mothers: Evidence from the June CPS*. Paper presented at the Population Association of America Annual Meeting, Chicago.

Leira, A. (1999). Cash-for-child care and daddy leave. In P. Moss & F. Deven (Eds.), *Parental leave: Progress or pitfall? Research and Policy Issues in Europe* (pp. 267–292). Brussels: CBGS Publications.

Lindberg, L. (1996). Women's decisions about breast-feeding and maternal employment. *Journal of Marriage and the Family, 58*(1), 239–251.

Mayer, S. (1997). *What money can't buy: The effect of parental income on children's outcomes.* Cambridge, MA: Harvard University Press.

Meyers, M., Rosenbaum, D., Ruhm, C., & Waldfogel, J. (2004). Inequality in early childhood education and care: What do we know? In K. Neckerman (Ed.), *Social inequality* (pp. 223–270). New York: Russell Sage Foundation.

Morris, P., Huston, A., Duncan, G., Crosby, D., & Bos, J. (2001). *How welfare and work policies affect children: A synthesis of research.* New York: Manpower Demonstration Research Corporation.

Moss, P., & Deven, F. (Eds.). (1999). *Parental leave: Progress or pitfall? Research and policy issues in Europe.* Brussels: CBGS Publications.

Organization for Economic Cooperation and Development. (2001a). *Starting strong: Early childhood education and care.* Paris: Author.

Organization for Economic Cooperation and Development. (2001b). *Employment outlook.* Paris: Author. Retrieved January 22, 2004, from *http://www.oecd.org*

Organization for Economic Cooperation and Development. (2003a). *Education at a glance for 2003.* Paris: Author. Retrieved February 13, 2004, from *http://www.oecd.org*

Phillips, D., & Mekos, D. (1993, October 28–30). *The myth of child care regulation: Rates of compliance in center-based child care settings.* Paper presented at the annual research conference of the Association for Public Policy Analysis and Management, Washington, DC.

Phillips, D., Voran, M., Kisker, E., Howes, C., & Whitebrook, M. (1994). Child care for children in poverty: Opportunity or inequity? *Child Development, 65,* 772–792.

Roe, B., Whittington, L., Fein, S., & Teisl, M. (1996, May). *The conflict between breast-feeding and maternal employment.* Paper presented at the Population Association of American Annual Meeting.

Ronsen, M. (1999). Assessing the impact of parental leave: Effects on fertility and employment. In P. Moss & F. Deven (Eds.), *Parental leave: Progress or pitfall? Research and policy issues in Europe* (pp. 193–225). Brussels: CBGS Publications.

Ross, K. (1998, April). *Labor pains: The effects of the Family and Medical Leave Act on recent mothers' returns to work after childbirth.* Paper presented at the Population Association of America Annual Meeting, Chicago.

Ruhm, C. (1998). The economic consequences of parental leave mandates: Lessons from Europe. *Quarterly Journal of Economics, 113*(1), 285–318.

Ruhm, C. (2000). Parental leave and child health. *Journal of Health Economics, 19*(6), 931–960.

Salmi, M., & Lammi-Taskula, J. (1999). Parental leave in Finland. In P. Moss & F. Deven (Eds), *Parental leave: Progress or pitfall? Research and policy issues in Europe* (pp. 85–122). Brussels: CBGS Publications.

Sawhill, I., & Thomas, A. (2001). *A tax proposal for working families with children.* Welfare Reform and Beyond Brief No. 3. Washington, DC: Brookings Institution.

Shonkoff, J., & Phillips, D. (Eds.). (2000). *From neurons to neighborhoods: The science of early childhood development.* Washington, DC: National Academy Press.

Sleebos, J. (2003). *Low fertility rates in OECD countries: Facts and policy responses.* (OECD Social, Employment, and Migration Working Papers No. 15). Paris: OECD. Retrieved February 10, 2004 from *http://www.oecd.org*

Smith, N., & Pylkkanen, P. (2004, April 1–3). *Career interruptions due to parental leave: A comparative study of Denmark and Sweden.* Paper presented at the annual meeting of the Population Association of America, Boston.

Smolensky, E., & Gootman, J. (Eds.). (2003). *Working families and growing kids: Caring for children and adolescents.* Washington, DC: National Academy Press.

Tanaka, S. (2005). Parental leave and child health across OECD countries. *Economic Journal, 115,* F7–F28.

Vandell, D., & Wolfe, B. (2002). *Child care quality: Does it matter and does it need to be improved?* Washington, DC: Office of the Assistant Secretary for Planning and Evaluation, US Department of Health and Human Services.

Waldfogel, J. (1999a, October). Family leave coverage in the 1990s. *Monthly Labor Review*, pp. 13–21.

Waldfogel, J. (1999b). The impact of the Family and Medical Leave Act. *Journal of Policy Analysis and Management, 18*(2), 281–302.

Waldfogel, J. (2001a, September). Family and medical leave: Evidence from the 2000 surveys. *Monthly Labor Review*, pp. 17–23.

Waldfogel, J. (2001b). Family-friendly policies for families with young children. *Employee Rights and Employment Policy Journal, 5*(1), 273–296.

Waldfogel, J. (2001c). International policies toward parental leave and child care. *The Future of Children, 11*(1), 99–111.

Waldfogel, J. (2002). Child care, women's employment, and child outcomes. *Journal of Population Economics, 15,* 527–548.

Waldfogel, J. (2004). A cross-national perspective on policies to promote investments in children. In A. Kalil & T. DeLeire (Eds.), *Family investments in children's potential: Resources and parenting behaviors that predict children's success* (pp. 237–262). Mahwah, NJ: Lawrence Erlbaum Associates.

29

Promoting Social Competence in Early Childhood: Classroom Curricula and Social Skills Coaching Programs

Karen L. Bierman and Stephen A. Erath

Beginning in the preschool years, peer relations provide an important context for socialization. As play partners, peers offer companionship, entertainment, and unique opportunities for interpersonal learning (Hartup, 1983). In order to sustain friendly exchanges, children are challenged to master the "golden rule" of reciprocity; they must learn to negotiate, cooperate, and compromise (Parker, Rubin, Price, & DeRosier, 1995). Preschool peer interactions are grounded in fantasy play that stimulates imagination and allows children to explore and consolidate their understanding of various social roles, social routines, and conventions (Mize & Ladd, 1990; Parker et al., 1995). Thus, interactions with peers motivate and support the development of critical social skills, enhance interpersonal understanding, and foster feelings of social self-worth (Hartup, 1983; Parker et al., 1995).

Children who are delayed in their acquisition of social skills, and who enter grade school with low levels of social competence and poorly regulated social behaviors are at heightened risk for significant school difficulties, which can escalate in adolescence and contribute to problems ranging from emotional difficulties (anxiety, depression) to antisocial behaviors (substance use, delinquent activities) (Parker et al., 1995). In his description of peer rejection processes, Coie (1990) describes a negative developmental spiral linking poor peer relations with later developmental dysfunction. In his model, initial social skill deficits contribute to a child's difficulty gaining acceptance by peers. Left out or actively ostracized by peers, rejected children spend more time playing alone or interacting in limited ways with younger and less skillful peers, further restricting their opportunities to learn age-appropriate social skills (Coie, 1990). In addition, peer rebuff and social isolation contribute to feelings of loneliness, insecurity, and anger (Boivin, Hymel, & Bukowski, 1995), which can increase disruptive behaviors and aggressive reactions. In this way, initial skill deficits can escalate over time, due both to restricted learning opportunities, and to the negative impact of peer censure.

From a developmental perspective, the preschool years represent an ideal time for interventions aimed at supporting social-emotional development and peer interaction competencies. Normatively, first friendships are established during the preschool years, and most children that age are highly motivated to move beyond adult–child interactions and begin to explore and take pleasure in the cooperative and shared fantasy play offered by peers (Fabes, Gaertner, & Popp, this volume; Gottman, 1983; Howes, 1987). Friendships tend to be much more fluid than in middle childhood, allowing children to recover more easily from social blunders, without the damage to their social reputations that will occur in later years. In addition, the skills needed for effective interaction and friendship formation during the preschool years are behaviorally based, increasing the ease with which interventions to promote social competence can be implemented by teachers or parents. Peer problems become more complicated with age, due to the increasing role played by social reputations, complex peer group structures, and children's social-cognitive and self-system biases (Bierman, 2004). Educational and therapeutic interventions designed to foster social competence during the preschool years may provide children with the competencies they need to establish supportive friendships and peer group acceptance at school entry, as well as a foundation to build upon to meet future challenges for increased self-regulation and social integration that occur in the later elementary and adolescent years.

Goals of Social Competence Interventions

The chapter by Fabes et al. in this volume provides a comprehensive review of the development of social competence during the preschool years. In this chapter, we focus specifically on how developmental research on social competence can inform intervention design, beginning with the identification of social skills which serve as the targets for intervention efforts.

Defining social competence in early childhood

Designing educational programs or interventions to promote social competence requires, as a first step, the operationalization of the construct "social competence," and the identification of the skills to be targeted for promotion. Empirical trials conducted over the last fifty years have contributed to important theoretical advances in the conceptualization of social competence and target skill identification (Bierman, 2004; Weissberg & Greenberg, 1998). Initial attempts to promote preschool social competence emerged in the late 1960s and 1970s and focused on promoting discrete social behaviors (e.g., increasing rates of social initiation and interaction) with modeling and the manipulation of environmental contingencies. While effective in increasing the rates with which specific behaviors were displayed, for the most part these early programs failed to promote sustained improvements in children's social functioning and peer acceptance (Dodge & Murphy, 1984).

As developmental research exploring the dynamics of early friendships and the correlates of peer acceptance accumulated, it became clear that, although effective social interaction during early childhood is grounded in identifiable patterns of social behavior, these behaviors must be displayed in ways that are sensitive to interpersonal cues and context in order to have the desired positive effect on social partners. Sroufe (1996) described social competence as an "organizational" construct involving the capacity to regulate and adapt behavior in dynamic interpersonal situations. Similarly, other theorists have defined social competence in terms of a child's capacity to successfully navigate social relationships: for example, to organize his or her social behavior in a sensitive and responsive fashion, in order to elicit positive responses (and avoid negative responses) from others in a variety of different social contexts and in a manner consistent with prevailing cultural norms (Bierman & Welsh, 2000; Dodge & Murphy, 1984; Parker et al., 1995). According to this definition, a repertoire of socially appropriate behaviors is necessary but not sufficient for effective social interaction. Social competence also requires the more complicated process of behavioral and social regulation, in which social behavior is displayed in a manner that is responsive to ongoing social feedback and stimuli. As such, social competence is affected by social information processing, emotion regulation, motivation and self-efficacy, as well as by behavioral repertoire (Bierman & Welsh, 2000; Fabes et al., this volume; Sroufe, 1996).

Parallel to the growing sophistication of understanding reflected in these operational definitions of social competence, empirical research has contributed to progressions in the criteria used to select skill domains targeted for promotion in social competence interventions. Early social competence promotion programs often took what LaGreca (1993) has described as a "molecular" approach to identifying target skills, focusing on discrete behaviors, such as maintaining eye contact or smiling, that are related to sociability. In contrast, she advocates a "molar" approach to skill identification, targeting broader domains of social behavior selected on the basis of empirical evidence of association with valid measures of peer acceptance and positive social functioning. Often called the "competence correlates" approach to target skill identification, this approach emphasizes two criteria for the selection of target skills: (1) they are social interaction *strategies* represented by multiple behavioral exemplars (e.g., cooperative strategies, represented by behaviors such as taking turns and sharing materials), and (2) they have been linked empirically with peer acceptance. By defining target skills in terms of interaction strategies, illustrated by a variety of behavioral examples, social competence interventions focus on building child capabilities for flexible and socially sensitive behavioral responding (Ladd & Mize, 1983). Examples of target skill domains that fit these criteria for preschool children follow.

Prosocial, cooperative play skills

Well-liked preschoolers participate in pretend play and share toys in a reciprocal manner (Eisenberg & Fabes, 1992). They approach others with positive affect and friendly overtures, and they respond positively to peer initiations (Denham & Burton, 2004; Eisenberg & Fabes, 1992). They are able to sustain interactive, reciprocal play, attending to their play partner, and coordinating their social initiations and responses (Hartup, 1983). Sharing materials, taking turns, initiating and responding to play invitations foster high-quality friendships during shared activities, when children identify common ground interests and develop a mutual affective bond (Gottman, 1983; Hartup, 1983). Cooperative play skills in preschool also predict to positive school engagement at elementary school entry (Ladd & Price, 1987), and continue to promote positive peer relations throughout middle childhood, when positive social behaviors, including agreeability and cooperative behaviors (being perceived by peers as helpful, friendly, and nice), are the dominant predictors of peer acceptance (Coie, Dodge, & Kupersmidt, 1990). Hence, prosocial and cooperative play skills represent an important target skill domain for preschool interventions promoting social competence.

Language and communication skills

Language skills and the capacity to communicate effectively have a large impact on peer relations during the preschool years (Fabes et al., this volume). For example, language and vocabulary skills predict peer play competence and popularity among preschoolers (Mendez, Fantuzzo, & Cicchetti, 2002). Functional communication skills support the identification of common ground and reciprocal interactions. Indeed, the ability to clearly direct an initiation and to respond contingently to the initiations of others is linked with social acceptance and likeability among preschoolers (Kemple, Speranza, & Hazen, 1992). Suggesting and elaborating joint play themes, asking questions, and responding to requests for clarification also facilitate sustained and coordinated interaction, and predict positive peer experiences and emerging friendships (Gottman, 1983).

By kindergarten, the capacity to communicate effectively during group entry becomes an additional correlate of peer acceptance (Putallaz, 1983). Well-liked kindergartners first "hover" around a peer group activity, getting a sense of the situation and choosing an appropriate time for entry. They might make a relevant comment about the ongoing activity, and they watch for an opportunity to enter without disrupting the play of others (e.g., at the end of someone's turn), then ask permission to join in. Children who have trouble with group entry – either because they approach others with intrusive, disruptive strategies, or because they "hover" for sustained periods of time without being able to take the subsequent steps toward entry, often have few opportunities for positive peer interactions and face corresponding difficulties gaining peer acceptance (Putallaz, 1983). Thus, communication skills, particularly sharing information about oneself and one's feelings, establishing common ground by listening to social partners and making topic-relevant comments, asking questions to elicit information from others, and recognizing the turn-taking sequences involved in conversation, represent a second competence skill domain associated with preschool social competence.

Emotional understanding and regulation

Emotional understanding includes knowledge about emotions, such as the ability to accurately identify emotional expressions, and to recognize events that are likely to elicit particular emotional reactions. Emotional understanding predicts teacher-rated social competence as well as peer sociometric ratings of acceptance in preschool (Denham & Burton, 2004). Children who are sensitive to the feelings of others and able to assess social situations with accuracy also tend to be well liked by their peers in grade school (Bierman & Welsh, 2000). Indeed, the ability to recognize and label emotional expressions in preschool predicts parent and teacher ratings of social behavior and adjustment in middle childhood (Izard et al., 2001).

Emotional understanding provides an important foundation for the effective regulation of emotion. Observational research documents that socially competent preschoolers regulate affect and behavior when excited or upset (Eisenberg & Fabes, 1992) and can inhibit their behavioral impulses through self-distraction in tasks that require delay of gratification (Raver, Blackburn, & Bancroft, 1999); conversely, observed lapses of emotion regulation and high rates of emotional outbursts predict low teacher ratings of social competence and low levels of peer-nominated acceptance (Denham & Holt, 1993). Preschool play often involves mild frustrations (e.g., waiting in line, sharing a prized toy) and can be very stimulating emotionally, both exciting and disappointing. Well-liked children are able to weather the emotional ups and downs of peer interaction, maintaining their own emotional equilibrium and recovering from mild set-backs and disappointments (Eisenberg & Fabes, 1992). In contrast, children who are often irritable and unhappy, easily annoyed by others, and emotionally reactive in the face of conflict or frustration are less rewarding as playmates and have more difficulty gaining acceptance by their peers (Eisenberg & Fabes, 1992). These empirical findings support targeting emotional understanding and regulation in preschool social competence promotion programs.

Aggression control and social problem-solving skills

Preschool children who show high levels of aggressive and oppositional behavior find it difficult to gain acceptance by their peers (Denham & Holt, 1993). In fact, argumentative children are likely to experience increased peer rejection across the course of the preschool years (3½ to 4½ years old) (Ladd, Price, & Hart, 1988), along with increasing rates of aggressive peer retaliation and initiation (Olson, 1992). Aggressive peer responding can, in turn, fuel escalations in aggressive behavior. For example, when Patterson, Littman, and Bricker (1967) observed peer interactions over the course of a preschool year, they identified two groups of aggressive children. One group consisted of children who exhibited high rates of aggressive behavior at the beginning of the school year and successfully used their aggression throughout the year to dominate peers and control resources in the classroom. A second group of children were initially victimized by others, but "turned the tables" later in the year, by modeling aggressive behavior and successfully dominating others. These studies suggest that, in addition to teaching and supporting alternative strategies for anger control and conflict management, preschool interventions also need to make sure that aggressive strategies are not "effective" in gaining dominance or resource control over peers. A failure to learn aggression control in preschool can have negative effects for later social adjustment. For example, Ladd and Price (1987) found that children who behaved aggressively in preschool were more likely to be disliked by peers and described as hostile toward others by teachers when they moved on into kindergarten.

In contrast to the findings for aggressive behavior, children who are able to regulate their anger and manage conflicts verbally are at an advantage in terms of their peer relations. For example, constructive anger reactions (e.g., non-abusive verbalizations) at ages 4–6 predicted teacher reports of socially appropriate behavior (high prosocial and low aggressive-disruptive) four years later (Eisenberg et al., 1999). Similarly, social problem-solving skills, which enable children to use their verbal skills to identify conflicts, generate alternative solutions, and negotiate with their peers, enhance friendship quality among preschool children (Gottman, 1983), promote acceptance by the peer group (Youngstrom et al., 2000), and thereby warrant inclusion in social competence promotion programs.

A developmental framework

Although the identification of target skill domains is a necessary step for intervention planning, it is important to recognize that the various skill domains described here (prosocial cooperation, language and communication skills, emotion understanding and regulation, and anger management) are intertwined developmentally (Greenberg, Kusche, & Speltz, 1991). For example, as preschoolers begin to use language to describe internal affective states, their capacity for empathy increases, and they find new ways to cope with unpleasant emotions by labeling them and sharing them verbally with others. Language skills also allow the child to understand and comply with the requests of others, and the capacity to offer alternatives, thereby providing a foundation for mutually rewarding cooperation and social problem solving. Conversely, positive peer exchanges motivate children to inhibit the impulsive and aggressive behaviors that might alienate their peers, fueling the identification of cause–effect links between their behavior and the interpersonal consequences.

Most children display aggressive behaviors when they are first learning to get along with others (age 2–3). Normatively, however, rates of aggression decrease sharply during the preschool years, as children develop the verbal, emotional, and social skills that allow them to inhibit their first impulses, comply with social protocol, and "use their words" to voice dissatisfaction and resolve disagreements (Ladd, 1990; Vitaro, Tremblay, Gagnon, & Boivan, 1992). Hence, elevated rates of aggression are less likely to disturb peer relations during the preschool years than in elementary school (Hartup, 1983). In fact, aggression focused on accessing resources or attaining social dominance has shown positive associations with peer acceptance in some studies (Vaughn, Vollenweider, Bost, Azria-Evans, & Snider, 2003). As Vaughn et al. (2003) noted, children who are highly sociable in preschool naturally encounter more frequent conflicts of interest and negative interactions (as well as positive interactions). Theorists suggest that some of the aggressive exchanges that occur around resource control and dominance during the preschool years represent normative opportunities for learning to manage conflict and promoting social-emotional learning (Shantz & Hartup, 1992). However, children who display frequent aggressive behaviors that do not decline with accumulating opportunities for learning self-regulation and conflict resolution are likely to face peer difficulties in elementary school. Hence, preschool interventions may serve social development best when they focus primarily on the promotion of the social skills that will allow children to inhibit their aggressive impulses in favor of more civil ways of interacting with others, rather than focusing primarily on the external control of aggressive behaviors (Zigler, Taussig, & Black, 1992).

Promoting Social-Emotional Learning and Social Competence

Instructional approaches to foster social-emotional learning

A rapidly growing research base suggests that the skills that comprise social competence during the preschool years (e.g., cooperative play skills, communication skills, emotional understanding and regulation, aggression control, and social problem-solving skills) can be promoted with instructional approaches applied in school settings (Elias et al., 1997). Whether this instruction is undertaken by the classroom teachers and directed toward the whole class, or undertaken by a therapist working with children who have special needs, the instructional process is similar, and consists of four training components (Ladd & Mize, 1983).

First, instructions, models, and rationales are provided to illustrate the targeted social skill strategy and exemplar behaviors, and demonstrate the positive impact of that skill strategy on one's friendships and peer relations. At the preschool level, presentations of target skills typically involve modeling via stories, videotaped examples, and/or puppet scenarios, with interactive instruction and guided discussion. The purpose is to provide children with knowledge about the skill, a label for the skill, and an understanding of its functional value. By providing a few varied behavioral examples of each skill domain (e.g., taking turns, sharing materials, and helping someone are different ways to cooperate), the goal is to teach children general strategies for social interaction, giving them a repertoire of specific behaviors that they can apply flexibly to fit particular social situations (Ladd & Mize, 1983).

Second, learning to use social skill strategies requires multiple opportunities to practice with guidance and support. Structured opportunities to practice skills are often offered to help children try out new social skills, such as role-plays or scripted socio-dramatic play. Supported opportunities to extend skill performance in naturalistic social contexts are also critical for generalization of the skills to everyday peer interactions. During the initial phases of skill learning, children are dependent upon adults to provide cues for skill performance, and to scaffold or model "in-the-moment" how a skill could be applied. Adults can help children attend to social cues, gradually reducing the amount of support they provide over time, as children become more spontaneous and confident in their skill performance.

Third, performance feedback contributes to skill acquisition in important ways. When children are first learning new behaviors, teacher praise or redirection provides important feedback for behavioral shaping. For the consolidation of social skills, an additional goal is to increase children's sensitivity to and responsivity to the social feedback provided by others, particularly their peers. Hence, adults can help clarify subtle social cues by eliciting feedback during ongoing social interactions, to help young children understand the impact of their behavior on their own feelings and the feelings of their peers. By enhancing the child's self-monitoring and social awareness, the goal is to promote empathic and socially responsive behavioral choices.

Fourth, the generalization of social competence requires a supportive and ordered classroom context, in which positive social behaviors are rewarding to children and aggressive behaviors are neither necessary nor useful for resource control. In addition, flexible use of multiple skills in natural peer interaction settings may benefit from engaging in dialogue with the teacher to support flexible social problem solving when disagreements arise – identifying and assessing social problems, generating and evaluating responses, and making positive behavioral choices, thus linking across the social skill domains (Denham & Burton, 2004).

These instructional techniques have been incorporated in social-emotional curricula designed for teachers to use in preschool classrooms, and they have also been utilized in social skill training programs designed for use with children with special needs. In the next sections, we first consider classroom-based social-emotional learning programs designed for delivery by teachers to the entire class as a regular part of their preschool curriculum. We give examples of two such programs that have been through a randomized trial with preschool children and demonstrated positive effects. Then, we examine social skill training (coaching) programs, which are social-emotional learning programs designed for delivery by therapists with children who have documented delays or deficits in their social behavior and peer acceptance. Again, we highlight interventions that have documented positive effects in randomized trials. Finally, we discuss specific issues in designing interventions for aggressive children who have concurrent social skill deficits, and describe how social-emotional classroom and coaching interventions have been combined with parent-training and behavior management strategies to address the multiple needs of this high-risk group of preschool children. We also discuss environmental support strategies that can be used to enhance the generalization and maintenance of coaching interventions.

Preschool Curricula Designed to Promote Social-Emotional Learning in the Classroom

Teacher-led curriculum-based programs targeting student social-emotional learning have been implemented at multiple developmental levels (Weissberg & Greenberg, 1998). During the preschool years, teacher-led classroom curricula may be particularly appropriate and effective, both because of the developmental significance of social-emotional learning during those years, and because of the central role that early childhood educators play as sources of socialization and support for young children. Developmental research suggests that teacher–child relationships provide a critical context for social-emotional development of children during the preschool and early elementary years, and influence social-emotional learning in both formal and informal ways (Pianta, 1999). For example, the quality of a teacher's direct interactions with a child (his or her sensitivity, warmth, responsiveness to child affect) is associated with that child's observed social competence and on-task behavior in the kindergarten classroom (Pianta, 1999). Similarly, high levels of teacher sensitivity and support are associated with reduced rates of aggressive and off-task behavior in "socially bold" kindergarten students (Rimm-Kaufman et al., 2002). Teacher warmth and conflict management styles may also provide important models for preschool and early elementary children that influence their approach to peers and promote self-regulation of behavior and attention (Denham & Burton, 1996; Pianta, 1999). Indeed, training teachers in the provision of warm support and effective (non-punitive) classroom management processes has positive effects on children's prosocial behavior and reduced aggression during the preschool and early elementary years (see Webster-Stratton, Mihalic, Fagan, Arnold, Taylor, & Tingley, 2001). In addition to pro-moting child social competence by providing warmth, sensitive responding, and model-ing of non-aggressive conflict management, teachers can also foster social-emotional learning through the use of explicit curricula and teaching strategies, as in the two curriculum-based programs described next.

I Can Problem Solve

The "I Can Problem Solve" (ICPS) program is one of the oldest examples of an empiri-cally based social competence promotion program developed for preschool children (Shure, 1992). Designed for preschool and kindergarten children, the contemporary version of this preschool curriculum includes skill presentation lessons and guided prac-tice activities, which utilize pictures, role-playing, puppets, and group interaction to teach social skills associated with emotion understanding and social problem solving (Shure, 1992). During the first ten to twelve lessons, children learn word concepts to help them describe social sequences (e.g., some vs. all, if/then, same/different). The second unit (comprised of twenty lessons) focuses on identifying one's own feelings and recognizing the feelings of others. Students practice identifying people's feelings in problem situations, and are shown how behaviors can affect others' feelings and responses. In the third set of fifteen lessons, teachers utilize role-playing games and dialogue to promote social problem-solving skills. Teachers introduce hypothetical problem situations that commonly occur in preschool settings, and ask children to generate and act out possible solutions, in order to encourage generative thinking and help children understand the consequences linked with various choices.

A randomized trial evaluating ICPS with preschool and kindergarten children revealed a positive impact of the program on the promotion of social problem-solving skills, especially the ability to think about multiple alternative solutions to social problems, which was its major focus. In addition, children were rated by teachers as less impulsive in the classroom, more able to cope with frustration, and less withdrawn. The behavioral impact of the program was sustained for at least one year (Shure & Spivac, 1980, 1982). These program findings support the premise that helping young children to develop their cognitive capacities to recognize and assess social problems, and to generate and evaluate multiple potential responses, can foster self-regulation and positive social interaction in the classroom (Weissberg & Greenberg, 1998). At the same time, the ICPS program does not provide comprehensive coverage of the competence correlate skill domains associated with positive peer relations; some of the more recently developed preschool social-emotional curricula incorporate social problem-solving skills along with other friendship skills, as in the following example.

Promoting Alternative Thinking Strategies (PATHS) – preschool version

The Promoting Alternative Thinking Strategies (PATHS) Curriculum (Conduct Problems Prevention Research Group, 1999; Greenberg & Kusche, 1998; Kusche & Greenberg, 1995) was developed originally for elementary-school students. The recently developed preschool version of PATHS (Domitrovich, Greenberg, Cortes, & Kusche, 1999) targets skills in five specific domains: (1) cooperative friendship skills (helping, sharing, taking turns, being a fun and friendly play partner), (2) emotional awareness and communication (being able to identify and label one's own and others feelings, understanding the impact of common events and behaviors on feelings, listening skills), (3) self-control/emotion regulation (inhibition of impulsive reactivity when angry or upset, calming down), (4) self-esteem (complimenting oneself and others), and (5) social problem solving (being able to sequence calming down, problem identification, generating alternative solutions, and selecting a positive solution). Preschool PATHS units are divided into thirty-three brief lessons that are delivered by teachers during the classroom circle time. Skill concepts are taught with modeling stories, illustrated with pictures, and sometimes acted out with puppets or role-plays. Central to the program are key characters, such as Twiggle the Turtle and Henrietta the Hedgehog, who provide graphic models of skill techniques.

For example, when Twiggle the Turtle gets very upset, he learns to stop himself from acting out and to pull into his shell to calm down first. Then he is able to explain his feelings, listen to his friends, and find a way to solve the problem. Following Twiggle's example, children are taught to tell themselves to stop when they are very upset and to do "turtle" by placing their arms across their chest and taking a few moments to calm down. Once calm, they are encouraged to explain how they felt and what was bothering them, as the first step in effective self-regulation and social problem solving. Henrietta the Hedgehog, a second puppet, is a friend of Twiggle's, and helps to model friendship concepts and social problem solving in the curriculum. For example, in a story, Henrietta learns that she feels good when she is able to share things with her friend, Twiggle, and it makes her happy when she sees her friend smile. During a PATHS lesson, Henrietta talks about her sharing ideas with the children in the class, describing what she learned when she shared with Twiggle: "Every time you share with someone, you are showing that you care about him or her. That will make the other person feel happy and it will make you feel happy too." She invites the children to think about their sharing experiences and ideas. In a follow-up practice activity on sharing, each child is given a small bag of stickers and asked to notice how he/she and classmates feel when they share the stickers with each other. In this way, the PATHS puppets become models and coaches in the preschool classroom, encouraging self-regulation and prosocial skills to build a supportive peer community.

Connected with each lesson are ideas for formal and informal extension activities that teaching staff can use throughout the day as ways to generalize the key concepts of the curriculum. Linking with literacy support, each lesson also identifies several children's books that teachers can read during story time to reinforce specific social-emotional and friendship themes, thus giving children additional opportunities to talk about the skill concepts and explore models for their use. Teachers are encouraged to provide emotion coaching throughout the day, modeling feeling statements themselves when appropriate, helping children notice the feelings of peers, and prompting children to describe their own feelings. Teachers are also shown how to use naturally occurring "teachable moments," such as peer disagreements or conflicts, to dialogue with children about their assessment of the problem, their feelings, their friend's feelings, and possible strategies for solving problems in positive ways.

The professional development model for teachers includes both initial training in the curriculum and ongoing consultation and support provided by PATHS consultants, designed to enhance integration of PATHS concepts and techniques throughout the day. PATHS consultants also provide teachers with suggestions in the area of effective classroom management (e.g., establishing clear rules and directions; providing positive and corrective feedback for appropriate behavior; applying natural response cost procedures to reduce problem behaviors; and strengthening positive relations with children and parents).

Three randomized controlled trials have demonstrated positive effects for regular education and special education students receiving the PATHS curriculum in grades 1–3. Significant effects included improvements in teacher-rated behaviors (e.g., self-control, frustration tolerance, emotional understanding, and reduced aggression), observer ratings (on-task behavior, student engagement), student self-reports (emotion recognition and social problem-solving skills, reduced depressive symptoms), and peer sociometric ratings (lower levels of aggression, higher mean levels of positive friendship nominations) (Conduct Problems Prevention Research Group, 1999; Greenberg & Kusche, 1998; Greenberg, Kusche, Cook, & Quamma, 1995). Thus far, one randomized trial has been conducted on the preschool version of the PATHS Curriculum. Teacher and parent ratings of social competence at the end of one year in Head Start were higher for children who received PATHS than for children in the control group. Children who received PATHS also exhibited significantly greater emotional identification and knowledge skills (on standardized assessments) compared to control children (Domitrovich et al., 1999).

Social Competence Coaching Programs for Children with Skill Delays and Deficits

Classroom curricula designed to promote the social-emotional competence of all preschool students as part of a comprehensive educational program, such as the ICPS and PATHS programs, thus show much promise. In addition, however, focused remedial and therapeutic support is often needed to help children who enter preschool with significant social-emotional delays or learning difficulties (such as developmental delays, language delays, or attention deficits) that put them at particular risk for peer difficulties. These children often need additional services that provide more intensive instructional support, guided practice, and feedback in order to remediate their skill delays and to promote their social adjustment (Odom & Brown, 1993).

Social skill training programs designed for children with significant social problems have been studied more intensively at the elementary school level than at the preschool level (Bierman, 2004). The most effective programs appear to be those that incorporate all four instructional components described above (e.g., skill presentation, guided practice, performance feedback, and support for skill generalization). Social skill training programs that utilize these four strategies in the context of peer pairs or small groups are called "coaching" programs. Initial studies suggest that coaching may be a useful strategy for remediating social skill deficits and promoting social competence among special needs preschool children, as well as grade-school children (Mize & Ladd, 1990; Odom et al., 1999).

The earliest programmatic research in this area with preschool children involved modeling programs designed in the 1970s for socially withdrawn preschool children (see Gresham, 1981, for a review). Particularly when children were shown films of models who were similar to them physically, and when modeling films included personal narrations that explicitly instructed and reinforced children for trying out the new behaviors, these programs produced short-term increases in children's rates of social interaction (Gresham, 1981). However, this early research also suggested that gains in the areas of behavior and peer acceptance were limited when intervention consisted only of brief modeling tapes. Hence, researchers began to expand upon these programs, including instructions and modeling of social skill concepts and behaviors in programs that also utilized more comprehensive coaching in social skill domains associated with social competence.

Coaching children in cooperative play skills

For example, in 1990, Mize and Ladd designed a coaching program that included modeling and instructions, but also included additional components associated with social skill acquisition: for example, guided opportunities for skill practice with supportive performance feedback. In their study, Mize and Ladd (1990) identified preschool children who were poorly accepted (either neglected or rejected) by peers and who also showed evidence of behavior problems during classroom observations. Children qualified for the intervention if their behavior involved elevated aggressive behavior and/or low levels of communication skills (e.g., leading, asking questions, commenting on ongoing play, and supporting peers). An adult coach worked with pairs of high-risk children for eight 30-minute sessions outside of the classroom, and with individual children for two 20-minute sessions within the classroom. In their intervention, short puppet plays were used to model skill concepts. Then, guided socio-dramatic play was used to provide a context for skill practice and reinforcement, as the adult coach encouraged children to try out the skills and praised and supported skill performance. The intervention program also included video play-backs of interactions between peer partners to enhance self-monitoring, and programmed generalization by arranging additional play sessions with non-intervention children. In this study, coached children displayed higher rates of the targeted social skills after intervention compared to children in the control condition. However, coaching did not have a significant impact on levels of aggressive behavior observed in the classroom, or on peer sociometric "like most" or "like least" nominations.

Additional evidence regarding the promise of coaching programs for preschool children with developmental delays comes from a study conducted by Guglielmo and Tryon (2001). In this randomized trial evaluation, three intervention conditions were compared: (1) nineteen children received coaching using selected units of the Taking Part, Introducing Social Skills to Children program (Cartledge & Kleefeld, 1991) plus additional classroom reinforcement for target skill behaviors; (2) nineteen children received classroom reinforcement for target skills (without additional coaching); and (3) twenty children served as a control group. The coaching program was conducted for sixteen days, and utilized two lessons (on sharing, and joining group activities) selected from the Taking Part program, which has a total of six units comprised of five to seven skills in each unit. Each session included an introduction to the skill concept, modeling activities in which the skill was illustrated in puppet play, followed by role-play practice for the children. Coaching plus classroom reinforcement of target skills produced significant increases in sharing compared to either of the other conditions. Coaching and the classroom reinforcement conditions both produced elevated levels of positive group interaction compared with the control group. Although this study focused on only two skills over a relatively brief intervention period, it supports the utility of coaching as a useful intervention for preschool children, and also highlights the utility of classroom reinforcement as a generalization procedure.

A third randomized trial conducted by Odom and his colleagues (1999) also suggests that coaching may be beneficial for preschool children with mild to moderate developmental delays (e.g., mental retardation, behavior disorders, communication disorders). Odom et al. compared the effects of coaching developmentally delayed children, coaching their typically developing peers, and arranging the environment to support positive interaction. In the child-focused coaching sessions, small groups (three to four) of developmentally delayed children met with teachers for 10–15 minutes per day for twenty-five days. These sessions targeted the play skills of initiating play, sharing, agreeing, leading a game, and trying a new way. In these groups, teachers introduced, demonstrated, and discussed the social skills concepts, and then had children role-play the social skills. Typically developing peer partners then joined the group, and teachers provided prompts and praise for ongoing skill performance. In the peer coaching sessions, typically developing kindergarten children met with teachers for ten sessions. Teachers coached these peers in skills for initiating social initiations with children with disabilities (e.g., share, share request, play organizer, assistance, assistance request, persistence). Environmental arrangements included the use of structured activities and supports in the classroom setting to enhance opportunities for peer play for the developmentally delayed students. Odom et al. found that coaching (directed at the developmentally delayed children or their peers) had a significant impact increasing the quality of child social interactions (assessed with observer ratings) and social competence (assessed with teacher ratings). Environmental arrangements were needed to produce effects on peer sociometric ratings.

These three studies all suggest that coaching children in play skills may have positive effects on their social behavior, and further suggest that generalization activities in the classroom context (selective reinforcement and environmental engineering of opportunities for peer play) play an important role in promoting changes in peer acceptance. Each of these programs focused on cooperative play and communication skills – two important competence correlates for preschool children. However, owing to the developmental interplay that occurs in social-emotional development, many children with significant peer problems have deficits that include additional skill domains – emotional understanding and regulation, anger management and social problem solving – as well as the positive play and communication skills (Bierman, 2004). Children who present with high rates of aggressive-disruptive behaviors, along with skill deficits in social-emotional skills, have particularly complex intervention needs.

Comprehensive intervention programs for aggressive children

Many of the children who display high rates of aggressive-disruptive behavior in the preschool setting also have significant delays in areas of emotional understanding, emotion regulation, language and communication skills, and social problem-solving skills (Bierman, 2004). Their behavior problems often emerge across home and school settings, and impede their ability to form positive relationships with peers, as well as teachers. Hence, researchers are finding that effective prevention and intervention programs for aggressive-disruptive children need to address both their social-emotional deficits and their aggressive behavioral excesses, and need to support positive socialization practices by parents and teachers (see Webster-Stratton & Reid, this volume). As a consequence, multi-component interventions for aggressive-disruptive children often include a social-emotional learning intervention (classroom curriculum and/or therapeutic social skills training program) as one component. For example, Webster-Stratton and Reid (this volume) reviewed the Montreal Longitudinal Experimental Study, which utilized the classroom ICPS program (Shure, 1992) to enhance the social-emotional learning of the targeted aggressive children, along with parent-focused interventions. Similarly, the Fast Track study (also reviewed in Webster-Stratton & Reid, this volume) included the PATHS curriculum in elementary classrooms to promote the social-emotional learning of all children, while providing aggressive children with a set of additional intervention components.

Not only do aggressive-disruptive children typically require a multi-component intervention that includes behavioral management as well as social skills training, but the range of the social-emotional deficits they have also requires that a more comprehensive set of skills be targeted in coaching programs. In particular, emotional understanding and regulation, anger management, and social problem solving require emphasis, along with prosocial and communication skills (Bierman, 2004).

A good example of an expanded coaching program that has proven effective in improving the behaviors of preschool and early-elementary children (ages 4 to 8) with aggressive-disruptive conduct problems is one developed recently by Carolyn Webster-Stratton and her colleagues (Webster-Stratton, Reid, & Hammond, 2001). The Incredible Years Dinosaur Social Skills and Problem Solving Curriculum targets skills for positive peer interaction and friendship development, emotional understanding and expression, anger management, interpersonal problem solving, and appropriate classroom behavior. The program is delivered in weekly two-hour sessions with small groups of five to six children for approximately twenty-one weeks. Videotaped vignettes of children in stressful situations model coping strategies and problem-solving skills, stimulate discussion about common interpersonal problems, and provide a starting point for role-plays and re-enactments. Child-sized puppets also participate as group members to elicit discussion and enlist children's assistance in solving problems. In addition, materials such as cue cards, books, stickers, and prizes are used to enhance interest and learning (Webster-Stratton, Reid, & Hammond, 2001).

Two randomized trials have evaluated the impact of the Dinosaur Curriculum on preschool and early-elementary children with conduct problems. One, conducted by Webster-Stratton, Reid, and Hammond (2001), compared the effects of the Dinosaur Curriculum with a wait-list control group for ninety-nine children with early-onset conduct problems, aged 4–8. Following eighteen- to twenty-two weekly clinic sessions, children receiving the Dinosaur Curriculum had fewer externalizing problems than children in the control group, as assessed by a combined index comprised of parent and teacher reports. The Wally Social Problem-solving measure, an interview with children, revealed that children who had received the Dinosaur Curriculum showed enhanced social problem-solving skills compared with children on the waiting list. In another trial, families of ninety-seven children with early-onset conduct problems were randomly assigned to receive the Dinosaur Curriculum, a parent training program, the combination of Dinosaur Curriculum and parent training, or a wait-list control group (Webster-Stratton & Hammond, 1997). The Dinosaur Curriculum, used alone or in combination with parent training, produced significant improvements in social problem-solving skills (as measured in child interviews) and conflict management skills (as measured by observations of play interactions with best friends). Parent training (used alone or in combination with Dinosaur Curriculum) produced greater effects on problem behaviors at home. The positive effects of the Dinosaur Curriculum and parent training were maintained at one-year follow-up (Webster-Stratton & Hammond, 1997). This study suggests that comprehensive coaching programs for young children with aggressive behavior problems and concurrent social-emotional skill deficits can enhance their social competencies. Furthermore, these studies suggest that social competence coaching programs are one useful intervention component for aggressive-disruptive children, but that their impact is greatest when they are integrated with additional intervention components, such as classroom behavior management and parent training programs.

Promoting Generalized and Sustained Competencies

Whether social competence promotion efforts involve classroom curricula or therapeutic coaching programs for high-risk children, research suggests that strategies that foster the generalized use of competencies in natural peer settings warrant further development and evaluation. There may be important conditions in the preschool setting that are necessary for social competence interventions to take hold. For example, one study of the PATHS curriculum (Conduct Problems Prevention Research Group, 1999) found that effects on children's social competence were greatest in elementary classrooms that were well ordered and characterized by relatively high levels of positive student engagement. Hence, training teachers in effective classroom management may both foster child social competence directly (Webster-Stratton, Mihalic et al., 2001) and provide an important foundation to support the effectiveness of more explicit social-emotional learning curricula or coaching programs.

Teacher attention to and contingent responding that supports child skill performance in the classroom may also play a critically important role in supporting generalized use of those social skills in ongoing peer interactions. Studies which have manipulated teacher attention have demonstrated its powerful impact on child behavior. For example, Allen, Hart, Buell, Harris, and Wolf (1964) instructed a preschool teacher to attend to and praise a withdrawn child whenever he interacted with peers but to ignore him when he was playing alone. Under these conditions, the child's rate of social interaction increased dramatically from 10% to 60%. Similarly, investigators asked teachers to selectively praise the cooperative behaviors displayed by aggressive children and documented corresponding increases in child cooperative peer interactions and reductions in aggressive exchanges (Pinkston, Reese, LeBlanc, & Baer, 1973).

Teachers may also enhance generalized skill performance by organizing the classroom in a way that creates naturalistic opportunities for high-risk children to become involved positively with peers (see review by Gresham, 1981). Labeled "environmental arrangements" by Odom et al. (1999), systematic efforts by teachers to create play opportunities for children, by introducing play activities, assigning play roles if necessary, and prompting children in interaction, are often used to increase the social integration of developmentally delayed children in preschool settings. Several studies have shown the effectiveness of environmental arrangements on rates of play. For example, Strain and his colleagues demonstrated that socially withdrawn preschool children were more interactive when teachers helped them identify opportunities to play with peers (Strain, 1977) and when teachers organized socio-dramatic play that included explicit roles for these children (Strain & Weigerink, 1976). Furman, Rahe, and Hartup (1979) found that providing opportunities for dyadic play sessions with younger peers was another form of organized peer opportunity that enhanced the positive social interaction of socially withdrawn preschoolers, by giving them an opportunity to take a more assertive, leadership role than they took ordinarily in the larger classroom peer context. In some cases, coaching peers to initiate interactions with and respond positively to target children has also proven effective in increasing rates of social interaction among preschoolers, as illustrated by the buddy training program evaluated by English, Goldstein, Shafer, and Kaczmarek (1997). In this program, teachers coached and then prompted and reinforced peers for initiating and sustaining play with their developmentally delayed peers. This kind of buddy support can enhance rates of positive peer interaction in the classroom (Fantuzzo et al., 1988).

Used alone, it is unlikely that environmental arrangements can remediate social skill deficits in target children without additional program components that coach children directly in those skills. Yet such systematic efforts to support skillful interactions in the classroom setting may be critical to promote generalized and sustained improvements, and warrant inclusion in comprehensive social competence promotion programs (Fantuzzo et al., 1988).

Summary and Future Directions

In summary, classroom-based and social skills coaching programs have proven effective in promoting the social-emotional competencies of preschool children, contributing to their school readiness and future social adjustment. Building upon research on peer relations and social-emotional development, programs with sustained effects target social competence as an "organizational construct," recognizing the importance of helping children develop behavioral and social regulation skills by attending to their social information processing, emotion regulation, motivation and self-efficacy, as well as building their behavioral repertoires. Critical skill domains associated empirically with social competence in the preschool years include: (1) prosocial, cooperative play skills, (2) language and communication skills, (3) emotional understanding and regulation, and (4) aggression control and social problem-solving skills. These skills can be promoted with classroom curricula and with therapeutic coaching programs. In each type of program, four components are used to promote competence: (1) instructions and modeling, (2) multiple practice opportunities, (3) performance feedback, and (4) strategic classroom engineering designed to support the generalization and maintenance of skills in naturalistic peer interactions.

The available empirical research provides a solid basis for guiding educational policy and practice. First, evidence documenting the important role of social-emotional competence and positive peer relations for school readiness and later school adjustment suggests that all teachers should receive training in the developmental research and research-based educational practices that support preschool children in this important area of developing competence. Second, in addition to training, empirically supported social-emotional curricula should be available to preschool teachers, enabling them to integrate these research-based educational strategies into their general preschool curricula. Third, therapeutic support programs designed for children with special needs (e.g., developmental delays, learning difficulties, social withdrawal) should incorporate empirically supported social skill coaching procedures into intervention plans. Fourth, therapeutic programs for highly aggressive preschool children should involve multiple components, including social skill coaching, along with classroom management and parent management training, to provide maximum support for social-emotional skill remediation as well as aggression control for these children.

In addition, although empirical evidence supports the promise of social-emotional learning programs during the preschool years, research is needed to further extend and evaluate these programs. For example, one important area for further research involves the optimal design of social competence promotion programs for preschool children. In general, investigators have adapted instructional techniques, developed originally for grade-school children, by providing shorter skill instructions, making a greater use of puppets or dolls to illustrate skill concepts, shortening or simplifying role-plays, or replacing role-plays with skill practice in the context of socio-dramatic play. Social competence promotion programs would benefit from a more specific examination and comparison of format options, to identify strategies for skill concept introduction and practice that produce the greatest engagement and learning among preschool children, given their motivational orientation, attention span, and cognitive skills.

Although recent research has included evaluations that compare the efficacy of "stand-alone" classroom-based or social skill coaching programs with multi-component, nested programs (e.g., programs that combine teacher-led classroom curricula with therapist-delivered coaching programs for high-risk children), further research of this kind is needed. In addition, strategies that may enhance the generalization and long-term maintenance of social skills require further study. Modifications of the classroom environment, classroom management practices, and teacher–child relationships all hold promise for extending the impact of social skills training programs, and further investigation of these factors would be useful. Also useful would be research focused on clarifying the mechanisms of action that account for the positive effects of social competence promotion programs at the preschool level, to provide a foundation for ongoing program development and improvement.

Finally, the value of linking social competence promotion programs at school with parent-focused early intervention programs also warrants further research. Parents play a critical role in fostering child social-emotional learning and self-regulation. Webster-Stratton's research (Webster-Stratton & Hammond, 1998) suggests that parent training can be linked effectively with school-based intervention programs to promote cross-situational behavioral improvements for young children with early-starting conduct problems. Future research may clarify whether parent-focused programs can promote child social competence when used in coordination with classroom-based programs or for children with other types of social-emotional disabilities.

References

Allen, K. E., Hart, B., Buell, J. B., Harris, R. W., & Wolf, M. M. (1964). Effects of social reinforcement of isolate behavior of a nursery school child. *Child Development, 34,* 511–518.

Bierman, K. L. (2004). *Peer rejection: Developmental processes and intervention strategies.* New York: Guilford.

Bierman, K. L., & Welsh, J. A. (2000). Assessing social dysfunction: The contributions of laboratory and performance-based measures. *Journal of Clinical Child Psychology, 29,* 526–539.

Boivin, M., Hymel, S., & Bukowski, W. M. (1995). The roles of social withdrawal, peer rejection, and victimization by peers in predicting loneliness and depressed mood in childhood. *Development and Psychopathology, 7,* 765–785.

Cartledge, G., & Kleefeld, J. (1991). *Taking part, introducing social skills to children.* Circle Pines, MN: American Guidance Service.

Coie, J. D. (1990). Toward a theory of peer rejection. In S. R. Asher & J. D. Coie (Eds.), *Peer rejection in childhood* (pp. 365–401). Cambridge: Cambridge University Press.

Coie, J. D., Dodge, K. A., & Kupersmidt, J. G. (1990). Peer group behavior and social status. In S. R. Asher & J. D. Coie (Eds.), *Peer rejection in childhood* (pp. 17–59). Cambridge: Cambridge University Press.

Conduct Problems Prevention Research Group. (1999). Initial impact of the Fast Track prevention trial for conduct problems: II. Classroom effects. *Journal of Consulting and Clinical Psychology, 67,* 648–657.

Denham, S. A., & Burton, R. (1996). A social-emotional intervention for at-risk four-year olds. *Journal of School Psychology, 34,* 225–246.

Denham, S. A., & Burton, R. (2004). *Social and emotional prevention and intervention programming for preschoolers.* New York: Kluwer Academic/Plenum Publishers.

Denham, S. A., & Holt, R. W. (1993). Preschoolers' likeability as a cause or consequence of their social behavior. *Developmental Psychology, 29,* 271–275.

Dodge, K. A., & Murphy, R. R. (1984). The assessment of social competence in adolescents. *Advances in Child Behavior Analysis and Therapy, 3,* 61–96.

Domitrovich, C. E., Greenberg, M. T., Cortes, R., & Kusche, C. (1999). *Manual for the Preschool PATHS Curriculum.* Pennsylvania State University.

Eisenberg, N., & Fabes, R. A. (1992). Emotion, regulation, and the development of social competence. In M. S. Clark (Ed.), *Review of personality and social psychology: Vol. 14. Emotion and social behavior* (pp. 119–150). Newbury Park, CA: Sage.

Eisenberg, N., Fabes, R. A., Murphy, B. C., Shepard, S., Guthrie, I. K., Mazsk, P., Poulin, R., & Jones, S. (1999). Prediction of elementary school children's socially appropriate and problem behavior from anger reactions at age 4–6 years. *Journal of Applied Developmental Psychology, 20,* 119–142.

Elias, M. J., Zins, J. E., Weissberg, R. P., Frey, K. S., Greenberg, M. T., Haynes, N. M., Kessler, R., Schwab-Stone, M. E., & Shriver, T. P. (1997). *Promoting social and emotional learning: Guidelines for educators.* Alexandria, VA: Association for Supervision and Curriculum Development.

English, K., Goldstein, H., Shafer, K., & Kaczmarek, L. (1997). Promoting interactions among preschoolers with and without disabilities: Effects of a buddy skills-training program. *Exceptional Children, 63,* 229–243.

Fantuzzo, J. W., Jurecic, L., Stovall, A., Hightower, A. D., Goins, C., & Schachtel, D. (1988). Effects of adult and peer social initiations on the social behavior of withdrawn, maltreated preschool children. *Journal of Consulting and Clinical Psychology, 56,* 34–39.

Furman, W., Rahe, D. F., & Hartup, W. W. (1979). Rehabilitation of socially withdrawn children through mixed-age and same-aged socialization. *Child Development, 50,* 915–922.

Gottman, J. M. (1983). How children become friends. *Monographs of the Society for Research in Child Development, 48*(2, Serial No. 201).

Greenberg, M. T., & Kusche, C. A. (1998). Preventive intervention for school-aged deaf children: The PATHS Curriculum. *Journal of Deaf Studies and Deaf Education, 3,* 49–63.

Greenberg, M. T., Kusche, C. A., Cook, E. T., & Quamma, J. P. (1995). Promoting emotional competence in school-aged deaf children: The effects of the PATHS Curriculum. *Development and Psychopathology, 7,* 117–136.

Greenberg, M. T., Kusche, C. A., & Speltz, M. (1991). Emotional regulation, self control, and psychopathology: The role of relationships in early childhood. In D. Cicchetti & S. L. Toth (Eds.), *Rochester Symposium on Developmental Psychopathology: Vol. 2. Internalizing and externalizing expressions of dysfunction* (pp. 21–66). Hillsdale, NJ: Erlbaum.

Gresham, F. M. (1981). Social skills training with handicapped children: A review. *Review of Educational Research, 51,* 139–176.

Guglielmo, H. M., & Tryon, G. S. (2001). Social skills training in an integrated preschool program. *School Psychology Quarterly, 16,* 158–175.

Hartup, W. W. (1983). The peer system. In E. M. Hetherington (Ed.), *Handbook of child psychology: Vol. 4. Socialization, personality, and social development* (4th ed., pp. 102–196). New York: Wiley.

Howes, C. (1987). Social competence with peers in young children: Developmental sequences. *Developmental Review, 7,* 252–272.

Izard, C. E., Fine, S., Schultz, D., Mostow, A., Ackerman, B., & Youngstrom, E. (2001). Emotion knowledge as a predictor of social behavior and academic competence in children at risk. *Psychological Science, 12,* 18–23.

Kemple, K., Speranza, H., & Hazen, N. (1992). Cohesive discourse and peer acceptance: Longitudinal relations in the preschool years. *Merrill-Palmer Quarterly, 38,* 364–381.

Kusche, C. A., & Greenberg, M. T. (1995). *The PATHS Curriculum.* Seattle, WA: Developmental Research & Programs.

Ladd, G. W. (1990). Having friends, keeping friends, making friends, and being liked by peers in the classroom: Predictors of children's early school adjustment? *Child Development, 61,* 1061–1100.

Ladd, G. W., & Mize, J. (1983). A cognitive-social learning model of social skill training. *Psychological Review, 90,* 127–157.

Ladd, G. W., & Price, J. M. (1987). Predicting children's social and school adjustment following the transition from preschool to kindergarten. *Child Development, 58,* 1168–1189.

Ladd, G. W., Price, J. M., & Hart, C. H. (1988). Predicting preschoolers' peer status from their playground behaviors. *Child Development, 59,* 986–992.

LaGreca, A. M. (1993). Social skills training with children: Where do we go from here? *Journal of Clinical Child Psychology, 22,* 288–298.

Mendez, J. L., Fantuzzo, J., & Cicchetti, D. (2002). Profiles of social competence among low-income African American preschool children. *Child Development, 73,* 1085–1100.

Mize, J., & Ladd, G. W. (1990). Toward the development of successful social skills training for preschool children. In S. R. Asher & J. D. Coie (Eds.), *Peer rejection in childhood* (pp. 274–308). New York: Cambridge University Press.

Odom, S. L., & Brown, W. H. (1993). Social interaction skills interventions for young children with disabilities in integrated settings. In C. Peck, S. Odom, & D. Bricker (Eds.), *Integrating young children with disabilities into community programs* (pp. 39–64). Baltimore: Brookes.

Odom, S. L., McConnell, S. R., McEvoy, M. A., Peterson, C., Ostrosky, M., Chandler, L. K., Spicuzza, R. J., Skellenger, A., Creighton, M., & Favazza, P. C. (1999). Relative effects of interventions supporting the social competence of young children with disabilities. *Topics in Early Childhood Special Education, 19,* 75–91.

Olson, S. L. (1992). Development of conduct problems and peer rejection in preschool children: A social systems analysis. *Journal of Abnormal Child Psychology, 20,* 327–350.

Parker, J. G., Rubin, K. H., Price, J. M., & DeRosier, M. E. (1995). Peer relationships, child development and adjustment: A developmental psychopathological perspective. In D. Cicchetti & D. Cohen (Eds.), *Developmental psychopathology: Vol. 2. Risk disorder and adaptation* (pp. 96–161). New York: Wiley.

Patterson, G. R., Littman, R. A., & Bricker, D. (1967). Assertive behavior in children: A step toward a theory of aggression. *Monographs of the Society for Research in Child Development, 32*(5, Serial No. 18b).

Pianta, R. C. (1999). *Enhancing relationships between children and teachers.* Washington, DC: American Psychological Association.

Pinkston, E. M., Reese, N. M., LeBlanc, J. M., & Baer, D. M. (1973). Independent control of a preschool child's aggression and peer interaction by contingent teacher attention. *Journal of Applied Behavior Analysis, 6,* 115–124.

Putallaz, M. (1983). Predicting children's sociometric status from their behavior. *Child Development, 54,* 1417–1426.

Raver, C. C., Blackburn, E. K., & Bancroft, M. (1999). Relations between effective emotional self-regulation, attentional control, and low-income preschoolers' social competence with peers. *Early Education and Development, 10,* 333–350.

Rimm-Kaufman, S. E., Early, D. M., Cox, M. J., Saluja, G., Pianta, R. C., Bradley, R. H., & Payne, C. (2002). Early behavioral attributes and teachers' sensitivity as predictors of competent behavior in the kindergarten classroom. *Journal of Applied Developmental Psychology, 23,* 451–470.

Shantz, C. U., & Hartup, W. H. (1992). Conflict and development: An introduction. In C. U. Shantz & W. H. Hartup (Eds.), *Conflict in child and adolescent development* (pp. 1–11). Cambridge: Cambridge University Press.

Shure, M. B. (1992). *I Can Problem Solve: An interpersonal cognitive problem-solving program: Kindergarten and primary grades.* Champaign, IL: Research Press.

Shure, M. B., & Spivac, G. (1982). Interpersonal problem-solving in young children: A Cognitive approach to prevention. *American Journal of Community Psychology, 10*(3), 341–355.

Shure, M. B., & Spivac, G. (1980). Interpersonal problem solving as a mediator of behavioral adjustment in preschool and kindergarten children. *Journal of Applied Developmental Psychology, 1,* 29–44.

Sroufe, L. A. (1996). *Emotional development: The organization of emotional life in the early years.* Cambridge: Cambridge University Press.

Strain, P. S. (1977). An experimental analysis of peer social initiations on the behavior of withdrawn preschool children: Some training and generalization effects. *Journal of Abnormal Child Psychology, 5,* 445–455.

Strain, P. S., & Weigerink, R. (1976). The effects of sociodramatic activities on social interaction among behaviorally handicapped preschool children. *Journal of Special Education, 10,* 71–75.

Vaughn, B. E., Vollenweider, M., Bost, K. K., Azria-Evans, Snider, J. B. (2003). Negative interactions and social competence for preschool children in two samples: Reconsidering the interpretation of aggressive behavior for young children. *Merrill-Palmer Quarterly, 49,* 245–278.

Vitaro, F., Tremblay, R. E., Gagnon, D., & Boivan, M. (1992). Peer rejection from kindergarten to grade 2: Outcomes, correlates, and prediction. *Merrill-Palmer Quarterly, 38,* 382–400.

Webster-Stratton, C., & Hammond, M. (1997). Treating children with early onset conduct problems: A comparison of child and parenting interventions. *Journal of Consulting and Clinical Psychology, 65,* 93–101.

Webster-Stratton, C., Mihalic, S., Fagan, A., Arnold, D., Taylor, T., & Tingley, C. (2001). *Blueprints for violence prevention, book eleven: The incredible years: Parent, teacher and child training series.* Boulder, CO: Center for the Study and Prevention of Violence.

Webster-Stratton, C., Reid, J., & Hammond, M. (2001). Social skills and problem-solving training for children with early-onset conduct problems: Who benefits? *Journal of Child Psychology and Psychiatry and Allied Disciplines, 42,* 943–952.

Weissberg, R. P., & Greenberg, M. T. (1998). School and community competence-enhancement and prevention programs. In I. Siegel & A. Renninger (Eds.), *Handbook for child psychology: Vol. 4. Child psychology in practice* (5th ed., pp. 877–954). New York: Wiley.

Youngstrom, E., Wolpaw, J.-M., Kogos, J. L., Schoff, K., Ackerman, B., & Izard, C. (2000). Interpersonal problem solving in preschool and first grade: Developmental change and ecological validity. *Journal of Clinical Child Psychology, 29,* 589–602.

Zigler, E., Taussig, C., & Black, K. (1992). Early childhood intervention: A promising preventative for juvenile delinquency. *American Psychologist, 47,* 997–1006.

30

Treatment and Prevention of Conduct Problems: Parent Training Interventions for Young Children (2–7 Years Old)

Carolyn Webster-Stratton and M. Jamila Reid

Early-onset oppositional, defiant, and aggressive behaviors in young children are serious problems, which, when left untreated, lead to more serious and costly antisocial behaviors (i.e., conduct disorder, substance abuse, mental illness, delinquency, and violence). Research has identified an array of risk factors, processes, and possible behavioral targets for reducing delinquency (Snyder, 2001). The children at greatest risk of engaging in antisocial acts in adolescence are those who exhibit high levels of conduct problems at earlier ages. The risk of later problems is further increased if the child with early-onset conduct problems is exposed to additional risk factors such as deviant peers, low school bonding, teachers with poor classroom management skills, harsh or inconsistent parenting, or low parental monitoring. Consequently, effective interventions designed to treat or prevent conduct problems must lead to a clear change in one or more of these risk factors.

A number of child and family risk factors contribute to the development of early-onset conduct problems in a cumulative and synergistic manner (Hawkins & Weiss, 1985; J. B. Reid & Eddy, 1997). Our model, as outlined in Figure 30.1, derived from a model described by John Reid and Mark Eddy (1997), begins in the toddler period. Children with impulsive and volatile temperaments often overwhelm parents and interfere with developing positive parent–child interactions. Parents may respond with harsh or inconsistent discipline strategies, which exacerbate child behavior problems. Thus ineffective parenting results in increased child behavior problems, which, in turn, makes the child increasingly difficult to parent. When children with these family and child risk factors enter school, the developmental model becomes more complex. Teachers are more critical of, and provide less teaching and support to, the children who are inattentive, uncooperative, and fail to follow their directions (Shores & Wehby, 1999). Parents may be uninvolved or feel unwelcome in the school setting, eroding the bonds between the home and school. Over time, rejected children form deviant peer groups that reinforce antisocial behaviors. Thus, early home problems spill over into the school and peer group settings. Research indicates that the more risk areas children are exposed to, the greater the likelihood of a negative behavioral outcome later in life (Hawkins, Catalano, & Miller, 1992). As can be seen in Figure 30.1, cascading domains of risk factors make early prevention/intervention imperative.

This review identifies and describes empirically supported prevention and intervention parent programs (Mrazek & Haggerty, 1994) that target risk behaviors in early childhood (ages 2–7 years). The review covers selective prevention programs (targeting children at risk because of socio-familial and environmental factors) and indicated interventions (targeting children diagnosed with oppositional defiant disorder or conduct disorder). We focus this review on parent programs because of the substantial work showing that parent-mediated interventions are the most promising approach for preventing the escalation of conduct problems (for review see Brestan & Eyberg, 1998; Taylor & Biglan, 1998). Included in this review are parent interventions that also incorporate child and classroom or teacher training components as adjuncts to parent training. These multi-focused interventions seek to address multiple risk factors across settings. We conclude by outlining key features of effective programs and policy implications for implementing empirically supported programs.

The Importance of Early Intervention

Longitudinal studies consistently confirm the relation between early-onset conduct problems and later delinquency, substance abuse, and antisocial behavior (Moffitt, 1993; Patterson, DeBaryshe, & Ramsey, 1989; Tremblay, Mass, Pagani, & Vitaro, 1996). Eron (1990) concluded that, without intervention, aggressive tendencies crystallize around age 8 years of age. Other research indicates that if children with aggressive behavior problems are not treated by age 8, their problems become less responsive to intervention in later years and are more likely to become a chronic disorder (Bullis & Walker, 1994; Francis, Shaywitz, Stuebing, Shaywitz, & Fletcher, 1991). Additionally, the earlier intervention is offered, the more positive the child's behavioral adjustment at home and at school, and the greater chance of preventing later delinquency and drug abuse (Taylor & Biglan, 1998).

Characteristics of Empirically Validated Interventions

To be included in this review, programs had at least one (preferably two) published, randomized control-group trial documenting effectiveness compared to an alternate treatment or no treatment. Effectiveness was measured by direct reductions in parental

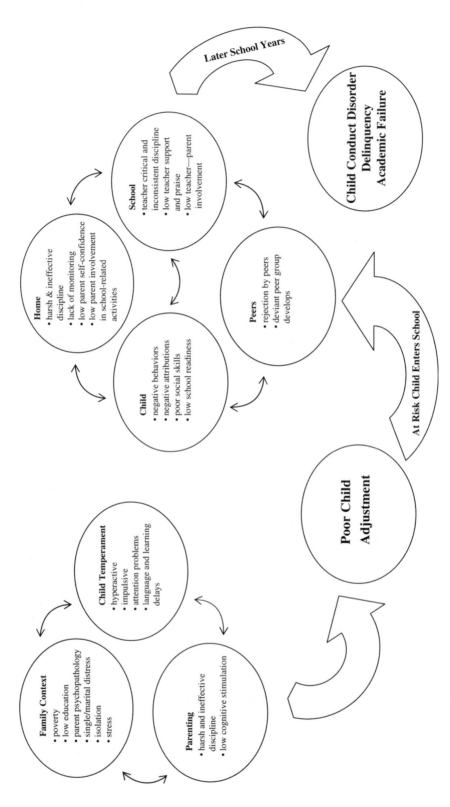

Figure 30.1 Model of linking risk factors: unfolding chain of events in development of conduct disorder.

Toddler Years

Family Context
- poverty
- low education
- parent psychopathology
- single/marital distress
- isolation
- stress

Child Temperament
- hyperactive
- impulsive
- attention problems
- language and learning delays

Parenting
- harsh and ineffective discipline
- low cognitive stimulation

Poor Child Adjustment

Preschool/Kindergarten Years   Later School Years

Home
- harsh & ineffective discipline
- lack of monitoring
- low parent self-confidence
- low parent involvement in school-related activities

Child
- negative behaviors
- negative attributions
- poor social skills
- low school readiness

School
- teacher critical and inconsistent discipline
- low teacher support and praise
- low teacher—parent involvement

Peers
- rejection by peers
- deviant peer group develops

At Risk Child Enters School

Later School Years

Child Conduct Disorder Delinquency Academic Failure

behavior that has been linked to child conduct problems (e.g., harsh parenting) or in child conduct problems. Programs were also only included if they were replicable by others (e.g., programs are well described using manuals or other treatment guidelines). Table 30.1 presents a summary of included parent programs.

Cognitive Behavioral Parent Training Programs for Children with Conduct Problems (Ages 2–7 Years)

Parent training programs based on cognitive social learning theory can counteract the *parent and family risk factors* by helping parents to develop positive relationships with their children and by teaching them to use non-violent discipline methods that reduce children's conduct problems and promote their self-confidence, prosocial behaviors, problem-solving skills, and academic success. These programs can also help parents to become actively involved in school and to promote parent–teacher communication.

Parent training content

Most parent training programs draw extensively from the pioneering work of Patterson and Reid (Patterson, 1974; J. B. Reid, Taplin, & Loeber, 1981) and Connie Hanf (Hanf, 1970; Hanf & Kling, 1973). In these approaches, parents are guided to increase their positive interactions with their children through the use of child-directed activities, praise, and other rewards, while ignoring mild inappropriate behavior. Parents are also taught to set clear and predictable limits, use warnings, give appropriate consequences (loss of privileges, Time-Out), monitor effectively, and use problem-solving strategies with children.

Parent training process

A clinically sophisticated therapeutic approach is needed when conducting parent training. Therapists must be supportive, caring, and demonstrate genuine understanding of what it is like to be a parent of a child with behavior problems (Patterson & Chamberlain, 1994; Webster-Stratton, 1996). Therapists must also provide adequate structure to the therapy process (Alexander & Parsons, 1982; Alexander, Waldron, Newberry, & Liddle, 1988). They must be an effective "coach" – educating, supporting, and problem-solving difficult issues and exploring resistance, all with a high level of sensitivity, compassion, and understanding of child development principles (Webster-Stratton & Herbert, 1994). They must be able to draw the parents into the collaborative process of developing solutions together (Cunningham, Davis, Bremmer, & Dunn, 1993). Effective therapists also engage parents in role-playing new parenting skills and practicing at home (Knapp & Deluty, 1989).

Therapists working with parents must also be skilled at responding to a range of non-parenting issues, because it is likely that up to one-third of their time spent with

Table 30.1 Summary of empirically validated prevention programs for young children (0–8 years) that are designed to prevent later development of substance abuse, violence, and delinquency: parent- and family-focused interventions

Program type and name	Age of children	Target and format of intervention	No. of hours	Populations studied		Child outcome
				Selective intervention (S)	Indicated intervention (I)	
Home visiting (Barnard et al., 1988; Kitzman, 1997; Olds et al., 1997)	Prenatal and infants	• Individual parent education	60–90 min., every other week during pregnancy until child age 2 years	X		↓ Child arrests at 15 and ↓ Child injuries
Living with Children (Patterson, 1975; Patterson et al., 1982)	3–12 years	• Family skills training	15–20 hours per family		X	↓ Conduct problems
Helping the Non-compliant Child (Forehand & MacMahon, 1981)	3–8 years	• Individual parent skills training	6–12 hours per family		X	↓ Non-compliance
Parent–Child Interaction Therapy (Eyberg & Boggs, 1989; Schuhmann et al., 1998)	2–6 years	• Individual parent and child training	14 hours per family		X	↓ Conduct problems

Program	Age	Format	Duration			Target outcome
Synthesis training (Wahler et al., 1993)	5–9 years	• Individual parent skills training	36 1-hour sessions/family over 9 months		X	↓ Aversive behaviors
Positive Parenting Program (Triple P) (Sanders, 1992)	7–14 years	• Individual parent skills training and • Self-administered	6–12 hours per family		X	↓ Conduct problems
Incredible Years Parenting Program (Webster-Stratton, 1982a, 1982b, 1990a)	2–8 years	• Group parent training and • Self-administered	20–44 hours per group (12–14)	X	X	↓ Child conduct problems
Community-based program (Cunningham et al., 1995)	2–5 years	• Large group parent training	24 hours per group (18–28)	X	X	↓ Behavior problems
DARE to be You (Miller-Heyl et al., 1998)	2–5 years	• Group parent training	20–4 hours per group	X		↓ Oppositional behavior
Focus on Families (Catalan & Haggerty, 1999)	7–11 years	• Group parent training and home visits	53 hours	X		↓ Parental use of drugs

parents may be focused on issues other than parenting (Olds, Eckenrode, & Henderson, 1997). Intervention strategies designed specifically to address marital difficulties, depression, anger management, and social isolation have all been shown to improve parental attendance (Prinz, Blechman, & Dumas, 1994) as well as the effectiveness of parent training for families experiencing these parenting problems (Dadds, Schwartz, & Sanders, 1987; Wahler, Cartor, Fleischman, & Lambert, 1993; Webster-Stratton, 1994). Although not all parents will need to address these issues, the ability to integrate these aspects into the therapy process clearly enhances the effectiveness of parenting interventions.

Empirically supported programs: individual family format

Living with Children. One of the first parent training programs for treating children with conduct disorders (age 6 and up) was developed by Patterson, Reid and colleagues at the Oregon Social Learning Center (Patterson, 1976). A therapist meets individually with parents to train them in five main management areas: tracking, positive reinforcement, discipline, monitoring, and problem solving. Marital and other issues are addressed as they arise. The length and course of treatment varies according to the need, with an average of 15–20 hours of therapy per family.

The first randomized controlled trial evaluating this approach compared it to usual eclectic approaches offered in applied mental health settings (Patterson, Chamberlain, & Reid, 1982). Children of parents who received the parent training exhibited significantly fewer problems than those whose families received usual care. Other researchers have evaluated variations on this program, including some treatment modifications (Sayger, Horne, Walker, & Passmore, 1988) and work with divorcing mothers and sons (Forgatch & DeGarmo, 1999).

Helping the Non-compliant Child. This individual parent training program, designed to treat non-compliant children age 3–8, was developed by Hanf (Hanf & Kling, 1973) and later modified and evaluated by McMahon and Forehand (Forehand, Steffe, Furey, & Walley, 1983). Parents are taught a series of skills, including non-directive play, contingent praise and attention, how to deliver clear commands, and to use Time-Out. Experimental studies of this approach have demonstrated improvements in children's compliant behavior compared with a control group (e.g., Peed, Roberts, & Forehand, 1977). The effectiveness of this intervention has been enhanced by additional parent training components: training in the principles upon which the management strategies are based (McMahon, Forehand, & Griest, 1981); self-control training for parents (Wells, Forehand, & Griest, 1980); and problem solving for single mothers on non-parenting issues (Pfiffner, Jouriles, Brown, Etscheidt, & Kelly, 1990). A long-term follow-up study compared twenty-six children (age 2–7) who received treatment with matched community controls. No differences were found between the children with early conduct problems and the community group, indicating that treatment effects were maintained (Long, Forehand, Wierson, & Morgan, 1994).

Parent–Child Interaction Therapy. Parent–Child Interaction Therapy (PCIT), developed by Eyberg (Schuhmann, Foote, Eyberg, Boggs, & Algina, 1998), is another treatment program for young children (2–6) with conduct problems, also derived from Hanf's child-directed play (Hanf & Kling, 1973). Treatment is offered to individual parent–child dyads using bug-in-the-ear coaching, in which the parent wears a small microphone in his or her ear while playing with his or her child and the therapist coaches through a one-way mirror. This treatment (Eyberg, Boggs, & Algina, 1995) is an integration of traditional play therapy and current behavioral thinking about child management. While the importance of behavior management is maintained, skills for child-directed play (describe, reflect, imitate, praise) are also a major focus of intervention. After learning child-directed interaction play (CDI), which fosters a positive parent–child relationship, parents are taught parent-directed interaction (PDI), which focuses on using clear, direct commands, and imposing consistent consequences for misbehavior (Eisenstadt, Eyberg, McNeil, Newcomb, & Funderburk, 1993). Treatment ends when parents have mastered the skills, presenting problems have been resolved, and the child no longer meets the *Diagnostic and Statistical Manual of Mental Disorders* criteria for oppositional defiant disorder (ODD).

Einsenstadt and colleagues (1993) evaluated the effectiveness of each stage of PCIT with twenty-four families of young children with behavior problems. Results showed significant improvements in children's conduct problems and positive interactions with parents (Eyberg & Boggs, 1989; Eyberg et al., 1995; Hembree-Kigin & McNeil, 1995) that were maintained one to two years later (Hood & Eyberg, 2003). Other studies showed generalization to the school setting (Funderburk et al., 1998; McNeil et al., 1991) and improvements three to six years later (Hood & Eyberg, 2003).

Synthesis training. Synthesis training was specifically designed for socio-economically disadvantaged, stressed, and depressed mothers (Wahler et al., 1993). This model was developed to address stresses outside of the parent–child relationship that impact mothers' ability to cope with childrearing challenges. Mothers are taught to deal effectively with child issues by learning to discriminate between child-specific and other life stressors. The goal is to help the parent become sensitive to the differences in these situations by first exploring their similarities.

In an evaluation of this approach, families of twenty-three children were randomly assigned to parent training only, parent training and synthesis training, or parent and synthesis training plus friendship liaison (e.g., mother brought a close friend). Mothers attended weekly sessions spread over nine months. Mothers who received synthesis training exhibited significantly fewer indiscriminant reactions to their children, and, by follow-up, their aversive behavior had also improved, compared with those who received parent training only. The addition of a close friend did not impact the outcome (Wahler et al., 1993).

Positive Parenting Program (Triple P). Another individual, family-based approach to parent training is the Triple P (Sanders & Dadds, 1993). Parents are taught to give descriptive praise and other reinforcement for appropriate behavior, as well as a correction procedure, including Time-Out, for certain deviant behaviors. Sessions combine parent–child interaction with parent–therapist feedback and discussion. Six sessions are devoted to managing child behavior at home, three sessions focus on managing misbehavior in public, and two sessions address partner support and problem solving.

A randomized controlled trial treated the families of children with behavior problems with one of two versions of the above intervention. One version included the "partner support training" sessions, and one omitted these sessions. Both treatment approaches resulted in short-term improvements in children's behavior for all families. At a four-month follow-up, families with high discord only maintained these gains if they had received the partner support training. Families with low discord maintained gains in both treatment conditions (Dadds et al., 1987). The Triple P has also been evaluated in a randomized controlled study (Sanders, Markie-Dadds, Tully, & Bor, 2000) as a self-administered program for families living in rural Australia. Families read the book *Every Parent: A Positive Approach to Children's Behavior* (Sanders, 1992) and receive six weekly telephone consultation sessions with a therapist. Parents receiving the self-administered parent training reported significant reductions in their child's conduct problems compared to a waiting-list control group (Connell, Sanders, & Markie-Dadds, 1997).

Empirically supported programs based on group format

Two of the programs reviewed above have been adapted for use in group format. Both have been evaluated in randomized controlled trials, showing that the group format produced significant changes in parent and child behavior compared with controls. One trial (Christensen, Johnson, Phillips, & Glasgow, 1981) evaluated a group-based version of Living with Children (Patterson & Guillon, 1968). A second trial (Pisterman, McGrath, Firestone, & Goodman, 1989) evaluated a group-based version of Helping the Non-compliant Child (Forehand & McMahon, 1981). Additionally, there are several parent programs, described below, that were specifically designed to be delivered in group format.

The Incredible Years (IY) Parenting Series. This series, developed by Webster-Stratton, is delivered in a group format and includes child behavior management training as well as other cognitive behavioral and emotional approaches such as mutual problem-solving strategies, self-management principles, and positive self-talk. This content is embedded in a relational framework including parent group support and a collaborative relationship with the group leader. There are two versions of the Incredible Years BASIC program, one for preschool children (ages 2–6 years) and one for early school-age children (ages 5–10 years). The content of both versions utilizes videotape examples to foster group discussion about such matters as child-directed play skills involving parent coaching in social skills, emotion language and problem solving, differential attention, encouragement, praise, effective commands, Time-Out, consequences, monitoring, and problem solving. The school-age program adds training in ways to support children's academic skills such as reading and homework activities. The BASIC program lasts for twelve to fourteen weeks (2–2½ hours per week). A supplemental ADVANCED parenting program (Webster-Stratton, 1990b) was developed to address specifically a number of life stressors (depression, marital discord) in greater depth. This ADVANCED program teaches parents to cope with upsetting thoughts and depression, to give and get support from others, and to communicate and problem solve with adults. This additional ten- to fourteen-week program enhances the effects of BASIC by promoting children's and parents' conflict management skills and self-control techniques (Webster-Stratton, 1994). Recommended treatment for children with conduct problems is the combination of the BASIC plus the ADVANCED programs (twenty-four weeks total).

The efficacy of the IY parent program as a treatment program for children (ages 3–8 years) with conduct problems has been demonstrated by the program developer in six published randomized trials (Webster-Stratton, 1981, 1982a, 1982b, 1984, 1990a, 1994; Webster-Stratton & Hammond, 1997; Webster-Stratton, Reid, & Hammond, 2004). The program has been replicated by independent investigators with families of children with conduct problems (Scott, Spender, Doolan, Jacobs, & Aspland, 2001; Spaccarelli, Cotler, & Penman, 1992; Taylor, Schmidt, Pepler, & Hodgins, 1998). Two of these replications were "effectiveness" trials: that is, they were conducted in applied mental health settings with therapists who worked at the center (rather than with research therapists) (Taylor & Biglan, 1998). The Taylor study found that parents who received the IY group parenting program were more satisfied with service and felt that it was more suited to the unique problems they were facing than did the families who received eclectic and flexible individual therapy.

The BASIC parent program has also been evaluated as a prevention program with low-income, primarily minority, Head Start families (Miller & Rojas-Flores, 1999; Webster-Stratton, 1998; Webster-Stratton, Reid, & Hammond, 2001). All studies found that, following intervention, experimental mothers were more consistent and less harsh than control mothers. Their children also showed fewer behavior problems. These results were maintained at one-year follow-up. The program strengthened parenting skills and reduced behavior problems with low-income African-American mothers of toddlers in Chicago child care centers (Gross, Fogg, Webster-Stratton, Garvey, & Grady, 2003).

The IY parent program has also been shown to be effective as a self-administered program, in two randomized control studies (Webster-Stratton, 1990a; Webster-Stratton, Kolpacoff, & Hollinsworth, 1988).

Coping Skills Parenting Program. Another group-based parenting program for parents of young children is the Coping Skills Parenting Program developed by Charles Cunningham (Cunningham, Bremner, & Boyle, 1995). The curriculum includes problem solving, attending to and rewarding prosocial behavior, transitional strategies, when–then strategies, ignoring, disengaging from coercive interactions, advanced planning for difficult situations, and Time-Out. Mixed groups of parents of diagnosed and typically developing children meet weekly for twelve sessions. The program uses a coping problem-solving model in which parents view videotape models of ineffective parenting strategies for dealing with common child management problems and then generate solutions. Leaders model solutions suggested by participants, and parents role-play the solutions and set homework goals. This community program was evaluated in a randomized controlled trial, comparing it to individual family parent training (with similar content) offered at a clinic or to a no-treatment control. Native English speakers and any family whose children exhibited moderate behavior problems were equally likely to participate in the groups or the clinic-based training. However, families for whom English was a second language and families with a child exhibiting severe problems were more likely to participate in the group format. Families who attended the parenting groups reported significantly greater improvement in child behavior post-test and after a six-month follow-up. The parenting groups were significantly less expensive than the clinic-based intervention offered to the same number of families.

DARE to be You. This is a twelve-week group prevention program for parents of 2- to 5-year-old children in high-risk families, designed to promote parents' self-efficacy, effective childrearing strategies, understanding of developmental norms, social support, and problem-solving skills. Along with the parent group, there are ten parent–child activity sessions to practice session objectives. The program has been evaluated in a randomized control design with a low-income population and has been replicated with multi-ethnic populations (Ute Mountain Ute, Hispanic, Anglo). Parents reported significant changes in self-appraisals, democratic childrearing practices, and children's oppositional behavior (Miller-Heyl, MacPhee, & Fritz, 1998).

Focus on Families. Focus on Families is another group parenting program, designed specifically for recovering heroin addicts currently receiving methadone treatment. Topics include: family goal setting, relapse prevention, family communication skills, family management skills, creating family expectations about drugs and alcohol, teaching children skills, and helping children succeed in school. A randomized controlled trial evaluation revealed positive effects on parenting practices, increased coping ability for parents, and fewer relapses in using illegal drugs (Hawkins, Catalano, & Miller, 1992).

Summary of Parent-Focused Interventions

Individual family-based, group-based, and self-administered parent training programs have been shown to improve parenting practices and reduce conduct problems in children. Generalization of behavior improvements from the clinic setting to the home over reasonable follow-up periods (one to four years) and to untreated child behaviors has also been demonstrated (Taylor & Biglan, 1998; Webster-Stratton & Hammond, 1990). Studies of children with conduct problems typically find that approximately two-thirds of children show behavior in the normal range on standardized measures following family/parent intervention (Webster-Stratton, 1990c; Webster-Stratton, Hollinsworth, & Kolpacoff, 1989). Despite these promising findings, there is mixed evidence on generalization of improvements from home to school; improvements in the child's behavior at home are not necessarily reflected in improved behavior according to teachers' reports, particularly if teachers are not involved in the intervention (Taylor & Biglan, 1998). Characteristics of those families whose children fail to improve or fail to improve with parent training programs include considerable marital discord, high negative life stress, depression, and severe poverty (Webster-Stratton & Hammond, 1990, 1999).

Because of these findings, broader-based treatment approaches that include attention to interpersonal parent issues (e.g., depression and marital conflict) and family stressors by offering training in communication, anger management, and problem solving have demonstrated modest but significant improvements over and above what can be gained from parent training, which strictly focuses on parent skills.

Multi-focused Interventions: Combining Parent Training with Classroom Intervention

Historically, parent training has not been seen by school personnel as an essential element in school service delivery. However, school-based programs have several advantages over traditional mental health settings. First, school-based programs are ideally placed to strengthen the parent–teacher–child links. Second, offering parent interventions in schools eliminates the stigma and some of the practical barriers (e.g., transportation, insurance, child care) that can be associated with traditional mental health services. Third, preventive school programs can be offered in early grades before children's minor behavior problems have escalated into severe symptoms that require referral and extensive clinical treatment. A final advantage of interventions delivered in school is the sheer number of high-risk families and children who can be reached at comparatively low cost. Mounting evidence from several randomized control, longitudinal prevention programs shows that multi-modal (parent–child–teacher) interventions delivered through schools can significantly lower later delinquency, substance abuse, and school adjustment problems. Because these interventions were offered as complete intervention packages, behavior change cannot be attributed to a single treatment component; therefore they are included here as multi-focused interventions. See Table 30.2 for a summary.

First Step

This school-based selective prevention program (Walker et al., 1998) is designed for at-risk kindergarten children with early signs of antisocial behavior patterns. This program combines the CLASS program (described below) for acting-out children (Hops et al., 1978), with a six-week (one hour per week) home-based parenting program in which parents are taught to provide adequate monitoring and reinforcement to build child social competencies. The CLASS program (Hops et al., 1978) is a "game" played every day at school for a month, initially for 20 minutes per day, and gradually expanding to the whole day. During the first five days, the consultant visits the classroom and sits beside the child to constantly monitor on-task behavior using a card signal. Then the teacher takes over the management of the card system. When the child receives enough points, the entire

Table 30.2 Summary of empirically validated prevention programs for young children (0–8 years) that are designed to prevent later development of substance abuse, violence, and delinquency: multi-focused interventions

Program type and name	Age of children	Target and format of intervention	No. of hours	Populations studied Universal intervention (U)	Selective intervention (S)	Indicated intervention (I)	Child outcome
First Step (CLASS) (Walker et al., 1998)	5 years	• Home-based parent skills training+ • Program consultants+ • Individual child training in class	6 weeks, 1 hour per week 2½ hours daily for 3 months (50–60 hours)			X	↓ Aggression, ↑ Academic engagement
Montreal Program (Tremblay et al., 1995)	7–9 years	• Lunchtime child social skills peer training • Home-based individual parent skills training	9 sessions 1st year; 10 sessions 2nd year 17 sessions over 2 years			X	↓ Delinquency at age 15, less fighting at age 12
Fast Track (Conduct Problems Prevention Group)	6–12 years	• Classroom-based skills training (U) • Individual home-based for parents (S & I) • Group parent training (S & I) • Tutoring and social skills training for children (S & I)	6 years	X	X	X	↓ Conduct problems

Program	Age	Components	Dosage			Outcomes
Linking the Interests of Family and Teacher (LIFT) (Reid et al., 1999)	7–11 years	• Group parent training at school (S) • Classroom-based child skills training (U) • Playground program	Once a week, 6 weeks 20 1-hour sessions twice a week		X	↓ Physical aggression
Seattle Social Development Project (Hawkins & Weiss, 1985)	7–11 years	• Academic, social skills, and problem-solving training • Teacher training • Optional parent skills training	1st–5th grades 1st–3rd grades		X	↓ Violence at age 18 ↓ Aggression
Incredible Years Teacher Training (Webster-Stratton et al., 1999)	4–8 years	• Group teacher training (U) • Group parent training (S & I) • Small group child training (I)	36–50 hours, for children, teachers, and parents	X	X	↓ Classroom aggression with peers and teachers ↓ Conduct problems at home

class wins a prize. Three randomized controlled trials have shown that this program (without the parent component) results in significantly higher levels of appropriate behavior in the classroom, and that benefits maintain a year later with a new teacher (Hops et al., 1978; Walker, Retana, & Gersten, 1988). In a randomized evaluation of First Step (CLASS plus the six-week parent program), forty-six high-risk kindergartners were randomly assigned to the intervention or wait-list control. One year later, intervention students were significantly more adapted, more engaged, and less aggressive than controls. Follow-up results indicated that effects lasted over time (Epstein & Walker, 1999).

The Montreal Longitudinal Experimental Study

This school-based prevention program for high-risk boys includes classroom social-cognitive skills training based on the work of Shure and Spivack (1982) and a home-based parent training program based on the work of the OSLC (Patterson, Reid, Jones, & Conger, 1975). Tremblay and colleagues (Tremblay et al., 1996; Tremblay, Pagani, Masse, & Vitaro, 1995; Tremblay et al., 1992) identified 366 disruptive boys at age 6, and randomly assigned them to an experimental group that received a school-based small-group social skills program or a control condition. Coaching, peer modeling, role-playing, and positive reinforcement methods were used to teach anger management and peer problem solving. Parents were offered home-based parent training once every three weeks over a two-year span. (The average number of sessions was 17.4.) Follow-up when children were 12 showed that boys in the experimental condition had higher academic achievement, had committed less burglary and theft, and were less likely to get drunk or be involved in fights than controls. These effects increased as follow-up period lengthened.

Fast Track

This comprehensive, multi-component program provided continuous services to first- to fifth-grade children exhibiting aggressive behaviors. The six-year intervention included a classroom management component, socio-cognitive skills training, emotional regulation skills training (Kusche & Greenberg, 1994), academic tutoring, home visiting, parent–child relationship enhancement, and parent training (based on the parent programs of Forehand & McMahon and Webster-Stratton). Also included in this intervention were weekend friendship enhancement groups. Mid-intervention data at one and three years showed reductions in conduct problems and special education resource use (Conduct Problems Prevention Research Group, 1999a, 1999b, 1999c).

Linking the Interests of Families and Teachers (LIFT)

Linking the Interests of Families and Teachers (LIFT) is a school-based universal prevention program, developed by John Reid and colleagues, for elementary-school-aged children and their families. Two versions of the program are available: the first is tailored to meet the needs of children and their families as they begin elementary school; the second is tailored for the transition to middle school. The core of the program is a six-week parent training that promotes consistent and effective parental discipline techniques as well as close and appropriate supervision. This is combined with classroom-based small-group interpersonal skills training program (ten weeks, total of 20 hours). During recess, a version of the Good Behavior Game (Kellam, Ling, Merisca, Brown, & Ialongo, 1998) is used to encourage the use of positive skills during unstructured activities (children receive credit for good behavior toward class rewards). A controlled study of LIFT showed post-intervention reduction of playground aggression, improved classroom behavior, and reductions in maternal criticisms at home (J. B. Reid, Eddy, Fetrow, & Stoolmiller, 1999).

Parent programs that include teacher training

To promote students' social and academic competence and reduce levels of aggressive and antisocial behavior, teachers must be well trained in effective classroom management strategies. Integrated school-wide approaches that provide consistent classroom discipline plans and individualized behavior plans for children with conduct problems can be highly effective (Cotton & Wikelund, 1990; Gottfredson, Gottfredson, & Hybl, 1993; Knoff & Batsche, 1995). Programs that train teachers in classroom management strategies have consistently demonstrated short-term improvements in disruptive and aggressive behavior in the classroom for approximately 78% of disruptive students (Stage & Quiroz, 1997).

The Seattle Social Development Project. This preventive intervention combines teacher and parent training and is offered to all families through the public schools (Hawkins, Catalano, Morrison et al., 1992). Teachers are trained in proactive classroom management, interactive teaching, and cooperative learning. First-grade teachers were also trained to implement the ICPS curriculum developed by Shure and Spivack (1982). In the first and second grades, the "Catch 'Em Being Good" program was offered to parents. The program targets improved parental monitoring, clear parental expectations, positive reinforcement, and consequences for misbehavior. The program evaluation consisted of 643 students (first- to- fifth-graders) from high crime areas in Seattle. Schools were assigned to intervention or control conditions. The six-year follow-up (Hawkins, Catalano, Kosterman, Abbott, & Hill, 1999) with children who received the full school-based intervention (i.e., started in first grade and received all five years) indicated that intervention students reported fewer violent delinquent acts, lower first drinking age, less sexual activity, and fewer pregnancies by 18 years, and better school achievement and bonding.

Incredible Years (IY) Parents and Teachers Series. In a randomized control prevention study in Head Start, Webster-Stratton and colleagues (2001) evaluated the effects of the IY Teacher Training program combined with the IY Parenting program. Head Start classrooms were randomly assigned to intervention or control conditions (272 mothers and 61 teachers participated). Parents received the BASIC parent training, and all teachers received six days of training. The teacher training focused on classroom management skills, relationship building with students and parents, and promotion of social and emotional competence in the classroom. The positive parenting results found in a prior prevention study were replicated (Webster-Stratton, 1998). In addition, intervention teachers promoted more parent involvement and positive classroom atmosphere and were more positive and less harsh than control teachers. Students in the intervention classrooms exhibited significantly less non-compliance and physical aggression than students in control classrooms. Intervention children were more engaged, more socially competent, and had better school readiness than control children. Most of these improvements were maintained one year later (Webster-Stratton et al., 2001).

This same teacher training program was evaluated for children (4–8 years old) with diagnosed conduct problems (Webster-Stratton et al., 2004). Participating teachers were observed to use fewer inappropriate and harsh discipline strategies and to be more nurturing and positive than non-intervention teachers. In conditions where families received more than one treatment (e.g. parent + teacher training, or child + teacher training), significant changes occurred across more domains (i.e., parent, child, peer relationships, and teacher) than conditions where only one treatment was delivered. At the two-year follow-up, teacher training added significantly to the parent and child training in terms of children's school functioning (M. J. Reid, Webster-Stratton, & Hammond, 2003). Two years after treatment, significantly more children from the teacher training conditions were in the normal range according to teacher report. These data suggest that intervention across multiple domains (teachers, parents, and children) is beneficial to children who have pervasive conduct problems.

Key Features of Effective Programs

There are several excellent literature reviews indicating that cognitive-behavioral interventions are helpful for prevention and treatment of conduct disorders (Brestan & Eyberg, 1998; Taylor & Biglan, 1998; Taylor, Eddy, & Biglan, 1999). These reviews can be used to evaluate the appropriateness of particular parenting programs for a target population. A number of key program elements can be pulled from the empirically validated programs reviewed above: (1) focus on skills enhancing and participant strengths (not deficits), (2) broad-based content that includes cognitive, behavioral, and affective components, (3) at least 20 hours of intervention, (4) collaborative process and delivery by skilled therapists, (5) use of performance training methods (e.g., videotape methods, live modeling, role-play or practice exercises, weekly home practice activities) rather than didactic lecture format, (6) promotion of parent–teacher partnerships, (7) sensitivity to barriers for low socio-economic families and provisions to overcome these barriers (child care, transportation, easily accessible intervention location), and (8) empirical validation in control and comparison group studies that use multiple assessment methods and provide follow-up data.

Summary of Effective Parent Interventions for Children Ages 2–7 Years

As demonstrated by the existing research, effective interventions for at-risk children or children exhibiting conduct problems may involve several domains of risk factors. Parent intervention continues to be the single most effective avenue for preventing conduct problems and promoting social competence in young children. These parent programs are particularly effective when they address not only child behavior management training, but also broader parenting and life-stress issues (e.g., parent communication, problem solving, stress management, collaboration with schools). In addition, as indicated by the above review, parent programs may be enhanced by interventions that offer additional components delivered to teachers or the children themselves. This review focuses on programs for children ages 2–7 years that have been shown to be effective using rigorous evaluation standards. Given the powerful potential of these programs, prevention and early intervention staff should be trained in empirically validated interventions (Brestan & Eyberg, 1998) and should consider strategies to effectively integrate these into a mental health prevention plan for children. Services that are flexible in format (individual, group, or self-administered treatment) and readily available (offered through mental health agencies, schools, churches, and community centers) will allow for dissemination of these programs to families that are at high risk because of life circumstances as well as to families who have a child with risk factors such as attention deficit hyperactivity disorder, peer and conduct problems, and developmental delays.

Policy Implications: Principles for Implementing Empirically Supported Prevention Programs

As research begins to guide prevention services, there are a number of principles that can guide the selection and implementation of empirically supported interventions. The application of these principles will bridge the fields of science and practice. First, prevention/intervention is most effective if it is implemented early. By age 3, high levels of conduct problems place children at substantially elevated risk of later problems (Olweus, 1978). Additionally, family-based intervention is more effective when children are younger (Dishion, Patterson, & Kavanagh, 1992). Children older than 8 years are less responsive to intervention and their behavior problems are more likely to become chronic (Bullis & Walker, 1994; Francis et al., 1991).

Second, programs should be developmentally based and target reductions in risk factors (e.g., harsh parent or teacher discipline practices) as well as increase protective factors (i.e. children's social, emotional, and academic competence) (Mrazek & Haggerty, 1994). This comprehensive model could be the single most important step in preventing and reducing conduct problems before they "cascade" (Patterson, Reid, & Dishion, 1992) across developmental periods and result in cumulating and intensifying risk factors.

Third, intervention should be targeted to reach populations that are at elevated risk for the development of child behavior problems. Such populations include teenage single parents, families living in poverty, foster parents, divorcing parents, and families with a child exhibiting early conduct problems. A recent cost–benefit analysis identified behavioral parent training offered to families with a child exhibiting early conduct problems as one of the most cost-effective ways to reduce crime (Greenwood, Model, Rydell, & Chiesa, 1996).

Fourth, prevention is best seen on a continuum of service with treatment. In practice, applied settings would be best served if their prevention and early intervention services reflected this continuum, rather than creating artificial distinctions between them. An enlightened application of this model includes the recognition that the most effective prevention of one problem (e.g., delinquency or drug abuse) may be the treatment of another earlier problem (e.g., early conduct problems). When making decisions about what programs would best serve a community, one must consider which prevention and early intervention services are already available. Rather than creating separate service providers who offer prevention, and others who offer highly similar early intervention, we should make sure that the continuum of prevention and early intervention services works effectively.

Fifth, one of the most consistent lessons learned in the dissemination of empirically validated programs is that implementing them effectively requires a considerable amount of work and skill. In fact, attempts to replicate effective programs with only minimal initial training and little ongoing consultation with the program developers have often failed to achieve the effects obtained in the published studies (Kitzman, Cole, Yoos, & Olds, 1997). As a result, some programs have developed rigorous training and certification processes to ensure that the interventions are offered with fidelity when disseminated.

Sixth, one of the most effective ways to facilitate the wide-scale adoption of empirically supported prevention programs is for government agencies and private foundations to fund their dissemination. Biglan and colleagues (Biglan, Mrazek, Carnine, & Flay, 2003) have recommended that the early prevention and intervention community come to a consensus about the minimum level of evidence that programs should have for such dissemination.

Conclusions

The field of prevention/early intervention has made tremendous advances over the past few decades. Much has been learned about treating early-onset conduct problems: the most significant risk factor for delinquency, violence, and substance abuse. Numerous interventions have been developed that can reduce early risk factors and increase protective factors, resulting in a reduction of later conduct problems. The cost of doing this early prevention/intervention far outweighs the costs and risk of a child continuing on a trajectory that leads to delinquency, violence, and substance abuse problems.

Notes

This chapter was supported in part by the NIH/National Center for Nursing Research, Grant No. 5 R01 NR01075 and NIH/National Institute on Drug Abuse, Grant No. 5 R01 DA12881.

The first author of this chapter has disclosed a potential financial conflict of interest because she disseminates one of these treatments and stands to gain from a favorable report. Because of this, she has voluntarily agreed to distance herself from certain critical research activities (i.e., recruiting, consenting, primary data handling, and analysis), and the University of Washington has approved these arrangements.

References

Alexander, J. F., & Parsons, B. V. (1982). *Functional family therapy*. Monterey, CA: Brooks/Cole.

Alexander, J. F., Waldron, H. B., Newberry, A. M., & Liddle, N. (1988). *Family apporaches to treating delinquents*. Newbury Park, CA: Sage.

Barnard, K. E., Magyary, D., Sumner, G., Booth, C. L., Mitchell, S. K., & Spieker, S. (1988). Prevention of parenting alterations for women with low social support. *Psychiatry, 51*, 248–253.

Biglan, A., Mrazek, P. J., Carnine, D., & Flay, B. R. (2003). The integration of research and practice in the prevention of youth problem behaviors. *American Psychologist, 58*(6–7), 443–440.

Brestan, E. V., & Eyberg, S. M. (1998). Effective psychosocial treatments of conduct-disordered children and adolescents: 29 years, 82 studies, and 5,272 kids. *Journal of Clinical Child Psychology, 27*, 180–189.

Bullis, M., & Walker, H. M. (Eds.). (1994). *Comprehensive school-based systems for troubled youth*. Eugene, OR: University of Oregon, Center on Human Development.

Catalano, R. G., Haggerty, K. P., & Fleming, C. B. (1999). *Children of substance abusing parents: Current findings from the Focus on Families Project*. Seattle: University of Washington.

Christensen, A., Johnson, S. M., Phillips, S., & Glasgow, R. E. (1981). Cost-effectiveness in behavioral family therapy. *Behavior Therapy, 11*, 208–226.

Conduct Problems Prevention Research Group. (1999a). Initial impact of the Fast Track prevention trial for conduct problems: I. The high-risk sample. *Journal of Consulting and Clinical Psychology, 67*, 631–647.

Conduct Problems Prevention Research Group. (1999b). Evaluation of the first 3 years of the Fast Track Prevention Trial with children at high risk for adolescent conduct problems. *Journal of Abnormal Child Psychology, 30*, 19–35.

Conduct Problems Prevention Research Group. (1999c). Initial impact of the Fast Track prevention trial for conduct problems: II. Classroom effects. *Journal of Consulting and Clinical Psychology, 67*, 648–657.

Connell, S., Sanders, M. R., & Markie-Dadds, C. (1997). Self-directed behavioral family intervention for parents of oppositional children in rural and remote areas. *Behavior Modification, 21*, 379–408.

Cotton, K., & Wikelund, K. R. (Eds.). (1990). *Schoolwide and classroom discipline*. Portland, OR: Northwest Regional Education Laboratory.

Cunningham, C. E., Bremner, R., & Boyle, M. (1995). Large group community-based parenting programs for families of preschoolers at risk for disruptive behaviour disorders: Utilization, cost effectiveness, and outcome. *Journal of Child Psychology and Psychiatry, 36*, 1141–1159.

Cunningham, C. E., Davis, J. R., Bremmer, R., & Dunn, K. W. (1993). Coping modeling problem-solving versus mastery modeling: Effects on adherence, in-session process, and skill acquisition in a residential parent-training program. *Journal of Consulting and Clinical Psychology, 61*, 871–877.

Dadds, M. R., Schwartz, M. R., & Sanders, M. R. (1987). Marital discord and treatment outcome in behavioral treatment of child conduct disorders. *Journal of Consulting and Clinical Psychology, 16*, 192–203.

Dishion, T. J., Patterson, G. R., & Kavanagh, K. (1992). *An experimental test of the coercion model: Linking theory, measurement, and intervention.* New York: Guilford.

Eisenstadt, T. H., Eyberg, S. M., McNeil, C. B., Newcomb, K., & Funderburk, B. (1993). Parent–child interaction therapy with behavior problem children: Relative effectiveness of two stages and overall treatment outcome. *Journal of Clinical Child Psychology, 22*, 42–51.

Epstein, M. H., & Walker, H. M. (1999). Special education: Best practices and first step to success. In B. Burns, K. Hoagwood, & M. English (Eds.), *Community-based interventions for youth with serious emotional disorders* (pp. 179–197). Oxford: Oxford University Press.

Eron, L. D. (1990). Understanding aggression. *Bulletin of the International Society for Research on Aggression, 12*, 5–9.

Eyberg, S. M., & Boggs, S. R. (1989). Parent training for oppositional-defiant preschoolers. In C. E. Schaeffer & J. M. Brienmeister (Eds.), *Handbook of parent training* (pp. 105–132). New York: Wiley.

Eyberg, S. M., Boggs, S., & Algina, J. (1995). Parent–child interaction therapy: A psychosocial model for the treatment of young children with conduct problem behavior and their families. *Psychopharmacology Bulletin, 31*, 83–91.

Forehand, R. L., Steffe, M. A., Furey, W. A., & Walley, P. B. (1983). Mother's evaluation of a parent training program completed three and one-half years earlier. *Journal of Behavior Therapy and Experimental Psychiatry, 14*, 339–342.

Forehand, R. L., & McMahon, R. J. (1981). *Helping the noncompliant child: A clinician's guide to parent training.* New York: Guilford Press.

Forgatch, M. S., & DeGarmo, D. S. (1999). Parenting through Change: An effective prevention program for single mothers. *Journal of Consulting and Clinical Psychology, 67*(5), 711–724.

Francis, D. J., Shaywitz, S. E., Stuebing, K. K., Shaywitz, B. A., & Fletcher, J. M. (1991). Analysis of change: Modeling individual growth. *Journal of Consulting and Clinical Psychology, 59*, 27–37.

Funderburk, B. W., Eyberg, S. M., Newcomb, K., McNeil, C. B., Hembree-Kigin, T., & Capage, L. (1998). Parent–child interaction therapy with behavior problem children: Maintenance of treatment effects in the school setting. *Child and Family Behavior Therapy, 20*, 17–38.

Gottfredson, D. C., Gottfredson, G. D., & Hybl, L. G. (1993). Managing adolescent behavior: A multiyear, multischool study. *American Education Research Journal, 30*, 179–215.

Greenwood, P. W., Model, K. E., Rydell, C. P., & Chiesa, J. (1996). *Diverting children from a life of crime: Measuring costs and benefits.* Santa Monica, CA: Rand.

Gross, D., Fogg, L., Webster-Stratton, C., Garvey, C. W. J., & Grady, J. (2003). Parent training with families of toddlers in day care in low-income urban communities. *Journal of Consulting and Clinical Psychology, 71*(2), 261–278.

Hanf, C. (1970). *Shaping mothers to shape their children's behavior.* Unpublished manuscript. Portland, OR: University of Oregon Medical School.

Hanf, C., & Kling, J. (1973). *Facilitating parent–child interactions: A two-stage training model.* Portland, OR: University of Oregon Medical School.

Hawkins, J. D., Catalano, R. F., Kosterman, R., Abbott, R., & Hill, K. G. (1999). Preventing adolescent health-risk behaviors by strengthening protection during childhood. *Archives of Pediatrics and Adolescent Medicine, 153,* 226–234.

Hawkins, J. D., Catalano, R. F., & Miller, Y. (1992). Risk and protective factors for alcohol and other drug problems in adolescence and early adulthood: Implications for substance abuse prevention. *Psychological Bulletin, 112,* 64–105.

Hawkins, J. D., Catalano, R. F., Morrison, D. M., O'Donnell, J., Abbott, R. D., & Day, L. E. (1992). The Seattle Social Development Project: Effects of the first four years on protective factors and problem behaviors. In J. McCord & R. E. Tremblay (Eds.), *Preventing antisocial behavior: Intervention from birth through adolescence* (pp. 162–195). New York: Guilford.

Hawkins, J. D., & Weiss, J. G. (1985). The social developmental model: An integrated approach to delinquency prevention. *Journal of Primary Prevention, 6,* 73–95.

Hembree-Kigin, T. L., & McNeil, C. B. (1995). *Parent–child interaction therapy.* New York: Plenum Press.

Hood, K. K., & Eyberg, S. M. (2003). Outcomes of parent–child interaction therapy: Mothers' reports of maintenance three to six years after treatment. *Journal of Clinical Child & Adoloescent Psychology, 32*(3), 419–429.

Hops, H., Walker, H. M., Hernandez, D., Nagoshi, J. T., Omura, R. T., Skindrug, K., & Taylor, J. (1978). CLASS: A standardized in-class program for acting out children. II. Field test evaluations. *Journal of Educational Psychology, 70,* 636–644.

Kellam, S. G., Ling, X., Merisca, R., Brown, C. H., & Ialongo, N. (1998). The effect of the level of aggression in the first grade classroom on the course and malleability of aggressive behavior into middle school. *Development and Psychopathology, 10,* 165–185.

Kitzman, H. (1997). Effect of prenatal and infancy home visitation by nurses on pregnancy outcomes, childhood injuries, and repeated childbearing: A randomized controlled trial. *Journal of the American Medical Association, 278,* 644–652.

Kitzman, H. J., Cole, R., Yoos, H. L., & Olds, D. (1997). Challenges experienced by home visitors: A qualitative study of program implementation. *Journal of Community Psychology, 25,* 95–109.

Knapp, P. A., & Deluty, R. H. (1989). Relative effectiveness of two behavioral parent training programs. *Journal of Clinical Child Psychology, 18*(4), 314–322.

Knoff, H. M., & Batsche, G. M. (1995). Project ACHIEVE: Analyzing a school reform process for at-risk and underachieving students. *School Psychology Review, 24,* 579–603.

Kusche, C. A., & Greenberg, M. T. (1994). *The PATHS Curriculum.* Seattle, WA: Developmental Research and Programs.

Long, P., Forehand, R., Wierson, M., & Morgan, A. (1994). Does parent training with young noncompliant children have long-term effects? *Behavior Research and Therapy, 22,* 101–107.

McMahon, R. J., Forehand, R., & Griest, D. L. (1981). Effects of knowledge of social learning principles on enhancing treatment outcome and generalization in a parent training program. *Journal of Consulting and Clinical Psychology, 49*(4), 526–532.

McNeil, C. B., Eyberg, S., Eisenstadt, T. H., Newcomb, K., & Funderburk, B. W. (1991). Parent–child interaction therapy with behavior problem children: Generalization of treatment effects to the school setting. *Journal of Clinical Child Psychology, 20*(2), 140–151.

Miller, L. S., & Rojas-Flores, L. (1999). *Preventing conduct problems in urban, Latino preschoolers through parent training: A pilot study.* New York: New York University Child Study Center.

Miller-Heyl, J., MacPhee, D., & Fritz, J. J. (1998). DARE to be You: A family-support, early prevention program. *Journal of Primary Prevention, 18*(3), 257–285.

Moffitt, T. E. (1993). Adolescence-limited and life-course-persistent antisocial behavior: A developmental taxonomy. *Psychological Review, 100,* 674–701.

Mrazek, P. J., & Haggerty, R. J. (1994). Illustrative preventive intervention research programs. In

P. J. Mrazek & R. J. Haggerty (Eds.), *Reducing risks for mental disorders: Frontiers for preventive intervention research* (pp. 215–313). Washington, DC: National Academy Press.

Olds, D. L., Eckenrode, J., & Henderson, C. R. (1997). Long-term effects of home visitation on maternal life course and child abuse and neglect: 15-year follow-up of a randomized trial. *Journal of the American Medical Association, 278,* 637–643.

Olweus, D. (1978). *Aggression in the schools: Bullies and whipping boys.* Washington, DC: Hemisphere Press.

Patterson, G. R. (1974). Interventions for boys with conduct problems: Multiple settings, treatments, and criteria. *Journal of Consulting and Clinical Psychology, 42*(4), 471–481.

Patterson, G. R. (1975). *Families: Applications of social learning to family life.* Champaign, IL: Research Press.

Patterson, G. R. (1976). *Living with children: New methods for parents and teachers.* Champaign, IL: Research Press.

Patterson, G. R., & Chamberlain, P. (1994). A functional analysis of resistance during parent training therapy. *Clinical Psychology Science and Practice, 1*(1), 53–70.

Patterson, G. R., Chamberlain, P., & Reid, J. B. (1982). A comparative evaluation of a parent training program. *Behavior Therapy, 13,* 638–650.

Patterson, G. R., DeBaryshe, B. D., & Ramsey, E. (1989). A developmental perspective on antisocial behavior. *American Psychologist, 44*(2), 329–335.

Patterson, G. R., & Guillon, M. E. (1968). *Living with Children: New methods for parents and teachers.* Champaign, IL: Research Press.

Patterson, G. R., Reid, J. B., Jones, R. R., & Conger, R. W. (1975). *A social learning approach to family intervention* (Vol. 1). Eugene, OR: Castalia.

Patterson, G. R., Reid, J. B., & Dishion, T. (1992). *Antisocial boys: A social interactional approach* (Vol. 4). Eugene, OR: Castalia Publishing.

Peed, S., Roberts, M., & Forehand, R. (1977). Evaluations of the effectiveness of a standardized parent training program in altering the interaction of mothers and their noncompliant children. *Behavior Modification, 1,* 323–350.

Pfiffner, L. J., Jouriles, E. N., Brown, M. M., Etscheidt, M. A., & Kelly, J. A. (1990). Effects of problem-solving therapy on outcomes of parent training for single-parent families. *Child and Family Behavior, 12,* 1–11.

Pisterman, S., McGrath, P. J., Firestone, P., & Goodman, J. T. (1989). Outcome of parent-mediated treatment of preschoolers with attention deficit disorder with hyperactivity. *Journal of Consulting and Clinical Psychology, 57*(5), 628–635.

Prinz, R. J., Blechman, E. A., & Dumas, J. E. (1994). An evaluation of peer coping skills training for childhood aggression. *Journal of Clinical Child Psychology, 23*(2), 193–203.

Reid, J. B., & Eddy, J. M. (1997). The prevention of antisocial behavior: Some considerations in the search for effective interventions. In D. M. Stoff, J. Breiling, & J. D. Maser (Eds.), *The handbook of antisocial behavior* (pp. 343–356). New York: Wiley.

Reid, J. B., Eddy, J. M., Fetrow, R. A., & Stoolmiller, M. (1999). Description and immediate impacts of a preventive intervention for conduct problems. *American Journal of Community Psychology, 27*(4), 483–517.

Reid, J. B., Taplin, P., & Loeber, R. (1981). A social interactional approach to the treatment of abusive families. In R. B. Stuart (Ed.), *Violent behavior: Social learning approaches to prediction management and treatment* (pp. 83–101). New York: Brunner/Mazel.

Reid, M. J., Webster-Stratton, C., & Hammond, M. (2003). Follow-up of children who received the Incredible Years Intervention for Oppositional-Defiant Disorder: Maintenance and prediction of 2-year outcome. *Behavior Therapy, 34,* 471–491.

Sanders, M. R. (1992). *Every parent: A positive guide to children's behavior.* Sydney: Addison-Wesley.

Sanders, M. R., & Dadds, M. R. (1993). *Behavioral family intervention.* Needham Heights, MA: Allyn and Bacon.

Sanders, M. R., Markie-Dadds, C., Tully, L. A., & Bor, W. (2000). The Triple P-Positive Parenting Program: A comparison of enhanced, standard and self-directed behavioural family intervention for parents of children with early onset conduct problems. *Journal of Consulting and Clinical Psychology, 68,* 624–640.

Sayger, T. V., Horne, A. M., Walker, J. M., & Passmore, J. L. (1988). Social learning family therapy with aggressive children: Treatment outcome and maintenance. *Journal of Family Psychology, 1,* 261–285.

Schuhmann, E., Foote, R., Eyberg, S. M., Boggs, S., & Algina, J. (1998). Parent–child interaction therapy: Interim report of a randomized trial with short-term maintenance. *Journal of Clinical Child Psychology, 27,* 34–45.

Scott, S., Spender, Q., Doolan, M., Jacobs, B., & Aspland, H. (2001). Multicentre controlled trial of parenting groups for child antisocial behaviour in clinical practice. *British Medical Journal, 323*(28), 1–5.

Shores, R. E., & Wehby, J. H. (1999). Analyzing classroom social behavior of students with EBD. *Journal of Emotional and Behavioral Disorders, 7,* 194–199.

Shure, M. B., & Spivack, G. (1982). Interpersonal problem-solving in young children: A cognitive approach to prevention. *American Journal of Community Psychology, 10*(3), 341–356.

Snyder, H. (2001). Epidemiology of official offending. In R. Loeber & D. Farrington (Eds.), *Child delinquents: Development, intervention and service needs* (pp. 25–46). Thousand Oaks, CA: Sage.

Spaccarelli, S., Cotler, S., & Penman, D. (1992). Problem-solving skills training as a supplement to behavioral parent training. *Cognitive Therapy and Research, 16,* 1–18.

Stage, S. A., & Quiroz, D. R. (1997). A meta-analysis of interventions to decrease disruptive classroom behavior in public education settings. *School Psychology Review, 26,* 333–368.

Taylor, T. K., & Biglan, A. (1998). Behavioral family interventions for improving child-rearing: A review for clinicians and policy makers. *Clinical Child and Family Psychology Review, 1*(1), 41–60.

Taylor, T. K., Eddy, J. M., & Biglan, A. (1999). Interpersonal skills training to reduce aggressive and delinquent behavior: Limited evidence and the need for an evidence-based system of care. *Clinical Child and Family Psychology Review, 2*(3), 169–182.

Taylor, T. K., Schmidt, F., Pepler, D., & Hodgins, H. (1998). A comparison of eclectic treatment with Webster-Stratton's Parents and Children Series in a children's mental health center: A randomized controlled trial. *Behavior Therapy, 29,* 221–240.

Tremblay, R. E., Mass, L. C., Pagani, L., & Vitaro, F. (1996). From childhood physical aggression to adolescent maladjustment: The Montreal Prevention Experiment. In R. D. Peters & R. J. MacMahon (Eds.), *Preventing childhood disorders, substance abuse and delinquency* (pp. 268–298). Thousand Oaks, CA: Sage.

Tremblay, R. E., Pagani, K. L., Masse, L. C., & Vitaro, F. (1995). A biomodal preventive intervention for disruptive kindergarten boys: Its impact through mid-adolescence. Special Section: Prediction and prevention of child and adolescent antisocial behavior. *Journal of Consulting and Clinical Psychology, 63,* 560–568.

Tremblay, R. E., Vitaro, F., Bertrand, L., LeBlanc, M., Beauchesne, H., Boileau, H., & David, L. (1992). Parent and child training to prevent early onset of delinquency: The Montreal Longitudinal-Experimental study. In J. McCord & R. E. Tremblay (Eds.), *Preventing antisocial behavior: Interventions from birth through adolescence* (pp. 117–138). New York: Guilford.

Wahler, R. G., Cartor, P. G., Fleischman, J., & Lambert, W. (1993). The impact of synthesis teaching and parent training with mothers of conduct disordered children. *Journal of Abnormal Child Psychology, 12,* 425–440.

Walker, H. M., Kavanagh, K., Stiller, B., Golly, A., Steverson, H., & Feil, E. (1998). First step to success: An early intervention approach for preventing school antisocial behavior. *Journal of Emotional and Behavioral Disorders, 6,* 66–80.

Walker, H. M., Retana, G. F., & Gersten, R. (1988). Replication of the CLASS program in Costa Rica. *Behavior Modification, 12,* 133–154.

Webster-Stratton, C. (1981). Modification of mothers' behaviors and attitudes through videotape modeling group discussion program. *Behavior Therapy, 12,* 634–642.

Webster-Stratton, C. (1982a). The long term effects of a videotape modeling parent training program: Comparison of immediate and 1-year followup results. *Behavior Therapy, 13,* 702–714.

Webster-Stratton, C. (1982b). Teaching mothers through videotape modeling to change their children's behaviors. *Journal of Pediatric Psychology, 7*(3), 279–294.

Webster-Stratton, C. (1984). Randomized trial of two parent-training programs for families with conduct-disordered children. *Journal of Consulting and Clinical Psychology, 52*(4), 666–678.

Webster-Stratton, C. (1990a). Enhancing the effectiveness of self-administered videotape parent training for families with conduct-problem children. *Journal of Abnormal Child Psychology, 18,* 479–492.

Webster-Stratton, C. (1990b). *The Incredible Years parent training program manual: Effective communication, anger management and problem-solving (ADVANCE).* Seattle, WA: Incredible Years.

Webster-Stratton, C. (1990c). Long-term follow-up of families with young conduct problem children: From preschool to grade school. *Journal of Clinical Child Psychology, 19*(2), 144–149.

Webster-Stratton, C. (1994). Advancing videotape parent training: A comparison study. *Journal of Consulting and Clinical Psychology, 62*(3), 583–593.

Webster-Stratton, C. (1996). Parenting a young child with conduct problems: New insights using grounded theory methods. In T. H. Ollendick & R. S. Prinz (Eds.), *Advances in clinical child psychology* (pp. 333–355). Hillsdale, NJ: Lawrence Erlbaum Associates.

Webster-Stratton, C. (1998). Preventing conduct problems in Head Start children: Strengthening parenting competencies. *Journal of Consulting and Clinical Psychology, 66*(5), 715–730.

Webster-Stratton, C., & Hammond, M. (1999). Marital conflict management skills, parenting style, and early-onset conduct problems: Processes and pathways. *Journal of Child Psychology and Psychiatry, 40,* 917–927.

Webster-Stratton, C., & Hammond, M. (1990). Predictors of treatment outcome in parent training for families with conduct problem children. *Behavior Therapy, 21,* 319–337.

Webster-Stratton, C., & Hammond, M. (1997). Treating children with early-onset conduct problems: A comparison of child and parent training interventions. *Journal of Consulting and Clinical Psychology, 65*(1), 93–109.

Webster-Stratton, C., & Hammond, M. (1999). Marital conflict management skills, parenting style, and early-onset conduct problems: Processes and pathways. *Journal of Child Psychology and Psychiatry, 40,* 917–927.

Webster-Stratton, C., & Herbert, M. (1994). *Troubled families – problem children: Working with parents: A collaborative process.* Chichester: Wiley & Sons.

Webster-Stratton, C., Hollinsworth, T., & Kolpacoff, M. (1989). The long-term effectiveness and clinical significance of three cost-effective training programs for families with conduct-problem children. *Journal of Consulting and Clinical Psychology, 57*(4), 550–553.

Webster-Stratton, C., Kolpacoff, M., & Hollinsworth, T. (1988). Self-administered videotape therapy for families with conduct-problem children: Comparison with two cost-effective treatments and a control group. *Journal of Consulting and Clinical Psychology, 56*(4), 558–566.

Webster-Stratton, C., Reid, M. J., & Hammond, M. (2001). Preventing conduct problems, promoting social competence: A parent and teacher training partnership in Head Start. *Journal of Clinical Child Psychology, 30*(3), 283–302.

Webster-Stratton, C., Reid, M. J., & Hammond, M. (2004). Treating children with early-onset conduct problems: Intervention outcomes for parent, child, and teacher training. *Journal of Clinical Child and Adolescent Psychology, 33*(1), 105–124.

Wells, K. C., Forehand, R., & Griest, D. L. (1980). Generality of treatment effects from treated to untreated behaviors resulting from a parent training program. *Journal of Consulting and Clinical Psychology, 9*, 217–219.

Author Index

Subject Index